lonely planet

Portugal

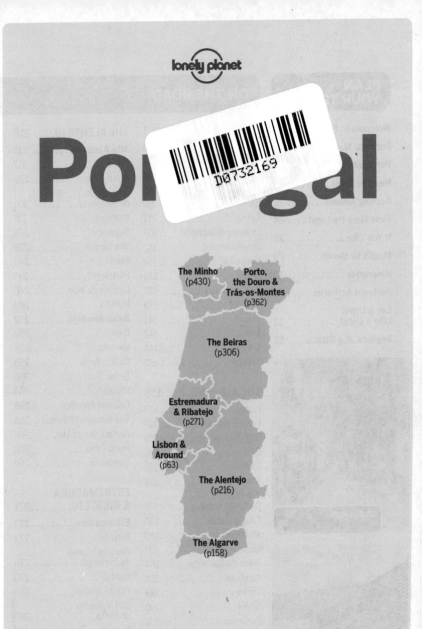

The Minho
(p430)

**Porto,
the Douro &
Trás-os-Montes**
(p362)

The Beiras
(p306)

**Estremadura
& Ribatejo**
(p271)

**Lisbon &
Around**
(p63)

The Alentejo
(p216)

The Algarve
(p158)

Gregor Clark, Duncan Garwood, Catherine Le Nevez, Kevin Raub,
Regis St Louis, Kerry Walker

PLAN YOUR TRIP

ÓBIDOS P276

VINEYARDS, ALTO DOURO
P405

ON THE ROAD

Contents

Welcome to Portugal

Medieval castles, cobblestone villages, captivating cities and golden beaches: the Portugal experience can be many things. History, great food and idyllic scenery are just the beginning...

Ghosts of the Past

Celts, Romans, Visigoths, Moors and Christians all left their mark on the Iberian nation. Here, you can gaze upon 20,000-year-old stone carvings in Foz Côa, watch the sunset over mysterious megaliths outside Évora or lose yourself in the elaborate corridors of Unesco World Heritage Sites in Tomar, Belém, Alcobaça or Batalha. You can ponder the rise and fall of ancient civilisations in the Celtic Citânia de Briteiros or the ancient Roman Cidade de Ammaia, and explore Portugal's most enchanting settings in palaces set above mist-covered woodlands, craggy clifftop castles and stunningly preserved medieval town centres.

The Portuguese Table

Freshly baked bread, olives, cheese, red wine or crisp *vinho verde* (young wine), chargrilled fish, *cataplana* (seafood stew), smoked meats – the Portuguese have perfected the art of cooking simple, delicious meals. Sitting down to table means experiencing the richness of Portugal's bountiful coastline and fertile countryside. But you don't have to sit; you can take your piping-hot *pastel de nata* (custard tart) standing at an 1837 patisserie in Belém, or wander through scenic vineyards sipping the velvety ports of the Douro Valley.

Cinematic Scenery

Outside the cities, Portugal's beauty unfolds in all its startling variety. You can go hiking amid the granite peaks of Parque Nacional da Peneda-Gerês or take in historic villages of the little-explored Beiras. Over 800km of coast offers more places to soak up the splendour. Gaze out over dramatic end-of-the-world cliffs, surf stellar breaks off dune-covered beaches or laze peacefully on sandy islands fronting calm blue seas. You'll find dolphin watching in the lush Sado Estuary, boating and kayaking along the meandering Rio Guadiana, and memorable walks and bike rides all across the country.

Rhythms of Portugal

Festivals pack Portugal's calendar. Drink, dance and feast your way through all-night revelries such as Lisbon's Festa de Santo António or Porto's Festa de São João. There are kick-up-your-heels country fairs in the hinterlands, and rock and world-music fests all along the coast. Any time is right to hear the mournful music of fado in the Alfama, join the dance party in Bairro Alto or hit the bars in Porto, Coimbra and Lagos. Rural Portugal has its own age-old musical traditions, from the Alentejo's polyphonic *Cante Alentejano* to the *pauliteiros* (stick dancers) of Miranda do Douro.

Why I Love Portugal

By Regis St Louis, Writer

I'm enamoured of the scenery, the rhythms of village life and Portugal's outstanding (and underrated) food and wine. I love exploring the hidden beaches along the Costa Vicentina, taking picturesque walks in the Serra da Estrela (where I still bump into shepherds during a day's outing), and roaming in less-visited corners of the Alentejo – such a magical place for discovering the traditional soul of Portugal. But it's the Portuguese themselves who make this country so special. Despite the sometimes dour exterior (it's just a facade!), they're among the kindest and most warm-hearted people on earth.

For more about our writers, see p544

Above: Palácio Nacional da Pena (p124), Sintra

Portugal

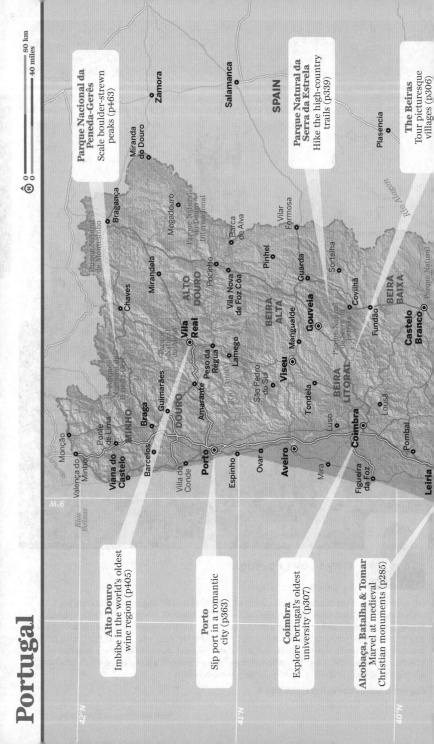

Parque Nacional da Peneda-Gerês
Scale boulder-strewn peaks (p463)

Parque Natural da Serra da Estrela
Hike the high-country trails (p339)

The Beiras
Tour picturesque villages (p306)

Alto Douro
Imbibe in the world's oldest wine region (p405)

Porto
Sip port in a romantic city (p363)

Coimbra
Explore Portugal's oldest university (p307)

Alcobaça, Batalha & Tomar
Marvel at medieval Christian monuments (p285)

80 km
40 miles

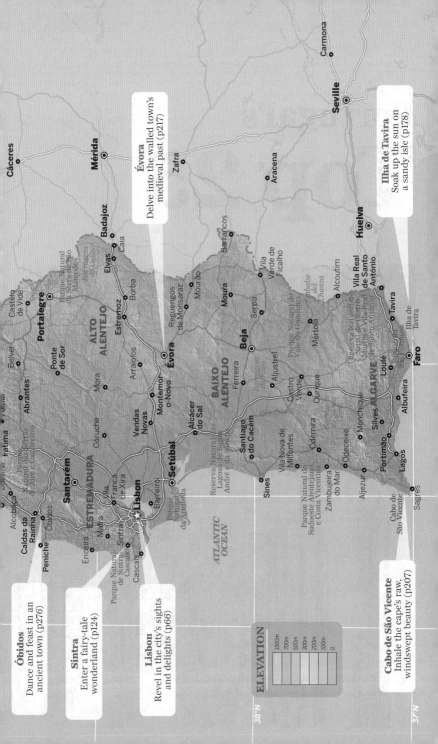

Óbidos
Dance and feast in an ancient town (p276)

Sintra
Enter a fairy-tale wonderland (p124)

Lisbon
Revel in the city's sights and delights (p66)

Évora
Delve into the walled town's medieval past (p217)

Ilha de Tavira
Soak up the sun on a sandy isle (p178)

Cabo de São Vicente
Inhale the cape's raw, windswept beauty (p207)

ELEVATION

1500m
700m
500m
300m
200m
100m
0

ATLANTIC OCEAN

38°N

37°N

Cáceres
Mérida
Badajoz
Caia
Elvas
Castelo de Vide
Belver
Portalegre
Parque Natural da Serra de São Mamede
Borba
Estremoz
ALTO ALENTEJO
Arraiolos
Mora
Ponte de Sor
Abrantes
Coruche
Vendas Novas
Montemor-o-Novo
Évora
Reguengos de Monsaraz
Mourão
Zafra
Seville
Carmona
Aracena
Huelva
Vila Verde de Ficalho
Barrancos
Moura
Serpa
Beja
BAIXO ALENTEJO
Ferreira
Aljustrel
Castro Verde
Ourique
Mértola
Alcoutim
Vila Real de Santo António
Tavira
Ilha de Tavira
Faro
Loulé
Albufeira
Silves ALGARVE
Monchique
Portimão
Lagos
Odeceixe
Aljezur
Sagres
Cabo de São Vicente
Parque Natural do Sudoeste Alentejano e Costa Vicentina
Zambujeira do Mar
Odemira
Vila Nova de Milfontes
Sines
Santiago do Cacém
Alcácer do Sal
Reserva Natural das Lagoas de Santo André e da Sancha
Setúbal
Barreiro
Parque Natural da Arrábida
Lisbon
Vila Franca de Xira
Santarém
ESTREMADURA
Mafra
Sintra
Cascais
Parque Natural de Sintra-Cascais
Ericeira
Peniche
Óbidos
Caldas da Rainha
Alcobaça

Portugal's
Top 25

The Alfama

1 Lisbon's Alfama district (p70), with its labyrinthine alleyways, hidden court-yards and curving, shadow-filled lanes, is a magical place in which to lose all sense of direction and delve into the soul of the city. You'll pass breadbox-sized grocers, brilliantly tiled buildings and cosy taverns filled with easy-going chatter, accompanied by the scent of chargrilled sardines and the doleful rhythms of fado drifting in the breeze. Round a bend and catch sight of steeply pitched rooftops leading down to the glittering Tejo, and you'll know you're hooked...

Nightlife in Lisbon

2 Lisbon's dizzying nightlife is a mix of old-school drinking dens, brassy jazz clubs and stylish lounges. The challenge is where to begin. You can start the evening with sunset drinks on a panoramic terrace overlooking the city, then head to Príncipe Real for exciting eats and early-evening craft cocktails or microbrews. Then wander downhill to Cais do Sodré, a former red-light district turned hipster playground, or to Bica for a lively local bar scene. At the end of the night there's always riverside Lux-Frágil (p109), still one of Portugal's best nightspots. Below right: Revellers on Rua Nova do Carvalho

Sintra

3 Less than an hour by train from the capital, Sintra (p124) feels like another world. It is sprinkled with stone-walled taverns and has a whitewashed palace looming over it. Forested hillsides form the backdrop to the village's storybook setting, with imposing castles, mystical gardens, strange mansions and centuries-old monasteries hidden among the woodlands. The fog that sweeps in by night adds another layer of mystery, and cool evenings are best spent fireside in one of Sintra's many charming B&Bs. Top: Castelo dos Mouros (p124), Sintra

Porto

4 It would be hard to dream up a more romantic city than Portugal's second largest. Laced with narrow pedestrian laneways, Porto (p363) is blessed with baroque churches, epic theatres and sprawling plazas. Its Ribeira district (pictured above) – a Unesco World Heritage Site – is a short walk across a landmark bridge from centuries-old port wineries in Vila Nova de Gaia. Though some walls are crumbling, a sense of renewal – in the form of modern architecture, cosmopolitan restaurants, burgeoning nightlife and a vibrant arts scene – is palpable.

Historic Évora

5 The Queen of the Alentejo and one of
Portugal's most beautifully preserved
medieval towns, Évora (p217) is an enchanting place to spend several days delving into the past. Inside the 14th-century
walls, Évora's narrow, winding lanes lead
to striking architectural works including
an elaborate medieval cathedral and cloisters, Roman ruins and a picturesque town
square. Its historic and aesthetic virtues
aside, Évora is also a lively university
town, and its many attractive restaurants
serve up some excellent, hearty Alentejan
cuisine.

Cabo de São Vicente

6 There's something thrilling about
standing at Europe's most southwestern edge, a headland of barren cliffs
(p207) to which Portuguese sailors bid
a nervous farewell as they sailed past,
venturing into the unknown during Portugal's golden years of exploration. The
windswept cape is redolent of history – if
you squint hard (really hard), you will see
the ghost of Vasco da Gama sailing past.
These days, a fortress and lighthouse
perch on the cape, and a museum beautifully highlights Portugal's maritime navigation history.

Drinking In the Douro

7 The exquisite Alto Douro wine country (p405) is the oldest demarcated wine region on earth. Its steeply terraced hills, stitched together with craggy vines that have produced luscious wines for centuries, loom either side of the Rio Douro. Whether you get here by driving the impossibly scenic back roads, or by train or boat from Porto, take the time to hike, cruise and taste. Countless vintners receive guests for tours, tastings and overnight stays, and if you find one that's still family-owned, you may sample something very old and special. Top: vineyards near Pinhão (p406)

Ilha de Tavira

8 Ilha de Tavira (p178) has the lot for sunseekers, beach bums, nature lovers (and naturists): kilometre after kilometre of golden beach (think sand, sand, sand, as far as the eye can see), a designated nudist area, transport via miniature train, busy restaurants and a campground. To top it off, it's part of the protected Parque Natural da Ria Formosa. Outside high season (July and August), the island feels wonderfully remote and empty, but be warned: during high season the hordes descend.

Megaliths Around Évora

9 Spiritual, magical, historical, incredible – the many ancient megaliths (p229) around Évora will make your hair stand on end. As a traveller, you will more often than not have these sites to yourself – and what better way to ponder the mysteries of places so ancient they cannot fully be explained? How did such massive rocks get hauled into place? Were they fertility symbols or proprietorial land boundaries? They beg questions, yet – refreshingly in a world of reasoning – provide few answers. Somehow, their appeal lies in not knowing. Above left; Cromeleque dos Almendres (p230)

Parque Natural da Ria Formosa

10 This special spot (p164) feels like the middle of the wilderness, yet it's right off the Algarvian coast. Enclosing a vast area of *sapais* (marshes), *salinas* (salt pans), creeks and dune islands, the protected lagoon system stretches for an incredible 60km and encompasses 18,000 hectares. It's a major hotspot for birdwatchers, as it's a key stopover on the migration between Europe and Africa. And it's all accessible from various towns – have a boat drop you at a deserted beach, or amble along the nature trail among the precious wetland birdlife.

Fado

11 Born in a working-class Lisbon neighbourhood, the melancholic music of fado has been around for centuries. Despite its years, fado remains a living art, heard in tiny family-run restaurants, like A Baiuca (p112), and elegant music halls alike. A lone, powerful voice coupled with the 12-string Portuguese *guitarra* are all the tools needed to bring listeners to tears, as songs recall broken hearts, unfulfilled dreams and the lost days of youth. In fado, raw emotion often conveys more than mere lyrics can; even non-Portuguese speakers find themselves moved by great *fadistas*.

Staying in a Pousada

12 Portugal has its share of boutique hotels and lavish beach resorts, but some of its most memorable lodging is found inside its lavish *pousadas* (upmarket inns). The settings are historic and jaw-dropping: clifftop mansions, 300-year-old castles and former monasteries – like the one in the Convento dos Lóios (p224) – are among the 40 *pousadas* across the country. Where else can you lodge in antique-filled rooms where dukes once slept? Pulling aside curtains, you'll gaze upon rolling vineyards, mountains or the glimmering coastline. Top: Pousada Mosteiro de Guimarães (p444)

Beaches of the Algarve

13 Sunseekers have much to celebrate when it comes to beaches. Along Portugal's south coast, the Algarve (p158) is home to a wildly varied coastline. There are sandy islands reachable only by boat, rugged rarely visited beaches and people-packed sands near buzzing nightlife. Days are spent playing in the waves, taking long oceanfront strolls and surfing memorable breaks. For endless days of sun and refreshing ocean temperatures, come in summer; but to escape the crowds, plan a low-season visit, when prices dive Bottom: Benagil Caves (p188), Carvoeiro

Alcobaça, Batalha & Tomar

14 These medieval Christian monuments – all Unesco World Heritage Sites – constitute one of Portugal's greatest national treasures. Each has its own magic: the haunting roofless shell of the unfinished Capelas Imperfeitas at Batalha's Mosteiro de Santa Maria da Vitória (p287; pictured above); the great kitchen at Alcobaça's monastery, where a multistorey chimney and fish-stocked river once tended to the appetites of countless monks; and the labyrinthine courtyards and mysterious 16-sided chapel of the Knights Templar at Tomar's Convento de Cristo.

Villages of the Beiras

15 From schist-walled communities spilling down terraced hillsides to spiky-edged sentinels that once guarded the eastern border against Spanish incursions, the inland Beiras (p306) are filled with picturesque villages: Piódão, Trancoso, Sortelha, Monsanto, Idanha-a-Velha... Today mostly devoid of residents but not yet overwhelmed by mass tourism, they are some of the country's most peaceful and appealing destinations. String a few together into the perfect road trip – or, better yet, don your walking shoes. Bottom: Sortelha (p338)

Óbidos

16 Wandering through the tangle of ancient streets and whitewashed houses of Óbidos (p276) is enchanting at any time of year, but come during one of its festivals and you'll be in for a special treat. Whether attending a jousting match or climbing the castle walls at the medieval fair, searching for the next Pavarotti at the Festival de Ópera or delving into the written world at Folio – Portugal's newest international literature festival – you couldn't ask for a better backdrop.

Azulejos

17 Some of Portugal's most captivating works of art are out on the streets – free viewing for anyone who strolls past. A great legacy of the Moors, the *azulejo* (hand-painted tile) was adopted by the Portuguese and put to stunning use over the centuries. Exquisite displays cover Porto's train station and iconic churches, with larger-than-life stories painted on the ceramic surfaces. Lisbon has even more eye candy, with *azulejo*-adorned buildings all over town. The best place to start the hunt: Museu Nacional do Azulejo (p70), home to *azulejos* dating back 400 years.

Pastries

18 One of the great culinary wonders of Portugal, the cinnamon-dusted *pastel de nata* (custard tart), with its flaky crust and creamy centre, lurks irresistibly behind pastry counters across the country; the best are served piping hot in Belém (p106), and draw foodies from all across the globe. Of course, when it comes to dessert, Portugal is more than a one-hit wonder, with a dazzling array of regional sweets – from the jewel-like Algarve marzipan to Sintra's heavenly almond-and-egg *travesseiros* to Serpa's cheesecake-like *queijadas*. Above left: *Pastéis de nata*

Festivals

19 There's always something to celebrate in Portugal. If you want Easter processions, head to Braga (p432). Romantics will love Lisbon's mid-June Festa de Santo António, with ubiquitous parties and locals plying sweethearts with poems and pots of aromatic basil. In August, catch Viana do Castelo's Romaria de Nossa Senhora d'Agonia, where *gigantones* (giants) parade down sawdust-painted streets alongside gold- and scarlet-clad women. And, in winter, young lads wear masks and colourful garb in Trás-os-Montes' villages during the pagan-derived **Festa dos Rapazes**. Top right: Festa de Santo António (p30)

Coimbra

20 Portugal's atmospheric college town, Coimbra (p307) rises steeply from the Rio Mondego to a medieval quarter housing one of Europe's oldest universities. Students roam the narrow streets clad in black capes, while strolling fado musicians give free concerts beneath the Moorish town gate or under the stained-glass windows of Café Santa Cruz. Kids can keep busy at Portugal dos Pequenitos theme park (p315), while grown-ups will appreciate the upper town's student-driven nightlife and the medieval lanes of the steeply stacked historic centre. Bottom right: Torre da Universidade and Paço das Escolas (p313)

VAFLYA/SHUTTERSTOCK ©

Braga

21 Portugal's third-largest city enjoys terrific restaurants, a vibrant university and raucous festivals, but when it comes to historic sites it is unparalleled. Here's the remarkable 12th-century cathedral, there's a 14th-century church. Braga (p432) has not one but two sets of Roman ruins, countless 17th-century plazas and an 18th-century palace turned museum. Then there's that splendid baroque staircase: Escadaria do Bom Jesus do Monte (p433) the target of penitent pilgrims who come to make offerings at altars on the way to the mountaintop. Above left: Escadaria do Bom Jesus do Monte (p433)

Seafood

22 Always a seafaring people, the Portuguese know a thing or two about cooking fish. Taste the culinary riches of Portugal's coast in dishes such as *caldeirada de peixe* (fish stew layered with tomatoes, potatoes and rice), *açorda de camarãoes* (a tasty stew of shrimp, garlic and coriander thickened with breadcrumbs) or *cataplana* (shellfish stewed with wine, garlic and tomatoes in a traditional domed copper pan). Algarve luminaries like A Eira do Mel (p208) are memorable settings for enjoying a seafood feast. Top right: Caldeirada de peixe

Parque Natural da Serra da Estrela

23 Portugal's highest mountains (p339) blend rugged scenery, outdoor adventure and vanishing traditional ways. At Torre, the country's highest point (artificially pushed up to 2000m by the addition of a not-so-subtle stone monument!), you can slalom down Portugal's only ski slope. Hikers can choose from a network of high-country trails with stupendous vistas. Oh, and did we mention the furry sheepdog puppies that frolic by the roadside? You'll long to take one home. The region is also home to fascinating mountain villages that make good bases for outdoor adventures.

Barcelos Market

24 The Minho is famous for its sprawling outdoor markets, but the largest, oldest and most celebrated is the Feira de Barcelos (p439), held every Thursday in this ancient town on the banks of the Rio Cávado. Most outsiders come for the yellow-dotted *louça de Barcelos* ceramics and the gaudy figurines à la local potter Rosa Ramalho, while rural villagers are more interested in the clucking chickens, hand-embroidered linen, handwoven baskets and hand-carved ox yokes. There are fine bases to stay in the area, including a 16th-century convent surrounded by vineyards.

Parque Nacional da Peneda-Gerês

25 The vast, rugged wilderness of Portugal's northernmost park (p463) is home to dramatic peaks and rolling hillsides covered with wildflowers. Its age-old stone villages seem lost in time and, in remote areas, wolves still roam. As always, the best way to feel nature's power is on foot along one of more than a dozen hiking trails. Some scale peaks, a few link to old Roman roads, others lead to castle ruins or waterfalls.

Need to Know

For more information, see Survival Guide (p507)

Currency
Euro (€)

Language
Portuguese

Visas
Generally not required for stays of up to 90 days; some nationalities will need a Schengen visa.

Money
ATMs are widely available, except in the smallest villages. Credit cards are accepted in midrange and high-end establishments.

Mobile Phones
Local SIM cards can be used in unlocked European, Australian and quad-band US mobiles.

Time
GMT/UTC in winter, GMT/UTC plus one hour in summer.

When to Go

Warm to hot summers, mild winters

The Douro
GO May–Sep

The Beiras
GO Jun & Sep

Lisbon
GO May & Jun

The Alentejo
GO May–Sep

The Algarve
GO Jun & Sep

High Season (Jul–Aug)

➡ Accommodation prices increase 30%.

➡ Expect big crowds in the Algarve and coastal resort areas.

➡ Sweltering temperatures are commonplace.

➡ Warmer ocean temperatures.

Shoulder (Apr–Jun & Sep–Nov)

➡ Wildflowers and mild days are ideal for hikes and outdoor activities.

➡ Lively festivals take place in June.

➡ Crowds and prices are average.

➡ Colder ocean temperatures.

Low Season (Dec–Mar)

➡ Shorter, rainier days with freezing temperatures at higher elevations.

➡ Lower prices, fewer crowds.

➡ Attractions keep shorter hours, and many beach lodgings close for winter.

➡ Frigid ocean temperatures, but big waves for surfers.

Useful Websites

Lonely Planet (www.lonely planet.com/portugal) Destination information, hotel bookings, traveller forum and more.

Portugal Tourism (www.visit portugal.com) Portugal's official tourism site.

Portugal News (www. theportugalnews.com) The latest news and gossip in Portugal.

Wines of Portugal (www. winesofportugal.info) Fine overview of Portugal's favourite beverage, covering wine regions, grape varieties and wine routes.

Important Numbers

Country Code	☎351
International Access Code	☎00
Ambulance, Fire & Police	☎112

Exchange Rates

Australia	A$1	€0.62
Canada	C$1	€0.66
Japan	¥100	€0.81
New Zealand	NZ$1	€0.60
UK	£1	€1.16
USA	US$1	€0.88

For current exchange rates see www.xe.com.

Daily Costs
Budget: Less than €50

➡ Dorm bed: €15–22

➡ Basic hotel room for two: from €35

➡ Lunch special at a family-run restaurant: €8–10

➡ Second-class train ticket from Lisbon to Faro: from €23

Midrange: €50–120

➡ Double room in a midrange hotel: €50–100

➡ Lunch or dinner in a midrange restaurant: €22–40

➡ Admission to museums: €3–8

Top end: More than €120

➡ Boutique hotel room: from €120

➡ Dinner for two in a top restaurant: from €80

➡ Three-day surf course: €150

Opening Hours

Opening hours vary throughout the year. We provide high-season opening hours; hours will generally decrease in the shoulder and low seasons.

Banks 8.30am–3pm Monday to Friday

Bars 7pm–2am

Cafes 9am–7pm

Clubs 11pm–4am Thursday to Saturday

Restaurants noon–3pm and 7–10pm

Shopping malls 10am–10pm

Shops 9.30am–noon and 2–7pm Monday to Friday, 10am–1pm Saturday

Arriving in Portugal

Aeroporto de Lisboa (Lisbon) Metro trains head downtown (€1.50, €1.33 with a Zapping card, 20 minutes, frequent departures 6.30am to 1am). AeroBus (€3.60) departs every 20 minutes from 7am to 11pm. A taxi to the centre takes 15 minutes (around €16, plus €1.60 for luggage).

Aeroporto Francisco Sá Carneiro (Porto) Metro do Porto violet line E (direction Estádio do Dragão) links to downtown Porto (one-way €2, around 45 minutes). Alternatively, daytime taxis cost €20 to €25 to the centre and take an hour.

Aeroporto de Faro (Faro) Proximo city buses 14 and 16 run to the bus station (€2.25) every 30 minutes from June to August, slightly less frequently in low season. From the bus station, it's an easy stroll to the centre. A taxi costs around €20 (20 minutes).

Health

➡ Good healthcare is readily available, and for minor illnesses pharmacists can give valuable advice and sell over-the-counter medication. Most pharmacists speak some English. They can also advise when more specialised help is required and point you in the right direction.

➡ Citizens of the EU are eligible for free emergency medical treatment if they have a European Health Insurance Card (EHIC), which replaces the no-longer-valid E111 certificate. It will not cover you for nonemergencies or emergency repatriation.

➡ Citizens from other countries should find out if there is a reciprocal arrangement for free medical care between their country and Portugal. If you do need health insurance, consider a policy that covers you for the worst possible scenario, such as an accident requiring an emergency flight home. Find out in advance if your insurance plan will make payments directly to providers or reimburse you later for overseas health expenditures.

For much more on **getting around**, see p518

Getting Around

For more information, see Transport (p516)

Travelling by Car

Nothing beats the freedom of having your own car in Portugal, especially if you fancy exploring the country's wealth of beautiful rural villages, beaches and remote natural areas. You'll do best to walk or use public transport in larger cities such as Lisbon, Porto, Braga and Coimbra, where a car is more of a hindrance than a help – but once you leave the city behind, you'll appreciate Portugal's extensive network of efficient motorways and scenic back roads.

Major toll routes, such as the A1 from Lisbon to Porto and the A2 between Lisbon and Faro, are modern, fast, well-signposted and extremely well-maintained. With speed limits ranging up to 120km/h, these motorways allow you to travel the entire country from north to south in less than six hours. At the other end of the spectrum, Portuguese back roads can be slow, narrow and meandering, but often offer fabulous scenery by way of compensation.

Car Hire

International rental agencies are well-represented in Portugal, with offices at Portugal's three main airports (Lisbon, Porto and Faro) and in several city centres. Advance reservations made through travel booking websites usually offer the best deals.

Tolls

Portugal has an extensive network of toll motorways. While there are still some staffed toll booths, there's a growing trend toward electronic tolls, with cameras

RESOURCES

Automobile Associations

Automóvel Club de Portugal (ACP; ☑219 429 113, 24hr emergency assistance 808 222 222; www.acp.pt), Portugal's national auto club, provides road information and maps at its offices throughout the country, along with emergency breakdown assistance to members of affiliated clubs from other countries (bring your home country membership card).

Road Maps

Road maps of Portugal, such as Michelin's 1:400,000 map, are available at bookstores in major cities and at service stations along Portugal's motorways.

Road Conditions

For information on current driving conditions, road work projects, speed camera locations and a handy toll calculation tool, see this Portuguese-language website: www.estradas.pt.

recording your license plate number at regular intervals as you drive past. If you're renting a car and planning to drive even part of your journey on motorways, it's advisable to purchase a Via Verde pass (usually available for a small surcharge). This allows you to drive through the fast 'Via Verde' lane at toll booths around the country. Individual toll charges will be automatically calculated and billed to your credit card by the rental agency.

Parking

Metered street parking is widely available in Portugal's cities and towns, often supplemented by free parking in peripheral streets or at lots outside the city centre. Rates are generally reasonable (typically €1 or less per hour – pay at the machine and leave the ticket under your windscreen). More expensive, enclosed garage parking is also an option in larger cities.

Hazards

Once behind the wheel of a car, some otherwise mild-mannered Portuguese change personality. Aggressive driving, such as tailgating at high speeds and overtaking on blind corners, is not uncommon. Portugal has one of the highest road accident rates in Europe, though the situation has improved in recent years thanks to a zero-tolerance police crackdown on accident-prone routes and alcohol limits.

No Car?

Train

Portugal's rail network, operated by Comboios de Portugal (www.cp.pt) is less extensive than in some European countries, but it's still an enjoyable, practical alternative to driving, especially on main routes such as the Lisbon-to-Porto line,

which connects the two cities in three hours. Several other key destinations are easily reached by train, including Coimbra, Braga, Évora, Faro and the scenic Douro Valley wine country.

Bus

Buses are the most efficient – and sometimes only – option for reaching Portugal's interior towns and cities. A variety of companies – including the large carriers Rede Expressos and Rodonorte – offer competitive fares aboard comfortable coaches.

Bicycle

While there are few dedicated bike routes in Portugal, cycling is a scenic way to get around the country, especially in rural areas such as the Serra da Estrela and Parque Nacional da Peneda-Gerês. Free or low-cost bike sharing programs offer an attractive option in several Portuguese cities.

PLAN YOUR TRIP GETTING AROUND

DRIVING FAST FACTS

➡ Drive on the right.

➡ Seatbelt required for driver and all passengers.

➡ Maximum speed 120km/h on motorways, 50km/h in towns and villages.

➡ Blood alcohol limit 0.05% (0.02% for new drivers licensed within the past 3 years).

➡ Minimum driving age 18 years (16 years for motorbikes up to 125cc).

ROAD DISTANCES (KM)

	Lisbon	Porto	Faro	Coimbra	Évora
Lisbon	---				
Porto	317	---			
Faro	296	585	---		
Coimbra	202	123	468	---	
Évora	138	368	244	251	---

First Time Portugal

For more information, see Survival Guide (p507)

Checklist

➡ Check whether you can use your phone in Portugal and ask about roaming charges.

➡ Book your first night's accommodation.

➡ Check the calendar to see which festivals to visit (or avoid!).

➡ Organise travel insurance.

➡ Check airline baggage restrictions.

➡ Inform your debit-/credit-card company of your travel plans.

What to Pack

➡ Good walking shoes for the cobblestones

➡ A smart outfit and shoes

➡ Phrasebook

➡ Electrical adaptor and phone charger

➡ Earplugs for thin-walled guesthouses and noisy weekend nights

➡ Hat, sunglasses, sunscreen

➡ Swimming towel

➡ Rain jacket (especially in winter)

➡ English-language reading material

Top Tips for Your Trip

➡ Portugal's *mercados* (markets) are a great way to sample the country's culinary bounty of breads, cheeses, olives, smoked meats, fruit and vegetables.

➡ Get off Portugal's main highways and take to the back roads, where you'll find sleepy villages, roadside fruit stands and tiny lanes leading to remote beaches.

➡ You'll earn respect and smiles if you learn a few phrases in Portuguese. Don't try to use Spanish, which can rub some folks the wrong way. You're better off just using English.

➡ Don't be put off by the sometimes dour-looking Portuguese. Make the effort to approach and engage people, and you'll find an incredibly hospitable and warm-hearted country.

What to Wear

Portugal is fairly casual, though most Portuguese tend to wear trousers (rather than shorts) outside resort areas. For upscale outings, smart casual is sufficient – no restaurant, theatre or concert hall will insist on jackets or ties. Nights can get windy or chilly, so bring a lightweight jacket in summer, and expect rain and cooler temperatures in winter.

Sleeping

While you can usually find a room on the spot, it's worthwhile booking ahead, especially for July and August.

Guesthouses Small, often family-run places, some set in historic buildings; amenities range from simple to luxurious.

Pousadas Unique accommodation inside former castles, monasteries and estates.

Turihab Properties Stay in characterful manor houses, restored farmhouses or self-contained stone cottages.

Hostels Portugal's growing nationwide network of hostels includes many in Lisbon and Porto.

Private rooms and apartments Loads of online listings throughout Portugal.

Eating

Settling down to a meal with friends is one of life's great pleasures for the Portuguese, who take pride in simple but flavourful dishes honed to perfection over the centuries. Seafood, roast meats, freshly baked bread and velvety wines are key staples in the everyday feast that is eating in Portugal.

Bargaining

Gentle haggling is common in markets (less so in produce markets); in all other instances you're expected to pay the stated price.

Tipping

Bars Not expected.

Hotels One euro per bag is standard; gratuity for cleaning staff is at your discretion.

Restaurants In touristy areas, 10% is fine; few Portuguese ever leave more than a round-up to the nearest euro.

Snack bars Not expected.

Taxis Not expected, but it's polite to round up to the nearest euro.

Language

English is spoken in larger cities and in popular tourist areas (especially the Algarve), but is less common in rural areas and among older Portuguese. Many restaurants have English-language menus, though smaller family-run places typically do not (but may have English-speaking staff on hand to help out). Smaller museums are likely to have signs in Portuguese only. The Portuguese always appreciate the effort: a few key words, such as *'bom dia'*, *'boa tarde'*, *'obrigado/obrigada'* and *'por favor'*, can go a long way.

When is admission free?
Quando é grátis a entrada?
kwang·doo e graa·teesh a eng·traa·da

Try to plan your sightseeing in Portugal around free-admission days (often Sunday mornings).

Can I have a half-serve, please?
Podia servir-me meia-dose, por favor?
poo·dee·a ser·veer·me may·a·do·ze poor fa·vor

Much Portuguese cuisine is served in massive portions – it's often worth ordering a half-serve, especially if you're on a budget.

Can I get this without meat?
Este prato pode vir sem carne?
esh·te praa·too po·de veer seng kaar·ne

Vegetarians aren't generally well catered for in Portugal, and they may need to be creative in requesting their dishes.

Where can we go for 'street fado'?
Onde é que há fado vadio?
ong·de e ke aa faa·doo va·dee·oo

For an authentic, spontaneous approach to music, seek out places where locals take turns singing the 'Portuguese blues'.

5 **Where can I find an art exhibition?**
Onde é que há alguma esposição de arte?
ong·de e ke aa alg·goo·ma shpoo·zee·sowng de aar·te

There are always interesting cultural happenings in major Portuguese cities, including free fringe-art exhibitions.

Etiquette

Greetings When greeting females or mixed company, an air kiss on both cheeks is common courtesy. Men give each other a handshake.

Visiting churches It is considered disrespectful to visit churches as a tourist during Mass. Taking photos at such a time is definitely inappropriate.

'Free' appetisers Whatever you eat, you must pay for, whether or not you ordered it. It's common practice for restaurants to bring bread, olives, cheese and other goodies to the table, but these are never free and will be added to your bill at the end. If you don't want them, a polite 'No, thank you' will see them returned to the kitchen.

If You Like...

Food

Renowned for its seafood, hearty country cooking and many regional specialities, Portugal offers plenty of temptation for the food-minded traveller. Celebrated new chefs have brought attention to a host of dining rooms, while those who enjoy the simple things – olives, cheeses, roast meats, fish sizzling on the grill, freshly baked bread – will enjoy memorable meals in traditional restaurants all across the country.

Alma A celebrated, Michelin–starred restaurant serving up some of the best meals in Portugal. (p98)

Food festivals The Algarve elevates its seafood and regional delicacies to high art in these food-minded celebrations. (p171)

Vila Joya Overlooking the beach, this two-Michelin–starred restaurant is one of Portugal's finest. (p187)

Cataplana This decadent seafood stew is a south-coast speciality; it's available across the Algarve and almost always feeds two. (p172)

DOC Serves delectable haute cuisine in a beautiful setting on the Douro. (p408)

Wine & Port

Home to some of the oldest vineyards on earth, Portugal has some fantastic (and deliciously affordable) wines. Each region has its enticements, from full-bodied Alentejan reds to Minho's refreshing *vinho verde* (young wine), along with the famous ports from the Douro. Stylish wine bars and bucolic vineyards provide memorable settings in which to taste Portugal's great fruits of the vine.

BA Wine Bar do Bairro Alto Sample the country's finest quaffs at this atmospheric spot in Lisbon. (p109)

Herdade do Esporão An acclaimed winery outside Reguengos de Monsaraz, with vineyards dating back hundreds of years. (p231)

Casa da Ínsua Drinking in the velvety reds of the Dão region at this celebrated winery and five-star hotel near Viseu. (p354)

Casa de Mateus At this shop inside a palace, drink in the grandeur while sipping distinctive and rare Alvarelhão. (p411)

Solar do Vinho do Porto With views over the Douro, this elegant garden bar serves an astounding variety of ports. (p109)

Douro Vineyards Breathtaking views from 18th-century manors and velvety rich wines make the Douro a requisite stop for wine lovers. (p405)

Graham's Port-wine lodges are two a penny in Gaia, but Graham's stands out with its stellar cellar tours, tastings and big views. (p378)

Beaches

With 830km of coastline, Portugal has sun-kissed shores of every type, from festive, people-packed coves to remote, windswept shores that invite endless wandering.

Ilha de Tavira This sandy island off the southern coast is a remarkable getaway. (p178)

Figueira da Foz Admiring the striking confluence of sand and sea in Portugal's widest beach. (p323)

Praia de São Jacinto For a seaside escape in northern Portugal, head to this wild beach backed by dunes west of Aveiro. (p330)

Vila Nova de Milfontes Star of the Alentejo coastline is this lovely and vibrant village overlooking several pretty beaches. (p265)

Costa da Caparica Just across the Tejo from Lisbon is 8km

of pretty coastline with stylish beach bars sprinkled along it. (p148)

Lagos This popular Algarve resort town offers a mix of lively surfing beaches and secluded sandstone-backed shorelines further out of town. (p195)

Architecture & Design

Taking in Portugal's wildly varied architecture involves delving into the past as you gaze upon medieval monasteries, imposing hilltop castles and ancient ruins.

Sé Velha Peel back the centuries while walking through Coimbra's magnificent Romanesque cathedral. (p311)

Fortaleza de Sagres Contemplate Portugal's seafaring past from this clifftop perch over the Atlantic. (p205)

Casa da Música Rem Koolhaas' stunning music hall, completed in 2005, is an architectural gem. (p392)

Mosteiro dos Jerónimos Dom Manuel I's fantastical tribute to the great explorers of the 15th century. (p79)

Convento de Cristo Former headquarters of the Knights Templar, this Unesco World Heritage Site is stunning to behold. (p301)

Conímbriga The best-preserved Roman ruins on the Iberian Peninsula provide a window into the rise and fall of the once great empire. (p321)

Palácio Nacional de Mafra The construction of this exuberant palace with its 1200 rooms nearly bankrupted the nation. (p142)

Biblioteca Joanina An amazing work of baroque interior design in Coimbra. (p311)

PLAN YOUR TRIP IF YOU LIKE...

Top: Mosteiro dos Jerónimos (p79), Lisbon

Bottom: Camilo beach (p195), Lagos

Music

The national music of Portugal is undoubtedly fado, that stirring, melancholic sound that's so prevalent in Lisbon (its birthplace) and Coimbra. Other genres also have their followers, and you can catch live rock, jazz and a wide range of world sounds.

Alfama The birthplace of fado has many authentic places in which to hear it live – as well as tourist traps to avoid. (p112)

Á Capella Coimbra also has a fado-loving heart; this converted 14th-century chapel is the best place to hear it live. (p319)

Festival do Sudoeste One of Portugal's biggest music fests erupts each August in the seaside town of Zambujeira do Mar. (p31)

Casa da Música Rem Koolhaas' concert hall is both an architectural masterpiece and a vibrant set piece for year-round music events. (p392)

Art

In the Portuguese art world, quality trumps quantity. You may not find massive art institutions here, but you will find galleries showcasing unique works from the past and present – including home-grown Portuguese legends.

Museu Calouste Gulbenkian One of Lisbon's finest museums houses an epic collection of magnificent artwork from East and West. (p78)

Museu Coleção Berardo In Belém, this museum hosts some of Portugal's most daring exhibits. (p80)

Casa das Histórias Paula Rego Cascais' best exhibition space celebrates the artwork of Paula Rego, one of Portugal's finest postwar painters. (p133)

Serralves Porto's art lovers never miss the cutting-edge exhibits inside this art-deco mansion in the park. (p380)

Museu da Tapeçaria de Portalegre Guy Fino Be dazzled by colour at this fine tapestry museum in the Alentejo. (p243)

Museu de Lamego This museum houses a superb collection of works by 16th-century luminary Grão Vasco. (p402)

Nightlife

When the sun goes down, things start to get interesting. Whether you want to party like a rock star or sip cocktails with a more laid-back, bohemian crowd, you'll find these and dozens of other scenes in Portugal.

Lagos Packed with music-filled bars and lounges, Lagos is the nightlife centre of the Algarve. (p195)

Forte São João Baptista In a striking 17th-century fort, this hotel, restaurant and nightclub throws some of the best summer parties in the north. (p399)

Cais do Sodré Lisbon's nightlife epicentre has colourful bars, tapas joints and DJ-spinning clubs that stay open till the early morning. (p95)

Porto Nightlife has exploded in recent years, with revellers packing the bar- and gallery-lined streets near Rua das Carmelitas. (p363)

Historic Villages

Portugal is home to many enchanting villages, where a stroll along peaceful cobblestone lanes is like a trip back in time.

Óbidos Medieval architecture, lively festivals and charming guesthouses await in this fortified town an hour north of Lisbon. (p276)

Mértola Set high above the Rio Guadiana, this remarkably well-preserved Alentejo town is considered an open-air museum. (p256)

Monsanto A forlorn village surrounding an age-old, boulder-strewn castle, Monsanto has great walking trails through the rolling countryside nearby. (p336)

Miranda do Douro This remote fortress town on the border with Spain has an imposing 16th-century castle and street signs in the ancient language of Mirandês. (p425)

Castelo de Vide Wander the medieval Jewish quarter and take in sweeping views over the surrounding cork and olive groves. (p246)

Month by Month

January

A peaceful month to visit, though the weather can be patchy and cool. Dia de Reis (Three Kings' Day) brings the Christmas festivities to a close on 6 January.

February

Winter sees fewer crowds and lower prices along with abundant rainfall, particularly in the north. Coastal temperatures are cool but mild, while inland there are frigid days. Many resorts remain shuttered until spring.

🎭 Carnaval

Portugal's Carnaval features much merrymaking in the pre-Lenten celebrations. Loulé boasts the best parades, but Lisbon, Nazaré and Viana do Castelo all throw a respectable bash.

🍷 Essência do Vinho

Oenophiles are in their element at this wine gathering (www.essenciadovinho porto.com), held in late February in the sublime setting of Palácio da Bolsa. Some 3000 wines from 350 producers are available for tasting. (p368)

April

Spring arrives, bringing warmer temperatures and abundant sunshine in both the north and the south. Late April sees a profusion of wildflowers in the south.

🎭 Semana Santa

The build-up to Easter is magnificent in the Minho's saintly Braga. During Holy Week, barefoot penitents proceed through the streets, past rows of makeshift altars, with an explosion of jubilation at the cathedral on the eve of Easter.

May

Lovely sunny weather and the lack of peak-season crowds make May an ideal time to visit. The beaches of the Algarve awake from their slumber and see a smattering of travellers passing through.

🎭 Queima das Fitas

Join the mayhem of the Burning of the Ribbons at the University of Coimbra (Portugal's Oxford), as students celebrate the end of the academic year with concerts, a parade and copious amounts of drinking.

🎭 Festa do Mar

Celebrating the age-old love of the sea (and the patron saints of fishers), this lively festival brings a flotilla of fishing boats to Nazaré's harbour, as well as a colourful parade of elaborately decorated floats. There's plenty of eating and drinking.

🎭 Fátima Romaris

Hundreds of thousands make the pilgrimage to Fátima each year to commemorate the apparitions of the Virgin that occurred on 13 May 1917. The pilgrimage also takes place on 12 and 13 October. (p493)

June

Early summer is one of the liveliest times to visit, as the festival calendar is packed. Warm, sunny days are the norm, and while tourism picks up, the hordes have yet to arrive.

Serralves em Festa

This huge cultural event (www.serralvesemfesta.com) runs for 40 hours nonstop over one weekend in Porto in June. Parque de Serralves hosts the main events, with concerts, avant-garde theatre and kids' activities. Other open-air events happen all over town.

Fado no Castelo

Lisbon's love affair with fado reaches a high point at this annual songfest held at the cinematic Castelo de São Jorge over three evenings in June. (p71)

Festa do Corpo de Deus

This religious fest happens all across northern Portugal on Corpus Christi but is liveliest in Monção, with an old-fashioned medieval fair, theatrical shows and over-the-top processions.

Festival Med

Loulé's world-music festival (www.festivalmed.pt), held over three days, brings more than 50 bands playing an incredible variety of music. World cuisine accompanies the global beats.

Vaca das Cordas & Corpus Christi

Ponte de Lima gets rowdy during this unusual event, which features a bull on a rope let loose on the streets. A more solemn event follows, with religious processions along flower-strewn streets.

Festas de Junho

Amarante goes wild for its favourite saint and patron of lovers, São Gonçalo. All-night music, fireworks, markets and processions mark the occasion.

Festa de Santo António

The lively Festival of St Anthony is celebrated with fervour in Lisbon's Alfama and Madragoa districts, with feasting, drinking and dancing in some 50 *arraiais* (street parties).

Festa de São João

St John is the favourite up north, where Porto, Braga and Vila do Conde celebrate with elaborate processions, music and feasting, while folks go around whacking each other with plastic hammers.

Festas Populares

Celebrating the feast days of São João and São Pedro, Évora hosts a lively 12-day event that kicks off in late June. There's a traditional fairground, art exhibitions, gourmet food and drink, cultural events and sporting competitions.

July

The summer heat arrives, bringing sunseekers who pack the resorts of the Algarve. Lisbon and Porto also swell with crowds, and prices peak in July and August.

Mercado Medieval

Don your armour and head to the castle grounds for this lively two-week medieval fair (www.mercadomedievalobidos.pt) in Óbidos. Attractions include wandering minstrels, jousting matches and plenty of grog. Other medieval fairs are held in Silves and other castle towns.

Festival dos Canais

In mid-July, Aveiro becomes an arts capital, with concerts, huge street installations, circus art shows and surreal parades. In all the city hosts more than 200 performances with artists from over a dozen countries.

MEO Marés Vivas

Over a weekend in late July, Afurada dusts off its party clothes to host the MEO Marés Vivas (www.maresvivas.meo.pt), which draws a massive crowd from Porto and beyond with an impressive roster of rock and pop stars.

August

The mercury soars in August, with sweltering days best spent at the beach. This is Portugal's busiest tourist month, and reserving ahead is essential.

⭐ Festas Gualterianas

The old city of Guimarães brings revellers from across the region to its colourful processions, with allegorical floats, folk dancing, fireworks and bands.

⭐ Festival do Sudoeste

The Alentejan Glastonbury, in Zambujeira do Mar, attracts a young, surfy crowd with huge parties and big-name bands headlining (https://sudoeste.meo.pt).

✕ Festival do Marisco

Seafood-lovers should not miss this grand culinary fest (www.festivaldomarisco.com) in Olhão. Highlights include regional specialities like chargrilled fish, *caldeirada* (fish stew) and *cataplana* (a kind of shellfish hotpot); there's also live music.

⭐ Romaria de Nossa Senhora d'Agonia

The Minho's most spectacular festival (www.viana festas.com), in Viana do Castelo, has elaborate street paintings, folk-costume parades, drumming, giant puppets and much merrymaking.

⭐ Feira de São Mateus

Folk music, traditional food and fireworks rule the day at St Matthew's Fair (www.feirasaomateus.pt) in Viseu, which runs for six weeks. There's also live music, including major international bands.

⭐ Folkfaro

A musician's treat, Folkfaro (www.folkfaro.com) brings local and international folk performers to the city of Faro for staged and impromptu performances across town. Street fairs accompany the event.

⭐ Festival Internacional de Folclore de Gulpilhares

Traditional groups and costumed dancers perform at the International Folk Festival of Gulpilhares, a week-long event in early August. (p379)

⭐ Festa de Nossa Senhora dos Remédios

Head to Lamego, in the Douro, for a mix of religious devotion and secular revelry from late August to midSeptember. Rock concerts and all-night celebrations coincide with pious processions winding through the streets.

September

Peak tourist season officially runs until mid-September, when ongoing warm weather ensures beaches remain packed. Things cool down a bit and prices dip as the crowds dissipate by late September.

⭐ Nossa Senhora da Nazaré

The festival of Our Lady of Nazaré brings much life to this eponymous town in Estremadura, with rich

processions, folk music and dancing, bullfights and other competitions. (p283)

⭐ Feiras Novas

One of Portugal's oldest ongoing events, the New Fairs festival has a massive market and fair, with folk dances, fireworks and brass bands at Ponte de Lima.

October

The weather is cooling and rains are a possibility (especially in the north). However, it's a great time for outdoor activities in the south and in central Portugal.

December

December means rain and colder temperatures. Few travellers venture south, where many resorts close for the winter. Christmas and New Year's Eve bring merriment to the somewhat dreary season.

⭐ Festa dos Rapazes

Just after Christmas, the 'Festival of the Lads' is a rollicking time of merrymaking by young unmarried men, who light bonfires and rampage around in rags and wooden masks. Catch it in Miranda do Douro.

⭐ New Year's Eve

The best place to ring in the Ano Novo is Lisbon, with fireworks, free concerts and DJs down by the Tejo.

Plan Your Trip
Itineraries

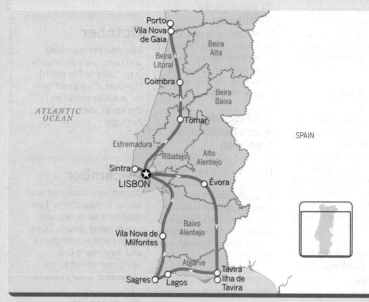

Highlights of Portugal

This grand journey takes you from the vibrant Portuguese capital to the sunny beaches of the Algarve and up north to striking, riverside Porto. Along the way, you'll visit Unesco World Heritage Sites, stroll medieval town centres and sample the varied cuisines of the north, south and centre.

Start in **Lisbon**, spending two days exploring the city's enchanting neighbourhoods, atmospheric restaurants and fado-filled taverns. Take vertiginous tram rides, and visit the city's hilltop castle, museums and historic sites. On day three, head to nearby **Sintra**, with its fairy-tale woodlands and palaces. Next, enjoy two days exploring fascinating **Évora** and its nearby megaliths. From there, go south and spend a day in peaceful **Tavira**, one of the Algarve's prettiest towns, then take the ferry out to the car-free **Ilha de Tavira**. Continue west to beach- and nightlife-loving **Lagos**. Don't miss the pretty beaches (Batata, Dona Ana and Camilo) south of town. Keep going west until you hit laid-back **Sagres**, where you can visit its dramatically sited fort, surf good waves and contemplate the endless clifftop views. Return

Funicular, Lisbon

north to Lisbon, stopping en route at the coastal town of **Vila Nova de Milfontes**, a great spot for superfresh seafood grilled to perfection. You can eat it right on the waterfront. Spend a day in **Tomar**, a sleepy river town that is home to the staggering Convento de Cristo. Then head to **Coimbra** for two nights. This venerable university town is packed with medieval convents and churches and lively bars (during term time). Spend your last two

days in **Porto**, Lisbon's rival in beauty. Enjoy a day exploring the Ribeira, visiting avant-garde galleries and museums, and taking in the nightlife in the city centre. Then cross the river to **Vila Nova de Gaia** for an introduction to the country's great ports. If time allows, finish with a boat trip along the Rio Douro, passing through dramatic gorges flanked by steeply terraced, centuries-old vineyards.

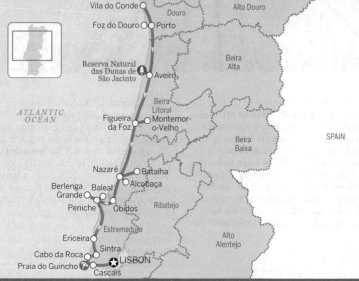

Vila do Conde

Foz do Douro — Porto

Douro

Alto Douro

Beira Alta

Reserva Natural das Dunas de São Jacinto — Aveiro

Beira Litoral

ATLANTIC OCEAN

Figueira da Foz — Montemor-o-Velho

Beira Baixa

SPAIN

Nazaré — Batalha

Alcobaça

Berlenga Grande — Baleal

Peniche — Óbidos

Ribatejo

Ericeira

Estremadura

Alto Alentejo

Cabo da Roca — Sintra

Praia do Guincho — ★ LISBON

Cascais

3 WEEKS Exploring the Atlantic Coast

Scenic shorelines, captivating towns and staggering architectural monuments set the stage for this memorable journey down the Atlantic coast.

PLAN YOUR TRIP ITINERARIES

Begin in **Porto**, the port-wine capital at the mouth of the Douro. Spend two days exploring its historic centre, museums, parks and gardens, plus the beach neighbourhood of **Foz do Douro**. On the third day go north to the seaside town of **Vila do Conde**, a quick and popular beach getaway. Next, head south to **Aveiro**, for rides along its scenic canals from high-prowed *moliceiros* (traditional boats). For a fine day trip from here, take a bus and ferry out to the **Reserva Natural das Dunas de São Jacinto**, a scenic nature reserve and birdwatching site. The popular resort town of **Figueira da Foz** is the next stop; you'll find prime surfing, a touch of nightlife and wide people-packed beaches, with more isolated sands out of town. After a day of sunbaking, make an inland day trip to the striking mountaintop castle of **Montemor-o-Velho**. The picturesque and fun-loving beach town of **Nazaré** is next, and here you can frolic in the waves, enjoy traditional seafood restaurants and take the funicular to a clifftop promontory for superb views. Nazaré is also a good base for exploring the architecturally stunning monasteries (and Unesco World Heritage Sites) in **Alcobaça** and **Batalha**. From there, head south to **Óbidos**, with its cobblestone lanes and upmarket inns. Go west back to the coast to reach **Peniche**, where you'll find excellent beaches, particularly in nearby **Baleal**. From Peniche, be sure to take a boat out to the remote island of **Berlenga Grande**. You can even stay overnight (reserve well ahead). Continue south to **Ericeira**, a whitewashed village perched atop sandstone cliffs. Explore the beaches, feast on seafood, then continue on to the fairy-tale setting of **Sintra**, where picturesque guesthouses make a fine overnight stay. Take the road to the coast, and follow it out to the dramatically set **Cabo da Roca** and down to the windswept beach of **Praia do Guincho**. The next stop is the pretty village of **Cascais**, home to narrow pedestrian lanes, lively outdoor restaurants and leafy gardens. End your journey in **Lisbon**, spending a few days exploring Portugal's vibrant capital.

Top: Ribeira (p363), Porto
Bottom: Baleal beach (p273), Peniche

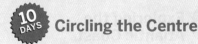

10 DAYS | Circling the Centre

Dramatic scenery, frozen-in-time villages and clifftop castles make for a charming journey on this loop around Portugal's often overlooked interior.

From **Lisbon** head 200km southeast to the historic village of **Castro Verde**. Visit the royal basilica in town then the LPN Interpretative and Environmental Centre, a great spot for bird-watching some 5km north of town. Drive east to **Mértola**, a picturesque medieval settlement perched high above the placid Rio Guadiana. Wander the old streets, go kayaking on the river and overnight in one of the area's charming inns. From Mértola, drive north to **Beja**, a lively town with a walled centre, intriguing museums and a 13th-century castle. For a break from the heat, head to **Praia Fluvial de Monsaraz** and cool off in refreshing Alqueva Lake, then head up to looming **Monsaraz**, a jaw-droppingly beautiful medieval village. From there, it's a short hop to **Évora**, the most vibrant town in the Alentejo – its large cobblestone centre is packed with history (don't miss the Bone Chapel and Roman temple). Évora has great traditional restaurants and makes a good base for visiting nearby Neolithic sites. Head northeast to the marble town of **Vila Viçosa**, home to a staggering palace and peaceful town centre. Next up is **Castelo de Vide**, a wildly remote-feeling town set on a clifftop. Nearby, you can stop in **Marvão** for more magnificent views from a cobblestone village. Continue to **Monsanto**, a photogenic castle-in-the-sky town. Leave early for the two-hour drive to **Vila Nova de Foz Côa**, gateway to some of Iberia's most extensive petroglyphs. From here, it's an easy detour to the vineyards along the Douro. Otherwise, head southwest into the **Parque Natural da Serra da Estrela**, a scenic, mountainous area with great hiking and tranquil guesthouses where you can soak up the scenery – **Manteigas** makes a great base. After a day or two in the mountains, head west to the lively university town of **Coimbra**. Visit the historic campus, stroll the riverbank, feast on hearty Portuguese cooking and catch live Coimbra-style fado. Visit **Conímbriga**, southwest of Coimbra, for a look at Roman ruins, then continue to **Santarém**, with its Gothic architecture, atmospheric restaurants and panoramic views, before finishing the tour in Lisbon.

Top: Mértola (p256)
Bottom: Templo Romano (p221), Évora

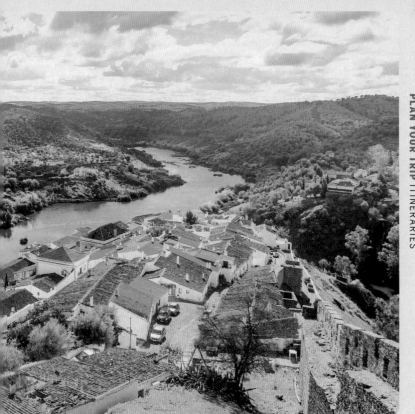

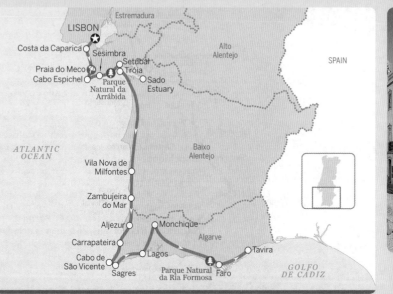

STOCKPHOTOSART/SHUTTERSTOCK ©

2 WEEKS Southern Beauty

This trip will give you a chance to see spectacular contrasts in scenery by following Portugal's southern rivers, beaches and ridges.

From **Lisbon** head to the **Costa da Caparica**, taking in the festive beaches near the town, and then escaping the crowds on wilder beaches to the south. Next head down to **Praia do Meco** for more sandy action and some great seafood. Keep going south to reach the desolate cliffs of **Cabo Espichel**. A good place to stay for the night is at a rural guesthouse outside **Sesimbra**, a fishing village turned resort with open-air restaurants and family-friendly beaches. On the next day, continue east, stopping for a picnic on the forest-lined shores of **Parque Natural da Arrábida**. At night, stay in **Setúbal** for more seafood feasting and a wander through the sleepy old-town quarters. The next day, book a dolphin-watching boat trip along the **Sado Estuary**. From Setúbal, take the ferry across to handsomely sited **Tróia**. Continue south to overnight in **Vila Nova de Milfontes**, a lovely seaside town with fine beaches and charming places to stay. Next is **Zambujeira do Mar**, a tiny village perched above a pretty beach. Follow the coast to **Aljezur**, with its unspoilt, cliff-backed sands, and into the rustic town of **Carrapateira**, with more wild, untouched beaches, plus cafes and guesthouses catering to the surf-loving crowd.

Head south, and you'll reach the southern coast at pretty, laid-back **Sagres**, another surfers' town. Visit Sagres' sea-cliff fortress, followed by the surreal cliffs of **Cabo de São Vicente**.

Go east to **Lagos**, one of the Algarve's liveliest towns, with loads of good sleeping, eating and drinking options. Afterwards, go inland to **Monchique**, with its densely wooded hillsides that offer picturesque walking, cycling and pony-trekking opportunities, and then stop at Termas de Monchique Spa. Back on the coast, stay overnight in the old town centre of lively **Faro**, before journeying out to the **Parque Natural da Ria Formosa**, a lagoon system full of marsh, creeks and dune islands. From there, head to **Tavira**, set with genteel 18th-century buildings straddling the Rio Gilão.

VAL THOERMER/SHUTTERSTOCK ©

Top: Cabo Espichel (p149)
Bottom: Tavira (p172)

Off the Beaten Track: Portugal

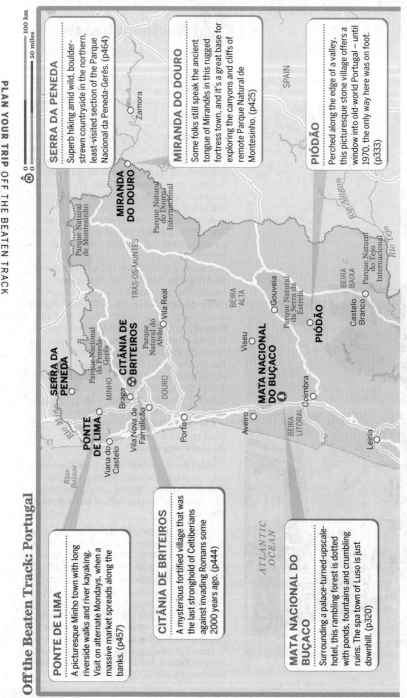

SERRA DA PENEDA

Superb hiking amid wild, boulder-strewn countryside in the northern, least-visited section of the Parque Nacional da Peneda-Gerês. (p464)

MIRANDA DO DOURO

Some folks still speak the ancient tongue of Mirandês in this rugged fortress town, and it's a great base for exploring the canyons and cliffs of remote Parque Natural de Montesinho. (p425)

PIÓDÃO

Perched along the edge of a valley, this picturesque stone village offers a window into old-world Portugal – until 1970, the only way here was on foot. (p333)

PONTE DE LIMA

A picturesque Minho town with long riverside walks and river kayaking. Visit on alternate Mondays, when a massive market spreads along the banks. (p457)

CITÂNIA DE BRITEIROS

A mysterious fortified village that was the last stronghold of Celtiberians against invading Romans some 2000 years ago. (p444)

MATA NACIONAL DO BUÇACO

Surrounding a palace-turned-upscale-hotel, this rambling forest is dotted with ponds, fountains and crumbling ruins. The spa town of Luso is just downhill. (p320)

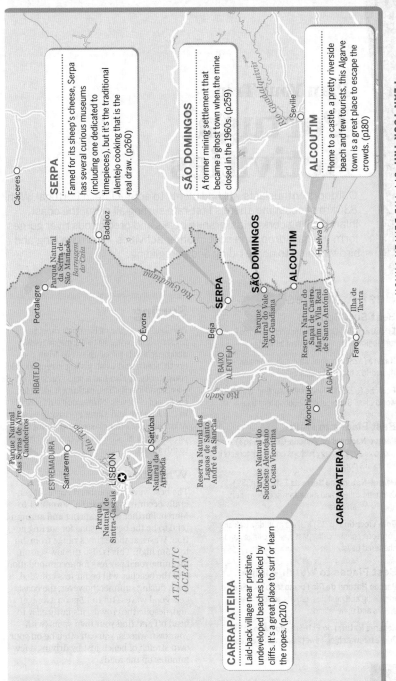

SERPA
Famed for its sheep's cheese, Serpa has several curious museums (including one dedicated to timepieces), but it's the traditional Alentejo cooking that is the real draw. (p260)

SÃO DOMINGOS
A former mining settlement that became a ghost town when the mine closed in the 1960s. (p259)

ALCOUTIM
Home to a castle, a pretty riverside beach and few tourists, this Algarve town is a great place to escape the crowds. (p180)

CARRAPATEIRA
Laid-back village near pristine, undeveloped beaches backed by cliffs. It's a great place to surf or learn the ropes. (p210)

Plan Your Trip

Portugal Activities

Outdoors enthusiasts will find plenty to appreciate in Portugal. With 830km of coastline, there's first-rate surfing all along the coast. Inland, rolling cork fields, granite peaks and precipitous river gorges form the backdrop for a host of other activities – from walking and birdwatching to horse riding and paragliding.

Best Activities

Best Surf Spots

Ericeira (p144) Outstanding breaks on the Praia da Ribeira d'Ilhas just north of town.

Nazaré (p281) Famous waves, including some of the world's biggest breaks.

Peniche (p273) Unforgettable surfing, whether on world-class Supertubos or consistent Baleal.

Best Places to Walk

Parque Nacional da Peneda-Gerês (p463) Stone villages, craggy hilltops and thick forests in Portugal's north.

Parque Natural da Serra da Estrela (p339) Dramatic valleys and mountain scenery where shepherds still roam.

Rota Vicentina (p213) Make a multiday trek along gorgeous coastal cliffs, past sleepy villages and sheltered bays.

Best Places to Watch Wildlife

Parque Natural da Ria Formosa (p164) See migrating and nesting seabirds amid marshes, creeks and dune islands.

Reserva Natural do Estuário do Sado (p152) Prime birdwatching in wetlands near Setúbal.

Surfing

Portugal has some of Europe's most impressive surf, with 30 to 40 major reefs and beaches. It picks up swells from the north, south and west, giving it remarkable consistency. It also has a wide variety of waves and swell sizes, making it ideal for surfers of all levels. Numerous surf schools in the Algarve and along Portugal's western Atlantic coast offer classes and all-inclusive packages for all skill levels, from beginners to advanced.

When to Surf

The best waves in southern Portugal generally occur in winter from November to March. Further north, spring and autumn tend to be the best seasons for surfing action. Waves at these times range from 2m to 4.5m high. This is also the low season, meaning you'll pay less for accommodation, and the beaches will be far less crowded. Even during summer, however, the coast gets good waves (1m to 1.5m on average) and, despite the crowds, it's fairly easy to head off and find your own spots (with your own wheels, you can often be on your own stretch of beach just by driving a few minutes up the road).

WORLD CHAMPIONSHIP WAVES

In 2009 Portugal's surf scene got a real shot in the arm when Supertubos beach near Peniche was chosen as one of 10 stops on the ASP World Tour, the most prestigious international competitive surfing event. For 12 days in October, the beach was packed with surfers from around the world showing off their best moves. The event's organisers apparently liked what they saw – Supertubos has hosted the international contest (today known as the MEO Rip Curl Pro Portugal) nearly every year since then.

Supertubos isn't the only spot in Portugal with legendary breaks. Some 60km north of Peniche, you'll find some of the world's tallest waves, thanks to a deep-water canyon connected to the shoreline. Pro Brazilian surfer Rodrigo Koxa set the world record for the largest wave ever ridden in 2017, when he surfed a wave 24.38m (80ft) high.

Essential Gear

The water temperature here is colder than it is in most other southern European countries, and even in summer you'll probably want a wetsuit. Board and wetsuit hire are widely available at surf shops and surf camps; you can usually score a discount if you rent long-term – otherwise, you'll be paying around €20 to €30 per day for a board and wetsuit, or €15 to €25 per day for the board only.

Prime Spots

One of Portugal's best breaks is at Ericeira (p145), Europe's only World Surfing Reserve. It covers a stretch of some 4km of ocean, with seven world-class waves. South of there, Nazaré (p284) is also famous around the globe for hosting some of the tallest waves ever ridden (over 23m).

Other fabled surf spots include Peniche (p273), where you can count on good waves with just about any wind. Praia do Guincho, near Cascais, sometimes hosts international championships. Another break that's famous among the global surfing community is Carrapateira (p210) in the western Algarve. Schools and clubs head over this way from Lagos and further afield to take advantage of the crashing waves. Nearby, the area around Praia do Penedo is a good choice for beginners.

There are countless other good surf spots up and down the coast including, but by no means limited to, the following, from north to south: Viana do Castelo, Praia da Barra, Costa Nova, Figueira da Foz, Costa da Caparica, Sesimbra, Vila Nova de Milfontes and Zambujeira.

Surf Schools & Operators

There are dozens of schools that can help you improve your surfing game. Most offer weekly packages including simple accommodation (dorms, bungalows or camping), meals and transport to the beach.

Recommended surf camps north of Lisbon include Ericeira's Rapture Surf Camp (p144) and the camps at Baleal (p274).

In the Algarve you'll have your pick of countless operators, many of them concentrated around Lagos, Sagres and Carrapateira.

Online Resources

For information on wave conditions, competitions and more, surf on over to one of these helpful sites:

www.magicseaweed.com International site with English-language surf reports for many Portuguese beaches.

www.surfingportugal.com Official site of the Portuguese Surfing Federation.

www.surftotal.com Portuguese-language site with news about the national surf scene, and webcams showing conditions at a dozen popular beaches around Portugal.

Diving

Portugal offers some of the best diving in Europe. The mainland is home to eight marine protected areas and has over 940km of coastline. You'll find rich sea life and countless wrecks to explore, with wide-ranging appeal for both experienced and novice divers (the 3000 hours of sunshine per year only adds to the appeal).

Portugal Outdoors

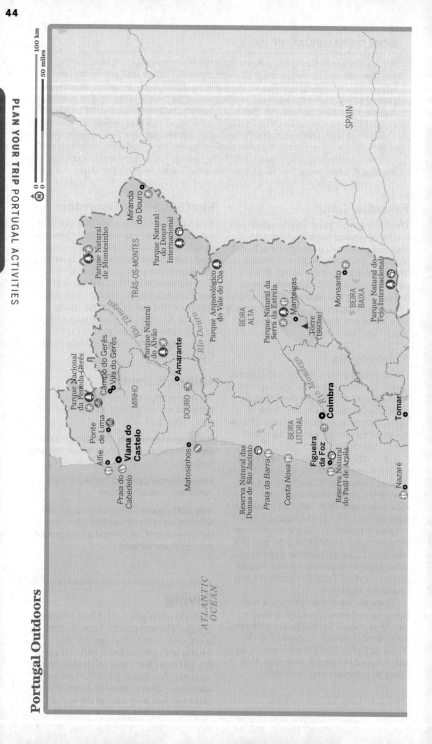

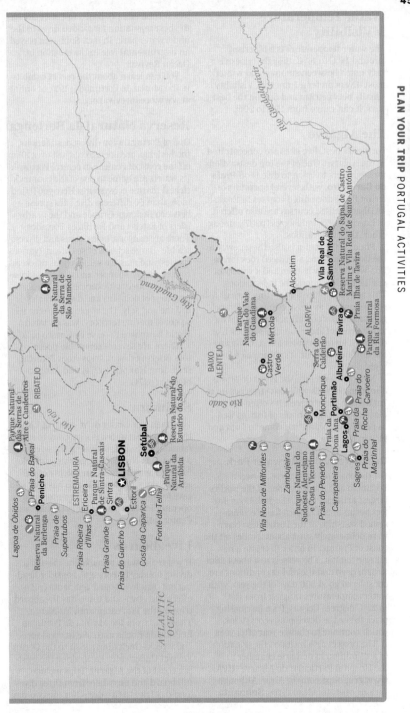

Water Temperature & Visibility

The water temperature is a bit crisp (around 14°C to 16°C, though it doesn't vary much between summer and winter); most divers prefer a 5mm suit. Visibility is usually between 4m and 6m; on the best days, it can range from 15m to 20m.

The Algarve

Portugal's best dive sites are concentrated in the Algarve. One of the top destinations for beginners to learn to dive is off **Praia do Carvoeiro**, with several operators offering PADI-accredited courses in English. PADI-accredited courses are also offered in Lagos (p197) and Sagres (p207), among other Algarve locations.

Praia da Carvoeira is also the gateway to the Pedra da Torre, a terraced rock formation with a sandy bottom and a variety of sea life hidden among the indentations. This is a good place for spotting various fish species as well as crustaceans, nudibranch, gorgonians (soft coral), anemones and different types of algae – at times it feels like diving in an underwater forest. Owing to the minimal current, it's a fine place for night dives.

Near Praia da Luz, the Porto de Mos is a submerged rock wall that stretches up to 7m high in some places. It's often a good place to see large schools of fish, as well as pods of dolphins that come to hunt and play in the area.

Ocean Revival Underwater Park

Off the coast of the Algarve, between Portimão and Alvor, lies one of the world's largest artificial reefs. The ambitious project began in 2012, when four decommissioned warships of the Portuguese Navy were deliberately sunk about 2 miles off the coast of Prainha in order to create a new marine habitat. The vessels rest about 26m to 32m deep and the diving conditions are considered good 300 days of the year, with water temperatures ranging from 14ºC to 22ºC degrees Celsius. It's a fascinating place to see the developing ecosystems, which continue to change year after year.

The project also included the donation of a €1 million hyperbaric chamber to the Hospital Particular do Algarve (HPA; www.grupohpa.com) in Alvor. Although various operators lead dives, **Subnaúta** (www.subnauta.pt), based in Portimão, has the best reputation for guided dives to the underwater park. In fact, Subnaúta played an instrumental role in the creation of Ocean Revival.

You can learn about the reef at exhibits in the Museu de Portimão (p192), or online at www.oceanrevival.org.

Reserva Natural da Berlenga

One of Portugal's top diving destinations, the Berlenga archipelago sits just over 10km off the coast of Peniche in central Portugal. Its waters are home to one of the country's richest marine ecosystems. Here you'll find more than 60 different dive sites spread between Berlenga Grande and the nearby islets of Estelas and Farilhões-Forcados. There are canyons, holes, caves and diverse sea life – large schools of sea bream (various species) and massive sunfish, plus mackerel, conger, moray, snapper and rocky underwater walls dotted with gorgonians. It's also easy to spot dolphins and dwarf whales in June and July. The whole area (some 95 sq km of marine territory) was declared a World Biosphere Reserve by Unesco in 2011.

There are several reputable operators offering diving trips from Peniche, including Haliotis (p274) and AcuaSubOeste (p274).

Sesimbra

Less than a one-hour drive south of Lisbon, the town of Sesimbra is a gateway to some fabulous dive sites, including the wreck of a 170m-long Nigerian cargo ship, suitable for experienced divers, and plenty of rich sea life along the coast. It also has rock and cave formations. A highly recommended operator in the area is Anthia Diving Center (p150).

Liveaboards

If you really want to make the most of a diving holiday to Portugal, consider heading out on a liveaboard. Subnauta (p194) offers one-, two- and three-day liveaboard trips on the 18m catamaran *Xu-Nauta*. These sail from the Marina de Portimão in Praia da Rocha and take in coral reefs and wrecks (including a visit to the Ocean Revival Underwater Park) along the western coast of the Algarve. Trips include full board and anywhere from three dives (one-day trip) to five dives (for the two-day

GREAT OUTDOOR ADVENTURES FOR FAMILIES

➡ Mountain bike through the outback to see the Palaeolithic petroglyphs at Parque Arqueológico do Vale do Côa (p409).

➡ Kayak with your kids down the Rio Mondego (p315) from Penacova to Coimbra.

➡ Learn to surf with the whole family at Hooked Surf School (p135) in Costa da Caparica.

➡ Take the invigoratingly bouncy boat ride with Viamar (p274) from Peniche to Berlenga Grande, then stay overnight in a 17th-century fort converted into a hostel (p276).

➡ Look for dolphins (p207) – and learn about them from an on-board marine biologist – as you ply the Atlantic waters off the Algarve coast.

➡ Walk through a landscape of dramatic mountains and stone shepherds' huts as you climb the glacial Zêzere Valley, then cool off with icy water from a natural spring in Parque Natural da Serra da Estrela (p339).

➡ Scan the horizon for pirates from the 17th-century fort (p150), play king of the castle at the Moorish *castelo*, or build sandcastles of your own on the beach at Sesimbra.

➡ Take the narrow-gauge train to the lovely, wild beaches along Costa da Caparica (p148).

➡ See dinosaur footprints – yes, *real* dinosaur footprints! – at Cabo Espichel (p151) or Monumento Natural das Pegadas dos Dinossáurios (p296).

itinerary) to eight dives (for the three-day trip). One-two-three-day liveaboard, including dives, costs €130/260/365.

Windsurfing & Kitesurfing

Praia do Guincho (p135), west of Sintra, and the beaches near Portimão (p192) in the Algarve are both world-championship windsurfing sites. Other prime spots include (from north to south) Viana do Castelo's Praia do Cabedelo (p447); Lagoa de Óbidos, a pretty lagoon that draws both sailors and windsurfers; and (closer to Lisbon) the Costa da Caparica's Fonte da Telha. In the Algarve, Sagres (p207) attracts pros (its strong winds and fairly flat seas are ideal for free-riding), while Lagos (p195), Albufeira (p186) and Praia da Rocha (p193) cater to all.

Popular venues for windsurfing and kitesurfing lessons include the beaches around Viana do Castelo (p446), Foz do Arelho (p280), Peniche (p274), Praia do Guincho (p135), Lagos (p195) and Tavira (p175).

Boating

Along the coast, especially in the Algarve, pleasure boats predominate, offering everything from barbecue cruises to grotto tours to dolphin-spotting excursions. Inland, Portugal's rivers, lagoons and reservoirs offer a wide variety of boating opportunities, including kayaking, sailing, rafting and canoeing. Rivers popular for boating include the Guadiana, Mondego, Zêzere, Paiva, Minho and Tâmega.

Companies that rent boats and/or operate boat trips can be found in Lagos, Mértola, Barragem do Alqueva, Tomar, Coimbra, Ponte de Lima, Rio Caldo and Amarante, just to name a few.

Walking

Portugal's wonderful walking potential is all the better because so few people know about it. The fairly new Rota Vicentina (p213) offers fabulous views from multiday walks along the coast. The Algarve has some sublime hiking opportunities along the coast, particularly around Sagres, and in the hilly interior. Monchique makes an

SANTIAGO DE COMPOSTELA

Every year thousands of walkers from around the world hike the Camino de Santiago, the classic pilgrimage route from France to Santiago de Compostela, Spain. But what if you want to start in Portugal? Portuguese pilgrims have their own route to Santiago, less crowded but just as interesting for lovers of long-distance walking. Like its sister trail to the north, the Caminho Português has multiple starting points, but the best-known section originates in Porto. Information is available through www.caminhoportosantiago.com.

excellent base. There's also superb walking in the protected Serra do Caldeirão area north of Loulé. Northern Portugal has more mountainous terrain and several lovely, little-visited natural parks.

When to Walk

Summer temperatures can get stiflingly hot in some regions – particularly Trás-os-Montes, Beira Baixa, the Alentejo and the Algarve. To beat the heat, consider travelling in spring (April and May) or autumn (late September and October).

What to Take

Wherever you go, you'll want a hat, strong sun protection and some type of palliative for aching feet. A compass can come in handy, as trail maintenance and signposting are often spotty. Maps (or photocopies thereof) are best obtained at local *turismos* (tourist offices). If you're headed to the showery north, be sure to bring reliable rain gear.

Prime Spots

Southern Portugal offers some lovely hiking opportunities. One of the newest routes (opened in 2013) is the Rota Vicentina (p266), which consists of two signed long-distance trails in the Alentejo, one along the coast (120km), one inland (230km). Both offer picturesque scenery and there are opportunities to stay in guesthouses along the way.

Those interested in walking the breadth of the country should consider the Via Algarviana (p181), a 300km route following paved and unpaved roads between Alcoutim and Sagres that takes two to three weeks. Day hikers will find the Algarve equally rewarding, in places such as Monchique (p214) and Serra do Caldeirão (p184).

In the Beiras, the Parque Natural da Serra da Estrela (p339) forms a beautiful backdrop for walking, with both day hikes and multiday itineraries. In many places you're likely to have the trail to yourself. Especially beautiful is the Vale do Zêzere (p345), a glacial valley at the foot of Torre, Portugal's highest peak. A good base in this region is the mountain village of Manteigas. Also in the Beiras is the beautiful multiday GR-22 walking route, a 540km circuit of *aldeias históricas* (historic villages) including medieval hill towns such as Sortelha, Linhares and Monsanto.

Perhaps the country's best walking is in the far north, where Parque Nacional da Peneda-Gerês (p463) offers gorgeous hikes over mountainous terrain, encompassing forests, villages, high-altitude boulder fields, archaeological sites and ancient Roman milestones. A quiet base for adventure is Campo do Gerês (p469), while a busier touristy base (but with lots of services) is Vila do Gerês (p467). In neighbouring Trás-os-Montes, the natural parks of Montesinho (p422), Alvão (p413) and Douro Internacional (p428) also have some splendid trails connecting the region's remarkably picturesque stone villages.

Closer to civilisation, there are some great day hikes in prime tourist areas, including the walk along the top of Évora's 16th-century aqueduct (p224) and the climb from Sintra to its 9th-century Moorish castle (p124).

Walking Tours

If you love to walk but hate to plan, why not consider an organised walking tour? The companies listed here offer both group walking tours – complete with tour leader – and self-guided tours where you walk independently, following an itinerary provided by the tour company, with prearranged meals and lodging included in the price.

About 10km north of Sagres, walking-guide author Julie Statham runs **Portugal Walks** (☎+44 7393 479 489; www.portugal walks.com), which offers week-long packages (€860 to €980), as well as self-guided walks (14 days from €870) in mainland Portugal, plus Madeira and the Azores.

Another dependable Portuguese outfitter offering guided walks throughout the country is **A2Z Adventures** (☎911 122 293; www.a2z-adventures.com; Largo da Bica, Castelo Novo).

Ecotourism company Sistemas de Ar Livre (p153), in Setúbal, arranges activities including three-hour guided walks.

Three noteworthy outfitters based out of the UK also run tours. **ATG Oxford** (www.atg-oxford.co.uk) offers week-long guided walking holidays between Sintra and Cascais; **Headwater** (www.headwater.com) leads week-long walking trips as well as cycling jaunts; and **Ramblers Holidays** (www.ramblersholidays.co.uk) has guided seven- to 10-day walking holidays in the Minho, the Douro and the Algarve.

Resources

Many *turismos* and natural-park offices offer free brochures about local walks, although materials frequently go out of print due to insufficient funding. Other organisations that produce free maps of their own trails include Odiana (www.odiana.pt) in the Algarve and the Centro de Interpretação da Serra da Estrela (p341) in the town of Seia in the Serra da Estrela.

Portugal uses a system of coloured blazes to mark its trails. White and red are the colours of choice for the major multiday trails known as Grandes Rotas, while red and yellow blazes indicate Pequenas Rotas (shorter day hikes).

Cycling

Portugal has many exhilarating opportunities for mountain biking (*bicicleta todo terreno;* BTT). Monchique (p214) and Tavira (p172) in the Algarve, Sintra (p124) and Setúbal (p152) in central Portugal and Parque Nacional da Peneda-Gerês (p463) in the north are all popular starting points.

Bicycle trails are also growing in popularity. Rio Lima in the north has a handful of short greenways (ranging from 8km to 13.3km) that are popular with cyclists, walkers and runners. Another rail-to-trails initiative, the 49km Ecopista do Dão (www.ecopista-portugal.com) between Viseu and Santa Comba Dão in the Beiras, opened in 2011; there are even places to rent bikes near the start in Santa Comba Dão. Down south, the ambitious Ecovia do Litoral is a 214km cycling route across the Algarve that connects Cabo de São Vicente at Portugal's southwestern tip to Vila Real de Santo António on the Spanish border. For more information on the *ecovia* (walking

---

BEST READS BEFORE HITTING THE TRAIL

The following books, available online or at bookshops in Lisbon and Porto, are great planning aids for some of the country's best hikes:

➡ *Walking in Portugal: 40 Graded Short and Multi-day Walks Throughout the Country,* (2018) by Simon Whitmarsh and Andrew Mok – The most comprehensive, up-to-date guide for walking routes across the country.

➡ *Walking in the Algarve: 40 Coastal & Mountain Walks,* (revised 2014) by Julie Statham – An excellent guide authored by a British-born Algarve resident and tour leader.

➡ *Algarve: 5 Car Tours, 50 Long and Short Walks,* (revised 2016) by Brian and Eileen Anderson – Lots of useful information for exploring the southern coast.

➡ *Portugal Passo-a-Passo: 20 Passeios por Portugal,* (2004) by Abel Melo e Sousa and Rui Cardoso – A great little guide for anyone who reads Portuguese, with full-colour pictures and maps outlining 20 hikes around the country.

➡ *Guide to Walking Trails in the Algarve* (www.iltm.com/__novadocuments/62282) Published by Turismo de Portugal, this free downloadable guide has info on dozens of walks in the south.

and cycling path) and other *ecovias* around Portugal, the *Ecovias Portugal Road Book* with maps and other key info is available for purchase online at www.ecovias portugal.wix.com/ecoviasportugal.

Meanwhile, bike paths have become fixtures of the urban landscape around Lisbon and in northern cities such as Porto, Coimbra and Guarda; popular bike trails have also cropped up in coastal venues such as the Estremadura's Pinhal de Leiria (p292) and the Lisbon coast between Cascais and Praia do Guincho.

Cycling Tours

If you're looking for a good day trip or a longer cycling holiday, there are a number of excellent companies that can point you in the right direction.

In Lisbon, **Portugal Bike** (☑214 783 153; www.portugalbike.com; Rua Dom João V, 4, Caneças, Lisbon) has an excellent selection of bike tours. Trips go through the Algarve, the Minho or the Alentejo. There's also a route that follows the Camino de Santiago through northern Portugal and into Spain. Tours run six to 13 days and are available guided or self-guided.

Pedal Portugal (www.pedalportugal.com) is a well-established company offering both guided and self-guided bike tours throughout Portugal.

Based out of the USA, **Easy Rider Tours** (www.easyridertours.com) features several guided cycling itineraries in the Minho, Alentejo and Algarve, and along the Lisbon coast near Sintra.

From the UK, **Saddle Skedaddle** (www.skedaddle.co.uk) has both guided and self-guided tours lasting seven to nine days. Trips go through the eastern Beiras and the Alentejo (with a coastal and an inland route).

Wildlife Watching

Portugal boasts myriad spots to observe birds and other wildlife, especially in Atlantic coastal lagoons and the deep river canyons along the Spanish border. Birdwatching opportunities are especially good, with a wide variety of habitats and over 360 species that are regularly spotted. Portugal's leading ornithological society, **Sociedade Portuguêsa para o Estudo de Aves** (☑213 220 430; www.spea.pt; Av Columbano Bordalo Pinheiro 87, 3rd fl; ⊙9.30am-1pm & 2-6pm Mon-Fri), runs government-funded projects to map the distribution of Portugal's breeding birds. Portugal's long coastline is tailor-made for boat trips to view marine life, including dolphins, pelagic fish and even sea turtles.

Northern Portugal

In the north, you find the dramatic Tejo and Douro gorges, where vultures and eagles nest in the Parque Natural do Tejo Internacional (p335) and Parque Natural do Douro Internacional (p428). The latter is a mix of rocky outcroppings and riverside woodlands, where you can spot Egyptian vultures, Bonelli's eagles, Eurasian griffon vultures, golden eagles, Eurasian eagle owls and red kites, among many other species.

The Parque Natural de Montesinho (p422) is a mountainous area of scrubland, craggy hillsides, forests of oak and chestnut, and riverine woodlands. Its most iconic resident is the rust-coloured Iberian wolf – it is the last major refuge for this endangered animal. In the forests are roe deer, otters and wild boar. Bird species include the golden eagle, the royal eagle, Montagu's harrier and the black stork.

Portugal's only national park, the Parque Nacional da Peneda-Gerês (p463) is a mix of craggy peaks, mountain scrubland, and forests of pine and oak, along with rivers, lakes and marshland. Key species include the short-toed eagle, peregrine falcon, scops owl, red-backed shrike and rufous-tailed rock thrush.

The small, privately owned **Faia Brava Natural Reserve** (www.atnatureza.org) has granite cliffs where you can spot soaring griffon vultures, Egyptian vultures, Bonelli's eagles, royal eagles and black storks.

Central Portugal

Near Lisbon, the Sado Estuary is a prime birding hotspot with tidal mudflats, salt marshes, pine forests, meadowlands and pastures. Reserva Natural do Estuário do Sado (p152) is a good base for spotting some 250 avian species, including black-crowned night herons, glossy ibis, greater flamingos, kestrels, purple swamphens and great spotted cuckoos. The Sado Estuary is also a notable spot for dolphin watching, with recommended operators like Vertigem Azul (p153) offering cruises from Setúbal.

North of Lisbon, the Reserva Natural da Berlenga (p276) is an ideal place for observing seabirds: you can spot guillemots, great shearwaters, Wilson's storm-petrels, black-headed gulls, razorbills and even puffins on and near the rocky islands.

Other good places for birdwatching include Reserva Natural do Paúl de Arzila near Coimbra and the Dunas de São Jacinto (p328) near Aveiro.

In the Alentejo, Castro Verde is close to good birdwatching, and the surrounding region was listed as a Unesco Biosphere Reserve in 2017. Stop in the LPN Interpretative & Environmental Centre (p260) for details on trails offering the best wildlife watching. This area of open fields and grasslands has a surprising array of birdlife, including steppe birds such as the great bustard, Montagu's harrier and the black-bellied sandgrouse. With luck you might spot the very rare Iberian imperial eagle. There is also the odd sighting of the rare Iberian lynx.

Southern Portugal

Though best known for its beaches, the Algarve has diverse habitats, including salt marshes, dunes, tidal mudflats and lagoons. Inland lies a transitional area between coast and mountain.

Prime birdwatching spots include the Serra do Caldeirão, Parque Natural do Vale do Guadiana and the Reserva Natural do Sapal de Castro Marim e Vila Real de Santo António.

The Parque Natural da Ria Formosa (p164) is one of the best places in the Algarve for wildlife watching. Covering an area of tidal flats, coastal lagoons and dune-covered islands, the 160-sq-km hectare reserve teems with birdlife. Commonly spotted species include purple herons, European bee-eaters, Kentish plovers, marsh harriers and booted eagles.

The local environmental organisation Formosamar (p164) offers tours from Olhão in the Algarve, including a 2½-hour trip (€35 per person, minimum four people) in Parque Natural da Ria Formosa, employing marine biologists and raptor specialists as guides.

For birdwatching and other nature-oriented guided excursions in the Algarve, Natura Algarve (p165) offers boat-based trips through the Parque Natural da Ria Formosa.

UK-based Naturetrek (www.naturetrek. co.uk) runs a seven-day birdwatching excursion around southern Portugal starting at £1495.

Various companies in the Algarve offer dolphin-spotting trips, including Mar Ilimitado (p207), Algarve Water World (p198) and Dolphins Driven (p186).

Top birdwatching guides leading private tours all across the Algarve include João Jara of **Birds & Nature** (☏913 299 990; www.birds.pt; half/full day from €100/160) and British expat **Simon Wates** (☏282 639 418; www.algarvebirdman.com).

Rock Climbing, Paragliding & Adrenaline Sports

In the far north, the granite peaks of Parque Nacional da Peneda-Gerês (p463) are a climber's paradise. Other popular places are the schist cliffs at Nossa Senhora do Salto, east of Porto; the rugged 500m-tall granite outcropping of Cántaro Magro in the Serra da Estrela (p339); the limestone crags of Reguengo do Fetal near Fátima; the sheer rock walls of Penedo da Amizade, just below Sintra's Moorish castle; the dramatic quartzite ridge of Penha Garcia, near Monsanto in Beira Baixa; and Rocha da Pena (p185) in the Algarve.

Useful organisations for climbers include **Clube Nacional de Montanhismo** (☏917 827 472; www.cnm.org.pt; 2nd fl, Rua Formosa 303, Porto) and **Grupo de Montanha e Escalada de Sintra** (www.gmesintra.com).

Paragliding is also popular in the north. Two prime launch sites are Linhares (p358) in the Serra da Estrela and Alvados

ALTERNATIVE ACTIVITIES

Given Portugal's embarrassment of riches for walkers and water-sports enthusiasts, it's easy for other activities to get lost in the shuffle. Don't miss these other opportunities during your visit:

Skiing Yes, skiing! Believe it or not, Portugal has a downhill ski run. The country's highest peak, 1993m-high Torre in Parque Natural da Serra da Estrela (p341), offers basic facilities including three lifts and equipment rental. Alternatively, if you're really hard up, you can always hit the rather surreal 'dry ski' run at SkiParque (p341) east of Manteigas.

Photography Make a photo-taking pilgrimage to some of Portugal's stunning *miradouros* (scenic viewpoints). São Leonardo de Galafura (p407), overlooking northern Portugal's terraced port wine vineyards, is one of the finest, but you'll find plenty more, from Lisbon (p52) to the Ericeira World Surfing Reserve (p144) to the Rio Douro canyon (p429) along the Spanish border.

Foodie tours and courses Take a culinary-themed walking tour (p82) or hone your cooking skills with a Portuguese chef in Lisbon (p82) or the Algarve (p175).

Hot springs Soak in the spa at Termas de Luso (p321), Termas de Chaves (p417) or Termas de Monchique (p214).

Caving Explore a cave (p296) or two (p296) in the Parque Natural das Serras de Aire e Candeeiros.

---

in the Parque Natural das Serras de Aire e Candeeiros (p296).

Eco-aware, Sesimbra-based Vertente Natural (p150) offers trekking, canyoning, canoeing, diving and rappelling, while Porto-based **Detours** (☎966 054 152; www.detours.pt) offers waterfall treks and canyoning, as well as off-track tours around the Douro in 4WD vehicles.

Located outside Coimbra, **Capitão Dureza** (☎919 079 852; www.capitaodureza.com; Rua Principal 64, Telhado) is a one-stop shop for high-adrenaline activities including rafting, canyoning, abseiling (rappelling), mountain biking and trekking.

Porto-based **Trilhos** (☎225 504 604; www.trilhos.pt; Rua de Belém 94, Porto) ✈ is another reputable outfitter, offering climbing, caving, canyoning, trekking and other adventure sports.

Horse Riding

Horse riding is a fantastic way to experience Portugal's countryside. Lusitano thoroughbreds hail from Portugal, and experienced riders can take dressage lessons at the **Escola de Equitação de Alcainça** (www.eealcainca.pt), near Mafra, in Estremadura.

Otherwise, there are dozens of horse-riding centres – especially in the Alentejo, and in the Algarve at places such as Silves, Lagos and Albufeira. Northern Portugal also offers some pleasant settings for rides, including Campo do Gerês (p469) at the edge of Parque Nacional da Peneda-Gerês. Rates are usually around €20 to €30 per hour.

Switzerland-based **Equitour** (www.equitour.com) offers eight-day riding holidays (€1200 to €2000 per person), including accommodation and some meals. Its signature tour follows the Alentejo Royal Horse Stud Trail, with stays at grand country estates. Other destinations include the Alentejo coast and the rugged terrain of northern Portugal.

The Wyoming-based outfit **Equitours** (www.equitours.com), America's largest and oldest, offers a year-round classical dressage programme on Lusitano horses at the Escola de Equitação de Alcainça. Rates including accommodation plus up to three hours of riding per day start at US$220 in low season, and up to US$275 in high season. Equitours also offers several different multiday rides around the country from around US$1850 (for an eight-day trip along the Alentejo coast), including lodging and food.

Pastéis de nata (custard tarts)

Plan Your Trip

Eat & Drink
Like a Local

Settling down to a meal with friends is one of life's great pleasures for the Portuguese, who take pride in simple but flavourful dishes honed to perfection over the centuries. Seafood, roast meats, freshly baked bread and velvety wines are key staples in the everyday feast that is eating in Portugal.

The Year in Food

Spring

In late spring and early summer, you'll see signs advertising *caracois* (snails). These little delicacies are cooked in olive oil, garlic and herbs and are quite tasty. They go nicely with a cold beer.

Summer

Head to the market for bountiful fruits and vegetables: plump tomatoes, juicy peaches, *nísperos* (loquats), strawberries and other delights. Sardines, much loved along the coast (especially in Lisbon), are available from May through October, and are generally bigger and juicier in July and August.

Autumn

In September the Douro Valley begins its annual grape harvest; it's a festive time to visit and some wineries allow visitors to take part. It's also the season of pomegranates and persimmons.

Winter

During cold days Portuguese hunker down over hearty dishes such as *cozido à portuguesa,* a dish of mixed roast meats, potatoes, cabbage and carrots. Rich soups like *canja* (chicken soup) and *sopa de peixe* (fish soup) are also popular. In the Minho, January to March is the season for tender grilled eels.

Food Experiences

Meals of a Lifetime

Vila Joya (p187) Delightful two-Michelin–star restaurant by the sea.

Alma (p98) Brilliantly creative dishes in Lisbon by culinary superstar Henrique Sá Pessoa.

Botequim da Mouraria (p227) Fantastic traditional Alentejan cooking in a tiny bar-seating-only tavern in Évora.

Tasca do Celso (p267) Wonderful cuisine and a charming rustic ambience on the Alentejo coast in Vila Nova de Milfontes.

Restaurante O Barradas (p191) Some 3km from Silves, this delightful converted farmhouse restaurant sources organic fish, meat and fruits in season.

DOC (p408) Delectable fare and an unmatched wine list at an indoor-outdoor restaurant right on the Douro.

Mar à Vista (p145) Outstanding seafood in the coastal enclave of Ericeira.

Pedra de Sal (p322) A cosy dining room that serves phenomenal Iberian pork dishes.

Restaurante de Casa das Penhas Douradas (p346) Feast on sophisticated seasonal fare at this fabulous mountaintop restaurant in the high reaches of the Parque Natural da Serra da Estrela.

Belcanto (p98) Prepare for a dazzling meal at this celebrated restaurant of José Avillez in Lisbon.

Restaurant da Adraga (p132) Excellent fresh fish served just steps from the ocean in a famous but unfussy spot west of Sintra.

Restaurante António Padeiro (p287) An atmospheric place with legendary cooking in the historic town of Alcobaça.

O Paparico (p388) A slice of rustic romance, just north of Porto, serving wonderfully authentic Portuguese food.

Cheap Treats

Pastel de nata Custard tart, ideally served warm and dusted with cinnamon.

Travesseiro A rolled puff pastry filled with almond-and-egg-yolk custard. Find them in Sintra.

Tinned fish Sardines, mackerel and tuna served with bread, olives and other accompaniments are quite popular in Lisbon. Try Sol e Pesca (p97).

Francesinha Porto's favourite hangover snack is a thick open-faced sandwich covered in melted cheese.

Marzipan In the Algarve, this very sweet almond-infused confection is a local favourite.

Grilled chicken Rotisserie chicken is an art form in Portugal. Spice it up with piri-piri (hot sauce).

Bifana A bread roll served with a slice of fried pork inside. They're best in the Alentejo.

Ovos Moles Aveiro is famous for its eggy, sugary pastries.

Dare to Try

Tripe People from Porto aren't called *tripeiros* (tripe-eaters) for nothing. Try the surprisingly tasty *tripas à modo do Porto*, made of tripe, beans and sausage.

Arroz de cabidelo Rice soaked in chicken's blood may sound foul, but it's a bloody good delicacy. The pork variant is called *arroz de sarrabulho*.

Morcela Sausage made with pig's blood and perhaps rice and pork.

Caracois Smaller and less fancy than escargots, these are snails, plain and simple. Toothpick prying skills required.

Torresmos Slices of pig skin and fat served up deep-fried. Makes a great bar snack.

Food & Wine Festivals

Lisbon Restaurant Week (www.thefork.pt; ⊘late Feb-early Mar) This festival offers top-value set-price discounts at participating restaurants.

Essência do Vinho (www.essenciadovinhoporto. com; ⊘late Feb) A wine festival in Porto.

Festival Internacional do Chocolate (✆262 955 561; www.festival-chocolate.cm-obidos.pt; adult/child €6.50/free; ⊘Mar/Apr; ⊞) Chocolate lovers descend on the pretty medieval town of Óbidos in March.

Peixe em Lisboa (p85) A week of seafood feasting in April at top restaurants in Lisbon.

Festa de Santo António (Festival of St Anthony; www.lisboanarua.com/festasdelisboa; ⊘12-13 Jun) Lisbon's lively street party is a great opportunity to feast on chargrilled sardines and roast suckling pig.

Feira do Alvarinho (p455) In June or July, Monção in the Minho pays its respects to its most famous produce, the refreshing Alvarinho white wine.

Festival do Marisco (p171) A sinful seafood festival held in August in the Algarve.

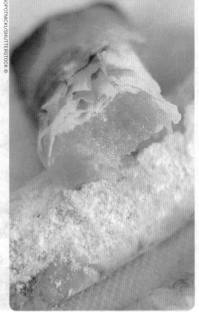

Travesseiro (almond custard pastry)

Cozinha dos Ganhões (Festival de Gastronomia Alentejana; Rua Engenheiro André de Brito Tavares; ⊘Nov or Dec) A lively culinary festival held in Estremoz.

Local Specialities

Bread remains integral to every meal, and it even turns up in some main courses. Be on the lookout for *açorda* (bread stew, often served with shellfish), *migas* (crumbled bread cooked up with pork and other meats) and *ensopados* (stews with toasted or deep-fried bread).

Seafood stews are superb in Portugal, particularly *caldeirada*, which is a mix of fish and shellfish in a rich broth, not unlike a bouillabaisse. *Bacalhau* (dried salt-cod) is bound up in myth, history and tradition, and is excellent in baked dishes.

Lisbon

Simplicity, pristine ingredients and creativity mark Lisbon's gourmet scene. Chefs such as Henrique Sá Pessoa at

---

PRICE RANGES

The following price ranges refer to a main course.

€ less than €10

€€ €10–20

€€€ more than €20

Cataplana (seafood stew)

TOP MARKETS

Every sizable town has a local produce market where you can assemble a feast of a picnic (breads, cheeses, olives, fruits, vegetables, smoked
meats and more) for very little cash.
Here are a few of our favourites:

➡ Mercado da Ribeira (p95), Lisbon

➡ Mercado do Livramento (p156),
Setúbal

➡ Mercado Municipal (p183), Loulé

➡ Mercado Municipal (p226), Évora

➡ Mercado Municipal Dom Pedro V
(p317), Coimbra

➡ Mercado Municipal (p437), Braga

➡ Mercado do Bolhão (p371), Porto

Alma (p98), João Rodrigues at Feitoria
(p107), José Avillez at Belcanto (p98) and
Ljubomir Stanisic at 100 Maneiras (p101),
among others, have put the Portuguese
capital on the gastronomic map with
ingredient-focused tasting menus that
often put a spin on comfort foods such as
slow-cooked suckling pig and *bacalhau*.

The Algarve

This is a shellfish zone, with hordes of
fresh clams, oysters, mussels, cockles and
whelks. Don't go past the seafood *cataplana* (a seafood stew) and *xerém* (corn mash
made with cockles).

The Alentejo

Warning to vegetarians: pork will confront
you at every repast. The culinary star is
porco preto, a high-quality 'black pork'
made from pigs that graze on acorns.
Bread also figures heavily; you'll find it
in gazpacho or *açorda*. During hunting
season, *perdiz* (partridge), *lebre* (hare)
and *javali* (wild boar) are popular. The
Alentejo also has surf-and-turf blends such
as *carne de porco à alentejana* (braised
pork with baby clams).

Estremadura & Ribatejo

Seafood dominates the culinary palate in
Estremadura; *caldeiradas de peixe* (fish
stews) rule the menus, closely followed by

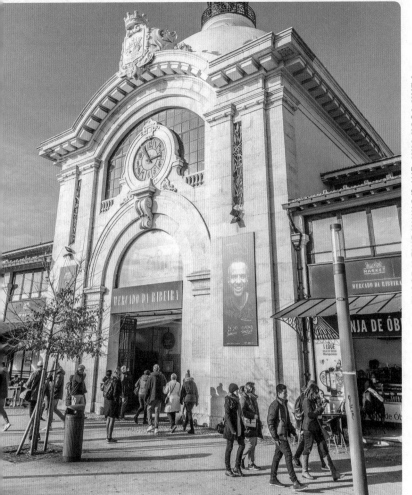

Top: Mercado da Ribeira (p95), Lisbon

Bottom: *Carne de porco à alentejana* (braised pork with baby clams)

Alma restaurant (p98), Lisbon

or white), *caldo verde* (Galician kale and potato soup), *broa de Milho* (golden corn loaf), thrifty *sopa seca* (dry soup) and seasonal eel-like lamprey, trout and salmon dishes.

escabeche (marinated vinegar fish stew) and *sopas de mariscos* (shellfish soups). Carnivores should head to Ribatejo – this is meat and tripe country.

The Beiras

There's plenty of *bacalhau* and *ovos moles*, egg cakes and *chanfana* (goat or lamb stews), plus Atlantic seafood. Sausages are popular, as are cheeses, especially Rabaçal cheese and *queijo serra da Estrela* (Serra cheese).

The Douro & Trás-os-Montes

The north is known for its pork dishes, *cabrito assado* (roast kid) and *posta de barrosã* (beef from a rare breed of cattle). The pork-free *alheira* (a bread and meat sausage) was invented by the Jewish people during the Inquisition. Crops of figs, cherries, almonds, chestnuts and oranges abound.

The Minho

The Minho produces the famous *vinho verde* (green wine – 'green' because it's made from immature grapes, either red

How to Eat & Drink

When to Eat

➡ *Café da manhã* (breakfast, 8am to 10am) is generally a simple affair with coffee and a bread roll or pastry.

➡ *Almoço* (lunch, noon to 3pm) can be a two-course fixed-price special, or something more casual, depending on the locale.

➡ *Jantar* (dinner, 7pm to 10pm) generally features more elaborate (and slightly pricier) dishes, though some places specialise in *petiscos* (sharing plates).

Where to Eat

Tasca (tavern) Old-fashioned place with daily specials, fair prices and a local crowd.

Churrasqueira (grill house) Specialising in chargrilled meats.

Marisqueira (seafood restaurant) Serves up fish and crustaceans, often priced by the kilo.

Cervejaria (beer house) Good for snacking and socialising.

Adega (wine tavern) Usually decorated with wine casks and boasting a rustic, cosy ambience; expect hearty, inexpensive meals.

Menu Decoder

Couvert The bread, olives and other nibbles brought to your table; note that these are not free.

Dose Portion, generally big enough for two people.

Ementa turística Tourist menu.

Meia dose Half-portion, big enough for one person.

Petiscos Tapas/snacks.

Postre Dessert.

Prato do dia Daily special or dish of the day.

Serviço Service charge.

Regions at a Glance

Lisbon & Around

History
Food & Wine
Nightlife

Ghosts of the Past

History is everywhere, from roofless cathedrals that bore witness to Europe's most devastating earthquake to the 1000-year-old castle on the hill. There are Roman ruins, medieval churches, 16th-century convents and more.

Culinary Powerhouses

Ever-inventive chefs showcase the bounty of field and ocean, and traditional restaurants serve Spanish, Italian, Indian, French and other cuisines. Cinematic views, al fresco meals and buzzing dining rooms complete the experience.

Music-Fuelled Nights

Nights out range from kerbside drinking in Bairro Alto to live fado shows in Alfama. Put your hands in the air at club Lux, listen to up-and-coming bands at Musicbox – the options are limitless.

p63

The Algarve

Beaches
Seafood
Activities

Captivating Coasts

Sun-kissed shores come in many forms in the Algarve: scenic coves, family-friendly bays, pounding surf. Beaches along the rugged west coast are more remote and natural. Those further east have bigger tourist infrastructures.

Seafood Feasts

Seafood plays a starring role in the Algarve – with superb *cataplanas* (seafood stews) and a vast range of grilled fish.

Outdoor Adventures

The Algarve offers a plethora of organised activities, especially for children, with water parks, horse riding and pirate-ship cruises. Also on offer are birdwatching, walking, thermal baths, surfing and boat trips.

p158

The Alentejo

Medieval Villages
Food & Wine
Scenery

Relics of the Past

Medieval villages proliferate in the Alentejo. Marvão, Monsaraz, Mértola, Estremoz and Elvas all have eye-catching, historic castles.

Traditional Cuisine

The Alentejo is known for its produce, especially *porco preto* (black pork). Vineyards cover the region, and there's a well-established network of wineries.

Mesmerising Landscapes

This region boasts great walks and scenic drives. Highlights include craggy mountains, rivers, gorges, and hillsides dotted with cork trees, olive groves and wildflowers. Parque Natural do Vale do Guadiana is particularly striking.

p216

Estremadura & Ribatejo

Architecture
Seafood
Surfing

Monasteries

A cluster of Unesco World Heritage Sites, Tomar, Batalha and Alcobaça are splendid religious monuments easily reached from Lisbon. With soaring arches, these medieval-Renaissance masterpieces are *the* reason to visit central Portugal.

Coastal Feasts

Fresh fish and shellfish abound along this region's coast; satisfy your seafood craving in coastal towns like Nazaré and São Martinho do Porto.

Legendary Breaks

Near Peniche, the waves of Baleal and Supertubos draw throngs from around the globe with world-class swell. Peniche has surf camps and make a great base for a surf holiday.

p271

The Beiras

Castles
Scenery
Culture

Fortified Frontier

The inland Beiras are filled with fortresses that once guarded the country's eastern frontier with Spain, from Folgosinho's fairytale minicastle to the elaborate star-shaped ramparts of Almeida.

Grand Views

The rocky heights of the Serra da Estrela are a revelation of cool air, magnificent vistas and great walks. Portugal's highest mountains see a stream of outdoor enthusiasts.

University Life

Portugal's oldest university town, Coimbra, wears its tradition proudly, as evidenced by its medieval architecture and the black capes still worn by students. One of the city's big events is the annual Queima das Fitas, held at school year's end.

p306

Porto, the Douro & Trás-os-Montes

Scenery
Wine & Port
Nightlife

Rivers & Rocks

Porto captivates with its pretty squares and riverside setting. Other stars include the stone villages and 30,000-year-old rock carvings at Vila Nova de Foz Côa.

Tastings & Wine Country

You can taste the world's best ports in Vila Nova de Gaia, then follow up with a wine-tasting ramble through vineyard country in the Douro and southern Trás-os-Montes.

Drinking & Revelry

Porto's bar-crammed Galerias is the party hub, with retro-cool bars and live-music haunts. Try Ribeira for mellow wine bars, and beachside Foz do Douro for drinks with Atlantic views.

p362

The Minho

History
Food & Wine
Activities

Medieval Gems

Head to medieval Guimarães to discover Portugal's birthplace. Even more stunning is Braga, with its 1000-year-old cathedral. Then there's the Celtic settlement of Citânia de Briteiros, atmospheric Viana do Castelo and the cinematic Valença do Minho citadel.

Fine Dining

Braga has first-rate restaurants, while Viana do Castelo and Guimarães also have gems. And the Minho produces some great wines, including the refreshing Alvarinho.

Surfing & Hiking

There's top surfing in Minho, particularly off Praia do Cabedelo. Parque Nacional da Peneda-Gerês has great hiking – choose from short or full-day hikes.

p430

On the Road

The Minho
(p430)

Porto,
the Douro &
Trás-os-Montes
(p362)

The Beiras
(p306)

Estremadura
& Ribatejo
(p271)

Lisbon &
Around
(p63)

The Alentejo
(p216)

The Algarve
(p158)

Top: Funicular, Chiado (p70)

Bottom: Lisbon skyline with Castelo de São Jorge (p71)

Lisbon & Around

POP 547,700

Best Places to Eat

➡ Alma (p98)

➡ Belcanto (p98)

➡ Cervejaria Ramiro (p95)

➡ Mercado da Ribeira (p95)

Best Places to Sleep

➡ Palácio Belmonte (p92)

➡ Casa do Príncipe (p93)

➡ Santiago de Alfama (p93)

➡ Lisbon Calling (p90)

Why Go?

Spread across steep hillsides that overlook the Rio Tejo, Lisbon has captivated visitors for centuries. Windswept vistas reveal the city in all its beauty: Roman and Moorish ruins, white-domed cathedrals, grand plazas lined with sun-drenched cafes. The real delight of discovery, though, is delving into the narrow cobblestone lanes.

As yellow trams clatter through tree-lined streets, *lisboêtas* stroll through lamplit old quarters, much as they've done for centuries. Gossip is exchanged over fresh bread and wine at tiny patio restaurants as fado singers perform in the background. In other parts of town, Lisbon reveals her youthful alter ego at bohemian bars and riverside clubs, late-night street parties and eye-catching boutiques selling all things classic and cutting-edge.

Just outside Lisbon, there's more – enchanting woodlands, gorgeous beaches and seaside villages – all ripe for discovery.

When to Go
Lisbon

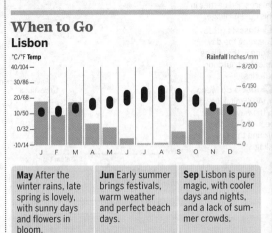

May After the winter rains, late spring is lovely, with sunny days and flowers in bloom.

Jun Early summer brings festivals, warm weather and perfect beach days.

Sep Lisbon is pure magic, with cooler days and nights, and a lack of summer crowds.

Lisbon & Around Highlights

① Alfama (p70) Getting lost in the narrow village-like lanes of this district, searching for the soul of fado.

② Bairro Alto (p70) Bar-hopping your way through the cobblestone streets of this nightlife-loving area.

③ Chiado (p70) Taking in the pleasant outdoor cafes and restaurants of this elegant neighbourhood.

④ Tram 28E (p90) Taking a rattling, rollercoaster ride through the city.

⑤ Mosteiro dos Jerónimos (p79) Gazing upon this Manueline fantasy.

⑥ Cais do Sodré (p95) Checking out the burgeoning new bar scene.

⑦ Sintra (p124) Striding through enchanted forests to above-the-clouds palaces and castles in this quaint village.

⑧ Cascais (p133) Spending the day taking in the village lanes and outdoor eateries.

⑨ Aldeia do Meco (p149) Frolicking in the waves off the beautiful beaches around this tiny village.

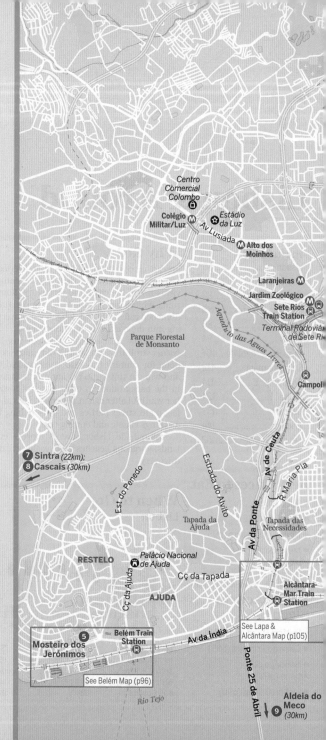

Lumiar

Quinta das
Conchas

Estádio
José de
Alvalade

Terminal
Campo Grande

Cidade
Universitária

Alvalade

Roma

Entrecampos

Roma-
Areeiro

Campo Grande

Av das Forças Armadas

Entrecampos
Train Station

Campo
Pequeno

Av Joao XXI

Areeiro

See Marquês de Pombal
& Around Map (p92)

Pç de
Espanha

Praça de
Espanha

São
Sebastião

Saldanha

Alameda

Parque

Picoas

Arroios

Parque
Eduardo
VII

Anjos

Marquês
de Pombal

Intendente

moreiras
hopping
enter

RATO

Rato

Av da Liberdade

Avenida

Martim
Moniz

ESTRELA

See Chiado & Bairro
Alto Map (p72)

Bairro Alto **2**

3 Chiado

Cais do
Sodre

Baixa-
Chiado

6

See Príncipe Real, Santos
& Estrela Map (p84)

APA

Santos
Train Station

See Baixa & Rossio
Map (p68)

4 Tram 28E

Alfama **1**

Terreiro
do Paço

8ª Colina
Taproom

Lux-Frágil

Santa Apolónia
Train Station

See Alfama, Castelo
& Graça Map (p76)

Av Infante Dom Henrique

Museu Nacional
do Azulejo

Est de Chelas

Olaias

Bela
Vista

Chelas

Av do Santo Condestável

Dois
Corvos

Aeroporto
de Lisboa

Av de Berlim

Av Almirante Gago Coutinho

Cabo
Ruivo

Gare do Oriente
Train Station

See Parque das Nações
Map (p108)

Rio Tejo

N
0   1 km
0   0.5 miles

CACILHAS

LISBON

History

Imperial riches, fires, plague, one of the most destructive and deadly earthquakes in recorded human history, revolutions, coups, Europe's longest dictatorship and the most severe financial crisis since the Great Depression – Lisbon has certainly had its ups and downs. But come hell or high water, Europe's second-oldest capital soldiers on, improbably emerging from each crisis better and more beautiful than before.

It's said that Ulysses was here first, but the Phoenicians definitely settled here some 3000 years ago, calling the city Alis Ubbo (Delightful Shore). Others soon recognised its qualities: the Greeks, the Carthaginians and then, in 205 BC, the Romans, who stayed until the 5th century AD. After some tribal chaos, the city was taken over by North African Moors in 714. They fortified the city they called Lissabona and fended off the Christians for 400 years.

But in 1147, after a four-month siege, Christian fighters (mainly British crusaders) under Dom Afonso Henriques captured the city. In 1255, Afonso III moved his capital here from Coimbra – it proved far more strategic given the city's excellent port and central position.

In the 15th and 16th centuries Lisbon boomed as the opulent centre of a vast empire after Vasco da Gama found a sea route to India. The party raged on into the 1800s, when gold was discovered in Brazil. Merchants flocked to the city, trading in gold, spices, silks and jewels. Frenzied, extravagant architecture held up a mirror to the era, as seen in Manueline works such as Belém's Mosteiro dos Jerónimos.

At 9.40am on All Saints' Day, 1 November 1755, Lisbon was forever changed. Three major earthquakes hit, as residents celebrated Mass, in what is considered one of the most powerful earthquake sequences in recorded human history, measuring between an estimated 8.5 and 9.1 on the moment magnitude scale. But the devastation didn't end with the astonishing 3½ to six minutes of initial rattling. With Lisbon's churches full of worshippers with candles, an even more catastrophic fire began to rage after the rumbling subsided, and it wasn't contained for five days. Making things even worse, the waters of the Rio Tejo had receded from the seismic

disruption and a disastrous 9m-high tsunami wiped out hundreds who had gathered in the seemingly safe open space of Praça do Comércio (throngs of unsuspecting locals had also run out to the river bed to gather fish). All said and done, it was estimated that as many as 100,000 of Lisbon's 270,000 inhabitants died. Much of the city was ruined, never to regain its former status. Dom João I's chief minister, the formidable Marquês de Pombal, immediately began rebuilding in a simple, cheap, earthquake-proof style that created today's formal grid around the Pombaline downtown area known as Baixa.

In 1908 amid social and economic turmoil, the Portuguese monarchy came to an abrupt and violent end when King Dom Carlos I, along with his heir apparent, Prince Royal Dom Luís Filipe, Duke of Braganza, were assassinated in Lisbon's Terreiro do Paço. Two bloodless coups followed: the first in 1926 put an end to the Portuguese First Republic, and the second in 1974 ended Europe's longest dictatorship in what has become known as the Revolution of the Carnations. In 1974 and 1975 there was a massive influx of refugees from the former African colonies, a demographic change that added to the city's cultural richness.

After Portugal joined the European Community (EC) in 1986, massive funding fuelled redevelopment, a welcome boost after a 1988 fire in Chiado. Streets became cleaner and investment improved facilities. Lisbon has spent recent years in and out of the limelight, as 1994 European City of Culture and host of Expo '98, the 2004 European Football Championships and the 2018 Eurovision Song Contest. Though the global recession had stalled many major development projects over the last half-decade or so, jackhammers have returned to city projects, such as the continued expansion of the metro, including a new €216-million plan to create a circular line linking the southern terminus at Cais do Sodré (Green line) with Rato on the Yellow line. As the 2010s bow out, Lisbon is now enjoying what is perhaps its most significant shining moment, mainly thanks to a notable increase in tourism, which has spawned a multimillion-euro cruise-ship terminal and waves of new restaurants, bars, museums and other cultural attractions. In 2018 alone 15 new hotels opened across the city.

◉ Sights

◉ Baixa & Rossio

After the devastating earthquake of 1755, Baixa was reborn as a grid – the world's first ever – as envisioned by the Marquês de Pombal. Wide commercial streets were laid, with grand plazas, fountains and a triumphal arch evoking the glory of Portuguese royalty. Today the main drag, pedestrianised Rua Augusta, buzzes with bag-toting shoppers, camera-wielding tourists and shrill-voiced buskers. For a taste of the trades that once flourished here, stroll down streets named after *sapateiros* (shoemakers), *correeiros* (saddlers), *douradores* (gilders), *fanqueiros* (cutlers) and even *bacalhoeiros* (cod-fishing vessels).

★ **Praça do Comércio** PLAZA
(Terreiro do Paço; Map p68; Praça do Comércio) With its grand 18th-century arcades, lemon-on-meringue facades and mosaic cobbles, the riverfront Praça do Comércio is a square to out-pomp them all. Everyone arriving by boat used to disembark here, and it still feels like the gateway to Lisbon, thronging with activity and rattling trams.

At its centre rises the dashing equestrian statue of Dom José I (Map p68), hinting at the square's royal roots as the pre-earthquake site of Palácio da Ribeira. In 1908 the square witnessed the fall of the monarchy, when anarchists assassinated Dom Carlos I and his son (perhaps most astonishing, however, was its use as a car park in the 1980s!).

The biggest crowd-puller is Verissimo da Costa's triumphal **Arco da Rua Augusta** (Map p68; Rua Augusta 2-10; €3; ☺9am-8pm), crowned with bigwigs such as 15th-century explorer Vasco da Gama; come at dusk to see the arch glow gold.

★ **Núcleo Arqueológico da Rua dos Correeiros** RUINS
(Map p68; ☏211 131 004; http://ind.millennium bcp.pt; Rua Augusta 96; ☺10am-noon & 2-5pm Mon-Sat) **FREE** Hidden under the Millennium BCP bank building are layers of ruins dating from the Iron Age, discovered on a 1991 parking-lot dig. Fascinating archaeologist-led tours, run by Fundacão Millennium (booking ahead year-round is highly advisable), descend into the depths – in English or Portuguese (departing on the hour and depending on bookings). The extremely well-done site is now rightfully a National Monument.

LISBON IN...

Two Days

Take a ride on tram 28E from Praça do Comercio (p67), hopping off to scale the ramparts of Castelo de São Jorge (p71). Sample some of Portugal's finest drops at Wine Bar do Castelo (p110) before strolling the picturesque lanes of Alfama and stopping for lunch at O Zé da Mouraria (p101). In the afternoon, continue on to the fortress-like Sé de Lisboa (p71) cathedral en route to shopping in pedestrianised Baixa. Round things out with a fado-fuelled evening back in lantern-lit Alfama.

On day two, breakfast on pastries in Belém, then explore the fantastical Mosteiro dos Jerónimos (p79), the riverfront Torre de Belém (p80) and the avant-garde Museu Coleção Berardo (p80). Head for dinner at 100 Maneiras (p101) and bar-crawling back in Bairro Alto. End the night with some bohemian mixology at Pensão Amor (p108) in Cais do Sodré.

Four Days

Spend the morning window-shopping and cafe-hopping in well-heeled Chiado (p70). Stop to admire the dramatic ruined rooftop at Convento do Carmo (p70) before lunching at Mercado da Ribeira (p95). Consider a walking or street-art tour for the afternoon, or – if you're traveling with children – visit the excellent Oceanário de Lisboa (p82) and Pavilhão do Conhecimento (p82). Tonight, book a table with a view at Chapitô à Mesa (p102).

On day four, catch the train to Sintra (p124) for walks through boulder-speckled woodlands to fairy-tale palaces. Back in Rossio this evening, toast your trip with cherry liqueur at A Ginjinha (p107) and a seafood feast at Cervejaria Ramiro (p95).

Baixa & Rossio

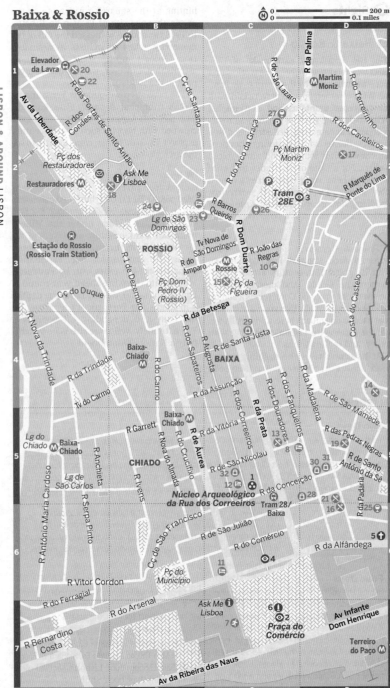

Map labels:

Elevador da Lavra
R das Portas de Santo Antão
Av da Liberdade
R dos Condes
Pç dos Restauradores
Restauradores
Ask Me Lisboa
Cç de Santano
Cç do Duque
Cç do Duque
Estação do Rossio (Rossio Train Station)
R de Dezembro
Lg de São Domingos
ROSSIO
R do Amparo
Pç Dom Pedro IV (Rossio)
R Barros Queiroz
Tv Nova de São Domingos
Rossio
Pç da Figueira
R de São Lazaro
R da Palma
Martim Moniz
R do Terreirinho
R dos Cavaleiros
Pç Martim Moniz
R Marquês de Ponte do Lima
Tram 28E
R do Arco da Graça
R Dom Duarte
R João das Regras
R da Betesga
R da Santa Justa
Baixa-Chiado
BAIXA
R dos Sapateiros
R Augusta
Costa do Castelo
R Nova da Trindade
R da Trindade
Tv do Carmo
R do Carmo
R da Assunção
R da Prata
R dos Correeiros
R dos Douradores
R dos Fanqueiros
R da Madalena
R de São Mamede
R das Pedras Negras
R de Santo António da Sé
Lg do Chiado
Baixa-Chiado
R Garrett
Baixa-Chiado
R da Vitória
R de São Nicolau
R da Conceição
R da Padaria
CHIADO
R Anchieta
Lg de São Carlos
R Ivens
R Nova do Almada
R do Crucifixo
R de Aurea
Núcleo Arqueológico da Rua dos Correeiros
Tram 28/Baixa
R António Maria Cardoso
R Serpa Pinto
Cç de São Francisco
R de São Julião
R do Comércio
R da Alfândega
Pç do Município
R Vitor Cordon
R do Ferragial
R do Arsenal
Ask Me Lisboa
Praça do Comércio
Av Infante Dom Henrique
R Bernardino Costa
Terreiro do Paço
Av da Ribeira das Naus

Baixa & Rossio

★**Igreja de São Domingos** CHURCH
(Map p72; www.patriarcado-lisboa.pt; Largo de São Domingos; ⊙7.30am-7pm) FREE It's a miracle that this baroque church dating to 1241 still stands, having barely survived the 1755 earthquake, then fire in 1959. Its sea of tea lights illuminates gashed pillars, battered walls and ethereal sculptures in its musty yet enchanting interior. Note the Star of David memorial outside, marking the spot of a bloody anti-Semitic massacre in 1506.

Elevador de Santa Justa VIEWPOINT
(Map p72; www.carris.pt/en/elevators; cnrs Rua de Santa Justa & Largo do Carmo; return trip €5.30; ⊙7am-11pm Mar-Oct, to 9pm Nov-Feb) If the lanky, wrought-iron Elevador de Santa Justa seems uncannily familiar, it's probably because the neo-Gothic marvel is the handiwork of Raul Mésnier, Gustave Eiffel's apprentice. It's Lisbon's only vertical street lift, built in 1902 and steam-powered until 1907. Get here early to beat the crowds and zoom to the top for sweeping views over the city's skyline.

Bear in mind, however, that some call the €5.30 fee Santa *Injusta!* You can save €3.80 by entering the platform from the top (behind Convento do Carmo via Bellalisa restaurant) and paying just €1.50 to access the viewing platform.

Ribeira das Naus WATERFRONT
(Map p72) This riverfront promenade between Praça do Comércio and Cais do Sodré is a focal point along Lisbon's continually regenerating waterfront. With broad views over the Rio Tejo, it's a fine place for strolling, lounging, reading, cycling or kicking back with a coffee at the kiosk. This is the closest Lisbon gets to an urban beach.

Rossio PLAZA
(Map p72; Praça Dom Pedro IV) Simply known as Rossio to locals, Praça Dom Pedro IV has 24-hour buzz. Shoeshiners, lottery-ticket sellers, hash-peddlers and office workers drift across its wave-like cobbles, gazing up to its ornate fountains and Dom Pedro IV (Brazil's first emperor), perched high on a marble pedestal.

And these cobbles have seen it all: witch burnings and bullfights, rallies and 1974 revolution carnations. Don't miss Estação do Rossio, a frothy neo-Manueline station with horseshoe-shaped arches and swirly turrets. Trains depart here for Sintra.

Ascensor da Glória FUNICULAR
(www.carris.pt/pt/ascensores-e-elevador; Praça dos Restauradores; return €3.80; ⊙7.15am-11.55pm Mon-Thu, to 12.25am Fri, 8.45am-12.25am Sat, 9.15am-11.55pm Sun) Lisbon's second-oldest funicular has been shuttling folk from Praça dos Restauradores to Rua São Pedro

de Alcântara since 1885. From the *praça* (square), it climbs up to a superb viewpoint atop one of Lisbon's seven hills, Miradouro de São Pedro de Alcântara, and is a less tiring way of getting to Bairro Alto.

◉ Chiado & Bairro Alto

Framed by the ethereal arches of Convento do Carmo, well-heeled Chiado harbours old-world cafes with literary credentials, swish boutiques, grand theatres and elegant 18th-century town houses. Designer divas seeking Portuguese couture, art buffs hunting Rodin originals, and those content to people-watch from a cafe terrace flock here.

Sidling up to Chiado is the party-loving Bairro Alto, whose web of graffiti-slashed streets is sleepy by day. The district comes alive at twilight when hippie chicks hunt for vintage glitz in its retro boutiques and revellers hit its wall-to-wall bars and bistros.

★ **Convento do Carmo & Museu Arqueológico** RUINS
(Map p72; www.museuarqueologicodocarmo.pt; Largo do Carmo; adult/child €4/free; ☺10am-7pm Mon-Sat Jun-Sep, to 6pm Oct-May) Soaring above Lisbon, the skeletal Convento do Carmo was all but devoured by the 1755 earthquake, and that's precisely what makes it so captivating. Its shattered pillars and wishbone-like arches are completely exposed to the elements. The Museu Arqueológico shelters

---

DON'T MISS

MUSEU NACIONAL DO AZULEJO

You haven't been to Lisbon until you've seen the tiles at this **museum** (☎218 100 340; www.museudoazulejo.pt; Rua Madre de Deus 4; adult/child €5/free; ☺10am-6pm Tue-Sun). Housed in a sublime 16th-century convent, the museum covers the entire *azulejo* spectrum, from early Ottoman geometry to zinging altars, scenes of lords a-hunting and Goan intricacies. Star exhibits include a 36m-long panel depicting pre-earthquake Lisbon, a Manueline cloister with web-like vaulting and exquisite blue-and-white *azulejos*, and a gold-smothered baroque chapel. Food-inspired *azulejos* – ducks, pigs and the like – adorn the restaurant opening onto a vine-clad courtyard.

---

archaeological treasures, such as 4th-century sarcophagi, griffin-covered column fragments, 16th-century *azulejo* (hand-painted tile) panels and two gruesome 16th-century Peruvian mummies.

★ **Igreja & Museu São Roque** CHURCH, MUSEUM
(Map p72; www.museu-saoroque.com; Largo Trindade Coelho; church free, museum adult/child €2.50/free, 10am-2pm Sun free; ☺2-7pm Mon, 10am-7pm Tue, Wed & Fri-Sun, 10am-8pm Thu, shorter hours in winter) The plain facade of 16th-century Jesuit Igreja de São Roque belies its dazzling interior of gold, marble and Florentine *azulejos* – bankrolled by Brazilian riches. Its star attraction is **Capela de São João Baptista**, a lavish confection of amethyst, alabaster, lapis lazuli and Carrara marble. The **museum** adjoining the church is packed with elaborate sacred art and holy relics.

★ **Miradouro de São Pedro de Alcântara** VIEWPOINT
(Map p72; Rua São Pedro de Alcântara; ☺viewpoint 24hr, kiosk 10am-midnight Sun-Wed, to 2am Thu-Sat) Hitch a ride on vintage Ascensor da Glória (p69) from Praça dos Restauradores, or huff your way up steep Calçada da Glória to this terrific hilltop viewpoint. Fountains and Greek busts add a regal air to the surroundings, and the open-air kiosk doles out wine, beer and snacks, which you can enjoy while taking in the castle views and live music.

◉ Alfama, Castelo & Graça

Unfurling like a magic carpet at the foot of Castelo de São Jorge, Alfama is Lisbon's Moorish time capsule: a medina-like district of tangled alleys, palm-shaded squares and skinny, terracotta-roofed houses that tumble down to the glittering Rio Tejo. The cobbles have been worn smooth by theatre-going Romans, bath-loving Moors who called it *al-hamma* (Arabic for 'springs'), and stampeding Crusaders.

Here life is literally inside out: women dish the latest *mexericos* (gossip) over strings of freshly washed laundry, men gut sardines on the street then fry them on open grills, matrons spontaneously erupt into wailful fado, kids use chapel entrances as football goals, babies cry, budgerigars twitter, trams rattle and in the noon heat the web of steep lanes falls into its siesta slumber.

Add some altitude to your sightseeing by edging north to Graça, where giddy *miradouros* (lookouts) afford sweeping vistas, and the pearly white Panteão Nacional and Mosteiro de São Vicente de Fora punctuate the skyline.

★ Castelo de São Jorge   CASTLE

(Map p76; www.castelodesaojorge.pt; adult/student/child €8.50/4/free; ⊙9am-9pm Mar-Oct, to 6pm Nov-Feb) Towering dramatically above Lisbon, these mid-11th-century hilltop fortifications sneak into almost every snapshot. Roam its snaking ramparts and pine-shaded courtyards for superlative views over the city's red rooftops to the river. Three guided tours daily (in Portuguese, English and Spanish), at 10.30am, 1pm and 4pm, are included in the admission price (additional tours available).

These smooth cobbles have seen it all – Visigoths in the 5th century, Moors in the 9th century, Christians in the 12th century, royals from the 14th to 16th centuries, and convicts in every century.

Inside the Tower of Ulysses, a camera obscura offers a unique 360-degree view of Lisbon, with demos every 20 minutes. There are also a few galleries displaying relics from past centuries, including traces of the Moorish neighbourhood dating from the 11th century at the Archaeological Site. But the standout is the view – as is the feeling of travelling back in time amid fortified courtyards and towering walls. There are a few cafes and restaurants to while away time in as well.

Bus 737 from Sé or Praça da Figueira goes right to the gate. Tram 28E also passes nearby. A set of escalators traversing the hill from Praça Martim Moniz opened in 2018.

Jardim da Cerca da Graça   PARK

(Map p76; Calçada Do Monte 46; 🏃) Closed for centuries, this 1.7-hectare green space opened again in 2015 and is Lisbon's second-biggest park, offering a lush transition between the neighbourhoods of Graça and Mouraria. There are superb city and castle views from several points and a shady picnic park along with a playground, an orchard and a peaceful kiosk with a terrace.

Load up on wine and cheese and call it an afternoon here!

Museu do Aljube   MUSEUM

(Map p76; www.museudoaljube.pt; Rua de Augusto Rosa 42; adult/child €3/free, free Sun until 2pm;

GET LOST IN THE ALFAMA

There's no place like labyrinthine Alfama for ditching the map and getting lost in sun-dappled alleys and squares full of beauty and banter. Its narrow *becos* (cul-de-sacs) and *travessas* (alleys) lead you on a spectacular wild goose chase past chalk-white chapels and tiny grocery stores and patios shaded by orange trees. The earthy, working-class locals, *alfacinhas*, fill the lanes with neighbourly chatter, wafts of fried fish and the mournful ballads of fado. Experiencing Alfama is more about luxuriating in the everyday than ticking off the big sights. Take a serendipitous wander through the lanes fanning out from Rua de São Miguel, Rua de São João da Praça and Rua dos Remédios.

⊙10am-6pm) Both poignant and haunting, this new and highly important museum has turned the former Portuguese dictatorship's political prison of choice into a museum of truth and consequence, memorial and remembrance – it's a must-see. Disturbing tales of authoritarian dictatorship are found over three floors (beginning with the *Ditadura Militar* in 1926, and evolving into the *Estado Novo*, or New State, from 1933 to 1974), including those of government torture, eavesdropping, oppression, coercion, informing and censorship.

Museu de Artes Decorativas   MUSEUM

(Museum of Decorative Arts; Map p76; www.fress. pt; Largo das Portas do Sol 2; adult/child €4/free; ⊙10am-5pm Wed-Mon) Set in a petite 17th-century palace, this museum creaks under the weight of treasures including blingy French silverware, priceless Qing vases and Indo-Chinese furniture – a collection amassed by a wealthy Portuguese banker from the age of 16. It's worth a visit just to admire the lavish apartments, embellished with baroque *azulejos,* frescoes and chandeliers.

Sé de Lisboa   CATHEDRAL

(Map p76; Largo de Sé; ⊙9am-7pm Tue-Sat, to 5pm Sun & Mon) FREE The fortress-like Sé de Lisboa is one of Lisbon's icons, built in 1150 on the site of a mosque soon after Christians recaptured the city from the Moors. It was sensitively restored in the 1930s. Despite the masses outside, the rib-vaulted interior, lit

LISBON & AROUND

Chiado & Bairro Alto

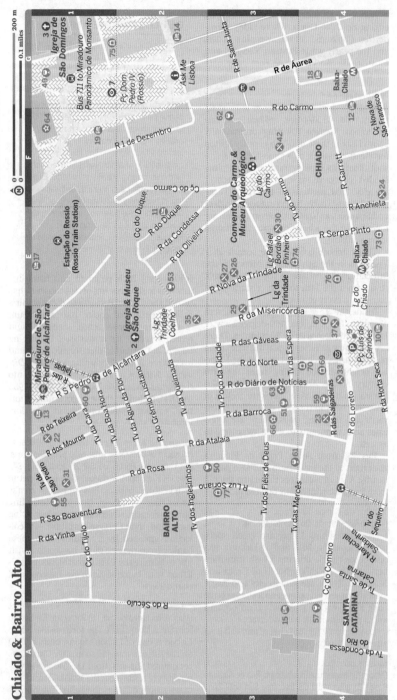

Igreja de São Domingos 3

Bus 711 to Miradouro Panorâmico de Monsanto

Pc Dom Pedro IV (Rossio) 7

Ask Me Lisboa

R de Aurea

R do Carmo

Estação do Rossio (Rossio Train Station)

Cç do Carmo

Convento do Carmo & Museu Arqueológico 1

Igreja & Museu São Roque 2

CHIADO

Baixa-Chiado

Miradouro de São Pedro de Alcântara 4

R da Misericórdia

Pç Luís de Camões

BAIRRO ALTO

SANTA CATARINA

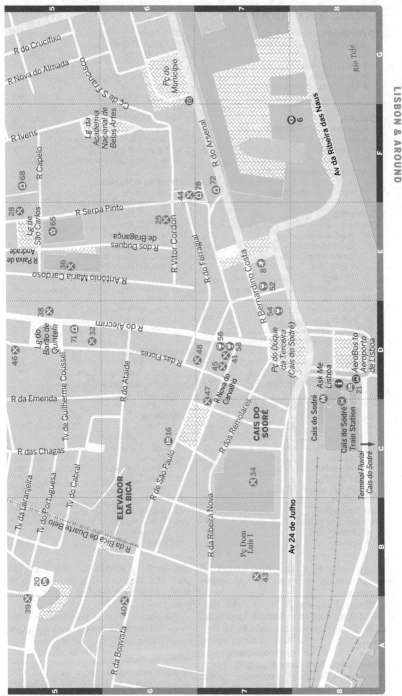

R do Crucifixo

R Nova do Almada

Cc de S Francisco

Pç do Município

R Ivens

Lg da Academia Nacional de Belas Artes

R do Arsenal

Av da Ribeira das Naus

Rio Tejo

R Capelo

68

6

28

R Serpa Pinto

Lg de São Carlos

65

44

78

72

25

R dos Duques de Bragança

R Vitor Cordon

R de Ferragial

R Paiva de Andrade

36

R António Maria Cardoso

R Bernardino Costa

8

52

38

Lg do Barão de Quintela

R do Alecrim

32

71

54

46

R das Flores

48

56

45

41

58

R da Emenda

R do Ataíde

R Nova do Carvalho

47

Tv de Guilherme Coussel

CAIS DO SODRÉ

Pç do Duque da Terceira (Cais do Sodré)

AeroBus to Aeroporto de Lisboa

R das Chagas

16

R dos Remolares

Ask Me Lisboa

21

Tv do Portuguesa

Tv do Cabral

R de São Paulo

Cais do Sodré

Cais do Sodré Train Station

Tv da Laranjeira

ELEVADOR DA BICA

34

Terminal Fluvial Cais do Sodré

Tv do Duarte Belo

R da Bica de

R da Ribeira Nova

Pç Dom Luís I

Av 24 de Julho

20

39

43

40

R da Boavista

Chiado & Bairro Alto

by a rose window, is calm. Stroll around the cathedral to spy leering gargoyles above the orange trees.

History buffs shouldn't miss the less-visited **Gothic cloister** (Map p76; Largo de Sé; €2.50; ◷ 10am-5pm Mon, to 6.30pm Tue-Sat May-Sep, 10am-5pm Mon-Sat Oct-Apr), which opens onto a deep pit full of archaeological excavations going back more than 2000 years. However, €5-million renovation works expected to last at least two years have

temporarily shuttered the area since late 2017. The **Treasury** (Map p76; Largo de Sé; €2.50; ◷ 10am-5pm Mon-Sat) showcases religious artwork.

The plaza in front of the church is home to one of Lisbon's most adorable kiosks, Quiosque Lisboa.

Museu do Fado   MUSEUM
(Map p76; www.museudofado.pt; Largo do Chafariz de Dentro; adult/child €5/3; ◷ 10am-6pm Tue-Sun)

Fado was born in Alfama. Immerse yourself in its bittersweet symphonies at Museu do Fado. This engaging museum traces fado's history from its working-class roots to international stardom.

Mosteiro de São Vicente de Fora   CHURCH

(Map p76; Largo de São Vicente; adult/child €5/free; ⊙10am-6pm Tue-Sun) Graça's Mosteiro de São Vicente de Fora was founded in 1147 and revamped by Italian architect Felipe Terzi in the late 16th century. Since the adjacent church took the brunt of the 1755 earthquake (the church's dome crashed through the ceiling of the sacristy, but emerged otherwise unscathed), elaborate blue-and-white *azulejos* dance across almost every wall, echoing the building's architectural curves.

Panteão Nacional   MUSEUM

(Map p76; www.panteaonacional.gov.pt; Campo de Santa Clara; €4; ⊙10am-6pm Tue-Sun, to 5pm Oct-Mar) Perched high and mighty above Graça's Campo de Santa Clara, the porcelain-white Panteão Nacional is a baroque beauty. Originally intended as a church, it now pays homage to Portugal's heroes and heroines, including 15th-century explorer Vasco da Gama and *fadista* (fado singer) Amália Rodrigues.

Lavishly adorned with pink marble and gold swirls, its echoing dome resembles an enormous Fabergé egg. Trudge up to the 4th-floor viewpoint for a sunbake and vertigo-inducing views over Alfama and the river.

Fundação José Saramago – Casa dos Bicos   NOTABLE BUILDING

(Map p76; www.josesaramago.org; Rua dos Bacalhoeiros 10; adult/child €3/free; ⊙10am-6pm Mon-Sat) The pincushion facade of Casa dos Bicos, the eccentric 16th-century abode of Afonso de Albuquerque, former viceroy to India, grabs your attention with 1125 diamond-shape spikes *(bicos)*. The *casa* houses a small museum dedicated to José Saramago (1922–2010), Portugal's most famous writer; and a newly added ground-floor excavation of Roman ruins (which are free to visit).

⊙ Príncipe Real, Santos & Estrela

West of Bairro Alto, these serene and affluent tree-fringed neighbourhoods slope down to the Rio Tejo, and are dotted with boutique hotels, art galleries, vine-clad courtyards and antique shops. This offbeat corner of Lisbon harbours a handful of must-sees including a neoclassical basilica, exotic gardens and the neoclassical Palácio da Assembleia da República, home to Portugal's parliament.

★ Basílica da Estrela   CHURCH

(Map p84; Praça da Estrela; basilica free, nativity scene €2, roof €3; ⊙basilica 9.30am-1pm & 3-7.30pm, terrace 10am-6.40pm, presépio 10-11.30am & 3-5pm, closed Mon, Sat & Sun morning, Wed afternoon) The curvaceous, sugar-white dome and twin belfries of Basílica da Estrela are visible from afar. The echoing interior is awash with pink-and-black marble, which creates a kaleidoscopic effect when you gaze up into the cupola. The neoclassical beauty was completed in 1790 by order of Dona Maria I (whose tomb is here) in gratitude for a male heir.

Museu da Marioneta   MUSEUM

(Puppet Museum; Map p84; www.museuda marioneta.pt; Rua da Esperança 146; adult/child €5/3, free before 2pm Sun; ⊙10am-6pm Tue-Sun; 📷) Discover your inner child at the surprisingly enchanting Museu da Marioneta, a veritable Geppetto's workshop housed in the 17th-century Convento das Bernardas. Alongside superstars such as impish Punch and his Portuguese equivalent Dom Roberto are rarities: Vietnamese water puppets, Sicilian opera marionettes and intricate Burmese shadow puppets. Check out the fascinating exhibit of the making of the animation film *A Suspeita*.

Casa Museu de Amália Rodrigues   MUSEUM

(Map p84; www.amaliarodrigues.pt; Rua de São Bento 193; adult/child under 5yr €6/free; ⊙10am-6pm) A pilgrimage site for fado fans, this is where the Rainha do Fado (Queen of Fado) Amália Rodrigues (1920-99) lived; note the *calçada portuguesa* (Portuguese sidewalk design) announcing 'Amália'. Short tours take in portraits, glittering costumes and crackly recordings of her performances.

Jardim da Estrela   GARDENS

(Map p84; Praça da Estrela; ⊙7am-midnight; 📷) **FREE** Seeking green respite? Opposite the Basílica da Estrela, this 1852 green space is perfect for a stroll, with paths weaving past pine, monkey-puzzle and palm trees, rose and cacti beds, and the centrepiece – a giant banyan tree. Kids love the duck ponds and animal-themed playground. There are several open-air cafes where you can recharge.

Alfama, Castelo & Graça

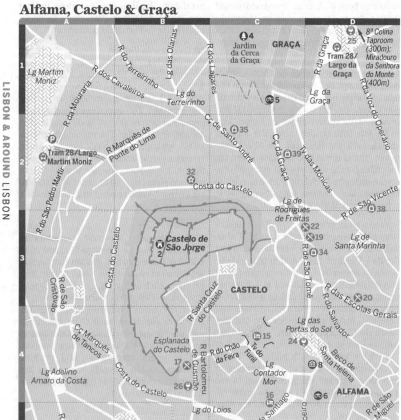

Jardim do Príncipe Real   PLAZA
(Map p84) Shaded by a giant cedar tree, this is a relaxing shady plaza with an al fresco cafe for watching the world go slowly by. The surrounding district is perfect for lazy days spent exploring markets, antique stores, edgy boutiques and design stores. Creatives, hipsters and the gay community love this boho-flavoured pocket of Lisbon.

◉ Lapa & Alcântara

Near the scenic but gratingly noisy suspension bridge (and Golden Gate Bridge

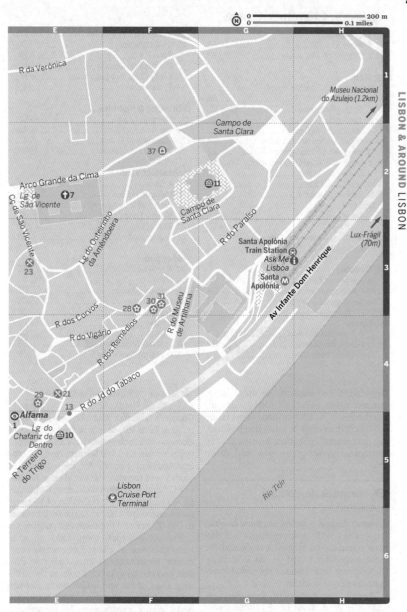

lookalike) Ponte 25 de Abril, the reborn Alcântara dock is sprinkled with outdoor restaurants and drinking spots. For sightseers, the star attraction is the impressive Museu do Oriente. Getting here on westbound tram 28E or 25E is fun. You can also take the riverside bike path from Cais do Sodré.

Museu do Oriente MUSEUM
(www.museudooriente.pt; Doca de Alcântara; adult/child €6/2, free 6-10pm Fri; ⊙10am-6pm Tue-Thu, Sat & Sun, to 10pm Fri) The beautifully designed Museu do Oriente highlights Portugal's ties with Asia, from colonial baby steps in Macau to ancestor worship.

Alfama, Castelo & Graça

The cavernous museum occupies a revamped 1940s *bacalhau* (dried salt-cod) warehouse – a €30-million conversion. Strikingly displayed in pitch-black rooms, the permanent collection focuses on the Portuguese presence in Asia, and Asian gods.

◎ Marquês de Pombal & Around

Up north, Lisbon is racing headlong into the 21st century with gleaming high-rises, dizzying roundabouts, shopping malls and the Parisian-style boulevard Av da Liberdade. The contrast with Lisbon's old-world riverfront districts is startling.

Though often overlooked, these parts reveal some gems: from René Lalique jewellery at Museu Calouste Gulbenkian's Coleção do Fundador and Hockney masterpieces at Coleção Moderna, to hothouses in Parque Eduardo VII and the lofty arches of Aqueduto das Águas Livres.

★ **Museu Calouste Gulbenkian – Coleção do Fundador**   MUSEUM
(Founder's Collection; Map p92; www.gulbenkian. pt; Av de Berna 45A; Coleção do Fundador/Coleção Moderna combo ticket adult/child €10/free, temporary exhibitions €3-6, free Sun from 2pm; ⊙10am-6pm Wed-Mon) Famous for its outstanding quality and breadth, the world-class Founder's Collection at Museu Calouste Gulbenkian showcases an epic collection of Western and Eastern art – from Egyptian treasures to Old Master and Impressionist paintings.

The chronological romp kicks off with highlights such as gilded Egyptian mummy masks, Mesopotamian urns, elaborate Persian carpets, Qing porcelain (note the grinning *Dogs of Fo*) and a fascinating Roman gold-medallion collection. Going west, art buffs admire masterpieces by Rembrandt *(Portrait of an Old Man)*, Van Dyck and Rubens (including the frantic *Loves of the Centaurs*). Be sure to glimpse Rodin's passionate *Eternal Springtime* sculpture. The grand finale is the collection of exquisite

René Lalique jewellery, including the other-worldly *Dragonfly*.

Admission includes the separately housed Coleção Moderna, which is situated in a sculpture-dotted garden and contains a stellar collection of 20th-century Portuguese and international art.

Casa-Museu Medeiros e Almeida
MUSEUM

(Map p92; www.casa-museumedeirosealmeida.pt; Rua Rosa Araújo 41; adult/child €5/free, free 10am-1pm Sat; ⊙10am-5pm Mon-Sat) Housed in a stunning early-19th-century mansion, this little-known museum presents António Medeiros e Almeida's exquisite fine- and decorative-arts collection. Highlights include Han ceramics and Ming- and Qing-dynasty porcelain, Thomas Gainsborough paintings, a 300-strong stockpile of watches and clocks (one of the best private collections in Europe), and a dinner service that once belonged to Napoléon Bonaparte.

Mãe d'Água
HISTORIC BUILDING

(Mother of Water; Map p92; www.epal.pt/EPAL/menu/museu-da-água; Praça das Amoreiras 10; adult/child €3/1.50, Sun free; ⊙10am-12.30pm & 1.30-5.30pm Tue-Sun) The king laid the Aqueduto das Águas Livres' final stone at Mãe d'Água, the city's massive 5500-cu-metre main reservoir. Completed in 1834, the reservoir's cool, echoing chamber is a fine place to admire 19th-century technology. Climb the stairs for a view of the aqueduct and the surrounding neighbourhood. Admission is €5 if there's an exhibition on.

◉ Belém

As well as Unesco World Heritage–listed Manueline stunners such as Mosteiro dos Jerónimos and the whimsical Torre de Belém, this district 6km west of Lisbon's centre offers a tranquil botanical garden, fairy-tale golden coaches, Lisbon's tastiest *pastéis de nata* (custard tarts) and a whole booty of other treasures. The best way to reach Belém is on the zippy tram 15E from Praça da Figueira or Praça do Comércio.

★Mosteiro dos Jerónimos
MONASTERY

(Map p96; www.mosteirojeronimos.pt; Praça do Império; adult/child €10/5, free Sun until 2pm for Portuguese citizens/residents only; ⊙10am-6.30pm Tue-Sun Jun-Sep, to 5.30pm Oct-May) Belém's undisputed heart-stealer is this Unesco-listed monastery. The *mosteiro* is the stuff of pure fantasy: a fusion of Diogo de Boitaca's creative vision and the spice and pepper dosh of Manuel I, who commissioned it to trumpet Vasco da Gama's discovery of a sea route to India in 1498.

Wrought for the glory of God, Jerónimos was once populated by monks of the Order of St Jerome, whose spiritual job for four centuries was to comfort sailors and pray for the king's soul. When the order was dissolved in 1833, the monastery was used as a school and orphanage, until about 1940.

Entering the church through the western portal, you'll notice tree-trunk-like columns that seem to grow into the ceiling, which is itself a spiderweb of stone. Windows cast a soft golden light over the church. Superstar

---

DON'T MISS

A WONDROUS ART COLLECTION

Set in a lemon-fronted, 17th-century palace, the Museu Nacional de Arte Antiga (National Museum of Ancient Art; www.museudearteantiga.pt; Rua das Janelas Verdes; adult/child €6/free, with themed exhibitions €10/free, free Sun until 2pm for Portuguese citizens/residents only; ⊙10am-6pm Tue-Sun) is Lapa's biggest draw. It presents a star-studded collection of European and Asian paintings and decorative arts. Keep an eye out for highlights such as Nuno Gonçalves' naturalistic *Panels of São Vicente*, Albrecht Dürer's *St Jerome*, Lucas Cranach's haunting *Salomé*, as well as period furniture pieces such as King Afonso V's ceremonial 1470s armchair and the elaborate lacquered wood, silver-gilt and bronze late-16th-century casket. Other gems include the golden wonder that is the *Monstrance of Belém*, a souvenir from Vasco da Gama's second voyage, and 16th-century Japanese screens depicting the arrival of the Namban (southern barbarians), namely big-nosed Portuguese explorers.

Biannual temporary themed exhibitions (priced separately, at around €6) are reached via a second entrance also on Rua das Janelas Verdes, as are the stone-arched cafe and wonderfully peaceful gardens with river views.

GREAT ESCAPES

Some of Lisbon's greenest and most peaceful *praças* (town squares) are perfect for a crowd-free stroll or picnic. A few of our favourites:

Praça da Alegria Swooping palms and banyan trees shade tranquil Praça da Alegria, which is actually more round than square. Look out for the bronze bust of 19th-century Portuguese painter and composer Alfredo Keil.

Praça do Príncipe Real A century-old cedar tree forms a giant natural parasol at the centre of this palm-dotted square, popular among grizzled card players by day and the gay scene by night. There's a kids' playground and a relaxed cafe with al fresco seating.

Praça das Flores Centred on a fountain, this romantic, leafy square has cobbles, pastel-washed houses and Paris levels of doggy do.

Campo dos Mártires da Pátria Framed by elegant buildings, this grassy square is dotted with pine, weeping willow and jacaranda trees, with a pond for ducks and a pleasant indoor-outdoor cafe. *Lisboêtas* in search of cures light candles before the statue of Dr Sousa Martins, who was renowned for his healing work among the poor.

Vasco da Gama is interred in the lower chancel, just left of the entrance, opposite venerated 16th-century poet Luís Vaz de Camões. From the upper choir, there's a superb view of the church; the rows of seats are Portugal's first Renaissance woodcarvings.

There's nothing like the moment you walk into the honey-stone Manueline cloisters, dripping with organic detail in their delicately scalloped arches, twisting auger-shell turrets and columns intertwined with leaves, vines and knots. It will simply wow. Keep an eye out for symbols of the age, such as the armillary sphere and the cross of the Military Order, plus gargoyles and fantastical beasties on the upper balustrade.

If you plan to visit both the monastery and the **Museu Nacional de Arqueologia** (National Archaeology Museum; Map p96; museuarqueologia.pt; Praça do Império; adult/child €5/free, free Sun to 2pm for Portuguese citizens/residents only; ⊙10am-6pm Tue-Sun), you can save a little by purchasing a €12 admission pass valid for both.

★**Museu Nacional dos Coches**　　MUSEUM
(Map p96; www.museudoscoches.pt; Av da Índia 136; €8, combined ticket with Antigo Picadeiro Real €10, free Sun to 2pm for Portuguese citizens/residents only; ⊙10am-6pm Tue-Sun) Cinderella wannabes delight in Portugal's most visited museum, which dazzles with its world-class collection of 70 17th- to 19th-century coaches in an ultramodern (and some might say inappropriately contrasting) space that debuted in 2015. Don't miss Pope Clement XI's stunning ride, the scarlet-and-gold *Coach of the Oceans*, or the old royal riding school,

Antigo Picadeiro Real (Old Royal Riding School; Map p96; www.museudoscoches.pt; Praça Afonso de Albuquerque; €4, combined ticket with Museu Nacional dos Coches €10, free Sun to 2pm for Portuguese citizens/residents only; ⊙10am-6pm Tue-Sun), across the street.

★**Museu Coleção Berardo**　　MUSEUM
(Map p96; www.museuberardo.pt; Praça do Império; adult/student/child under 6yr €5/2.50/free, free Sat; ⊙10am-7pm) Culture fiends can get their contemporary-art fix at Museu Coleção Berardo, the star of the Centro Cultural de Belém. The ultrawhite, minimalist gallery displays billionaire José Berardo's eye-popping collection of abstract, surrealist and pop art, including Hockney, Lichtenstein, Warhol and Pollock originals.

Temporary exhibitions are among the best in Portugal. Also in the complex is a cafe-restaurant that faces a grassy lawn, a bookshop and a museum store.

Torre de Belém　　TOWER
(Map p96; www.torrebelem.pt; Av de Brasília; adult/child €6/3, free Sun until 2pm for Portuguese citizens/residents only; ⊙10am-6.30pm Tue-Sun May-Sep, to 5.30pm Oct-Apr) Jutting out onto the Rio Tejo, this Unesco World Heritage–listed fortress epitomises the Age of Discoveries. You'll need to breathe in to climb the narrow spiral staircase to the tower, which affords sublime views over Belém and the river.

Museu de Arte,
Arquitetura e Tecnologia　　MUSEUM
(MAAT; Art, Architecture & Technology Museum; Map p96; www.maat.pt; Av de Brasília, Central Tejo; admission with/without Central Tejo €9/5; ⊙11am-

7pm Wed-Mon) Lisbon's latest riverfront star is this low-rise, glazed-tiled structure that intriguingly hips and sways into ground-level exhibition halls. Visitors can walk over and under its reflective surfaces, which play with water, light and shadow, and pay homage to the city's intimate relationship with the sea.

Museu da Presidência da República   MUSEUM
(Museum of the Presidency of the Republic; Map p96; www.museu.presidencia.pt; Praça Afonso de Albuquerque, Palácio de Belém; adult/child €2.50/free, with Palácio de Belém €5; ⊙10am-6pm Tue-Sun) Portugal's small presidential museum is worth a look for its fascinating state gifts exhibit – note the outrageous 1957 offering from Brazil's Juscelino Kubitschek, a massive tortoiseshell depicting hand-painted Brazilian scenes, plus Saudi swords and a gorgeous traditional Japanese dance scene. Don't miss the official presidential portrait of Mário Soares, either – that guy looked like fun!

Palácio Nacional da Ajuda   PALACE
(www.palacioajuda.gov.pt; Largo da Ajuda; adult/child €5/free, free Sun until 2pm for Portuguese citizens/residents only; ⊙10am-6pm Thu-Tue) Built in the early 19th century, this staggering neoclassical palace served as the royal residence from the 1860s until the end of the monarchy (1910). You can tour private apartments and state rooms, getting an eyeful of gilded furnishings and exquisite artworks dating back five centuries, as well as the queen's chapel, home to Portugal's only El Greco painting.

It's a long uphill walk from Belém, or you can take tram 18E or several buses from downtown, including 760 from Praça do Comércio.

Palácio de Belém   HISTORIC BUILDING
(Belém Palace; Map p96; ☑213 614 980; www.presidencia.pt; Praça Afonso de Albuquerque; adult/child €5/free; ⊙10.30am-4.30pm Sat) The salmon-slabbed 16th-century Belém Palace is Portugal's official presidential residence and office (though the country's previous president, Cavaco Silva, chose to live in his own home). Tours in Portuguese, English and French are available on Saturday only, with just 150 spots up for grabs (book in advance via phone or email). Alternatively, the small but fascinating Museu da Presidência da República (p81) is open most of the week.

Jardim Botânico Tropical   GARDENS
(Map p96; www.iict.pt/jbt; Largo dos Jerónimos; adult/child €2/1; ⊙10am-8pm May-Aug, shorter hours in winter) Far from the madding crowd, these botanical gardens bristle with hundreds of species, from date palms to monkey-puzzle trees. Spread across 7 hectares, it's a peaceful, shady retreat on a sweltering summer's day. A highlight is the Macau garden, complete with mini pagoda, where bamboo rustles and a cool stream trickles.

Padrão dos Descobrimentos   MUSEUM
(Discoveries Monument; Map p96; www.padraodos-descobrimentos.pt; Av de Brasília; adult/child €6/3; ⊙10am-7pm Mar-Sep, to 6pm Oct-Feb) The monolithic Padrão dos Descobrimentos, looking like a caravel ship frozen in midswell, was inaugurated in 1960 on the 500th anniversary of Henry the Navigator's death. The 56m-high limestone giant is chock-full of Portuguese bigwigs. At the prow is Henry, while behind him are explorers Vasco da Gama, Diogo Cão, Fernão de Magalhães (Ferdinand Magellan) and 29 other greats.

Do take the lift (or puff up 267 steps) to the windswept miradouro for 360-degree views over the river. The mosaic in front of the monument charts the routes of Portuguese mariners.

⊙ Parque das Nações

A shining model of urban regeneration, Parque das Nações has almost single-handedly

---

WATER FEATURE

The 109 arches of the Aqueduto das Águas Livres (Aqueduct of the Free Waters; ☑218 100 215; www.epal.pt; Campolide; ⊙10am-5.30pm Tue-Sun) lope across the hills into Lisbon from Caneças, more than 18km away; they are most spectacular at Campolide, where the tallest arch is an incredible 65m high. Built between 1731 and 1799, by order of Dom João V, the aqueduct brought Lisbon its first clean drinking water. Its more sinister claim to fame is as the site where 19th-century mass-murderer Diogo Alves pushed his victims over the edge.

Another of the best places to see the aqueduct is in the leafy Praça das Amoreiras next to the Mãe d'Água (p79).

propelled Lisbon into the 21st century since Expo '98 was held in the city. Here you'll find an impressive aquarium, riverside gardens, public-art installations and an abundance of outdoor dining options.

To reach Parque das Nações, take the train or metro to Gare do Oriente and follow the signs to the waterfront. The riverside promenade is great for cycling adventures. To rent your own set of wheels, there are well-worn bikes at the reception of **Marina Parque das Nações** (Map p108; ☑218 949 066; www. marinaparquedasnacoes.pt; bike hire per 1/4/8hr €5/10/12; ☺9am-6pm) or you can head to **Ring-A-Bike** (Map p108; ☑219 444 081, 964 442 027; www.ringabike.pt; Rua do Armistício 24, Moscavide; bike hire 1/4/8hr from €5/10/20; ☺9am-9pm), 1.6km northwest of Parque das Nações in Moscavide. For a bird's-eye view of the park, take a ride on the **Teleférico** (Telecabine Lisboa; Map p108; www.telecabinelisboa. pt; Passeio do Tejo; one-way adult/child €3.95/2; ☺10.30am-8pm Jun–mid-Sep, 11am-6pm or 7pm rest of the year), which glides above the river's edge.

★ Oceanário de Lisboa
AQUARIUM

(Map p108; www.oceanario.pt; Doca dos Olivais; adult/child €15/10, incl temporary exhibition €18/12; ☺10am-8pm, to 7pm in winter) The closest you'll get to scuba diving without a wetsuit, Oceanário is mind-blowing. With 8000 marine creatures splashing in 7 million litres of seawater, no amount of hyperbole does it justice. Huge wrap-around tanks make you feel as if you're underwater, as you eyeball zebra sharks, honeycombed rays, gliding mantas and schools of neon fish.

Pavilhão do Conhecimento
MUSEUM

(Pavilion of Knowledge; Map p108; www.pavconhecimento.pt; Largo José Mariano Gago 1; adult/child €9/6; ☺10am-6pm Tue-Fri, 11am-7pm Sat & Sun; ☒) Kids won't grumble about science at the interactive Pavilhão do Conhecimento, where they can run riot in the adult-free unfinished house, get dizzy on a high-wire bicycle or have fun whipping up tornadoes and blowing massive soap bubbles.

⚘ Activities

Kiss the Cook
COOKING

(☑968 119 652; www.kissthecook.pt; Rua Rodrigues de Faria 103, LX Factory; classes €65) If you're into Portuguese food in a big way and fancy picking up a few tips and tricks from the experts, why not pass by Kiss the Cook? Here you can prepare (and devour)

traditional dishes. The cookery classes are totally hands-on, and the price includes lunch and wine.

ViniPortugal
WINE

(Map p68; www.winesofportugal.info; Praça do Comércio; ☺11am-7pm Apr-Oct, closed Sun Nov-Mar) Under the arcades on Praça do Comércio, this viticultural organisation offers €6 themed wine tastings, if booked in advance. Otherwise, pop in and grab a €3 enocard, which allows you to taste at least three Portuguese wines, from Alentejo whites to full-bodied Douro reds (glasses are €1 to €8).

Culinary Backstreets
FOOD & DRINK

(☑963 472 188; www.culinarybackstreets.com/ culinary-walks/lisbon; 3/6hr tour €83/118) *Eat Portugal* co-author Célia Pedroso leads epic culinary walks through Lisbon, a fantastic way to take in some of the best treats in town. Try *ginjinha* (cherry liqueur) then *pastéis de nata* (custard tarts) and artisanal sheep cheese, paired with killer local wines. Tours are mostly available Tuesday to Saturday. Expect tantalising multiple foodgasms followed by a debilitating food coma.

Sandemans New Lisbon
WALKING

(Map p72; www.newlisbontours.com; ☺10am, 11am & 2pm) For the inside scoop on the city, Sandemans' fun, informative and free 2½-hour walking tours of downtown Lisbon are hard to beat. You'll do the rounds of all the major landmarks and get versed in history and city tips as you stroll. The tours begin at the scheduled times (book online) at the monument on Praça Luís de Camões.

Lisbon Walker
WALKING

(Map p76; ☑218 861 840; www.lisbonwalker. com; Rua do Jardim do Tabaco 126; 3hr walk adult/ child €15/free; ☺10am) This excellent company, with well-informed, English-speaking guides, offers themed walking tours of Lisbon. Note that these normally depart at 10am from the northwest corner of Praça do Comércio (p67).

Lisbon Explorer
WALKING

(☑966 042 993; www.lisbonexplorer.com; private group tours €160) Top-notch English-speaking guides peel back the many layers of Lisbon's history during the three-hour walking tours offered by this highly rated outfit. Fees do not include admissions but often include public-transport costs during the tour. Tours typically depart from Praça do Comércio or

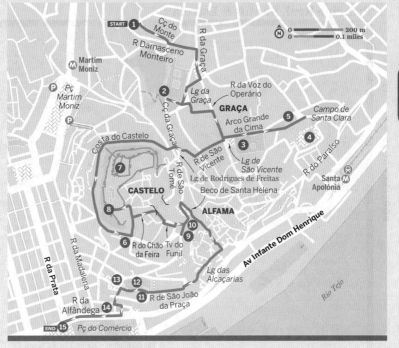

City Walk
Exploring the Alfama

START MIRADOURO DA SENHORA DO MONTE
END PRAÇA DO COMÉRCIO
LENGTH 3KM; TWO TO THREE HOURS

This scenic route starts on tram 28E from Largo Martim Moniz or the Baixa, taking in the city's best tram route *and* avoiding uphill slogs. Take the tram up to Largo da Graça. From here, stroll north and turn left behind the barracks for breathtaking views from Lisbon's highest lookout, ❶ **Miradouro da Senhora do Monte** (p90). Next, walk south and turn right to pine-shaded ❷ **Miradouro da Graça** (p90), where central Lisbon spreads out before you. Retrace your steps and head east to admire the exquisitely tiled cloisters of ❸ **Mosteiro de São Vicente de Fora** (p75), and the cool, echoing ❹ **Panteão Nacional** (p75). If it's Tuesday or Saturday, make a detour to the buzzy ❺ **Feira da Ladra** (Map p76; www.cm-lisboa.pt; Campo de Santa Clara; ⊙9am-5pm Tue & Sat) to hunt for buried treasure. Otherwise, go west along Arco Grande da Cima until you reach Largo de Rodrigues de Freitas. Take the Costa do Castelo fork, continuing west to skirt the castle battlements. Pass in front of ❻ **Solar dos Mouros**, then turn left up to the ❼ **Castelo de São Jorge** (p71) and its ❽ **viewpoint**. Next, head down the steep lanes to Largo das Portas do Sol, and another fine vista from ❾ **Miradouro de Santa Luzia** (p90). From here wander northward, past whitewashed ❿ **Igreja de Santa Luzia** and turn right into the atmospheric lane of Beco de Santa Helena, threading through labyrinthine Alfama to Largo das Alcaçarias. Take Rua de São João da Praça westward, pausing for a bite at ⓫ **Cruzes Credo Café** (Map p76; Rua Cruzes da Sé 29; mains €3.50-14; ⊙noon-midnight; 🛜), before continuing on to the ⓬ **Sé de Lisboa** (p71) and ⓭ **Igreja de Santo António**. Continue downhill, stopping for a look at the facade of ⓮ **Igreja da Conceição Velha** (Map p68; www.paroquiasaonicolau.pt; Rua da Alfândega 108; ⊙10am-2pm & 3-8pm Mon-Fri, to 6pm Sat & Sun) FREE, before ending at ⓯ **Praça do Comércio** (p67), Europe's largest square.

Príncipe Real, Santos & Estrela

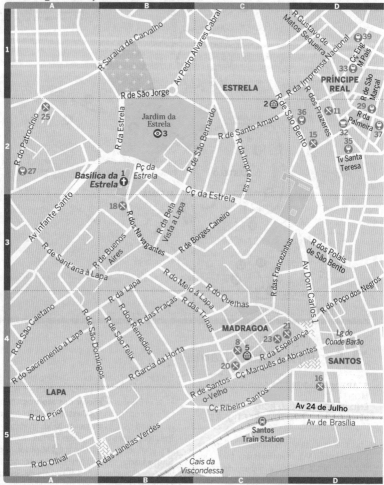

other central locations. You'll receive the meeting point upon booking.

Lisbon Bike Tour CYCLING
(Map p92; ☑ 912 272 300; www.lisbonbiketour.com; adult/child €32.50/15; ☺ 9.30am-1pm) It's all downhill on this 3½-hour guided bike ride from Marquês de Pombal to Belém.

The company also does bikes tours of Monsanto, Sintra and Arrábida on request.

We Hate Tourism Tours TOURS
(☑ 913 776 598; www.wehatetourismtours.com; Rua Rodrigues de Faria 103, 4th fl, LX Factory; per person from €30; ☺ 2-6pm) One memorable

way to explore Lisbon is aboard an open-topped UMM (a Portuguese 4WD once made for the army). In addition to the weekend King of the Hills tour, this alternative outfit organises innovative lunch and dinner tours, longer city tours and excursions to Sintra and Cascais.

You can always find these folks hanging out and drinking wine at their quirky HQ inside LX Factory.

HIPPOtrip TOURS
(☑ 211 922 030; www.hippotrip.com; Doca de Santo Amaro; adult/child €25/15; ☺ 9am-6pm) This fun 90-minute tour takes visitors on a land

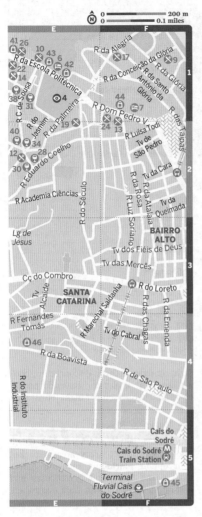

and river excursion in an amphibious vehicle that drives straight into the Rio Tejo! It begins and ends at Doca de Santo Amaro. From April to September, tours depart at 10am, noon, 2pm, 4pm and 6pm (the last departure falls off the schedule from October to March).

🎉 Festivals & Events

Indie Lisboa   FILM
(📋 213 158 399; www.indielisboa.com; ⊙ Apr & May) This spring filmathon brings 10 days of indie features, documentaries and shorts to Lisbon's big screens.

Peixe em Lisboa   FOOD & DRINK
(📋 222 088 500; www.peixemlisboa.com; Pavilhão Carlos Lopes, Parque Eduardo VII; ⊙ Apr) Seafood lovers won't want to miss this week-long culinary extravaganza, put on by a dozen restaurants (with Michelin-star chefs).

Dias da Música   MUSIC
(📋 213 612 400; www.ccb.pt; ⊙ Apr) Classical-music buffs see world-renowned orchestras perform at this three-day festival held in April at Centro Cultural de Belém (CCB; Map p96; 📋 213 612 400; www.ccb.pt; Praça do Império; ⊙ 8am-8pm Mon-Fri, 10am-6pm Sat & Sun).

Somersby Out Jazz   MUSIC
(📋 213 421 546; www.ncs.pt/outjazz; ⊙ May-Sep) One of the best free events of summer, Out Jazz happens on Sundays from May through September (and in Cascais one Saturday per month), with a band playing at a different park around the city each week. DJs follow the live music. Bring a picnic blanket and join the festive summer crowds.

Rock in Rio – Lisboa   MUSIC
(www.rockinriolisboa.sapo.pt/lisboa/pt-PT; Parque da Bela Vista; ⊙ May) This Brazilian import, which bounces between Rio, Madrid, Las Vegas and Lisbon, is one of the world's largest music festivals and tends to arrive in the Portuguese capital with the world's biggest bands in tow every other year, including 2020 and 2022.

Headliners have included Muse, Bruno Mars and The Killers.

Fado no Castelo   MUSIC
(www.castelodesaojorge.pt; Praça de Armas, Castelo de São Jorge; ⊙ Jun) Lisbon's love affair with fado takes centre stage at this newly inaugurated annual song-fest held at the cinematic Castelo de São Jorge (p71) over three evenings in June, with a different singer performing each night in the square at the castle entrance. Admission is free; a limited number of tickets are available and must be picked up in advance.

Festival ao Largo   MUSIC
(www.festivalaolargo.pt; Largo de São Carlos; ⊙ late Jun-late Jul) Free outdoor performances – classical concerts, ballet and opera – are held in front of the Teatro Nacional de São Carlos (p114).

NOS Alive   MUSIC
(www.nosalive.com; Passeio Marítimo de Algés; ⊙ Jul) This three-day music and arts shindig, held annually along the river in Algés, is one

Príncipe Real, Santos & Estrela

of the best and most popular events on the European summer festival circuit.

Super Bock Super Rock　　　　　MUSIC
(www.superbocksuperrock.pt; ⊗ Jul) One of Portugal's premier music festivals, held in July. Past editions have included Iggy Pop, Queens of the Stone Age, Arctic Monkeys, The Killers, The Strokes, Arcade Fire, Noel Gallagher's High Flying Birds, Blur, Metallica, Massive Attack and Kendrick Lamar.

Jazz em Agosto　　　　　　　　MUSIC
(☏ 217 823 000; www.gulbenkian.pt/jazzem agosto; ⊗ Aug) Both established and fresh talent are welcomed to the stage at this soulful jazz fest, held at **Fundação Calouste Gulbenkian** (Map p92; ☏ 217 823 000; www.gulben kian.pt; Av de Berna 45A).

🛏 Sleeping

Lisbon has an array of boutique hotels, upmarket hostels and both modern and old-fashioned guesthouses. Be sure to book ahead for high season (July to September). A word to those with weak knees and/or heavy bags: many guesthouses lack lifts, meaning you may have to haul your luggage up three flights or more. If this is disconcerting, book a place with an elevator. Rates do not include a €2 per person per night tourist tax.

🛏 Baixa & Rossio

Sandwiched between Alfama and Bairro Alto, this central touristy area is packed with options, including high-end hotels, modest and upper-end guesthouses and first-rate hostels. You can walk everywhere and there's great public transport.

★**Lisbon Destination Hostel**　HOSTEL €
(Mapp72; ☏ 213466457;www.followyourdestination. com; Rossio train station, 2nd fl; dm €25, s/d without bathroom from €36/54, d from €107; @ ⊛) Housed in Lisbon's loveliest train station, this world-class hostel has a glass ceiling that lights the spacious plant-filled common area. Rooms are crisp and well kept, and there are loads of activities (bar crawls, beach day trips, etc). Facilities include a shared kitchen, game consoles, movie room (with popcorn) and a 24-hour self-service bar. The breakfast with crêpes and fresh fruit is top-notch.

Home Lisbon Hostel
HOSTEL €

(Map p68; ☑ 218 885 312; www.homelisbonhostel.com; Rua São Nicolau 13; dm €30-34, d €110-140; @ 🐱) In the heart of Baixa, this high-security hostel is one of the best maintained you'll come across. Facilities are above and beyond, from the professional-grade bar/reception to dark hardwood bunks spread across various floors with privacy curtains that might as well be luxury drapes. It's a family-run oasis, with the doting matriarch, known affectionately as Mamma, even cooking for guests.

It has won the Hoscar for Best Hostel in the World five years running. A new floor, acquired in 2018, houses private rooms.

Living Lounge
HOSTEL €

(Map p72; ☑ 213 461 078; www.livinglounge-hostel.com; Rua do Crucifixo 116, 2nd fl; dm/s/d €25/37/64; ❄ @ 🐱) The Living Lounge is steeped in style – vintage barber chairs, suspended tables, vinyl on the speakers – and offers spick-and-span mixed dorms with lockers, various hang lounges, friendly staff and excellent amenities (full kitchen, bicycle hire, an obvious emphasis on cocktails). The nightly dinners and wide range of tours provide a fine opportunity to meet other travellers.

Travellers House
HOSTEL €

(Map p68; ☑ 210 115 922; www.travellershouse.com; Rua Augusta 89; dm €30-32, d without bathroom €80, d €90-100; ❄ @ 🐱) Travellers enthuse about this superfriendly hostel set in a converted 250-year-old house. As well as cosy dorms and a wealth of comfortable private rooms (some more minimalist than others), there's a retro lounge with beanbags, an internet corner and a communal

kitchen. CCTV and heaters keep everyone safe and warm.

★ Lisbon Story Guesthouse
GUESTHOUSE €€

(Map p68; ☑ 218 879 392; www.lisbonstoryguesthouse.com; Largo de São Domingos 18; d €80-100, without bathroom €50-70, apt €110-120; @ 🐱) 🍃 Overlooking Largo de São Domingos, Lisbon Story is a small, extremely welcoming guesthouse with nicely maintained, light-drenched rooms, all of which sport Portuguese themes (the Tejo, tram 28E, fado etc), plus working antique radios, record players and the like. The lounge, with throw pillows and low tables, is a great place to chill.

My Story Tejo
HOTEL €€

(Map p68; ☑ 218 866 182; www.mystoryhotels.com/mystorytejo; Rua dos Condes de Monsanto 2; s/d from €115/123; ❄ 🐱) Formerly a broom-maker's and the modest Hotel Lisboa Tejo, this 135-room hotel was phenomenally upgraded by the local My Story chain in 2018. It's now a fantastic three-star property with modern rooms (light hardwood and teal accents, and walls fashioned from reclaimed wooden pillars from the building's pre-earthquake foundations), and is one of the best-value options you'll find.

A restaurant and bar have also been added. Don't miss the Roman *poço* (well) near the entrance.

My Story Rossio
BOUTIQUE HOTEL €€€

(Map p72; ☑ 213 400 380; www.mystoryhotels.com/mystoryrossio; Praça Dom Pedro IV 59; s/d from €157/167; ❄ 🐱) This upstart local chain gets a gold star for its central location right on Rossio. Carpeted hallways depicting Google Maps views of Lisbon lead to rooms (and bathrooms) that tend to be cramped (you'll be happier in a roomier superior),

---

Where to Stay in Lisbon

0 —————— 2 km
0 —————— 1 mile

Príncipe Real, Santos & Estrela

Príncipe Real is tops for hip local fashion, shopping and restaurants. Santos and Estrela are ideal for avoiding the central bustle.

Best For LGBT+ travellers; local life

Transport Frequent buses and trams

Price Midrange and top end

Lapa & Alcântara

Gentrified bairros with en vogue bars, clubs and restaurants. Less popular for overnighting than the more bustling areas.

Best For Leafy Lapa backstreets

Transport Half-hour by tram to the centre

Price Mostly top end

Belém

Close to Lisbon's top Unesco-listed sights. Limited sleeping options.

Best For Quiet nights
Transport Eight minutes by train or 30 by tram to central Lisbon

Price Mostly midrange

Basílica d.
Estrela

Lapa &
Alcântara

Belém
Mosteiro dos
Jerónimos

Parque das Nações
Near Oceanário de Lisboa but far from other sights.

Best For Contemporary architecture; chain hotels

Transport 20-minute metro to centre; three bus stops to airport

Price Midrange

Parque das Nações

Oceanário de Lisboa

Marquês de Pombal & Around
Home to Lisbon's finest restaurants and boutiques – but its high-rises can lack charm.

Best For High culture; upscale tastes

Transport Easy metro access

Price Top end

Marquês de Pombal

Alfama, Castelo & Graça
Steep Graça and Castelo offer dramatic views. Alfama is Lisbon's most cinematic neighbourhood, but it can be noisy.

Best For Boutique hotels; history lovers

Transport Central with good connections

Price Mostly top end

ncipe Real, Santos & Estrela

Alfama, Castelo & Graça

Castelo de São Jorge

Convento do Carmo

Baixa & Rossio

Chiado & Bairro Alto

Praça do Comércio

Chiado & Bairro Alto
Chiado boasts top-end trendies, boutique options galore and world-class shopping. Bairro Alto oozes historical charm but is rowdy-nightlife central.

Best For Luxury hotels; great hostels

Transport Central with good connections

Price Budget and top end

Baixa & Rossio
Very central but very touristy; the 24-hour buzz can disrupt sleep.

Best For Urban hubbub

Transport Great public transport links

Price All budgets

DON'T MISS

HITCH A RIDE ON TRAM 28

Vintage **tram 28E** (Map p68; Largo Martim Moniz) offers the ultimate tour of Lisbon's blockbuster sights – from Basílica da Estrela, across the backstreets of Baixa, through the winding, postcard-perfect lanes of Alfama and up to the hilltop *bairro* of Graça – all for the price of a €2.90 ticket. The route from Campo de Ourique to Martim Moniz – the best direction both for getting a seat and because it dumps you in central Lisbon at the end – is 45 minutes of astonishing views and absurdly steep climbs. The fun begins at **Cemitério dos Prazeres** (www.cm-lisboa.pt/equipamentos/equipamento/info/cemiterio-dos-prazeres; Praça São João Bosco; ⊙9am-6pm May-Sep, to 5pm Oct-Apr) – the **tram** (www.carris.pt/pt/electrico/28E/descendente; Praça São João Bosco) is nearby – a particularly atmospheric burial ground, before rambling through the residential neighbourhood of Estrela (p75) and its magnificent Basílica da Estrela (p75) and pretty Jardim da Estrela (p75). It continues on through the district of Santa Catarina before arriving in upmarket Chiado (p70), passing its quaint beating heart, Praça Luís de Camões, along the way. The tram then crosses east through the heart of Baixa (p67), where just a few blocks south of the tramway, Lisbon's triumphant and striking main square, Praça do Comércio (p67), sits flanking the Rio Tejo. Just imagine: this massive square, with its Instagram-ready grand 18th-century arcades, lemon-meringue facades and mosaic cobbles, was used as a car park as recently as 1990!

Getting back on board tram 28, you'll then take a turn towards its most exciting bit – the start of its rattling climb to Alfama (p70), where passengers lean perilously out of the window for an in-motion shot of the Sé de Lisboa (p71) or hop out for postcard-perfect views from **Miradouro de Santa Luzia** (Map p76; Largo Santa Luzia). The final stretch negotiates impossibly narrow streets and hairpin bends up to Graça (p70), where most folk get out to explore Mosteiro de São Vicente de Fora (p75) and to take even more photos of impossibly pretty cityscapes at **Miradouro da Graça** (Map p76; Largo da Graça) and **Miradouro da Senhora do Monte** (Rua da Senhora do Monte) – the highest of Lisbon's lookouts. The tram then circles around to the north and begins its rickety descent into the multicultural area of Martim Moniz.

but travellers enjoy hi-tech mod-cons such as TV/mirror hybrids, plus quirky themes (Fado, Amor, Lisboa) and value for money.

Pousada de Lisboa BOUTIQUE HOTEL €€€
(Map p68; ☑210 407 650; www.pestana.com/en/hotel/pousada-lisboa; Praça do Comércio 31; r €235-440; ❄@🖥❄) Location, location, location! Portugal's Pestana chain hit the jackpot in 2015 with this privileged position on Praça do Comércio. A €70-million renovation turned the former Ministry of Internal Affairs into a cosy *pousada* (upmarket inn) with museum-like qualities. Sculptures throughout represent epic moments in Portuguese history and, yes, you can sit on those 13th-century *liteiras* (litters).

Internacional Design Hotel BOUTIQUE HOTEL €€€
(Map p72; ☑213 240 990; www.idesignhotel.com; Rua da Betesga 3; s/d from €175/195; 🅿❄@🖥) This high-concept hotel has four types of rooms, each conjuring a radically different aesthetic. Urban rooms have brightly coloured artwork and duvets; Tribu rooms have

wood details and burlap wallpaper; Zen aim for simple elegance; while Pop feature eye-catching art and bubblegum-coloured floors and walls. The best? Room 407 (Pop), with its tiny balcony staring straight over Rossio.

🛏 Chiado & Bairro Alto

Bairro Alto is nightlife central, meaning you won't get much rest amid the late-night revelry. Well-heeled Chiado has high-quality top-end and budget options, but little in between. The hip Santa Catarina district has a few options.

★**Lisbon Calling** HOSTEL €
(Map p72; ☑213 432 381; www.lisboncalling.net; Rua de São Paulo 126, 3rd fl; dm from €20, d with/without bathroom from €75/55; @🖥) This fashionable, unsigned backpacker favourite near Santa Catarina features original frescoes, *azulejos* and hardwood floors – all lovingly restored by friendly Portuguese owners. The bright, spacious dorms and a brick-vaulted kitchen are easy on the eye, but the private

rooms – specifically room 1812 – will floor you: boutique-hotel-level dens of style and comfort that thunderously out-punch their price point.

Lisbon Calling has also opened a second location with five suites near Av da Liberdade.

Sunset Destination Hostel
HOSTEL €
(Map p72; ☑ 210997735; www.followyourdestination. com; Cais do Sodré train station; dm €27-34, d without bathroom €73-81, d from €87; ❄ @ ? ☎) This beautifully designed river-facing hostel is awash in antiquated art-deco swank. It has comfy dorm rooms with electronic lockers and a high-style dining room, but it outclasses its peers with its rooftop pool terrace (with winter dome bar) and impressive river views. Organised street-art tours, pub crawls and fado excursions provide dependable good times.

Independente
HOSTEL €
(Map p72; ☑ 213 461 381; www.theindependente. pt; Rua de São Pedro de Alcântara 81; dm €22-28, ste without/with view €170/195; ❄ @ ?) On the edge of the Bairro Alto, this superstylish hostel has 11 dorm rooms (with six to 12 beds in each) and four mid-century-modern-leaning minimalist suites with balconies overlooking the Rio Tejo. There are two great restaurants here: Decadente (p100) – modern Portuguese, creative cocktails – and the more chef-driven and pricier Insólito (mains €20).

Light sleepers beware: noise can be an issue.

★ Casa Balthazar
GUESTHOUSE €€€
(Map p72; ☑ 213 243 000; www.casabalthazar lisbon.com; Rua do Duque 26; d €190-380; P ❄ ? ☎) Tucked down a quiet lane, Casa Balthazar has undeniable appeal, with spacious, beautifully furnished rooms that bridge art deco with the 21st century, plus friendly service and a grassy courtyard with a pool. Each of the 17 rooms has been appointed with high-end fittings (iPod docks, big flat-screen TVs, luxury bedding), and pricier rooms have magnificent views (some with private Jacuzzi terraces).

★ Palácio Verride
BOUTIQUE HOTEL €€€
(Map p72; ☑ 211 573 055; www.verridesc.pt; Rua de Santa Catarina 1; d €500-1500, ste €3000; P ❄ @ ? ☎) The 19-room Palácio Verride, dating to the 1750s, was once the stomping ground of Count Verride, whose former dining room now makes up the extraordinary

Queen Suite, awash in original *azulejos*, hand-painted silk wallpaper and one of Portugal's most lavish bathtubs. Elsewhere, custom-designed furniture and heated wooden flooring offer a contemporary Nordic-ish counterpoint to marble and pre-earthquake luxury.

Criatura, the casual dining option, is decked out with custom Vista Alegre tableware and a photo exhibition on loan from Museu Coleção Berardo, while Suba, the fine-dining rooftop restaurant, sits on a towering lookout that offers downtown Lisbon's only 360-degree city view. The whole thing is a discerning bastion of Scandinavian-evoking style, while not losing sight of its historic past.

Bairro Alto Hotel
BOUTIQUE HOTEL €€€
(Map p72; ☑ 213 408 288; www.bairroaltohotel. com; Praça Luís de Camões 2; r from €380; P ❄ ?) On a pretty square is Lisbon's most storied luxury hotel, dating from 1921. It reopened in early 2019 after a massive €30 million redesign by Pritzker Prize–winning architect Eduardo Souto de Moura, who oversaw 32 new rooms, a redesigned reception and an entirely new 5th-floor restaurant (BAHR, by lauded chef Nuno Mendes) with a panoramic terrace for food and sundowners.

Late Birds
GUESTHOUSE €€€
(Map p72; ☑ 933 000 962; www.thelatebirds lisbon.com; Tv André Valente 21-21A; d from €161; ❄ @ ? ☎) Billed as a 'gay urban resort', this fabulous Bairro Alto place is better described as a high-style guesthouse where gay couples (and those that are straight but not narrow) can feel welcome and comfortable. The design-forward public spaces (sexy lounge, small pool and garden patio) are perfectly minimalist, and the 16 whitewashed rooms all have desktop iMacs.

Hotel do Chiado
HOTEL €€€
(Map p72; ☑ 213 256 100; www.hoteldochiado. com; Rua Nova do Almada 114; s/d from €195/210; P ❄ ?) Fusing 19th-century charm with 21st-century cool, the well-located 39-room Hotel do Chiado offers carpeted, well-appointed rooms that come in three styles: classics (small and boxy, with no views), superiors (brighter and roomier, with French balconies) and premiums (top-floor rooms that open onto grassy, bougainvillea-clad terraces with river and castle views). The 7th-floor bar (open 11am to 10.30pm) offers superb vistas.

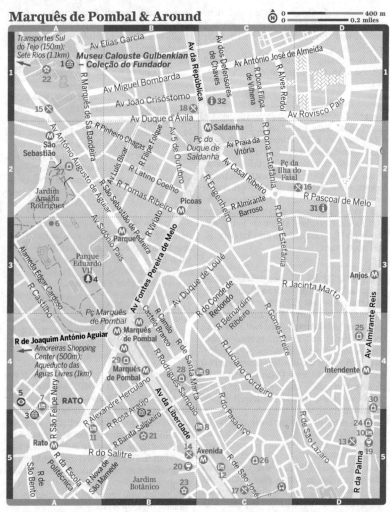

Alfama, Castelo & Graça

Alfama's cobbled lanes generally offer peaceful slumber, though choose wisely or else you might find yourself being serenaded to sleep by a warbling *fadista*. On its hilltop perch above Lisbon, leafy Graça has dramatic views.

Largo Residencias   GUESTHOUSE €
(Map p92; ☎218 885 420; www.largoresidencias. com; Largo de Intendente 19; with/without bathroom s €50/35, d €70/50; ☜) Cool and quiet, this artsy multifloored guesthouse sits in the thick of it on Largo de Intendente. Rooms are simple but feature beds custom-made from reclaimed wood, plus piecemeal antiques and other flea-market furniture and accoutrements. There's a bohemian cafe on the ground floor.

★**Palácio Belmonte**   BOUTIQUE HOTEL €€€
(Map p76; ☎218 816 600; www.palaciobelmonte. com; Páteo Dom Fradique 14; ste €500-3000; P ✳ ☜ ⛢) Nestled beside Castelo de São Jorge, this 15th-century palace, formerly belonging to the family of Brazil explorer Pedro Álvares Cabral, turns on the VIP treatment with its 10 suites, named after Portuguese luminaries and lavishly adorned with

Marquês de Pombal & Around

LISBON & AROUND LISBON

18th-century *azulejos,* silks, marble and antiques.

There's a pool framed by herb gardens and adjacent sauna, a wood-panelled library where classical music plays, and numerous other luxuries, including the privilege of sleeping amid original castle walls and towers. A *sous-vide*-oriented restaurant, Leopold, is open to nonguests and serves nightly changing set menus (€45) to rave reviews.

★**Memmo Alfama**   BOUTIQUE HOTEL €€€
(Map p76; ☎210 495 660; www.memmoalfama.com; Tv Merceeiras 27; d €200-350, ste €300-450; ❄☞❀) Slip down a narrow alley to reach this gorgeous Alfama boutique option, a stunning conversion of a shoe-polish factory and former bakery. The rooms are an ode to whitewashed minimalism and staff are as sleek as the decor, with their uniform-issued retro New Balance sneakers and hipster aura. The view down to the Rio Tejo from the roof terrace is phenomenal.

★**Santiago de Alfama**   BOUTIQUE HOTEL €€€
(Map p76; ☎213 941 616; www.santiagodealfama.com; Rua de Santiago 10; d/ste from €285/660; ❄☞❀) In 2015 Dutch hospitality dreamer

Heleen Uitenbroek turned a ruined 15th-century palace into luxury sleeps at this 19-room bastion of style. It's airy and awash in light pinewoods and contemporary art, and exquisite attention to detail is everywhere, from the Santiago-cross-inspired tile flooring and textured bathroom tiling to an encased glass hallway revealing uncovered Roman steps.

🛏 Príncipe Real, Santos & Estrela

Leafy neighbourhoods and plenty of style set the scene for an overnight stay in the top-notch boutique hotels in this area. It's ideal for escapists who prefer pin-drop peace to central bustle – yet can still have quick access to nearly everywhere.

★**Casa do Príncipe**   B&B €€
(Map p84; ☎218 264 183; www.casadoprincipe.com; Praça do Príncipe Real 23; d €108-209; ❄☞) Perfectly located and exquisitely restored (and accordingly priced to shock!), this 14-room B&B is housed inside what was once the same 19th-century neo-Moorish palace as Embaixada (p118) next door. Original frescoes, *azulejos* and ornate moulded

ceilings adorn the hardwood halls and spacious rooms, which are themed after the life of King Dom Pedro V. Indeed, you'll sleep like royalty here yourself.

Memmo Príncipe Real BOUTIQUE HOTEL €€€
(Map p84; ☑ 213 514 368; www.memmohotels.com; Rua Dom Pedro V 56; d €300-450; ✳@✳☞) Príncipe Real's hottest hotel is this 41-room cradle of cool steeped in a corresponding high-design ethos with its sister property in Alfama. Rooms contrast vintage furniture with modern artworks, many featuring terraces complete with outdoor firepits, a real coup for a city-centre hotel. Similarly impressive 180-degree city views beckon from the private rooftop terrace and pool.

🛏 Marquês de Pombal & Around

Lisbon Dreams GUESTHOUSE €€
(Map p92; ☑ 213 872 393; www.lisbondreamsguesthouse.com; Rua Rodrigo da Fonseca 29; s/d without bathroom €65/70, d €105; ✳@☞) 🍴 On a quiet street lined with jacaranda trees, eco-leaning Lisbon Dreams offers excellent value for its 19 bright, modern rooms with high ceilings and excellent mattresses. The green apples are a nice touch, and there are attractive common areas to unwind in. All bathrooms are shared except one, but are spotlessly clean.

★Casa Amora GUESTHOUSE €€€
(Map p92; ☑ 919 300 317; www.casaamora.com; Rua João Penha 13; d €130-150, apt €160-180, ste €200; ✳☞) 🍴 Casa Amora has 11 beautifully designed guest rooms and studio apartments, with eye-catching art and iPod docks. There's a lovely garden patio where the first-rate breakfast is served out of a Smeg-filled kitchen. It's located in the peaceful neighbourhood of Amoreiras, a few steps from one of Lisbon's prettiest squares.

★Valverde BOUTIQUE HOTEL €€€
(Map p92; ☑ 210 940 300; www.valverdehotel.com; Av da Liberdade 164; d €302-410, ste €446-646; P✳@☞✳) Exquisite Valverde feels like a boutique town house (which it once was). Its facade is not showy, but once inside, an urban oasis of discerning design and personalised service is subtly unveiled. Reached by black-dominated, hushed hallways, the 25 rooms elicit style, form and function, and are awash in cultured European art and unique mid-century-modern pieces.

Inspira Santa Marta HOTEL €€€
(Map p92; ☑ 210 440 900; www.inspirasantamartahotel.com; Rua de Santa Marta 48; s/d from €144/154; ✳@☞) 🍴 The 89-room Inspira Santa Marta is an ecofriendly designer hotel set in a converted 19th-century building. Rooms are stylish but functional, with different feng shui themes, including earth-toned Terra rooms and cork-floored Arvore (tree) rooms with sky-blue details. An inviting Mediterranean brasserie showcases locally grown ingredients, plus there's a spa, a bar with a fireplace and a games room.

Hotel Britania HOTEL €€€
(Map p92; ☑ 213 218 200; www.heritage.pt; Rua Rodrigues Sampaio 17; d €125-400; P✳@☞) Art deco rules the waves at the 33-room Britania, a boutique gem near Av da Liberdade. Architect Cassiano Branco put his modernist stamp on the rooms with chrome lamps, plaid fabrics and shiny marble bathrooms. Hobnob over a G&T at the bar, chat with the affable staff and let this time capsule take you back to the 1940s.

🛏 Belém

Pensão Residencial Setúbalense GUESTHOUSE €€
(Map p96; ☑ 213 636 639; www.setubalense.pt; Rua de Belém 28; s/d not incl breakfast from €50/70; ✳☞) A short toddle east of the Mosteiro dos Jerónimos, this 17th-century guesthouse has 80 spartan but modern rooms – some have floral fabrics, newer rooms don't – with tiled floors and decent bathrooms. Corridors are a tad dark, but *azulejos* and potted plants add a homely touch.

There is no breakfast, but you're steps from the pastries of Antiga Confeitaria de Belém (p106). It's a holiday, right?

Jerónimos 8 BOUTIQUE HOTEL €€
(Map p96; ☑ 213 600 900; www.jeronimos8.com; Rua dos Jerónimos 8; s €80-220, d €90-240; ✳☞) Belém's first boutique hotel, 65-room stylish Jerónimos 8 has clean lines, floor-to-ceiling windows and designer flourishes aplenty. Slick rooms are dressed in cream and caramel hues with natural fabrics (four include balconies with monastery views). Chill in the pepper-red bar or grab a drink and take it to the 2nd-floor deck.

🍴 Eating

Creative new-generation chefs at the stove, first-rate raw ingredients and a generous pinch of world spice have transformed Lisbon into a buzzing culinary capital. Reservations, even early in the week and in low season, are a good idea – getting turned away without them is all too common.

✖ Baixa & Rossio

Many of Baixa's old-school bistros and outdoor cafes heave with tourists, but tiptoe away from the main drag, Rua Augusta, and you'll find some gems in streets such as Rua dos Correiros and Rua dos Sapateiros.

★ Mercado da Baixa MARKET €

(Map p68; www.adbaixapombalina.pt/mercado-da-baixa; Praça da Figueira; ⊙10am-10pm Fri-Sun last weekend of month) This tented market/glorious food court has been slinging cheese, wine, smoked sausages and other gourmet goodies since 1855. It's fantastic fun to stroll the stalls, eating and drinking yourself into a gluttonous mess.

Nova Pombalina PORTUGUESE €

(Map p68; www.facebook.com/anovapombalina; Rua do Comércio 2; sandwiches €3-4.50; ⊙7am-7.30pm Mon-Sat) The reason this bustling traditional restaurant is always packed around noon is its delicious *leitão* (suckling pig) sandwich, served on freshly baked bread in 60 seconds or less by the lightning-fast crew behind the counter.

★ Pinóquio PORTUGUESE €€

(Map p68; ☑213 465 106; www.restaurantepinoquio.pt; Praça dos Restauradores 79; mains €17-26; ⊙noon-midnight; 🖘) Busy Pinóquio is easy to miss as it's tucked into a *praça* corner partially obstructed by a souvenir kiosk. Dressed in white tablecloths against peagreen walls, it's distinctly old school, with indomitable waiters slinging a stunning slew of classic dishes: *arroz de pato* (duck rice), seafood *feijoada*, *arroz de bacalhau* (codfish rice), and pork chops with almonds and coriander.

Ask in-the-know Portuguese foodies about their favourite home-grown restaurant and their nose will be growing if they don't say Pinóquio. Prices are higher here, but they're worth it. Reserve a table.

Tasca Kome JAPANESE €€

(Map p68; ☑211 340 117; www.kome-lisboa.com; Rua da Madalena 57; mains €8-23, sushi plates from €15; ⊙noon-2.30pm & 7-10pm Tue-Thu, noon-3pm & 7-10pm Fri, 12.30-3pm & 7-10pm Sat; 🖘) This blink-and-you'll-miss-it Japanese *tasca* is one of Lisbon's few turning out authentic cuisine from the Land of the Rising Sun. The menu doesn't overwhelm with options; instead, there's exquisite sushi, *tonkatsu* (breaded pork cutlets), *aji tataki* (horse mackerel with ginger and chives), *nasu dengaku* (fried aubergine with miso) and daily-changing specials that bridge cultures (pork stew with daikon, for example).

Bebedouro TAPAS €€

(Map p68; ☑218 860 376; www.facebook.com/bebedourowineandfood; Rua de São Nicolau 24; tasting plates €18-40; ⊙noon-11.45pm Wed-Mon; 🖘) Wine-bottle lights illuminate stylish Bebedouro, where full-bodied Douro wines are nicely paired with tasting platters of regional cheese and sausage, creative salads and *petiscos* (tapas or small plates). The small, shotgun-style place has just five tables and five bar seats plus a little pavement terrace.

There's a good buzz, friendly service and it's one of the few that isn't fussy about folks who just want a nice glass of wine.

★ Cervejaria Ramiro SEAFOOD €€€

(Map p92; www.cervejariaramiro.pt; Av Almirante Reis 1; seafood per kg €12-91; ⊙noon-12.30am Tue-Sun) Opened in 1956, Ramiro has legendary status among Lisbon's seafood lovers. Here you can feast on rich plates of giant tiger prawns, *percebes* (goose barnacles), lobster, crab and clams, and even juicy steak sandwiches.

Despite the high prices, the atmosphere is bustling and informal, with garrulous crowds – albeit more tourists than locals these days – quaffing more beer than wine. Ramiro doesn't take reservations after 7.30pm, so arrive early and prepare to queue.

Solar dos Presuntos PORTUGUESE €€€

(Map p68; ☑213 424 253; www.solardospresuntos.com; Rua das Portas de Santo Antão 150; mains €16-27.50, seafood per kg €29-98; ⊙12.30-3.30pm & 7-11pm Mon-Sat; 🖘) Don't be fooled by the smoked *presunto* (ham) hanging in the window, this iconic restaurant is renowned for its excellent seafood too. Start with the *pata negra* (cured ham), *paio* smoked sausage and cheese *couvert* (stew), then dig into a fantastic lobster *açorda*, delectable seafood paella or crustacean curry.

✖ Chiado & Cais do Sodré

★ Mercado da Ribeira MARKET €

(Map p72; www.timeoutmarket.com; Av 24 de Julho; ⊙10am-midnight Sun-Wed, to 2am Thu-Sat,

Belém

Belém

◎ Top Sights

◎ Sights

⬤ Sleeping

⊗ Eating

⬤ Drinking & Nightlife

⬤ Entertainment

traditional market 6am-2pm Mon-Sat; 🛱) Doing trade in fresh fruit and veg, fish and flowers since 1892, this domed market hall has been the word on everyone's lips since *Time Out* transformed half of it into a gourmet food court in 2014. Now it's Lisbon in chaotic culinary microcosm: Garrafeira Nacional wines, Café de São Bento steaks, Manteigaria Silva (p114) cold cuts and Michelin-star chef creations from Henrique Sá Pessoa.

Follow the lead of locals and come for a browse in the morning followed by lunch at one of 40 kiosks. Need tips for navigating the chaos? Top chefs (Pessoa, Alexandre Silva, Miguel Laffan etc) occupy the northern back row. The kiosks along the western and eastern sides have counter-style seating that open out to a far less crowded corridor on their opposite sides (great for solo diners); and a few, such as seafooder Marisqueira Azul, offer outdoor seating facing pretty Praça Dom Luís. Bar stalls hold court in the middle of the market – prepare to go to war for a spot. Some famed restaurants, such as **Pap'Açorda** (Map p72; 🕿 213 464 811; www.papacorda.com; mains €16-36; ☉noon-midnight Sun, Tue & Wed, to 2am Thu-Sat; 🛱), are a bit hidden on the 1st floor.

Ao 26 – Vegan Food Project   VEGAN €
(Map p72; 🕿 967 989 184; www.facebook.com/ao26veganfoodproject; Rua Vítor Cordon 26; mains €5.50-7.50; ☉12.30-6.30pm & 7.30-11pm Tue-Sat; 🛱🌱) So good it even lures in devout carnivores, this small, hip and bustling place offers two elaborate, daily-changing chalkboard specials (eg Manchurian meatballs with tomato, coconut and masala). There's a fixed menu of loaded lentil burgers, beet burgers and veg sandwiches on *bolo do caco*

(round bread cooked on a basalt stone slab), plus Lisbon craft beer.

Pistola y Corazon
MEXICAN €

(Map p72; www.pistolaycorazon.com; Rua da Boavista 16; tacos €7-10; ⊙6pm-midnight Mon & Sat, noon-3pm & 6pm-midnight Tue-Fri, noon-3pm & 7pm-1am Sun; 🛜) This lively hipster taqueria is a godsend of authentic Mexican street tacos (*carnitas, cochinita pibil, carne asada, al pastor* etc), served among tweaked *El Tri* kitsch (Frida Kahlo rocking a Daft Punk T-shirt!). The creative mescal- and tequila-laced cocktail list is equally outstanding. Write your name on the wait list – it's always packed.

On Sundays, don't miss breakfast, with *chilaquiles,* huevos rancheros and all your favourite Mexican morning delights.

Landeau
SWEETS €

(Map p72; www.landeau.pt; Rua das Flores 70; cake €3.70; ⊙noon-7pm; 🛜) The Portuguese love to self-proclaim their product to be the best this or the best that in the world, but this don't-miss cafe puts its chocolate where its mouth is, serving up as flawless a piece of chocolate cake as you'll ever encounter.

Gelato Davvero
GELATO €

(Map p84; www.facebook.com/gelatodavvero; Av Dom Carlos I 39; small/medium/large ice cream €2/3/4; ⊙noon-8pm Mon-Wed, to midnight Thu-Sat, 1-8pm Sun; 🛜) Owner Filippo Licitra defected from Lisbon's Gelataria Nannarella and his rival *gelataria,* Davvero, boasts 35 or so changing flavours, so there's room for wackiness (avocado, curried mango), but the creamilicious classics are all here. There are other locations in Belém (Map p96; Praça do Império, Centro Cultural de Belém; ⊙noon-8pm Sun & Mon, to 9pm Tue-Thu, to 11pm Fri & Sat) and near the cruise-ship terminal.

O Trevo
PORTUGUESE €

(Map p72; Praça Luís de Camões 48; snacks €0.80-2.75; ⊙7am-11.30pm Mon-Sat) Despite a posh address on Praça Luís de Camões, O Trevo is a bustling and surly local joint deeply rooted in the daily grind. Working-class *lisboêtas* go for the *bifanas* – thinly sliced pork, precooked in boiling seasoned lard and slapped on the griddle, served between two slices of warmed *biju* bread with mustard and/or chilli oil (€1.90 to €2.15).

Sol e Pesca
PORTUGUESE €

(Map p72; www.facebook.com/solepesca; Rua Nova do Carvalho 44; tinned fish €2-16.80; ⊙noon-2am Sun-Thu, to 3am Fri & Sat) Rods, nets, hooks and fish charts give away this tiny bar's former life as a fishing-tackle shop. Cabinets are stacked with vintage-looking tins of sardines, tuna, mackerel and other preserved delicacies. Grab a chair, order a tin or two, add bread, olives and wine, and you have the makings of a fine and quite affordable meal.

Povo
PORTUGUESE €

(Map p72; 🗹213 473 403; www.povolisboa.com; Rua Nova do Carvalho 32; small plates €7.50-16; ⊙6pm-2am Sun-Wed, to 4am Thu-Sat) On bar-lined Rua Nova do Carvalho, Povo serves tasty Portuguese comfort food in the form of *petiscos.* There's also outdoor seating, plus live performances at 8pm Tuesday to Sunday, often by in-house *fadista* Marta de Sousa (Thursdays are best).

Self-Service do ACISJF
PORTUGUESE €

(Map p72; www.juntanacionalacisjf.blogspot.pt; Tv do Ferragial 1, 2nd fl; meals €6.50; ⊙noon-3pm Mon-Fri) Known on the street as Cantina das Freiras, this small, sunny cafeteria inside a Catholic association is run by sweet nuns dressed as lunch ladies. They dish up a daily soup (the gazpacho is great), several mains of the beef, sardines or codfish variety, and fresh fruit for dessert. The river views from the sun-drenched terrace are astounding. Buzz 'Self-Service' for entrance.

Mini Bar
FUSION €€

(Map p72; 🗹211 305 393; www.minibar.pt; Rua António Maria Cardoso 58; small plates €2.80-14.50, tasting menus €45-55; ⊙7pm-2am; 🛜) Trendy and fun, Mini Bar is the most approachable and hippest entry point into the innovative cuisine of Michelin-starred chef José Avillez, who has several restaurants in the vicinity. Billed as a gourmet bar amid theatre-inspired decor, it's a trendy mash-up of nightlife and fine dining, where you'll enjoy exceptional craft drinking alongside small, chef-driven *petiscos.*

Taberna Tosca
TAPAS €€

(Map p72; 🗹218 034 563; www.tabernatosca.com; Praça São Paulo 21; tapas €4-13; ⊙noon-midnight, to 2am Fri-Sat) A peaceful retreat from the nearby Rua Nova do Carvalho mayhem, Tosca is an enticing spot for Portuguese tapas and bold Douro reds (but don't be afraid to spring for a pitcher of fabulous port sangria). Open-air seating is on leafy Praça São Paulo in front, opposite an 18th-century church, making it feel like a hidden Lisbon highlight.

Vicente by Carnalentejana
PORTUGUESE €€

(Map p72; ☑ 218 066 142; www.carnalentejana.pt/restaurantes; Rua das Flores 6; mains €10.50-17; ⊘12.30-3pm & 7.30-11.30pm; ☎) This sexy restaurant dishes up succulent beef and pork dishes made with ultrapremium Carnalentejana DOP-certified meat from the Alentejo, along with wines, cheeses, olive oils and other treats produced by the same artisanal farmers. In this former coal shop turned carnivore's den of decadence, the original low-slung stone walls, exposed air ducts and filament light bulbs are notably atmospheric.

Queijaria
CHEESE €€

(Map p84; ☑ 213 460 474; www.queijaria.wix.com/queijaria; Rua do Monte Olivete 40; 1/3/5 cheese tastings €4.70/11.70/14.70; ⊘noon-8pm Tue-Fri, from 10am Sat, 10am-4pm Sun; ☎) What started as Lisbon's only dedicated cheese shop has evolved into a fantastic place to sample over 60 top homemade cheeses from small regional producers otherwise inaccessible in the capital. Plop yourself down for a creamy, barnyardy five-cheese plate paired with wines or craft beer (serving two; €42.50 to €47.50). No regrets!

Taberna da Rua das Flores
PORTUGUESE €€

(Map p72; ☑ 213 479 418; Rua das Flores 103; small plates €2.50-15; ⊘noon-midnight Mon-Sat) You'll have to get past the owner's unfortunate 'My way or the highway' attitude, but if you do, this tiny throwback tavern does a daily-changing, locally sourced chalkboard menu of creative small plates, all market-fresh and fantastic. Sweet staff offer in-depth, mouth-watering descriptions for each dish, which are chased with Lisbon-area-only wines and select cocktails mixed with hardcore Portuguese firewaters.

Mercantina
PIZZA €€

(Map p72; ☑ 231 070 013; www.mercantina.pt; Rua da Misericórdia 114; pizza €8-14, pasta €11-13.50; ⊘noon-3.30pm & 7.30-11.30pm Mon-Thu, 12.30-3.30pm & 7pm-midnight Fri-Sun; ☎) You'll find some of Lisbon's best pizza – uncut, certified by Napoli's strict *Associazione Verace Pizza Napoletana* – at this cosy Chiado hotspot whose hardwood-heavy decor vaguely approaches ski-lodge territory. The spicy *diavola* (tomato, mozzarella, ventricina sausage, Parmesan and basil) and *mercantina* (tomato, mozzarella, ham, salami, mushrooms and Parmesan) are both show-stoppers, but don't discount the phenomenal lasagne. Reserve ahead online.

Palácio Chiado
GASTRONOMY €€

(Map p72; www.palaciochiado.pt; Rua do Alecrím 70; mains €7-28; ⊘noon-midnight Sun-Wed, to 2am Thu-Sat; ☎) This ravishing former home of Portuguese barons is one of Lisbon's most stunning addresses for foodies, a gourmet food court wrapped in exquisitely renovated 18th-century packaging. A breathtaking grand staircase, swamped by original stained glass and archetypal frescoes, invites you to explore multiple gastronomic concepts and bars spread over two floors, from burgers and grills to sparkling wine and seafood.

Sacramento
PORTUGUESE, MEDITERRANEAN €€

(Map p72; ☑ 213 420 572; www.sacramentodochiado.com; Calçada Sacramento 40; mains €15-25; ⊘12.30-3pm & 7.30pm-midnight Mon-Fri, 7pm-2am Sat & Sun; ☎) If you drop your *cêntimos* at one touristy restaurant in Lisbon, choose contemporary Sacramento, a fun and festive place gorgeously set inside a former 17th-century palace. Both the decor (soothing maroon and chocolate-framed mirrors and suspended red luminaires) and the food (lovely wild mushrooms with presunto ham, a perfectly charred octopus *à lagareiro*) are real crowd-pleasers.

★ Alma
MODERN PORTUGUESE €€€

(Map p72; ☑ 213 470 650; www.almalisboa.pt; Rua Anchieta 15; mains €32-36, tasting menus €110-120; ⊘noon-3pm & 7-11pm Tue-Sun; ☎) Two-Michelin-starred Henrique Sá Pessoa's flagship Alma is one of Portugal's destination restaurants and, in our humble opinion, Lisbon's best gourmet dining experience. The casual space exudes understated style amid the original stone flooring and gorgeous hardwood tables, but it's Pessoa's outrageously good nouveau Portuguese cuisine that draws the foodie flock from far and wide.

★ Belcanto
PORTUGUESE €€€

(Map p72; ☑ 213 420 607; www.belcanto.pt; Largo de São Carlos 10; mains €49.50, tasting menu €165-185, with 5/9 wines €100/120 extra; ⊘12.30-3pm & 7-11pm Tue-Sat; ☎) José Avillez' two-Michelin-starred cathedral of cookery wows diners with painstaking creativity, polished service and a first-rate sommelier. Standouts among Lisbon's culinary adventure of a lifetime include suckling pig with orange purée; sea bass with seaweed and bivalves; and Avillez' masterstroke, the Garden of the Goose that Laid the Golden Eggs (egg, crunchy bread

LISBON FOR CHILDREN

Even little things in Lisbon spark the imagination – from bumpy rides on bee-yellow trams to gooey *pastéis de nata*(custard tarts). There are free or half-price tickets for little ones at major sights, half-portions at many restaurants and free transport for under-fives.

Parque das Nações

Parque das Nações is prime kiddie territory, where little nippers love to spot toothy sharks and sea otters at the eye-popping Oceanário de Lisboa (p82), experience zero-gravity and ride the high-wire bicycle at the hands-on Pavilhão do Conhecimento (p82), and get utterly soaked at the splashy Jardins d'Água (Water Gardens; Map p108; www.cm-lisboa.pt/equipamentos/equipamento/info/jardins-da-agua; Rua da Pimenta; ⊙24hr.

Parque Eduardo VII

Most of Lisbon's squares and parks have playgrounds for little tykes to let off excess energy, including Parque Eduardo VII (Map p92; Alameda Edgar Cardoso; ⊙24hr) FREE and an animal-themed one at Jardim da Estrela (p75).

Museu de Marinha

Go west to relive the nautical adventures of the Age of Discoveries in Belém's barge-stuffed Museu de Marinha (Naval Museum; Map p96; http://ccm.marinha.pt/pt/museu; Praça do Império; adult/child €6.50/3.25, free 1st Sun of month; ⊙10am-6pm Tue-Sun May-Sep, to 5pm Oct-Apr).

Museu da Marioneta

Kids can marvel at the puppets in Lapa's enchanting Museu da Marioneta (p75).

Around Lisbon

When the weather warms up, take the train to Cascais (p133) for some ice-cream-licking, bucket-and-spade fun. Kids can make finny friends on a dolphin-watching tour in Setúbal (p152), and play king or queen of the castle in the fantastical turrets and wood-lands of Sintra (p124).

---

and mushrooms). Paired wines sometimes date to the '70s!

★ **Bistro 100 Maneiras**　FUSION €€€
(Map p72; ☑910 307 575; www.restaurante 100maneiras.com; Largo da Trindade 9; mains €21-39; ⊙noon-2am Mon-Sat; 🗢) The Bosnian mastermind behind Bairro Alto's 100 Maneiras (p101) also oversees this creatively charged Chiado bistro. Start with the name-sake 100 Maneiras Strong cocktail in the beautiful downstairs bar, then head upstairs for beautifully prepared dishes showcasing high-end Portuguese ingredients. Classics such as truffled mushroom risotto with wild shrimp are astounding, and options for braver souls include lamb brains.

Sala de Corte　STEAK €€€
(Map p72; ☑213 460 030; www.saladecorte.pt; Praça D Luís I 6-12; steaks €18-32; ⊙noon-3pm & 7pm-midnight Mon-Fri, noon-midnight Sat & Sun; 🗢) From its latest and far more prominent location on pretty Praça Dom Luís, the not-

to-be-missed 'cut room' dishes out succulent, perfectly seasoned imported beef in six cuts (entrecôte, *picanha,* sirloin, chateaubriand etc). These are chargrilled in a small, world-class Josper grill/oven hybrid, then prepped and beautifully presented on wooden planks in an intimate open kitchen.

✕ Bairro Alto & Santa Catarina

Manteigaria　PASTRIES €
(Map p72; www.facebook.com/pg/manteigaria. oficial; Rua do Loreto 2; pastel de nata €1; ⊙8am-midnight) Baking *pastéis de nata* (custard tarts) really *is* like rocket science in Lisbon. This born-again butter factory gets it just right – crisp tarts that flake just so are filled with luscious cream and served with good strong coffee and smiles at this bright, modern cafe. This isn't Lisbon's most famous *pastel de nata,* but some say it's the best.

A Cultura do Hamburger BURGERS €

(Map p72; www.facebook.com/aculturadoham burguer; Rua das Salgadeiras 38; burgers €7-9.50; ☺noon-midnight Mon-Fri, from 12.30pm Sat & Sun; ⏶) In what is surely a legendary culinary coup, the owners of A Cultura do Chá woke up one morning and flipped the script. A Cultura do Hamburger was born in the same quiet Bairro Alto nook, with no tea in sight. Instead, some of Lisbon's most perfectly charred burgers emerge among these stone walls and arches and reclaimed-door tables.

★ Bairro de Avillez PORTUGUESE €€

(Map p72; ☎215 830 290; www.bairrodoavillez. pt; Rua Nova da Trindade 18; small plates €2-16.50, mains €7-18.50; ☺noon-midnight; ⏶) Step into the latest culinary dream by Portugal's most famous chef – Michelin-starred maestro José Avillez – who has set up his gastronomic dream destination: a 'neighbourhood' featuring several dining environments, including everything from a traditional tavern to an avant-garde gourmet cabaret.

Once inside, your first stop is a traditional Portuguese *taberna* (unoriginally named Taberna) with *petiscos* (tapas) and exquisite charcuterie and cheese plates. Next up is Páteo, a seafood and fish-driven food court with classic Portuguese dishes, then you'll see Beco (Map p72; ☎210 939 234; www.becocabaretgourmet.pt; tasting menus €95; ☺8.30-10.45pm Wed-Sat; ⏶) – well, not really, it's hidden away in an 18th-century chapel. It serves up an exclusive surprise gourmet menu accompanied by a sexy cabaret show. And, in case you're tired of Portuguese cuisine, there's the excellent Cantina Peruana (Map p72; ☎215 842 002; www.cantinaperuana.pt; small plates €4-10; ☺12.30-3pm & 7pm-midnight; ⏶) and Pisco Bar one floor above.

★ Boa-Bao ASIAN €€

(Map p72; ☎919 023 030; www.boabao.pt; Largo Rafael Bordalo Pinheiro 30; small plates from €6.50, mains €12-19; ☺noon-11.30pm Sun-Wed, to 12.30am Thu-Sat; ⏶) The food at this trendy spot will transport you to Laos, Cambodia, Malaysia and Vietnam, but the ceramic swallows draped across the exposed brick archway (the most famous artwork of Rafael Bordalo, the artist for which the beautiful Chiado plaza is named) are undeniably Portuguese.

American, Belgian and Dutch owners have brought a sorely needed laundry list of traditional (no fusion!) Asian dishes to Lisbon with raging success. Dishes from the Malaysian curry soup to the steamed sea bass with lime, chilli, garlic and bok choy to the lemongrass and basil crème brûlée are revelations in a city where finding a decent stir-fry is a tear-your-hair-out exercise in frustration. Throw in some of the city's best craft cocktails (from €8.50) and you've got yourself an evening.

Pharmacia MEDITERRANEAN €€

(Map p72; ☎213 462 146; www.chef-felicidade.pt; Rua Marechal Saldanha 2; tapas €10-15; ☺noon-1am; ⏶) At this wonderfully quirky restaurant in Lisbon's apothecary museum, chef Susana Felicidade (Algarvian grandmother-trained!) dispenses tasting menus and tapas singing with flavours that are both market-fresh and Mediterranean influenced. Appetisers served in test tubes, cabinets brimming with pill bottles and flacons – it's all part of the pharmaceutical fun. The terrace is a great spot for cocktails.

Flor da Laranja MOROCCAN €€

(Map p72; ☎964 781 122; Rua da Rosa 206; mains €14-16; ☺7-11.30pm Mon-Sat; ⏶) Casablanca native Rabea Esserghini runs a one-woman show at the wonderful Flor da Laranja. Service is slow, but the cosy North African ambience and delicious Moroccan cuisine more than make up for it. Top picks include dolmas, mouth-watering couscous dishes, lamb, shrimp and veggie tagines, chicken with lemon confit, and fresh berry crêpes for dessert.

Decadente PORTUGUESE €€

(Map p72; ☎213 461 381; www.thedecadente.pt; Rua de São Pedro de Alcântara 81; mains €11-18; ☺noon-3pm & 7pm-midnight Mon-Fri, noon-4pm & 7pm-midnight Sat-Sun, bar to 2am Fri-Sat; ⏶) This beautifully designed restaurant inside a boutique hostel (p91) overlooks the stunning Miradouro de São Pedro de Alcântara and has touches of industrial chic, geometric artwork and an enticing back patio. It serves inventive dishes showcasing high-end Portuguese ingredients at excellent prices. The changing three-course lunch menu (€13) is first-rate. Start with creative cocktails in the front bar.

Jardim dos Sentidos VEGETARIAN €€

(Map p84; ☎213 423 670; www.jardimdosentidos. com; Rua Mãe d'Água 3; mains €9-11.50, lunch buffet €8.90; ☺12.30-3.30pm & 7-10pm Mon-Fri, 7-11pm Sat; ⏶🖋) Vegetarian-minded diners flock to this attractive restaurant and wellness centre with a back garden/spa, an

CRISTO REI

The sleepy seaside suburb of Cacilhas lies just across the Rio Tejo from Lisbon. Its star attraction – visible from almost everywhere in Lisbon – is the 110m-high **Cristo Rei** (www.cristorei.pt; Alto do Pragal, Av Cristo Rei, Almada; adult/child €5/2.50; ☉9.30am-6.30pm Jul & Aug, to 6pm Sep-Jun). Perched on a pedestal, the statue of Christ with outstretched arms is a slightly more baroque version of Rio de Janeiro's Christ the Redeemer. It was erected in 1959 to give thanks to God for sparing Portugal from the horrors of WWII. A lift zooms you up to a platform, from where Lisbon spreads magnificently before you. It's a fantastic place for photos.

To reach the statue from Lisbon, take the breezy commuter ferry from Terreiro do Paço terminal across the Rio Tejo to Cacilhas (€1.25, 15 minutes), then bus 101 (€1.45). And make an afternoon of it: *lisboêtas* also flock to Cacilhas for the *cervejarias* (beer halls) serving fresh seafood and refreshing brews, and the fine views of the sun setting over the river.

extensive lunch buffet and à la carte dinners. Among the globally inspired vegetarian offerings: portobello mushroom lasagne, Mexican chilli, veggie and nut stroganoff, plus a substantial tea menu.

★**100 Maneiras**   FUSION €€€
(Map p72; ☑910 307 575; www.restaurante100maneiras.com; Rua do Teixeira 35; tasting menu €60, with classic/premium wine pairing €95/120; ☉7pm-2am; ☎) How do we love 100 Maneiras? Let us count the 100 ways... The 10-course tasting menu changes twice yearly and features imaginative, delicately prepared dishes. The courses are all a surprise – part of the charm – though somewhat disappointingly, the chef will only budge so far to accommodate special diets and food allergies. Reservations are essential for the elegant and small space.

🍴 Alfama, Castelo & Graça

★**Ti-Natércia**   PORTUGUESE €
(Map p76; ☑218 862 133; Rua Escola Gerais 54; mains €5.50-12; ☉7pm-midnight Tue-Fri, noon-3pm & 7pm-midnight Sat) 'Aunt' Natércia and her downright delicious Portuguese home cooking is a tough ticket: there are a mere six tables and they fill up fast. She'll talk your ear off (and doesn't mince words – some have been rubbed the wrong way, vegetarians in particular should avoid) while you devour her excellent take on the classics. Reservations are essential. Cash only.

Marcelino Pão e Vinho   PORTUGUESE €
(Map p76; Rua do Salvador 62; mains €4-9; ☉10am-2am Thu-Tue; ☎) What this narrow cafe lacks in space it makes up for in atmosphere, with local artworks on the walls,

occasional live music, traditional hats suspended from the ceiling and wine-crate-lined walls. It's a cosy spot for refreshing sangria, and salads, cheeseboards, sandwiches, quiches and tapas, including a fun meat grill flamed up tableside in traditional crockware.

Páteo 13   PORTUGUESE €
(Map p76; www.facebook.com/pateo13; Calçadinha de Santo Estêvão 13; mains €7.50-9.50; ☉noon-10pm Tue-Thu, to 11pm Fri-Sun, closed Nov-Feb; ☎) Follow the scent of chargrilled fish to this local favourite tucked away on a small, festively decorated plaza in Alfama. Join buzzing crowds hunkered over picnic tables and feast on barbecued seafood and meats, washing it all down with ever-flowing Alentejan reds.

★**O Zé da Mouraria**   PORTUGUESE €€
(Map p68; ☑218 865 436; Rua João do Outeiro 24; mains for 2 €16.50-33.50; ☉noon-4pm Mon-Sat; ☎) Don't be fooled by the saloon-like doors, there's a typical Portuguese *tasca* (tavern) inside: homey local cuisine, blue-and-white-tiled walls, chequered tablecloths – and it's one of Lisbon's best. The house-baked cod loaded with chickpeas, onions, garlic and olive oil is rightfully popular, and daily specials (duck rice on Wednesday!) make return trips tempting. Service is a lost cause, however.

Portions are huge – a half dose *('meia porção')* is usually big enough for two. Walk-ins are welcome but booking ahead is recommended. Cash only.

Prado   PORTUGUESE €€
(Map p68; ☑210 534 649; www.pradorestaurante.com; Tv das Pedras Negras 2; small plates €4.50-14;

CERCA VELHA: LISBON'S MEDIEVAL WALL

There are vestiges of Lisbon's medieval defensive wall scattered about Alfama and around – but you might walk right past them if you aren't paying attention or don't know where to look. Enter Lisbon city hall, which has teamed up with the Museu de Lisboa and Centro de Arqueologia de Lisboa to create the free walking tour, *Muralhas de Lisboa: Cerca Velha*, based on intense historical and archaeological investigations of the city's pre-1147 fortified defence system (and later construction of the Fernandina wall from 1373–75).

There are 16 signposted points of interest along the circular 1500m path, beginning and ending near Castelo de São Jorge from Rua do Chão da Feira, down to the water and back around up to Porta de Alfofa. Notable stops include No 2 (Pátio Dom Fradique) – this 186m stretch of the wall is the longest intact section – and No 4 (Rua Norberto de Araújo), where the only Islamic portion of the wall is visible.

You'll need to pick up the city hall's very helpful brochure and map, available in several languages at Fundação José Saramago – Casa dos Bicos (p75), and Castelo de São Jorge (p71), among other points.

⊘ noon-3.30pm & 7-11pm Wed-Sat, noon-5pm Sun; 🐾) 🍴 This all-organic small-plates newcomer comes courtesy of chef António Galapito, after his stint at Taberna do Mercado (Michelin-star chef Nuno Mendes' Portuguese restaurant in London). Beautifully presented plates explode with fresh, clean flavours and change daily (the only dishes repeated are the cockles with spinach, coriander and fried bread, and the Barrosã beef tartar with grilled galega cabbage).

Os Gazeteiros
EUROPEAN €€
(Map p76; ☑939 501 211; www.osgazeteiros.pt; Rua das Escolas Gerais 114-116; prix-fixe dinners €35; ⊘7.30-10pm Tue-Sat; 🐾) 🍴 French chef David Eyguesier honed his skills at Poïs Café, then at his own underground restaurant at home before opening this sorely needed Alfama gem, whose name loosely translates as 'the Truants' (he 'skipped' culinary school!). His daily-changing, market-fresh four-course set menus delight under a spiderweb of modern lighting, beautiful geometric cabinetry and an open kitchen. No microwave, no freezer!

Chapitô à Mesa
PORTUGUESE €€
(Map p68; ☑218 875 077; www.chapito.org; Rua Costa do Castelo 7; mains €19-21; ⊘noon-midnight Mon-Fri, 7.30-11pm Sat & Sun; 🐾) At this circus school's casual cafe, the decidedly creative menu of Chef Bertílio Gomes is served alongside views worth writing home about. His modern takes include classic dishes (*bacalhau à Brás*, pork cheeks with clams, baked octopus with sweet potatoes and tomato frittata) that go swimmingly with a drop of Quinta da Silveira Reserva wine.

Santa Clara dos Cogumelos
INTERNATIONAL €€
(Map p76; ☑218 870 661; www.santaclaradoscogumelos.com; Campo de Santa Clara 7; petiscos €4.50-11, mains €12-25; ⊘7.30-11pm Tue-Sun & 1-3pm Sat; 🐾🍴) Mushroom fans unite! This Italian-owned, Italian-executed restaurant in the old Campo de Santa Clara market hall is simply magic. The menu devotes proper patronage to the humble *cogumelo* (mushroom). The organic shiitake *à bulhão pato* (with garlic and coriander), porcini risotto with black trumpets, orange peel, rosemary and walnuts, and the porcini ice cream with glazed chestnuts are all outstanding.

Princesa do Castelo
CAFE, VEGAN €€
(Map p76; www.facebook.com/princesadocastelorestaurantevegetariano; Rua do Salvador 64A; mains €10.50; ⊘12.30-10pm Tue-Sun; 🐾🍴) 🍴 This chirpy, cash-only vegan cafe, run by a good-vibes Bangalorean, positively radiates good health with vegetarian, vegan, macrobiotic and sattvic dishes that play up the wild and the organic. Every day is different (there might be Mexican quinoa chilli with fried bananas, or tomato peanut rice with edamame aubergine curry), and the cafe offers Lisbon's only vegan *pastéis de nata*.

Claras em Castelo
PORTUGUESE €€
(Map p76; ☑218 853 071; Rua Bartolomeu de Gusmão 31; mains €12-15; ⊘10.30am-1am Thu-Tue) Just steps from Castelo de São Jorge's entrance, this tiny restaurant enjoys a loyal following for its warm service and solid home cooking. Dishes such as *bacalhau com nata* (cod in a creamy sauce) pair nicely with reasonably priced wines. Booking ahead is advisable.

A Travessa do Fado　　　PORTUGUESE €€
(Map p76; www.facebook.com/ATravessaDoFado; Largo do Chafariz de Dentro 1; mains €7.50-14.50; ⏰11am-11pm Wed-Sun, closed Jan; 🐾) Non-touristy restaurants are hard to come by in Alfama, but this one, the more casual sister restaurant to high-end A Travessa (Map p84; 🖉213 902 034; www.atravessa.com; Tv do Convento das Bernardas 12; mains €24.50-35; ⏰7.30pm-midnight Mon-Sat; 🐾), gets a nod for its sun-drenched, flower-draped terrace – a nice spot for chasing classics such as stuffed squid or sea-bass rice with a refreshing *vinho verde* (young wine). There's also fado on Wednesday and Friday (at 8.30pm) on the 2nd floor.

✖ Príncipe Real, Santos & Estrela

⭐**Gelataria Nannarella**　　　GELATO €
(Map p84; www.nannarella.pt; Rua Nova da Piedade 68; small/medium/large €2.50/3/3.50; ⏰noon-10pm) Seatless Nannarella is squeezed into little more than a doorway and serves up Lisbon's best gelato. Roman transplant Constanza Ventura churns out 34 perfect, spatula-slabbed flavours of traditional gelato/sorbet daily (18 fixed, 10 daily-changing, four seasonal) to anxious lines of *lisboêtas*. Nailing both consistency and flavour, this sweet, sweet stuff seemingly emerges straight from Ventura's kitchen.

⭐**Bettina & Niccolò Corallo**　　　SWEETS €
(Map p84; www.claudiocorallo.com; Rua da Escola Politécnica 4; chocolate per kg from €90; ⏰11am-7pm Tue-Sat) Few chocolates command such undying devotion, but this family-run transplant from São Tomé and Príncipe elicits freakish enthusiasm for its thin artisan chocolate bars. Indeed, in ginger, orange, sea-salt and pepper, sesame, and toffee and sea-salt varieties, this is heart-stoppingly good stuff. Try a free sample with the excellent espresso (€1) before committing.

⭐**Frangasqueira Nacional**　　　PORTUGUESE €
(Map p84; www.facebook.com/frangasqueira; Tv Monte do Carmo 19; chicken/ribs per kg €10.60/13; ⏰6-10pm Tue, noon-2.30pm & 6-10pm Wed-Fri, noon-3pm & 6pm-2am Sat & Sun) This tiny, mostly takeaway-only grill (the new location now spares space for two tables) does splendid chicken, ribs, crioula sausage and turkey kebabs worth lining up for. Grab a bird to go along with house-cut potato chips and spiced olives, all of which can make for

a wondrously carnivorous picnic in nearby Jardim do Príncipe Real.

O Tachadas　　　STEAK €
(Map p84; 🖉213 976 689; www.facebook.com/restaurante.tachadas; Rua da Esperança 178; mains €5.60-15.75; ⏰9am-3pm & 6.30-11pm; 🐾) On closer inspection, this seemingly undistinguished *tasca* near Santos train station reveals some very serious carnivorous happenings. There are other things on the menu, but this patron-packed grillhouse is all about thick, juicy, way-too-cheap steaks slapped on the *churrasco* by a meticulous grillman and served table-side on wooden planks known as *tábuas*.

Coyo Taco　　　MEXICAN €
(Map p84; 🖉210 529 201; http://coyotaco.pt; Rua Dom Pedro V 65; tacos €7.50-9; ⏰noon-midnight Sun-Wed, to 2am Thu-Sat; 🐾) Straight outta Miami, where it is reportedly Barack Obama's favourite taqueria, Coyo brings fierce taco authenticity to one of Lisbon's most gourmand streets. Handmade tortillas stuffed with duck carnitas, chicken and pork *al pastor* and *cochinita pibil*, along with excellent shrimp quesadillas and easy-drinkin' margaritas (served out of a window to the street), help fill a long-empty Mexican niche.

Chutnify　　　INDIAN €
(Map p84; 🖉213 461 534; www.chutnify.com; Tv da Palmeira 42; mains €4.50-15, tasting menu €28; ⏰noon-3pm & 7pm-midnight Tue-Fri, 1-4pm & 7pm-midnight Sat & Sun; 🐾) A transplant from Berlin's hip Prenzlauer Berg district, this artsy and modern Indian place strikes the perfect balance between real-deal South Indian street food (sometimes with innovative twists) and hipster decor.

The *dosas* (rice and lentil Indian-style crêpes) are legit – both the classic *masala dosa* (with potatoes) and the more creative duck *dosa*. The Indian chef isn't afraid to add a bit of fury to the curries (lamb, chickpea, chicken, fish, aubergines etc) if you ask, and everything is a bit less greasy and healthier than in the motherland (noticeably less ghee, no greasy residue after hand-devouring those dosas!). There's even Kingfisher Indian beer.

Cantinho Lusitano　　　PORTUGUESE €
(Map p84; 🖉218 065 185; www.cantinholusitano.com; Rua dos Prazeres 52; petiscos €5.15-8.50; ⏰7-11pm Tue-Sat; 🐾) Sharing is what this unassuming little place is all about. Its appealing menu of *petiscos*, such as Azeitão

cheese, chorizo, garlic shrimps, *pica-pau* beef and fava-bean salad, pairs nicely with Portuguese wines, and husband-and-wife team Silvia and João are consummate hosts. Reservations are a good idea at all times.

Tapisco
FUSION €€

(Map p84; ☏ 213 420 681; www.tapisco.pt; Rua Dom Pedro V 81; tapas €5-18, mains €16-29; ⊙noon-midnight; ☎) Michelin-starred Lisbon chef Henrique Sá Pessoa's venture into Príncipe Real may seem obvious (trans-Iberian tapas) but in reality Spain and Portugal don't often share more than the peninsula. Washing down *tapiscos* (Spanish tapas and Portuguese *petiscos* – get it?) with traditional vermouth never felt so novel.

Highlights on the small plates side include a wonderful vinaigrette-marinated *bacalhau* and La Bomba de Lisboa (fried mashed potato balls with alheira sausage, topped with a spicy sauce). Heartier winners like the perfectly seared tuna loin and crockery-served shrimp *açorda* (a porridge-like bread 'soup') top off a fun night at this casual and cool choice.

ZeroZero
PIZZA €€

(Map p84; ☏ 213 420 091; www.pizzeriazerozero.pt; Rua da Escola Politécnica 32; pizza €10-19; ⊙noon-midnight Sun-Thu, to 1am Fri & Sat; ☎) Just arriving at your table here is a memorable ride, sliding past an enormous illustration from Ana Gil, a beautiful prosecco bar and minimalist copper lamps and muted grey walls leading to an impressive, oak-fired pizza oven. Attention to Italian detail is fierce, and the thin-crusted, uncut pies make an impression. And the patio is a bougainvillea-draped haven for pizza lovers.

Taberna da Esperança
FUSION €€

(Map p84; ☏ 213 962 744; www.tabernadaesperanca.com; Rua da Esperança 112-114; small plates €7-12, mains €17-19; ⊙7.30pm-2am Tue-Fri, 11-4pm & 7pm-midnight Sat & Sun) In a cosy, atmospheric dining room, Taberna da Esperança wows diners with flavourful dishes that blend Alentejan recipes with a modern edge. The inventive menu changes often and features plates designed for sharing. Favourites include fava beans with sausages, sautéed mushrooms with chestnuts, and *bacalhau* rice with rosemary. Reserve ahead. Cash only for nonresidents.

Tasca da Esquina
FUSION €€

(Map p84; ☏ 210 993 939; www.tascadaesquina.com; Rua Domingos Sequeira

41C; mains €16-21.50, tasting menu 4/5/6/8 courses €23.50/29.50/35.50/42, with wine €35.50/47.50/57.50/64; ⊙12.30-3.30pm & 7.30-11.30pm; ☎) Headed by celebrated chef Vitor Sobral, the 'tavern on the corner' serves rich and inventive dishes featuring classic Portuguese ingredients. It's a small place in cool and contained Campo de Ourique, with a sizzling grill in front and a cheery sunroom where well-dressed diners fill the tables most days.

Petiscaria Ideal
FUSION €€

(Map p84; ☏ 213 971 504; www.petiscariaideal.com; Rua da Esperança 100; small plates €3-9, mains €9-14; ⊙7pm-2am Mon-Sat; ☎) This small, buzzing spot serves delicious *petiscos* – fava, ham and Serra cheese toast, pork stew with pepper compote, *alheira* sausage-stuffed portobello mushrooms – followed by sweet endings like *medronho*-spiked chocolate mousse or pear crumble. The walls are clad with mismatching *azulejos*, dining is at long communal tables, and there's a spirited rock 'n' roll vibe to the place.

Mercearia do Século
PORTUGUESE €€

(Map p84; ☏ 216 062 070; www.facebook.com/merceariadoseculo; Rua de O Século 145; mains €12.50-14.80; ⊙7-11.30pm Tue-Sat; ☎) Anthropologist and Portuguese-cookbook writer Fernanda runs this sweet little deli and grocery store with love and an eye for careful sourcing. Daily-changing mains are wholesome and big on unorthodox flavours – be it pork confit with clams and carrots or marinated rabbit with cabbage and sweet potato. You can also stock up on foodie gifts – fig bread, preserves, honey and more.

Loco
PORTUGUESE €€€

(Map p84; ☏ 213 951 861; www.loco.pt; Rua dos Navigantes 53B; dégustation €96-126; ⊙7-11pm Tue-Sat) ✐ Near the Basílica da Estrela (p75), Lisbon's latest hot table comes courtesy of chef Alexandre Silva, whose bold and modern take on Portuguese cuisine taps both tradition and travel on its way to a personality-rich gastronomic adventure. It offers a daily-changing, description-free tasting menu (you choose 18 'moments' with or without a cheese option), each steeped in sustainability and seasonality.

✖ Lapa & Alcântara

★ Último Porto
SEAFOOD €€

(☏ 308 808 939; Estação Marítima da Rocha do Conde de Óbidos; mains €8.50-17; ⊙8am-4.30pm

Lapa & Alcântara

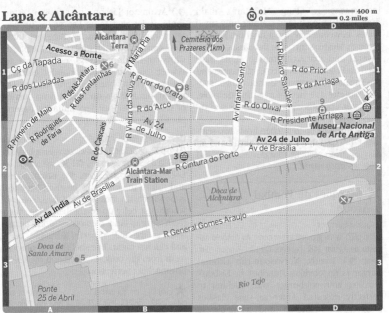

Lapa & Alcântara

Mon-Sat) An absolute local's secret for a reason, this top seafooder takes an act of God to find. Hidden among the shipping-container cranes of the Port of Lisbon, its fantastically simple grilled fish paired with top Alentejan and Douro wines draws locals in droves. With shipping containers and departmental port buildings framing the ambience, María do Céu oversees a parking-lot-style grill.

Seabass, cuttlefish, grouper, sole and more – seasoned with nothing but salt – are charred to perfection and served with boiled potatoes and *grelhos* (rapini greens),

all without a tourist in sight. Technically it's across from the Museu Nacional de Arte Antiga, but you'll need a schooner to reach it from here! Google Maps is also not your friend (it tries to take you through a restricted area). To find it, walk down Rua Cintura Porto Lisboa along the marina, turn left, and go to the end of the dock.

★ Izcalli Antojeria MEXICAN €€€
(☏ 211 914 991; www.izcalli.pt; Rua Alcântara 13A; small plates €7.50-13; ⊘ 7-10.30pm Tue-Wed, 12.30-3pm & 7-10.30pm Thu-Sat) Sitting

inconspicuously along Alcântara's main drag, this tiny, cash- and counter-only small plates newcomer is an authentic journey through Mexico's intricate flavours. Chef Ivo Tavares and margarita maven Paola have lived and cooked in Mexico City, Oaxaca and the Yucatán; their two-team show incontestably satiates the need for authentic mole, *al pastor* and other gourmet versions of regional street staples.

The intimate open kitchen hosts two seatings (7pm and 9pm). Reserve ahead and go easy on the excellent margaritas – the bill adds up *muy rapido*.

✖ Marquês de Pombal & Around

Ground Burger   BURGERS €
(Map p92; www.groundburger.com; Av António Augusto de Aguiar 148; burgers €9-12; ⊘ noon-midnight; 🛜) Trendy, Norwegian-run Ground Burger is an obvious standout in Lisbon's ongoing gourmet-burger war, sticking to perfectly executed American-style classics (cheese, bacon-cheese and chilli-cheese burgers) and great hand-cut chips and onion rings. The local and international craft-beer list is probably Lisbon's most impressive for such a restaurant. It's tucked away almost discreetly around the side of an office building near Museu Calouste Gulbenkian (p78).

There's a second outlet in Mercado da Ribeira (p95).

Versailles   PASTRIES €
(Map p92; Av da República 15A; pastries €0.85-2.30; ⊘ 7.30am-11.45pm; 🛜) With a marble chandelier and icing-sugar stucco confection, this sublime patisserie is where well-coiffed ladies come to gossip and devour cream cakes (or scones with jam), espresso with *sortidos Húngaros* (chocolate-covered cookies) and house-spawned chocolate cake (served disc-shaped; it's oh, so decadent!).

As Velhas   PORTUGUESE €€
(Map p84; 📞 213 422 490; Rua da Conceição da Glória 21; mains €18-23; ⊘ noon-3pm & 7-10pm) No airs, no graces, just hearty helpings of Portuguese soul food served by delightfully old-school servers. The monkfish and clams in garlic and coriander sauce is superb, as is the grilled goat. Don't skip that dessert cart!

Jesus é Goês   INDIAN €€
(Map p92; 📞 211 545 812; Rua de São José 23; mains €8-18.50; ⊘ noon-3pm & 7-11pm Tue-Sat;

🛜) At one of Lisbon's best Indian restaurants, jovial chef Jesus Lee whips up contemporary Goan delicacies. Rice-sack table-cloths and colourful murals (note the playful Christian-Hindu imagery) set the scene for starters such as onion-coriander chickpea fritters or potato bhaji with puri, followed by mushroom and chestnut or shrimp curries, or 11-spices goat – all fiery-fantastic. Reserve ahead – it's tiny. Cash only.

Cervejaria Ribadouro   SEAFOOD €€
(Map p92; 📞 213 549 411; www.cervejariaribadouro.pt; Rua do Salitre 2; mains €11-30, seafood per kg €42.50-147; ⊘ noon-1.30am; 🛜) Bright, noisy and full to the gills, this bustling beer hall is popular with local seafood fans, some of whom just belly up to the bar, chase their fresh shrimp and *tremoços* (lupin beans) with an ice-cold *imperial* (draught beer) and call it a night. The shellfish are plucked fresh from the tank, weighed and cooked to lip-smacking perfection.

★ Horta dos Brunos   PORTUGUESE €€€
(Map p92; 📞 213 153 421; Rua Ilha do Pico 27; mains €25-30; ⊘ noon-3pm & 7-11pm Mon-Sat) Chef Pedro Filipe's somewhat unknown and unassuming gourmet *tasca*, a favourite among moving and shaking politicians and in-the-know gastronauts, does some of Lisbon's best work. There's a menu, but stick to your server's rundown of what's cooking daily, such as extraordinary tuna, cuttlefish *à lagareiro* and succulent lamb chops, all beautifully presented and modern in execution. There are top-end French wines, too.

✖ Belém

★ Antiga Confeitaria de Belém   PASTRIES €
(Pastéis de Belém; Map p96; www.pasteisdebelem.pt; Rua de Belém 84-92; pastries from €1.10; ⊘ 8am-11pm Oct-Jun, to midnight Jul-Sep) Since 1837 this patisserie has been transporting locals to sugar-coated nirvana with heavenly *pastéis de Belém*. The crisp pastry nests are filled with custard cream, baked at 200°C for that perfect golden crust, then lightly dusted with cinnamon. Admire *azulejos* in the vaulted rooms or devour a still-warm tart at the counter and try to guess the secret ingredient.

Go early on a midweek day to avoid nasty lines.

Pastelaria Restelo   BAKERY €
(www.pastelariaocareca.pt; Rua Duarte Pacheco Pereira 11D; croissants €1.20; ⊘ 8am-8pm Mon

& Wed-Sat, 8.30am-8pm Sun) Better known as Pastelaria O Careca ('The Bald Guy') among locals, this simple *pastelaria* flanking a small plaza has been dishing out Lisbon's sweetest croissants since 1954. It's definitely worth heading a few blocks inland from the tourist onslaught along Belém's waterfront for the doughy, sugar-coated goodness.

Alecrim & Manjerona
CAFE €

(Map p96; www.facebook.com/alecrim manjeronamercearia; Rua do Embaixador 143; light meals & lunches €2.75-8; ☉10am-6pm Mon-Fri) Tucked away from the crowds on a side street, Alecrim & Manjerona ('Rosemary & Marjoram') is a cute grocery store, cafe, deli and wine bar rolled into one. Besides delicious homemade cakes and tarts, it rustles up wallet-friendly specials – from quiches to *bacalhau espiritual* (codfish gratin).

Enoteca de Belém
PORTUGUESE €€

(Map p96; ☑213 631 511; www.travessada ermida.com; Tv do Marta Pinto 10; mains €17-20; ☉1-11pm; ☎) Tucked down a quiet lane just off Belém's main thoroughfare, this casual wine bar serves modernised Portuguese classics (fantastic octopus, Iberian pork), matched by an excellent selection of full-bodied Douro reds and refreshing Alentejan whites. The experience – led by well-trained servers particularly adept at gravitating you towards a beverage that marries with your tastes – is distinctively memorable.

★ Feitoria
MODERN PORTUGUESE €€€

(Map p96; ☑210 400 208; www.restaurante feitoria.com; Altis Belém Hotel, Doca do Bom Sucesso; mains €39-40, tasting menus €85-135, with wine €130-195; ☉7.30-10pm Mon-Sat; ☎) A defining dining experience awaits at chef João Rodrigues' slick, contemporary, Michelin-starred restaurant overlooking the riverfront. Rich textures and clean, bright flavours dominate throughout three tasting menus, which showcase Portugal's rich and vibrant bounty. Pigeon with wild mushrooms, foie gras and truffles, Algarve scarlet shrimp and Iberian pork neck exhilarate with every bite.

✗ Parque das Nações

★ Casa Bota Feijão
PORTUGUESE €

(Map p108; ☑218 532 489; www.restaurante botafeijao.pt; Rua Conselheiro Lopo Vaz 5; half/whole portions €8.50/12; ☉8am-8pm Mon-Fri) Don't be fooled by the nondescript decor and railroad-track views – when a tucked-away place is this crowded with locals at lunch-time midweek, it must be doing something right. Everyone's here for one thing and one thing only: Bairrada-style *leitão* – suckling pig spit-roasted on an open fire until juicy and meltingly tender, doused in a beautiful, peppery garlic sauce.

★ Old House
CHINESE €€€

(Map p108; ☑218 969 075; www.theoldhouse portugal.pt; Rua Pimenta 9; mains €9.90-45; ☉noon-3pm & 7pm-midnight; ☎) Transport yourself to China at this authentic Szechuan powerhouse (tamed for local tastes), an up-scale Chinese chain restaurant that chose Parque das Nações for its first foray outside the motherland. The daunting list of specialities, including Beijing duck (half/whole €28/52), hotpots (the veggie version with noodled tofu is outstanding) and plenty of garlic- and pepper-loaded dishes, is a welcome taste-bud change-up.

Fifty Seconds
GASTRONOMY €€€

(Map p108; ☑211 525 380; www.fiftyseconds experience.com; Cais das Naus, Myriad by Sana Hotel; tasting menu €120-150, with wine €180-210; ☉12.30-3pm & 7-11pm Tue-Sat; ☎) This hot newcomer is named for the time it takes the lift to whisk foodies up the long-unused, 120m-high Vasco de Gama Tower at the Myriad by Sana Hotel. Superstar chef Martín Berasategui masterfully marries Basque-grounded fusion with Portuguese ingredients – cod brandade with camomile and yuzu mayo, pork cannelloni with smoked aubergine tortellini – at Lisbon's most exciting new gastronomic experience.

The sexy, 360° panoramic space sees Berasategui bring his eight–Michelin–starred CV to shake things up in one of Lisbon's less impressive food neighbourhoods.

🍷 Drinking & Nightlife

🍷 Baixa & Rossio

★ A Ginjinha
BAR

(Map p72; Largo de Saõ Domingos 8; ☉9am-10pm) Hipsters, old men in flat caps, office workers and tourists all meet at this microscopic *ginjinha* (cherry liqueur) bar for that moment of cherry-licking, pip-spitting pleasure (€1.40 a shot).

TOPO Martim Moniz
COCKTAIL BAR

(Map p68; www.facebook.com/pg/topolisboa; Centro Comercial Martim Moniz, 6th fl, Praça

Parque das Nações

N 0 ——— 500 m
0 ——— 0.25 miles

Fábrica Coffee Roasters   COFFEE
(Map p68; www.fabricacoffeeroasters.com; Rua das Portas de Santo Antão 136; ⊙9am-9pm) Keep on walking past the touristy restaurants along pedestrianised Rua das Portas de Santo Antão to this sublime coffee temple, where serious caffeine is served amid a hodgepodge of exposed brick, hardwood floors and mismatched vintage furniture. Single-origin arabica beans from Brazil, Ethiopia and Colombia are roasted in-house and churned into distinctly third-wave cups of joe. Connoisseurs rejoice!

☕ Chiado & Bairro Alto

★**Park**   BAR
(Map p72; www.facebook.com/parklisboaofficial; Calçada do Combro 58; ⊙1pm-2am Tue-Sat, to 8pm Sun; 🛜) If only all multistorey car parks were like this... Take the lift to the 5th floor, and head up and around to the top, which has been transformed into one of Lisbon's hippest rooftop bars, with sweeping views reaching right down to the Rio Tejo and over the bell towers of Igreja de Santa Catarina.

The vibe is cool and creative, and DJs spin hip hop, jazz and house at all hours. Plopping yourself down on the sunset-facing wooden chairs in the late afternoon is a Lisbon must.

★**Pensão Amor**   BAR
(Map p72; www.pensaoamor.pt; Rua do Alecrím 19; ⊙2pm-3am Sun-Wed, to 4am Thu-Sat) Set inside

Martim Moniz; ⊙12.30pm-midnight Sun-Wed, to 1am Thu, to 2am Fri & Sat) This hipster hangout is an excellent rooftop lounge with extraordinary views over lively Praça Martim Moniz and the whole of Lisbon. It features loungey open-air wooden benches for cocktails (€8 to €14), coffee and light bites, and a covered indoor lounge. It's all set to a vibey soundtrack, often courtesy of DJs.

A **second location** (Map p72; Terraços do Carmo; ⊙12.30pm-midnight Sun-Wed, to 2am Thu-Sat) in Chiado is equally atmospheric but lacks the edge of the original.

Rooftop Bar   BAR
(Map p68; www.hotel-mundial.pt; Praça Martim Moniz 2, Hotel Mundial; ⊙4-11pm) Grab a table at sundown on the Hotel Mundial's roof terrace for a sweeping view of Lisbon and its hilltop castle. The backlit bar, white sofas and ambient sounds set the stage for evening drinks and sharing plates.

a former brothel, this cheeky bar pays homage to its lascivious past with colourful wall murals, a library of erotically tinged works and a small stage where you can sometimes catch burlesque shows.

★ BA Wine Bar do Bairro Alto   WINE BAR
(Map p72; ☎ 213 461 182; bawinebar@gmail.com; Rua da Rosa 107; ⊘ 6-11pm Tue-Sun; ☎) Reserve ahead unless you want to get shut out of Bairro Alto's best wine bar, where the genuinely welcoming staff will offer you three fantastic tasting choices based on your wine proclivities (wines from €5; tasting boards for one/four €13/47). The cheeses (from small artisanal producers) and charcuterie (melt-in-your-mouth black-pork *presuntos*) are not to be missed, either. Reservations are essential.

Duque Brewpub   CRAFT BEER
(Map p72; www.duquebrewpub.com; Duques da Calçada 49; ⊘ 3pm-midnight Sun-Wed, to 1am Thu, to 2am Fri & Sat; ☎) Lisbon's inaugural brewpub features 12 taps of Portuguese-only craft brews, a few of which are dedicated to on-site suds (under the banner of Cerveja Aroeira), brewed in true craft-beer style: no two batches are the same. Additional taps feature invitees such as Dois Corvos, Musa and Letra.

Tasca Mastai   BAR
(Map p72; www.facebook.com/tascadomastai; Rua da Rosa 14; ⊘ 1pm-midnight Tue-Sun; ☎) This artsy, Italian-run bar-cafe is a refreshing change of pace for Bairro Alto – the long list of speciality Aperol spritzes are worth the trip (try the tart and appley Hugo, summer-drink perfection in a glass). It's a small, corner spot, with old sewing tables and tightly spun corrugated-cardboard bar stools. Bruschettas help soak up all those cocktails.

O Bom O Mau e O Vilão   COCKTAIL BAR
(Map p72; www.thegoodthebadandtheuglybar.com; Rua do Alecrím 21; ⊘ 7pm-2am Mon-Thu, to 3am Fri & Sat) 'The Good, the Bad and the Ugly' is an artsy drinking den sprung from a refurbished Pombaline town house. It's divided among several rooms draped in contemporary artworks and period furnishings. DJs throw down funk, soul, acid jazz and vintage beats to an eclectic, easy-on-the-eyes crowd that is mingle-friendly and more highbrow than average for the neighbourhood.

Loucos & Sonhadores   BAR
(Map p72; Rua da Rosa 261; ⊘ 10pm-4am Mon-Sat) This smoky, bohemian drinking den feels secreted away from the heaving masses on nearby streets. With kitschy decor, free (salty) popcorn and a wide range of tunes, it's a great place for eclectic conversation in the various rooms rather than downing shots.

Solar do Vinho do Porto   WINE BAR
(Map p72; www.ivdp.pt; Rua São Pedro de Alcântara 45; ⊘ 11am-midnight Mon-Fri) The glug, glug of a 40-year-old tawny being poured is music to port-lovers' ears here. Part of an 18th-century mansion, this low-lit, beamed cavern is ideal for nursing a glass from the 180-plus inventory of Portugal's finest. Ports by the glass cost €2.80 to €13.50.

Crafty Corner   CRAFT BEER
(Map p72; www.facebook.com/craftycorner lisboa; Tv Corpo Santo 15; ⊘ 4pm-2am Mon-Sat, to 11.45pm Sun; ☎) An Irishman well versed in Cais do Sodré bars (he owns **Hennessy's Irish pub** (Map p72; www.hennessys-pub.com; Rua Cais do Sodré 32-38; ⊘ noon-2am Sun-Thu, to 3am Fri & Sat; ☎) as well) has stepped up the neighbourhood's bar game with this refined lounge dedicated to Lisbon craft beer. There are 12 taps and plenty of atmospheric ambience: leather sofas in the loft, stools fashioned from emptied kegs and original wooden ceilings.

🍷 Alfama, Castelo & Graça

★ Memmo Alfama   BAR
(Map p76; www.memmoalfama.com; Tv das Merceeiras 27; ⊘ noon-midnight; ☎) Wow, what a view! Alfama unfolds like origami from the stylishly decked roof terrace of the Memmo Alfama hotel (p93). It's a perfect sundowner place, with dreamy vistas over the rooftops, spires and down to the Rio Tejo (and, unfortunately, the new cruise-ship terminal). Cocktails cost €7.50 to €10.

★ Lux-Frágil   CLUB
(www.luxfragil.com; Av Infante D Henrique, Armazém A, Cais de Pedra; ⊘ 11pm-6am Thu-Sat) Lisbon's ice-cool, must-see club, glammy Lux hosts big-name DJs spinning electro and house. It was started by late Lisbon nightlife impresario Marcel Reis and is part-owned by John Malkovich. Grab a spot on the terrace to see the sun rise over the Rio Tejo, or chill like a king or queen on the throne-like giant interior chairs.

LOCAL KNOWLEDGE

GINJINHA BARS

Come dusk, the area around Largo de São Domingos and the adjacent Rua das Portas de Santo Antão buzzes with locals getting their cherry fix in a cluster of *ginjinha* (cherry liqueur) bars. A Ginjinha (p107) is famous as the birthplace of the sugary-sweet tipple, thanks to a quaffing friar from Igreja de Santo António who revealed the secret to an entrepreneurial Galician by the name of Espinheira. Order your €1.40 *ginjinha sem* (without) or – our favourite – *com* (with) the alcohol-soaked cherries. Other postage-stamp-sized bars nearby include Ginjinha Sem Rival (Map p68; www.facebook.com/ginjasem-rivaleeduardino; Rua das Portas de Santo Antão 7; ⊙8am-midnight Mon-Fri, from 9am Sat & Sun) and Ginjinha Rubi (Map p68; Rua Barros Queirós 27; ⊙7am-10.30pm Mon-Sat).

★ **Wine Bar do Castelo**　　　WINE BAR

(Map p76; ☑218 879 093; www.facebook.com/winebardocastelo; Rua Bartolomeu de Gusmão 13; ⊙1-10pm) Located near the entrance to the Castelo de São Jorge (p71), this laid-back wine bar serves more than 150 Portuguese wines by the glass (€4 to €30), along with gourmet smoked meats, cheeses, olives and other tasty accompaniments. Nuno, the multilingual owner, is a welcoming host and a fount of knowledge about all things wine-related.

★ **Outro Lado**　　　CRAFT BEER

(Map p68; www.facebook.com/OutroLado Lisboa; Beco do Arco Escuro 1; ⊙3pm-midnight Tue-Thu, to 2am Fri & Sat, 2-11pm Sun; 🛜) An Egyptian-Polish couple took over and seriously upgraded Lisbeer, one of Lisbon's loungiest and least beer-geeky craft-beer bars, in late 2018. Sé's Outro Lado now offers 15 artisanal brews on draught and 200 or so by the bottle/can, with an emphasis on Portugal's rising scene and the freshest options from Europe, the USA and Canada.

It's a great spot to get hopped up on a well-rounded selection of beers not seen everywhere else while kicking back on retro-style plush sofas and armchairs in the various well-lit rooms.

Portas do Sol　　　BAR

(Map p76; www.portasdosol.pt; Largo das Portas do Sol; ⊙10am-1am Sun-Thu, to 2am Fri & Sat; 🛜) Near one of the city's iconic viewpoints, this spacious sun-drenched terrace has a mix of sofas and white patio furniture, where you can sip cocktails (€7) while taking in magnificent river views. DJs bring animation to the darkly lit industrial interior on weekends.

Chapitô　　　BAR

(Map p68; ☑218 875 077; www.chapito.org; Costa do Castelo 7; ⊙terrace 7am-1pm, restaurant 7pm-

2am; 🛜) There are fantastic views from this bar at an alternative theatre/circus school occupying a former female prison. It's a top choice for sundowners or late-night drinks overlooking the city. More serious foodies will want to book a table at Chapitô à Mesa (p102) – mains €19 to €21 – the restaurant in the hands of Bertílio Gomes, one of the city's top chefs.

8ª Colina Taproom　　　CRAFT BEER

(www.oitavacolina.pt; Rua Damasceno Monteiro 8a; ⊙noon-11pm Tue-Thu & Sun, to 1am Fri & Sat) One of the top brewers in Lisbon's microbrew scene, 8ª Colina's long-awaited taproom opened with spectacularly framed castle views straight from its 10 taps in 2018. The minimalist, slate-grey space is a nod to industrial design; and there's good pub grub (pulled pork, banh mi, bratwurst) to pair with its lagers, IPAs and porters.

Nearby, you can grab a pint in its five-tap kiosk (Map p76; www.oitavacolina.pt; Largo da Graça; ⊙noon-10pm Sun & Tue, 3-9pm Wed, 3-10pm Thu, 3pm-midnight Fri, noon-midnight Sat).

🍷 Príncipe Real, Santos & Estrela

★ **Foxtrot**　　　BAR

(Map p84; www.barfoxtrot.com; Tv Santa Teresa 28; ⊙6pm-2am Mon-Thu, to 3am Fri & Sat, 8pm-2am Sun; 🛜) A cuckoo-clock doorbell announces new arrivals to this dark, decadent slither of art-nouveau glamour, in the bar business since 1978. Foxtrot keeps the mood mellow with jazzy beats and intensely attentive mixology detailed on a tracing-paper menu (cocktails €7 to €15). It's a wonderfully atmospheric spot for a drink.

★ **Cinco Lounge**　　　LOUNGE

(Map p84; www.cincolounge.com; Rua Ruben António Leitão 17; ⊙9pm-2am) Take an award-winning London-born mixologist, Dave Palethorpe, add a candlelit, turquoise-kissed setting and give it a funky twist – *et voilà* – you have Cinco Lounge. Come here to converse, sip legendary cocktails (€7.50 to €15) or join a cocktail-mixing workshop. Cash only.

Cerveteca Lisboa
CRAFT BEER

(Map p84; www.cervetecalisboa.com; Praça das Flores 62; ☺3.30pm-1am Sun-Thu, to 2am Fri & Sat; 🛜) Lisbon's best craft-beer bar is a boozy godsend: 14 oft-changing taps (including two hand pumps) focusing on local and Northern European artisanal brews, including numerous local microbreweries. Not only will hopheads rejoice at IPAs from Lisbon including standouts such as Dois Corvos and 8ª Colina, but having choice alone inspires cartwheels. *Adeus*, tasteless lagers!

The Bar
COCKTAIL BAR

(Map p84; Tv Monte do Carmo 1; ☺7pm-midnight Tue-Thu, to 2am Fri & Sat; 🛜) Australian Teresa Ruiz runs a one-woman cocktail show at this fantastic bar that puts tasty spins on classics in a heavily concreted environment spruced up with an eye-catching she-wolf street mural by Tamara Alves. Negronis are her thing (traditional, with mezcal or with Aperol) but there's something for everyone.

Copenhagen Coffee Lab
CAFE

(Map p84; www.cphcoffeelab.pt; Rua Nova da Piedade 10; ☺8am-7pm Mon-Fri, from 9.30am Sat; 🛜) Serious caffeine aficionados should make a beeline for this Danish import just off lovely Praça das Flores, where properly trained baristas know their way around strong espressos and creamy flat whites, plus a bastion of fiendish preparation methods (V60, Aeropress etc). The clean-lined, blindingly white space screams Denmark, but sometimes you have to transport yourself for java transcendence.

A Paródia
BAR

(Map p84; www.aparodia.com; Rua do Patrocínio 26B; ☺9pm-2am; 🛜) This delightful bar time warps you back to the more glamorous age of art nouveau, with its dark wood, red velvet walls, soft lamp lighting and vintage knick-knacks. It's a wonderfully cosy and intimate place for a tête-à-tête over cocktails (€7 to €9), with jazz playing in the background.

Lost In
BAR

(Map p84; www.facebook.com/lostin.esplanada; Rua Dom Pedro V 56; ☺4pm-midnight Mon, from 12.30pm Tue-Sat) For drinks and light bites with knockout views of the castle and downtown Lisbon, head to the Indo-chic patio at Lost In, shaded by colourful parasols and an enclosed terrace. There's live jazz on Thursday evenings.

🍷 Lapa & Alcântara

Bosq
CLUB

(📞210 938 029; www.facebook.com/bosqlx; Rua Rodrigues de Faria 103, LX Factory; ☺11pm-6am Fri & Sat) This hypercool two-storey nightclub features a 120-sq-metre vertical garden above the upstairs bar and duelling environments that bounce between dance, R&B and hip-hop. Lisbon's bold and beautiful flock here to dance under the guise of nightlife-ready animal portraits and 3D wallpaper.

Quimera Brewpub
BREWERY

(www.quimerabrewpub.com; Rua Prior do Crato 6; ☺5pm-midnight Wed-Thu, to 1am Fri & Sat, to 11pm Sun; 🛜) An American-Brazilian couple launched Lisbon's second brewpub in 2016 with 12 beers, including rarer choices such as Belgian blonde ale, American dark lager and experimental brews, along with a few taps devoted to invited *lisboêta* suds from Dois Corvos, 8ª Colina, Lince and more. Downing proper pints within the Palácio

---

OFF THE BEATEN TRACK

CUTTING-EDGE CRAFT BREWS

One of the anchors that established artsy Marvila as Lisbon's 'it' neighbourhood, **Dois Corvos** (www.doiscorvos.pt; Rua Capitão Leitão 94; ☺2-11pm Sun-Thu, to 1am Fri & Sat; 🛜) is an informal taproom that packs in craft enthusiasts downing hoppy IPA and strong barrel-aged brews within earshot of the brewery floor. Seattle microbrewer Scott Steffens and team brew Portugal's best craft beer, sold fresh from the 17 taps here (more planned, one nitro) and considerably cheaper than elsewhere.

Creature IPA and Finisterra Porter are particularly worth the trip, as are experimental, one-off beers and the odd resurrected style from across Europe. There's growler service as well. Catch buses 728, 781 or 782 from Cais de Sodre/Praça do Comercio/Santa Apolonia.

das Necessidades' stone-walled 18th-century carriage tunnel feels vaguely medieval.

♟ Marquês de Pombal & Around

★ Red Frog
COCKTAIL BAR

(Map p92; www.facebook.com/redfrogspeakeasy; Rua do Salitre 5A; ⊙6pm-2am Mon-Thu, to 3am Fri & Sat) In true speakeasy fashion, Red Frog is accessed via a 'Press for Cocktails' doorbell and a list of rules. Enter a sophisticated mixology world of craft cocktails and appropriate glassware, dress and behaviour. The exquisite seasonal cocktail menu (€10 to €14.50) is perfectly balanced, and the dark and classy room, plus the intriguing secret one, are perfect accompaniments. Connoisseurs only.

Casa Independente
BAR

(Map p92; www.casaindependente.com; Largo do Intendente 45; ⊙5-11pm Tue-Fri, to midnight Sat) There's always something going on at this creative space overlooking a sleepy plaza just north of Largo Martim Moniz. You can wander through rooms looking at strange and curious artworks, hit the plant-filled back patio (joining the smokers), or nurse drinks in quiet corners of this rambling old space.

♟ Belém

A Margem
FUSION

(Map p96; ☑914 736 191; www.amargem.com; Doca do Bom Sucesso; ⊙10am-1am Apr-Oct, to 7.30pm Nov-Mar) Well positioned near the river's edge, this small, sun-drenched cube of glass and white stone boasts an open patio and large windows facing the Tejo and dramatic sunsets over the Torre de Belém. Locals come for fresh salads, cheese plates, bruschetta and other light bites (salads €10 to €14) that go nicely with a sundowner (wines €3.50 to €5).

Sunglasses are essential. To get here, follow the river's edge 200m west from the Padrão dos Descobrimentos (p81). On weekends you'll need to settle in up to 90 minutes early for a prime spot at sunset.

☆ Entertainment

Fado

Mesa de Frades
LIVE MUSIC

(Map p76; ☑917 029 436; www.facebook.com/mesadefradeslisboa; Rua dos Remédios 139A; prix-fixe shows €50; ⊙8pm-2.30am Mon-Sat) A magical place to hear fado, tiny Mesa de Frades used to be a chapel. It's tiled with exquisite *azulejos* and has just a handful of tables, including a dark and sexy mezzanine level. Shows begin at around 10.30pm.

Tasca Bela
LIVE MUSIC

(Map p76; ☑926 077 511; www.facebook.com/bela.vinhosepetiscos; Rua dos Remédios 190; ⊙8.30pm-3am Tue-Sun) This intimate spot features live fado on Wednesday, Friday, Saturday and Sunday, and eclectic cultural fare (jazz, poetry readings) on other nights. Although there is a €19 minimum spend, unlike most fado houses you won't have to buy a pricey meal, as it's an appetisers-and-drinks kind of place. Fado begins at 9.30pm.

Senhor Fado
LIVE MUSIC

(Map p76; ☑914 431 971; www.sr-fado.com; Rua dos Remédios 176; ⊙8pm-2am Wed-Sat) Small and lantern-lit, this is a cosy spot for *fado vadio* (street fado). *Fadista* Ana Marina and guitarist Duarte Santos make a great double act.

A Baiuca
LIVE MUSIC

(Map p76; ☑218 867 284; Rua de São Miguel 20; ⊙8pm-midnight Thu-Mon) On a good night, walking into A Baiuca is like gatecrashing a family party. It's a special place with *fado vadio*, where locals take a turn and spectators hiss if anyone dares to chat during the singing. There's a €25 minimum spend, which is as tough to swallow as the food, though the fado is spectacular. Reserve ahead.

Parreirinha de Alfama
LIVE MUSIC

(Map p76; ☑218 868 209; www.parreirinhadealfama.com; Beco do Espírito Santo 1; minimum €30; ⊙8pm-2am Tue-Sun) Owned by fado legend Argentina Santos, this place offers good food amid candlelit ambience; it attracts an audience that often falls hard for the top-quality *fadistas* (three singers and two guitarists per night, sometimes appearing straight out of the crowd). Book by 4pm.

A Tasca do Chico
LIVE MUSIC

(Map p72; ☑961 339 696; www.facebook.com/atasca.dochico; Rua do Diário de Notícias 39; ⊙7pm-1.30am Sun-Thu, to 3am Fri & Sat) This crowded dive (reserve ahead), full of soccer banners and spilling over with people of all ilks, is a fado free-for-all. It's not uncommon for taxi drivers to roll up, hum a few bars, and hop right back into their cabs, speeding off into the night.

LGBT+ LISBON

The gay and lesbian community had much to celebrate in 2010, with the passing of a bill that legalised gay marriage. The big events worth looking out for are Lisbon Pride (www.portugalpride.org) in June, and the Festival Internacional de Cinema Queer (www.queerlisboa.pt) in late September.

The Scene

The kings and queens of Lisbon's gay and lesbian scene are the bear-leaning bars of hip Príncipe Real and the street-party atmosphere of more varied venues around Bairro Alto's so-called 'gay corner' at Rua da Baroca and Tv da Espera ('Hope Alley'). It's worth being in town for hot parties like venue-jumping Conga Club (www.facebook.com/pg/congaclub-party), visits by the global franchise Matinée (www.facebook.com/MatineeGroup), or the summer-long Hot Season Festival between June's Lisboa Pride (www.ilga-portugal.pt/lisboapride) and September's QueerLisboa Film Festival (www.queerlisboa.pt).

The edgier and more glamorous nightspots, especially Lux-Frágil (p109), draw a mixed gay-straight crowd, while those open to more hardcore adventures could consider WoofX (www.facebook.com/Woofx) or newcomer Chains (www.facebook.com/chainsbarclub). For more listings and events, check out *Time Out* (http://timeout.sapo.pt), with its gay section updated weekly; Lisbon Gay Circuit (www.lisbongaycircuit.com); Lisbon Beach (www.lisbonbeach.com), which has gay-centric tours; and the members of Variações (www.variacoes.pt), the new Portuguese LGBTI Chamber of Commerce and Tourism.

For summer fun, head to Costa da Caparica, where Praia de Bela Vista (south towards Fonte da Telha) is a popular hotspot, along with Praia do Meco and Praia da Adiça (Nato).

WoofLX (Map p84; www.facebook.com/wooflx; Rua da Palmeira 44A; ☺10pm-4am) Príncipe Real's bear-ish gay bar (though it attracts all shapes and sizes). It's part of the Woof empire that includes the naughtier, more hardcore option WoofX.

Corvo (Map p84; Calçada Miguel Pais 18; ☺4pm-2am Tue-Thu, to 3am Fri & Sat) This hipster-ish newcomer in Príncipe Real is positioning itself as a fashionable option.

Bar TR3S (Map p84; www.areismarcos.wix.com/tr3slisboa; Rua Rubén a Leitão 2; ☺4pm-2am Sun-Thu, to 3am Fri & Sat) Bears and their friends flock to this hopping bar, especially for its daily happy hour and outdoor seating.

Shelter Bar (Map p84; www.facebook.com/shelterbarlisboa; Rua da Palmeira 43A; ☺6pm-2am Sun-Thu, to 3am Fri & Sat) One of Príncipe Real newer gay bars, it's a good bet for craft beer, Italian-style bites and happy-hour specials.

Clube da Esquina (Map p72; www.facebook.com/clubedaesquina.bairroalto; Rua da Barroca 30; ☺7pm-2am Mon-Thu, to 3am Fri & Sat, 9pm-2am Sun; 🐾) The anchor of Lisbon's 'gay corner' in Bairro Alto, it nonetheless draws a mixed crowd, while bars one block in all four directions (Mathilde, Side Bar, Espaço 41 and others) attract a more gay clientele.

Posh (Map p84; www.facebook.com/poshclublisbon; Rua de São Bento 157; ☺midnight-6am Fri & Sat) This nightclub with slick aspirations opened in 2018, with drag, electronic music and national and international stars.

Construction (Map p84; www.facebook.com/construction.lisbon; Rua Cecílio de Sousa 84; ☺midnight-6am Thu-Sun) A top club among thirty-somethings, with somewhat industrial design, pumping house music and a dark room.

Finalmente (Map p84; www.finalmenteclub.com; Rua da Palmeira 38; ☺midnight-6am) This popular club has a tiny dance floor, nightly drag shows and wall-to-wall crowds.

Purex (Map p72; www.facebook.com/purexclub; Rua das Salgadeiras 28; ☺10pm-2am Tue-Thu, to 3am Fri & Sat) One for the women, this unsigned Bairro Alto spot draws a lesbian and mixed crowd, with DJ nights and a small dance floor.

Trumps (Map p84; 🖀915 938 266; www.trumps.pt; Rua da Imprensa Nacional 104B; ☺midnight-5am Thu, to 6am Fri & Sat) Lisbon's hottest younger-leaning gay club with cruisy corners, a sizeable electro-house and pop-fuelled dance floor, and events from live music to drag.

LISBON & AROUND LISBON

Portugal's most famous fado singer, Mariza, brought us here in 2005. It's legit.

Football

Estádio da Luz
STADIUM

(Estádio do Sport Lisboa e Benfica; 🎫 707 200 100; www.slbenfica.pt; Av General Norton de Matos; tour/museum €12.50/10) SL Benfica play at this 65,000-seat stadium in the northwestern Benfica district, which also houses the club's well-done museum (https://museubenfica.slbenfica.pt), where you can visit the soaring bald eagle mascot, Vitória. The stadium hosted the 2014 Champions League final and was voted the most beautiful stadium in Europe the same year by French sporting newspaper, *L'Équipe*. Seeing a match here is epic.

Stadium tours are available. The nearest metro station is Colégio Militar-Luz.

Music, Theatre & Dance

★ Hot Clube de Portugal
JAZZ

(Map p92; 🎫 213 460 305; www.hcp.pt; Praça da Alegria 48; ⊘ 10pm-2am Tue-Sat) As hot as its name suggests, this small, poster-plastered cellar (and newly added garden) has staged top-drawer jazz acts since the 1940s. It's considered one of Europe's best.

Zé dos Bois
LIVE MUSIC

(ZDB; Map p72; www.zedosbois.org; Rua da Barroca 59; cover €6-10; ⊘ expositions 6-11pm Wed-Sat, concerts from 10pm) Focusing on tomorrow's performing-arts and music trends, Zé dos Bois is an experimental venue with a graffitied courtyard and an eclectic line-up of theatre, film, visual arts and live music.

Teatro Taborda
THEATRE

(Map p76; 🎫 218 854 190; www.teatrodagaragem.com; Costa do Castelo 75) This cultural centre showcases contemporary dance, theatre and world music, and is the residence of experimental theatre company Teatro da Garagem. It also has spectacular views from its cafe (open 5pm to midnight Tuesday to Friday, from 3pm on weekends).

Teatro Nacional de São Carlos
THEATRE

(Map p72; 🎫 213 253 045; www.saocarlos.pt; Rua Serpa Pinto 9; ⊘ box office 1-7pm Mon-Fri) Teatro Nacional de São Carlos is worth visiting just to see the sublime gold-and-red interior (email ahead for €5 guided tours), and it has opera, ballet and theatre seasons. The summertime Festival ao Largo (p85) features free outdoor concerts on the plaza facing the theatre.

Teatro Nacional de Dona Maria II
THEATRE

(Map p72; 🎫 800 213 250; www.teatro-dmaria.pt; Praça Dom Pedro IV; ⊘ box office 11am-10pm Wed-Fri, 2-10pm Sat, 10.30am-7pm Tue & Sun) Rossio's graceful neoclassical theatre has a somewhat hit-and-miss schedule. Guided tours on Mondays (except August) are at 11am (€8).

Cinema

Cinemateca Portuguesa
CINEMA

(Map p92; 🎫 213 596 266; www.cinemateca.pt; Rua Barata Salgueiro 39; films €3.20) Cinemateca Portuguesa screens offbeat, art-house, world and old movies.

It's worth popping in even without intentions of seeing a film – there is a fascinating permanent exhibition of Golden Age of Hollywood–era movie equipment, including numerous antique movie cameras, plus a cinema-centric bookshop and an artsy-leaning cafe (Map p92; www.cinemateca.pt; mains €7.50-12.50; ⊘ 12.30pm-1am Mon-Sat; 🖱).

🛍 Shopping

🛍 Baixa & Rossio

★ Garrafeira Nacional
WINE

(Map p68; 🎫 218 879 080; www.garrafeiranacional.com; Rua de Santa Justa 18; ⊘ 9.30am-7.30pm Mon-Fri, to 7pm Sat) This Lisbon landmark has been selling Portuguese wine since 1927 and is easily the best spot to pick up a bevy of local wines and spirits. It is especially helpful and will steer you towards lesser-known boutique wines and vintage ports in addition to the usual suspects. The small museum features vintages dating to the 18th century.

★ Typographia
CLOTHING

(Map p68; www.typographia.com; Rua Augusta 93; ⊘ 10am-7pm) With stores in Porto and Madrid as well, this high-design T-shirt shop is one of Europe's best. It features a select, monthly changing array of clever and artsy, locally designed T-shirts (€23.95), which no one else will be wearing back home.

★ Manteigaria Silva
FOOD

(Map p72; www.manteigariasilva.pt; Rua Dom Antão de Almada 1D; ⊘ 9am-7.30pm Mon-Sat) Specialising in the best of the best and in business for more than a century, Manteigaria Silva does a brisk trade in staunchly curated Portuguese ham, cheese, wine and *bacalhau*.

Retrox   VINTAGE
(Map p92; www.facebook.com/retroxcoisas
vintage; Rua dos Anjos 4C; ⊘noon-7pm Tue-Sat)
Stylish Brazilian Josiane Lima has assem-
bled a collection of vintage kitsch from the
'50s to the '70s, from Portugal and abroad, at
this hip Intendente shop. The ever-changing
bounty might feature Abba 45s, West German scales, Cuban cigar boxes, framed 1940
Comboios de Portugal train schedules or
old-school Japanese Super 8 cameras.

Napoleão   WINE
(Map p68; www.napoleao.co.pt; Rua dos Fanqueiros 70; ⊘9.30am-8pm Mon-Sat, 3-7pm Sun) Of
the two Napoleão shops on this corner, this
friendly, English-speaking cellar specialises
in Portuguese-only wines, ports and spirits. There are hundreds of bottles to choose
from (as well as other home-grown gourmet
products) and it ships worldwide.

A Vida Portuguesa   GIFTS & SOUVENIRS
(Map p92; www.avidaportuguesa.com; Largo do
Intendente 23; ⊘10.30am-7.30pm) The second
outlet of Catarina Portas' made-in-Portugal
boutique has turned a 19th-century ceramics factory into another must-visit shop, this
time also helping revitalise the Intendente
neighbourhood.

Espaço Açores   FOOD
(Map p68; Rua de São Julião 58; ⊘10am-2pm &
3-7pm Mon-Sat) The closest you can get to
actually visiting the Azores in Lisbon is this
attractive shop, where a taste of the islands
comes in the form of cheeses, honeys, preserves, passion-fruit liqueurs and, apparently, the oldest tea produced in Europe.

Anjos70   MARKET
(Map p92; www.anjos70.org; Regueirão Dos Anjos
70; ⊘11am-7pm first Sat & Sun of the month, closed
Aug) This rambling alternative market takes
place on the first weekend of each month
and draws a young, eclectic crowd of freaks
and geeks who gobble up alternative designs and vintage clothing, jewellery, rare vinyl, funky and performance art, handmade
soaps, artisan chocolates and tea – with DJs
and a bar fuelling the fun. No two days are
the same.

Queijaria Nacional   FOOD
(Map p68; Rua da Conceição 8; ⊘10am-8pm) A
one-stop cheese shop with varieties from all
over Portugal – from pungent and creamy
Serra da Estrela offerings to Azores and
Alentejo varieties. You can also pair cheese

CATWALK QUEENS

Make way for Lisbon's catwalk kings and
queens, revamping wardrobes with their
majestic collections:

Fátima Lopes (Map p92; ☎213 240
550; www.fatimalopes.com; Rua Rodrigues
Sampaio 96; ⊘9am-6pm Mon-Fri) Divas
love Fátima's immaculate collection of
figure-hugging, Latin-inspired threads
– from slinky suits to itsy-glitzy prom
dresses and hot-pink ball gowns.

Luís Onofre (Map p92; www.luisonofre.
com; Av da Liberdade 247; ⊘10am-7pm
Mon-Sat) For sexy women's shoes fit for
a princess, it doesn't get any bigger than
Luis Onofre, whose designs have graced
the feet of Michelle Obama, Naomi
Watts and Paris Hilton

Storytailors (p117) Daring designs
from Luís Sanchez and João Branco
that skirt traditional gender roles.

Nuno Gama (p117) Portugal's catwalk
king, whose locally steeped designs feature coats of arms and *azulejo* (painted
tile) patterns.

and charcuterie with Portuguese wines during a tasting here.

🏠 Chiado & Bairro Alto

⭐ **A Vida Portuguesa**   GIFTS & SOUVENIRS
(Map p72; www.avidaportuguesa.com; Rua Anchieta 11; ⊘10am-8pm Mon-Sat, from 11am Sun) A
flashback to the late 19th century with its
high ceilings and polished cabinets, this former warehouse and perfume factory lures
nostalgics with its all-Portuguese products,
from retro-wrapped Tricona sardines to
Claus Porto soaps, and heart-embellished
Viana do Castelo embroideries to Bordalo
Pinheiro porcelain swallows. There's also a
location in Intendente (p115).

⭐ **Loja das Conservas**   FOOD
(Map p72; www.facebook.com/lojadasconservas;
Rua do Arsenal 130; ⊘10am-8pm Mon-Sat, from
noon Sun) What appears to be a gallery is
on closer inspection a fascinating temple to
tinned fish (or *conservas* as the Portuguese
say) – the result of an industry on its death-
bed revived by a savvy marketing about-
face and new generations of hipsters. The
retro-wrapped tins, displayed along with

DON'T MISS

FACTORY OF THE ARTS

Set in a converted 19th-century industrial complex, LX Factory (www.lxfactory.com; Rua Rodrigues de Faria 103) is Lisbon's coolest hub of creativity. In 2007 some 23,000 sq metres of abandoned warehouses were transformed into spaces for art studios, galleries, and printing and design companies. Creative restaurants, bars and shops have added to the energy, and today LX Factory is a great spot to check out an alternative side of Lisbon. It's liveliest on weekend nights, though it's also worth stopping by the open-air market (vintage clothes, crafts) held on Sundays from 11am to 7pm. Get there on tram 15E or 18E.

Other highlights:

Kiss the Cook (p82) Offers cooking classes (the chef speaks English).

Kare Design (www.kare-design.com; ⊙ noon-8pm Tue-Fri, from 11am Sat, 10am-2pm Sun) Imaginative home-design store.

Ler Devagar (p118) Great bookshop and cosy cafe. Don't miss the wild exhibits on upper floors.

1300 Taberna (🖉 213 649 170; www.1300taberna.com; mains €13-26; ⊙ 12.30-3pm & 8pm-midnight Tue-Sat; 🔊) An excellent restaurant featuring creative takes on Portuguese fare.

Landeau (www.landeau.pt; cake €3.70; ⊙ noon-7pm Sun-Thu, to 11pm Fri & Sat; 🔊) Wondrously gooey, perfectly moist, just-sweet-enough pieces of chocolate-cake perfection.

Rio Maravilha (🖉 966 028 229; www.riomaravilha.pt; small plates €5-22.50, menus €25-45; ⊙ 6pm-2am Tue, 12.30pm-2am Wed-Thu, 12.30pm-3am Fri-Sat, 12.30-8pm Sun) Chef Diogo Noronha's good-time Portuguese-Brazilian *petiscos* come with outstanding river views.

the history of each canning factory, are artworks.

★ **Loja do Burel**   CLOTHING
(Map p72; www.burelfactory.com; Rua Serpa Pinto 15B; ⊙ 10am-8pm Mon-Sat, 11am-7pm Sun) Once a clothing staple of Serra da Estrela mountain-dwelling shepherds, Burel, a Portuguese black wool, was all but left to disappear until this company single-handedly resurrected the industry, giving it a stylish makeover fit for 21st-century fashion. The colourful blankets, handbags, jackets, hats and other home decor items aren't like anything anyone has back home.

Cork & Company   GIFTS & SOUVENIRS
(Map p72; www.corkandcompany.pt; Rua das Salgadeiras 10; ⊙ 11am-7pm Mon-Sat, from 5pm Sun) 🖉 At this elegantly designed shop, you'll find cork put to surprisingly imaginative uses, with well-made and sustainable cork handbags, pens, wallets, journals, candleholders, hats, scarves, place mats, umbrellas, iPhone covers and even chaise longues!

Fábrica Sant'Ana   ARTS & CRAFTS
(Map p72; www.santanna.com.pt; Rua do Alecrím 95; ⊙ 9.30am-7pm Mon-Sat) Handmaking and

painting *azulejos* (from €5) since 1741, this is the place to get some eye-catching porcelain tiles for your home.

Underdogs Public Art Store   ART
(Map p84; www.under-dogs.net; Rua da Cintura do Porto de Lisboa, Armazém A; ⊙ 11am-7pm Tue-Sun) Witness the strength of street knowledge at this part gallery, part Montana-street-art paint store and cafe behind Cais do Sodré. Underdogs specialises in high-profile public art and offers Lisbon's best public-art tours on a sporadic, by-appointment-only basis (tours from €35). Good coffee is available, too.

Oficina Irmãos Marques   ART
(Map p72; www.oficinairmaosmarques.com; Rua Luz Soriano 71; ⊙ 10.30am-6.30pm Wed-Sat, by appointment Mon & Tue) Even if you don't buy anything, it's worth popping into the gallery/workshop of Brazilian-born Gezo Marques, mainly for his striking woodwork, which channels the maze-like tapestries of Brazilian favela construction into one-of-a-kind cabinetry and wood art. You'll also find provocative paintings, *objets d'art*, chandeliers and unique interior-design pieces – perhaps easier to lug home than a chest of drawers.

Nuno Gama   FASHION & ACCESSORIES

(Map p72; www.nunogama.pt; Rua Nova da Trindade 1B; ⊙10.30am-7.30pm Mon-Sat) One of the country's most feted fashion designers, Nuno Gama is Portugal's catwalk king. His sleek flagship store showcases Nuno's hallmarks, including a love of blue, contemporary, figure-hugging tailoring, as well as a subtle use of heritage motifs, such as coats of arms and *azulejo* patterns. There's also a barber shop here should you fancy revamping your locks.

A Carioca   FOOD

(Map p72; Rua da Misericórdia 9; ⊙9am-7pm Mon-Fri, to 1pm Sat) Little has changed since this old-world store opened in 1924: brass fittings still gleam, the coffee roaster is still in action, and home blends, sugared almonds and toffees are still lovingly wrapped in green paper.

Louie Louie   MUSIC

(Map p72; www.louielouie.biz; Rua Nova da Trinidade 8; ⊙10.30am-7pm Mon-Sat) Clued-up DJs head for this music store that stocks second-hand vinyl and the latest house, dance and electronica grooves.

Storytailors   CLOTHING

(Map p72; www.storytailors.pt; Calçada do Ferragial 8; ⊙11am-7pm Tue-Sat) Mirror, mirror...undoubtedly one of Lisbon's fairest boutiques is this chandelier-lit enchanted forest of fashion, where design duo Luís Sanchez and João Branco bewitch with fairy-tale dresses, floaty ruffle skirts, quirky reversible coats and their latest catwalk creations (for women, men and the gender-fluid).

El Dorado   VINTAGE, CLOTHING

(Map p72; ☑213 423 935; Rua do Norte 23; ⊙1-9pm Mon-Thu, to 11pm Fri & Sat, 3-9pm Sun) A gramophone plays vinyl classics as divas grab vintage styles, from psychedelic prints to 6in platforms and pencil skirts, at this Bairro Alto hipster place. There's also a great range of club wear.

🏠 Alfama, Castelo & Graça

★**Cortiço & Netos**   HOMEWARES

(Map p76; www.corticoenetos.com; Calçada de Santo André 66; ⊙10am-1pm & 2-7pm Mon-Sat) A wonder wall of fabulous *azulejos* greets you as you enter this very special space. It's the vision of brothers Pedro, João, Ricardo and Tiago Cortiço, whose grandfather dedicated more than 30 years to gathering, storing and selling discontinued Portuguese industrial tiles. Reviving the family trade, the brothers are experts on the *azulejo* and how it can be interpreted today.

★**A Arte da Terra**   GIFTS & SOUVENIRS

(Map p76; www.aartedaterra.pt; Rua de Augusto Rosa 40; ⊙11am-8pm) In the stables of a centuries-old bishop's palace, A Arte da Terra brims with authentic Portuguese crafts including Castello Branco embroideries, nativity figurines, hand-painted *azulejos*, fado CDs and quality cork goods (umbrellas, aprons, writing journals). Some goods are beautifully lit in former troughs.

O Voo da Andorinha   GIFTS & SOUVENIRS

(Map p76; www.facebook.com/ovooda andorinha; Rua do Barão 22; ⊙11am-7.30pm Mon-Sat) Candy-bright beads, hand-stitched swallows, embroidered accessories and quirky furnishings made with recycled castaways such as cassette tapes, floppy discs, computer keys and old vinyl – you'll find all of this and more at this adorable boutique representing some 50 Lisbon-area artists near the cathedral.

It shares space with Joana Candeias (backpacks), Amores de Tóquio (Asian-influenced women's clothing) and Adonis Jewellery (contemporary ornaments inspired by Lego pieces, flowers, sewing needles etc).

Garbags   FASHION & ACCESSORIES

(Map p76; www.garbags.eu; Rua São Vicente 17; ⊙11am-7pm) A second outlet of the eco-friendly **Graça shop** (Map p76; www.garbags. eu; Calçada da Graça 16; ⊙10am-8pm) 🍃 hawking all manner of gear (wallets, phone cases, handbags) fashioned from recycled coffee sacks, potato-chip bags, juice containers and other materials.

Coises do Alberto   ARTS & CRAFTS

(Map p76; Rua do Salvador 83; ⊙11am-7.30pm Mon-Sat, 2-7pm Sun) Creative Angolan Alberto's small Alfama studio will get your attention as you stroll by. A peek in reveals his artistic 'things' *(coises):* a retro array of vintage suitcases and travel cases covered in old newspaper and magazines clippings and glazed for protection. Leave the cork magnets to less savvy travellers and get yourself something unique.

Loja dos Descobrimentos   ARTS & CRAFTS

(Map p76; www.loja-descobrimentos.com; Rua dos Bacalhoeiros 14A; ⊙9am-7pm Mon-Sat) Watch artisans carefully painting handmade *azulejos* at this workshop and store near the Casa dos Bicos. Fruits and flowers, boats, culinary motifs or geometric styles – the tiles are available in myriad colours and designs.

Fabula Urbis BOOKS
(Map p76; www.fabula-urbis.pt; Rua de Augusto Rosa 27; ⊙11am-1.30pm & 3-8pm Thu-Sat) A great little bookshop that celebrates works about Portugal, both by home-grown and expat authors. All the best books by Lobo Antunes, Saramago, Pessoa, Richard Zimler and Robert C Wilson are here – available in English, French, Spanish, Italian, German and, of course, Portuguese.

🅰 Príncipe Real, Santos & Estrela

★ Embaixada SHOPPING CENTRE
(Map p84; www.embaixadalx.pt; Praça do Príncipe Real 26; ⊙noon-8pm Mon-Fri, 11am-7pm Sat & Sun, restaurants to 2am) Take an exquisite 19th-century neo-Moorish palace and fill it with fashion, design and concept stores on the cutting edge of cool and you have one of Lisbon's most exciting new shopping experiences: Embaixada. Centred on a grand sweeping staircase and courtyard are boutiques selling everything from vintage records to organic cosmetics, eco-homewares, contemporary Portuguese ceramics and catwalk styles.

There's a wonderful gin-centric bar (Gin Lovers) and cafe (Less) in the atrium, and a good steakhouse hidden below, to the back – Atalho Real (Map p84; ☑213 460 311; www.grupoatalho.pt; Calçada do Patriarca 40, Embaixada; mains €7-15; ⊙noon-11pm Sun-Wed, to midnight Thu-Sat; 🐟).

Solar ANTIQUES
(Map p84; www.solar.com.pt; Rua Dom Pedro V 70; ⊙10am-7pm Mon-Fri, to 1pm Sat) Hawking antique *azulejos* for seven decades, Solar offers row after row and pile after pile of precious Portuguese tiles dating from the 1500s to 1900s, many of which were salvaged from old churches and palaces.

Verso Branco DESIGN
(Map p84; www.versobranco.pt; Rua da Boavista 132-134; ⊙11.30am-8pm Tue-Sat) 'Free verse' is the name of this split-level design store, where Fernando has a story for every object. The high-ceilinged space showcases Portuguese contemporary arts, crafts and furnishings, from Burel's quality wool creations to limited-edition La.Ga bags by designer Jorge Moita – the beautifully crafted bags made from Tyvek weigh just 40g and can hold 55kg.

Casa Pau-Brasil DESIGN
(Map p84; Rua da Escola Politécnica 42; ⊙noon-8pm Mon-Sat, to 6pm Sun) Inside the 18th-century Castilho Palace, this high-design Brazilian concept store divvies up space among 18 Brazilian brands and designers, including Granado cosmetics, iconic furniture by Sérgio Rodrigues, swimwear by Lenny and interior design by Campana. Brazilian accents fill the trendy space.

Loja Real DESIGN
(Map p84; www.facebook.com/lojareal.Lisboa; Praça do Príncipe Real 20; ⊙10.30am-8pm) A showcase largely for Portuguese designers, Loja Real features a wide assortment of unique, high-quality products that run the gamut of home decor (cushions, teapots, vases), fashion (clothing, jewellery) and artwork to items for children (clothing, books and toys). The emphasis is on 'slow retail': nothing is mass-produced or made with plastics or cheap materials.

🅰 Lapa & Alcântara

LX Market MARKET
(www.lxmarket.com.pt; Rua Rodrigues de Faria 103, LX Factory; ⊙11am-8pm Sun) Vintage clothing, antiques, crafts, food, and weird and wonderful plants – the LX Factory market is the place to find them. Live music keeps the Sunday shoppers entertained.

Ler Devagar BOOKS
(☑213 259 992; www.lerdevagar.com; Rua Rodrigues de Faria 103, LX Factory; ⊙11am-9pm Sun-Mon, to 11pm Tue-Thu, to 1am Fri & Sat) Late-night bookworms and anyone who enjoys a good read will love this floor-to-ceiling temple of books. Foreign-language titles and books on art and culture are well represented.

Portugal Gifts GIFTS & SOUVENIRS
(www.portugalgifts.com.pt; Rua Presidente Arriaga 60; ⊙10am-7pm Mon-Fri) This craft shop puts a contemporary spin on Portuguese souvenirs, with everything from Barcelos cockerel mugs to *azulejo* coasters and chocolate sardines.

🏠 Marquês de Pombal & Around

Carbono   MUSIC
(Map p92; www.carbono.com.pt; Rua do Telhal 6B; ⊙11am-7pm Mon-Sat) The staff may be grumpy here, but it's hard not to like Carbono, with its impressive selection of new and second-hand vinyl and CDs. World music – West African boogaloo, Brazilian tropicalia – is especially well represented.

ℹ Information

DANGERS & ANNOYANCES

Lisbon generally enjoys a low crime rate, but petty theft is on the rise.

➡ Mind your wallet on trams – major hotspots for pickpockets – and other tourist hubs such as Rua Augusta.

➡ Pay attention at night around Anjos, Martim Moniz and Intendente metro stations, where muggings have occurred. Take care in dark alleys around Alfama and Graça.

➡ Ignore hash and cocaine offers from shady characters in Baixa, especially around Rossio, Praça do Comércio and Bairro Alto – the drugs are fake anyway.

➡ Always keep your wits about you in Cais do Sodré, which has seen an increase in snatch-and-grabs.

EMERGENCY

Police	☎112
Fire	☎112
Ambulance	☎112
Lisbon Tourist Police	☎213 421 623

INTERNET ACCESS

The majority of cafes and restaurants in Lisbon offer free wireless access, though it's not always obvious, as few bother changing the name of their wi-fi network from the default ones that come with the router to their business name. Ask your server.

MEDIA

Popular Portuguese newspapers include Diário de Notícias (www.dn.pt) and the tabloid bestseller Correio da Manhã (www.cmjornal.pt). The Portugal News (www.theportugalnews.com) is an English-language daily.

MEDICAL SERVICES

Medical services are readily available. There are no special requirements other than for EU citizens who want to receive free emergency

---

SHOPPING MALLS

When you need a break from the heat, step into air-conditioned splendour. All of the following malls have cinemas, food courts and, of course, shops:

Centro Comercial Colombo (www.colombo.pt; Av Lusíada; ⊙9am-midnight)

Amoreiras Shopping Center (Complexo das Amoreiras; ☎213 810 200; www.amoreiras.com; Av Duarte Pacheco; ⊙10am-11pm)

El Corte Inglés (Map p92; www.elcorte-ingles.pt; Av António Augusto de Aguiar 31; ⊙10am-10pm Mon-Thu, to 11.30pm Fri & Sat, to 8pm Sun)

Dolce Vita Tejo (www.dolcevitatejo.pt; Av Cruzeiro Seixas 5 e 7, Amadora; ⊙10am-11pm Sun-Thu, to midnight Fri & Sat)

---

medical treatment – they need to show their European Health Insurance Card.

MONEY

International credit cards – referred to as Visa, even when they're MasterCard and others! – can be problematic. Some smaller family-run businesses will only accept debit cards that are Portuguese-issued. ATMs are everywhere, but avoid Euronet's holiday-ruining fees and conversion rates – use feeless Multibanco, Portugal's principle ATM network.

POST

Correios, Telégrafos e Telefones (CTT; www.ct.pt) is the national postal service of Portugal.

Main Post Office (CTT; Map p68; www.ctt.pt; Praça dos Restauradores 58; ⊙8.30am-10pm Mon-Fri, 9am-6pm Sat) There's also a **central post office** (CTT; Map p72; www.ctt.pt; Praça do Município 6; ⊙8.30am-6pm) near Praça do Comércio and a handy **branch** (CTT; Map p72; www.ctt.pt; Praça Luís de Camões 20; ⊙9am-6pm Mon-Fri) in Chiado.

TOURIST INFORMATION

Ask Me Lisboa (Map p68; ☎213 472 134; www.askmelisboa.com; Rua do Jardim do Regedor 50; ⊙10am-8pm) This branch near Praça dos Restauradores provides tourist info, left luggage and charged internet access.

Ask Me Lisboa (Map p68; ☎210 312 810; Praça do Comércio; ⊙9am-8pm) Another helpful branch.

Ask Me Lisboa also runs several information points, which are handy places for maps and quick information, at Aeroporto de Lisbo (p123); Mosteiro dos Jerónimos (Map p96;

☑213 658 435; Jardim Vasco da Gama; ⊙10am-6pm Tue-Sat); **Belém Tower** (Map p96; ☑910 517 886; Jardim da Torre de Belém; ⊙9am-6pm); **Santa Apolónia** (Map p76; ☑912 409 142; Door 48, Santa Apolónia train station; ⊙7.30am-1pm & 2-4.30pm); **Rossio** (Map p72; ☑910 517 914; Praça Dom Pedro IV; ⊙10am-1pm & 2-6pm); **Parque das Nações** (Map p108; ☑910 518 028; Alameda dos Oceanos; ⊙9am-8pm); and the newest at **Cais do Sodré** (Map p72; ☑912 484 108; www.visitlisboa.com; Praça do Duque de Terceira, Estação Cais do Sodré; ⊙9am-1pm & 2-6pm). These are all run by the city's official tourism arm, Turismo de Lisboa, but bear in mind it is member-driven so not impartial when it comes to recommendations.

Instituto da Conservação da Natureza e da Biodiversidade (ICNB; Map p92; ☑213 507 900; www.icnf.pt; Av da República 16) Portugal's governmental body responsible for the management of protected and state-forested areas.

ℹ️ Getting There & Away

AIR

Situated around 6km north of the centre, the ultramodern **Aeroporto de Lisboa** (Lisbon Airport; ☑218 413 500; www.ana.pt/pt/lis/home; Alameda das Comunidades Portuguesas) operates direct flights to major international hubs including London, New York, Paris and Frankfurt. Low-cost carriers (Norwegian, easyJet, Ryanair, Transavia, Blue Air and Wizz Air) leave from the less efficient Terminal 2 – you'll need to factor in extra time for the shuttle ride if arriving at the airport on the metro.

BOAT

The city's new **Lisbon Cruise Port** (☑213 936 595; www.lct.pt; Av Infante D Henrique) debuted in 2017 at a cost of €77 million. The **Transtejo ferry line** (☑808 203 050; www.transtejo.pt) has several riverfront terminals. Services are less frequent on weekends and may increase in summer.

Terminal Fluvial Cais do Sodré (Map p84; ☑213 500 115; www.ttsl.pt; Rua da Cintura do Porto de Lisboa) offers services to Cacilhas (€1.30, 10 minutes, every 10 minutes, 5.35am to 1.40am Monday to Friday, from 5.40am Saturday and Sunday, Sala 3), Montijo (€2.80, 30 minutes, 6.30am to 11.15pm Monday to Friday, to 9pm Saturday, 10am to 9.30pm Sunday, Sala 1) and Seixal (€2.45, 30 minutes, 6.35am to 11.15pm Monday to Friday, 7am to 10pm Saturday, 8.30am to 9.30pm Sunday, Sala 2).

Terminal Fluvial Terreiro do Paço (☑213 500 115; www.ttsl.pt; Rua da Cintura do Porto de Lisboa) offers services to Barreiro (€1.25, 30 minutes, every 10 to 30 minutes, 5.45am

to 2am) for rail connections to the Algarve, the Alentejo and Setúbal.

Estação Fluvial de Belém (Map p96; ☑808 263 050; www.ttsl.pt; Av Brasília) offers services to Trafaria and Porto Brandão (€1.20, every 30 to 60 minutes, 7am to 9.40pm), about 3.5km and 5km, respectively, from Costa da Caparica town.

BUS

Information and tickets for international departures are scarce at weekends, so try to avoid that last-minute Sunday dash out of Portugal.

Sete Rios

Lisbon's main long-distance bus terminal is **Terminal Rodoviário de Sete Rios** (Praça General Humberto Delgado, Rua das Laranjeiras), adjacent to both Jardim Zoológico metro station and Sete Rios train station. The big carriers, **Rede Expressos** (☑707 223 344; www.rede-expressos.pt; ⊙info booth 9am-1pm & 2-6pm Mon-Sat, 10am-2pm & 3-7pm Sun) and **Eva** (☑707 223 344; www.eva-bus.com), run frequent services from here to almost every major town in Portugal. You can buy your ticket up to one month in advance (use Window 1 for international tickets) sometimes with a discount of as much as 30%.

Intercentro/Internorte (Map p108; ☑707 200 512; www.intercentro.pt; Av Dom João II, Gare do Oriente; ⊙9am-6pm) runs coaches to destinations all over Europe, beginning at Sete Rios and stopping at Gare do Oriente 15 minutes later. In addition to Madrid (from €40, 9¼ hours, 9pm), there are direct connections to several points in Galicia, including Vigo (€34, 9¼ hours, 7.30am) Santiago de Compostela (€50, 10¼ hours, 7.30am) and Coruña (€58, 12 hours, 7.30am), as well as to Sevilla (€45, 7¾ hours, 1.30pm and 9.45pm), Málaga (€71, 10¾ hours, 9.45pm) and Paris (€95, 27 hours, 9am Monday to Friday plus 12.45pm Saturday).

Domestic services:

TO	COST (€))	TIME (HR)	FREQUENCY
Coimbra	13.80	2½	49 daily
Évora	11.90	1¾	27 daily
Faro	18.50	4	19 daily
Porto	19	4¼	40 daily

Gare do Oriente

The large terminal **Gare do Oriente** (Oriente Station; Map p108; Av Dom João II) concentrates on services to the north and on to Spain and beyond. On the 1st floor are bus-company booths (mostly open from 9am to 5.30pm Monday to Saturday, and to 7pm Friday, closed for lunch; smaller operators only open just before arrival or departure).

BIKING THE TEJO

With its steep, winding hills and narrow, traffic-filled lanes, Lisbon may not seem like the ideal place to hop on a bicycle, though the city added a biking/jogging path in 2010, to the delight of pedallers. Coursing along the Rio Tejo for nearly 7km, the path connects Cais do Sodré with Belém, and has artful touches, including the poetry of Pessoa printed along parts of it. It passes beside a rapidly changing landscape, taking in ageing warehouses that are being converted into open-air cafes, restaurants and nightspots, as well as the Museu de Arte, Arquitetura e Tecnologia (MAAT). An additional path connecting Santa Apolónia with Parque das Nações, a 8km jaunt, was opened in 2013. The newest part of the path extends along the waterfront for another 5km from Belém to the Fortress of Caxias.

A handy place to rent bikes is **Bike Iberia** (Map p72; ☑ 969 630 369; www.bikeiberia. com; Largo Corpo Santo 5; bike hire per hour/day from €5/15, e-bike €20/35; ☺ 9.30am-5.30pm), a short stroll from Cais do Sodré. True enthusiasts will also want to pick up their indispensable and extremely well done *Lisbon Bike Map* (€5; €3 for customers), which not only details all the bike trails in the Lisbon region, but notes terrain, inclines, points of interest and traffic etiquette.

Those looking for a longer ride can bike out to Belém, catch the ferry to Trafaria, and then continue on another bike path (separate from traffic) that runs for about 6km down to the pretty beach of Costa da Caparica. Nature lovers should explore Parque Florestal de Monsanto, situated around 8.5km northwest of Cais do Sodré – self-guided GPS tour options are available from Bike Iberia.

The biggest companies operating from here are **Renex/Rede Expressos/Citiexpress** (Map p108; ☑ 218 956 836; www.rede-expressos. pt; ☺ 7am-1pm), which heads to the Algarve, Coimbra, Porto, Minho, and Guimarães; and Spanish operator **Avanza** (Map p108; ☑ 218 940 250; www.avanzabus.com; ☺ 8.30am-1pm & 2-8.15pm Mon-Fri, 8.30am-11am & 5-8.15pm Sat & Sun), which heads to Madrid (€24 to €45, 8½ hours, 9.15am and 8.15pm daily, plus 12.15pm Monday to Friday).

Additional international companies include Flixbus (www.flixbus.com) and Iberocoach (www.iberocoach.com).

Domestic services:

TO	COST (€))	TIME (HR)	FREQUENCY
Braga	20	4½	10 daily
Coimbra	13.80	2½	4 daily
Guimarães	19.50	5½	3 daily
Lagos	19	4½	8 daily
Porto	19	3½	10 daily

Terminal Campo Grande

Regional operators in the north – including **Mafrense** (☑ 707 201 371; www.mafrense.pt) for Ericeira and Mafra – operate from **Terminal Campo Grande** (Rodoviária de Lisboa; ☑ 217 928 180; www.rodoviariadelisboa.pt; Campo Grande 382) outside Campo Grande metro station.

CAR & MOTORCYCLE

Motorbikes, ranging from 50cc to 1000cc, are available for hire from **LX Rent** (☑ 917 249 806; www.lxrentascooter.pt; Campo das Cebolas 21; ☺ 9.30am-6.30pm). Prices start at €32 for 24 hours. **Free Spirit Campers** (☑ 915 085 269; www.freespiritcampers.com; per day €80-120) rents fully equipped converted Fiat Ducato camper vans.

Easy Tours (☑ 915 100 242; www.lisboa. easytours.pt; Alameda dos Oceanos 37; ☺ 9am-7pm Mon-Sat) rents full-size electric cars from €50 per day including insurance. Charging is free, as is parking for electric vehicles within Lisbon city limits.

Otherwise, the big-name car-hire companies are all on hand at Lisbon's airport and around town – **Europcar** (☑ 218 875 472; www.europcar.com; Av Infante D Henrique, Santa Apolónia; ☺ 9am-1pm & 2.30-6.30pm) has a handy office at Santa Apolónia railway station – though you can often save by using local agencies; most offer pick-up and delivery services to the Palácio Foz tourist office on Praça dos Restauradores. Tourist offices have loads of car-rental flyers so you can compare prices – staff will even call and book a vehicle for you. Rates vary wildly, from as low as €8 per day in low season to over €60 in high season.

➡ **Autojardim** (☑ 218 463 187; www.autojardimrentacar.pt; Rua Severiano Falcão 2; ☺ 8am-8pm)

➡ **Avis** (☑ 218 435 550; www.avis.com.pt; Aeroporto de Lisboa; ☺ 6am-1am)

ⓘ LISBOA CARD

If you're planning on doing a lot of sightseeing, the Lisboa Card represents excellent value. It offers unlimited use of public transport (including trains to Sintra and Cascais), entry to all key museums and attractions, and discounts of up to 50% on tours, cruises and other admission charges. It's available at Ask Me Lisboa tourist offices (p119), including the one at the airport (p123). The 24-/48-/72-hour adult versions cost €20/34/42. You validate the card when you want to start using it.

➔ **Europcar** (☑ 218 401 176; www.europcar.pt; Aeroporto de Lisboa; ☺ 24hr)

➔ **Hertz** (☑ 219 426 300; www.hertz.pt; Aeroporto de Lisboa; ☺ 6am-1pm)

TRAIN

Lisbon is linked by train to other major cities. Check the website of **Comboios de Portugal** (☑ 707 210 220; www.cp.pt) for schedules – cheaper promo fares are often available online.

Lisbon has several major train stations. Express services from Gare do Oriente:

TO	COST (€))	TIME (HR)	FREQUENCY
Coimbra	23.50-33.70	2	10-20 daily
Évora	12.40-16.50	1½	3-4 daily
Faro	21.90-30.70	3	3-6 daily
Porto	25-43.60	3	7-20 daily

Do not forget to validate your ticket/transport card on both regional and local Comboios de Portugal (CT) trains (at some train stations, it's possible to hop on the train without doing so) – the fine is 100 times the price of your journey if caught (and checks are frequent!).

ⓘ Getting Around

TO/FROM THE AIRPORT
Metro

The Aeroporto metro station allows convenient access to downtown. Change at Alameda (green line) to reach Rossio and Baixa.

Bus

The **AeroBus** (www.aerobus.pt; one-way adult/child €3.60/2) departs from outside the Arrivals Hall. Line 1 (from 7.30am to 11pm) goes via Martim Moniz, Praça do Comércio, **Cais do Sodré** (Map p72), Rossio, Restauradores, Av da Liberdade, Marquês de Pombal and Saldanha. Line 2 (from 7.40am to 10.45pm) goes via Saldanha, Marquês de Pombal and Sete Rios (for bus terminal access). You'll save 10% by purchasing your tickets online in advance.

Taxi

Expect to pay about €16 for the 15-minute taxi ride into central Lisbon, plus €1.60 if your luggage needs to be placed in the boot. Avoid long queues by flagging down a taxi outside the Departures Hall. Make sure the driver switches on the taxi meter, that you hold them to the route (follow along with Google maps, if possible) and that you pay the listed fare – taxis in Lisbon are notorious for fleecing tourists, especially from the airport.

You'll find cheaper fares with Uber and other ride-share services, which pick up passengers outside the Departures entrance at Terminal 1 (not Arrivals) – and eliminate the potential rip-off factor.

CAR & MOTORCYCLE

Lisbon can be quite stressful to drive around, thanks to heavy traffic, maverick drivers and narrow one-way streets and tram lines. There are two ring roads useful for staying out of the centre: the inner Cintura Regional Interna de Lisboa (CRIL) and the outer Cintura Regional Externa de Lisboa (CREL).

Once in the centre, you'll find parking is the main issue. Spaces are scarce (600,000 car drivers fight for 200,000 spaces daily), parking regulations are complex, pay-and-display machines are often broken and car-park rates can be expensive (daily charges range from €15 to €45). Street parking is enforced Monday to Friday (8am to 8pm) and on Saturday (8am to 6pm) in three types of zones: red (per hour €1.60) has a two-hour maximum, while yellow (per hour $1.30) and green (per hour $0.80) have four-hour maximums. On Sunday, parking is usually free. EMEL (www.emel.pt) manages Lisbon's parking and has extensive, Portuguese-only information on its website and an app that can be used to pay and monitor parking meters (for residents only).

There are a few good places for free parking. Campo de Santa Clara, near Alfama, is good on every day except Saturday and Tuesday, when the Feira da Ladra takes over the lot. You can also find free parking on Av 24 de Julho west of Cais do Sodré. Theft is a risk, so always lock up and don't leave any valuables inside.

The cheapest, closest paid car parks are found south of the centre near the coast around Santa Apolónia and Doca de Santo Amaro.

PUBLIC TRANSPORT
Bus, Tram & Funicular

Carris (☎ 213 500 115; www.carris.pt) runs all transport in Lisbon proper except the metro. Its buses run from about 5am or 6am to about 10pm or 11pm; there are some night-bus services. Pick up a transport map, *Rede de Transportes de Lisboa,* from tourist offices. The Carris website has timetables and route details.

Buses are especially useful for neighbourhoods not serviced by the metro or trams, such as Príncipe Real and Marvila.

Take **bus 711** (Map p72; Praça Dom Pedro IV) from Rossio to get to Miradouro Panorâmico de Monsanto (walk the final 650m).

Metro

The **metro** (☎ 213 500 115; www.metrolisboa.pt; single/day ticket €1.50/6.40; ⊙ 6.30am-1am) is useful for short hops, and to reach the Gare do Oriente and nearby Parque das Nações.

Buy tickets from metro ticket machines, which have English-language menus. The Lisboa Card is also valid.

Entrances are marked by a big red 'M'. Useful signs include *correspondência* (transfer between lines) and *saída* (exit to the street). There is some impressive contemporary art on the metro, including Ângelo de Sousa at Baixa-Chiado and Friedensreich Hundertwasser at Oriente.

Watch out for pickpockets in rush-hour crowds.

TAXI

Taxis in Lisbon are reasonably priced and plentiful. If you can't hail one, try the ranks at Rossio and Praça dos Restauradores, near stations and ferry terminals, and at top-end hotels, or call **Rádio Táxis** (☎ 218 119 000; www.taxislisboa.pt) or **Cooptáxis** (☎ 217 932 756; www.auto-coope.pai.pt).

The fare on the meter should read €3.25 for the daytime flagfall. You will be charged extra for luggage, and an additional 20% for journeys between 9pm and 6am, plus more if they cross municipalities or if you call. Lisbon taxis have a well-deserved dubious reputation of fleecing foreigners (the airport route is the main culprit – use a ride-share service or book a prepaid taxi with **Ask Me Lisboa** (☎ 218 450 660; www.askmelisboa.com; Aeroporto de Lisboa, Arrivals Hall; ⊙ 7am-midnight) to avoid problems). Follow along the route watching Google maps or another app, and if you think you may have been cheated, get a receipt from the driver, note the registration number and contact the **tourist police** (Esquadra de Turismo; ☎ 213 400 090, 213 421 623; www.psp.pt; Praça dos Restauradores, Palácio Foz; ⊙ 24hr).

Taxi apps and ride-share services such as Uber (www.uber.com), Cabify (www.cabify.

ℹ TICKETS & TRANSPORT CARDS

You'll pay more for transport if you buy your ticket on board rather than purchasing a prepaid card. On-board one-way prices are €2 for buses and €3 for trams. One-way tickets for funicular rides are not available; these are €3.80 return.

The following are the most commonly used passes by visitors; there are many more, depending on your specific needs/time frames.

Viva Viagem/7 Colinas cards These are €0.50 from metro-station kiosks (add credit in €5 denominations). Cards may then be loaded with day passes and/or Zapping fares for use on a variety of transport companies.

Zapping Allows for pay-as-you-go fares of €1.33 with metro and €1.35 with Carris (buses and trams, with a hour-long re-entry period); add credit of denominations between €5 and €40. Zapping also works with Comboios de Portugal (€1.90), as well as **Transportes Sul do Tejo** (☎ 211 126 200; www.tsuldotejo.pt; Praça de Espanha), Fertagus and Transtejo/Soflusa, among others, with various discounted fares and included transfer periods.

Day passes Costing €6.40 and allowing unlimited travel over a 24-hour period on the entire bus, tram and metro network (€10.55 if you want to include Comboios de Portugal as well). If you're going to take more than five trips on the bus or metro on any given day, this is the best and easiest choice.

Lisboa Card Good for most tourist sights as well as bus, tram, funicular and metro travel.

Bilhete Train & Bus A hop-on, hop-off, one-day travel card valid on Comboios de Portugal trains and Scotturb suburban buses between Lisbon, Sintra, Cascais and Azambuja for €15.50.

com), 99Taxis (www.99taxis.com), Taxify (www.taxify.eu) and MyTaxi (https://pt.mytaxi.com) are available.

AROUND LISBON

Sintra

With its rippling mountains, dewy forests thick with ferns and lichen, exotic gardens and glittering palaces, Sintra is like a page torn from a fairy tale. Its Unesco World Heritage–listed centre, Sintra-Vila, is dotted with pastel-hued manors folded into luxuriant hills that roll down to the blue Atlantic.

Celts worshipped their moon god here, the Moors built a precipitous castle, and 18th-century Portuguese royals swanned around its dreamy gardens. Even Lord Byron waxed lyrical about Sintra's charms: 'Lo! Cintra's glorious Eden intervenes, in variegated maze of mount and glen', which inspired his epic poem *Childe Harold's Pilgrimage*.

It's the must-do side trip from Lisbon, which many do in a day, but this can feel rushed and, if time's not an issue, there's more than enough allure to seize you here for a few days.

◎ Sights

★ **Palácio Nacional de Sintra**   PALACE
(Map p129; www.parquesdesintra.pt; Largo Rainha Dona Amélia; adult/child €10/8.50; ⊙9.30am-7pm) The star of Sintra-Vila is this palace, with its iconic twin conical chimneys and lavish, whimsical interior, which is a mix of Moorish and Manueline styles, with arabesque courtyards, barley-twist columns and 15th- and 16th-century geometric *azulejos* that are among Portugal's oldest.

Of Moorish origins, the palace was first expanded by Dom Dinis (1261–1325), enlarged by João I in the 15th century (when the kitchens were built), then given a Manueline twist by Manuel I in the following century.

Highlights include the octagonal **Sala dos Cisnes** (Swan Room), adorned with frescoes of 27 gold-collared swans, and the **Sala das Pegas** (Magpie Room), with its ceiling emblazoned with magpies. Lore has it that the queen caught João I kissing one of her ladies-in-waiting. The cheeky king claimed the kisses were innocent and all *'por bem'* ('for the good'), then commissioned one magpie for every lady-in-waiting.

Other standouts are the wooden Sala dos Brasões, bearing the shields of 72 leading 16th-century families, the shipshape **Galleon Room** and the Palatine **chapel** featuring an Islamic mosaic floor. Finally, you reach the restored **kitchen** of twin-chimney fame, where you can almost hear the crackle of a hog roasting on a spit for the king.

★ **Castelo dos Mouros**   CASTLE
(Map p126; www.parquesdesintra.pt; adult/child €8/6.50; ⊙9.30am-8pm) Soaring 412m above sea level, this mist-enshrouded ruined castle looms high above the surrounding forest. When the clouds peel away, the vistas over Sintra's palace-dotted hill and dale, across to the glittering Atlantic are – like the climb – breathtaking. The 10th-century Moorish castle's dizzying ramparts stretch across the mountain ridges and past moss-clad boulders the size of small buses.

Tickets and info are available at the entrance (open 10am to 6pm).

The best walking route here from Sintra-Vila is not along the main road but the quicker, partly off-road route via Rua Marechal Saldanha. The steep **trail** (Map p129) is around 2km, but quiet and rewarding.

★ **Palácio Nacional da Pena**   PALACE
(Map p126; www.parquesdesintra.pt; combined ticket with Parque da Pena adult/child €14/12.50; ⊙9.45am-7pm) Rising from a thickly wooded peak and often enshrouded in swirling mist, Palácio Nacional da Pena is a wacky confection of onion domes, Moorish keyhole gates, writhing stone snakes and crenellated towers in pinks and lemons. It is considered the greatest expression of 19th-century romanticism in Portugal.

Ferdinand of Saxe Coburg-Gotha, the artist-husband of Queen Maria II, and later Dom Ferdinand II, commissioned Prussian architect Ludwig von Eschwege in 1840 to build the Mouresque-Manueline epic (and as a final flourish added an armoured statue representing a medieval knight overlooking the palace from a nearby peak). Inspired by Stolzenfels and Rheinstein castles and Potsdam's Babelsberg Palace, a flourish of imagination and colour commenced.

The eclectic, extravagant interior is equally unusual, brimming with precious Meissen porcelain, Portuguese-style furniture, trompe l'œil murals and Dom Carlos' unfinished nudes of buxom nymphs.

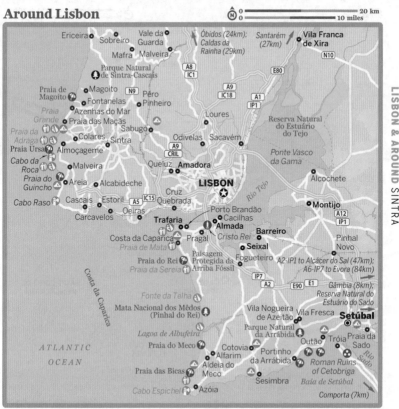

There are daily guided tours at 2.30pm. Buses depart from the entrance to the palace every 15 minutes (€3); otherwise it's a 10- to 15-minute walk uphill.

Parque da Pena   GARDENS
(Map p126; ☎219 237 300; www.parquesde sintra.pt; adult/child €7.50/6.50, combined ticket with Palácio Nacional da Pena €14/12.50; ⊘9.30am-8pm) Nearly topped by King Ferdinand II's whimsical Palácio Nacional da Pena (only Cruz Alta, at 529m, is higher), these romantic gardens are filled with tropical plants, huge redwoods and fern trees, camellias, rhododendrons and lakes (note the castle-shaped duck houses for web-footed royalty!).

While the crowds descend on the palace, another less-visited but fascinating site within the park is the *Snow White & the Seven Dwarfs*–evoking **Chalet da Condessa d'Edla** (adult/child €9.50/8.50), an alpine-inspired summer getaway cottage commissioned by King Ferdinand II and his future second wife, Elise Hensler (the Countess of Edla).

Buses to the park entrance leave from Sintra train station and near Palácio Nacional de Sintra, among other spots around town. A taxi costs around €10 oneway. The steep, zigzagging walk through pine and eucalyptus woods from Sintra-Vila is around 3km to 4km.

Palácio & Parque de Monserrate   PALACE
(www.parquesdesintra.pt; adult/child €8/6.50; ⊘9.30am-7pm) At the centre of a lush, 30-hectare park, a manicured lawn sweeps up to this whimsical, Moorish-Gothic-Indian *palácio*, the 19th-century romantic folly of English millionaire Sir Francis Cook. The wild and rambling gardens were created in the 18th century by wealthy English merchant Gerard de Visme, then enlarged by landscape painter William Stockdale (with help from London's Kew Gardens).

Sintra

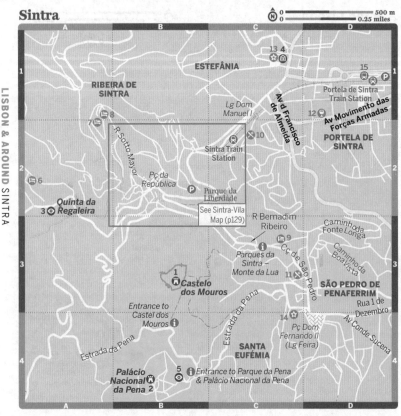

Sintra

◉ Top Sights
1 Castelo dos Mouros	B3
2 Palácio Nacional da Pena	B4
3 Quinta da Regaleira	A2

◉ Sights
4 Museu das Artes de Sintra	C1
5 Parque da Pena	B4

⌂ Sleeping
6 Almaa	A2
7 Casa do Valle	A2
8 Casa Miradouro	A1
9 Hotel Sintra Jardim	C3

⊗ Eating
10 Dom Pipas	C2

11 Nau Palatina	C3

⊖ Drinking & Nightlife
12 Saloon Cintra	D1

⊛ Entertainment
13 Centro Cultural Olga Cadaval	C1
14 Taverna dos Trovadores	C4

ℹ Transport
Bus 440 to Azenhas do Mar	(see 15)
Bus 441 to Colares/Praia das Macãs/Praia Grande & Azenhas do Mar	(see 15)
15 Bus Station (Portela de Sintra Interface)	D1

Its wooded hillsides bristle with exotic foliage, from Chinese weeping cypress to dragon trees and Himalayan rhododendrons. Seek out the Mexican garden nurturing palms, yuccas and agaves, and the bamboo-fringed Japanese garden abloom with camellias.

The park is 3.5km west of Sintra-Vila.

Convento dos Capuchos MONASTERY
(Capuchin Monastery; ☑219 237 300; www.par-quesdesintra.pt; adult/child €7/5.50; ☺9.30am-8pm) Hidden in the woods is this bewitchingly hobbit-hole-like convent, which was originally built in 1560 to house friars, who lived in incredibly cramped conditions, in tiny cells with low, narrow doors. Byron mocked the monastery in his poem *Childe Harold's Pilgrimage,* referring to recluse Honorius, who spent a staggering 36 years here (before dying at age 95 in 1596).

It's often nicknamed the Cork Convent, as its minuscule cells are lined with cork. Visiting here is an *Alice in Wonderland* experience, as you squeeze through to explore the warren of cells, chapels, kitchen and cavern. The monks lived a simple, touchingly well-ordered life in this idyllic yet spartan place, hiding up until 1834 when it was abandoned after all religious orders were abolished. Worthwhile audio guides are available for €3.

You can walk here – the monastery is 7.3km from Sintra-Vila (5.1km from the turn-off to Parque da Pena) along a remote, wooded road. There is no bus connection to the convent. Taxis charge around €35 return; arrange ahead for a pick-up.

Museu das Artes de Sintra MUSEUM
(MU.SA; Map p126; www.cm-sintra.pt/musa-museu-das-artes-de-sintra; Avenida Heliodoro Salgado; adult/child €1/free; ☺10am-8pm Tue-Fri, from 2pm Sat & Sun) This museum features a small and manageable collection of contemporary and modern art, around 80% of which is dedicated to local works. The permanent collection features some of Portugal's best-known artists, most notably sculptor Dorita de Castel-Branco and painters Columbano Bordalo Pinheiro and António Carneiro.

🏃 Activities

Sintra is a terrific place to get out and stride, with waymarked hiking trails (look for red and yellow stripes) that corkscrew up into densely wooded hills strewn with giant boulders. Justifiably popular is the gentle 50-minute trek from Sintra-Vila to Castelo dos Mouros. You can continue to Palácio Nacional da Pena (another 15 minutes). From here you can ascend Serra de Sintra's highest point, the 529m Cruz Alta (High Cross), named after its 16th-century cross, with amazing views all over Sintra. It's possible to continue on foot to São Pedro de Penaferrim and loop back to Sintra-Vila. Detailed hiking (and mountain biking) routes can be downloaded from Active Sintra (www.activesintra.com).

Horse riding is available in the Parque da Pena, from 30-minute teasers (€15) to six-hour excursions (€100).

Go2Sintra Tours CYCLING
(Map p129; ☑917 855 428; www.go2cintra.com; Avenida Dr Miguel Bombarda 37; ☺10am-7pm) Offers highly recommended electric-bike tours (from €35) as well as eBike rental (take our word for it – you'll want the motorised option in Sintra!). A full day's rental with support starts at €30. Its office is across from the Sintra train station inside the SintraCan shop.

Also offers wi-fi–equipped Twizy e-vehicles that can go all the way to the coast (€25 to €75).

✨🎷 Festivals & Events

Festival de Sintra CULTURAL
(www.festivaldesintra.pt; ☺May or Jun; 📋) Usually in May or June, the three-week-long Festival de Sintra features classical recitals, ballet and modern dance, world music and multimedia events, plus concerts for kids.

🛏 Sleeping

It's worth staying overnight, as Sintra has some magical guesthouses, from quaint villas to lavish manors. Book (way) ahead in summer. Check out www.sintrainn.net/en for an extensive list of available accommodation.

★ Moon Hill Hostel HOSTEL €
(Map p129; ☑219 243 755; www.moonhillhostel.com; Rua Guilherme Gomes Fernandes 17; dm €19-22, d with/without bathroom €75/55; ✳@⬤) ◗ This design-forward, minimalist newcomer easily outshines the competition. Book a bed in a four-bed mixed dorm (with lockers), or a boutique-hotel-level private room, with colourful reclaimed-wood headboards and wall-covering photos of enchanting Sintra forest scenes (go for 10 or 14 for Palácio Nacional da Pena views; 12 or 13 for Moorish castle views). Either way, you're sleeping in high style.

Nice Way Sintra HOSTEL €
(Map p129; ☑219 249 800; www.nicewaysintra.com; Rua Sotto Mayor 22; dm €18-22, d with/without bathroom €70/60; 🅿@⬤) In a rambling but recently refreshed mansion (and annex) north of Sintra-Vila's main square, you'll

find stylishly outfitted rooms with heaters, great countryside views and a lovely garden with a full bar and multiple hang spaces. There's an intriguing, old-fashioned shared kitchen and a friendly vibe, making it a good place to meet other travellers. Free walking tours are available.

Almaa
HOSTEL €

(Map p126; ☑ 919 850 805; www.almaasintrahostel.com; Caminho dos Frades 1; dm €20, d with/without bathroom €64/56; @ 🛜) 🏄 Sustainably minded Almaa is an idyllic spot to recharge, with a quirky design scheme (featuring recycled furniture) and an attractive setting. The surrounding 3.5 hectares of lush grounds have walking paths and an old spring-fed reservoir for swimming. It's not without imperfections (a little mould-proof paint would work wonders) but as the name in Portuguese suggests, it has soul.

More recent add-ons include an activity room for yoga, meditation, qigong and other spiritual practices. It's a 10-minute walk from the village centre.

★ Sintra 1012
B&B €€

(Map p129; ☑ 918 632 997; www.sintra1012.com; Rua Gil Vicente 10 & 12; dm €25, d €65-120, villas €120-150; ❄ @ 🛜) You'll probably need to go to war to book one of the eight spacious and smart rooms in this highly recommended guesthouse run by a young Portuguese-American couple. Behind original medieval walls, it's a modern, minimalist retreat which, in Roman times, was Sintra's first theatre. Today it's all comfort and class, right down to the basement studio, an astonishing deal (€65).

A new free-standing villa was added in 2017 with a mixed four-bed dormitory, a castle-view rooftop and three private rooms.

Villa Mira Longa
B&B €€

(Map p129; ☑ 219 244 502; www.villamiralonga.com; Estrada da Pena 4; d €115-135; P 🛜) A fabulous and gay-friendly choice, this restored 1898 baby-blue villa is a short walk from Sintra-Vila's centre and offers comfortable rooms (the best with panoramic views) and beautiful common areas (including an antique-filled dining room and an exquisitely manicured garden). The kind Belgian-Brazilian hosts have a wealth of knowledge about Sintra and spread a first-rate breakfast.

Casa Miradouro
GUESTHOUSE €€

(Map p126; ☑ 914 232 203; www.casa-miradouro.com; Rua Sotto Mayor 55; d without breakfast €90-120; 🛜) Lovely Belgian Charlotte is your consummate host at this imposing Battenberg cake of a house, built in 1893, with eight elegant, stuccoed rooms with bathrobes, Egyptian-cotton sheets and panoramic views. The best have small balconies with storybook-castle views. Breakfast is €10.

Casa do Valle
B&B €€

(Map p126; ☑ 219 244 699; www.casadovalle.com; Rua da Paderna 5; d €98-133; P @ 🛜 ❄) Just downhill from the historical centre of Sintra-Vila, Casa do Valle has spacious rooms set around a garden with an inviting pool and communal kitchen. Some rooms lack an en suite. It has fine views of the lush hillsides rising above the valley, friendly multilingual service courtesy of the Finnish owner, and two monstrous Great Danes.

Hotel Sintra Jardim
GUESTHOUSE €€

(Map p126; ☑ 219 230 738; www.hotelsintrajardim.pt; Tv Avelares 12; s/d from €80/90; P @ 🛜 ❄) This stately 1880s manor with a swirly staircase overlooks rambling gardens and offers partial castle views from some of its 16 rooms (they are bright, high-ceilinged affairs but slightly underwhelming – the real coups here are the gardens and spectacular pool). Wake up to birdsong and a hearty breakfast.

✖ Eating

Café Saudade
CAFE €

(Map p129; www.facebook.com/CafeSaudade; Avenida Dr Miguel Bombardo 6; mains €5.50-8; ⊙ 8.30am-7pm; 🛜) This former bakery, where Sintra's famous *queijadas* (crisp pastry shells filled with a marzipan-like mix of fresh cheese, sugar, flour and cinnamon) were made, has cherub-covered ceilings and a rambling interior. It's a fine spot for pastries (the massive scones are a travel highlight in the making), lighter fare or an evening glass of wine.

Casa Piriquita
PASTRIES €

(Map p129; www.piriquita.pt; Rua das Padarias 1-5; travesseiros €1.40; ⊙ 9am-8pm Thu-Tue) This busy fifth-generation cafe is a popular destination for inexpensive bites as well as Sintra's famous *queijadas* and *travesseiros* (puff pastries filled with almond-and-egg-yolk cream). If you're here on a Wednesday, Piriquita II just up the street at Rua das Padarias 18 is open.

Sintra-Vila

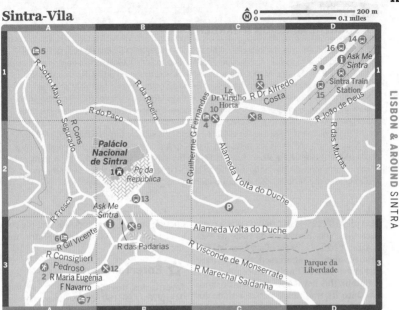

Sintra-Vila

Nau Palatina PORTUGUESE €€

(Map p126; ☎219 240 962; www.facebook.com/barnaupalatina; Calçada São Pedro 18, São Pedro de Penaferrim; tapas €1.50-11.90; ⏰6pm-midnight Tue-Sat; ☎) Sintra's friendliest and most welcoming restaurant is a travel-highlight star in the making. Congenial owner Zé's creative tapas are as slightly off-centre as his location, a worthwhile 1km walk from Sintra centre in São Pedro de Penaferrim. Spice Route undertones are weaved throughout the small but tasty menu of tidbits, strongly forged from local and regional ingredients.

INcomum PORTUGUESE €€

(Map p129; ☎219 243 719; www.incomumbyluissantos.pt; Rua Dr Alfredo Costa 22; mains €12.50-15.50, tasting menu €37.50; ⏰noon-midnight Mon-Fri & Sun, from 4.30pm Sat; ☎) Chef Luis Santos shakes up Sintra's culinary scene with his modern upgrades to Portuguese cuisine, served amid the muted greys and greens of his synchronic dining room. INcomum quickly establishes itself as the anti-traditional choice among serious foodies, first by dangling an unbeatable €11 three-course-lunch carrot, then by letting the food seal the deal.

A SURREAL MANSION & GARDENS

Exploring the Quinta da Regaleira (Map p126; www.regaleira.pt; Rua Barbosa du Bocage; adult/child €6/4, tours €12/8; ⊙ 9.30am-7pm Apr-Sep, to 5pm Oct-Mar) is like delving into another world. This neo-Manueline extravaganza was dreamed up by Italian opera-set designer Luigi Manini under the orders of Brazilian coffee tycoon António Carvalho Monteiro, aka 'Monteiro dos Milhões' ('Moneybags Monteiro'). Enter the villa to begin the surreal journey, with ferociously carved fireplaces, frescoes and Venetian-glass mosaics. Keep an eye out for mythological and Knights Templar symbols.

The playful gardens are fun to explore – footpaths wriggle through the dense foliage to follies, fountains, grottoes, lakes and underground caverns. All routes seem to eventually end at the revolving stone door leading to the initiation well, Poço Iniciático, plunging some 27m. You walk down the nine-tiered spiral (three by three – three being the magic number) to mysterious hollowed-out underground galleries, lit by fairy lights.

Tascantiga   PORTUGUESE €€

(Map p129; ☑ 219 243 242; www.facebook.com/tascantigasintra; Escadinhas da Fonte da Pipa 2; tapas €2.20-12; ⊙noon-10pm Mon-Sat; ☜) Nestled along a staircased thoroughfare just above Sintra's lovely 14th-century Pipa Fountain, this newcomer puts a little more love into its traditional *petiscos* than the next guy, serving well-presented and modern takes on traditional small plates. The grilled portobello mushroom smothered in arugula, smoked ham and São Jorge cheese stands out, but it's hard to go wrong whatever you choose.

The colourful outdoor tables are also a wonderful spot for a bottle of wine – they're located just far enough from the tourist frenzy to feel a bit secret.

Dom Pipas   PORTUGUESE €€

(Map p126; www.restaurantedompipas.pt; Rua João de Deus 62; mains €9.50-16.75; ⊙noon-3pm & 7-10pm Tue-Sun; ☜) A consistently buzzing local favourite, Dom Pipas serves excellent Portuguese dishes amid *azulejos* and rustic country decor. It's behind Sintra's train station (left out of the station, first left, then left again to the end) – a fair way outside the hubbub.

🍷 Drinking & Nightlife

Saloon Cintra   BAR

(Map p126; www.facebook.com/barsaloon.cintra; Avenida Movimento das Forças Armadas 5, Portela de Sintra; ⊙8pm-2am Mon-Fri, from 3pm Sat & Sun; ☜) Sintra's best bar isn't in Sintra-Vila, but that shouldn't stop seasoned drinkers from checking it out. A potpourri of antiques and Portuguese bric-a-brac hovering over numerous mismatched vintage sofas makes for an atmospheric spot to take in the Belgian-heavy beer list (including Mc Chouffe on tap), good cocktails and the cool local crowd. It's 700m east of Sintra train station.

☆ Entertainment

Taverna dos Trovadores   LIVE MUSIC

(Map p126; ☑ 967 050 536; www.tavernadostrovadores.pt; Praça Dom Fernando II 18, São Pedro de Penaferrim; ⊙ noon-3.30pm & 7-10.30pm Mon-Sat, bar to 2am Fri & Sat) This atmospheric restaurant and bar features live music (folk and acoustic) on Friday and Saturday nights – an institution that's been around for more than two decades. Concerts run from 11pm to 2am. Nearby, its new Sabores de Sintra offers dinner and fado. It's in São Pedro de Penaferrim.

**Centro Cultural
Olga Cadaval**   PERFORMING ARTS

(Map p126; ☑ 219 107 110; www.ccolgacadaval.pt; Praça Francisco Sá Carneiro) Sintra's major cultural venue stages concerts, theatre and dance.

ℹ️ Information

There's an ATM at the train station and in the tourism office as well as others scattered about town.

Sintra offers free wi-fi access points around town.

Near the centre of Sintra-Vila, **Ask Me Sintra** (Map p129; ☑ 219 231 157; www.visitlisboa.com; Praça da República 23; ⊙ 9.30am-6pm) is a helpful multilingual office with expert insight into Sintra and the surrounding areas. There's also a small branch at **Sintra train station** (Map p129; ☑ 211 932 545; Av Miguel Bombarda; ⊙9am-7pm), often overrun by those arriving by rail.

Cintramédica (☏ 219 100 080; www.cintra-medica.pt; Tv da Portela, Edifício Cintramédica, Portela de Sintra; ⊙7am-9pm Mon-Fri, to 1pm Sat) A recommended private medical clinic. Consultations without insurance are €80.

Parques da Sintra – Monte da Lua (Map p126; ☏ 219 237 300; www.parquesdesintra.pt; Largo Sousa Brandão; ⊙ 9.30am-6pm Apr-Oct, 10am-5pm Nov-Mar), which manages the majority of top Sintra sites, has a friendly information and ticket centre (along with a smaller one next to the Sintra-Villa post office).

Police (Guarda Nacional Republicana; ☏ 213 252 620; www.gnr.pt; Rua João de Deus 6)

ℹ Getting There & Away

Scotturb (Map p129) runs buses 403 and 417, which leave regularly for Cascais (€4.25, one hour), the former via Cabo da Roca (€4.25). Bus 418 heads to Estoril (€4.25, 40 minutes). Most services leave from **Sintra train station** (Estacão Sintra; www.cp.pt) – which is *estação* on timetables – and travel via Portela de Sintra. Scotturb's useful **information office** (Map p129; ☏ 219 230 381; www.scotturb.com; Avenida Dr Miguel Bombarda 59; ⊙9am-8pm) is opposite the station.

Mafrense (☏ 261 816 152; www.mafrense.pt) has buses heading to Mafra (€3.50, 50 minutes) and Ericeira (€3.50, one hour) from the **Portela de Sintra Interface** (Map p126; Largo Vasco da Gama) on the north side of Portela de Sintra train station.

Comboios de Portugal (p122) runs trains (€2.25, 40 minutes) half-hourly between Sintra and Lisbon's Rossio station (hourly on weekends), and every 20 minutes to Lisbon's less-convenient Oriente station (half-hourly on weekends). If arriving by train, go to the last stop – Sintra – from where it's a pleasant 1km, sculpture-peppered walk into the village.

ℹ Getting Around

BUS

From the train station it's a 1km walk into Sintra-Vila, or you can grab the hop-on, hop-off **bus 435** (€5). This bus continues on to Quinta da Regaleira, and Palácio and Parque de Monserrate.

A handy **Scotturb** bus for accessing the Castelo dos Mouros is **bus 434** (€6.90), which runs frequently from the train station via Sintra-Vila to the castle (10 minutes), Palácio Nacional da Pena (15 minutes) and back. One ticket gives you hop-on, hop-off access (in one direction; no backtracking).

You can also purchase a daily €12 hop-on, hop-off Scotturb ticket that works across the entire network and is valid in any direction until midnight. Be prepared to wait – even in winter the bus lines outside major attractions can be long.

CAR

Sintra's local government took drastic steps in late 2018 to relieve the traffic congestion in the historic centre – the area is now restricted to residents, city buses, emergency and commercial vehicles and taxis. Parking is limited around town but 1000 new spaces were being planned at time of research, in addition to the reconfiguration of traffic flow and entry points. For parking near town, there's a free car park below Sintra-Vila; follow the signs by the *câmara municipal* (town hall) in Estefânia. Alternatively, park at Portela de Sintra Interface and take the bus. For detailed parking info in English, see www.cm-sintra.pt/car-parking-in-sintra.

TAXI & RIDE-SHARE

Taxis are available at the train station or opposite Sintra-Vila post office. They are metered – flagfall is €3.25 during the week and €3.90 on weekends. Count on about €8 one-way to Palácio Nacional da Pena from central Sintra-Vila; if you want the driver to wait, the meter runs at €15 per hour; expect to pay about €35 for a return visit to Convento dos Capuchos (Uber is a far better deal – between €8 and €12 one way from Palácio Nacional de Sintra, for example).

TRAM

From 19 June to 24 September, Sintra's restored electric tram, the **Elétrico de Sintra** (www.cm-sintra.pt; one-way €3), offers access to the coast, running from Rua Alves Roçadas near Portela de Sintra train station and arriving at Praia das Maçãs 45 minutes later. In summer, trains depart hourly from 10.10am to 6pm (from 9.20am on weekends). The last tram back leaves the beach at 7pm. In 2018, the train returned for winter hours as well.

LOCAL KNOWLEDGE

SWEET DREAMS

Sintra is famous for its luscious sweeties. **Fábrica das Verdadeiras Queijadas da Sapa** (Map p129; www.facebook.com/queijadasdasapa; Alameda Volta do Duche 12; pastries from €0.85; ⊙ 9am-6pm Tue-Fri, 9.30am-6.30pm Sat & Sun) has been fattening up royalty since 1756 with bite-sized *queijadas*. Since 1952, Casa Piriquita (p128) has been serving another kind of sweet dream: the *travesseiro* (pillow), a light puff pastry turned, rolled and folded seven times, then filled with delicious almond-and-egg-yolk cream and lightly dusted with sugar.

West of Sintra

Precipitous cliffs and crescent-shaped bays pummelled by the Atlantic lie just 12km west of Sintra. Previous host of the European Surfing Championships, Praia Grande lures surfers and bodyboarders to its big sandy beach with ripping breakers, and you can clamber over the cliffs to spot dinosaur fossils. Family-friendly Praia das Maçãs has a sweep of gold sand, backed by a lively little resort. Azenhas do Mar, 2km further, is a cliffhanger of a village, where a jumble of whitewashed, red-roofed houses tumble down the crags to a free saltwater pool (only accessible when the sea is calm).

En route to the beaches, quaint Colares makes a worthwhile pit stop with its panoramas, stuck-in-time village charm and wines dating to the 13th century. The vines grown today are the only ones in Europe to have survived the 19th-century phylloxera plague, saved by their deep roots and sandy soil. To taste or purchase some of the venerable wines, visit **Adega Regional de Colares** (☑ 219 291 210; www.arcolares.com; Alameda Coronel, Linhares de Lima 32; tastings €4-10.65, tours €15; ☉ 9am-1pm & 2-6pm Mon-Fri, 9am-1pm Sat), which also offers tours with the winemaker if arranged in advance.

Wild and wonderful **Cabo da Roca** (Rock Cape) is a sheer 150m cliff, facing the roaring sea, 18km west of Sintra. It's mainland Europe's westernmost point and a terrific sunset spot. A steady trickle of visitors come to see the **lighthouse** (open for up to 15 people Wednesdays at 2pm, 3pm and 4pm only, though a hostel and cafe are planned for the future after Parques da Sintra – Monte da Lua (p131) struck a new management deal in 2017 with the maritime authorities. Although you can buy an €11 'I've-been-there' certificate at the **Posto de Turismo** (☑ 219 280 081; www.sintraromantica.net; ☉ 9am-7.30pm May-Sep, to 6.30pm Oct-Apr), it still has an air of rugged, windswept remoteness, best seen on a 10km-loop hike (maps available at Turismo).

Just before reaching Cabo da Roca, there's a small sign indicating the turn-off to Praia Ursa. From here it's a 20-minute descent along a treacherous path (take care!) to a beautiful deserted beach (bring your own food and drinks). There may be a few nudists here in summer. From here you can continue walking along the coast another 5km to Praia Grande.

🛏 Sleeping

Quinta Beira-Mar B&B €

(☑ 918 899 441; www.quintabeiramar.com; Rua Da Vigia No 12, Praia Pequena; d €75, dm/s/d without bathroom €25/30/65; ☉ closed Jan & Feb; 🕾 ☒) Friendly half-English Suzanna oversees this six-room working farm complete with horses, ducks, dogs and cats. It feels like the countryside yet is steps from Praia Pequena, Praia Grande and Praia das Maçãs. Wooden-accented rooms are spacious while bathrooms are surprisingly modern. It's a cosy option for those who want a rural element to their sun-worshipping. Horse riding is available.

Suzanna also rents out surfboards and wetsuits.

Arribas Sintra Hotel HOTEL €€€

(☑ 219 289 050; www.arribashotel.com; Avenida Alfredo Coelho 28, Praia Grande; d €120-200, ste from €200; 🅿 ✳ @ 🕾 ☒) While this 59-room, scallop-shaped relic of a family hotel doesn't inspire confidence from the road, its sea views over Praia Grande and 100m-long, 5-million-litre ocean-water pool are quite a show. Its light, breezy rooms were stylishly updated in 2016 and feature fridges, TVs and balconies that are ideal for watching surfers ride the waves.

🍴 Eating

Many cafes and seafood restaurants are scattered along Praia Grande; Praia das Maçãs also has a few options. Cafes framing the sunset are prevalent in Azóia near Cabo da Roca.

★ Restaurant da Adraga SEAFOOD €€

(☑ 219 280 028; www.restaurantedaadraga.com; Rua da Praia da Adraga S/N, Praia da Adraga; seafood per kg €37-100; ☉ 12.30-10.30pm; 🕾) This legendary seafood restaurant sits on the edge of a small beach below Almoçageme. No fancy techniques or overdressed dining room here – just incredibly fresh fish and seafood cooked to perfection, served in a casual, yellow-tableclothed setting with framed sea views. Call ahead to reserve a table by the window. Parking can be tough in summer.

Restaurante Central PORTUGUESE €€

(☑ 219 290 071; Rua da Liberdade 100, Colares; mains €7.75-14.75; ☉ 12.30-3.30pm & 7.15-10pm, closed Wed dinner & Thu; 🕾) Drawing a healthy mix of village old-timers and hip travellers, the authentic Portuguese cuisine of Mrs

Dalila takes centre stage at this simple but charming local haunt. You'll find staples such as whole *bacalhau* and *bitoque* (steak and egg with fries) along with a daily changing array of excellent dishes.

Azenhas do Mar
SEAFOOD €€€

(☏ 219 280 739; www.azenhasdomar.com; Azenhas do Mar; mains €18-35, seafood per kg €47-175; ⏱12.30-10pm; 🐟) Shake the table and your plate might just fall into the sea at this top seafooder perched above the saltwater pool in Azenhas do Mar. The sea views are stunning, especially from the deck. Skip the overpriced and underwhelming tuna tartare and spend that €22 on the delicious grilled octopus. An off-peak Uber from Sintra costs between €8 and €12.

❶ Getting There & Away

Bus 441 (Map p126; www.scotturb.com; Portela de Sintra Interface) from Sintra's Portela Interface runs frequently via Colares to Praia das Maçãs (€4.25, 25 minutes) and on to Azenhas do Mar (€4.25, 30 minutes), sometimes stopping at Praia Grande (€4.25, 25 minutes) six times daily (more in summer). **Bus 440** (Map p126) also runs from Sintra to Azenhas do Mar (€4.25, 35 minutes). Between June 18 and September 23, the Elétrico de Sintra (p131) (€3) goes from Sintra to Praia das Maçãs via Colares seven times daily between 9.20am and 6pm.

Bus 403 to Cascais runs regularly via Cabo da Roca (€4.25, 45 minutes, 9am to 9pm) from Sintra station.

Cascais

Cascais (kush-*kaish*) has rocketed from sleepy fishing village to much-loved summertime playground of wave-frolicking *lisboêtas* since King Luís I went for a dip in 1870. Its trio of golden bays attracts sun-worshipping holidaymakers, who come to splash in the ice-cold Atlantic. Don't expect to get much sand to yourself at the weekend, though.

There's plenty of post-beach life in the European Youth Capital 2018, too, with winding lanes leading to small museums, cool gardens, a shiny marina and a pedestrianised old town dotted with designer boutiques and al fresco fish restaurants. After dark, lively bars fuel the party. There's also great surfing at Praia do Guincho, 9km northwest, and running or cycling along the shoreline path.

◉ Sights

Palácio da Cidadela de Cascais MUSEUM
(☏ 213 614 980; www.museu.presidencia.pt; Cidadela de Cascais, Avenida Dom Carlos I; adult/child €4/free; ⏱10am-1pm & 2-6pm) Commissioned as a summer palace in 1870 by King Dom Luís I, this captivating museum remains the official residence of visiting heads of state in Portugal. When Putin isn't present, it's yours for the touring. Contemporary Portuguese tapestries, rare Lincrusta wall coverings, striking hardwood ceilings and fascinating gilded wood dragon/cherub chandeliers stand out among myriad Asian and European antiques.

Duna da Cresmina VIEWPOINT
(Núcleo de Interpretação; ☏ 918 847 421; www.dunadacresmina.com; Rua da Areia; ⏱9am-sunset) 🌿 Built in 2013, this nature interpretation centre was built to educate (and protect) the fragile flora and fauna of the coastal dune system around Guincho. To lure folks in, they built a cafe serving excellent crepes, salads and *tostas* with a postcard-ready outdoor terrace that dramatically frames 180-degree views of Cabo Raso, Praia da Cresmina and Praia do Guincho.

Walk off lunch on the well-built plankway system that extends into the dunes (guided tours available in advance). It's 6km northwest of Cascais on the way to Guincho; and bus 415 from Cascais passes by.

Boca do Inferno VIEWPOINT
Atlantic waves pummel the craggy 'Mouth of Hell', 2km west of Cascais. It's about a 20-minute walk along the coast, or you can catch the BusCas (427) from Cascais station (€1, every 10 to 15 minutes). Expect a mouthful of small splashes unless a storm is raging.

Casa das Histórias Paula Rego MUSEUM
(www.casadashistoriaspaularego.com; Avenida da República 300; adult/child €5/free; ⏱10am-6pm Tue-Sun, free 1st Sun of month) 🌿 This museum showcases the disturbing, highly evocative paintings of Portugal's finest postwar artists. Biannually changing exhibits span Rego's career, from early work with collage in the 1950s to the twisted fairy tale–like tableaux of the 1980s, and up to the disturbing realism of more recent years.

Cidadela de Cascais FORTRESS
(Av Dom Carlos I) The citadel is where the royal family used to spend the summer. Today it houses a luxury hotel – the **Pestana**

Cascais

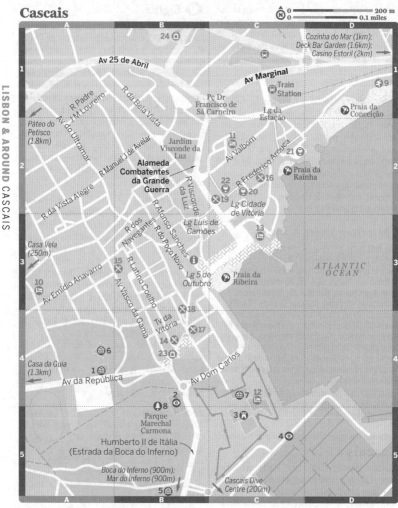

Cidadela Cascais (☎214 814 300; www.
pestana.com; d from €251; ✳@🛜➡) – a courtyard restaurant, bookshop, art gallery, chapel and the Palácio da Cidadela de Cascais.
Beyond lies the modern **Marina de Cascais**
(☎214 824 800; www.mymarinacascais.com; Casa
de São Bernardo; ⏱reception 9am-8pm) with its
postcard-perfect lighthouse, sleek yachts
and lounge bars.

Parque Marechal
Carmona   PARK
(www.cm-cascais.pt/equipamento/parque-mare
chal-carmona; Avenida Rei Humberto II; ⏱8.30am-
8pm Apr-Sep, to 6pm Oct-Mar) This wild park
provides a shady retreat from the seaside
crowds, with a duck pond, birch and pine
trees, palms and eucalyptus, rose gardens
and flowering shrubs.

The grounds harbour the **Museu Condes
de Castro Guimarães** (www.cm-cascais.pt/
equipamento/museu-condes-de-castro-guimaraes;
adult/child €4/free, free 1st Sun of month; ⏱10am-
6pm Tue-Sun), the whimsical early-19th-cen-
tury mansion complete with castle turrets
and Arabic cloister. The lavishly decorated
interior houses 17th-century Indo-Portuguese cabinets, oriental silk tapestries and
350-year-old *azulejos*.

Cascais

Centro Cultural de Cascais CULTURAL CENTRE (www.fundacaodomluis.pt; Avenida Rei Humberto II de Itália; adult/child €5/free; ☺10am-6pm Tue-Sun, free 1st Sun of month) Formerly a barefooted Carmelite convent, this centre hosts contemporary exhibitions and cultural events.

Museu do Mar Rei Dom Carlos MUSEUM (https://museumar.cascais.pt; Rua Júlio Pereira de Mello; adult/child €3/free; ☺10am-6pm Tue-Sun, free 1st Sun of month) The small, brightly accented Museu do Mar spells out Cascais' maritime history with costumes, tools, nets and boats, accompanied by quotes (in English) from the fisherfolk.

🏖 Beaches

Cascais' three sandy bays – Praia da Conceição, Praia da Rainha and Praia da Ribeira – are fine for a sunbake or a tingly Atlantic dip, but don't expect much towel space in summer.

The best beach is wild, windswept Praia do Guincho, 9km northwest, a mecca for surfers and windsurfers, with its massive crashing rollers. The strong undertow can be dangerous for swimmers, but Guincho still lures nonsurfers with powder-soft sands, fresh seafood and magical sunsets.

🏃 Activities

If you're keen to ride the waves, grab your boardies and check out the surfing courses available at **Moana Surf School** (☎964 449 436; www.moanasurfschool.com; Estrada do Abano, Praia do Guincho; private lesson per hour €50, group lesson €30, 4-lesson course €85), which also rents boards and wetsuits. **Guincho Surf School** (☎914 024 400, 917 535 719; www.guincho surfschool.com; Praia do Guincho; 1/2/5 group lessons €30/50/100, private lessons €50/90/135) also offers classes. South African-run **Hooked Surf School** (☎913 615 978; www.hookedsurf.com; introductory lesson €25, 4 lessons €80) holds classes here as well.

But Cascais is not limited to water sports. **Cascais Routes** (☎919 860 899; www.cascaisroutes.pt; tours from €40) specialises in land adventures such as rock climbing and mountain biking.

Cascais Dive Center DIVING (☎919 913 021; www.cascaisdive.com; Marina de Cascais, Loja 123; 1-/2-tank dive incl equipment €55/85; ☺9am-6pm May-Sep, 10am-12.30pm & 2.30-5pm Oct-Apr) At the Marina de Cascais (p134), this outfit can take you scuba diving around the Cascais coastline and beyond with equipment rental and courses.

Surf N Paddle WATER SPORTS (☎933 258 114; www.surfnpaddle.com; Praia da Duquesa; ☺9am-7pm Apr–mid-Oct, to 5.30pm mid-Oct–Mar) Open all year at Praia da Duquesa, midway between Cascais and Estoril, you can rent stand-up paddleboards and surfboards and/or take classes in both.

🎉 Festivals & Events

Festival de Estoril Lisboa MUSIC (www.festorilisbon.com; ☺Jul) This festival, founded in 1975 as the Festival de Música da Costa do Estoril, brings classical and jazz concerts to both Cascais and Estoril in July. Some concerts are free.

LAZY DAYS

Need an escape from the crowds of central Lisbon? Hop aboard A Linha – the local nickname for the Cais do Sodré–Cascais suburban train line – and you'll soon reach a bevy of beautiful beaches, charming towns and restaurants with fine dining and memorable sea views.

BREAK FOR THE BEACH

As the comboio (train) hugs the sand-adjacent tracks heading west from Cais do Sodré, it doesn't take long to leave Lisbon's urban sprawl behind. Dozens of beaches come into view, including Praia de Carcavelos, Praia da Parede, Praia da Torre and Praia da Conceição, all within a 40-minute ride from the city.

DINING INSIDE & OUT

Fresh seafood in the numerous beachfront eateries and inland tavernas that pepper the landscape from the city to Cascais is well worth seeking out. It's hard to go wrong, but A Pastorinha (www.apastorinha.com) and Taverna do Rogério (www.tavernado rogerio.com) in Carcavelos, Villa Tamariz Utopia in Estoril, and Bar das Avencas and Restaurante Sociedade in Parede should be on your list.

VILLAGE CHARMS

From the small-town village atmosphere of Carcavelos to the upscale enclaves of Estoril and Cascais, A Linha is chock-full of suburban escapes that feel miles away from the capital. Here you can explore family-run shops and atmospheric small-town taverns or sip away an afternoon with a bica (espresso) or glass of fine Portuguese wine in a charming outdoor cafe.

1. Praia da Conceicao (p135), Cascais
2. Cascais town centre (p133)
3. Praia do Tamariz, Estoril (p141)

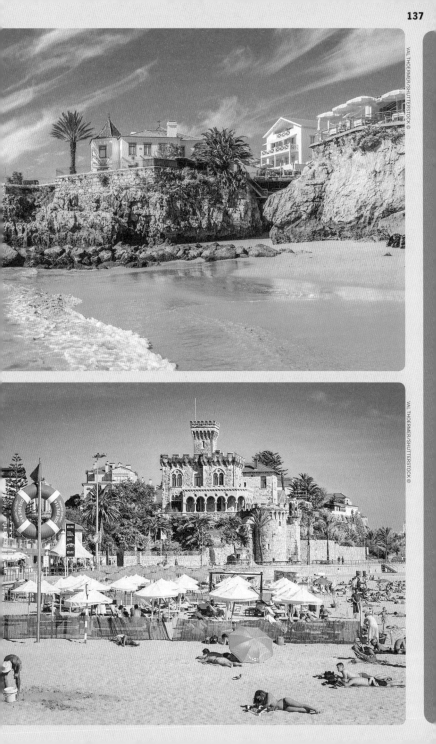

Festas do Mar CULTURAL

(www.facebook.com/FestasdoMar; ⊘Aug) This free, 10-day festival in late August celebrates Cascais' maritime heritage and *lusofonia* (the Portuguese speaking community) in general with outdoor concerts, nautical parades and fireworks.

🛌 Sleeping

Ljmonade Hostel HOSTEL €

(☏916 880 056; www.ljmonade.com; Rua Manuel Joaquim Gama Machado 4-6; dm from €25, d with/without bathroom €85/65; 🛜) In a quiet neighbourhood some 900m southwest of the train station, this Ukrainian-run hostel has the best traveller vibe of Cascais' budget options. Dorms come in four-, six- or seven-bed varieties (mixed and separate) but low, vaulted ceilings may be tough on basketball and volleyball players. A sunny terrace, big shared kitchen and free nightly wine are big pluses here.

Orbitur Guincho CAMPGROUND €

(☏214 870 450; www.orbitur.pt; EN 247-6, Lugar de Areia; bungalows €66, sites per adult/tent/car €7.40/8.40/7.50; ❄🛜⊜) Set back behind the dunes of Praia do Guincho, 9km from Cascais, this pine-shaded site is one of the Lisbon area's finest. It has a new swimming pool, restaurant, tennis court and even solar-powered showers in some cases. It gets busy in July and August. Buses run frequently to Guincho from Cascais.

FREE WHEELS

For a spin out along the coast, take advantage of BiCas (☏214 647 767; www.mobicascais.pt; ⊘8am-8pm), Cascais' free bike-hire scheme. Over 1200 new bikes were introduced in 2018 and are available from 8am to 8pm daily from 76 stations around the municipality, including as far away as Parede and Estoril. You'll need to register via the app (use '123456789' in place of the Portuguese tax ID known as a 'NIF'), select a time frame in the store section of the app and follow the instructions for unlocking your bike. There's a bicycle path that runs the entire 9km stretch from Cascais to Guincho. A shorter route is along the attractive seafront promenade to Estoril, 2km east.

★**Casa Vela** GUESTHOUSE €€€

(☏218 093 996; www.casavelahotel.com; Rua dos Bem Lembrados 17; d from €155; 🅿❄🛜⊜) The friendly Casa Vela has it all: 29 bright and attractive rooms with modern furnishings in decor schemes set to spice, colonial or garden themes in two upscale residential homes; deceptively large and grand gardens with trickling fountains, hidden nooks and two tranquil pools; and a Portuguese-by-birth, Mozambican-by-upbringing manager, João Paulo, who is the epitome of jovial hospitality. Paradise found.

Villa Cascais BOUTIQUE HOTEL €€€

(☏214 863 410; www.thealbatrozcollection.com; Rua Fernandes Tomás 1; d €250-340; ❄@🛜) If you like your hotels with a jolting dose of personality, the newly made-over, so-very-blue Villa Cascais (blue walls, blue couches and blue ceilings!) should sit quite well. Striking brass staircases lead to 11 beautiful and spacious rooms in three colours (two of which are not blue), each with discerning lounge furniture. Trendy, bright and beautiful.

Pergola House B&B €€€

(☏214 840 040; www.pergolahouse.pt; Avenida Valbom 13; s/d from €93/150; ❄🛜) An oasis of calm with a lush garden and bougainvillea-draped facade, this century-old manor is a family heirloom. A marble staircase sweeps up to 12 classically elegant rooms with stucco, dark-wood trappings and sparkling bathrooms; several have garden-facing balconies. Relax in the antique-filled sitting room, maybe with a glass of complimentary port in the evening.

🍴 Eating

You'll find a glut of restaurants with al fresco seating along pedestrianised Rua Frederico Arouca and cobbled Largo Cidade de Vitória. For seafood and sunsets, make for the ocean-facing restaurants in Guincho.

Os Bordallos BURGERS €

(Rua Marques Leal Pancada 430; burgers €5.80-12; ⊘noon-3pm & 7-11pm Tue-Sat, noon-3pm Sun; 🛜) Humbly tucked away in the narrow alleyways above town, this cosy joint does good gourmet Portuguese-style burgers amid a bit of history – it's owned by and named after a descendant of Rafael Bordalo Pinheiro, a famous Portuguese cartoonist and ceramist (that's his work on the wall). Service is a delight, too. Save room for the lime tart.

QUELUZ
....

Versailles' fanciful cousin-once-removed, the powder-puff **Palácio de Queluz** (www.parquesdesintra.pt; Largo Palácio de Queluz; adult/child €10/8.50; ☺9am-7pm Apr-Oct, to 6pm Nov-Mar) was once a hunting lodge, converted in the late 1700s to a royal summer residence. It's surrounded by queen-of-hearts formal gardens, with oak-lined avenues, fountains (including the Fonte de Neptuno, ascribed to Italian master Bernini) and an *azulejo*-lined canal where the royals went boating.

The palace, whose facade was restored to its original 'enamel blue' during a massive 2015 restoration, was designed by Portuguese architect Mateus Vicente de Oliveira and French artist Jean-Baptiste Robillon for Prince Dom Pedro in the 1750s. Pedro's niece and wife, Queen Maria I, lived here for most of her reign, going increasingly mad. Her scheming Spanish daughter-in-law, Carlota Joaquina, was quite a match for eccentric British visitor William Beckford. On one occasion she insisted that Beckford run a race with her maid in the garden and then dance a bolero, which he did 'in a delirium of romantic delight'.

Inside it's like a chocolate box, with a gilded, mirror-lined Throne Room and Pedro IV's bedroom where he slept under a circular ceiling, surrounded by *Don Quixote* murals. The palace's vast kitchens house a palatial restaurant, **Cozinha Velha** (☎214 356 158; www.pousadas.pt; mains €17-30; ☺12.30-3pm & 7.30-10pm), where you can feast on original palace recipes such as steamed Dover sole.

Once you've seen the palace, live the life: the Royal Guard of the Court quarters have been converted into the dazzling **Pousada Palácio de Queluz** (☎214 356 158; www.pousadas.pt; s/d from €95/130; ✴☎), with high-ceilinged rooms that will make you feel as if you're at home with the royals.

Queluz (keh-*loozh*) is 12km northwest of Lisbon and makes an easy day trip. Frequent trains from Lisbon's Rossio station stop at Queluz-Belas (€1.60, 18 minutes).

Santini ICE CREAM €

(www.santini.pt; Alameda dos Combatentes da Grande Guerra 102; 2/3/4 scoops €2.90/3.90/5.50; ☺11am-midnight) All hail Lisbon's favourite gelato (it's not the area's best, but the Portuguese are immensely nostalgic for it). Santini's creamy, rich, 100% natural version is made to the age-old family recipe of Italian immigrants, dating to 1949. Join the line at this conveniently located outlet, grab a cone and eat quickly before it melts.

★ Bar do Guincho PORTUGUESE €€

(☎214 871 683; www.bardoguincho.pt; Estrada do Abano, Praia do Guincho; mains €9-18; ☺noon-7pm Sun & Tue-Thu, noon-11.45pm Fri & Sat, later hours Jul & Aug; ☎) Sweeping the awards for most dramatic location in Cascais, this good-time bar-restaurant sits tucked behind a craggy ridge on the northern end of Guincho. From the sand, you would never know it's there, but it is – and it is packed! Revellers gobble up the beach-friendly burgers, seafood and salads washed down with cold *cerveja* (beer). Settle in for the afternoon.

★ Café Galeria House of Wonders CAFE €€

(www.facebook.com/houseofwonders; Largo da Misericórdia 53; meals €4.75-14.75; ☺9am-10pm;

☎🍴) 🌿 This fantastically whimsical, Dutch-owned cafe is tucked away in the old quarter. Its astonishingly good Middle Eastern/Mediterranean vegetarian plates, refreshing juices (€4), fabulous cakes (always at least one vegan and gluten-free option), welcoming ambience and artwork-filled interior are unmissable.

Upstairs in the main space, Cascais' best rooftop is delightful for al fresco dining, as is the sea-level terrace in the space next door, which serves an à la carte menu. A true traveller's delight.

5 Sentidos PORTUGUESE €€

(☎961 571 194; www.restaurante5entidos.com; Largo Assunção 6; mains €13-24; ☺noon-3pm & 6.30pm-midnight Sun-Thu, to 1am Fri & Sat; ☎) In a colourful and cosy home known around town as Casa do Largo (the site of a legendary bar of the same name), 5 Sentidos is popular with expats and in-the-know tourists, who come for sophisticated meat and seafood dishes that go beyond *bitoques* and grilled fish.

Páteo do Petisco PORTUGUESE €€

(☎214 820 036; www.facebook.com/pateodopetiscocascais; Travessa das Amoreiras 5; tapas

€2-9.90, mains €8.50-14; ⊘noon-11.30pm Tue-Sun) To escape the high prices and tourist masses in the old town, head out to this local favourite in the Torre neighbourhood. It's a buzzing place, with a friendly, tavern-like vibe and good-value Portuguese-style tapas – ideal for sharing with friends. It's about 3km northwest of the old town centre, best reached by Uber (around €2 to €3 from Cascais station). Reserve ahead.

If you don't feel like making the trek, it serves an identical menu at its newer location inside Mercado da Vila.

Confraria Sushi   JAPANESE €€

(☑214 834 614; www.facebook.com/confraria cascais; Rua Luís Xavier Palmeirim 14; salads €13-15, sushi combos €13-48; ⊘noon-midnight Sun-Thu, to 2am Fri & Sat; 🛜) It's hard to know where to look first at this bright, art-slung cafe, with hipster servers and candlelight at night. It's jazzed up with flower prints, zebra stripes and technicolour glass chandeliers. It's a fun spot for sushi and salads, albeit pricey – you're paying for an added cool quotient here. There are a handful of tables on the sunny patio.

Apeadeiro   PORTUGUESE €€

(Avenida Vasco da Gama 252; mains €8.50-16; ⊘noon-3pm & 7-10pm Tue-Sat, noon-3pm Sun) With simple decor, this sunny neighbourhood restaurant is known for its superb chargrilled fish and other souped-up Portuguese classics at reasonable prices.

Casa da Guia   INTERNATIONAL €€

(www.facebook.com/casadaguia; Avenida Nossa Senhora do Cabo 101; ⊘hours vary; 🛜) Among palm and pine trees, this lush waterfront complex contains a handful of shops, cafes and restaurants with outdoor terraces overlooking the deep blue Atlantic. It's located on the main coastal road, about 3km west of the historic centre (and 1.3km west of Boca do Inferno (p133)).

Mar do Inferno   SEAFOOD €€€

(☑214 832 218; www.mardoinferno.com; Avenida Rei Humberto II de Itália; seafood per kg €49-138; ⊘noon-11pm Tue-Thu; 🛜) Near the Boca do Inferno, this humble-looking place serves superb seafood dishes to ocean views. Its mouth-watering mixed platters for two (€39.50 to €88 – it'll do the cheapest one for one person) are legendary. The service can be hit or miss. Reserve ahead to score a table on the terrace.

🍷 Drinking & Nightlife

The pub-like bars huddling around Largo Luís de Camões fill with a good-time crowd after sunset.

Crow Bar   BAR

(www.facebook.com/crowbarcascais; Travessa da Misericórdia 1A; ⊘3pm-2am Tue-Sun, from 8.30pm Mon; 🛜) Sitting unsuspectingly above one of the most atmospheric and touristy streets in Cascais is this alternative watering hole, a dive bar with a rock and roll attitude. No sea views. No sunsets. But damn fine for a cold one.

O Luain's   IRISH PUB

(www.facebook.com/oluainscascais; Rua da Palmeira 4A; ⊘noon-2am; 🛜) For the craic in Cascais, it has to be this cheery Irish watering hole. Pull up a stool for Guinness, Premiere League footy or live jam sessions on weekends (nightly in summer).

Esplanada Rainha   BAR

(www.facebook.com/esplanadarainha.cascais; Largo da Praia da Rainha; ⊘10am-8pm Fri-Wed) For sundowners with a sea view, head to this outdoor place with a pleasant vista overlooking Praia da Rainha beach.

🛍 Shopping

Mercado da Vila   MARKET

(www.facebook.com/MercadodavilaCASCAIS; Rua Padre Moisés da Silva 29; ⊘6.30am-5pm Mon-Sat) Completely revamped and modernised in recent years, Cascais' municipal market tempts with not only fresh local produce such as juicy Algarve nectarines, glossy olives, wagon wheel–sized cheeses and bread on various days (check the schedule online), but also with a new line-up of bars, restaurants and gourmet takeaway stalls surrounding an inviting outdoor plaza.

Ceramicarte   FINE ART

(☑214 840 170; www.ceramicarte.pt; Largo da Assunção 3; ⊘10.30am-1.30pm & 3-6pm Mon-Fri, 10.30am-1pm Sat) This eye-catching gallery showcases Luís Soares' bright, abstract, fused-glass creations, from jewellery to tableware.

ℹ Information

Cascais Visitor Centre (Turismo; ☑912 034 214; www.visitcascais.com; Praça 5 de Outubro 45A; ⊘9am-8pm May-Sep, to 6pm Oct-Apr) The official Cascais tourist information is set up in glossy new digs on the main square.

Hospital de Cascais (☏214 653 000; www.hospitaldecascais.pt; Avenida Brigadeiro Victor Novais Gonçalves; ☻24hr) Located 6km north of Cascais in Alcabideche. Offers emergency service with English-speaking doctors.

Tourist Police Station (PSP Esquadra de Turismo; ☏214 863 929; www.psp.pt; Largo Mestre Henrique Anjos; ☻9am-9pm) In the plaza across from Praia da Ribeira.

ⓘ Getting There & Away

The **train station** (www.cp.pt; Largo da Estação) and nearby **bus station** (☏214 699 125; www.scotturb.com; Av Dom Pedro) are about 250m north of the main pedestrianised drag, Rua Frederico Arouca.

Scotturb runs the Cascais bus system. Bus 417 goes about hourly from Cascais to Sintra (€4.25, 40 minutes). For a more scenic view take bus 403 (€4.25, 1¼ hours), which goes via Cabo da Roca (30 minutes).

Comboios de Portugal (p122) trains run from Lisbon's Cais do Sodré station to Cascais via Estoril (€2.25, 40 minutes, every 20 to 30 minutes, 5.30am to 1.30am).

It's only 2km to Estoril, so it doesn't take long to walk the seafront route.

ⓘ Getting Around

Buses 405 and 415 go to Guincho (€3.25, 20 minutes, about hourly from 6.50am to 7.50pm). Scotturb's 427 (BusCas; €1) leaves every 10 to 20 minutes from just outside the train station and wiggles its way around most of the town's most important tourist sites.

For a taxi, call 214 659 500.

Estoril

With its swish hotels, turreted villas and glitzy casino, Estoril (shtoe-*reel*) once fancied itself as the Portuguese Riviera. The rich and famous came here to frolic in the sea, stroll palm-fringed landscaped gardens and fritter away their fortunes. Though it still has a whiff of faded aristocracy, those heady days of grandeur have passed. Today, Estoril remains a well-to-do, less touristy option than Cascais with a nice beach and casino. While some overnight guests may end up wishing they'd stayed in livelier Cascais, those looking for more peace and quiet will find a burgeoning guesthouse scene that yields some of the area's most memorable options.

Estoril was where Ian Fleming hit on the idea for *Casino Royale,* as he stalked Yugoslav double-agent Dusko Popov at the casino. During WWII, the town heaved with exiles and spies (including Graham Greene, another British intelligence man and author).

◉ Sights

Estoril's sandy Praia de Tamariz tends to be quieter than the bays in Cascais and has showers, cafes, beachside bars and a free ocean swimming pool, east of the train station.

Estoril has a world-famous golf scene, including the nationally acclaimed **Clube de Golf do Estoril** (www.clubegolfestoril.com).

Casino Estoril　　　　　　　　　　CASINO
(☏214 667 700; www.casino-estoril.pt; Avenida Dr Stanley Ho; ☻3pm-3am) Bond fans after a spritz of espionage head for glitzy Casino Estoril. Fritter away your euros on a high-stakes poker tournament or check out the spangly Las Vegas–style shows. There's a first-rate Chinese restaurant on the ground floor (mains €11 to €18).

ⓘ Sleeping

★**Blue Boutique Hostel**　　　　HOSTEL €
(☏214 820 132; www.blueboutiquehostel.com; Avenida Marginal 6538; dm from €25, d with/without bathroom €99/69) You can't miss this gorgeous aquamarine belle of the ball, a sky-blue bright mansion restored into a top hostel. The design-forward space, with marble staircases, retro furniture and local art installations, offers an above-bar shared kitchen, colourful dorms with lockers and a near wrap-around porch. There's an emphasis on water sports (surfing, windsurfing and stand-up paddleboarding) but why leave?

Hotel Smart　　　　　　　GUESTHOUSE €€
(☏214 682 164; www.hotel-smart.net; Rua Maestro Laçerda 6; s/d from €70/75; P※@శ☜) The affable Bandarra family runs this 26-room colonial-orange guesthouse with pride – think manicured lawns, a clean swimming pool, gleaming marble floors and modernised bathrooms (part of a 2016 renovation). The light-filled rooms have lots of polished wood and tiny balconies.

✕ Eating & Drinking

Pastelaria Garrett　　　　　PORTUGUESE €
(☏214 680 365; Avenida de Nice 54; snacks €1-11; ☻8am-7pm Wed-Mon) A block west of the park, this handsomely set *pastelaria* and restaurant is one of Lisbon's most storied, a

destination bakery when it comes to *Bolo Rei* (€23.50; a Christmas-like fruitcake served year-round), *palmiers cobertos* (€1.15; puff pastry covered with sweet egg icing) and croissants (€1.10), but everything is good, including the pricier savoury lunch fare.

Cozinha do Mar PORTUGUESE €€
(☑ 214 689 317; Avenida São Pedro 9; mains €8-17; ⊙ noon-3pm & 7-10.30pm Mon-Sat) This small, classy locals' haunt also receives its share of tourists who come for great-value Portuguese staples such as grilled fish, *dourada* (sea bream) cooked with rock salt (€14), *bacalhau à Brás* (€10; salted cod with eggs and potatoes) and *açorda de camarão* (€12; shrimp over mashed day-old bread with garlic and herbs) served over kitschy seashell tablecloths. Friendly service.

It's about a 350m walk north of Monte Estoril station.

Deck Beer Garden BEER GARDEN
(www.deckbeerlab.pt; Arcadas do Parque 21; ⊙ 8am-2am Thu-Tue; 🛜) The owner of a decades-old *restaurante típico* facing Estoril's pretty Jardim do Estoril realised he needed to get hip to craft brewing to keep up with the cool kids. The result is a clash of two eras: the artisanal draught brews are a work in progress but are surely better summer-heat beaters than Super Bock.

The outdoor seating is ideal, and when all else fails, there's Lagunitas IPA as well.

Mafra

Mafra, 39km northwest of Lisbon, makes a superb day trip. It is home to Palácio Nacional de Mafra, Portugal's extravagant convent-palace hybrid with 1200 rooms. Nearby is the beautiful former royal park, Tapada Nacional de Mafra, once a hunting ground and still teeming with wild animals and plants.

The monumental palace facade dominates the town. Opposite is a pleasant square, Praça da República, which is lined with cafes and restaurants.

◉ Sights

Palácio Nacional de Mafra PALACE
(☑ 261 817 550; www.palaciomafra.pt; Terreiro Dom João V; adult/child €6/free, free Sun to 2pm for Portuguese citizens/residents only; ⊙ palace 9.30am-5.30pm Tue-Sun, basilica 9.30am-1pm & 2-5pm) Wild-spending Dom João V poured pots of Brazilian gold into this baroque palace, covering a mind-boggling 4 sq km and comprising a monastery and basilica. Begun in 1717 and finished by 1746, the exuberant mock-marble confection is the handiwork of German master Friedrich Ludwig, who trained in Italy and clearly had a kind of Portuguese Vatican in mind.

No expense was spared: around 45,000 artisans worked on building its 1200 rooms and two bell towers, which shelter the world's largest collection of bells (97 in total, 92 of which are original).

When the French invaded Portugal in 1807, Dom João VI and the royals skedaddled to Brazil, taking most of Mafra's furniture with them. Imagine the anticlimax when the French found nothing but 20 elderly Franciscan friars. General Junot billeted his troops in the monastery, followed by Britain's Duke of Wellington and his men. From then on the palace became a military haven. Even today, much of it is occupied by the military as an academy.

On a self-guided visit, you'll take in treasures such as the antler-strewn hunting room, a striking infirmary, the gorgeous Blessing Room, awash in colourful Lioz stone, and a walled bed for mad monks (maybe sent over the edge by all those corridors!). The biggest stunner is the 83.6m-long barrel-vaulted library, housing some 36,000 book volumes encasing an as-yet-uncounted 100,000-plus 15th- to 18th-century books, many handbound by the monks. It's an appropriate fairy-tale coda to all this extravagance that they're gradually being gnawed away by rats. The basilica of twin bell-tower fame is strikingly restrained by comparison, featuring multihued marble floors and Carrara marble statues.

Aldeia Típica José Franco AMUSEMENT PARK
(Estrada Nacional 116; ⊙ 9.30am-7pm Jun-Oct, to 6pm Nov-May) FREE At the village of Sobreiro, 4km northwest of Mafra (take any Ericeira-bound bus), sculptor José Franco has created an enchanting miniature, vaguely surreal craft village of windmills, watermills and traditional shops. Kids love it here; as do some adults, especially when they discover the rustic *adega* (winery) serving red wine and snacks. Most folks, however, bring a picnic.

Tapada Nacional de Mafra FOREST
(☑ 261 814 240; www.tapadademafra.pt; Portão do Codeçal; activities €6.50-12; ⊙ 9.30am-7pm

WORTH A TRIP

A WOLF IN THE WOODS

There's no need to be afraid of the wolves at the Centro de Recuperação do Lobo Ibérico (Iberian Wolf Recovery Centre; ☑ 917 532 312; www.grupolobo.pt; Vale da Guarda, Picão; adult/concession €6/4; ⊙ 4pm & 6pm Sat & Sun May-Sep, 3pm & 4.30pm Sat & Sun Oct-Apr), located near Malveira, 10km east of Mafra. The centre is home to around 13 wolves that can no longer live in the wild. Visits are by 90-minute guided tours with prebooking only (English is always the latter of the two time slots).

Set in a forested valley, the centre aims to boost the rapidly dwindling numbers of the Iberian wolf population (now just 250 in the wild in Portugal, along with an additional 2000 in Spain) by affording them safe shelter in a near-to-natural habitat inside five 1-hectare enclosures. As the wolves are free to roam in their large enclosures, there's no guarantee that you'll spot them, but encounters are frequent. There are volunteering opportunities as well. The sanctuary is best reached by private transport (call ahead for directions as GPS will take you an impassable way). Cash only; no access for strollers or wheelchairs.

Jul-Sep, to 6pm Oct-Jun) The 819-hectare Tapada Nacional de Mafra is where Dom João V used to go a-hunting. Enclosed by an original 21km wall, the grounds are now an environmentally aware game park, home to free-roaming wild boar and red deer, plus smaller numbers of foxes, badgers and eagles.

To appreciate the different ecosystems, hike through its woodlands of Portuguese oak, cork oak and pine; don't miss the 350-year-old cork oak saved from fire in 2003. The 4.8km trail is a good introduction to the park, but you have a greater chance of spotting animals on one of the more remote 7km to 9km routes. Also on the grounds is a simple but pleasantly furnished guest-house (singles/doubles €60/70). On weekends, many activities are on offer, including archery (as well as on-again, off-again horse riding and wagon rides). You can also take a tourist 'train' around the park.

The Tapada is about 7km north of Mafra, along the road to Gradil. It's best reached by private transport, as buses are erratic; from Mafra, an off-peak Uber runs to €6 to €9 one-way.

🛏 Sleeping & Eating

★ Aldeia da Mata Pequena   INN €€
(☑ 219 270 908; www.aldeiadamatapequena.com; Rua São Francisco de Assis; €75-160; ☜) Located 9km south of Mafra, this unique rural tourism option is the forward-thinking vision of *lisboêta* Diogo Batalha, who managed to buy and restore 18 ruined structures of a 300-year-old village, 14 of which so far have been turned into fabulous, historically

accurate stone cottages, each with a kitchen, living room and sleeping area.

The details are extraordinary: all of the houses contain original *salgadeiras* (meat-salting boxes) while others – formerly wineries, barns or bakeries – retain original elements such as stables-turned-living-rooms and a massive wine press as a design centrepiece. There's *ginjinha* (cherry liqueur) in the room, piping hot Mafra bread at your doorstep in the morning and a tiny, independently operated *petiscos* restaurant on premises. You'll share the tiny village with cats, a pig, rabbits, peacocks, goats and a donkey. It sits in an extraordinary countryside location and is best reached by private car. There is a two-day minimum (or 50% surcharge for one night when reserved less than five days in advance), but you'll want to stay forever.

★ João da Vila Velha   PORTUGUESE €
(☑ 261 811 254; Rua Pedro Julião 4; mains €7-12; ⊙ noon-3pm & 7-10pm Fri-Wed) Located just enough off the tourist path, old school chef João runs this authentic and colourful neighbourhood *tasca*. There's a wealth of simple but honestly cooked classics (octopus, *bacalhau* etc) and a good bit of wilder and gamier meat dishes (wild boar, rabbit and the like). Standouts include a wild-boar *chanfana* (stew) and a curried-shrimp *moqueca* (stew).

★ Cabana do Peixe   SEAFOOD €€
(☑ 219 661 420; Av 9 de Julho 5, Venda do Pinheiro; mains for 2 €30-38; ⊙ noon-3pm & 7.30pm-1.30am Tue-Sat, noon-3pm Sun; ☜) It's worth the schlep 15km east of Palácio Nacional de Mafra for creatively tweaked *cataplanas*

(seafood stews in copper cookware), seafood rices, *massadas* (seafood stews with pasta) and fresh fish at this rustic-chic seafooder. Above-and-beyond service contemplates the notable attention to detail (seasoned olives served in mini-*cataplanas*, artistic *saco de pano* bread bags), and the food is fantastic.

Adega de Covento PORTUGUESE **€€**
(☑261 814 185; www.adegadoconvento.pt; Rua Moreira 11; mains €9-19; ☺11am-11pm Thu-Mon, to 3pm Tue; ☎) This classy option, a short walk from the palace but tucked away down a seldom-used side street, does an incredibly tender and tasty octopus rice (*arroz de polvo*) on special and a host of other classic menu staples. Portions are hefty and more gourmet than expected, with an emphasis on seafood (but plenty of *carne* as well).

ⓘ Information

Posto de Turismo (☑261 817 170; www.cm-mafra.pt; Avenida das Forças Armadas 28; ☺10am-1pm & 2-6pm) Mafra's tourist information centre is just off the south side of the palace and full of information, maps and helpful staff.

ⓘ Getting There & Around

Mafra's main bus terminal is at **Parque Intermodal** (www.mafrense.pt; Santa Casa Misericórdia 8), 1.2km west of the palace, but buses also stop in front of the palace and at the parking lot/bus station **Parque Intermodal do Alto da Vela** (Avenida das Forças Armadas S/N), 500m south of the palace (but there is little advantage to walking the extra 500m to get here).

Regular **Mafrense** (☑707 201 371) buses to Sintra (€3.30, one hour) and Lisbon's Campo Grande terminal (€6.25, 75 minutes, at least hourly) leave from the **bus stop** (Avenida das Forças Armadas S/N) across from the palace in front of the Mafricentro shop.

For Ericeira (€2.40, 25 minutes, at least hourly), go to the **bus stop** (Avenida das Forças Armadas S/N) on the palace side of the street next to Posto de Turismo.

Mafra's train station is 6km away from the town centre but, with infrequent transport, it's not a recommended option (though an off-peak Uber costs €6 to €9 from the station to the town centre). Go to Malveira station instead for easier connections (20 minutes) to Mafra.

There is a **taxi point** (☑261 815 512; Praça da República S/N) on Praça da República, just off the north side of the palace in front of the Cartório Notarial.

Ericeira

Picturesquely draped across sandstone cliffs above the blue Atlantic, sunny, whitewashed Ericeira is popular with *lisboêtas* seeking a quick weekend getaway. It's equally renowned for spectacular ocean vistas and excellent seafood restaurants, and is a mecca for surfers, who come here for the great waves and camaraderie (it is in fact a Save the Waves Coalition World Surfing Reserve). The town's old centre is clustered around Praça da República, with the sprawl of newer development spreading south and north.

'Ericeira' comes from *Ouriceira,* which means a place flush with *ouriços* (sea urchins). Fans of the purple version of the spiny delicacy will be delighted during the season (late October to April) and during the city's Festival do Ouriço-do-Mar in April.

◉ Sights & Activities

As well as the small Praia dos Pescadores in the heart of town, there are three beaches within walking distance of the centre. Praia do Sul, also called Praia da Baleia, is easiest to get to and has a protected pool for children. Praia do Norte (also called Praia do Algodio) and Praia de São Sebastião lie to the north. Some 6km north is unspoilt Praia de São Lourenço, while Praia Foz do Lizandro, a big bite of beach backed by a small car park and a couple of restaurants, is 3km south.

★ **Miradouro Ribeira d'Ilhas** VIEWPOINT
(N247) If you dropped dead of a heart attack a moment after ogling this jaw-dropping view above Ribeira d'Ilhas and Alibabá beaches – and the surfers tackling the waves of the Ericeira World Surfing Reserve – you'd die happy. Absolutely stunning. Further words unnecessary.

Rapture Surf Camp SURFING
(☑919 586 722; www.rapturecamps.com; Foz do Lizandro 6; surf lessons €30, board & wetsuit rental per day €20, dm/d with shared bathroom incl half-board €39/100) Standing out among the surf camps in Ericeira, Rapture offers nicely chilled digs near the beach at Foz do Lizandro and lessons with proficient instructors.

Activity Surf Center SURFING
(www.activitysurfcenter.com; Rua de Santo António 3A; per day surfboard/wetsuit hire €20/10; ☺9am-1pm & 2-7pm May-Sep, 10am-7pm Oct-Dec & Mar-Apr) Rents out surfboards, paddleboards,

bodyboards and wetsuits; and morphs into a bar at night.

🛏 Sleeping

Ericeira is well equipped with everything from bygone-era beach hotels to sea-view boutique offerings and a boatload of surf camps. Book ahead in July and August. During the low season, expect discounts of 30% to 50% (though many establishments are closed in January and February).

Residencial Fortunato   GUESTHOUSE €
(☑261 862 829; www.pensaofortunato.com; Rua Dr Eduardo Burnay 45; s/d €47/52, d with ocean view €62; [P]🔊) One of the best budget options around, this well-run, well-kept place has light, bright and all-white rooms with cutesy and retro touches in a nice location at the end of the main pedestrian thoroughfare. The best digs upstairs have small terraces with lovely sea views (€10 extra) – which might ease the pain of the disappointing breakfast.

Ericeira Camping   CAMPGROUND €
(☑261 862 706; www.ericeiracamping.com; N247, Km49.4; sites per adult/tent/car €5.50/6.50/3.50, bungalows from €70; [P]🔊) On the coastal highway 800m north of Praia de São Sebastião, this high-quality site has two-, four- and six-bedroom bungalows, teepees and 100 tent sites among loads of trees, as well as a playground, disabled access and a popular skatepark next door.

⭐Blue Buddha Beachhouse   GUESTHOUSE €€
(☑910 658 849; www.bluebuddhahostel.com; Rua Florêncio Granate 19; d/tr/q from €65/81/96; 🔊) The nearest thing to your own modern beach house, this delightful spot has seven bright, white and very smart rooms, plus an ocean vista to die for. A spacious communal living room with couches, cable TV and mod cons adds to the appeal, plus there's a guest kitchen. Multilingual proprietress Luzia knows the lot, from surfing spots to the latest bars.

⭐Residencial Vinnus   GUESTHOUSE €€
(☑261 866 933; www.vinnusguesthouse.com; Rua Prudêncio Franco da Trindade 19; without breakfast s/d/tr/q €50/65/75/75; 🔊) Bright, with trendy, contemporary decor, the centrally located Residencial Vinnus offers great value, with simple and comfortable whitewashed rooms. It's worth the extra investment for the spacious ones with kitchenette, but the pretty corner doubles have great light. Excellent

overall, with a good attitude. In summer you might cop street noise from nearby bars.

🍽 Eating

Casa da Fernanda   PASTRIES €
(Largo das Ribas 29; ouriço €0.95; ⊗8am-9pm) For a sweet little treat, pop into this simple *pastelaria* for Ericeira's best *ouriço* – a small, muffin-like almond cake with a crusty top that hails from here. €0.95 well spent!

Casa das Três   CAFE €
(Rua de Santo António 12A; breakfast €1.60-6.50, mains €5-10; ⊗9am-11pm Mon-Sat, to 6pm Sun Mar-Dec; 🔊) 🍴 This barely larger than a hole-in-the-wall cafe is hyper-focused on its mission of bringing third wave java – single-origin Panamanian, Ethiopian, Costa Rican speciality coffees – to Ericeira, roasted by 7g near Porto. It succeeds. Great for a pre- or post-surf caffeine fix espresso or flat white from a mini La Marzocco (from €1.10).

But don't discount the food: DIY buddha bowls and other vegan-friendly treats such as avocado toasts. Cash only.

⭐Mar à Vista   SEAFOOD €€
(☑261 862 928; Largo das Ribas 16; seafood per kg €18-120; ⊗noon-10pm Thu-Tue) Crustaceans of every kind are on display at this hearty frill-free local *marisqueira* known for its shellfish (no fish, no meat). Phenomenal crabs (both *santola* and *sapateira*) are eaten from the shell, while lobsters (both *lavagante* and *lagosta*) can be whipped up into memorable seafood rices, *massadas*, *açordas* and *cataplanas*.

Excellent starters include *doses* of oysters, clams or garlic shrimp, all accompanied by

Ericeira

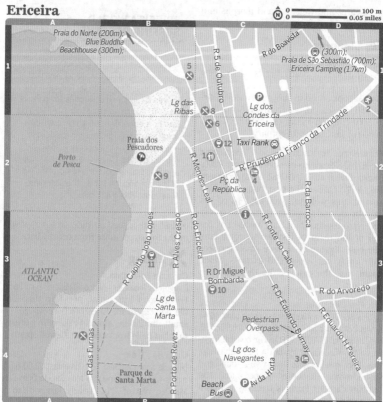

Ericeira

🏃 Activities, Courses & Tours
1 Activity Surf Center.............................C2
2 Go Out...D1

🛏 Sleeping
3 Residencial Fortunato.......................D4
4 Residencial Vinnus............................C2

🍴 Eating
5 Casa da Fernanda..............................B1
6 Casa das Três....................................C2
7 Esplanada Furnas..............................A4
8 Mar à Vista..C1
9 Mar das Latas....................................B2

🍷 Drinking & Nightlife
10 Jukebox...C3
11 Ouriço...B3
12 Tubo..C2

beer on tap or a fresh white wine. Cash only. Reserve ahead!

★ **Clube Naval**
Praia da Assenta   SEAFOOD €€
(📞 261 855 077; Rua do Facho 22, Assenta; seafood per kg €12-42; ⏰ noon-3pm & 7-11pm Wed-Mon; 🛜) Hidden down a steeply zigzagging road clinging to sea cliffs 14km north of Ericeira, this low-key find was opened by a family of fisher-folk in 1998. Punters line up for simply but fantastically prepared fresh catches such as sea bream, snapper, goldenfish, grouper, turbot, shrimp, cuttlefish (you name it, they might have caught it today!) barbecued over hot coals. Fantastic.

Mar das Latas   PORTUGUESE €€
(📞 912 218 423; www.facebook.com/mar.das. latas; Rua João Lopes 24A; mains €15-18; ⏰ bar 4pm-midnight, restaurant 7pm-midnight, closed Wed; 🛜) Ericeira's happening happy hour goes down on the sidewalk at this sophisticated bistro, which does well-curated wines and tapas with sunset sea views from the bar; and worthwhile, creatively approached

Portuguese dining in the modern restaurant. Dishes such as Gomes de Sá *pataniscas* (cod fritters) and a grilled veggie *moqueca* reveal a daring but welcome desire to be different.

Esplanada Furnas SEAFOOD €€€
(261 864 870; www.restaurantefurnasericeira. com; Rua das Furnas 2; fish per kg €42-59; ☺noon-4pm & 7-11.30pm;) As close to the sea as you can get without a boat, Furnas is all about freshly caught fish and spectacular ocean views. It'll show you the catch of the day right as you enter and then barbecue your choice on the spot. The per-kilogram price on the chalkboard covers the fish plus a side of potatoes.

It will split a whole fish for solo travellers, too (which is rare and can get pricey).

Drinking & Nightlife

Tubo BAR
(Travessa da Esperança 3; ☺6pm-2am Fri & Sat Nov-May, 6pm-2am daily Jun-Oct) Popular among the twenty- to thirty-somethings, this post-surf bar – and its severed VW bus – spills out onto the street. There's live music every Wednesday and in summer from 10pm a DJ sets the mood.

Jukebox BAR
(www.jukeboxericeira.com; Rua Dr Miguel Bombarda 7; ☺8pm-2am Mon-Sat;) This laid-back little spot blasts '80s alternative music (with occasional live music). It is known for mixing a decent cocktail.

Ouriço CLUB
(927 378 882; www.facebook.com/discoteca ourico; Rua Capitão João Lopes 9; ☺11pm-6am Mon-Sat Jul & Aug, 11pm-6am Fri & Sat Sep-Jun) One of Portugal's oldest discos, catering to night owls of all ages, with a mix of pop, dance, oldies and dance-floor standards.

Information

Ask Me Ericeira (910 518 029; www.cm-mafra.pt; Praça da República 17; ☺10am-1pm & 2-6pm) Offers useful maps of town, information on surfing (ask for the *Surf Guide* booklet), and maps and brochures for Lisbon and beyond.

Getting There & Away

Mafrense (www.mafrense.pt) buses stop at the **bus station** (261 268 717; Rua dos Bombeiros Voluntários 3) 500m north of the *praça* (town square), off the national road N247. Ask at Ask Me Ericeira for timetables.

Bus connections to northern destinations such as Peniche and Coimbra are best made through Torres Vedras (€4, one hour, six to 10 on weekdays, three on Saturday and one on Sunday). Other destinations, with services roughly hourly, are Lisbon–Campo Grande station (€6.25, 1¼ hours), Mafra (€2.40, 25 minutes) and Sintra (€3.50, 50 minutes).

Getting Around

Though regular local buses going to Torres Vedras (€4) go past Praia das Ribeira d'Ilhas (around €1), and any Sintra-bound bus passes Praia Foz do Lizandro (around €1), the dedicated **Beach Bus** (€1) operates from July to mid-September between 9.05am and 7.05pm from stops at the bus station (and a few minutes later on Largo dos Navegantes near more centrally located Hotel Vila Galé) and heads to both beaches.

You can rent bicycles from **Go Out** (925 307 317; www.goout.com.pt; Rua Prudêncio Franco da Trindade 1, Amar Hostel; per day/week bicycle €15/84, scooter €30/175; ☺10am-8pm Nov-May, to 10pm Jun-Oct).

There's a **taxi rank** (Largo das Condes de Ericeira) on Rua Prudêncio Franco da Trindade, near the post office.

SETÚBAL PENINSULA

As the mercury rises, the promise of sun, sand and mouth-watering grilled fish lures *lisboêtas* south to the Setúbal Peninsula for weekends of seaside fun. Beach bums make for the Costa da Caparica's 8km sweep of golden sand to surf the chilly Atlantic and unwind over sundowners in beachside cafes. Further south sits Cabo Espichel, a vertiginous cape thrashed by the Atlantic, where you can trace the footprints of dinosaurs.

The main hub of the region is the vibrant port of Setúbal, a fine place to munch *choco frito* (fried cuttlefish) and spot bottlenose dolphins on a cruise of the marshy Sado Estuary (across which lies gorgeous and upscale Comporta). To the west lies Parque Natural da Arrábida, lined with scalloped bays flanked by sheer cliffs that are home to birds of prey. It leads to the cobbled backstreets of the fishing town of Sesimbra, overshadowed by a Moorish castle.

Costa da Caparica

Costa da Caparica's seemingly never-ending beach attracts sun-worshipping *lisboêtas* craving all-over tans, surfers keen to ride

Atlantic waves, and day-tripping families seeking clean sea and soft sand. It hasn't escaped development, but head south and the high-rises soon give way to pine forests and mellow beach-shack cafes. The town has the same name as the coastline, and is a cheery place with shops and lots of inflatable seaside tack, done up in 2009 under a now-bankrupt government-sponsored revitalisation project that was responsible for building the town's 24 boxy seaside bar and restaurant structures.

Beaches

The beaches of Costa da Caparica can be divided into three sections: the North (São João da Caparica), which skews more middle-to-upper class and trendy (and carries a parking charge of €4 per day); the Vila, which includes the town beaches from Praia do Norte in the north to Nova Praia in the south; and the South, which begins at Saúde and carries on to Fonte da Telha and is best accessed by the Transpraia train in summer, which operates on a narrow-gauge railway running the length of the southern beaches (you can jump off at any one of over 20 stops).

Beaches nearer to town, including Praia do Norte and Praia do Santo Antonio, are great for families (as is the South's Praia da Cabana do Pescador at stop 12, which boasts a playground), while the further out in either direction are younger and trendier. Praia 19 (stop 19) is a more secluded gay and nudist haven.

Activities

Among the best surfing spots for beginners are São João da Caparica, Praia da Mata and Praia da Sereia. Locals prefer Praia do Barbas and bodyboarders tend towards Cova do Vapor for its big barrels. Fonte da Telha and Praia da Bela Vista are the best beaches for windsurfing and kitesurfing.

Centro Internacional de Surf   SURFING
(☑912 530 689; www.caparicasurf.com; Praia do CDS; group/private lessons €25/50; ⊙9am-6pm Jan-Nov) The main surfing school. In addition to individual lessons, group packages of five (€90) and 10 (€150) lessons, as well as private packages of five lessons (€200), are available.

Nshark   CYCLING
(☑927 738 803; www.facebook.com/Nshark; Avenida 1 de Maio 33; per hour/day €3/9; ⊙9am-

1pm & 4-8pm Tue-Sat) Rents the most reliable bikes in town, for both adults and children year-round.

Sleeping

★**Lost Caparica Surf House**   B&B €€
(☑918 707 779; www.lostcaparica.com; Rua Dr Barros de Castro 17; dm/s/d with shared bathroom €25/50/55; ☞) Your charming and stylish host Filipa has turned this former architect's home into an upscale surfers' crash pad. Her keen eye for vintage design ensures a mid-century modern ethos throughout the space, a welcome retreat for weary but discerning sand addicts. Hot outdoor showers, an open-air solarium and a modern guest kitchen are highlights. The six-bed dorm has a fireplace.

Surf lessons, surf guiding, yoga and massages are on offer, as is puppy time with the adorable beagle, Serra.

Residencial Mar e Sol   GUESTHOUSE €€
(☑212 900 017; www.residencialmaresol.com; Rua dos Pescadores 42; s/d/tr €49/53/65; ❋@☞) The friendly, family-run Mar e Sol offers renovated rooms (simple but comfy) in warm hues with parquet floors. This family also has a gastronomy empire: it runs popular Italian restaurant Napoli (☑212 903 197; www.facebook.com/restaurantenapolicostacaparica; Rua dos Flores 1; mains €9-14.50, pizzas €7.50-12.50; ⊙noon-3pm & 7-11.30pm; ☞) on the premises; and Portugal's first burger joint, Sandwich Bar (www.facebook.com/sandwichbarcosta caparica; Praça da Liberdade 5; burgers €5.50-6.50; ⊙11am-2am), opened in 1974, next door, among others. There is bike hire too (summer only).

Eating & Drinking

In Costa da Caparica town, seafood restaurants line Rua dos Pescadores.

Clássico Beach Club   TAPAS €€
(☑927 194 906; www.facebook.com/Classico Portugal; Praça da Liberdade 7; mains €7-21; ⊙noon-7pm Mon-Fri, to 9pm Fri & Sat; ☞) One of the best beach bars in São João, stylishly built by a trendy Lisbon chef but taken over by Brazilians, who have shaken up the beach food scene with Bahian *moquecas*, tapioca crepes and croquettes, and other homeland specialities; and well-made cocktails (€8 to €11). It has one of the trendiest vibes as well, without being too pretentious.

There's a DJ on summer weekends.

★ O Mercado PORTUGUESE €€

(📞 218 235 099; www.facebook.com/omercadocc; Avenida 1 de Maio 36D; mains €10-16; ⏰ 12.30-3pm & 7.30-10pm Tue-Sat; 🛜) Oozing rustic charm, this savvy Portuguese-fusion gastropub is a pleasant escape from beach-bum Babylon. The select menu ranges from classics *(bitoque à portuguesa)* to modern takes on beef cheeks and pork belly, with occasional Peruvian flourishes. There's a good wine list and better beers on offer than usual. A nice night out.

Da Wave CAFE €€

(www.da-wave.com; Praia Nova; mains €2.80-15; ⏰ 11.30am-7.30pm Oct-Mar, to 2am Apr-Sep; 🛜) One of many open-sided cafe-restaurants along the beach, Da Wave has a laid-back, hippie seaside-diner vibe, with its aqua trim and reggae soundtrack. American-style breakfasts, sandwiches, pizzas and juices make up the menu, though it's mainly frequented for sunset cocktails (€5.50).

Bar Waikiki BAR

(📞 212 962 129; www.waikiki.com.pt; Praia da Sereia; ⏰ 9am-7.30pm Mon-Thu, to 6am Fri & Sat Apr-Oct; 🛜) Nicely on its own, this beachfront bar is popular with surfers and has a cool lounge vibe. While not renowned for food, its late-night disco on summer weekends is requisite partying in Costa da Caparica. It's stop 15 on the train.

ℹ Information

Posto de Turismo (📞 212 900 071; www.m-almada.pt; Frente Urbana de Praias, Edifício da Polícia Marítima; ⏰ 9.30am-1pm & 2-5.30pm Mon-Sat Apr-Sep, 9.30am-1pm & 2-5.30pm Mon-Fri Oct-Mar) Very helpful staff in the modern brown and concrete building on the beach.

ℹ Getting There & Away

Transportes Sul do Tejo (www.tsuldotejo.pt) runs buses 153 and 161 every 45 to 60 minutes in summer to Costa da Caparica from Lisbon's Praça de Espanha (€3.35, 40 minutes) and Praça do Areeiro (€4.25, one hour), respectively. Service drops off quite a bit in winter. The **bus terminal** (📞 707 508 509; www.tsuldotejo.pt; Praça Padre Manuel Bernardes 14C) is 600m south of Praça da Liberdade.

The best way to get here is by ferry to Cacilhas from Lisbon's Cais do Sodré (€1.25, 10 minutes, every 10 minutes, 5.35am to 1.40am), where buses 124 and 135 run to Costa da Caparica town (€3.25, 20 minutes, every 30 to 60 minutes).

Those who prefer to cycle can do a bike-ferry-bike combo from Lisbon. Take the bike path along the Tejo out to Belém, board the ferry to Trafaria, and continue another 3km by bike from there along a bike path to Costa da Caparica.

ℹ Getting Around

The **Transpraia** train (adult/child €8/4 return, cheaper if you go a shorter distance) along the beach runs every half-hour from 9am to 7.30pm departing from Praia Nova (Praia da Saúde) and making more than 20 stops before reaching Fonte da Telha, about 1km before the end of the county beach.

The town is also ideal for biking. Pick up wheels at Nshark (p148).

Aldeia do Meco

Famous for its seafood restaurants, this tiny village 12km northwest of Sesimbra is a popular weekend getaway due to its proximity to Praia do Meco and Lagoa de Albufeira, two of the peninsula's most stunning locales. Praia do Meco is an unspoilt sweep of golden sand, flanked by low-rise cliffs; try to catch one of its mesmerising sunsets. On its northern end, Lagoa de Albufeira is a postcard-perfect, beach-flanked lagoon popular for windsurfing and stand-up paddleboarding.

Beachfront **Bar do Peixe** (📞 212 684 732; fish per kg €25-55; ⏰ 10.30am-midnight Wed-Sun, closed mid-Nov–mid-Dec), along the Moinho do Baixo section of Praia do Meco, is a great seafood destination. Other top restaurants are scattered throughout the village, particularly on the main street Rua do Comércio.

Transportes Sul do Tejo (www.tsuldotejo.pt) buses 223 and 231 run from Sesimbra to Aldeia do Meco (€2.40, 25 minutes, six or so daily Monday to Saturday).

Cabo Espichel

At strange, bleak and extraordinary Cabo Espichel, frighteningly tall cliffs – some met by swathes of beach – plunge into piercing blue sea. The only buildings on the cape are a huge church, the 18th-century Nossa Senhõra do Cabo, flanked by two arms of desolately empty pilgrims' lodges, and the 1790 lighthouse.

It's easy to see why Wim Wenders used this windswept spot, with its lonely, brooding atmosphere, as a location when he was filming *A Lisbon Story.* It's worth your while trying to catch the Cabo Espichel Festival (p151) if you are visiting in September.

Transportes Sul do Tejo (www.tsuldotejo .pt) buses 201 and 205 to Cabo Espichel run direct from Sesimbra (€2.75, 25 minutes, 1.50pm and 2.50pm), while more frequent buses terminate at the village of Azóia (€2.40), about 3km before the cape.

Sesimbra

As well as fine sands, turquoise waters and a Moorish castle slung high above the centre, this former fishing village offers excellent seafood in its waterfront restaurants.

Though the beach gets packed in summer, the town has kept its low-key charm, with narrow lanes lined with terracotta-roofed houses, outdoor cafes and a palm-fringed promenade for lazy ambles. Cruises, guided hikes and scuba-diving activities here include trips to Cabo Espichel, where dinosaurs once roamed. It's 30km southwest of Setúbal, sheltering under the Serra da Arrábida at the western edge of the beautiful Parque Natural da Arrábida.

◎ Sights

Castelo de Sesimbra   CASTLE
(Rua Nossa Sra do Castelo 11; ⊘ 7am-8pm Apr-Oct, to 7pm Nov-Mar) FREE For sweeping views over dale and coast, roam the snaking ramparts of the Moorish castle, rising 200m above Sesimbra. It was taken by Dom Afonso Henriques in the 12th century, retaken by the Moors, then snatched back by Christians under Dom Sancho I.

The ruins harbour the 18th-century, chalk-white Igreja Santa Maria do Castelo (9am to 4pm); step inside to admire its heavy gold altar and exquisite blue-and-white *azulejos*. The shady castle grounds are ideal for picnics, and a few small historical exhibitions offer brief distractions. There's also a tourist information point for Geo-circuito de Sesimbra (www.cm-sesimbra. pt/geocircuito), which highlights important geological discoveries in the region. To get here from town, any outbound bus can drop you at the start of the pedestrian path, a 1km walk up to the Castelo.

Fortaleza de Santiago   CASTLE
(Rua da Fortaleza S/N; ⊘ 9am-10pm Apr–mid-Jun, to 2am mid-Jun–Sep, to 8pm Oct-Mar) FREE In the town centre, the grandest castle on the sand is 17th-century Fortaleza de Santiago,

once part of Portugal's coastal defences and the summertime retreat of Portuguese kings. It was reopened to much fanfare in 2014 and now includes the stunning Tap House (⊘ 11am-1am; ⊛), a small maritime museum (€3), tourist information and the renovated governor's quarters.

Audio tours are available for €3.

🏃 Activities

Sesimbra is a great place to get into the outdoors with a backyard full of cliffs for climbing, clear water for scuba diving, Atlantic waves for windsurfing, and kilometres of unspoiled coastal trails for hiking and cycling. Adrenaline junkies get their thrills with vigorous pursuits from canyoning to rappelling. Head out to Meira Pro Center (☑ 212 684 527; www.meiraprocenter.com; Marginal Lagoa de Albufeira S/N; ⊘ 10am-6pm) for gear.

Vertente Natural   ADVENTURE SPORTS
(☑ 210 848 919; www.vertentenatural.com; Porto de Abrigo 6; tours from €10; ⊘ 10am-6pm Jun-Sep) ✈ An eco-aware, one-stop shop for adventure sports, this Sesimbra-based outfitter offers trekking, canyoning, canoeing, diving, rappelling and its main event: coasteering (a climbing, jumping, rappelling, swimming hybrid along the coast; €35 to €50).

The summer office is seasonal, but activities are offered year-round from its headquarters in the village of Almoinha, 4km north of Sesimbra.

Anthia Diving Center   DIVING
(☑ 965 225 787; www.anthiadivingcenter.com; Porto de Abrigo, Loja 1; 1 dive incl equipment €50, tours from €35; ⊘ 9am-6pm) This friendly, highly recommended SSI-affiliated dive centre has legions of fans and is open year-round. In addition to diving, it offers dolphin tours from April to October.

Aquarama   CRUISE
(☑ 965 263 157; www.aquarama.com.pt; Avenida dos Náufragos; adult/child from €20/12; ⊘ Jun-Sep) Runs at least one trip per day to Cabo Espichel on a glass-bottomed, partially submerged boat. Check the daily schedule and buy tickets at the marina.

🎊 Festivals & Events

Senhor Jesus das Chagas   RELIGIOUS
(⊘ 4 May) On 4 May, a procession stops twice to bless the land and four times to bless the sea, carrying an image of Christ that is said to have appeared on the beach in the

16th century (usually kept in Misericórdia church).

Cabo Espichel Festival RELIGIOUS

(☉ Sep) Spectacularly set, this festival celebrates an alleged apparition of the Virgin Mary during the 15th century; an image of the Virgin is carried through the parishes, ending at the Cape. It takes place on the last Sunday in September.

🛏 Sleeping

Forte do Cavalo CAMPGROUND €

(📞 212 288 508; www.cm-sesimbra.pt; Parque Municipal de Campismo, Forte do Cavalo; campsites per adult/tent/car €3/3.10/2; ☉ closed Jan; 🛜) Camp under the pines at this hilltop municipal site, 1km west of town. It has outrageous sea views, a restaurant and a kids' playground.

Sana Sesimbra HOTEL €€€

(📞 212 289 000; www.sesimbra.sanahotels.com; Avenida 25 de Abril 11; d with/without sea view €190/160, ste from €250; 🅿❄🛜♨) Overlooking the sea, the modern Sana has attractive violet-trimmed rooms with big windows that overlook the ocean or the town and hills beyond (it's worth paying an extra €30 for the sea views). The newer rooftop pool, bar and hot tub add to the appeal – and stopping for a drink even if you don't stay here is a wise traveller decision.

It's in a good central location, a short stroll east of Fortaleza de Santiago.

🍴 Eating

Sea-foodies are in heaven in Sesimbra. Here, what swims in the Atlantic in the morning, lands on plates by midday. Check out the fish restaurants by the waterfront just east of the fort.

Isaías SEAFOOD €

(📞 914 574 373; Rua Coronel Barreto 2; mains €8-12; ☉ noon-4pm & 7-10pm Mon-Sat; 🛜) No menu, no frills, just *the* tastiest grilled fish and cheapest plonk in town at this *tasca* run with love and prowess by Senhor Isaías' surviving son Carlos, grandson Thiago and chip-maven Maria. Sole, sardines, swordfish (your boneless choice) – it's all uniformly delicious. Simple perfection.

★ Casa Mateus SEAFOOD €€

(📞 963 650 939; www.casamateus.pt; Largo Anselmo Braamcamp 4; mains €13-19; ☉ noon-3.30pm & 7-10pm Tue-Sun; 🛜) Upgrade from ubiquitous grilled fish at this cosy dining room drenched in hardwood and old stone. In 2013, husband, wife and son team Carlos, Cristina and Pedro resurrected a 55-year-old family business originally shuttered in 1982 – and took it to soaring new heights. They do wonderful, creative things with seafood.

The grouper with bacon, clams and sweet potatoes is stunning, but order envy will descend upon you over the seafood green curry and the razor clams with lemon, olive oil and cilantro. Whatever you do, don't skip the fascinating basil mousse for dessert, either. Reservations are a must on weekends and summer – it's a small place.

ℹ Information

The helpful **tourist office** (📞 212 288 540; www.visitsesimbra.pt; Fortaleza de Santiago; ☉ 9.30am-11.30pm), rebranded as Yes SeS!Mbra, is located inside Fortaleza de Santiago. A smaller **office** (Praia Moinho de Baixo; ☉ 10am-6pm Wed-Sun Jul & Aug) operates in July and August in Praia Moinho do Baixo (Praia do Meco).

ℹ Getting There & Away

Buses 207 and 260 operated by **Transportes Sul do Tejo** (www.tsuldotejo.pt) leave from Lisbon's Praça de Espanha (€4.45, 60 to 90 minutes); bus 230 from Setúbal (€3.75, 45 minutes); and bus 203 from Cacilhas (€4, around one hour). Buses 201 and 205 from Sesimbra make less frequent runs to the village of Azóia (€2.40, 20 minutes), about 3km before Cabo Espichel, and on to the cape just twice a day (€2.75, 25 minutes, 1.50pm and 2.50pm).

DINO PAWS

Step back 150 million years while hunting for the footprints of dinosaurs on the craggy limestone cliffs just north of Cabo Espichel. The clearly visible imprints are near the small cove of Praia dos Lagosteiros. Rare and remarkably well preserved, the tracks date to the Late Jurassic age when this area was the stomping ground of four-legged, long-necked, herbivorous sauropods. Apparently, they were first discovered in the 13th century by fishermen who believed they were made by a giant mule that carried Our Lady of the Cape. Kids and dinosaur fans should take a short ramble to see how many footprints they can find.

WORTH A TRIP

PARQUE NATURAL DA ARRÁBIDA

Thickly green, hilly and edged by gleaming, clean, golden beaches and chiselled cliffs, the Parque Natural da Arrábida stretches along the southeastern coast of the Setúbal Peninsula from Setúbal to Sesimbra. Covering the 35km-long Serra da Arrábida mountain ridge, this is a protected area rich in Mediterranean plants, from olive, pistachio and strawberry to lavender, thyme and camomile, with attendant butterflies, beetles and birds (especially birds of prey such as eagles and kestrels), and 70 types of seaweed. Its pine-brushed hills are also home to deer and wild boar.

Highlights of Parque Natural da Arrábida are the long, golden beaches of windsurfer hotspot Figueirinha and the sheltered bay of Galapo. Most stunning of all is Portinho da Arrábida, with fine sand, azure waters and a small 17th-century fort built to protect the monks from Barbary pirates.

Don't miss Convento da Arrábida (☑ 212 197 620; www.foriente.pt; Apartado 28; €5; ☺ Wed-Sun by appointment only), a 16th-century former monastery overlooking the sea just north of Portinho (call ahead to schedule a visit). It's burrowed into the hillside in dramatic fashion.

Public transport through the middle of the park is nonexistent; some buses serve the beach from July to September (around four daily to Figueirinha).

Your best option is to rent a car or motorcycle, or take an organised trip by jeep and/or boat. Be warned: parking is tricky near the beaches, even in low season.

The **bus terminal** (☑ 707 508 509; www.tsuldotejo.pt) is a straight-shot 250m north of the Fortaleza on Av da Liberdade.

Setúbal

The thriving port town of Setúbal (*shtoo-bahl*) makes a terrific base for exploring the region's natural assets. Top of the must-do list is a cruise to the marshy wetlands of the Sado estuary, the splashy playground of bottlenose dolphins, flocks of white storks (spring and summer), and wintering flamingos that make the water fizz like pink champagne. You can hike or bike along the dramatic, pine-brushed coastline of Parque Natural da Arrábida, or simply soak up rays on nearby sandy beaches.

Back in town, it's worth taking a stroll through the squares in the pedestrianised old town and clambering up to the hilltop fortress for views over the estuary. The fish reeled the Romans to Setúbal in 412, so it's no surprise that seafood here is delicious. On Avenida Luísa Todi, locals happily while away hours polishing off enormous platters of *choco frito* and carafes of white wine.

◉ Sights

Reserva Natural do Estuário do Sado   NATURE RESERVE
(www.icnf.pt) FREE This natural reserve protects the Sado Estuary, a biologically rich area of wetlands extending east and south of Setúbal. With more than 250 avian species, this is a prime spot for birdwatching. The little-visited Moinho de Maré da Mouriscas (www.mun-setubal.pt/pt/pagina/moinho-de-mare-da-mourisca/280; ☺ 9.30am-7.30pm Tue-Fri, 8.30am-8.30pm Sat & Sun Mar-Sep, 10am-6pm Tue-Fri, to 7.30pm Sat & Sun Oct, 10am-5pm Tue-Sun Nov-Feb) FREE, 8km east of Setúbal, has short walking trails and a bird observatory across the mudflats.

Casa da Cultura   CULTURAL CENTRE
(☑ 265 236 168; www.casadacultura-setubal.pt; Rua de Trás da Guarda 26; ☺ 10am-midnight Tue-Thu, to 1am Fri & Sat, to 10pm Sun) FREE This newish art space has a packed cultural calendar. Wander through changing exhibitions on the main floor, or stop in for an evening concert of jazz trios, classical quartets and world music. The cinema upstairs has a mix of European art-house fare, children's animated films and documentaries.

Prices are reasonable: exhibitions are free; films and concerts range from free to €7. Stop in the Cafe das Artes for a drink and to see what's on.

Convento de Jesus   CHURCH
(Rua Acácio Barradas 2; ☺ 10am-6pm Tue-Sat, 3-7pm Sun) FREE Setúbal's man-made wonder is this sand-coloured stunner, the first known example of Manueline architecture, adorned with gargoyles and twirling turrets.

Around the altar, 18th-century blue-and-white geometric *azulejos* contrast strikingly with the curling arches of the roof. Constructed in 1490, the church was designed by Diogo de Boitaca, better known for his later work on Belém's fantastical Mosteiro dos Jerónimos.

At time of research it was closed for extensive renovations and was due to re-open in 2019.

Castelo de São Filipe
CASTLE

(Estrada Castelo de São Filipe; ⊙10am-midnight Jun–mid-Sep, to 8pm Sun-Thu, to midnight Fri & Sat mid-Sep–May) FREE Worth the 500m schlep uphill to the west, the castle was built by Filipe I in 1590 to fend off an English attack on the invincible Armada. Converted into a *pousada* in the 1960s, its hulking ramparts afford precipitous views, and its chapel is festooned in blue-and-white 18th-century *azulejos*. It reopened in 2017 after stabilisation renovations.

Praça do Bocage
PLAZA

(Praça do Bocage) All streets in the pedestrianised old town seem to lead to this mosaic-cobbled square, presided over by the arcaded bright-purple town hall. It's a sunny spot for a wander amid the palms and fountains, or for coffee and people-watching on one of the pavement terraces.

Museu do Trabalho Michel Giacometti
MUSEUM

(www.patrimoniocultural.gov.pt/pt/museus-e-monumentos/rede-portuguesa/m/museu-do-trabalho-michel-giacometti; Largo Defensores da República; adult/child €1.50/free; ⊙9.30am-6pm Mon-Fri, 2-7pm Sat & Sun Jun–mid-Sep, 9.30am-6pm Tue-Fri, 2-6pm Sat & Sun mid-Sep–May) How does the sardine get in the tin and 1001 other fishy mysteries are solved at this quirky, rarely visited museum, set in a former sardine-canning factory. There's also an entire 1920s grocery store, transported from Lisbon wholesale.

English signage has been added, as well as poignant exhibitions on female factory workers, and young workers killed by the GNR (National Republican Guard, or police) while protesting workers' rights.

🏖 Beaches

While Setúbal itself is a little underwhelming, the coastal scenery outside town is spectacular. Don't miss the chiselled cliffs,

pine-brushed hills and picturesque beaches of Parque Natural da Arrábida.

Alternatively, it's an easy 20-minute ferry ride – look out for dolphins along the way – to Tróia (and its nouveau-rich playground of a marina) where the soft, sandy beaches are flanked by dunes.

☞ Tours

Cruises & Dolphin Watching

A highlight of any trip to Setúbal is the chance to spot resident bottlenose dolphins on a cruise of the Reserva Natural do Estuário do Sado (p152). The playful dolphins show off their dorsal fins to a happy-snappy crowd; listen for their high-pitched clicking. Plenty of companies run half-day trips around the estuary (leaving from Doca do Comércio, aka Doca das Fontainhas). Book ahead.

Vertigem Azul
WILDLIFE WATCHING

(☎265 238 000; www.vertigemazul.com; Rua Praia da Saúde 11D; adult/child €35/20; ⊙9am-1pm & 2-6pm) ✪ Offers sustainable three-hour dolphin-watching tours in the Sado estuary.

Troiacruze
BOATING

(☎962 405 933; www.troiacruze.com; ⊙9am-1pm & 2-5pm daily Apr-Oct, Mon-Fri Nov-Mar) Offers regular dolphin-spotting tours (€35) at 10.30am, 2.30pm and 5.30pm daily, plus summer sunset cruises; other cruises, such as sailing a galleon along the Sado estuary, are by reservation.

Rotas do Sal
WILDLIFE WATCHING

(☎938 122 190; www.rotasdosal.pt; tours from €15) Runs dolphin-spotting river tours as well as birdwatching and other cultural tours.

Walking Tours

Sistemas de Ar Livre
WALKING

(SAL; ☎265 227 685; www.sal.pt; per person from €8) ✪ This ecotourism company arranges activities including three-hour guided walks in or around Setúbal, Lisbon and Alentejo on weekends throughout summer.

Cycling Tours

GoperSports (☎265 501 621; www.gopersports.pt; Estrada de Palmela 15, Loja D; half/full day €10/15; ⊙10am-1pm & 3-7.30pm Mon-Fri, to 6pm Sat) offers several half-day bike tours in the surrounding nature.

Wine Tours

For detailed info on all the wine producers you can visit in the area, the tourist office

Setúbal

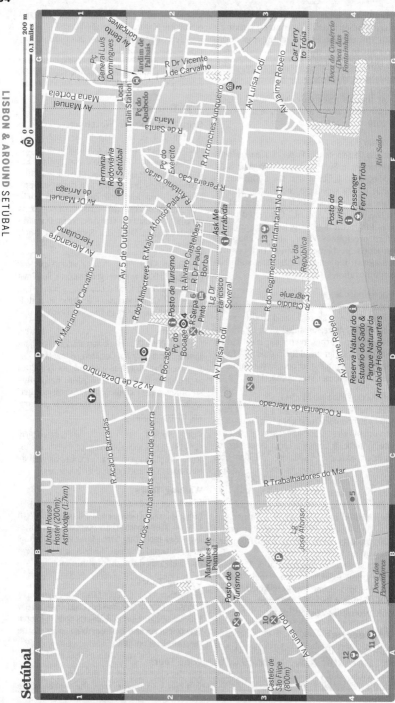

0 0 200 m
0 0.1 miles

Castelo de São Filipe (800m);

Urban House Hostel (200m); Astrolodge (1.7km);

Av dos Combatents da Grande Guerra

R Acácio Barradas

Av Mariano de Carvalho

Av Alexandre Herculano

Av Dr Manuel de Arriaga

Terminal Rodoviária de Setúbal

Pç General Luis Domingues

Av Bento Gonçalves

Jardim de Palhais

R Dr Vicente J de Carvalho

Av Manuel Maria Portela

Local Train Station

Pç do Quebedo

R de Santa Maria

Pç do Exército

R Arronches Junqueiro

Av Luisa Todi

Car Ferry to Tróia

Doca do Comércio (Doca das Fontainhas)

Rio Sado

Posto de Turismo

Passenger Ferry to Tróia

Pç da República

R do Regimento de Infantaria No 11

R Cláudio Lagrange

Av Jaime Rebelo

Reserva Natural do Estuário do Sado & Parque Natural da Arrábida Headquarters

R Ocidental do Mercado

R Trabalhadores do Mar

Doca dos Pescadores

Lg José Afonso

Pç Marques de Pombal

Av Luísa Todi

Av 22 de Dezembro

R dos Almocreves

R Major Afonso Pala

R António Pala

R Pereira Cao

Ask Me Arrábida

R Bocage

Pç do Bocage

R Dr Paulo Borba

R Álvaro Castelões

R Serpa Pinto

Lg Dr Francisco Soveral

Av Luísa Todi

Av 5 de Outubro

Posto de Turismo

Posto de Turismo

Posto de Turismo

Setúbal

usually has a free leaflet from the *Rota de Vinhos Península de Setúbal*. If not, check online at www.rotavinhospsetubal.com.

José Maria da Fonseca WINE
(☑266 197 500; www.jmf.pt; Rua José Augusto Coelho 11, Vila Nogueira de Azeitão; tours with tastings €3.20-10.50; ☺tours 10am-noon & 2.30-5.30pm Apr-Oct, to 4.30pm Nov-Mar, shop 10am-7pm Apr-Oct, to 5.30pm Nov-Mar) Wine lovers shouldn't miss the cellar tours of José Maria da Fonseca, the oldest Portuguese producer of table wine and Moscatel de Setúbal, in nearby Vila Nogueira de Azeitão. The winery is now run by the sixth generation of the family. From Setúbal, buses leave frequently to Vila Nogueira de Azeitão (20 minutes).

Tours are run in English and Portuguese (and sometimes Spanish and French). Booking ahead is essential in summer.

🛏 Sleeping

★**De Pedra e Sal Hostel & Suites** HOSTEL €
(☑265 418 353; www.depedraesal.com; Largo Dr Francisco Soveral 10; dm €25, d with/without bathroom €80/60; ✲☏) Setúbal's best hostel is flush with gorgeous hardwoods and subtle but well-thought-out design touches (Smeg refrigerators, seafaring art, fishing nets and globe-encased seashells). Dorm beds (book ahead – there are only 10) feature privacy screens, and the downstairs restaurant is very popular. Hip young owners can hook

you up with wine and coasteering tours, among others.

Urban House Hostel HOSTEL €
(☑917 813 089; www.facebook.com/urbanhouse.setubal; Avenida Gen Daniel de Sousa 75; dm €17.50; ☏☎) Inside a converted family home dating to the '60s a few clicks north of the centre, is this design-forward, nautical-themed hostel. Friendly owner Augusto runs a tight ship. There isn't a rowdy party vibe, but it's a good bet for those looking for longer-term accommodation surrounded by a thoughtfully curated, family atmosphere.

Astrolodge TENTED CAMP €€
(☑961 901 305; www.facebook.com/astrolodge1; Estrada das Machadas de Cima, Quinta Santo António do Galvão; €75-90; ☏☎🛒) It's not quite glamping but it's a step up from roughing it as well. Astrolodge features a dozen or so tented camps with comfy beds; excellent bathrooms (one in a shipping container) and a social, vaguely hippie-esque common area with wi-fi and charging station. It's nicely positioned between Setúbal and Parque Natural da Arrábida.

Tróia Design Hotel RESORT €€€
(☑265 498 000; www.troiadesignhotel.com; Marina de Tróia, Tróia; d from €189; ☏✲☎🛒) From its jarring, nonlinear glass facade to its ubermodern vibe, this 236-room luxury resort is Tróia's attempt at high style. It has a vertigo-inducing glass atrium and a gigantic high-heel art installation by Joana Vasconcelos, made with pots and pans. It can feel forced, but trendsetters won't baulk at the sleek rooms with deep, free-standing bathtubs and impressive sea views.

🍴 Eating

Head to the western end of Avenida Luísa Todi, where al fresco restaurants serve fresh-from-the-Atlantic seafood. Be sure to sample the local speciality, *chocos fritos* (fried cuttlefish) washed down with sweet Moscatel de Setúbal wine; and the *caldeiradas* are quite popular here as well.

O Pescador II SEAFOOD €
(☑265 533 369; www.facebook.com/opescador2; Travessia Álvaro Anes 8; mains €8-12.50; ☺noon-3pm Mon, noon-3pm & 7-10pm Wed-Sun; ☎) With tables sprawled along a lane a block or two back from the main drag, this simple but immensely authentic seafooder ain't much for manners and pleasantries, but you'd be

hard-pressed to find a better deal on simple seafood chargrilled over hot coals.

Taifa

THAI €

(☑265 231 642; www.facebook.com/taifa.setubal; Avenida Luísa Todi 558; mains €9-12; ☉11am-2am Sun & Tue-Thu, 1pm-4am Fri & Sat; ☎📶) A nice break from seafood, Taifa is a jazzy little cafe with outdoor tables and an eclectic menu that includes a limited but good menu of pad thai and red and green curries, Belgian beers and fragrant gin and tonics. The soundtrack is equally diverse, encompassing blues, folk, swing, soul and salsa.

Delice Garden

CAFE €

(www.facebook.com/delicegarden; Praça do Bocage; light meals €3-6; ☉8.30am-midnight, to 7pm winter; ☎) This cute little cafe offers the best vantage point for optimal people-watching and Instagram-ready plaza views. It does good crepes, bruschettas, croissants, pitchers of sangria and gin and tonics, etc.

Mercado do Livramento

MARKET €

(Avenida Luísa Todi 163; ☉7am-2pm Wed-Sun) Amid life-size statues of vendors (fruit sellers, fishmongers etc), you can assemble a first-rate picnic at this enticing cast-iron market: cheese, olives, bread, seasonal fruits and more.

🍷 Drinking & Nightlife

★Corktale

WINE BAR

(www.facebook.com/corktale; Rua Plácido Stichini 2; ☉6pm-2am Tue-Sun; ☎) This hip wine bar has lost a bit of lustre by no longer employing a sommelier, but its well-stocked inventory of 125 or so boutique wines means it's still got a lot going for it, and it is a great, somewhat sophisticated place for pairing experiences with regional cheeses and tapas (€4 to €8.50). Wines by the glass cater to all budgets (€4 to €25).

Roof61

COCKTAIL BAR

(www.facebook.com/roof61; Avenida Luísa Todi 61, 6th fl; ☉4pm-1am Tue-Thu, to 2am Fri & Sat, 3-9pm Sun; ☎) What a view! You can practically see beachgoers slathering on the sunscreen in Tróia from this upscale 6th-floor cocktail bar's open-air patio. DJs spin deep house from an epic retro yellow stereo cabinet, and the bartenders are adept at a bevy of house cocktails and great G&Ts (€7 to €12).

Absurdo

LOUNGE

(www.barabsurdo.com; Avenida José Mourinho 24; ☉4pm-midnight Tue-Thu, to 6am Fri & Sat; ☎) The trendiest spot in town is your weekend must, when the outdoor patio here rocks and rolls until sunrise. Absurdo is where you'll find Setúbal's bold and beautiful, sipping excellent cocktails and struggling to be heard over live cover/tribute bands (last Friday of the month) or DJs (every Friday and Saturday).

ℹ Information

Hospital São Bernardo (☑265 549 000; Rua Camilo Castelo Branco) Near the Praça de Touros, off Avenida Dom João II.

Police (Polícia de Segurança Pública; ☑265 522 022; www.psp.pt; Avenida Luísa Todi 350)

TOURIST INFORMATION

Ask Me Arrábida (Regional Turismo; ☑265 009 993; www.askmelisboa.com/arrabida; Travessa Frei Gaspar 10; ☉10am-1pm & 2-7pm Apr-Sep, 10am-1pm & 2-6pm Oct-Mar) Has a glass floor revealing the remains of a Roman garum (fish-condiment) factory. Hands out leaflets on the area.

Posto de Turismo (Casa da Baía - Centro de Promoção Turística; ☑265 545 010; www. visitsetubal.com.pt; Avenida Luísa Todi 468; ☉9am-midnight daily Jun–mid-Sep, to 8pm Sun-Thu, to midnight Fri & Sat mid-Sep–May) Excellent municipal tourism information about Setúbal and attractions in the surrounding countryside. You'll find smaller info points near the **passenger ferry** (www.visitsetubal.com.pt; Avenida Jaime Rebelo; ☉10am-1pm & 2-5pm) to Tróia and at **City Hall** (☑265 541 551; www. visitsetubal.com.pt; Praça do Bocage, Câmara Municipal; ☉9am-7pm Mon-Fri, 10am-1pm & 3-7pm Sat), Castelo de São Filipe, Moinho de Maré da Mouriscas and in Azeitão.

Reserva Natural do Estuário do Sado & Parque Natural da Arrábida Headquarters (☑265 544 140; www.icnf.pt; Praça da República; ☉9am-1pm & 2-6pm Mon-Fri) Stop here for information books and souvenirs.

ℹ Getting There & Away

BOAT

Passenger-only catamarans (☑265 235 101; www.atlanticferries.pt; adult/child return €4.15/2.80; ☎) to Tróia depart half-hourly to hourly every day (adult/child return €8.85/4.70) from 6.20am to 4am. Note that you will also need to purchase a Viva Viagem transport card (€0.50) if you don't already have one.

Car ferries (265 235 101; www.atlantic ferries.pt; car/additional passengers €15.50/3.60;) run from 7.30am to 11.15pm. Note that car ferries, catamarans and cruises all have different departure points.

BUS

Transportes Sul do Tejo (www.tsuldotejo. pt) bus 561 (express) runs between Setúbal and Lisbon's Praça de Espanha (€4, 45 to 90 minutes, half-hourly to hourly) – or bus 783 from Cacilhas (€4.25, 50 minutes, 11 daily Monday to Friday). Services drop off considerably in winter.

Setúbal's **bus terminal** (707 508 509; www.tsuldotejo.pt; Av Dr Manuel de Arriaga 2), operated by Transportes Sul do Tejo, is 650m or so north of Praça da República, but there are on-again, off-again plans in the works for a new terminal – Estação Intermodal de Setúbal – which will be joined with the train station at Praça do Brasil.

TRAIN

From Lisbon's Sete Rios station at least six IC trains run daily to Setúbal (€10 to €17.60, one hour), with a change at Pinhal Novo. You can also catch a frequent ferry from Lisbon's Terreiro do Paço terminal to Barreiro station (€2.90, 30 minutes, every 10 to 30 minutes, 5.45am to 2am), from where there are cheaper, frequent *urbano* (urban) trains to Setúbal (€2.25, 30 minutes).

ⓘ Getting Around

Most sights are within easy walking distance of the pedestrianised centre. The bus station is about 150m north of the centre; the main train station is 700m north of the centre. Frequent ferries shuttle across the Rio Sado to the Tróia peninsula from terminals around Doca do Comércio.

Cycling is a great way to discover the coast at your own pace. Hire a bike from GoperSports (p153).

Car-rental agencies include **Avis** (265 538 710; www.avis.com; Avenida Luísa Todi 96; 9am-1pm & 3-7pm Mon-Fri, 9am-1pm Sat).

LISBON & AROUND SETÚBAL

The Algarve

Why Go?

Soaring cliffs, sea caves, golden beaches and sandy islands draw over four million visitors to the Algarve each year. Surrounded on two sides by the Atlantic, it's a paradise for surfers, especially along the undeveloped west coast.

In the south, tourist hotspots harbouring massive conglomerations of holiday villas and brash resorts have action-packed activities – from splashy water parks to water sports – and vibrant nightlife spanning beach bars to sizzling nightclubs. Natural treasures here include the bird-filled lagoons and islands of the protected Parque Natural da Ria Formosa (p164), stretching for 60km from west of the capital, Faro, to the enchanting fishing village of Cacela Velha (p178).

Up in the hilly hinterland are historic castle towns and whitewashed villages, rolling countryside covered in cork, carob and almond trees and citrus orchards, rural farmhouse restaurants, and the wonderful Via Algarviana (p181) hiking trail crossing the region's breadth.

Best Places to Eat

➜ Vila Joya (p187)

➜ A Eira do Mel (p208)

➜ Restaurante O Barradas (p191)

➜ Kiosk Agapito (p213)

Best Places to Stay

➜ Vila Monte (p171)

➜ Pousada do Palácio de Estoi (p169)

➜ Casa d'Alagoa (p165)

➜ B&B Candelária (p185)

When to Go
Lagos

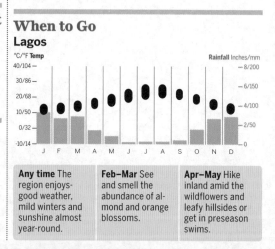

Any time The region enjoys good weather, mild winters and sunshine almost year-round.

Feb–Mar See and smell the abundance of almond and orange blossoms.

Apr–May Hike inland amid the wildflowers and leafy hillsides or get in preseason swims.

History

The Algarve has a long tradition of settlement. Phoenicians came first and established trading posts some 3000 years ago, followed by the Carthaginians. Next came the industrious Romans who, during their 400-year stay, grew wheat, barley and grapes and built roads and palaces. Check out the remains of Milreu, near Faro.

Then came the Visigoths and, in 711, the North African Moors. They stayed 500 years, although later Christians obliterated what they could of the era. Many place names come from this time and are easily recognised by the article 'al' (eg Albufeira, Aljezur, Alcoutim). The Syrian Moors called the region in which they settled (east of Faro to Seville, Spain) 'al-Gharb al-Andalus' (western Andalucía), later known as 'Algarve'. Another Arabic legacy is the flat-roofed house, originally used to dry almonds, figs and corn, and to escape the night heat. Trade, particularly in nuts and dried fruit, boomed and Silves was the mighty Moorish capital, quite independent of the large Muslim emirate to the east.

The Reconquista (Christian reconquest) began in the early 12th century, with the wealthy Algarve the ultimate goal. Though Dom Sancho I captured Silves and territories to the west in 1189, the Moors returned. Only in the first half of the 13th century did the Portuguese claw their way back for good.

Two centuries later the Algarve had its heyday. Prince Henry the Navigator chose the appropriately end-of-the-earth Sagres as the base for his school of navigation, and had ships built and staffed in Lagos for 15th-century explorations of Africa and Asia – seafaring triumphs that turned Portugal into a major imperial power.

While the huge seismic shock that hit Portugal in 1755 is usually known as the Lisbon earthquake, due to the massive damage and loss of life in the country's capital, its epicentre was actually 200km southwest of the Algarve. The region was devastated by the approximately 8.7-magnitude quake, and what was left along the coast was battered by the ensuing tsunami. Very few buildings survive from the pre-earthquake period, and those that did weather the quake generally needed extensive reconstruction. The Algarve is, hence, very rich in baroque architecture.

Since the arrival of Faro's international airport in the 1960s, tourism in the region has boomed, anchoring the local economy.

ⓘ Dangers & Annoyances

➜ Petty theft is prevalent. *Never* leave valuables unattended in the car or on the beach.

➜ Especially on the west coast, beware of dangerous ocean currents and strong winds. Check beaches' coloured flags: chequered means the beach is unsupervised, red means it's currently unsafe, yellow means paddle but don't swim, and green means it's safe to swim. Blue means the beach is safe and clean.

➜ Cliff instability is a problem, especially heading westwards from Lagos. Erosion is ongoing and serious rock falls and smaller landslides can occur. Heed the signs at the beaches and along the cliffs.

ⓘ Getting There & Away

Air Faro's international airport (p168) is the region's main gateway, with numerous flights, including by budget operators, serving the UK and Europe.

Bus A good bus network runs along the Algarve coast and to Loulé. From here, you can access inland Algarve, although services become more limited. Two big bus companies, Eva (www.eva-bus.com) and Rede Expressos (www.rede-expressos.pt), zip frequently between the Algarve and elsewhere in Portugal. Smaller lines include Frota Azul (www.frotazul-algarve.pt).

Car Most main towns have reliable car-hire outlets; companies can usually provide an electronic road-toll tag so tolls are automatically added to your rental bill. Comprehensive toll information, including a calculator and payment options, is listed at www.portugaltolls.com.

Train Trains (www.cp.pt) run along the coast between Faro and Vila Real de Santo António, and Faro and Lagos (and Loulé). Express trains run to/from the region's main towns to Lisbon.

Faro

POP 64,600

The Algarve's capital has a more distinctly Portuguese feel than most resort towns. Many visitors only pass through this underrated city, which is a pity, as it makes for an enjoyable stopover. It has an attractive marina, well-maintained parks and plazas, and a picturesque *cidade velha* (old town) ringed by medieval walls. The old town's winding, cobbled pedestrian streets, squares and buildings were reconstructed in a melange of styles following successive batterings – first by marauding British and then by two big earthquakes – and are home to museums, churches, a bone chapel and al fresco cafes.

The Algarve Highlights

① Cabo de São Vicente (p207) Catching technicolour sunsets from the cliffs of mainland Europe's most southwesterly point.

② Parque Natural da Ria Formosa (p164) Spotting rare birdlife in the marshes, salt pans, lagoons and dune islands of this 60km-long nature reserve.

③ Serra do Caldeirão (p184) Scaling the 479m-high limestone Rocha da Pena in this protected inland area.

④ Lagos (p195) Exploring seafaring Lagos' historic walled old town, brilliant beaches and spirited nightlife.

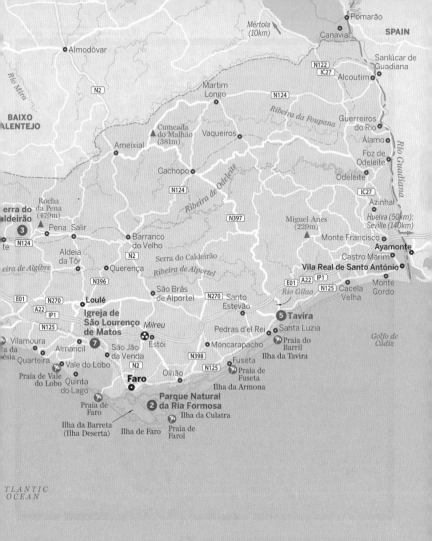

5 Tavira (p172) Wandering charming Tavira's hilltop castle ruins, riverbanks, cobbled alleyways and shaded squares.

6 Benagil Caves (p188) Cruising or kayaking to this sea cave with a hole in its roof outside Carvoeiro.

7 Igreja de São Lourenço de Matos (p184) Marvelling at the traditional blue-and-white-tiled interior of this baroque church near Loulé.

8 Carrapateira (p210) Riding the waves at the west coast's top surf spot.

Faro

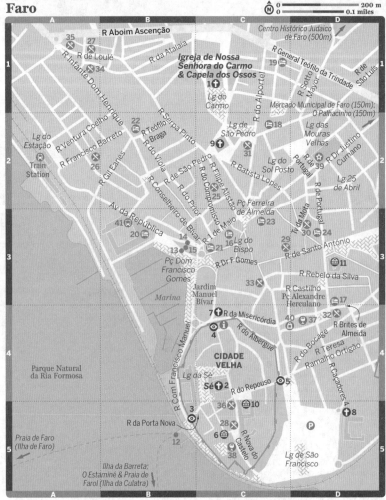

On Faro's doorstep are the lagoons of the Parque Natural da Ria Formosa and nearby beaches, including the islands of Ilha de Faro to the southwest and Ilha da Barreta (aka Ilha Deserta) to the south.

◉ Sights

◉ Cidade Velha

Enter the Cidade Velha (Old Town) through the neoclassical **Arco da Vila** (Rua da Misericórdia 8; ⊙ tower 9am-6pm) **FREE**, built in 1812 by order of Bishop Francisco Gomes do Avelar, who oversaw the city's reconstruction after the 1755 earthquake.

★ Sé   CATHEDRAL
(www.paroquiasedefaro.org; Largo da Sé; adult/child €3/free; ⊙10am-6pm Mon-Fri, 10am-1pm Sat Jun-Sep, 10am-5.30pm Mon-Fri, 10am-1pm Sat Oct-May) The centrepiece of the Cidade Velha, the *sé* was completed in 1251 but heavily damaged in the 1755 earthquake. What you see now is a variety of Renaissance, Gothic and baroque features. Climb the tower for lovely views across the walled town and estuary islands. The cathedral also houses the **Museu Capitular**, with an assortment of chalices, priestly vestments and grisly relics (including both forearms of St

Faro

THE ALGARVE FARO

Boniface), and a small 18th-century shrine built of bones.

The blocky, castle-like cathedral occupies what was probably the site of a Roman temple, then later a Visigoth cathedral and a Moorish mosque. Only the tower gate and several chapels remain of the original Romanesque-Gothic exterior – the rest was obliterated in 1755. The interior has very elaborate baroque side altarpieces, and the altar itself is flanked by matching vaulted Gothic chapels. The baroque pipe organ was built in 1715 by Johann Heinrich Hulenkampf.

Museu Municipal   MUSEUM
(☏ 289 870 827; www.cm-faro.pt; Praça Dom Afonso III 14; adult/child €2/free; ⊙10am-7pm Mon-Fri, 11.30am-6pm Sat & Sun Jun-Sep, 10am-6pm Mon-Fri, 10.30am-5pm Sat & Sun Oct-May) Faro's domed 16th-century Renaissance Convento de Nossa Senhora da Assunção, in what was once the Jewish quarter, houses the town's local history museum. Highlights include the 3rd-century *Mosaic of the Ocean*, found in 1976; 9th- to 13th-century domestic Islamic artefacts; and works by a notable Faro painter, Carlos Filipe Porfírio, depicting local legends. English-language leaflets detail key exhibits, including the *Paths of the Roman Algarve*, displaying monumental Roman-laid stones. The museum hosts regular fado (traditional song) performances.

◉ Elsewhere in Faro

★**Igreja de Nossa Senhora do Carmo & Capela dos Ossos**   CHURCH
(www.diocese-algarve.pt; Largo do Carmo; €2; ⊙church 9am-6pm Mon-Fri, 9am-1pm Sat Jun-Sep, 9am-5pm Mon-Fri, 9am-1pm Sat Oct-May, chapel 10am-1pm & 3-5.30pm Mon-Fri, 10am-1pm Sat year-round) One of the Algarve's most dazzling churches, this twin-towered baroque masterpiece was completed in 1719 under João V. After the 1755 earthquake, its spectacular facade was paid for with Brazilian gold, and the interior is gilded to the extreme, with numerous cherubs. Accessed through the church at the back, the 19th-century **Capela dos Ossos** is built from the bones and skulls of over 1000 monks as a reminder of earthly impermanence. It's quite a sight.

Museu Regional do Algarve   MUSEUM

(☑289 870 893; www.cm-faro.pt; Praça da Liberdade 2; adult/child €1.50/free; ◷10am-1.30pm & 2.30-6pm Mon-Fri) Three of the four halls at this worthwhile museum house exhibitions on rural life in the Algarve, including mock-ups of 19th-century shops and rooms, a real fishing boat, some impressively woven creations in wicker, bamboo and palm leaves, and lots of rag rugs and fishing nets. The fourth hall is always given over to a temporary show on a folksy local theme.

Igreja de São Francisco   CHURCH

(www.faro.ofs.pt; Largo de São Francisco; ◷8am-7pm) The foundations of this monastery's church were laid in 1679 and it was enlarged during the 18th and 19th centuries. Behind its blinding white facade are dazzling woodwork and a frenzied 18th-century baroque interior with hand-painted *azulejo* tiles on the walls and a barrel-vaulted ceiling depicting the life of St Francis.

Igreja de São Pedro   CHURCH

(www.paroquiasaopedro-faro.org; Largo de São Pedro; ◷8.30am-12.30pm & 3-7pm Mon-Sat, 9.30am-noon Sun) While the exterior of this 16th-century church is unassuming, the trinave interior has magnificent 18th-century *azulejos* and intricately carved woodwork, including a rococo altar.

Centro Histórico
Judaico de Faro   CEMETERY, MUSEUM

(Faro Jewish Heritage Centre; ☑289 829 525; www.cm-faro.pt; Estrada da Penha; admission by donation; ◷9.30am-12.30pm & 2-5pm Mon-Fri) The last vestiges of the first post-Inquisition Jewish presence in Portugal are found at this small Jewish cemetery. In use between 1838 and 1932, and restored in 1992, it has 76 beautiful marble gravestones. The site also has a tiny museum and re-created synagogue (complete with a reconstructed wedding and bar mitzvah). You're shown a DVD (in English), then given a detailed, interesting tour. It's behind the football stadium Estádio de São Luis, 1.3km northeast of the centre.

◉ Beaches & Nature Reserves

On the Ilha de Faro, 9km west, the town's beach, **Praia de Faro** (Ilha de Faro), has sweeping sand and windsurfing operators.

Ferries (p164) go out to **Praia de Farol** (on Ilha da Culatra) and **Ilha da Barreta**, a stunning, remote strip of sand just off the mainland where environmentally friendly restaurant Estaminé (p167) is built on boardwalks and run by solar power.

★ Parque Natural
da Ria Formosa   NATURE RESERVE

(www.icnf.pt) Encompassing 18,000 hectares, this sizeable system of lagoons and islands stretches for 60km along the Algarve coastline from west of Faro to Cacela Velha. It encloses a vast area of *sapal* (marsh), *salinas* (salt pans), creeks and dune islands. The marshes are an important area for migrating and nesting birds. You can see a huge variety of wading birds, along with ducks, shorebirds, gulls and terns. It's the favoured nesting place of the little tern and the rare purple gallinule.

🏃 Activities

San Lorenzo   GOLF

(☑289 396 522; www.sanlorenzogolfcourse.com; Quinta do Lobo; green fees €190) Past the airport, 19km west of Faro, this par-72 course is one of the Algarve's finest, with a stunning oceanside setting bordering the Ria Formosa, pine woodland and fairways planted with Bermuda grass. Club and buggy hire are available, as well as lessons.

🗘 Tours

★ Animaris   CRUISE

(☑918 779 155; www.ilha-deserta.com; Rua Comandante Francisco Manuel; return ferry/speedboat €5/10, 1hr boat trip from €27.50; ◷10am-4.45pm) 🖉 Animaris runs trips to Ilha da Barreta. Ferries take 45 minutes, while speedboats zip across in 15 minutes. Animaris also runs year-round guided boat trips through Parque Natural da Ria Formosa, dropping you at the island to return by ferry or speedboat at your own pace. Boats leave from the pier next to Arco da Porta Nova.

★ Formosamar   CRUISE, KAYAKING

(☑918 720 002; www.formosamar.com; Avenida da República, Stand 1, Faro Marina) 🖉 This recommended outfit promotes environmentally responsible tourism. Among its excellent tours are two-hour birdwatching trips around the Parque Natural da Ria Formosa (€25), dolphin watching (€45), cycling (€37) and a two-hour kayak tour negotiating some of the narrower lagoon channels (€35). All trips have a minimum number of participants (usually two to four).

WILDLIFE OF THE ALGARVE

With five special protection areas (a birding initiative), eight special areas of conservation, two natural parks and one natural reserve – not to forget its sea life – the Algarve is one of the most flora- and fauna-rich regions of the country. The purple gallinule (aka the western swamphen or sultana bird) is one of Europe's rarest and most nattily turned-out birds – a large violet-blue water creature with a red bill and legs. In Portugal it only nests in a patch of wetland spilling into the exclusive Quinta do Lago estate, at the western end of the Parque Natural da Ria Formosa (p164), 12km west of Faro. Look for it near the lake at the estate's São Lourenço Nature Trail.

Another eye-catching Algarve resident is the Mediterranean chameleon, a 20cm- to 35cm-long reptile with independently moving eyes, a tongue longer than its body and skin that mimics its environment. It's the only chameleon found in Europe, its habitat limited to Crete and the Iberian Peninsula. Your best chance of seeing this shy creature is on spring mornings in the Quinta Marim area of the Parque Natural da Ria Formosa or in Monte Gordo's conifer woods, now a protected habitat for the species.

Bird-lovers should consider a trip to the Serra do Caldeirão (p184) foothills. The dramatic Rocha da Pena, a 479m-high limestone outcrop, is a classified site because of its rich flora and fauna. Orchids, narcissi and native cistus cover the slopes, where red foxes and Egyptian mongooses are common. Among many bird species seen here are the huge eagle owl, the Bonelli's eagle and the buzzard.

There's a *centro ambiental* (environmental centre) in Pena village, and you can walk up to the top of Rocha itself.

Formosamar also hires kayaks (half/full day €35/45), bikes (€12/20) and fishing gear (€12/17). It has departures from Olhão and Tavira, too, and various ticket offices around the Faro waterfront.

Natura Algarve   CRUISE
(☑918 056 674; www.natura-algarve.com; Avenida da República, Stand 2, Faro Marina) 🖉 This ecoresponsible operator offers a range of trips, from all-day tours exploring the Ria Formosa (€52 excluding lunch, 5½ hours) to two-hour dolphin trips (€45), 2½-hour birdwatching trips (€35) and the popular 'Natura' trip – a 3½-hour interpretative tour covering history, traditions and the local economy (€30), exploring the canals as well as nearby Ilha da Culatra.

Lands   TOURS
(☑914 539 511; www.lands.pt; Avenida da República, Stand 3, Faro Marina) 🖉 Lands runs 45-minute solar boat tours (€15), two-hour kayak tours (€35) and guided walks including birdwatching (from €120 for up to four people), all with an environmental slant. It also hires out kayaks (half/full day €35/45) for you to explore Ria Formosa on your own. Four-hour sailing trips for up to six people cost €400.

🎋 Festivals & Events

Festa da Ria Formosa   FOOD & DRINK
(www.cm-faro.pt; ⊙late Jul-early Aug) This 11-day-long event held at the height of summer is one for seafood-lovers. Fishers and others set up stalls and prepare their wares, from crustaceans to other ocean delights, at the Largo de São Francisco. Concerts add to the fun atmosphere.

FolkFaro   MUSIC
(www.folkfaro.com; ⊙mid-Aug) The city's big folk festival features lots of dance (with local and international folk groups), live music and street fests over eight days at various venues around town.

Feira de Santa Iria   RELIGIOUS
(www.cm-faro.pt) Faro's biggest traditional event honours St Irene with fairground rides, stalls and entertainment. It takes place over nine days in the second half of October in a large parking area, the Largo de São Francisco, on the eastern side of the old town.

🛏 Sleeping

Faro has it all, from four-star comfort to crash-pad *residenciais,* hostels and campgrounds in the surrounding area. Outside high season, prices can more than halve.

★ Casa d'Alagoa   HOSTEL €
(☑289 813 252; www.farohostel.com; Praça Alexandre Herculano 27; dm/d from €22/92; 🛜) A renovated mansion on a pretty square houses this cool, laid-back hostel. Great facilities include a lounge with long, sociable tables and

ⓘ FINDING A BED

During July and August, thousands of Portuguese and foreign visitors flock to the Algarve. Faro airport – the region's main transport hub – receives multiple inbound flights daily. During this time, most visitors have prebooked package accommodation. For the independent traveller, it can be tricky to find a bed with no reservation; try to reserve a night or two in advance. Prices, too, are at their highest. In most places you can expect to pay considerably less in *mais tranquilo* (calmer) times. Check hotel websites for special deals.

beanbags, an upstairs terrace, barbecue and communal kitchen, plus on-site bike hire. There's a range of clean, spacious dorms (larger dorms have balconies) and en suite doubles.

Pensão Residencial Central   GUESTHOUSE €
(☏ 289 807 291; Largo do Bispo 12; s/d not incl breakfast €40/50; ⚶) The eight rooms at this small guesthouse are cool and tiled, and vary in size. They come with small bathrooms and gentle courtesy from the owners. Rooms with balconies overlook the pretty square; rooms at the back are quieter.

A Doca   GUESTHOUSE €€
(☏ 289 820 716; www.residencialadoca.com; Rua 1 de Maio 21; s/d/tr €60/65/90; ⊛⚶) This spotless guesthouse does the basics well – the wi-fi is strong, the beds comfortable and staff are on hand 24 hours a day. Simply furnished rooms are small – the double beds fill them out – but some have balconies, and the location, near the waterfront, is superb. Look for the blue sign with an anchor.

Hotel Eva   HOTEL €€€
(☏ 289 540 154; www.ap-hotelsresorts.com; Avenida da República 1; s/d/ste from €110/131/196; ⊛⚶⚱) Upmarket Eva has 134 spacious, contemporary rooms, with rates varying according to whether the view from the window is of the sea, marina or town; the best have balconies. Stunning views also extend from the rooftop, with a swimming pool and outdoor cocktail bar, though this level closes from November to April.

Hotel Faro   HOTEL €€€
(☏ 289 830 830; www.hotelfaro.pt; Praça Dr Francisco Gomes 2; d/ste/f from €144/295/325;

Ⓟ⊛⚶⚱) With an unbeatable location on the main square overlooking the marina, this modern cubist-style block has small but stylish rooms with large, comfortable beds. The top-floor gourmet restaurant and bar opens to a wraparound terrace that's ideal for a sunset cocktail; excellent breakfasts are also served here. There's a rooftop pool and a gym. Multilingual staff are professional and genuine.

✕ Eating

Faro's restaurants are big on seafood, though there are also plenty of alternatives spanning Portuguese and international cuisines. Faro's large **mercado municipal** (www.mercadomunicipaldefaro.pt; Largo Francisco Sá Carneiro; ⊘ stalls 7am-3pm Mon-Sat; ⚶) is in Largo Mercado.

A Venda   PORTUGUESE €
(Rua Do Compromisso 60; dishes €4-9; ⊘1-3pm & 7.30-11pm Tue-Sat) Homestyle Portuguese food at bargain prices – Monchique blood sausage stew; fava bean fritters with smoked paprika sauce – and a retro interior with an ancient tiled floor, mismatched furniture and antique glass display cases make this backstreet place a red-hot favourite with local students. DJs often spin on summer nights.

Gengibre e Canela   VEGETARIAN €
(Travessa da Mota 10; buffet €7.50; ⊘noon-3pm Mon-Sat; ⚶✐) Arrive early before this cosy spot fills to capacity (it doesn't take reservations) and its all-you-can-eat vegetarian buffet starts running low. Each day there are four main dishes (including a couple of curries) along with salads; wine and desserts are extra. Cash only.

Pastelaria Coelho   PORTUGUESE €
(Rua Brites de Almeida 2; mains €4.50-8; ⊘7.30am-12.30am) This deceptive spot looks like a *pastelaria* (pastry and cake shop) from the outside, yet inside it morphs into a restaurant, serving hearty Portuguese home cooking for a song, including tuna steaks, seafood *açorda* (stew) and roast pork. Locals rate it very highly.

★ Vila Adentro   PORTUGUESE €€
(☏ 933 052 173; www.vilaadentro.pt; Praça Dom Afonso III 17; mains €9-17.50, cataplanas €39-49; ⊘9am-midnight; ⚑) With tables on the square in Faro's old town and a dining room decorated with floor-to-ceiling *azulejos*, this Moorish 15th-century building is a romantic

spot for elevated Portuguese cuisine: pork, clam and lobster *cataplanas* (stew) for two, chargrilled octopus with fig and carob sauce, and tangerine-stuffed pork filet. Wines hail from around the country.

Restaurante Madeirense
MADEIRAN €€

(📞967 168 140; www.facebook.com/restaurante-madeirensefamilia; Rua 1 Dezembro 28; mains €8-17; ⊗noon-10.30pm Tue-Sun) For an exotic take on Portuguese cuisine, this small Madeiran restaurant bangs down plates loaded with specialities you'll only get on the Island of Eternal Spring. *Espada* (scabbard fish), *bolo de caco* (potato bread) and *pudim de maracuja* (maracuja pudding) are just some of the treats on offer; round things off with a *poncha* (sugar-cane liqueur) or sweet Madeira wine.

Restaurante O Murta
SEAFOOD €€

(📞289 823 480; www.facebook.com/OMurta; Rua Infante Dom Henrique 136; mains €8-13.50, cataplanas €25-35; ⊗noon-3.30pm & 7.30-10.30pm Mon-Sat) This simple place has been here for decades, so it must be doing something right. It grills quality meat and fish, and prepares excellent seafood dishes such as *açorda de marisco* (seafood stew in a bread bowl) and its signature *bacalhau* (salt-cod) dish, prepared with piri-piri and chilli, as well as *cataplanas* for two.

Faz Gostos
PORTUGUESE €€€

(📞914 133 668; www.fazgostos.com; Rua do Castelo 13; mains €12-25; ⊗noon-3pm & 6.30-10pm Sun-Fri, 6.30-10pm Sat; 🐾) Sophisticated twists on Portuguese classics at this stylish restaurant in the old town might include *xarém* (maize porridge) with Ria Formosa clams, steamed sea bass with olive oil–poached potatoes, cornbread-topped cod, or chorizo-stuffed pork loin with fig sauce, depending on what's in season. Presentation is exquisite. The cellar has over 250 Portuguese wines.

Estaminé
SEAFOOD €€€

(📞917 811 856; www.estamine.deserta.pt; Ilha da Barreta; mains €18-28; ⊗10am-6pm) 🐾 Built to look like a crab when viewed from above, this remote restaurant rises up on boardwalks from the Ilha da Barreta as its sole building. It's an entirely self-sufficient operation, using 100% solar power and desalinated water. Fresh-as-it-gets seafood dishes span Ria Formosa oysters, cracked crab and lobster to char-grilled prawns and fish, and aromatic stews.

🍷 Drinking & Entertainment

Fuelled by its 8000-strong student population, Faro's nightlife scene clusters in Rua do Prior and the surrounding alleys. Bars and clubs open most days till late, though things pick up considerably at weekends.

★ O Castelo
BAR

(www.facebook.com/OCasteloBar.CidadeVelha. Faro; Rua do Castelo 11; ⊗10.30am-4am Wed-Mon; 🐾) O Castelo is all things to all people: bar, restaurant, club and performance space. Its location atop the old town walls provides stunning Ria Formosa views, especially at sunset. Beers, wine and cocktails are accompanied by tapas such as flambéed chorizo and local cheeses.

Epicur
WINE BAR

(📞914 614 612; www.epicur.wine; Rua Alexandre Herculano 22; ⊗5pm-midnight Tue-Sat) Over 250 Portuguese wines are stocked at this stylish wine bar (which opened in 2018), 30 of them by the glass. All of the country's major wine regions are represented, including the Algarve. Pair them with *presunto* (charcuterie), tinned fish, local cheeses and Ria Formosa oysters. There are regular meet-the-winemakers events; you can also buy bottles to take home.

Teatro Lethes
THEATRE

(📞289 878 908; www.actateatro.org.pt/teatro lethes; Rua de Portugal 58; ⊗box office 2-6pm Tue-Fri, 8-9.30pm performance days) Faro's tiny and exquisite Italianate theatre hosts drama, music and dance performances. Adapted into a theatre in 1874 (from a building dating back to 1603), it was once the Jesuit Colégio de Santiago Maior. Check its website or ask the tourist office for a list of what's on; you can buy tickets online (though you'll need to print them).

🛍 Shopping

Chocolates de Beatriz
CHOCOLATE

(📞289 820 358; www.chocolatesdebeatriz.com; Rua Veríssimo de Almeida 5; ⊗10am-1pm & 3-7pm Tue-Sat) 🐾 Chocolates made in Odemira in the neighbouring Alentejo region are enticingly displayed in glass cabinets at this little shop. Dark, milk and white chocolates have fillings such as Portuguese-harvested sea salt, fig paste, *medronho* (strawberry-tree liqueur) or Algarve oranges. Walk through and you'll find a tiny cafe where you can sit down for a hot chocolate and treats on site.

88

88

THE ALGARVE FARO

Algarve Rock

DRINKS

(📞 289 815 203; www.algarverock.com; Unidade B, Parq Vale da Venda; ⏰ 9am-5pm Mon-Fri) 🍺 The Algarve's first craft brewery opened in 2018, producing organic, preservative-free, vegan brews inspired by the region, such as piri-piri pilsner and carob stout. It's located in an industrial estate 6.5km northwest of Faro. At the time of writing, tours and tastings (per person €25) were for groups only (call to confirm), but you can buy direct from the brewery.

ℹ️ Information

Turismo (www.visitalgarve.pt; Rua da Misericórdia 8; ⏰ 9.30am-1pm & 2-5.30pm; 📞) Efficient office at the edge of the old town.

Turismo de Aeroporto Internacional (📞 289 818 582; www.visitalgarve.pt; ⏰ 8am-11pm) Based at Faro airport and one of a series of offices run by Algarve Tourism around the region; good for basic information on arrival.

ℹ️ Getting There & Away

AIR

Faro Airport (FAO; 📞 289 800 800; www.aeroportofaro.pt; 📞) is 7km west of the centre.

TAP (Air Portugal; 📞 202 015 051; www.flytap.com) has multiple daily Lisbon–Faro flights (40 minutes).

Internationally there are many flights a day to/from regional airports across the UK and Europe, with additional seasonal and charter services in summer.

BUS

Buses arrive at and depart from the **bus station** (📞 289 899 760; Avenida da República 5), on the northern side of the marina. Most services are run by **Eva** (📞 289 899 760; www.eva-bus.com).

Destinations include the following.

Albufeira (€4.85, 55 minutes to 90 minutes, up to three per hour). Has express and slower services. Slower services include Portimão (€5.70, 1¾ hours) and Lagos (€6.05, 2¼ hours).

Lisbon (€20, 3¼ hours, six per day)

Loulé (€3.35, 40 minutes, at least hourly)

Olhão (€3.35, 20 minutes, up to four per hour)

São Brás de Alportel (€4.25, 40 minutes, 10 daily) via Estói (€3.35, 20 minutes)

Seville, Spain (€20, 3½ hours, two daily) via Huelva (€16, 2½ hours)

Vila Real de Santo António (€5.70, 1¾ hours, nine daily) via **Tavira** (€4.45, one hour)

CAR & MOTORCYCLE

The most direct route from Lisbon to Faro along the E1 takes about 2½ hours (depending on traffic). An alternative to the motorway is the often traffic-clogged A22/N120. Tolls apply on both routes; see www.portugaltolls.com for information including payment options.

Faro's easiest parking is in Largo de São Francisco (free).

Major car-hire agencies are at the airport.

Auto Jardim (📞 289 818 491; www.autocar-hire.net)

Auto Rent (📞 289 818 580; www.autorent.pt)

Guerin (📞 289 889 445; www.guerin.pt; Faro)

TRAIN

Faro's train station is 500m northwest of the centre.

There are five direct trains from Lisbon daily (€22.90, four hours). You can also get to Porto (€42.40, six to eight hours, four daily), sometimes changing at Lisbon.

Regional services include the following.

Albufeira (€3.35, 30 minutes, every two hours).

Lagos (€7.30, 1¾ hours, every two hours).

Vila Real de Santo António (€5.25, 1¼ hours, hourly) via Olhão (€1.45, 10 minutes).

ℹ️ Getting Around

TO/FROM THE AIRPORT

Faro Airport's manageable size and proximity to the town centre, just 7km to the airport's east, makes arriving here a breeze.

Próximo (📞 289 899 700; www.proximo.pt) city buses 14 and 16 run to the bus station (€2.25, 20 minutes, half-hourly June to August, slightly less frequently in low season). From here it's an easy stroll to the centre.

A taxi into town costs around €20 (20% more after 10pm and on weekends), plus around €2 for each luggage item.

BICYCLE

You can hire bikes (including kids' bikes) from Formosamar (p164) (per hour/day €6/20).

BOAT

Animaris (p164) operates year-round ferry services, both fast (€20 return) and slow (€10 return) to/from Ilha da Barreta. Schedules vary seasonally.

BUS

Buses for Praia de Faro (€2.30, 20 minutes, up to two per hour) depart alongside the bus station (p168).

TAXI

Ring 289 895 795 for a taxi or find one at the ranks outside the train and bus stations, and at the airport.

Estói & Milreu

POP 3500

Charming Estói is best known for its 18th-century rococo palace and gardens, which have been renovated into a *pousada*. Even if you're not staying here, you can visit its public areas and gardens.

The village centres on a pretty square dominated by a 16th-century church. Situated 850m west are the Roman ruins at Milreu.

Milreu Ruins   RUINS

(☑289 997 823; www.monumentosdoalgarve. pt; Rua de Faro; adult/child €2/free; ☺10.30am-1pm & 2-6.30pm May-Sep, 9.30am-1pm & 2-5pm Oct-Apr) Situated 900m west of Estói, these Roman villa ruins are so large and grand they were originally thought to have been a town. The villa, inhabited from the 1st century AD, has the characteristic peristyle form, with a gallery of columns around a courtyard. The highlight is the temple devoted to a water deity, the fish mosaics and former central pool. At the entrance is a small museum with a scale model of the temple in its glory days.

The fish mosaics in the bathing chambers (to the west of the villa's courtyard) provide a tantalising glimpse of the villa's former glory. The remains of the bathing rooms also include the *apodyterium* (changing room; note the arched niches and benches for clothes and postbath massage) and the *frigidarium,* which had a marble basin to hold cold water for cooling off after a bath.

Other luxuries included underground heating and marble sculptures (now displayed at Faro's Museu Municipal (p163)).

In the 6th century the temple was converted into a church, and a small mausoleum was added, and in the 8th century it was converted into a mosque. In the 10th century it collapsed, possibly due to an earthquake, and the site was abandoned. In the 15th century, a farmhouse was constructed within the abandoned site (the house, much modified, is still there today).

Faro–Estói buses stop at the site.

★ Pousada do
Palácio de Estoi   HISTORIC HOTEL €€€

(☑210 407 620; www.pousadas.pt; Rua São José; d/ste from €135/215; P 🕸 🛜 🌊) Built between the 1840s and 1909, this sumptuous rococo-style palace with a coral-pink facade is set in formal Versailles-style gardens.

Nonguests can visit its ornately frescoed drawing rooms opening to a terrace. Its 63 rooms are in a modern wing integrated into the hillside, topped by grass-covered roofs. There's a spa, indoor and outdoor pools, and an upmarket Portuguese/European restaurant.

★ Loja Canastra   FOOD & DRINKS

(www.facebook.com/canastraestoi; Rua do Pé da Cruz 59; ☺10.30am-2pm & 3-7pm Tue-Fri, 10am-2.30pm Sat) 🏷 Not only can you buy exquisite jams, chutneys, preserves, honeys, olive oils, carob powder and products, dried herbs, tinned fish, local wines and liqueurs (including carob, fig, almond and strawberry tree varieties) at this little emporium, the owner can provide fascinating insights into their origins and traditional (often medicinal) uses over the centuries.

ℹ️ Getting There & Away

Eva buses (www.eva-bus.com) run from Faro (€3.35, 25 minutes, 10 daily Monday to Friday, five Saturday, three Sunday), continuing on to São Brás de Alportel (€2.35, 10 minutes).

São Brás De Alportel

POP 10,700

The quiet country town of São Brás de Alportel (SBA) provides a welcome break from the coast. While there are few attractions in the town proper, it's a pleasant place to stroll. Excellent activities in the surrounding area include a guided cork walking route. SBA was a hotspot in the 19th-century heyday of cork, and there are still 10 prospering factories around the town. It lies in a valley in the olive-, carob-, fig- and almond-wooded Barrocal region, a lush limestone area between the mountains and the sea.

🅾️ Sights & Activities

★ Museu do Traje   MUSEUM

(☑289 840 100; www.museu-sbras.com; Rua Dr José Dias Sancho 61; adult/child €2/free; ☺10am-1pm & 2-5pm Mon-Fri, 2-5pm Sat & Sun) Encased in *azulejos*, this museum occupies a former cork magnate's mansion, which retains its original kitchen. It displays an ever-changing exhibition of local costumes, of which there are 15,000 in the museum store (free two-hour tours of the store take place on the last Tuesday of the month). The outbuildings have a presentation on the local cork industry, a huge collection of old carriages, an art gallery (hosting regular music events, including fado) and a cafe.

Nova Cortiça
FACTORY

(☑ 289 840 150; www.novacortica.pt; Parque Industrial da Barracha; tour €12.50; ☺ tours by reservation 10am-3.30pm Mon-Fri) On these fascinating cork factory tours, you'll learn about the tree's life cycle, harvesting and the manufacturing process, from drying to the production of wine and champagne corks. It also showcases other uses for the versatile material, such as clothing, footwear, bags and even furniture. Guided tours last 90 minutes and are in English and Portuguese.

Calçadinha de São Brás de Alportel
ROMAN SITE

(Rua Calçadinha Romana) Constructed during Roman times, this ancient road is thought to have linked Faro (Ossonoba) with Beja (Pax Julia). It was used by mules and shepherds until the 19th century. You can wander along two branches – one is 100m long, the other 500m. Contextual information is available at the interpretive centre Centro da Calçadinha (☑ 289 840 004; www.cm-sbras.pt; Rua do Matadouro 2; ☺ 9.30am-1pm & 2-5.30pm Mon-Sat) FREE, which can provide free guided tours on request.

Algarve Rotas
WALKING, TOURS

(☑ 965 561 166; www.algarverotas.com; tours/workshops from €15/28) English-speaking guides lead interactive cork tours that might include visiting a traditional cork factory, viewing cork stacks or planting your own cork tree. En route, you'll learn about the industry, from the extraction of cork from the trees to its production, processes and use. Workshops teach you to make cork items such as jewellery. Minimum two participants; meeting points vary.

🎎 Festivals & Events

Feira da Serra
FAIR

(http://feiradaserra.cm-sbras.pt; ☺ late Jul) This down-home country fair sells locally produced cheese and meats, cakes, wine and carob and almond liqueurs; there are also games for the kids and folkloric song and dance performances. It takes place over four days at sporting fields on the north side of town.

🛏 Sleeping & Eating

Hospedaria São Brás
GUESTHOUSE €€

(☑ 919 999 756; Rua Luís Bívar 27; s/d/tr/f €35/69/89/130; ✸ 🛜) In a tiled mansion-style town house, this guesthouse is jam-packed with antiques (including a gramophone), pretty *azulejos* and plants, opening to a vine-draped garden with a lemon tree. By contrast, bedrooms are sparsely furnished but comfortable (note that only some have air conditioning).

Pastelaria O Ervilha
CAFE €

(Largo de São Sebastião 7; pastries & cakes €1-3.60, sandwiches €2.50-4.50; ☺ 8am-8pm Tue-Sun; 🛜) Overlooking the square In the centre of town, this São Brás institution has been around since 1952. Pastries and cakes made on the premises include *tarte de alfarroba e amendôas* (carob, fig and almond tart) and *bolo de laranja* (orange syrup sponge); it also serves sandwiches and strong coffee.

Ysconderijo
INTERNATIONAL €€

(☑ 289 849 520; Rua Gago Coutinho 47; mains €13-19; ☺ kitchen 7-10pm, bar to midnight Tue-Sat) In a contemporary dining room with brick arches, timber tables and ivory-coloured chairs, Ysconderijo is popular with international visitors for elegantly presented dishes such as lamb cutlets with roast forest mushrooms, bacon-wrapped steak with sweet potato mash, and almond-crusted salmon. Reservations are recommended in summer, and you'll need to bring cash as you can't pay by card.

ℹ Information

Ponte de Informacão Turística (☑ 289 840 000; www.cm-sbras.pt; Rua Dr Victorino Passos Pinto 3; ☺ 9am-1pm & 2-5pm Mon-Fri) The municipality's tourist point is next to the public swimming pool.

Turismo (☑ 289 843 165; www.visitalgarve.pt; Largo de São Sebastião 23; ☺ 9.30am-12.30pm & 1.30-5.30pm Mon-Fri) Distributes maps and information on the region and town.

ℹ Getting There & Away

Buses run to/from Faro (€4.25, 40 minutes, nine daily) via Estói, (€1.35, 10 minutes) and to Loulé (€3.35, 25 minutes, up to four daily).

Olhão

POP 14,900

Olhão (pronounced *ol-yowng*) is the Algarve's biggest fishing port, with an active waterfront and pretty, bustling lanes in its old quarters. There aren't many sights, but the flat-roofed, Moorish-influenced neighbourhoods and North African feel make it a charming place to wander. The town's fish restaurants draw the crowds, as does the morning fish and vegetable market, best visited on Saturday.

Olhão is also a springboard for Parque Natural da Ria Formosa's sandy islands, Culatra and Armona, and the park's environmental centre at Quinta de Marim.

Sights & Activities

Fine beaches, sparsely sprinkled with holiday chalets, include those on the sandbank *ilhas* of Parque Natural da Ria Formosa: Ilha de Farol, Ilha da Culatra and Ilha da Armona. Ferries (p172) to the islands depart year-round from the pier just east of Jardim Patrão Joaquim Lopes, with frequent services in summer.

Monterosa Olive Oil   FARM
(☑289 790 441; www.monterosa-oliveoil.com; Horta do Felix, Moncarapacho; tours adult/child €7/3.50; ☺tours by reservation 10am Tue-Fri) Hour-long tours at this gold medal–winning olive oil producer take you around part of the 20-hectare estate showing you the five different varieties of olive trees that are handpicked in autumn, and the Roman-era press in a granite mill where the fruit is ground to a paste before the oil is extracted and filtered, finishing with a tasting. Even if you're not doing a tour, you can stop by its onsite shop to buy oils to take home.

Quinta de Marim   NATURE RESERVE
(www.natural.pt; Quelfes; ☺8am-8pm Mon-Fri, 10am-8pm Sat & Sun Jun-Sep 9am-noon & 2-5pm daily Oct-May) Situated 2.5km east of Olhão is the beautiful 60-hectare Centro Educação Ambiental de Marim (commonly known as Quinta de Marim). A 3km trail takes you through various ecosystems – dunes, salt marshes, pine woodlands – as well as to a wildlife rescue centre and a historic water mill. Chameleons and purple gallinule birds are among the rare local species. The Parque Natural da Ria Formosa headquarters and environmental centre are also here.

Festivals & Events

Festival do Marisco   FOOD & DRINK
(www.festivaldomarisco.com; ☺mid-Aug) One of southern Portugal's livelier festivals, this two-week seafood celebration features all the great Algarvian oceanic dishes, including *caldeirada* and *cataplana*. Bands add to the fun. It's held in the Jardim Pescador Olhanense, just west of the markets.

Sleeping

Pensão Bicuar   GUESTHOUSE €
(☑289 714 816; www.pensionbicuar.com; Rua Vasco da Gama 5; d with shared bathroom from €39.60, d/f from €44.10/52.20; ☺) Right in the heart of town, this guesthouse has a fantastic rooftop terrace with fiery sunset views, a handy guest kitchen and charming rooms with carved dark-wood furniture and patchwork quilts. Some rooms have bathrooms, others don't; a few have small balconies. The family room sleeps four, with two double beds.

O Tartufo   B&B €€
(☑289 791 218; www.otartufo.com; Sitio do Gião 41, Moncarapacho; d with shared bathroom from €90, d from €100, apt from €110; ☺mid-Apr–mid-Oct; ☐☺) An old *quinta* (farmhouse) has been converted into seven bohemian rooms (three of which share bathrooms) and a self-catering apartment. Guests have access to a communal kitchen. Surrounding the property, the lovely garden has hammocks, mosaic paths and fountains. It's 12km northeast of Olhão. Minimum stay is three nights.

★Vila Monte   BOUTIQUE HOTEL €€€
(☑289 790 790; www.vilamonte.com; Sitio dos Caliços, Moncarapacho; d/ste from €396/513; ☐☀☺☺) ☺ Set over nine hectares of olive groves, orange orchards and gardens blazing with bougainvillea, this stunningly designed farmhouse estate 11km northeast of Olhão has 55 rustic-contemporary guestrooms with terracotta floors, whitewashed walls and handwoven fabrics. There are two splendid restaurants (one tapas, one gastronomy) utilising estate-grown produce, two outdoor swimming pools, a tennis court and a shop selling regional products.

Eating

The seafront Avenida 5 de Outubro has a market and is lined with touristy seafood restaurants serving *cataplanas* and *xerém* (cornflour mash similar to polenta with clams, sardines and bacon); more local options hide in the old town's tangle of lanes.

Tacho à Mesa   PORTUGUESE €€
(☑961 624 577; www.facebook.com/tachoamesaolhao; Rua dos Lavadouros 46; mains €7-15, cataplanas €28-34; ☺11am-3pm Mon, 11am-3pm & 7.30-10.30pm Tue-Sat, closed Jan; ☺) A white, modern interior is the stylish setting for first-rate traditional cooking using fresh produce purchased twice daily from the markets. Menu highlights include aromatic

cataplanas, super-juicy *bochechas de porco* (pork cheeks) and other Algarvian-Alentejan dishes. Wines come from all over Portugal, with a few from Spain. Book ahead in summer.

Tasca o Galo PORTUGUESE €€
(✆964 709 746; Rua a Gazeta de Olhão 7; mains €8-18; ☺6pm-midnight Mon-Sat, closed Jan & Feb) Just back from the seafront, this converted merchant's store has just 22 seats, so advance bookings are a good idea. Begin with award-winning olive oil and bread before dining on homemade dishes like *cataplanas*, piri-piri prawns, roast rabbit loin with cherry jus, and charred Algarve orange with pepper honey and rosemary brittle for dessert.

🛍 Shopping

Mercados Municipais MARKET
(Avenida 5 de Outubro; ☺7am-2pm Mon-Sat) By the water, these two noble centenarian red-brick buildings are excellent examples of industrial architecture and house picturesque traditional fruit and fish markets that are worth a look at any time but are especially appealing on a Saturday morning. A string of simple seafood stalls and cafes makes them an atmospheric spot for a bite with water views.

ℹ Information

Turismo (✆289 713 936; www.visitalgarve.pt; Largo Sebastião Martins Mestre 6; ☺9am-5pm Tue-Thu, 9am-1pm & 2-5.30pm Fri-Mon) In the centre of the pedestrian zone.

ℹ Getting There & Away

BUS

Eva (www.eva-bus.com) buses run to Faro (€3.35, 20 minutes, up to two per hour), Lisbon (€20, 3¾ hours, four daily) and Tavira (€4.25, 40 minutes, every two hours).

TRAIN

Regular trains run to Faro (€1.45, 10 minutes, 10 daily) and east to Fuseta (€1.45, 10 minutes, hourly) and Tavira (€2.35, 25 minutes, hourly).

ℹ Getting Around

Handy municipal buses run 'green and yellow routes' around town, including to the campground and supermarkets.
Ferries (Avenida 5 de Outubro) run out to the *ilhas* from the pier at the eastern end of Jardim Patrão Joaquim Lopes.

Ilha da Armona (€6 return, 20 minutes) Hourly July and August, every two hours September to June.

Ilha da Culatra (€6 return, 30 minutes) Hourly July and August, every two hours September to June.

Ilha do Farol (€7 return, one hour) Hourly June to August, four daily September to May.

Tavira

POP 26,200

Set on either side of the meandering Rio Gilão, Tavira is arguably the Algarve's most charming town. The ruins of a hilltop castle, an old Roman bridge and a smattering of Gothic and Renaissance churches are among its historic attractions. An enticing assortment of restaurants and guesthouses makes it an excellent base for exploring the Algarve's eastern reaches.

Tavira is ideal for wandering; the warren of cobblestone streets hides leafy gardens and shady squares. There's a small, active fishing port and a modern market. Only 3km from the coast, Tavira is the launching point for the stunning, unspoilt beaches of Ilha de Tavira.

History

The Roman settlement of Balsa was just down the road from Tavira, near Santa Luzia (3km southwest). Ponte Romana, the seven-arched bridge the Romans built at Tavira (which was then called Tabira), was an important link in the route between Baesuris (Castro Marim) and Ossonoba (Faro).

In the 8th century the Moors occupied Tavira. They built the castle, probably on the site of a Roman fortress, and two mosques. In 1242 Dom Paio Peres Correia reconquered the town. Those Moors who remained were segregated into the *mouraria* (segregated Moorish quarter) outside the town walls.

As the Portuguese port closest to the Moroccan coast, Tavira became important during the Age of Discovery, serving as a base for expeditions to North Africa, with a hospital, and supplying provisions (especially salt, wine and dried fish). Its maritime trade also expanded, with exports of salted fish, almonds, figs and wine to northern Europe. By 1520 it had become the Algarve's most populated settlement and was raised to the rank of city.

Decline began in the early 17th century when the North African campaign was abandoned and the Rio Gilão became so silted up that large boats couldn't enter the port. Then the plague struck in 1645, followed by the 1755 earthquake.

After briefly producing carpets in the late 18th century, Tavira found a more stable income in its tuna fishing and canning industry, although this too declined in the 1950s. Today, tourists have taken the place of fish as the biggest source of town income.

◉ Sights

Enter the old town through the **Porta de Dom Manuel**, a stone archway that is one of the few surviving sections of the former city walls, built in 1520 when Dom Manuel I made Tavira a city.

◉ Old Town

Camera Obscura Tower   LANDMARK
(Torre da Tavira; www.torredetavira.com; Calçada da Galeria 12; adult/child €4/2; ⊙10am-5pm Mon-Fri, to 1pm Sat Jul-Sep, 10am-5pm Mon-Fri Feb-Jun, to 4pm Oct-Jan) Rising 100m high, the Torre da Tavira was formerly the town's water tower and now houses a camera obscura at the top, reached by a lift. A simple but ingenious object, the camera obscura reveals a 360-degree panoramic view of Tavira, its monuments and local events, in real time – all while you remain stationary.

Igreja de Santa Maria do Castelo   CHURCH
(www.diocese-algarve.pt; Calçada da Galeria; €2; ⊙10am-1pm & 2-5pm Mon-Fri 10am-1pm Sat) Built in Gothic style over a mosque, then rebuilt by an Italian neoclassicist following earthquake damage 500 years later, this church by the castle retains original elements – namely the main doorway, two side chapels and Arabic-style windows in the clock tower. Inside, a plaque marks the tomb of Dom Paio Peres Correia, who took the town back from the Moors, and those of the seven Christian knights whose killing by the Moors precipitated the final attack on Tavira.

Igreja da Misericórdia   CHURCH
(www.diocese-algarve.pt; Largo da Misericórdia; church incl museum €2, fado performances €8; ⊙10am-12.30pm & 3-6.30pm Tue-Sat Jul & Aug, 9.30am-12.30pm & 2-5.30pm Tue-Sat Sep-Jun, fado performances 3.15pm Sat year-round) Built between 1541 and 1551, this church is the Algarve's most important Renaissance monument, with a magnificent carved, arched doorway. Inside, the restrained Renaissance arches contrast with the cherub-festooned baroque altar and enormous panels of *azulejos* depicting the works of mercy. Fado performances are sublime here.

Behind is a museum with salvers, chalices, and a hall with an interesting 18th-century applewood ceiling and elegant furniture.

Castelo   CASTLE
(Largo Abu-Otmane; ⊙8am-5pm Mon-Fri, 9am-7pm Sat & Sun, to 5pm winter) FREE Tavira's ruined castle rises high and mighty above the town. Possibly dating back to Neolithic times, the structure was rebuilt by Phoenicians and later taken over by the Moors; most of what now stands is a 17th-century reconstruction. The interior contains an exotic botanic garden, and the octagonal tower affords fine views over Tavira. Note that the ramparts are without railings, so parents beware.

Ruínas Fenícias de Tavira   ARCHAEOLOGICAL SITE
(www.cm-tavira.pt; Calçada Dom Paio Peres Correia 4; ⊙24hr) FREE Astonishing archaeological remains found on this site just below the *castelo* date from the 8th century BC through to the 18th century AD. Digs have unearthed part of a Phoenician wall circa 800 BC, an ox-hide altar from the 4th century BC thought to be Turdetanian (the pre-Roman Iberian civilisation), Moorish foundations from the 12th century AD and a 17th-century Portuguese mansion.

Palácio da Galeria   MUSEUM
(Museu Municipal de Tavira; ☑281 320 540; www.cm-tavira.pt; Calçada da Galeria; adult/child €2/1, with Núcleo Islâmico €3/1.50; ⊙10am-12.30pm & 3-6pm Tue-Sat Apr-Oct, 9.15am-4.30pm Tue-Sat Nov-Mar) With oyster-grey baroque window mouldings and 16 hipped, terracotta-tiled roofs, this whitewashed, 16th-century palace now hosts a variety of exhibitions on a wide range of artistic and historical topics.

◉ Elsewhere in Tavira

Ponte Romana   BRIDGE
This seven-arched Roman Bridge that loops away from Praça da República may actually pre-date the Romans but is so named because it linked the Roman road from Castro Marim to Tavira. The structure you see dates from a 1667 reconstruction; it's been car-free since flood damage in 1989, but remains accessible to pedestrians.

Tavira

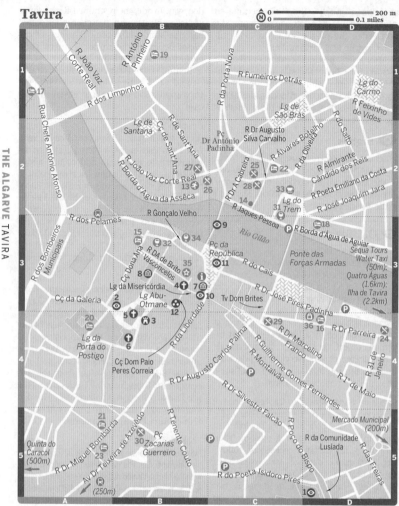

Núcleo Islâmico
MUSEUM

(☎281 320 570; www.cm-tavira.pt; Praça da República 5; adult/child €2/1, with Palácio da Galeria €3/1.50; ⊙9.15-12.30pm & 1.30-4.30pm Tue-Sun) Built around the remains of an Islamic-era structure, this small 21st-century museum exhibits impressive Islamic pieces discovered in various excavations around the old town. One of the most important finds on display is the Tavira vase, an elaborate ceramic work with figures and animals around the rim. Multilingual handouts are available at reception.

The top floor of the museum is dedicated to temporary exhibitions with a local theme.

Praça da República
SQUARE

For centuries this town square on the riverfront served as a promenade and a marketplace, where slaves were traded along with fish and fruit. Today a large part has been remodelled as an amphitheatre, and is covered with tables that spill from the square's many cafes.

Quatro Águas
AREA

You can walk 2km east along the river, past the fascinating, snowlike salt pans to Quatro Águas. The salt pans produce tip-top table salt and attract feeding birds in summer, including flamingos. It's the jumping-off point

Tavira

THE ALGARVE TAVIRA

for ferries to Ilha de Tavira and has a couple of simple seafood restaurants.

Santa Luzia   VILLAGE
The fishing village of Santa Luzia is effectively a district of Tavira these days, and it's a great place to wander to get a feel for typical Algarve life. Overlooking the channel that separates the mainland from the Ilha de Tavira, the village is famous for its *polvo* (octopus), which you can try in several restaurants. You'll often see fishers mending nets in their storage huts. Boat trips also leave from the waterfront here.

🏃 Activities

Kitesurf Eolis   KITESURFING
(☑ 962 337 285; www.kitesurfeolis.com; Rua Capitão Baptista Marçal 41, Cabanas de Tavira; ☉ 4hr kitesurfing lesson €100, 2hr kitebugging €65) Based at Cabanas de Tavira, 6km east of Tavira, this highly professional operator has kitesurfing classes, as well as 'kitebugging' (land-yacht–style kiting along the sand, aka 'blokarting') and SUP (stand-up paddleboarding) lessons and equipment hire.

Monte Rei   GOLF
(☑ 281 950 960; www.monte-rei.com; Sitio do Pocinho Sesmarias, Vila Nova de Cacela; green fees €218; ☉ 8am-6pm) Overlooking the Serra do Caldeirão mountains, Portugal's top-rated course, par-72 Monte Rei was created by golfing legend Jack Nicklaus. Designed to blend into the surrounding landscapes, it has rolling fairways lined with native grasses, trees and shrubs, sculpted white-sand bunkers, and lakes bordering 11 of its 18 holes. It's 15km northeast of Tavira.

🍴 Courses

⭐ **Taste Algarve**   COOKING
(☑ 281 098 209; www.tastealgarve.com; Monte do Álamo; 4hr class incl lunch or dinner from €75) 🌱
If you've fallen in love with Algarvian cooking, you can learn how to make specialities such as *petiscos, cataplanas* and local pastries at small-group classes (English available) run by this cookery school. It also runs food-oriented tours of local producers, market visits and foraging tours such as clam collecting in the Ria Formosa.

It also makes up gourmet picnic baskets by request, and has onsite guesthouse accommodation (doubles from €110) on its organic farm.

🧭 Tours

Passeios Ria Formosa   CRUISE
(☑ 962 156 922; www.passeios-ria-formosa.com; Avenida 28 de Maio, Cabanas de Tavira; ☉ 1hr cruise

€12.50, 90-min flamingo tour €20, 4hr octopus tour €30) Wildlife-spotting cruises from Cabanas de Tavira include an hour-long tour of the Ria Formosa protected area, a 90-minute flamingo-spotting tour and a four-hour octopus tour, stopping at Santa Luzia. The company also runs various boat trips departing directly from Santa Luzia, as well as Olhão and Fuseta.

🛏 Sleeping

Pousada de Juventude Tavira HOSTEL €
(📞 281 326 731; www.pousadasjuventude.pt; Rua Dr Miguel Bombarda 36; dm/d from €17.60/44; ☺ Jan-Nov; 🛜) Perfectly located for walking around town, just 100m south of the Castelo, this modern hostel is handy for budget travellers. Spacious dorms have only four beds, and private rooms have en suite bathrooms. Facilities include a sociable living room decked out in a Moorish theme, a self-catering kitchen and a guest laundry.

Casa Beleza do Sul GUESTHOUSE €€
(📞 960 060 906; www.casabelezadosul.com; Rua Dr Parreira 43; d/studio/ste not incl breakfast from €70/80/90; 🛜) A beautiful 19th-century town house now houses this chic guesthouse, comprising a double room, studio and three suites with original tiled floors and modern bathrooms. All except the double have a kitchenette. The sunlounger-lined roof terrace has river views, while the shaded patio provides welcome respite from the heat. Two suites have pull-out sofa beds for families. Breakfast costs €7.50.

Calçada Guesthouse GUESTHOUSE €€
(📞 926 563 713; www.calcadaguesthouse.com; Calçada de Dona Ana 12; d not incl breakfast €85-105; ❄🛜) 🧺 On a cobbled laneway in the town centre, this whitewashed guesthouse's six bedrooms are individually styled with colourful bedspreads and details like maps on the walls. Two have small wrought-iron balconies. Unwind in the hammock overlooking Tavira's rooftops on the sunny roof terrace. Minimum stay is four nights June to September, two nights March to May and in October.

Hotel Vila Galé Albacora HOTEL €€
(📞 281 380 800; www.vilagale.pt; Quatro Águas; s/ste from €95/124; ☺ Mar-Oct; 🅿❄🛜🏊) Overlooking Ilha de Tavira 4km east of town, this four-star, 162-room property has been converted from, and ingeniously incorporates, an entire former tuna village, complete with the original school and chapel. Along with sleek modern rooms (the former tuna workers' living premises), there are indoor and outdoor pools, a spa, two restaurants and two bars. Kids under 12 stay free.

Hotel Residencial Princesa do Gilão HOTEL €€
(📞 281 325 171; www.hotelprincesadogilao. com; Rua Borda d'Água de Aguiar 10; d/tr from €90/110; ❄🛜) 🧺 Right on the river, this late-20th-century hotel has tight but neat rooms with lemon-yellow walls and plain-tiled floors brightened by colourful fabrics. Ask for a room on the river side with a small balcony, as the views are worth waking up to. Breakfast is served at the in-house bar/cafe, which has a pavement terrace. Staff are terrifically helpful.

⭐ Maria Nova HOTEL €€€
(📞 281 001 200; www.ap-hotelsresorts.com; Rua António Pinheiro 17; d/f from €122/180; 🅿❄🛜🏊) Tavira's best hotel is set on a hill; it's worth paying extra for a south-facing room, with views from the balcony over the vast, free-form pool (and poolside bar), palm-planted gardens and the town. Contemporary, sand-toned rooms are up-to-the-minute; there's also an indoor pool spa, gym, gourmet restaurant and panoramic rooftop bar. Parking is first come, first served.

Pousada Convento de Tavira HISTORIC HOTEL €€€
(📞 210 407 680; www.pousadas.pt; Rua Dom Paio Peres Correia; d/ste from €190/315; 🅿❄🛜🏊) Dating from the 16th century, this landmark sunflower-yellow former convent near the Castelo is now an upmarket hotel with streamlined rooms featuring splashes of poppy-red, an outdoor pool, organic spa and a restaurant serving contemporary regional cuisine at both lunch and dinner. Ask staff to show you the excavations that have revealed the remains of Moorish-era houses.

Quinta da Lua BOUTIQUE HOTEL €€€
(📞 964 696 417; www.quintadalua.com.pt; Bernardinheiro; d/ste from €246/375; ☺ Apr-Nov; 🅿❄🛜🏊) Orange and carob groves surround this tranquil converted manor house 6km west of Tavira. Palms shade the large saltwater swimming pool, set amid extensive gardens aromatically planted with rosemary, lavender and olive trees. Some of its eight bright, stylish rooms have contemporary, cotton-canopied four-poster beds. Breakfast is served poolside in fine weather.

From June to September, there's a minimum three-night stay.

🍴 Eating

Portuguese and international restaurants line Rua Dr José Pires Padinha's waterfront and fan out across both banks of the river. In the fishing village of Santa Luzia, 3km southwest of Tavira, *marisqueiras* (seafood restaurants) serve the local speciality, *polvo*. Many places reduce their hours or close altogether in winter.

Pastelaria Tavirense CAFE, PASTRIES €
(Travessa Dom Brites; pastries €1.20-3.50; ⊙7am-midnight; 🛜) Beloved by its namesake *tavirense* (Tavira locals), this corner *pastelaria* has the full spectrum of Portuguese *pastéis* (custard-filled pastries), *bolos* (cakes), *tortas* (filled, rolled sponge) and *sonhos* (traditional doughnuts), along with strong coffee. You can dine on-site or take away.

Casa Simão PORTUGUESE €
(☑281 321 647; www.facebook.com/Restaurante Simao; Rua João Vaz Corte Real 10; mains €6-12; ⊙noon-2pm & 6-10pm Mon-Sat mid-Dec–Oct) Filled with locals, this old-style, family-run restaurant concentrates on honest, down-to-earth dishes such as *javali estufado* (wild-boar stew) and grilled fish and meat (served with coriander rice and tomato salad), plus, at lunch, a choice of three daily specials.

★ O Tonel PORTUGUESE €€
(☑963 427 612; Rua Dr Augo Silva Carvalho 6; tapas €3.50-7.50, mains €9-16; ⊙6.30-10pm Mon-Sat) Contemporary Portuguese cuisine is complemented by a striking dining room of scarlet walls and *azulejos*. Begin with *petiscos* like chorizo sautéed in Medronho (local brandy) or clam-and-mackerel pâté served in a tin with crusty bread, before moving on to mains such as almond-crusted pork or carob-marinated lamb. Wines come from all over Portugal. Book ahead.

Luzzo Pizzeria PIZZA €€
(☑281 327 016; www.facebook.com/luzzo tavira; Rua João Vaz Corte Real 28; pizzas €7-15.75; ⊙noon-3pm & 7-11pm; 🛜🌱) *Tuti trufi* (truffle oil and black-truffle shavings), *siffredi* (with *ventricina* spicy sausage, arugula and balsamic) and the house-speciality *luzzo* (portobello mushrooms, crispy bacon and caramelised pineapple) are just some of the enormous thin-crust pizzas pulled from the wood-fired oven at this fabulous spot. Dine in the plant-filled interior or pick up pizzas to take away.

Aquasul EUROPEAN €€
(☑281 325 166; Rua Dr Augo Silva Carvalho 11; mains €9-20.50; ⊙6.30-10pm Tue-Sat Mar–mid-Dec; 🛜🌱) Behind a rose-covered facade, mosaics and local artworks line the walls of this popular spot, while mismatched tables are topped with tiles, marble and brightly painted timbers. Dishes change seasonally and might include roast duck breast with port wine reduction, and porcini and white-truffle ravioli (around a quarter of the menu is vegetarian).

🍷 Drinking & Entertainment

Most bars are on the northern bank, with a smattering across the river along Rua Dr José Pires Padinha.

Sítio Cafe CAFE
(www.facebook.com/sitiocafetavira; Largo do Trem; ⊙8.30am-2am Mon-Thu, 8.30am-3am Fri, 6.30pm-3am Sat; 🛜) One of the few summer hotspots with any atmosphere out of season, Sítio is divided into three parts: outside, light-inside and neon-lit dark-inside. Drinks span house wine and beer to sangria and cocktails. During the day, stop by for a coffee or light meal.

Tavira Lounge BAR
(☑281 381 034; Rua Gonçalo Velho 16-18; ⊙noon-2am Mon-Sat Jun-Sep, reduced hours Oct-May; 🛜) By day it's a cafe-restaurant, by night a cafe-bar. At all times, it's a relaxed place to kick back with a smoothie or cocktail. Its inviting spaces include a contemporary timber-furnished interior, a glass-encased terrace and al fresco tables overlooking the river.

Pessoa's Cafe BAR
(www.facebook.com/PessoaSCafe; Rua Jacques Pessoa 22; ⊙noon-11pm Wed-Sun early Jan-Oct; 🛜) Abstract oils and watercolours cover the walls of Pessoa's, but in summer the best seats are on the sunny, south-facing riverside terrace, so get in early. Wines, beers and local liqueurs pair with *queijo* (cheese) and *charcutaria* platters. Acoustic or folk music occasionally plays.

★ Fado Com História TRADITIONAL MUSIC
(☑966 620 877; www.fadocomhistoria.com; Rua Damião Augo de Brito Vasconcelos 4; adult/child €8/free; ⊙shows 12.15pm, 3.15pm & 5.15pm Mon-Fri, 12.15pm & 5.15pm Sat, museum 10am-6pm Mon-Sat) If you haven't experienced fado, this comprehensive introduction is even more

CACELA VELHA

Enchanting, small and cobbled, Cacela Velha (pop 127) is a huddle of bright-bordered whitewashed cottages. The town has a pocket-sized fort, orange and olive groves, and gardens blazing with colour. Situated 11km east of Tavira, above a glittering stretch of sea, it has a couple of excellent cafe-restaurants, splendid views and a meandering path down to the long, white beach. Busy in summer, it's a quiet retreat during the rest of the year.

On the beachfront 1.4km by road from Cacela Velha, seafood specialist A Fábrica do Costa (281 951 467; Rua de Fábrica; mains €16-35, cataplanas €40-55; noon-3pm & 7-10.30pm Jun-Aug, hours vary Sep-May) has a stunning outlook over the bobbing boats on the estuary and to the sand island beyond. Maritime fare includes succulent oysters and rich *cataplanas* for two. Cash only.

Buses to/from Tavira (€3.35, 10 minutes, hourly Monday to Friday, every two hours Saturday) stop 1.8km north of Cacela Velha on the N125.

worthwhile. Space is limited, so buy your ticket a couple of hours ahead. The 35-minute show begins with an interesting film about fado's roots and history, followed by three live songs with explanations in English. On Saturdays, the 3.15pm performance takes place at the Igreja da Misericórdia (p173).

ℹ Information

SOS Clinic (281 380 660; www.sosmedicos.pt; Rua Almirante Cândido dos Reis 226; 8am-midnight) Private clinic. Between midnight and 8am doors are closed, but ring in an emergency as there's a 24-hour phone service.

Turismo (281 322 511; www.visitalgarve.pt; Praça da República 5; 9am-1pm & 2-5pm) Provides local and some regional information.

ℹ Getting There & Away

BUS

The bus station (p179) has the following services:

Faro €4.45, one hour, 11 daily Monday to Friday, seven Saturday and Sunday.

Huelva, Spain €15, 1½ hours, two daily.

Lisbon €20, 4¼ hours, five daily.

Seville, Spain €19, three hours, two daily.

Vila Real de Santo António €4.45, 40 minutes, 10 daily Monday to Friday, six Saturday and Sunday.

TRAIN

Trains run daily to Faro (€3.20, 35 minutes, 12 daily) and Vila Real (€2.70, 30 minutes, 13 daily).

ℹ Getting Around

BICYCLE

Abílio Bikes (281 323 467; www.abiliobikes.com; Rua João Vaz Corte Real 23; per day city/

mountain/electric bike €8/13/35; 9.30am-1pm & 3-7pm Mon-Sat Jun-Oct, 9.30am-1pm & 3-7pm Mon-Fri, 9.30am-1pm Sat Nov-May) Hires all kinds of bikes. Weekly discounts are available.

TAXI

For a taxi, contact **Taxi Gilao** (917 330 513; www.taxigilao.com).

Ilha de Tavira

The Parque Natural da Ria Formosa's islands stretch along the coast from Cacela Velha to just west of Faro, and this is one of the finest. Made up of dunes, white-sand beaches and a strip of woodland, it's a real hideaway reached via a footbridge or by boat.

Praia da Ilha de Tavira   BEACH

This huge white-sand beach at the island's eastern end, opposite Tavira, has operators for water sports (such as windsurfing and kitesurfing), beach bars and a campground in summer. Outside the peak months of July and August, it feels wonderfully remote and empty.

Praia do Barril   BEACH

(train 8.30am-10pm Jun-Sep, 9am-5pm Oct-May) At this glorious beach, you'll find several cafes and beach bars, and the remnants of a fishing settlement, with a poignant cemetery of anchors from the former tuna-fishing fleet.

Mini Train Pedras d'el Rei   RAIL

(one-way €2; every 20min 8am-7pm May-Sep, reduced services 9am-7pm Oct-Apr) This little train runs on narrow rails for 1km (eight minutes) through sandflats and marshland to Praia do Barril.

ⓘ Getting There & Away

Silnido (☑ 918 278 934; www.silnido.com; Estrada das Quatro Águas; ⊙ 8am-midnight Jul & Aug, 8am-7pm Mar-Jun, Sep & Oct, 9am-4.45pm Nov-Feb) ferries make the 10-minute hop to the *ilha* from Quatro Águas, 2km southeast of Tavira. Sailing schedules vary seasonally. From June to September, it also runs a direct service from Rua Dr José Pires Padinha in central Tavira (€2 return, 20 minutes one-way, 10am to 5.30pm).

The **Sequa Tours water taxi** (☑ 966 615 071; www.sequatours.com/watertaxiservice.html; Rua Dr José Pires Padinha; one-way per boat Tavira–Quatro Águas €15, Tavira–Ilha de Tavira €18; ⊙ 24hr Jun–mid-Sep, 8am-midnight Mar-May & mid-Sep–Oct) service from Tavira to Quatro Águas (five minutes) or the Ilha de Tavira (10 minutes) carries up to six people.

A bus goes to Quatro Águas from the **Tavira bus station** (Rua dos Pelames; €2, 10 minutes, five daily July to mid-September only). A taxi to Quatro Águas costs €6.

For Praia do Barril, take a bus from Tavira to Pedras d'el Rei (€2, 15 minutes, six daily Monday to Friday, fewer on weekends). At Pedras d'el Rei, cross the footbridge to pick up the Mini Train Pedras d'el Rei (p178), which runs on narrow rails for 1km (eight minutes) through sandflats and marshland to the beach.

Vila Real De Santo António

POP 19,200

Perched on the edge of wide Rio Guadiana, low-key Vila Real de Santo António's small pedestrian centre is architecturally impressive: it was founded after the 1755 earthquake to defend the region from neighbouring Spain, and was expanded in 1774 by the Marquês de Pombal using the same grid pattern of streets as Lisbon's Baixa district. The town's square named in his honour – Praça Marquês de Pombal – is the lively focal point of the centre. Cobbles radiate out from a statue of King Don José I, who was on the throne at the time of Pombal's efforts.

The impressive fortress of Castro Marim lies 4km to the north, and the large, sandy Monte Gordo beach is 4km to the southwest. With cheaper prices across the river in Spain, easily reached by car ferry or road, many travellers base themselves on the Spanish side and visit the area as a day trip.

Residência Matos Pereira   GUESTHOUSE €
(☑ 281 543 325; www.residenciamatospereira.com; Rua Dr Sousa Martins 57; s/d not incl breakfast from €21/27; ❄ 🅿 🛜) Within an impossible-to-miss emerald-green building, this family home has small, traditionally furnished rooms, each very different, some with a terrace. The green colour scheme extends to the little roof terrace; guests also have use of a shared kitchenette. Minimum stay is two nights. Cash only.

Grand Beach Club   INTERNATIONAL €€
(☑ 281 543 025; www.grandhousealgarve.com; Ponta da Areia; mains €10.50-26; ⊙ 10am-7pm Sun-Thu, to midnight Fri & Sat; 🛜 🅿) At the edge of the Atlantic and Rio Guadiana river mouth, with its own small beach (and a pool), Portugal's most southeasterly restaurant opens to a wraparound deck strewn with tables and sunloungers. Iberian black pork ribs with barbecue sauce, grilled steaks with green chimichurri sauce, gourmet pizzas, burgers on homemade brioche buns, organic salads and barbecued fish all feature.

ⓘ Information

Turismo (☑ 281 544 495; www.cm-vrsa.pt; Avenida Infante Dr Henrique, Monte Gordo; ⊙ 9am-6pm Tue-Thu, 9am-1pm & 2-6pm Fri-Mon Jun-Sep) In summer there's a tourist office 4km southwest of Vila Real De Santo António.

ⓘ Getting There & Away

BOAT

Buy tickets for the ferry to Ayamonte, Spain, from this waterfront **office** (www.rioguadiana.net; Avenida da República 118; pedestrian/bicycle/motorcycle/car one-way €1.90/1.20/3.50/5.50; ⊙ 9.30am-9pm Mon-Sat, 10am-8pm Sun Jul–mid-Sep, shorter hours mid-Sep–Jun). Ferries run every 30 minutes in summer and hourly the rest of the year. Note: there is a one-hour time difference between Portugal and Spain.

BUS

Eva buses (www.eva-bus.com) serve the following destinations:

Faro €5.75, 1¾ hours, nine daily.

Lisbon €20, 4¾ hours, five daily.

Monte Gordo €2.35, 10 minutes, four daily.

Seville, Spain €18, two hours, one daily.

Tavira €4.50, 40 minutes, nine daily.

TRAIN

Vila Real is the eastern terminus of the Algarve line.

Trains run to Faro (€5.25, 65 minutes, 12 daily) via Tavira (€2.70, 30 minutes)

Castro Marim

POP 2200

Slumbering in the shadows of a 14th-century castle, Castro Marim is a picturesque village that sees few foreign visitors. It has a quaint, tree-shaded centre, a few cafes and impressive fortifications. These afford views across the surrounding salt pans, the bridge to Spain and the marshes of the Reserva Natural do Sapal de Castro Marim (p180), which is famous for its flamingos. Walkers will find some wonderful trails in the area.

Castelo
CASTLE

(www.cm-castromarim.pt; Travessa do Castelo; adult/child €1.10/free; ⊙9am-7pm Apr-Sep, to 5pm Oct-Mar) Castro Marim's huge castle has an intriguing borderland history. Much of the area was destroyed in the 1755 earthquake, but the ruins of the main fort are still impressive. Inside the evocative, derelict castle walls stands a 14th-century church, the Igreja de Santiago, where Prince Henry the Navigator is said to have prayed. A small museum displays local artefacts dating back to the Iron Age. Most unforgettable are the views across the salt flats and into Spain.

In the 13th century, Dom Afonso III built this castle over Moorish and Roman foundations in a dramatic and strategic position for spying on the Spanish frontier. In 1319 it became the first headquarters of the religious military order known as the Order of Christ, formerly the Knights Templar. Until they moved to Tomar in 1334, they used this castle to keep watch over the estuary of the Rio Guadiana and Spain.

Most of the grand stretch of ruins today, however, dates from the 17th century, when Dom João IV ordered the addition of vast ramparts. At the same time, Forte de São Sebastião, a smaller fort (closed to the public), was built on a nearby hilltop.

A medieval fair takes place in and around the castle over the last weekend in August.

Reserva Natural do Sapal de Castro Marim e Vila Real de Santo António
NATURE RESERVE

(www.cm-castromarim.pt; Sapal de Venta Moinhos, Apartado 7; ⊙9am-12.30pm & 2-5.30pm Mon-Fri) Established in 1975, this nature reserve is mainland Portugal's oldest, covering 20 sq km of marshland and salt pans bordering the Rio Guadiana. Winter visitors include greater flamingos, spoonbills and Caspian terns; in spring it's busy with white storks. September is the best time to see European chameleons, when they descend from the trees to lay their eggs in the conifer woodlands.

Walking trails with interpretive signs fan out from the park's headquarters, located 1.8km south of Castro Marim.

ⓘ Information

Turismo (☑281 531 232; www.visitalgarve.pt; Mercado Local, Rua de São Sebastião; ⊙9.30am-1pm & 2-5.30pm Mon-Fri) Small office housed in the village's tiny whitewashed market building.

ⓘ Getting There & Away

Buses from Vila Real run to Castro Marim (€2.30, eight minutes, eight daily). Weekend buses are extremely limited.

If coming from the west by train, don't get off at the station called Castro Marim – it's 5km southwest of the village. Instead, alight at Vila Real and connect to Castro Marim by bus.

Alcoutim

POP 2900

Strategically positioned along the idyllic Rio Guadiana – a major trading route from 219 BC until the 16th century, when it began silting up – Alcoutim (ahl-ko-*teeng*) is a small village just across the river from the Spanish town of Sanlúcar de Guadiana.

Fortresses above both villages remind visitors of testier times. Phoenicians, Greeks, Romans and Arabs have barricaded themselves in the hills here, and centuries of tension have bubbled across the river, which forms the Algarve's entire eastern boundary. In the 14th century, Dom Fernando I of Portugal and Don Henrique II of Castile signed a tentative peace treaty in Alcoutim.

Today this remote village is struggling to stay on the map, its population slowly diminishing despite tax incentives for residents. Nevertheless, if you're passing between the Algarve and Alentejo it's worth a quick visit for its riverside beach and fascinating castle and churches.

Castelo
CASTLE

(☑281 540 509; www.cm-alcoutim.pt; Largo do Castelo; €2.50; ⊙9.30am-7pm Jun-Aug, to 5.30pm Sep-May) Alcoutim's flower-ringed, 13th-century *castelo* has sweeping views over the village rooftops and river. Inside the grounds is the Núcleo Museológico de Arqueologia (Archaeological Museum), displaying ruined

WALKING ACROSS THE ALGARVE

Offering an alternative perspective on the Algarve while taking in some of the region's most beautiful scenery,, the 300km-long Via Algarviana (www.viaalgarviana.org) walking trail crosses the breadth of Portugal from Alcoutim to Cabo de São Vicente, passing through the wooded hillsides of the Serra do Caldeirão and Monchique.

The Via Algarviana is fairly well marked (with red-and-white way signs). It's divided into 14 sections, covering up to 30km per day over two weeks. At the start of each stage is an information panel; starting point GPS coordinates are provided in the route guide, available as a free download at www.viaalgarviana.org (run by environmental group Al-margem) and at tourist offices throughout the region.

The best times to walk the trail are between March and May; hunting season takes place on Thursday and Sunday from mid-August to February – be careful on these days. Be sure to carry enough water at all times, particularly in the warmer months as water often isn't available en route.

medieval castle walls and other artefacts, and an exhibition on Islamic board games.

The entrance fee to the castle also includes entry to the tiny themed museums (*núcleos museológicos*) in Alcoutim and around.

Praia Fluvial　　　　　　　　　　BEACH
(www.cm-alcoutim.pt) The main attraction for most day trippers is this sandy riverside beach on a narrow tributary of the Rio Guadiana, equipped with a cafe, palm-leaf umbrellas and a lifeguard in summer. The setting is lovely. From the bridge on Rua Dom Fernando, follow the signs 400m west to Praia Fluvial.

Brisas do Guadiana　　　　GUESTHOUSE €
(☑ 967 531 064; www.facebook.com/hospedaria.brisasdoguadiana; Rua Maria Eduarda de Freitas; s/d €35/45; ❄ ☏) On top of the hill behind the castle, this smart yellow-painted place has five spic-and-span rooms, some with views across the river to Spain, and a cosy guest lounge with a roaring open fire in cooler weather.

O Soeiro　　　　　　　　PORTUGUESE €
(☑ 281 546 241; Rua do Município 4; mains €6.50-12; ⊙ noon-2.30pm Mon-Fri Jun-Aug, hours vary Sep-May) Opening to a terrace with views of the river, this cheap and cheerful family-run lunch spot is a good bet for its charcoal-grilled chicken, sizzling pork steaks and sardines (all served with salad and chips). Waiting times can be lengthy in summer; opening hours vary substantially the rest of the year.

❶ Information

Turismo (☑ 281 546 179; www.cm-alcoutim.pt; Rua 1 de Maio; ⊙ 9.30am-1pm & 2-5.30pm Tue-Sat; ☏) Just above the riverside, this office distributes maps and other information.

❶ Getting There & Away

Without your own wheels, Alcoutim is tricky to reach. Bus services run to/from Vila Real de Santo António (€4.25, 1¼ hours, one on Monday, Wednesday and Friday); on Monday and Friday these go to/from Beja (€5.25, two hours) via Mértola (€4.75, 50 minutes).

Loulé
POP 26,800

One of the Algarve's largest inland towns, and only 16km northwest of Faro, Loulé (lo-*lay*) is a handy base from which to explore the hinterland. A busy commercial centre, it's a fast-growing place in which service employees live while working in the Algarve.

Loulé has an attractive old quarter and Moorish castle ruins, and its history goes back to the Romans. A few of Loulé's artisan traditions still survive; artisans make wicker baskets, copperworks and embroidery in hole-in-the-wall workshops about town. Its small university lends it some verve, as does its wild Carnaval (p183) and annual music festival, Festival Med (p183).

◉ Sights

Nossa Senhora da Conceição　　CHAPEL
(Rua Dom Paio Peres Correia; ⊙ 9am-6pm Mon-Fri, to 2pm Sat) Situated opposite Loulé's castle, the mid-17th century chapel of Nossa Senhora da Conceição possesses three impressive elements: a heavily gilded baroque altar, floor-to-ceiling *azulejos* and a whitewashed stucco ceiling. During excavations, an Islamic door dating from the 3rd century was

Loulé

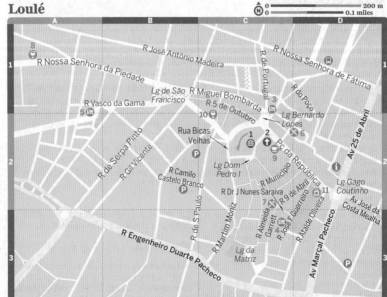

Loulé

uncovered under the floor, where it now remains, protected by glass.

Museu Municipal   MUSEUM
(Castelo; ☏ 289 400 885; www.museudeloule.pt; Rua Dom Paio Peres Correia 17; €1.62; ☺ 10am-6pm Tue-Fri, to 4.30pm Sat Jun-Sep, 9.30am-5.30pm Tue-Fri, 9.30am-4pm Sat Oct-May) Loulé's restored castle is the setting for its municipal museum. The archaeology section's *homo erectus* kicks things off, and via dusty collections of pottery and bone you'll arrive at the Roman and Islamic periods. Medieval house ruins can be viewed under a glass floor, and the admission fee includes entry to a stretch of square-towered **castle walls** and the **Cozinha Tradicional Algarvia**, a re-creation of a traditional Algarve kitchen,

featuring a hearth, archaic implements and burnished copper.

🏃 Activities

Dom Pedro   GOLF
(☏ 289 310 333; www.dompedrogolf.com; Volta do Medronheiro, Vilamoura; green fees from €155) In the sprawling resort of Vilamoura, 15km southwest of Loulé, Dom Pedro has five high-standard golf courses, including the par-72 Victoria course – the longest 18-hole course in Portugal. Designed by Arnold Palmer, and featuring natural wetlands, lakes and carob, almond and olive trees, it has hosted the Portugal Masters every year since 2007.

✨ Festivals & Events

Carnaval de Loulé
CARNIVAL

(www.cm-loule.pt; ⊘ Feb or Mar) Just before Lent, Loulé celebrates Carnaval over three days. Exuberant festivities include parades with tractor-drawn floats, live music and a grand ball. Friday is the children's parade and Sunday's the big one.

Festival Med
MUSIC

(www.festivalmed.pt; ⊘ late Jun) This three-day world-music festival has gained a reputation as a quality event and now attracts strong line-ups of international performers, as well as dance, handicrafts exhibitions and street theatre.

🛏 Sleeping & Eating

Hospedaria Dom Fernando
GUESTHOUSE €

(🖉 964 026 277; www.domfernandoloule.com; Rua José Fernandes Guerreiro 58; d/tr/f from €50/60/70; ❄🕾) Painted a bright buttercup yellow, this sound choice has 20 simple rooms in an excellent location behind the market. The best rooms, on the top floor, open to private terraces. Family rooms have two double beds; triples have a double and a single. Breakfast is served at the restaurant next door.

★ Allons-y Guesthouse
GUESTHOUSE €€

(🖉 969 870 585; Rua de São Domingos 13; d/tr from €63/73; ❄🕾) The high point (in all senses) of this town-centre guesthouse is its top-level terrace overlooking Loulé's rooftops and castle, with potted plants and a pergola-shaded area where homemade breakfasts are served. Charming guestrooms have high ceilings, antique-style furniture and herringbone floors; all are en suite except one, which has a private but external bathroom.

Loulé Jardim Hotel
HOTEL €€

(🖉 289 413 094; www.loulejardimhotel.com; Praça Manuel de Arriaga 25; s/d/ste from €55/65/115; 🅿❄🕾🏊) Overlooking a pretty square, this late-19th-century building has 52 spacious, airy rooms in contemporary creams and beiges. Book ahead for the suite with a large private terrace, which requires a two-night minimum stay. There's a small saltwater pool with sunloungers, and breakfast, served in a glass-roofed atrium, is a substantial affair.

Colheita Fresca
TAPAS €

(🖉 289 070 608; www.facebook.com/colheita fresca; Rua Dr Joaquim Nunes Saraiva; tapas €3-10;

⊘ 9am-9pm Mon-Fri, to 10pm Sat) 🍴 Produce from Loulé's magnificent Mercado Municipal (p183) is utilised in *petiscos* such as *ostras* (oysters) served with a squeeze of grapefruit, *chouriço assado* (flambéed chorizo) and *moelas estufadas* (garlic- and tomato-stuffed chicken gizzards), served in an arched-brick dining room and accompanied by Portuguese wines. Cash only.

Bocage
PORTUGUESE €

(🖉 289 412 416; www.restaurantebocage.com; Rua Bocage 14; mains €6-12; ⊘ noon-3.30pm & 6.30-10pm Mon-Sat) On the corner of a quiet lane just off the main drag, this traditional, family-run restaurant serves solid plates of market-sourced grilled fish and meat in a cosy, wood-lined dining room. Get here early at lunchtime, as it fills up fast with locals.

🍷 Drinking & Nightlife

Café Calcinha
CAFE

(🖉 289 415 763; www.facebook.com/cafecalcinha; Praça da República 67; ⊘ 8am-11pm; 🕾) Loulé's oldest cafe is a replica of an old Brazilian coffee shop, opened in 1927 and virtually unchanged since, with a gorgeous art-deco interior and marble-topped tables. Live fado occasionally takes place. The statue outside depicts António Aleixo, an early-20th-century poet and a former regular of the cafe, sitting at his own bronze table.

Taberna dos Frades
WINE BAR

(Rua Condestável Dom Nuno Alvares Pereira 8; ⊘ 3pm-2am Sun-Wed, 10am-2am Thu-Sat; 🕾) Decorated in rustic style, with wine barrels on the pavement out front and striking cross-vaulted ceilings, this *taberna* serves Portuguese wines by the glass, a wide range of gins and local cheeses and charcuterie. It regularly hosts live fado nights, and the atmosphere is nearly always great.

Bar Marroquia
BAR

(www.facebook.com/marroquiabar; Rua Nossa Senhora da Piedade 120; ⊘ 8pm-midnight Sun-Thu, to 2am Fri & Sat; 🕾) Arabic-themed Bar Marroquia has an inviting interior with a fireplace and pool table with a red baize. Seasonal fruit mojitos, caipirinhas and punches served in giant glass bowls are specialities. Occasional live music spans flamenco, fado and jazz.

🛍 Shopping

Mercado Municipal
MARKET

(Praça da Republica; ⊘ 6.30am-3pm Mon-Sat) Loulé's most impressive piece of architectural

ALMANCIL

It's worth making a detour to Almancil, 13km northwest of Faro and about 9km south of Loulé, to visit the marvellous **Igreja de São Lourenço de Matos** (Church of St Lawrence of Rome; www.diocese-algarve.pt; Rua da Igreja, Almancil; €2; ⏱10am-1pm & 3-6pm Mon, 3-6pm Tue-Sat). This baroque masterpiece was built on the site of a ruined chapel after locals, while digging a well, implored Saint Lawrence for help and then struck water.

Constructed by brothers Antão and Manuel Borges, it's smothered in *azulejos* – even the ceiling – depicting the saint's life and death. In the 1755 earthquake, only five tiles fell from the roof.

Buses from Loulé (€2.35, 15 minutes, up to two per hour) stop 2.5km west in Almancil's centre.

heritage is its art-nouveau market, a 1908 revivalist neo-Arab confection with four cupolas at the four corners and Moorish features picked out in raspberry-red against cream-coloured walls. Inside you'll find a fish market, cheap cafes and local produce such as orange-blossom honey, fig 'cheese' (not cheese at all) and Cliff Richard's Algarve-produced wine.

ℹ Information

Turismo (☑289 463 900; www.visitalgarve. pt; Avenida 25 de Abril 9; ⏱9.30am-1pm & 2-5.30pm Mon-Fri) In the centre of town, just off the main street.

ℹ Getting There & Away

Bus The **bus station** (☑289 416 655; Rua Nossa Senhora de Fátima) is on the town centre's northern edge.

Daily connections include the following:
Albufeira €4.45, 50 minutes, five daily.
Faro €3.35, 40 minutes, two per hour Monday to Friday, fewer on weekends.
Lisbon €20, four hours, four to five daily.

Train If you're arriving by train, be aware that the station is 7km southwest of town (take any Quarteira-bound bus).

ℹ Getting Around

Parking is limited in central Loulé – park in one of the four parking areas on the edge of town.

Serra do Caldeirão

Starting around 10km north of Loulé, Serra do Caldeirão is a beautiful protected area of undulating hills, cork trees and harsh scrubland. The area is renowned for its bird varieties. It's an excellent place to hike – the Via Algarviana passes through – and a great spot to base yourself to meander through some quaint villages and enjoy the local cuisine. A feature of the region is its *fontes* (traditional water sources, many of which comprise exquisite taps and fountains).

Alte & Salir
POP 4800

Perched on a hillside on the edge of the Serra do Caldeirão, **Alte**, 45km northwest of Loulé, is a quaint and very pretty little village of flower-filled streets, whitewashed buildings and several *fontes*. The *fontes* were traditionally used for the mills and former wells; a main *fonte*, Fonte Grande, passes through dykes, weirs and watermills. *Artesanatos* (handicrafts shops) are dotted around town, as are several restaurants and cafes.

The small, sleepy and authentic village of **Salir**, 14km to the east of Alte, harbours castle walls dating from the 12th century, and a 17th-century church.

◉ Sights

Fábrica de Brinquedos　　WORKSHOP
(www.projectotasa.com/project/artisans/da-torre; Rua de Torre, Torre, Fonte Santa; ⏱9am-1pm Mon-Fri) 🖉 The hamlet of Torre's school fell into disuse when there weren't enough children. There wasn't much work around, either, so three local women decided to put the building to use. It's now a heart-warming workshop where they handcraft charming, old-fashioned toys such as cars, motorcycles, carriages, aeroplanes, spinning tops, building blocks and puzzles from carob, almond, gorse and olive wood. It's 3.5km northwest of Alte via Estrada de Santa Margarida and Rua das Valinhas.

Pólo Museológico de Salir　　MUSEUM
(☑289 489 137; www.museudeloule.pt; Largo Pedro Dias, Salir; ⏱9am-5pm Mon-Fri) **FREE** Within the area encompassed by what remains of Salir's ruined castle, this little museum has a glass floor above the 12th-century Moorish foundations. Other local archaeological finds include Neolithic menhirs (standing

stones), Iron Age stelae (stone carvings) and Roman pottery. You can also pick up tourist information here.

Pólo Museológico Cândido Guerreiro e Condes de Alte   MUSEUM

(⌨ 289 478 058; www.museudeloule.pt; Rua Condes de Alte, Alte; ⊙ 9am-5pm Mon-Fri) **FREE** This museum–cultural space pays homage to Alte's famous poet, Cândido Guerreiro, along with the Counts of Alte who once lived here. It displays books and paraphernalia, and also provides tourist information.

🛏 Sleeping & Eating

Alte has a couple of decent cafes and restaurants and its *fontes* make scenic picnic spots; there's a small supermarket in the village.

Quinta do Coração   GUESTHOUSE €

(⌨ 289 489 959; www.algarveparadise.com; Carrasqueiro; s/d €35/55, studio €65, 2-person cottage €70; P 🛇 🗑 🗲) 🅿 On a wooded hill 6.7km northeast of Salir, this converted farmhouse is encircled by eucalyptus, olive and cork trees. Accommodation is rustic; the studio and cottage have kitchenettes, but, unlike the guestroom, don't include breakfast. There's a two-night minimum stay for the cottage. Kids under 10 stay free. Superb hiking nearby includes the long-distance Via Algarviana trail.

Casa da Mãe   GUESTHOUSE €€

(⌨ 289 489 179; www.casadamae.pt; Almeijoafra; s/d/tr/f/apt from €37.50/65/85/110/135; P 🛇 🗑) Farmhouse Casa da Mãe has simple, great-value rooms and apartments, some with views of Salir, 1.2km to the south. Surrounding the complex, the shady gardens centre on a sunlounger-lined swimming pool. Home-cooked breakfasts include oranges from the orchard, eggs from the owners' chickens and fresh herbs from the vegetable plot. The Via Algarviana hiking trail passes close by.

ℹ Information

Tourist information is available at Salir's Pólo Museológico de Salir (p184).

ℹ Getting There & Away

Buses depart Loulé for Alte (€3.85, 50 minutes, every two hours Monday to Friday, two on Saturday, one Sunday) via Salir (€2.55, 30 minutes). There are also direct services between Loulé and Alte (€3.75, 45 minutes, twice daily on weekdays, one on Saturday).

Querença

POP 750

Querença is one of the region's prettiest villages, with whitewashed buildings set around a square graced by an early 16th-century church.

◉ Sights

Pólo Museológico da Água   MUSEUM

(⌨ 289 422 495; www.cm-loule.pt; Rua Prof Dr Manuel Viegas Guerreiro; ⊙ 9am-1pm & 2-5pm Mon-Fri) **FREE** On the village square, this small museum has a model of a waterwheel as well as information panels (in Portuguese) on water use. There's also a tourist office here, and it holds the keys to the church opposite. Despite official opening hours, you'll often find staff members here at weekends.

🛏 Sleeping & Eating

★ B&B Candelária   B&B €€

(⌨ 969 097 399; www.casa-candelaria.com; Monte Seco; d/f €75/112.50; P 🛇) Surrounded by olive, carob and almond trees, this rustic farmhouse has thick adobe walls providing natural coolness in summer and warmth in winter, heavy timber furniture and an open fireplace in the guest kitchen/lounge area. Its five tile-floored guestrooms are petite but comfortable; the family room sleeps four. The rooftop has sunloungers, hammocks and glorious valley views.

WALKS IN THE SERRA DO CALDEIRÃO

The Serra do Caldeirão's most worthwhile short walk is climbing **Rocha da Pena** (www.walkalgarve.com; Rua de Rocha da Pena), a 479m-high limestone rock, via a well-signposted 4.7km circuit (allow two to three hours return). Museums in Salir, Alte and Querença stock a basic map-guide. Carry water and snacks (the only refreshment stops are small shop-cafes at the base and in Pena village) and heed seasonal forest fire warnings.

The area has 450 plant species, including native daffodils and bee orchids. Among the birdlife you might see are the short-toed snake-eagle, Iberian green woodpecker and Egyptian vulture.

THE ALGARVE SERRA DO CALDEIRÃO

THE ALGARVE ALBUFEIRA

It's 14km west of Querença, 16km southeast of Alte and 18km southwest of Salir.

Tasquinha do Lagar
PORTUGUESE €

(🖉912 730 795; Rua da Escola; mains €8.50-10; ⊙noon-3pm & 6.30-10pm Thu-Tue, closed Nov) On the left as you come to the village proper from the south, this whitewashed place with a timber extension cooks hearty, no-frills country fare. Dishes change daily but regularly feature heart-warmers such as *borrego no forno* (roast lamb), *bochechas de porco* (pigs cheeks stewed in port) or *leitão* (suckling pig).

★ Monte da Eira
PORTUGUESE €€

(🖉289 438 129; www.restaurantemontedaeira. com; N396, Clareanes; mains €8-16, 2-/3-course lunch menu €14.50/17.50; ⊙12.30-2.30pm & 7-10.15pm Tue-Sat, 12.30-3pm Sun; 🛜🏵) A former threshing mill's stables have been converted to house this charming restaurant with white-clothed tables spread over several rooms and two outdoor terraces. Refined rustic specialities, such as *estfado de javali* (wild boar stew with local herbs) and *caçarola de coelho e ameixas* (rabbit and plum casserole), are complemented by hundreds of Portuguese wines. It's 4km south of Querença.

ⓘ Getting There & Away

There's no public transport to Querença – you'll need your own wheels to get here.

Albufeira

POP 40,800

Once a scenic fishing village, Albufeira gained popularity for its sharp, red-gold sand beaches. Today, it's devoted to mass-market tourism, particularly cheap package deals, and has all but lost the vestiges of its past. Fishing boats are now moored at the ultramodern marina southwest of the centre, and the old town – with its pretty cobblestone streets and Moorish influences – is concealed by gaudy signs, English menu boards and rowdy bars.

Even if this isn't your sort of place, Albufeira has good transport links to lovely beaches, such as Praia da Galé (p186) to the west. There are loads of activities and there's a relaxed holiday atmosphere away from the British pubs. To explore the pretty inland villages and the area's high-quality rural restaurants, you will need your own transport.

◉ Sights & Activities

In-town beach **Praia do Peneco**, through the tunnel near the Turismo (p188) is usually packed sardine-style with sunloungers.

Beyond the town are beautifully rugged coves and bays, though most are heavily developed and often crowded. **Buses** (Rua Bairro dos Pescadores) serving beaches to the east depart from above the escalators by the old fishing quarter. For western beaches, buses depart from Albufeira's main bus station (p188).

While beaches are the biggest draw, there are plenty of other diversions in the area, from water parks to boat trips and horse riding.

Fiesa
SCULPTURE

(🖉282 317 084; www.fiesa.org; Pêra; adult/child €9.90/4.90; ⊙10am-midnight mid-Jul–mid-Sep, to 10pm Jun–mid-Jul, to 7pm Mar–May & mid-Sep–early Nov) Fiesa is the world's biggest sand-sculpture contest. Artists are given 45,000 tonnes of sand to sculpt, and their truly amazing creations (up to 12m high and illuminated at night) can be admired throughout the season. It's 13km northwest of Albufeira, just off the N125 in the inland area of Pêra.

Praia da Falésia
BEACH

One of the Algarve's most impressive beaches is this 6km-long strip of sand backed by stunning cliffs in several shades of ochre. Starting 8.5km east of Albufeira, the strand gets very crowded in summer, especially when the tide is in, but in low season it's all yours.

Praia da Galé
BEACH

Beginning 9km west of Albufeira, Praia da Galé is long (5km), sandy and less crowded than many other beaches in the area.

Aquashow
WATER PARK

(🖉289 315 129; www.aquashowpark.com; N396, Quarteira; adult/child €29/19; ⊙10am-6.30pm Aug, to 6pm Jul, to 5.30pm Jun & Sep, to 5pm May) In Quarteira, 20km east of Albufeira, this is a huge complex with all the usual water-park attractions (wave pool, slides and sunbathing areas), roller coasters and an on-site hotel. Book online for discounted admission.

Dolphins Driven
CRUISE, KAYAKING

(🖉913 113 094; www.dolphins.pt; Marina de Albufeira; tours adult/child €35/20; ⊙Apr-Oct) Dolphins Driven runs three excellent excursions from Albufeira: a 2½-hour exploration of the

THE ALGARVE FOR KIDS

The Algarve is a fun, kid-focused area with loads of attractions, family-friendly beaches and cultural activities. Try thrilling water parks such as Slide & Splash (p189) and Krazy World (☑282 574 134; www.krazyworld.com; Estrada Algoz-Messines; adult/child €17/10; ☺10am-6.30pm Jul & Aug, to 6pm late Mar-Jun, Sep & Oct, to 5.30pm Nov-late Mar, closed most weekdays Jan & Feb); the great zoo (☑282 680 100; www.zoolagos.com; Barão de São João; adult/child €18/14; ☺10am-7pm Apr-Sep, to 5pm Oct-Mar; ♿) in Lagos; and, at Silves, the imagination-firing castle (p190).

There are some excellent museums, too: in São Brás de Alportel there's a simple cork display in the Museu do Traje (p169), and in Portimão the wonderful Museu de Portimão (p192) re-creates a former fish cannery.

Many towns along the coast run boat trips, and several have little trains.

Albufeira has a plethora of agencies in the area selling a variety of trips, from horse riding to cruising on pirate ships. Most boat trips leave from the marina. Other kid-oriented activities include the following:

Albufeira Riding Centre (☑961 269 526; www.albufeiraridingcentre.com; Vale Navio 151; 30min/1hr/2hr group rides per person €20/30/50, 30min lesson €25; ☺by reservation) On the road to Vilamoura. Offers one- to three-hour horse rides for all ages and abilities.

Aqualand (☑282 320 230; www.aqualand.pt; N125, Sítio das Areias, Alcantarilha; adult/child €29/21; ☺10am-6pm Jul-Sep, to 5pm Jun) Huge loop-the-loop slide and rapids.

Aquashow (p186) In Quarteira, 10km east of Albufeira, with parrots, reptiles and a wave pool.

local sea caves and dolphin-watching; three-hour dolphin spotting off the coast; and a 2½-hour kayak trip into the local caves.

🛏 Sleeping & Eating

Dianamar GUESTHOUSE €€
(☑289 587 801; www.dianamar.com; Rua Latino Coelho 36; d/tr from €75/95; ☺Apr-Oct; ☎) Removed from the central hubbub, but just 150m southwest of the beach, Dianamar has simply furnished rooms – some with balconies and two with sea views – with lovely details such as fresh flowers. Stunning views also extend from the communal roof terrace. Rates include excellent, very generous breakfasts and afternoon teas.

Vila Joya SPA HOTEL €€€
(☑289 591 795; www.vilajoya.com; Estrada da Galé; s/ste from €340/690; ᴾ❄☎☲) Just 8km west of Albufeira, yet a planet away in every respect, luxurious Vila Joya is right on the beachfront near Praia da Galé. Pool areas, lush green lawns, views of the sea and a spa with a sauna, steam bath, outdoor Jacuzzi and beauty treatment rooms create an ultra-relaxing environment. Its restaurant has two Michelin stars.

Veneza PORTUGUESE €€
(☑289 367 129; www.restauranteveneza.com; Estrada de Paderne 560A, Mem Moniz; mains €11-22;

☺7.30-10.30pm Wed, 12.30-3pm & 7.30-10.30pm Thu-Mon; ☎) Famed for its *cataplana* – here, a delicious pork and clam combination – Veneza also turns out superb dishes such as *polvo à lagereiro* (tender octopus with baked potatoes). Its wine cellar is one of the region's finest, with over 1000 references. It's 11km north of Albufeira; you'll need a car to get here.

★ **Vila Joya Restaurant** GASTRONOMY €€€
(☑289 591 795; www.vilajoya.com; Estrada da Galé; degustation menu €185; ☺sittings 1-2pm & 7.30-8.45pm; ☎) Helmed by Austrian chef Dieter Koschina, this fine-dining restaurant in the Vila Joya resort was Portugal's first to gain two Michelin stars. Koschina draws on a variety of culinary influences and premium Portuguese produce to create exquisite dishes such as confit *bacalhau* with goat's-milk yoghurt and beetroot coulis, or roast goose liver with smoked eel and caviar.

Dom Carlos PORTUGUESE €€€
(☑289 541 224; Rua Alves Correia 100; 5-course menu €49; ☺7.15-11pm Wed-Sun Apr-Oct) Higher-end restaurants tend to be out of town, but here you can splash out and still walk back to your hotel. The elegant but intimate interior, dressed in white and pale blue, feels worlds away from the frenzied centre, and the five-course menus (no à la carte) utilise

market-sourced produce in intricately presented dishes.

❶ Information

Experience Shop (🖉966 130 256; Avenida da Liberdade 63; ☺10am-11pm May-Sep) A handy one-stop shop for booking any experience in the Albufeira area, including all theme parks, dolphin watching, bike hire and 4WD safaris.

Municipal Tourism Office (🖉289 515 973; www.cm-albufeira.pt; Estrada de Ferreiras; ☺9am-5pm Mon-Sat) Helpful local tourist office with maps and info.

Turismo (🖉289 585 279; www.visitalgarve.pt; Rua 5 de Outubro 8; ☺9.30am-7pm daily Jul & Aug, 9.30am-1pm & 2-5.30pm Mon-Fri Sep-Jun) Algarve Tourism office with information on the town and surrounding attractions; by the tunnel that leads to the beach.

❶ Getting There & Away

BUS

The **main bus station** (🖉289 580 611; Rua Paul Harris 63) is 2km north of town. Passengers travelling to Lisbon can purchase tickets at a more conveniently located **ticket shop** (Avenida da Liberdade 127; ☺6.45am-7.45pm Mon-Fri, from 8am Sat & Sun), outside of which buses leave for the main bus station (€1.40) every 30 minutes from 7am to 10pm.

Key destinations include the following:
Faro €4.85, 1½ hours, up to two per hour.
Lagos €5.70, 80 minutes, hourly.
Lisbon €20, three hours, six daily.
Loulé €4.25, 40 minutes, seven daily.
Silves €4.45, 45 minutes, seven daily.

Two buses per day also head to Huelva in Spain (€16, three hours, via Faro) and on to Seville (€20, 4½ hours).

TRAIN

Services from Albufeira:
Faro €3.35, 35 minutes, nine daily.
Lagos €4.85, 1¼ hours, nine daily.

❶ Getting Around

To reach the train station, take the red-line Giro city bus (per trip/day ticket €1.40/4) to the main bus station, then the yellow line.

From the ticket shop, the red line leaves half-hourly for Praia de São Rafael and the marina.

Eva buses (www.eva-bus.com) operates local services. Prices vary according to distance, with reduced services outside high season.

For car hire, try **Auto Jardim** (🖉965 046 640; www.autocarhire.net; Avenida da Liberdade, Edifício Brisa; ☺8.30am-6.30pm Jul & Aug,

hours vary Sep-Jun) or **Auto Prudente** (🖉289 542 160; www.auto-prudente.com; Estrada de Santa Eulália, Edifício Ondas do Mar, Loja 1).

Carvoeiro

POP 2700

Carvoeiro is a cluster of whitewashed buildings atop gold-tinged cliffs and backed by gentle hills. Shops, bars and restaurants rise steeply from the small arc of beach that is the focus of the town, with holiday villas sprawling across the hillsides beyond. It's prettier and more laid-back than many of the Algarve's bigger resorts, but its diminutive size means that it gets full to bursting in summer.

◉ Sights

The town's handkerchief-sized sandy beach, Praia do Carvoeiro, is surrounded by the steeply mounting town. On the coastal road 800m east is the bay of Algar Seco, a favourite stop on the tour-bus itinerary thanks to its dramatic rock formations.

If you're looking for a stunning swimming spot, continue 2.2km further east along the main road, Estrada do Farol, to Praia de Centianes, where the secluded cliff-wrapped beach is almost as dramatic as Algar Seco.

★ **Benagil Caves**   CAVE
(Algar de Benagil; Praia de Benagil) One of the Algarve's – and Portugal's – most emblematic sights, this huge natural seaside cave has a hole in its ceiling through which streaming sunlit illuminates the sandstone and beach below. The only way to access the interior is via the water. Numerous companies along the coast, such as Taruga Tours (p189), run boat trips, and hire kayaks and SUPs (stand-up paddleboads) to paddle here yourself. Swimming to the caves is discouraged due to strong tides and currents, and high watercraft traffic. From the cliffs above, you can look down to see the hole in the cave's roof.

Praia da Marinha   BEACH
One of a few nearby beaches with karst rock stacks, Praia da Marinha is among the most beautiful. It's 7.5km east of Carvoeiro; the nicest way to reach it is via the Percurso dos Sete Vales Suspensos (p189) path.

🏃 Activities

Golfers can take their pick: there's the **Pestana Gramacho** (🖉282 340 900; www. pestanagolf.com; Rua do Pestana Golf Resort; green fees high/low season €110/73; ☺7am-9pm Jun-

Aug, to 6pm Sep-May) and **Pestana Vale da Pinta** (☑282 340 900; www.pestanagolf.com; Rua do Pestana Golf Resort; green fees high/low season €110/73; ☺7am-9pm Jun-Aug, to 6pm Sep-May), both at Pestana Golf Resort; and **Vale de Milho** (☑282 358 502; www.valedemilho golf.com; Rua de Vale de Milho; green fees €16; ☺8am-sunset) near Praia de Centianes.

Slide & Splash WATER PARK
(☑282 340 800; www.slidesplash.com; Vale de Deus 125, Estômbar; adult/child €27/20; ☺10am-6.30pm Jul & early–mid-Sep, to 5.30pm Jun, to 5pm Apr, May & mid-late Sep) Set over 7 hectares, 8km north of Carvoeiro, this water park is widely considered Portugal's best, thanks to the sheer quantity of slides, toboggans and pools, along with reptile and birds-of-prey shows, and multiple restaurants. There's enough here to keep kids and adults entertained for most of a day, though with no family ticket available it can be expensive.

Percurso dos Sete Vales Suspensos WALKING
One of the Algarve's most memorable walks, this clifftop route connects the beaches east of Carvoeiro. Beginning at Praia Vale Centianes, 2.3km east of town, it heads 5.7km to Praia da Marinha, with its spectacular rock stacks, via the beach at Benagil.

Divers Cove DIVING
(☑282 356 594; www.divers-cove.com; Quinta do Paraíso; 1-day discovery course €135, 1 dive with/without gear €50/35, 6 dives €250/175; ☺9am-7pm Mon-Sat, 10am-7pm Sun) This multilingual, family-run diving centre provides equipment, dives and PADI certification.

Taruga Tours CRUISE, KAYAKING
(☑969 617 828; www.tarugatoursbenagilcaves. pt; Praia de Benagil; 30/75min boat tours €15/25, 90min kayak/SUP hire €30/60; ☺9.30am-6.30pm May-Sep, 10.30am-4.30pm Oct-Apr) Taruga's boat trips visit the extraordinary Benagil Caves (p188); longer tours take you past other cliff-side caves and through natural arches. It also rents kayaks and stand-up paddleboards (SUPs) to reach the caves under your own steam. Book well ahead in summer. It's 6km east of Carvoeiro; park at the top of the hill on the eastern side of the beach.

🛏 Sleeping & Eating

★**O Castelo** GUESTHOUSE €€
(☑919 729 259; www.ocastelo.net; Rua do Casino 59; d not incl breakfast with/without sea view from €90/55, f not incl breakfast from €150;

⚹🔊) Right on the beach, this guesthouse is gleamingly maintained. Most of the 12 rooms with colourful, contemporary striped bed linens have a terrace or balcony with sea (and sunrise) views, and can accommodate an extra bed. The family room, with a double bed and two singles, also has a kitchenette.

Le Crô Portugal TAPAS €€
(☑910 983 443; Estrada do Farol 77; tapas €4.50-7.50, mains €8-13.50; ☺12.30-3pm & 6.30-10pm Thu-Tue; ✍) Run by husband-and-wife team Hugo and Marina, this tiny wine bar–style place turns out terrific *petiscos* such as sea bass ceviche, chorizo and squid, and marinated anchovies. Plentiful vegetarian options include local cheeses and olives, and aubergine-stuffed figs. It stocks a connoisseur's selection of wines, most from the surrounding area. Cash only.

A Marisqueira SEAFOOD €€
(☑282 358 695; www.facebook.com/amarisqueira .carvoeiro; Estrada do Farol 95; mains €7-20.50; ☺noon-2.30pm & 6.30-10pm Mon-Sat) You'll smell the smoky aromas of this well-established seafood restaurant before you see it, as almost everything is cooked over a flaming charcoal grill – sardines, sole, sea bream, squid and prawns included. It's 600m up the main road east of Praia do Carvoeiro.

Restaurante Boneca Bar BAR
(☑282 358 391; www.facebook.com/Restaurante BonecaBar; Estrada do Algar Sêco; ☺10am-midnight) Hidden in the rock formations at Algar Seco, 750m east of the beach in Carvoeiro (just below the cliff-side car park and reached by a steep staircase), this long-standing place is a glorious spot for a cocktail, beer or wine, particularly at sunset.

Portuguese dishes include grilled sardines and pork steaks.

🛍 Shopping

★**Porches Pottery** CERAMICS
(☑282 352 858; www.porchespottery.com; N125, Porches; ☺9am-6pm Mon-Fri, 10am-2pm Sat) ✍ Watch artists hand-painting traditional *azulejo* tiles at this pottery stocking a vast array of ceramics, from fridge magnets to plates, bowls, vases, lamps and pots. International shipping is available. Opening to a bougainvillea-draped front terrace, its enchanting on-site cafe is clad in classic blue-and-white tiles, and serves light dishes (sandwiches, quiches, salads, cakes) on its own crockery at tile-topped tables.

It's 9km northeast of Carvoeiro.

ℹ Information

Turismo (☏ 282 357 728; www.visitalgarve.
pt; Largo da Paia; ⊘ 9.30am-1pm & 2-5.30pm
Tue-Sat) Just back from the beach in the centre
of town.

ℹ Getting There & Away

Buses run on weekdays between Carvoeiro and
Portimão (€3.35, 35 minutes, eight daily) and
Lagoa (€2.35, 10 minutes, up to two per hour).

ℹ Getting Around

Parking is difficult in summer – it's best to head
to Estrada do Farol and walk.

Silves

POP 10,900

Silves' winding backstreets of whitewashed
buildings topped by terracotta roofs climb
the hillside above the banks of the Rio
Arade. Crowning the hill, hulking red-stone
walls enclose one of the Algarve's best-preserved castles. Situated 17km northeast of
Portimão, the town makes a good base if
you're after a less hectic, noncoastal Algarvian pace.

History

The Rio Arade was an important route into
the interior for the Phoenicians, Greeks and
Carthaginians, who wanted the copper and
iron action in the southwest of the country.
With the Moorish invasion from the 8th
century, the town gained prominence due to
its strategic hilltop, riverside site. From the
mid-11th to the mid-13th centuries, Shelb (or
Xelb), as it was then known, rivalled Lisbon
in prosperity and influence: according to the
12th-century Arab geographer Idrisi, it had a
population of 30,000, a port and shipyards,
and 'attractive buildings and well-furnished
bazaars'.

The town's downfall began in June 1189,
when Dom Sancho I laid siege to it, supported by mostly English crusaders, who had
been persuaded (with the promise of loot)
to pause in their journey to Jerusalem and
give Sancho a hand. The Moors holed up
inside their impregnable castle, but after
three hot months of harassment they ran
out of water and were forced to surrender.
Sancho was all for mercy and honour, but
the crusaders wanted the plunder they were
promised, and stripped the Moors of their
possessions (including the clothes on their
backs) as they left, tortured those remaining
and wrecked the town.

Two years later the Moors recaptured the
town. It wasn't until 1249 that Christians
gained control once and for all. By then,
however, Silves was a shadow of its former
self. The silting up of the river – which
caused disease and stymied maritime trade
– coupled with the growing importance of
the Algarvian ports hastened the town's decline. Devastation in the 1755 earthquake
seemed to seal its fate. But in the 19th century, local cork and dried-fruit industries
revitalised Silves, hence the grand bourgeois
architecture around town. Today tourism
and agriculture are its lifeblood.

◉ Sights

★**Castelo**   CASTLE
(☏ 282 440 837; www.cm-silves.pt; Rua da Cruz de
Portugal; adult/child €2.80/1.40, joint ticket with
Museu Municipal de Arqueologia €3.90; ⊘ 9am-
10pm Jul & Aug, to 8pm Sep–mid-Oct, to 7pm Jun,
to 5.30pm mid-Oct–May) This russet-coloured,
Lego-like castle – originally occupied in the
Visigothic period – has great views over the
town and surrounding countryside. What
you see today dates mostly from the Moorish
era, though the castle was heavily restored in
the 20th century. Walking the parapets and
admiring the vistas is the main attraction,
but you can also gaze down on the excavated
ruins of the Almohad-era palace. The whitewashed 12th-century water cisterns, 5m
deep, now host temporary exhibitions.

★**Sé**   CATHEDRAL
(Rua da Sé; by donation; ⊘ 9am-12.30pm &
2-5.30pm Mon-Fri year-round, plus 9am-1pm Sat
Jun-Aug) Just below the castle is the *sé*, built
in 1189 on the site of an earlier mosque,
then rebuilt after the 1249 Reconquista and
subsequently restored several times following earthquake damage. In many ways, this
is the Algarve's most impressive cathedral,
with a substantially unaltered Gothic interior of dramatically high, ribbed vaulted
ceilings, stained glass and intricately carved
tombs. The Christ sculpture, the *Senhor dos
Passos,* is one of the main processional figures of the town's Easter celebrations.

Museu Municipal de Arqueologia   MUSEUM
(☏ 282 444 838; www.cm-silves.pt; Rua das Portas
de Loulé 14; adult/child €2.10/1.05, joint ticket with
Castelo €3.90; ⊘ 10am-6pm) Near the defensive walls, this archaeological museum has
a mix of interesting finds from the area. The

modern building was constructed around an 18m-deep Moorish well with a spiral staircase heading into the depths that you can follow for a short stretch. Otherwise, this is another Algarve museum that starts at the prehistoric beginning but soon moves on to the Almohad period of the 12th and 13th centuries.

🏇 Activities

Country Riding Centre HORSE RIDING
(📞917 976 992; www.countryridingcentre.com; Rua de Pinheiro e Garrado, Pinheiro e Garrado; 1/3hr rides from €40/85, 30min private lesson €30; ⏰9am-1pm & 3.30-7pm Mon-Sat, by appointment Sun) Signposted 5km northeast of Silves, this riding centre provides lessons and rides for all levels, from one hour to multiday trips – packages including accommodation and lunches start at €990 for five nights. Pony rides for kids cost €25 for 30 minutes.

🎊 Festivals & Events

Feira Medieval CULTURAL
(www.cm-silves.pt; ⏰mid-Aug) Silves' Medieval Fair takes place over 10 days at venues around town. Its important events and people are represented, from Silves governor Al-Mu'tamid, who reigned from 1069 to 1091, to the town being awarded its charter. Period costumes, dances, jesters, feasts, traditional food and handicrafts all evoke life in the 11th to 13th centuries.

🛏 Sleeping

Casa das Oliveiras B&B €
(📞282 342 115; www.casa-das-oliveiras.com; Rua de Vala, Montes da Vala; s/d from €45/55; 🅿🛜❄) Run by British owners, this B&B has five simply furnished rooms and a relaxed rural setting. Room 3 has a private terrace, while rooms 1, 2 and 4 open onto the paved pool area. It's 7.5km southeast of Silves. There's a three-night minimum stay in July and August. Cash only.

Quinta da Figueirinha APARTMENT €
(📞282 440 700; www.qdf.pt; Figueirinha; 2-/4-/6-person apt not incl breakfast from €58/92/132; 🅿🛜❄) 🍃 This 36-hectare organic farm and botanic garden 4.7km east of Silves has six apartments with full kitchens; some have washing machines. You can self-cater or breakfast can be arranged for €8. Guests are free to wander the orchards and pick oranges, lemons, clementines and grapefruits. Four above-ground swimming pools are dotted around the grounds.

Duas Quintas GUESTHOUSE €€
(📞282 449 311; www.duasquintas.com; Santo Estevão; d/studio €110/135; 🅿🛜❄) Set amid 6 hectares of orange groves, with views over the rolling hills from the terrace, this restored farmhouse has six partially antique-furnished rooms (including a spacious three-person studio with a kitchenette and washing machine), a communal lounge room, terraces and landscaped natural pool. Cots and high chairs are available for tots. It's 6km northeast of Silves along the N124.

🍴 Eating & Drinking

Pastelaria Rosa CAFE, PASTRIES €
(www.darosa.pt; Largo do Município; pastries €1.50-4, dishes €3-8.50; ⏰7.30am-10pm Mon-Sat; 🛜) Wrought-iron chairs fill the traditional blue-and-white tiled interior and pavement terrace at this atmospheric cafe. House-baked treats include *bolos de arroz* (orange rice-flour cakes) and *folhados de maçã* (apple and almond pastries); it also serves breakfast (fruit salad with yoghurt, cinnamon toast) and light lunches (sandwiches, salads and savoury pastries such as *rissóis de carne* with spicy minced beef).

★Restaurante O Barradas PORTUGUESE €€
(📞282 443 308; www.obarradas.com; Palmeirinha; mains €12.50-26.50, cataplanas €45-46; ⏰6-10pm Thu-Tue) 🍃 The star choice for foodies is this converted farmhouse 4.5km south of Silves, which utilises sustainably sourced fish and organic meat and vegetables in creations like slow-cooked suckling pig, char-grilled octopus with sweet potato, and fava bean and chorizo stew. The owner is a winemaker, whose wares appear on the wine list alongside vintages from Portugal's finest wineries.

Recanto dos Mouros PORTUGUESE €€
(📞282 443 240; www.recantodosmouros.com; Rua Estrada do Monte Branco; mains €9-16; ⏰noon-3pm & 6.30-11pm Thu-Tue) As the crowds of locals attest, this farmhouse restaurant surrounded by citrus orchards is *bom preço-qualidade* (good value for money), serving hearty Algarvian dishes such as *coelho à caçador* (red wine–braised rabbit) and *javali no pote com castanhas* (wild boar with chestnuts). Views stretch south from the terrace to the castle.

Marisqueira Rui SEAFOOD €€
(📞282 442 682; www.marisqueirarui.pt; Rua Conselheiro Vilarinho 27; mains €14-35; ⏰noon-11pm Wed-Mon) With a huge live tank, Silves' best

seafood restaurant is a favourite with locals for its cockles, clams, crabs, Olhão oysters and whole fish, served at communal tables in a cork-lined interior. Head to the awning-shaded terrace on the laneway in summer.

Café Inglês　　　　　　　　　　　　BAR
(☑ 282 442 585; www.cafeingles.com.pt; Rua do Castelo 11; ◷ 10am-5pm Tue & Wed, to 11.30pm Thu-Sun; ☏) Located below the castle entrance, Café Inglês has a wonderful, shady terrace for a coffee or ice-cold beer (pub-style food is also available). One of the Algarve's liveliest venues north of the coast, it has live jazz, fado and African music at weekends.

❶ Information

Centro de Interpretaçao do Património Islâmico (☑ 282 440 800; www.cm-silves.pt; Largo do Município; ◷ 10am-1pm & 2-5pm Mon-Fri) Municipal tourist office within the Islamic history interpretative centre.

Turismo (☑ 282 098 927; www.visitalgarve.pt; Parque Ribeirinho de Silves; ◷ 9.30am-1pm & 2-5.30pm Tue-Sat) Next to the main car park and bus stops.

❶ Getting There & Away

BUS

Buses leave from the riverfront, with direct services to Albufeira (€4.45, 40 minutes, seven daily) and Portimão (€3.45, 35 minutes, eight daily Monday to Friday only), which has connections to towns along the coast.

TRAIN

The train station is 2km south of the town, and you'll need to take a local bus (€1, seven minutes, up to five daily) or a taxi, as it's along a major highway.

Train services from Silves:
Lagos €2.95, 30 minutes, nine daily.
Faro €5.20, one hour, nine daily.

❶ Getting Around

Much of Silves' hilly, compact centre is easily navigated on foot; many streets are pedestrianised areas only. Drivers are advised to park in the large car park on the town side (north) of the river and southwest of the town centre (no charge).

Portimão

POP POP 55,600

Dating back to the time of the Phoenicians, Portimão is the Algarve's second-most-populous city. Most visitors only pass through the city en route to Praia da Rocha, but while it's rough around the edges, it has a long waterfront promenade and an excellent museum in a former fish cannery. You can also take a boat trip up the Rio Arade or go skydiving from its aerodrome.

Portimão was an important trading link for Phoenicians, Greeks and Carthaginians (Hannibal is said to have visited). The Romans called it Portos Magnus, and it was fought over by Moors and Christians. In 1189 Dom Sancho I and a band of crusaders sailed up the Rio Arade from here to besiege Silves. Almost destroyed in the 1755 earthquake, it regained its role as a fishing and canning centre in the 19th century. The last cannery closed in the 1970s.

Portugal's recession in the early 1980s hit Portimão hard and the city has struggled to recover economically, particularly as tourists head to the coast instead. Since the 1990s, vast shopping malls on the city's outskirts have also reduced the prosperity of the centre. Efforts being made to improve Portimão's fortunes include the 2011 expansion of its riverside promenade.

Operators running boat trips up the coast and/or the Rio Arade, visiting caves along the way, include **Santa Bernarda** (☑ 967 023 840; www.santa-bernarda.com; Ribeirinha; adult/child from €35/20). Other activities include parachute jumping with **Skydive Algarve** (☑ 914 266 832; www.skydivealgarve.com; Aerodomo Municipal de Portimão, Montes de Alvor; tandem skydive €150, per dive €31; ◷ by reservation 8.30am-6pm), or golfing at **Penina Golf Resort** (☑ 282 420 200; www.penina.com; N125, Penina; green fees €127), 7.5km northwest of Portimão.

★ **Museu de Portimão**　　　　　　MUSEUM
(☑ 282 405 230; www.museudeportimao.pt; Rua Dom Carlos I; adult/child €3/free; ◷ 2.30-6pm Tue, 10am-6pm Wed-Sun Sep-Jul, 7.30-11pm Tue, 3-11pm Wed-Sun Aug) Housed in a 19th-century fish cannery, the ultramodern, award-winning Museu de Portimão is the city's number-one draw. The museum focuses on three areas: archaeology, underwater finds and, the most fascinating, a re-creation of the fish cannery (mackerel and sardines). You can see former production lines, complete with sound effects – clanking and grinding and the like. An excellent video (in Portuguese) of the fishing industry reveals each step in the process.

Festival da Sardinha　　　　FOOD & DRINK
(www.festivaldasardinha.pt; ◷ Aug) Portimão's sardine festival is a five-day celebration of

Portugal's favourite fish, accompanied by associated music, dance and festivities. It's held at the old fishing quarter, the Zona Ribeirinha de Portimão.

Alameda Hostel HOSTEL €
(☑ 968 696 499; www.alamedahostel.com; Rua do Comércio 9; dm/tw from €18/40; ✳ 🛜) On a pedestrianised street in the city centre, reached by a tiled staircase, this hostel is basic but clean and bright, and puts you within easy walking distance of everything. Female-only dorms are available. There's a small rooftop terrace and two kitchens for self-caterers. Cash only.

Clube Naval de Portimão SEAFOOD €€
(☑ 282 417 529; www.clubenavaldeportimao.com; Zona Ribeirinha; mains €14-24; ⊙ noon-3pm & 7-11pm Tue-Sun; 🛜) On the waterfront near the Museu de Portimão, the Naval Club has a fancy upstairs restaurant, Restaurante do Cais, with unsurpassed views over the river from its terrace. Choose from the day's catch or go for monkfish skewers, prawns sautéed in garlic and chilli or oysters in season. The downstairs snack bar is great for a waterside coffee or beer.

Bar Marginália LIVE MUSIC
(www.facebook.com/barmarginalia; Rua Arco Maravilhas 35; ⊙ 10pm-2am Wed & Thu, to 3am Fri & Sat; 🛜) Reached via an arched stone tunnel off Rua Professor José Buísel, this charismatic backstreet bar is Portimão's best venue for live music, with weekend concerts (normally on the heavier side of the spectrum, such as metal, rock and grunge).

❶ Information

Turismo Municipal (☑ 282 402 487; www.visitalgarve.pt; Largo 1 de Dezembro 3; ⊙ 9.30am-12.30pm & 1.30-5.30pm Mon-Fri) Housed in the city's theatre, Teatro Municipal de Portimão ('Tempo').

❶ Getting There & Away

BUS

Buses run by Frota Azul (www.frotazul-algarve.pt) and Eva buses (www.eva-bus.com) depart from the **bus station** (Avenida Guanaré).

Services include:

Albufeira €4.75, one hour, up to two per hour.
Cabo São Vicente €6.55, 1½ hours, one daily.
Faro €5.70, 1¾ hours, seven daily.
Lagos €4, 35 minutes, up to two per hour.
Lisbon €20, 3¼ hours, six daily.

HIDDEN BEACHSIDE BAR

Descend 33 shallow steps, then take a lift through the sandstone and walk through an underground tunnel to reach Caniço (☑ 282 458 503; www.canico restaurante.com; Aldeamento Prainha 5, Alvor; ⊙ 10am-4am Mar-Nov; 🛜), a hidden bar opening onto a little beach wedged between soaring cliffs about 6km southwest of Portimão. Sangria, punches, cocktails and champagne are highlights of the drinks list. DJs spin nightly, when dancing takes place on the sand and the cliffs are illuminated with neon lights.

Barbecued fish is the speciality of its restaurant, along with classic cataplanas.

Loulé €5.70, 1¾ hours, three daily Saturday and Sunday only.
Monchique €4.60, 45 minutes, nine daily Monday to Friday, six Saturday and Sunday.
Silves €3.45, 35 minutes, eight daily Monday to Friday only.

TRAIN

The train station is on Rua do Moinho, 700m north of the centre.

Trains to/from Lisbon (€28.85, 4½ hours, five daily) require a change in Tunes. Direct services go to Silves (€1.55, 15 minutes, nine daily) and Lagos (€2.05, 20 minutes, 10 daily).

❶ Getting Around

Local bus 33 shuttles between Praia da Rocha and Portimão's Largo do Dique (€1.60) every half-hour. The walk is miserable, passing the deserted port and convent ruins en route, though many do it.

If you have your own wheels, the easiest parking is a free area along the Ribeirinha riverfront.

Praia da Rocha

POP 200

Just 3km south of Portimão, Praia da Rocha has one of the Algarve's best beaches, backed by ochre-red cliffs and the small 17th-century Fortaleza da Santa Catarina (Avenida Tomás Cabreira).

Behind the beach looms the built-up resort catering to summer visitors, when the tiny population swells to over 4000, with high-rise condos and luxury hotels sprouting along the cliffside. The main thoroughfare is a tightly packed row of restaurants, bars, clubs and a well-known casino. Peer beyond the concrete facade and you'll see vestiges of an elegant past, including some late 19th-century and early 20th-century mansions, which are now atmospheric guesthouses.

The Marina de Portimão, painted autumnal colours (to match the cliffs) is at the beach's eastern end, just inside the river mouth.

Activities

Subnauta
DIVING

(☎ 935 577 000; www.subnauta.pt; Rua Engenheiro José Bívar, edifício Scorpius, Praia da Rocha; 1/2 dives €50/75) One of the top dive operators in the Algarve, Subnauta offers a wide range of diving trips, including multiday excursions on its 18m liveaboard. It also offers diving courses.

Sleeping & Eating

Praia da Rocha's popularity means prices are high and accommodation is almost impossible to find during the high season if you don't have a prior reservation.

The marina has a row of cafes, restaurants and fast-food outlets, some of which face the beautiful Praia Meia Grande.

Hotel da Rocha
HOTEL €€

(☎ 282 424 081; www.hoteldarocha.com; Avenida Tomás Cabreira; d/f from €115/195; P ❋ 🛜 ≋) Close to the beach strip, this high-rise couldn't have a better location. Its 158 rooms are huge, light and contemporary, with fridges, microwaves and balconies; family rooms sleep four. It's worth the upgrade to the ones that face the sea, though the balconies can be noisy with traffic and revellers.

★ Bela Vista
HISTORIC HOTEL €€€

(☎ 282 460 280; www.hotelbelavista.net; Avenida Tomás Cabreira; d/ste from €368/671; ⊙ Mar-Dec; P ❋ 🛜 ≋) This exquisite spot – a renovated 1918-built mansion with two modern wings containing 39 rooms and six suites – was overhauled by Portuguese interior-designer Graça Viterbo, blending contemporary and antique furnishings. There's a L'Occitane spa with an indoor pool, sauna, Turkish steam bath and treatment rooms, a magnificent outdoor pool overlooking the beach, and a Michelin-starred, evening-only restaurant serving elevated Portuguese cuisine.

Albergaria Vila Lido
GUESTHOUSE €€€

(☎ 282 241 127; www.vilalido.pt; Avenida Tomás Cabreira; d/ste from €120/200; ⊙ Apr-Nov; ❋ 🛜) Footsteps from the beach and fortress, this sturdy white, blue-trimmed, converted 19th-century mansion has superwelcoming hosts and bright rooms, some of which have terracotta-tiled balconies and sea views. There's a small, grassy garden with sunloungers and a fountain; breakfast is served on the terrace overlooking the Atlantic or in the chestnut-beamed dining room.

F Restaurante
PORTUGUESE €€

(☎ 919 115 512; www.facebook.com/restaurantef; Avenida Tomás Cabreira; mains €15-22; ⊙ 2.30-10.30pm Mar-Dec; 🛜) Classier than most restaurants on the strip, F has superb views over the beach from the covered terrace and contemporary Portuguese dishes such as cornbread-crumbed octopus, mackerel ceviche with tiger milk (a citrus marinade) and sweet potato, or slow-cooked suckling pig stuffed with Algarve oranges.

Marisqueira Praia da Rocha
PORTUGUESE €€

(☎ 282 416 541; https://restaurant-marisqueira-praia-da-rocha.business.site; Rua Bartolomeu Dias; mains €9-16, cataplanas €37-39; ⊙ 11am-11pm Feb-Dec) An unusually traditional restaurant for Praia da Rocha, this low-key place serves classic Portuguese fare: *sardinhas grelhadas* (salt-seasoned grilled sardines), *arroz de tamboril* (monkfish and coriander rice) and *cozida à Portuguesa* (pork and cabbage stew). The exotic fish in the aquariums are not for consumption. The nicest seats are in the umbrella-shaded courtyard.

Drinking & Nightlife

Most of Praia da Rocha's bars have satellite TVs screening sporting matches, live music and karaoke. Many are owned or run by foreign residents. These and the town's plethora of Irish pubs are open all day (and nearly all night). You'll find more bars at the marina.

Nana's Bar
BAR

(Estrada da Rocha; ⊙ noon-4am; 🛜) The best bar in town by some distance, Nana's has much more local character than the others, pours better drinks (local wines, craft beers and generous cocktails) and keeps it real with Portuguese lingua franca.

ℹ Information

Turismo (☎ 282 419 132; www.visitalgarve. pt; Avenida Tomás Cabreira; ⊙ 9am-12.30pm & 1.30-5.30pm Jun-Sep) Large office strategically positioned on the strip.

ℹ Getting There & Away

Praia da Rocha's bus terminus is opposite the Fortaleza da Santa Catarina.

City bus 33 heads to Portimão (€1.60, 10 minutes, every 30 minutes).

Eva buses run to/from Lisbon (€20, 4½ hours, six daily).

Lagos

POP 22,000

As tourist towns go, Lagos (*lah-goosh*) has got the lot. The port town, which launched many naval excursions during Portugal's extraordinary Age of Discovery, lies along the bank of the Rio Bensafrim. Its old town's pretty, cobbled lanes and picturesque squares and churches are enclosed by 16th-century walls. Beyond the walls is a modern but not overly unattractive sprawl and some truly fabulous beaches.

With a huge range of activities spanning water sports, boat trips and horse riding, excellent restaurants and a pumping nightlife, it's not surprising that people of all ages are drawn here.

History

Phoenicians and Greeks set up shop at this port (which later became Roman Lacobriga) at the mouth of the muddy Rio Bensafrim. Afonso III recaptured it from the Moors in 1241, but it wasn't until 1249 that he claimed it definitively. In 1415 a giant fleet set sail from Lagos under the command of the 21-year-old Prince Henry the Navigator to seize Ceuta in Morocco, thereby setting the stage for the Age of Discovery.

The shipyards of Lagos built and launched Prince Henry's caravels, and Henry split his time between his trading company here and his navigation school at Sagres. Local boy Gil Eanes left Lagos in 1434 as commander of the first ship to round West Africa's Cape Bojador. Others continued to bring back information about the African coast, along with ivory, gold and slaves. Lagos has the dubious distinction of having hosted (in 1444) the first sale of Africans as slaves to Europeans, and the town grew into a slave-trading centre.

It was also from Lagos in 1578 that Dom Sebastião, along with the cream of the Portuguese nobility and an army of Portuguese, Spanish, Dutch and German buccaneers, left on a disastrous crusade to Christianise North Africa, which ended in a debacle at El-Ksar el Kebir in Morocco. Francis Drake inflicted heavy damage on Lagos a few years later, in 1587.

Lagos was the Algarve's high-profile capital from 1576 until 1755, when the earthquake flattened it.

Today tourism drives the economy.

◉ Sights

Meia Praia (Map p200), the vast expanse of sand east of the marina, starts 1km by foot (via a footbridge) or 2km by road from central Lagos, reachable by train year-round and by boat in summer. South of town, the beaches – **Batata**, **Pinhão**, **Dona Ana** and **Camilo**, among others – are smaller and more secluded, lapped by calm waters and punctuated with amazing grottoes, coves and towers of coloured sandstone.

★ **Ponta da Piedade**   VIEWPOINT
(Point of Piety; Map p200) Protruding 2.5km south of Lagos, Ponta da Piedade is a wedge of headland with contorted, polychrome sandstone cliffs and towers, complete with a lighthouse and, in spring, hundreds of nesting egrets, with crystal-clear turquoise water below. The surrounding area blazes with wild orchids in spring. On a clear day you can see east to Carvoeiro and west to Sagres. The only way to reach it is by car or on foot.

Museu de Cera dos Descobrimentos   MUSEUM
(Map p200; ☏ 282 039 650; www.museucera descobrimentoscom; Urbanizaço, Marina da Lagos; adult/child €6/4; ⊙ 10am-7pm Jul & Aug, to 6pm Apr-Jun & Sep, to 5pm Oct-Mar) Unlike typical celebrity-filled wax museums, this one has 22 historic wax figures representing 16 different points in time during Portugal's Age of Discovery. They include Prince Henry the Navigator, Gil Eanes, Pope Alexander VI and Ferdinand Magellan (the first navigator credited with sailing across the Pacific). It's engaging for kids and adults alike; information panels are in English and Portuguese.

Centro Ciênia Viva de Lagos   MUSEUM
(Map p196; ☏ 282 770 000; www.lagos.cienciaviva. pt; Rua Dr Faria e Silva 34; adult/child €5/2.50; ⊙ 10am-6pm Tue-Sun) Young adventurers will especially love this science museum devoted to Portuguese seafaring in the 15th and 16th centuries. Its main exhibit covers the age of navigation from the astrolabe (an ancient instrument used to calculate latitude using the sun and stars in day and night skies)

Lagos

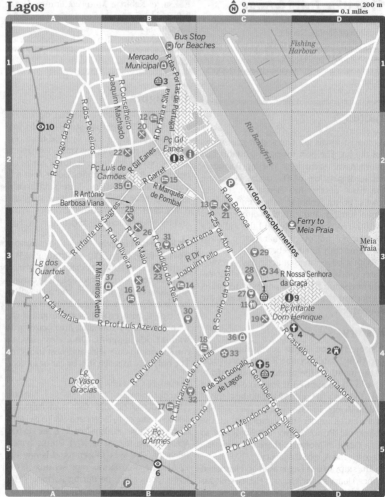

to today's GPS systems. Kids can also operate a solar-powered lighthouse, move sailboats around a pool with an air blower, use sonar and look through a periscope in a submarine.

Igreja de Santo António
CHURCH

(Map p196; Rua General Alberto da Silveira; adult/child incl museum €3/1.50; ⊙ 9.30am-12.30pm & 2-5pm Tue-Sun) A baroque extravaganza, this little church bursts with gilded, carved wood and beaming cherubs. The dome and *azulejo* panels were installed during repairs after the 1755 earthquake. Enter the church from the adjacent Museu Municipal.

Museu Municipal
MUSEUM

(Map p196; ☑ 282 762 301; www.cm-lagos.com; Rua General Alberto da Silveira; adult/child €3/1.50; ⊙ 9.30am-12.30pm & 2-5pm Tue-Sun) The town museum holds a bit of everything: swords and pistols, landscapes and portraits, minerals and crystals, coins, Moorish pottery, miniature furniture, Roman mosaics, African artefacts, stone tools, model boats, the original 1504 town charter and an intriguing model of an imaginary Portuguese town. Exhibits are scattered randomly through the museum, with limited explanations, making it unwittingly like a treasure hunt. The museum

Lagos

is also the entry point for the baroque Igreja de Santo António.

🏃 Activities

Lagos is a popular surfing centre and has good facilities; surfing companies head to the west coast for bigger waves.

Numerous boat operators have ticket stands at the marina or along the promenade opposite. Competition is fierce (expect plenty of hustle) but they run some fun outings. Local fishers offering jaunts to the grottoes by motorboat trawl for customers along the promenade and by the Fortaleza da Ponta da Bandeira.

Lagos Surf Center   SURFING
(Map p196; ☑ 282 764 734; www.lagossurfcenter. com; Rua da Silva Lopes 31; 1-/3-/5-day courses €60/165/250) This surf school travels along the Algarve to locations with suitable swells. Private lessons per day cost €120. It also rents out wetsuits (€5 per day) and boards (€10 to €25) and offers beach kayaking and stand-up paddleboarding (per half/full day €30/50). Children must be accompanied by a family member over 14 years of age.

Algarve Water Sport   WATER SPORTS
(Mapp200;☑960460800;www.algarvewatersport. com; Estrada da Albarderia; water sports lessons/ equipment hire per day from €55/35, 7-day surf camp incl accommodation & sports from €675) Small-group windsurfing, kite-surfing, stand-up paddleboarding and surfing lessons and equipment hire are all available from this long-established operator. Rates include transfers from your own accommodation to wherever the wind or waves are best on the day, and an 'all action guarantee', so if conditions aren't favourable for one activity, you can switch to another.

Blue Ocean   DIVING
(Map p200; ☑ 964 665 667; www.blue-ocean-divers.de; Hotel Âncora Park, Estrada de Porto de Mós 837; 1/10 dives €35/270, with gear €55/450) Blue Ocean runs out to eight different dive sites, including reefs, wrecks and caves. Night dives are possible by request; beginners can take a half-day discovery experience (€30). It also organises snorkelling trips (per half-day €30) and kayak safaris (half/full day €30/45). Lessons take place in the pool at the Hotel Âncora Park.

Tiffany's   HORSE RIDING
(☑282 697 395; www.teamtiffanys.com; Vale Grifo, Almádena; 1hr/3hr/full-day rides €33/85/140; ☺9am-dusk) Located 8.5km west of Lagos, this riding centre runs rides from one hour through to all-day forest trips that include a picnic. Lessons lasting 90 minutes cost €75;

there are also 20-minute pony rides for kids (€15). You'll need your own transport to get here.

Tours

Mountain Bike Adventure · MOUNTAIN BIKING

(Map p200; ☎918 502 663; www.themountain bikeadventure.com; Porta da Vila; half-/full-day tours from €40/80) Bike enthusiasts will have some fun with this company, which runs a range of outings from shorter scenic trips to mountain-to-coast trips and full-on technical rides with shoots, drops and jumps. The meeting point is on the southern side of Porta da Vila, from where buses with trailers take you up into the hilly hinterland.

Algarve Water World · WILDLIFE, CRUISE

(Map p200; ☎938 305 000; www.algarvewater world.com; Marina de Lagos; adult/child 90min tour €40/25, 75min grotto tour €15/7.50; ☺Mar-Oct) This small outfit offers excellent dolphin-spotting trips on a 7.4m rigid inflatable named the *Dizzy Dolphin*. Along with three species of dolphins (common, bottlenose and risso), you'll often spot sharks, turtles, orcas and fin whales. Grotto trips aboard the *Captain Nemo* take you to caves, cliffs and beaches.

Outdoor Tours · OUTDOORS

(☎282 969 520; www.outdoor-tours.com; Rua Francisco Bivar 142A, Mexilhoeira Grande; tours from €28) This Dutch-run company runs downhill and off-road mountain biking (€55), kayaking (€28) and walking trips (day walks €42) between Lagos and Serra de Monchique. Departure points vary, depending on the activity. Kids must be aged 12 and above.

Kayak Adventures · KAYAKING

(Map p200; ☎917 716 202; www.kayakadventures lagos.com; Cais da Solara, Avenida dos Descobrimentos; 2½hr kayaking trip €30; ☺Mar-Oct) Kayaking trips from Praia da Batata give you an up-close perspective of the caves and fissures in the cliffs along the Ponta da Piedade. Advance online bookings are essential.

Bom Dia · CRUISE

(Map p200; ☎282 764 670; www.bomdia-boattrips. com; Marina de Lagos) Lagos' oldest boat tour operator runs trips on traditional schooners, including a five-hour barbecue cruise with a chance to swim (adult/child €55/30), a two-hour grotto trip (€27.55/12.50) and a three-hour family fishing trip (adult/child €40/25, plus fishing licence per person €5).

Sleeping

Sol a Sol · HOSTEL €

(Map p196; ☎282 085 377; www.solasolhostel.com; Rua Lançarote de Freitas 22; dm/d from €20/50; ☏) Well located for nightlife, this central *residencial*-turned-hostel has private rooms with tiny balconies and views over the town, and tightly packed dorms, both single-sex and mixed. Views also extend from its roof terrace, which has a barbecue.

When it fills up, guests might be relocated to its sister property, the **Old Town Lagos Hostel** (☎282 088 309; www.oldtownlagoshostel. com; Rua da Oliveira 70; dm €13-23; ☏).

★ Lagos Atlantic Hotel · HOTEL €€

(Map p200; ☎282 761 527; www.facebook.com/ lagosatlantic.hotel; Estrada do Monte Carapeto 9; d/f from €115/125; P❄☀) Most of the spacious rooms at this pristine, stylish hotel, which opened in 2018, face south and open to balconies overlooking the pool. Family rooms have pull-out sofa beds; kids under 12 stay free. Handy amenities include shaded lock-up parking and a barbecue area.

It's peacefully located 1.7km southwest of town and 500m uphill from the long, family-ly-friendly beach, Praia de Porto de Mós.

Hotel Mar Azul · GUESTHOUSE €€

(Map p196; ☎282 770 230; www.hotelmarazul.eu; Rua 25 de Abril 13; d not incl breakfast from €70; ☀☏) Central, well-run and delightfully welcoming, this little gem is one of Lagos' best-value spots, with tidy, compact white rooms with chocolate-toned accents, some with small balconies. The simple breakfast costs €5 extra.

Vila Galé Lagos · RESORT €€€

(Map p200; ☎282 771 400; www.vilagale.com; Rua Sophia de Mello Breyner Andresen, Meia Praia; d/f/ ste from €155/202/217; P❄☀☏) Opposite the beach, this vast place lays on all the creature comforts for resort-loving visitors, with two huge pools (one indoor, one outdoor), three restaurants, a spa and tennis and basketball courts. Its 130 rooms and suites are spacious and contemporary, with white, grey and red hues. Family rooms sleep four; kids under 12 stay and eat for free.

Hotel Marina Rio · HOTEL €€€

(Map p200; ☎282 780 830; www.marinario.com; Avenida dos Descobrimentos 388; d from €215; P❄☀☏) Opposite the footbridge leading to the marina, this ideally positioned hotel completed renovations in 2019. Rooms open onto balconies, but the best views are from the rooftop terrace, which has a small swimming pool.

🍴 Eating

Stock up on fresh produce at Lagos' **covered market** (www.cm-lagos.pt; Avenida dos Descobrimentos; ⊘ 8am-2pm Mon-Sat).

Bar Quim
PORTUGUESE €

(☑ 282 763 294; Quinta da Praia, Meia Praia; dishes €4.50-13; ⊘ 10am-10pm daily Jul & Aug, 10am-10pm Fri-Wed May, Jun, Sep & Oct; 🛜) Right on the sand, this is the best of the places to eat on Meia Praia. It's a fair stroll along the beach, but it's well worth it for the welcoming service, delicious fish soup and house-speciality spicy prawns cooked in a single pot with olive oil, garlic, coriander and chilli.

Mimar Café
CAFE €

(Map p196; Rua António Barbosa Viana 27; tapas €2-6.50, dishes €4.50-11; ⊘ 8am-midnight Mon-Sat Jun-Aug, to 10pm Sep-May; 🛜) One of the town's best-value casual cafes, Mimar is excellent for coffee and breakfasts (eg omelettes, croissants) and lunch dishes like toasties, burgers and steak sandwiches. By night it morphs into a tapas and wine bar serving *petiscos* such as *azeitonas* (marinated olives), *caracóis* (garlic snails), *chouriço* (flambéed chorizo) and *pastéis de bacalhau* (cod fritters) alongside all-Portuguese wines.

Café Gombá
CAFE €

(Map p196; ☑ 282 762 188; https://pastelaria-gomba.negocio.site; Rua Cândido dos Reis 56; dishes €0.80-4; ⊘ 8am-7pm Mon-Sat year-round, Sun mid-Jun–mid-Sep; ✸) Around since 1964, this traditional cafe-bakery is a local favourite for cakes and sweets including *pastéis de nata*, *bolas de berlim* (custard-filled doughnut-like pastry balls) and *pastéis de laranja* (sticky orange cake made from Algarve oranges). Pick them up to take away or dine on site.

Bora Café
CAFE €

(Map p196; Rua Conselheiro Joaquim Machado 17; dishes €4-8.50; ⊘ 8.30am-6pm Mon-Sat; 🛜🍽) Tiny Bora is the ideal place for your healthy fruit and veggie fix, with omelettes, soups, salads, sandwiches (such as beetroot, sweet potato and hummus) and delicious *batidos* (fruit shakes – try the kiwi and coconut flavour). Most dishes, though not all, are vegetarian. Tables spill out onto the cobbles.

O Camilo
SEAFOOD €€

(Map p200; ☑ 282 763 845; www.restaurante-camilo.pt; Praia do Camilo; mains €11.50-23.50; ⊘ noon-4pm & 6-10pm Jun-Sep, to 9pm Oct-May; 🛜) Perched above pretty Praia do Camilo, this sophisticated restaurant is renowned for its high-quality seafood dishes. Specialities include razor clams, fried squid, lobster and oysters in season, along with grilled fish. The 40-seat dining room is light, bright and airy, and the large 28-seat terrace overlooks the ocean. Bookings are a good idea any time and essential in high season.

Arribalé
PORTUGUESE €€

(Map p196; ☑ 918 556 618; www.arribale.com; Rua da Barroca 40; mains €10.50-18.50; ⊘ 7-11pm Mon-Sat) Tucked away on an atmospheric street that was Lagos' original sea wall, this pretty, tiled place does a short, simple menu of seafood and grilled meat. The owners are friendly, quality is high, and there's an appealing, homey vibe. There aren't many tables, so it's worth booking. Cash only.

Casinha do Petisco
SEAFOOD €€

(Map p196; Rua da Oliveira 51; mains €9-17, cataplanas €32-38; ⊘ noon-3pm & 6-11pm Tue-Sat Jul & Aug, 6-11pm Tue-Sat Oct-Jun) Blink and you'll miss this tiny traditional restaurant. Cosy and simply decorated, it concentrates on seafood grills and shellfish dishes, including *camarão e amêijoas* (one-pot clam and prawn dish), *lulas fritas com alho* (garlic-sautéed squid) and two-person *cataplanas*. It fills to the gills in high summer, but maintains a strong local following out of season.

A Forja
PORTUGUESE €€

(Map p196; ☑ 282 768 588; Rua dos Ferreiros 17; mains €8.50-22.50, cataplanas €30-35; ⊘ noon-3pm & 6.30-10pm Mon-Sat) Hearty, top-quality traditional food served in a bustling environment at great prices sees this buzzing *adega tipica* (wine bar) pull in the crowds. Daily specials are always reliable, as are simply prepared fish dishes such as grilled sole, turbot and mackerel, and two-person *cataplanas*.

Atlântico
PORTUGUESE €€€

(Map p200; ☑ 282 792 086; www.atlanticorestaurante.com; Pinhal da Meia Praia L6, Meia Praia; mains €19-32; ⊘ noon-3pm & 6-10pm; 🛜) In summer, the stunning terrace overlooking the beach is the place to be, but the wood-panelled interior with a beautiful timber bar is also wonderfully atmospheric. Both Portuguese and international dishes feature on the menu, including sizzling steaks, poultry (eg chicken Kiev) and flambéed crepes. Its wine collection has bottles as old as 1856. Kids' dishes cost €11 to €15.

Around Lagos

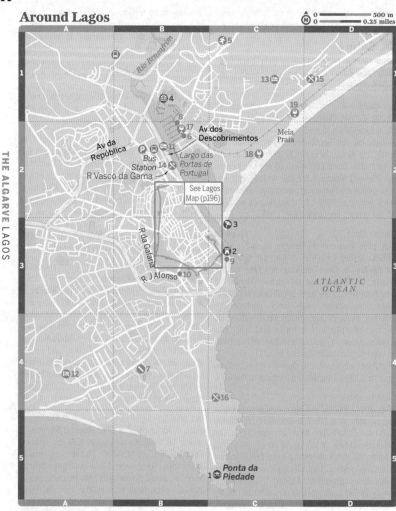

Drinking & Nightlife

★ The Garden

BEER GARDEN

(Map p196; www.facebook.com/thegardenlagos; Rua Lançarote de Freitas 48; ⊙ bar 1pm-midnight, kitchen to 10pm May-Nov; ☏) Filled with flowering hibiscus, bougainvillea and citrus trees, with a mural of a barrelling wave, this fabulous beer garden is a brilliant spot to lounge with a beer or cocktail on a sunny afternoon. The aromas of barbecuing meat and seafood will make you want to stay for a meal. Look for the kissing snails painted on the outside wall.

Its tortoiseshell cat, Burney, is otherwise known as 'the boss'.

★ Bon Vivant

BAR

(Map p196; www.bonvivantbarinlagos.com; Rua 25 de Abril 105; ⊙ 4pm-3.30am Mon-Thu, to 4am Fri-Sun; ☏) Spread across five levels, including two underground rooms and a roof terrace, each with its own bar, cherry-red-painted Bon Vivant shakes up great house cocktails including the signature Mr Bonvivant (jenever, absinthe, strawberry-infused Aperol and bitters). Happy hour runs from 5pm to 9pm; DJs spin nightly downstairs.

Around Lagos

Red Eye Bar   BAR
(Map p196; Rua Cándido dos Reis 63; ☺8pm-2am)
This straight-up rock 'n' surf bar makes a top
spot to kick off the night (happy hour runs
from 8pm to 10pm), with a pool table, darts
and fun-loving staff.

Bahia Beach Bar   BAR
(Map p200; www.bahiabar.pt; Estrada de São
Roque, Meia Praia; ☺10.30am-11pm daily Jul & Aug,
10.30am-7pm Tue-Sun May, Jun, Sep & Oct; ☏)
An essential hang-out on the sand at Meia
Praia, busy Bahia has homemade sangria,
fruit-based cocktails, Algarve and Alentejo
wines, gourmet dining (poultry pie with foie
gras; lobster and cod terrine) and live music
at weekends.

Inside Out   BAR
(Map p196; www.facebook.com/InsideoutFace;
Rua Cândido dos Reis 19; ☺8pm-4am; ☏) This
late opener has good DJs and a lively atmosphere, fuelled by enormous fishbowl
cocktails; you'll often see people (or find
yourself) dancing on the tables.

Amuras Bar   BAR
(Map p196; Passeio dos Descobrimentos, Marina de
Lagos; ☺10am-3am; ☏) One of half a dozen
bar-restaurants overlooking the marina and
the town beyond, this breezy spot is especially popular for a sundowner in its interi-
or framed by floor-to-ceiling glass or on its
terrace to catch the sunset. Live music plays
most nights in summer and from Thursday
to Sunday the rest of the year.

Grand Café   CLUB
(Map p196; Rua da Senhora da Graça 2; ☺10pm-6am
Jun-Oct, to 4am Nov-May; ☏) This classy place
has three bars, nightly DJs and lots of gold

leaf, kitsch, red velvet and cherubs. Given its
central location, it's a popular spot to end up.

☆ Entertainment

Stevie Ray's   JAZZ, BLUES
(Map p196; ☏914 923 885; Rua da Senhora da Graça
9; ☺9pm-6am; ☏) This intimate, two-level,
candlelit joint is the best live-music bar in
town, with blues, jazz and occasional rock
acts. Admission is free, but a €5 minimum
spend on drinks is required.

Centro Cultural   PERFORMING ARTS
(Map p196; ☏282 770 450; www.facebook.com/
CentroCulturaldeLagos; Rua Lançarote de Freitas 7;
☺3-11pm Wed-Sat Jul & Aug, 10am-6pm Tue-Sat Sep-
Jun; ☏) Lagos' main venue for performances
stages everything from choirs and live music
gigs to theatre, opera, comedy and dance, and
also hosts contemporary-art exhibitions.

🛍 Shopping

★ Mar d'Estórias   CONCEPT STORE
(Map p196; www.mardestorias.com; Rua Silva Lopes
30; ☺10am-7pm Mon, 10am-10pm Wed-Sat) ✎
Portuguese handicrafts at this artisan emporium include ceramics, blankets, scarves
and bags, along with stationery, cookbooks
and music, while gourmet goods span olive
oils, honey, cheeses, preserves, tinned fish,
sweets, beers, wines and liqueurs. On the
mezzanine, the in-house cafe serves *petiscos*
and platters, as well as full meals; you can
also dine on its panoramic roof terrace.

ℹ Information

Turismo (Map p196; ☏282 763 031; www.visit
algarve.pt; Praça Gil Eanes 17; ☺9.30am-1pm
& 2-5.30pm) Helpful office on the main square.

LAZY DAYS

The Algarve is awash with adrenaline-pumping activities, from horse riding, mountain biking and hiking to water sports galore. While Lagos has all those and more, it's also a perfect place to unwind, with stunning beaches, superb shopping and the region's best nightlife.

BEACHES

Lagos' best-known beach is lively **Meia Praia** (p195), a 4km-long sweep of golden sand, easily reached on foot, by car or a summer ferry. Smaller, more secluded alternatives with grottoes, coves, coloured sandstone cliffs and calm waters are just south of town; try Batata, Pinhão, Dona Ana and Camilo, for starters.

SHOPPING

While wandering Lagos' walled old town, you'll find intriguing shops selling local specialities, including cork (fashioned into everything from hats to shoes and bags); beautiful *azulejos*; local liqueurs like fig or carob; and tinned sardines. Artisan emporium **Mar d'Estórias** (p201) is a one-stop shop and has a fantastic in-house cafe.

NIGHTLIFE

Lagos' after-dark scene is the best in the Algarve, spanning beach bars for a feet-in-the-sand sundowner to classy bar-restaurants, wine bars, dive bars, rock bars and nightclubs with DJs filling the dance floors. Two of the best venues are al fresco hangout **The Garden** (p200), a surfer favourite with fruit trees, street-art-style murals and a barbecue, and all-rounder **Bon Vivant** (p200), set over five levels, with a great rooftop terrace and knock-out house cocktails.

1. Lagos town centre (p195)
2. Bon Vivant (p200)
3. Praia de Dona Ana (p195)

ℹ Getting There & Away

BUS

Buses run by Eva (www.eva-bus.com) and Rede Expressos (www.rede-expressos.pt) use the **bus station** (Rua Mercado de Levante). Destinations include the following:

Albufeira €5.70, 1¼ hours, six daily.

Aljezur €4, 50 minutes, four daily Monday to Friday, one daily Saturday.

Cabo de São Vicente €4.30, one hour, one daily Monday to Friday.

Faro €6.05, 2¼ hours, six daily.

Lisbon €20, 3¾ hours, six express services daily.

Portimão €4.45, 25 minutes, six daily.

Sagres €4, one hour, up to two per hour.

Seville (Spain) €21, 5½ hours, two daily.

TRAIN

Lagos is at the western end of the Algarve line. Direct connections include the following:

Faro (€7.40, 1¾ hours, nine daily), via Albufeira (€4.85, one hour).

Vila Real de Santo António (€10.60, 3¼ hours, seven daily).

Trains go daily to Lisbon (all requiring a change at Tunes; €22.15, four hours, five daily).

ℹ Getting Around

BOAT

In summer, locals run a **boat** (one way €1; ☉ sunrise-sunset Jun-Oct) to and fro across the estuary to the Meia Praia side from a landing near the Forte da Ponta da Bandeira.

BUS

Local Onda bus 2 (www.aonda.pt) links the city centre with all the surrounding beaches – the main town-centre **stop** is near the market on the riverfront. Bus 1 circles the city in an anticlockwise direction. The tourist office can provide information.

Tickets start from €1.20; travel to the beaches is €1.60. A day ticket costs €3.60. Buses run from Monday to Saturday between 7am and 8pm, with reduced services on Sunday.

CAR & MOTORCYCLE

Drivers are advised to leave their cars in one of the free car parks on the outskirts of Lagos (look for the large parking signs). An alternative is the underground car park on Avenida dos Descobrimentos, but this road can get congested in summer. Street parking spaces close to the centre are metered – watch out or you'll be wheel-clamped.

Local agencies offering competitive car- and scooter-hire rates include the following.

Auto Jardim (☑ 282 769 486; www.autocar-hire.net; Rua Victor Costa e Silva 18A; ☉ 10am-1pm & 3-5pm)

Luzcar (☑ 282 761 016; www.luzcar.com; Largo das Portas de Portugal 10; ☉ 9am-1pm & 3-6pm)

Motorent (☑ 965 525 468; www.motorent.pt; Rua Victor Costa e Silva; per day bicycle/motorcycle/scooter hire from €13/45/35; ☉ 9am-1pm & 3-7pm)

TAXI

You can call for a taxi (282 460 610) or find one on Rua das Portas de Portugal where buses stop.

Salema

POP 280

Set on a wide bay 18km west of Lagos, this charmingly small coastal resort has an easy-going atmosphere and is surrounded by developments that manage not to overwhelm it. It's ideal for families, and there are several small, secluded beaches within a few kilometres – Praia da Salema by the village, Praia da Figueira to the west and Boca do Rio to the east.

Salema Eco Camp CAMPGROUND €

(☑ 282 695 201; www.salemaecocamp.com; M537, Praia de Salema; sites per adult/tent/car €5.50/6/4.50, tipi/studios/apt from €45/60/90; P ⊕ ☎ ⚤) ⚡ Utilising solar power, this eco-friendly campground 1.5km north of Salema has a peaceful, tree-filled setting with abundant birdlife. Teepees sleep two or four people. Studios (for two) and apartments (for four) have en suite bathrooms, kitchenettes and private terraces. Pizzas and toasties are served at the on-site cafe. Wi-fi in public areas only. There's a designated nudist camping area.

A Maré GUESTHOUSE €€

(☑ 282 695 165; www.the-mare.com; Praia de Salema; s/d/tr/apt from €75/85/100/110; ☉ mid-Jan–mid-Dec; ⊕ ☎) A 100m stroll from the beach, this blue-and-white beach house has bright rooms, some with sea views, a pretty garden and a guest kitchen. Five-person apartments have a balcony and kitchenette but, unlike the rooms, don't include breakfast. There's a three-night minimum stay in July and August (five-night minimum for apartments), and a two-night minimum at other times.

Água na Boca PORTUGUESE €€

(☑ 282 695 651; Rua dos Pescadores 82; mains €12-18; ☉ 5-11pm Mon-Sat; ☎) A top-notch choice in Salema, Água na Boca has a dining room opening to a terrace with retractable glass and a well-stocked wine cellar. The menu changes daily but might include grilled octopus with sweet potato, whole sea bass, barbecued Iberian pork ribs or lamb rump.

Restaurante O Lourenço   SEAFOOD €€
(📞282 698 622; www.facebook.com/lourenco salema; Rua 28 de Janeiro 11; mains €9-15, cataplanas €25-35; ⊗noon-3pm & 6-10pm Mon-Sat) Compact and unpretentious, with more seating on a covered terrace situated across the street, this place is recommended for its seafood: the day's catch will be brought out on a stainless steel platter for you to select from. Seasonally changing dishes could include grilled turbot and chickpea salad, Medronho-braised clams, piri-piri lobster or a pork-and-squid *cataplana* for two.

ℹ Getting There & Away

Buses connect Salema with Lagos (€2.90, 30 minutes, seven daily) and Sagres (€3.15, 35 minutes, seven daily). Many more stop at the crossroads, from where it's a 2km walk along the main road – these services are marked on timetables as 'Salema(x)'.

Sagres

POP 1900

Overlooking some of the Algarve's most dramatic scenery, the small, elongated village of Sagres has an end-of-the-world feel, with its sea-carved cliffs high above the frothing ocean strung with wind-whipped fortresses that connect it to Portugal's rich nautical past. It's the only place in the world where white storks are known to nest on cliff faces.

Situated 1.5km east of the square, past holiday villas and restaurants, is the port, still a centre for boat building and lobster fishing, and the marina. Outside town are the striking cliffs of Cabo de São Vicente (p207), the southwesternmost point of the European mainland, and splendid beaches that are increasingly popular with surfers.

Sagres has milder temperatures than other parts of the Algarve, with Atlantic winds keeping the summers cool.

History

Sagres is where Prince Henry the Navigator built a new, fortified town and a semi-monastic school of navigation that specialised in cartography, astronomy and ship design, steering Portugal towards the Age of Discovery.

At least, that's according to history and myth. Henry was, among other things, governor of the Algarve and he had a residence in its primary port town, Lagos, from where most expeditions set sail. He certainly did put together a kind of nautical think tank, though how much thinking went on out at Sagres is uncertain. He definitely had a house somewhere near Sagres, where he died in November 1460.

In May 1587 the English privateer Francis Drake, in the course of attacking supply lines to the Spanish Armada, captured and wrecked the fortifications around Sagres. The Ponta de Sagres was refortified following the earthquake of 1755, after which there was little of verifiable antiquity left standing.

◉ Sights

There are four good beaches a short drive or long walk from Sagres: Praia da Mareta, just below the town; lovely Praia do Martinhal to the east; Praia do Tonel on the other side of the Ponta de Sagres, which is especially good for surfing; and the isolated Praia de Beliche, on the way to Cabo de São Vicente.

Fortaleza de Sagres   FORTRESS
(📞282 620 142; www.monumentosdoalgarve.pt; adult/child €3/1.50; ⊗9.30am-8pm May-Sep, to 5.30pm Oct-Apr) Blank, hulking and forbidding, Sagres' fortress offers breathtaking views over the sheer cliffs, and all along the coast to Cabo de São Vicente. Legend has it that this is where Prince Henry the Navigator established his navigation school. It's quite a large site, so allow at least an hour to see everything.

Inside the gate is a huge, curious stone pattern that measures 43m in diameter. Named the *rosa dos vento*s (literally, a pictorial representation of a compass), this strange configuration is believed to be a mariner's compass or a sundial of sorts. Excavated in 1921, the paving may date from Prince Henry's time but is more likely to be from the 16th century.

The precinct's oldest buildings include a cistern tower to the east, a house and the small, whitewashed, 16th-century Igreja de Nossa Senhora da Graça (www.promontoriodesagres.pt; Fortaleza de Sagres; ⊗9.30-8pm May-Sep, to 5.30pm Oct-Apr), a simple barrel-vaulted structure with a gilded 17th-century altarpiece. Take a closer look

Sagres

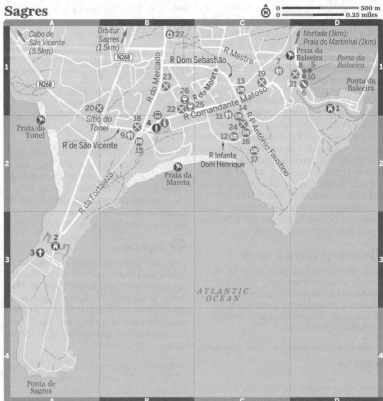

Sagres

⊙ Sights
1 Fortaleza da Baleeira	D1
2 Fortaleza de Sagres	A3
3 Igreja de Nossa Senhora da Graça	A3
4 Statue of Henry the Navigator	B2

⊕ Activities, Courses & Tours
5 Cape Cruiser	D1
6 DiversCape	D1
7 Free Ride Sagres Surfcamp	C1
8 Mar Ilimitado	D1
9 Sagres Natura	B2
10 Sea Xplorer Sagres	D1
11 Wave Sensations	C1

⊟ Sleeping
12 Aparthotel Navigator	C2
13 Casa Azul	C1
14 Casa do Cabo de Santa Maria	C2
15 Mareta View Boutique B&B	B2
16 Pontalaia	C2
17 Pousada do Infante	C2

⊗ Eating
18 A Casínha	B2
19 A Grelha	C1
20 A Sagres	A1
21 A Tasca	D1
22 Mum's	B1
23 Three Little Birds	B1
24 Vila Velha	C2

⊕ Drinking & Nightlife
25 Agua Salgada	B1
26 Dromedário	B1
Pau de Pita	(see 26)

⊕ Shopping
27 Mercado Municipal 25 de Abril	B1

at the tiled altar panels, which feature elephants and antelopes.

Many of the gaps you see between buildings are the result of a 1960s spring clean of

17th- and 18th-century ruins that was organised to make way for a reconstruction (later aborted) that was to coincide with the 500th anniversary of Henry's death.

Its visitors centre contains a gift shop, an exhibition centre and a cafe.

It's a great walk around the perimeter of the promontory; information boards (in English and Portuguese) shed light on the rich flora and fauna of the area. Don't miss the limestone crevices descending to the sea, or the labyrinth art installation by Portugal's famous sculptor-architect Pancho Guedes.

Near the southern end of the promontory is a lighthouse. Death-defying anglers balance on the cliffs below the walls, hoping to land bream or sea bass.

Cabo de São Vicente NATURAL FEATURE
(N258) Europe's southwesternmost point is a barren headland 6km northwest of Sagres' town centre that was the last piece of home that Portuguese sailors once saw as they launched into the unknown. It's a spectacular spot: at sunset you can almost hear the hissing as the sun hits the sea. A red **lighthouse** (☑282 624 606; www.faros.pt; N268; adult/child €1.50/1; ☉10am-6pm Apr-Oct, to 5pm Oct-Mar) houses a small but excellent museum showcasing Sagres' role in Portugal's maritime history.

The cape – a revered place even in the time of the Phoenicians and known to the Romans as Promontorium Sacrum – takes its present name from a Spanish priest martyred by the Romans.

Before reaching the lighthouse, you'll pass the ruined fortress **Fortaleza do Beliche** (N268).

🏃 Activities

Surfing is possible at all beaches except Praia do Martinhal and nearby Praia da Baleeira. Several places offer surfing and bodyboarding lessons.

Sagres Natura SURFING
(☑282 624 072; www.sagres-surfcamp.com; Rua São Vicente; ☉Mar–mid-Dec) This highly recommended surf school runs full-day group lessons (€55 including gear) and also hires bodyboards (€15 per day), surfboards (€20) and wetsuits (€10). It has bikes for hire (€10), and the same company also runs a surf-equipment shop and hostel (dorm from €17.50). A one-week surf camp including lessons, equipment, accommodation, breakfast and a barbecue party starts at €410.

Free Ride Sagres Surfcamp SURFING
(☑916 089 005; www.frsurf.com; Hotel Memmo Baleeira, Sítio da Baleeira; 1-/3-/5-day lessons €60/165/255, board or wetsuit hire per day €15) One of several surf schools in the area, this set-up offers lessons, packages and hire, as well as free transport from Sagres and Lagos to wherever the surf's good that day. It also runs stand-up paddleboard tours around the cliffs and beaches (€35, 1½ hours).

DiversCape DIVING
(☑965 559 073; www.diverscape.com; Porto da Baleeira) The PADI-certified DiversCape organises dives of between 12m and 30m around shipwrecks, caves and canyons. A dive and equipment costs €50/250/400 for one/six/10 dives, while the four-day PADI open-water course is €400. Beginners' courses (from €80) are available, and there are even sessions for children aged over eight (€60).

👉 Tours

★Mar Ilimitado WILDLIFE, CRUISE
(☑916 832 625; www.marilimitado.com; Porto da Baleeira) 🦈 Mar Ilimitado's team of marine biologists lead a variety of highly recommended, ecologically sound boat trips, from dolphin spotting (€35, 1½ hours) and seabird watching (€45, 2½ hours) to excursions up to Cabo de São Vicente (€25, one hour). Incredible marine life you may spot includes loggerhead turtles, basking sharks, common and bottlenose dolphins, orcas and minke and fin whales.

Walkin'Sagres WALKING
(☑925 545 515; www.walkinsagres.com) Multilingual Ana Carla explains the history and other details of the surrounds on her tours. Walks head through pine forests to the cape's cliffs, and vary from shorter 7.7km options (€25, three hours) to a longer 15km walk (€40, four hours). There's also a 2.5km weekend walk for parents with young children (adult/child €15/free, 1½ hours).

Sea Xplorer Sagres WILDLIFE, CRUISE
(☑918 940 128; www.seaxplorersagres.com; Porto da Baleeira; ☉tours Jun-Aug, fishing year-round) Leaving from the harbour in Sagres, Sea Xplorer boat trips include dolphin watching (€35, two hours), the cliffs of Cabo São Vicente from the sea (€35, one hour) and fishing (€50 including equipment, four hours).

Cape Cruiser WILDLIFE, CRUISE
(☑919 751 175; www.capecruiser.org; Porto da Baleeira) Boat trips run by Cape Cruiser include

dolphin watching (€35, 1½ hours), seabird watching (€45, 2½ hours), trips to Cabo São Vicente (€25, 1½ hours) and various fishing excursions.

🛏 Sleeping

Orbitur Sagres
CAMPGROUND €

(☑ 282 624 371; www.orbitur.com; Cerra das Moitas; sites per adult/tent/car €7.40/10.40/7.20, cabins from €60; P ☎) Situated 2.5km north of town, off the road to Cabo de São Vicente, and just 1km east of Praia do Beliche, this is a well-maintained campground with lots of shady pine trees. Cabins sleep up to seven people (some have en suite bathrooms, kitchenettes and terraces). There's a kids' playground, games room and barbecue area, plus bike hire.

Casa Azul
GUESTHOUSE €€

(☑ 282 624 856; www.casaazulsagres.com; Rua Dom Sebastião; d/apt from €110/176; ☀ ☎) As azure-blue as its name suggests, inside Casa Azul has bright, breezy rooms done out in vivid colours, such as lemon yellow or lime green. Sleeping up to five people, apartments are ideal for families, with facilities including kitchenettes, washing machines and terraces. Minimum stay is two nights.

It's attached to its own surf school, Wave Sensations (☑ 282 624 856; www.wavesensations.com; Rua Comandante Matoso).

Pontalaia
APARTMENT €€

(☑ 282 620 280; www.pontalaia.pt; Rua Infante Dom Henrique; apt from €82; P ☀ ☎ ☎) Airy apartments with blonde-wood finishes and stylish furnishings at this small, condo-like complex sleep up to four people. All have balconies and some have partial sea views. A large sun terrace surrounds the pool; there's also a sauna and fitness room on site.

Casa do Cabo de Santa Maria
GUESTHOUSE €€

(☑ 282 624 722; Rua Patrão António Faustino; d/apt not incl breakfast from €60/90; P ☎) This welcoming guesthouse is excellent value for money. Traditional Portuguese tiles and furniture fill its spotless rooms and four-person, kitchenette-equipped apartment. Some, including the apartment, have balconies.

Pousada do Infante
BOUTIQUE HOTEL €€€

(☑ 282 620 240; www.pousadas.pt; Rua Patrão António Faustino; d/ste from €150/230; P ☀ @ ☎ ☎) On the promontory's clifftop, this modern *pousada* occupies a never-to-be-outbuilt position. All rooms and suites (with king-size beds and whirlpool baths) have balconies, but those at the front face the car park, so it's definitely worth paying extra for one overlooking the fortress and ocean to take in the dazzling sunsets and swimming pool (romantically floodlit at night).

Mareta View Boutique B&B
BOUTIQUE HOTEL €€€

(☑ 282 620 000; www.maretaview.com; Beco D Henrique; s/d from €111/124; ☀ ☎) On the old plaza, the Mareta View brings sleek and classy attitude to Sagres, with 18 white- and aquamarine-hued rooms (eight of which have glorious sea views from private terraces), and reed umbrellas strewn across the lawns and by the Jacuzzi (though there's no pool). Breakfasts are excellent.

🍴 Eating

There are cafes and restaurants on Praça de República and a couple on the sands of Praia do Martinhal. Good-value, more typically Portuguese restaurants popular with locals cluster on and around Rua Comandante Matoso just before it reaches the harbour.

Pick up beach picnic supplies at the municipal market (www.cm-viladobispo.pt; Rua do Mercado; ⊙ 8am-2pm Mon-Sat).

★ A Eira do Mel
PORTUGUESE €€

(☑ 282 639 016; Estrada do Castelejo, Vila do Bispo; mains €11-22, cataplanas €27-35; ⊙ noon-2.30pm & 7.30-10pm Tue-Sat) A rustic former farmhouse 9km north of Sagres is the atmospheric setting for José Pinheiro's lauded slow-food cooking. Seafood is landed in Sagres, with meats, vegetables and fruit sourced from local farms. Dishes such as octopus *cataplana* with sweet potatoes, spicy piri-piri Atlantic wild shrimp, rabbit in red wine, and *javali* are accompanied by regional wines.

★ A Tasca
SEAFOOD €€

(☑ 282 624 177; Porto da Baleeira; mains €13-30, tapas €3.50-16, seafood platters €60-115; ⊙ 12.30-3pm & 6.30-10pm Thu-Tue) Seafood doesn't come fresher than at this converted fish warehouse, with a timber-decked terrace overlooking the marina and Ilhotes do Martinhal offshore. Inside, the vaulted interior's walls are inlaid with glass bottles, ceramic plates, shells and pebbles. A live tank sits alongside the bar. Daily-changing platters and *cataplanas* are specialities.

Three Little Birds
CAFE €€

(☑ 282 624 432; www.three-little-birds.org; Rua do Mercado; dishes €9-14; ⊙ 5-11pm Feb-Nov; ☎ ✎)

Sagres' coolest cafe makes everything from scratch – tortillas, corn chips and brioche buns included – for its tacos, nachos and burgers (eg piri-piri chicken with bacon jam and grilled pineapple, or cod with lime aioli, avocado and cucumber salsa), all with veggie options. Drinks include 20 craft beers and gin-based cocktails. Live reggae, funk and soul plays on Saturdays in summer.

Mum's INTERNATIONAL €€
(📞 968 210 411; www.mums-sagres.com; Rua Comandante Matoso; mains €15-23; ⏰ kitchen 7pm-midnight, bar to 2am Wed-Mon; 🛜🥗) 🍴 Eclectically decorated with retro TVs and radios, toasters, bottles, books and framed photos, this cosy spot on the main drag serves mostly vegetarian dishes (such as marinated tofu with chestnut purée, roasted beetroot and wild berry sauce) and some seafood (eg cornbread-crusted cod with Parmesan foam). Staff are happy to recommend wine pairings. Cash only.

Vila Velha INTERNATIONAL €€€
(📞 282 624 788; www.vilavelha-sagres.com; Rua Patrão António Faustino; mains €12.50-29.50; ⏰ 6.30pm-midnight Tue-Sun) In an elegant old house accessed by a lovely, mature front garden, upmarket Vila Velha offers consistently good seafood mains (go for the catch of the day), plus meat dishes such as wine-stewed rabbit, garlic- and herb-crusted lamb cutlets, and sirloin steak with wild mushroom sauce. Book ahead in high season.

🍷 Drinking & Nightlife

The centre of Sagres' postsurfing scene is Rua Comandante Matoso, which has a closely packed string of places where you can get everything from a coffee to a caipirinha. Cafes by day, they're also good dining options and lively bars by night.

Pau de Pita CAFE
(Rua Comandante Matoso; ⏰ 10am-3am; 🛜) Natural timber features throughout the rustic-chic interior of this lively cafe-bar, which has a great postsurf vibe. The upper level has a sun-drenched terrace overlooking the sea, while the ground floor has a toasty wood-burning stove and opens out to a laneway with picnic tables. Coffees, juices and smoothies are available, along with cocktails and beers.

Dromedário BAR
(📞 282 624 219; Rua Comandante Matoso; ⏰ 10am-2am Sun-Wed, to 3am Thu-Sat; 🛜) Founded in 1985, Sagres' original cafe-bar is still its best, and a cool spot to hang out after a day on the waves. Spot its namesake *dromedário* (camel) painted on its facade and tiled in mosaics on its bar. Creative cocktails include watermelon-and-ginger martinis; DJs spin regularly and gourmet burgers come in veggie varieties.

Agua Salgada BAR
(📞 282 624 297; Rua Comandante Matoso; ⏰ 10am-2am Sun-Wed, to 3am Thu-Sat; 🛜) One of Sagres' liveliest bars, sky-lit Agua Salgada has a party vibe thanks to DJs and occasional live gigs. Fresh fruit forms the basis of its extensive range of cocktails (eg a 'kiwi colada').

ℹ️ Information

Turismo (📞 282 624 873; www.visitalgarve.pt; Rua Comandante Matoso 75; ⏰ 9.30am-1pm & 2-7pm daily Jul & Aug, 9.30am-1pm & 2-5.30pm Tue-Sat Sep-Jun) On a patch of green lawn, 100m east of Praça da República.

ℹ️ Getting There & Away

The **bus stop** (Rua Comandante Matoso) is by the *turismo*. You can buy tickets on the bus.

Buses travel to/from Lagos (€4, one hour, hourly Monday to Friday, fewer on weekends) via Vila do Bispo (€2.20, 20 minutes) and Salema (€2.55, 30 minutes). There are weekday services to Cabo de São Vicente (€2.10, 10 minutes, two daily Monday to Friday).

ℹ️ Getting Around

Hire bicycles from Sagres Natura (p207) or **Maretta Shop** (📞 282 624 535; www.marettashop.com; Rua Comandante Matoso; per day bike hire €8-25, scooter hire €29; ⏰ 10am-8pm).

North of Sagres

Spectacular beaches along the Algarve's western coast are backed by beautiful wild vegetation and are wonderfully undeveloped thanks to building restrictions imposed to protect the **Parque Natural do Sudoeste Alentejano e Costa Vicentina**. The reserve contains at least 48 plant species found only in Portugal, and around a dozen or so found only within the park. The region is also home to otters, foxes and wildcats, and some 200 bird species, including ospreys, enjoy the coastal wetlands, salt marshes and cliffs. Although the seas can be dangerous, the area has a growing reputation for some of Europe's finest surf.

Carrapateira

Surf-central Carrapateira is a tranquil, pretty, spread-out village, with two nearby beaches whose lack of development and strong swells attract a hippy, surf-dude crowd. The coast along here is wild, with copper-coloured and ash-grey cliffs covered in speckled yellow and green scrub, backing creamy, wide sands.

◉ Sights & Activities

Carrapateira's two fabulous beaches are **Praia da Bordeira**, 1.7km by road north-west of town (1.3km on foot), and **Praia do Amado** (2.2km southwest). They're linked by a stunning 5.5km hike (or drive), with lookouts over the beaches and the rocky coves and cliffs between them.

For surfing courses (packaged with accommodation) contact **Algarve Surf School** (☑ 962 846 771; www.algarvesurfschool.com; Praia do Amado; day-long group lesson €50, week-long package from €305) or **Amado Surf-camp** (☑ 927 831 568; www.amadosurfcamp.com; Praia do Amado; day-long group lesson €60, week-long package from €255).

Praia de Vale Figueira   BEACH
One of the more remote west-coast beaches, this wide, magnificent stretch of sand has an ethereal beauty, backed by stratified cliffs hazy in the ocean spray. It's reached by a rough, partly paved road that runs some 5km from the main road at a point 10km north of Carrapateira (take the northern of the two turn-offs). There are no facilities.

**Museu do Mar e da Terra da
Carrapateira**   MUSEUM
(☑ 282 970 000; www.cm-aljezur.pt; Rua do Pescador; adult/child €2.70/1.10; ☉ 10am-noon & 1.30-4.30pm Tue-Sat Jun-Sep, 11am-6pm Tue-Sat Oct-May) The Carrapateira Land & Sea Museum is a must for visitors – surfers or otherwise. Up a steep hill 200m east of the town square, its contemporary design space has small exhibits covering everything from the fishing industry to the daily life of locals, and intriguing photographic collages depicting the Carrapateira of yesteryear (there's minimal English labelling). The vista from the museum's viewing window over the dunes is sublime.

🛌 Sleeping

Despite the number of camper vans you see around the place, camping here is definitely illegal and also damages the fragile dune system. Accommodation is available at surf schools, guesthouses and a boutique hotel.

Pensão das Dunas   GUESTHOUSE €
(☑ 282 973 118; www.pensao-das-dunas.pt; Rua da Padaria 9; not incl breakfast d with/without bathroom from €50/40, tr from €55, 2-/3-/4-person apt from €70/85/100; 🛜) Draped in bougainvillea, this pretty guesthouse on the western side of town has four simple rooms and six apartments in a riot of colours, with equally bright bathrooms, overlooking a flower-filled courtyard. Breakfast costs €7.50. From March to October, there's a minimum two-night stay.

Casa Fajara   BOUTIQUE HOTEL €€
(☑ 282 973 134; www.casafajara.com; Urbanização Quinta da Barrada 6; d/f from €115/175; ☉ closed Dec & Jan; 🅿 ✳ 🛜 🏊) A secluded hideaway, whitewashed boutique property Casa Fajara provides real relaxation. Immaculate rooms vary in size and outlook; all have balconies and some have kitchenettes. Family rooms sleep four. First-rate facilities include a pool lined by timber sunloungers and a lawn tennis court. From the turn-off to Praia da Bordeira, it's 750m in the opposite (eastern) direction to the beach.

Monte do Sapeiro   B&B €€
(☑ 282 973 108; www.montedosapeiro.pt; Vilarinha; d €80-110; 🅿 ✳ 🛜) With full-length, east-facing windows to catch the sunrise, these two contemporary rooms open to grassy lounging areas with scents of rose and lavender from the gardens, and views of fields beyond. Guests can use the communal kitchen, barbecue and bicycles. It's 5.7km southeast of Carrapateira. Minimum stay is one week in July and August, and two nights at other times.

Casa Bamboo   GUESTHOUSE €€
(☑ 969 009 988; https://casa-bamboo-bb.business.site; Estrada da Praia; d/tr/apt from €60/85/90; 🛜) 🔌 On the main road 500m southeast of Praia da Bordeira, this eco-friendly, rammed-earth and wood building has four brightly coloured rooms and a communal terrace and garden with views of the beach. Its open-plan apartment, sleeping up to four people, is equipped with a kitchenette, private terrace and its own barbecue.

✖ Eating

Cafes and snack bars line the tiny town square.

Microbar Carrapateira   CAFE €

(Largo do Comercio 7; dishes €6-12; ⊘10am-10pm Jul & Aug, to 9pm Mar-Jun & Sep) Umbrellas shade the tables at this summer cafe on the town's cobbled square. It's a lively pre- or postsurf hang-out for bruschetta, burgers. vibrant salads, coffee (soy milk available) and cake, or just an ice-cold *imperial* (small draught beer) or cocktail in the sun.

Sítio do Forno   SEAFOOD €€

(☑282 973 914; www.sitiodofornoalgarve. restaurant; Estrada da Praia, Praia do Amado; mains €10-22, cataplanas €37-40; ⊘noon-10pm Tue-Sun, closed mid-Dec–mid-Jan; 🛜🚗) High on the cliff overlooking Praia do Amado, what was a tiny fisher's cabana has evolved into this large restaurant, where magnificent ocean views unfurl from the terrace – sunsets here are magnificent. Enormous *cataplanas* serve two, with seafood specials changing daily according to the catch.

Sítio do Rio   SEAFOOD €€

(☑282 973 119; Estrada da Praia, Praia da Bordeira; mains €9-16; ⊘noon-midnight Wed-Mon, closed mid-Dec–mid-Jan; 🛜) 🌿 On Praia da Bordeira's dunes, with stone walls around its terrace to keep the sand out, and direct boardwalk access to the beach, this great-value restaurant also has an atmospheric timber-ceilinged interior with driftwood on the walls. Fish grilled over charcoal is the house speciality, with herbs and vegetables sourced from its own organic garden.

ℹ Getting There & Away

One bus a day on weekdays links Carrapateira with Aljezur (€3.25, 25 minutes), where you can change for Lagos.

Aljezur

POP 3400

Straddling a narrow river, Aljezur is split between its western Moorish section, with a collection of cottages below a ruined 10th-| century hilltop castle, and eastern section, known as Igreja Nova (New Church), which is 600m up a steep hill. Nearby beaches are surfing hotspots. The surrounding countryside, which is part of the natural park, is a tangle of yellow, mauve and green wiry gorse and heather.

◉ Sights

Wonderful, unspoilt beaches near Aljezur include **Praia da Arrifana** (10km southwest, near a tourist development called Vale da Telha), a dramatic, curved black-cliff-backed bay with one restaurant, balmy pale sands and some big northwest swells (a surfer's delight); and **Praia do Monte Clérigo**, 8.5km northwest. **Praia da Amoreira**, 6km away, is a wonderful beach where the river meets the sea. More difficult to reach but worth the effort is the remote **Praia de Vale Figueira**, 15km southwest of Aljezur via rugged dirt roads.

Museu Municipal   MUSEUM

(www.cm-aljezur.pt; Largo 5 de Outubro; €2.20; ⊘9am-1pm & 2-6pm Tue-Sat Jun-Sep, to 5pm Tue-Sat Oct-May) This small but likeable museum has three rooms. Downstairs is an archaeological collection displaying everything from Stone Age axes to a 16th-century whipping post, while across the hall the Islamic section has a good selection of locally produced ceramics. Upstairs is an ethnographic display with everything from clocks to carts. Information is in Portuguese.

Your ticket here grants admission to Aljezur's three other municipal museums: the Museu de Arte Sacra, the Museu Antoniano and the Casa Museu Pintor José Cercas.

Castelo   CASTLE

(Rua dom Paio Pires Correia; ⊘24hr) FREE On the site of an Iron Age fort, the polygonal castle was built by the Moors in the 10th century, conquered by the Christians in 1249, then abandoned in the late 15th century. The walls and a couple of towers survive, as well as a cistern. Sweeping views of the surrounding area extend from the rock in its centre and ramparts.

Ruinas da Fortaleza de Arrifana   FORTRESS, RUINS

(Rua Serpa Pinto 32) A boardwalk leads through the remaining gate of this 1635-built fortress. Largely wiped out by the tsunami following the 1755 earthquake, the fortress was rebuilt several times before being abandoned in the early 19th century. Aside from the gate and crumbling walls, very little remains today, but the clifftop views are magnificent – a coin-operated telescope provides close-ups.

⯅ Activities

Surfing lessons are available at schools, including **Arrifana Surf School** (☑961 690

THE ALGARVE NORTH OF SAGRES

249; www.arrifanasurfschool.com; Praia da Arrifana; 1-/3-/5-day course €55/150/225, surfboard/wetsuit hire per half day €20/10; ⊙ closed Feb).

A 19.5km taster of the 350km-long hiking route Rota Vicentina (p213) runs north from Aljezur to Odeceixe.

Algarve Adventure OUTDOORS
(📞913 533 363; www.algarve-adventure.com; Praia do Monte Clérigo; 4hr rock-climbing course beginner/advanced from €60/120) The energetic team at Algarve Adventure can take you rock climbing along the coast and in the Algarve's hilly interior. Prices include transport and gear. The company also runs a local surf school (half-/full-day lesson with gear €35/60) and rents equipment (surfboard/wetsuit per day €25/10) and mountain bikes (half/full day from €15/20).

Hostel-style accommodation is available (dorm/double €25/50).

Burros e Artes TOURS
(📞967 145 306, 282 995 068; www.burros-artes.blogspot.com; Vale das Amoreiras; self-guided donkey trek per day from €60, 1-/3-/7-day guided tours from €85/490/895) Fans of slow travel will enjoy covering 10km to 15km per day on foot through stunning landscapes, accompanied by your *burro* (donkey), which carries your luggage. This company coordinates trips including accommodation, food and optional multilingual guides; alternatively go it alone, in which case the added fun is tending to the donkey (there are strict rules regarding its care).

🛏 Sleeping

Pousada da Juventude HOSTEL €
(📞282 997 455; www.pousadasjuventude.pt; Urbanização Vale da Telha, Praia da Arrifana; dm/d/tr from €18/38/48; P ≋) Brilliantly situated 900m east of Praia da Arrifana, this hostel has a striking grey-and-yellow colour scheme incorporating designer plastic furniture such as surfboard-shaped coffee tables, and light, bright rooms (some with private bathrooms, air conditioning and/or sea views). Great facilities include a sunny ocean-view terrace, above-ground pool, a storeroom for surf gear, and a washing and drying room.

Amazigh Hostel HOSTEL €
(📞282 997 502; www.amazighhostel.com; Rua da Ladeira 5; dm/d/tr/q from €12/49/60/75; 🛜) A surfer favourite, this hostel is clean and intelligently designed, with inbuilt lockers under the bunks, steel staircases, surfboard and gear storage, a tiled living area opening to a sun terrace, and a communal kitchen. It's all about the waves here, with tips on local conditions and summer transport to nearby beaches.

Parque de Campismo Serrão CAMPGROUND €
(📞282 990 220; www.campingserrao.com; Herdade do Serrão; per adult/tent/car €5.50/5/4, 2-/3-/4-person apt €75/85/95; P 🛜 ≋) Located 4.5km north of Aljezur, this tranquil, shaded site has wheelchair access, tennis courts, a playground, a restaurant, bar and grocery store, plus bike hire. Apartments have small private patios and kitchenettes.

🍴 Eating & Drinking

Cafe-bars overlook the main square around Igreja Nova. In Praia da Arrifana there's a string of seafood restaurants on the road above the beach.

Mó Veggie Bistro VEGETARIAN, VEGAN €
(📞925 289 246; www.facebook.com/MoVeggie Bistro; Rua João Dias Mendes 13; dishes €5.50-11; ⊙12.30-4pm & 6.30-10pm Tue-Sat Apr-Nov; 🛜 📶) A former wheat mill now houses this brilliant split-level bistro with raw timbers, comfy sofas and suspended lighting. All dishes are vegetarian and many are vegan. Yoga workshops and live music gigs regularly take place.

O Paulo SEAFOOD €€
(📞934 975 250; www.restauranteopaulo.com; Rua Serpa Pinto 32, Arrifana; mains €9-25; ⊙kitchen 9.30am-10pm, bar to midnight Apr-Nov, hours vary Nov-Mar; 🛜) Adjacent to the ruined fortress of Arrifana, O Paulo has a romantic covered terrace with majestic clifftop views as far as Cabo de São Vicente. The vistas are hard to live up to, but it does, with tanks of live lobsters and crabs, superfresh fish and delicacies such as razor clams and traditional brine-boiled goose barnacles (a local speciality).

★ O Sargo BAR
(📞912 995 839; Praia do Monte Clerigo; ⊙9am-10pm Thu-Tue Mar–mid-Nov) Directly across the beach, with glass walls buffering the wind and sand, O Sargo is a great place to slake your postsurf thirst, with cold-pressed juices, craft beers, ciders, local wines, and white and red sangrias. Live music plays on weekends from June to September; the bar also hosts regular full-moon parties.

Ocean-fresh food includes ceviche, grilled octopus and fantastic salads such as scallop and prawn.

🔒 Shopping

Mercado Municipal   MARKET
(Rua 25 de Abril; ⊙8am-2pm Mon-Sat) Located
near the bridge, the small covered market is
a good place to buy fresh fruit and veggies,
cured meats and locally caught seafood.

❶ Information

Turismo (☑282 998 229; www.visitalgarve.
pt; Rua 25 de Abril 62; ⊙9.30am-1pm & 2-7pm
daily Jul & Aug, 9.30am-1pm & 2-5.30pm Tue-
Sat Sep-Jun) Helpful office on the main road
through town.

❶ Getting There & Away

Eva (www.eva-bus.com) buses run between
Aljezur and Lagos (€4, 50 minutes, four on
weekdays, one on Saturday). One bus runs on
weekdays to/from Carrapateira (€1.85, 30
minutes) en route to Vila do Bispo (€3.25, 55
minutes), where you can connect to Sagres.

Rede Expressos (www.rede-expressos.pt)
buses run north to Lisbon (€17.60, 3¾ hours, two
daily) and south to Lagos (€7.60, 35 minutes,
two daily), and Portimão (€8.70, 55 minutes, two
daily). No buses run to/from Praia da Arrifana.

If you're driving, there's a free car park opposite the *turismo*.

Odeceixe

POP 950

Around Odeceixe the countryside rucks
up into rolling, large hills. The Algarve's
northernmost coastal settlement before the
Alentejo is an endearing small town clinging
to the southern side of the Ribeira de Seixe
valley that divides the two regions. Sleepy
for most of the year, it gets packed in high
summer, including surfers hitting its beach.

⊙ Sights & Activities

Rota Vicentina   HIKING
(www.rotavicentina.com) This 350km-long
walking route enters the Algarve at Odeceixe and continues right down the west
coast to Cabo de São Vicente. The day walk
from Odeceixe south to Aljezur (19.5km)
is an easy introduction, heading through
mostly flat local farmland.

Praia de Odeceixe   BEACH
Flanked by imposing cliffs, this beach has
a superb setting at a river mouth, allowing
you to rinse off the salt in fresh water. It's
also a good family option, as smaller kids
can paddle on the peaceful river side of the
strand. Located 3.5km west of Odeceixe.

Odeceixe Surf School   SURFING
(☑963 170 493; www.odeceixesurfschool.
com; Praia de Odeceixe; 1-/3-/5-day courses
€60/165/250, half-day surfboard/wetsuit hire
€20/10; ⊙10.30am-7pm) This friendly set-up
offers surfing classes (board and wetsuit
hire included) and half-, full- and multiday
gear hire. There are sites both on and just
above the beach; look for the octopus sign.
It will transport you to whatever local beach
has the best waves that day, and arrange
packages with accommodation.

🛏 Sleeping

**Parque de Campismo
São Miguel**   CAMPGROUND €
(☑282 947 145; www.campingsaomiguel.
com; N120, São Miguel; sites per adult/tent/car
€6.75/9/5.70, bungalows from €95; ▣ 🛜 🐾) This
family-oriented campground is 2km northeast of Odeceixe. Shaded by pines, it has
well-spaced sites and great facilities, including a proper restaurant, large pool area, two
tennis courts and a small grocery store. Bungalows with en suite bathrooms sleep up to
five people. Wi-fi is in the games room only.

Casa Hospedes Celeste   GUESTHOUSE €€
(☑282 947 150; www.casahospedesceleste.com;
Rua Nova 9; s/d from €50/60) Host Celeste's
traditional guesthouse has a great location
right in the town centre. Its eight rooms are
clean and bright, with small TVs. Cash only.

Agapito Beach House   APARTMENT €€€
(☑926 771 356; www.agapito.pt; Rua da Prai, Praia
de Odeceixe; apt €130; 🛜) Just 15m from the
beach, this pair of four-person apartments
share a great roof terrace with a barbecue
and cabana-shaded picnic tables. Both have
full kitchens, washing machines and breezy
marine-hued fabrics. Kids are welcome (but
not pets). Minimum stay is four nights.

Casa Vicentina   INN €€€
(☑282 947 447; www.casavicentina.pt; Monte Novo;
d €100-170; ▣ 🛜 🐾) Set on 17 hectares planted
with oak, cork and pine trees, Casa Vicentina's rooms are arranged around a lush green
lawn with a pool and lily ponds, and a fenced
kids' playground. Some rooms have kitchenettes and most have terraces. It's well signposted 6.5km southwest of Odeceixe.

🍴 Eating

★Kiosk Agapito   CAFE €
(☑926 771 356; www.agapito.pt; Rua da Praia, Praia
de Odeceixe; dishes €3.50-12.50; ⊙9am-11pm

early Jan-Oct) 🏊 Overlooking the surf, this new-generation beach cafe with aqua-and-white tiles and terrace-only seating uses local produce in breakfasts, sharing platters, open-faced toasties, burgers and huge salads. Live music plays Saturdays in July and August.

Chaparro
PORTUGUESE €€

(☑282 947 304; Rua da Estrada Nacional 8; mains €7.50-15; ⊙10am-3.30pm & 6pm-midnight Fri-Wed) Chaparro is a great choice for no-nonsense Portuguese char-grilled meat and seafood, particularly the house-speciality, octopus with sweet potato. Watch your food cook on the huge grill in the yellow-walled dining room or head out to the terrace when the mercury is high. Reserve ahead in high summer.

Taberna do Gabão
PORTUGUESE €€

(☑282 947 549; www.facebook.com/tabernagab ao; Rua do Gabão 9; mains €9.50-23.50; ⊙noon-2.30pm & 6-10pm Wed-Mon) Traditional dishes from the neighbouring Alentejo region – such as *pezinhos de porco* (roast pig trotters) and *ensopado de borrego* (lamb stew) – are served in a charming, old-fashioned wooden dining room and small courtyard with frescoed walls depicting local history and landscapes. It's hidden in a narrow backstreet in the town centre.

ⓘ Getting There & Away

Express buses run between Lagos and Odeceixe (€4.55, 80 minutes, four on weekdays) via Aljezur (€2.75, 35 minutes).

Monchique

POP 4800

High above the coast, in the forested Serra de Monchique mountain range, the hamlet of Monchique makes a scenic base for exploring the surrounding area, with some excellent options for walking, biking and canoeing.

Caldas de Monchique is 6km to the south – it has been a popular spa town for over two millennia.

Fires regularly affect this area during summer, causing widespread damage, though the countryside regenerates quickly.

◉ Sights & Activities

A series of brown signs starting near the bus station directs pedestrians up into the town's narrow old streets and major places of interest.

Traversed by the Via Algarviana (p181), Monchique makes a great base for hiking, the Trilha dos Moinhos is a 10.3km circuit of the hills above town. From the top of Fóia, there are loop trails of 6.5km and 17km. Caldas de Monchique, Picota and Monchique are linked by an 18km circular trail.

Termas de Monchique Spa
SPA

(☑282 910 910; www.monchiquetermas.com; Rua de Caldas de Monchique; adult/hotel guest €20/15, treatments from €20; ⊙mid-Feb–Dec) In the wooded valley below Caldas de Monchique is this famed spa. Admission allows access to the sauna, steam bath, swimming pool with hydromassage jets, and the thermal spa, whose alkaline waters are rich in fluoride and bicarbonate. You can then indulge in beauty treatments, from a purifying facial to a hot-stone massage in an outdoor cabana.

Alternativtour
OUTDOORS

(☑965 004 337; www.alternativtour.com; Sítio das Relvinhas; tours €50-75) Alternativtour runs guided walks, mountain-biking tours, canoeing trips and combined mountain-biking and canoeing trips. Tours require a minimum of two people; per-person prices decrease the larger the group gets. Bike hire costs €20 per day.

🛏 Sleeping

Monchique has some characterful guest-houses and a hotel, but limited availability makes booking ahead a must for most of the year. There's more accommodation around Caldas de Monchique, including private rooms and villas, and the spa resort's hotels.

Vilafoîa
HOTEL €€

(☑282 910 110; www.vilafoia.com; Corte Pereiro Apartado 241; s/d/f/ste/cottage from €95/105/168/133/168; 🅿❉🅑☎♨) 🏊 Situated 2.5km southwest of town, this rural hotel has an enchanting location in a hillside cork grove, with splendid views extending from the contemporary rooms' balconies or terraces south over the Algarvian coast. A couple of cottages 50m up the hill have kitchenettes. The saltwater pool overlooks the coast.

Albergaria do Lageado
HOTEL €€

(☑282 912 616; www.albergariadolageado.com; Rua de Caldas de Monchique; s/d from €60/75; ⊙May-Oct; ❉♨☎) In Caldas de Monchique, Albergaria do Lageado is an attractive hotel with a red-sloped roof and a cosy ambience. It has simply furnished rooms and a small thermal pool surrounded by plants. Sierra de Monchique meats such as wild boar, and seafood delivered daily from the coast, are highlights of its tiled in-house restaurant. Packages including board are available.

Termas de Monchique Hotels HOTEL €€€
(www.monchiquetermas.com; Rua de Caldas de Monchique; d/f/ste from €120/190/260; ◉mid-Feb–Dec; P❋♠☎) All four hotels in the Termas de Monchique complex have the same room rates. There are 105 rooms in total; suites come with balconies. You can book weekend or week-long packages that include spa treatments, with half- and full-board options at the hotels' restaurants, which range from casual, health-conscious dining to high-end gastronomy. Prices are cheaper in low season.

🍴 Eating & Drinking

Local specialities include *presunto* (smoked ham), *morcela* (blood sausage) and *chouriça* (chorizo). On the road to Fóia, many restaurants serve excellent piri-piri chicken.

Óchálá CAFE €
(Rua do Dr Samora Gil 12; dishes €1.50-7; ◉10am-6pm Mon-Fri; ☎🖉) Light and bright, with red-and-white tiled floors, a timber bar and local art for sale on the walls, this cafe is a great weekday stop for soups, quiches and sandwiches. It also serves traditional cakes and pastries such as *malassadas* (deep-fried dough balls rolled in sugar and cinnamon) and a *bolo xadrez* (chessboard chocolate-and-vanilla sponge iced in chocolate).

Café Império PORTUGUESE €
(📞282 912 290; Largo dos Chorões; mains €6-14; ◉12.30-3pm & 6-9.30pm Wed-Mon; ☎) Locals adore this place in Caldas de Monchique for what's considered the best piri-piri chicken in the region (ask for extra sauce if you like it hot). While you tuck in, enjoy the lovely views of the valley.

★ Jardim das Oliveiras PORTUGUESE €€
(📞913 081 349; www.jardimdasoliveiras.com; Sitio do Porto Escuro; mains €12-18; ◉noon-3.30pm & 6.30-9.30pm Mon & Wed-Sat, 12.30-3.30pm Sun; 🚗) High up in the hills, this local secret has dining rooms with crackling open fires, farming implements and black-and-white photos, and a magical garden with tables amid the olive and cork trees. Daily specials cooked in the wood-fired oven or over coals might include *cabrito assado* (roast baby goat), *ensopado de borrego* (lamb stew) or *pezinhos de porco* (pigs' trotters).

WORTH A TRIP

FÓIA

The 902m Fóia peak, 5.5km west of Monchique, is the Algarve's highest. The road to the summit climbs through eucalyptus and pine trees and opens up views over the hills. On clear days you can see to the corners of the western Algarve – Cabo de São Vicente to the southwest and Odeceixe to the northwest.

Perched on the cliff edge with expansive views from the glassed-in dining room and terrace, the rustic restaurant **O Luar da Fóia** (📞282 911 149; www.facebook.com/LuarDaFoia; Estrada da Fóia; mains €13.50-20; ◉10am-11pm Tue-Sun) serves traditional Portuguese dishes utilising local produce, with excellent-value wines. It's 1km southwest of Monchique on the road to Fóia. Book ahead.

Barlefante BAR
(Travessa das Guerreiras 7; ◉noon-2am Mon-Fri, 1pm-4am Sat; ☎) Monchique's coolest hangout, in converted horse stables on the side of a hill, has an ivy-clad interior courtyard, and outdoor tables on the narrow alley. DJs or live music acts play most evenings. Look for the irreverent tiled sign of the rear of an *elefante* (elephant) out front.

🛍 Shopping

Casa dos Arcos HOMEWARES
(📞282 911 071; Rua da Estrada Velha; ◉10.30am-7pm Mon-Sat) 🖉 Carpenter José Leonardo Salvador has been crafting traditional Monchique chairs aka 'scissor chairs' from alder (a type of birch wood) since the 1960s, following on from his father and grandfather..

ℹ Information

Turismo (📞282 911 189; www.visitalgarve.pt; Largo de São Sebastião; ◉9.30am-1pm & 2-5.30pm Mon-Fri) Has some information on the Via Algarviana and other trails in the area.

ℹ Getting There & Away

Frota-Azul (www.frotazul-algarve.pt) buses run to/from Portimão (€4.45, 45 minutes, nine daily Monday to Saturday only) via Caldas de Monchique.

ℹ Getting Around

The bus trip between Caldas de Monchique and Monchique costs €1.40 and takes just five minutes.

The Alentejo

Best Places to Eat

➡ Tasca do Celso (p267)

➡ Gadanha Mercearia e Restaurante (p237)

➡ Taberna Típica Quarta Feira (p228)

➡ Confraria (p248)

➡ Terra Utópica (p258)

Best Places to Stay

➡ Albergaria do Calvario (p226)

➡ The Place (p232)

➡ Train Spot (p250)

➡ Convento da Provença (p245)

➡ São Lourenço do Barrocal (p233)

Why Go?

You'll be bewitched – Portugal's largest region, covering a third of the country, truly captivates. Think dry, golden plains, rolling hillsides and lime-green vines. A rugged coastline, traditional whitewashed villages, marble towns and majestic medieval cities. Plus a proud if melancholic people, who valiantly cling to their local crafts.

Centuries-old farming traditions – and cork production – continue here. Alentejo's rich past offers Palaeolithic carvings, fragments from Roman conquerors and solid Visigothic churches. There are Moorish-designed neighbourhoods and awe-inspiring fortresses built at stork-nest heights.

And the cuisine? Alentejo is the destination for traditional food. Gastronomic delights are plentiful – pork, game, bread, cheese, wine, and seafood along the coastline. Birdlife and rare plants are prolific, and walking opportunities abound.

The world is (finally) catching on to Alentejo. Get there before everyone else does.

When to Go

Évora

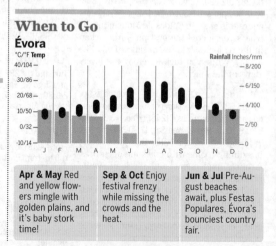

Apr & May Red and yellow flowers mingle with golden plains, and it's baby stork time!

Sep & Oct Enjoy festival frenzy while missing the crowds and the heat.

Jun & Jul Pre-August beaches await, plus Festas Populares, Évora's bounciest country fair.

History

Prehistoric Alentejo was a busy place, and even today it is covered in megaliths. But it was the Romans who stamped and shaped the landscape, introducing vines, wheat and olives, building dams and irrigation schemes and founding huge estates called *latifúndios* to make the most of the region's limited rivers and poor soil.

The Moors, arriving in the early 8th century, took Roman irrigation further and introduced new crops such as citrus and rice. By 1279 they were on the run to southern Spain or forced to live in *mouraria* (segregated Moorish quarters) outside town walls. Many of their hilltop citadels were later reinforced by Dom Dinis, who created a chain of spectacular fortresses along the Spanish border.

Despite Roman and Moorish development, the Alentejo remained agriculturally poor – increasingly so when the Age of Discoveries led to an explosive growth in maritime trade, and seaports became sexy. Only Évora flourished, under the royal patronage of the House of Avis, but it too declined once the Spanish seized the throne in 1580.

During the 1974 revolution Alentejo suddenly stepped into the limelight: landless rural workers who had laboured on the *latifúndios* for generations rose in support of the communist rebellion and seized the land from its owners. Nearly 1000 estates were collectivised, although few succeeded and all were gradually reprivatised in the 1980s. Most are now back in the hands of their original owners.

Today the Alentejo remains among Europe's poorest and emptiest regions. Portugal's entry into the EU (and its demanding regulations), increasing mechanisation, successive droughts and greater opportunities elsewhere have hit the region hard: young people have headed for the cities, leaving villages – and their traditions – to die out. Although its cork, olives, marble and granite are still in demand, and the deep-water port and industrial zone of Sines is of national importance, this vast region contributes only a small fraction to the gross national product.

Locals are still waiting for the benefits promised by the construction of the huge Barragem do Alqueva (Alqueva Dam) and its reservoir.

ALTO ALENTEJO

POP 522,000

The northern half of the Alentejo is a medieval gem, with a scattering of walled fortress towns (such as Elvas and Estremoz) and remote clifftop castles (such as Marvão and Castelo de Vide). Only a handful of visitors to Alto Alentejo travel beyond Évora, so once outside the city you'll see traditional life at its most authentic.

Évora

POP 56,700

One of Portugal's most beautifully preserved medieval towns, Évora is an enchanting place to delve into the past. Inside the 14th-century walls, Évora's narrow, winding lanes lead to striking architectural works: an elaborate medieval cathedral and cloisters; the cinematic columns of the Templo Romano (near the intriguing Roman baths); and a picturesque town square, once the site of some rather gruesome episodes courtesy of the Inquisition. Aside from its historic and aesthetic virtues, Évora is also a lively university town, and its many attractive restaurants serve up hearty Alentejan cuisine. Outside town, Neolithic monuments and rustic wineries make for fine day trips.

Évora climbs a gentle hill above the Alentejo plain. Around the walled centre runs a ring road from which you can enter the town on one of several 'spoke' roads. The town's focal point is Praça do Giraldo, 700m from the bus station to the southwest.

History

The Celtic settlement of Ebora had been established here before the Romans arrived in 59 BC and made it a military outpost, and eventually an important centre of Roman Iberia, when it was known as 'Ebora Liberalitas Julia'.

After a depressing spell under the Visigoths, the town got its groove back as a centre of trade under the Moors. In AD 1165 Évora's Muslim rulers were hoodwinked by a rogue Portuguese Christian knight known as Giraldo Sem Pavor (Gerald the Fearless). The well-embellished story goes like this: Giraldo single-handedly stormed one of the town's watchtowers by climbing up a ladder of spears driven into the walls. From there he distracted (some say killed) municipal sentries while his companions took the town with hardly a fight.

The Alentejo Highlights

1 Évora (p217)
Sampling the history, culture and cuisine of this historically rich Unesco World Heritage–listed city.

2 Vila Nova de Milfontes (p265)
Exploring gorgeous beaches by day, and feasting on seafood in moonlit plazas by night.

3 Marvão (p249)
Gazing out over the countryside from one the Alentejo's enchanting hilltop fortress villages.

4 Rota Vicentina (p266) Admiring the view over sea cliffs along one of Portugal's most captivating multiday treks.

5 Cromeleque dos Almendres

(p230) Watching the shadows play on the mysterious megaliths outside Évora.

6 Mértola (p256)

Strolling with the spirits of past civilisations and religions in this peaceful riverside enclave.

7 Monsaraz

(p231) Admiring the views from this lofty mountaintop village, then taking a dip in nearby Alqueva Lake.

8 Vila Viçosa

(p238) Wandering the corridors of a former palace and medieval castle, then dining on Alentejan fare in a traditional restaurant.

Évora

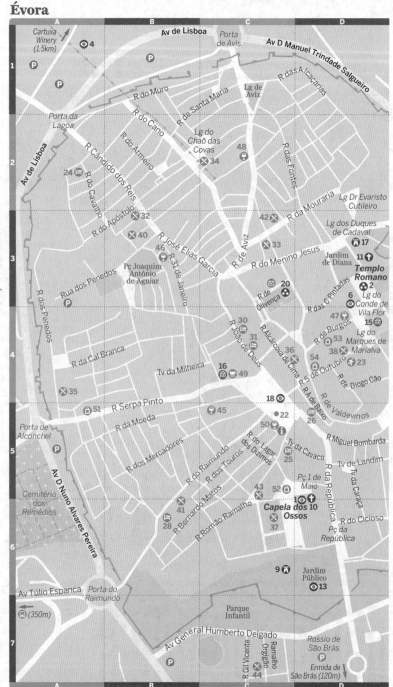

Cartuxa
Winery
(1.5km)

Av de Lisboa

Porta
de Avis

Av D Manuel Trindade Salgueiro

R das Alcaçarias

Porta da
Lagoa

R do Muro

R de Santa Maria

R do Cano

Lg de
Aviz

Lg do
Chão das
Covas

Porta
de Avis

R das Fontes

Av de Lisboa

R Cândido dos Reis

R do Armeiro

Lg Dr Evaristo
Cutileiro

R do Cavalo

R do Apóstolo

R da Mouraria

Lg dos Duques
de Cadaval

R José Elias Garcia

Pç Joaquim
António
de Aguiar

R 31 de Janeiro

R de Aviz

R do Menino Jesus

Jardim
de Diana

Templo
Romano

Rua dos Penedos

R de
Olivença

Lg do
Conde de
Vila Flor

R dos Penedos

R da Cal Branca

R João de Deus

R Alcárcova de Baixo

R das C Pintadas

Lg do
Marques de
Marialva

Tv da Milheira

R de Burgos

R 5 de Outubro

R de Diogo Cão

Porta de
Alconchel

R Serpa Pinto

R da Moeda

R A de Baixo

R de Valdevinos

R Miguel Bombarda

Cemitério
dos
Remédios

Av D Nuno Alvares Pereira

R dos Mercadores

R do Raimundo

R dos Touros

R do Lagar
dos Dízimos

Tv da Cavaco

Tv de Landim

Pç 1 de
Maio

R da República

Tv da Caraça

Capela dos
Ossos

R Bernardo Matos

R Romão Ramalho

R do Cicioso

Pç da
República

Av Túlio Espanca

Porta do
Raimundo

(350m)

Parque
Infantil

Jardim
Público

Av General Humberto Delgado

R Gil Vicente

Ramalho
Orgião

Rossio de
São Brás

Ermida de
São Brás (120m)

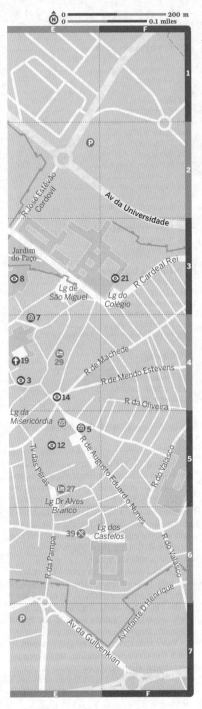

Évora's golden age was from the 14th to 16th centuries, when it was favoured by the Alentejo's own House of Avis, as well as by scholars and artists. Declared an archbishopric in 1540, it got its own Jesuit university in 1559.

When Cardinal-King Dom Henrique, last of the Avis line, died in 1580 and Spain seized the throne, the royal court left Évora and the town began wasting away. The Marquês de Pombal's closure of the university in 1759 was the last straw. French forces plundered the town and massacred its defenders in July 1808.

Ironically, it was decline itself that protected Évora's very fine old centre – economic success would have led to greater redevelopment. Today its population is smaller than it was in the Middle Ages.

◉ Sights

★ Templo Romano
RUINS

(Temple of Diana; Largo do Conde de Vila Flor) Once part of the Roman Forum, the remains of this temple, dating from the 2nd or early 3rd century AD, are a heady slice of drama right in town. It's among the best-preserved Roman monuments in Portugal, and probably on the Iberian Peninsula. Though it's commonly referred to as the Temple of Diana, there's no consensus about the deity to which it was dedicated, and some archaeologists believe it may have been dedicated to Julius Caesar.

How did these 14 Corinthian columns, capped with Estremoz marble, manage to survive in such good shape for some 18 centuries? The temple was apparently walled up in the Middle Ages to form a small fortress, and then used as the town slaughterhouse. It was uncovered late in the 19th century. These unwitting preservation techniques worked, as the imposing colonnade is stunningly complete.

★ Capela dos Ossos
CATACOMB

(Chapel of Bones; Praça 1 de Maio; adult/student €5/3.50; ⊙9am-6.30pm Jun-Sep, to 5pm Oct-May) One of Évora's most popular sights is also one of its most chilling. The walls and columns of this mesmerising *memento mori* (reminder of death) are lined with the bones and skulls of some 5000 people. This was the solution found by three 17th-century Franciscan monks for the overflowing graveyards of churches and monasteries.

There's black humour to the way the bones and skulls have been arranged in

Évora

patterns, and the whole effect is strangely beautiful, though probably not one you'd be inspired to re-create at home. An inscription over the entrance translates as 'We bones that are here await yours'. Above the chapel, a museum contains works of religious art and a terrace with views over town. The former Chapter House (which currently contains the ticket counter for the chapel) contains a fine collection of *azulejos* (hand-painted tiles).

Sé CATHEDRAL
(Largo do Marquês de Marialva; €2.50 cathedral & cloister, with towers €3.50, with museum €4.50; ☉9am-5pm) Guarded by a pair of rose granite towers, Évora's fortress-like medieval cathedral has fabulous cloisters and a museum jam-packed with ecclesiastical treasures. It was begun around 1186, during the reign of Sancho I, Afonso Henriques' son; there was probably a mosque here before. It was completed about 60 years later. The flags of

Vasco da Gama's ships were blessed here in 1497.

You enter the cathedral through a portal flanked by 14th-century stone apostles, flanked in turn by asymmetrical towers and crowned by 16th-century roofs. Inside, the Gothic influence takes over. The chancel, remodelled when Évora became the seat of an archdiocese, represents the only significant stylistic change since the cathedral was completed. Golden light filters through the window across the space.

The cool cloister is an early-14th-century addition. Downstairs are the stone tombs of Évora's last four archbishops. At each corner of the cloister, a dark, circular staircase (at least one will be open) climbs to the top of the walls, from where there are good views.

Climb the steps in the south tower to reach the choir stalls and up to the museum, which demonstrates again the enormous wealth poured into the church, with ecclesiastical riches, including a revolving jewelled reliquary (containing a fragment of the true cross). Encrusted with emeralds, diamonds, sapphires and rubies, it rests on gold cherubs and is flanked by two Ming vases and topped by Indo-Persian textiles.

Igreja de São Francisco   CHURCH
(www.igrejadesaofrancisco.pt; Praça 1 de Maio; ⊙9am-6.30pm Jun-Sep, to 5pm Oct-May) Évora's best-known church is a tall and huge Manueline-Gothic structure, completed around 1510 and dedicated to St Francis. Legend has it that the Portuguese playwright Gil Vicente is buried here.

Exuberant nautical motifs celebrating the Age of Discoveries deck the walls and reflect the confident, booming mood of the time. It's all topped by a cross of Christ's order and dome.

Praça do Giraldo   PLAZA
The city's main square has seen some potent moments in Portuguese history, including the 1483 execution of Fernando, Duke of Bragança; the public burning of victims of the Inquisition in the 16th century; and fiery debates on agrarian reform in the 1970s. Nowadays it's still the city's focus, host to less dramatic activities such as sitting in the sun and drinking coffee.

The narrow lanes to the southwest were once Évora's *judiaria* (Jewish quarter). To the northeast, Rua 5 de Outubro, climbing to the *sé* (cathedral), is lined with handsome town houses wearing wrought-iron balconies, while side alleys pass beneath Moorish-style arches.

Museu do Évora   MUSEUM
(☑266 730 480; Largo do Conde de Vila Flor; adult/child €3/free; ⊙9.30am-5.30pm Tue-Sun) Adjacent to the cathedral, in what used to be the archbishop's palace (built in the 16th century), is this elegant museum. The cloistered courtyard reveals Islamic, Roman and medieval remains. In polished rooms upstairs are former Episcopal furnishings and a gallery of Flemish paintings. Most memorable is *Life of the Virgin,* a 13-panel series originally part of the cathedral's altarpiece, created by anonymous Flemish artists working in Portugal around 1500.

Fórum Eugénio de Almeida   MUSEUM
(☑266 748 300; www.fea.pt; Largo do Conde de Vila Flor; adult/child €2/free, Sun free; ⊙10am-6pm Tue-Sun) In a building that once housed the Holy Office of Inquisition, this centre of arts and culture hosts some of Évora's most thought-provoking art exhibitions throughout the year. Also part of the foundation is the Casas Pintadas, a small collection of outdoor murals facing a little garden.

Casas Pintadas   HISTORIC SITE
(€1; ⊙10am-6pm Tue-Sun) Painted on the garden walls of an open-vaulted gallery are a series of unusual 16th-century murals that were once part of a noble's residence. Recently restored, these paintings depict creatures real and imagined, such as birds, hares, foxes, a basilisk, a mermaid and a harpy. Access is via the Fórum Eugénio de Almeida.

Coleção de Carruagens   MUSEUM
(Carriage Collection; Largo Dr Mário Chicò 4; €1, Sun free; ⊙10am-1pm & 3-7pm Tue-Sun Jun-Sep, 10am-12.30pm & 1.30-6pm Tue-Sun Oct-May) Part of the Eugénio de Almeida Foundation, this pint-sized museum houses an intriguing collection of old carriages. It's hidden away behind the Sé and is largely overlooked by most visitors.

Aldeia da Terra   ART STUDIO
(☑266 746 049; www.aldeiadaterra.pt; Rua de São Manços 19; adult/child €2/1; ⊙10am-6pm) The artist Tiago Cabeça has created this wondrous miniature world of Portugal moulded in clay and peopled with humorous and irreverent characters. You'll find recognisable Alentejo imagery – castles, painted-white villages, cathedrals – and the interiors of tiny houses and lanes where Cabeça's characters are captured in all their adorable, big-eyed whimsy.

Igreja de São João   CHURCH
(Church of St John the Evangelist; ☑967 979 763; www.palaciocadaval.com; Rua Augo Filipe Simões; church €4, church & palace €8; ⊙10am-12.30pm & 2-5pm Tue-Fri & Sun, 2-5pm Sat) The small, fabulous Igreja de São João, which faces the Templo Romano (p221), was founded in 1485 by one Rodrigo Afonso de Melo, count of Olivença and the first governor of Portuguese Tangier, to serve as his family's pantheon. It is still privately owned, by the Duques de Cadaval, and notably well kept.

Behind its elaborate Gothic portal is a nave lined with fantastic floor-to-ceiling *azulejos* produced in 1711 by one of Portugal's best-known tile-makers, António de Oliveira Bernardes. The grates in the floor expose a surprising underworld: you can see a deep Moorish cistern that pre-dates the church and an ossuary full of monks' bones. In the sacristy beyond are fragments of even earlier *azulejos*.

After exploring the church, head next door to the Palácio Cadaval (Palace of Cadaval; www.palaciocadaval.com; incl Igreja de São João €8; ⏰ 10am-12.30pm & 2-5pm Tue-Fri & Sun, 2-5pm Sat) with its collection of illuminated manuscripts, Arraiolos carpets and 18th-century paintings of Portuguese royals.

Convento dos Lóios   NOTABLE BUILDING
(Largo do Conde de Vila-Flor) The former Convento dos Lóios, to the right of Igreja de São João (p223), has elegant Gothic cloisters topped by a Renaissance gallery. A national monument, the convent was converted into a top-end pousada (p226) (upmarket inn) in 1965. If you want to wander around, wear your wealthy-guest expression – or have dinner at its upmarket restaurant.

Jardim Público   GARDENS
(⏰ 8am-9pm May-Aug, to 7pm Mar, Apr, Sep & Oct, to 5.30pm Nov-Feb) For a lovely tranquil stroll, head to the light-dappled public gardens (with a small outdoor cafe) south of the Igreja de São Francisco. Inside the walls of the 15th-century Palácio de Dom Manuel is the Galeria das Damas (Ladies' Gallery; ⏰ 10am-noon & 2-6pm Mon-Fri, 2-6pm Sat), an indecisive hybrid of Gothic, Manueline, neo-Moorish and Renaissance styles. It's open when there are temporary art exhibitions.

From the town walls you can see, a few blocks to the southeast, the crenellated, pointy-topped Arabian Gothic profile of the Ermida de São Brás (Chapel of St Blaise; Avenida Dr Barahona).

Aqueduto da Água de Prata   LANDMARK
(Aqueduct of Silver Water) Jutting into the town from the northwest is the beguilingly named Aqueduto da Água de Prata, designed by Francisco de Arruda (better known for Lisbon's Tower of Belém) to bring clean water to Évora. It was completed in the 1530s. At the end of the aqueduct, on Rua do Cano, the neighbourhood feels like a self-contained village, with houses, shops and cafes built right into its perfect arches, as if nestling against the base of a hill.

It's possible to walk for around 8.5km alongside the aqueduct, starting outside town, on the road to Arraiolos. There are three access points; the tourist office provides maps. Unfortunately, it heads in one direction only, so transport back can be a problem if you don't have your own wheels.

Take plenty of liquids – ironically, there's no potable water along the way.

Universidade de Évora   UNIVERSITY
(🖉 266 740 800; Rua do Cardeal Rei; €3; ⏰ main building 9am-8pm Mon-Fri, to 6pm Sat) Just outside the walls to the northeast is the university's main building (Colégio do Espírito Santo), a descendent (reopened in 1973) of the original Jesuit institution founded in 1559 (which closed when the Jesuits got shooed out by Marquês de Pombal in 1759). Inside are arched, Italian Renaissance–style cloisters, the Mannerist-style Templo do Espírito Santo and beautiful *azulejos*.

Largo da Porta de Moura   PLAZA
The Moura Gate Sq stands just southeast of the cathedral. Near here was the original entrance to town. In the middle of the square is a strange-looking, globular 16th-century Renaissance fountain. Among the elegant mansions around the square is Casa Cordovil (Largo da Porta de Moura), built in Manueline-Moorish style. Have a look across the road to the west at the extraordinary knotted Manueline stone doorway of the Igreja do Carmo (Our Lady of Carmo Church; Rua Dom Augo Eduardo o Nunes).

Museu Relogio   MUSEUM
(🖉 266 751 434; www.museudorelogio.com; Rua Serpa Pinto 6; €2; ⏰ 2-5.30pm Tue-Fri, 10am-12.30pm & 2-5.30pm Sat & Sun) This is one of two watch museums that houses one family's extraordinary private collection (the other is in Serpa). You name it – if it ticks, chimes, beeps and tells the time in some form or another, it's here.

Termas Romanas   RUINS
(Praça do Sertório; ⏰ 9am-5.30pm Mon-Fri) FREE
Inside the entrance hall of the *câmara municipal* (town hall) are more Roman vestiges, only discovered in 1987. These impressive Roman baths, which include a *laconicum* (heated room for steam baths) with a superbly preserved 9m-diameter circular pool, would have been the largest public building in Roman Évora. The complex also includes an open-air swimming pool, discovered in 1994.

🏃 Activities

Rota dos Vinhos do Alentejo   WINE
(Wine Route of the Alentejo; 🖉 266 746 498; www.vinhosdoalentejo.pt; Rua 5 de Outubro; wine tasting €3; ⏰ 11am-7pm Mon-Fri, to 1pm Sat) Head here to sample some of the great wines of the Alentejo. Every week new wines are on

WINE ROUTE OF THE ALENTEJO

Wines here, particularly the reds, are fat, rich and fruity. But tasting them is much more fun than reading about them, so drop in on some wineries. The Rota dos Vinhos do Alentejo (Wine Route of the Alentejo) splits the region into three separate areas – the Serra de São Mamede (dark reds, full bodied, red fruit hints); Historic (smooth reds, fruity whites) around Évora, Estremoz, Borba and Monsaraz; and the Rio Guadiana (scented whites, spicy reds). Some wineries also have accommodation options.

You'll see brown signs all over the Alentejo announcing that you are on the wine trail, and you can pick up the booklet that lists wineries and their details at any local tourist office. Otherwise visit the helpful Rota dos Vinhos do Alentejo headquarters.

offer, with more than 70 wineries represented. You can taste six or so varieties on hand for a minimal fee. Bottles will set you back anywhere from €4.50 to €65.

👉 Tours

Ebora Megalithica TOURS
(☑ 964 808 337; www.eboramegalithica.com; per person €25, maximum 7 people; ⊘ tours 10am & 2.30pm Mon-Sat) If you're interested in the megaliths – Almendres, Zambujeiro and the Menir dos Almendres – this three-hour tour is a must. Young archaeology enthusiast Mário Carvalho makes the megalithic sites accessible in every sense, providing the where, what, why and how. He succeeds in making the experience an educational yet relaxed one.

Tuk 2 You HISTORY
(☑ 962 804 959; www.facebook.com/tuk2you; 15/60/90min tour €15/30/45) Frederico (Fred) Telho Rasquila takes visitors on a fun, fact-filled tour around Évora aboard his shiny white tuk-tuk (motorised rickshaw) – ideal for negotiating the narrow lanes of the historical centre. Fred offers a range of tours, from short 15-minute overviews of the city, to more in-depth 90-minute historical surveys. The tuk-tuk accommodates two adults and one child.

Évora Local Tours CULTURAL
(☑ 961 792 740; www.facebook.com/evoralocal tours; per person €30) The highly knowledgeable Andreia Sousa runs fascinating three-hour tours that take visitors by 4WD out to a cork farm outside town. There you'll get a close-up look at this age-old sustainable industry, and its relation to traditional agriculture, wildlife and regional gastronomy.

Cartuxa Winery WINE
(☑ 266 748 383; www.cartuxa.pt; Estrada da Soeira; from €5; ⊘ tours 10.30am, 11.30am, 3pm & 4.30pm) For a taste of history, Cartuxa is one of the oldest wineries in the Alentejo. Run by local philanthropic foundation Eugénio de Almeida, it produces good wines at all prices, plus olive oils and other products. You must reserve a tour (strictly at times given); prices start at €5 and then depend on how many wines you want to taste.

Agia WALKING
(☑ 963 702 392; www.alentejoguides.com; adult/child €15/free, minimum 2 people; ⊘ 10am) Agia offers daily two-hour guided walking tours of Évora, departing from outside the *turismo* (p229) on Praça do Giraldo.

🎏 Festivals & Events

Queima das Fitas FIESTA
(⊘ early Jun) Like the famous celebrations in Coimbra, the Queima das Fitas features a riotous end-of-year celebration for University of Évora students finishing the term. Expect a week of outdoor concerts and DJ-fuelled dance parties.

Feira de São João CULTURAL
Évora's biggest, bounciest annual bash, and one of Alentejo's best country fairs, features processions, concerts, special exhibitions, hands-on activities for kids, and plenty of feasting and drinking. The big day is 29 June, feast day of São Pedro, with events happening the week prior.

🛏 Sleeping

Hostel Namaste HOSTEL €
(☑ 266 743 014; www.hostelnamasteevora.pt; Largo Doutor Manuel Alves Branco 12; dm/s/d €17/30/45; ☏) In the historic Arabic quarter, you'll find bright rooms decorated with splashes of art and colour, and there's a lounge, library, kitchen and bike hire.

Stay Inn Ale-Hop HOTEL €
(☑ 910 852 255; Rua João de Deus 86; d €55-65, q €75; ✳ ☏) In the heart of town, this place

offers spacious, attractively set modern rooms, the best of which have big windows over the street. There's a kitchen for guests (with free coffee and tea) and a small terrace. It's located above the Ale-Hop store; check in at the shop.

Casa dos Teles GUESTHOUSE €
(☑266 702 453; www.casadosteles.com; Rua Romão Ramalho 27; s/d €35/38, with shared bathroom €30/34; ❃☜⛅) These eight mostly light and airy rooms are simply furnished but good value for their central location and the friendly welcome. The quarters are clean and quiet, though the vibe might seem a little sombre for some.

Évora Inn HOSTEL €€
(☑266 744 500; www.evorainn.com; Rua da República 11; s/d/tr/q €40/50/80/95; ☜) This friendly 10-room guesthouse in a 120-year-old building brings a serious dose of style to Évora. Pop art adorns the rooms and corridors, along with eye-catching wallpaper, modular chairs, a bold colour scheme and unusual features (including a telescope in the Mirante room up top).

Moov Hotel HOTEL €€
(☑220 407 000; www.hotelmoov.com; Rua do Raimundo 99; d €53-83; ❃☜) Once home to Évora's first bullring, Moov Hotel features attractive modern rooms with a minimalist design and a lounge adorned with black-and-white photos of prancing ponies and handsome horsemen. The multilingual staff are friendly.

★**Albergaria do Calvario** BOUTIQUE HOTEL €€€
(☑266 745 930; www.albergariadocalvario.com; Travessa dos Lagares 3; r €118-155; ⓟ❃☜) Unpretentiously elegant, discreetly attentive and comfortable, this beautifully designed guesthouse has an ambience that travellers adore. The kind-hearted staff provide the best service in Évora, and breakfasts are outstanding, with locally sourced seasonal fruits, homemade cakes and egg dishes.

Gorgeous lounge areas are decked out with a tasteful melange of antique and modern furniture. Comfortable beds, marble-filled bathrooms, first-rate heating and air conditioning, and a pleasant garden patio area ensure a homey, don't-want-to-leave kind of stay. It's in a delightful part of town, near Porta Lagoa and the aqueduct. Excellent insider tips for exploring the Alentejo.

Valeriana GUESTHOUSE €€€
(☑266 755 126; www.valerianaguesthouse.pt; Rua João de Deus 50; r €100-155; ⓟ❃☜) Valeriana

hits all the right notes with seven beautifully furnished rooms and posh common areas, including a stylish lounge and a rooftop terrace with views. The rooms don't stint on luxury, and the best have king-sized beds with French doors overlooking the pedestrian street out front. Good breakfasts and an honesty bar add to the value.

Noble House BOUTIQUE HOTEL €€€
(☑266 247 290; www.thenoblehouse.pt; Rua da Freiria de Baixo 16; r €110-250; ⓟ❃☜) Set in a 14th-century building, this boutique charmer has 24 handsomely designed rooms, some with vaulted ceilings and vestiges of Évora's distant past – including one room with a fragment of the original wall built by the Romans. You can relax in the lounge bar after a day of exploring or take a bit of sun on the small terrace.

Pousada Convento de Évora HERITAGE HOTEL €€€
(☑266 730 070; www.pestana.com; Largo do Conde de Vila Flor; r €140-240, ste €255-325; ❃@☜⛅) Occupying the former Convento dos Lóios (p224) opposite the Templo Romano (p221), this beautiful *pousada* has a historic air, though the rooms are furnished in a contemporary style and set around a pretty cloister. There's a flash restaurant (mains €17 to €24) on the ground floor of the cloister.

✗ Eating

Pick up cheeses, olives, smoked meats, fruit and vegetables at Evora's **Mercado Municipal** (Municipal Market; Praça 1 de Maio; ⏰7am-6pm Tue-Sat, to 2pm Sun).

Salsa Verde VEGETARIAN €
(☑266 743 210; www.salsa-verde.org; Rua do Raimundo 93A; small plate €5, per kg €15; ⏰noon-3pm & 7-9.30pm Mon-Fri, noon-3pm Sat; ☜☝) Vegetarians (and Portuguese livestock) will be thankful for this veggie-popping paradise. Pedro, the owner, gives a wonderful twist to traditional Alentejan dishes such as the famous bread dish, *migas,* prepared with mushrooms. Low-playing bossa nova and a cheerful, airy design make a fine complement to the dishes – all made from fresh, locally sourced products (organic when possible).

Vinarium Wine & Tapas TAPAS €
(☑968 217 574; www.facebook.com/vinarium evora; Praça Primeiro de Maio 27; tapas €3.50-5; ⏰noon-10pm Thu-Tue) In a thoughtfully designed space across from the municipal

market, Vinarium is a must for wine lovers. Here you can sample fine quaffs from the Alentejo, which pair nicely with baked cheese and oregano, baked octopus, chickpeas with cod and other small sharing plates. *Provas* (tastings) of three to six wines (for €5 and €7) offer excellent value.

Chão das Covas
PORTUGUESE €

(☑266 706 294; www.facebook.com/chaodas-covascafe; Largo do Chão das Covas; sharing plates €5-7, mains €8-11; ⊙7-11pm Tue, noon-3pm & 7-11pm Wed-Sun) Tucked away on a small plaza beside the aqueduct, this friendly, boxcar-sized eatery serves up tasty home-cooked Alentejan classics that change by day, as well as good-value *petiscos* (tapas/snacks) like fried squid, roasted peppers, cheese platters and the like. It's a fine place to linger, with a barrel-vaulted ceiling, black-and-white photos of Évora, and terrace seating on warm days.

Fábrica dos Pasteis
PORTUGUESE €

(☑266 098 424; Rua Alcárcova de Cima 10; pastries €1-1.50; ⊙10am-8pm Tue-Sun) Take a stroll along the narrowest lane in town to find this gem of a bakery, which fires up the best *pastéis de nata* (custard tarts) for miles around, as well as good *salgados* (savoury meat-, cheese-, or chicken-filled pasties). Thick stone walls and a fado soundtrack add atmosphere to the cavernous, low-lit space.

Pastelaria Conventual Pão de Rala
BAKERY €

(Rua do Cicioso 47; pastries €1.50-3; ⊙7.30am-8pm; ☎) The *azulejo*-covered walls (complete with a bakery scene) and low-playing fado create a fine setting for nibbling on heavenly pastries and convent cakes, all made on the premises. Don't miss the *pão de rala* (an egg-yolk, sugar, lemon-zest and almond cake) – it's sweet stuff and wonderfully sinful.

Momentos
PORTUGUESE €€

(☑925 161 423; Rua Cinco de Outubro 61; mains €18-22; ⊙7-10.30pm Mon & Wed-Fri, 12.30-3pm & 7-10.30pm Sat & Sun; ☑) Jorge, the affable proprietor of Momentos, takes great pride in the bounty of the Alentejo, which he showcases each night on his changing blackboard menus. He works with small farmers, and you'll find flavour-packed organic vegetables accompanying black pork, oven-baked lamb and other delicacies. The chef can also whip up special dishes for vegetarians and vegans.

Bistro Barão
PORTUGUESE €€

(☑266 706 180; Rua da Zanguela 8; mains €15-25; ⊙6.30-10pm Mon, 12.30-3pm & 6.30-10pm Tue-Sat; ☑) This tiny family-run restaurant serves exquisitely prepared Portuguese dishes using high-quality products. Start with sauté shrimp with garlic or stuffed mushrooms, before moving on to black-pork tenderloin, lightly breaded octopus, grilled ribs and other hearty main courses.

With just a handful of tables, this place fills up quickly. Reserve ahead.

Botequim da Mouraria
PORTUGUESE €€

(☑266 746 775; Rua da Mouraria 16A; mains €15-18; ⊙12.30-3pm & 7-10pm Mon-Sat) Poke around the old Moorish quarter to find some of Évora's finest food and wine – gastronomes believe this is Évora's culinary shrine. Owner Domingos will guide you through the menu, which also features an excellent variety of wines from the Alentejo. There are no reservations and just nine stools at a counter.

It is extremely popular, and lines are long. To have any chance of getting a seat, arrive before it opens.

Vinho e Noz
PORTUGUESE €€

(☑266 747 310; Ramalho Orgião 12; mains €12-17; ⊙noon-10pm Mon-Sat) This unpretentious place is run by a delightful family and offers professional service, a large wine list and good-quality cuisine. It's been going for over 30 years and is one of the best-value places in town.

Standout dishes include *secreto de porco alentejano* (grilled Alentejan pork loin), lamb chops with mint, and the celebrated wild boar with chestnuts.

Dom Joaquim
PORTUGUESE €€

(☑266 731 105; www.restaurantedomjoaquim.pt; Rua dos Penedos 6; mains €14-18; ⊙noon-3pm & 7-10.45pm Tue-Sat, noon-3pm Sun) Housed in a renovated building with stone walls and modern artwork, this restaurant offers fine dining in a smart, contemporary setting. Chef Dom Joaquim serves excellent traditional cuisine including meats (game and succulent, fall-off-the-bone lamb) and seafood dishes, such as *caçao* (dogfish).

Restaurante O Fialho
PORTUGUESE €€

(☑266 703 079; www.restaurantefialho.pt; Travessa dos Mascarenhas 16; mains €16-24; ⊙noon-3pm & 7-10pm Tue-Sun) An icon of Évora's culinary scene, O Fialho has been wowing diners since 1945 – as evidenced by the photos of visiting dignitaries lining the walls.

Amid wood panelling and white tablecloths, professional staff serve up first-rate Alentejan cuisine. The appetisers steal the show, along with the extensive wine list.

⭐ **Taberna Típica**
Quarta Feira PORTUGUESE €€€
(☑ 266 707 530; Rua do Inverno 16; dinner per person incl starters, house wine & dessert €30; ⊙ 7.30-10pm Mon, 12.30-3pm & 7.30-10pm Tue-Sat) Don't bother asking for the menu since there's just one option on offer at this jovial eatery tucked away in the Moorish quarter. Luckily it's a stunner: slow-cooked black pork so tender it falls off the bone, plus freshly baked bread, grilled mushrooms (and other starters), dessert and ever-flowing glasses of wine – all served for one set price. Reserve ahead.

Arched ceilings, checked tablecloths and the warm smile of the young owner João make this family-run place a favourite with out-of-towners.

🍷 **Drinking & Nightlife**

Culpa Tua BAR
(Praça Joaquim António de Aguiar 6; ⊙ 5pm-2am Tue-Sat, to midnight Sun) Gin lovers from near and far gather over refreshing, goblet-sized gin and tonics at this friendly, easy-going spot north of Praça Giraldo. There's a small terrace in front.

MolhóBico BAR
(☑ 927 133 869; Rua de Aviz 91; ⊙ 6pm-3am Tue-Sun) Opened in 2018, MolhóBico is the new hotspot in town, with decent cocktails and frequent live music. The low-ceiling pub-like space packs standing-room-only crowds most weekends. With smoking allowed inside, it becomes quite a tobacco den as the evening progresses.

Enoteca Cartuxa WINE BAR
(www.cartuxa.pt; Rua Vasco da Gama 15; ⊙ 10am-10pm Mon-Sat, noon-3pm Sun) Around the corner from the Templo Romano (p221), this bright, modern wine bar serves up quality pours from the well-known Cartuxa (p225) vineyard. You can pair those wines with a wide range of sharing plates – sauté shrimp, grilled mushrooms, cheese boards or heartier plates of roast meats or seafood.

Bardamoeda Gastropub BAR
(☑ 266 785 047; Rua da Moeda 55; ⊙ 7.30pm-3am Tue-Sun; 🛜) Nestle in under the attractive vaulted ceilings of this cool spot and order a great meal at a reasonable price (mains €7

to €10) and a drink, anything from beer on tap to spirits. It sometimes has live acoustic music.

Sociedade Harmonia Eborense BAR
(☑ 266 746 874; Praça do Giraldo 72, 2nd fl; €3; ⊙ 4-7pm & 10pm-2am Mon-Sat) Join the bohemian crowd in the vintage drawing rooms of this cultural space, which hosts occasional concerts, art exhibitions and film screenings. At other times, you can play billiards, or hang out on the spacious terrace enjoying the views over the plaza.

Nada Mais Cafe CAFE
(☑ 919 706 135; Rua Serpa Pinto 6; ⊙ 9am-10pm) Set in the cloisters of the old Palácio Barrocal, this tiny cafe and drinking spot has outdoor tables in the courtyard where you can recharge with a drink after a day exploring. Tasty veg-friendly snacks too (gazpacho, *tostas,* lasagna).

🛍️ **Shopping**

Rua 5 de Outubro has rows of *artesanatos* (handicrafts shops) selling pottery, knick-knacks and cork products. A couple of shops on the outside of the modern Mercado Municipal (p226) sell pottery.

Bookmark Évora BOOKS
(www.thebookmarkevora.com; Rua Serpa Pinto 94; ⊙ 10am-7pm; 🛜♿) When you need a break from sightseeing, retreat to this delightful bookshop, owned by expat and author Julie Hodgson. You'll find a good selection of affordable books in various languages, a special room for Harry Potter fans, and steaming cups of tea.

Fonte de Letras BOOKS
(www.facebook.com/fontedeletras; Rua Vasco da Gama 8; ⊙ 10am-7pm Mon-Fri, to 6pm Sat) This small bookstore stocks intriguing titles, including a few English-language versions of books by Portuguese authors. Don't miss the gumball machine in front that sells tiny poems (in Portuguese and English) instead of candy (a mere €0.50)

Gente da Minha Terra FOOD, GIFTS & SOUVENIRS
(☑ 964 956 259; www.facebook.com/gentedaminhaterraevora; Rua 5 de Outubro 39; ⊙ 10am-7pm) On a boutique-lined street leading off the main plaza, this is a great one-stop shop for gifts. The shelves are packed with quality olive oils, *azulejos,* textiles, ceramics and pretty packages of tinned sardines and other preserves.

Feiras no Largo   MARKET
(Praça 1 de Maio; ⊗8am-2pm Sat & Sun) Each weekend sees the Feiras no Largo, one of four different markets held in the city. Expect antiquities, used books art and collectables.

ℹ Information

There are several banks with ATMs on and around Praça do Giraldo, including **Caixa de Crédito Agrícola** (Praça do Giraldo 13; ⊗8.30am-3pm Mon-Fri).

Branch Post Office (Largo da Porta de Moura 34; ⊗9am-12.30pm & 2-6pm Mon-Fri)

Main Post Office (Rua de Olivença; ⊗9am-6pm Mon-Fri)

PSP Police Station (☑266 760 450; Rua Francisco Soares Lusitano) Near Templo Romano.

Turismo (☑266 777 071; www.cm-evora. pt; Praça do Giraldo 73; ⊗9am-7pm Apr-Oct, 9am-6pm Mon-Fri, 10am-2pm & 3-6pm Sat & Sun Nov-Mar) This central tourist office offers a great town map. Staff are more helpful if you have specific questions.

ℹ Getting There & Away

BUS

The **bus station** (Terminal Rodoviário; ☑266 738 120; Avenida São Sebastião) is 600m west of the walled centre.

TO	COST (€)	TIME (HR)	FREQUENCY
Beja	express 8	1½hr	7 to 9 daily
Coimbra	18.10	4½hr	2 to 5 daily (or change in Lisbon)
Elvas	express 12	1¼hr	3 daily
Estremoz	express 8	30-50min	2 to 4 daily
Faro (via Albufeira)	17	4hr	3 to 4 daily
Lisbon	12	1½-2hr	hourly
Portalegre	12.20	1½hr	1 to 3 daily
Reguengos de Monsaraz	express 7	45min	2 daily Mon-Fri, 1 daily Sat-Sun
Vila Viçosa	9.10	1hr	3 daily

TRAIN

Évora station (Estação de Evora; ☑266 742 336; Largo da Estação) is outside the walls, 600m south of the Jardim Público (p224). There are daily trains to/from Lisbon (€13.70, two hours, three to four daily). Trains also go to/from Beja (change in Casa Branca; €7.40, 2½ hours, two to four daily), Lagos (€25 to €28, 4¼ to five hours, two to three daily) and Faro (€26.20, 3½ to 4½ hours, two to three daily).

ℹ Getting Around

BICYCLE

Loja D'Bike (☑266 707 707; www.d-bike. pt; Rua Horta das Figueiras 69; per day €15; ⊗10am-1.30pm & 3-7.30pm Mon-Sat) offers bike rental.

CAR & MOTORCYCLE

If you're driving it's best to park outside the walls at a signposted car park (eg at the southern end of Rua da República in Parking Rossio de São Brás). Spaces inside the walls are limited and usually metered, and driving here can be tricky due to a web of narrow streets. Pricier hotels have some parking.

On the outskirts of town, in the direction of Viana, **Europcar** (☑266 742 627; www.europcar. com; Rua Horta das Figueiras 140; ⊗9am-1pm & 2.30-7pm Mon-Fri, 9am-1pm Sat) has cars for hire.

TAXI

Taxis (☑266 735 735; www.radiotaxisevora.pt) congregate in Praça do Giraldo. On a weekday you can expect to pay about €6 from the train station to Praça do Giraldo.

Around Évora

Megaliths are found all over the ancient landscape that surrounds Évora. These prehistoric structures, built around 5000 to 7500 years ago, dot the European Atlantic coast, but here in Alentejo there is an astounding amount of Neolithic remains. Dolmens (Neolithic stone tombs; *antas* in Portuguese) were probably temples and/or collective tombs, covered with a large flat stone and usually built on hilltops or valleys, near water lines. Menhirs (individual standing stones) point to fertility rites – as phallic as skyscrapers, if on a smaller scale; and cromlechs *(cromeleques),* organised sets of standing stones, seem to incorporate basic astronomic orientations related to seasonal transitions (equinoxes and solstices). You can see more megaliths around Reguengos de Monsaraz, Elvas and Castelo de Vide.

◉ Sights

Anta Grande do Zambujeiro   ARCHAEOLOGICAL SITE
(Great Dolmen of Zambujeiro; Herdade da Mitra) The Great Dolmen of Zambujeiro, 13km

ARRAIOLOS: THE GREAT CARPETS OF PORTUGAL

About 20km north of Évora is the small town of Arraiolos (pop 7400), famed for its exquisite *tapetes* (carpets). These handwoven works have been in production here since the 12th century and show a marked influence from Persian rugs. It seems half the town is involved in this artistry, and on a casual stroll through town, you might encounter several locals stitching in front of their homes. Rug patterns are based on abstract motifs, *azulejo* designs or flower, bird or animal depictions.

Shops selling *tapetes* are abundant, and you can pay anything from €50 for a tiny runner to €2000 for the most beautiful pieces, which feature more elaborate designs. Just off the main plaza, Rua Alexandre Herculano is lined with carpet (and souvenir) shops.

The village itself dates from the 2nd or 3rd century BC and is laid out along traditional lines, with whitewashed blue-trimmed houses topped with terracotta roofs and the ruins of a castle overlooking the town. The plain facade of the Igreja da Misericórdia hides a beautiful interior with a golden altar and 18th-century azulejo-lined walls.

Take a peek at the centuries-old dye chambers in the main square, which is also where you'll find the turismo (Tourist Office; ☑ 266 490 254; www.cm-arraiolos.pt; Praça do Município 27; ☺ 10am-1pm & 2-6pm Tue-Sun).

Arraiolos makes an easy day trip from Évora, but if you fancy staying overnight, there's the flashy Pousada Convento Arraiolos (☑ 266 419 340; www.pousadas.pt; off N370; d €120-260; P ❋ ☺ ☂ ☒) in a 16th-century former convent just outside town.

southwest of Évora, is Europe's largest dolmen. Under a huge sheet-metal protective shelter in a field of wildflowers and yellow broom, stand seven stones and a 'closing slab' that connects the chamber with the corridor. Each is 6m high and together they form a huge chamber around 5m in diameter.

Unfortunately the entrance is blocked and you cannot enter; but you can peer in from the high mound behind. Archaeologists removed the capstone in the 1960s. Most of the site's relics are in the Museu do Évora (p223).

Cromeleque dos Almendres
ARCHAEOLOGICAL SITE

(Almendres Cromlech; Herdade dos Almendres) Set within a beautiful landscape of olive and cork trees stands this huge, spectacular oval of standing stones, 15km west of Évora. It is the Iberian Peninsula's most important megalithic group and an extraordinary place to visit. The site consists of a huge oval of some 95 rounded granite monoliths – some of which are engraved with symbolic markings – spread down a rough slope.

The megaliths were erected over different periods, it seems, with basic astronomic orientations, and were probably used for social gatherings or sacred rituals back in the dawn of the Neolithic period.

Two and a half kilometres before Cromeleque dos Almendres stands Menir dos Almendres (Herdade dos Almendres), a single stone about 4m high, with some very faint carvings near the top. Look for the sign; to reach the menhir you must walk a few hundred metres from the road.

Gruta do Escoural
CAVE

(☑ 266 857 000; grutadoescoural@cultura-alentejo.pt; M370; €3; ☺ by appt) Around 27km west of Évora, the Escoural Caves contain several cave paintings and rock carvings that date back more than 13,000 years. One-hour guided visits help illuminate some of the mysteries of these faintly visible works. Tours typically happen at 10.30am and 2.30pm Tuesday to Saturday, but you must book ahead. Get in touch at least 24 hours in advance.

ⓘ Getting There & Away

To get to this area, your only options are to rent a car or bike (though note that about 5km of the route is rough and remote), hire a taxi for the day (around €60) or go on a guided tour, such as those offered by the recommended Ebora Megalithica (p225).

With your own wheels, head west from Évora on the old Lisbon road (N114) for 10km, then turn south for 2.8km to Guadalupe, then follow the signs to the Cromeleque dos Almendres (4.3km).

Return to Guadalupe and head south for 5km to Valverde, home of the Universidade de Évora's school of agriculture and the 16th-century Convento de Bom Jesus. Following the signs to Anta Grande do Zambujeiro, turn into the school's farmyard and on to a badly potholed track. After 1km you'll see the Great Dolmen.

Reguengos de Monsaraz

POP 7200

This small working-class town, once famous for its sheep and wool production, is a stopping point and transport hub for Monsaraz. It's also close to the pottery centre of São Pedro do Corval, as well as an impressive half-dozen dolmens and menhirs (out of around 150 scattered across the surrounding plains). It's worth a day trip for its excellent wineries alone, particularly the renowned Herdade do Esporão.

Herdade do Esporão   WINE

(☑266 509 280; www.esporao.com; Apartado 31; winery tour & tasting from €15; ☉10am-7pm daily, restaurant closed Mon Nov-Mar) There are several wineries around Reguengos (part of the wine route), including the acclaimed Herdade do Esporão, 7km south of town. Under the direction of oenologist David Baverstock, it produces a wide variety of wines for domestic and overseas markets. There are tours through the extraordinary wine cellars, among the largest in Portugal.

Parts of the cellars were sourced from the same factory that supplied the underground in Lisbon. It's worth splurging at the wine cellar shop or the restaurant. Reservations are essential for dining at the restaurant (meals around €50), and recommended for booking a tour (which are sometimes booked solid by groups; there's typically one English-language tour each day). If you show up without a reservation, you can still enjoy wine tasting in the wine bar. Charcuterie, cheeses and other snacks are available.

The small on-site museum features the original artwork done for the wine labels of Esporão's annual reserve collection; each year a famous Portuguese artist is given the honour. The property's border was defined in 1267 and it has vestiges of Roman times.

Fabrica Alentejana
de Lanificios   ARTS & CRAFTS

(☑266 502 179; www.mizzete.pt; Rua Mendes; ☉10am-4.30pm Mon-Fri) This is the last remaining hand-loom producer of *mantas alentejanas* (handwoven woollen floor rugs). The owner and/or weavers are happy to show you around. The factory is southeast of the *praça* (take the road to Monsaraz and turn right at Rua Mendes) and the factory's shop (p234) is in Monsaraz.

ⓘ Getting There & Away

Buses run to Évora (€7, 45 minutes, several daily) and direct to Lisbon (€14.30, 2½ hours, one to two daily). There's also a bus to Monsaraz (€3.50, 35 minutes, two to three daily weekdays).

Monsaraz

POP 780 (CASTLE 40)

Perched high over the surrounding countryside, tiny Monsaraz is a charming village with a looming castle at its edge, great views over the Alqueva Dam and olive groves sprinkling the landscape. Its narrow streets are lined with uneven-walled, whitewashed cottages. Today, the village prospers on tourism, with a handful of restaurants, guesthouses and artisan shops. It's worth coming to taste a slice of traditional Portugal, wander the slumbering streets and sample Alentejan cuisine. It's at its best as it wakes up in the morning, in the quiet of the evening or during a wintry dusk.

Settled long before the Moors arrived in the 8th century, Monsaraz was recaptured by the Christians under Giraldo Sem Pavor (Gerald the Fearless) in 1167, and then given

> **DON'T MISS**
>
> ### SÃO PEDRO DO CORVAL
>
> Known for its fine pottery traditions, the tiny village of São Pedro do Corval, 5km east of Reguengos de Monsaraz, has dozens of pottery workshops where you can see both the potters and artists in action and purchase a few pieces of cheap and cheerful plates, pots, jugs, candlesticks and floor tiles.
>
> With more than 20 *olarias* (pottery workshops), the village is one of Portugal's largest pottery centres. It's difficult to recommend one *olaria* over another; wander along Rua da Primavera and the nearby streets (follow the '*olarias*' signs) and ask at the Reguengos and Monsaraz tourist offices for a map locating the *olarias*. Buses between Reguengos and Monsaraz stop here.

WORTH A TRIP

ÉVORAMONTE

Thirty-two kilometres northeast of Évora, this tiny village (pop 570) with its quaint 16th-century castle and fine views across the low hills makes an interesting detour.

The Castelo (Rua da Convenção 7; adult/student €2/1, free Sun morning; ⊗10am-1pm Wed-Sun, 2-5pm Tue-Sun, closed 2nd weekend every month) dates from 1306, but was rebuilt after the 1531 earthquake. Exterior stone carving shows unwarlike small bows, the symbol of the Bragança family – the knot symbolises fidelity. The interior is neatly restored, with impressively meaty columns topped by a sinuous arched ceiling on each cavernous floor, though there isn't much to see inside. The roof provides sweeping panoramas.

A handsome new guesthouse and restaurant near the castle has helped revive this once-sleepy village. Run by a friendly, well-travelled couple from South Africa and Scotland, the Place (☑927 603 884; www.evoramonte.com; Rua de Santa Maria 26; r/ste €80/120; 🐾) offers four stylish modern rooms, trimmed with artwork and set with all mod cons (high-quality mattresses, marble-filled bathrooms). The best have striking views over the Alentejan countryside. Hosts Mitch and Vicki make guests feel right at home, and have a wealth of knowledge on the region. Even if you don't stay for the night, it's well worth stopping in the restaurant (☑927 603 884; mains €9-14; ⊗11am-8pm Tue-Sun Apr-Oct, to 5.30pm Wed-Sun Nov-Mar) for a meal or a drink on the terrace, with its magnificent views.

Most visitors have their own wheels. However, there are two buses a day travelling between Évora and Évoramonte (€4, 70 minutes) on weekdays. Schedules change depending on whether school is in session.

to the Knights Templar as thanks for their help. The castle was added in 1310.

⊙ Sights

Observatório do Lago Alqueva　OBSERVATORY
(☑960 361 906; www.olagoalqueva.pt; CM 1127, Courela da Coutada; adult/child €14/10; ⊗9.30pm Tue-Sat Apr-Oct, 6.30pm Tue-Sat Nov-Mar) Offers two-hour open-air sessions taking in the marvellous star-filled skies of the Alentejo. You'll get an overview of constellations visible with the naked eye, then use telescopes to view some of the planets and moons in the solar system, and peer at distant galaxies and nebulae. Entertaining and knowledgeable guides also touch on mythology and history. Bring warm clothes, as it can get chilly at night even in summer.

The observatory is about 3km east of Monsaraz (head north towards Telheiro, then take CM 1127 towards Alqueva Lake, following signs for Centro Naútico).

Igreja de Nossa Senhora da Lagoa　CHURCH
(Largo Dom Nuno Álvares Pereira; ⊗9.30am-12.30pm & 2-6pm Apr-Sep, 9.30am-1pm & 2-5.30pm Oct-Mar) The parish church, near the turismo (p235), was rebuilt after the 1755 earthquake and again a century later. Inside is an impressive nave and a 14th-century marble tomb carved with 14 saints. An 18th-century *pelourinho* (stone pillory) topped by a Manueline globe stands outside.

Museu do Fresco　MUSEUM
(Fresco Museum; Praça Dom Nuno Álvares Pereira; €1 incl Casa da Inquisação; ⊗9.30am-1pm & 2-5.30pm) Housed inside a fine Gothic building beside the parish church, this museum includes a rare example of a 14th-century secular fresco. The striking work depicts a good judge (with angels perched behind his shoulder) and a bad judge, the latter appropriately two-faced (with a demon on his left shoulder).

A collection of photographs depict life in rural Alentejo from the early 1900s to the 1950s – and cover the period of mass emigration from the countryside (in the 1960s, Monsaraz alone lost 4500 inhabitants). Unfortunately, the explanatory signage is in Portuguese only.

Castelo　CASTLE
(Largo do Castelo; ⊗24hr) The weather-beaten castle at the southwestern end of the village was one in the chain of Dom Dinis' defensive fortresses along the Spanish border. It's now converted into a small bullring, and its ramparts offer a fine panoramic view over the Alentejan plains.

Praia Fluvial de Monsaraz　BEACH
(CM 1127, Telheiro) When you need a break from the heat, head down to this beach on the edge of Alqueva Lake. You can go for a swim (there are lifeguards in summer), hire kayaks and other gear from the Centro

Naútico or grab a drink and a bite in the restaurant. There's also a children's playground. If you lack wheels, Sem-Fim provides transport by van from Monsaraz (€15 per person).

It's 5km east of Monsaraz.

Menhir do Outeiro ARCHAEOLOGICAL SITE
(Outeiro Monsaraz) FREE Situated 6km north of Monsaraz is the granite, 5.6m-tall Menhir do Outeiro, one of the tallest megalithic monuments ever discovered.

🏃 Activities

Centro Náutico de Monsaraz WATER SPORTS
(☑962 653 711; CM 1127, Telheiro; per hour kayak/paddleboard/sailboat from €10/10/20; ⏰10am–11pm) On the shore of Alqueva Lake, this nautical centre hires out kayaks, paddleboards, or tiny sailboats for a leisurely jaunt out on Europe's largest artificial body of water. You can also arrange sailing excursions (per hour €10) – though there's a six-person minimum. The centre has a beach (p232) and a cafe, both of which draw quite the crowd on warm days.

Veleiro Sem-Fim BOATING
(☑962 653 711; www.sem-fim.com; Rua das Flores 6A, Telheiro; per person €10-20) A great way to explore the Barragem do Alqueva dam is by boat. Capitão Tiago runs excellent voyages in his 17m Dutch sailboat, including a standard two-hour trip (€20 per person) with the chance to swim and visit some of the islands. You can also do two-day trips, camping at one of the islands along the way (€150).

Alqueva Cruzeiros BOATING
(☑961 544 559) Leads regular boat trips out on Alqueva Lake. Boats depart from the Centro Náutico de Monsaraz.

🎉 Festivals & Events

Museu Aberto MUSIC
(Open Museum) Monsaraz heaves during its week-long Museu Aberto music festival, held in July in even-numbered years.

Festa de Nosso Senhor Jésus dos Passos CULTURAL
Bullfights and processions feature in this festival around the second weekend of September.

🛏 Sleeping

Dom Nuno GUESTHOUSE €€
(☑964 304 078; www.dnunoth.com; Rua José Fernandes Caeiro 6; s/d from €50/70; 🛜) Inside the old walls, this delightful, family-run guesthouse was one of Monsaraz' first lodging options when it opened in 1983. Today this historic building (a pharmacy in the 1700s) is run by the second generation, and it offers eight spacious rooms with thick walls, terracotta floors and bright, modern bathrooms. The best rooms have views over the countryside. Good breakfasts.

Vila Planicie GUESTHOUSE €€
(☑266 557 021; www.vilaplanicie.pt; Rua da Barrada 13, Telheiro; r €75-120; P✳🛜♨) Down in Telheiro, roughly 2km from Monsaraz, this pleasant guesthouse has spacious, nicely appointed rooms (some have kitchenette) with terracotta floors and windows overlooking the vineyards next door. The pools (take your pick; there are two) are a lovely spot to cool off in summer.

Casa Pinto B&B €€
(☑266 557 076; www.casapinto.net; Praça Dom Nuno Álvares Pereira 10; r €70-100; ✳🛜) A touch of class and the downright quirky pervades this five-room guesthouse. Each room has a design theme based around former Portuguese colonies, from Macau to Mombasa. We're talking serious embellishments, from a stone-walled waterfall shower (Mombaça) to lovely Buddha statues (Dili) and much more besides. Fabulous terrace views and pleasant living spaces.

Casa Saramago FARMSTAY €€
(☑266 557 494; www.casasaramago-monsaraz.com.pt; Rua de Reguengos 9A, Telheiro; s/d €50/80; P✳🛜♨) Based in Telheiro, at the foot of Monsaraz, this delightfully converted blue and white *quinta* (estate) is great value for money. Rooms are tastefully decorated in old-style furniture. The Portuguese owners are friendly and accommodating. Rooms in the former *celeiros* (silos) have verandas and face Monsaraz.

São Lourenço do Barrocal BOUTIQUE HOTEL €€€
(☑266 247 140; www.barrocal.pt; r €290-600; P✳🛜) Set on a 780-hectare estate of olive groves and vineyards, 7km west of Monsaraz, this rural tourism stay offers countryside charm that doesn't stint on high-end comforts. What was once a self-contained farming village has been transformed into lovely boutique accommodation, and the excellent restaurant uses many products grown or raised on-site.

THE ALENTEJO MONSARAZ

WORTH A TRIP

MEGALITHS AROUND MONSARAZ

Neolithic megaliths are scattered throughout the landscape around Monsaraz – it is great to explore and discover them (they're signposted, but finding each one is an adventure) amid the tangles of olive groves and open fields of wildflowers. Most spectacular is **Cromeleque do Xerez**, an ensemble with the triumphant 7-tonne menhir at its centre. The rocks once stood 5km south of Monsaraz but were moved before flooding by the massive Barragem do Alqueva. A remaining highlight is the **Menhir de Bulhoa**, another phallic stone with intriguing carved circles and lines; it's 4km north of Monsaraz off the Telheiro–Outeiro road. A map outlining the region's megalithic circuit is available at the tourist office (p235).

Eating

O Gaspacho CAFE €

(☎926 784 825; Rua Direita 7; sandwiches €4-5; ⏱10am-10pm Sat-Thu; 📶✍) A small, cheerfully decorated cafe where you can try owner Gabriel's excellent signature gazpacho. It goes well with the creative small plates on hand, including cheese platters, salads (like red pepper with mackerel), Spanish-style tortilla and tasty *tibornas* – open-faced sandwiches made with fresh bread, olive oil and quality ingredients (like black pork or shredded codfish).

Cafe-Restaurante Lumumba PORTUGUESE €

(☎266 557 121; Rua Direita 12; mains €8-11; ⏱noon-2.30pm & 7.30-10pm Tue-Sun) This small place has a more local, less touristy clientele who come for filling, inexpensive staples. Don't let duelling TVs and neon lights deter you, head to the terrace for a meal with a view.

Sabores de Monsaraz PORTUGUESE €€

(☎969 217 800; www.saboresdemonsaraz.com; Largo de S Bartolomeu 5; mains €12-15; ⏱7.30-10.30pm Tue, 12.30-3.30pm & 7.30-10.30pm Wed-Sun; 👪) Perched high above the plains, with views reaching as far as Spain, this stone-built tavern is a rustic, wonderfully family-friendly spot. Good honest Alentejano home cooking stars on the menu, with dishes like meltingly tender black pork and *migas com bacalhau e coentros* (codfish with bread and coriander).

Don't pass up dessert – the rich *sericaia* (an egg-custard tart) with sugared plums is quite good.

Taverna Os Templarios PORTUGUESE €€

(☎266 557 166; Rua Direita 22; mains €10-15; ⏱noon-3pm & 7-10.30pm Wed-Mon) Step back in time with this Knights Templar–themed eatery, complete with iron chandeliers, wall-mounted weapons and banners strung from the rafters. The food is classic Alentejan fare, and it's one of Monsaraz' more reliable restaurants. Don't miss the view over the lake from the back terrace.

Sem Fim PORTUGUESE €€

(☎266 557 471; www.sem-fim.com; Rua das Flores 6A, Telheiro; mains €11-20; ⏱11am-2am Thu-Tue; 📶✍) In Telheiro this former olive-oil factory has been transformed into an atmospheric eating and drinking space. The changing menu features a small selection of good Alentejo classics as well as options for vegetarians.

Shopping

Ervideira FOOD & DRINKS

(☎266 950 010; www.ervideira.pt; Travessa Dom Dinis; ⏱11am-7pm) Set in the former primary school, this welcoming shop sells wines by Ervideria, a 160-hectare vineyard that's been run by the same family since the 1880s. You can sample some unusual wines (try the Invisível, so named for its transparent colour), or even linger on the terrace upstairs over a glass (€3 to €5) or a bottle (from €9).

Casa Tial FOOD

(Rua de Santiago 33; ⏱10am-7pm Thu-Tue Oct-Jul, daily Aug & Sep) Run by a French expat, this charming little shop is a fine spot to browse for gifts, with artfully wrapped tins of sardines, high-quality olive oils, unique wines, handsomely packaged liqueurs (like the limoncello-stylel Limontejo) and rich chocolates. You can also stop by for espresso and desserts (try a *delicia de Monsaraz*, made with squash, almond, orange and cinnamon).

Loja da Mizette ARTS & CRAFTS

(☎266 557 159; www.mizzete.pt; Rua do Celeiro; ⏱10am-6pm Oct-May, to 7.30pm Jun-Sep) Here you can purchase handsome Alentejano *mantas* (woollen rugs and blankets) that are still made entirely by handloom. The factory in Reguengos where these are produced – the Fabrica Alentejana de Lanificios (p231) – is the only one still in existence.

❶ Information

Turismo (☑ 927 997 316; Rua Direita 24; ⊘ 9.30am-12.30pm & 2-6pm Apr-Sep, 9.30am-1pm & 2-5.30pm Oct-Mar) Inside the old walls and stocked with some regional information, including bus timetables and basic maps of the area's megalithic monuments.

❶ Getting There & Away

Buses run to/from Reguengos de Monsaraz (€3.50, 35 minutes, two to three daily week-days). The last bus back to Reguengos, where you can pick up connections to Évora, is around 5.30pm (check as this changes).

Estremoz

POP 7500

Along with neighbouring Borba and Vila Viçosa, the very authentic, active town of Estremoz is one of the region's well-known marble hotspots and is worth visiting. The region's marble – rivalling that in Carrara, Italy – is used all over the place: even the cobbles are rough chunks of marble.

Ringed by an old protective wall, Estremoz has a centre set with orange tree-lined lanes, a 13th-century hilltop castle enclosed in an old quarter, and peaceful plazas (the main one being Rossio Marquês de Pombal, or 'the Rossio'). This simple provincial town is a busy trading centre, with lots of shops selling farm tools, though visitors can also load up on crafts, earthenware pottery and gourmet delights – all of which are available at the great market that fills the huge central square on Saturday. The town also boasts some excellent eateries.

❍ Sights

❍ Lower Town

On the fringes of the Rossio are imposing old churches, former convents and, just north of the square, monastic buildings converted into cavalry barracks. Opposite these, by Largo General Graça, is a marble-edged water tank, called the **Lago do Gadanha** (Lake of the Scythe) after its scythe-wielding statue of Neptune. Some of the prettiest marble streets in town are south of the Rossio, off Largo da República.

Palácio dos Marqueses da Praia e Monforte MUSEUM

(Rua da Vasco da Gama 13; ⊘ 9am-12.30pm & 2-5.30pm) **FREE** This former royal palace was recently restored and reopened to the public in 2015. It houses a changing array of exhibitions showcasing talented artists from the Alentejo – easily the best works in Estremoz – with three to four shows annually. Regardless of what's on, it's well worth strolling the marble-lined corridors, past stained-glass windows beneath lovely decorative ceilings.

❍ Upper Town

The upper town is surrounded by dramatic zigzagging ramparts and contains a gleaming white palace. The easiest way to reach it on foot is to follow narrow Rua da Frandina from Praça Luís de Camões and pass the inner castle walls through the Arco da Frandina.

Paço Reial PALACE

(Royal Palace; Largo Dom Dinis; ⊘ 9am-7pm) **FREE** At the top of the upper town is the stark, glowing-white, fortress-like former royal palace, now the Pousada de Rainha Santa Isabel (p237). Dom Dinis built the palace in the 13th century for his new wife, Isabel of Aragon. Visitors are welcome to view the public areas of the *pousada* and climb the keep, which offers a superb panorama of the old town and surrounding plains.

After Isabel of Aragon's death in 1336 (Dinis had died 11 years earlier), the palace was used as an ammunition dump. An inevitable explosion, in 1698, destroyed most of the palace and the surrounding castle, though in the 18th century João V restored the palace for use as an armoury. The 27m-high keep, the **Torre das Três Coroas** (Tower of the Three Crowns), survived and is still the dominant feature. It's so called because it was apparently built by three kings: Sancho II, Afonso III and Dinis.

The holes at the keep's edges were channels for boiling oil – a good way of getting rid of uninvited guests.

Museu Municipal MUSEUM

(☑ 268 339 219; Largo Dom Dinis; €1.55; ⊘ 9am-12.30pm & 2-5.30pm Tue-Sun) This museum is housed in a beautiful 17th-century almshouse near the former palace. Pretty hand-painted furniture sits alongside endearing, locally carved wooden figures (charming rural

Estremoz

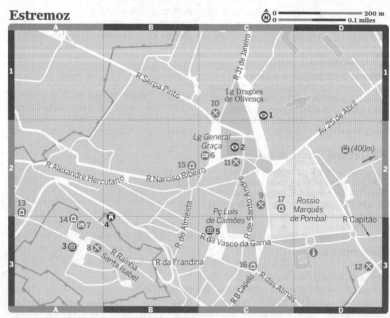

Estremoz

scenes by Joaquim Velhinho) and a collection of typical 19th-century domestic Alentejan items.

🎊 Festivals & Events

Feira Internacional de Artesanato e Agro-Pecuária de Estremoz   FERIA
(FIAPE; Rua Engenheiro André de Brito Tavares; ☺ Apr) The town's biggest event is this baskets, ceramics, vegetables and livestock bonanza, held for several days at the end of April.

🛏 Sleeping

Hotel O Gadanha   HOTEL €
(☎ 268 339 110; Largo General Graça 56; s/d/tr €25/40/55; ✸ 🖥) This whitewashed house is excellent value. It has bright, fresh, white and clean rooms (with satellite TV and even hairdryer) overlooking the square (several rooms have castle views instead). Disappointingly, there are no single rates Friday to Sunday. It's popular, so it's worth reserving ahead.

★**Pousada de Rainha Santa Isabel** HERITAGE HOTEL €€€
(☎268 332 075; www.pousadas.pt; Largo Dom Dinis; d €120-190; ✳☎☀) In the restored former palace (p235), this lavish *pousada* offers spacious rooms with antique furnishings and views over the Alentejo plains. There are lovely palace gardens, a pool with views, and common areas set with museum-quality tapestries.

Casa Azimute BOUTIQUE HOTEL €€€
(☎968 396 999; www.casa-azimute.pt; Estrada da Folgada; d €130-160; P✳☎☀) Some 4km west of Estremoz, this striking Belgian-owned guesthouse offers a peaceful getaway overlooking the bucolic countryside. The design incorporates an ultra-modern aesthetic with regional accents, in rooms of varnished concrete floors, huge floor-to-ceiling windows, hand-painted tiles and locally made textiles.

✗ Eating

★**Gadanha Mercearia e Restaurante** PORTUGUESE €€
(☎268 333 262; www.merceariagadanha.pt; Largo Dragões de Olivença 84A; sharing plates €8-15, mains €18-24; ⊙10am-11pm Tue-Sat, to 5pm Sun) This foodie-loving spot brilliantly merges traditional local products with contemporary touches. Extraordinary *petiscos* include *linguiça de porco preto* and *farinheira* with quail eggs (*farinheira* is a local speciality made of pork fat, herbs and flour). The daily lunch menu is highly recommended.

Alecrim PORTUGUESE €€
(☎268 324 189; www.facebook.com/alecrimestremoz; Rossio Marquês de Pombal 31; mains €15-20; ⊙9am-11pm Thu-Tue) Alecrim is a fine place for a meal, no matter the time of day. Come at lunchtime for excellent multicourse daily specials (creamy codfish dishes and tender Alentejan pork), or stop by in the morning for croissants, eggs or pancakes. By evening, you can nibble on creative tapas plates or heartier servings of roast lamb with grilled vegetables.

Sabores das Maltezas PORTUGUESE €€
(☎965 788 403; www.facebook.com/saboresdasmaltezas; Largo General Graça 30; mains €8-15, tapas €4-8; ⊙10am-9pm Wed-Mon; ☀) Across from the Lago do Gadanha, this small, cheery cafe serves big, creatively topped salads, *tostas* (open-faced sandwiches) and soups as well as heartier dishes such as pork, steak and a variety of burgers (including salmon, lamb and veggie burgers). Open around the clock, it's good for an afternoon coffee, wine or dessert, when other places are closed.

Venda Azul PORTUGUESE €€
(☎961 941 394; Largo de São José 26; mains €9-15; ⊙noon-2.30pm & 7-10pm Mon-Sat) Just south of the main square, Venda Azul serves delicious Alentejan fare at unbeatable prices – a feast for two, including wine and dessert, costs less than €30. Never mind the bustling, unpretentious atmosphere, this place is universally loved by locals and visitors alike. Call ahead to be sure of scoring a table. The *porco preto* (black Iberian pig) is legendary.

A Cadeia INTERNATIONAL, PORTUGUESE €€
(☎268 323 400; www.cadeiaquinhentista.com; Rua Rainha Santa Isabel; sharing plates €6-18, mains €14-19; ⊙12.30-3pm & 7.30-10pm) Unlock your purses at this place, housed in the former judicial jail, which dates from the 16th century; the two storeys of the quadrangle separated male and female prisoners. The restaurant serves *petiscos* and main dishes. There's also an area for coffee and drinks under the building's arch and a classy, romantically lit bar upstairs.

🛍 Shopping

The *turismo* can provide a list of artisans who work with cork, clay, wood and iron, making figurines, bells, sculptures and unique pieces. Those who make *bonecas,* the clay dolls for which the town is famous, include Irmãs Flores (☎268 323 350; Largo da República 16; ⊙9am-1pm & 2-7pm Mon-Sat), Afonso Ginja (☎268 081 618; afonsoginja@gmail.com; Rua Direita 5; ⊙9am-1pm & 3-7pm) and Fátima Estróia (Rua Narciso Ribeiro; ⊙10am-6pm Mon-Fri, to 2pm Sat).

Ela Pedra ART
(☎963 273 440; Largo Dom Dinis 13; ⊙10am-8pm Tue-Sun Jun-Sep, 11am-5.30pm Oct-May) Near the Paço Reial, this sunny gallery has a beautiful collection of drawings, watercolours, oil paintings and, most of all, works in marble. They range in size from palm-sized carvings (including hearts and open-winged swallow, something of a symbol of Portugal) to large-format pieces. The kind-hearted owner, Filipa André, will happily ship anywhere in the world.

Saturday Market

MARKET

(Rossio Marquês de Pombal; ⊙8am-1.30pm) The weekly Saturday market provides a great display of Alentejan goodies and Estremoz specialities, from goat's- and ewe's-milk cheeses, to a unique style of unglazed, ochre-red pots.

ℹ️ Information

Turismo (☑268 339 200; www.cm-estremoz. pt; Casa de Estremoz, Rossio Marquês de Pombal; ⊙9am-12.30pm & 2-5.30pm) Handy office on the southern side of the Rossio.

ℹ️ Getting There & Away

All buses stop at and depart from a small modern **bus station** (Terminal Rodoviário de Estremoz; ☑268 324 266; Avenida Rainha Santa Isabel), located off Avenida 25 de Abril (behind the *azulejo*-covered former train station).

TO	COST (€))	TIME (HR)	FREQUENCY
Elvas	9	60-80 min	5 daily Mon-Fri
Évora	8	1¼hr	6 daily Mon-Fri, one Sat
Évoramonte	4.60	21min	4 daily Mon-Fri
Portalegre	8	45min	at least 2 daily Mon-Fri
Vila Viçosa	3	30min	3 daily Mon-Fri

Regular buses also head further afield to Faro (€19, change in Albufeira or Évora) in the Algarve, and Lisbon (€16, at least six daily).

Vila Viçosa

POP 5050

If you visit just one marble town in the region, Vila Viçosa is the one to hit. It features Praça da República, a long attractive plaza set with orange trees, a marvellous marble palace (one of the country's largest) and a castle.

This was once home to the Bragança dynasty, whose kings ruled Portugal until it became a republic – Dom Carlos spent his last night here before his assassination; it was also the birthplace of Catarina de Bragança (1638), who married Charles II to become Queen of England (and after whom Queens in New York was named). There are many sites and sights of marble (and nonmarble), and a friendly laid-back citizenry who are proud of their sparkling town.

◉ Sights

Paço Ducal

PALACE

(☑268 980 659; www.fcbraganca.pt; Terreiro do Paço; adult/child €7/free; ⊙2-5pm Tue, 10am-1pm & 2-5pm Wed-Sun, to 5pm Jun-Sep) The dukes of Bragança built their palace in the early 16th century when the fourth duke, Dom Jaime, grew tired of his uncomfortable hilltop castle. The wealthy family, originally from Bragança in Trás-os-Montes, settled in Vila Viçosa in the 15th century. After the eighth duke became king in 1640, it changed from a permanent residence to just another royal palace, but the family maintained a special fondness for it and Dom João IV and his successors continued to visit.

The palace's best furniture went to Lisbon after Dom João IV ascended the throne, and some went on to Brazil after the royal family fled there in 1807, but there are still some stunning pieces on display, such as a huge 16th-century Persian rug in the Dukes Hall. Lots of royal portraits put into context the interesting background of the royal family.

The private apartments hold a ghostly fascination – toiletries, knick-knacks and clothes of Dom Carlos and his wife Marie-Amélia are laid out as if the royal couple were about to return (Dom Carlos left one morning in 1908 and was assassinated in Lisbon that afternoon).

A Portuguese-speaking guide leads the compulsory hour-long tours. English tours are offered at 11am on Wednesday, Thursday and Friday.

Other parts of the Ducal Palace, including the 16th-century cloister, house more museums containing specific collections and with separate admission fees (armoury/coach collection/Chinese porcelain/treasury €3/3/2.50/2.50).

Museu de Arqueologia & Museu de Caça

MUSEUM

(Archaeological Museum & Game & Hunting Museum; Avenida Duques de Bragança; €3; ⊙2-5pm Tue, 10am-1pm & 2-5pm Wed-Sun, to 6pm Jun-Sep) Inside the historic **castelo** FREE looming above Vila Viçosa is an intriguing collection of relics, plus some less appealing animal skins and assorted taxidermy. Nevertheless, a visit to these museums is a must – if only to wander through the castle itself (think

USING YOUR MARBLES

The Alentejo's marble towns gleam with rosy-gold or white stone, and the effect is enhanced by the houses, which have a Hollywood-smile brightness. As if locals hadn't found enough uses for the stone stuff, with their marble doorsteps, pavements, drinking fountains and shoes (OK, we made that last one up), a process has been cooked up to create marble paint: marble is recrystallised limestone, so if you heat marble chips in a clay oven for three days they turn into calcium oxide, which is mixed with water to become whitewash. Cheaper than paint. People take pride in the whiteness of their houses and retouch them annually.

While we're on the subject of colour, apparently the yellow borders keep away fever, while blue is the bane of flies (you can add these colours to the oxide). The blue theory may have some truth, or at least it has international adherents – in Rajasthan (India) local people also apply pale blue to their houses to ward off mosquitoes.

'secret' tunnels, giant fireplaces and wonderful vaulted ceilings). The extraordinary (and underpromoted) archaeological collection is housed in the castle's many rooms and spans various eras from the Palaeolithic to the Roman. It even has ancient Egyptian treasures.

**Igreja de Nossa Senhora
da Conceição** CHURCH
(☉8.30am-12.30pm & 2.30-6.30pm) Within the castle walls is this brilliantly tiled 15th-century church. It is also known as *Solar da Padroeira,* Home of the Patron Saint – the Virgin's image is within. It was here that in 1646 Dom João IV offered the kingdom to Nossa Senhora Da Conceição, who became then the patron saint of Portugal. From that time on, the kings of Portugal never wore the crown again, as it was now the Virgin's. Celebrations take place on 8 December.

🛏 Sleeping

Hospedaria Dom Carlos GUESTHOUSE €
(☑268 980 318; hospedariadcarlos@hotmail.com; Praça da República 25; s/d/tr €30/40/50; 🌐🛜) In an excellent location on the main square, the Dom Carlos offers tidy and comfortable rooms with wood finishing and fine views over the plaza. The towels (and mattresses) are a bit stiff, but it's a peaceful spot.

Casa do Colégio Velho GUESTHOUSE €€
(☑268 889 430; www.casadocolegiovelho.com; Rua Dr Couto Jardim 34; d €80-100, ste €110-140; 🛜🛝) You'll feel like Catarina de Bragança herself in one of the seven plush rooms in this former family residence, home to the Jesuits in the 17th century. Decoration embraces a melange of styles, including modern art deco and even rare rose marble in one of the bathrooms. The *casa* overlooks a lovely, neat garden, with lilies and a pool.

Solar dos Mascarenhas HOTEL €€
(☑268 886 000; www.solardosmascarenhas.com; Rua Florbela Espanca 125; s/d €75/85, ste €115-150; 🌐🛜🛝) In a heritage building in the centre of town, this upscale charmer has stylish, contemporary rooms filled with natural light and boasting spotless marble bathrooms. There's an enticing lounge area filled with lavender sofas. The small pool is refreshing on hot days, and by night you can retire to the bar for wine or cocktails.

Herdade da Ribeira de Borba INN €€
(☑268 980 709; www.herdaderibeiradeborba.com; Ciladas; d/bungalow/ste/villa €80/90/135/210; 🌐🛝) Six kilometres east of Vila Viçosa and on a working farm (think rural tranquility, walks, birdwatching), this lovely option offers everything from fully outfitted two-bedroom villas with kitchen to bungalows set in futuristic geodesic domes with private terrace overlooking olive groves. Perfect for longer-term stays.

★**Pousada Convento
Vila Viçosa** BOUTIQUE HOTEL €€€
(☑268 980 742; www.pousadas.pt; Terreiro do Paço; d €110-230; 🌐🛜🛝) Next to the Paço Ducal, this former royal convent was once the 'House of the Ladies of the Court'. Today this regal spot offers spacious rooms – one with original frescoes – terraces and classic furnishings. Rooms open on to a striking inner courtyard.

It's an atmospheric place to wander at any time of day, particularly at night, when candles light up the old stone-walled corridors and lounge rooms with lavishly painted ceilings and artwork adorning the walls.

🍴 Eating & Drinking

Taverna dos Conjurados PORTUGUESE €€
(📞268 989 530; Largo 25 de Abril 12; mains €10-26; ⊙12.30-3pm & 7.30-10pm Tue-Sun Apr-Oct, weekends only Nov-Mar) More upmarket than the average taverna, this inviting eatery serves excellent regional cooking. The attentive host is proud of his classic Portuguese dishes, with some recipes going back to the Dukes' times (complete with time-consuming preparation). Salted codfish, duck with plum sauce, and stewed partridge with saffron sauce are favourites.

Adega 7160 TAPAS €€
(📞268 094 862; Rua Cristóvão de Brito Pereira 12; mains €10-16; ⊙12.30-3pm & 6-11pm Tue & Wed, 12.30pm-midnight Thu-Sun) Amid huge wine jars and painted Alentejan ceramics, Adega 7160 serves traditional regional dishes with a modern twist. Start off with roasted pumpkin soup with toasted almonds (or gazpacho in summer) followed by rich black-pork cheeks with saffron or a tender oven-baked octopus. You can also make a meal of the appealing tapas selection, matched with wines from the Alentejo.

Os Cucos PORTUGUESE €€
(📞268 980 806; Mata Municipal; mains €9-13; ⊙noon-3pm & 7.30-10pm; 🐾) Hidden in the leafy gardens south of the Praça República, this is the pick for quality food and shady location. It has an airy, semicircular interior, and you can eat snacks at garden tables. The changing daily specials – *arroz de pato* (duck with rice) on Saturday, *borrego assado* (roast lamb) on Wednesday – feature unique regional dishes.

Craft BBS BAR
(📞268 035 451; www.facebook.com/craftbbs portugal; Avenida Duques de Bragança 9; ⊙11am-midnight Sun-Thu, to 2am Fri & Sat) This new craft-beer bar serves up five or so microbrews on tap from the Alentejo craft-brewer Libata. The friendly bartender will let you sample before committing, and you can order some delicious – and massive! – burgers (including a good veggie option) to go with those pints of frothy American stout.

ℹ️ Information

Turismo (📞268 889 317; www.cm-vilavicosa. pt; Praça da República 34; ⊙9am-12.30pm & 2.30-5.30pm) For town maps and information.

ℹ️ Getting There & Away

There are limited buses to/from Évora (€9.10, one hour, two to three on weekdays), and Estremoz (€3, 35 minutes, two to three on weekdays).

Elvas
POP 23,800

Elvas' claim to fame is that it boasts the largest group of bulwarked dry-ditch land fortifications in the world. The impressive fortifications zigzagging around this pleasant little town – declared a Unesco World Heritage Site in 2012 – reflect an extraordinarily sophisticated military technology. Its moats, fort and heavy walls would indicate a certain paranoia if it weren't for Elvas' position, only 15km west of Spain's Badajoz. Inside the stout town walls, you'll find a lovely town plaza, some quaint museums and very few foreign visitors – aside from the occasional flood of Spanish day trippers. Although there's not much to hold your attention beyond a day, Elvas is an interesting place to visit, with its evocative frontier-post atmosphere, narrow medina-like streets and extraordinary, forbidding walls and buttresses. It also has a few good eateries.

History

In 1229 Elvas was recaptured from the Moors after 500 years of fairly peaceful occupation. The following centuries saw relentless attacks from Spain, interrupted by occasional peace treaties. Spain only succeeded in 1580, allowing Felipe II of Spain (the future Felipe I of Portugal) to set up court here for a few months. But the mighty fortifications were seldom breached: in 1644, during the Wars of Succession (1640–68), the garrison held out against a nine-day Spanish siege and, in 1659, just 1000 – an epidemic had wiped out the rest – withstood an attack by a 15,000-strong Spanish army. The fortifications saw their last action in 1811, when the Duke of Wellington used the town as the base for an attack on Badajoz during the Peninsular War.

👁️ Sights

Torre Fernandina TOWER
(Fernandina Tower; 📞268 636 470; Rua da Cadeia; ⊙3-6pm Tue, 10am-1pm & 3-6pm Wed-Sun) FREE
The Fernandina Tower was the result of alterations undertaken in the 14th century to the second Muslim wall. It served as a jail

Elvas

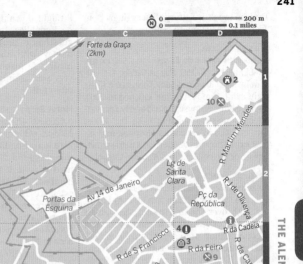

Forte da Graça (2km)

Elvas

⊚ Sights
1 Aqueduto da Amoreira	B3
2 Castelo	D1
3 Museu de Arte Contemporânea de Elvas	D3
4 Torre Fernandina	D3

⊨ Sleeping
5 Garcia de Orta	D4

6 Hotel Dom Luís	A4
7 Hotel São João de Deus	C3

⊗ Eating
8 Adega Regional	D3
9 Mercato	D3
10 Pedras do Castelo	D1

from the end of the 15th century. These days you can climb the spiral staircase to the top for wonderful views. Note: the lighting is poor and it's a steep and winding climb up three levels.

Aqueduto da Amoreira LANDMARK

It took an unsurprising 100 years or so to complete this breathtakingly ambitious aqueduct. Finished in 1622, the huge cylindrical buttresses and several tiers of arches stalk from 7km west of town to bring water

to the marble fountain in Largo da Misericórdia. It's best seen from the Lisbon road, west of the centre.

Castelo CASTLE

(Rua da Parada do Castelo; adult/student/child €2/1/free; ⊙ 9.30am-1pm & 2-5.30pm Tue-Sun) You can walk around the battlements at the castle for dramatic views across the baking plains. The original castle was built by the Moors on a Roman site and rebuilt by Dom

Dinis in the 13th century, then again by Dom João II in the late 15th century.

Museu de Arte Contemporânea de Elvas
GALLERY

(MACE; ☑ 268 637 150; Rua da Cadeia; €2; ⊘ 1-5pm Tue, from 10am Wed-Sun) A must-see if the right exhibition is showing. Opened in 2007, the museum is housed in a cleverly renovated baroque-style building from the 1700s, formerly the Misericórdia Hospital, and offers exhibitions of modern Portuguese artists from the collection of António Cachola.

Forte da Graça
FORT

(☑ 268 625 228; Monte de Nossa Senhora da Graça; €5, guided tour €8; ⊘ 10am-5pm Tue-Sun) Looming high over the arid countryside, about 3km north of town, this old military fort has a commanding presence. From the castelo (p241), the fort is just visible on a distant hillside. Partially restored in 2015, the thick-walled corridors provide a window into the past – particularly if you take part in one of the 80-minute guided tours (call ahead to arrange an English guide). There are splendid views over Elvas and the surrounding countryside.

Forte de Santa Luzia
FORT

(☑ 268 628 357; €2; ⊘ 1-5pm Tue, from 10am Wed-Sun) Dating from the 1640s, this miniature, zigzag-walled fort lies just 1.4km south of the main *praça* (town square). Today it houses a military museum with displays of weaponry dating to the 18th century.

🧭 Tours

Agia
WALKING

(☑ 933 259 036; www.alentejoguides.com; walking tour €120-150) This licensed guide association organises half-day walking tours that explore Elvas' historic sites. Contact Agia in advance for meeting places and times.

🎊 Festivals & Events

Festas do Senhor da Piedade e de São Mateus
MUSIC

Elvas starts to tap its blue suede shoes in late September, celebrating the Festas, with everything from agricultural markets and bullfights to folk dancing and religious processions (especially on the last day).

🛏️ Sleeping

Garcia de Orta
GUESTHOUSE €

(☑ 968 809 512; www.rgarciadeorta.com; Avenida Garcia de Orta 3A; s/d/tr/q €30/40/45/63; ✳🏠) Straight downhill (400m) from the Praça da República, this welcoming, family-run guesthouse provides excellent value for money, with nine bright rooms set with quality furnishings. The whole place is very well maintained. Book ahead, as it's often full.

Hotel Santa Luzia
HOTEL €€

(☑ 268 637 470; www.slhotel-elvas.pt; Avenida de Badajoz; s/d from €80/90; ✳🏠⛱) Although it's a long (uphill) walk to the walled centre, this delightful 25-room hotel is otherwise hard to fault. It has handsome rooms with hand-painted Alentejo-style furniture, and extensive facilities, including an enticing pool, a tennis court and a good restaurant whose claim to fame is inventing the dish *bacalhau dourado* (cod, potatoes and eggs) back in 1947.

Rates are €10 cheaper weekdays.

Hotel São João de Deus
BOUTIQUE HOTEL €€

(☑ 268 639 220; www.hotelsaojoaodeus.com; Largo do Hospital; s/d from €60/75; ✳ @ ⛱) Spanish-owned and operated since 2004, this grand dame is a pleasant, although not always sympathetic, conversion of a 17th-century convent. Each room is different in size and decor – the larger ones are lovely, a couple of smaller ones less so. Most have handsome wood floors and heavy fabrics; one has a bedhead made of tiles.

Hotel Dom Luís
BOUTIQUE HOTEL €€

(☑ 268 636 710; www.hoteldluis-elvas.com; Avenida de Badajoz; s/d €55/70; ✳🏠) This modern 88-room establishment earns high marks for friendliness, with rooms set in a contemporary decor of light greys or browns. It's 700m west of the centre, just outside the town walls, and has a pleasant outdoor cafe with great views of the aqueduct.

🍴 Eating

On weekends the restaurants are packed at lunchtime with visitors arriving from Spain. Call ahead or go early to beat the crowds. For al fresco dining and snacks, head to one of the outdoor cafes on the Praça da República.

Pedras do Castelo
FUSION €€

(☑ 962 919 329; Rua da Parada do Castelo 4; mains €10-14, tapas €4-10; ⊘ noon-10pm Thu-Tue; ☑) Right across from the castle, this welcoming, easy-going spot is a great place to taste Alentejan delicacies – like *porco preto* or *bacalhau dourado*, as well as dishes with

Asian flavours – try the *jin jiao* (dumplings) stuffed with shrimp, meat or vegetables.

Mercato PORTUGUESE **€€**

(📞962 474 471; Rua da Feira 4; mains €8-14; ⊙noon-3pm & 6pm-midnight Tue-Sun) This lively, cheerfully decorated tavern serves traditional flavours with contemporary verve. Nicely turned out plates of garlic and olive-oil clams, or garlic prawns are great for sharing, as are the *tabuas* (boards) of local cheeses and cured meats. Aside from good wines by the glass, Mercato also serves Alentejo craft beer by the likes of duMato and Barona.

Adega Regional PORTUGUESE **€€**

(📞268 623 009; www.adegaregional-elvas.com; Rua João Casqueiro 22B; mains €10-14; ⊙noon-3pm & 7-10pm Wed-Mon; 🛜) Locals love this small place where it's all about the food – lashings of *plumas de porco preto* and *marisco* (shellfish) dishes of all kinds, or a good-value three-course daily meal for under €11.

ⓘ Information

Turismo (📞268 622 236; www.cm-elvas.pt; Praça da República; ⊙9am-7pm Apr-Sep, to 6pm Mon-Fri, 9am-12.30pm & 2-5.30pm Sat & Sun Oct-Mar) Usually has a town map and pamphlets.

ⓘ Getting There & Away

BUS

The **bus station** (Rodoviária de Elvas; 📞268 622 875; Rua do Patrimonio 1) is outside the city walls, on the road to Spain. It's an 800m walk mostly uphill (or a €6 taxi ride) to the main *praça*.

Estremoz €8.50, 45 minutes, three to six daily, or change at Vila Viçosa

Évora €12, 1¼ to 1¾ hours, three to four daily

Faro €22, 6½ hours, one daily with a transfer at Évora

Lisbon around €18, 2¾ to 3½ hours, seven daily

Portalegre €14, 1¼ hours, one to two on weekdays

TRAIN

The **train station** (Estação de Elvas; Largo da Estação, Fontainhas) is 3km northeast of the centre. From Elvas, one train runs daily across the border to Badajoz. There's also one train daily to Portalegre (€4.65, 45 minutes, one daily). This train continues on to Entroncamento, where you can transfer to a train bound for Lisbon (€16, 4½ hours) or Coimbra (€20, four hours).

ⓘ Getting Around

Drivers be aware: it's possible to find central parking, but it's not always easy (and most spots inside the walls are paid). If you don't like narrow one-way streets, park on the outskirts of town (or just inside Portas de Olivença).

Portalegre

POP 15,400 / ELEV 520M

Alto Alentejo's capital Portalegre is bunched up on a hilltop at the foot of Serra de São Mamede. This pretty, whitewashed, ochre-edged city makes for a charming, low-key, off-the-beaten-track experience. It's worth stopping here, at the very least, en route to mountaintop villages.

◎ Sights

Museu da Tapeçaria de Portalegre Guy Fino GALLERY

(Rua da Figueira 9; adult/child €2.10/1; ⊙9.30am-1pm & 2.30-6pm Tue-Sun) If there's one thing you must visit in Portalegre, it's this splendid museum. Opened in 2001, it contains brilliant contemporary creations from Portalegre's unique tapestry factory. It's named after the factory founder, who created an innovatory 'stitch' by hand weaving. The museum shows a selection of the 7000 colours of thread used.

French tapestry artist Jean Lurçat at first dismissed the technique, until the factory made a copy of one of his works – a cockerel – and asked him to identify the one made at Aubusson, in France. He chose the more perfect Portalegre copy – you can see them juxtaposed here. The huge tapestries are vastly expensive, and the museum includes works by some of the most famous names in Portuguese 20th-century art, including Almada Negreiros and Vieira da Silva. They are all hand-signed on the back by the artist, attesting their quality and authenticity.

Real aficionados can visit the **factory** (📞245 301 400; www.mtportalegre.pt; Rua de Iria Gonçalves 2; ⊙9am-5pm Mon-Fri) where the tapestries are made (its walls are also adorned with fabulous examples). Photography is prohibited and advance reservations are required.

Museu e Fundação Robinson RUINS

(Rua D Iria Gonçalves Pereira 2; €2.10; ⊙10am-1pm & 2-5pm Mon-Fri) For an alternative view of Portugal, take a guided tour through an abandoned cork factory, winding through a

Portalegre

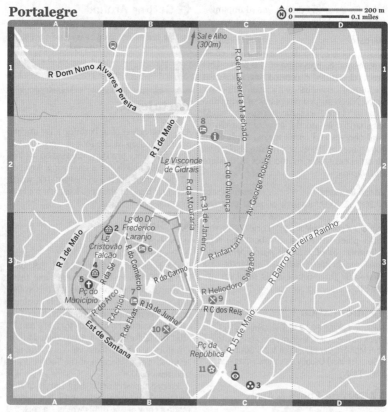

Portalegre

warren of rooms where old machinery lies rusting. Founded in 1835 by Englishman Thomas Reynolds, the factory was a major employer in Portalegre (with more than 2000 workers at its peak). Production declined in the second half of the 20th century, and the place closed for good in 2009.

Museu Municipal MUSEUM
(Rua José Maria da Rosa; adult/child €2.10/1; ⊙9am-1pm & 2-6pm Tue-Sun) The local museum exhibits religious art of the 17th and 18th centuries, including paintings and furniture from the Convento de Santa Clara (now a public library) and Monastero de São

Bernardo (now the National Guard School), along with private collections.

Sé
CATHEDRAL

(Praça do Município; ⊙2.30-6pm Tue, 9am-noon & 2.30-6pm Wed-Sun) In 1550 Portalegre became the seat of a new diocese and soon got its own cathedral. The pyramid-pointed, twin-towered 18th-century facade sombrely presides over the whitewashed Praça do Município. The sacristy contains an array of fine *azulejos*.

⭐ Festivals & Events

Festival One Man Band
MUSIC

Over one weekend in mid-October, this festival brings performers from Portugal and four or five other countries who show off their solo skills in blues, rock, folk and other styles. It typically happens in the Centro de Artes do Espectáculo de Portalegre (p246).

🛏 Sleeping

Hostel Portalegre
HOSTEL €

(☑968 580 588; www.hostelportalegre.pt; Rua Benvindo Ceia 2; dm/tw with shared bathroom €15/40; 🐞) Set in a converted house in a great central location, the Hostel Portalegre has spacious bunk rooms, and guests have free rein of the kitchen and lounge area. The friendly owners are happy to share their wealth of knowledge of Portalegre and the surrounding area. Contact them well in advance, as they don't live in the town.

Hotel Mansão Alto Alentejo
GUESTHOUSE €

(☑245 202 290; www.mansaoaltoalentejo.com.pt; Rua 19 de Junho 59; s/d €35/45; 🐞🐞) The stone staircase is steep, but it's the pick of the bunch for its bright rooms with traditional hand-painted Alentejan furniture and charming lounge area. It has a good, central location within easy walking distance to the top sights and restaurants in the old centre.

⭐ Convento da Provença
HERITAGE HOTEL €€

(☑245 337 104; www.provenca.pt; Monte Paleiros; s/d/ste €75/85/95; 🅿🐞🐞🐞) Mother Superior may not have approved of this out-of-town luxury sleeping option, but we do. This renovated former convent has an austere white exterior, but its interior is another story. Shiny sabres and suits of armour fill the grand lounge and entrance. Spacious rooms and suites are decorated with masculine hues and stylish wooden trimmings. All have lovely green views.

Quinta da Dourada
INN €€

(☑937 218 654; www.quintadadourada.pt; s €65, d €75-85, ste €85-100; 🅿🐞🐞🐞) Seven kilometres northeast of Portalegre, in the Parque Natural da Serra de São Mamede, this picture-perfect, modern-looking place is surrounded by glorious vegetation – lime trees and flowers. The individual rooms are smartly furnished and have granite floors.

Rossio Hotel
HOTEL €€

(☑245 082 218; www.rossiohotel.com; Rua 31 de Janeiro 6; s/tw €50/70, d €73-80; 🐞🐞) 🍃 This modern 15-room hotel earns high marks for its ecofriendly features, including solar panels, rainwater collection and low-energy LED lighting. The rooms are sleek and modern – if a touch on the minimalist side – with muted colour schemes and abundant natural light thanks to oversized windows. The best rooms have small balconies.

🍴 Eating

⭐ Solar do Forcado
PORTUGUESE €€

(☑245 330 866; Rua Cândido dos Reis 14; mains €11-16; ⊙12.30-3pm & 7.30-10.30pm Mon-Fri, 7-10pm Sat) The current owner is a former *forcado* (performer of a specific style of Portuguese bullfighting), as was his father, as attested by the many photos and paraphernalia that cover the walls of this atmospheric spot. Meat lovers should charge in here for hefty regional delights of *bovino* (bull meat), wild pig and deer, plus great *doces conventuais* (convent desserts). Incredible value.

Tomba Lobos
PORTUGUESE €€

(☑245 906 111; www.tombalobos.pt; Rua 19 de Julho 2; mains €15-19; ⊙noon-3pm & 7.30-10pm Tue-Sat, noon-3pm Sun) A stylish newcomer to Portalegre, Tomba Lobos serves beautifully prepared dishes that showcase the high-quality produce of the Alentejo. Roasted lamb, hare with white beans, and codfish rice are a few of the many standouts. Dining is in a cosy back room with vaulted brick ceilings, though there are also a few tables in front by the sleek marble-topped bar.

Sal e Alho
PORTUGUESE €€

(☑963 926 655; Avenida Piu XII, Lote 7; mains €13-20; ⊙noon-3pm Mon, noon-3pm & 7-10pm Tue-Sun) About a 10-minute walk (700m) north of the historical centre, Sal e Alho is famous in these parts for its hearty traditional cooking. Come for game meats – like *javali* (wild boar) or *febre* (hare) or signature plates of *porco preto.* It all goes nicely with the good wine selection.

🍷 Drinking & Entertainment

Pátio da Casa Café Concerto CAFE
(Rua Benvindo Ceia 1; ⊙ 10am-midnight Mon & Sun, from 1pm Tue-Fri, 2.30pm-1am Sat; 🛜) A bohemian air pervades this hidden glass-roofed patio cafe, with its chunky wooden tables and world music soundtrack. Changing artwork adorns the walls, and there's live music most weekends. At other times, it draws a local crowd who stop in for coffee or sangria, snacks (*tostas,* crepes, veggie burgers) and free wi-fi.

Centro de Artes do
Espectáculo de Portalegre THEATRE
(CAEP; ☏ 245 307 498; www.caeportalegre.blogspot.com; Praça da República 39) Overlooking Praça da República is Portalegre's major performance space, hosting fado singers, rock, jazz and acoustic groups, as well as dance and theatre. Ask at the tourist office (p246) for current shows.

ℹ️ Information

Turismo (☏ 245 307 445; Rua Guilherme Gomes Fernandes 22; ⊙ 9.30am-1pm & 2.30-6pm) Helpful staff dole out information and a town map. Also has free internet access.

ℹ️ Getting There & Away

BUS

The **bus station** (☏ 245 330 723; Avenida do Brasil 49) has regular services to the following destinations.

TO	COST (€)	TIME (HR)	FREQUENCY
Castelo Branco	11.40	1¼hr	1 daily
Castelo de Vide	6	20min	2 daily Mon-Fri
Elvas	14	1¼hr	1 daily Mon-Fr
Estremoz	8	50min	2 to 6 daily
Évora	12.20	1½hr	1 to 3 daily
Lisbon	15	4hr	4 daily
Marvão	6	35min	1 daily

TRAIN

Portalegre's **train station** (Estação de Portalegre; off IP2) is 12km south of the centre. A free shuttle bus provides transport from the station.

From Portalegre, you can catch trains southwest to Elvas (€4.65, 45 minutes, one daily) and on to Badajoz in Spain (€9, 70 minutes). Heading east, you can reach Castelo Branco (€12.30, three hours, one daily) with a transfer at Abrantes, or Lisbon (€14.10, four hours, one daily) or Coimbra (€18, 3¼ hours, one daily), transferring at Entroncamento.

Castelo de Vide

POP 3300 / ELEV 570M

High above lush, rolling countryside, Castelo de Vide is one of Portugal's most attractive and underrated villages. Its fine hilltop vantage point, dazzlingly white houses, flower-lined lanes and proud locals are reason alone to visit. There aren't many attractions in town, but there doesn't need to be. Absorb this pleasant place for a day and a night; at dusk and early morning you can experience the town at its most disarming. You'll see elderly women crocheting on doorsteps, children playing in the narrow streets and neighbours chatting out of upper-storey windows.

Castelo de Vide is famous for its crystal-clear mineral water, which spouts out of numerous pretty public fountains; several of these are surrounded by hedged gardens.

👁 Sights

Synagogue & Museum MUSEUM
(Rua da Judiaria; ⊙ 9am-1pm & 2-5pm Tue-Sun Sep-May, to 6pm Jun-Aug) FREE Reopened in 2009 after being converted into a museum, the site comprises the original synagogue – two rooms (one for women and one for men), a wooden tabernacle and Holy Ark for Torah scrolls. The remaining rooms (part of the village home from which the synagogue was originally converted) house a superb collection of items illustrating the history of the local Jewish communities. Following Manuel I's convert-or-leave edict in 1496, many Jews returned to Spain, though some headed to Évora.

Casa da Inquisição MUSEUM
(Rua Nova 24) Under construction at research, this museum will delve into the dark era of the Inquisition. It's set inside a restored 17th-century mansion.

Castelo CASTLE
(Rua Bartolomeu Álvares de Sant; ⊙ 9.30am-5pm Sep-May, to 6pm Jun-Aug) FREE Originally Castelo de Vide's inhabitants lived within the castle's sturdy outer walls; even now

Castelo de Vide

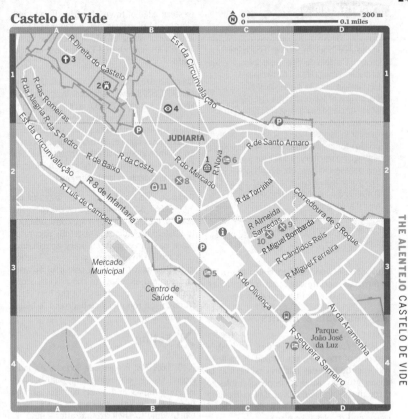

Castelo de Vide

there remains a small inner village with a church, the 17th-century **Igreja da Nossa Senhora da Alegria** (Rua Direita do Castelo). You can take in some brilliant views from here over the town's red roofs, surrounded by green and olive hills.

Judiaria   HISTORIC SITE
(off Rua da Fonte) By the castle is a small *judiaria* – the former Jewish district. A sizeable community of Jews settled here in the 12th century, then larger waves came in the early 15th century after the expulsion of the Jews from Spain. At first they didn't have an exclusive district, but Dom Pedro I restricted them to specific quarters. The highlight of this area is the synagogue & museum.

🏃 Activities

Keen walkers should ask at the tourist office (p249) for walking-trail maps such as those headed to Torrinha and Serra de São

WORTH A TRIP

MIGHTY MEGALITHS

In the wild, boulder-strewn landscape around Castelo de Vide are dozens of ancient megaliths. The two most impressive are the **Anta da Melriça**, northwest of town, and the 7m-high **Menhir da Meada**, around 13km north of town. This is supposedly the tallest menhir in the Iberian Peninsula – a large phallus for keeping the fields fertile and acting as a territory marker (one of the few believed to have done both jobs). The so-called **Parque Megalítico dos Coureleiros** is a collection of five different arrangements.

These megaliths are best accessed by car. Ask for a map from the tourist office.

Paulo. These wonderful three- to four-hour sojourns around the area pass old churches, fountains, and megaliths and dolmens.

Festivals & Events

Easter Festival RELIGIOUS
(☉Mar or Apr) Castelo de Vide's big bash – and one of the most traditional of its festivals – is the four-day fair on Good Friday to Easter Monday when a couple of lambs go through the highs and lows of blessings and slaughter. Processions, folk dances, band music and revelry take place.

Carnaval CARNIVAL
(☉Feb/Mar) This festival is great fun, with everyone out to watch processions of those in their homemade fancy dress. The revelry dates to the Middle Ages, and provides locals with the opportunity to rack up a few sins before Quaresma (Lent).

Sleeping

Inatel HOTEL €
(☑245 900 200; www.inatel.pt; Rua Sequeira Sameiro 6; s/d from €35/50; ☜) Overlooking a leafy park in the town centre, this Portuguese chain offers excellent value for money. Rooms have terracotta floors, heavy carved-wood furniture, comfortable beds and spacious bathrooms (the vanity mirror is a nice touch). Grab a table in the back of the breakfast room for pretty mountain views.

Casa de Hóspedes Machado GUESTHOUSE €
(☑245 901 515; www.casamachado.com.pt; Rua Luís de Camões 33; s/d/tr €25/30/35; ☜) On the western edge of town, this friendly and efficiently run place has airy, modern and spotless rooms, some of which offer fine views. There's a small, shared kitchen and outdoor patio.

Casa Amarela GUESTHOUSE €€
(☑245 905 878; www.casaamarelath.pt; Praça Dom Pedro V 11; s/d from €80/90; ❀ ☜) This beautifully restored 18th-century building on the main square, with views over the *praça,* is a luxurious choice. It has stone staircases and common areas filled with antiques. The 11 rooms drip with rich fabrics and feature massive, marble-filled bathrooms.

Casa da Rua Nova APARTMENT €€€
(☑967 567 310; www.casadaruanova.com; Rua Nova 36; r €90-130; ❀ ☜) A welcome addition to Castelo de Vide, this tastefully decorated place has three contemporary apartments, each with a living room and small kitchen unit. Rooms are set with colourful artwork and contain elements of the original stone walls. Book the penthouse for the best views (though the roomier one-bedroom is better for families).

Eating

Pirolito TAPAS €
(☑925 619 748; Rua Almeida Sarzedas 20; tapas around €6; ☉noon-midnight Tue-Sun) A stylish new tapas and wine bar has arrived in Castelo de Vide, making it all the more worthwhile to stick around after sundown. Small plates of shrimp with garlic, octopus salad, fried chicken and Spanish-style tortilla – plus cheese and sausage boards – go nicely with the affordable local wines.

★ Confraria PORTUGUESE €€
(☑245 905 106; Rua Santa Maria 10; mains around €14; ☉10am-10pm Tue-Sun) This outstanding restaurant serves up delectable plates of regional fare showcasing whatever is fresh and seasonal. The menu is limited and mostly meat-centric (think tender beef cheeks, wild partridge, hare with white beans, and rich roast pork), but plates are beautifully turned out, and the wines (over 40 from this part of the Alentejo) are outstanding.

O Miguel PORTUGUESE €€
(☑245 901 882; Rua Almeida Sarzedas 32-34; mains €9-14; ☉noon-2.30pm & 7.30-10pm Mon-Sat) This long-standing down-to-earth spot whips up regional dishes including *migas de batata* (potato dumplings), tripe and traditional flavours of the season in a convivial

atmosphere. Set lunches for around €9 are served on weekdays.

🛍 Shopping

Toca do Chocolate   FOOD
(Rua Mouzinho da Silveira 14; ⊘3-7pm Wed-Fri, 11am-1pm & 3-7pm Sat & Sun, closed Sun Oct-Apr) If you have a weakness for chocolate, don't miss this heavenly shop and cafe hidden on a narrow lane on the way to the castle. You'll find plenty of temptations here, from rich hot chocolate to chocolate-covered fruit, decadent tarts and even chocolate liqueurs. There's also a good tea selection (including Azorean varieties), microbrews and wine.

ℹ Information

Turismo (🖉 245 908 227; www.cm-castelo-vide.pt; Praça Dom Pedro V; ⊘9am-1pm & 2-5pm Nov-Apr, 9am-1pm & 3-6pm May-Oct) Stocks some reasonable printed matter, including maps and leaflets.

ℹ Getting There & Away

From the **bus stop** (🖉 245 901 510) at Praça Valência de Alcántara, buses run to/from Portalegre (€6, 20 minutes, two daily) and Lisbon (€17, 4¼ hours, two daily). For Marvão you must change in Portagem. Ask at the turismo for bus times.

Marvão

POP 110 / ELEV 862M
On a jutting crag high above the surrounding countryside, the narrow lanes of Marvão feel like a retreat far removed from the settlements below. The whitewashed village of picturesque tiled roofs and bright flowers has marvellous views, a splendid castle and a handful of low-key guesthouses and restaurants. Since the 16th century, the town has struggled to keep inhabitants, and today the friendly locals survive mainly on tourism. It's worth spending a night here.

Arriving by car or bus you'll approach Portas de Ródão, one of the four village gates, opening on to Rua de Cima, which has several shops and restaurants. Drivers can park outside, or enter this gate and park in Largo de Olivença, just below Rua de Cima.

History

Not surprisingly, this garrison town just 10km from the Spanish frontier has long been a prized possession. Romans settled here, and Christian Visigoths were on the scene when the Moors arrived in 715. It was probably the Moorish lord of Coimbra, Emir Maraun, who gave the place its present name.

In 1160 Christians took control. In 1226 the town received a municipal charter, the walls were extended to encompass the whole summit and the castle was rebuilt by Dom Dinis.

Marvão's importance in the defence against the Castilians was highlighted during the 17th-century War of Restoration, when further defences were added. But by the 1800s it had lost its way, a garrison town without a garrison, and this lack of interest is why so many 15th- and 16th-century buildings have been preserved. Its last action was at the centre of the tug-of-war between the Liberals and Royalists; in 1833

WORTH A TRIP

ROMAN RUINS

The excellent little Roman museum **Cidade de Ammaia** (🖉 245 919 089; www.ammaia.pt; Estrada da Calçadinha 4; €3; ⊘9am-12.30pm & 2-5.30pm) lies between Castelo de Vide and Marvão in São Salvador de Aramenha. From São Salvador head 700m south along the Portalegre road, then turn left, following the signs to Ammaia. This fascinating museum is packed with treasures. Start with the seven-minute film (with English subtitles) that give a vivid depiction of this ancient city of 2000 inhabitants.

In the 1st century AD this area was a huge Roman city called Ammaia, flourishing from the area's rich agricultural produce (especially oil, wine and cereals). Although evidence was found (and some destroyed) in the 19th century, it wasn't until 1994 that thorough digs began.

At Cidade de Ammaia you can see some of the finds, including engraved lintels and tablets, jewellery, coins and some incredibly well-preserved glassware. You can also follow paths across the fields to where the forum and spa once stood and see several impressive columns.

the Liberals used a secret entrance to seize the town – the only time Marvão has ever been captured.

⊙ Sights

Castelo
CASTLE

(Rua do Castelo; adult/student €1.90/1; ⊙10am-7pm) The formidable castle, built into the rock at the western end of the village, dates from the end of the 13th century, but most of what you see today was built in the 17th century. The views from the battlements are staggering. There's a huge vaulted cistern (still full of water) near the entrance, and it's landscaped with hedges and flower beds. The *torre de menagem* (keep) has displays on the castle's history even pre-dating its 13th-century founding.

Museu Municipal
MUSEUM

(☑245 909 132; Largo de Santa Maria; adult/student €1.90/1; ⊙10am-12.30pm & 1.30-5pm Tue-Sun) Just southeast of the castle, the Igreja de Santa Maria provides graceful surroundings for this one-room museum. Its renovated exhibition hall offers a brief overview of regional history from the Paleolithic era to more recent centuries.

☆ Activities

Rail Bike Marvão
OUTDOORS

(☑912 987 639; www.railbikemarvao.com; Largo da Alfândega, Beirã; 2/4hr trips from €20/45) New in 2018, this New Zealand–owned outfit offers scenic trips along a disused train line using customised, two-person pedal-powered rail bikes. You'll see cork and olive fields, farmhouse ruins and perhaps some wildlife. The four-hour trip takes you to the old train station of Castelo de Vide for a picnic lunch before making the return journey (32km return).

It's in Beirã, about 11km north of Marvão, and right next door to the Train Spot guesthouse.

Caballos Marvão
HORSE RIDING

(☑653 348 948; www.caballosmarvao.com; Abegões; ⛨) For equestrian adventures, get in touch with this friendly, professionally run outfit, which offers a wide range of outings. You can head out on a one-hour ride (€25) through typical Alentejan scenery, explore the little-visited landscapes along the Rio Sever or ride along old smuggler routes past vulture colonies near the Spanish border (€150, five hours).

The stables are about 5km northeast of Marvão. Call for directions.

Piscina Fluvial
SWIMMING

(Portagem) A favourite local way to cool off in summer is to take a dip in the Rio Sever. On warm days, you can swim in a protected stretch of the river in Portagem, which is about 6km southwest of Marvão. There's also a cafe with outdoor seating overlooking the swimming area.

☆ Visiting Megaliths

You can make a brilliant 30km round-trip via Santo António das Areias and Beirã, visiting nearby *antas* (dolmens). You'll pass through a fabulously quiet landscape of cork trees and rummaging pigs. Some megaliths are right by the roadside, while others require a 300m to 500m walk. Be sure to bring refreshments: there's no village en route. You can continue north of Beirã to visit the megaliths in the Castelo de Vide area.

☆ Walking

Ask at the tourist office for instructions on the interesting 7.5km circuit walk from Marvão to Portagem via Abegoa and Fonte Souto (or 2.5km direct to Portagem), following a medieval stone-paved route. Note: the return journey is steep.

⊨ Sleeping

★ Train Spot
GUESTHOUSE €€

(☑963 340 221; www.trainspot.pt; Largo da Alfândega, Beirã; r with shared/private bathroom €45/65; ℗ ✿) Some 11km north of Marvão in the tiny village of Beirã, this extraordinary place offers lodging in a beautifully converted building that was once part of the now inactive train station. It's a designer's dream, with lovely tile-work, a spacious lounge with fireplace and intriguing details (including a bicycle dangling from the ceiling).

The rooms are bright and quite comfy. The patio faces on to the old train tracks. The guesthouse makes a fine base for exploring the area. There are lesser-known megaliths and lovely walks (or horse rides) in the countryside nearby.

★ Quinta do Barrieiro
GUESTHOUSE €€

(☑936 721 199; www.quintadobarrieiro.pt; Estrada Reveladas; r €55-130, 6-person apt €150-230; ℗ ✿ ✿ ✿) Special occasion anyone? Bah! You shouldn't need an excuse to come to this rural tourism abode. This superb place, made up of several *casinhas* (little houses) and rooms, provides comfort, creativity and the outdoors (there are some great walks around the property and to a dam).

The garden is full of the owner's sculptures, as are the light and airy communal living areas. Continental breakfasts are excellent and cost €15 per double room. Ring for directions as it's 15km south of Marvão, 13km north of Portalegre.

Estalagem de Marvão GUESTHOUSE €€
(☑968 147 862; www.estalagemdemarvao.com; Rua do Espírito Santo 1; s/d/tr €48/60/80; ❋☎) In the heart of the village, you'll find six simple but attractively decorated rooms with wood floors and kind staff. The inn also operates a small shop, where you can browse gourmet food items and a few crafts. There's also a communal terrace with views.

Hotel El Rei Dom Manuel HOTEL €€
(☑245 909 150; www.turismarvao.pt; Largo de Olivença; s €60, d €70-85; ☎) The pick for reliability. This charming, friendly and professional hotel has comfortable rooms with tiled floors, drapes and puffy pillows. The best rooms are the suites with a view. Breakfast is served in the hotel restaurant.

Casa da Árvore GUESTHOUSE €€
(☑245 993 854; www.casadaarvoremarvao.com; Rua Dr Matos Magalhães 3; s/d from €50/65; ❋☎) This elegant guesthouse has five country-home-style rooms and an attractive, comfortable lounge area with a stunning view. Great for kicking back after pounding the streets. It's worth paying a bit extra (€10) for a room with a veranda.

Dom Dinis GUESTHOUSE €€
(☑245 909 028; www.domdinis.pt; Rua Dr Matos Magalhães 7; d €56-80; ❋☎) Dom Dinis has nine smallish but modern rooms with whitewashed walls and heavy wood furnishings. The largest has a balcony with lovely views over the castle walls. Even if you don't score a room with a view, you can enjoy the sweeping expanse from the terrace.

Pousada de Marvão HERITAGE HOTEL €€€
(☑245 993 201; www.pousadas.pt; Rua 24 de Janeiro 7; r €120-190; ❋☎) Inside a whitewashed building that once housed a factory, this 31-room guesthouse has attractive rooms with hand-painted Alentejan furniture and terracotta or polished wood floors. The best rooms have great views, while cheaper digs

have small windows and feel a bit cramped. The fine restaurant gives a panoramic expanse of the valley below.

✖ Eating & Drinking

O Castelo PORTUGUESE €
(☑245 993 060; www.facebook.com/cafelounge marvao; Rua Dr Matos Magalhães 7; mains €5-10; ⊙9am-11pm; ☎) This friendly cafe has outdoor tables and a cosy interior where you can warm up by the fireplace on chilly afternoons. It has appetisers and other lighter fare – *tostas,* sandwiches, soups, plus hot chocolate, Alentejan wines, beer and the like.

★ Restaurante Sever PORTUGUESE €€
(☑245 993 318; Estrada Rio Sever, Portagem; mains €13-20; ⊙noon-3pm & 7-10pm; ☎☑) The pick of the restaurants for miles around, this smart place is in a beautiful location, just over the bridge in Portagem, on the Rio Sever. It comes highly recommended by locals and serves first-class Alentejan cuisine. Specials include roast leg of lamb and wild rabbit with mushrooms. The grilled vegetables are great for vegetarians.

Natural Bar CAFE
(www.facebook.com/naturalcocktailbar; Travessa do Chabouco 7A; 10am-10pm) This charming new spot has a lovely terrace with views over the Alentejo countryside, and serves up fresh juices, cocktails, craft beer and wines by the glass, as well as *tostas,* salads and other snacks. There's live music most weekend nights.

ℹ Information

Turismo (☑245 909 131; www.cm-marvao. pt; Rua de Baixo; ⊙10am-5pm; ☎) After the main gate entrance (not to be confused with a small information booth on the left as you enter the walls) is the helpful *turismo,* which has a complete list of accommodation and restaurant options.

ℹ Getting There & Away

Buses run between Portalegre and Marvão (45 minutes, two daily on weekdays). There is also a service to/from Castelo de Vide (22 minutes), but it may require a change of bus at Portagem, a key road junction 6km southwest of Marvão.

For taxi trips, contact the owner of the restaurant **Varanda do Alentejo** (☑245 909 002; Praça do Pelourinho 1). A taxi to Castelo de Vide costs around €16.50; it's €7.50 to Portagem and €30 to Portalegre.

THE ALENTEJO MARVÃO

BAIXO ALENTEJO

POP 125,000

The southern half of the Alentejo is packed with history. The scenic hilltop town of Mértola has an old centre that's something of a living museum, with its archaeological sites dating back to the Islamic period. Beja has Roman and Visigoth ruins, including recently excavated sites that will be showcased in a new museum; Moura has its share of artefacts and a small Moorish street pattern. For something a little different, don't miss the abandoned mining buildings of São Domingos.

Beja

POP 23,500

Baixo Alentejo's principal town is easy-going, welcoming and untouristed, with a walled centre and some beguiling sights, all of which are within an easy walk of each other; these often follow old Roman routes. Often dismissed as Évora's 'plainer cousin', Beja has an inferiority complex, but it shouldn't. Its inexpensive guesthouses, quaint plazas and excellent eateries make for a relaxing stop and a very genuine Portuguese experience.

Beja is at the heart of the regional tourist area called Planície Dourada (Golden Plain) – meaning it's surrounded by a sea of wheat fields. On Saturday there's the bonus of a traditional market, spread around the castle.

◉ Sights

★ **Museu Regional de Beja** MUSEUM
(Convento de Nossa Senhora da Conceição; Largo da Conceição; adult/child €2/free; ⊙9.30am-12.30pm & 2-5.30pm Tue-Sun) Beja's must-see attraction is set in a 15th-century Franciscan convent and the backdrop to an unlikely romance between a nun and soldier that inspired *Letters of a Portuguese Nun*. A romantic setting, the convent is a delicate balance between no-nonsense Gothic and Manueline flights of fancy. The interior is lavish, with a rococo chapel of 17th- and 18th-century gilded woodwork. Also on display are Roman lamps, glass bottles and stelae, and 16th-century paintings.

The chapter house is incongruously Arabian, with a beautiful ceiling painted with unfurling ferns, 16th-century tiles and a carved doorway. The cloister has some splendid 16th- and 17th-century *azulejos*.

The admission fee includes entry to the Museu Visigótico.

Centro de Arqueologia e Artes MUSEUM
(Praça da República) Under construction at time of research, this new museum will house some of the great archaeological finds unearthed in Beja in recent years. Pieces date to the Iron Age (the 7th century BC) and include relics from Islamic and medieval times, though the highlight will be the Roman collection. In fact, the museum will incorporate features of a Roman temple and a Roman forum discovered here in 2008.

The opening date has been pushed back several times, and is currently slated for late 2020.

Castelo CASTLE
(Rua Dom Dinis; ⊙9.30am-12.30pm & 2-5.30pm) FREE Dom Dinis built this castle on Roman foundations in the late 13th century. You can climb up the Torre de Menagem for fine views over the roofs of town. The turismo (p256) is located here.

Museu Visigótico MUSEUM
(Largo de Santo Amaro; adult/student €2/1; ⊙9.30am-12.30pm & 2-5pm Tue-Sun) Found just beyond the castle, the unusual Visigothic museum is housed in the former Igreja de Santo Amaro, parts of which date from the early 6th century, when it was a Visigothic church – meaning it's one of Portugal's oldest standing buildings. Inside, the original columns display intriguing, beautiful carvings. The admission fee includes entry to the Museu Regional de Beja.

**Núcleo Museológico
da Rua do Sembrano** RUINS
(Rua do Sembrano; ⊙9.30am-12.30pm & 2-5.30pm) FREE This modern museum contains more than meets the eye – the exhibition is underfoot and displayed through a glass floor. Iron Age finds were discovered here during building works in the 1980s, and the site was deemed important enough to excavate and protect. Peer through the glass floor at 2200-year-old remains, over which were laid subsequent Roman walls, indicating that this location was important for millennia.

⎵ Sleeping

Hospedaria Rosa do Campo GUESTHOUSE €
(☑284 323 578; www.rosadocampo.pt; Rua da Liberdade 12; s/d/tr from €35/45/55; ✳ 🛜) This sparkling guesthouse has polished floors

Beja

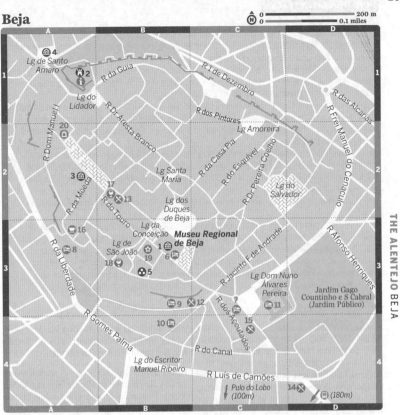

Beja

(wood or granite) and spacious rooms, each utterly spotless and with a small refrigerator. The owner loves a bit of greenery, keeping plants in the foyer and in most of the rooms (with wisteria growing up the outside of the building). Incredible value.

ALVITO

Situated 38km northwest of Beja and 37km southwest of Évora in Baixa Alentejo, beautiful Alvito (pop 1250) is well worth visiting, at least for half a day. Be aware, though, such is its appeal, it's the kind of place you get to and wish you'd packed your toothbrush. The town was the home of the Portuguese barons; the first baron, Dom João Fernandes da Silveira, decided to make Alvito an artistic landmark.

You can visit parts of a 15th-century former castle, now a luxury **pousada** (☑ 284 480 700; www.pousadas.pt; Largo do Castelo; d €85-135, ste €145-170; P ❄ ☎ ☎), and several important churches. The 16th-century **Ermida de Sao Sebastião** has some extraordinary revived frescoes.

Throughout the village, you can see beautiful Manueline features – pick up a map from the **turismo** (☑ 284 480 808; www.cm-alvito.pt; Rua dos Lobos 13; ⊙ 9am-12.30pm & 2-5.30pm Mon-Fri, 10am-12.30pm & 2-5.30pm Sat) and play 'spot the Manueline doorway' (these are stunning).

Public transport is very limited in these parts. It's most convenient to arrive with your own wheels.

If you decide to stay the night, our pick is the delightful **Horta do Padre** (☑ 916 261 027, 962 013 059; hortadopadre@gmail.com; Quinta da Esperança, Apartado 16; d €40-50, house €150; ☎) ✿ , a renovated blue-and-white traditional Alentejan farmhouse 1km east of Alvito's centre (direction down Estrada de São Roman), with comfortable rooms and excellent breakfasts. The multilingual owners Fernanda and Lino are passionate about preserving Portuguese traditional practices and are founts of knowledge about the region.

Hospedaria Dona Maria　　　HOTEL €
(☑ 284 327 602; www.hospedariadonamaria.com; Largo Dom Nuno Álvares Pereira 12; s/d/ste €33/43/50; ❄☎) In a pretty, half tile-covered building just outside the walls, the Hospedaria Dona Maria has trim, modern, but somewhat small rooms, with comfy mattresses, tiny desks and a light colour scheme – apart from the lavender duvets and pillows that add a dash of colour. The service is friendly and there's a decent Italian restaurant on the ground floor.

Beja Hostel　　　GUESTHOUSE €
(☑ 939 317 472; www.hostelfreimanuel.com; Rua Alexandre Herculano 7; s €23, d €30-45, q €50; ❄☎) This new guesthouse in the centre of town is a good choice for budget travellers. Despite the name, there are no dorms, just clean and simple private rooms (some with private bathroom), with an appealing lounge, pool table and cafe.

Hotel Bejense　　　GUESTHOUSE €€
(☑ 284 311 570; www.hotelbejense.com; Rua Capitão João Francisco de Sousa 57; s/d €45/55; ❄☎) This pleasant family-run option has bright rooms, each slightly different in design – some have murals, others elaborately painted bedheads. Front rooms have small balconies, and the hallways are trimmed with tiles. You might have flashbacks to

your childhood while walking up the stairs, which are lined with family photos. Breakfast is a small but excellent buffet.

Hotel Santa Bárbara　　　GUESTHOUSE €€
(☑ 284 312 280; Rua de Mértola 56; s/d €42/50; ❄☎) This reliable and good-value choice has neat, motel-style rooms with artwork and colourful throws on the bed. Front rooms have balconies over the lane. In winter you can warm up beside the small fireplace in the lounge. It's well located in the pedestrianised town centre.

Pousada Convento de Beja　　　POUSADA €€€
(☑ 284 313 580; www.pousadas.pt; Largo Dom Nuno Álvares Pereira; s/d €135/145; P ☎ ☎) Located in the 13th-century São Francisco Convent, this *pousada* provides gorgeous rooms, formerly cells, and a restaurant (open all day) with a magnificent vaulted ceiling. A Gothic chapel, former chapter house and pleasant lounge areas add to the unique and luxurious atmosphere.

🍴 Eating

Sabores do Campo　　　VEGETARIAN €
(☑ 284 320 267; Rua Bento de Jesus Caraça 4; per kg €14; ⊙ noon-9.30pm Mon-Thu, to 3pm Fri; ☑) If you're a vegetarian, or simply need a break from pork and codfish, this cheerful cafeteria-style eatery will come as a godsend.

Fresh fruit (papaya, mango, strawberries), stuffed mushrooms, oven-baked enchiladas, cabbage-wrapped 'sausage' (from soy), vegetarian lasagna and honey-drizzled filo pastry filled with goat's-milk cheese and walnuts are just a few of the recent hits of the ever-changing daily menu.

Taberna do Arrufa
TAPAS €

(📞967 229 487; www.facebook.com/tabernadoarrufa; Travessa das Francas 3, Cuba; tapas €4-8; ⏰noon-2am Thu-Mon, from 5pm Wed) Located 20km north of Beja, this eating and drinking den blends old-fashioned charm with bohemian style. Sharing plates are the name of the game, with Serpa cheese, roasted pork cheeks, grilled octopus, steaming pots of clams and sweet-potato fries best washed down with a jug of the local wine.

Smiles
CAFE €

(Rua da Infantaria 17; snacks €1.50-3; ⏰7.30am-7pm Mon-Fri, to 1pm Sat) This charming little spot whips up soups and *rissois* (meat or veg-filled croquettes), but it's the desserts that warrant the trip – think chocolate tort drizzled with caramel, vegan banana cake and strawberry tart. Indie rock plays softly in the background, there's art on the walls and the kind-hearted staff make decent coffees.

Luiz da Rocha
CAFE €

(📞284 323 179; www.luizdarocha.com; Rua Capitão João Francisco de Sousa 63; snacks €2-4; ⏰8am-11pm Mon-Sat, to 8pm Sun) Founded in 1893, this is one of Beja's oldest cafes and best-known institutions. It gathers a chatty neighbourhood crowd day and night and is justly famous for its cakes: *trouxas de ovos* (literally 'sweet egg yolks') and *porquinhos de doce* (sweet little pigs). There's a more polished sit-down restaurant upstairs that serves Alentejan staples (mains €8 to €11).

Pulo do Lobo
PORTUGUESE €€

(📞284 327 898; www.facebook.com/restaurantepulodolobo; Praceta Rainha Dona Leonor 6; mains €8-18; ⏰noon-3pm & 7-11pm Mon-Sat) A short walk south of the historic centre, buzzing Pulo do Lobo is extremely popular with locals. They come from across the city for mouthwateringly fresh seafood and some of Beja's best *porco preto* (black-pork) dishes. It's an easy-going, unfussy affair – a classical Bejan *tasca* (tavern).

Os Infantes
PORTUGUESE €€

(📞936 171 317; www.facebook.com/osinfantesrestaurante; Rua dos Infantes 16; mains €10-16; ⏰12.30-3pm & 7-11pm Wed-Sun; 📶) Inside this cavernous space, you can dine on updated versions of classical Alentejan recipes as well as creative dishes with international accents. Salad with grapes, Azorean cheese and walnuts, codfish with cream and spinach, seared duck breast with port-wine reduction are a few of the many temptations.

🍷 Drinking & Nightlife

Porta 15
COCKTAIL BAR

(📞966 295 978; Rua do Sembrano 15; ⏰5pm-4am Mon-Sat) An atmospheric spot for a cocktail, Porta 15 has soaring arched brick ceilings, friendly bartenders and a small stage flanked by Egyptian-style sarcophagi. There's live music most weekends (low-key one- or two-person bands) from around 11pm.

Oficina os Infantes
BAR

(📞966 651 380; www.facebook.com/oficina osinfantes; Rua dos Infantes 14; ⏰10pm-4am Tue-Sat) The liveliest spot in town for a drink is this upstairs space tucked along a narrow lane near the Praça da República. You can catch live bands and DJ sets most weekends.

Estoriastantas
CAFE

(📞964443202; www.facebook.com/estoriastantas; Rua das Portas de Aljustrel 22; ⏰9.30am-5.30pm Mon-Fri, 10am-2pm Sat) Chequered floors, vintage furnishings and quirky

THE ALENTEJO BEJA

LOVE LETTERS FROM BEJA

A series of scandalous, passionate 17th-century love letters came from Beja, allegedly written by one of the nuns of Convento de Nossa Senhora da Conceição (p252), Mariana Alcoforado, to French cavalry officer Count Chamilly. The letters immortalised their love affair while the count was stationed here during the time of the Portuguese war with Spain.

The *Letters of a Portuguese Nun* first emerged in a French translation in 1669 and subsequently appeared in English and many other languages. Funnily enough, the originals were never found.

In 1972 three Portuguese writers, Maria Isabel Barreno, Maria Teresa Horta and Maria Velho da Costa, published *The Three Marias: New Portuguese Letters*, a collection of stories, poems and letters that formed a feminist update of the letters – for which they were prosecuted under the Salazar regime.

artwork draw a creative crowd to this charming cafe and cultural space. Estoriastantas hosts regular workshops in engraving, illustration, painting and other fields, and there are always a few vintage curios for sale.

☆ Entertainment

Pax Julia Teatro Municipal   CINEMA, THEATRE
(☑ 284 315 090; www.paxjuliateatromunicipal.blog spot.com; Largo de São João 1) This cinema and theatre hosts regular concerts, dance performances and film screenings. A programme guide is available at the theatre's box office.

🛍 Shopping

Igreja de Misericórdia   ARTS & CRAFTS
(Praça da República; ☉ 10am-1pm Mon-Sat, 2-5.30pm Mon-Fri) An *artesenato* cooperative has a range of goods for sale within the Igreja de Misericórdia – a unique style of store. You'll find hand-painted ceramics, cork products, strawberry preserves and more.

❶ Information

Turismo (☑ 284 311 913; Rua Capitão João Francisco de Sousa 25; ☉ 9.30am-12.30pm & 2-6pm) Located within the castle premises. Provides a city map but not much else.

❶ Getting There & Away

BUS

From the **bus station** (Terminal Rodoviário de Beja; ☑ 284 313 620) buses run to regional towns and villages. Weekends see fewer services. The bus station is in the southern part of town, about 600m from the historic centre.

Buses run from Beja to local destinations and those further afield.

Albufeira (€14, two hours, three daily)
Évora (€8, 1¼ hours, four to nine daily)
Faro (€14.20, three hours, three daily)
Lisbon (€13.30, three hours, four to 14 daily)
Mértola (€11, 70 minutes, three daily, weekdays)
Serpa (€6, 35 minutes, three daily)

CAR & MOTORCYCLE

Drivers are advised to park their cars in the clearly marked car parks outside the walled centre, such as the free lot off Rua Ramalho Ortigão, a few blocks south of the centre.

TRAIN

Trains head to Lisbon (€14 to €18, three hours, three daily). You change to a connecting train at Casa Branca.

Mértola

POP 2100

Spectacularly set on a rocky spur, high above the peaceful Rio Guadiana, the cobbled streets of medieval Mértola are a delightful place to roam. A small but imposing castle stands high, overlooking the jumble of dazzlingly white houses and a picturesque church that was once a mosque. A long bout of economic stagnation in this remote town has left many traces of Islamic occupation intact, so much so that Mértola is considered a *vila museu* (open-air museum). To let Mértola's magic do its thing, you need more than a quick visit here. Every two years in May, Mértola comes to life during the town's Islamic Festival.

History

Mértola follows the usual pattern of settlement in this area: Phoenician traders, who sailed up the Guadiana, then Carthaginians, then Romans. Its strategic position, as the northernmost port on the Guadiana and the final destination for many Mediterranean routes, led the Romans to develop Mértola (naming it Myrtilis) as a major agricultural and mineral-exporting centre. Cereals and olive oil arrived from Beja, copper and other metals from Aljustrel and São Domingos. It was a rich merchant town.

Later the Moors, who called it Martulah and made it a regional capital, further fortified Mértola and built a mosque. Dom Sancho II and the Knights of the Order of Santiago captured the site in 1238. But then, as commercial routes shifted to the Tejo, Mértola declined. When the last steamboat service to Vila Real de Santo António ended and the copper mines of São Domingos (the area's main employer) closed in 1965, its port days were over.

◉ Sights

Parque Natural do Vale do Guadiana   NATURE RESERVE
Created in 1995, this zone of hills, plains and deep valleys around Serpa and Mértola shelters the Rio Guadiana, one of Portugal's largest and most important rivers. Among its rich flora and fauna are several rare or endangered species, including the black stork (sightings of the shy creatures are rare), lesser kestrel (most likely around Castro Verde and at Convento do São Francisco), Bonelli's eagle, royal owl, grey kite,

horned viper and Iberian toad. The park also has prehistoric remains.

Ask at the park headquarters (p259), in smart premises by the *câmara municipal* (town hall), for details of walking trails and where to spot wildlife – they can advise you and provide you with a basic map.

Alcáçova
ARCHAEOLOGICAL SITE

(⊙ 9.15am-12.30pm & 2-5.15pm Tue-Sun) **FREE** This site contains the ruins of what was once a thriving Islamic neighbourhood. Some 20 dwellings were here, each with a classic Mediterranean layout – a main entry patio, kitchen, storage area, sleeping quarters and latrine. You can wander around the site on raised platforms, with signage (in English and Portuguese) pointing out key details.

Also on the site are the ruins of a portico with mosaic tiles that was once part of a 5th-century Episcopal Palace. Below lies an impressive 32m-long underground gallery dating from the same period. Shortly after the Reconquista by the Knights of Santiago in the 13th century, the neighbourhood was destroyed and turned into a cemetery.

Castelo
CASTLE

(⊙ 9am-6pm Tue-Sun) **FREE** Above the parish church looms Mértola's fortified castle, most of which dates from the 13th century. It was built upon Moorish foundations next to an Islamic residence, the *alcáçova* (citadel), which itself overlaid the Roman forum. For centuries the castle was considered western Iberia's most impregnable fortress. From the walls, there are ultrafabulous views – the *alcáçova* is on one side, and the old town and the river on the other.

The castle's tower, the **Torre de Menagem** (adult/student/child €2/1/free; ⊙ 9.15am-12.30pm & 2-5.15pm Tue-Sun), has exhibitions related to the history of Mértola, with several worthwhile (if dramatically scored) videos in both English and Portuguese on Mértola's strategic location and the Reconquista.

Igreja Matriz
CHURCH

(Rua da Igreja; ⊙ 9.15am-12.30pm & 2-5.15pm Tue-Sun) Mértola's striking parish church – square, flat-faced and topped with whimsical little conical decorations – is known because in a former incarnation it was a mosque, one of the few in the country to have survived the Reconquista. It was reconsecrated as a church in the 13th century. Look out for an unwhitewashed cavity in the wall, behind the altar; in former times this served as the mosque's *mihrab* (prayer niche).

Note also the goats, lions and other figures carved around the peculiar Gothic portal and the typically Moorish horseshoe arch in the north door.

Attached to the church is a small underground **museum** (head out the rear door of the church and turn right) that has displays of items dating back to the Moorish period found during excavations – including lovely Islamic tiles, 6th-century marble pediments and carved, twisted columns.

Casa Islâmica
HISTORIC SITE

(⊙ 9.15am-12.30pm & 2-5.15pm Tue-Sun) **FREE** Next to the *alcáçova* (citadel), this interpretation centre is an accurately sized replica of an Islamic residence dating from the 12th century. Key features include an open central patio with a rainwater collection tank in the centre, small sleeping alcoves, a storage area, kitchen with fireplace and a toilet that was linked to the sewers that emptied outside the town walls.

Casa Romana
RUINS

(Roman House; Largo Luís de Camões; ⊙ 9am-1pm & 2-6pm Mon-Fri, 9.45am-1pm & 2-5.45pm Sat & Sun) **FREE** The enchanting Casa Romana is located in the cellar of the *câmara municipal* (town hall). The clever display allows visitors to walk 'through' the foundations of the Roman house upon which the building rests, and brings it to life with its small collection of pots, sculpture and other artefacts.

Museu Paleocristão
RUINS

(Palaeo-Christian Museum; Rossio do Carmo; ⊙ 9am-12.30pm & 2-5.30pm Tue-Sun) **FREE** This museum, north of the old town, features a partly reconstructed line of 6th-century Roman columns and poignant funerary stones, some of which are beautifully carved with birds, hearts and wreaths. It was the site of a huge palaeo-Christian basilica, and the adjacent cemetery was used over the centuries by both Roman-era Christians and medieval Moors.

Museu Islâmico
MUSEUM

(Largo de Misericórdia; adult/student €2/1; ⊙ 9am-12.30pm & 2-5.30pm Tue-Sun) At the southern end of the old town, the Islamic Museum is a small but dramatic display of inscribed funerary stones, jewellery, pots and jugs from the 11th to 13th centuries.

🐾 Tours

Beira Rio Náutica
KAYAKING

(📋 913 402 033; www.beirarionautica.pt; Rua Dr Afonso Costa 108; kayak rental 1hr/day from €6/18,

THE ALENTEJO MÉRTOLA

bike rental per day from €10) You can rent kayaks for trips down the lazy river at Beira Rio Náutica. It also offers boat tours (minimum four; from €10 per person) and you can hire bicycles here.

✦ Festivals & Events

Festival Islâmico de Mértola   RELIGIOUS
(www.festivalislamicodemertola.com) Mértola comes to life every two years in May (dates change but it's in odd-numbered years) during the town's Islamic Festival, when it is decorated to resemble a souk. Music, handicrafts and festivities continue for several days.

🛏 Sleeping

Casa Rosmaninho   GUESTHOUSE €
(☎934 187 455; www.casarosmaninho.com; Rua 25 de Abril 23; r €35-45; 🛜) Inside a yellow, two-storey house in the town centre (just outside the old walls), you'll find four cheerfully decorated rooms (purple being the colour accent of choice) that are good value for money. The small roof terrace has fine views of the castle. Ana, the host, does a great job of making guests feel at home.

Casa do Funil   GUESTHOUSE €
(☎934 187 455; www.casadofunil.com; Rua Prof Batista da Graça 19; d €35-45, q €65; 🛜) Just inside the old walls, this appealing place has four lovely rooms with wood floors, nice furniture and shuttered windows with views over the river. Rui and Paola make their guests feel at home, and they can advise on outdoor activities (birdwatching, canoeing, day trips) in the area.

Casa da Tia Amalia   HOSTEL €
(☎918 918 777; www.casadatiaamalia.com; Estrada dos Celeiros 16, Além Rio; dm/d with shared bathroom €19/43; 🛜) Across the river from Mértola in Além Rio, this delightful guesthouse offers sweeping views of the village and the castle rising above it. The rooms have homey touches, and the living room (with fireplace) is a fine spot to relax. There's also a four-bed dorm (and a shared kitchen), making it a good option for budget travellers.

Hotel Museu   HOTEL €
(☎913 402 033; www.hotelmuseu.com; Rua Dr Afonso Costa 112; d €50-60, ste €65; ❄🛜) On the road leading down to the river, this sleek, modern hotel has attractive, comfortably furnished rooms with black-and-white print on the wall and big windows – the best of which offer sweeping views over the riverside. Roman ruins were found in the foundations and anyone can visit (thus the hotel name).

Residencial Beira Rio   GUESTHOUSE €
(☎913 402 033; www.beirario.pt; Rua Dr Afonso Costa 108; s/d/tr from €35/40/55; ❄🛜) Beira Rio offers simple, colourful rooms. Those with river views are slightly more expensive but they have breezy terraces.

O Monte do Alhinho   FARMSTAY €€
(☎286 655 414; www.omontedoalhinho.com; Estrada Nacional 265; s/d €50/60; ❄🛜🏊) Try the appealing O Monte do Alhinho, 8km from Mértola on the road to São Domingos. This tastefully converted farmhouse-hacienda has massive rooms, fluffy white towels and a superb kitchen, where breakfast (€5 per person) features an onslaught of Alentejan delights.

🍴 Eating & Drinking

★ Terra Utópica   FUSION €€
(☎962 813 980; Rua Dom Sancho II, 41; mains €10-16; ⊙noon-2.30pm & 7-10pm Tue-Sun) The most atmospheric place for a meal in the old town, Terra Utópica has two small antique-filled dining rooms (one with a roaring fire on cold nights) and a terrace with magnificent views.

The menu is small but well executed with a mix of classic Portuguese fare (oven-baked codfish, grilled black pork) and a few surprises, including a variant of jambalaya (rice with chicken and vegetables, though lacking the heat of the New Orleans–style dish).

Café-Restaurante Alentejo   PORTUGUESE €€
(☎286 655 133; Rua Grande 3, Moreanes; mains €9-14; ⊙11.30am-3pm & 7-9.30pm Tue-Sun) This attractive place in Moreanes, 10km from Mértola on the way to São Domingos, is almost a museum thanks to its antique exhibits (including the local clients themselves!). It serves great-value, hearty helpings of true Alentejan cuisine, with standout dishes like *javali* (boar), *veado* (venison) and *migas com entrecosto* (a bread dish with ribs).

Tamuje   PORTUGUESE €€
(☎286 611 115; Rua Dr Serrão Martins 34; mains €9-14; ⊙noon-3pm & 7-11pm Mon-Sat) This welcoming two-room restaurant serves up excellent traditional plates, all made with care. Grilled pork ribs, fried squid with garlic, fava beans with pork and game meat (wild

SÃO DOMINGOS

The ghost town of São Domingos, 15km east of Mértola, consists of desolate rows of small mining cottages. Once the mine closed in the 1960s, many miners emigrated or moved to Setúbal. But the nearby village is set amid beautiful countryside and next to a huge lake, where you can swim or rent a paddleboat or canoe.

The São Domingos mine itself is over 150 years old – though mining had been taking place here since Roman times – and is a deserted, eerie place to explore, with crumbling old offices and machinery. The rocks surrounding it are clouded with different colours, and the chief mine shaft is filled with deep, unnatural dark-blue water, shot through with substances that don't bear thinking about (read: contaminated). Locals have no fondness for the firm that established the mines, which kept its workers in line with a private police force.

On the main road leading into town, the Cine Teatro da Mina de São Domingos (Rua Catarina Eufémia, €1; ⏰ 2-5.30pm Tue-Sun) provides a suitable introduction to life during the mining days. Tucked away on one of the narrow streets of the village, Casa do Mineiro (Rua Santa Isabel 31-33; ⏰ 9am-12.30pm & 2-5.30pm Mon-Fri, plus Sat & Sun Jun & Aug) FREE re-creates a typical miner's cottage.

São Domingos is best visited with your own transport.

boar, rabbit venison) are among the standouts. Don't overlook the rich desserts.

It's on the road leading to the old town, about 200m east of the main entrance gate.

Casa Amarela
TAPAS €€

(☎286 094 102; www.facebook.com/espacocasaamarelamertola; Estrada dos Celeiros 25, Além Rio; mains €12-15; ⏰ 6.30pm-midnight Wed-Fri, noon-4pm & 6.30pm-midnight Sat & Sun) This place makes a great spot for inventive Portuguese fare. Outdoor tables on the veranda have magnificent views of Mértola – all of it, since Casa Amarela is across the river in Além Rio. There's generally live music every other Saturday night.

Restaurante Alengarve
PORTUGUESE €€

(☎286 612 210; Avenida Aureliano Mira Fernandes; mains €9-14; ⏰ noon-3pm & 7-10pm Thu-Tue; 🐕) Run by the same family for over 40 years, this place is well loved by locals and extremely consistent for its homestyle Alentejan dishes. There's outdoor seating on the front patio.

Lancelote
BAR

(Rua Nossa Senhora da Conceição 3; ⏰ 10pm-2am Thu-Sat) This vaguely medieval-feeling bar has friendly barkeeps and eclectic decor (colourful paintings and a wall of skeleton keys), with a shaded wooden terrace attached (no views, though).

ℹ️ Information

Parque Natural do Vale do Guadiana Headquarters (☎286 610 090; Rua Don Sancho II; ⏰ 9am-noon & 2-5pm Mon-Fri) In smart premises by the town hall. Has hiking-trail maps and information on the fauna and flora of the 600-sq-km park.

Turismo (☎286 610 109; Rua da Igreja 31; ⏰ 9am-12.30pm & 2-5.30pm mid-Sep–Jun, 9.30am-12.30pm & 2-6pm Jul–mid-Sep) Just inside the walled town, this place has a town map, list of *quartos* (private rooms) and free internet access. Also stocks brochures outlining nine different *percurso pedestres* (walking trails) in the area, varying from one- to five-hour walks.

ℹ️ Getting There & Away

Rede Expressos (☎286 611 127; www.redeexpressos.pt; Avenida Aureliano Mira Fernandes) has services to Lisbon (€17, four hours, one daily) and Vila Real de Santo António/Monte Gordo (€11, 1½ hours, one daily). Rodoviária do Alentejo (www.rodalentejo.pt) runs to Beja (€7, 70 minutes, three daily Monday to Friday) and Vila Real de Santo António (€6, two hours, one daily Monday to Friday) via Alcoutim (50 minutes).

Buses depart from Aureliano Mira Fernandes, about 700m east of the old town.

Castro Verde

POP 5200

The thriving village of Castro Verde has a big history – once an ancient hill fort, it soon grew into a settlement. The town is near the site where the Battle of Ourique was fought (1139), when Afonso Henriques defeated the Moors and declared himself the first King

DON'T MISS

ENTRADAS

The tiny village of Entradas (pop 640) is a photo-stop must. Entradas' main street features tiny, whitewashed homes and is a wonderful example of a working rural village. The name is said to have come from the fact that it was the *entrada* (gateway) to the Campos de Ourique, sought-after winter pastures for herds and herders.

In the village centre, the beautifully laid out **Museu da Ruralidade** (☑ 286 915 329; Rua da Santa Madalena 328; ⊙ 10am-12.30pm & 2-6pm Wed-Sun) **FREE** showcases elements of local cultural and agricultural practices.

Entradas is 15km northeast of Castro Verde and 36km south of Beja. You'll need your own wheels to get here.

of Portugal. These days, its inhabitants are fiercely proud of the local traditions and the unique beauty of their surrounding countryside. In fact, a 57,000-hectare swathe of the region was declared a Unesco Biosphere Reserve for its golden (cereal grain) fields, natural grasslands and endemic bird species, including the Iberian Imperial eagle, one of the most endangered birds of prey in the world.

The town's big annual fair – **Feira de Castro** – is held on the third weekend of October. It's worth the detour here, especially if en route from Beja to Mértola or the Algarve.

Museu da Lucerna   MUSEUM
(Largo Vítor Prazeres; ⊙ 10am-12.30pm & 2-5.30pm Tue-Sun) **FREE** Set in a former factory, this museum houses a beautiful collection of ancient Roman oil lamps from the 1st century that were found in the region. You can also purchase fully functioning replicas of the lamps for under €10.

LPN Interpretative
& Environmental Centre   BIRDWATCHING
(League for the Protection of Nature; ☑ 286 328 309; www.lpn.pt; Herdade de Vale Gonçalinho; ⊙ 9am-1pm & 2-6pm Tue-Sat) 🦅 This environmental organisation is responsible for overseeing the protected area (85,000 hectares) known as the steppe – the flat, grassy land that distinguishes this area – and for implementing protection measures for the incredible steppe birds, including the great bustard and

lesser kestrels. Staff at the information office are particularly welcoming; you can view displays and pick up information.

This is the place for birdwatchers, and the departure point for walks in the steppe; ask at the office. It's around 8km northeast of Castro Verde (on E802, the main road to Beja).

Casa do Alentejo   PORTUGUESE €€
(☑ 286 327 132; www.facebook.com/casadoalentejo castroverde; Largo da Feira; €9-12; ⊙ noon-3pm & 7-11pm) A stylish addition to Castro Verde, the Casa do Alentejo fires up delicious regional produce, including chargrilled *porco preto* (black pork) and other first-rate cuts of meat as well as seafood on weekends. There's outdoor dining on the terrace.

ℹ️ Information

Turismo (☑ 286 328 149; www.cm-castro-verde.pt; Rua Dom Afonso I; ⊙ 9am-12.30pm & 2-5.30pm Tue-Fri, 10am-1pm & 3-6pm Sat & Sun) Has maps, information, and a selection of local products for sale.

ℹ️ Getting There & Away

Castro Verde is connected by bus to Beja (€9, one hour, three to four daily), Évora (€13.30, 2¼ hours, two to four daily) and Lisbon (€16, three to 4½ hours, two to four daily).

Serpa
POP 7200

Planted among the rolling hills of vineyards and dusty fields, Serpa is a sleepy, atmospheric town of bleached-white walls and narrow cobblestone streets, with a small, pretty plaza at its medieval heart. Locals are renowned for their love of food, and several factory outlets produce the town's culinary jewel, *queijo Serpa*, a cheese made from curdled sheep's milk.

It's worth a quick visit, or even an overnight stay if you want to experience life in the Portuguese slow lane.

◉ Sights

Walls still stand around most of the inner town. Along the west side (follow Rua dos Arcos) run the impressive remains of an 11th-century aqueduto. At the southern end is a huge 17th-century wheel pump (aka *noria*), once used for pumping water along the aqueduct to the nearby **Palácio dos Condes de Ficalho** (Largo dos Condes de Ficalho).

Castelo
CASTLE

(Largo dos Santos Próculo e Hilarião; ⊙9am-12.30pm & 2-5.30pm Tue-Sun) `FREE` Dating from the 14th century, this imposing castle affords long views from the battlements: flat plains, the aqueduct, town walls, rooftops and orange trees, and the slow life of Serpa residents. Inside the walls, the free **Museu Municipal de Arqueologia de Castelo** houses a small collection of archaeological exhibitions, with information covering the Neolithic, Roman and Islamic presence in Serpa.

Museu Etnográfico
MUSEUM

(Ethnographic Museum; Largo do Corro; ⊙9am-12.30pm & 2-5.30pm Tue-Sun) `FREE` No traditional rural trade is overlooked in this exquisite exploration of Alentejan life. Occupying the former town market (in use from 1887 to 1986), the museum beautifully presents restored items donated by locals. Polished tools used by former wheelwrights, saddle makers, cheese makers, barrel makers and ironmongers – among others – are on display.

At research time, the museum was closed for long-term renovations.

Museu do Relógio
MUSEUM

(Watch Museum; ☑284 543 194; www.museu-dorelogio.com; Rua do Assento 31; adult/under 10yr €2/free; ⊙2-5.30pm Tue-Fri, 10am-12.30pm & 2-5.30pm Sat & Sun) The Watch Museum houses an amazing collection of watches and clocks – shared with its sister museum in Évora (p224), dating from a 1630 Edward East clock to the museum's own present-day wristwatch model. Napoleonic gilded timepieces and Swiss cuckoo clocks are among the 2000 pieces ticking away in the cool surroundings of the former Convento do Mosteirinho.

★ Festivals & Events

Festas de Senhora de Guadalupe RELIGIOUS
(⊙Mar or Apr) Celebrations of Serpa's patron saint take place over Easter from Good Friday to the following Tuesday – there is a pilgrimage to bring the saint's image down to the parish church, and on the last day a procession takes it back to the chapel. On Easter Tuesday, roast lamb is the traditional meal.

Noites na Nora THEATRE
(www.facebook.com/noitesnanora) This festival features nightly local theatre and music shows on a terrace tucked behind the aqueduct. It usually runs for two weeks in July, but check with the tourist office as dates can change.

🛏 Sleeping

Hotel Pulo do Lobo HOTEL **€**
(☑284 544 664; Estrada de São Brás 9A; s/d €35/45; 🌢🅿🛜) Handy to the bus station, this sparkling place and its house-proud owners provide plain but modern rooms. Excellent value if you don't mind being slightly

---

THE SONG OF THE ALENTEJO

One of the great but little-known musical forms of Portugal, Cante Alentejano is a powerful choral tradition with deep roots – dating back to Renaissance-style Gregorian chants of the 15th century or perhaps even earlier (some scholars believe it a cultural legacy of the Islamic presence in the country). Though popular in the first half of the 20th century, it had fallen out of fashion in the post–WWII years. All that is slowly changing, as word has gotten out about this once endangered art form. In 2014 Unesco recognised Cante Alentejano as an Intangible Cultural Heritage of Humanity (just as fado had been honoured in 2011), which has sparked interest both far and near in rediscovering this music.

Cante Alentejano is sung by a choir without instrumentation, with two soloists singing in different keys. It is traditionally associated with rural life – the farmers and labourers of the Alentejo – who sing of hardships, lost love, loneliness, poverty and other topics overflowing with *tristeza* (sadness). Despite the sorrowful themes, the many voices singing polyphonic works create a moving experience, full of power and even joy. Choirs consist of up to 30 singers and can be all male or all female but are rarely mixed.

The Baixo Alentejo remains the epicentre of the resurgence of Cante Alentejano. A new cultural centre, Casa do Cante (☑284 544 720; www.casadocante.pt; Rua dos Cavalos 12; ⊙10am-1pm & 2-6pm Tue-Sun) `FREE`, in Serpa is a good place to learn about this tradition (check the website for choral events in other parts of the Alentejo). If you can track it down, check out Sérgio Tréfaut's film *Alentejo, Alentejo*, an award-winning feature-length documentary from 2014 that explores this rich music.

Serpa

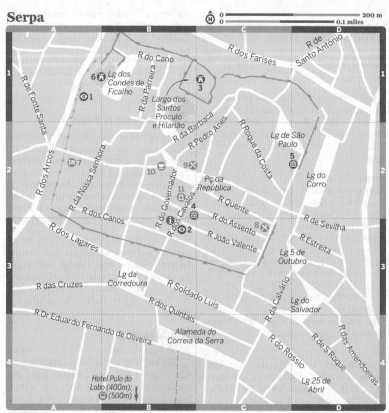

out of the centre (about 1km south of the main square).

Cantar do Grilo   GUESTHOUSE €€
(☑ 284 595 415; www.cantardogrilo.com; Vale de Milhanos; d €90; 🎧 ➿) In the sunbaked countryside, some 19km south of Serpa, this delightful *turismo rural* option is a great place to unwind, with four comfy, modern rooms, a saltwater pool and deck fringed with olive trees, and two kind-hearted hosts who go out of their way to make guests feel at home.

Casa da Muralha   GUESTHOUSE €€
(☑ 284 543 150; Rua das Portas de Beja 43; s/d/ste €55/65/75; 🎧) Set along a narrow cobblestone lane near the aqueduct, the friendly Casa da Muralha has clean, well-maintained rooms set with traditional Alentejan furnishings, and a pretty courtyard garden complete with palm and orange trees.

🍴 Eating & Drinking

Restaurante O Alentejano   PORTUGUESE €€
(☑ 284 544 335; Praça da República; mains €9-14; ⏰ noon-3pm & 7-10.30pm Tue-Sun) This

handsome place, above a cafe of the same name, in a former mansion, serves delicious traditional cuisine.

Go for the daily specials – anything from braised hare in red wine to oven-baked lamb.

Molhó Bico PORTUGUESE €€
(🖉 284 549 264; Rua Quente 1; mains €10-15; ⊙noon-3pm & 7-10pm Thu-Mon, noon-3pm Tue) With its wagon-wheel lights, huge wine urns and friendly ambience, this enticing place pulls a crowd. Eating here is a pure, traditional gastronomic experience – the kitchen odours will hit you as soon as you enter its arched, rustic space. Hearty half-portions are available.

Serpa Lovers CAFE
(🖉 284 544 707; Rua das Portas de Beja 2) A friendly cafe, gallery and shop, where you can browse for regional goodies, or recharge over coffee, Moroccan mint tea and sweets (or salads and cheese platters). The friendly owner speaks English and French, and is happy to share the magic of the Alentejo with visitors.

🛍 Shopping

Casa de Artesenato FOOD
(🖉 969 706 366; Rua dos Cavalos 33; ⊙10am-1pm & 2-7pm) Among the craft shops around town, this is one of the best, with painted ceramics, wooden cutting boards, oils, honey, herbs and handicrafts.

ℹ Information

Turismo (🖉 284 544 727; www.cm-serpa.pt; Rua dos Cavalos 19; ⊙10am-1pm & 2-6pm) Provides a map of the old town with good listings, and sells CDs of local folk music and local handicrafts.

ℹ Getting There & Away

BUS

The **bus station** (🖉 284 544 740; Avenida Capitães de Abril) is 1km south of town; head south along Avenida da Paz to get here. Buses run to/from Lisbon (€15.20, four hours, three to four daily) via Beja (€6). There are no direct buses to Évora (head to Beja first).

CAR & MOTORCYCLE

If arriving by car it's best to park outside the wall, or risk tight gateways into the old town and breathtakingly narrow streets.

Moura
POP 8400

This pleasant working-class city, a flattish fortified town, has an ageing castle, graceful buildings and a well-preserved Moorish quarter. Well placed near water sources and rich in ore, Moura has been a farming and mining centre and a fashionable spa in previous incarnations. More recent developments? The world's largest solar-power generation plant is nearby, and it's the nearest large town to the Barragem do Alqueva, 15km to the north.

The Moors' 500-year occupation came to an end in 1232 after a Christian invasion. Despite the Reconquista, Moorish presence in the city remained strong – they only abandoned their quarter in 1496 (after Dom Manuel's convert-or-leave edict).

The town's name comes from a legend related to the 13th-century takeover. Moorish resident Moura Salúquiyya opened the town gates to Christians disguised as Muslims. They sacked the town, and poor Moura flung herself from a tower.

⊙ Sights

Castelo CASTLE
(off Praça Sacadura Cabra; ⊙9am-5.30pm) FREE
The castle offers fabulous views across the countryside. One of the towers is the last remnant of a Moorish fortress. Rebuilt by Dom Dinis in the 13th century and again by Dom Manuel I in 1510, the castle itself was largely destroyed by the Spanish in the 18th century. There's a ruined convent inside the walls.

You can visit the *torre de menagem* (keep) on guided visits only (daily at 10am, 11.30am, 3pm and 4.30pm). It contains a small collection of weaponry, some dating to the 16th century. You can also climb up the winding steps for a fine view over the castle and the arid landscape just beyond town.

Jardim Dr Santiago & Spa GARDENS
(Praça Sacadura Cabral; ⊙8am-midnight Jun-Sep, to 8pm Apr & May, to 6pm Oct-Mar; 🖨) The lovely, shady Jardim Dr Santiago, at the eastern end of Praça Sacadura Cabral, is a delightful place. There are good views, a bandstand and shady, flowering trees. It's a favourite spot for elderly men to sit and chat, particularly after a soak in the thermal bath at the

entrance to the garden. There's also a small playground in the northwest corner.

You can join the locals for a soak in a basic bath (open weekdays), but don't expect any luxury (it's basically a bathtub in a dimly lit room). Bicarbonated calcium waters, said to be good for rheumatism, burble from the richly marbled Fonte das Três Bicas (Fountain with Three Spouts) by the entrance to the *jardim*.

Lagar de Varas do Fojo   MUSEUM

(Museu do Azeite; Rua João de Deus 20; ⊙9am-12.30pm & 2-5.30pm Tue-Sun) FREE With a system of production similar to that of Roman times, an oil press here re-creates the oil-pressing factory that functioned on this spot between 1841 and 1941, with giant wooden and stone-wheel presses, vats and utensils.

Jardim das Oliveiras   GARDENS

(Rua São João de Deus 17; ⊙9am-12.30pm & 2-5.30pm Tue-Sun) FREE Opposite the Lagar de Varas do Fojo, the Jardim das Oliveiras is home to various varieties of olive trees and herbs, and reflective space. It's dedicated to Miguel Hernández, a Spanish poet and revolutionary who, upon fleeing Spain, entered the Moura district, only to be returned by Salazar to Franco's troops. He later died in prison.

Mouraria   AREA

(Poço Árabe; near Primeira Rua da Mouraria) The old Moorish quarter lies at the western end of Praça Sacadura Cabral. It's a well-preserved, tight cluster of narrow, cobbled lanes and white terraced cottages with chunky or turreted chimneys.

Museu Alberto Gordillo   MUSEUM

(☑285 253 579; Rua da Vista Alegre; ⊙9am-12.30pm & 2-5.30pm Tue-Sun) FREE A small one-of-a-kind jewellery museum dedicated to the fascinating works of the avant-garde artist Alberto Gordillo. On display are around 50 pieces, some of which are more like sculptures than mere pretty adornment for the body. Gordillo, who was born in Moura in 1943, is considered one of the pioneers of modern Portuguese jewellery. You can also arrange visits here to the Casa dos Poços (Travessa da Mouraria 11; ⊙9.30am-12.30pm & 2.30-5.30pm Tue-Sun) FREE, which has a pocket collection of Moorish ceramics and other remains.

🛏 Sleeping & Eating

Hotel Santa Comba   HOTEL €

(☑285 251 255; Praça Sacadura Cabral 34; s/d/tr €31/41/55; ❄) In a great location overlooking the main square, the Hotel Santa Comba has pleasant rooms with painted wrought-iron beds, heavy woven drapes and bedspreads, and some rather curious artwork. The nicest rooms have French doors with decorative balconies that open on to the square. The pretty breakfast room/lounge has striking ornate ceilings.

Hotel de Moura   HOTEL €€

(☑285 251 090; www.hoteldemoura.com; Praça Gago Coutinho 1; s €45-55, d €55-65; ❄ 🖥) Overlooking a leafy plaza, Hotel de Moura has comfortable rooms set with solid wooden furnishings; be sure to get a room in the front with a view on to the greenery. The lounge with a small bar in this handsome tile-covered building (a former convent) is inviting: arched brick ceilings, big windows and rustic Alentejan decorations on the walls.

Rates are lower on weekdays.

Taberna o Liberato   PORTUGUESE €

(☑285 254 171; Segunda Rua da Mouraria 3; sharing plates €5-8; ⊙noon-3.30pm & 6.30pm-midnight Mon-Sat) Just off the main square, Praça Sacadura Cabral, this cosy tavern is a lively spot for a bite and a drink. There's not much of a menu, but the owner whips up delicious tapas plates – including a very rich *presunto* (cured ham) – served with his first-rate wine selection.

★ Vermelhudo   PORTUGUESE €€

(☑968 483 023; Rua da Latoa 1; mains €10-16; ⊙noon-3pm & 7.30pm-midnight Mon-Sat) Locals and visitors alike receive a warm welcome at this cosy traditional eatery on the western fringes of the old centre. Family recipes from the owner Fernanda Vermelhudo are beautifully prepared, and she pays homage to her rural upbringing in Pedrogueiros with village photos and poetry adorning the walls.

ℹ Information

Centro de Interpretação de Alqueva (CIAL; ☑284 315 100; www.cm-moura.pt; ER 255, Barragem de Alqueva; ⊙10am-12.30pm & 2-5pm) Information and exhibitions on the Alqueva Dam.

Turismo (☑285 251 375; www.cm-moura.pt; ⊙9am-12.30pm & 2-5.30pm) Located on the castle grounds. It has information and internet access and sells a few regional handicrafts.

❶ Getting There & Away

Buses run to/from Beja (around €5.50, one hour, six daily weekdays) via Serpa (€4, 40 minutes). Rede Expressos runs to Lisbon (€16.20, 3¼ hours, daily) via Évora (€11, 1½ hours); these leave from a bus stop on the Largo de São Francisco, about 400m south of Rua da República.

COASTAL ALENTEJO

POP 102,000

Coastal Alentejo (Alentejo Litoral in Portuguese) has undeniable appeal. Beautiful beaches, whitewashed villages and seafood feasts are among the chief draws. This is also a great place for outdoor lovers, with first-rate surfing, kayaking and mountain biking, as well as scenic walks along the coast – including two well-marked walking treks totalling 400km that go all the way down to Cabo de São Vicente in the Algarve.

Vila Nova De Milfontes

POP 5050

One of the loveliest towns along this stretch of the coast, Vila Nova de Milfontes has an attractive, whitewashed centre, sparkling beaches nearby and a laid-back population who couldn't imagine living anywhere else. Milfontes remains much more low-key than most resort towns, except in August when it's packed to the hilt with surfers and sun-seekers (up to 50,000 people in town). It's located in the middle of the beautiful Parque Natural do Sudoeste Alentejano e Costa Vicentina and is still a port (Hannibal is said to have sheltered here) alongside a lovely, sand-edged limb of estuary.

◎ Sights

Praia da Franquia   BEACH

(Avenida Marginal) The main beach in Vila Nova de Milfontes is where the sea meets the Rio Mira. Sectioned-off areas allow for safe swimming, though you'll still need to be mindful of strong currents. You can also hire kayaks and SUP boards on the beach.

Praia do Malhão   BEACH

If you have your own transport, head 7km north of town to the fantastic Praia do Malhão, backed by rocky dunes and covered in fragrant scrub. The sea can be quite wild

here, but the rugged coast is strikingly empty of development. To get here, travel 2.5km to Bruinheras, turn left at the roundabout just before the primary school, then travel another 3km.

Praia do Farol   BEACH

(Avenida Marginal) The 'Lighthouse Beach' just west of town is sheltered but gets busy. Beaches on the other side of the estuary are less crowded. Be careful of the strong river currents running through the estuary.

Praia das Furnas   BEACH

On the left bank of the Rio Mira, Praia das Furnas is a long stretch of fine sand backed by small rocky cliffs. The sandbars in the area make for some relaxing frolicking in the waves – a good option for families. You can drive here, and you can also take the Maresia Milfontes ferry from Vila Nova de Milfontes.

🏃 Activities

SW SUP   WATER SPORTS

(☑963 551 232; www.swsup.pt; Praia da Franquia; 1hr/2hr/half-day tour €25/35/60, SUP rental per 1hr/half-day €15/35) This outfit has a sterling reputation for its SUP lessons and most importantly tours, with scenic trips heading up the Rio Mira on the incoming tide to scenic spots such as the cliff-backed Pego das Pias.

Surf Milfontes   SURFING

(☑300 505 996; www.surfmilfontes.com; Rua Antonio Mantas 26; 1/5 surf lessons €40/160; ☉10am-7pm) Offers surf lessons as well as surf-and-stay packages based in the hostel Hike & Surf Lodge (p266), a few blocks away. You can also hire boards and wetsuits (€30 for one day, €120 for five days).

Maresia Milfontes   BOATING

(☑964 200 944; Largo de Brito Pais; return boat trip from €5; ☉9am-6pm) From the dock near Largo de Brito Pais, this outfit offers hourly trips across the Rio Mura from Vila Nova de Milfontes to Praia das Furnas aboard a traditional fishing boat. You can also arrange longer trips upriver to Odemira (from €40 per person).

🛌 Sleeping

★ Casa Amarela   GUESTHOUSE €

(☑283 996 632; www.casaamarelamilfontes.com; Rua Dom Luís Castro e Almeida; dm €18-20, d €35-65, tr €80, q €92.50; @ 🛜) This cheery yellow place is set with eclectic knick-knacks

THE ALENTEJO VILA NOVA DE MILFONTES

WALKING THE ALENTEJO: THE ROTA VICENTINA

The Rota Vicentina comprises two walking trails – one coastal and one inland – and runs along the southwest coast to Cabo de São Vicente. The coastal walk (referred to as 'the fishermen's trail') begins in Porto Côvo. It uses paths forged by beachgoers and fisherfolk and passes through some of the harsher, yet stunning, coastal scenery and wilderness. The inland route (dubbed the 'historical way') is equally appealing. It runs through the Parque Natural do Sudoeste Alentejano e Costa Vicentina, plus rural towns and villages, cork-tree forests and valleys.

Both trails are made up of sections, and it's never more than 25km between villages, where you can lodge for the night (thus no need to bring camping gear). The Fishermen's Trail has four sections, totalling 120km, and the walk is slightly more difficult, with some passages on dunes and thigh-tiring sands. At times it runs along the cliffs, mostly single track, and only walkers are allowed. The longer Historical Way has 12 sections totalling 230km. Trails are wider and generally the walk is easier; mountain bikes are permitted.

Private companies have cottoned on to the route, providing luggage transfer between each night's lodging, but there's nothing to stop you from doing it alone, if you're prepared to carry your things. Numerous accommodation options are along both routes. For further information see www.rotavicentina.com.

belonging to the genial English-speaking owner, Rui. In the main building are seven bright rooms, a lounge space and kitchen for guests. Nearby, the handsomely furnished annex has 17 appealing rooms with brick floors, blonde woods and artwork from Rui's world travels. The spacious courtyard is a lovely place to unwind.

Hike & Surf Lodge
HOSTEL €

(☑ 965 839 839; www.surfmilfontes.com/hike-andsurflodge.html; Rua São Sebastião 24; d €65, dm/d with shared bathroom €22/50; @☎) In the heart of town, the friendly Hike & Surf Lodge offers bright, well-maintained private rooms and six-bed dorms. You can arrange surf lessons and hire gear (surfboards, SUP boards), and it's a good place to meet other travellers. There's also an outdoor space and a communal kitchen (with coffee and tea always available).

Sol da Vila
GUESTHOUSE €

(☑ 962 574 157; www.soldavila.com; Rua Custódio Brás Pacheco 4; d/apt €55/90; ☎) A centrally located, unpretentious spot with bright, spotless rooms and a lovely patio with a prolific lemon tree. The friendly owner on the premises can provide tips on exploring the town. Three apartments are also available. Bike rental is €10 per day.

Mil Reis
GUESTHOUSE €€

(☑ 283 998 233; www.milreismilfontes.com; Largo Rossio 2; d from €75; ✽☎) In a great location in the centre of Vila Nova, Mil Reis has attractively decorated rooms trimmed with artwork and comfy beds. The best feature

is the rooftop terrace, with fine views over the houses down to the seaside. The friendly staff and ample breakfasts add to the appeal.

Casa do Adro
GUESTHOUSE €€

(☑ 283 997 102; www.casadoadro.com.pt; Rua Diário de Notícias 10; d €90-120; ✽☎) Set in a 17th-century house, this special option is chock-a-block with antiques and artwork. It has six elegantly furnished bedrooms, some with private balcony or shared terrace. Hospitality abounds and foodies will love the breakfasts – and you can turn up to this scrumptious spread at any time in the morning (a nice touch).

Eating & Drinking

18 e Piques
CAFE €

(www.facebook.com/18epiques; Largo do Rossio 18; sandwiches €3.50-5; ☉9am-7pm Tue-Sun; ☎✎) Everyone's favourite lunch spot, 18 e Piques whips up delicious toasted sandwiches on fabulous freshly baked bread – combos range from goat's cheese, walnuts and honey to smoked salmon, rocket and homemade yoghurt sauce. You can also stop in for snacks like guacamole and hummus, good coffees and craft beer from Lisbon microbrewer Dois Corvos. Don't overlook the enticing dessert counter.

Padaria de Dona Ercília
BAKERY €

(Strada R393, Venda Fria; bread from around €2; ☉8am-8pm May-Sep, to 7pm Oct-Apr) Bread lovers and those who appreciate traditional culinary practices shouldn't miss this simple *padaria* (bakery) in the tiny village of

Venda Fria, 4.5km from Vila Nova de Milfontes. Dona Ercília Joaquina has baked bread here every day for over 20 years. You can't enter the kitchen for photographs, but you can pick up some steaming loaves straight from the oven.

Mabi
CAFE, ICE CREAM €
(Largo de Santa Maria 25; ice cream from €2; ⊙8am-10pm Tue-Sun) Famed for its ice cream, Mabi is one of the icons of town, and it serves up creamy rich decadence to an often packed house. This buzzing bakery and dessert spot also offers massive croissants and other snacks.

A Portuguesa
PORTUGUESE €€
(Rua dos Carris 1; light meals €5-12; ⊙10am-10pm Mon-Sat; 🗲) This sunny, handsomely designed cafe is a showcase for high-quality Portuguese produce. You can stop in for light meals (creative salads, sandwiches, cheese and charcuterie boards) or desserts, coffee and wines or craft beers. The terrace is a fine choice on clear days.

A Portuguesa also functions as a small market, and it's a good place to pick up wines, Azorean teas, *medronho* (a traditional Portuguese brandy) and other edible souvenirs for the trip home.

Ritual
TAPAS €€
(🗲283 998 648; www.facebook.com/ritualrestaurantetapasbar; Rua Barbosa Viana 4; tapas €6-16, mains €12-18; ⊙6-11pm Mar-May & Sep & Oct, from noon Jun-Sep; 🗲) With its tall ceilings and colonial-like ambience, Ritual is one of the most atmospheric settings for a meal in town. The eclectic tapas menu features creative combinations like sun-dried tomato hummus, garlic and ginger sauté shrimp, and cured sausage fired in *aguardente* (distilled spirits). The global influence extends to main courses, including Thai curry, fresh gnocchi and salmon tataki.

Porto das Barcas
PORTUGUESE €€
(🗲283 997 160; Estrada do Canal; mains €12-22; ⊙noon-3pm & 6-11pm Wed-Mon) With a wonderful outlook over the water and cliffs, this is a great place to kick back for a seafood lunch. Its light and airy ambience in a dreamy location are winners, and the seafood is first rate. It's 2.5km north of town along the canal road.

Restaurante A Fateixa
SEAFOOD €€
(🗲283 996 415; Largo do Cais; mains €11-16; ⊙noon-3pm & 7-10pm Thu-Tue) A Fateixa has good grills and seafood dishes – try the *tamboril* (monkfish) rice for two – and it has breezy outdoor tables. It's excellent value given its perfect setting down by the river.

★ Tasca do Celso
PORTUGUESE €€€
(🗲283 996 753; www.tascadocelso.com; Rua dos Aviadores; mains €17-32; ⊙noon-3pm & 7-11pm Tue-Sun) *The* choice. Locals and travellers from far and wide rave about the excellent cuisine produced in the kitchen of this charming, 'upmarket rustic' blue-and-white building. You're safe trying anything here, though the seafood is outstanding (and priced accordingly). Great service, open fires and an appealing bar area too. Reservations essential at night.

Riverside Pub
BAR
(🗲965 842 897; Avenida Marginal, Edifício Milfontes; ⊙9am-2am Tue-Sun; 🗲) Above Praia da Franquia (p265), about a 10-minute (700m) walk west of the centre, the wood-panelled Riverside Pub is good any time for drinks and a meal. The raised deck offers fine views over the water, and the burgers (€8 to €13) and other bites are quite good.

Manjedoura & Lua Cheia
BAR
(🗲283 998 282; Cerca do Arneirão; ⊙10pm-4am Wed-Sat) One of Vila Nova's best spots for a night out, this place has fun parties (including the odd costume event), with DJs spinning wide-ranging sounds. There's also a pool table and a small garden, where you can take a break from the dance floor.

ℹ Information

Turismo (🗲283 996 599; Rua António Mantas; ⊙9am-1pm & 3-6pm Oct-May, 9am-6pm Jun-Sep; 🗲) Off the main road (Rua Custódio Brás Pacheco), opposite the **police station** (🗲283 990 020; Rua António Mantas 28). There's free wi-fi and a computer if you need to get online.

ℹ Getting There & Away

Vila Nova has two bus connections daily on weekdays to/from Odemira (€6, 20 minutes). **Rede Expressos** (🗲283 107 069; www.rede-expressos.pt) buses run daily from Lisbon (€16, 3½ hours, three daily, more in summer) via Setúbal (€14.20) and at least once daily to/from Portimão (€13.10, two hours) and Lagos (€13, two hours). There are summer services to Sagres (€13, two hours). The ticket agent for Rede Expressos is located in the sewing shop on Travessa dos Amadores. The bus stop is on Rua da Praça, about 600m north of the centre.

Zambujeira Do Mar

POP 900

Enchantingly wild beaches backed by rugged cliffs form the setting of this sleepy seaside village. The main street terminates at the cliff, and from there paths lead to the attractive sands below. Quieter than Vila Nova, Zambujeira attracts a backpacker, surfy crowd, though in August the town is a party place and hosts the massive music fest, Festival Sudoeste. The high-season crowds obscure Zambujeira's out-of-season charms: fresh fish in family-run restaurants, blustering clifftop walks and a dramatic, empty coast.

Activities

A 3km-long walking and biking path runs between Zambujeira do Mar and Porto de Pesca. For something more demanding, you can hit the Rota Vicentina trail along the coast: it's a 22km walk north to Almograve, or 18km south to Odeceixe.

Sleeping

Hakuna Matata HOSTEL €
(☑918 470 038; www.facebook.com/hostel. hakunamatata; Rua Dr Jaurez 1B; dm/d from €20/50; ☜) A great option for budget travellers, this charming spot has three- and six-bed dorms, as well as private rooms with both shared and private facilities. Guests have access to the kitchen and lounge, and you can rent bikes. It's in a good location, a short walk to the village centre and the beach.

Rosa dos Ventos GUESTHOUSE €€
(☑283 961 391; www.rosadosventoszambujeira. com; Rua Nossa Senhora do Mar; d €60-85; ✸☜) A short walk from the town centre (and 75m from the cliff over the ocean), this well-maintained guesthouse has airy modern rooms painted in light hues (including some in pastel shades), with minifridge and other mod cons, and set around a patio. Some rooms have partial ocean views.

★ **Herdade do Touril** INN €€€
(☑283 950 080; www.herdadedotouril.pt; off CM 1158; r from €135; @☜☒) Four kilometres north of Zambujeira do Mar is this upmarket *quinta* (estate) building with rooms and apartments of the fluffy-pillow variety. Some are within the original building (built in 1826), others are converted farm cottages. The rustic and contemporary design of this tranquil place has an African safari-lodge feel – without the lions of course.

Eating

Marisqueira Costa Alentejana SEAFOOD €€
(☑283 961 508; Rua Miramar 8; mains €12-20; ☉noon-3pm & 7-11pm Tue-Sun) Everyone's favourite seafood restaurant in town serves up mouthwatering octopus, rice dishes, tender crab and other plates of uberfresh seafood. Wash it down with a first-rate bottle of Cortes de Cima.

A Barca SEAFOOD €€
(☑283 961 186; Entrada da Barca, Porto de Pesca; meals €10-19; ☉noon-3pm & 7-11pm Tue-Sun) The owner's father used to cook lunch for the local fisherfolk after they came into port; these days, the former kiosk is an upmarket restaurant that serves great fish and *marisco* (shellfish) dishes to discerning diners. Lovely outdoor area and view of the sea, but (of course) expect the odd seagull.

Restaurante Sacas SEAFOOD €€
(☑283 961 151; Entrada da Barca, Porto de Pesca; mains €10-18; ☉noon-3pm & 7-10pm Thu-Tue) A family team add colour to this fun, laid-back 'cabana' – Dona Ana Maria creates her own seafood dishes. The fresh fish and shellfish more than make up for the car-park view (many years ago the cabana was at the base of the cliffs, but the original building was destroyed by rough seas).

ℹ Information

Turismo (☑283 961 144; ☉10am-6pm Tue-Sat) A small office on the main street, which closes to traffic from July to mid-September.

ℹ Getting There & Away

Rede Expressos (www.rede-expressos.pt) buses connect Zambujeira with Vila Nova de Milfontes (€9, 45 minutes, two to five daily) and Lisbon (€17, three to four hours, two to four daily). You can buy tickets at **Pastelaria Doce Tentaçao** (Rua da Palmeira 101). Buses also run to Odemira (40 minutes) and Beja (three hours, one on weekdays); for these you buy your ticket on the bus.

Porto Côvo

POP 1050

The appealingly 'traditional cute' Porto Côvo is worth a quick visit if you have the time. Perched on low cliffs with views over the sea, Porto Côvo is a former fishing village with a pretty square, cobbled streets lined with sun-bleached houses and a popular beach. It gets packed in high season.

In summer, a boat shuttles between Porto Côvo and the diminutive island of Ilha do Pessegueiro (Fishermen's Island; per person €10). Diving trips can be arranged through Ecoalga (✆964 620 394; www.ecoalga.com; Rua dos Pescadores 15).

Tasca do Xico   PORTUGUESE €€
(✆962 284 363; www.facebook.com/taskadoxico; Rua Candido da Silva 55; mains €10-17; ⊗noon-3pm & 7-10pm Tue-Sun) Much loved by locals, Tasca do Xico serves some of the best seafood in town. Go early (or reserve ahead) to score one of the tables in back overlooking the water.

ℹ Information

Turismo (✆269 959 120; Rua do Mar 4; ⊗9am-noon & 1-5pm Mon-Fri year-round & 1-7pm Sat & Sun Jun-Aug) Located on the southern edge of the old town, across the road from a fine lookout.

ℹ Getting There & Away

During summer at least five buses a day travel to/from Lisbon (€16, three hours). There are also regular connections to Vila Nova de Milfontes (around €6, 20 minutes).

Comporta

Hippie-chic Comporta – once one of Iberia's best off-the-beaten-path beach destinations – may no longer solely be the private playground of refined jet-set designers such as Jacques Grange, Christian Louboutin and Philippe Starck, but this development-restrained gourmet seaside village and surroundings remain on the one hand one of the most authentic Portuguese beach experiences you can find around Lisbon; and on the other, one of Portugal's most highly cultured and noticeably upscale sea and sun destinations. Comporta's cork tree, sand dune and rice-field–draped landscape will lure you not only for its idyllic scenery but for its palatable opulence as well.

Comporta is located along the less developed southern end of the Tróia Peninsula, which sits across Sado Estuary from Setúbal some 121km southwest of Lisbon by road (shortened considerably by the car ferry).

◉ Sights & Activities

★ Cais Palafítico da Carrasqueira   PIER
(Carrasqueira) Built in the 1950s and 1960s, this ramshackle, zigzagging, interlocking pier on wooden stilts is one of Europe's last surviving of its kind. At sunset, it's deluged with professional photographers and amateur smartphone shutterbugs, who come for one of Portugal's most cinematic photo ops. You can wander the wharf, flush with colourful fishing huts and moored wooden boats, all in the muddy flats of the Sado Estuary.

★ Cavalos na Areia   HORSE RIDING
(✆919 002 545; www.cavalosnaareia.com; EN-261, Km6; €65-80) This highly recommended outfit does an epic 90-minute horse ride through the rice fields, sand dunes and beaches of Comporta. From June to September, tours leave at 8.30am, 9.30am and 11.30am (11am and 3pm the rest of the year).

⊨ Sleeping

Verde e Mar   HOTEL €€
(✆265 497 485, 967 765 553; verdeemar1@gmail.com; Rus dos Pinheiros, Lote 121, Brejos da Carregueira de Cima; s/d/tr €75/85/100; ❄️🛜) These motel-style sleeps don't inspire much from the outside, but the 14 rooms here are actually quite modern and well-kept; smallish but with TVs, and some with balconies. In pricey Comporta, it's a good deal, especially when you cast your eyes on the fantastic rooftop garden patio – perfect for breakfast or a bottle of wine or three.

It's in Brejos da Carregueira de Cima, a small village 7.6km south of Comporta village.

★ Sublime Comporta   BOUTIQUE HOTEL €€€
(✆269 449 376; www.sublimecomporta.pt; EN 261-1, Grândola; d/ste from €360/480; P❄️🛜♨️) One of Portugal's top sleeps, Sublime stays true to its name, revamping a former rice-storing warehouse tucked away in a dramatic landscape of cork trees and umbrella pines surrounded by sand dunes, rice fields and vineyards. Its 22 environmentally unobtrusive, pinewood villas cradle 76 rooms steeped in luxurious furnishings with massive windows that frame the cinematic surroundings.

✕ Eating

★ Cavalariça Comporta   FUSION €€€

(📞 930 451 879; www.cavalaricacomporta.com; Rua do Secador 9; small plates €9.50-13, mains €14-27; ⊗ 7.30-10.30pm Wed-Fri, 1-3pm & 7.30-10.30pm Sat & Sun; 🐾) Seasonally inspired Cavalariça, in the heart of Comporta village, wins hearts for bucking tradition in favour of creating a modern, foodie-focused dining experience in a casual atmosphere (most notable for its spacious six-seater, nautical-themed banquettes). Small plates such as cottage cheese gnocchi with sweetcorn and jalapeño are real regional highlights; and friendly staff know their wines. Trust them.

Comporta Café   SEAFOOD €€€

(📞 265 497 652; www.comportacafe.com.pt; Praia da Comporta, Grândola; mains €14-26, fish per kg €56.50-67.50; ⊗ 11am-10.30pm Sun-Thu, 9am-11pm Fri & Sat; 🐾) Trendy Comporta Café sits right on the main beach and is an idyllic little spot for everything from cocktails to an elevated beach lunch. Kitchen creativity looms here more so than many (veggie tagliatelle, grilled sea bass with cockles risotto, grilled duck breast with caramelised apples), and whiling away an afternoon on the patio is tough to beat.

Restaurant Dona Bia   PORTUGUESE €€€

(📞 265 497 557; EN 261 S/N, Torre; mains for 2 €26-48, fish per kg €28-55; ⊗ noon-4pm & 7.30-10.30pm; 🐾) In tiny Torre, 3.5km south of Comporta village, this regional favourite will surprise you with everything from its shabby-chic decor and charming tableware to excellent seafood and duck rices or grilled fish. The turbot with coriander rice is particularly recommended, but bring a dining partner: the menu is not friendly whatsoever to solo diners.

ℹ Information

Posto de Turismo (📞 269 750 429; www.visitgrandola.com; Av 18 de Dezembro S/N, ⊗ 9.30am-1.30pm & 2.30-5.30pm Jul-Sep, 9.30am-1.30pm & 2.30-5.30pm Sat & Sun Jun) In Carvalhal, 14km south of Comporta village.

ℹ Getting There & Away

Comporta is not easily reachable on public transport, so having your own wheels is key for exploring the area. It's a 121km drive the long way round from Lisbon; but you can cut 52km off that ride by catching the car ferry (p157) across the Sado River estuary from Setúbal to Tróia (car and driver €15.50, additional passenger €3.60) and continuing on from there.

Estremadura & Ribatejo

Best Places to Eat

➡ Casinha Velha (p291)
➡ Estrela do Mar (p293)
➡ Ja!mon Ja!mon (p279)
➡ Alcoa (p286)
➡ Ao Largo (p291)

Best Places to Stay

➡ Casa das Marés (p274)
➡ Casa da Alcáçova (p299)
➡ Casa d'Óbidos (p278)
➡ Casa Lagoa (p280)

Why Go?

Stretching from the Rio Tejo to the Atlantic Ocean, Estremadura and Ribatejo constitute Portugal's heartland, but their central importance goes beyond geography. These fertile lands have formed the backdrop for every major chapter in Portuguese history, from the building of key fortified settlements in the 12th century to the release of Salazar's political prisoners in 1974. Two of medieval Portugal's critical battles for autonomy – against the Moors at Santarém and the Spaniards at Aljubarrota – were fought and won here, and remain commemorated in the magnificent monasteries at Alcobaça and Batalha, both Unesco World Heritage Sites. A third Unesco site, Tomar's Convento de Cristo, was long the stronghold of the Knights Templar.

These days the region draws visitors not only to these renowned monasteries, but also to its vineyards, beaches, castles and historic villages – and Fátima, modern Portugal's premier religious shrine.

When to Go

Leiria

Apr & May Beat summer heat (and crowds) with a springtime visit to the region's World Heritage Sites.

Jun & Sep For warm beaches at cooler prices, visit the coast in early summer or autumn.

Oct World-class waves at Peniche, Nazaré and other prime surf spots.

Estremadura & Ribatejo Highlights

❶ Batalha (p287) Travelling back in time at this village's awe-inspiring monastery. Alcobaça, too!

❷ Convento de Cristo (p301) Marvelling at the 12th-century spiritual headquarters of the Knights Templar in Tomar.

❸ Óbidos (p276) Conquering this picturesque village on a 1560m walk around the top of its imposing medieval wall.

❹ Castelo de Almourol (p300) Surveying the Rio Tejo from the crenellated heights of this 12th-century castle.

❺ Parque Natural das Serras de Aire e Candeeiros (p296) Wandering around the limestone walls of this natural park.

❻ Nazaré (p281) Surfing and sunning in Estremadura's most picturesque beach resort.

❼ Peniche (p273) Watching the pros in action at this prime surfing destination.

ESTREMADURA

Running up the Atlantic coast from the mouth of the Rio Tejo almost to the Rio Mondego, Estremadura has long been a land of plenty, its rolling hills and valleys offering up some of Portugal's richest farmland. For proof, visit the elaborate kitchens that fattened up the monks at Alcobaça's extraordinary monastery. The coast is blessed with miles-long strands of beach, which catch some of Europe's best surf.

Estremadura earned its name the same way as Spain's Extremadura: for a time, it represented the furthest reaches of the Reconquista.

Peniche

POP 14,700

Popular for its long, fabulous town beach, nearby surf strands and also as a jumping-off point for the beautiful Ilhas Berlengas nature reserve, Peniche is spectacularly set on a headland surrounded by sea. It remains a working port, giving it a slightly grittier, more 'lived in' feel than its resort neighbours. The seaside fort where Salazar's regime detained political prisoners is a must-see for anyone interested in Portuguese history; artisan lovers will enjoy Peniche's speciality, handmade lace known as *Renda de Bilros* (bobbin lace), and you can watch the nimble fingers of women at work; and outdoors enthusiasts will love the beaches and the spectacular, heavily eroded limestone cliffs that jut out from the tip of the headland at Cabo Carvoeiro like a jagged jigsaw piece timelessly waiting for a never-to-come unification.

⊙ Sights

★ Baleal   BEACH

About 5km to the northeast of Peniche is this scenic island-village, connected to the mainland village of Casais do Baleal by a narrow causeway (note:it's accessed through a car park). The fantastic sweep of sandy beach here offers some fine surfing. Surf schools dot the sands, as do several bar-restaurants.

★ Headland   AREA

While in Peniche, make sure you do the 8km circuit of the whole headland (walking is hot going, however, as much of it is on the road). At Cabo Carvoeiro, the very tip, there's a lighthouse and spectacular views of a rock

stack and the Berlenga islands, as well as an excellent restaurant.

Fortaleza de Peniche   FORT

(🖉 262 780 116; Campo da República; ⊙ 9am-12.30pm & 2-5.30pm Tue-Fri, from 10am Sat & Sun) **FREE** Dominating the south of the peninsula, Peniche's imposing 16th-century fortress was used in the 20th century as one of dictator Salazar's infamous jails for political prisoners. By the entrance where prisoners once received visitors – the stark booths with glass partitions are preserved – is the Núcleo-Resistência, a grim but fascinating display about those times, including Resistance leaflets and prisoners' poignant, beautifully illustrated letters to their children.

At the time of research he fort was closed for the building of Portugal's new Museu da Resistência e Liberdade (Resistance and Freedom Museum).

Museu da Renda de Bilros   MUSEUM

(Rua Nossa Senhora da Conceição 1; ⊙ 10am-1pm & 2-6pm Tue-Sun) **FREE** For those interested in the Peniche tradition of bobbin lace, this museum, inaugurated in 2016, offers an interesting glimpse into this traditional coastal lace textile technique with a short introductory film (four minutes) and small but well-done exhibitions on its history, production, bobbins from around the world and modern adaptations. Stop here first before heading over to see the work in action at the Escola de Rendas de Bilros.

Escola de Rendas de Bilros   FACTORY

(Rua Alexandre Herculano 70; ⊙ 9am-12.30pm & 2-5.30pm Mon-Fri) At this school attached to Peniche's turismo building, you can watch the nimble (and chatty) ladies in action as the organised 'chaos' of their bobbins produces exquisite lace.

🏃 Activities

🏄 Surfing

Long renowned as a prime surfing destination, Peniche burnished its celebrity status when **Supertubos** beach, south of town, was selected as a stop on the ASP World Tour, the most prestigious international circuit of competitive surfing.

Meanwhile, **Baleal** is a paradise of challenging but, above all, consistent waves that make it an ideal learners' beach.

Peniche is full of surf hostels and surf schools. Depending on the season, surf camps at Baleal charge in the vicinity of €275 to €545 for a week of classes, including equipment and shared self-catering lodging. You can also take individual two-hour classes for around €35 and rent boards with wetsuits (€25 per day). Well-established operators include **Baleal Surfcamp** (☑262 769 277; www.balealsurfcamp.com; Rua Amigos do Baleal 2; 2-/3-/7-day course with lodging €180/255/528) and **Peniche Surfcamp** (☑962 336 295; www.penichesurfcamp.com; Avenida do Mar 162, Casais do Baleal; ⊙1/2/10 surf classes €30/50/145).

🏊 Diving

There are good opportunities for diving, especially at Berlenga. Expect to pay about €65 to €75 (less around Peniche) for two dives with **AcuaSubOeste** (☑918 393 444; www.acuasuboeste.com; Armazém 3, Avenida do Porto de Pesca; 2 dives €70; ⊙9-10am & 5-7pm) or **Haliotis** (☑262 781 160; www.haliotis.pt; Casal da Ponte S/N, Atouguia da Baleia; 2-tank dive €75; ⊙9am-1pm & 2-6pm). Both also offer a range of PADI certification courses.

🏄 Kitesurfing

Kitesurfing is big in Peniche. On the far side of high dunes about 500m east of the walled town, **Peniche Kite & Surf Center** (☑919 424 951; www.penichesurfcenter.com; Avenida Monsenhor Bastos, Praia de Peniche de Cima; ⊙9.30am-8pm Mar-Oct) offers surfing and kitesurfing lessons with equipment for €40 per lesson (minimum two people, three lessons).

👉 Tours

Berlinga Viva TOURS
(☑926 852 046; Marina do Peniche, Cais de Belengas, Office No 8; ⊙8am-8pm) An association of local tour boats organising cruises on demand throughout the year (depending on conditions). In addition to the standard trips to Reserva Natural da Berlenga in speedy good-time rigid-hulled inflatable boats, it also runs trips to Cabo Carvoeiro (€9.50 per person) and the rarely booked Farilhões, the twin outer islands of the Berlenga chain (€44 per person).

Viamar TOURS
(☑262 785 646; www.viamar-berlenga.com; Largo da Ribeira Velha 2, Marina de Peniche; day round-trip adult/child €20/12; ⊙8.30am-1pm & 3-6pm Jun & Sep, 8.15am-1pm & 3-7pm Jul & Aug) Viamar

does the 45-minute trip to Berlenga Grande three times daily during July and August, at 9.30am, 11.30am and 5.30pm, returning at 10.30am, 4.30pm and 6.30pm. During the remainder of the season there's one sailing daily, departing at 10am, returning at 4.30pm. Tickets tend to sell out quickly in summer, as only 300 visitors are allowed each day. All sailings are weather-dependent.

🛏 Sleeping

Peniche Hostel HOSTEL €
(☑969 008 689; www.penichehostel.com; Rua Arquitecto Paulino Montês 6; dm €15-18, d €45; @@🐱) A colourful, driftwood-inspired staircase leads to this older-style little hostel run by friendly staff, only steps from the tourist office and a five-minute walk from the bus station. Bright and whimsically decorated rooms have a modern hippie element. Front rooms have windows, while one smaller, more claustrophobic option only has an interior window.

Residencial Rimavier GUESTHOUSE €
(☑916 809 456; www.rimavier.com; Rua Castilho 6; s/d €35/45; 🐱) This immaculate *pensão* has small but spruce rooms, nautically themed linens and hallways decorated with lovely tile paintings of Peniche. Note: prices do not include breakfast, and you'll have to head elsewhere for your morning java fix.

★ Casa das Marés B&B €€
(☑Casa 1 262 769 200, Casa 2 262 769 255, Casa 3 262 769 379; www.casadasmares1.com; Praia do Baleal; d/ste €70/120; 🐱) At the picturesque, windswept tip of Baleal stands one of the area's most unusual accommodation options. Three sisters originally inherited this dramatically perched house from their parents and divided it into three parts – each of which now serves as its own little B&B run by two surviving brothers-in-law and one of the sisters.

Breezy, inviting rooms all have great close-up sea views, and the sound of the breaking waves below is magical. Each of the downstairs sitting areas are different, but cosy, and the entire place is loaded with character. Worth reserving ahead (no English at No 3, FYI).

Residencia Maciel GUESTHOUSE €€
(☑262 784 685; www.residencialmaciel.com; Rua José Estevão 38; s/d from €53/65; ❋🐱) This place comprises three accommodation

options within the same block: simpler São João, the original Maciel and a modernised Maciel II opposite. We like the original Maciel: it's older in style but has generous-sized rooms and carpeted hallways (head here for all check-ins). Breakfast is served in a pleasant dining room near Maciel's reception. The owner is proud and welcoming.

★**Surfers Lodge**   DESIGN HOTEL €€€
(☑262 700 030; www.surferslodgepeniche.com; Avenida do Mar 132, Ferrel; s/d/f €109/179/330; ❋ ☏) This hip spot is all about the design. And experience. Given its apparent target (surfers who are riding a money wave, and are happy to spend it), it redefines the image of the hippie dude living out of a combi van. The funky decor incorporates polished concrete and recycled woods, and comprises clean lines, whites and natural hues.

✖ Eating

Os Americanos   INTERNATIONAL €€
(☑262 789 046; www.intelligentartstudio. zenfolio.com; Rua José Estevão 29-31; mains €15; ⊙6pm-midnight Tue-Sun; ☏) There's no sugarcoating what's going down at this wildly popular restaurant inside Residencial Maciel II – an American couple (with Portuguese and Russian roots) satiate homesick crowds with mostly American-style classics (sirloin steak, chicken cordon bleu, lamb chops, duck breast) with occasional Italian and Portuguese flourishes. Ignore the distracting menu font – the food is solid, especially the fish specials (no bones!).

Taberna do Ganhão   PORTUGUESE €€
(☑988 451 600; Largo dos Amigos do Baleal, Baleal; mains €5-16; ⊙10am-10pm Thu-Tue; ☏) This 'new-school tavern' is a reconstituted 'old-school tavern' where fishermen bought wine and groceries (plus it was the first in the area to have a telephone). The current owners have reinvigorated its spirit by maintaining its red-and-white-checked tables and elevated traditional daily plates (sweet and sour fried chicken on Tuesday, cuttlefish with garlic on Friday and so on).

★**Nau dos Corvos**   PORTUGUESE €€€
(☑262 783 168; www.naudoscorvos.com; Marginal Norte, Cabo Carvoeiro; mains €17-23; ⊙noon-3pm & 7-10.30pm) It's just you and the sea out here at Cabo Carvoeiro, 2.5km from town at the tip of the peninsula. As you gaze out at the Atlantic from the windy rooftop viewing platform, it's nice to know that under your

feet is an excellent, upmarket seafood restaurant (Peniche's best). It boasts some of the best sunset views in Portugal.

🍷 Drinking & Nightlife

The area around Igreja de São Pedro is the old town's drinking hub (think four walls, cold beer and a home stereo system). For nightlife, you're really better off in Baleal, where you'll find several laid-back surfer bars right on the beach.

★**Base**   COCKTAIL BAR
(www.thebasebar.com; Rua Infante Dom Henrique, Lote 2; ⊙6pm-2am Mon-Sat Feb-Oct, 6pm-2am Wed-Sat Nov-Dec; ☏) Connoisseurs of the cocktail will want to burrow themselves into the palette lounges at this in-the-know bar tucked away inside a residential complex – it's easily Peniche's best for creative mixology. Pair a sunset perch on the grassy lawn in front with refreshing cocktails such as Gin Garden (gin, lemon, mint, soda) mixed to perfection.

ℹ Information

Posto de Turismo (☑262 789 571; www. cm-peniche.pt; Rua Alexandre Herculano 70; ⊙9am-1pm & 2-5pm)

ℹ Getting There & Away

BUS

Peniche's **bus station** (☑968 903 861; Rua Dr Ernesto Moreira) is served by served mainly by Rodoviária do Oeste (www.rodoviariadooeste. pt) and Rede Expressos (www.rede-expressos. pt) as well as Intercentro (www.internorte.pt) and Rápida Azul. Destinations include Coimbra (€14.70, 2¾ hours, hourly), Leiria (€12.80, two hours, three to four daily), Lisbon (€9, 1½ hours, every one to two hours) and Óbidos (€3.30, 40 minutes, six to eight daily).

CAR & MOTORCYCLE

Driving into Peniche, the main highway (N114/IP6) reaches a roundabout shortly before town, where you can bear left towards the centre, right for Baleal and the eastern beaches, or straight for 3km along the northern cliffs to Cabo Carvoeiro and its lighthouse. Most days you can find ample free parking on the road that runs along the harbour.

ℹ Getting Around

From the bus station, it's a 10-minute walk west to the historic centre. The fort, harbour and Avenida do Mar – where you'll find most of the seafood restaurants – are a short distance south.

Local buses connect Peniche's bus terminal with Baleal (€1.90, 10 minutes, 2.30pm, 3.30pm and 5pm) but only during the summer. Bikes are a handy way to get around; hire them at **Wildside Campers** (⏵262 785 318; www.wildsidecampers.com; Avenida Monsenhor Bastos 33; rental per day/week €15/70; ⊙10am-1pm & 2-7pm).

Reserva Natural da Berlenga

Sitting about 10km offshore from Peniche, Berlenga Grande is a spectacular, rocky and remote island, with twisting, shocked-rock formations and gaping caverns. It's the only island of the Berlenga archipelago you can visit – the group consists of three tiny islands surrounded by clear, calm, dark-blue waters full of shipwrecks that are great for snorkelling and diving.

In the 16th century Berlenga Grande was home to a monastery, but now the most famous inhabitants are thousands of nesting seabirds, especially guillemots. The birds take priority over human visitors: the only development that has been allowed includes housing for a small fishing community and a lighthouse. Paths are clearly marked to stop day trippers trespassing on the birds' domain.

Linked to the island by a narrow causeway is the 17th-century Forte de São João Baptista, now one of the country's most dramatic (but barren) hostels.

🛏 Sleeping

If you want to sleep on the island, you'll need to reserve ahead; places can be prebooked solid as early as May. For camping, reservations must be made via email – the Posto de Turismo (p275) in Peniche can assist.

Forte de São João Baptista CAMPGROUND €
(⏵918 025 300; www.facebook.com/aaberlenga; Grande Berlenga; s/d/tr from €25/45/65; ⊙Jun–mid-Sep) The original fort (built in 1666) was later remodelled as an inn but was then abandoned for many years. This is a dramatic but dead-basic spot that's essentially 'camping with walls': you sleep in rooms, but must bring all your own linen, food and drinking water. Wonderful bucket-nozzle showers from cistern water are on offer; bathrooms are shared.

Payment is inconveniently required in advance via bank transfer, but the outlook and nature experience is simply beautiful. Bring a torch, as the generator goes off at midnight, and keep in mind the fort is reachable only via a 45-minute, 360-step hike or by water taxi (€3).

Mar e Sol HOTEL €€
(⏵919 543 105, 262 750 331; www.restaurantemaresol.pt; Grande Berlenga; tw/q €80/110; ⊙May-Sep) The decent if simple six rooms here would seem overpriced anywhere else, but when you consider the location just a few steps above Berlenga's boat dock and directly adjacent to its only restaurant, things appeal more. Prices halve at the beginning and end of the season.

❶ Getting There & Away

Peniche-based Viamar (p274) is the longest-established of several harbourside outfits, all making the 45-minute trip to the island on roughly the same schedule and for the same round-trip fare. Viamar sails a large ferry three times daily during July and August, at 9.30am, 11.30am and 5.30pm, returning at 10.30am, 4.30pm and 6.30pm. During the remainder of the season there's one trip per day, departing at 10am and returning at 4.30pm. Berlinga Viva (p274) makes the trip in 25 minutes with its speed demon rigid-hulled inflatable boats (imagine a turbo steeplechase on a supersonic horse, a highly entertaining and recommended ride!).

Tickets tend to sell out quickly in summer, as only 300 visitors are allowed each day. All sailings are weather-dependent; some include harbour porpoise sightings.

If you're prone to seasickness, choose your day carefully – the crossing can be rough.

Óbidos

POP 3100 / ELEV 80M

Surrounded by a classic crenellated wall, Óbidos' gorgeous historic centre is a labyrinth of cobblestoned streets and flower-bedecked, whitewashed houses livened up with dashes of vivid yellow and blue paint. It's a delightful place to pass an afternoon, but there are plenty of reasons to stay overnight, as there's excellent accommodation, including a hilltop castle now converted into one of Portugal's most luxurious *pousadas*.

Hill-town aficionados looking to savour Óbidos' 'lost in time' qualities may find the main street ridiculously touristy, especially on weekends and during festivals. There are pretty bits outside the walls too.

The main gate, Porta da Vila, leads directly into the main street, Rua Direita, lined with chocolate and sour cherry–liqueur shops, but the joy of Óbidos is wandering among its nooks and crannies within; and along its imposing wall above.

History

When Dom Dinis first showed Óbidos to his wife Dona Isabel in 1228, it must have already been a pretty sight because she fell instantly in love with the place. The king decided to make the town a wedding gift to his queen, initiating a royal tradition that lasted until the 19th century.

Any grace it had in 1228 must be credited to the Moors, who had laid out the streets and had only recently abandoned the strategic heights. The Moors had chased out the Visigoths, who in turn had evicted the Romans, who also had a fortress here.

Until the 15th century Óbidos overlooked the sea; the bay gradually silted up, leaving the town landlocked.

◉ Sights

Óbidos' dramatic, fully-intact Moorish wall (Muro de Óbidos) imposingly surrounds the historic centre of town and stretches in a completed loop of 1560m, all of which can be walked across the top, at a height of 13m in some spots (not including the towers). There are four staircases accessing the wall, but most folks climb up either at Porta da Vila or the castle. There are no guardrails, so take care, especially with children or anyone unsteady on their feet or prone to vertigo.

The town castle **Castelo de Óbidos** `FREE`, one of Dom Dinis' 13th-century creations, is a stern edifice, with lots of towers, battlements and big gates. Converted into a palace in the 16th century (some Manueline touches add levity), it's now a deluxe pousada (p278).

Porta da Vila   HISTORIC SITE
(Rua Josefa de Óbidos 2) The main gate of Óbidos' historic centre bears the King João IV-ordered inscription, 'A Virgem Nossa Senhora foi concebida sem pecado original' ('The Virgin Mary was conceived without original sin'). The gate features a chapel and a gorgeous blue-and-white-tiled baroque balcony. It dates to around 1380.

Igreja de Santa Maria   CHURCH
(Praça de Santa Maria; ⊙ 9.30am-12.30pm & 2.30-7pm summer, to 5pm winter) The town's elegant main church, near the northern end of Rua Direita, stands out for its interior, with a wonderful painted ceiling and walls done up in beautiful blue-and-white 17th-century *azulejos*. Paintings by the renowned 17th-century artist Josefa de Óbidos are to the right of the altar. There's a fine 16th-century Renaissance tomb on the left, probably carved by French sculptor Nicolas Chanterène.

Museu Municipal   MUSEUM
(Rua Direita 97; ⊙ 10am-1pm & 2-6pm Tue-Sun) `FREE` Located in an 18th-century manor house just next to Igreja de Santa Maria, the town's museum houses a small collection of paintings spanning several centuries. The highlight is a haunting portrait by Josefa de Óbidos, *Beneficiado Faustino das Neves* (1670), remarkable for its dramatic use of light and shade.

Aqueduto de Óbidos   HISTORIC SITE
(Óbidos Aqueduct; N114) The impressive 3km-long aqueduct, southeast of the main gate, dates from the 16th century.

✸ Festivals & Events

Mercado Medieval   FAIR
(☎ 262 955 561; www.mercadomedievalobidos.pt; adult/child €7/free) This two-week medieval fair – held during late July/early August inside the castle grounds and below the town's western wall – includes live entertainment, jousting matches (yes, on horses!), plenty of grog and pigs roasting on spits, and the chance to try your hand at scaling the town walls with the help of a harness and rope.

🛏 Sleeping

Although touristy, Óbidos has an excellent array of accommodation, from atmospheric *pousadas* to cosy guesthouses and some cutting-edge boutique hotels.

Hostel Argonauta   HOSTEL €
(☎ 262 958 088, 963 824 178; www.hostelargonauta.com; Travessia Adelaide Ribeirete 14; dm/d €28/49; ☎) In a pretty spot just outside the walls, this feels more like a friend's place than a hostel. Run with good cheer by a Spanish couple who whip up eggs at breakfast, it has an arty, colourful dorm with wood-stove heating and beds as well as bunks; there's also a cute double with a great view.

BUDDHA EDEN

What have the Taliban got to do with a rural winery 12km south of Óbidos? Well, when they blew up the Buddhas of Bamiyan in Afghanistan in 2001, the millionaire art collector José Berardo was so incensed at the wanton destruction of culture that he decided to do something to balance it out and created a large sculpture park on the grounds of his winery. The result, **Bacalhôa Buddha Eden** (www.buddhaeden.com; Quinta dos Loridos, Carvalhal; €5; ⊘9am-6pm), is an astonishing sight.

The wildly out of place, thoroughly fascinating park features monumental Buddhist statues standing proudly above the cork trees, a phalanx of electric blue terracotta warriors looking down on a duck-filled lake, modern contemporary sculpture among the vines, and a little tourist train (adult/child €4/free) doing the rounds for the sore of foot. It's a great place to relax, and there's a cafe here, as well as a wine shop. To make a day of it, there's an appealing restaurant in the nearby village – **Mãe d'Água** (www.restaurante maedagua.com; Rua 13 Maio 26, Sobral do Parelhão; mains €10.50-16.50; ⊘noon-4pm & 7pm-late Tue-Sun) does confident modern Portuguese fare in a contemporary setting within a noble old building.

To get here, take the A8 motorway south from Óbidos and exit at junction 12, then follow signs for Carvalhal.

Casa do Relógio
GUESTHOUSE €

(☑262 959 282; www.casadorelogio.com; Rua do Vale; d/tr €50/80; ☜) Just east of the town walls this 18th-century house (named for a nearby sundial) has eight smallish but spotless rooms that have had a nearly-not-quite-there decor update. There's a pretty shared terrace and it's good value for money – especially when you consider the free laundry service. Cash only.

★ Casa d'Óbidos
HOTEL €€

(☑262 950 924; www.casadobidos.com; Quinta de São José; s/d €75/90, 2-/4-/6-person apt €90/140/175; P☜☜☜) In a whitewashed 1887 villa below town, this delightful option features spacious, breezy rooms with good modern bathrooms and period furnishings, plus a tennis court, swimming pool and lovely grounds with sweeping views of Óbidos' bristling walls and towers. Breakfast is served at a common dining table (fresh bread and breakfast fixings are delivered every morning to the apartments).

Hostel Vila d'Óbidos
HOSTEL €€

(☑262 955 360; www.senhorasrainhas.com; Largo de São Pedro 1; dm €25, d with/without bathroom €80/60; ☜) Across the street from pricier **Casa das Senhoras Rainhas** (☑262 955 360; www.senhorasrainhas.com; Rua Padre Nunes Tavares 6; d/ste from €145/199; ☒☜) and sharing the reception and breakfast room, this spiffy new option lacks a hostel vibe (you're on your own here, with keypad access), but small, stylish rooms with dramatic wall-to-ceiling cityscape scenes and wonderful bathrooms with rain-style showers are great value for Óbidos. The second-floor lounge has epic wall views.

Literary Man
DESIGN HOTEL €€

(☑262 959 217; www.theliteraryman.pt; Rua Dom João de Ornelas; r from €90; ☜) Billed as one of the first 'literary' hotels around, this place, housed in a beautiful former convent, is remarkable for its concept. It has a library-bar-cafe-hotel-lounge, whose decor is a melange of funk and traditional, and wall-to-wall books (some 60,000, most for sale for €5). Thirty contemporary and minimalist rooms feature polished concrete and recycled wood, most with bathtubs.

Hotel Real d'Óbidos
HOTEL €€€

(☑262 955 090; www.hotelrealdobidos.com; Rua Dom João de Ornelas; d from €120; P☒☜☜) Medieval mania abounds, with suits of armour, shields riveted to the walls and staff in tunics, but modern comforts aren't lacking. Just outside the town walls, this is an atmospheric and well-equipped aristocratic dwelling converted to a small upmarket hotel. Rooms are spacious and comfortable, and the summertime pool is great, as are superior rooms with dark, rustic hardwood accents.

Pousada do Castelo
HISTORIC HOTEL €€€

(☑210 407 630; www.pousadas.pt; Paço Real; d/ste from €200/320; ☒☜) One of Portugal's most unusual *pousadas* occupies the town's forbidding 13th-century castle. The rooms are within two sections – the castle (traditional decor), and the attached building known as 'the cottage' (more modern interiors). Each room is different – some with working wood fireplaces, original wood beams and *azulejos*. All castle bathrooms were redone in 2016.

✖ Eating

Senhor da Pedra
PORTUGUESE €

(☑ 914 604 362; Largo do Santuário; mains €6-9.50; ⏰ 11.30am-10pm Mon-Sat, 11am-4pm Sun) Behind the striking church of Senhor da Pedra below town, this simple white-tiled eatery (the one on the right as you look at the row of restaurants) is a recommended place to try low-priced authentic Portuguese cuisine. It's a classic affair with mum in the kitchen and dad on the tables. Don't expect fast service.

★ Ja!mon Ja!mon
PORTUGUESE €€

(☑ 916 208 162; Rua da Biquinha S/N; mains €10-14; ⏰ noon-3pm & 7-10pm Tue-Sat, noon-3pm Sun) With the cheery Andre, his family and a young, enthusiastic staff at the helm, the hospitality is oh-so Portuguese (read: happy and generous) at this excellent *tasca* (tavern) featuring a wonderful terrace with lush hillside views.

Fresh bread is baked in the wood-fired oven, and each day brings a small selection of daily specials – one meat, one fish, one veg – along with well-executed staples such as *bacalhau a lagareiro* (salted cod with olive oil, onions and potatoes), ox tail or pork cheeks.

★ Poço dos Sabores
PORTUGUESE €€

(☑ 262 950 086; www.facebook.com/pocodos sabores; Rua Principal 83B, Usseira; mains €13-22; ⏰ 12.30-2.30 & 7.30-10.15pm Tue-Sun Sep-Jun, 12.30-2.30pm Jul & Aug; ☎) Ditch the tourist onslaught in Óbidos for this village charmer 5km away in Usseira, where Joaquim and sister Angela combine restaurant skills honed in France and Switzerland to create a modern Portuguese destination worth shuffling your itinerary for. The decor is full of village character (walls stacked with memorabilia, bric-a-brac, arts and crafts). The food? At once classic but creative.

Tasca Torta
PORTUGUESE €€

(☑ 262 958 000; Rua Direita 81; mains €9-19; ⏰ 12.30-2.25pm & 7-10.25pm) A pleasant hum, appealing aromas and colourful plates sum up this stylish, contemporary spot. There's a cosy line of tables down one side, a kitchen on the other, and black-and-white photos of Portuguese fishermen. Everything from delicious salmon and spinach lasagna to a trilogy of seafood (salted cod, octopus and fish) pleases palates. Delicious starters are arranged on a slate plate.

🍷 Drinking & Nightlife

Belgituda
PUB

(www.belgituda.com; Estrada Nacional 8; ⏰ 6pm-late Thu-Sun, closed late Dec–mid-Feb; ☎) With over 70 types of Belgian beer by the bottle, this bar just outside the walls is the place in Óbidos for those who set the beer bar higher than Sagres and Super Bock. But the quirky Belgian owner is threatening to close – let's not let him!

Esplanada Santa Maria
CAFE

(Praça de Santa Maria; ⏰ 10am-8pm) In the shadow of Santa Maria church and a couple of 500-year-old Japanese maple trees, this cash only, open-air esplanade offers some of Óbidos' most atmospheric tipple tables. No fancy mixology here – just cold Estrella Damm on draught and a few select standard cocktails (*porto tonicos*, caipirinhas, gin and tonics; €7.50) – served out of a made-over shipping container.

ℹ Information

Posto de Turismo (☑ 262 959 231; www.obidos.pt; Rua da Porta da Vila S/N; ⏰ 9.30am-7.30pm May-Sep, to 6pm Oct-Apr) Just outside Porta da Vila, near the bus stop, with helpful multilingual staff offering town brochures and maps in five languages, plus information on concerts and more.

ℹ Getting There & Away

BUS

Rodoviária do Oeste (www.rodoviariadooeste.pt) buses stop on the main road just outside Porta da Vila. There are frequent departures for Peniche (€3.30, 40 minutes) and Lisbon (€7.85, 65 minutes) from the **bus stop** (☑ 262 767 676) on the west side of Rua da Praça; and to Caldas da Rainha (€1.90, 20 minutes) from the **bus stop** (☑ 262 767 676) on the east side.

CAR & MOTORCYCLE

There are five car parks in Óbidos outside the gates, two of which are fee-charging (€1.20 to €1.60 per hour, €5 to €6.60 per day maximum). The best and biggest free **car park** (N114) is behind Caixa Geral de Depósitos, 220m southeast of Porta da Vila. There is also free parking along the outside of the wall, but don't leave it

ESTREMADURA & RIBATEJO ÓBIDOS

anywhere near a portal or gate – the police will be on it in seconds.

TRAIN

There are at least six daily trains to Lisbon (€8.90 to €9.05, 2½ hours) mostly via connections at Mira Sintra-Meleças station on the suburban Lisbon line. The **train station** (www.cp.pt; Estrada da Estação S/N) is located outside the northeastern section of the castle walls, 1.1km north of Porta da Vila. It's a pretty, but uphill, walk to town.

Foz do Arelho

POP 1300

With a vast, lovely beach backed by a river-mouth estuary ideal for windsurfing, Foz do Arelho remains remarkably undeveloped. It makes a fine place to laze in the sun, and outside July and August it'll often be just you and the local fishers. The beach has a row of relaxed bars and restaurants; the town is a 15-minute walk inland.

🏃 Activities

Escola de Vela da Lagoa WATER SPORTS
(☑962 568 005, 262 978 592; www.escoladavelada-lagoa.com; Rua Engenheiro Luís Paiva e Sousa 105; ⏱10am-sunset Jun-Sep, Fri-Mon Oct-Mar, Thu-Mon Apr, Wed-Mon May) Hires out sailboats (€16 per hour), canoes (€12), SUP (€10 per hour) and windsurfing boards (from €15) and catamarans (from €20). Gives windsurfing and sailing lessons (two hours, €60/90 for one/two) and group kayak lessons (three hours, €16 per person). From the Foz do Arelho village, it's 2.8km: turn left on the road that follows the lagoon's inland edge past the rock called 'Penedo Furado' and continue.

🛏 Sleeping & Eating

★Casa Lagoa B&B €€
(☑962 319 861; casalagoafda@gmail.com; Rua Francisco Almeida Grandela 57; d €70-90; ❄ 🛜 🏊) Côte d'Azur escapees Laetitia, Hervé and their awesome dog, Janisse, run this stylish, discerning B&B just 850m from the sand. Six earth-toned rooms boast superstar showers, terraces with lagoon views and a splash of Portuguese art for colour. Hervé runs a serious SUP operation (rentals and excursions), and Laetitia handles hospitality and the to-die-for breakfast (these are ex-bakers!).

Água d'Alma HOTEL €€
(☑262 979 610; www.aguadalma.pt; Rua dos Camarções 3; s/d from €58/68; 🅿 ❄ 🛜) A

family-run boutique gem up the hill originally started in the 1950s as a simple *pension* and transformed in 2016 into one of the region's sleekest options. The hip bar and terrace hosts local art and is great for a refreshing *porto tónico* (port and tonic). The minimalist rooms are decorated in muted grey tones. Breakfast is better than most.

★Távola PORTUGUESE €€
(www.tavoladepedra.pai.pt; Rua Francisco Almeida Grandela 135A; mains €8-15; ⏱noon-3pm & 7-10.30pm Wed-Mon Oct-Mar; 🛜) In the village, at the entrance from the east, this place serves up the town's best local cooking, with tasty copper *cataplanas* (seafood stews) served on cork boards, good-quality meat dishes and, on winter Saturdays, an Angolan *moamba* (chicken stew). The attached bar-cafe at the front is decked out in contemporary decor while the back ambience is more traditional.

❶ Getting There & Away

In summer, at least eight daily Rodoviária do Oeste (www.rodoviariadooeste.pt) buses connect the beach at Foz do Arelho with Caldas da Rainha (€2.30, 25 minutes), from where you can connect to larger towns.

To alleviate the serious parking issue at the beach, the free open-top Fozbus runs from 10:45am to 9pm on weekends in July and August (daily from August 1 to 19), connecting outlying car parks with the beach.

São Martinho do Porto

POP 2700

In contrast to nearby Nazaré, São Martinho do Porto is no party town, but a happy place where families and older paddlers enjoy the gentle lap of the waves on the omega-shaped bay ringed by sheltered, safe, sandy beaches.

🛏 Sleeping

Colina do Sol CAMPGROUND €
(☑262 989 764; www.colinadosol.org; Serra dos Mangues; sites per adult/car €3.25/3, tents €3.50-7.50; 🅿 🛜 🏊) This friendly campsite is 2km north of town, and about the same distance from the beach, with disabled access, a children's playground, mini-golf, a pool and some sections shaded by pine trees. It's a nicer pick than the municipal park, though the latter is on the beachfront.

Palace do Capitão
B&B €€

(✉ 262 985 150; www.hotelpalacecapitao.com; Rua Capitão Jaime Pinto 6; d €80-110, ste €150; P ✳ 🛜) This perfectly preserved, if ever-so-slightly tired 19th-century sea captain's home directly across from the beach is a place of distinction, with much of its original Victoriana still intact. Rooms are all different and beautiful. Room 4 (the captain's former bedroom) is lovely and light. The upstairs suite (room 6) has a sun terrace, accessed by a whimsical spiral staircase.

Hotel Atlântica
HOTEL €€

(✉ 262 980 151; www.hotelatlantica.pt; Rua Miguel Bombarda 6; s/d €50/60; 🛜) In a modern building, this welcoming place has spotless white-and-blue rooms with tiled floors to match. Rooms have low beds, little balconies and a summery feel. Ultra-friendly, helpful owners and reception staff. Downstairs, the restaurant has a great terrace and serves simple but good fish and meat dishes. Room rates drop dramatically outside July and August.

✗ Eating

Seafood eateries line São Martinho do Porto's quay and beachfront. You are safe to take your pick; all prepare fresh seafood, and the quality is good.

Pastelaria A Concha
CAFE €

(Rua José Bento da Silva 41; cakes from €0.90; ⏰ 8am-8pm Fri-Wed) In São Martinho do Porto's upper village, not far from the church, you'll find this nondescript little cafe that has served up big, sweet flavours since 1950. All cakes are made on the premises. Does a killer *pastel de nata* (custard tart).

A Nova Gaviota
PORTUGUESE €€

(✉ 911 046 829; Rua José Bento da Silva; mains €9-16; ⏰ noon-2pm & 7pm-midnight; 🛜) A modern *tasca* adorned with photos of VW vans on the walls, this upper village hotspot is a great place to escape tourists and the menus that cater solely to them. Top plates here include the monkfish rice as well as the house steak – with mushrooms, *alheira* (garlicky poultry or game sausage) and an egg. Best to make a reservation.

Restaurante Royal Marina
INTERNATIONAL €€

(✉ 262 989 959; www.restaurante-royal-marina. eu; Rua Cândido dos Reis 30A; mains €15-20.50; ⏰ 12.30am-4pm & 7-11pm Fri-Tue; 🛜) A Swiss owner-chef runs the kitchen, and his friendly Portuguese wife runs the floor. This unpretentious spot on the quay has a slightly antiquated maritime feel and serves up great seafood. And it whips up international treats such as *nasi goreng*. It is happy to cater to vegetarians.

ℹ Information

Posto de Turismo (✉ 262 989 110; www. cm-alcobaca.pt; Rua Vasco da Gama; ⏰ 9.30am-12.30pm & 2-5.30pm) In the heart of the village; in the same building is an elevator that takes you up to the top of the town (free of charge).

ℹ Getting There & Away

BUS

Rede Expressos (www.rede-expressos.pt) runs between five and seven buses daily to/from Lisbon (€10.90, 1½ hours).

Rodoviária do Oeste (www.rodoviariadooeste. pt) has buses heading to Óbidos (€3.15, 45 minutes), Batalha (€4.45, 1¼ hours), Alcobaça (€3.50, 45 minutes) and Nazaré (€2.40, 30 minutes).

TRAIN

The **train station** (www.comboios.pt; Largo 28 de Maio) is about 700m southeast of the centre. There are three daily trains northbound to Leiria (€4.25, 40 to 45 minutes) and around three southbound to Caldas da Rainha (€1.60, 15 minutes), with onward connections in both directions.

Nazaré
POP 10,500

With a warren of narrow, cobbled lanes running down to a wide, cliff-backed beach, Nazaré is Estremadura's most picturesque coastal resort. The sands are packed wall-to-wall with multicoloured umbrellas in July and August, but the party atmosphere isn't limited to the summer beach scene – Nazaré is one of Portugal's top draws for New Year's Eve and Carnaval celebrations as well.

The town centre is jammed with seafood restaurants, bars and local women in traditional dress (in summer, they're hawking rooms for rent, especially near seafront Avenida da República). To get a different perspective, take the funicular up to Promontório do Sítio, where picture-postcard coastal views unfold from the cliffs.

Nazaré often hits the headlines for the record-breaking feats of gutsy surfers who ride monster winter waves that roll in north of town at Praia do Norte.

Nazaré

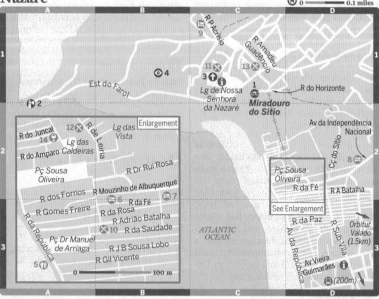

Nazaré

◎ Sights

Promontório do Sítio　　　　　HISTORIC SITE

Until the 18th century the sea covered the present-day site of Nazaré; locals lived at this clifftop area 110m above the beach. Today this tourist-filled promontory is popular for its tremendous views, the lighthouse and its religious associations. From Travessa do Elevador, north of the Turismo, a funicular climbs up the hill to Promontório do Sítio; it's nice to walk back down, escaping the crowds of trinket-sellers. There are plenty of places to stay and eat up on the clifftop too.

On a foggy day in 1182, local nobleman Dom Fuas Roupinho was in pursuit of a deer when the animal disappeared off the edge of the Sítio precipice. Dom Fuas cried out to the Virgin, whose sculpture was venerated in a nearby cave, for help, and his horse miraculously stopped right at the cliff's edge; the mark of one of its horseshoes is still visible. In what is a much-repeated story in the Iberian peninsula, Dom Fuas built the small Hermida da Memória chapel on the edge of the drop-off to commemorate the event and house the sculpture. It was later visited by a number of VIP pilgrims, including Vasco da Gama. The statue is now housed in the grander church across the square.

★ Miradouro do Sítio   VIEWPOINT
(Largo do Horizonte) As you exit the funicular at the top of Promontório do Sítio, make a quick left and walk 50m to the Sitío viewpoint – an outstanding aerial view of Nazaré and its immense beaches (100m wide, 6km long). A vista you won't soon forget.

Farol da Nazaré   LIGHTHOUSE
(Estrada do Farol, Sítio; €1; ⊙10am-8.30pm, last entrance at 8pm) This picturesque lighthouse (famous for its backdrop when surfers hit the high seas) sits at São Miguel Arcanjo fort and is a lovely place to visit, especially as the sun is setting. In addition to a small explanation of the geological reasons for the ocean's towering waves, its halls house the Surfer Wall exhibition, a gallery of surfboards of famed international surfers who have conquered Praia do Norte's mighty seas (not all unscathed – see Italian surfer Alessandro Marcianò's split board!).

Igreja de Nossa Senhora da Nazaré CHURCH
(Largo de Nossa Senhora da Nazaré, Sítio; ⊙10am-7pm Apr-Sep, to 6pm Oct-Mar) [FREE] The 17th-century, baroque Igreja de Nossa Senhora da Nazaré, decorated with attractive Dutch *azulejos,* is on the Promontório do Sítio and holds the much-venerated sculpture of the Virgin, said to have been made by Joseph himself in Nazareth when Jesus was a baby: hence the name of the town. For €1, you can get close to the statue itself – it's not too often that you get the chance to appear in the middle of an altarpiece.

★ Activities

Nazaré Surf School   SURFING
(☑916 386 907; www.nazaresurfschool.pt; Avenida da República S/N, Edificio S Miguel; 1/5/10 private classes €50/225/400; ⊙10am-7pm) You can learn how to tap into your inner Garrett McNamara (or not) with this recommended surf school.

★ Festivals & Events

★ Carnaval   MARDI GRAS
(www.carnavaldanazare.pt) One of Portugal's brashest Mardi Gras celebrations, held in February and/or March, with lots of costumed parades and general irreverence. Many people dress up and the nights go loud and long.

Festa do Mar   RELIGIOUS
Held on the first Sunday afternoon in May, this festival features a parade with floats dedicated to local patron saints and a procession of decorated boats that leave the harbour and head around Nazaré's beachfront.

Nossa Senhora da Nazaré   RELIGIOUS
This annual pilgrimage, held in Sítio on 8 September (with celebrations until 24 September), sees a religious Mass in the sanctuary and a procession with the image of Our Lady in the streets of Sítio. As Nazaré's big religious festival, it also features sombre processions, folkloric dances and bullfights.

🛏 Sleeping

You'll likely be hit up by local women (elderly women, often widows of fishermen, known as *chambristas*) – offering rooms for rent. It never hurts to bargain and see what the going rate is. Expect a 30% to 50% discount on rates outside July and August.

★ Lab Hostel   HOSTEL €
(☑262 382 339; www.labhostel.pt; Rua de Rio Maior 14; dm €17.50-18.50, d €55-100; ☏) One of Portugal's band of growing 'glostels' (glamorous hostels) – stylish, minimal design, attention to detail and some of the whitest, brightest and cleanest rooms around make this worth a look. There's a female dorm and a family room – and breakfast is included. It was a former laboratory (the owner's father-in-law was a pharmacist), and old chemist jars and bottles make for fun *objets d'art.*

Cute loft rooms are the only ones with air-conditioning, but are not for tall people.

★ Vila Turística
Conde Fidalgo   GUESTHOUSE, APARTMENT €
(☑262 552 361; www.facebook.com/VilaConde Fidalgo; Avenida da Independência Nacional 21a; d €35-55, apt €45-75; ☏) Built around a series of flower-strewn courtyards and patios, this pretty family-run complex a few blocks up from the beach was a former fishermen's colony. Delightful English-speaking owner Ana offers 10 clean, colourful and comfortable rooms with minifridges, plus a dozen apartments of varying sizes. Breakfast is €5 extra, served in your room or on the terrace outside.

Orbitur Valado   CAMPGROUND €
(☑262 561 111; www.orbitur.pt; Rua dos Combatentes do Ultramar 2; sites per adult/tent/car €5.20/5.45/4.80; P☏☀) This shady, well-equipped year-round Orbitur site has a restaurant, bar and excellent swimming pool, as well as bungalows and fixed tents

THE BIGGEST WAVE

A tiny black dot on a massive wall of water: footage of surfers riding monster waves at Nazaré has captivated the world in recent years. Given the right conditions, the big ones here can be over 30m high – think an eight-storey office building. The official world record of 23.77m for the biggest wave surfed was set here in 2011 by Garrett McNamara, only to be broken in 2017 by Rodrigo Koxa, who manhandled an 24.38m monster here (fellow Brazilian Maya Gabeira set the female record at Nazaré with her 20.7m triumph in 2018). The waves are so fast and tall that surfers get towed in by jet-ski.

Why so big? Storms and winds in the Atlantic can generate mighty waves by themselves, but Nazaré has a peculiarity that multiplies this potential: an offshore underwater canyon some 5km deep pointing right at Praia do Norte beach. The energy of the ocean swells is concentrated by this feature, producing the massive waves.

available. It's 2km east of town, off the Alcobaça road.

Zulla – Nazaré Surf Village
BOUTIQUE HOTEL €€

(918 966 800, 935 972 003; www.zulla.pt; Rua Padre Acrisio, Sítio; dm €20, s/d €30/60, apt with/without kitchen €90/70; ❄️🛜🅿️) A local female surfer duo have converted this American motor-court–style hotel into a hip surfer's haven in Sítio, with boutique furnishings across well-equipped dorm rooms, private doubles and apartments, all surrounding a sociable pool. In summer it draws families, while the winter brings nothing but serious surfers. The Terrace Bar (12.30pm to 8.30pm) is Sítio's hippest happy hour.

Magic Art Hotel
HOTEL €€

(262 569 040; www.hotelmagic.pt; Rua Mouzinho de Albuquerque 58; s/d €75/80; 🅿️❄️🛜) Close to the action, this hotel has gone for the standard current trend, the more ritzy and chic modern look. Clean-lined, well-equipped, lavender-accented white rooms with artily presented photos of old-time Nazaré sometimes contrast with appealing black-slate bathrooms (otherwise the white theme continues).

🍴 Eating & Drinking

Conchinha da Nazaré
SEAFOOD €

(262 186 156; Rua de Leiria 17D; mains €7-12; noon-4pm & 7-11pm, closed Wed in winter) One of the most authentic experiences around, this simple place on a backstreet square serves good-value seafood, including wood-grilled fish and delicious *açorda de marisco* (thick bread stew with seafood; €14). Many nights there are more locals than tourists.

★ Casa Pires
SEAFOOD €€

(Largo de Nosso Sra da Nazaré 45, Sítio; fish per kg €38.50-52, mains €11-16; noon-3.30pm & 7-10.30pm Tue-Sun) Many locals think that this is the only place in Nazaré to eat grilled sardines. Enough said. When sardines are out of season, though (read: frozen), you can always opt for a different grilled fish instead. Stick to the suggestions of whatever is going that day.

★ A Tasquinha
SEAFOOD €€

(262 551 945; Rua Adrião Batalha 54; mains €7.50-17.50; noon-3pm & 7-10.30pm Tue-Sun Carnival-New Year) This exceptionally friendly family affair has been running for 50-plus years, serving high-quality seafood in a pair of snug but prettily tiled dining rooms. Solo travellers delight: *arroz de marisco* (shellfish rice) for one person (€17.50)!

Sitiado
PORTUGUESE €€

(262 087 512; Rua Amadeu Guadêncio 2, Sítio; tapas €4.50-9.80, mains €9-16.50; noon-3.30pm & 7-11.45pm; 🛜) A modern *tasca* not content with following the crowd, this pleasant Sítio hotspot does elevated classic tapas along with a fun menu of Portuguese-bent surprises (braised smoked ham with fried eggs, beef with coriander, stewed chicken gizzards, black pudding with caramelised onions) and is one of Nazaré's few destinations with an emphasis on *cerveja artesanal* (craft beer).

Casa O Santo de Anibal Portugal
BAR

(262 085 128; Rua do Juncal 11; noon-11.30pm Jun-Sep, noon-11.30pm Tue-Sun Oct-May) An immensely enjoyable *cervejaria* (beer house) serving beer, wine and tasty seafood snacks (appetisers from €6) – especially recommended are the garlicky steamed *ameijoas* (clams). Grab a table on the pavement, or eat under the stone arches of the cosy interior rooms beside the bustling bar.

ℹ️ Information

Posto de Turismo (☎️262 561 194; www.
cm-nazare.pt; Avenida Vieira Giumarães,
Edifício do Mercado Municipal; ⏰9.30am-1pm
& 2.30-6pm Oct-Apr, to 7pm May, Jun & Sep,
9am-8pm Jul & Aug) In the front offices of
the food market as well as next door to Igreja
de Nossa Senhora da Nazaré in **Sítio** (☎️930
424 860; www.cm-nazare.pt; Largo de Nossa
Senhora da Nazaré, ⏰9.30am-1pm & 2.30-
6pm Oct-Apr, to 7pm May, Jun & Sep, 9am-8pm
Jul & Aug). Helpful, multilingual staff.

ℹ️ Getting There & Away

BUS

Rodoviária do Oeste (www.rodoviariadooeste.
pt) and **Rede Expressos** (www.rede-expressos.
pt) serve the following destinations several
times daily from Nazaré's **bus station** (☎️967
449 860; Avenida do Município), a couple of
blocks in from the ocean: Alcobaça (€2.30,
20 minutes), Leiria (express/local €7/4.45,
35 to 75 minutes), Lisbon (€12, 1¾ hours) and
Peniche (€10, 70 minutes).

TRAIN

The nearest train station is in **Valado da Frades**,
6km east of Nazaré.

ℹ️ Getting Around

A funicular, in operation since 1889, connects
the beach with Promontório do Sítio 110m
above. The trip costs €1.50 per ride or €5 for a
six-trip package.

Ascensor – Praia (Travessa do Elevador;
adult/child €1.50/1; ⏰7.30am-midnight Oct-
Jun, to 2am Jul-Sep)

Ascensor – Sítio (Rua do Horizonte 20; adult/
child €1.50/1; ⏰7.30am-midnight Oct-Jun, to
2am Jul-Sep)

Alcobaça

POP 17,800

Only 100km north of Lisbon, the little town
of Alcobaça has a charming if touristed centre with a little river and bijou bridges. All,
however, yields centre stage to the magnificent 12th-century Mosteiro de Santa Maria
de Alcobaça, one of Portugal's memorable
Unesco World Heritage Sites.

👁️ Sights

⭐ **Mosteiro de Santa
Maria de Alcobaça**   MONASTERY
(☎️262 505 120; www.mosteiroalcobaca.pt; Praça
25 de Abril; €6, with Tomar & Batalha €15, free first
Sun of the month to 2pm for residents, church free;

⏰9am-7pm Apr-Sep, to 6pm Oct-Mar) One of
Iberia's great monasteries utterly dominates
the town of Alcobaça. Hiding behind the imposing baroque facade lies a high, austere,
monkish church (free entry) with a forest of
unadorned 12th-century arches. But make
sure you visit the rest too: the atmospheric
refectory, vast dormitory and other spaces
bring back the Cistercian life, which, according to sources, wasn't quite as austere here
as it should have been.

The monastery was founded in 1153 by
Afonso Henriques, first king of Portugal,
honouring a vow he'd made after the Reconquista of Santarém in 1147. The monastery
estate became one of the richest and most
powerful in the country, apparently housing 999 monks, who held Mass nonstop in
shifts.

In the 18th century, however, it was the
monks' growing decadence that became
famous, thanks to the writings of 18th-cen-
tury travellers such as William Beckford,
who, allowing for his tendency to exagger-
ate, was shocked at the 'perpetual gorman-
dising...the fat waddling monks and sleek
friars with wanton eyes...'. The party ended
in 1834 with the dissolution of the religious
orders.

Much of the original facade of the
church was altered in the 17th and 18th
centuries. However, once you step inside,
the combination of Gothic ambition and
Cistercian austerity hits you immediately: the nave is a breathtaking 106m long
but only 23m wide, with huge pillars and
truncated columns. It is modelled on the
French abbey of Clairvaux.

Occupying the south and north transepts
are two intricately carved 14th-century
tombs, the church's greatest possessions,
which commemorate the tragic love story of Dom Pedro and Dona Inês de Castro.
Although the tombs themselves were badly
damaged by rampaging French troops in

ℹ️ MULTI-MONASTERY
TICKET

If you're planning to visit the monasteries at Alcobaça and Batalha, as well
as the Convento de Cristo in Tomar,
you can get (from any one of them) a
combined ticket for €15 (a saving of €3)
that will let you in to all three and is valid
for a week.

LOVE, POLITICS & REVENGE

As moving as *Romeo and Juliet* – and far more gruesome – is the tragic story of Dom Pedro. Son of the king, Dom Afonso IV, Pedro fell madly in love with his wife's Galician lady-in-waiting, Dona Inês de Castro, with whom he had several children. Even after the death of Pedro's wife, his father forbade Pedro from marrying Inês, wary of her Spanish family's potential influence. Suspicious nobles continued to pressure Dom Afonso IV until finally he sanctioned Inês' murder in 1355, unaware that the two lovers had already secretly married.

Two years later, when Pedro succeeded to the throne, he exacted his revenge by ripping out and eating the hearts of Inês' murderers. He then exhumed and crowned her body, and ordered the court to pay homage to his dead queen by kissing her decomposing hand.

The couple are buried in elaborate tombs in the Mosteiro de Santa Maria de Alcobaça (p285). Inês' tomb rests not on lions, but on the animal-like figures of the men who assassinated her.

search of treasure in 1811, they still show extraordinary narrative detail. The tombs are inscribed Até ao Fím do Mundo (until the end of the world) and, on Pedro's orders, placed foot to foot so that, when the time comes, they can rise up and see each other straight away.

Nearby, look at the remarkable clay figures in the chapel of St Bernard and the unusual arching in the ambulatory.

The grand kitchen, described by Beckford as 'the most distinguished temple of gluttony in all Europe', owes its immense size to alterations carried out in the 18th century, including a water channel built through the middle to divert wild fish right into the kitchen.

The adjacent refectory, huge and vaulted, is where the monks ate in silence while the Bible was read to them from the pulpit, reached by a photogenic arched staircase. The monks entered through a narrow door on their way to the refectory; those too fat to pass through were forced to fast.

The beautiful **Claustro do Silencio** (Cloister of Silence) dates from two eras: Dom Dinis built the intricate lower storey, with its arches and traceried stone circles, in the 14th century; the upper storey, typically Manueline in style, was added in the 16th century.

Off the northwestern corner of the cloister is the 18th-century **Sala dos Reis** (Kings' Room), so called because statues of practically all the kings of Portugal line the walls. Below them are *azulejo* friezes depicting stories relevant to the abbey's construction. Upstairs, make sure you see the vast vaulted dormitory.

✯ Festivals & Events

Cistermúsica MUSIC
(www.cistermusica.com) Now in its second decade, the Cistermúsica festival is held from late June to late July, and features classical concerts in the Alcobaça monastery and other local venues.

🛏 Sleeping & Eating

★Hostel Rossio Alcobaça HOSTEL €
(✍ 262 598 237; www.hostelrossioalcobaca.pt; Praça 25 de Abril 15; dm €16-17, d with/without bathroom from €40/32; 🛜) There are not many places left where you can enjoy a view of one of the world's top monastery sites from your hostel room. This spot, bang on the main plaza, has been delightfully restored. Clean, bright, minimalist-style rooms are set around a hexagonal design. Way-too-hip-for-Alcobaça owner Clara is a delight, as are the shared kitchen and terrace.

★Challet Fonte Nova BOUTIQUE HOTEL €€€
(✍ 262 598 300; www.challetfontenova.pt; Rua da Fonte Nova 8; s/d/ste €85/120/130; 🅿 ❄ 🛜) Set amid pretty gardens, this elegant, charming 19th-century chalet has grand common areas with gleaming wood floors, carpets and period furnishings. The main house is especially attractive: sumptuously decorated rooms with big plush beds, tall French windows, and a downstairs self-serve bar with billiard table. There's also a whitewashed modern annexe with suites and a small spa complex.

★Alcoa BAKERY €
(www.pastelaria-alcoa.com; Praça 25 de Abril 44; pastries €1.30-3; ⊗ 8am-7.30pm) You may

have seen it in Lisbon, but this heralded *pastelaria* (pastry shop) hails from Alcobaça, sitting front and centre across from the monastery hawking some of Portugal's most decadent *doces conventuais* (conventual sweets) since 1957. Loosen your belt: these award-winning cash-only pastries pack a wallop of sugar and satisfaction.

Superstars here include *cornucópias* (egg sweet in a hard-shell cone), *coroa de abadessa* (our favourite; a small cake made with almonds, hazelnuts, caramelised squash, sugars and egg yolks) and *torrão real* (more almonds, more eggs, more sugar but caramel!).

★**Restaurante António Padeiro**   PORTUGUESE €€
(📞262 582 295; www.facebook.com/restauranteantoniopadeiro.alcobaca; Rua Dom Maur Cocheril 27; mains €10-17; ⊙noon-3pm & 7-10pm) If the monks had not pigged out at the Alcobaça monastery (their gluttony was eventually noticed), they would have flocked to this wonderful, elegant-but-not-snobby spot. It's clocked up 70 years and for good reason. It boasts a superb atmosphere (traditional trinkets minus the kitsch), superquality fare from the kitchen and ultraprofessional service. The owners know their cuisine. As do the regular locals.

O Cabeço   PORTUGUESE €€
(📞914 500 202; www.ocabeco.pt; Rua Dona Elvina Machado 65; mains €9-16; ⊙12.30pm-2pm & 7.30-10pm Tue-Sat) This lovely spot, located on a hill behind Alcobaça in Bemposta, is an understated, modern, wooden-and-stone cabana with country-garden surrounds. It serves Portuguese dishes with contemporary flair, and is the perfect place to escape the monastery and plaza crowds. Warning: you'll want to spend time here. Reserve ahead.

Sabores da India   NORTH INDIAN €€
(📞920 109 137; www.facebook.com/saboresdaindiaofficial; Rua Mariana Coelho Bernardo 19; mains €8-19; ⊙11am-midnight Wed-Mon) This unexpected gem is the perfect cure to the Bacalhau Blues. Tucked away 1km or so outside the tourist zone in a residential complex, the flavours and colours of Punjab come alive in fiery curries, biryanis and tandoori dishes, all authentic and all immensely satisfying if you have been overdosing on Portuguese cuisine.

ℹ️ Information

Posto de Turismo (📞262 582 377; www.cm-alcobaca.pt; Rua 16 de Outubro 39-5; ⊙9am-12.30pm & 2-5.30pm Mon-Fri, 10am-12.30pm & 2-6pm Sat & Sun) In a street near the main plaza; very helpful and providing assistance in multiple languages.

ℹ️ Getting There & Away

Coming from Leiria it's possible to see both Batalha and Alcobaça in a single, carefully timed day on **Rodoviária do Oeste** (www.rodoviariadooeste.pt) buses. Note: most buses run less frequently on weekends. Destinations include Batalha (€3.30, 40 minutes, 11 per weekday), Leiria (€4 to €7, 50 minutes, seven per weekday), Porto do Mós (€3.30, 35 minutes, one to three per weekday), Nazaré (€2.30, 20 minutes, 18 daily). **Rede Expressos** (www.rede-expressos.pt) services Lisbon (€12, two hours, seven per weekday).

Batalha

POP 8500 / ELEV 120M

Towering above the rush-orange rooftops of tiny Batalha, the Unesco-listed Santa Maria da Vitória monastery transports visitors to another world, where solid rock has been carved into forms as delicate as snowflakes and as pliable as twisted rope. Among the supreme achievements of Manueline architecture, it draws admirers of architecture, history, religion and warfare from far and wide.

⊙ Sights

★**Mosteiro de Santa Maria da Vitória**   MONASTERY
(📞244 765 497; www.mosteirobatalha.pt; Largo Infante Dom Henrique; €6, with Alcobaça & Tomar €15, church free; ⊙9am-6.30pm Apr-Sep, to 6pm Oct-Mar) The extraordinary monastery of Batalha was built to commemorate the 1385 Battle of Aljubarrota (fought just south of here). Most of the monument was completed by 1434 in Flamboyant Gothic, but Manueline exuberance steals the show, thanks to additions made in the 15th and 16th centuries (the 'unfinished chapels').

At the Battle of Aljubarrota, around 6500 Portuguese, commanded by Dom Nuno Álvares Pereira and supported by a few hundred English soldiers, repulsed a 30,000-strong force of Juan I of Castile, who had come claiming the throne of João d'Avis. João called on the Virgin Mary for help and vowed to build a superb monastery in return for victory. Two years later he made good on his promise, as work began on this magnificent house of worship.

The glorious limestone exterior bristles with pinnacles and parapets, flying buttresses and balustrades, and late-Gothic carved windows, as well as octagonal chapels and massive columns. The spectacular western doorway's layered arches pack in apostles, angels, saints and prophets, all topped by Christ and the Evangelists.

The vast, vaulted Gothic interior is plain, long and high (the highest in Portugal), warmed by light from the deep-hued stained-glass windows. Some of the interior was originally painted. To the right as you enter is the intricate Capela do Fundador (Founder's Chapel), an achingly beautiful, lofty, star-vaulted square room lit by an octagonal lantern. In the centre is the joint tomb (the first pantheon to be built in Portugal) of João I and his English wife, Philippa of Lancaster, whose marriage in 1387 cemented the alliance that still exists between Portugal and England. The tombs of their four youngest sons line the south wall of the chapel, including that of Henry the Navigator (second from the right).

Afonso Domingues, master of works during the late 1380s, built the fabulous Claustro Real (Royal Cloister) in a Gothic style, but it's the later Manueline embellishments by the great Mateus Fernandes that really take your breath away. Every arch is a tangle of detailed stone carvings of Manueline symbols, such as armillary spheres and crosses of the Order of Christ, entwined with writhing vegetation, exotic flowers and marine motifs – corn and shells. Three graceful cypresses echo the shape of the Gothic spires atop the adjacent chapter house. (And we challenge you to spot the ancient graffiti on the walls!)

Anything would seem austere after the Claustro Real, but the simple Gothic Claustro de Dom Afonso V is like being plunged into cold water – sobering you up after all that frenzied decadence. Between the two cloisters is an interpretation centre.

To the east of the Claustro Real is the early-15th-century chapter house, Sala do Capítulo, containing a beautiful 16th-century stained-glass window. The huge vault was considered so potentially dangerous that prisoners on death row were employed to remove its supports. A guard of honour watches over the tomb of unknown soldiers (a Mozambican soldier and Flemish soldier from WWI).

The roofless Capelas Imperfeitas (Unfinished Chapels) are perhaps the most astonishing aspect of Batalha. Only accessible from outside the monastery, the octagonal mausoleum with its seven chapels was commissioned in 1437. However, the later Manueline additions by the architect Mateus Fernandes overshadow everything else.

Although Fernandes' plan was never finished, the staggering ornamentation is all the more dramatic for being open to the sky. Most striking is the 15m-high doorway, a mass of stone-carved thistles, ivy, flowers, snails and all manner of 'scollops and twistifications', as William Beckford noted. Dom Duarte can enjoy it for all eternity: his tomb, and that of his wife, lie opposite the door.

Batalha de Aljubarrota

Centro de Interpretação HISTORIC SITE
(www.fundacao-aljubarrota.pt; Avenida Nuno Álvares Pereira 120; adult/student/child/family €7/5/3.50/20; ⊙10am-5.30pm Tue-Sun) For Portuguese people Aljubarrota conjures up a fierce sense of national pride, a 1385 battle where they defied the odds to defeat the Castilian force and established the foundations for the Portuguese golden age. The entry fee to the modern interpretation centre here, 3km south of Batalha, might seem steep until you see the multimedia show, a no-expenses-spared blood-and-thunder half-hour medieval epic (showing at 11.30am, 3pm and 4.30pm, audio guide €3) that brings the whole thing to vivid life.

MCCB MUSEUM
(Museu da Comunidade Concelhia da Batalha; www.museubatalha.com; Largo Goa, Damão e Diu 4; adult/child €2.50/1.80; ⊙10am-1pm & 2-6pm Wed-Sun) This modern, award-winning municipal museum in the centre of town is well worth the visit, taking you through the prehistory and history of the region, including some well-presented Roman remains and sections on the Battle of Aljubarrota and Mosteiro de Santa Maria da Vitória's construction.

🍽 Sleeping & Eating

Pensão Gládius GUESTHOUSE €
(📱 244 765 760, 919 103 044; Travessia Doutor José Taibner 1; s/d without breakfast €25/30; 🛜) In the square right next to the monastery, friendly older proprietor Dona Eglantina runs this snug but attractive place (one of the 'old world' guesthouses that's independent of

'official' lists). It's got a vaguely alpine feel, with flower-filled window boxes and four spotless, modern rooms tucked under the eaves. The '80s time warp of a bar below can be fun.

⭐ **Hotel Casa do Outeiro**   HOTEL €€
(☑ 244 765 806; www.hotelcasadoouteiro. com; Largo Carvalho do Outeiro 4; s/d/tr/f from €64/69/89/153; P❄🅰🄿) This modern 23-room hotel with a guesthouse feel is awash in the whimsical and colourful artwork of the owner, who also makes some of the arts and crafts in the lobby shop. The rooms are all modern, commodious and attractive – set in bright colour schemes and many with balconies framing astonishing monastery views across the orange rooftops.

The excellent breakfast with homemade jams (also made by the owner) and a welcome drink on arrival are sweet bonuses. And did we mention the swimming pool, minigym and pool table? Rooms with view of the monastery cost €10 to €15 more.

⭐ **Burro Velho**   PORTUGUESE €€
(☑ 244 764 174; www.burrovelho.com; Rua Nossa Sra do Caminho 6A; mains €8.50-16.50; ⊗ noon-3pm & 7-10pm Mon-Sat, noon-3pm Sun; 🐾) Batalha's best, a bustling place serving up great modern Portuguese fare – seafood rices for two (€28 to €65), fresh catches of the day and a *bulhão pato*-style (with olive oil, coriander and garlic) salted cod 'cheeks' starter that will redefine your enthusiasm for *bacalhau*. Carry on later (until 2am; same menu) at the newer and trendier wine bar next door.

ℹ Information

Posto de Turismo (☑ 244 765 180; www. descobrirbatalha.pt; Praça Mouzinho de Albuquerque; ⊗ 10am-1pm & 2-6pm) The very helpful, enthusiastic Nelia has worked here for years and knows the lot. It faces the back of the monastery.

ℹ Getting There & Away

Buses with **Rodoviária do Lis** (www. rodoviariadolis.pt) and **Rede Expressos** (www. rede-expressos.pt) leave from the **bus stop** on Rua do Moinho da Via, near the Intermarché supermarket, behind the police station. Express services go to major cities, including Lisbon (€11.40, two hours) four to five times daily – buy tickets online or at **Cafe Frazão** (Rua António Cândido da Encarnação 22; ⊗ 6am-9pm Mon-Sat, to 1pm Sun) behind the church nearby. For

Alcobaça, Fátima, Leiria, Nazaré and Tomar, connections are few and schedules change frequently, though with forward planning it can be done. Tickets are purchased on board. See helpful Nelia at the Posto de Turismo (p289) for the rundown.

A **taxi** (Rua Doña Filipa de Lencastre) to Fátima costs around €18 (weekdays) to €22 (weekends).

Leiria

POP 55,000

Leiria is an agreeable mixture of medieval and modern, a lively university town built at the foot of a promontory fortified since Moorish times. The town's dramatically sited castle is a commanding presence above the narrow streets and red-tiled roofs of the historic centre, built along the lazy curves of the Rio Lis.

Dom Afonso III convened a *cortes* (Portugal's early parliament) here in 1254; Dom Dinis established his main residence in the castle in the 14th century; and in 1411 the town's sizeable Jewish community built Portugal's first paper mill. Modern-day Leiria has a pleasant, low-key urban buzz and makes a convenient base for visiting nearby sights, including Alcobaça, Batalha, Fátima and the Pinhal de Leiria – all easily accessible by bus.

◉ Sights

Castelo de Leiria   CASTLE
(www.cm-leiria.pt; Largo de São Pedro; adult/child €2.10/free; ⊗ 9.30am-6.30pm Apr-Sep, to 5.30pm Oct-Mar) Inside the castle walls is a peaceful garden, overgrown with tall trees, and the ruined but lovely Gothic Igreja de Nossa Senhora da Penha, originally built in the 12th century and rebuilt by João I in the early 15th century. It has beautiful leaflike carvings over one arch (and don't miss the fascinating *marcas de canteiro*, unique insignias chiselled on the bricks to indicate which builder laid it and was due payment by the king).

The castle's most spectacular feature, however, is a gallery with stone seats. It provides a fantastic vantage point over the town's roofs, though the structure is largely the result of restoration. The castle sits upon a clifftop site that got its first *castelo* in the time of the Moors; it was captured by Afonso Henriques in 1135. Be sure to climb the recently re-opened tower; it exhibits replicas

Leiria

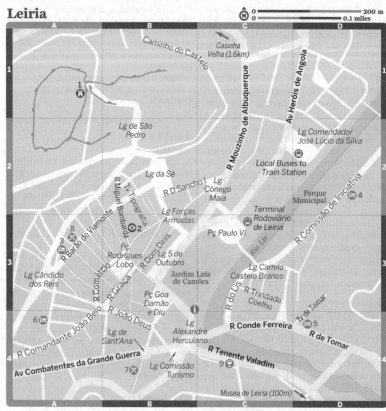

Leiria

⊙ Sights
1	Castelo de Leiria	A1
2	Centro de Diálogo Intercultural de Leiria	B3

🛏 Sleeping
3	Atlas Hostel	A3
4	Eurosol Residence	D2
5	Hotel Dom Dinis	D4

6	La Palma	A4

⊗ Eating
7	Ao Largo	B4
8	Tasca 7	A3

⊕ Drinking & Nightlife
	Atlas Hostel	(see 3)
9	Mulligan's	C4

of medieval costumes, including armour, helmet and swords.

Museu de Leiria　　　　MUSEUM
(☑ 244 839 677; www.cm-leiria.pt; Santo Agostinho Convent, Rua Tenente Valadim 41; adult/child €2.10/free, incl Museu do Moinho de Papel €5; ☉ 9.30am-5.30pm) Opened in November 2015, this lovely museum celebrates Leiria and its region. Housed in the former Santo Agostinho Convent, the exhibits span everything from the geological (a rock shelter in the Lapedo Valley from 10,000 years ago) to information on the Leiria city and diocese. The mishmash of themes and eras is saved by the excellent curation with distinct installations, plus descriptions in English. Audio guides are available in English, French and Spanish.

Centro de Diálogo Intercultural de Leiria　　　　HISTORIC SITE
(CDIL; www.cm-leiria.pt; Rua Miguel Bombarda 15; ☉ 9.30am-12.30pm & 2-5.30pm Mon-Fri,

2-5.30pm Sat) FREE The gorgeously restored 18th century Igreja da Misericórdia was built in late-Mannerist style on the plot of land where an even older cathedral dating to 1544 once stood and, before that, Leiria's medieval synagogue, which catered to a thriving Jewish quarter here from the 13th to 15th centuries. Today, the space is the centrepiece of the city's new Centre for Intercultural Dialogue dedicated to highlighting the value of the coexistence of Christianity, Judaism and Islam.

🛏 Sleeping

Atlas Hostel   HOSTEL €

(☑ 917 460 810; www.atlashostel-leiria.com; Rua Barão de Viamonte 59; dm €18, d with/without bathroom €42/32; 🛜) Leiria's first hostel, co-owned by the bassist in the city's biggest alternative band (Nice Weather for Ducks), is chock-full of character – from original hardwood flooring to a bevy of antiques and art (exhibitions change monthly). Four and six-bed dorms follow suit. It's a bohemian-leaning, internationally minded gathering space that transforms into the city's coolest bar (p292) in the evenings.

The same owners also opened La Palma, which might be better for those who actually want to sleep!

La Palma   HOSTEL €

(☑ 917 460 810; www.facebook.com/Lapalmahostelleiria; Rua Artur de Paiva 16; d with/without bathroom €42/32; 🛜🏊) Sharing a phone number and reception with its sibling, Atlas, this more upscale hostel inhabits a 120-year-old mansion with an epic central wooden staircase. Original hardwood flooring, crown mouldings and dark blue walls adorned with Moroccan rugs are both austere and bohemian.

There is a guest kitchen on both floors and a small but sure-to-be-emphatically-used pool.

Hotel Dom Dinis   HOTEL €

(☑ 244 815 342; www.hotelddinis.pt; Rua de Tomar 3; s/d/tr €35/45/57; 🅿❄🛜) Just across the river from the old town, this modern, compact place offers simple but spot-on rooms and renovated common areas (lobby, breakfast room, reception). Some rooms have balconies and wonderful views over the river and up to the castle. The roof terrace is a super spot on a sunny day.

Eurosol Residence   APARTMENT €€

(☑ 244 860 460; www.eurosol.pt; Rua Commisão de Iniciativa 13; s/d studio apt €69/79, 1-/2-bedroom apt €89/145; 🅿❄🛜🏊) Downtown Leiria's high-end option has comfortable if unexceptional business-class (studio, one- and two-bedroom) mini-apartments with kitchens, many with pleasant views across parkland to the castle. The rooftop bar and terrace affords spectacular castle views.

🍴 Eating & Drinking

Tasca 7   PORTUGUESE €

(☑ 962 238 621; Rua Maria da Fonte 1-3; meals €6.50-8; ⊙ noon-3pm & 5pm-midnight) A mere block and a half from the main square but feeling like a million miles away, Estrela (don't call her 'Doña!') offers just two dishes per day at her simple, five-table *tasca*. There's no menu (and no English!) but Estrela is as sweet as her *pudim* (not crotchety like so many at traditional restaurants) and runs through the dishes slowly.

Think baked chicken, *bacalhau espiritual* (baked salted cod with cream, onions, carrots and cheese) and other home-cooked deliciousness. 'Meals' include starter, beer or wine, dessert and coffee. At dinner, she does a changing menu of *petiscos*, all revealed verbally. Go here now. Cash only.

★ Ao Largo   PORTUGUESE €€

(☑ 911 555 323; www.facebook.com/aolargoleiria; Rua Dr Correia Mateus 36; tapas €1-7, mains €8-13; ⊙ 12.30-3.30pm & 7-11pm Tue-Thu, to midnight Fri & Sat, 12.30-4pm Sun; 🛜) Leiria's most enjoyable spot comes courtesy of friendly wine-lover Miguel, who opened a restaurant with his sister and his girlfriend, combined their skills as a journalist, teacher and designer with a common love of food and drink, and created a wonderful modern *tasca* that excels at everything it does. Don't miss the mushroom *feijoada* and the signature sesame-crusted tuna with honey mustard.

Even the *couvert*, with local Giesta cheese spiced in olive oil, is creative and fantastic. Let Miguel guide your wine picks as well. Reservation essential.

★ Casinha Velha   PORTUGUESE €€€

(☑ 244 855 355; www.casinhavelha.com; Rua Professores Portelas 23; mains €17.50-21.50; ⊙ noon-3pm & 7.30-10pm Mon & Wed-Sat, 12.30-3pm Sun; 🛜) The best culinary experience in central Portugal begins insanely: an epic cow's, sheep's and goat's cheese cart, arranged regionally, along with black pork sausages, awaits at your table – you cut your own portions and pay what you cut (per kg €70, served with homemade pumpkin jam, bread and olive oil).

Mains? Let's just say this: wow! The duck served in the *arroz de pato* (duck rice), with bacon, pineapple and dried fruits, is raised on the restaurant's own farm. The baked baby goat is also massively popular. The sommelier is a master, neatly pairing every bite with a memorable wine choice. Wait... save room for dessert (the *creme de leite*, the Portuguese version of crème brûlée, is a beautiful mess on a plate). You won't forget this meal in a hurry – this is what people are talking about when they rave about Portuguese cuisine. It's 2.2km north of the main square in the sleepy suburbs.

★ **Atlas Hostel**   BAR
(www.atlashostel-leiria.com; Rua Barão de Viamonte 59; ⊘8am-2am; 🛜) Leiria's coolest hostel somehow harvested the city's hankering for a culturally minded space for forward-thinking international hipsters, yielded its common areas to a cavalcade of artists, musicians, alterna-hipsters, punk-rock misfits and other bohemian types, and transformed it into the city's most interesting bar. Check its calendar monthly for live gigs, which can get a bit mad.

Mulligan's   IRISH PUB
(www.mulligans.pt; Rua Tenente Valadim 10; ⊘6.30am-2am Mon-Sat; 🛜) This convivial Irish pub has plenty of Jameson and Bushmills, along with a decent selection of craft beer, including extensive stock of Lisbon's 8ª Colina, its own IPA and red ale, and a few Belgian stragglers.

ℹ Information

Posto de Turismo (📞 244 848 770; www. turismodocentro.pt; Jardim Luís de Camões; ⊘9.30am-5.30pm Mon-Fri, 9.30am-1pm & 2-5.30pm Sat & Sun) Leiria's tourism information is run by the region, not the municipality. Provides a free town map.

ℹ Getting There & Away

BUS
Rodoviária do Lis (www.rodoviariadolis.pt) and **Rede Expressos** (www.rede-expressos. pt) both serve the **bus station** (📞 244 822 505; Largo 5 de Outubro) in the heart of town. Buses run every hour or two to Alcobaça (€4 to €7, 50 minutes), Batalha (€2.20, 20 minutes),

Coimbra (€9.20, 50 minutes), Fátima (€3.30 to €6, 25 to 45 minutes), Lisbon (€12.60, two hours) and Nazaré (€4.45 to €7, 35 minutes to 1¼ hours).

TRAIN
Leiria is on the train line that runs about three times daily from Figueira da Foz (€7.05, one hour, two daily) to the Mira Sintra-Meleças station near Lisbon (€10.65, 2½ to 3½ hours, three daily). The **train station** (www.cp.pt; Largo da Estação) is 4km northwest of the town centre; local Bus 1 'Circular Urbana Sentido Estação' runs to the train station frequently from Largo Comendador José Lúcio da Silva (€1.30, 10 minutes). A taxi costs about €5 to €6.

Local Buses to Train Station (📞 244 735 735; www.mobilis.pt; Largo Comendador José Lúcio da Silva)

Pinhal de Leiria

First planted by a forward-looking monarch some 700 years ago, the Pinhal de Leiria was once a vast forest of towering pines whose fragrance and stippled shade made this one of the loveliest stretches of Portugal's Atlantic coast.

However, over 86% of the 100 sq km protected area along the coast was lost in a devastating fire in October 2017, and 49 people, 1500 homes and 500 businesses were lost. Many of the narrow roads and well-maintained bike paths cutting through the forest are now blocked, although you can still access three really excellent beaches and three resort towns: São Pedro de Moel, 20km west of Leiria, which survived mostly unscathed; Praia da Vieira, 16km north of São Pedro along the coastal highway; and Pedrógão, 2km further north.

🛏 Sleeping & Eating

São Pedro de Moel's accommodation is the most appealing of the three towns.

Orbitur – Săp Pedro do Moel   CAMPGROUND €
(📞 244 599 168; www.orbitur.pt; Rua Volta do Sete 2430, São Pedro de Moel; sites per adult/tent/car €5.70/6.65/5.90; 🅿🛜⛱) In among the pine trees but in the centre of town, this well-equipped, pretty site includes a swimming pool, disabled facilities and a playground. Two-/four-/five-person bungalows cost €73.40/82.50/91.50 in June.

Hotel Mar e Sol   HOTEL €€
(📞 244 590 000; www.hotelmaresol.com; Avenida da Liberdade 1, São Pedro de Moel; r €90-135;

⊞ ✳ 🛜) This well-refurbished hotel is comfortable and sparkling clean, with minimalist modern decor. It's showing ever-so-slight signs of wear, but is in a great position; the best rooms, with balconies and grand views over the heaving sea, cost €35 to €45 extra. There's a rooftop sun-deck, and a gym and spa complex (costing extra).

O Pai dos Frangos PORTUGUESE €€
(☑244 599 158; www.facebook.com/paidos frangos; Praia Velha; ⊘10am-late Jun-Sep, 10am-10pm Tue-Sun Oct-May; 🛜) 'The Father of Chickens' sits in splendid isolation right on the fabulous sands of Praia Velha, 1km north of São Pedro de Moel. Specialties include *arroz de marisco* (saucy seafood rice) and *terramar* (a massive dish of beef, lobster, clams and french fries for a minimum of two people; €25 per person). Plus, yes, there's grilled chicken.

★ Estrela do Mar SEAFOOD €€€
(☑244 599 245; Avenida Marginal, São Pedro de Moel; mains €7.50-28, fish per kg €25-130; ⊘noon-2am Jul & Aug, noon-3pm & 6-11pm Sep-Jun) In an utterly memorable position on the water, this classic seafood place scores top marks for location: the dining room is right over the waves above São Pedro's town beach. Prices here partly reflect the unbeatable view, but the quality and atmosphere are great. And there's *massada* (lobster stew with pasta and tomatoes).

ℹ Information

You'll find seasonal tourism offices in **São Pedro de Moel** (www.cm-mgrande.pt; Praça 25 de Abril; ⊘10am-1pm & 2-6pm Tue-Sun Jul-Sep) and **Praia da Vieira** (☑969 281 960; Av dos Pescadores; ⊘9am-9pm Jul & Aug, 9am-noon & 2-7pm Sep-Jun), the latter working out of reception at Parque de Campismo da Praia da Vieira for the foreseeable future. Outside the summer high season, you'll find Marinha Grande's main branch inside the Museu do Vidro.

ℹ Getting There & Away

From Leiria there are at least nine daily buses Monday to Saturday to São Pedro de Moel (€3.15, 40 minutes) and Praia da Vieira (€3.35, 45 minutes); from Marinha Grande to São Pedro de Moel, at least 12 from Monday to Saturday (€2.20, 15 minutes). Buses drop off considerably on Sunday.

If driving from Leiria, follow signs for Marinha Grande first.

Fátima
POP 11,600 / ELEV 320M

Whatever your beliefs, you can't help but be impressed by the vast reserves of faith that every year lead as many as six million people to the glade where, on 13 May 1917, the Virgin Mary is said to have first appeared to three awestruck peasant children. Where sheep once grazed there are now two huge basilicas on opposite ends of a vast 1km-long esplanade.

Before this event, there was nothing here (little can grow on limestone, which is what the area is made up of). These days, it's another story.

For Catholic pilgrims Fátima has a magnetic appeal like few places on earth, and whatever your faith, or otherwise, a trip here will provide you with new insights into Portugal's religious culture.

Fátima is packed with boarding houses and restaurants for the pilgrim masses, plus hundreds of shops crowded with glow-in-the-dark Virgins and busts of the Pope.

⊙ Sights

★ Santuário de Fátima CHRISTIAN SITE
(☑249 539 600; www.fatima.pt; Apartado 31) **FREE** It's difficult to believe that a century ago, this was rocky pastureland outside an insignificant village. This vast complex is now one of Catholicism's major shrines; the focus of enormous devotion and pilgrimage. At the eastern end is the 1953 Basílica de Nossa Senhora do Rosário de Fátima, a triumphantly sheer-white building with colonnade reminiscent of St Peter's. Nearby, the Capela das Aparições (Chapel of the Apparitions) marks the site where the Virgin appeared five times in 1917.

At the precinct's western end is the Basílica da Santíssima Trindade. In between is a massive space where the crowds gather.

The Capela das Aparições is the focus of the most intense devotion. Supplicants who have promised penance (for example, in return for helping a loved one who is sick, or to signify a particularly deep conversion) shuffle on their knees across the vast esplanade, following a long marble runway polished smooth by previous penitents). Near the chapel is a blazing pyre where people light candles in prayer (most just toss them in the fire due to heat and space concerns). The candles themselves range in price from €0.50 to €2.70, sold on the honour system, and candle lighting queue wait times can top half a day on the holiest of days. The sound of hundreds of candles is like a rushing waterfall.

Inside the older church, the Basílica de Nossa Senhora do Rosário de Fátima, attention is focused on the tombs of the three children, Os Três Pastorinhos (the three little shepherds): Francisco (died 1919, aged 11) and Jacinta (died 1920, aged 10), both victims of the flu epidemic, were beatified in 2000 and canonised in 2017. Lúcia, the third witness of the apparition, entered a convent in Coimbra in 1928, where she died in 2005. Her beatification is underway.

The new basilica, Basílica da Santíssima Trindade, was inaugurated in 2007, and, while impressive, has something of a conference-centre feel. A central passageway hung with golden angels leads to a long etched-glass window spelling out scriptural verses in dozens of languages. Running around the edges of the monumental, round marble structure are 12 9m bronze doors, each with a biblical quote dedicated to one of Jesus' disciples. Inside, the impersonal feel is redeemed by Irish artist Catherine Green's striking altarpiece depicting a wild-haired and gaunt Crucifixion, backed by Slovenian artist Marko Ivan Rupnik's beautiful mosaic work.

At the sanctuary entrance is a segment of the Berlin Wall, a tribute to 'God's part in the fall of communism'.

Masses are held (in Portuguese) regularly, often in the Capelinha das Aparições; and there is a beautiful nightly candlelight procession at 10pm from April to October – check at the information booth near the chapel.

Museu de Arte Sacra e Etnologia   MUSEUM
(☏ 249 539 470; www.consolata.pt; Rua Francisco Marto 52; adult/child €4.50/2.50; ⊙ 10am-1pm & 2-6pm Tue-Sun Apr-Oct, to 5pm Nov-Mar) The most interesting of Fátima's several religious exhibitions and museums, this has a wide display of religious art and artefacts from around the world, as well as small but interesting exhibitions on African tribal weaponry.

Grutas da Moeda   CAVE
(☏ 244 703 838; www.grutasmoeda.com; Rua das Grutas da Moeda, São Mamede; adult/child €6/3, combo ticket with Centro de Interpretação €9/3; ⊙ 9am-5pm Oct-Mar, to 6pm Apr-Jun, to 7pm Jul-Sep) These underground caves, 2km northwest of Fátima, are part of the surrounding limestone massif. They were discovered in

1971 when two hunters chased a fox that disappeared into a hole. Visitors can enter the caves (which are atmospherically lit and are an extraordinary 18°C), descending via steps to a depth of 45m on a 350m circuit. It won't ping the 'wow, the best thing ever' scale, though it's interesting. Tours are fully guided (English, German and French guides available; 35 minutes).

🛏 Sleeping & Eating

Hotel Coração de Fátima   BOUTIQUE HOTEL €
(☏ 249 531 433; https://coracaodefatima.fatima-hotels.com; Rua Cónego Manuel Nunes Formigão 14; s/d/tr from €40/50/70; P ❄ 🛜) This chic place, revamped in 2016, offers a dazzle of personality by Fátima standards. The style of the plush and colourful lobby carries on to the rooms, which boast contemporary window treatments, design-forward and bright decor and modern bathrooms. Front desk staff are some of central Portugal's most helpful and enthusiastic; and it sits about 50m off the southeastern flank of the sanctuary.

★ O Crispim   PORTUGUESE €€
(☏ 249 532 781; www.ocrispim.com; Rua S João Eudes 23; meat per kg €21-34, seafood per kg €39-72.50; ⊙ noon-4pm Tue, noon-4pm & 7-11pm Wed-Sun; 🛜) It's worth seeking this place out for an atmosphere full of good cheer without any ostentatious piety. It's a comfortably rustic sort of place serving house wine in wooden tankards, and whose speciality is grilled meats – Iberian pork, and succulent veal from the north of Portugal (Mirandela), flame-grilled on the back patio. Prices are by weight, but are reasonable.

ℹ Information

Fátima's **tourist information post** (☏ 249 531 139; www.turismodocentro.pt; Avenida Dr José Silva 213; ⊙ 9am-1pm & 2-5pm) is set up in a modern building near the sanctuary – look for the 12m-high red heart (the world's largest steel heart), erected in 2017 to commemorate the town's 100th anniversary.

The Santuário de Fátima itself has its own dedicated **tourist information** (☏ 249 539 600; www.fatima.pt; Apartado 31; ⊙ 9am-6.30pm May-Oct, to 6pm Nov-Apr) as well.

ℹ Getting There & Away

The focus of the pilgrimages, the district known as Cova da Iria, is just east of the A1 motorway. Several major roads ring the area, including Avenida Dom José Alves Correia da Silva to the south, where the **bus station** (☑ 249 531 611) is located. Parking lots in the vicinity are free.

Fátima's train station is 21km east: buses are a much better option.

BUS

Fátima (sometimes called Cova da Iria on timetables) is a stop on most major north–south bus runs and is better connected than many towns due to its worldwide popularity among Catholics. **Rede Expressos** (www.rede-expressos.pt) serves Coimbra (€11.50, one to 1¼ hours), Lisbon (€12.80, 1½ hours), Porto (€18, two hours) and Santarém (€9.60, 50 minutes). **Rodoviária do Tejo** (www.rodotejo.pt) has buses heading to Batalha (€2.45, 20 minutes), Leiria (€3.30, 25 to 45 minutes) and Tomar (€4, 45 minutes). **Alsa** (www.alsa.com) heads to Salamanca (Spain; €45, 8 hours). Weekend services are severely limited.

Porto de Mós

POP 6000 / ELEV 260M

Dominated by a 13th-century hilltop castle, Porto de Mós is an untouristy town on the little Rio Lena that makes a good launch pad for exploring the mountains and caves of the adjacent Parque Natural das Serras de Aire e Candeeiros.

Porto de Mós was a major Roman settlement, whose residents used the Lena to ferry millstones from a nearby quarry. The region remains an important centre for quarrying the black-and-white stones used in *calçada portuguesa,* the mosaic-style pavements seen throughout Portugal.

◎ Sights & Activities

Castelo de Porto de Mós　　　CASTLE
(www.municipio-portodemos.pt; Rua do Castelo 3; over/under 25yr €1.50/0.80; ☺10am-12.30pm & 2-6pm Tue-Sun May-Sep, to 5.30pm Oct-Apr) The green-towered castle was originally a Moorish stronghold. Conquered definitively in 1148 by Dom Afonso Henriques, it was largely rebuilt in 1450 and again after the 1755 earthquake. These days it's too pristine to be convincingly medieval, but is fun to climb around and has pleasant views across the valley to the Serras de Aire e Candeeiros. Stick around until closing and watch them lock up with a key the size of your forearm.

Ecopista　　　WALKING
(www.municipio-portodemos.pt) Opened in 2012, this neat gravel trail heads along former railway tracks from the days when small trains shunted coal from the Mina São Pedro. It's

QUINTA DE RIO ALCAIDE

For a peaceful retreat from Estremadura & Ribatejo's bustling beaches and Unesco World Heritage sites, head for the **Quinta de Rio Alcaide** (☑968 434 115, 244 482 207; www.quintarioalcaide. com; Rua do Catadouro 528, Rio Alcaide; d €45-60; 🅿🌊). About 1km southeast of sleepy Porto de Mós, this rustic inn set in a converted 18th-century paper mill boasts a charming array of rooms and apartments, including one in a hilltop windmill, and another that, in 1973, was the meeting place for Portuguese captains plotting the Revolution of the Carnations. Even the smallest room (Lagar) is atmospheric – with stone walls and plenty of space – a perfect hideaway for hermits! The grounds feature a pool, citrus trees, hiking trails and cascading stream.

around 13km along a circular track carved into the mountainside and providing great views over Porto de Mós and surrounds.

🛏 Sleeping & Eating

Dom Lambuças　　　PORTUGUESE €
(☑925 470 951; Rua Monsenhor José Cacela, Alcaria; meals €6-8.50; ☺11am-late Wed-Mon; 🖳) In the small village of Alcaria, this welcoming and very genuine old-school *petisqueiria* (place selling huge portions of *petiscos,* or tapas) with its red awnings gets the thumbs up for all things local and of high quality. For lunch, a few simple, home-cooked meals change daily; in the evenings, snacks and tapas. Fabulous value.

Adega do Luis　　　PORTUGUESE €€
(☑964 103 287; www.adegadoluis.pt; Rua Principal 650, Livramento; mains €8.75-16; ☺12.30-3pm & 7-10pm Wed-Mon) Some 3km southeast of Porto de Mós, this delightful (if touristy) place with high ceilings, stone walls and a roaring fire in the brick oven serves grilled bacon, lamb chops, roasted goat, Iberian pork and *picanha* (rump steak), with pear tart for dessert.

ⓘ Information

Posto de Turismo (☑244 499 600; www. municipio-portodemos.pt; Alameda Dom Afonso Henriques, Jardim Municipal; ☺10am-1pm & 2-6pm Mon-Sat) Near the town's main roundabout in the building marked 'Espaço Jovem'; pick up the yearly updated *Percursos Pedestres e BTT*, a useful booklet on walks and bike paths in Parque Natural das Serras de Aire e Candeeiros and around.

ℹ Getting There & Away

Rodoviária do Lis (www.rodoviariadolis.pt) runs two to three buses each weekday to/from Leiria (€3.30, 45 minutes) via Batalha (€2.30, 15 minutes). There are also up to three daily buses to Alcobaça (€3.30, 35 minutes). The **bus stop** (Av Francisco Sá Carneiro) is next to Mercado Municipal (the handwritten schedule is inside the market, next to the vet office).

Parque Natural das Serras de Aire e Candeeiros

With its barren limestone heights crisscrossed by hiking trails, this natural park east of Porto de Mós is a popular and very beautiful place for outdoor pursuits.

Once the haunt of dinosaurs, the park is famous for its cathedral-like caves, but above ground it's also scenic, particularly the high Planalto de Santo António (starting 2km south of the Grutas de Santo António). Gorse- and olive-grove-covered hills are divided by an irregular grid of dry-stone walls and threaded by cattle trails, all making for tempting rambles.

◉ Sights

Monumento Natural das Pegadas dos Dinossáurios ARCHAEOLOGICAL SITE
(☑ 249 530 160; www.pegadasdedinossaurios. org; Estrada de Fátima, Bairro; adult/child €3/2; ☺ 10am-12.30pm & 2-6pm Tue-Sun, to 8pm Sat & Sun Mar-Sep; 🅼) On the N357 10km south of Fátima in the village of Bairro, this extraordinary quarry is one of the most important locations for sauropod prints in the world, with more than a thousand individual prints. Visits start with a 20-minute video in Portuguese, followed by a 1.5km walk around the quarry, first seeing the prints from above then walking among them.

These, the oldest and longest sauropod tracks in the world, record walks in the mud 175 million years ago. The dinos would have been stepping through carbonated mud, later transformed into limestone. As you walk across the slope you can clearly see the large elliptical prints made by the hind feet and the smaller, half-moon prints made by the forefeet.

Fórnea CANYON
(www.municipio-portodemos.pt; Chão das Pias) FREE Don't miss stunning Fórnea, Europe's largest natural amphitheatre (around 1km in diameter) in the middle of the limestone park. You can enter from two directions but must go on foot. The first entrance is signed at Alcaria road. Park at the snack bar; it's a 20-minute walk to the base. To enter from the top side for incredible views, head to Chão das Pias village. A sign shows the way (best to ask); the site is due east – a 300m walk.

Grutas de Mira de Aire CAVES
(☑ 244 440 322; www.grutasmiradaire.com; Avenida Luciano Justo Ramos 470, Mira de Aire; adult/child €6.80/4; ☺ 9.30am-8pm Jul & Aug, 9.30am-7pm Jun & Sep, 9.30am-6pm Apr-May, 9.30am-5.30pm Oct-Mar; 🅼) Portugal's largest cave system, 14km southeast of Porto de Mós, is very commercial and old-fashioned, although the caves themselves are impressive. The 45-minute tour's spiralling 110m descent leads through psychedelically lit chambers to a final cavern containing a lake with a rather hokey fountain display. There's also a children's zoo and an aquapark here. There are three Rodotejo buses weekdays from Porto de Mós (€2.65, 35 minutes).

Grutas de Alvados & Grutas de Santo António CAVES
(☑ 249 841 876; www.grutasalvados.com; Estrada das Grutas – Alto de Alvados; adult/child per cave €6/3.80, both caves €9.40/6.40; ☺ 10am-6.30pm Jul & Aug, to 5pm Sep-Jun) Discovered in 1964, these caves are the spiky smaller cousins of Mira de Aire, with similarly disco-flavoured lighting. These caves are about 15km southeast of Porto de Mós, and 2km and 3.5km, respectively, south of the N243 from Porto de Mós to Mira de Aire.

Outside high season, you must go to Grutas de Santo António first to arrange a visit to Grutas de Alvados.

⛏ Sleeping

Pousada de Juventude Alvados HOSTEL €
(☑ 244 441 202; www.pousadasjuventude.pt; Barreira de Água, Alvados; dm €14, d €38, f with/without bathroom €65/56; ☺ Dec-Oct; 🅿🛜) This friendly, sparkling, modern (if institutional) place 8km southeast of Porto de Mós has four-bed dorms and doubles with

private bathrooms, as well as kitchen and wheelchair-accessible facilities. The helpful and long-standing manager, Joana, can give you the rundown of what's in the area. Buses from Leiria (€4, 55 minutes) stop out front twice daily on weekdays. The 6pm check-in is infuriating, however.

Cooking & Nature Emotional Hotel DESIGN HOTEL €€€
(☑244 447 000; www.cookinghotel.com; Rua Asseguia das Lages 181, Alvados; d €159-169; P✴⛄❄) This boutique hotel is located in Alvados, a quaint rural village. Each of the rooms is whimsically decorated in line with an emotion: Meditation, Melancholy, Fun, Nostalgia etc. It's clever, though the design elements are hardly understated. The result is a blast of design gimmicks from the sublime (unique rooms with vistas) to the less so (plaques in English lettering).

❶ Information

The **Park Headquarters** (ICNF; Instituto da Conservação da Natureza e das Florestas; ☑243 999 480; www.icnf.pt; Rua Dr Augo César Silva Ferreira; ◷9am-noon & 2-7pm Mon-Fri) is in the town of Rio Maior, south of the park. There's also good info at tourist information (p295) in Porto de Mós.

❶ Getting There & Away

Parque Natural das Serras de Aire e Candeeiros can be tricky to get to: this is one spot you might like to explore with your own wheels.

RIBATEJO

Literally meaning 'Above the Tejo', Ribatejo is the only Portuguese province that doesn't border either Spain or the open ocean. A string of Templar castles are proof of its strategic importance, though these days its clout is economic, thanks to industry along the Tejo and the rich agricultural plains that spread out from the river's banks. This is also bull country – most of Portugal's fighters are bred in and around the capital, Santarém.

Santarém

POP 29,200 / ELEV 110M

Contemplating the staggering views from Santarém's Portas do Sol atop the old town walls, it's easy to understand why Roman,

Visigoth, Moorish and Portuguese armies all wanted to claim this strategic stronghold above the Rio Tejo. Dom Afonso Henriques' storming of these heights in 1147 marked a turning point in the Reconquista and quickly became the stuff of Portuguese national legend.

A group of beautiful Gothic buildings recalls Santarém's glory days, though it was quickly eclipsed by Lisbon. These days the traditional centre is worth a visit, with its venerable stores and workshops still functioning amid a general air of genteel decay, plus the heart-lifting vistas. What it lacks in accommodation options it makes up for with its atmospheric restaurants.

History

One of the most important cities of Lusitania under Julius Caesar, and prized by the Moors under the name Xantarim for almost 400 years, Santarém already had centuries of history under its belt before passing to Portuguese rule in 1147. So great was Dom Afonso Henriques' joy at conquering this legendarily impenetrable citadel that he built the magnificent Mosteiro de Santa Maria de Alcobaça in gratitude.

◉ Sights

★**Casa Museu Passos Canavarro** MUSEUM
(☑243 325 709; www.fundacaopassoscanavarro.pt; Largo da Alcáçova 1; adult/child €5/free; ◷10am-1pm & 3-6pm Tue-Sun) Right by the Portas do Sol and sharing some of the same privileged views, this is a unique place to

Santarém

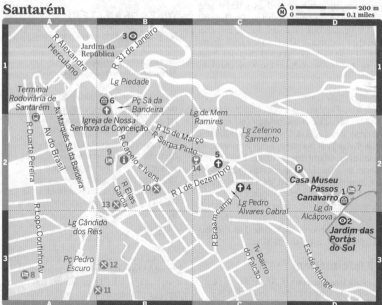

Santarém

◎ Top Sights
1 Casa Museu Passos Canavarro D2
2 Jardim das Portas do Sol D3

◎ Sights
3 Convento de São Francisco B1
4 Igreja da Santa Maria Graça C2
5 Igreja de Marvila C2
6 Museu Diocesano de Santarém B1

🛏 Sleeping
7 Casa da Alcáçova D2

8 Cereal Vitória Hotel A3
9 Santarém Hostel B2

✕ Eating
10 Pigalle B2
11 Taberna do Quinzena B3
12 Taberna O Balcão B3
13 Tascá B2

◉ Drinking & Nightlife
14 Ponto G C2

visit for lovers of art and beauty. The historic house, once home to 19th-century liberal politician Passos Manuel, is stocked with artistic treasures and curios, from Japanese furniture and *netsuke* (miniature sculptures) to 16th-century maps and collections of 20th-century art.

★ **Jardim das Portas do Sol**   GARDENS
(Garden of the Gates of the Sun; Largo do Alcáçova 1; ⊙8am-11pm May-Sep, to 8pm Oct-Apr) **FREE** Occupying the site of the Moorish citadel, the Portas do Sol garden offers utterly majestic views over the Rio Tejo and the great spread of plains emanating from it. The garden's shady walks make a fine option for a picnic

or afternoon linger. It's particularly spectacular at sundown.

Igreja de Marvila   CHURCH
(Largo de Marvila; ⊙9am-12.30pm & 2-5.30pm Wed-Sun) **FREE** Dating from the 12th century but with 16th-century additions, this endearing little church has a fine, twisted Manueline doorway, while the interior is completely awash in brilliant, dramatically patterned *azulejos* dating from the 17th century.

Museu Diocesano de Santarém   MUSEUM
(www.museudiocesanodesantarem.pt; Praça Sá da Bandeira; €4; ⊙10am-1pm & 2-6pm Mon & Wed-Fri, to 7pm Sat & Sun) This small but excellent museum, in a former Jesuit college

adjoining the cathedral, holds a lovely collection of restored religious artworks from its diocese. Around 200 works span the 13th to 19th centuries, and descriptions are in English. The oldest piece is a tempera painting of the Annunciation, and there is a most remarkable statue of Christ, depicted in a rare pose, half on and half off the cross.

Convento de São Francisco   MONASTERY
(Rua 31 de Janeiro; €2; ⊗9am-12.30pm & 2-5.30pm Wed-Sun) This restored 13th-century Franciscan monastery is a fine example of Portuguese Gothic. Especially lovely is the cloister, with graceful twinned columns and arches. It's also a venue for temporary exhibitions.

Igreja da Santa Maria Graça   CHURCH
(Largo Pedro Álvares Cabral; ⊗9am-12.30pm & 2-5.30pm Wed-Sun) **FREE** This early-15th-century church, with its delicately carved facade of multilayered arches, is a Santarém jewel. Inside, a rose window spills light across the beautifully spare interior of stone columns and white walls. Note the tombs of Pedro Álvares Cabral (the 'discoverer' of Brazil, who lived in Santarém) and Dom Pedro de Menezes, the first governor of the *Ceuta e do Império* (City and of the Empire; Vila Real).

Igreja de Nossa Senhora
da Conceição   CATHEDRAL
(Sé; Praça Sá da Bandeira; with Museu Diocesano de Santarém €4; ⊗10am-1pm & 2-6pm Mon & Wed-Fri, to 7pm Sat & Sun) **FREE** This baroque, 17th-century Jesuit church, built on the site of the former royal palace, looms over the town's most impressive square, Praça Sá da Bandeira. The church now serves as the town's cathedral. Inside is a lush ceiling bursting with angels, plus a number of elaborately gilded altars. Unless a mass is underway, entry is via the recently opened Museu Diocesano de Santarém.

★ Festivals & Events

Feira Nacional da Agricultura   FAIR
(www.feiranacionalagricultura.pt; Quinta das Cegonhas, Centro Nacional de Exposições) Promoting agricultural and food products, this is famous nationwide for its merriment, concerts, horse races, bullfights and night-time bull-running. It lasts 10 days in the first half of June and mostly takes place 2km west of the town centre.

🛏 Sleeping

★ Santarém Hostel   HOSTEL €
(⊘243 322 256; www.santaremhostel.blogspot.pt; Rua Eng António Júnior 26; dm/s/d/q €15/30/40/70) One of Portugal's best 'glostels' (glamorous hostels); helpful owner Mario runs a great ship, from the neat, airy, brightly decorated rooms (each with en suite), to the massive home-away-from-home lounge room complete with TV, guitar and designer sofas. There's also a sunny patio and cosy bar (with Mario's amazing guitar collection). A top location in the historic centre.

Understandably, it's heaven for walkers on the Santiago de Camino (Portugal) path. Worth coming to Santarém for this alone.

Cereal Vitória Hotel   GUESTHOUSE €
(⊘243 309 130; www.cerealvitoriahotel.com; Rua Segundo Visconde de Santarém 21; s/d/tr €30/50/65; ❋ 🛜) You'll either love, hate or be puzzled by – likely the latter! – this hip boutique hotel's grain theme, but you can never accuse it of not instilling a sense of place! Beyond the oats, wheat and barley imagery, the soft green colour scheme and crafty-curated decor, this place is welcoming, stylish and, above all, very nice value for central Portugal.

★ Casa da Alcáçova   HISTORIC HOTEL €€€
(⊘243 304 030; www.alcacova.com; Largo da Alcáçova 3; r €125-175, apt €125-200; 🅿❋🛜🏊) With the atmosphere of a stylish country retreat, but right in the city, this secluded manor house is set by its own section of the city walls, offering spectacular views from the ramparts and many of the rooms. The lovely interior is crammed with antiques and heirlooms – perhaps not to everyone's taste, but nonetheless extraordinary.

Extras include a lovely pool area and a summer lounge with the foundations of a Roman temple in the middle of it. Two new apartments offer a more modern stay and a bit more seclusion away from the main house.

🍴 Eating & Drinking

★ Taberna do Quinzena   PORTUGUESE €
(www.quinzena.com; Rua Pedro de Santarém 93; mains €7-9; ⊗10am-midnight Mon-Sat) The theme of this fabulous, atmospheric neighbourhood hang-out is *forcadeiros* (Portuguese bullfighters), and it celebrates these through its posters, photos and paraphernalia. But as far

as the cuisine goes – look at the walls' worth of awards. Daily-changing dishes are delicious and local – grilled pork or fish, washed down with cheap, local Ribatejo wine straight from the barrel.

Taberna O Balcão
PORTUGUESE €€

(☑ 243 055 883; www.facebook.com/tabernaobalcao; Rua Pedro de Santarém 73; mains €12.50-17; ☺ noon-11pm Mon-Thu, to midnight Fri & Sat; 🗟) This place has the flavour of Ribatejo, from traditional Portugal recipes to modern dishes such as a Black Angus burger. The decor – a mix of modern and old – is done with flair: marble-topped tables, ceramic plates on the walls, and stunning retro-Ribatejan tiles. It's traditional with a modern twist and appeals to those who enjoy, well, nice things.

Tascá
TAPAS €€

(☑ 243 306 118; www.facebook.com/TASCAnanet; Rua Arco de Manços 8; petiscos €5-7.50, mains €7-14; ☺ noon-2am; 🗟) Bright, fun and contemporary, this loosely Spanish-themed bar attracts a trendy, younger crowd. It does innovative *petiscos* from its open kitchen. Most of the socialising goes on around the barrels or on the great terrace outside, especially during important football matches. Good looking crowd, great food.

Pigalle
PORTUGUESE €€

(☑ 243 046 865; www.facebook.com/Pigalle2016; Rua Capelo e Ivans 15; dishes €8.50-18; ☺ noon-3.30pm & 7-11pm Tue-Sat; 🗟) Informal and cosy, this is Santarém's most foodie-friendly restaurant, where chef Andre churns out jazzed up *petiscos* and heavier plates based on traditional recipes but with a more gourmand focus alongside fine Portuguese wines to match. Think stuffed pork cheeks with sweet potato puree, and curried shrimp with cockles and *malagueta* chilli peppers.

Ponto G
BAR

(www.facebook.com/ponto.g.santarem; Praça Visconde Serra do Pilar; ☺ 4pm-2am Mon-Sat, to 9pm Sun; 🗟) A friendly, bearded beer lover runs Santarém's refuge from commercial lagers, which features eight or so German and Belgian beers on draught along with another 150 in bottles, including a rotating menu of 30 or so Portuguese craft beers. It occupies a lovely, aqua-tiled corner building with sidewalk tables with views to Igreja de Marvila.

❶ Information

Posto de Turismo (☑ 243 304 437; www.cm-santarém.pt; Rua Capelo e Ivens 63; ☺ 10am-6pm Mon-Fri, 9.30am-1pm & 2-5.30pm Sat & Sun)

❶ Getting There & Away

The **train station** (www.cp.pt; Estrada da Estação de Caminhos de Ferro) is 2.4km northeast of the city centre and steeply downhill from the centrally located **bus station** (☑ 243 333 200; www.rodotejo.pt; Avenida do Brasil). **Scala Bus** (www.scalabus.pt) No 2 runs regularly between the two stations on weekdays and Saturday mornings (€1.40, 10 minutes) as well as Sundays from July to September. Taxis charge about €5.

BUS

Rede Expressos (www.rede-expressos.pt) heads to Lisbon (€7.60, one hour) nearly a dozen times per day. **Rodoviária do Tejo** (www.rodotejo.pt) runs at least two times daily to Coimbra (€14.70, 2¼ hours, 12.30pm and 6.20pm) and once to Leiria (€12.80, 1¼ hours, 5.30pm); **Rodoviária do Lis** (www.rodoviariadolis.pt) heads to Fátima (€9.60, 45 minutes, 10.15am and 4.45pm). Service drops off on weekends.

TRAIN

Very frequent IC (€11.90 to €13.70) and local (€6.20 to €6.85) trains go to Lisbon (45 minutes to one hour).

Constância & Castelo de Almourol

POP 1000

Constância's compact cluster of whitewashed houses, cobbled lanes and narrow staircases spills picturesquely down a steep hillside to the confluence of the Rios Tejo and Zêzere. It's a sleepy, pretty village whose leafy riverfront promenade, main square and gardens make a lovely place for lunch or a stroll before moving on to the biggest draw in these parts, nearby Castelo de Almourol.

◎ Sights

Castelo de Almourol
CASTLE

(Praia do Ribatejo; ☺ 10am-1pm & 2.30-7.30pm Tue-Sun Mar-Oct, to 5.30pm Nov-Feb) Like the stuff of legend, 10-towered Castelo de Almourol stands tantalisingly close to shore but just out of reach in the Rio Tejo. The castle is 5km from Constância. **Boats** (€2.50, five minutes) leave every 10 minutes from a riverside landing directly opposite the castle. Once on the island, a short walk leads up to the ramparts, where you're free to linger as long as you like.

The island, almost jumping distance from land, was once the site of a Roman fort; the castle was built by Gualdim Pais, Grand Master of the Order of the Knights Templar, in 1171. It's no surprise that Almourol has long caught the imagination of excitable poets longing for the Age of Chivalry.

Buses run between Constância and Tancos, passing within 2.5km of the castle.

🛏 Sleeping

Hostel 18   HOSTEL €
(☑ 962 612 594; www.hostel18.pt; Praça Alexandre Herculano 18; dm/d €15/30; ❄ 🛜) This smart hostel unravels over three floors from a well-curated common ground floor brimming with a bevy of antiques along with modern sofas and other amenities. Whitewashed dorm beds feature built-in lockers and are light and airy, while the walls throughout are peppered with family documents and heirlooms. Some private rooms are small but feature Tejo views.

Casa João Chagas   GUESTHOUSE €
(☑ 249 739 403; www.casajoaochagas.com; Rua João Chagas, Constância; s/d €35/50; P ❄ 🛜) Set in the former town hall (more modern) and another building opposite (more classic but with modernisation plan in the works), this excellent place offers large, simple, refurbished rooms with comfortable beds and a good attitude. It's right in the centre of things just off the main square near the river.

ℹ Information

Posto de Turismo (☑ 249 730 052; www.cm-constancia.pt; Avenida das Forças Armadas; ⏱ 10am-5pm Mon-Fri, 10am-1pm & 2-6pm Sat & Sun) In the municipal offices in the centre of town.

ℹ Getting There & Away

By public transport, a combined visit to Constância and Castelo de Almourol is possible but somewhat tricky. Bus and train routes can be joined into a loop with the insertion of an intermediate rail leg between Constância's Praia do Ribatejo station and Almourol station (€1.45, three minutes); however, there's a substantial walk involved at the Constância end of this short train journey.

BUS

Constância is easily reached by buses from Tomar (€2.90, 40 minutes). **Rodoviária do Tejo** (www.rodotejo.pt) runs four buses on weekdays

to Tancos (€2.10, 20 minutes, 7.20am, 10.40am, 2.15pm and 5.50pm) from a **bus stop** (Estrada Nacional 3) near the town Gal petrol station, but the nearest bus stop along the route is still about a 2.5km walk to the boat landing. You are better off in a taxi from Praça Alexandre Herculano (€10 to €15).

CAR & MOTORCYCLE

If driving your own vehicle, exit the A23/IP6 at Constância and follow signs to the castle.

TRAIN

To visit the castle only, take a local train (changing at Entroncamento) from Tomar (€3.30, 40 minutes) or Santarém (€4.10, 35 minutes, limited direct services) to tiny **Almourol station** (www.cp.pt; Praia do Ribatejo), then walk 1km downhill to the ferry landing. The train station nearest Constância – known as **Praia do Ribatejo** – is 2km outside town, so the bus is a better option if you're only visiting Constância.

Tomar

POP 16,000

Tomar is one of central Portugal's most appealing small towns. With its pedestrian-friendly historic centre, its pretty riverside park frequented by swans, herons and families of ducks, and its charming natural setting adjacent to the lush Mata Nacional dos Sete Montes (Seven Hills National Forest), it wins lots of points for aesthetics.

But to understand what makes Tomar truly extraordinary, cast your gaze skyward to the crenellated walls of the Unesco World Heritage–listed Convento de Cristo, which forms a beautiful backdrop from almost any vantage point. Eight-and-a-half centuries after its founding, this venerable headquarters of the legendary Knights Templar is a rambling concoction of Gothic, Manueline and Renaissance architecture that bears extravagant witness to its integral role in centuries of Portuguese history, from the founding of Portugal as a nation state to the Age of Discoveries.

👁 Sights

★ Convento de Cristo   MONASTERY
(www.conventocristo.pt; Rua Castelo dos Templários; adult/under 12yr €6/free, with Alcobaça & Batalha €15; ⏱ 9am-6.30pm Jun-Sep, to 5.30pm Oct-May) Wrapped in splendour and mystery, the Knights Templar held enormous power in Portugal from the 12th to 16th centuries, and largely bankrolled the Age of Discoveries. Their headquarters sit on wooded slopes

Tomar

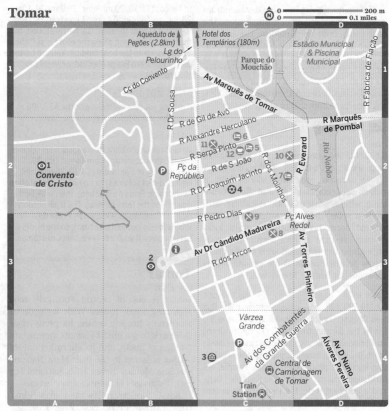

above the town and are enclosed within
12th-century walls. The Convento de Cristo
is a stony expression of magnificence, founded in 1160 by Gualdim Pais. It has chapels,
cloisters and choirs in diverging styles, added over the centuries by successive kings
and Grand Masters.

The **Charola**, the extraordinary 16-sided
Templar church, thought to be in imitation
of the Church of the Holy Sepulchre in Jerusalem, dominates the complex. Its eastern
influences give it a very different feel to most
Portuguese churches; the interior is otherworldly in its vast heights – an awesome
combination of simple forms and rich em-
bellishment. It's said that the circular design
enabled knights to attend Mass on horseback. In the centre stands an eerily Gothic
high altar, while wall paintings date from
the early 16th century. A huge funnel to the
left is an ancient organ pipe (the organ itself
is long gone).

Dom Manuel was responsible for tacking the nave on to the west side of the Charola and for commissioning a two-level **choir**. The *coro alto* (upper choir) is a fabulous Manueline work, with intricate decor on the vaulting and windows. The main western doorway into the nave is a splendid example of Spanish *plateresque* style.

Seeming to have grown from the wall, the **Janela Manuelina** (Manueline Window) on the church's western side is the most famous and fantastical feature of the monastery. It's the ultimate in Manueline extravagance, a celebration of the Age of Discoveries: a Medusa tangle of snaking ropes, seaweed and cork boats, atop of which floats the Cross of the Order of Christ and the royal arms and armillary spheres of Dom Manuel. It's best seen from the roof of the adjacent Claustro de Santa Bárbara. Follow signs to the *janela*. Unfortunately obscured by the Claustro Principal is an almost-equivalent window on the southern side of the church.

Two serene, *azulejo*-decorated cloisters to the east of the Charola were built during the time when Prince Henry the Navigator was Grand Master of the order in the 15th century. The **Claustro do Cemitério** (Burial-Ground Cloisters) contains two 16th-century tombs and pretty citrus trees, while the two-storey **Claustro da Lavagem** (Ablutions Cloisters) affords nice views of the crenellated ruins of the Templars' original castle.

The elegant Renaissance **Claustro Principal** (Great Cloisters) stands in striking contrast to the flamboyance of the monastery's Manueline architecture. Commissioned during the reign of João III, the cloisters were probably designed by the Spaniard Diogo de Torralva but completed in 1587 by an Italian, Filippo Terzi. These foreign architects were among several responsible for introducing a delayed Renaissance style into Portugal. The Claustro Principal is arguably the country's finest expression of that style: a sober ensemble of Greek columns and pillars, gentle arches and sinuous, spiralling staircases.

★**Aqueduto de Pegões**   LANDMARK
FREE This astonishing aqueduct, striding towards the monastery from the northwest, was built between 1593 and 1613 to supply water to thirsty monks. Its 180 arches, some of which are double-decker, are thought to have been designed by Filippo Terzi. It's best seen just off the Leiria road, 2.3km from town, where it winds along a dramatic turn. You are free to climb about the top at will.

Mata Nacional dos Sete Montes   GARDENS
(Praça do Infante D Henrique; ⊙8am-8pm) These bucolic 39-hectare gardens – linked to the Convento de Cristo – were founded by the Order of Christ and once served as a contemplative space and apple orchard for the monastic order. Indeed today it is a finely manicured and peaceful walled forest well worth exploration.

Museu Luso-Hebraico Abraham Zacuto   SYNAGOGUE
(www.cm-tomar.pt; Rua Dr Joaquim Jacinto 73; ⊙10am-noon & 2-5pm Tue-Sun winter, 10am-noon & 3-6pm summer) FREE On a charming cobbled lane in the old town, you'll find the country's best-preserved medieval synagogue. Built between 1430 and 1460, it was used for only a few years before Dom Manuel's convert-or-leave edict of 1497 forced most Jews to do the latter. The synagogue subsequently served as prison, chapel, hayloft and warehouse until classified as a national monument in 1921.

Museu dos Fósforos   MUSEUM
(Avenida General Bernardo Faria; ⊙10am-noon & 2-5pm Tue-Sun) FREE This museum, reached via the lovely courtyard of the Convento de São Francisco, contains Europe's largest collection of matchboxes. Amassed by local 'phillumenist' Aquiles da Mota Lima, the 43,000-plus matchboxes from 127 countries around the world depict everything from bullfighters to bathing beauties, dinosaurs and French cuisine.

★ Festivals & Events

Festa Templaria Tomar   CULTURAL
(www.festatemplaria.pt) A fun medieval fair, celebrating the Templars, with lots of costumes, lectures, handicrafts and the like. Held annually on different dates (check the website).

🛏 Sleeping

★**Hostel 2300 Thomar**   HOSTEL €
(☑249 324 256; www.hostel2300thomar.com; Rua Serpa Pinto 43; dm/s/d/tr/q €18/30/45/60/80; ☎) One of the country's funkiest hostels, this cleverly renovated mansion right in the heart of town celebrates Portugal, with each room brightly decorated in a particular national theme: from the Lisbon tram to sardines. Airy dorms (and doubles), lockers,

THE ORDER OF THE KNIGHTS TEMPLAR

Founded in about 1119 by French crusading knights to protect pilgrims visiting the Holy Land, the Templars got their name when King Baldwin of Jerusalem housed them in his palace, which had once been a Jewish temple. The Knights soon became a strictly organised, semireligious gang. Members took vows of poverty and chastity, and wore white coats emblazoned with a red cross – a symbol that eventually came to be associated with Portugal itself. By 1139 the Templars were the leading defenders of the Christian crusader states in the Holy Land.

In Portugal, Templar knights played a key role in expelling the Moors. Despite vows of poverty, they accepted land, castles and titles in return for military victories. Soon the order had properties all over Europe and the Middle East. This geographically dispersed network enabled them to take on another influential role: bankers to kings and pilgrims.

By the early 14th century, the Templars had grown so strong that French King Philip IV – eager for their wealth or afraid of their power – initiated an era of persecution (supported by the French pope Clement V). He arrested all of the knights, accusing many of heresy and seizing their property. In 1314 the last French Grand Maître (Master) was burned at the stake.

In Portugal, Dom Dinis followed the trend by dissolving the order, but a few years later he cannily re-established it as the Order of Christ, though now under the royal thumb. It was largely thanks to the order's wealth that Prince Henry the Navigator (Grand Master from 1417 to 1460) was able to fund the Age of Discoveries. In the 16th century, Dom João III took the order into a humbler phase, shifting it towards monastic duties. In 1834, with the dissolution of the monasteries, the order's lands were confiscated, but it still lives on to some extent: these days the Grand Master is the Portuguese president.

modern bathrooms and a cool and fun living space are enough to convert any luxury lover into a backpacker instead.

This is a standout for budget travellers. Even a light breakfast is included. Dorm beds are €5 off for Camino de Santiago walkers.

Camping Redondo
CAMPGROUND €

(☑249 376 421; www.campingredondo.com; Rua Casal Rei 6, Poço Redondo; sites per adult/tent/car €4/5/2.50, 4-person chalets from €55; P🔊❄) This lovely Dutch- and British-run campground with four chalets plus two additional stone cottages is 9km northeast of Tomar at Poço Redondo. Amenities include a bar, pool and sun terrace (plus kid-friendly things such as a games room and playground). Consult the website for transport details and driving directions in English.

Residencial União
GUESTHOUSE €

(☑249 323 161; www.residencialuniao.pt; Rua Serpa Pinto 94; s/d from €35/45; 🔊) Tomar's most atmospheric budget choice, this once-grand townhouse on the main pedestrian drag features large and sprucely maintained rooms with antique furniture and fixtures. Especially pleasant are the elegant breakfast room, serve-yourself bar and kindly

owners. It's better value in summer than winter, when it can feel a little chilly.

★Thomar Story
BOUTIQUE HOTEL €€

(☑249 327 268; www.thomarstory.pt; Rua João Carlos Everard 53; s/d/tr €43/50/65; ❄🔊) A major refurbishment of an old house has created 12 light and pleasant rooms along the lines of the current trend in Portugal: funky wall decorations and mirrors, bright accessories and modern bathrooms. The interior of each in some way reflects Tomar, from the town's convent to its synagogue. Breakfast costs €5. The best rooms have small patios and kitchenettes.

Hotel dos Templários
HOTEL €€

(☑249 310 100; www.hoteldostemplarios.pt; Largo Cândido dos Reis 1; s/d from €75/92; P❄🔊❄) At the river's edge, just outside the historic centre, this spacious, efficient hotel offers excellent facilities, including gym, sauna, and indoor and outdoor pools (the last adjacent to a small but stylish hotel bar). The rooms are large and very comfortable; most have balconies, some of which overlook the river.

Quinta do Valle
HOTEL €€

(☑249 381 165, 966 814 613; www.quintadovalle.com; Quinta do Valle; 1-/2-bedroom apt from €79/119; P🔊❄) With parts dating back to the 15th century, this manor house 8km south of Tomar has been turned into rustic accommodation, with large grounds, chapel, swimming pool and quaint one- and two-bedroom apartments featuring fireplaces and kitchenettes. It's got a lovely out-of-the-way feel and is a venue for utter relaxation. Breakfast is available for €7.50 extra per person.

✖ Eating & Drinking

Amor Lusitano PORTUGUESE €
(www.amorlusitano.pt; Avenida Dr Cândido Madureira 19-21; sandwiches €1.20-4.50, petiscos €2.80-4.90; ⊙9am-9pm Sun-Thu, to 11.45pm Fri & Sat) This charming spot is part cafe, part wine bar, and celebrates all things *Lusitano* (Portuguese). This is the place to come for *doces conventuais* (convent sweets; €1 to €1.20) or a good selection of Portuguese wine. It's the kind of place that you come for a cup of tea and *pão de ló* (sponge cake), and stay for a tipple.

Casa das Ratas PORTUGUESE €€
(⊘249 315 237; Rua Dr Joaquim Jacinto 6; mains €7.50-12.50; ⊙noon-3pm & 7-10pm Tue-Sat, noon-3pm Sun) One of Tomar's fun experiences, where old meets new. Housed in a former *adega* (winery), the eatery is lined with wine vats. As grain was once here too, it used to attract rats (thus the name), but besides the jokey ones you'll see hanging off electric wires, you'll see nothing but delicious share plates and good wine.

Calça Perra PORTUGUESE €€
(⊘249 321 616; www.calcaperra.pt; Rua Pedro Dias 59; mains €12-18; ⊙11am-3pm & 6.30pm-midnight Mon-Sat, noon 10.30am-3pm Sun in summer; 🔊) At this charming backstreet eatery you can partake in the elegant dining room or the breezy, intimate courtyard below. Speciality, well-presented fish dishes such as *dourada grelhada* (grilled bream), *bife de atum* (tuna steak) and *açorda de peixe* (a bread-filled fish stew) are the highlights, along with reliable meat dishes.

Restaurante Tabuleiro PORTUGUESE €€
(⊘249 312 771; www.restaurantetabuleiro.wordpress.com; Rua Serpa Pinto 140; mains €15.80;

⊙noon-3pm & 7-10pm Mon-Sat; 🛉) Just off Tomar's main square, this family-friendly local hang-out features warm, attentive service, good traditional food and ridiculous (read: more-than-ample) portions. A great spot to experience local fare. The cod pie is a standout.

Café Paraíso CAFE
(www.cafeparaisotomar.com; Rua Serpa Pinto 127; ⊙8am-late Mon-Sat, to 8pm Sun) More than 100 years old and frozen in time since its renovation in 1946, this old-fashioned, high-ceilinged, cash-only deco cafe serves as a refuge for anyone in need of a mid-afternoon snack (from €2.50) and a shot of caffeine or whisky.

☆ Entertainment

Fatias de Cá THEATRE
(⊘960 303 991; www.fatiasdeca.net) This Tomar-based theatre company presents highly innovative and entertaining monthly performances (more in summer) of works such as *The Name of the Rose* and *The Tempest,* often in amazing locations.

❶ Information

Posto de Turismo (⊘249 329 823; www.cm-tomar.pt; Avenida Dr Cândido Madureira; ⊙9.30am-6pm Apr-Sep, 10am-5pm Oct-Mar) Offers a good town map, an accommodation list and information about a historical trail.

❶ Getting There & Away

The **bus station** (⊘249 312 738; Avenida dos Combatentes da Grande Guerra) and **train station** (www.cp.pt) are next door to each other, about 500m south of the posto de turismo. You will also find several large car parks here.

BUS

Regular services go to Lisbon (€9.50, 1¾ hours) with **Rede Expressos** (www.rede-expressos.pt). **Rodoviária do Tejo** (www.rodotejo.pt) services Fátima (€4, one hour), Leiria (€4.45, 1½ hours), Batalha (€5.90, one hour), Alcobaça (€7.25, one hour) and Nazaré (€7.85, one hour).

TRAIN

Trains run to Lisbon (€9.80 to €11.10, 1¾ to two hours) via Santarém (€5.20, 40 to 55 minutes), every hour or two between 8am and 10pm.

The Beiras

Best Places to Eat

➡ Pedra de Sal (p322)

➡ Restaurante de Casa das Penhas Douradas (p346)

➡ Sete Restaurante (p317)

Best Places to Stay

➡ Casa das Penhas Douradas (p346)

➡ Aveiro Rossio Hostel (p331)

➡ Universal Boutique Hotel (p325)

➡ Casas do Côro (p360)

Why Go?

With few big-name destinations to boast of, the Beiras often slip under the radar. But this wonderfully varied region, traditionally divided into the Beira Litoral, Beira Alta and Beira Baixa, is a fascinating and beautiful part of the country.

The headline act is Coimbra, a cultured city renowned for its historic university. To the west, the Atlantic crashes in on wild sandy beaches, luring surfers and sunseekers to resorts such as high-rise Figueira da Foz.

Move inland and the crowds thin as the landscape becomes increasingly dramatic. Stoical schist villages cling to wooded slopes, while winding roads snake up Portugal's highest mountains in the Serra de Estrela. Below, vineyards flourish in the lush Dão valley.

Continue east and you'll come to the far-flung borderlands. Few people venture this far, but make the effort and you'll discover a strange, almost otherworldly area of sun-browned plains, medieval castles and hilltop fortress towns.

When to Go
Coimbra

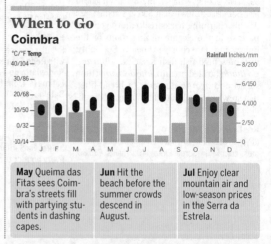

May Queima das Fitas sees Coimbra's streets fill with partying students in dashing capes.

Jun Hit the beach before the summer crowds descend in August.

Jul Enjoy clear mountain air and low-season prices in the Serra da Estrela.

BEIRA LITORAL

From salt pans and unspoiled Atlantic beaches to castles, lush forests and one of Portugal's most important ancient sites, Beira Litoral is rich in natural beauty and historical interest. The region's main gateway is the spirited university town of Coimbra, while to the north Aveiro charms with its pretty canals. On the western coast, Figueira da Foz is a favourite summer resort, renowned for its huge beach and top surfing.

Coimbra

POP 143,400

Rising scenically from the Rio Mondego, Coimbra is an animated city steeped in history. It was Portugal's medieval capital for more than a century and it's home to the country's oldest and most prestigious university. Its steeply stacked historic centre dates to Moorish times and is wonderfully atmospheric, with its dark cobbled lanes and monumental cathedral. On summer evenings, the city's old stone walls reverberate with the haunting metallic notes of the *guitarra* (Portuguese guitar) and the full, deep voices of fado singers.

The city is at its best during university term time, when the students bring a youthful energy to the streets, thronging bars and partying at weekends. Their presence also adds a political edge – witness the graffiti scrawled outside the *repúblicas* (communal student dwellings) addressing the political issues of the day.

History

Coimbra's origins date to antiquity when it started life as the Roman town of Aeminium. It thrived under the Moors, who ruled it from the early 8th century until their expulsion by Christian forces in 1064. A later golden age saw it serve as Portugal's capital from 1139 to 1255, when King Afonso III decided he preferred Lisbon.

The Universidade de Coimbra, Portugal's first university (and among Europe's oldest), was actually founded in Lisbon by Dom Dinis in 1290 but settled here in 1537. It attracted a steady stream of teachers, artists and intellectuals from across Europe. The 16th century was a particularly heady time thanks to Nicolas Chanterène, Jean de Rouen (João de Ruão) and other French artists who inspired a school of sculpture that influenced styles all over Portugal.

Today Coimbra's university remains Portugal's most prestigious – and one of its most traditional. Students still attend class in black robes and capes – often adorned with patches signifying course, home town or other affiliation – while a rigorously maintained set of rites and practices called the *codigo de praxe* governs all aspects of university life.

◉ Sights

Many of Coimbra's headline sights are in the hilltop university area and the upper old town. This atmospheric district cascades down the hill in a tangle of steep cobbled lanes, medieval towers and graffiti-daubed student houses. The new town, known as the 'Baixa', sits at the foot of the hill by the Rio Mondego. Its main pedestrianised drag, Rua Ferreira Borges and Rua Visconde da Luz, traverses the area, joining the two focal squares, Largo da Portagem and Praça 8 de Maio.

◉ Upper Town

Crowned by the university, Coimbra's historic upper town rises from the banks of the Rio Mondego. This was the heart of the city in Moorish times and later served as the seat of Portugal's early kings. The best way to access the area from the lower town is through the Arco de Almedina just off Rua Ferreira Borges. This leads to the steep, stepped Rua Quebra Costas (Backbreaker Street). Continue up this and eventually you'll emerge at the university.

For a glimpse of student life, stroll along any of the alleys around the Sé Velha (p311) or below the Sé Nova (p313) . Flags, offbeat art and graffiti mark the cramped houses known as *repúblicas*, each housing a dozen or so students from the same region or faculty.

★ **Universidade de Coimbra**   UNIVERSITY
(☑ 239 242 744; www.uc.pt/turismo; Pátio das Escolas; adult/child incl Paço das Escolas, Biblioteca Joanina, Capela de São Miguel & Museu da Ciência €12.50/free, without Biblioteca €7/free; ⊙ 9am-7.30pm Mar-Oct, 9am-1pm & 2pm-5pm Nov-Feb) Coimbra's Unesco-listed university, one of the world's oldest, was originally founded in Lisbon in 1290. It was subsequently relocated several times before being permanently established in Coimbra in 1537. Its showpiece centre is the Pátio das Escolas, a vast courtyard surrounded by majestic

The Beiras Highlights

1 Coimbra (p307) Admiring the baroque splendours of the hilltop university before losing your heart to fado music.

2 Manteigas (p344) Hiking the soaring peaks and forest trails that surround this tranquil mountain town.

3 Viseu (p350) Sipping fine Dão wine on a pretty plaza in the cobbled centre.

4 Monsanto (p336) Marvelling at the sweeping views and mighty boulders that litter this craggy clifftop village.

5 Aveiro (p328) Jumping on a traditional *moliceiro* (seaweed-harvesting vessel) to cruise this elegant canal-side town.

6 Piódão (p333) Zigzagging your way up terraced slopes to the most isolated of the Beiras' schist villages.

7 Almeida (p361) Striding the martial ramparts of this frontier fortress town.

8 Conimbriga (p321) Conjuring up a vanished civilisation at these extensive Roman ruins.

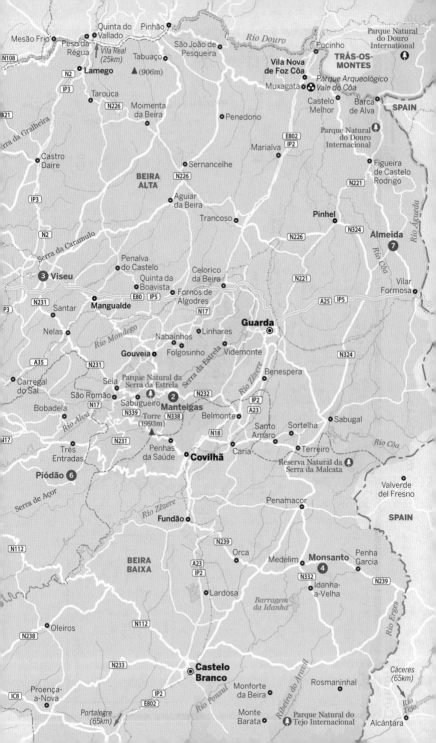

Coimbra

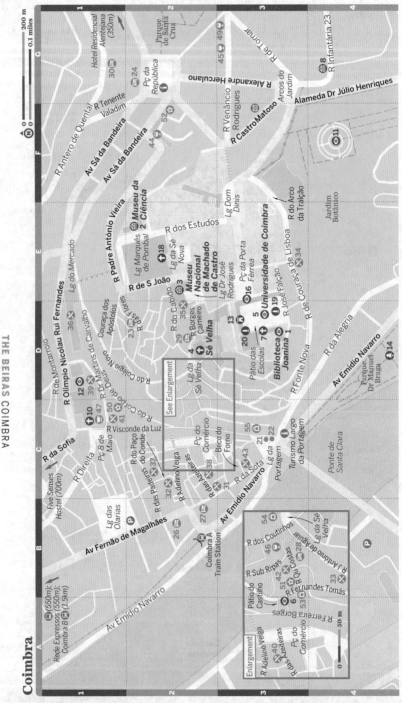

Map labels (key features):

- Parque de Santa Cruz
- R Alexandre Herculano
- R de Tomar
- R Infantária 23
- Hotel Residencial Alentejana (350m)
- Pç da República
- R Tenente Valadim
- R Antero de Quental
- Av Sá da Bandeira
- R Venâncio Rodrigues
- R Castro Matoso
- Arcos do Jardim
- Alameda Dr Júlio Henriques
- R de Montarroio
- R de Dias
- R Olímpio Nicolau Rui Fernandes
- Lg do Mercado
- R Padre António Vieira
- Museu da Ciência
- R dos Estudos
- Lg Marquês de Pombal
- Lg da Sé Nova
- Jardim Botânico
- R do Arco da Traição
- Lg Dom Dinis
- R de Martins de Carvalho
- Couraça dos Apóstolos
- R das Flores
- R de S João
- Museu Nacional de Machado de Castro
- Pç da Porta Férrea
- R Dr José Rodrigues
- R de Couraça de Lisboa
- Universidade de Coimbra
- R José Falcão
- R da Sofia
- R Direita
- Pç 8 de Maio
- R de Colégio Novo
- R do Corpo de Deus
- R do Cabido
- R Borges Carneiro
- Sé Velha
- Lg da Sé Velha
- Pátio das Escolas
- Biblioteca Joanina
- R Fonte Nova
- R da Alegria
- Av Emídio Navarro
- Parque Dr Manuel Braga
- Five Senses Hostel (700m)
- R Visconde da Luz
- Lg das Olarias
- R do Paço do Conde
- R das Padeiras
- R Adelino Veiga
- R das Azeiteiras
- Pç do Comércio
- Beco do Forno
- R da Sota
- Lg da Portagem
- Turismo Largo da Portagem
- Ponte de Santa Clara
- Av Fernão de Magalhães
- Coimbra A Train Station
- Rede Expressos (550m); Coimbra B (1.5km)
- Av Emídio Navarro

Enlargement:

- R Adelino Veiga
- R das Azeiteiras
- Pç do Comércio
- R Ferreira Borges
- Pátio do Castilho
- R Fernandes Tomás
- R Qu Costas
- R Sub Ripas
- R J António de Aguiar
- R dos Coutinhos
- Lg da Sé Velha

Scale bars:
- 200 m / 0.1 miles
- 50 m

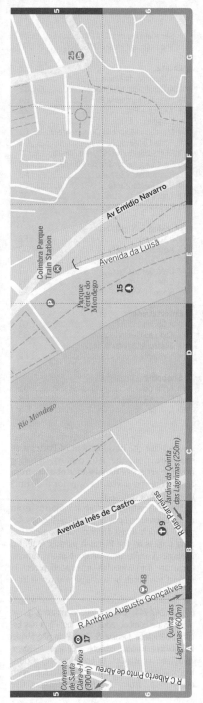

16th- to 18th-century buildings. These include the Paço das Escolas (p313), Torre da Universidade (p313), Prisão Acadêmica (p313), Capela de São Miguel (p313) and Biblioteca Joanina.

★ **Biblioteca Joanina** LIBRARY
(Baroque Library; ☎ 239 242 744; www.uc.pt/turismo; Pátio das Escolas, Universidade de Coimbra; adult/under 26yr/child incl Paço das Escolas, Capela de São Miguel & Museu da Ciência €12.50/10/free; ☺ 9am-7.30pm Mar-Oct, 9am-1pm & 2pm-5pm Nov-Feb) The university's baroque library is Coimbra's headline sight. Named after King João V, who sponsored its construction between 1717 and 1728, it features a remarkable central hall decorated with elaborate ceiling frescoes and huge rosewood, ebony and jacaranda tables. Towering gilt chinoiserie shelves hold some 40,000 books, mainly on law, philosophy and theology. Curiously, the library also houses a colony of bats to protect the books – they eat potentially harmful insects.

Note admission to the library is strictly regulated, with entry in groups at set times. At your allotted time – given when you buy your ticket – you enter through a side door and wait to be admitted to the main hall. While waiting you can peek down into the cells of the Prisão Acadêmica (p313).

★ **Sé Velha** CATHEDRAL
(Old Cathedral; ☎ 239 825 273; www.sevelha coimbra.org; Largo da Sé Velha, Rua do Norte 4; €2.50; ☺ 10am-6pm Mon-Sat, 1-6pm Sun) Coimbra's 12th-century cathedral is one of Portugal's finest examples of Romanesque architecture. The main portal and facade are particularly striking, especially on warm summer evenings when the golden stone seems to glow in the soft light. Its construction was financed by Portugal's first king, Afonso Henriques, and completed in 1184 at a time when the nation was still threatened by the Moors, hence its crenellated exterior and narrow, slit-like lower windows. Interior highlights include an ornate late-Gothic retable and a lovely 13th-century cloister.

Inside, the high, barrel-vaulted nave retains its main Romanesque features; side altars and well-preserved Gothic tombs of bishops are backed by bright Andalusian tiles. Over the main altar, the flamboyant gilt retable depicts the Assumption of Mary. Contrast this with the grey tones of the Renaissance Capela do Santíssimo Sacramento alongside.

THE BEIRAS COIMBRA

Coimbra

★Museu Nacional
de Machado de Castro   MUSEUM
(☏ 239 853 070; www.museumachadocastro.pt; Largo Dr José Rodrigues; adult/child €6/3, cryptoportico only €3; ☉ 2pm-6pm Tue, 10am-6pm Wed-Sun) This great museum is a highlight of central Portugal. Housed in a 12th-century bishop's palace, it stands over the city's ancient Roman forum, remains of which can be seen in the maze of spooky tunnels under the building – the *cryptoporticus*. Once you emerge from this, you can start on the fascinating art collection, which runs the gamut from Gothic religious sculpture to 16th-century Flemish painting and ornately crafted furniture.

Particularly spectacular is the vast recreation of a chapel from the Convento de São Domingos, but highlights abound. These include a section of the delicate cloister of São João de Almedina and some exquisite alabaster pieces from England. Sculptural works trace the development of Portuguese sculpture from the 11th century, showing how the arrival of Renaissance masters from across Europe paved the way for a distinctive Coimbra tradition.

You can admire terracotta figures from a 16th-century *Last Supper* by the mysterious French artist Hodart and some stunning panels by the Flemish painter Quentin Metsys. A collection of gold monstrances, furniture and Moorish-influenced pieces is almost too much by the time you reach it.

★Museu da Ciência   MUSEUM
(☏ 239 242 744; www.museudaciencia.org; Largo Marquês de Pombal; adult/child incl Paço das Escolas, Biblioteca Joanina & Capela de São Miguel €12.50/free, without Biblioteca €7/free; ☉ 10am-7pm Tue-Sun Mar-Oct, to 6pm Nov-Feb) Coimbra's science museum is wonderful, with everything from kid-friendly interactive

machines to early scientific instruments, fossils and skeletons. The eclectic collection is spread over three sections in two buildings: the chemistry labs where the ticket office is, and, over the road, the physics and natural history galleries. Highlights include a section on light and matter and a riveting display of exquisitely crafted physics apparatus, many dating from the 17th to 19th centuries.

Sé Nova
CATHEDRAL

(New Cathedral; ☑239 823 138; Largo da Sé Nova; €1; ☺8.30am-6.30pm) The landmark 'new' cathedral, started by the Jesuits in 1598 and completed a century later, dominates the square of the same name high in the old town. Its facade gives onto an interior adorned with gilt side panels and an ornate baroque altarpiece. It also features a gallery of reliquaries featuring bones and worse from minor saints and bishops, including St Francis Xavier and St Luke (so it's claimed!). Climb to the platform for uplifting city views.

Porta Férrea
GATE

The university's main entrance is the Iron Gate, a 17th-century confection designed by architect António Tavares in 1634 on the orders of Rector D Álvaro da Costa. It stands on the same spot as the original gateway to Coimbra's Moorish citadel and was the first major work following the acquisition of the Royal Palace by King Felipe I in 1597.

Each side of the gate features one of the university's founding monarchs: King Dinis on the outside and João III on the courtyard side. Above them stands the figure of Wisdom, the insignia of the university, while female figures represent the university's early faculties – Medicine and Law (exterior) and Theology and Canons (interior).

Statue of João III
STATUE

(Pátio das Escolas, Universidade de Coimbra) Lording it over the main university square, King João III turns his back to the sweeping city views behind him and faces his great centre of learning. It was he who re-established the university in Coimbra in 1537 and invited big-shot scholars to teach here in what had previously been a royal palace.

Torre da Universidade
TOWER

(Pátio das Escolas; €2; ☺9am-7.30pm Mar-Oct, 9am-1pm & 2pm-5pm Nov-Feb) Another of the university's signature landmarks, this 18th-century tower – and its clock and bells – regulates academic life. Built between 1728 and 1733, on the premise that there could be no order

without a clock, it was cursed as '*a cabra*' ('goat'; or 'bitch' in contemporary lingo) as it rang out to end the day's classes, signifying the curfew (in the days when students had to be home by 7pm or face prison) and that there would be classes the following day.

Paço das Escolas
PALACE

(Schools Palace; ☑239 242 744; www.uc.pt/turismo; Pátio das Escolas, Universidade de Coimbra; adult/child incl Biblioteca Joanina, Capela de São Miguel & Museu da Ciência €12.50/free, without Biblioteca €7/free; ☺9am-7.30pm Mar-Oct, 9am-1pm & 2pm-5pm Nov-Feb) Housed in a former royal palace, this is the historic heart of the university, where traditional academic ceremonies are still held. The main ceremonial hall is the Sala dos Capelos (named after the cape awarded to graduating doctorate students), a former exam room hung with portraits of Portugal's kings and crimson quilt-like decoration. The Sala do Exame Privado (Private Examination Room) is where graduates would be secretly examined at night.

Capela de São Miguel
CHURCH

(www.uc.pt/turismo; Pátio das Escolas, Universidade de Coimbra; adult/child incl Paço das Escolas, Biblioteca Joanina & Museu da Ciência €12.50/free, without Biblioteca €7/free; ☺9am-7.30pm Mar-Oct, 9am-1pm & 2pm-5pm Nov-Feb) Part of the main university complex, this ornate 16th-century chapel has a brightly painted ceiling, lavish tilework, Manueline features and a gilded 18th-century organ with about 2000 pipes. Concerts are still held here on occasion.

Prisão Acadêmica
HISTORIC BUILDING

(☑239 242 744; www.uc.pt/turismo; Universidade de Coimbra; adult/child incl Paço das Escolas, Biblioteca Joanina, Capela de São Miguel & Museu da Ciência €12.50/free; ☺9am-7.30pm Mar-Oct, 9am-1pm & 2pm-5pm Nov-Feb) This former prison for misbehaving students sits in the basement of the Biblioteca Joanina (p311). Originally located beneath the Sala dos Capelos, it was later transferred back to the medieval jail beneath the library (incredibly, the university was able to operate its own separate laws). In 1834, after the liberal revolution in Portugal, the prison was used as a deposit for books and illuminated manuscripts from convents and monasteries.

⊙ Baixa & Around

Igreja de Santa Cruz
CHURCH

(Praça 8 de Maio; adult/child €3/free; ☺9.30am-4.30pm Mon-Sat, 1-5pm Sun) Overlooking the

THE BEIRAS COIMBRA

TOP VIEWS IN COIMBRA

Coimbra's picturesque hillside setting means there are some great viewpoints. Our picks:

➡ Loggia (p317), restaurant of the Museu Nacional de Machado de Castro

➡ Torre da Universidade (p313)

➡ Convento de Santa Clara-a-Nova (p314)

➡ Ponte de Santa Clara

graceful Praça 8 de Maio, this is one of Coimbra's oldest churches, dating to the 12th century. Little remains of the original Romanesque structure, and it owes much of its current look to a 16th-century makeover. Step through the Renaissance porch and flamboyant 18th-century arch to the echoing tiled interior where you'll find the elaborate tombs of Portugal's first kings, Afonso Henriques and Sancho I. Also impressive is its restrained Manueline cloister.

Behind the church is the Jardim da Manga (Rua Olímpio Nicolau Rui Fernandes), once part of the cloister, and its curious fountain: a lemon-yellow, four-buttressed affair.

◉ Praça de República & Around

Leafy Praça da República is a lively hub, particularly in the early evening when students converge on its numerous bars and cafes for a leisurely drink or two. The surrounding neighbourhood, laid out in the 19th century and still dominated by prim bourgeois homes from the period, provides a relaxing break from the high density of the university and Baixa area.

Jardim Botânico   GARDENS
(☑ 239 855 215; www.uc.pt/jardimbotanico; ☉ 9am-8pm Apr-Sep, 9am-5.30pm Oct-Mar) FREE A serene place to catch your breath, the lovely university-run botanic garden sits in the shadow of the 16th-century Aqueduto de São Sebastião. Founded by the Marquês de Pombal, the garden combines formal flower beds, meandering paths and elegant fountains.

Casa Museu Bissaya Barreto   MUSEUM
(☑ 239 853 800; www.cmbb.pt; Rua Infantaria 23; adult/child & senior €2.50/1.25; ☉ 11am-1pm & 3-6pm Tue-Fri year-round & 3-6pm Sat & Sun May-Sep) Bissaya Barreto was a local surgeon,

scholar and obsessive hoarder of fine arts, and his late-19th-century mansion is now a small museum. A guide (not necessarily English-speaking) accompanies guests through rooms jam-packed with Portuguese sculpture and painting, Chinese porcelain, old *azulejos* and period furniture.

◉ Along & Across the River

The area to the west of the Rio Mondego harbours a couple of historic convents, as well as a romantic garden and kid-friendly theme park.

Stretching south from the Ponte de Santa Clara, the right bank of the river is flanked by two verdant parks: Parque Dr Manuel Braga and the Parque Verde do Mondego.

Jardins da Quinta das Lágrimas   GARDENS
(Rua Vilarinho Raposo; adult/under 15yr/family €2.50/1/5; ☉ 10am-5pm Tue-Sun mid-Oct–mid-Mar, 10am-7pm mid-Mar–mid-Oct) According to legend, this lovely pocket of parkland is where Dona Inês de Castro (aka Portugal's Juliet to the Infante Pedro's Romeo) was murdered on the orders of King Afonso IV, Pedro's father. Nowadays it's home to a five-star hotel, but anyone can take a turn about the romantic grounds and track down the Fonte dos Amores (Lovers' Fountain), which reputedly marks the spot where Inês was struck down. Look also for a sequoia tree planted by the Duke of Wellington.

Convento de Santa Clara-a-Nova   CONVENT
(☑ 239 441 674; www.rainhasantaisabel.org; Calçada de Santa Isabel; €2; ☉ 9am-6.45pm Mon-Sat, to 6pm Sun Nov-Feb, 9am-7pm Mon-Sat, to 6.30pm Sun Mar-Oct) On the west side of the river, this imposing convent was built in the 17th century to replace the original Convento de Santa Clara-a-Velha, which often suffered flooding. It's devoted almost entirely to Queen Isabel (Coimbra's patron saint), whose remains are encased in a silver casket above the altar. Paintings along the aisles illustrate her life story. Also of note is the convent's attractive 18th-century cloister.

Convento de Santa Clara-a-Velha   CONVENT
(☑ 239 801 160; Rua das Parreiras; adult/student €4/2; ☉ 10am-7pm Tue-Sun Apr-Sep, to 6pm Oct-Mar) This Gothic convent was founded in 1330 by the saintly Queen Isabel, Dom Dinis' wife; it served as her final resting place until flooding forced her to be moved uphill. The adjacent museum displays archaeological finds and shows two films, one about the

nuns who lived here, the other documenting the 20-year renovation that cleared the river ooze that had buried it since the 17th century.

Portugal dos Pequenitos   AMUSEMENT PARK
(☑239 801 170; www.portugaldospequenitos. pt; Rossio de Santa Clara; adult/under 13yr/family €9.95/5.95/26.75; ⊙9am-8pm Jun–mid-Sep, 10am-7pm Mar–May & mid-Sep–mid-Oct, 10am-5pm mid-Oct–Feb; ⊕) The brainchild of local collector Bissaya Barreto, this is a cute theme park where kids clamber over, into and around micro versions of Portugal's most famous monuments, while parents clutch cameras at the ready. There are also three minimuseums dedicated to marine life, furniture and clothing.

🏃 Activities

Several organisations offer tours on foot or tuk-tuk, as well as kayaking and other outdoor pursuits. Many tours start at Largo da Portagem near the river.

Go Walks   WALKING
(☑910 163 118; www.gowalksportugal.com; Rua Visconde da Luz 75; tours per person €25-40) Offers various themed walking tours – from fado to Jewish Coimbra – led by enthusiastic, knowledgeable students who speak good English (French and Spanish also bookable). It also runs tours further afield in central Portugal.

Tuk a Day   TOURS
(☑964 486 445, 962 826 855; per person €15; ⊙9am-7pm) Travellers love these 1¼-hour tuk-tuk tours of Coimbra. The multilingual drivers know their stuff and are highly entertaining guides. Minimum three people. Tours begin at Largo da Portagem.

O Pioneiro do Mondego   KAYAKING
(☑239 478 385; www.opioneirodomondego.com; per person €22.50-24.50) Take to the waters of the Mondego river on a kayak tour. Routes include the 18km stretch between Penacova and Torres de Mondego (three to four hours) and the 25km descent between Penacova and Coimbra (four to five hours). Pick-ups in Coimbra are available on request.

⭐🎉 Festivals & Events

Festival das Artes   ART
(www.festivaldasartes.com; ⊙mid-Jul) From classical concerts in the park to jazz on the river, music takes to the streets of Coimbra for this annual arts festival. Events, which include film projections, dance performances and exhibitions, are held in the Quinta das Lágrimas gardens and atmospheric venues across town.

Festa da Rainha Santa   RELIGIOUS
(www.rainhasantaisabel.org; ⊙Jul) Held in early July in even-numbered years, this festival commemorates Santa Isabel. On a Thursday night candlelit procession, her statue is carried from the Convento de Santa Clara-a-Nova across the Ponte de Santa Clara and on to the Igreja do Mosteiro de Santa Cruz; a second procession the following Sunday returns her to the convent.

🛏 Sleeping

★Serenata Hostel   HOSTEL $
(☑239 853 130; www.serenatahostel.com; Largo da Sé Velha 21; dm €16, d €49-60, f €71; ❋ 🛜) Occupying an elegant town house overlooking Coimbra's old cathedral, this fabulous hostel sits in the heart of the historic centre. Rooms, spread over three floors, come in an array of shapes and sizes, ranging from 10-bed dorms to spacious family rooms. White

---

FIRED UP

In the first week of May, Coimbra celebrates the end of the academic year with the Queima das Fitas (www.facebook.com/queimadasfitascoimbra). This bacchanalian weeklong party takes its name – literally the 'Burning of the Ribbons' – from the student custom of ritually torching the colour-coded ribbons they wear to represent their faculties.

Festivities kick off at midnight on the first Friday with the Serenata Monumental, a hauntingly beautiful fado performance on the steps of the Sé Velha (p311). The programme continues with sports events, black-tie balls, concerts at the so-called Queimodromo across the Ponte de Santa Clara, and a beer-soaked parade called the Cortejo dos Grelados from the university down to Largo da Portagem.

In their rush to sponsor the various festivities, Portuguese breweries provide ultra-cheap beer, which is distributed and drunk in liberal quantities.

walls and artistic stencils create a modern feel, while high ceilings and creaking wood floors add a period touch.

Great lounge areas, a kitchen and secluded sun terrace complete the happy picture.

Despertar Saudade — GUESTHOUSE $
(☑ 239 167 500; www.despertarsaudade.com; Praça da República 8; s €45, d €60-65; ❈ ☎) In a town house overlooking Praça da República, this friendly lodging makes an excellent base. Its rooms are smallish but immaculately laid out with blond parquet and functional modern decor. There's also an airy kitchen where you can make your own breakfast with the supplies provided, and a small back courtyard.

Quebra-Luz — GUESTHOUSE $
(☑ 912 278 779; www.quebra-luz.com; Rua Quebra Costas 18; d €43-55; @ ☎) Right on the old town's 'back-breaking' stairs, this friendly, homely place makes a good central base. It's a bright, second-floor apartment with four simply furnished rooms and a central kitchen. Note that two rooms share a bathroom and one has an exterior private bathroom. Note also you'll have to drag your luggage here – there's no lift and no nearby parking.

Hotel Botânico de Coimbra — HOTEL $
(☑ 239 714 824; www.hotelbotanicocoimbra.pt; Bairro de São José 15; s/d/tr/q €38/49/69/85; ❈ ☎) This immaculate two-star is a little way out of the centre near the botanic gardens. It's worth the walk, though, with spotless rooms furnished with polished wood floors, crimson bedspreads and plain white walls. A warm welcome awaits and there's easy street parking in the vicinity. Excellent value for money.

★ The Luggage Hostel & Suites — HOSTEL $$
(☑ 239 820 257; www.theluggagehostel.com; Rua Antero de Quental 125; d €50-70, ste €85-99; ☎) Housed in a white 1920s villa, complete with garden and columned portico, The Luggage is a hostel in name only. At the time of research its dorms were about to be transformed into private rooms, adding to the lovely, high-ceilinged rooms already on offer. Throughout, the decor is fantastic, marrying creaking parquet floors and original window fittings with hip, vintage furniture and city views.

★ Five Senses Hostel — HOSTEL $$
(☑ 918 383 840, 239 094 135; www.fivesenseshostel.com; Rua da Figueira da Foz 51; dm €23, d €55-80, f €100-140; ❈ ☎) Handily located for the bus station, yet still accessible to the historic centre on foot, this modern boutique-style hostel impresses. It has a range of rooms, from four-bed dorms to family rooms, each spacious and bright with cool white decor and original furniture. Guests also have run of a kitchen and lovely outdoor patio.

Casa Pombal — GUESTHOUSE $$
(☑ 239 835 175; www.casapombal.com; Rua das Flores 18; s/d €55/65, with shared bathroom €40/54; ❈ ☎) In a lovely old-town location, this snug guesthouse squeezes tons of charm into a small space. Interiors boast dark wood floors, ceramic tiles and aquamarine blues, while rooms are cosy and individually decorated – two boast magnificent views. Breakfast is good and the friendly staff can provide multilingual advice.

Hotel Vitória — HOTEL $$
(☑ 239 824 049; www.hotelvitoria.pt; Rua da Sota 9-13; s €45-55, d €55-75, tr €67-90; ❈ ☎) With attractive rooms and a prime location near the action, the friendly family-run Vitóriais a great choice. Its light-filled rooms are clean and unfussy, sporting unadorned white walls and earthy brown tones, while those on the 3rd floor also come with views of the old town or river. To eat in-house, there's a restaurant on the ground floor, open noon to 3pm and 7pm to 10pm.

Hotel Residencial Alentejana — HOTEL $$
(☑ 239 825 903; www.residencialalentejana.com; Rua Dr António Henriques Seco 1; s €48-62, d €55-69; ❈ ☎) A characterful, old-fashioned two-star run by kindly owners. It's a little out from the centre but well placed for the student-driven bar life on Praça da República. Rooms are high-ceilinged and warmly furnished with heavy wood furniture.

★ Quinta das Lágrimas — LUXURY HOTEL $$$
(☑ 239 802 380; www.quintadaslagrimas.pt; Rua António Augusto Gonçalves; r €160-450; P ❈ ☎) Coimbra's sole five-star hotel is charmingly ensconced in the romantic Jardim Quinta das Lágrimas (p314) on the west bank of the Mondego. Choose between classic, richly furnished rooms in the original 18th-century palace, or go for something more minimalist in the modern annex. There's a formal fine-dining restaurant for gourmet dinners, and a fully equipped spa.

Hotel Oslo — HOTEL $$$
(☑ 239 829 071; www.hoteloslo-coimbra.pt; Avenida Fernão de Magalhães 25; s €55-156 d €75-

156; P✳🛜) Near Coimbra A train station, this is a comfortable, business-like hotel. Rooms come in shades of beige and are smart and well-maintained, while the 5th-floor breakfast room and bar (open 8pm to 1am) command memorable rooftop views. Free parking is a further bonus. Check the website for deals for longer stays.

🍴 Eating

Coimbra is packed with restaurants, bars, cafes and takeaways catering to all budgets. Hotspots include the area between Praça do Comércio and Coimbra A train station, which is full of characterful, old-school Portuguese eateries, and the upper town, which boasts a number of contemporary tapas-style places.

Justiça e Paz
CAFETERIA $

(☑239 822 483; www.justicaepaz.com/restaurante-e-bar.php; Rua de Couraça de Lisboa 30; fixed-price menus €5.50-7; ⊙8.30am-11.30pm Mon-Fri, 9am-7pm Sat) Part of the university's law faculty, this busy cafeteria is one of Coimbra's best-kept secrets. An excellent option for the budget traveller, it's open to everyone and serves a selection of daily dishes, cheap snacks and drinks. Best of all, it has a lovely sun terrace with views over the city's botanic garden.

Adega Paço dos Condes
PORTUGUESE $

(☑239 825 605; Rua do Paço do Conde 1; mains €5.50-13; ⊙11am-midnight Mon-Sat) Drawing a mixed crowd of students, locals and visitors, this unpretentious family-run grill is a reliable choice for a good-value fill-up. Don't expect culinary fireworks, just honest helpings of char-grilled meat or fish with salad and chips. There's a long list of daily specials, which are often your best way forward.

Porta Larga
SANDWICHES $

(☑239 823 619; Rua das Padeiras 35; sandwiches €4.50; ⊙9am-8pm Mon-Sat) Meat lovers should make a beeline for this workaday eatery renowned for its *leitão* (spit-roasted pork). For a taste on the hoof, go for a *sandes de leitão* (sandwich) at the bar with a refreshing beer.

Mercado Municipal Dom Pedro V
MARKET $

(Rua Olímpio Nicolau Rui Fernandes; ⊙7am-7pm Mon-Sat) A colourful stop for self-caterers, this market is full of lively fruit and veg stalls, fishmongers and butchers shops displaying the full range of Portuguese cuts (hooves, claws and all).

⭐Sete Restaurante
MODERN PORTUGUESE $$

(☑239 060 065; www.facebook.com/sete restaurante; Rua Dr. Martins de Carvalho 10; mains €11-19; ⊙1-4pm & 7-midnight Wed-Mon) Squeezed into a corner behind the Igreja de Santa Cruz (p313), this intimate restaurant is one of the most popular in town. Its casual wine bar vibe, personable service and modern take on Portuguese cuisine ensure it's almost always buzzing. Book ahead to avoid disappointment.

⭐Loggia
MODERN PORTUGUESE $$

(☑239 853 076; www.loggia.pt; Largo Dr José Rodrigues, Museu Nacional de Machado de Castro; mains €13-18; ⊙10am-6pm Tue & Sun, to 10.30pm Wed-Sat) As much as its confident modern cuisine, the Loggia's big draw is its setting, on a panoramic terrace overlooking the old town. There's open-air seating for romantic sunset dinners, or you can sit inside and admire the views from its glass-walled dining room. Its lunch buffet (€9.50) is great value.

Tapas Nas Costas
TAPAS $$

(☑239 157 425; Rua Quebra Costas 19; tapas €4-7.50; ⊙11am-midnight Tue-Sat, to 4pm Sun) All the rage right now, this sophisticated spot boasts a prime location on the steep steps up the historic centre. Refined decor and friendly service set the tone for fine Portuguese wines and gourmet tapas such as *costeletinhas de borrego* (lamb chops with honey and almonds). Reservations a must.

Zé Manel dos Ossos
PORTUGUESE $$

(☑239 823 790; Beco do Forno 12; mains €8-16; ⊙12.30-3pm & 7.30-10pm Mon-Sat) Tucked down a nondescript alley, this hole-in-the-wall gem, papered with scholarly doodles and scribbled poems, is much loved for its hearty meat specialities. Typical of its culinary approach is *feijoada de javali*, a thick casserole of wild boar, beans and black pudding. Come early or be prepared to wait in line.

A Cozinha da Maria
TASCA $$

(☑968 650 253; www.facebook.com/cozinhada maria/; Rua das Azeiteiras 65; mains €10-15; ⊙noon-3pm & 7-11pm) With its low wood-beamed ceiling, tiled walls and rustic decor, this is the very picture of a traditional backstreet *tasca* (tavern). In keeping with the look, the cuisine is orthodox, featuring much-loved classics such as fortifying *chanfana à serrana* (stewed highland goat) and *bacalhau à brás* (fried flaked cod).

THE BEIRAS COIMBRA

Fangas Mercearia Bar
TAPAS $$

(☑ 934 093 636; Rua Fernandes Tomás 45-49; tapas €5.90-14; ⊙ 12.30-4pm & 7-11.30pm Sun-Wed, to 12.30am Thu-Sat) Top-quality produce is used to create delightful *petiscos* (tapas) at this bright, casual eatery. It's an animated spot with Paul Klee–inspired wallpaper and a convivial buzz and there's a delicious array of tapas to choose from – sausages, stuffed mushrooms, spicy prawns. Down the road you can get more of the same at its bigger twin, Fangas Maior (same hours).

Restaurante Giro Churrasqueira
PORTUGUESE $$

(☑ 239 833 020; www.restaurantegiro.com; Rua das Azeiteiras 39; mains €9-16; ⊙ noon-3.30pm & 6-10pm Mon-Sat) This local favourite, an intimate back-alley restaurant, specialises in tasty traditional Portuguese fare. The menu features many regional staples, but the stars of the show are the grilled meats and fish, served quickly and in hefty portions.

Restaurante Zé Neto
PORTUGUESE $$

(☑ 239 826 786; Rua das Azeiteiras 8; mains €7-14; ⊙ noon-3pm & 7pm-11pm Mon-Sat) This marvellous family-run place specialises in homemade Portuguese standards such as *chanfana* (goat) cooked in red wine, and *dobrada* (tripe) served with beans and rice. It's well known locally and fills quickly, particularly at weekends, when you'd do well to reserve ahead.

Restaurante Jardim da Manga
PORTUGUESE $$

(☑ 239 829 156; Rua Olímpio Nicolau Rui Fernandes; mains €9-14.50; ⊙ 8am-midnight Sun-Fri) This bright and breezy cafeteria-style restaurant serves up tasty meat and fish dishes, with pleasant outdoor seating beside the Jardim da Manga fountain. Helpings are generous, and the complimentary glass of sweet Douro wine rounds things off nicely.

🍷 Drinking & Nightlife

Coimbra has some action-packed bars. In the old town, around Praça da Sé Velha, students spill on to the cobblestones outside classic pubs, while the area around Praça da República is chock-full of bars, cafes and clubs.

★ Galeria Santa Clara
BAR

(☑ 239 441 657; www.galeriasantaclara.com; Rua António Augusto Gonçalves 67; ⊙ 2pm-2am Sun-Thu, to 3am Fri & Sat) Arty tea room by day and chilled-out bar by night, this is a terrific place to hang out. Inside, it's all mismatched vintage furniture, books and chandeliers, while out back the garden terrace boasts lovely views back over the river to the historic centre. The atmosphere is laid-back, and it can feel like a house party when things get going.

Café Santa Cruz
CAFE

(☑ 239 833 617; www.cafesantacruz.com; Praça 8 de Maio; ⊙ 7am-2am) Coimbra's historic showpiece cafe is set in a beautiful high-vaulted former chapel, with stained-glass windows and graceful stone arches. Outside, a terrace grants lovely views over Praça 8 de Maio. Don't miss the *crúzios,* egg- and almond-based conventual cakes for which the cafe is famous.

Aqui Base Tango
BAR

(☑ 916 882 731; www.facebook.com/aquibasetango; Rua Venâncio Rodrigues 8; ⊙ 4pm-6am Mon-Sat) This offbeat house is one of Coimbra's most enticing hangouts, a quirky space with original decor and a relaxed, inclusive vibe. Music ranges from jazz to alternative rock, and there's always something going on. Gay-friendly, too. Check its Facebook page for upcoming events.

Noites Longas
CLUB

(☑ 965 076 429; Rua Almeida Garrett 11; ⊙ 11pm-6am Mon-Sat) This alternative club plays mainly rock and metal, loudly and into the early hours. It's not subtle – think standing room only and sweaty dancing – but it's a reliable local favourite. Gay-friendly.

Bar Quebra Costas
BAR

(☑ 239 841 174; Rua Quebra Costas 45; ⊙ noon-3am Mon-Sat, to 9pm Sun) This Coimbra classic has a sunny, cobbled terrace, an artsy interior, friendly service, and a chilled-out jazzy soundtrack. It's perfectly placed for people-watching over an ice-cold beer after a day pounding the streets.

AAC Bar
BAR

(Bar Associação Académica de Coimbra; www.facebook.com/baraac; Rua Padre António Vieira 1; ⊙ 10am-4am Mon-Fri, from 3pm Sat & Sun) Join the black-caped students at their union bar, where beers are cheap and everyone is welcome. The esplanade out back, with wood decking and a grassy lawn, makes an agreeable refuge.

☆ Entertainment

★ Fado ao Centro
FADO

(☑ 239 837 060; www.fadoaocentro.com; Rua Quebra Costas 7; show incl drink €10; ⊙ show 6pm)

At the bottom of the old town, this friendly cultural centre is a good place to acquaint yourself with fado. The evening 6pm show includes plenty of explanation, in Portuguese and English, about the history of the music and the meaning of each song. It's tourist-oriented, but the performers enjoy it and do it well.

You can chat with the musicians afterwards over a glass of port (included).

Á Capella   FADO

(☑239 833 985; www.acapella.com.pt; Rua do Corpo de Deus; entry with/without drink €10/5; ⊙7pm-2am, shows 9.30pm) A 14th-century chapel turned intimate cocktail lounge, this place hosts nightly performances by the city's most renowned fado musicians. Shows cater directly to a tourist crowd, but the music is excellent and the intimate setting creates a wonderful atmosphere, abetted by heart-rendingly good acoustics .

Teatro Académico
de Gil Vicente   THEATRE, CONCERT VENUE

(TAGV; ☑239 855 630; www.tagv.pt; Praça da República; ⊙box office 5-10pm Mon-Sat) This university-run auditorium is an important venue, staging a varied programme of theatre, cinema, dance and music.

🛍 Shopping

Comur   FOOD

(www.comur.com; Largo da Portagem 25; ⊙10am-10pm) Canned fish becomes baroque art at this bright, hard-to-miss shop. The interior, a blast of kitsch gold, camp frescoes and red carpet, is crammed with elaborately designed cans of sardines and all manner of preserved fish. But while the packaging is gleefully over-the-top, the fish is high quality, produced at the historic Comur cannery near Aveiro.

Anthrop   DESIGN

(☑963 705 464; www.facebook.com/Anthrop.portugal; Rua Fernandes Tomás 2-6; ⊙11am-7.30pm Mon-Fri, 2-7.30pm Sat) Ceramicist Célia Guerreiro set up this shop to promote Portuguese designers. The result is a browser's delight, with a small but well-curated selection of clothes, homeware, artisanal jewellery, handcrafted bags and original soaps, some made from olive oil and goat's milk.

Carlos Tomás   CERAMICS

(☑239 812 945; carlostomas_ceramicaartesanal@hotmail.com; Largo da Sé Velha 4; ⊙9am-8pm) Lovely hand-painted ceramics by Senhor Tomás. If you can't find anything from the stacks of mugs, jars, plates tiles, objets d'art on sale, he can do custom-made orders to your designs.

ℹ Information

MEDICAL SERVICES

Hospital da Universidade de Coimbra (☑239 400 400; www.chuc.min-saude.pt; Praceta Prof. Mota Pinto) Located 1.5km northeast of the centre.

POST

Post Office (Rua Castro Matoso 12c; ⊙9am-7pm Mon-Fri) Up the road from Praça da República.

TOURIST INFORMATION

These offices offer good town maps as well as what's-on listings.

Turismo Largo da Portagem (☑239 488 120; www.turismodecoimbra.pt; Largo da Portagem; ⊙9am-6pm Mon-Fri, 9.30am-1pm & 2-5.30pm Sat & Sun) Coimbra's main tourist office. Can provide information on the city and surrounding areas.

Turismo Praça República (☑939 010 084; www.turismodecoimbra.pt; Praça da República; ⊙9.30am-6pm Mon-Fri) On the east side of town.

ℹ Getting There & Away

BUS

From the **bus station** (Av Fernão de Magalhães; ⊙ticket office 8am-10pm), a 15-minute walk northwest of the centre, **Rede Expressos** (☑239 855 270; www.rede-expressos.pt) runs at least a dozen buses daily to Lisbon (€14.50, 2½ hours) and Porto (€12.50, 1½ hours), as well as direct services to Braga (€14, 2¾ hours, six daily), and Faro (€28, six to 8½ hours, two daily).

Regional destinations served include Seia (€10, 1¾ hours, five to seven daily) and Viseu (€8.50, 1¼ hours, at least hourly), where you can pick up onward connections to Guarda.

TRAIN

Coimbra has two train stations: **Coimbra-B** and the more central **Coimbra A** (called just 'Coimbra' on timetables). Long-distance trains stop at Coimbra-B, 2km north of the city centre, from where local trains connect with Coimbra A – this connection is included in the price of tickets to/from Coimbra.

Coimbra has regular services to Lisbon (AP/IC €23.20/19.50, 1¾/two hours, hourly) and Porto (€17/13.40, one/1¼ hours, at least hourly). Trains also serve Figueira da Foz (€2.75, 1¼ hours, hourly weekdays, fewer on weekends) and Aveiro (€5.20, one hour, at least hourly).

ⓘ Getting Around

BICYCLE

Bike and electronic bikes are available to rent from **By Bike** (☑ 919 080 216; www.facebook.com/bybikecoimbra; bike per hr/half-day/day €5/10/15, E-bikes €10/20/30).

BUS

Coimbra's bus service is run by **SMTUC** (☑ 800 203 280; www.smtuc.pt). Tickets can be bought on board, at the **SMTUC office** (Largo do Mercado; ⊙ 7am-7pm Mon-Fri, 8am-1pm Sat) by the Elevador (p320), at official kiosks, and at some *tabacarias* (tobacconists-slash-newsagents). A single ticket costs €1.60. There are also multiuse tickets (three/five/10 trips €2.20/3.15/5.80; day ticket €3.50).

Useful routes include:

27, **28** and **29** From Coimbra-B train station to Praça da República via the main bus station.

103 From Coimbra A station up to the university.

Electric buses on the **Linha Azul** (blue line) run a circular route through the historic centre from Largo da Portagem.

CAR

If you come by car, be prepared for snarled traffic and limited parking. There are car parks at the Mercado Municipal Dom Pedro V and, over the river, on Praça das Cortes de Coimbra near the Ponte de Santa Clara. Nearer the university, street parking is available around Praça da República.

You can hire cars from **Hertz** (☑ 219 426 300; www.hertz.pt; Edifício Tricana, Rua Padre Estevão Cabral, Shop 6; ⊙ 9am-1pm & 2-7pm Mon-Fri, 9am-1pm Sat).

ELEVADOR DO MERCADO

The **Elevador** (Largo do Mercado; ticket €1.60; ⊙ 7.30am-9pm Mon-Sat, 10am-9pm Sun) – an elevator and funicular connected by a walkway – takes you from the market up to the university district. It'll save you a steep uphill climb. Use city bus tickets.

Around Coimbra

Luso & Mata Nacional do Buçaco

A retreat from the world for almost 2000 years, the Mata Nacional do Buçaco (National Forest of Buçaco or Bussaco) sits on the slopes of the Serra do Buçaco, some 30km north of Coimbra. The forest, which is now a walled 105-hectare reserve, has an astounding 700 plant species, from huge Mexican cedars to tree-sized ferns, and its own fairy-tale royal palace. A network of paths criss-crosses the woodland, whose beauty has inspired reams of poetry over the ages. Generations of writers have enshrined the forest in the national imagination with breathless hymns to its natural and spiritual beauty.

Access to the forest is through the quaint spa town of Luso at the foot of the Serra. The town, famed for its thermal waters, has some decent accommodation, or you can visit on an easy day trip from Coimbra.

History

The Luso and Buçaco area probably served as a Christian refuge as early as the 2nd century AD, although the earliest known hermitage was founded by Benedictine monks in the 6th century. In 1628 Carmelite monks embarked on an extensive programme of forestation – they planted exotic species, laid paths and built high stone walls around the woods. The forest became so renowned that in 1643 Pope Urban VIII decreed that anyone damaging the trees would be excommunicated.

The peace was eventually shattered in 1810, when Napoleon's forces were soundly beaten here by an Anglo-Portuguese army led by the British general Arthur Wellesley, the future Duke of Wellington (the battle is re-enacted every 27 September). In 1834, when religious orders throughout Portugal were abolished, the forest became state property.

◉ Sights

★**Mata Nacional do Buçaco**   FOREST
(☑ 231 937 000; www.fmb.pt; per car/cyclist/pedestrian €5/free/free; ⊙ 8.30am-7pm Mon-Fri, to 8pm Sat & Sun) Sprawling out from the Palacio do Buçaco (p321), this aromatic forest is littered with crumbling chapels, fountains, ponds and exotic trees. There is a network of well-signposted trails leading to features such as the lush **Vale dos Fetos** (Valley of the Ferns) and the **Fonte Fria**, a monumental stone staircase near a picturesque pond. Another lovely route is the **Via Sacra**, which passes a series of chapels as it wends its way up to the Cruz Alta, a hilltop cross offering wonderful views.

From Luso, you can access the forest on foot – it's a steep uphill walk from the southern end of Avenida Emídio Navarro – or by car through the Portas das Ameias some 900m from the centre.

CONÍMBRIGA

Set in the lush countryside southwest of Coimbra, Conímbriga Roman Ruins (☑ 239 949 110; www.conimbriga.pt; Condeixa-a-Velha; ruins & museum adult/child €4.50/free; ⊘ 10am-7pm Mar–Oct, to 6pm Nov–Feb) is Portugal's largest and most impressive Roman site. Ancient Conímbriga was an important city in the Roman province of Lusitania and its ruins are extensive and wonderfully well preserved. Highlights include villas paved with elaborate floor mosaics – in particular the Casa dos Repuxos (House of Fountains) – and a 3rd-century defensive wall.

To get your head around Conímbriga's fascinating history, start (or finish) at the small museum near the entrance. Here you can browse finds unearthed at the site, including mosaics, sculptural fragments, coins, jewellery and everyday household items. There's also a scale model of the forum which puts flesh on the skeletal remains you'll see outside.

Conímbriga's origins date to Celtic times (*briga* is a Celtic term for a defended area). But it was under the Romans, who arrived in the 2nd century BC, that it blossomed, thanks, in part, to its strategic position on the main route between Lisbon (Olisipo) and Braga (Bracara Augusta). After a golden age in the 1st and 2nd centuries, it eventually fell prey to barbarian attacks and, in 468 AD, it was captured by Germanic Suebi forces. Many citizens fled to nearby Aeminius (Coimbra) – thereby saving the city from destruction.

As you enter the ruins, you'll soon find a massive wall rising in front of you. Dating to the 3rd century, this was built to keep out the by-now threatening barbarians and originally ran right through the city centre – much of the city's residential area was simply abandoned.

Under the walls are a series of mosaic-floored villas, including the Casa dos Esqueletos (House of Skeletons) and Casa da Cruz Suástica (House of the Swastika) – to the Romans the swastika was a symbol of good luck. Over the wall, the Casa de Cantaber was the city's largest private villa.

You'll find the most impressive mosaics in the 1st-century Casa dos Repuxos. These vivid illustrations, set around a small central garden, depict the four seasons and various hunting scenes.

Other highlights include the remnants of the Grandes Termas do Sul (Great Southern Baths) one of the city's several baths complexes; part of a 3km-long aqueduct; and the forum, which was originally surrounded by covered porticoes.

To get to the site by public transport, Transdev (☑ 225 100 100; www.transdev.pt) runs buses from near Coimbra A station to the ruins (€2.55, 45 minutes, three times daily). You'll need to check the precise hours, though, as they change seasonally. Coimbra's turismo (p319) can provide timetables.

Palacio do Buçaco PALACE
(Mata Nacional do Buçaco) Originally a royal summer retreat, this lavish palace, now home to the Palace Hotel do Buçaco (p322), was built in 1907 on the site of a 17th-century Carmelite monastery. It's an extraordinary sight, over the top in every way. Its exterior of turrets and spires is surrounded by rose gardens and box hedges, while inside, neo-Manueline carvings and archways crown grand staircases and *azulejos* showing scenes from *Os Lusiados* (The Lusiads). These depict Portuguese armies winning sea battles as their stupefied opponents look on in dismay.

Note that access to the palace, which is 2km up from the Portas das Ameias, is limited to hotel and restaurant guests.

Convento de Santa Cruz do Buçaco CONVENT
(www.fmb.pt; ⊘ closed for restoration) Tucked away behind the Palace Hotel do Buçaco (p322), this is what remains of the convent where Arthur Wellesley rested after he had led his Anglo-Portuguese army to victory at the Battle of Bussaco in 1810. The atmospheric interior has decaying religious paintings, some guns from the battle, and a much-venerated image of *Nossa Senhora do Leite* (Our Lady of the Milk), with a raft of ex-voto offerings.

🏃 Activities

Termas de Luso SPA
(☑ 231 937 910; www.termasdeluso.pt; Rua Álvaro Castelões; ⊘ 9am-1pm & 2-7pm Mon-Fri, 9am-1pm

& 3-8pm Sat, 9am-1pm & 3-7pm Sun) Just the ticket after a long walk in the forest, the Termas de Luso welcomes drop-in visitors for hammams and baths (from €25 for 30 minutes), as well as therapies ranging from hydro-massages (€20) to facials (€50). Or just fill up your water bottle for free at the natural spring fountain in the adjacent square.

Sleeping & Eating

Alegre Hotel HOTEL $
(☑231 930 256; www.alegrehotels.com; Rua Emídio Navarro 2, Luso; s €50-60, d €55-65; P ☎ ☒) Hard to miss, with its flags and pink facade, this grand 19th-century townhouse charms with its elegant old-world feel and spacious rooms. These come with creaking wood floors, plush drapes and polished period furniture. Its appeal is further enhanced by the pretty vine-draped garden with pool.

Palace Hotel do Buçaco HISTORIC HOTEL $$$
(☑231 937 970; www.almeidahotels.pt/pt/hotel-coimbra-portugal; Mata Nacional do Buçaco; s €148-199, d €169-225; P) Originally a royal hunting lodge, this Gothic-Manueline palace in the Buçaco forest is a delightfully ostentatious place to stay. Common areas are stunning – particularly the lobby area and grand staircase – though some of the guest rooms feel a little musty. Don't expect mod cons – there's no air-con, and wi-fi is only available in communal areas – but do expect a dreamy setting and memorable meals.

★**Pedra de Sal** PORTUGUESE $$
(☑231 939 405; www.restaurantepedradesal.com; Rua Francisco A Dinis 33, Luso; mains €9-20; ☉noon-3pm & 7-10pm Wed-Mon) Winningly done out in dark wood, this cosy wine-bar-restaurant is the best in Luso by far. Its menu covers the usual array of meat and fish dishes; however, it's the succulent cuts of Iberian pork and expertly grilled steaks that stand out. The wine list and service are also excellent. Book ahead at weekends.

ℹ Information

Turismo (☑231 939 133; Rua Emídio Navarro 136, Luso; ☉9am-1pm & 2.30-5.30pm) Has accommodation information, internet access, town and forest maps.

ℹ Getting There & Away

BUS

Three weekday buses run from Coimbra's bus station to Luso (€3.75, 40 minutes), with two continuing on to Buçaco (€4, 50 minutes). Note, however, only one bus makes the return journey. Timetables are seasonal so it always pays to check times beforehand.

CAR

If driving from Coimbra, the most scenic route is via the lovely, foresty N235 off the main IP3.

TRAIN

Three daily trains run from Coimbra-B to Luso-Buçaco (€2.55, 25 minutes), but only the first (departing at 12.25pm) is a practical option for a day trip – the others don't give you enough time in Luso.

From Luso-Buçaco station it's a 15-minute walk to the centre of Luso.

Montemor-o-Velho

POP 3150

Some 25km west of Coimbra, the small town of Montemor-o-Velho is home to one of the area's great landmarks: a formidable hilltop castle dating from Moorish times. The *castelo* is pretty much the only sight in town, but it's well worth a detour, if nothing else for the fine views it commands.

◉ Sights

Castelo do Montemor-o-Velho CASTLE
(☉9.30am-6pm Apr-Sep, 9.30am-5.30pm Oct-Mar) FREE Perched atop a rugged hilltop, this medieval castle dominates the surrounding landscape. Originally dating to the 10th century, it was the scene of much fighting during the Reconquista as Moors and Christians sought to conquer it. It eventually fell to Ferdinand I of Castile and León in 1064 and less than a century later, Ferdinand's great-grandson Afonso Henrique claimed it for his new Kingdom of Portugal.

Over the centuries the castle was modified several times, and most of the current structure dates to the 14th century.

Nowadays, you can walk the crenellated battlements and survey the lush rice fields by the Rio Mondego far below. Inside little remains except for part of the 13th-century Paço das Infantas (Princesses' Palace) and the Igreja de Santa Maria de Alcáçova, a small Romanesque church with a 16th-century Manueline interior. Note the gold altarpiece, actually a 17th-century addition, and adjacent tiled chapel.

ℹ Information

Turismo (☑239 680 380; www.cm-montemorvelho.pt; Castelo do Montemor-o-Velho;

⊙ 9.30am-6pm Apr-Sep, 9.30am-5.30pm Oct-Mar) Up at the *castelo*.

❶ Getting There & Away

Regular trains run from Coimbra-B to Alfarelos station (€2.20, 35 minutes, at least hourly) some 5km southeast of Montemor-o-Velho. From there, a taxi up to the castle will cost around €7.

Alternatively, Moisés Correia de Oliveira (www.moises-transportes.pt) buses between Coimbra (around €4, one hour) and Figueira da Foz (around €3, 30 minutes) stop in Montemor-o-Velho five to eight times daily, less often on Sundays.

Figueira da Foz

POP 62,100

Popular with Portuguese holidaymakers for over a century, the beach resort of Figueira da Foz (fi-*guy*-ra da *fosh*) continues to attract big summer crowds – including Spaniards lured by easy motorway access, and surfers drawn to championship-calibre waves at nearby Cabedelo. For most visitors, the star attractions are Figueira's outlandishly wide beach and Las Vegas-style casino. Out of season the town has a more tranquil charm, but thanks to its many restaurants and bars it's not a lonely experience. In summer it's another matter: sizzling bodies and candy-striped beach huts fill every square inch of sand, and evenings are upbeat.

◉ Sights & Activities

Praia da Figueira   BEACH

Figueira da Foz's main beach is one of Portugal's largest, a vast expanse of yellow sand. It gets packed to the gills in summer, but has all the services, from bars to beach sports and water activities.

To the north is the adjacent beach, Praia de Buarcos.

Historically, Figueira's beach was one of the first to promote tourism, as you'll see from old black-and-white photos around town and in many establishments.

Museu Municipal Dr Santos Rocha   MUSEUM

(☑ 233 402 840; Rua Calouste Gulbenkian; adult/child €2/free; ⊙ 9.30am-6pm Tue-Fri, 2-7pm Sat & Sun summer, 9.30am-5pm Tue-Fri, 2-7pm Sat winter) FREE This modern museum, beside the Parque das Abadias, houses a wonderfully eclectic collection of local archaeological finds, Roman coins, medieval statues, outlandish Indo-Portuguese furniture, objects

documenting Portugal's early African explorations and weapons from across the ages.

At the time of research, parts of the museum were closed for building work and admission was free.

Núcleo Museológico do Sal   MUSEUM

(☑ 966 344 488; Armazéns de Lavos; adult/child €1/free; ⊙ 10am-12.30pm & 2.30-6.45pm Wed-Sun summer, 10am-12.30pm & 2-4pm Thu-Sun winter) In the wetlands south of the city, this small museum charts the centuries-old history of salt production in the area. Old photos and models illustrate production techniques, while outside a network of boardwalks traverse the geometrically divided saltpans. Look out for wetland birds and a pair of giant pink flamingos.

Realistically, you'll need your own wheels to get to the museum, which is about 9km outside Figueira.

Serra da Boa Viagem   AREA

For those with wheels, this wooded headland carpeted in pines, eucalypts and acacias is a fine place for panoramas, picnics and cool walks. To get there it's a simple 4km drive from town: take the coastal road to Buarcos, turn right at the end and follow signs for the Parque Aventura.

Escola de Surf da Figueira da Foz   SURFING

(☑ 918 703 363; www.surfingfigueira.com; Praia Do Cabedelo 36, São Pedro; ⊙ 10am-7pm) Over the Rio Mondego by the Praia Do Cabedelo, this surf school offers lessons (group/individual €30/40) and kit rental (surfboard/stand-up paddleboard €20/30 per day).

⚜ Festivals & Events

Festas da Cidade   FIESTA

(⊙ Jun) Figueira's main annual bash sees two weeks of concerts, sports events, parades and fireworks.Highlights include the traditional processions held on 23 and 24 of June.

RFM Somnii   MUSIC

(www.rfm.sapo.pt/somnii) Thousands of fans take to Figueira's sands for this three-day festival of electronic dance music. Held in early July, it draws big-name DJs and top international acts.

🛏 Sleeping

Figueira has plenty of accommodation catering to all budgets. That said, you'll need to book for high season in July and August. In summer, you may be approached by locals offering private rooms: while informal, they

THE BEIRAS FIGUEIRA DA FOZ

Figueira da Foz

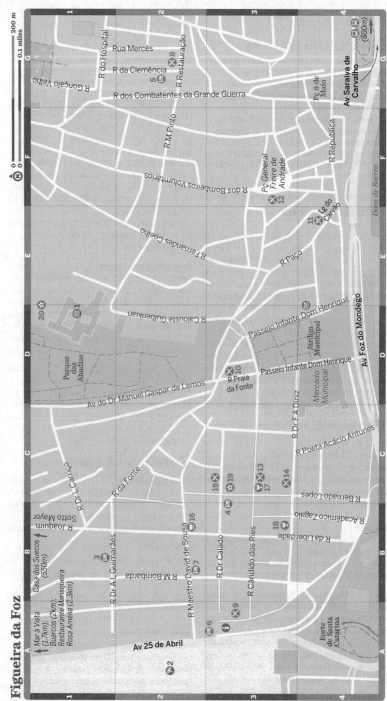

Map key / labels:

G
- R do Hospital
- Rua Mercês
- R da Clemência
- R Gonçalo Velho
- R Restauração
- 5
- 8
- R dos Combatentes da Grande Guerra
- Pç 8 de Maio
- Av Saraiva de Carvalho
- (600m)

F
- R M Pinto
- R dos Bombeiros Voluntários
- R Fernandes Coelho
- Pç General Freire de Andrade
- 12
- R República
- R Paço
- Lg do Carvão
- 11
- Doca de Recreio

E
- 20
- 1
- R Calouste Gulbenkian
- Passeio Infante Dom Henrique
- Jardim Municipal
- Passeio Infante Dom Henrique
- Av Foz do Mondego

D
- Parque das Abadias
- Av do Dr Manuel Gaspar de Lemos
- R Praia da Fonte
- 10
- Mercado Municipal
- R D F A Diniz

C
- R Dr L Carriço
- R da Fonte
- R Poeta Acácio Antunes
- 15
- 19
- 13
- 17
- 14
- R Bernado Lopes

B
- Casa dos Suecos (550m)
- R Joaquim Sotto Mayor
- R Dr A L Guimarães
- R M Bombarda
- 3
- 16
- R Maestro David de Sousa
- 7
- R Dr Calado
- 4
- R Académico Zagalo
- R da Liberdade
- 18
- R Cândido dos Reis
- 9
- 6
- 1

A
- Mar à Vista (1.7km); Buarcos (2km); Restaurante Marisqueira Rosa Amélia (2.3km)
- Av 25 de Abril
- 2
- Forte de Santa Catarina

- 200 m
- 0.1 miles

Figueira da Foz

⊙ Sights
1 Museu Municipal Dr Santos Rocha.......D1
2 Praia da Figueira.................................A2

🛏 Sleeping
3 Hotel Aviz...B1
4 Hotel Wellington..................................B3
5 Paintshop Hostel.................................G2
6 Sweet Atlantic Hotel............................A3
7 Universal Boutique Hotel.....................B2

⊗ Eating
8 A Grega...G2
9 Emanha Geladeria................................A3
10 Núcleo Sportinguista..........................D3

11 Pizzeria Claudio...................................E4
12 Praça 18..F3
13 Restaurante Caçarola I.........................C3
14 Volta e Meia...C3
15 Wine Bar by Cristal..............................C3

⊙ Drinking & Nightlife
16 A Pharmácia..B2
17 Nb Club...C3
18 Zeitgeist Caffé.....................................B3

⊕ Entertainment
19 Casino Figueira....................................C3
20 Centro de Artes e Espectáculos...........D1

are often decent deals. Expect discounts of up to 40% in winter.

★ Paintshop Hostel
HOSTEL $

(☎ 233 436 633; www.paintshophostel.com; Rua da Clemência 9; dm/d €20/50; @ 🛜) Set in a characterful blue house in the old part of town, this excellent hostel is a laid-back, sociable place with excellent facilities for backpackers and surfers. Beds are in colourful, high-ceilinged dorms or quiet private rooms, while communal areas include a kitchen and bar area. Bikes, surfboards and wetsuits are available for hire, and the laundry service (€5) is a godsend for road-weary travellers.

In high season, there are weekly barbecues and other events so you've got an instant social scene, led by the helpful English owners, who offer great advice on everything from biking routes to nightlife.

Orbitur Gala
CAMPGROUND $

(☎ 233 431 492; www.orbitur.pt; Praia de Gala; per person/tent/car €7.10/9.60/6.60; P 🛜 🏊) The best of the local campgrounds, this flat, shady spot is well equipped and has direct access to a nearby beach. It is, however, some way from the town centre, across the Rio Mondego, and you'll need your own transport to get there. Outside the summer high season, prices drop considerably.

Hotel Aviz
HOTEL $

(☎ 233 422 635; Rua Dr A L Guimarães 16; s €25-50, d €35-65; ✳🛜) Run by a charming, well-travelled couple, this old-school hotel is one of the best deals in town. Situated two blocks back from the beach, its rooms come with lovely wood floors, high ceilings and some nice period details. Reserve ahead in summer.

★ Universal Boutique Hotel
BOUTIQUE HOTEL $$

(☎ 233 090 110; www.universalboutiquehotel.pt; Rua Miguel Bombarda 50; d €70-100; ✳🛜) A lovely boutique hotel, only a few blocks back from the beach. Its interiors are stylish, from the ground-floor lounge bar to the carpeted guest rooms spread across four colour-themed floors. Throughout, contemporary architectural touches such as 'hanging' balustrades and a glass floor add to the look.

Casa dos Suecos
GUESTHOUSE $$

(☎ 233 040 483; www.casadossuecos.com; Rua Joaquim Sotto Mayor 73A; s/d/f €70/80/110; P 🛜 🏊) A large white villa surrounded by manicured lawns and a swimming pool, Casa dos Suecos is a tranquil spot. Rooms feel Scandinavian – clean lines and blonde woods – and provide great value if you don't mind being out of the thick of things. There's also an excellent restaurant serving classic Portuguese cuisine (mains €14-17; weekday lunch menu €10).

Hotel Wellington
HOTEL $$

(☎ 233 426 767; www.hotelwellington.pt; Rua Dr Calado 25; s €55-85, d €65-95, f €120-140; P ✳🛜) In the heart of the action near the casino, this business-like three-star offers immaculate rooms in shades of beige with lots of natural light and huge beds. If you're coming by car, the off-street parking (€7 per night) is another plus, well worth the price.

Sweet Atlantic Hotel
HOTEL $$$

(☎ 233 408 900; www.sweethotels.pt; Avenida 25 de Abril 21; d/f €140/185; P ✳ @ 🛜 🏊) Occupying a landmark glass tower on the seafront road, this excellent hotel boasts airy, modern rooms, ocean views and a long list of four-star services. These include an in-house restaurant and a spa with sauna, Turkish bath, pool and massages.

✕ Eating

★ Praça 18
CAFE $

(📞 914 418 757; Praça General Freire de Andrade 18; mains €4.50-9; ⊙ noon-2.30pm & 7-10pm Mon-Thu, to 10.30pm Fri, noon-3pm & 7-10.30pm Sat; 🖊) This cool retro-hip cafe features mismatched vintage furniture, blackboards and a menu that lists everything from gourmet hamburgers to salads and snacks. It's very popular and often full, meaning that service can be slow-ish, but there's a friendly, laid-back vibe, and the food is generally worth the wait.

Emanha Geladeria
ICE CREAM $

(Avenida 25 de Abril 62-64; ice cream from €2.25; ⊙ 8am-midnight winter, to 2am summer) A stop at this seafront *geladeria* is a rite of passage for any ice-cream fan. Choose from the array of classic flavours or push the boat out and go for goat's cheese, perhaps topped with a squirt of cream. It's on the terrace above the *turismo*.

Mar à Vista
SEAFOOD $

(Rua 5 de Outubro, Buarcos; mains €7-12; ⊙ 11am-8pm) Head to Buarcos at the northern end of the beachfront for a fishy fill-up at this humble, old-school tavern. A favourite with holidaymakers, its prime sea-facing tables are a lovely spot to try the local *sardinhas assadas* (grilled sardines) – as many as you can eat.

A Grega
PORTUGUESE $

(📞 233 420 665; Rua Restauração 30; mains €7-11; ⊙ 12.30-3pm & 7-10pm Tue-Sun) This modest neighbourhood restaurant excels in tasty grilled dishes, both fish and meat. Standouts include toothsome grilled squid and an Argentine-style *parrillada* (mixed grill; €17) that two will struggle to finish.

Pizzeria Claudio
PIZZA $

(📞 233 427 072; Largo do Carvão 11e; pizzas from €5.60-10.40; ⊙ noon-2.30pm & 7-10.30pm Tue-Sun) Take a break from *bacalhau* and *bife* (steak) with a pizza from this long-standing favourite. It gets very busy in summer so expect lines out the door. Also does takeaway.

Núcleo Sportinguista
PORTUGUESE $

(📞 233 434 882; Rua Praia da Fonte 14; mains €8-8.50; ⊙ noon-3pm & 7-10pm) Hearty portions of homestyle Portuguese cooking and a relaxed TV-on-in-the-corner vibe await at this long-standing restaurant. Sit down to football on the box – it's a supporters' club for Sporting Lisbon – and piled-high plates of grilled meat and fish accompanied by pitchers of refreshing *vinho verde* (semi-sparkling wine).

★ Volta e Meia
PORTUGUESE $$

(📞 233 418 381; www.voltaemeia.com; Rua Dr Francisco António Diniz 64; fixed-price lunch menu €8, mains €9-15; ⊙ noon-3pm & 7-11pm Tue-Sun) A casual cafe-restaurant with light floral decor and uplifting messages chalked on blackboards, this is a charming spot for a relaxed meal. The menu runs the gamut from salads and soups to vegetarian pasta and meat staples such as Portuguese-style pork (stewed with olives and vinegar-doused vegetables), all prepared with care and attractively served.

★ Wine Bar by Cristal
INTERNATIONAL $$

(📞 233 043 837; Rua Dr Calado 24; tapas €6.50-16; ⊙ 7pm-4am Tue-Sun) This cosy wine-bar-restaurant is the hottest ticket in town. Tapas and other dishes are served creatively and with pizzazz, while oenophiles can take their pick from the extensive list. There's also a great choice of cocktails and spirits (gin lovers are in for a treat). It's not a big place so reservations are recommended.

Restaurante Marisqueira Rosa Amélia
SEAFOOD $$

(📞 233 412 288; Av D João II 2, Buarcos; mains from €10; ⊙ 12.30-3pm & 7.30-10pm, closed Tue & Sun dinner) In the Hotel Tamargueira in Buarcos, this renowned seafood restaurant is the domain of traditional 'fisherwoman' and town personality Dona Rosa Amelia. Speciality of the house are her bountiful platters of *mariscos* (shellfish).

Restaurante Caçarola I
PORTUGUESE $$

(📞 233 424 861; Rua Cândido dos Reis 65; specials €8-10, mains €12.50-18.50; ⊙ 10am-2am) In business for more than 40 years, Caçarola draws a mixed bag of loyal locals and hungry visitors. What they come for are the good-value *combinados do dia* (daily lunch specials) and fantastic seafood dishes peppered with clams, shrimps, shellfish and locally-sourced fish. Seating is in the blue-tiled interior or glass sidewalk pavilion.

🍷 Drinking & Nightlife

Zeitgeist Caffé
BAR

(📞 966 310 564; Rua Dr Francisco António Diniz 82; ⊙ 8pm-2am Mon-Thu, to 4am Fri & Sat) With its lava lamps, subdued red lighting and retro '70s look, Zeitgeist is one of several popular hangouts in the bar-heavy area around Rua Académico Zagalo. There's regular live music and DJs in a wide range of styles.

A Pharmácia CAFE
(☑233 094 536; Rua da Liberdade 96; ☺8.30am-7pm Tue-Sat, to 1pm Sun) If coffee and cake sounds good, hotfoot it to this lovely relaxed cafe. Tea addicts can choose from a decent selection of infusions, while caffeine aficionados will not be disappointed by the excellent espresso-based coffees. Brownies, scones and cakes provide sweet sustenance.

Nb Club CLUB
(☑916 455 943; www.facebook.comnbclubfig; Rua Bernardo Lopes; ☺Sat 11pm-late & special events) Figueira's best-known nightclub, housed in the town's ex-casino, draws an energetic, party-loving crowd. DJs keep the tempo high on the dancefloors, spinning everything from funk to hip-hop, house and drum 'n' bass

☆ Entertainment

Casino Figueira CASINO
(☑233 408 400; www.casinofigueira.pt; Rua Dr Calado 1; ☺3pm-3am Sun-Thu, 4pm-4am Fri & Sat) Shimmering in neon and acrylic, Figueira's landmark casino is the epicentre of the resort's nightlife. Crawling with cash-laden holidaymakers, it has roulette and slot machines, as well as a restaurant and sophisticated bar. Dress rules apply at night so avoid beachwear, flip-flops and trainers.

Centro de Artes e Espectáculos ARTS CENTRE
(☑233 407 200 233 407 200; www.cae.pt; Rua Calouste Gulbenkian; ☺ticket office 1-7.30pm Mon-Fri, 2-7pm Sat) Behind the Museu Municipal Dr Santos Rocha (p323), CAE hosts big-name bands, theatre performances and arthouse cinema. Check the website or pick up a schedule at the turismo.

❶ Information

Biblioteca Municipal (Rua Calouste Gulbenkian; ☺9.30am-6.30pm Mon-Fri, 2-7pm Sat) Free internet at the town library.

Post Office (Passeio Infante Dom Henrique; ☺9am-6pm Mon-Fri) Near the Jardim Municipal (Municipal Garden).

Turismo (☑233 422 610; Avenida 25 de Abril 19; ☺9.30am-1pm & 2-5.30pm) Run by helpful staff. Has good maps and a useful listings magazine, *Agenda*.

❶ Getting There & Away

The **train station** (Avenida Saraiva de Carvalho) and **bus station** are right next to each other, 1.5km east of the beach.

BUS
Figueira is served by two long-distance bus companies.

Moisés Correia de Oliveira (☑233 426 703; www.moises-transportes.pt) has up to seven weekday buses (fewer on weekends), via Montemor-o-Velho, to Coimbra (€4.50, 1½ hours).

Rede Expressos (☑968 903 826; www.rede-expressos.pt) runs to Lisbon (€15.20, 2¾ hours, five to seven daily) and Aveiro (€8.30, 1¼ hours, two to four daily).

TRAIN
Train connections to/from Coimbra (€2.75, 1¼ hours, hourly weekdays, fewer on weekends).

Praia de Mira
POP 3150

For a few days of sunny, windblown torpor, head to Praia de Mira, the best-known resort on the largely undeveloped 50km coastline between Figueira da Foz and Aveiro. Sandwiched between a glorious sandy beach and a placid lagoon, it's a small place that while lively in summer has little to distract you from sun, surf and seafood.

⚑ Activities

Secret Surf School SURFING
(☑915 480 890; www.secretsurfschool.com; 1/5/10 classes per person €20/80/145; ☺daily Jul & Aug, Mon-Sat Sep-Jun) Operating out of Duna Bar on the beach, Secret Surf offers kit rental and two-hour surf lessons. Expect €50 for a private lesson, €20 for a group session.

⏚ Sleeping

Orbitur CAMPGROUND $
(☑231 471 234; www.orbitur.pt; Estrada Florestal 1-Km 2, Dunas de Mira; per adult/tent/car €6.80/7.25/6.80, two-person bungalow €89; ☺Mar-Oct; ℗ 🐾) This neat, shady campsite is about 1.5km out of town, set among trees at the southern end of the lagoon. It's well equipped and has a range of accommodation options, including wooden bungalows sleeping from two to five people. Prices drop markedly outside the August high season.

Maçarico Beach Hotel HOTEL $$$
(☑231 471 114; www.macaricobeachhotel.com; Rua Raúl Brandão 17; d €85-175, with sea view €115-195;

P ✳ 🛜 🖥) With its sudoku-like facade and a glitzy lobby, this seafront four-star is a stylish choice. Rooms, in cooling whites, browns and nautical blues, are neat and modern, with some offering fantastic sea views. The rooftop pool has more great vistas.

✗ Eating & Drinking

Salgáboca SEAFOOD $$
(🖉231 471 158; www.facebook.com/www.salgaboca.pt; Rua Furriel Henriques da Costa 19; mains €10-30; ⊘10.30am-4.30pm & 6.30pm-2am) There's usually a good buzz at this modern restaurant just off the seafront. The name means 'salty mouth' so there's no prize for guessing the menu: seafood galore. Staff speak English and other languages and are happy to work through the menu, which features everything from steamed clams to grilled Atlantic mackerel.

Restaurante Caçanito SEAFOOD $$
(🖉911 106 259; Av Arrais Batista Cera; mains €10-15; ⊘10am-2am Apr-Sep, 10am-6pm Sun-Thu, to 10pm Fri & Sat Oct-Mar) Fresh fish on the beach. It's a simple formula but one that has served the ever-popular Caçanito well over the years. Housed in an unadorned wood and glass cube on the sand, this modest outfit wins universal acclaim for its sunset views and fantastic char-grilled seafood.

Marisqueira Tezinho SEAFOOD $$
(🖉231 471 162; Av da Barrinha 9; mains €10-25; ⊘10am-3.30pm & 6.30-10pm, closed Tue Sep-Jun) Bustling and laid-back, this is one of several eateries facing on to the lagoon. The oars and nautical paraphernalia hint at what to expect: fresh-off-the-boat fish and a range of briny seafood platters.

Sixties Irish Pub IRISH PUB
(🖉919 358 897; Travessa Arrais Manuel Patrão 14; ⊘8pm-2am Mon-Thu, to 4am Fri & Sat, 3pm-2am Sun) Tucked into an alley a block from the beachfront, this snug pub has Guinness on tap and an inviting lively atmosphere.

ⓘ Information

Turismo (🖉231 480 550; www.cm-mira.pt; Avenida da Barrinha; ⊘9am-1pm & 2-5pm) On the lagoon at the southern end of town, it shares a traditional wooden house with a small ethnographic exhibition.

ⓘ Getting There & Away

Praia de Mira is 7km west of Mira, itself 35km north of Figueira da Foz.

Transdev (🖉225 100 100; www.transdev.pt) buses serve Praia de Mira from Coimbra (€5.25, 1½ hours, three to four times daily) and Aveiro (€4.25, 1¼ hours, three on weekdays). Services from Figueira da Foz (€6.10, 1¼ hours, one on weekdays) require a change of bus at Mira.

Aveiro

POP 78,450

Situated on the edge of an extensive coastal lagoon system, Aveiro (uh-vey-roo) is a prosperous town with a good-looking centre and a youthful, energetic buzz. It's occasionally dubbed the Venice of Portugal thanks to its small network of picturesque canals. But where the Italian city has gondolas, Aveiro has *moliceiros*.

There are several beaches within easy striking distance, and the nearby São Jacinto nature reserve provides walking and birdwatching – Aveiro's name is possibly derived from the Latin *aviarium* (place of birds).

History

A prosperous seaport in the early 16th century, Aveiro was battered by a ferocious storm in the 1570s that blocked the mouth of the Rio Vouga, closing it to ocean-going ships and creating fever-breeding marshes. Over the next two centuries, Aveiro's population shrank by three-quarters. But in 1808 the Barra Canal forged a passage back to the sea, and within a century Aveiro was rich again, as evidenced by the spate of art nouveau houses that still define the town's old centre. Salt harvested here was taken to Newfoundland to preserve cod that came back as *bacalhau*.

◉ Sights

★ **Reserva Natural das Dunas de São Jacinto** NATURE RESERVE
(www.natural.pt/portal/en/Infraestrutura/Item/176; ⊘9am-1pm & 2-5pm) This gloriously tranquil nature reserve extends north from São Jacinto, between the sea and the placid lagoon west of Aveiro. A network of trails runs through the pine woods and dunes, including an 8km (three-hour) loop, while various hides offer the chance for birdwatching – the best period for this is November to February. Access to the reserve is free but you should register at the interpretative centre (p333) 1.5km north of the ferry on the N327 road.

Aveiro

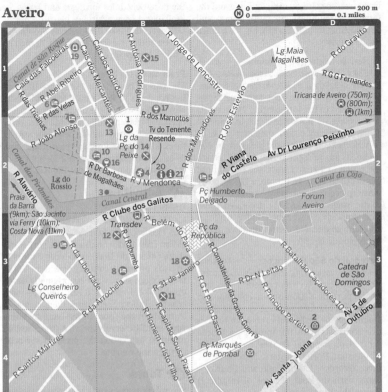

Aveiro

⊙ Sights
1 Mercado do Peixe	B2
2 Museu de Aveiro/Santa Joana	D4

✪ Activities, Courses & Tours
3 Aveitour	B2
4 Oficina do Doce	B2

🛏 Sleeping
5 Aveiro Palace Hotel	C2
6 Aveiro Rossio Bed & Breakfast	A1
7 Aveiro Rossio Hostel	A2
8 Hotel Aveiro Center	B3
9 Hotel das Salinas	A3
10 Hotel Moliceiro	B2

✪ Eating
11 Ki	B3
12 Maré Cheia	B3
13 O Bairro	B2
14 O Batel	B2
Restaurante Mercado do Peixe	(see 1)
15 Tasca Palhuça	B1

🍷 Drinking & Nightlife
16 Casa de Chá	B2
17 Má Ideia	B1

✪ Entertainment
18 Teatro Aveirense	B3

🛍 Shopping
19 Cais à Porta	A1

ℹ Information
20 Espaço Turismo & Museus	B2
21 Regional Turismo	B2

To get to the reserve from Aveiro, take a bus to Forte da Barra (return €5.05) and then the ferry to São Jacinto (return passenger/car €3.30/9.30). Check schedules at www.aveirobus.pt. By car, you can avoid the ferry by circumnavigating the lagoon and approaching from the north, but it's a much longer journey.

Museu de Aveiro/Santa Joana   MUSEUM

(📞 234 423 297; www.facebook.com/museuaveiro; Avenida Santa Joana; adult/child €5/free; ⊙ 10am-12.30pm & 1.30-6pm Tue-Sun) This fine museum, housed in the 15th-century Mosteiro de Jesus, owes its finest treasures to Princesa Joana (later canonised), daughter of Afonso V. In 1472, 11 years after the convent was founded, Joana 'retired' here and, though forbidden to take full vows, she stayed until her death in 1490. Her tomb, a 17th-century masterpiece of inlaid marble mosaic, takes centre stage in a lavishly decorated room (the remodelled lower choir stalls), while an adjacent gold-leafed chapel displays *azulejos* depicting her life.

Catedral de São Domingos   CATHEDRAL

(www.paroquiagloria.org; Rua Batalhão Caçadores 10; ⊙ 9am-7pm) Aveiro's cathedral was formerly part of a Dominican convent and contains a Manueline stone cross of Saint Domingo. The cathedral's sober white interior contrasts with the impressive facade centred on a portal flanked by two pairs of unusual Doric pilasters. Note also the three figures – Faith, Hope and Charity – along with the coat of arms of Infante D Pedro (the King's son).

Mercado do Peixe   MARKET

(Largo da Praça do Peixe; ⊙ 7am-1pm Tue-Sat) Right in the centre of town, Aveiro's covered fish market is a fun place to watch the local fishmongers sell their daily wares. If you want to taste as well as look, head upstairs to the market's restaurant, the **Restaurante Mercado do Peixe** (📞 234 351 303; www.restaurantemercadodopeixeaveiro.pt; Largo da Praça do Peixe; mains €12-22; ⊙ noon-3pm & 7.30-11pm, closed Mon & Sun dinner).

⊙ Beaches

★ Praia de São Jacinto   BEACH

Sandwiched between crashing Atlantic breakers and endless sand dunes, this magnificent beach forms the western flank of the São Jacinto nature reserve. To get here, you'll need to take a bus from Aveiro to Forte da Barra (return €5.05) and then the ferry to São Jacinto (return passenger/car €3.30/9.30). The beach is then 1.5km west of

the port. Schedules for boats and buses are available at www.aveirobus.pt.

Drivers can take the long way around the lagoon and arrive from the north, though it's a much longer trip.

Praia da Costa Nova   BEACH

The closest beaches to Aveiro are the surfing hangouts of **Praia da Barra** and **Costa Nova**, 13km west of the town. Both are developed and busy in summer; Costa Nova is the prettier of the two with its beachside strip of cafes, kitsch gift shops and picturesque candy-striped cottages. Buses (€2.55, hourly) go from Aveiro's Rua Clube dos Galitos.

🏃 Activities

Oficina do Doce   FOOD

(📞 234 098 840; www.oficinadodoce.com; Rua João Mendonça 23; tours adult/child €2.75/1.75; ⊙ 9am-7pm) Part living museum, part workshop, Oficina do Doce introduces visitors to Aveiro's proudest culinary tradition – *ovos moles:* eggy, sugary sweets originally developed by local nuns. You can watch as modern-day confectioners work their magic, or learn about the process first-hand by filling your own. Reserve your visit (tours are 45 minutes) by visiting the premises, or book through the website.

🖝 Tours

Several companies run canal trips in the *moliceiros*. You'll find them pitching for business down by the central canal.

Aveitour   BOATING

(📞 916 658 100; www.aveitour.com; ⊙ boat tour adult/child €10/5) Offers a range of walks and guided tours, including 45-minute boat tours of the local canals.

O Cicerone   WALKING

(📞 234 094 074; www.o-cicerone-tour.com; from per person €22.50) Year-round, O Cicerone leads various (half- and full-day) walking tours in Aveiro and surrounds.

⁂ Festivals & Events

Ria de Aveiro   CULTURAL

Aveiro celebrates its canals and *moliceiros* in summer, usually in July or August. Highlights include folk dancing and a *moliceiros* race, plus competitions for the best *moliceiro* paintings.

Feriado Municipal   RELIGIOUS

Aveiro makes merry for five days in honour of the town's patron saint, Santa Joana.

THE BEIRAS AVEIRO

ALIANÇA UNDERGROUND MUSEUM

Between Aveiro and Coimbra, in the village of Sangalhos in the Bairrada wine-producing region, the magnificent **Aliança Underground Museum** (☑ 234 732 045, 916 482 226; www.bacalhoa.pt; Rua do Comércio 444, Sangalhos; guided tour €3; ☺ tours 10am, 11.30am, 2.30pm, 4pm) is part *adega* (winery), part art museum. Guided tours take you beneath the winery to a vast 1.5km network of tunnels housing an extraordinary collection of African and Portuguese art. Also down here are cellars crammed with huge oak barrels of maturing wines and brandies.

Exhibit highlights include a haunting collection of funerary objects from Niger and a marvellous selection of contemporary Zimbabwean Shona sculpture. Other key 'stops' – maps of the museum are set out like the London Underground – are the fossil and mineral collections, and the display of Portuguese ceramics. These include a range of *azulejos* (hand-painted tiles) and quirky animals by former ceramics company Bordallo Pinheiro (still an icon in Portugal).

The scale of the wine production is also impressive – the largest oak barrels, all specially made on-site, are capable of holding 17,000 litres of brandy.

Tours, which must be booked in advance, are available in English, Spanish, French and German, and include a glass of sparkling wine.

A key event is the traditional procession through the city centre on 12 May.

Feira de Março   FIESTA
(www.facebook.com/feirademarcooficial; Parque de Feiras e Exposições de Aveiro; ☺ 25 Mar–25 Apr) This big annual festival dates back five and a half centuries. A major showcase for local businesses, it features a programme of concerts, ranging from folk music to rock gigs.

🛏 Sleeping

★ Aveiro Rossio Hostel   HOSTEL $
(☑ 234 041 538; www.aveirorossiohostel.com; Rua João Afonso de Aveiro 1; dm €21-25, r with/without bathroom €75/54; ✺ @ ☎) One of a trio of solid Rossio accommodation options, this hostel has an inclusive laid-back vibe and stylish, colourful decor, with family heirlooms, recycled furniture and scavenged objects. Dorm rooms, all mixed, come with individual reading lamps, and there are a couple of air-con rooms under the eaves with beds rather than bunks.

There's a small back patio for lounging, and breakfast often includes organic fruit from the owner's family farm.

Tricana de Aveiro   GUESTHOUSE $
(☑ 234 423 366; Avenida Dr Lourenço Peixinho 259; d/tr €60/70) A good budget choice, this handsome art nouveau guesthouse is opposite the old train station, about a 15-minute walk from the centre. The owners, who also run the ground-floor *pastelaria* (pastry and cake shop), have fixed up the bright,

high-ceilinged rooms simply but tastefully. No credit cards and no English spoken.

★ Aveiro Rossio Bed & Breakfast   B&B $$
(☑ 234 043 859; www.aveirorossiohostel.com; Rua das Velas 20; d €70-120, f €85-160; ✺ ☎) More a boutique guesthouse than a traditional B&B, this cracking place has got the lot: a convenient central location, welcoming staff and nine modern guestrooms. Sunlight pours into the pristine white rooms equipped with speakers to which you can connect your smartphone. There's also an attractive open-plan kitchen and lounge area.

Hotel das Salinas   HOTEL $$
(☑ 234 404 190; www.hoteldassalinas.com; Rua da Liberdade 10; d €80-120, apt €95-140; ☎) Seemingly larger inside than out, this hotel is a stylish bolthole. Long corridors, floored with mosaic tiles and lined with poems and paintings, lead to modern, minimalist-white rooms and nine studio apartments furnished with kitchenettes and plasma TVs. A good breakfast is served in the pleasant indoor-outdoor patio.

Hotel Aveiro Center   HOTEL $$
(☑ 234 380 390; www.hotelaveirocenter.com; Rua da Arrochela 6; s €60-90, d €75-110; ✺ ☎) This small hotel is a short stroll from the heart of town and has a quiet backstreet location. Rooms, in the main hotel and nearby annex, are smartly furnished with polished wood floors and modern functional furniture, and there's a bar and small outdoor patio. The English-speaking staff are helpful.

WORTH A TRIP

MUSEU MARÍTIMO DE ÍLHAVO

The wonderful Museu Marítimo de Ílhavo (☑ 234 329 990; www.museumaritimo.cm-ilhavo.pt; Avenida Dr Rocha Madahil; adult/child €6/3; ⏱10am-6pm Tue-Sat, 2-6pm Sun) is in a modern, award-winning building in the town of Ílhavo, 8km south of Aveiro. It covers the history of Portugal's maritime identity, from cod fishing (with superb fishing vessels from the 19th and 20th centuries) to oil paintings on the bows of the *moliceiros* (the traditional seaweed-harvesting boats). A highlight is the codfish (*bacalhau*) aquarium, showcasing the Atlantic cod, which the Portuguese have been fishing (and munching on) for centuries. Combined entry with the associated Santo André ship museum costs €8.

Aveiro Palace Hotel HOTEL $$

(☑234 423 001; www.hotelaveiropalace.com; Rua Viana do Castelo 4; s €61-89, d €69-105; P❄@🛜) Aveiro's most central hotel, and one of its smartest, overlooks the canal in the heart of town. Its four-star rooms, the best of which have *ria* (canal) views, are comfortable and soberly-decorated. There's a pretty 1st-floor lounge, and you can leave your car for only €6 a day in the nearby underground parking.

Hotel Moliceiro HOTEL $$$

(☑234 377 400; www.hotelmoliceiro.com; Rua Dr Barbosa de Magalhães 15; s/d €115/150; ❄@🛜) A prime canal-side location combines with attentive service, polished public areas and bright carpeted rooms at this elegant central set-up. Higher-grade rooms add views over the park and canal, as well as zippier decor.

✗ Eating

Tasca Palhuça PORTUGUESE $

(☑234 423 580; Rua Antónia Rodrigues 28; mains €7; ⏱9am-11pm Sun-Fri) As authentic as they come, this modest family-run place is largely shielded from travellers due to its side-street location. We think it's great – the type of place where clients have stuck to their (regular) seats longer than the tiles have been glued to the walls. The cuisine is meaty, fishy and plentiful.

Ki VEGAN $

(☑915 552 205; www.kimacrobiotico.com; Rua Capitão Sousa Pizarro 15; fixed-price menu €9; ⏱10am-6pm Mon-Fri; ✒) A vegetarian restaurant is a rare sight in this part of the country, so vegans will delight at finding Ki, a colourful backstreet eatery serving organic vegan food. Nothing flashy, just simple healthy dishes, perhaps wholemeal rice and lentils, plus soups and tea. Desserts cost an extra €3.

★ A Peixaria SEAFOOD $$

(☑234 331 165; www.restauranteapeixaria.pt; Rua Mestre Jorge Pestana, São Jacinto; mains €14-18; ⏱noon-3pm & 7-10pm Tue-Sun) It might not be the easiest to get to but there's never a shortage of diners at this no-frills fish restaurant, reckoned by many to be the best in the area. Situated a block back from the waterfront in São Jacinto, it specialises in locally caught Atlantic fish, served fresh and simply cooked.

Maré Cheia SEAFOOD $$

(Rua José Rabumba 8-12; mains €14-35; ⏱noon-3pm & 7-10.30pm Thu-Tue) *Maré cheia* means 'high tide' in Portuguese, but '*cheia*' (full) applies equally to this popular seafood eatery. You'll often have to elbow your way through a crowd of locals just to get your name on the waiting list. Its giant seafood platters are magnificent, or try the local *enguias* (eels), served fried, grilled or *caldeirada* (stewed).

O Bairro PORTUGUESE $$

(☑234 338 567; www.obairro.pt; Largo da Praça do Peixe 24; mains €15-22; ⏱12.30-3pm & 7.30-11pm Thu-Sun) Classic Portuguese cuisine gets a fusion makeover at this smart, tiled eatery near the fish market. Bag a table in the spacious, light-filled interior and go for innovative dishes such as tiger prawns (*camarão*) served with lime and risotto, or lamb (*cordeiro*) with a pistachio crust.

O Batel PORTUGUESE $$

(☑234 484 234; Travessa do Tenente Resende 21; mains €15-19; ⏱noon-3pm & 7.30-11.30pm Mon-Sat) On a narrow sidestreet off busy Rua do Tenente Resende, this woody, nautically-themed restaurant is worth tracking down. Its daily specials are backed up by a seafood-heavy menu with some leftfield choices – anyone for prawn curry with fruit? Service is professional and friendly.

🍷 Drinking & Entertainment

Má Ideia CRAFT BEER

(www.facebook.com/maideia.aveiro; Rua dos Marnotos 56; ⏱3pm-2am) With books to browse, art on the walls and a laid-back cafe vibe, this is the place for craft beer in Aveiro. Choose from the selection of international guest beers, lovingly curated by the knowledgeable English-speaking owner, and settle down for an evening's tasting. Also serves tapas-style food.

Casa de Chá
BAR

(Rua Dr Barbosa de Magalhães 9; ☉10am-2am Tue-Fri, 12.30pm-3am Sat, 12.30-9pm Sun; 🐝) With its elegant walled courtyard and classy location in Aveiro's landmark art nouveau building, this cafe absolutely looks the part. Stop by for tea and a snack during the day or come late for cocktails and *caipirinhas* (national cocktail of Brazil, made with cachaça, limes, sugar). It's at its liveliest on warm summer nights.

Teatro Aveirense
THEATRE

(✆234 400 920; www.teatroaveirense.pt; Rua Belém do Para; ☉box office 9.30am-12.30pm & 2-6pm Mon-Fri, 2-6pm Sat) Celebrating over 125 years at the heart of Aveiro's cultural scene, this historic theatre stages regular concerts, dance performances and plays.

🛍 Shopping

★ Cais à Porta
CONCEPT STORE

(✆234 063 085; www.facebook.com/caisaporta; Cais das Falcoeiras 6; ☉10am-8pm) This warehouse concept store down by the canalside is a browser's delight. Carrying a selection of Portuguese brands and artisanal wares, it stocks everything from men's shirts and sunglasses to frocks, bags, costume jewellery, shoes, original prints and locally distilled liqueurs. It's well worth searching out.

ℹ Information

Dunas de São Jacinto Interpretative Centre (✆960 335 438, 234 331 282; www.icnf.pt; Estrada Nacional 327; ☉9am-1pm & 2-5pm Mon-Sat) A small information centre that acts as a reception for the Reserva Natural das Dunas de São Jacinto.

Espaço Turismo & Museus (✆234 406 486; c/o Museu da Ciudade, Rua João Mendonça 8; ☉10am-12.30pm & 3.30-6pm) A space in the Museo da Ciudade with leaflets and a small shop selling postcards, books, T-shirts and the like.

Hospital Infante Dom Pedro (✆234 378 300; www.chbv.min-saude.pt; Av Artur Ravara)

Police Station (✆234 400 290; Praça Marquês de Pombal)

Post Office (Praça Marquês de Pombal; ☉8.30am-6.30pm Mon-Fri)

Regional Turismo (✆234 420 760; www.turismodocentro.pt; Rua João Mendonça 8; ☉9am-7pm Mon-Fri, to 6pm Sat & Sun Jun-Sep, 9am-6pm Mon-Fri, 9.30am-1pm & 2-5.30pm Sat & Sun Oct-May) In an art nouveau building on the main canal. Has town maps and information on Portugal's central region.

ℹ Getting There & Away

BUS

Catch buses at the **stop** on Rua Clube dos Galitos or the **bus station** east of the centre.

Rede Expresso (✆234 383 479; www.rede-expressos.pt) has services to/from Lisbon (€16, three to four hours, six to 12 daily), Coimbra (€6, 45 minutes, four daily), Figueira da Foz (€8.30, 45 minutes to 1¼ hours, two to three daily) and Viseu (€8.30, one hour, five to six daily).

Transdev (www.transdev.pt; Rua Clube dos Galitos 12; ☉ticket & information office 8.30am-12.30pm & 2-6pm) runs a slower but cheaper coastal service to Figueira da Foz (€5.55, two hours, three a day on weekdays) via some intermediate beaches.

TRAIN

Trains run from the modern station, which has superseded the beautiful old tiled one alongside. Aveiro is within Porto's *urbano* network, which means there are commuter trains there at least every half-hour (€3.50, one hour); pricier IC/AP links (€11.90/14.50, 30 to 40 minutes) are only slightly faster.

There are also at least hourly links to Coimbra (regional/intercity/AP €5.20/11.90/14.50, 30 to 60 minutes) and hourly IC (€20.60, 2½ hours) and AP (€26.70, two hours) trains to Lisbon.

ℹ Getting Around

BICYCLE

Loja BUGA (Bicicleta de Utilização Gratuita de Aveiro; Praça do Mercado 2; ☉9am-7pm Mon-Fri, 10am-1pm & 2-7pm Sat & Sun) Provides bikes for use within the town limits, all for free. Bike quality can vary a bit. Leave ID such as your driving licence or passport.

BUS

Catch buses to the coast at the stop on Rua Clube dos Galitos.

Piódão

POP 180 / ELEV 690M

A trip to the tiny village of Piódão (pee-*oh*-downg) takes you deep into the Serra de Açor (Goshawk Mountains), a remote range of vertiginous ridges, deeply cut valleys rivers and virgin woodland. There, set among steeply terraced slopes, the village sits in glorious isolation, its grey schist houses clinging to the verdant hills.

Until the 1970s the only way to reach Piódão was on horseback or by foot. Nowadays, visitors drive in, and the village has become something of a tourist attraction. It remains a wonderfully atmospheric spot, though. As you wander its tiny lanes note the many doorways with crosses over them – these were said to offer protection against curses and thunderstorms.

◎ Sights & Activities

Igreja Nossa Senhora Conceição
CHURCH

(⏱ 10am-1pm & 2-6pm mid-Jun–mid-Sep, 9am-1pm & 2-5pm mid-Sep–mid-Jun, closed Mon & Tue) Resembling a strange, Disney-like vision of what a quaint village church should look like, Piódão's white church stands out like a beacon against the grey schist of the surrounding houses. It's believed to have been built on the site of a former chapel, though the current building, funded by locals, dates to the early 19th century.

Hiking Trails
HIKING

A signposted network of hiking trails connects Piódão to the nearby villages of Foz d'Égua (3.5km or 2.8km depending on which path you take, 45 to 55 minutes) and Chãs d'Égua (4km, one hour). Foz d'Égua has some lovely old stone bridges, schist houses and a precarious-looking footbridge over the river gorge. Chãs d'Égua is home to more than 100 examples of rock art from the Neolithic to the Iron Age.

⛏ Sleeping & Eating

Casa de Xisto Piódão
COTTAGE $$

(www.casadexistopiodao.com; Rua Francisco Pacheco; for 1/2/4 people €76/90/120) This tall, narrow house hidden in a quiet corner near the O Fontinha restaurant, sleeps up to six people. It's a homely affair and while there's not a lot of space, it's colourful and cosy. Minimum two-night stay.

Casa da Padaria
B&B $

(☑ 235 732 773; www.casadapadaria.com; Rua Cónego Manuel Fernandes Nogueira; s/d €55/60) A picture-perfect rural hideaway, this handsome B&B has an exceptionally friendly host, great breakfasts and attractive, rustic

guestrooms. It's in a former bakery on the far side of the village from where you arrive.

O Fontinha
PORTUGUESE $

(☑ 235 731 151; Rua Eugénio Correia; mains €8-10; ⏱ noon-3pm & 7-9pm) This modest, no-frills restaurant, in a traditional schist house, is good for no-nonsense mountain food such as grilled trout and *bife de vaca* (steak).

ℹ Information

There's no ATM in the village.

Turismo (☑ 235 732 787; www.visitarganil. pt; Largo Cónego Manuel Fernando Nogueira; ⏱ 10am-1pm & 2-6pm mid-Jun–mid-Sep, 9am-1pm & 2-5pm mid-Sep–mid-Jun) On the main village square.

ℹ Getting There & Away

The only public transport is a bus from Arganil (41km to the west) to Piódão (€4.30, 1½ hours) on Thursdays and Sundays. Check current times with Piódão's *turismo*, as they change.

The area's breathtaking views, narrow roads and sheer drops make for some white-knuckle driving in certain parts.

BEIRA BAIXA

Beira Baixa (Lower Beira) closely resembles the neighbouring region of Alentejo, with its ferocious summer heat and endless rolling plains. This tough boulder-strewn land is home to sprawling agricultural estates and humble farming hamlets, as well as several stunning fortress villages. For centuries, these remote strongholds stood guard against incursions from across the Spanish border. Highlights include the haunting hillside village of Monsanto and Sortelha with its dramatically-sited medieval castle.

Castelo Branco

POP 35,200

Provincial capital Castelo Branco is a lively place with plenty going on. It boasts some impressive modern architecture and a few excellent museums, as well as an authentic, if slightly run-down, medieval centre. The modern town, which features an attractive series of tree-lined squares and boulevards, makes a good jumping-off point for exploring the Beiras' southern reaches and outlying villages such as Monsanto and Idanha-a-Velha.

PARQUE NATURAL DO TEJO INTERNACIONAL

Still one of Portugal's wildest landscapes, Parque Natural do Tejo Internacional (www2.icnf.pt/portal/ap/p-nat/pnti), a 264-sq-km natural park, shadows the Rio Tejo and the watersheds of three of its tributaries. While not aesthetically remarkable, it shelters some of the country's rarest bird species, including black storks, Bonelli's eagles, royal eagles, Egyptian vultures and griffon vultures.

The Centro Interpretação Ambiental (☑272 346 068; Rua da Bela Vista; ☺9.30am-noon & 2-5.30pm Mon-Fri) in Castelo Branco provides a great introduction to the area.

The best-marked hiking trail, the 10.5km Rota dos Abutres (Route of the Vultures), descends from Salvaterra do Extremo (60km east of Castelo Branco) into the dramatic canyon of the Rio Erges.

Drivers can get a taste of the park's natural beauty by following the unnumbered road between Monforte da Beira and Cegonhas (southeast of Castelo Branco), which passes through a beautiful cork-oak forest on either side of the Ribeira do Aravil. It doesn't appear on all maps: pass through Monforte da Beira if coming from Castelo Branco, and turn right after 2km. Alternatively, a signposted turn-off to the park just short of Monforte takes you down a rough, circular route through part of the park, but the way is not well indicated.

◉ Sights

Centro de Cultura Contemporânea de Castelo Branco
CULTURAL CENTRE

(☑272 348 170; www.facebook.com/oficialcentrodeculturacontemporaneacb; Campo Mártires da Pátria; adult/child €2/free; ☺10am-1pm & 2-6pm Tue-Sun) FREE Castelo Branco's modernist cultural centre has quickly established itself as town landmark since it was inaugurated in 2013. The cutting-edge building, designed by the Barcelona-based Josep Lluis Mateo and Portuguese architect Carlos Reis de Figueiredo, provides a stunning space for temporary exhibitions with its cantilevered floors extending over the town plaza.

Museu Cargaleiro
MUSEUM

(☑272 337 394; www.fundacaomanuelcargaleiro.pt; Rua dos Cavaleiros 23; adult/child €2/free; ☺10am-1pm & 2-6pm Tue-Sun) This extraordinary museum is spread over two buildings, a mid-18th-century house in Rua dos Cavaleiros (Knights Street) and a clashing contemporary building nearby. On display are many works by Manuel Cargaleiro (1927–), a celebrated Portuguese ceramicist and painter whose style has been influenced by the Paris School of Artists. You'll also find paintings by other Portuguese and international artists.

Museu de Francisco Tavares Proença Júnior
MUSEUM

(Paço Episcopal; ☑272 344 277; Largo Dr José Lopes Dias; adult/under 10yr €3/free; ☺10am-1pm & 2-6pm Tue-Sun) Occupying the so-ber 18th-century bishop's palace, this long-standing museum has an excellent display of local archaeological finds. Its highlight, however, is its collection of *colchas*, silk-embroidered linen bedspreads and coverlets inspired by silks and motifs brought back by Portuguese explorers. For centuries Castelo Branco was famous for these elaborately designed spreads, and you can see many locally made examples alongside a stunning selection of Asian originals.

Jardim do Paço Episcopal
GARDENS

(Rua Bartolomeu da Costa; admission €2; ☺9am-5pm Oct-Apr, to 7pm May-Sep) This delightful retreat is the garden of the former bishop's palace, an 18th-century baroque whimsy of clipped box hedges, pools and grand staircases. Scattered around its manicured confines are numerous stone figures, representing the virtues, seasons, kings, saints, months and continents, among other things. Notice how the statues of Portugal's Spanish-born kings Felipe I and II are smaller than those of the Portuguese-born monarchs.

At the bottom of the kings' stairway, there's a hidden, clap-activated fountain. This strange folly was supposedly built by a loutish 18th-century bishop who liked to surprise maidens by soaking their petticoats.

⊨ Sleeping & Eating

★ Império do Rei
HOTEL $

(☑272 341 720; www.imperiodorei.pt; Rua dos Prazeres 20; s €25-28, d €43-46, tr €62-65, f €77-80; ᴘ❋ᴥ) The best-value stay in town.

THE BEIRAS CASTELO BRANCO

Friendly staff extend a warm welcome at this modest hotel in a quiet backstreet behind the cathedral. Rooms come with big, comfy beds and blown-up photos of regional scenes such as a Monsanto boulder house or freshly harvested olives. You'll also find in-room information about the local area in Portuguese and English.

Retiro do Caçador PORTUGUESE $
(☑ 272 343 050; Rua Ruivo Godinho 15; mains €7-13; ⊙ noon-3pm & 7-10.30pm Mon-Sat) The clue's in the name – Hunter's Retreat – and the mounted boars' heads on the stone wall. This small, much frequented rustic restaurant is all about the joys of meat, everything from deer stew to *javali* (wild boar) and Iberian pork, cooked simply and served in generous portions.

O Pinguim PORTUGUESE $
(☑ 272 343 236; Rua Dadrá 7A; mains €7.50-10; ⊙ 9am-midnight Mon-Sat) Friendly, fast and efficient, this is the sort of place where you join the locals for simple, home-cooked fare with the TV on in the corner. The menu holds few surprises but everything is fresh – the fish dishes are excellent – and the home-made desserts are lovely.

ℹ Information

Biblioteca Municipal (Campo Mártires da Pátria; ⊙ 10am-6.30pm Mon-Fri) Free internet in the public library.

Turismo (☑ 272 330 339; www.cm-castelo-branco.pt; Av Nuno Álvares 30; ⊙ 9.30am-7.30pm Mon-Fri, 9.30am-1pm & 2.30-6pm Sat & Sun) Helpful office near the town's main square.

ℹ Getting There & Away

Both the bus station and train station are south of the centre, at the bottom end of Avenida Nuno Álvares.

BUS

From the **bus station** (Rua Poeta João Roiz) you can take **Rede Expressos** (☑ 272 320 997; www.rede-expressos.pt) and **Citi Express** (www.citiexpress.eu) buses to:

Covilhã (€6, 50 minutes, almost hourly daily)
Guarda (€10.50, 1½ to two hours, up to 17 daily)
Coimbra (€13.80, two to 2½ hours, up to six daily)
Lisbon (€14.20, 2¾ to 3¾ hours, up to 11 daily)

TRAIN

Castelo Branco is on the Lisbon–Covilhã line. From the **train station**, three daily IC trains to Lisbon (€15, three hours) are supplemented by four slower regional services (€14.55, four hours). Up to seven IC/regional services also serve Covilhã (€6.70/6.45, 50 minutes/one hour).

Monsanto

POP 830 / ELEV 600M

Like an island in the sky, the stunning village of Monsanto towers high above the surrounding plains. Steep cobbled lanes lead to the heart of the village, where red-roofed stone houses sit wedged between giant grey boulders. It's a strange and unique sight. To fully appreciate Monsanto's rugged isolation, climb the shepherds' paths to the abandoned hilltop castle, whose crumbling walls command vertiginous views in all directions. Walkers will also appreciate the network of hiking trails threading through the wooded expanses below.

◉ Sights

Castelo CASTLE
FREE This formidable stone fortress seems to grow out of the boulder-littered hilltop. There's not a lot left inside the walls but it's a beautiful site, windswept and full of lizards and wild flowers. Immense vistas take in Spain to the east and the Barragem da Idanha dam to the southwest.

There was probably a fortress here even before the Romans arrived, but after Dom Sancho I booted out the Moors in the 12th century it was beefed up. Dom Dinis fortified it, but after centuries of attacks from across the border it finally fell into ruin.

Just below the castle stands what's left of the Romanesque **Capela de São Miguel**, with its cluster of tombs carved into solid rock eerily lying just outside the chapel portal.

Miradouro do Forno VIEWPOINT
Get your camera ready. This viewing balcony commands huge views over the village's red roofs down to the baking plains below. It also looks up to an alarmingly balanced boulder known locally as the *Penedo do Pé Calvo*.

☂ Activities

Several long-distance hiking trails pass through Monsanto, including the trans-

European GR-12 and the GR-22, a 565km circuit of Portugal's historic villages. For a lovely, relatively easy walk (one hour return), descend the GR-12 along the stone road to the Capela de São Pedro de Vir-a-Corça, a medieval chapel surrounded by giant boulders. From there you can either double back or continue onto Idanha-a-Velha, a beautiful but exposed 10km away. Note the full walk is best undertaken in cooler weather.

Festivals & Events

Festa das Cruzes CULTURAL

On 3 May (or the nearest weekend) Monsanto bursts into life for this festival, held to honour Nossa Senhora dos Cruzes and commemorate the invasion of the Moors.

According to local lore, the starving villagers threw their last calf over the walls, taunting their besiegers as if they had plenty to spare. The hoodwinked attackers promptly abandoned the siege. These days, young girls throw baskets of flowers instead, after which there's dancing and singing by the castle walls.

Sleeping & Eating

Casa Pires Mateus GUESTHOUSE $

(☎277 314 018; www.piresmateus.pt; Rua Fernando Namora 4; d from €60; ❄️📶) This old family house has been converted into a spotless, comfortable abode, with six rustic, stone-walled rooms. One is considerably smaller but costs less (from €50), while several have great rooftop views. Lovely host but little English is spoken. Good breakfasts.

Casa da Tia Piedade GUESTHOUSE $

(☎966 910 599; www.casadatiapiedade.com; Rua da Azinheira 21; d/q not incl breakfast €60/90; ❄️📶) A cosy retreat tucked away in a quiet back lane. Run by a kind, hospitable couple it comes with a panoramic terrace, kitchen/lounge and two bedrooms (the smaller one has a view). Only one is let at a time unless you're a group, so the exterior bathroom is private. Breakfast is available for an extra €5.

Monsanto Geo-Hotel Escola DESIGN HOTEL $$

(☎277 314 061; www.monsantoghe.com; Rua da Capela 1; s €57-110, d €71-125; ❄️📶) This hip hotel brings a dash of contemporary design to Monsanto's granite-grey centre. Occupying a renovated mansion, it has 10 spacious rooms, each a picture of understated cool. Plain white walls are paired with polished wood floors, colourful accents and memorable views. The friendly and welcoming staff are a further plus.

Adega Típica O Cruzeiro PORTUGUESE $$

(☎936 407 676; Rua Fernando Namora 4; mains €10-13; ⏲12.30-3pm & 7-9pm Thu-Mon, 12.30-3pm Tue) Just below the village proper, this likeable place is a rather surprising find, situated as it is in a modern municipal building. The panoramic dining area boasts spectacular views over the plains below, and the superfriendly staff serve tasty dishes from a seasonal menu.

Petiscos e Granitos PORTUGUESE $$

(Rua Pracinha 16; mains €12.50-16; ⏲12.30-4pm & 7.30-10pm Tue-Sun) Wedged within gigantic boulders, Petiscos e Granitos' back terrace provides a fantastic backdrop for a *copo de vinho* (glass of wine) at sunset, with incomparable views over the plains below. Its food offerings are traditional, with an array of delicious game dishes as well as *bacalhau* and grilled octopus.

Information

Turismo (☎277 314 642; www.cm-idanhanova.pt; Rua Marquês da Graciosa; ⏲9.30am-1pm & 2-5.30pm Tue-Sun) See the website for details of accommodation in the area (in Portuguese).

Getting There & Away

Without a car, Monsanto can be difficult to reach. **Transdev** (☎272 320 997; www.transdev.pt) has one direct daily bus from Castelo Branco (€5.95, one hour), leaving at 5.15pm Monday to Friday, 12.25pm on Saturday and 11.40am on Sunday. The return bus then departs Monsanto at 7.15am the following morning. However, schedules change according to school term

WORTH A TRIP

PENHA GARCIA

A good side trip from Monsanto takes you 12km east to the village of Penha Garcia. It's a picturesque spot capped by a hilltop castle from where you can look down onto a steeply banked rocky gorge and glassy reservoir. To explore further, a signposted 3km circular path, the **Rota dos Fósseis**, leads from the village church down into the canyon, where you'll find several old mills and millers' houses as well as some fabulous fossil finds.

You can also walk to Penha Garcia along the GR-12 path from Monsanto.

times so check at the *turismo* in either Monsanto or Castelo Branco for the latest timetable.

Idanha-a-Velha

POP 60

Idanha-a-Velha is the very definition of a sleepy backwater, a tiny, almost-deserted stone hamlet nestled in a quiet valley of patchwork farms and olive groves. But it wasn't always so, and the village has an extraordinary history.

It was founded by the Romans in the 1st century BC and grew to become an important ancient city (Civitas Igaeditannorum or Egitania) – hence the surviving Roman ramparts. It subsequently flourished under the Visigoths, who built a cathedral and made it their regional capital. According to local legend the Visigoth King Wamba was born here. After a period of Muslim occupation in the 8th century, the Knights Templar arrived in the late 1100s. Later a 15th-century plague is said to have devastated the town, driving survivors to found Idanha-a-Nova about 20km to the southwest. Today a small population of shepherds and farmers live amid the Roman, Visigothic and medieval ruins.

◉ Sights

Ruins
RUINS

FREE The only remaining vestige of the defences the Knights Templar built in the 13th century is the **Torre de Menagem**. Also known as the Torre dos Templários, this rectangular tower, now surrounded by clucking hens, sits atop what was probably the pedestal of a Roman temple. Other Roman remains include a gracefully arched bridge on the east side of the village, and the old wall and gate on the north side.

Catedral
CATHEDRAL

(Sé; Rua da Sé; ⊙10am-12.30pm & 2.30-4.30pm Tue-Sun) **FREE** Tucked into a corner of the walled village sits the 6th-century Visigothic cathedral, surrounded by a jigsaw puzzle of scattered archaeological remains. The church has undergone heavy restoration, but its early roots are evident everywhere: foundation stones bearing Latin inscriptions, Moorish brick arches, salvaged Roman columns and Visigothic elements such as the baptistry visible through glass near the entrance. The best preserved of the frescoes within features São Bartolomeu with a demon at his feet.

Lagar de Varas
HISTORIC BUILDING

(Rua da Sé; ⊙9.30am-1pm & 2-5.30pm Tue-Sun) **FREE** This a 19th-century stone barn near the cathedral houses an impressive olive-oil press made in the traditional way with huge tree trunks providing the crushing power. In the same complex you'll find a tiny **epigraphic museum** (closed for maintenance at the time of research) densely packed with more than 200 stones bearing Latin inscriptions.

🛌 Sleeping

Idanha-a-Velha has no accommodation. Monsanto (16km northeast) and the hill town of Idanha-a-Nova (20km southwest) are your best bets for a place to bed down. The latter has a comfortable **hostel** (☑277 208 051; www.pousadasjuventude.pt; Praça da República 32; dm €9.35-16.50, d €25-40, f €44-70; ⊙closed mi-Dec–mid-Jan; 🛜) in a prime position.

ℹ Information

Turismo (☑277 914 280; www.cm-idanhanova.pt; Rua da Sé; ⊙9.30am-1pm & 2-5.30pm Tue-Sun) Friendly office in the heart of the village.

ℹ Getting There & Away

Realistically you'll need your own transport to get to Idanha-a-Velha. There is a weekday bus to the village from Castelo Branco (€5.25, 1½ hours) via Idanha-a-Nova but it departs at 5.15pm and drops you off at 6.44pm. The return service is not until the next morning. Alternatively, you can reach the village by hiking a 10km trail from Monsanto or getting a taxi from Idanha-a-Nova (around €30).

Sortelha

POP 450 / ELEV 760M

Perched on a rocky promontory, Sortelha is the oldest of a string of fortress settlements on the frontier east of Guarda and Covilhã. The hilltop village, which has changed little over the centuries, is wonderfully photogenic, with its stout granite cottages, cobbled streets and formidable medieval walls. Most spectacular of all is its 12th-century castle, teetering dramatically on the brink of a steep cliff.

You arrive in the lower modern part of the village. From here, it's a short drive, or 10-minute walk up to the medieval centre – follow signposts for the '*castelo*'.

The town holds a medieval fair in the last weekend of September. You can join in the fun by hiring clothes and spending coins from the era.

◎ Sights

★ Historic Centre   VILLAGE

FREE The entrance to the fortified village is a grand Gothic gate. From the square inside, a cobbled lane leads up to the heart of the village, with a *pelourinho* (stone pillory) signalling the remains of a small castle to the left and the parish church to the right. Higher still is the bell tower – climb it for bird's-eye views. For a more adventurous walk, take to the ramparts that surround the village, though beware precarious stairways and big steps.

As you walk, keep your eyes open for the weather-worn Arabic script over the door of the Casa Árabe at the top of the village. Outside the nearby gate, look out for the Old Lady's Head, a huge boulder with an uncanny resemblance to a sharp-chinned witch. And at the castle entrance, look for the *mata-cães,* the holes in the veranda through which hot oil was poured to repel the enemy.

🛏 Sleeping & Eating

Casa da Lagariça
& Casa da Calçada   COTTAGE $$

(☏ 271 388 116; www.casalagarica.com; Calçada de Santo Antão 11; d €60-80; 🅿) These cute stone cottages just below the old town make a fine base. The larger, Lagariça, sleeps up to eight people, with three double rooms and a lounge with sofa-bed; the smaller, Casa da Calçada, has two doubles. Both come with fully equipped kitchens but breakfast is included. You can rent a room or the whole house, with discounts available for longer stays.

O Celta   PORTUGUESE $$

(☏ 271 388 291; Rua Dr Vitor Manuel Pereira Neves 10; mains €7.50-9, fixed-price menu €16; ⊙ noon-3pm & 7-9pm Wed-Mon) On the main road through the modern village, O Celta (The Celt) serves up a cheerful farmhouse atmosphere and filling country staples, including a flavoursome *ensopada de borrego* (lamb stew). A small cafe is at the front, and the helpful owner is used to tourists with queries.

Restaurante Dom Sancho   PORTUGUESE $$

(☏ 271 388 267; Largo do Corro; mains €13-18; ⊙ noon-2.30pm & 7-9.30pm, closed Sun dinner & Mon) The only restaurant in the old village, Dom Sancho sits just inside the main Gothic gate. It's touristy but the traditional food is spot on – mainly game and hearty stews – and its snug, stone-walled dining room is an attractive place to dine. For lighter snacks and drinks, try the bar downstairs (with cosy fireplace in winter).

🍷 Drinking & Nightlife

Bar Boas Vindas   BAR

(⊙ 8am-1am) This stone house with rustic decor and a cat curled up by the fire is a great place to hole up in winter. In the warmer months, you can sit out on its sunny terrace and munch on ham and cheese sandwiches, ideal for a simple lunch. The bar's signposted from the top of the village.

❶ Information

Turismo (☏ 271 381 072; www.cm-sabugal.pt; Largo do Corro; ⊙ 10am-1pm & 2-6pm summer, 9.30am-1pm & 2-5.30pm winter) Located inside the old town gates.

❶ Getting There & Away

You really need your own wheels to get to Sortelha. The only bus service is on school days, on a bus that takes kids to and from Sabugal.

PARQUE NATURAL DA SERRA DA ESTRELA

Portugal's oldest and largest protected area, the Parque Natural da Serra da Estrela encompasses 888 sq km of the country's highest mountains. At its centre, rising above a wild, boulder-strewn *planalto* (high plateau), is Torre (1993m), continental Portugal's highest peak. Below, steep mountain roads inch past icy lakes and vast granite outcrops as they corkscrew down thickly wooded valleys. The Serra's rushing rivers – including the Mondego and Zêzere, which have their sources here – historically provided hydropower to spin and weave the local wool into cloth. Nowadays traditional shepherding is giving way to a service economy catering to weekending tourists.

To explore the park, which offers fine hiking and some limited winter skiing, you can base yourself in the attractive mountain town of Manteigas or, in the park's western reaches, in Seia. To the south, and just outside the park proper, Covilhã is the area's largest town.

Parque Natural da Serra da Estrela

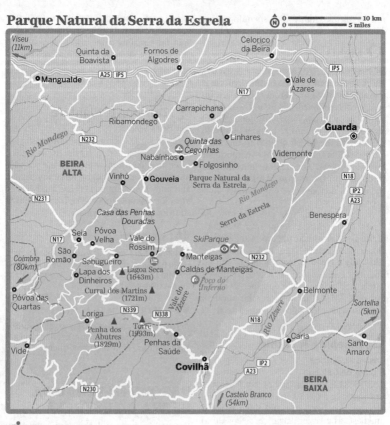

0   10 km
0   5 miles

🏃 Activities

🏃 Wildlife Watching

The park is an important natural habitat, harbouring a rich array of flora and fauna. Look out for otters, wild cats, boars, peregrine falcons, eagle owls and rare black storks. Among the park's endemic animals is the Iberian rock lizard, one of 33 species of reptiles and amphibians to inhabit the mountains.

The park's flora is interesting too, ranging from sweet chestnut and holm oaks to plants known for their medicinal properties such as mountain thrift (*Armeria transmontana*), great yellow gentian (*Gentiana lutea*) and juniper (*Juniperus communis*).

🏃 Walking

An extensive network of trails traverses the Serra da Estrela, offering superb hiking.

Despite this, surprisingly few people get off the main roads, and even in summer you'll often feel you have the park to yourself.

The best hiking period is May through to October. April is beautiful with hillsides covered in wildflowers but it's still cold and it can also be wet. Winter is harsh, with snow at the higher elevations from November or December to April or May.

Whenever you come, be prepared for extremes: scorching summer days give way to freezing nights, and chilling rainstorms blow through with little warning. Mist is a big hazard not only because it obscures walking routes and landmarks, but also because it can stealthily chill you to the point of hypothermia.

Routes run the gamut from multiday treks to family-friendly day hikes. Some of the most accessible walks are in the area around Manteigas, where the Trilhos Verdes (p345) network has 16 routes, ranging from simple country strolls to tough uphill trails.

Check the website for route descriptions and maps.

Further resources include the turismo (p343) at Seia and the Centro de Interpretação da Serra da Estrela (p341). Multilingual staff there are experts on hiking in the Serra and are goldmines of route information.

Within a zone of special protection, camping and fires are strictly prohibited except at designated sites, all of which are on the main trails.

🎿 Skiing & Other Activities

Skiing in the park is available at the Serra da Estrela Ski Resort (p347) on Torre. The ski season runs from December to April, with the best conditions usually in February.

SkiParque (☑ 275 980 090; www.skiparque. pt; Largo Relva da Reboleira Sameiro, Sameiro; ski kit rental & one-/two-hour lift pass €15/19; ☉ 10am-6pm), east of Manteigas, offers a range of activities, including summertime 'dry skiing', rock climbing, mountain biking and hiking.

ℹ️ Information

There are park offices at Manteigas (headquarters), Seia, Gouveia and Guarda. Local *turismos* can also provide information.

The **Centro Interpretativo do Vale Glaciar do Zêzere** (CIVGLAZ; ☑ 275 981 113; www. civglaz-manteigas.pt; adult/child €1/0.50; ☉ 10.30am-12.30pm & 2-5pm Mon-Fri, from 10am Sat & Sun mid-Sep–mid-May, 10.30am-12.30pm & 2-5.45pm Mon-Fri, 10am-12.30pm & 2.30-6pm Sat & Sun mid-May–mid-Sep) at Manteigas provides a wonderful introduction to the surrounding glacial valley, along with maps and walking info. The best available map for the central *planalto* is the 1:25,000 *Parque Natural da Serra da Estrela* (€14) published by Adventure Maps. Another good one is the 1:30,000 map that comes with a Portuguese booklet called *Rotas e Percursos da Serra da Estrela* (€11), which describes various walking routes.

ℹ️ Getting There & Away

Buses run daily from Coimbra to Seia and Guarda, and from Porto and Lisbon to Guarda and Covilhã.

Once in the area, there are regular, though infrequent, bus services around the edges of the park but none directly across it.

Trains serve Guarda and Gouveia from Lisbon and Coimbra-B. There are also services from Lisbon to Covilhã.

Roads are generally good but driving can be hairy thanks to mist, stiff winds, and wet or icy roads at high elevations. The Gouveia–Manteigas N232 road is one of the most tortuous in all of Portugal. Be prepared for traffic jams around Torre on weekends.

Seia

POP 6350 / ELEV 532M

With its high-rise blocks and modern suburbs, Seia is not an immediately inviting prospect. But scratch beneath the surface and you'll discover it's not without its charms. Seia has sweeping views over the surrounding lowlands and a few interesting museums. Nearby, there are some attractive rural lodgings in the verdant hills, ideal for a tranquil getaway. Further afield, the village of Sabugueiro is a popular day trip and Torre, mainland Portugal's highest peak, is a gripping 29km drive away.

👁 Sights

Centro de Interpretacão da Serra da Estrela   MUSEUM

(CISE; ☑ 238 320 300; www.cise.pt; Rua Visconde Molelos; adult/child €4/2.50; ☉ 10am-6pm Tue-Sun) In a park to the west of the town centre, this centre provides an excellent introduction to the Serra da Estrela region. A nine-minute film in English or Portuguese takes you flying around the mountains' main points of interest, while multimedia displays include an interactive scale model of the Serra. It also has helpful information on hiking and is a good place to buy maps.

Museu do Brinquedo   MUSEUM

(Toy Museum; ☑ 238 082 015; www.cm-seia.pt/ index.php/museus/museu-do-brinquedo; Largo de Santa Rita; adult/child €3/2; ☉ 10am-6pm Tue-Sun) This museum, housed in a lovely converted mansion, traces the history of Portuguese toys, from the Victorian to the contemporary, providing an interesting cultural study of Portuguese society, past and present. On display are over 8000 toys made of everything from paper and clay to wood and cork, as well as factory-made dolls and cars.

Museu do Pão   MUSEUM

(☑ 238 310 760; www.museudopao.pt; Rua de Santa Ana, Quinta Fonte do Marrão; adult/child €5/3; ☉ 10am-6pm Tue-Sun) This popular museum, set in a huge complex with mill wheels, a restaurant and rustic buildings, celebrates the history of traditional bread making. The highlight is a traditional-style

THE BEIRAS SEIA

WORTH A TRIP

SABUGUEIRO

An easy 15-minute drive up from Seia, Sabugueiro is reputed to be Portugal's highest village. Standing at 1050m, it's a typical mountain settlement, with white, red-roofed houses and a compact stone centre set above a small river.

However, its most obvious feature, and the one that draws tourists from far and wide, is its rash of souvenir shops. These gaudy stores, strung along the main road, all sell the same things: smoked ham, rye bread, juniper-berry firewater, woolly slippers, fluffy toy dogs, and, of course, *queijo da serra*. This local cheese has long been a signature speciality but it's now mostly made with milk from outside the Serra da Estrela due to diminishing local supply and skyrocketing demand. Don't let that deter you, though, it's still delicious. If you like yours runny, ask for cheese that's *amanteigado*.

A taxi from Seia up to Sabugueiro will cost around €12.

shop where you can stock up on *pão* (bread) and other local specialities. The museum is 1km northeast of the centre on the road to Sabugueiro.

🛏 Sleeping

★ Casas da Ribeira COTTAGE $$

(📞 238 311 221; www.casasdaribeira.com; Póvoa Velha; cottages 2-person €60-70, 4-person €80-120; 🖥) Close to Seia's services but feeling a million miles away, this cluster of traditional granite cottages sits in a secluded hamlet above town. The six rustic houses are all snug and well set up for the chill mountain air, with kitchens and stone fireplaces (firewood included). A delicious breakfast with home-baked bread is provided. There's normally a two-night minimum stay.

From Seia, climb the Sabugueiro road for about 5km, then turn left 1km to Póvoa Velha. Call ahead.

Casa das Tílias HERITAGE HOTEL $$

(📞 964 008, 585 927 186 125; www.casadastilias.com; Rua das Tilias, São Romão; d €59-79, tr €84-106, apt for 2/4 people from €79/138; 🅿🖥🏊) In São Romão, 4km from Seia, this is a gorgeous retreat, complete with walled garden and outdoor pool. The central manor house, dating to the 19th-century and sporting plenty of polished wood, high ceilings and stucco work, has six rooms. An adjacent modern annex houses three self-catering apartments, sleeping from two to six people.

Casa do Vidoeiro APARTMENT $$

(📞 238 085 502; www.casadovidoeiro.com; Av Dr Joaquim Guilherme Correira de Carvalho 14; d €59-69; 🅿❄🖥) An excellent choice if you decide to use Seia as your base for the Serra da Estrela. Casa do Vidoeiro has four smart modern apartments in a town house five

minutes' walk from the centre. At the time of research building work was underway to add new rooms and a studio flat.

Hotel Eurosol Seia-Camelo HOTEL $$

(📞 238 310 100; www.eurosol.pt; Av 1 de Maio 16; s €47-84 d €57-120; 🅿❄🖥🏊) The most central of Seia's hotels, situated just off the main drag. Big and business-like in look, it offers a warm welcome and spacious carpeted rooms, some with views. Facilities are also good, with free off-street parking, an in-house restaurant and an outdoor pool with bar service. Two-night minimum stays on winter weekends.

🍴 Eating

Restaurante Regional da Serra PORTUGUESE $$

(📞 238 312 717; Av dos Combatentes da Grande Guerra 14; mains €8-13; ⏰ noon-3pm & 7-9.30pm) Lunching visitors and locals out for their weekend meal create a cheerful buzz at this laid-back bar-restaurant. It's known for its hearty mountain cuisine, so keep it regional with *queijo da Serra* (mountain cheese) for your starter and *chanfana à serrana* as the main event.

Taberna da Fonte PORTUGUESE $

(📞 238 082 304; Largo da Misericórdia 1; mains €7.50-9; ⏰ 9.30am-10pm Tue-Sun) With a prime position looking up to the Igreja de Misericordia and an attractive slate-floored interior, this central place is a good spot for a taste of Serra cuisine. That means plenty of ham and cheese, sausages and *morcela* (black pudding) and rich daily specials of *chanfana* and *bacalhau*.

Restaurante Borges PORTUGUESE $$

(📞 238 313 010; Travessa do Funchal 7; mains €10-14; ⏰ noon-3pm & 7-10pm, closed Wed dinner &

Thu) Tucked away in a tight corner near the tourist office, this friendly, country-style restaurants offers large portions of traditional Portuguese fare. There's *bacalhau* and *bife* (steak), as well as the house speciality *joelinhos de porco* (pork knuckles), a regular crowd-pleaser.

❶ Information

Parque Natural da Serra da Estrela Office (☑ 238 001 060; www.icnf.pt; Praça da República 28; ⊙ 9am-1pm & 2-5pm Mon-Fri) This park office is in the centre of town. There's better information at the park interpretative centre (p341), though.

Turismo (☑ 238 317 762; www.cm-seia.pt; Rua Pintor Lucas Marrão; ⊙ 9am-12.30pm & 2-5.30pm Mon-Sat, 9am-1pm Sun) Very helpful and centrally located. English and French is spoken.

❶ Getting There & Away

From the **bus station** (☑ 238 313 102; Avenida Dr Afonso Costa), **Marques** (☑ 238 312 858; www.marques.pt) has buses to Gouveia (€2.75, 40 minutes, three per weekday), Viseu (€4.40, 65 minutes, three per weekday), and local villages. Note that fewer buses run on Sundays.

Rede Expressos (☑ 238 313 102; www. rede-expressos.pt) has direct buses to Lisbon (€18.50, 4¼ hours, four daily), Coimbra (€10, 1¾ hours, five to seven daily), Guarda (€10.30, 70 minutes, two to three daily) and Covilhã (€12.80, 1¾ hours, two daily).

Gouveia

POP 3470 / ELEV 650M

Pleasantly laid out with parks and public gardens, the small hillside town of Gouveia offers sufficient accommodation, food and transport to be a good base for the Serra da Estrela's northwestern reaches. Several interesting churches, including the central Igreja de São Pedro, clad in gorgeous *azulejos*, keep the eyes keen, as do several quirky museums.

◉ Sights

Museu Municipal de Arte Moderna Abel Manta MUSEUM (www.cm-gouveia.pt; Rua Direita 45; ⊙ 9.30am-12.30pm & 2-6pm) FREE This fascinating modern-art museum pays homage to Abel Manta, a (controversial) Portuguese modernist painter, who was born in Gouveia in 1888. Around 23 of his works are on display, along with paintings by other well-known Portuguese artists.

❚ Sleeping & Eating

Casas do Toural COTTAGE $$ (☑ 927 971 221; www.casasdotoural.pt; Rua Direita 74; cottages 2-person €65-85, 4-person €120-145; ❄❒) This gorgeous ensemble of rustic cottages surrounds an immaculately kept hillside farm-garden in the centre of town. Rooms feature exposed stone walls, tiled floors, kitchens, fireplaces and living rooms. For longer-term guests, owner Maria José offers guided hikes into the Serra da Estrela. Apartments are self-catering, but if you want breakfast, it's available for €5. Minimum stays of two nights.

Quinta das Cegonhas CAMPGROUND, APARTMENTS $$ (☑ 238 745 886; www.cegonhas.com; Nabaínhos; sites 2 adults, tent & car €21.50, d €55, 3-/4-person apt €63/85; ⓟ❄❒) Run by hospitable Dutch owners on a 17th-century *quinta* (country estate), this laid-back set-up has various options: terraced tent sites, private rooms or self-catering apartments. Information boards provide details of local hikes but if you'd rather just sit back and relax, head to the pool and lounge area. Sociable evening meals are available.

The camping ground is in Nabaínhos, 6km northeast of Gouveia towards Folgosinho.

★**Madre de Água** BOUTIQUE HOTEL $$$ (☑ 238 490 500; www.quintamadredeagua.pt; Vinhó; s €95-100, d €120-150, ste €140-200; ⓟ❄❒) A fabulous rural retreat, this contemporary four-star is set on verdant farmland 6km west of Gouveia. The 10-room hotel, a good-looking mix of exposed stone, honey-blonde wood floors, plate-glass walls and hip modern design, is part of a farm company that also produces its own wine, olive oil and cheese, as well as breeding horses.

One wing of the hotel is given over to a restaurant that serves gourmet meals (mains €15-21) – it's open daily for lunch (12.30 to 3pm) and dinner (7.30-10pm).

Restaurante O'Flor PORTUGUESE $$ (☑ 238 492 336; Rua Cardeal Mendes Belo 14; mains €10-16; ⊙ noon-3pm & 7-10pm) A traditional family-run restaurant, complete with exposed stone walls, blue ceramic tiles and framed pictures, O'Flor is a cut above many similar-looking places. Alongside boar, lamb and pork cooked in various ways, it serves some excellent fish dishes, including a wonderful fried *bacalhau*.

A SHEPHERD'S BEST FRIEND

As much a part of the Serra da Estrela's landscape as hilltop castles and rocky peaks are the bushy-tailed dogs that lounge around its mountain villages.

The indigenous Cão da Serra da Estrela, or **Estrela mountain dog** (EMD), is a muscular beast, as handsome as it is strong, smart, loving and loyal.

Widely recognised as one of the most ancient breeds on the Iberian Peninsula, the EMD is thought to have descended from dogs brought over by the Romans or Visigoths. Over the centuries, shepherds chose the best dogs to guard their sheep and goats.

The EMD is today a popular Portuguese pet, but its traditional use has declined drastically. Ironically, though, the wolf-recovery organisation Grupo Lobo (http://lobo.fc.ul.pt) has become a leading advocate for reviving the EMD's role. Conservationists worldwide now see the use of shepherd dogs as one of the best ways of protecting flocks whilst also promoting wolf recovery.

ℹ Information

Turismo (☑ 238 083 930; www.cm-gouveia. pt; Jardim da Ribeira; ☉ 9.30am-12.30pm & 2-6pm) On a green square just below the market building.

Vergílio Ferreira Municipal Library (Praça de São Pedro; ☉ 9.30am-12.30pm & 2-6pm Mon-Fri, 9.30am-1pm Sat) For free internet access.

ℹ Getting There & Away

BUS

Rede Expressos (☑ 238 493 675; www.re-de-expressos.pt) and **Marques** (www.marques. pt) buses stop at Gouveia's **bus station** (☑ 238 493 675; Rua Cidade da Guarda), some 500m north of the centre. Marques runs to Seia (€2.75, 40 minutes, three per weekday) and Guarda (€4.55, 1½ hours, one daily at 7.30am). Rede Expressos serves Coimbra (€12.20, two hours, three daily) and Lisbon (€18.50, 4½ to five hours, three daily).

TRAIN

The Gouveia railway station, 14km north near Ribamondego, is on the Beira Alta line between Coimbra-B (€9.10, 1¾ hours, two to three daily) and Guarda (€5.75, 50 minutes, three to five daily). A taxi between Gouveia and the station will cost around €12.

Manteigas

POP 2870 / ELEV 775M

Cradled at the foot of the Vale do Zêzere, Manteigas feels more like a mountain town than any of the other main gateways to the Serra da Estrela. There are no modern high-rises here, just white, red-roofed houses clinging to verdant slopes, and wooded peaks looming silently on the horizon. Nearby, hot sulphur-rich waters bubble away at the Caldas de Manteigas.

The town has some good accommodation, making it an excellent base for exploring the surrounding mountains. Walking trails traverse the nearby slopes, leading past terraced meadows and stone shepherds' huts. For more dramatic scenery, the drive up to Torre, some 22km away, is a real white-knuckle ride.

◉ Sights

Burel Factory   MUSEUM
(☑ 926 542 095; www.burelfactory.com; Amieiros Verdes; ☉ shop 10am-5pm Mon-Fri, 10am-1pm Sat, tours 11am Mon-Sat) FREE The burel factory originally opened in 1960 and employed 1000 people at its height (burel is a wool fabric similar to felt). After a decline in the industry it was forced to close in the noughties, but thanks to an injection of capital it has since started up again. You can now tour part of the factory and see the production process before buying products at the adjacent shop.

Tours are free but you'll need to reserve a spot by emailing factory@burelfactory.com.

Around 20 people churn out the most amazing products, from exquisite blankets to bags, knapsacks, shoes and homeware, incorporating the factory's original and very retro designs. And FYI: Microsoft helped make burel fashionable again when the software company used burel wall coverings to insulate its offices in Lisbon.

Poço do Inferno   WATERFALL
This waterfall, which descends the steep gorge of Ribeira de Lenadres, is a magnificent spectacle, particularly in spring. To get there from Manteigas, drive about 4km along the main road towards Torre. Just beyond Caldas de Manteigas, turn left and climb a further 6km to the falls through a lush evergreen forest. Alternatively, there's a popular walking route to the falls – check www.manteigastrilhosverdes.com for details.

🏃 Activities

⭐ Trilhos Verdes   WALKING
(www.manteigastrilhosverdes.com) This excellent 200km network of marked trails in the Manteigas area comprises 16 themed features known as 'Trilhos Verdes'. These range from the popular 2.5km Poço do Inferno walk to serious 20km treks through the mountains. Maps and route information are available at the park office (p346) in Manteigas and via the website listed.

Vale do Zêzere   WALKING
The relatively easy hike takes you through the magnificent, glacier-scoured Vale do Zêzere (Zêzere Valley), one of the Serra da Estrela's most significant natural features. It's a highlight of any trip to Manteigas, although be warned: the trail is shadeless and baking hot in clear summer weather.

To get to the start point from Manteigas, follow the N338 for 2.8km towards Caldas de Manteigas, leaving the road at the 'Roteiro Rural Palhotas' sign just beyond the spa hotel.

From there, a part-cobbled, part-dirt road leads upstream through irrigated fields dotted with typical stone *casais* (huts). About 4km along, the unpaved road crosses the Rio Zêzere just above a popular swimming hole.

The trail then follows the Rio Zêzere upstream along its eastern bank, climbing gradually through a wide-open landscape dotted with stone shepherds' huts and backed by spectacular views of the looming mountains on either side. Eventually the path narrows and steepens as you scramble up to meet the N338 (11km from Manteigas).

Once at the N338, you can continue uphill on the paved road 1.1km to the Covão da Ametade, a lovely shaded picnic spot. Thirsty day trippers should descend 900m along the road to Fonte Paulo Luís Martins, a crystalline spring whose delightfully cold water (constantly 6°C) is bottled in Manteigas and sold nationally. If you've left a car at the swimming hole, you can walk the 3.2km back along the N338, although it's usually easy to hitch a ride from someone filling bottles at the springs.

Penhas Douradas   WALKING
A medium-difficulty walk from Manteigas goes to Penhas Douradas, on a ridge high above the village. The track climbs northwest out of town via Rua Dr Afonso Costa to join a sealed, switchback forestry road and, briefly, a loop of the Seia-bound N232.

Branch left off the N232 almost immediately, on another road to the Meteorological Observatory. From there it's a short, gentle ascent to Penhas Douradas.

When you get there, don't miss the stunning panorama from the Miradouro do Fragão de Covão (viewpoint); just follow the signs. You can also drive up the N232 just for the view.

Walking back the same way makes for a return trip of about eight hours.

🛏 Sleeping

Covão da Ponte   CAMPGROUND $
(www.skiparque.pt/en/services/4-camping; sites per adult/tent/car €2.50/2.50-3/2; ☺end Jun-Sep; ℗) At this lovely shaded spot on the Mondego, you can wade, picnic or simply relax by the river's tranquil headwaters. Hikers can also explore the surrounding fields and mountains on three loop trails of varying lengths. To get here, take the N232 5.4km uphill from Manteigas, then continue an additional 5km from the signposted turn-off. The poorly marked park entrance is on the right.

There's an intermittently open snack bar as well as cold showers.

Pensão Serradalto   PENSION $
(☑ 275 981 151; paragem_serradalto@hotmail.com; Rua 1 de Maio 15; s €25, d €35-45; ☎) A reliable budget choice in the town centre, Serradalto offers eight basic rooms with wood floors and older furnishings, plus fine valley views from a sunny, grapevine-shaded terrace. There's a good, old-school Portuguese restaurant downstairs, also with amazing vistas (closed Tuesday; mains €10 to €15).

⭐ SerraVale   GUESTHOUSE $$
(☑ 275 982 825; www.serravale.pt; Quinta de Santo António; s €50 d €60-75; ❋☎) Run by the superhospitable Elsa, this charming guesthouse is set in a typical mountain stone house. Its four attractive rooms – two doubles and two larger suites – are colour themed and tastefully decorated with wooden window shutters, modern bathrooms and inspiring quotations stencilled on the walls.

Outside, there's a small garden where you can relax over an evening beer; it has views of the town centre.

⭐ Casa das Obras   GUESTHOUSE $$
(☑ 275 981 155; www.casadasobras.pt; Rua Teles de Vasconcelos; r €58-80; ☎❋) Live like nobility at this glorious 18th-century mansion, the

pick of the town centre accommodation. The manor house has been in the same family for centuries and is a picture of old-world charm with its stone-flagged floors, grand fireplace and original period furniture. It's no shrine, though, and you're made to feel very at home.

The antique-filled rooms are stylish, but the real joy comes from the public areas, including a wonderful breakfast room where you all eat around a lord-of-the-manor-style long table, and a games room with a billiard table. There's also a pool in a grassy courtyard across the street.

★Casa das
Penhas Douradas   DESIGN HOTEL $$$
(☑275 981 045; www.casadaspenhasdouradas.pt; Penhas Douradas; s €127-152, d €150-185, ste €250-280; P✳@☎❄) Make it up to this fantastic mountain hideaway and you won't want to leave. Everything about the place is just so right, from its panoramic setting to the minimalist Scandinavian-inspired chalet design and impeccable service (evening drinks, afternoon teas). And that's before you've even plunged into the heated pool or grabbed a spa treatment (the massages are amazing).

For meals, it's hard to go past the hotel's gourmet restaurant (also open to the public), yet less fancy snacks are available. When you eventually decide to hit the outdoors, there are marked trails and a lake nearby. Rooms vary from the more modestly priced attic rooms in the original building to a stylish, airy suite, but all are immaculate and most offer stirring views.

🍴 Eating & Drinking

★**Restaurante de Casa
das Penhas Douradas**   GASTRONOMY $$
(☑275 981 045; www.casadaspenhasdouradas.pt; Penhas Douradas; fixed-price lunch/dinner menu €28/38; ☺1-3pm & 8-10pm) This smart restaurant, part of the fabulous Casa das Penhas Douradas hotel, is a world away from traditional village life. Its streamlined Scandinavian-style decor sets the scene for sophisticated modern cuisine based on seasonal local ingredients such as kid goat, trout, juniper berries and wild mushrooms. The fixed-price lunch menu comprises a starter, main and dessert, while dinner is a five-course feast.

Gourmet picnics are also available to order. Penhas Douradas is a winding 12km northwest of Manteigas.

Restaurant Vale do Zêzere   PORTUGUESE $$
(☑275 982 002; www.hotelvaledozezere.com; Estrada da Lapa, Quinta de Santo António; mains €8.50-11.50; ☺noon-2.30pm & 7-9pm, closed Tue dinner & Wed) Over the river from the centre in the hotel of the same name, this casual family-run restaurant scores across the board. The food is excellent – try the *medalhão de vitela* (veal steak) garnished with cheese and juniper berries – service is brisk, and its often crowded dining room creates a pleasant buzz, even in seemingly quiet periods.

Santa Luzia   PORTUGUESE $$
(☑963 968 013; Rua Dr Esteves Carvalho 4; mains €9-15; ☺noon-3pm & 7-9pm) The crisp reds and whites of the dining area blend seductively with the dark wood tables at this main-street eatery. The menu is typical of these parts, featuring country specialities like locally-caught trout, roast *cabrito* (goat), and *javali* (wild boar), all to be enjoyed over uplifting valley views.

Granittus   BAR
(Rua Bernardo Marcos Leitão 2; ☺3pm-late) With a wooden terrace for al fresco drinking and a colourful interior complete with log fire, pool table, darts board and cheap drinks, this animated bar is pretty much it as far as Manteigas nightlife goes.

❶ Information

Centro de Interpretativo do Vale Glaciar do Zêzere (p341) Provides a vivid introduction to the Zêzere Valley; it's on the N338 at the southern approach to town.

Parque Natural da Serra da Estrela Office Headquarters (☑275 980 060; www.icnf.pt; Rua 1 de Maio 2; ☺9am-12.30pm & 2-5.30pm Mon-Fri) In the centre of town, it has leaflets on walking routes in the Manteigas area but little else.

Manteigas Welcome Center (☑275 981 129; www.cm-manteigas.pt; Rua Dr Esteves de Carvalho 2; ☺9am-12.30pm & 2-5.30pm Tue-Sat) The helpful tourist office is on the main road near the petrol station.

❶ Getting There & Away

By car, there are three main approaches to Manteigas: from the west (Seia or Gouveia) via the tortuous N232; from the southwest (Torre) along the snaking N338 and the Zêzere valley; from the east (Belmonte) along a relatively flat stretch of the N232.

Transdev (transdev.pt) runs two weekday buses to/from Guarda (1¼ hours, €4.30).

Torre

Torre is mainland Portugal's highest mountain. Its summit, which is accessible by road, stands at 1993m. But while the journey up is spectacular and the surrounding *planalto* (high plateau) wild and windswept, Torre's summit is a rather peculiar place: a tarmacked roundabout with two ageing golf-ball radar domes and drab shopping arcades. At its centre is a 7m-high tower erected by João VI in the early 19th century so Portugal could claim its highest point was exactly 2000m.

The main reason to make the tortuous drive up to the top is to ski in winter (December to mid-April) or simply to admire the thrilling scenery. The road from Manteigas is particularly breathtaking, crawling up the glacial Zêzere valley before traversing the **Nave de Santo António** – a highland sheep pasture – and climbing through a surreal moonscape of crags and gorges. Visible near the top is the **Cántaro Magro**, a fearsome rock formation that rises 500m from the valley below.

🏃 Activities

Serra da Estrela Ski Resort   SKIING
(🖉275 094 779; www.skiserradaestrela.com; Torre, Estrada Nacional 339; day pass per adult/child/family €25/15/70; ☺lifts 9am-4.30pm ski season, 10am-6pm summer) This small ski station has three lifts serving a small set of pistes, including a black run and several beginners' slopes. Gear rental is available, including skis, poles and boots (€25 per day) and snowboards (€15 per day). For lessons reckon on on €45 for a one-hour individual session.

A chairlift is operational in summer, providing half-hour panoramic rides for €5.

🛈 Getting There & Away

By car, there are three main approaches to Torre: from Seia on the N339; from Covilhã on the N339; or from Manteigas on the N338. All roads involve steep climbs and endless switchbacks.

A taxi from Seia will cost around €40 return.

Penhas da Saúde

A collection of roadside chalets, hotels and restaurants, Penhas da Saúde straddles the N339 mountain road at an elevation of 1500m. As the nearest place to Torre with accommodation, it's at its busiest in the winter ski season.

🛏 Sleeping & Eating

Pousada da Juventude   HOSTEL $
(🖉275 335 375; www.pousadasjuventude.pt; Estrada Nacional 339; dm €11-15, d €31-52; 🅿 @ 🛜)
Penhas' popular mountaintop hostel has a communal kitchen, giant stone fireplaces and a games room featuring billiards and table tennis. The deluxe doubles in the annex are especially inviting, but those in the main building are cosy too. Dorms have eight berths and plenty of space. Book well ahead in winter.

Varanda da Estrela   PORTUGUESE $$
(🖉963 447 873; www.varandadaestrela.pt; Penhas da Saúde; mains €12-16.50; ☺noon-3pm & 7.30-10pm Wed-Tue) This warming restaurant, decked out in wood and stone in classic chalet style, is an inviting spot to feast on authentic mountain food. That means Serra de Estrela's trademark cheese, locally-sourced *javali* (wild boar) and earthenware bowls of delicious juniper-spiked rice. The restaurant is just off the N339 road through Penhas.

🛈 Getting There & Away

In July and August, **Autotransportes do Fundão** (🖉275 336 448) runs a daily bus service from Covilhã's bus station to Penhas (€2.30). You'll need to check times as they change between seasons.

A taxi from Covilhã to Penhas will cost €16 one-way.

Covilhã

POP 51,800 / ELEV 700M

Sprawled over a hillside, Covilhã is the main southern gateway to the Serra da Estrela mountains. The town was once an important textile centre, but most of its 18th-century factories have now been replaced by high-rise apartment blocks. These days it's the Universidade da Beira Interior that energises the city, adding an air of modern urban vitality to its steeply stacked historic streets.

⊙ Sights

Museu de Lanifícios   MUSEUM
(Museum of Wool-Making; 🖉275 241 411; www.museu.ubi.pt; Rua Marquês d'Ávila e Bolama; adult/16-25yr €5/2.50, free Sun; ☺9.30am-noon & 6pm Tue-Sun) Covilhã used to be the centre of one of Europe's biggest wool-producing re-

Covilhã

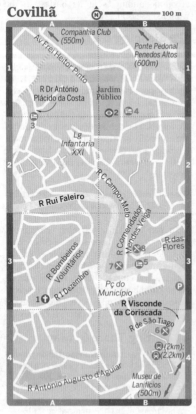

with the cartoonish works of street art that appear on several nearby walls.

The church is not open to the public.

Jardim Público PLAZA
(Av Frei Heitor Pinto) Commanding fabulous views, the leafy Jardim Público, north of Praça do Município, is a popular local haunt and a pleasant spot for a sunset drink at the Covilhã Jardim Café-Bar (p349).

Ponte Pedonal Penedos Altos BRIDGE
This striking footbridge spans the valley east of the old town, connecting the centre with the town's outer suburbs. Zigzagging over the valley floor, the 52m-high structure, accessible by a free lift from the Jardim Público, was designed by João Luís Carrilho da Graça and opened to rave architectural reviews in 2009.

🛏 Sleeping

Hotel Covilhã Jardim HOTEL **$**
(☎ 275 322 140; www.hotelcovilhajardim.com; Jardim Público 40; s €30-38, d €48-55; ❄ 🤚) This welcoming family-run two-star offers excellent value for money and a prime position on the municipal gardens. Its simply furnished white rooms get lots of sunlight and have fine views over the park in front or valley behind. The pleasant cafe downstairs is another plus.

⭐ **Casa com História** GUESTHOUSE **$$**
(☎ 275 322 493, 968 310 610; www.casacomhistoria.pt; Rua Dr António Plácido da Costa 25; d/f €75/140; 🤚) The pick of Covilhã's accommodation, this revamped mansion coolly blends contemporary design with creaking wood floors and old timber beams. Each guest room has a unique touch, from

gions, but stray outside the centre and you'll see the town's ghostly mills standing empty and forlorn. This interesting museum, housed in the former royal textile factory, traces the area's proud but vanishing history of wool production and cloth dyeing.

A map shows the 100-plus wool producers that once thrived in this region, while other displays illustrate how carmine and indigo dyes from the New World were used to colour Portuguese military uniforms. And even if yarn makes you yawn, you may be impressed by the gigantic old looms and dyeing vats.

Igreja de Santa Maria CHURCH
(Rua 1 Dezembro) In the heart of Covilhã's gritty historic centre, the 16th-century Igreja de Santa Maria is a startling sight. Its facade is entirely clad in blue and white *azulejos* depicting episodes from the life of the Virgin Mary. This traditional creation, actually a 20th-century addition, contrasts markedly

enlarged photographic wallpaper to bright, refurbished furniture. The communal library-lounge area is lovely, and there's a large, homely kitchen for breakfast.

Hotel Solneve   HOTEL **$$**
(📋 275 323 001; www.solneve.pt; Rua Visconde da Coriscada 126; s €33-55, d €50-80; 🅿 ❋ 🛜) Just off Covilhã's main square, this landmark pink hotel makes a good central base, with its spacious, light-filled rooms and good facilities. These include a decent in-house restaurant and convenient underground parking (€2.50). A good-value choice.

🍴 Eating & Drinking

ComFusão   PORTUGUESE **$$**
(📋 275 098 902; Rua de São Tiago 13; mains €6-14; ☺ 4pm-2am Mon-Sat) Housed in a rustic wood and stone building, this bar-restaurant is a popular student hangout, good for a beer and a simple meal, perhaps a hamburger or grilled steak and chips.

Restaurante Zé do Sporting   PORTUGUESE **$$**
(📋 275 334 127; Rua Comendador Mendes Veiga 19; mains €8-14; ☺ 11.30am-3pm & 6.30-11pm, closed Mon & Sun dinner) A local favourite, the vine-covered terrace of this cheerfully boisterous restaurant heaves at weekends as families and groups of friends crowd in for a filling homestyle feed. Speciality of the house is the grilled meat, with reliable crowd-pleasers such as *coelho* (rabbit) and *cabrito* (kid).

Pastelaria Restaurante Montiel   CAFE **$$**
(📋 275 322 086; Praça do Município 33-37; snacks €2-5, mains €10-14; ☺ cafe 7am-1am, restaurant noon-3pm & 5-10pm) Montiel's cafe is something of a social hub (if a smoky one), drawing in locals for a relaxed drink and tasty snack – it has fabulous *empadas* (pies), sausage rolls and the like. Upstairs, the restaurant cooks up warming regional staples such as grilled kid with rosemary, and *bacalhau* in various guises.

Covilhã Jardim Café-Bar   CAFE
(📋 275 322 140; Jardim Público 40; ☺ 8am-2am) With comfy couches inside and tree-shaded tables on its parkside terrace, this lively cafe is an enjoyable place to kick back over a cool beer and watch the world go by.

Companhia Club   CLUB
(📋 935 182 488; www.facebook.com/companhia club; Rua da Indústria 33; ☺ midnight-6am Thu-

Sat) This sleek club is one of a cluster of popular late-night student haunts in the abandoned-looking mill zone to the north of the centre. Check its Facebook page for upcoming parties and events. To get there, head along Avenida Frei Heitor Pinto past the *turismo* and veer right down Rua da Indústria.

ℹ Information

Turismo (📋 275 319 560; www.turismodocentro.pt; Av Frei Heitor Pinto; ☺ 9am-12.30pm & 2-5.30pm Mon-Sat) In a pink building near the Jardim Público. Has a good town map and a few dusty pamphlets, but is of limited help.

ℹ Getting There & Away

BUS

From the **bus station** (📋 275 313 506; Av da Anil), **Rede Expressos** (📋 275 336 700; www.rede-expressos.pt) and **Citi Express** (📋 275 336 700; www.citiexpress.eu) buses run to:

Guarda (€6, 45 minutes, at least hourly, fewer on Sundays)

Castelo Branco (€6, 50 minutes, almost hourly daily)

Lisbon (€15.20, 3¾ hours, seven to 10 daily)

Porto (€16.60, 3¾ hours, eight to 13 daily)

TRAIN

From the **train station** (Largo da Estação dos Caminhos de Ferro), three daily IC trains run to/from Lisbon Oriente (€17.70, 3¾ hours) via Castelo Branco (€6.80, 50 minutes). Three regional services also serve Castelo Branco (€6.45, one hour).

ℹ Getting Around

From the train and bus stations, it's a punishing 2km climb to Praça do Município, the town centre. A taxi from either station will cost about €6, or you can catch a **Covibus local bus** (📋 275 098 097; www.covibus.com; tickets €1.30): take No 10 or 11 for Praça do Município.

STREET ART

You don't have to visit a museum to enjoy great art in Covilhã. The city's walls boast an impressive, and increasingly varied, display of murals and artworks by artists from across the world. These were mostly created under the auspices of the Wool Festival de Arte Urbana da Covilha (www.facebook.com/woolfest), an annual initiative started in 2011.

BEIRA ALTA

The tablelands and su-baked plains of the Beira Alta (Upper Beira) stretch north to the Douro valley and east to the Spanish border. Historically, the province was the frontline in Portugal's defences against its Iberian neighbour, and its remote outer reaches are home to several heavily fortified fortress-towns. These are the main draw for travellers, along with the cultured cities of Viseu and Guarda.

Viseu

POP 99,270

A charming provincial centre, Viseu is one of the Beiras' most appealing cities. Interest is chiefly focused on its hilltop centre, a walled enclave of quaint plazas and cobbled alleyways capped by a monumental cathedral. For art lovers there are Renaissance treasures to savour in the Museu Grão Vasco, while gourmets can luxuriate in rich red wines from the nearby Dão region, one of Portugal's top wine-producing areas.

Down in the new town, action is centred on Praça da República, aka the 'Rossio', a leafy square graced with fountains and beds of colourful flowers.

History

Viseu's history dates to ancient times. It thrived under the Romans despite strong opposition from the local Lusitanian tribes led by warrior-chief Viriato (Viriathus). Legend holds that the rebel leader eventually took refuge in a nearby cave before being captured in 139 BC.

In later centuries Viseu was conquered and reconquered during the struggles between Christians and Moors. It was definitively captured by Fernando I, king of Castilla y León, in 1057.

Afonso V completed Viseu's sturdy walls in about 1472. The town soon spread beyond them, and grew fat from agriculture and trade. An annual 'free fair', declared by João III in 1510, continues today as one of the region's biggest agricultural and handicraft expositions.

◉ Sights

Most of Viseu's sights are clustered in the medieval walled centre. From the old town, Rua Augusto Hilário runs southeast through the former judiaria (14th- to 16th-century Jewish quarter) to connect with Rua Direita, a lively strip flanked by shops, souvenir stands, restaurants and town houses.

Viseu's handsome main square, the Adro da Sé, is overlooked by a trio of impressive buildings – the cathedral, the Paço de Três Escalões (home of the Museu Grão Vasco) and the Igreja da Misericórdia (church/museum free/€1.50; ⊙10am-12.30pm & 2-5.30pm, museum closed Mon) – with the Passeio dos Cónegos, an elevated colonnaded porch attributed to Italian architect Francesco da Cremona, on its southern flank.

Just below, attractive Praça de Dom Duarte was the city's principal square until the 19th century. Standing in the centre is a statue of Dom Duarte, the Portuguese monarch who was born in Viseu in 1391.

★ Museu Grão Vasco   MUSEUM

(☎232 422 049; Adro da Sé; adult/child €4/free; ⊙2-6pm Tue, 10am-1pm & 2-6pm Wed-Sat, 10am-2pm & 3-6pm Sun) Adjoining the cathedral, the granite Paço de Três Escalões (Palace of Three Steps) was originally built as the bishop's palace. It's now a splendid museum showcasing an important collection of works by local-born Vasco Fernandes, aka Grão Vasco (the Great Vasco; c 1475–1543), one of Portugal's seminal Renaissance artists.

There are two principal floors, one with religious art and 19th-century Portuguese works (check out the moustached lady by José de Almeida Furtado). The top floor displays Vasco's majestic canvases and works by other bright lights of the so-called Viseu School. Vasco's colleague, collaborator and rival Gaspar Vaz merits special attention. They spurred each other on to produce some of Portugal's finest artwork. After five centuries their rich colours and luminous style are still as striking as ever.

★ Catedral de Viseu   CATHEDRAL

(Sé; Adro da Sé; ⊙9am-1pm & 2-5.30pm Mon-Sat, 9am-noon & 2-6.30pm Sun) FREE Viseu's cathedral is a striking hybrid of architectural styles. Originally built in the 13th century, it now has a 17th-century Mannerist facade and a soaring 16th-century columned interior. Particularly impressive is the vaulted Manueline ceiling with ribs carved to resemble knotted strands of rope. The rounded arches of the lower level, like the double-tier cloister outside, are early examples of Italian-inspired Renaissance architecture. Note also the azulejo (hand-painted tile) panels and

Viseu

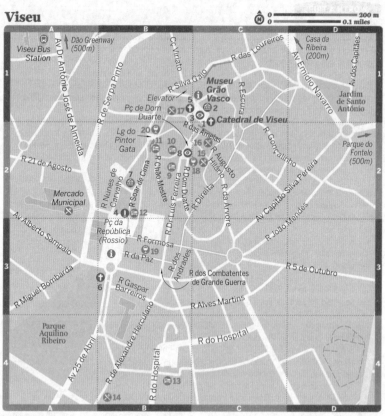

Viseu

amazing Romanesque-Gothic portal, redis-covered during restoration work in 1918.

Stairs in the northern transept lead to the **Museu de Arte Sacra**. The museum itself is a lacklustre assemblage of vestments and religious paraphernalia, but its lofty setting offers a nice perspective on the church's ar-chitecture.

Azulejos   PUBLIC ART
The north side of Praça da República is adorned with a series of striking *azulejo*

WORTH A TRIP

BELMONTE

With its excellent museums and secret Jewish history, the charming hilltop town of Belmonte is well worth a visit.

There have been Jews in Portugal since ancient times, and it's estimated that 10% of the country's population was Jewish during the period of Moorish rule. Later, Jews remained vital to the young Portuguese state, serving as government ministers and filling key roles in Henry the Navigator's school of overseas exploration.

However, when Portugal began to embrace Spain's Inquisitorial zeal from the 1490s onwards, thousands of Jews fled to the Beiras and Trás-os-Montes, where the Inquisition had yet to establish itself. But it wasn't long before the Inquisitors made their presence felt even there, and Jews once again faced conversion, expulsion or death. To continue practising as a Jew meant doing so in secret.

In the 1980s it was revealed that a group of Jewish families in Belmonte had been doing exactly that, observing their customs in secret for more than 500 years. To keep the community intact, traditions had been passed down orally from mother to daughter and marriages arranged only between Jewish families. Each Friday night members would descend into basements to pray and celebrate the sabbath. Now that the community is out in the open, it has embraced male-dominated Orthodox Judaism, though the female elders have not forgotten the secret prayers they so doggedly transmitted down the centuries.

To learn more, head to the Museu Judaico de Belmonte (Rua Portela 4, adult/child €4/3; ☺9.30am-1pm & 2.30-6pm Tue-Sun mid-Apr–mid-Sep, 9am-12.30pm & 2-5.30pm Tue-Sun mid-Sep–mid-Apr) which has a well-presented display of Jewish artefacts with some history about the 20th century re-establishment of Judaism in Portugal.

For a change of scene, the fabulous Museu dos Descobrimentos (☏275 088 698; Rua Pedro Alvares Canral 68; adult/child €5/3; ☺9.30am-1pm & 2.30-6pm Tue-Sun mid-Apr–mid-Sep, 9am-12.30pm & 2-5.30pm Tue-Sun mid-Sep–mid-Apr) focuses on Portugal's past as a seafaring nation and its discovery of and relationship with Brazil – the explorer Pedro Álvares Cabral, the 'discoverer' of Brazil, was born in Belmonte.

See www.cm-belmonte.pt for more details on visiting Belmonte.

Weekday buses run to Belmonte from both Covilhã (€3.30, 40 minutes to 1¼ hours) and Guarda (€3.50, 35 minutes to 1¼ hours).

panels depicting scenes from regional life. The blue, white and yellow illustrations were painted in 1931 by Joaquim Lopes (1886–1956).

Parque do Fontelo
PARK

This 10-hectare haven of woodland and verdant space sprawls beyond the Portal do Fontelo. Here you'll find the 16th-century Antigo Paço Episcopal (former Bishop's Palace), now occupied by the Welcome Center – Solar do Vinho do Dão, together with lovely shaded paths, the local sports stadium and a recreation complex.

Museu Almeida Moreira
MUSEUM

(☏232 427 471; Rua Soar de Cima; ☺2-6pm Tue, 10am-12.30pm & 2-6pm Wed-Sun) FREE The 19th-century, azulejo-adorned Museu Almeida Moreira is housed in the former home of art critic and collector Francisco António Almeida Moreira, founder of the Museu Grão Vasco (p350). It displays his eclectic collection of fine furnishings, paintings, ceramics, books and sculpture.

Casa da Ribeira
MUSEUM

(☏232 427 428; Largo Nossa Senhora da Conceição; ☺10am-1pm & 2-6pm Wed-Sun, 2-6pm Tue) FREE Housed in a smart stone house on the river Pavia, this small cultural centre focuses on the area's traditional way of life and artisanal skills. There's a display on the ground floor exhibiting various domestic objects as well as a typical river boat and a working wool loom, while upstairs is given over to temporary exhibitions.

Igreja Dos Terceiros
CHURCH

(Praça da República; ☺7am-7pm) FREE At the southern end of Praça da República is the late-18th-century Igreja dos Terceiros, all heavy, gilded baroque but apart from the luminous azulejos portraying the life of St Francis.

🏃 Activities

Welcome Center –
Solar do Vinho do Dão
WINE

(📞 232 410 060; www.rotavinhosdao.pt; Rua Aristides Sousa Mendes; ⏰ 10am-12.30pm & 2-6pm Tue-Fri, to 7pm Sat) This wonderful centre, housed in a 16th-century palace in the Parque do Fontelo, showcases the vineyards of the Dão region. You can learn about local producers as well as sampling and buying their wines. The Center also organises regular wine-related workshops and events.

Dão Greenway
WALKING, CYCLING

(Ecopista do Dão; www.ciclovia.pt) You can cycle or walk this 50km trail along a former rail track between Viseu and Santa Comba Dão. For further information and details of other routes in the area, pick up the Dão Greenway map at the Welcome Centre (p355).

Casa de Santar
WINE

(📞 919 662 839, 232 942 937; www.casadesantar. com; Av Viscondessa Taveiro, Santar; tours adult/child under 6 €15/free; ⏰ guided tours 10am, noon, 2pm, 4pm, 6pm (summer only) Tue-Sat, shop 10am-noon & 2-6pm Tue-Sat) One of the most accessible wineries from Viseu is Casa de Santar, some 16km southeast on the N231. Tours take in the mansion house of the Counts of Santar and Magalhães and its lovely gardens. Tastings are also available for €5 (for two wines and nibbles).

🎉 Festivals & Events

Feira de São Mateus
CULTURAL

(www.feirasaomateus.pt; ⏰ mid-Aug–mid-Sep) Viseu's biggest annual bash is this agricultural jamboree. Handicraft and food stalls are set up alongside amusement-park rides as concerts and fireworks provide the soundtrack. This direct descendant of the town's old 'free fair' still takes place in the riverside Campo da Feira de São Mateus, set aside for the event by João III in 1510.

🛏 Sleeping

⭐ Allgo Hostel
HOSTEL $

(📞 964 935 006; Rua Dr Luís Ferreira 87; dm €17-20, f €43-80; 📶) Occupying a tall town house overlooking Praça Dom Duarte, this new hostel – it opened in the summer of 2018 – squeezes in four dorms, sleeping from four to eight, and three private rooms, as well as a lovely kitchen. Space is tight but the pristine white walls and blonde wood floors ensure a light, airy feel.

Campismo
Moinhos do Dão
CAMPGROUND, COTTAGE $

(📞 232 610 586, 933 956 630; www.moinhosdodao. nl; Tibaldinho, Mangualde; sites per adult/child/car/tent €6/4/1.50/7; 🅿) This amazingly located, utterly tranquil spot sits at the end of a very rutted – walk if you value your vehicle – 1.6km dirt road 20km southeast of Viseu and offers camping on the banks of the Rio Dão, plus rustic indoor lodgings. Built amid a cluster of restored watermills, it's a place where you can truly get away from it all.

Meals are available, and you can buy organic fruit and veg fresh from the owners' garden.

Pensão Rossio Parque
PENSION $

(📞 232 422 085; www.pensaorossioparque. com; Rua Soar de Cima 55; s/d €30/35; 🅰🕻) A no-brainer for budget-minded travellers, this old-fashioned pension has modest, no-frills rooms above a popular restaurant. The best are those in front with grandstand views of the Rossio (Praça da República). Discounts are available for longer stays.

⭐ Casa da Sé
BOUTIQUE HOTEL $$

(📞 232 468 032; www.casadase.net; Rua Augusta Cruz 12; d standard €73-112, ste €135-155; 🅰🕻) Right in the heart of old Viseu, this handsome boutique hotel is owned by an antique dealer, so the charming 18th-century building is full of period furniture and *objets d'art*, all for sale should one take your fancy. Its 12 individually-decorated rooms are classically attired, and the helpful staff help create a warm, hospitable atmosphere.

⭐ Pousada de Viseu
POUSADA $$

(📞 210 457 320; www.pousadas.pt; Rua do Hospital; s €85-115, d €85-125; 🅿🕻🕸🕻🕻) This superbly refashioned *pousada* set in a monumental 19th-century hospital is a top luxury option. The original three floors, all with ridiculously high ceilings and spacious modern rooms, have been enhanced with a 4th floor dedicated to superior rooms with panoramic terraces. The enormous central courtyard, with bar, is a neoclassical delight, while the elegant former pharmacy has been converted into a cosy lounge. Indoor and outdoor pools, plus a gym and spa complex, complete the picture. Excellent value.

Palácio dos Melos
BOUTIQUE HOTEL $$

(📞 232 439 290; www.hotelpalaciodosmelos. pt; Rua Chão Mestre 4; s/d €70/90, ste €130; 🅿🕻🕸🕻) This friendly, central hotel enjoys a remarkable location, in a renovated

WINES OF THE DÃO REGION

The velvety reds of the Dão region, south and east of Viseu, have been produced for more than 2000 years, and are today among Portugal's best drops. Vineyards are mostly sheltered in valleys at altitudes of 200m to 900m just west of the Serra da Estrela, thus avoiding both rain from the coast and harsh summer heat from inland. This, together with the granitic soil, helps the wines retain their natural acidity. Dão wines are often called the Burgundies of Portugal because they don't overpower; rather they're subtle and full of finesse.

Some three dozen Dão vineyards and producers offer multilingual cellar tours and tastings; most require advance booking. Two popular wineries near Viseu are Casa da Ínsua (p354), 30km east on the IP5 and N329-1, and Casa de Santar (p353), 16km southeast on the N231. Both have fine grounds and lovely architecture, and the former is also a plush country hotel.

For those keen to learn about Dão wines, check out the Welcome Center – Solar do Vinho do Dão (p353) in Viseu. Here, you can sample Dão wines and get information on the region's excellent wine routes. Many of the wineries have excellent restaurants attached.

White Dão wines are available, though the full-bodied reds are generally better and more prolific. Do also try the sparkling whites from the separate, smaller Lafões region, northwest of Viseu.

mansion built into the city walls. Its public areas are elegant with high ceilings and period furniture while guest rooms come in a range of looks, from modern business-like to refined classical. All are comfortable and spacious, though.

Casa da Ínsua   HERITAGE HOTEL **$$**
(☑232 640 110; www.casadainsua.pt; Penalva do Castelo; r €95-195; 🅿❄🛜) Tiptoe away from civilisation for a night at the sublime Casa da Ínsua. This 18th-century manor and winery has been lovingly converted into a five-star hotel brimming with historical charm. Inside it's all creaking wooden floors, large stone fireplaces chandeliers and high-ceilinged rooms, while outside, the manicured gardens are a delight. For bon viveurs, there's also a wine-tasting room and a highly regarded restaurant.

✖ Eating

Churrasquiera Cacimbo   PORTUGUESE **$**
(☑232 422 894; Rua Alexandre Herculano 95; mains €6.25-10; ⏰9am-11.30pm) The Cacimbo is a lifesaver on Sunday evenings, when virtually every restaurant in central Viseu is closed. The dining room, next to its own busy takeaway, is a fairly charmless neon-white affair, but the food hits the spot. The speciality of the house is its excellent grilled meat served in generous portions.

O Hilário   PORTUGUESE **$**
(☑232 436 587; Rua Augusto Hilário 35; mains €7-11; ⏰9.30am-3pm & 7.30-10pm Mon-Sat; 🖉) An authentic slice of old Portugal, this homely restaurant is named after the 19th-century fado singer who once lived down the street. It's a cheerful, family-run place popular with visitors and locals alike for its mighty *doses* (daily specials) of stews, sausages and grilled steaks. Meat dominates the menu, but you'll also find a few fishy options and they'll even rustle up a vegetarian dish or two if asked.

Mercado Municipal   MARKET **$**
(Rua 21 de Agosto; ⏰6.30am-7pm Mon-Sat summer, to 6pm winter) Self-caterers will find fruit, vegetables and other goodies at Viseu's produce market. Things are at their liveliest on the ground floor, where the fruit and veg stalls are situated.

Restaurante A Colmeia   PORTUGUESE **$$**
(Rua das Ameías 12; mains €9-12; ⏰noon-2.30pm & 7.15-9.45pm Mon-Sat) For an atmospheric setting, few spots can rival Colmeia's summer terrace by the medieval walls. In the colder months, action reverts to the rustic white-washed interior, where hungry diners sit down to generous helpings of local staples. Try the mixed grill for a fabulous fill-up.

Paço dos Cunhas de Santar   PORTUGUESE **$$**
(☑232 945 452; www.facebook.com/pacodos cunhas; Largo do Paço, Santar; fixed-price menus lunch €12.50, 3-/4-/5-course €25/35/45; ⏰10am-6pm Tue-Thu, to 10pm Fri & Sat, to 4pm Sun) The Paço dos Cunhas de Santar, a historic winery on a 17th-century estate in Santar, sets an attractive stage for fine dining. The dining room is light and contemporary, and

the seasonal, creative cuisine beautifully complements the excellent wine. Several fixed-price menus are available, including a bargain weekday lunch menu.

Restaurante Muralha da Sé   PORTUGUESE **$$**
(☑232 437 777; www.muralhadase.pt; Adro da Sé 24; mains €14-22; ⊗noon-2.30pm & 7.15-10.30pm, closed Tue & Sun dinner) This unabashedly upper-crust spot under the looming Igreja da Misericórdia (p350) specialises in fine regional cuisine made with ingredients from the nearby Serra da Estrela. It further impresses with a fine wine list and cathedral-square views from the terrace.

★Tres Pipos   PORTUGUESE **$$$**
(☑232 816 851; www.3pipos.pt; Rua de Santo Amaro 966, Tonda; mains €11-25; ⊗noon-3pm & 7-10pm, closed Mon & Sun dinner) You'll need your own wheels but it's well worth searching out this convivial family-run restaurant in Tonda, a small village some 30km southwest of Viseu. Your reward will be a meal of brilliantly executed regional dishes served in an atmospheric dining room clad in old wood and exposed stone. The wine list is a further plus, offering a curated selection of local Dão labels.

If you want to take a bottle home with you, there's also a shop selling local *vinho* as well as regional honeys, preserves, sausages, oils and black earthenware from nearby Molelos.

🍷 Drinking & Nightlife

Palato Wine House   WINE BAR
(Praça de Dom Duarte 1; ⊗8pm-4am Mon-Sat) With its exposed stone walls and prime central location, this good-looking wine bar is a fine place to get to grips with the local *vinho*. It has a long list of Dão and Douro wines by the bottle, with many also available by the glass.

The Brothers   BAR
(☑232 440 391; Rua da Paz 26; ⊗8.30am-2am Mon-Sat, 2pm-2am Sun) A bistro-style cafe on an attractive pedestrian-only street, The Brothers has a bohemian, Parisian-style atmosphere, good beers and regular live music. In the warmer months, its outdoor tables are a favourite evening hangout.

The Irish Bar   PUB
(Largo do Pintor Gata 8; ⊗9am-2am Mon-Wed, to 4am Thu-Sat, 1pm-2am Sun) One of several bars near the cathedral, this classic pub offers Guinness on tap, occasional live music and

terrace seating on a charming square near the old town gate.

ℹ️ Information

Hospital de São Teotónio (☑232 420 500; Av Dom Duarte) Viseu's main hospital.

Welcome Center Viseu (☑232 420 950; www.turismodocentro.pt; Adro da Sé; ⊗9am-6pm Mon-Fri, 9am-1pm & 2-5.30pm Sat & Sun; 🛜) Viseu's main tourist office is on the cathedral square. As well as city maps, it has free wi-fi and internet, and a useful brochure on walks in and around Viseu. City information is also available from a **kiosk** (www.visitviseu.pt; Praça da República; ⊗10am-6pm summer, to 5pm winter) on Praça da República.

ℹ️ Getting There & Away

There is no train station in Viseu, but regular **Rede Expressos** (☑232 422 822; www.rede-expressos.pt) and **Citi Express** (☑232 422 822; www.citiexpress.eu) buses serve the following destinations from the **bus station** (Centro Municipal de Transportes; Av Dr Antonio José de Almeida):

Guarda (€9.10, one hour, up to 16 daily)
Coimbra (€8.50, 1¼ hours, at least hourly)
Vila Real (€10.50, 1¼ hours, eight daily)
Porto (€11.90, 1¾ hours, up to 19 daily)
Lisbon (€18.10, 3½ hours, four daily)

Guarda
POP 42,540 / ELEV 1056M

Forte, farta, fria, fiel e formosa (strong, rich, cold, loyal and handsome): such is the popular description of Portugal's highest fully fledged city. Perched on a steep hill, Guarda was founded in 1197 to guard young Portugal against both Moors and Spaniards (hence the name). Nowadays, its small, granite old town with its majestic cathedral is a delightful place to spend an afternoon.

The historic part of the city is at the top of the hill, roughly 5km from the main A25 road and train station. The bus station is closer to the action, about 800m southeast (downhill) of the old town.

👁️ Sights

Old Town   OLD TOWN
A handsome quarter of cobblestone lanes and huddled houses, Guarda's hilltop centre fans out from **Praça Luís de Camões**. This sloping square is flanked by 16th- to 18th-century mansions and the town's dramatic cathedral (p357). Plenty of medieval

THE BEIRAS GUARDA

Guarda

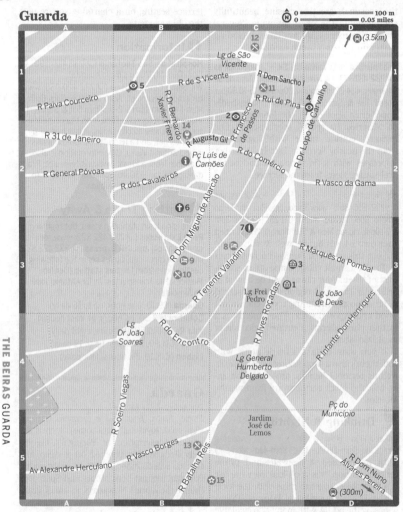

Guarda

⊙ Sights
1 Museu da Guarda	C3
2 Old Town	C1
3 Paço da Cultura	C3
4 Porta da Erva	D1
5 Porta d'El Rei	B1
6 Sé	B2
7 Torre dos Ferreiros	C3

🛏 Sleeping
8 Hotel Santos	C3
9 Solar de Alarcão	B3

🍴 Eating
10 O Bule	B3
11 Restaurante A Floresta	C1
12 Restaurante Belo Horizonte	C1
13 Restaurante O Caçador	B5

🍷 Drinking & Nightlife
14 Praça Velha	B2

🎭 Entertainment
15 Teatro Municipal da Guarda	C5

atmosphere survives in the narrow lanes to the north of the cathedral around Rua de São Vicente.

Of the old walls, towers and gates, the stalwart Torre dos Ferreiros (Blacksmiths' Tower; Rua Tenente Valadim) is still in good condition, rising to the east of the cathedral. To the north, you'll find two surviving gates, Porta d'El Rei and Porta da Erva. A walk between these two gates takes you through the heart of Guarda's historic judiaria (Jewish quarter). Sharp-eyed visitors will notice crosses and other symbols scratched into door frames: these identified the homes of marranos (Jews forced to convert to Christianity who continued to practice Judaism) during the dark days of the Inquisition.

Museu da Guarda   MUSEUM
(☑ 271 213 460; Rua Alves Roçadas 30; adult/child €2/free; ⊙ 9am-12.30pm & 2-5.30pm Tue-Sun) Housed in the severe 17th-century Episcopal Seminary, Guarda's main museum showcases an eclectic collection of archaeological finds, artworks and early books. Exhibits range from prehistoric flints to illustrated 16th-century tomes and contemporary Portuguese paintings.

In the adjacent 18th-century courtyard, the handsome Paço da Cultura (⊙ 9am-12.30pm & 2-5.30pm Tue-Sat) FREE stages temporary art exhibitions.

Sé   CATHEDRAL
(Praça Luís de Camões; admission €1, incl roof terrace €2; ⊙ 10am-1pm & 2-5.30pm Apr-Oct, 9.30am-1pm & 2-5pm Nov-Mar) Powerful in its sobriety, this grey Gothic edifice looms heavily over the central square. The earliest parts of the cathedral date from 1390 but it's dotted with Manueline and Renaissance ornamentation. The most striking feature in the immense, granite interior is the four-storey Renaissance altarpiece attributed to Jean de Rouen (João de Ruão).

Also impressive are the bird's-eye views of the city and surrounding landscape from the rooftop terrace, accessible by way of a narrow spiral staircase.

🛏 Sleeping

Senses Camping   CAMPGROUND
(☑ 915 707 050; www.sensescamping.com; Quinta da Rio, Faia; tent pitch €6-8 plus €4 per person, bell/safari tents €45/€85-95, tepees/yurts €65/95; P 🐾) Switch off from the outside world at this fantastic riverside retreat. About 8km outside Guarda, it has pitches

and ready-fixed bell and safari tents, as well as tepees and yurts, all spread over a verdant site on the banks of the Rio Mondego. There are also three guest rooms in a nearby farmhouse.

Communal meals are prepared with homegrown organic veggies, and there's a choice of activities on offer including yoga and massages.

★ Hotel Santos   HOTEL $
(☑ 271 205 400; www.hotelsantos.pt; Rua Tenente Valadim 14; s €30-40, d €40-60, f €60-80; 🐾) The best budget option in the historic centre, the friendly Santos offers value for money with spotless, light-filled rooms. Its labyrinthine interior resembles an Escher drawing with interconnecting walkways, stairs and glass walls, all elegantly incorporated into the town's medieval walls.

Solar de Alarcão   GUESTHOUSE $$
(☑ 962 327 177, 271 214 392; www.uk.solarde alarcao.pt; Rua Dom Miguel de Alarcão 25-27; d €60-80; P 🐾) Guarda's most refined choice, this beautiful 17th-century granite mansion has its own courtyard and loggia, and sits within hailing distance of the cathedral. It has a handful of genuine olde-worlde rooms, coloured in reds and golds and clad in antiques, drapes and polished wood furniture.

🍴 Eating

O Bule   CAFE $
(☑ 271 211 275; Rua Dom Miguel de Alarcão; ⊙ 8am-8pm Mon-Fri, 9am-8pm Sat, 10am-8pm Sun) If you fancy a coffee and a piece of cake, search out this cosy cafe near the cathedral. Here you can try some finger-licking local pastries, including delicious queijadas (sheep's milk tarts).

Restaurante O Caçador   SEAFOOD $$
(☑ 271 211 702; www.restauranteocacador.com; Rua Batalha Reis 121; mains €9-15; ⊙ noon-3pm & 7-10pm Tue-Sun) Despite its name (The Hunter), this popular restaurant is the place for seafood in Guarda. Locals flock to its glass-fronted dining room to feast on evergreen crowd-pleasers such as grilled squid and sea bass fresh in from Aveiro. Bookings recommended for dinner.

Restaurante Belo Horizonte   PORTUGUESE $$
(☑ 271 211 454; restaurantebelohorizonte.com; Largo de São Vicente 1; mains €9-15; ⊙ noon-3pm Tue-Sun & 7-10pm Tue-Sat) A cut above most of Guarda's midrange restaurants, Belo Horizonte has long been a local favourite. It does

a great line in regional specialities such as *cabrito grelhado* (grilled kid) and *morcelas da Guarda* (black-pudding–style sausage), as well as offering daily *bacalhau* specials.

Restaurante A Floresta PORTUGUESE $$
(☑ 271 212 314; Rua Francisco de Passos 40; mains €7-14; ☺ noon-4pm & 7-10pm) This snug family-run place is a reliable bet for huge helpings of hearty regional cuisine. That means heaving plates of grilled meats and sausages served with the ubiquitous combo of rice, salad and chips.

🍷 Drinking & Entertainment

Praça Velha BAR
(Rua Augusto Gil 17; ☺ 8am-3am Mon-Sat; 🛜) Hidden away in a tiny corner behind Praça Luís de Camões, this laid-back little bar is a fine spot for an evening drink, perhaps at one of the tables outside on the cobbled street.

Teatro Municipal da Guarda THEATRE
(☑ 271 205 240; www.tmg.com.pt; Rua Batalha Reis 12; tickets €3-10) Guarda's shiny theatre complex, just south of the historic centre, regularly hosts high-quality theatre, dance and music, including frequent international acts.

ℹ️ Information

Guarda Welcome Center (☑ 271 205 530; www.mun-guarda.pt; Praça Luís de Camões 21; ☺ 9am-5.30pm Mon-Fri, 9am-1pm & 2-5pm Sat & Sun winter, 9am-6pm Mon-Fri, 10am-1pm & 2-6pm Sat & Sun summer) Helpful office on the main square in the historic centre.

ℹ️ Getting There & Away

BUS

From the **bus station** (☑ 271 221 515; Rua Dom Nuno Álvares Pereira), **Rede Expressos** (☑ 271 221 515; www.rede-expressos.pt) and **Citi Express** (☑ 271 221 515; www.citiexpress.eu/agente/guarda) run services at least twice daily to the following destinations:

Covilhã (€6, 45 minutes)
Seia (€10.30, 70 minutes)
Viseu (€9.10, one to 1½ hours)
Trancoso (€8.60, 1½ hours)
Castelo Branco (€10.50, 1¾ hours)
Coimbra (€13.10, 2¾ hours)
Porto (€13.70, three hours)
Lisbon (€17.10, 4¾ hours)

Rede Expressos also has a weekday bus to Gouveia (€11.40, 1¾ hours, Monday to Saturday).

TRAIN

Guarda's modern **train station** (Largo 1 de Dezembro) is served by direct IC trains from Lisbon (€21.10, 4¼ hours, three daily) and Coimbra-B (€12.90, 2¼ hours, three daily). For Porto, change at Pampilhosa (frequent services).

ℹ️ Getting Around

Buses run by Transportes Urbanos da Guarda (www.mun-guarda.pt) between the train station and the centre (€1.10) are infrequent; you're probably better off taking a taxi (€6 to €7).

Linhares & Folgosinho

Two of the Serra da Estrela's prettiest towns lie high in the hills between Gouveia and Guarda. Neither has much tourist infrastructure, but that's part of their appeal.

Linhares, an attractive village of stone houses and steep cobbled lanes, is best known for its imposing 13th-century castle. Some 14km to the southwest, Folgosinho boasts a miniature castle – basically a clock tower emerging from a mound of rocks – and a pretty village square.

👁️ Sights

Castelo de Linhares CASTLE
(Rua do Castelo, Linhares; ☺ always open) FREE Visible for miles around, Linhares' 13th-century castle is a formidable sight, with its two crenellated keeps and impregnable walls. Not a lot remains inside the walls, but the dizzying views from the battlements are really quite something.

🛏️ Sleeping & Eating

Casa Pissarra GUESTHOUSE $
(☑ 271 776 180; www.casapissarra.com; Rua Direita, Linhares; r €35-45, house €90) A beautifully restored granite house, this rustic bolthole makes a lovely base for exploring Linhares and beyond. Both of its two rooms have heating, and there's a fully equipped kitchen and a living room with a stone fireplace. Two separate rooms with private bathroom are also available. The owner, Maria, speaks fluent English. Two-night minimum stay.

O Albertino PORTUGUESE $$
(☑ 238 745 266; www.oalbertino-folgosinho.com; Largo do Adro de Viriato 8, Folgosinho; mains €10-17; ☺ noon-4pm & 7-9pm, closed Mon & Sun lunch) With the smell of woodsmoke in the chill mountain air, O Albertino completes the scene perfectly: a cosy stone-walled restau-

rant specialising in delicious mountain food. Expect abundant farmhouse helpings of *leitão* (roast suckling pig) and gamey favourites like *feijoada de javali* (beans stewed with wild boar). Reservations recommended.

The restaurant also rents out rooms in the village from €50 (less outside high season).

Cova da Loba PORTUGUESE $$
(☎271 776 119; www.covadaloba.com; Largo da Igreja, Linhares; mains €12-18; ☺noon-3pm & 7-10pm, closed Wed & Thu lunch) A stone house on a hilltop square in tiny Linhares is not the most likely setting for creative contemporary cuisine. But that's what you'll get at Cova da Loba, a modish restaurant renowned for its gourmet approach to traditional Portuguese cooking.

ⓘ Information

Turismo (☎271 776 368; Rua Direita, Linhares; ☺9am-1pm & 2-7pm) Has an English-language leaflet with rudimentary information about Linhares and its castle.

ⓘ Getting There & Away

You really need your own transport to get to the villages. Linhares is signposted off the N17, but be alert as it's easy to miss the signpost.

Folgosinho is 14km southwest of Linhares, accessible by a small country road.

Trancoso

POP 3290 / ELEV 870M

A warren of cobbled lanes and grey houses huddled inside a ring of mighty 13th-century walls, Trancoso makes a charming retreat from the modern world. Now a sleepy little place, it was once an important fortress town, and it was here that Dom Dinis married the saintly Dona Isabel of Aragon in 1282.

The town's favourite son is Bandarra, a lowly 16th-century shoemaker and fortune-teller who put official noses out of joint by foretelling the end of the Portuguese monarchy. Sure enough, shortly after Bandarra's death, the young Dom Sebastião died, heirless, in the disastrous Battle of Alcácer-Quibir in 1558. Soon afterwards, Portugal fell under Spanish rule.

⊙ Sights

Old Town OLD TOWN
Trancoso's walled centre is a charming maze of picturesque squares, attractive churches

and narrow cobbled lanes. Several medieval gates puncture the walls, including the Portas do Prado and, to the south, the Portas d'El Rei (King's Gate), historically the main entrance into town – look for the coat of arms over the passageway. From either gate, it's a short walk to Largo Padre Francisco Ferreira, the handsome central square set around an octagonal 16th-century *pelourinho* (pillory). Nearby, the Igreja de São Pedro stands out, with its white baroque facade.

To the southeast is the judiaria, Trancoso's old Jewish quarter. Like many northern Portuguese towns, Trancoso acquired a sizeable Jewish community following the expulsion of the Jews from Spain in the late 15th century. As elsewhere along the border, you can generally spot Jewish houses by looking for a pair of doors: a smaller one for the private household and a larger one for a shop or warehouse. Among reminders of that time is a former rabbinical residence called the Casa do Gato Preto, marked with a Lion of Judah and other Jewish images.

Outside the northern walls, the 13th-century Capela de Santa Luzia is an attractive roadside feature, with its heavy Romanesque arches and unadorned dry-stone exterior.

Castelo CASTLE
(☺9am-12.30pm & 2-5.30pm Mon-Fri, 10am-1pm & 3-6pm Sat & Sun May-Oct, 9am-12.30pm & 2-5.30pm Mon-Fri, 10am-12.30pm & 2-5pm Sat & Sun Nov-Apr) FREE On a hill in the northeast corner of the historic centre is Trancoso's landmark castle, with its crenellated towers and the distinctively slanted walls of the Torre de Menagem, a squat Moorish tower you can climb for views over the town's rooftops and beyond.

Visigothic Tombs TOMB
FREE Across the road from the Portas do Prado by the courthouse car park, you'll find an untended mass of grey rocks, many of which have been shaped into eerie, body-shaped cavities. These were discovered during construction of the court in the 1960s, and are thought to be Visigothic tombs dating to the 7th or 8th century.

🎭 Festivals & Events

Feira Medieval de Trancoso CULTURAL
On the last weekend in June Trancoso revisits its past with lots of dressing up, a medieval market in the castle area, jousting and more. It's lots of fun.

THE BEIRAS TRANCOSO

AROUND THE PLANALTO

Remote and sparsely populated, the *planalto* (high plain) extends across the northeastern reaches of the Beira Alta. Its harsh landscape is littered with stone villages whose castles once represented Portugal's first line of defence against Spanish aggression. While Trancoso and Almeida are the quintessential *planalto* fortress-villages, three other places – Sernancelhe, Penedono and Marialva – are also well worth a gander if you have your own wheels. With a car, you can visit all three in a single, long day; without one you'd struggle to manage it, as bus services here are thin on the ground.

Located 30km northwest of Trancoso, Sernancelhe has a pristine historic centre fashioned out of warm, beige-coloured stone. Sights include the lovely 12th-century Igreja de São Jão Baptista (⊘ generally closed), whose facade is said to boast Portugal's only freestanding Romanesque sculptures, and several grand 17th- and 18th-century town houses, including the elegant Solar dos Cavalhos.

Heading northeast for another 16km, you arrive at little Penedono, with its small but splendid castle (☑ 254 508 174; www.cm-penedono.pt; ⊘ 9am-6pm Mon-Fri, 10am-12.30pm & 2.30-6pm Sat, 2.30-6pm Sun Apr-Jun & Sep-Oct, to 5pm Jul & Aug, to 3pm Nov-Mar) FREE. This irregular hexagon, with its picturesque crenellation, probably dates to the 14th century and commands fine views over the *planalto*.

Most impressive of all is Marialva, 25km southeast of Penedono. The cobbled upper part of the village is dominated by a forbidding, 12th-century castle (adult/child €1.50/free; ⊘ 10am-1pm & 2-6pm Jun-Sep, 9am-1pm & 2-5pm Oct-Mar) that guards over the rugged valley of the Rio Côa. Below its walls lies a haunting little village.

If you feel like lingering, consider an overnight stay at Casas do Côro (☑ 917 552 020; www.casasdocoro.pt; r €160-365; ☎ ☒). Marialva's cobbled centre provides the memorable setting for this luxurious set-up, one of central Portugal's standout hotels. In fact, much of the hilltop hamlet is given over to the hotel, whose antique-clad guest rooms occupy a series of traditional stone houses and modern chalet-like structures. Facilities include a spa, a private garden, a swimming pool and a restaurant where dinner is served for €67.50 per person. Nonguests can eat here too but should book at least 24 hours in advance.

🛏 Sleeping & Eating

Residencial Dom Dinis
GUESTHOUSE $
(☑ 271 811 525; www.domdinis.net; Av da República 10; s/d/tr €20/30/42; 🅿 🛜) In a drab apartment block outside the eastern walls, the Dom Dinis is an ever-reliable budget choice. It's decidedly no-frills but it's well placed for the historic centre and rooms are spotlessly clean and comfortably furnished.

Hotel Turismo de Trancoso
HOTEL $$
(☑ 271 829 200; www.hotel-trancoso.com; Rua Professora Irene Avillez; s/d/tr €45/65/94; 🅿 ❄ 🛜 ☒) A huge white complex 10 minutes' walk from the Portas d'El Rei, this cavernous four-star has modern, Nordic-style rooms with blonde wood and plenty of natural light. Facilities are good, including an indoor pool, a small gym and a restaurant. Deals are usually available online, with prices midweek or in winter especially attractive.

São Marcos Restaurante
PORTUGUESE $
(☑ 271 811 326; Rua Frei João de Lucena 7; mains €7-12; ⊘ noon-3pm & 6-10pm) With its pretty lace curtains, white tablecloths and woody decor, snug São Marcos is the very picture of an old-school Portuguese restaurant. In keeping with the decor, the menu sticks to the tried-and-tested with a selection of *bacalhau* staples and grilled and roasted meats, including an excellent *cordeiro* (lamb).

Dom Gabriel
PORTUGUESE $
(☑ 918 408 755; Av Engenheiro Frederico Ulrich 9A; mains €9-13.50; ⊘ 9am-11pm Tue-Sun) Just outside the city walls, this is the town's best-value restaurant for solid local fare. Meat dishes are well garnished and simply prepared – the steaks are excellent – or you can push the boat out and go for flavoursome grilled fish.

Restaurante Área Benta
PORTUGUESE $$
(☑ 966 310 789; Rua dos Cavaleiros 30A; mains €9-15; ⊘ 12.30-3pm & 7.30-10.30pm Tue-Sun) Ensconced in a traditional stone house off Largo Padre Francisco Ferreira, Área Benta is reckoned to be the best restaurant in town. Its spacious interior, complete with wood floors and exposed stone walls, provides the elegant setting for updated regional dishes prepared with seasonal ingredients.

🛍 Shopping

Casa da Prisca   FOOD & DRINKS
(☑271 811 196; www.casadaprisca.com; Rua da
Corredoura 1; ☉9am-7pm) Just inside Portas
d'El Rei, this richly-stocked deli is a treasure
trove of regional bounty: smoked meats and
local cheeses, preserves, olive oils, vinegars
and liqueurs. An unlikely sounding speciality is *sardinhas doces* (sweet sardines),
fish-shaped confections made with eggs, almonds, cinnamon and chocolate.

ℹ Information

Turismo (☑271 811 147; www.cm-trancoso.
pt/turismo; Avenida Heróis de São Marcos;
☉9am-12.30pm & 2-5.30pm Jun-Sep, 9am-
12.30pm & 2-5.30pm Mon-Fri, 10am-12.30pm
& 2-5pm Sat, 10am-12.30pm & 2-4.30pm Sun
Oct-May) Just outside Portas d'El Rei. Can
provide an English brochure about the village.

ℹ Getting There & Away

BUS

From Trancoso's **bus station** (Centro de Ca-
mionagem de Trancoso; ☑965 053 840; Av
Calouste Gulbenkian), just northwest of the
walled town, **Rede Expressos** (www.rede-ex-
pressos.pt) has services to Viseu (€6.70, 70
minutes, two daily), with connections via Celorico da Beira to Guarda (€8.60, 50 minutes to
1½ hours, two daily).

TRAIN

The closest train stations are at Celorico da
Beira, 27km to the south, and Vila Franca das
Navas, 16km southeast.

Almeida

POP 1300 / ELEV 760M

Some 15km from the Spanish border, Almeida is a remarkable example of a frontier
stronghold. The old village sits entirely within a vast, star-shaped fortress. This monumental structure, completed in 1641 over
an earlier medieval fort, was built to bolster
Portugal's defences in the tense period that
followed independence from Spain in 1640.

👁 Sights

Museu Histórico Militar de Almeida MUSEUM
(☑271 571 229; adult/child €3/free, incl Sala de
Armas & CEAMA €3.50/1; ☉9.15am-noon & 2-5pm
Tue-Fri, from 10am Sat & Sun) This interesting
little museum occupies the *casamatas*, a
series of underground rooms originally used
for storage and shelter in times of siege.
Nowadays they house displays of arms,

uniforms and military paraphernalia, with
each room dedicated to a different period.

🎆 Festivals & Events

**Recriação Histórica
do Cerco de Almeida**   CULTURAL
(☉late Aug) A lively re-enactment of a bloody
1810 battle which saw Almeida, defended
by English and Portuguese troops, fall to
French invaders. Held annually.

🛏 Sleeping & Eating

Residencial-Restaurante A Muralha HOTEL $
(☑271 571 744; www.amuralha.pt; Bairro de São
Pedro; s/d €25/40; P❄🐾) This functional
modern place sits 250m outside the Portas
de São Francisco on the main road into the
village. It's a modest affair with quiet rooms
and slightly faded decor, but the price is right
and the South African–Portuguese owner extends a warm welcome. Its restaurant serves
excellent local food (mains €9 to €14).

Hotel Fortaleza de Almeida   HOTEL $$
(☑271 574 283; www.hotelparadordealmeida.com;
s €73-98, d €85-125; P❄@🐾) This friendly
four-star, one of the only modern buildings
in the old town, sits on the site of a former
cavalry barracks near the north bastion. It
offers spacious rooms with lovely parquet
floors, heavy wood furniture and giant win-
dows and/or balconies, some with views
over to the Spanish hills. A restaurant and
terrace are added bonuses.

Casa de Pedra   APARTMENT $$
(☑919 625 138; www.casadepedra.com.pt; Praça
da Liberdade 9; apt €85-115; ❄🐾) In the heart
of the historic centre, Casa de Pedra (Stone
House) offers two apartments in a tastefully
restored 17th-century house. Both are full of
natural light and smartly styled with modern furnishings.

ℹ Information

Turismo (☑271 570 020; www.cm-almeida.
pt; Portas de São Francisco; ☉9am-12.30pm
& 2-5.30pm Mon-Fri, from 10am Sat & Sun)
Impressively located in an old guard-chamber
within the Portas de São Francisco; here you
can get a map of the fortress.

ℹ Getting There & Away

Nondrivers will almost certainly have to stay the
night due to limited bus connections. The most
useful bus route is the daily service to and from
Guarda (€5.25, 1½ hours). It stops at the square
outside Portas de São Francisco.

Porto, the Douro & Trás-os-Montes

Why Go?

It's the dynamic Rio Douro that brings diversity to the province it has defined, a province with granite bluffs, wine caves, medieval stone houses and steep, terraced vineyards. Romantic Porto, Portugal's second-largest city, is at its mouth; one of the world's oldest demarcated wine regions is close to the source; and scores of friendly villages in between have always relied on it for water, food and commerce. Alongside the river, the region also boasts intricately carved cathedrals, baroque churches, palatial *quintas* (estates), beaux arts boulevards and 18th-century wine cellars.

Sandwiched between the Rio Douro and the Spanish border in Portugal's extreme northeast corner, ruggedly beautiful Trás-os-Montes is named for its centuries-long isolation 'behind the mountains'. Life here unfolds at a different pace, dictated by harsh, pristine nature. Both its food and its people are hearty and no-frills, as you'll soon find out when travelling its towns and wilderness areas.

Best Places to Eat

➜ Flor dos
Congregados (p385)

➜ MUU (p386)

➜ DOC (p409)

➜ A Lareira (p429)

Best Places to
Sleep

➜ Canto de Luz (p381)

➜ Casa Agrícola da Levada
(p413)

➜ Casa do Romezal (p405)

➜ A Lagosta Perdida (p425)

When to Go
Porto

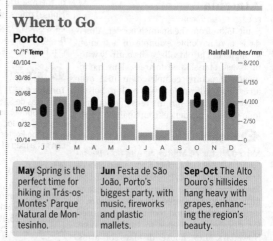

May Spring is the perfect time for hiking in Trás-os-Montes' Parque Natural de Montesinho.

Jun Festa de São João, Porto's biggest party, with music, fireworks and plastic mallets.

Sep-Oct The Alto Douro's hillsides hang heavy with grapes, enhancing the region's beauty.

PORTO

Opening up like a pop-up book from the banks of the Rio Douro, edgy-yet-opulent Porto entices with its historic centre, sumptuous food and wine, and charismatic locals.

Porto's charms are as subtle as the nuances of an aged tawny port, best savoured slowly on a romp through the hilly backstreets of Miragaia, Ribeira and Massarelos. It's the quiet moments of reflection and the snapshots of daily life that you'll remember most: the slosh of the Douro against the docks; the snap of laundry drying in river winds; the sound of port glasses clinking; the sight of young lovers discreetly tangled under a landmark bridge, on the rim of a park fountain, in the crumbling notch of a graffiti-blasted wall...

History

Porto put the 'Portu' in 'Portugal'. The name dates from Roman times, when Lusitanian settlements straddled the Rio Douro. The area was briefly in Moorish hands but was reconquered by AD 868 and reorganised as the county of Portucale, with Porto as its capital. British-born Henri of Burgundy was granted the land in 1095, and it was from here that Henri's son and Portuguese hero Afonso Henriques launched the Reconquista (Christian reconquest), ultimately winning Portugal its status as an independent kingdom.

In 1387 Dom João I married Philippa of Lancaster in Porto, and their most famous son, Henry the Navigator, was born here. While Henry's explorers groped around Africa for a sea route to India, British wine merchants – forbidden to trade with the French – set up shop, and their presence continues to this day, evidenced in port-wine labels such as Taylor's and Graham's.

Over the following centuries Porto acquired a well-earned reputation for rebelliousness. In 1628 a mob of angry women attacked the minister responsible for a tax on linen. A 'tipplers' riot' against the Marquês de Pombal's regulation of the port-wine trade was savagely put down in 1757. And in 1808, as Napoleon's troops occupied the city, Porto citizens arrested the French governor and set up their own short-lived junta. After the British helped drive out the French, Porto radicals were at it again, leading calls for a new liberal constitution, which they got in 1822. Demonstrations in support of liberals continued to erupt in Porto throughout the 19th century.

Wine profits helped fund the city's industrialisation, which began in earnest in the late 19th century, at a time when the elite in the rest of Portugal tended to see trade and manufacturing as vulgar. Today the city remains the economic capital of northern Portugal and is surpassed only by much-larger Lisbon in terms of economic and social clout.

◉ Sights

With the exception of the blockbuster Museu de Arte Contemporânea, Porto's must-sees cluster in the compact centre and are easily walkable. Many of the big hitters huddle in the Unesco-listed Ribeira district and Aliados, while hilltop Miragaia has some peaceful pockets of greenery and knockout views. For port-wine lodges aplenty, cross the river to Vila Nova de Gaia. What Foz do Douro lacks in trophy sights, it makes up for with its Atlantic breezes and coastal walks.

◉ Ribeira

★ Igreja de São Francisco   CHURCH
(Map p372; Jardim do Infante Dom Henrique; adult/child €6/5; ⊘9am-8pm Jul-Sep, to 7pm Mar-Jun & Oct, to 5.30pm Nov-Feb) Igreja de São Francisco looks from the outside to be an austerely Gothic church, but inside it hides one of Portugal's most dazzling displays of baroque finery. Hardly a centimetre escapes unsmothered, as otherworldly cherubs and sober monks are drowned by nearly 100kg of gold leaf. If you see only one church in Porto, make it this one.

High on your list should be the nave, interwoven with vines and curlicues, dripping with cherubs and shot through with gold leaf. Peel back the layers to find standouts such as the Manueline-style Chapel of St John the Baptist, the 13th-century statue of St Francis of Assisi and the 18th-century Tree of Jesse, a polychrome marvel of an altarpiece. The church museum harbours a fine, well-edited collection of sacred art.

In the eerily atmospheric catacombs, the great and the good of Porto were once buried. Look out for sculptural works by Italian master Nicolau Nasoni and prolific Portuguese sculptor António Teixeira Lopes.

Sé   CATHEDRAL
(Map p372; Terreiro da Sé; cloisters adult/student €3/2; ⊘9am-7pm Mon-Sat & 9.30am-12.30pm & 2.30-7pm Sun Apr-Oct, 9am-6pm Mon-Sat &

Porto, the Douro & Trás-os-Montes Highlights

① **Alto Douro** (p406) Wine-tasting your way around the picturesque vineyards of the region.

② **Ribeira** (p363) Losing yourself amid the medieval

alleys of this cinematic Porto neighbourhood.

③ **Amarante** (p400) Relaxing beside the Rio Tâmega and its medieval bridge in this charming town.

④ **Parque Arqueológico do Vale do Côa** (p409) Coming face to face with Palaeolithic artwork at this world-famous archaeological site.

5 Casa de Mateus (p411) Strolling the formal gardens and tasting fine wines at this stately 18th-century palace.

6 Parque Natural de Montesinho (p422) Hiking across a medieval bridge or climbing the park's heather-draped hills to 21st-century windmills.

7 Fisgas de Ermelo (p414) Swimming in natural pools above this dramatic waterfall in Parque Natural do Alvão.

8 Chaves (p417) Taking in the medieval tower and the 17th-century fortifications from the town's Roman bridge.

DRIVING TOUR: WINES OF THE DOURO

Wine lovers have their work cut out for them on this leisurely journey through the Douro Valley, one of the world's oldest demarcated wine regions. Drive through a landscape where steep terraced vineyards rise sharply from the Douro's banks and whitewashed quintas (estates) perch high in the hills.

❶ Porto

Begin in **Porto** (p370), gateway to the world-famous Douro Valley. Settle into the Douro's spirit with sunset drinks beneath Porto's iconic Ponte Dom Luís I bridge, followed by an evening out at the city's restaurants and wine bars.

The Drive > Cross the bridge to the Douro's southern bank, home to many of Portugal's most venerable wine producers.

❷ Vila Nova de Gaia

Spend an afternoon sampling countless varieties of port at **Vila Nova de Gaia's** (p371)

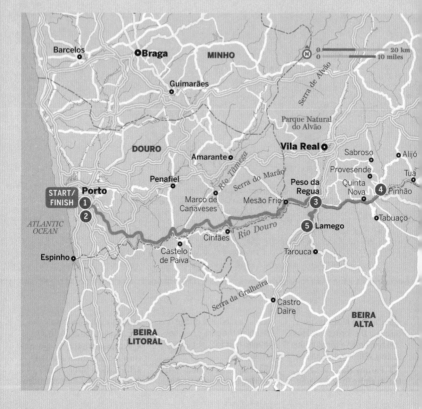

Vineyards near Pinhão (p406)

historic wine lodges. The recently spruced-up Graham's does great tours and tastings.

The Drive > Follow the curvy N108 upriver 125km to Peso da Régua, or zip across on the less scenic (but much faster) A4 and A24 motorways.

❸ Peso da Régua

In riverside **Peso da Régua** (p404), stop in at the wonderful Museu do Douro for far-reaching perspectives on the valley and its winemaking history. Next, head out for a tasting at the nearby Quinta do Vallado, a winery since 1716 and now a swanky little rural hotel where you can stay the night.

The Drive > Follow the N222 28km east to Pinhão, on one of Portugal's most stunning drives.

❹ Pinhão

The quaint riverside village of **Pinhão** (p407) makes a perfect base for a few nights. From the village, head out to explore the surrounding *Alto Douro* (Upper Douro), a spectacular area designated as a Unesco World Heritage Site in recognition of its centuries-old viticultural traditions. Quinta Nova, Quinta do Crasto and Quinta do Seixo all offer tastes of their wines paired with magnificent views.

The Drive > Double back west along the river, taking the N222 towards Peso da Régua, then continue south 13km on the A24 to Lamego.

❺ Lamego

On your way back to Porto, visit the foodie town of **Lamego** (p402), home to the hilltop shrine of Nossa Senhora dos Remédios and producer of a fine sparkling wine.

The Drive > Return to Porto via the A24 and A4 motorways (130km).

Porto

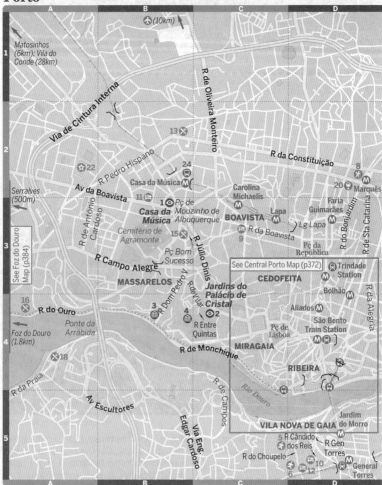

9am-12.30pm & 2.30-6pm Sun Nov-Mar) From Praça da Ribeira rises a tangle of medieval alleys and stairways that eventually reach the hulking, hilltop fortress of the cathedral. Founded in the 12th century, it was largely rebuilt a century later and then extensively altered during the 18th century. However, you can still make out the church's Romanesque origins in the barrel-vaulted nave.

History lends the cathedral gravitas – this is where Dom João I married his beloved Philippa of Lancaster in 1387, and where Prince Henry the Navigator was baptised in 1394, the fortune of far-flung lands but a distant dream.

★ **Palácio da Bolsa**   HISTORIC BUILDING
(Stock Exchange; Map p372; www.palaciodabolsa. com; Rua Ferreira Borges; tours adult/child €10/6.50; ⏲9am-6.30pm Apr-Oct, 9am-12.30pm & 2-5.30pm Nov-Mar) This splendid neoclassical monument (built from 1842 to 1910) honours Porto's past and present money merchants. Just past the entrance is the glass-domed **Pátio das Nações** (Hall of Nations), where the exchange once operated. But this pales in comparison with rooms deeper inside; to visit these, join one of the half-hour guided tours, which set off every 30 minutes.

The highlight is a stupendous ballroom known as the **Salão Árabe** (Arabian Hall),

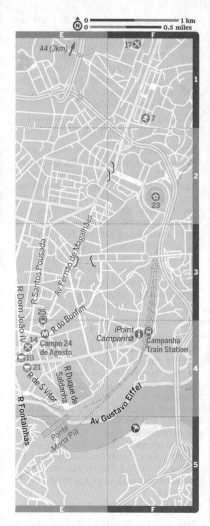

Porto

PORTO, THE DOURO & TRÁS-OS-MONTES PORTO

with stucco walls that have been teased into complex Moorish designs, then gilded with some 18kg of gold.

Museu da Misericórdia do Porto
CHURCH, MUSEUM
(MMIPO; Map p372; www.mmipo.pt; Rua das Flores 5; adult/child €5/2.50; ⊙10am-6.30pm Apr-Sep, to 5.30pm Oct-Mar) The Museu da Misericórdia do Porto harmoniously unites cutting-edge architecture, a prized collection of 15th- to 17th-century sacred art and portraiture, and one of Ribeira's finest churches, Igreja da Misericórdia. Bearing the hallmark of Italian baroque architect Nicolau Nasoni,

the church's interior is adorned with blue-and-white *azulejos* (hand-painted tiles). The museum's biggest stunner is the large-scale Flemish Renaissance painting *Fons Vitae* (Fountain of Life), depicting Dom Manuel I and family around a fountain of blood from the crucified Christ.

The museum centres on a sky-lit atrium, and a visit begins on the 3rd floor, gradually working down to the church (be sure to get a photogenic glimpse of it from the gallery). It showcases an impressive stash of religious art, most of which has ties to the Santa Casa da Misericórdia (Holy House of Our Lady of

Mercy), founded in 1499 by order of Dom Manuel I. This charitable organisation cared for the infirm, sick and poor for 500 years. On display are portraits of its benefactors, lab equipment (including electroshock apparatus to treat psychiatric disorders) and the treasures it amassed over centuries – sculpture, glass- and silverware, liturgical vestments etc.

The ultimate tribute to this old-meets-new medley is Portuguese artist Rui Chafes' eye-catching, curvaceous iron sculpture *My Blood is Your Blood* (2015), which hooks through the building to the facade.

Praça da Ribeira   PLAZA
(Map p372) Down by the Rio Douro, narrow streets open out onto a plaza framed by austerely grand, tiled town houses overlooking a picturesque stretch of the river. From here you have fine views of the port-wine lodges across the river, as well as the monumental, double-decker Ponte de Dom Luís I.

Ponte de Dom Luís I   BRIDGE
(Map p372) Completed in 1886 by a student of Gustave Eiffel, the bridge's top deck is now reserved for pedestrians, as well as one of the city's metro lines; the lower deck bears regular traffic, as well as narrow walkways for those on foot. The views of the river and old town are stunning, as are the daredevils who leap from the lower level.

Cais da Ribeira   AREA
(Map p372) This riverfront promenade is postcard Porto, taking in the whole spectacular sweep of the city, from Ribeira's pastel houses stacked like Lego bricks to the *barcos rabelos* (flat-bottomed boats) once used to transport port from the Douro. Early-evening buskers serenade crowds, and chefs fire up grills in the hole-in-the-wall fish restaurants and *tascas* (taverns) in the old arcades.

Jardim do Infante Dom Henrique   GARDENS
(Map p372; Rua Ferreira Borges) Presided over by the late-19th-century market hall Mercado Ferreira Borges and neoclassical Palácio da Bolsa (p368), these gardens are named after the centrepiece statue. Lifted high on a pedestal, the monument depicts Prince Henry the Navigator (1394–1460) – a catalyst in the Age of Discoveries and pioneer of the caravel (a small, fast ship), who braved the battering Atlantic in search of colonies for Portugal's collection.

Casa do Infante   HISTORIC BUILDING
(Map p372; Rua Alfândega 10; adult/child €2.20/free; ⏰10am-5.30pm Tue-Sun) In this handsomely renovated medieval town house, according to legend, Henry the Navigator was born in 1394. The building later served as Porto's first customs house. Today it boasts three floors of exhibits. In 2002 the complex was excavated, revealing Roman foundations and some remarkable mosaics – all of which are now on display.

👁 Aliados & Bolhão

★ Livraria Lello   HISTORIC BUILDING
(Map p372; www.livrarialello.pt; Rua das Carmelitas 144; €5; ⏰10am-7.30pm Mon-Fri, to 7pm Sat, 11am-7pm Sun; 🔁) Ostensibly a bookshop, but even if you're not after books, don't miss this exquisite 1906 neo-Gothic confection, with its lavishly carved plaster resembling wood and a stained-glass skylight. Feels magical? Its intricately wrought, curiously twisting staircase was supposedly the inspiration for the one in the Harry Potter books, which JK Rowling partly wrote in Porto while working here as an English teacher from 1991 to 1993.

The €5 entry is redeemable if you buy a book.

São Bento Train Station   HISTORIC BUILDING
(Map p372; Praça Almeida Garrett; ⏰5am-1am) One of the world's most beautiful train stations, beaux arts São Bento wings you back to a more graceful age of rail travel. Completed in 1903, it seems to have been imported from 19th-century Paris, with its mansard roof. But the dramatic *azulejo* panels of historical scenes in the front hall are the real attraction. Designed by Jorge Colaço in 1930, some 20,000 tiles depict historic battles (including Henry the Navigator's conquest of Ceuta), as well as the history of transport.

Avenida dos Aliados   AREA
(Map p372) Lined with bulging, beaux arts facades and capped by the stately câmara municipal (municipal council), this *avenida* recalls grand Parisian imitators such as Buenos Aires and Budapest. The avenue's central plaza was restored a few years back and often hosts pop-up book, comic and art festivals and exhibitions.

Torre dos Clérigos   TOWER
(Map p372; www.torredosclerigos.pt; Rua de São Filipe de Nery; €5; ⏰9am-7pm) Sticking out on Porto's skyline like a sore thumb – albeit a beautiful baroque one – this 76m-high tower was designed by Italian-born baroque master Nicolau Nasoni in the mid-1700s. Climb

its 225-step spiral staircase for phenomenal views over Porto's tiled rooftops, spires and the curve of the Douro to the port-wine lodges in Gaia. It also harbours an exhibition that chronicles the history of the tower's architects and residents.

Rua de Santa Catarina
AREA

(Map p372) This street is absurdly stylish and romantic, with trim boutiques, striped stone footpaths and animated crowds. It's home to Porto's most ornate tearoom, the art nouveau Café Majestic (p391), and the extraordinary *azulejo*-bedecked **Capela das Almas** (Map p372; ⊙ 7.30am-7pm Mon-Fri, 7.30am-1pm & 6-7pm Sat).

Mercado do Bolhão
MARKET

(Map p372; Rua Formosa) The 19th-century, wrought-iron Mercado do Bolhão closed its doors in spring 2018 for a major restoration project. No fixed date had been given for its reopening at the time of writing.

◎ Miragaia

★ Museu Nacional Soares dos Reis
MUSEUM

(Map p372; www.museusoaresdosreis.pt; Rua Dom Manuel II 44; adult/child €5/free; ⊙ 10am-6pm Tue-Sun) Porto's best art museum presents a stellar collection ranging from Neolithic carvings to Portugal's take on modernism, all housed in the formidable Palácio das Carrancas.

Miradouro da Vitória
VIEWPOINT

(Map p372; Rua São Bento da Vitória) Porto is reduced to postcard format at this viewpoint, perched high and mighty above a mosaic of terracotta rooftops that tumble down to the Douro. It's a highly atmospheric spot at dusk, when landmarks such as the Ponte Dom Luís I bridge are illuminated and the lights on Vila Nova de Gaia's wine lodges flick on one by one.

Igreja das Carmelitas
CHURCH

(Map p372; Rua do Carmo; ⊙ 7.30am-7pm Mon-Fri, 9am-6.45pm Sat & Sun) Blink and you might miss that this is a church in its own right, snuggled as close as it is to the Igreja do Carmo. The twin churches are separated only by a 1m-wide house, once the dividing line between the monks of Carmo and the Carmelite nuns. Dating to the 17th century, its modest classical facade belies its lavishly gilded nave.

Rua de São Bento da Vitória
AREA

(Map p372) With its cobblestones polished smooth by centuries of shoe leather, and pretty tiled houses with little wrought-iron balconies and window boxes brimming with pot plants, this narrow, gently curving street was the beating heart of Jewish Porto in late medieval times. Keep your eyes peeled for telltale sights of Jewish heritage, such as bronze Hamsa (protective hand) door knockers.

Centro Português de Fotografia
MUSEUM

(Portuguese Photography Centre; Map p372; www.cpf.pt; Campo dos Mártires da Pátria; ⊙ exhibition hall 10am-12.30pm & 2-6pm Tue-Fri, 3-7pm Sat & Sun) **FREE** This stately building (1767) once served as a prison and now houses a photography museum. You actually walk through the thick iron gates and into the cells to see the work, which lends the intriguing exhibits even more gravitas. On the 3rd floor is a collection of cameras spanning every decade; particularly fascinating are the espionage ones, discreetly hidden in everything from Pepsi cans to Marlboro packets.

Immediately south of the museum are the narrow, atmospheric lanes that were once part of Porto's *judiaria* (Jewish quarter).

Jardim da Cordoaria
PARK

(Map p372; Rua Campo dos Mártires da Pátria) This pleasantly leafy park is known simply as 'Cordoaria'. Check out the four haunting sculptures by Spain's Juan Muñoz. The romantic, narrow lanes that run north from the Cordoaria are the domain of Porto's hippest bars.

◎ Vila Nova de Gaia

Jardim do Morro
GARDENS

(Map p372; Avenida da República) The cable car swings up to this hilltop park, which can also be reached by crossing the upper level of Ponte de Dom Luís I. Shaded by palms, these gardens are all about the view. From here, Porto looks stunning, with the pastel-hued houses of Ribeira on the opposite side of the Douro and the snaking river below.

Espaço Porto Cruz
WINERY, MUSEUM

(Map p372; www.myportocruz.com; Largo Miguel Bombarda 23; ⊙ 11am-7pm Tue-Sun) This swanky port-wine emporium inside a restored 18th-century riverside building celebrates all things port. In addition to a shop where tastings are held (by the glass starting

Central Porto

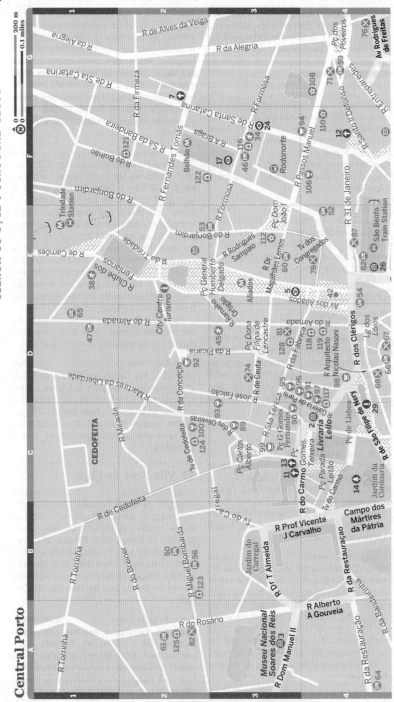

N
0 ____ 200 m
0 ____ 0.1 miles

CEDOFEITA

Museu Nacional Soares dos Reis

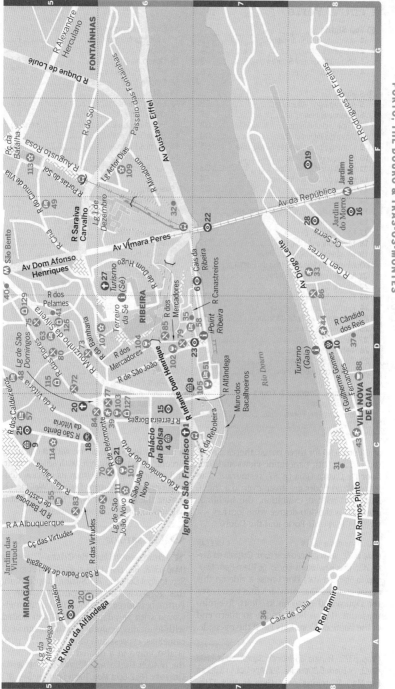

Central Porto

at €3 or €9.50 for three ports), there's a rooftop terrace with panoramic views and 3rd-floor De Castro Gaia (p387) restaurant. The 1st and 2nd floors are given over to a small, free, port-related exhibition, the highlight of which is the 360-degree wine journey – a virtual flight over Porto and the Douro.

Teleférico de Gaia   CABLE CAR
(Map p372; www.gaiacablecar.com; Calçada da Serra 143; one-way/return €6/9; ⊙10am-8pm May-Sep, to 6pm Oct-Mar) Don't miss a ride on this aerial gondola that provides fine views over the Douro and Porto on its short, five-minute jaunt. It runs between the southern end of the Ponte de Dom Luís I and the riverside.

Mosteiro da Serra do Pilar   MONASTERY
(Map p372; Rampa do Infante Santo; adult/child €4/2; ⊙10am-6.30pm Tue-Sun Apr-Oct, to 5.30pm Nov-Mar) Watching over Gaia is this 17th-

century hilltop monastery, with its striking circular cloister, church with gilded altar, and stellar river views from its cupola. Requisitioned by the future Duke of Wellington during the Peninsular War (1807–14), it still belongs to the Portuguese military.

◎ Massarelos

★**Jardins do Palácio de Cristal**   GARDENS
(Map p368; Rua Dom Manuel II; ⊙8am-9pm Apr-Sep, to 7pm Oct-Mar; ⊕) Sitting atop a bluff, this gorgeous botanical garden is one of Porto's best-loved escapes, with lawns interwoven with sun-dappled paths and dotted with fountains, sculptures, giant magnolias, camellias, cypress and olive trees. The park is also home to a domed **sports pavilion**, the hi-tech **Biblioteca Municipal Almeida Garrett** (⊙2-6pm Mon, 10am-6pm Tue-Sat; ☏)

and the **Museu Romântico** (Quinta da Macieirinha; Map p368; Rua de Entre Quintas 220; adult/
child weekdays €2.20/free, Sat & Sun free; ☺10am-
5.30pm Tue-Sun).

Museu do Carro Eléctrico   MUSEUM
(Tram Museum; Map p368; www.museudocarroelec-
trico.pt; Alameda Basílio Teles 51; adult/child €8/4;
☺2-6pm Mon, 10am-6pm Tue-Sun) Housed in an
antiquated switching-house, this museum
is a tram-spotter's delight. It displays dozens of beautifully restored old trams – from
early 1870s models once pulled by mules to
streamlined, bee-yellow 1930s numbers.

⊙ Boavista

★**Casa da Música**   LANDMARK
(Map p368; ☑220 120 220; www.casadamusica.
com; Avenida da Boavista 604-610; guided tour
€10; ☺English guided tours 11am & 4pm) At once
minimalist, iconic and daringly imaginative, the Casa da Música is the beating heart
of Porto's cultural scene and the home of the
Porto National Orchestra. Dutch architect
Rem Koolhaas rocked the musical world
with this crystalline creation – the jewel in
the city's European Capital of Culture 2001
crown.

The wonky cuboid conceals a shoebox-style concert hall lauded for some of the
world's best acoustics. If your curiosity has
been piqued, join one of the daily guided
tours.

Mercado Bom Sucesso   MARKET €
(Map p368; www.mercadobomsucesso.pt; Praça
Bom Sucesso; ☺10am-11pm Sun-Thu, to midnight
Fri & Sat) For a snapshot of local life and a
bite to eat, nip into Boavista's revamped
Mercado Bom Sucesso. A complete architec-
tural overhaul has brought this late 1940s

market hall bang up to date. Now bright, modern and flooded with daylight, the striking curved edifice harbours a fresh produce market, a food court, cafes and the slick design hotel, Hotel da Música.

◉ Foz do Douro

Parque da Cidade   PARK
(Avenida da Boavista; 🚼) The hum of traffic on the Avenida da Boavista soon fades as you enter the serene, green Parque da Cidade, Portugal's largest urban park. Laced with 10km of walking and cycling trails, this is where locals come to unplug and recharge, picnic, play ball, jog, cycle, lounge in the sun and feed the ducks on the lake.

Jardim do Passeio Alegre   GARDENS
(Map p384; Rua Passeio Alegre; 🚼) A joy for the aimless ambler, this 19th-century garden is flanked by graceful old buildings and dotted with willowy palms, sculptures, fountains and a bandstand that occasionally stages concerts in summer. Listen to the crash of the ocean as you wander its tree-canopied avenues. There's also crazy golf for the kids.

👉 Tours

★ Taste Porto   FOOD & DRINK
(📞 920 503 302; www.tasteporto.com; Downtown Food Tour adult/child €65/42, Vintage Food Tour €70/42; ⊙ Downtown Food Tour 10.45am & 4pm Tue-Sat, Vintage Food Tour 10am & 4.15pm Mon-Sat, Photo Food Experience 9.45am daily) Loosen a belt notch for Taste Porto's superb downtown food tours, where you'll sample everything from Porto's best slow-roast-pork sandwich to éclairs, fine wines, cheese and coffee. Friendly, knowledgeable guide André and his team lead these indulgent and insightful 3½-hour walking tours, which take in viewpoints and historic back lanes en route to restaurants, grocery stores and cafes.

★ Workshops Pop Up   COOKING
(Map p372; 📞 966 974 119; www.workshops-pop up.com; Rua do Almada 275; 3hr class incl lunch or dinner €35) This cool indie arts, crafts and interior design store hosts regular three-hour, hands-on cookery workshops, followed by lunch or dinner with wine pairing. Themes range from healthy snacks and Indian food to Cook and Taste Portugal, where you'll learn to cook Portuguese classics like *bacalhau à lagareiro* (codfish cooked in extra virgin olive oil) and *pastéis de nata* (custard tarts).

★ Other Side   TOURS
(Map p372; 📞 916 500 170; www.theotherside. pt; Rua Souto 67; ⊙ 9am-8pm) Well-informed, congenial guides reveal their city on half-day walking tours of hidden Porto (€19), a walking and food tour (€49), and wine tours (€55). They also venture further afield with full-day trips to the Douro's vineyards (€95), and to Guimarães and Braga (€85).

Porto Walkers   WALKING
(Map p372; 📞 918 291 519; www.portowalkers. pt; Praça da Liberdade, Avenida dos Aliados) Peppered with anecdotes and personality, these young, fun, three-hour guided walking tours are a great intro to Porto, starting at 10.45am daily. The tours are free (well, the guides work for tips, so give what you can). Simply turn up at the meeting point on Praça da Liberdade and look out for the guide in the red T-shirt.

Be My Guest   WALKING
(📞 938 417 850; www.bemyguestinporto.com; 3hr tours €20) To get better acquainted with Porto, sign up for one of Be My Guest's terrific themed walking tours of the city, skipping from an insider's peek at *azulejos* (hand-painted tiles) to belle époque architecture and urban art. Run by two incredibly passionate guides – Nuno and Fred – it also arranges four-hour cookery workshops (€35) and wine-tasting tours (€25). Meeting points vary. Check in advance.

Blue Dragon Tours   TOURS
(Map p372; 📞 222 022 375; www.bluedragon.pt; Avenida Gustavo Eiffel 280; tours from €18) This reputable outfit runs old town and riverside bike tours (€32.50), which make the link between the historic centre and the sea. It also offers several half-day walking tours, including the Best of Porto (€18) and a food and wine tour (€55), as well as two-hour Segway tours (€45) to tick off the highlights. Prices can depend on group sizes.

Worst Tours   WALKING
(Map p368; www.theworsttours.weebly.com; Praça do Marquês de Pombal) FREE A trio of out-of-work architects got together to offer free and fun offbeat tours of Porto on foot, each with a different theme – from romantic to trades and crafts. While the tours are technically free, tips are naturally very welcome; pay as much as you wish. Tours meet at Praça do Marquês de Pombal and last around two to three hours. Book ahead online.

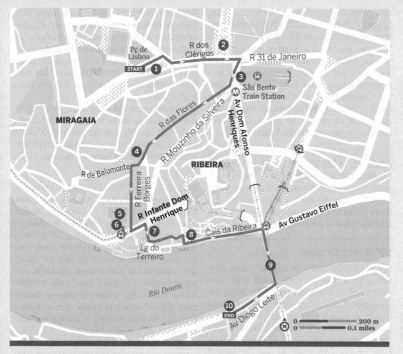

City Walk
Porto by Foot

START TORRE DOS CLÉRIGOS
FINISH VILA NOVA DE GAIA RIVERFRONT
LENGTH 2KM; TWO TO THREE HOURS

Begin at the baroque **1 Torre dos Clérigos** (p370), which offers unrivalled views over Porto from its 76m-high tower. Next, head down Rua dos Clérigos, passing the foot of grand **2 Avenida dos Aliados** (p370) and pausing to admire the avenue's beaux arts splendour. Just ahead, you'll see the French-inspired **3 São Bento Train Station** (p370). Check out the astounding *azulejos* (hand-painted tiles) in its main hall. Now cross over to Rua das Flores, a lovely street dotted with second-hand booksellers, old-fashioned stationers and some enticing cafes.

Near the end of the street is Nicolau Nasoni's baroque masterpiece, the **4 Igreja da Misericórdia** (p369), part of the stunning new Museu da Misericórdia do Porto. Cross Largo São Domingos to Rua Ferreira Borges, where you will pass the neoclassical **5 Palácio da Bolsa** (p368). You can check

out its main courtyard – once Porto's stock exchange – for free or stay on for a tour of its elaborate interior, including its spectacular gilded ballroom. Just next door is the **6 Igreja de São Francisco** (p363), with a severe Gothic facade hiding a jaw-dropping golden interior.

Head back up Rua Infante Dom Henrique and turn right on Rua da Alfândega, where you'll find the medieval **7 Casa do Infante** (p370), the birthplace of Henry the Navigator and the site of some remarkable Roman ruins. Continue into the shadowy Ribeira district, following narrow, medieval Rua de Fonte Taurina as it opens onto the lovely **8 Praça da Ribeira** (p370). From here, take a stroll along the Rio Douro, admiring Vila Nova de Gaia's port-wine lodges across the river. Next, walk across the Eiffel-inspired **9 Ponte de Dom Luís I** (p370) to Gaia's **10 waterfront esplanade**. Grab an outdoor table at one of the waterfront cafes and enjoy the splendid city views across the Douro over a well-deserved drink and some belly-filling *petiscos* (tapas).

efun GPS Tours TOURS
(Map p372; ☑ 914 173 671, 220 945 375; www.efungpstours.com; Rua Cândido dos Reis 55; ⊙ 10am-7pm)
Whether you want to explore Porto on foot or head further afield by minivan, eFun GPS Tours have got it nailed. Clued-up guides lead everything from three-hour walks of the historic centre (€19) to food-focused walking tours (€60) and Jewish heritage tours (€25), as well as excursions to Braga, Guimarães and deeper into the Douro Valley.

Living Tours TOURS
(Map p372; ☑ 228 320 992; www.livingtours.com; Rua Mouzinho da Silveira 352-4; ⊙ 9am-6pm) A great range of sightseeing options are on offer at this friendly agency, from half-day city tours (€40) to fado tours with dinner (€75), and day trips to the Douro and Minho (€98).

☞ River Cruises

Several outfits offer cruises in ersatz *barcos rabelos*, the colourful boats that were once used to transport port wine from the vineyards. Cruises last 45 to 55 minutes and depart at least hourly on summer days. You can board at Porto's Cais da Ribeira or Cais da Estiva, or at Vila Nova de Gaia's Cais de Gaia or Cais Amarelo. By far the largest carrier is **Douro Azul** (Map p372; ☑ 223 402 500; www.douroazul.com; Cais de Gaia; 6-bridges cruise adult/child €12/6; ⊙ 9.30am-6pm); **Barcadouro** (Map p372; ☑ 223 722 415; www. barcadouro.pt; Av Ramos Pinto 240, Cais de Gaia) and **Douro Acima** (Map p372; www.douroacima.pt; Rua dos Canastreiros 40; tours adult/child €15/7.50; ⊙ 10am-6.30pm Apr-Oct, to 4.30pm Mar) are also solid choices.

☞ Port Tasting

★**Graham's** WINE
(☑ 223 776 492, 223 776 490; www.grahams-port. com; Rua do Agro 141; tours incl tasting from €15; ⊙ 9.30am-6.30pm Apr-Oct, to 6pm Nov-Mar) One of the original British-founded Gaia wine cellars, established in 1820, Graham's has been totally revamped and now features a small museum. It's a big name and a popular choice for tours, which last around 30 minutes; they dip into atmospheric barrel-lined cellars and conclude with a tasting of three to eight port wines (tour prices vary according to quality).Reservations are essential.

★**Taylor's** WINE
(Map p368; ☑ 223 772 973; www.taylor.pt; Rua do Choupelo 250; tours incl tasting adult/child

€15/6; ⊙ 10am-6pm) Up from the river, British-run Taylor's boasts lovely, oh-so-English grounds with tremendous views of Porto. Its audio-guide tours, available in 11 languages, include a tasting of two top-of-the-range port wines (Chip Dry White and Late Bottled Vintage) – your reward for the short huff uphill.

The 300-year-old cellars are simply staggering, piled to the rafters with huge barrels, including the big one containing 100,000L of late bottled vintage. Private tours and tastings are also available on request.

Sandeman WINE
(Map p372; ☑ 223 740 533; www.sandeman.com; Largo Miguel Bombarda 3; museum free, guided tours incl tasting €12-40; ⊙ 10am-8pm Mar-Oct, 10am-12.30pm & 2-6pm Nov-Feb) Housed in an imposing granite building, Sandeman is a perfect first port of call for those who are new to port. It's free to visit the museum, showcasing port-related paintings and memorabilia whisking you back to 1790 when the young Scotsman George Sandeman started dabbling in the port and sherry trade. Guides dressed in black capes and hats lead the tours.

Tours conclude in a tasting, ranging from a tawny and ruby on the €12 tour to 10-, 20-, 30- and 40-year-old tawnies on the €40 one.

Cálem WINE
(Map p372; ☑ 916 113 451; www.calem.pt; Avenida Diogo Leite 344; tours incl tasting €12; ⊙ 10am-7pm May-Oct, to 6pm Nov-Apr) Making port since 1859, these award-winning wine cellars are among Porto's most attractive. Available in several languages, the informative, entertaining guided tours last around 30 minutes and include a video screening in one of the huge oak vats used for port ageing. A visit concludes with a tasting of two port wines – usually a ruby and a white.

⚑ Festivals & Events

Festa de São João RELIGIOUS
(St John's Festival) Porto's biggest party is the Festa de São João. For one night in June, on the 23rd, the city erupts into music, competitions and riotous parties; this is also when merrymakers pound each other on the head with squeaky plastic mallets (you've been warned).

Festa de São Pedro da Afurada FIESTA
(⊙ late Jun) The fishing village of Afurada pulls out all the stops for this festival in the

PORTO WITH CHILDREN

Exploring Porto with kids in tow can be child's play with a little know-how. What could be more family-friendly, after all, than screeching through the streets on a vintage tram, devising your own Harry Potter trail in the city that once inspired JK Rowling, hitting the beaches in Foz, or finding adventure in the footsteps of great Portuguese navigators?

Marionettes

Puppets on strings are in the spotlight at Ribeira's Museu das Marionetas (Map p372; www.marionetasdoporto.pt; Rua de Belomonte 61; €2; ⊙11am-1pm & 2-6pm).

Hands-on Activities

Check out the activity-driven family weekend workshops at Serralves' Museu de Arte Contemporânea (p380). The expansive gardens are also kid-friendly.

Shoreline Adventures

Hop aboard tram 1 to Foz for ice cream, lighthouse snapshots, a paddle in the Atlantic, and marine life encounters at the whopping Sealife Porto (www.visitsealife.com; 1 Rua Particular do Castelo do Queijo; adult/child €13.50/9.50; ⊙10am-6pm Mon-Fri, to 7pm Sat & Sun).

Budding Seafarers

Slip into the shoes of a swashbuckling explorer at the World of Discoveries (Map p372; www.worldofdiscoveries.com; Rua de Miragaia 106; adult/child €14/8; ⊙10am-6pm Mon-Fri, to 7pm Sat & Sun).

Day at the Park

Kids love letting off steam in Porto's biggest park (p376), and it's also perfect picnic territory.

---

days building up to 29 June. Dressed in traditional fishing garb, locals parade through the streets with statue-topped palanquins (covered litters) and give blessings to boats along the river. There's plenty of partying, with grilled sardines, *vinho,* live music, dancing and fireworks.

MEO Marés Vivas   MUSIC
(www.maresvivas.meo.pt; Antiga Seca do Bacalhau, Vila Nova de Gaia; ⊙late Jul) Over a weekend in mid-July, Afurada dusts off its party clothes to host the Marés Vivas (Living Tides), welcoming big rock and pop names to the stage. Headliners in recent years have included Keane, Snow Patrol, Sting and David Guetta. A one-/three-day pass costs €33/61.

Queima das Fitas   FIESTA
(www.queimadoporto.com; ⊙early May) Porto's black-caped students play a leading role in one of the city's biggest shindigs in early May with this week-long festival of gigs, entertainment, parades, parties, music, booze and all-round revelry. A huge draw is the Cortejo Académico on Tuesday, where floats and students in fancy dress squeeze their way through crowds onto Avenida dos Aliados.

Serralves Em Festa   CULTURAL
(www.serralves.pt; ⊙early Jun) This huge (free) celebration runs for 50 hours nonstop over one weekend in early June. Parque de Serralves hosts the main events, with concerts, avant-garde theatre and kiddie activities. Other open-air events happen all over town.

NOS Primavera Sound   MUSIC
(www.nosprimaverasound.com; Parque da Cidade; ⊙early Jun) Porto switches into party mode for NOS Primavera Sound, one of the biggest indie music festivals of the summer, drawing top-name acts to the stage over the course of a weekend in early June. Recent headliners include Neneh Cherry, Solange, Lorde and Nick Cave & the Bad Seeds. Tickets range between €95 and €150 for the full festival or €60 for the day.

The festival takes place in the chilled surrounds of Porto's Parque da Cidade.

**Festival Internacional
de Folclore de Gulpilhares**   MUSIC
(International Folk Festival of Gulpilhares; Gulpilhares) This vibrant week-long festival in early August attracts international folklore groups.

DON'T MISS

THE ART & GREENERY OF SERRALVES

Serralves (Map p384; www.serralves.pt; Rua Dom João de Castro 210; adult/child museums & park €10/free, park only €5/free, 10am-1pm 1st Sun of the month free; ⊙10am-7pm Mon-Fri, to 8pm Sat & Sun May-Sep, reduced hours Oct-Apr) is a fabulous cultural institution combining a museum, a mansion and extensive gardens. Cutting-edge exhibitions, along with a fine permanent collection featuring works from the late 1960s to the present, are showcased in the Museu de Arte Contemporânea, an arrestingly minimalist, whitewashed space designed by the eminent Porto-based architect Álvaro Siza Vieira. The delightful, pink Casa de Serralves is a prime example of art deco, bearing the imprint of French architect Charles Siclis. One ticket gets you into both museums.

The museums sit within the marvellous 18-hectare Parque de Serralves. Lily ponds, rose gardens, formal fountains and whimsical touches – such as a bright-red sculpture of oversized pruning shears – make for a bucolic outing in the city. The estate is 6km west of the city centre; take bus 201 from in front of Praça Dom João I, one block east of Avenida dos Aliados.

Fantasporto   FILM
(Porto International Film Festival; www.fantasporto. com; Rua do Bonjardim 143, Teatro Municipal Rivoli; ⊙late Feb/early Mar) Two weeks of fantasy, horror and just plain weird films in February/March.

🛏 Sleeping

🛏 Ribeira

Cats Hostel   HOSTEL €
(Map p372; ☎220 944 622; www.catshostels.com/ porto; Rua do Cativo 26-28; dm €14-19, d/q from €66/106; @🤶) Cats knows precisely what makes backpackers purr – the facilities are superb and the attractive rooms have thoughtful touches, including big lockers, good lighting and privacy curtains, plus each one comes with a bathroom and balcony. The open-air rooftop lounge is a great place for a sundowner.

Tiles Apartments   APARTMENT €
(Map p372; ☎936 224 536; portotilesapartment@ hotmail.com; Rua Mouzinho da Silveira 195; apt €40-100; 🤶) Cátia and David are your affable, clued-up hosts at this super-central apartment duo, glammed up with the namesake blue-and-white *azulejos*. The apartments are roomy, spotless, fitted with kitchenettes, and big enough to squeeze in four (each with a double and a sofa bed). A welcome decanter of port on arrival is a nice touch. Minimum two-night stay.

★Guest House Douro   BOUTIQUE HOTEL €€€
(Map p372; ☎222 015 135; www.guesthousedouro. com; Rua da Fonte Taurina 99-101; r €160-230; ✳@🤶) In a restored relic overlooking the

Rio Douro, these eight rooms have been blessed with gorgeous wooden floors, plush queen beds and marble baths; the best have dazzling river views. But it is the welcome that makes this place stand out from the crowd – your charming hosts Carmen and João bend over backwards to please.

★Porto River   APARTMENT €€€
(Map p372; ☎223 401 210; www.portoriver.pt; Rua dos Canastreiros 50; apt €100-175; ✳🤶) Down by the Rio Douro and right in the thick of the action, Porto River is a class act. The owners have waved a magic wand over this old stone warehouse to transform it into a hotel of understated luxury. The bustle outside fades in bright, minimalist Scandi-style apartments done out in natural fabrics and with attention-grabbing details.

🛏 Aliados & Bolhão

Rivoli Cinema Hostel   HOSTEL €
(Map p372; ☎968 958 637, 220 174 634; www.rivoli cinemahostel.com; Rua Dr Magalhães Lemos 83; dm/d/tr from €16/46/63; 🤶) Easygoing staff, spotless dorms and rooms jazzed up with cool movie-themed decor, a chilled lounge with DVDs, a roof terrace and an inflatable pool in summer – this hostel, lodged in a converted art deco building, really nails it. The atmosphere is nicely laid-back, and homemade treats appear at breakfast.

The Passenger   HOSTEL €
(Map p372; ☎963 802 000; www.thepassenger- hostel.com; Estação de São Bento, Praça Almeida Garrett; dm €22-27, d €55-90, tr €95-110, q €115- 190) A night spent at the station is no longer a miserable prospect since the opening of

this cool hostel in São Bento train station. Decorated with vintage furniture and one-of-a-kind Portuguese artworks, it sure is a step up from most backpacker digs. Besides upbeat staff, there's a shared kitchen and a bar with a Mac and piano.

Residencial Santo André GUESTHOUSE €
(Map p372; ☑222 000 115; www.residencial santoandre.pt; Rua Santo Ildefonso 112; d €39-58; ☎) A charming four-floor walk-up with spiralled staircase and 10 oddly curvaceous rooms, some with bathrooms. They're humble but spick and span, and it's the smaller rooms that catch the most light. Set on a quiet street, this is a splendid cheapie.

★Canto de Luz B&B €€
(Map p372; ☑225 492 142; www.cantodeluz.com; Rua do Almada 539; r €85-105; ☎) *Ah oui,* this French-run guesthouse, just a five-minute walk from Trindade metro, is a delight. Rooms are light, spacious and make the leap between classic and contemporary, with vintage furnishings used to clever effect. Your kindly hosts André and Brigitte prepare delicious breakfasts, with fresh-squeezed juice, pastries and homemade preserves. There's also a pretty garden terrace.

Vintage Guest House GUESTHOUSE €€
(Map p372; ☑916 052 529; www.portovintage guesthouse.pt; Rua do Almada 580; d €75-85, tr/q €140/160; ❋☎) *Bemvindo* (welcome) to one of Porto's most adorable digs – a town house lovingly restored to seamlessly unite the vintage (antique furnishings, stucco, *azulejos,* even the odd four-poster) with chic modernity (fancy linens, slick bathrooms, polished concrete). It sits on one of the city's most up-and-coming, characterful streets.

B The Guest GUESTHOUSE €€
(Map p372; ☑222 011 989; www.btheguest.com; Rua Formosa 331; d €74-120; ❋☎) Opposite Mercado do Bolhão, this boutique-chic guesthouse subtly fuses 19th-century architecture and 21st-century design. Splashes of colour and eye-catching fabrics lend warmth to the pared-down interiors. Opt for the front for views or the back for peace. The staff are incredibly friendly and breakfasts generous. The one drawback? There's no lift and stairs are steep.

In Porto Gallery GUESTHOUSE €€
(Map p372; ☑222 011 805; www.inporto.pt; Rua do Bonjardim 358; d €90-135; ❋☎) Architects and artists have pitched in to create this guest-

house, dotted with original works. Muted colours, luxurious fabrics and one-of-a-kind wall coverings dominate in rooms with names such as 'imagination', 'fantasy' and 'illusion'. Breakfast is served in the garden on fine days.

Hotel Teatro BOUTIQUE HOTEL €€€
(Map p372; ☑220 409 620; www.hotelteatro.pt; Rua Sá da Bandeira 84; d €132-370; ❋☎) This design hotel stands in the spot of the 1859 Teatro Baquet, a swanky hideaway done up by interior designer Nini Andrade Silva. The theatre theme prevails – the reception resembles a box office, while dark, slinky rooms and suites come with weighty curtains, large mirrors and highlights of bronze and gold.

InterContinental Porto HISTORIC HOTEL €€€
(Map p372; ☑220 035 600; www.ihg.com; Praça da Liberdade 25; d/ste from €225/338; ☐❋☎) In a painstakingly restored former palace on the central Praça da Liberdade, this is a top choice for business and leisure visitors, with classic decor that nods to the building's history, a full spectrum of amenities, including a restaurant, fitness centre and spa treatments, and outstanding service.

🏠 Miragaia

★Gallery Hostel HOSTEL €
(Map p372; ☑224 964 313; www.gallery-hostel. com; Rua Miguel Bombarda 222; dm/d/tr/ste from €20/59/75/80; ❋☎) A true travellers' hub, this hostel-gallery has clean and cosy dorms and doubles, a sunny, glass-enclosed back patio, a grassy terrace, a cinema room, a shared kitchen and a bar-cum-music-room. Throw in its free walking tours, homemade dinners on request, port-wine tastings and concerts, and you'll see why it's booked up so often – reserve ahead.

Poets Inn B&B €
(Map p372; ☑223 324 209; www.thepoetsinn.com; Rua dos Caldeireiros 261; d €40-70, apt €80-90; ☎) This laid-back B&B has a central but tucked-away location. Decorated by local artists, each of the doubles has a theme and some have fine city views. Most rooms share a bathroom. There's also a garden complete with hammock, a guest kitchen and a lounge with DVDs, plus a decent breakfast included in the price.

Maison Nos B&B B&B €€
(Map p372; ☑222 011 683; www.maisonnos. com; Rua Dr Barbosa de Castro 36; d €70-90;

☎) Stéphane and Baris go the extra mile to make you feel at home at their sweet, understated, stylish B&B, nuzzled within 14th-century walls in the Vitória district. The parquet-floored rooms are light and uniquely furnished – some with petite balconies, others with freestanding tubs. Fresh juice, homemade cake and strong coffee at breakfast kick-start the day perfectly.

Casa dos Caldeireiros
B&B €€

(Map p372; ☎914 573 774; www.caldeireiros portoflats.com; Rua dos Caldeireiros 191; d €75-90; ✳☎) Wow, what a view! Snuggled down a backstreet and occupying a 17th-century town house, Casa dos Caldeireiros affords lofty vistas over Porto's historic centre from many of its well-equipped studios, which retain original features such as beams and stone walls. Cartolina and Patio, with their private terraces, have the edge. There's a minimum two-night stay.

Yours Guesthouse
GUESTHOUSE €€

(Map p372; ☎222 033 082; www.yoursguest house.com; Rua dos Caldeireiros 131; d €85-60, q €101-154) Squirrelled away in one of the loveliest streets of old Porto, this guesthouse has bags of originality, with antiques speckling cheerfully decorated rooms, reached by a spiral staircase – the best have fine city views. Enjoy breakfast in the walled garden when the sun's out.

Pensão Favorita
GUESTHOUSE €€

(Map p372; ☎220 134 157; www.pensaofavorita.pt; Rua Miguel Bombarda 267; d €80-100, q €110-170; ☎) Pensão Favorita has inviting rooms of ample size with big windows, mid-century furnishings and wide plank floors. The rooms in the red-brick addition out the back overlook the garden; there's also a lounge and restaurant with outdoor seating, which does great lunch specials.

★ROSA ET AL Townhouse
BOUTIQUE HOTEL €€€

(Map p372; ☎916 000 081; www.rosaetal.pt; Rua do Rosário 233; ste €128-268; ☎) This gorgeously done-up town house in the thick of Porto's art district has suites with hardwood floors and freestanding claw-foot bathtubs, a lovely garden out back, and spa treatments on request. The restaurant serves one of Porto's finest brunches and afternoon tea at weekends.

★Torel Avantgarde
BOUTIQUE HOTEL €€€

(Map p372; ☎220 110 082; www.torelavantgarde. com; Rua da Restauração 336; d €190-385, ste

€320-550; ✳☎✳) High on a hill in Miragaia, this decadent five-star boutique hotel is a winner. Named after prominent avant-garde artists, designers and musicians – from Warhol to Nina Simone – the luxe rooms and suites are decorated in rich colours and fabrics, with bespoke murals, handwoven rugs and homestyle perks like Nespresso machines.

Vila Nova de Gaia

Gaia Porto Hostel
HOSTEL €

(Map p368; ☎224 968 282; www.hostelgaiaporto. pt; Rua Cândido dos Reis 374; dm €18-28, d €45-95; ☎) Down by the river and just a cork-pop away from the port-wine lodges, this hostel has fabulous views of the Rio Douro and Ribeira, and a secluded garden. A glass of port on arrival, generous breakfasts and bright dorms and doubles spruced up with murals seal the deal.

★Yeatman
RESORT €€€

(Map p368; ☎220 133 185; www.the-yeat man-hotel.com; Rua do Choupelo 88; d €255-315, ste €485-2370; ✳☎✳) Named after one of port producer Taylor's original founders, the Yeatman is Porto's only true five-star resort, terraced and tucked into the Gaia hillside with expansive Douro and Porto views. There's a two-Michelin–starred restaurant; huge, sumptuous guest rooms and suites with private terraces; a decanter-shaped pool; sunken Roman baths in the fantastic Caudalie spa; and it's close to everything else you could possibly wish for.

Massarelos

Porta Azul
GUESTHOUSE €€

(☎224 037 706; www.porta-azul.com; Rua Dom Manuel II 204; d €85-140; ☎) Pedro and Marta make you feel instantly at home at their neatly tended guesthouse, located in a 19th-century town house opposite the Jardins do Palácio Cristal. The wood-floored rooms are bright and well-kept – upgrade to a junior suite for extra space – and homemade goodies feature at breakfast.

Boavista

Hospedaria Boavista
GUESTHOUSE €

(Map p368; ☎226 098 376; Avenida da Boavista 880; d/tr €45/55; ☎) Eight spacious budget rooms await in your Porto grandma's house. The carpet may be industrial, but the

LOCAL KNOWLEDGE

THE ART OF THE TILE

Azulejos (hand-painted tiles) greet you on almost every corner in Porto. Among the delights of taking a stroll through the historic centre are the tiles you will encounter. Old and new, utilitarian and decorative, plain and geometrically patterned, they dance across the facades of medieval houses, the walls of cafes and bars, along metro-station tunnels and in opulent church interiors.

Some of the finest tiles grace Porto's churches. Among them is the large and exquisite panel of *azulejos* covering the Igreja do Carmo (Map p372; Rua do Carmo; ☺8am-noon & 1-6pm Mon & Wed, 9am-6pm Tue & Thu, to 5.30pm Fri, to 4pm Sat, to 1.30pm Sun). Silvestre Silvestri's 1912 magnum opus illustrates the founding of the Carmelite order and pays homage to Nossa Senhora (Our Lady).

On the Rua de Santa Catarina, the Capela das Almas (p371) catches your eye with the astonishing feast of *azulejos* festooning its facade; this stunning frieze by Eduardo Leite recounts the lives of various saints, including the death of St Francis and the martyrdom of St Catherine. The blue-and-white tiles evoke the classic 18th-century style, but actually date to 1929.

Rising high above Praça da Batalha, the elegant baroque Igreja de Santo Ildefonso (Map p372; Praça da Batalha; ☺3-6.30pm Mon, 9am-noon & 3-6.30pm Tue-Sun) is another *azulejo*-bedecked wonder. Some 11,000 blue-and-white tiles, by Jorge Colaço (1932), grace the facade, depicting scenes from the life of Santo Ildefonso and allegories from the Eucharist.

But Porto's crowning glory when it comes to tiles is undoubtedly the resplendent São Bento Train Station (p370), a veritable ode to *azulejo* art. Spelling out momentous events in Portuguese history, including the Battle of Valdevez (1140), the arrival of Dom João I and Philippa of Lancaster in Porto (1387) and the Conquest of Ceuta (1415), the friezes designed by Colaço in 1930 are so vivid and detailed you can almost hear the fanfare and the stampeding cavalry.

furniture is antique, the ceilings are high, the bathrooms gleaming and the beds are firm. Rooms overlook *senhora's* blooming veggie garden.

Casa do Conto   DESIGN HOTEL €€
(Map p368; ☏222 060 340; www.casadoconto. com; Rua da Boavista 703; ste €108-130; P✳🖃) Porto architects, artists and storytellers have pooled their creativity to totally make over a 19th-century town house in an up-and-coming corner of town. The result is the 'House of Tales', with a clever mix of stark concrete and granite interiors, and vintage furnishings. The higher you go, the better the view. Breakfast is superb, with fresh fruit, pastries and eggs.

🛏 Foz do Douro

Pousada da Juventude   HOSTEL €
(Map p384; ☏925 664 983, 226 163 059; www. pousadasjuventude.pt; Rua de Paulo da Gama 551; dm/d/apt €16/44/80; P@🖃) In a bright, modern building above the Rio Douro, this hostel offers handsome doubles with balconies and sweeping river views, well-maintained four-person dorms, and apartments.

There's a restaurant and a supermarket nearby, but no kitchen. The hitch: it's 4km from central Porto. Take bus 207 from Campanhã station or bus 500 from Aliados.

Casa das Laranjas   GUESTHOUSE €€
(Map p384; ☏965 445 624; www.casadaslaranjas-porto.com; Travessa das Laranjeiras 33; d €90-120; 🖃) This squat town house resides in the heart of Foz, just a short amble from the sea. Its bright, wood-floored, beautifully refurbished rooms sport naturalistic wall coverings and are kept immaculate; the best of the bunch have balconies. Homemade treats and fresh juice appear at breakfast.

🍴 Eating

🍴 Ribeira

Taberna do Largo   PORTUGUESE €
(Map p372; ☏222 082 154; Largo de São Domingos 69; petiscos €2-14; ☺5pm-midnight Tue-Thu, to 1am Fri, noon-1am Sat, to midnight Sun; 🖃) Lit by wine-bottle lights, this sweet grocery store, deli and tavern is run with passion by Joana and Sofia. Tour Portugal with your

Foz do Douro

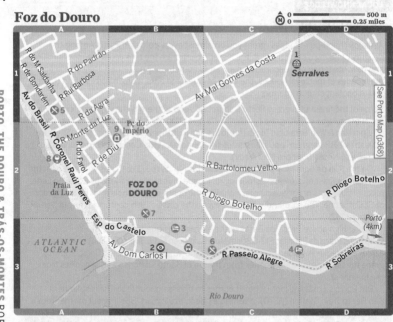

Foz do Douro

taste buds with their superb array of hand-picked wines, which go brilliantly with tasting platters of smoked tuna, Alentejo *salpicão* sausage, Azores São Jorge cheese, Beira *morcela* (blood sausage), *tremoços* (lupin beans) and more.

Da Terra　　　　　　　　　VEGETARIAN €
(Map p372; ☑ 223 199 257; www.daterra.pt; Rua Mouzinho da Silveira 249; buffet €9.95; ⓔnoon-11pm Wed, Thu, Sun & Mon, to 11.30pm Fri & Sat; ☑ ⓐ) Porto's shift towards lighter, super-healthy food is reflected in the buffet served at Da Terra. This popular, contemporary bis-tro puts its own spin on vegetarian and ve-gan food – from creative salads to Thai-style veggies and tagines. It also does a fine line in fresh-pressed juices and desserts. The web-site posts details of upcoming workshops and cookery courses.

Mercearia das Flores　　　　　　DELI €
(Map p372; Rua das Flores 110; petiscos €2.50-8.50; ⓔ11am-9pm Mon-Thu, to 10pm Fri-Sat, 11.30am-8pm Sun; ☎) This rustic-chic deli-catessen/food store serves all-day *petiscos* made with organic regional products on the three tables and two counters of its bright and airy interior. You can also order wines by the glass, tea from the Azores and locally brewed Sovina beer. Try the spicy sardines and salad on dark, sweet *broa* cornbread.

★Cantina 32　　　　　　PORTUGUESE €€
(Map p372; ☑ 222 039 069; www.cantina32.com; Rua das Flores 32; petiscos €3.50-20; ⓔ12.30-3pm & 6.30-10.30pm Mon-Sat; ☎) Industrial-chic meets boho at this delightfully laid-back haunt, with its walls of polished concrete, mismatched crockery, verdant plants, and vintage knick-knacks ranging from a

bicycle to an old typewriter. The menu is just as informal – *petiscos* such as *pica-pau* steak (bite-sized pieces of steak in a garlic-white-wine sauce), quail egg croquettes, and cheesecake served in a flower pot reveal a pinch of creativity.

Taberna dos Mercadores PORTUGUESE €€
(Map p372; ☑ 222 010 510; Rua dos Mercadores 36; mains €14-22; ☺ 12.30-3.30pm & 7-11pm Tue-Sun) The chefs run a tight ship in the open kitchen at this curvaceous, softly lit, bottle-lined tavern, sizzling, stirring and delivering superb Portuguese grub with a smile from noon to night. On the menu are spot-on dishes as simple as *polvo com arroz no forno* (octopus rice baked in the oven), *feijoada* (black bean one-pot), grilled fish and meats.

Jimão TAPAS €€
(Map p372; ☑ 220 924 660; www.jimao.pt; Praça da Ribeira 11; tapas €4.50-8.50; ☺ noon-10pm Wed-Mon) Many of the restaurants on Praça da Ribeira (p370) are tourist central, but Jimão is the real deal. Service is genuinely friendly, the upstairs dining room has a cracking view of Ribeira, and the tapas – garlicky *gambas* (prawns), codfish and octopus salad, sardine toasts and the like – are prepared with care and served with great wines.

Cantinho do Avillez GASTRONOMY €€
(Map p372; ☑ 223 227 879; www.cantinho doavillez.pt; Rua Mouzinho da Silveira 166; mains €18-40; ☺ 12.30-3pm & 7pm-midnight Mon-Fri, 12.30pm-midnight Sat & Sun) Rock star chef José Avillez' latest venture is a welcome fixture on Porto's gastro scene. A bright, contemporary bistro with a retro spin, Cantinho keeps the mood casual and buzzy. On the menu are seasonal Portuguese dishes with a dash of imagination: from flaked *bacalhau* (dried salt-cod) with melt-in-the-mouth 'exploding' olives to giant red shrimps from the Algarve with Thai spices.

O Comercial MODERN EUROPEAN €€
(Map p372; ☑ 918 838 649; www.ocomer cial.com; Palácio da Bolsa, Rua Ferreira Borges; 3-course set lunch/dinner €17/23; ☺ 12.30-3pm & 7.30-10.30pm Mon-Fri, 7.30-11.30pm Sat) A touch of class in the Palácio da Bolsa (p368), O Comercial has a whiff of romantic grandeur with its chandeliers, high ceilings and *azulejo*-clad walls. The service is polished and the menu places the accent on well-prepared Med-style classics, such as veal carpaccio with pesto, and tuna steak with port wine and onion sauce.

★DOP GASTRONOMY €€€
(Map p372; ☑ 222 014 313; www.doprestaurante. pt; Palácio das Artes, Largo de São Domingos 18; mains €25-28, tasting menus €80-90; ☺ 7.30-11pm Mon, 12.30-3pm & 7.30-11pm Tue-Sat; ☜) Housed in a grand edifice, DOP is one of Porto's most stylish addresses, with its high ceilings and slick, monochrome interior. Much-feted chef Rui Paula puts a creative, seasonal twist on outstanding ingredients, with dish after delicate, flavour-packed dish skipping from octopus carpaccio to cod with lobster rice.

✗ Aliados & Bolhão

★Cafe Santiago PORTUGUESE €
(Map p372; ☑ 222 055 797; www.caferestaurante santiago.com.pt; Rua Passos Manuel 226; mains €8-12; ☺ noon-11pm Mon-Sat) This is hands down one of the best places to try Porto's classic gut-busting treat, the *francesinha* – a thick, open-faced sandwich piled with cheese, sausage, egg and/or assorted meats, plus a tasty, rich beer sauce. This classic will set you back €9.75, which might seem pricey for a sandwich, but trust us: it's a meal in itself.

Cultura dos Sabores VEGETARIAN €
(Map p372; ☑ 222 010 556; Rua de Ceuta 80; buffet €12; ☺ noon-3.30pm & 6-11pm Tue-Sun; ☜♪) A hip, healthy addition to central Porto, this vegetarian and vegan restaurant can easily be spotted by the swings in its window. You can help yourself to the lunch and dinner buffet, which often includes hearty soups, salads, wild rice or pasta dishes. Herbal teas and detox juices are available.

★Flor dos Congregados PORTUGUESE €€
(Map p372; ☑ 222 002 822; www.flordos congregados.pt; Travessa dos Congregados 11; mains €8-16; ☺ 7-10pm Mon-Wed, noon-3pm & 7-11pm Thu-Sat) Tucked away down a narrow alley, this softly lit, family-run restaurant brims with stone-walled, wood-beamed, art-slung nooks. The frequently changing blackboard menu goes with the seasons.

All In Porto PORTUGUESE €€
(Map p372; ☑ 220 993 829; www.facebook.com/ allinporto; Rua Arquitecto Nicolau Nasoni 17; petiscos €8-22, tasting boards €12-16; ☺ noon-11pm) Wine-barrel tables, lanterns and funky Porto murals create a hip, laid-back space for sampling a stellar selection of Portuguese wines and nicely prepared *petiscos*. These range

from flame-grilled *chouriço* (spicy sausage) to spicy sardine roe, cheeses and *conservas* (canned fish). Quiet enough for conversing, it's also a chilled spot to begin or end an evening over drinks.

Tapabento
TAPAS €€

(Map p372; ☑222 034 115, 912 881 272; www.tapabento.com; Rua da Madeira 222; tapas & sharing plates €3-20, mains €14-27.50; ⊙7-10.30pm Tue, noon-4pm & 7-10pm Wed-Sun) There's a good buzz at split-level Tapabento, discreetly tucked behind São Bento train station. Stone walls, bright prints and cheek-by-jowl tables set the scene for outstanding tapas and Douro wines. Sharing is the way to go – be it fresh oysters with shallot vinaigrette, razor clams with garlic and coriander or Azores cheese with rocket and walnuts.

Dama Pé de Cabra
CAFE €€

(Map p372; ☑223 196 776; Passeio de São Lázaro 5; light bites & petiscos €2-7.50; ⊙9.30am-3.30pm Tue-Thu, 9.30am-3.30pm & 7.30-10pm Fri & Sat) The *bemvindo* is heartfelt at this cute, bottle-lined grocery-store-turned cafe. It's a cheerful spot for breakfast, brunch, coffee and cake, or a laid-back lunch of homemade breads with Portuguese hams and tangy cheeses.

★Euskalduna Studio
GASTRONOMY €€€

(Map p368; ☑935 335 301; www.euskaldunastudio.pt; Rua de Santo Ildefonso 404; 10-course tasting menu €95-110; ⊙7-10pm Wed-Sat) Everyone loves surprises, especially edible ones prepared with flawless execution, experimental finesse and a nod to the seasons. Just 16 lucky diners (eight at the green marble counter peeking into the kitchen and eight at oak tables) get to sample Vasco Coelho Santos' stunning 10-course menus that allow flavours and textures to shine.

More like a private dining experience and gastronomic event than just another good meal, Euskalduna already has insiders whispering 'Michelin star'. Vasco's credentials, including a stint behind the stove at the legendary El Bulli, speak of a chef aspiring to culinary greatness. And he achieves it. Book at least a week ahead.

★MUU
STEAK €€€

(Map p372; ☑914 784 032; www.muusteakhouse.com; Rua do Almada 149A; mains €22-32; ⊙7pm-midnight Wed-Mon) So you came for the steak, right? Wise decision. A welcome newcomer to Porto's food scene, MUU has carved out a name for itself with outstand-

ing cuts of beef. Homemade Scotch eggs and cheese gratins prelude the main act: a garlic-rubbed rib-eye, say, or tender Black Angus steak. Either way, you won't leave hungry.

The slickly urban decor has an industrial edge, with brick walls, statement lights and eye-catching crockery. Some of the steaks are big enough for sharing, and the upbeat staff can recommend gutsy red wines to go with them.

✖ Miragaia

Taberna de Santo António
PORTUGUESE €

(Map p372; ☑222 055 306; Rua das Virtudes 32; mains €8.50-12; ⊙noon-3pm & 7-10pm Tue-Sun) This family-run tavern prides itself on serving up honest Portuguese grub with a smile. It dishes up generous helpings of codfish, grilled sardines and *cozido* (meat and vegetable stew) to the lunchtime crowds. It's a friendly TV-and-tiles place in the traditional Portuguese mould, with pavement seating on warm days.

A Sandeira
SANDWICHES €

(Map p372; ☑223 216 471; www.asandeira.pt; Rua dos Caldeireiros 85; sandwiches €4.90, lunch menu €6; ⊙9am-midnight Mon-Sat; 🤝) Charming, boho-flavoured and lit by fairy lights, A Sandeira is a great bolthole for an inexpensive lunch. Chipper staff bring to the table creative salads such as smoked ham, rocket, avocado and walnuts, and Porto's best sandwiches (olive, feta, tomato and basil, for instance). The lunch menu including soup, a salad or sandwich and a drink is a steal.

Quintal Bioshop
DELI €

(Map p372; Rua do Rosário 177; snacks & mains €5-7, lunch €7.90; ⊙10.30am-8pm Mon-Sat; 🤝🖊) Tucked at the back of an organic grocery store, this bright, cheery deli opens onto a terrace and serves healthy, wholesome vegetarian food. It does fresh-pressed juices, creative sandwiches (try the goat's cheese, apple, walnut and honey) and salads. Or stop by for an organic tea with a slice of homemade cake between gallery hopping on Rua de Miguel Bombarda.

As 7 Maravilhas
INTERNATIONAL €

(Map p372; ☑222 032 116; www.as7maravilhas.com; Rua das Taipas 17C; tapas €2.50-6; ⊙6pm-midnight Wed-Fri, 1pm-midnight Sat & Sun; 🤝) A wood-floored gastropub with a pinch of boho flair, a dash of vintage charm and a generous helping of globetrotter, As 7

Maravilhas is a one-off. The friendly owners keep the good vibes and international beers flowing. These go very well with the tapas on offer, which reflect their well-travelled tastes – falafel, onion bhajis, *currywurst* and the like.

★**Belos Aires**   ARGENTINE €€
(Map p372; 223 195 661; www.facebook.com/belosairesrestaurante; Rua de Belomonte 104; mains €17-25; ⊙8-11.30am & 7pm-midnight Mon-Sat;) At the heart of this intimate part-Argentine, part-Portuguese restaurant is Mauricio, a chef with a big personality and an insatiable passion for his homeland, revealed as you watch him dashing around in the open kitchen. The market-fresh menu changes frequently, but you'll always find superb steaks and to-die-for *empanadas* (savoury turnovers). Save an inch for the chocolate brownie with *dulce de leche*.

Papavinhos   PORTUGUESE €€
(222 000 204; Rua de Monchique 23; mains €10-27.50; ⊙noon-3pm & 7-10pm Tue-Sun) This no-frills, family-run tavern extends a warm welcome and dishes up generous portions of home cooking. Try for a window table to see the river twinkle at night as you dig into classics such as clams in garlic and *bacalhau com broa* (codfish with cornbread) with a glass of crisp house white.

✖ Vila Nova de Gaia

Taberninha Do Manel   PORTUGUESE €€
(Map p372; 223 753 549; www.taberninhado manel.com; Avenida Diogo Leite 308; mains €11-18; ⊙11am-midnight Tue-Sun) Superfriendly service, big views across the Douro to Ribeira, and a menu crammed with well-executed Portuguese classics – Iberian pork, *petiscos*, *bacalhau* (dried-salt cold) in different guises – reel folk into Taberninha Do Manel. There's pavement seating for warm days and a rustic interior jam-packed with what looks like the contents of your grandmother's attic.

De Castro Gaia   INTERNATIONAL €€
(Map p372; 910 553 559; www.myportocruz.com; Largo Miguel Bombarda 23, Espaço Porto Cruz; petiscos €5-10, mains €10-16.50; ⊙12.30-3pm & 7.30-11pm Tue-Sat, 12.30-3pm Sun) Polished concrete, slatted wood and clean lines give this restaurant in the Espaço Porto Cruz a slick, contemporary look. The menu matches reasonably priced ports and wines with *petiscos* and mains such as octopus rice and

pork cheeks cooked in red wine and cumin. There are fine views across the Douro to the houses of old Porto spilling down the hillside.

★**Yeatman**   GASTRONOMY €€€
(Map p368; 220 133 100; www.the-yeatman-hotel.com; Yeatman Hotel, Rua do Choupelo 88; tasting menus €140-170, wine pairing €60-70; ⊙7.30-11pm) With its polished service, elegant setting and dazzling views over river and city, the two-Michelin–starred restaurant at the five-star Yeatman (p382) hotel is sheer class. Chef Ricardo Costa puts his imaginative spin on seasonal ingredients from lobster to pheasant – all skilfully cooked, served with flair and expertly matched with wines from the 1000-bottle cellar that is among the country's best.

★**Vinum**   PORTUGUESE €€€
(220 930 417; www.vinumatgrahams.com; Graham's Port Lodge, Rua do Agro 141; mains €24-29, menus €50-100; ⊙12.30-11pm) Vinum manages the delicate act of combining 19th-century port-lodge charm with contemporary edge. Peer through to the barrel-lined cellar from the pine-beamed restaurant, or out across the Douro and Porto's rooftops from the conservatory and terrace. Portuguese menu stunners include green ceviche fresh from Matasinhos fish market and dry-aged Trás-os-Montes beef, complemented by a stellar selection of wines and ports.

✖ Massarelos

O Antigo Carteiro   PORTUGUESE €€
(Map p368; 937 317 523; www.facebook.com/oantigocarteiro; Rua Senhor da Boa Morte 55; mains €14-19; ⊙noon-3pm & 7-11pm Tue-Sat, noon-3pm Sun;) Coyly tucked away on a lane back from the river, O Antigo Carteiro is as close as you'll get to eating in a Portuguese family home. Attentive, clued-up staff pair regional wines with well-executed classics – garlicky octopus, pork tenderloin, *bacalhau com broa* (codfish with cornbread crust) and the like.

★**Antiqvvm**   GASTRONOMY €€€
(Map p368; 912 024 754, 226 000 445; www.antiqvvm.pt; Rua de Entre Quintas 220; menus €45-130; ⊙noon-midnight Tue-Sat, to 3pm Sun) What a delight this tucked-away Michelin-starred restaurant is, ensconced in the revamped stone arcades of 19th-century Quinta da Macieirinha. Vítor Matos heads up the kitchen,

serving ingredient-driven dishes – truffle and Wagyu beef, and sea bass with algae and Azores saffron – with flair and artistry. With entrancing views out over Porto from the garden terrace, this is one for special occasions.

Boavista

Essência
VEGETARIAN €€

(Map p368; ✆ 228 301 813; www.essenciarestaurantevegetariano.com; Rua de Pedro Hispano 1190; mains €10.50-15; ⊙12.30-3pm & 8-10.30pm Mon-Thu, to midnight Fri & Sat; ✍) This bright, modern brasserie is famous Porto-wide for its generous vegetarian (and nonvegetarian!) dishes, stretching from wholesome soups and salads to curries, pasta dishes, risotto and *feijoada* (pork and bean casserole). There's a terrace for warm-weather dining.

Foz do Douro

Cafeína
MODERN EUROPEAN €€

(Map p384; ✆ 226 108 059; www.cafeina.pt; Rua do Padrão 100; 3-course lunch €18, mains €17-21; ⊙12.30-6pm & 7.30pm-12.30am Sun-Thu, to 1.30am Fri & Sat; ✍) Hidden coyly away from the seafront, Cafeína has a touch of class, with soft light casting a flattering glow across its moss-green walls, crisp tablecloths, lustrous wood floors and bookcases. The food is best described as modern European, simple as stuffed squid with saffron purée or rack of lamb in a herb and lemon crust, expertly matched with Portuguese wines.

Casa de Pasto da Palmeira
PORTUGUESE €€

(Map p384; ✆ 226 168 244; Rua do Passeio Alegre 450; small plates €4.50-14; ⊙noon-midnight) An adorable restaurant right on the waterfront, with two small colourful rooms featuring contemporary artwork and a few tables on the front patio. The creative small-size dishes change daily – think hake and shrimp *moqueca* (Brazilian fish stew) with banana and coriander, and *alheira* rolls with turnip sprouts.

★ Pedro Lemos
GASTRONOMY €€€

(Map p384; ✆ 220 115 986; www.pedrolemos.net; Rua do Padre Luís Cabral 974; tasting menus €110-130; ⊙12.30-3pm & 7.30-11pm Tue-Sat) One of Porto's two Michelin-starred restaurants, Pedro Lemos is sheer delight. With a love of seasonally sourced produce and robust flavours, the eponymous chef creates culinary fireworks using first-class ingredients from land and sea – be it ultra-fresh Atlantic

bivalves or Alentejano black pork cooked to smoky deliciousness with wild mushrooms. Choose between the subtly lit, cosy-chic dining room or the roof terrace.

Matosinhos

Dom Peixe
SEAFOOD €€

(✆224 927 160; www.dompeixe.com; Rua Heróis de França 241, Matosinhos; mains €8-20; ⊙noon-11pm; ▥) Out of all the authentic indoor-outdoor places on Matosinhos' 'fish restaurant row', Dom Peixe stands out as being one of the best. Snag a table on the terrace and go for the catch of the day grilled simply on an open-air barbecue. You won't be disappointed.

Boa Nova Tea House
GASTRONOMY €€€

(Casa de Cha; ✆ 229 940 066, 932 499 444; www.ruipaula.com; Avenida da Liberdade 1681, Leça da Palmeira, tasting menus €120-160; ⊙12.30-3pm & 7.30-11pm Tue-Sat) Designed by Portuguese architect titan Álvaro Siza Vieira and with star chef Rui Paula at the helm, this Michelin-starred restaurant perches alluringly on rocks above the crashing Atlantic. Massive boulders frame the white, low-rise building. The ingredients-driven tasting menus go with the seasons, but might include, say, monkfish with hazelnut and Champagne or Trás-os-Montes kid goat roasted to perfection.

Wine pairings are available for an extra €90 per head and, given the quality of the cellar, are worth considering. The restaurant is 20 minutes north of Porto along the coast. It's best reached by car or taxi.

Elsewhere Around Town

Taberna São Pedro
SEAFOOD €€

(Map p368; ✆986 732 466, 912 477 659; Rua Costa Goodofilm 84, Afurada; mains €10-15; ⊙10am-4pm & 7-11pm Mon-Sat, 10am-4pm Sun) Fado drifts up the *azulejo*-clad walls, toddlers tear through the dining room, plump and oily sardines (and other fresh fish) are roasted on sidewalk grills, and you can almost smell the tart snap of *vinho verde* (young wine) in the air. There's much to love in this forever-packed, salt-of-the-earth local seafood house. It's located one block inland from the ferry pier.

★ O Paparico
PORTUGUESE €€€

(Map p368; ✆225 400 548; www.opaparico.com; Rua de Costa Cabral 2343; menus €90-120; ⊙7.30-11pm Tue-Sat) It's worth the taxi hop north of town to O Paparico.

Portuguese authenticity is the name of the game here, from the romantically rustic interior of stone walls, beams and white linen to the menu that sings of the seasons. Dishes such as veal with wild mushrooms and monkfish are cooked with passion, served with precision and expertly paired with wines.

Drinking & Nightlife

Ribeira

⭐ **Prova**   WINE BAR
(Map p372; www.prova.com.pt; Rua Ferreira Borges 86; ⏱5pm-1am Wed-Sun; 📶) Diogo, the passionate owner, explains the finer nuances of Portuguese wine at this chic, stone-walled bar, where relaxed jazz plays. Stop by for a two-glass tasting (€5), or sample wines by the glass – including beefy Douros, full-bodied Dãos and crisp Alentejo whites. These marry well with sharing plates of local hams and cheeses (€14). Diogo's port tonics are legendary.

Wine Quay Bar   WINE BAR
(Map p372; www.winequaybar.com; Cais da Estiva 111; ⏱4-11pm Mon-Sat; 📶) Sunset is primetime viewing on the terrace of this terrific wine bar by the Rio Douro. As you gaze across to the graceful arc of the Ponte Dom Luís I and over to the port cellars of Vila Nova de Gaia, you can sample some cracking Portuguese wines and appetisers (cured ham, cheese, olives and the like).

Wine Box   WINE BAR
(Map p372; www.thewineboxporto.com; Rua dos Mercadores 72; ⏱10am-midnight Thu-Mon, 4pm-midnight Tue & Wed; 📶) Wine crates turn the interior into quite a feature at this uberhip, black-walled wine bar, with a good buzz and some 450 (at the last count) wines on the menu, some of which are available by the glass. *Petiscos* pair nicely with these. Service teeters on the indifferent, however, and the newfangled tablet menu can be hard to get the hang of.

Aliados & Bolhão

⭐ **Aduela**   BAR
(Map p372; Rua das Oliveiras 36; ⏱3pm-2am Mon, 10am-2am Tue-Thu, to 4am Fri & Sat, 3pm-midnight Sun) Retro and hip but not self-consciously so, chilled Aduela bathes in the nostalgic orange glow of its glass lights, which

illuminate the green walls and mishmash of vintage furnishings. Once a sewing machine warehouse, today it's where friends gather to converse over wine and appetising *petiscos* (€3 to €8).

⭐ **Era uma Vez em Paris**   BAR
(Map p372; Rua Galeria de Paris 106; ⏱11am-2am Mon-Wed, to 4am Thu-Sat) A little flicker of bohemian Parisian flair in the heart of Porto, Era uma Vez em Paris time warps you back to the more decadent 1920s. Its ruby-red walls, retro furnishings and frilly lampshades spin a warm, intimate cocoon for coffee by day and drinks by night. DJs keep the mood mellow with indie rock and funk beats.

⭐ **Terraplana**   CAFE
(Map p368; www.terraplanacafe.com; Avenida Rodrigues de Freitas 287; ⏱6pm-midnight Sun-Thu, to 3am Fri & Sat) Totally relaxed and boho-cool without trying, Terraplana is the bar of the moment in this neck of Porto. Murals adorn the artsy, stone-walled interior, and there's a pretty spot for summer imbibing. Besides inventive cocktails (around €10 a pop), they also have a solid selection of wines, gins and beers. These marry well with supertasty pizzas (€8.50 to €9.50).

Bonaparte Downtown   PUB
(Map p372; www.facebook.com/bonapartedowntown; Praça Guilherme Gomes Fernandes 40; ⏱5pm-2am Sun-Thu, to 3am Fri & Sat) Lanterns cast a warm glow across the cosy, knick-knack-crammed, wood-heavy interior at this pleasingly relaxed number, which morphs from a low-key spot to sip a predinner beer to a much livelier haunt later in the evening.

La Bohème   WINE BAR
(Map p372; www.facebook.com/laboheme.baixa; Rua Galeria de Paris 40; ⏱6pm-2am Tue-Thu, to 4am Fri & Sat, 7pm-2am Sun) With a high-ceilinged, Scandi-style pine interior, La Bohème is one of the most stylish, intimate bars on Rua Galeria de Paris. It's a nicely chilled choice for pairing fine wines with *petiscos*. DJs spin as the evening wears on.

Moustache   CAFE
(Map p372; www.moustache.pt; Praça Carlos Alberto 104; ⏱8am-8pm Mon-Wed, to 2am Thu-Sat, 2-8pm Sun; 📶) 🖊 Ease into the day gently or wind it out over drinks and mellow beats at this urban-cool cafe with cultural edge. The armchairs are perfect for dawdling over a robust coffee or smoothie and snacks such

PORT WINE

With its intense flavours, silky textures and appealing sweetness, port wine is easy to love, especially when matched with its proper accompaniments: cheese, nuts, dried fruit and dark chocolate. Ports are wonderfully varied, and even nonconnoisseurs can quickly learn to tell an aged tawny from a late-bottled vintage (LBV). For an insightful primer on port, hook onto a tasting at Touriga (p394) or Portologia (Map p372; www.vinologia.pt; Rua de São João 28-30; ☺11am-midnight), where the learned owners give an enlightening lesson with each glass they pour. Or sample fine ports by the glass at Prova (p389). From here, head across the Douro to Vila Nova de Gaia, the steep banks of which are speckled with grand port-wine lodges – Taylor's (p378), Graham's (p378), Croft (Map p368; ☏220 109 825; www.croftport.com; Rua Barão de Forrester 412; tours incl tasting €14; ☺10am-7.30pm), Ramos Pinto (Map p372; ☏967 658 980, 936 809 283; www.ramospinto.pt; Av Ramos Pinto 400; tours incl tasting €10; ☺10am-6pm May-Oct, reduced hours Nov-Apr) and Cálem (p378) included.

History

It was probably Roman soldiers who first planted grapes in the Douro Valley some 2000 years ago, but tradition credits the discovery of port itself to 17th-century British merchants. With their own country at war with France, the British turned to their old ally Portugal to meet their drinking habits. The Douro Valley was a particularly productive area, though its wines were dark and astringent. According to legend, the British threw in some brandy with grape juice, both to take off the wine's bite and to preserve it for shipment back to England – and, hey presto, port wine was born. In fact, the method may already have been in use in the region, though what's certain is that the Brits took to the stuff with a passion. Their influence has been long and enduring, evidenced by some of port's most illustrious names including Taylor's, Graham's and Cockburn's.

The Grapes

Port-wine grapes are born out of adversity. They manage to grow on the rocky terraces of the Douro with hardly any water or even soil, and their roots must reach down as far as 30m, weaving past layers of acidic schist (shale-like stone) to find nourishment. Vines endure both extreme heat in summer and freezing temperatures in winter. These conditions produce intense flavours that stand up to the infusions of brandy. The most common varietals are hardy, dark reds such as *touriga, tinto cão* and *tinto barroca*.

The Wine

Grapes are harvested in autumn and immediately crushed (sometimes still by foot) and allowed to ferment until alcohol levels reach 7%. At this point, one part brandy is added to every five parts wine. Fermentation stops immediately, leaving the unfermented sugars that make port sweet. The quality of the grapes, together with the ways the wine is aged and stored, determines the kind of port you get. The most common include the following:

Ruby – made from average-quality grapes, and aged at least two years in vats; rich, red colours and sweet, fruity flavours.

Tawny – made from average-quality grapes, and aged for two to seven years in wooden casks; mahogany colours, drier than ruby, with nuttier flavours.

Aged tawny – selected from higher-quality grapes, then aged in wooden casks for 10, 20, 30 or 40 years (reflected in the respective price). Subtler and silkier than regular tawny; drinks more like brandy than wine.

Vintage – made from the finest grapes from a single year (and only select years qualify), aged in barrels for two years, then aged in bottles for at least 10 years (and even beyond 100); dark ruby colours, fruity yet extremely subtle and complex.

Late-bottled vintage (LBV) – made from very select grapes of a single year, aged for around five years in wooden casks, then bottled; similar to vintage, but ready for immediate drinking once bottled, and usually smoother and lighter bodied.

as filled croissants and cakes. Products are mostly organic and fair trade, and it also has lactose-free options.

Museu d'Avó
BAR

(Map p372; Travessa de Cedofeita 54; ⊙8pm-4am Mon-Sat) The name translates as 'Grand-mother's Museum' and indeed it's a gorgeous rambling attic of a bar, crammed with cabinets, old clocks, *azulejos* and gramophones, with curios hanging from its rafters. Lanterns and candles illuminate young *tripeiros* (Porto residents) locked in animated conversation as the house beats spin. If you get the late-night munchies, it also whips up tasty *petiscos* (€2 to €8).

Café au Lait
BAR

(Map p372; www.facebook.com/aulait.cafe; Rua Galeria de Paris 46; ⊙10pm-4am Tue-Sat) Housed in a former textile warehouse, this narrow, intimate bar now stitches together a lively and unpretentious artistic crowd. Besides cocktails, there are snacks and salads, including vegetarian grub. DJs and occasional gigs amp up the vibe and add to the good cheer.

Galeria de Paris
BAR

(Map p372; www.facebook.com/restaurantegaleria deparis; Rua Galeria de Paris 56; ⊙8.30am-3am Sun-Thu, to 4am Fri & Sat) The original on the strip that's now synonymous with the Porto party scene, this whimsically decorated spot has toys, thermos flasks, old phones and other assorted memorabilia lining the walls. In addition to cocktails and draught beer, you'll find tapas at night.

Café Candelabro
CAFE

(Map p372; Rua da Conceição 3; ⊙10.30am-2am Mon-Fri, 4pm-2am Sat, 4pm-midnight Sun) Cool cafe-bar in a former bookstore, with a boho crowd and a retro vibe featuring black-and-white mosaic tile floors, bookcases with old books and magazines, and big windows opening out to the street. It gets busy with upbeat tunes and occasional gigs at weekends.

Café Majestic
CAFE

(Map p372; www.cafemajestic.com; Rua de Santa Catarina 112; ⊙9.30am-11.30pm Mon-Sat) Yes, we know, it's pricey and rammed with tourists brandishing selfie sticks, but you should at least have a drink at Café Majestic just so you can gawp at its beaux arts interior, awash with prancing cherubs, opulently gilded woodwork and gold-braided waiters.

Skip the so-so food and just go for coffee. There's a pavement terrace for sunny-day people-watching.

Livraria da Baixa
CAFE

(Map p372; www.facebook.com/livrariadabaixa; Rua das Carmelitas 15; ⊙10am-2am; 🐾) Part 1920s bookshop, part cafe-bar, this old-school charmer spills out onto the cobbled pavement – a terrific spot for people-watching and eavesdropping over tea or a glass of wine.

Duas de Letra
CAFE

(Map p368; www.duasdeletra.pt; Passeio de São Lázaro 48; ⊙10am-10pm Mon-Thu, to midnight Fri & Sat, 2-8pm Sun; 🐾) Artsy cafe overlooking a leafy square, with a low-key vibe, wooden ceilings, an exhibition space upstairs with rotating exhibits, and two patios. The snacks are delicious, and there's a great tea selection. The day special, including soup and a drink, goes for just €7.

📍 Miragaia

Pinguim Café
BAR

(Map p372; www.facebook.com/PinguimCafe; Rua de Belomonte 65; ⊙9pm-4am Mon-Fri, 10pm-4am Sat & Sun) A little bubble of bohemian warmth in the heart of Porto, Pinguim attracts an alternative crowd. Stone walls and dim lighting create a cosy, intimate backdrop for plays, film screenings, poetry readings, rotating exhibitions of local art, and G&T sipping. It's full to the rafters at weekends.

📍 Vila Nova de Gaia

360° Terrace Lounge
WINE BAR

(Map p372; www.myportocruz.com; Espaço Porto Cruz, Largo Miguel Bombarda 23; ⊙12.30pm-12.30am Tue-Thu, to 1.30am Fri & Sat, to 7pm Sun) From its perch atop the Espaço Porto Cruz, this decked terrace affords expansive views over both sides of the Douro and the city, fading into a hazy distance where the river meets the sea. As day softens into dusk, this is a prime sunset spot for sipping a glass of port or a cocktail while drinking in the incredible vista.

📍 Boavista

★ 7G Roaster
COFFEE

(Map p372; www.facebook.com/7groaster; Rua de França 26; ⊙10am-6pm Mon-Thu, to 7pm Fri-Sun) The baristas really know their stuff at this speciality coffee roasters. In the cool, monochrome, wood-floored space, you can sip a perfectly made espresso or go for brunch (€12), which includes everything from sheep's cheese to homemade granola, pastries and fresh-pressed juice. Sit on the terrace to gaze up at the vertical garden.

Bar Casa da Música BAR
(Map p368; www.casadamusica.com; Avenida da Boavista 604; ⊙12.30-3pm & 7.30-11pm Mon-Thu, to midnight Fri & Sat; 🛜) Situated on the top floor of Porto's most strikingly contemporary building, this bar is a fine place to sip a drink as the city starts to light up – the terrace commands great views. DJs occasionally work the decks at the twice-monthly Saturday clubbing sessions (11pm to 4am). See the website for more details.

🍷 Foz do Douro

Praia da Luz BAR
(Map p384; www.praiadaluz.pt; Avenida do Brasil; ⊙9am-2am) A worthwhile stop when out exploring Porto's coastline. It rambles over tiered wooden decks to its own private rocky cove, and while you could probably skip the food, you should definitely kick back and enjoy the view over a coffee or cocktail.

☆ Entertainment

☆ Music & Theatre

★Casa da Música CONCERT VENUE
(House of Music; Map p368; 🖂 220 120 220; www.casadamusica.com; Avenida da Boavista 604; ⊙box office 9.30am-7pm Mon-Sat, to 6pm Sun) Grand and minimalist, sophisticated yet populist, Porto's cultural behemoth boasts a shoebox-style concert hall at its heart, meticulously engineered to accommodate everything from jazz duets to Beethoven's Ninth.

The hall holds concerts most nights of the year, from classical and blues to fado and electronica, with occasional summer concerts staged outdoors in the adjoining plaza.

Maus Hábitos PERFORMING ARTS
(Map p372; www.maushabitos.com; 4th fl, Rua Passos Manuel 178; ⊙noon-midnight Tue, to 2am Wed & Thu, to 4am Fri & Sat, noon-5pm Sun) Maus Hábitos or 'Bad Habits' is an arty, nicely chilled haunt hosting a culturally ambitious agenda. Changing exhibitions and imaginative installations adorn the walls, while live bands and DJs work the small stage.

Teatro Municipal Rivoli THEATRE
(Map p372; 🖂 223 392 200; www.teatromunicipaldoporto.pt; Praça Dom João I; 🛜) This art deco theatre is one of the linchpins of Porto's evolving cultural scene. It traverses the whole spectrum from theatre to music, contemporary circus, cinema, dance and marionette productions.

Teatro Nacional São João THEATRE
(Map p372; 🖂 223 401 900; www.tnsj.pt; Praça da Batalha) The lavish, romantic Teatro Nacional São João was built in the style of Paris' Palais Garnier. One of Porto's premier performing-arts organisations, it hosts international dance, theatre and music groups.

Teatro Nacional São João – Mosteiro de São Bento da Vitória THEATRE
(Map p372; 🖂 223 401 900; www.tnsj.pt; Rua de São Bento da Vitória) Few theatre backdrops are more atmospheric than the Mosteiro de São Bento da Vitória, which harbours an offshoot of the Teatro Nacional São João. See the website for the full lineup, which traverses the cultural spectrum from plays to ballet and readings. Tickets generally cost between €7.50 and €15.

Coliseu do Porto CONCERT VENUE
(Map p372; 🖂 223 394 940; www.coliseu.pt; Rua Passos Manuel 137) This frayed, yet still stylish, art deco theatre hosts major gigs as well as grand theatre and dance productions. If something big is going on down here, you'll see posters all over town.

Hot Five Jazz & Blues Club JAZZ
(Map p372; 🖂 934 328 583; www.hotfive.pt; Largo Actor Dias 51; ⊙10pm-3am Wed-Thu, to 4am Fri & Sat, to 2am Sun) True to its name, this spot hosts live jazz and blues as well as the occasional acoustic, folk or all-out jam session. It's a modern but intimate space, with seating at small round tables, both fronting the stage and on an upper balcony. Concerts often start later than scheduled.

☆ Football

The flashy 52,000-seat Estádio do Dragão is home to heroes-of-the-moment **FC Porto** (Map p368; www.fcporto.pt; 🅜 Estádio do Dragão). It's northeast of the centre, just off the VCI ring road.

Boavista FC (Map p368; www.boavistafc.pt; Estádio do Bessa Século, Rua 1º de Janeiro) are FC Porto's worthy cross-town rivals. Their home turf is the Estádio do Bessa, which lies west of the centre just off Avenida da Boavista (take bus 3 from Praça da Liberdade). Check the local editions of *Jornal de Notícias* for upcoming matches.

☆ Fado

→ **O Fado** (Map p372; ☑ 222 026 937; www.ofado.com; Largo de São João Novo 16; ⊙ 8.30pm-1am Mon-Sat) Traditional Portuguese fado venue, where *fadistas* sing their melancholic hearts out.

→ **Casa da Mariquinhas** (Map p372; www. casadamariquinhas.pt; Rua de São Sebastião 25; ⊙ 8pm-1am Wed & Thu, to 2am Fri & Sat) Soulful renditions of fado in an intimate, stone-walled tavern.

→ **Fado in Porto** (Map p372; ☑ 223 746 660; www.fadoinporto.com; Av Diogo Leite 344; cover €21; ⊙ 6.30pm Tue-Sun Apr-Oct, 6pm Tue-Sun Nov-Mar) Sip port and hear *fadistas* sing the blues at the Cálem cellars.

🛍 Shopping

🛍 Ribeira

⭐ **Oliva & Co**   FOOD
(Map p372; www.facebook.com/pg/OlivaeCo; Rua Ferreira Borges 60; ⊙ 10am-7pm Sun-Fri, to 8pm Sat) Everything you ever wanted to know about Portuguese olive oil becomes clear at this experiential store, which maps out the country's six Protected Designation of Origin (PDO) regions producing the extra-virgin stuff. Besides superb oils and olives, you'll find biscuits, chocolate and soaps made with olive oil. Try before you buy, or join one of the in-depth tastings.

43 Branco   ARTS & CRAFTS
(Map p372; Rua das Flores 43; ⊙ 11am-7pm Mon-Sat) One-of-a-kind Portuguese crafts, fashion and interior design take centre stage at this new concept store, which brings a breath of fresh creativity to Rua das Flores. Here you'll find everything from filigree, gem-studded Maria Branco jewellery to funky sardine pencil cases, Porto-inspired Lubo T-shirts and beautifully packaged Bonjardim soaps.

Tradições   GIFTS & SOUVENIRS
(Map p372; Rua das Flores 238; ⊙ 10am-7.30pm) For Portuguese souvenirs, Tradições is the real deal. In this sweet, friendly shop, the owner knows the story behind every item – from bags beautifully fashioned

LGBT+ PORTO

Note that while there are no exclusive women's bars or clubs, all the places listed here are at least somewhat mixed.

Zoom (Map p372; www.facebook.com/ zoomporto; Rua Passos Manuel 40; ⊙ midnight-6am Fri & Sat) Located in an old warehouse, this is the gay dance hall of the moment, with some of the best electronic dance music in town and an often mixed crowd.

Pride Bar (Map p368; www.facebook. com/PrideBarPorto; Rua do Bonjardim 1121; ⊙ 11.30pm-6am Fri-Sun) Another favourite, with live music, drag shows and go-go boys. Open very late.

Café Lusitano (Map p372; www.cafelusitano.com; Rua José Falcão 137; ⊙ 9.30pm-2am Wed & Thu, 10pm-4am Fri & Sat) In a handsomely designed throwback to 1950s Paris, this intimate space hosts a mixed gay-straight crowd. Live music on Wednesday nights.

from Alentejo cork to Algarvian *flôr de sal* (hand-harvested sea salt), Lousã honey to Lazuli *azulejos*.

🛍 Aliados & Bolhão

⭐ **Workshops Pop Up**   ARTS & CRAFTS
(Map p372; ☑ 966 974 119; www.workshops-pop-up.com; Rua do Almada 275; ⊙ 1-7.30pm Sun-Fri, 10am-7.30pm Sat) Bringing a new lease of life to a restored smithy, this store is the brainchild of Nuno and Rita. It harbours an eclectic mix of pop-ups selling everything from original ceramics to vintage fashion, accessories and prettily wrapped Bonjardim soaps. It also runs three-hour cookery workshops (p376), some of which are in English.

⭐ **A Pérola do Bolhão**   FOOD & DRINKS
(Map p372; Rua Formosa 279; ⊙ 9.30am-7.30pm Mon-Fri, 9am-1pm Sat) Founded in 1917, this delightfully old-school deli sports Porto's most striking art nouveau facade and is stacked to the rafters with smoked sausages and pungent mountain cheeses, olives, dried fruits and nuts, wine and port. The beautiful *azulejos* depict flowers and two goddess-like women bearing *café* (coffee) and *chá* (tea) plants.

STREET ART IN PORTO

If only walls could speak... Well, in Porto they do – volumes. Their narrative is that of Porto's growing tribe of street artists, whose bold, eye-catching works emblazon facades. Hurled across crumbling ancient walls, empty storefront glass and neglected stucco, they lend artistic edge, urban grit and an element of the unexpected to the everyday. A far cry from graffiti scrawls, the spray-paint wonders reveal artistic flair and creative expression that transcend the conventional and stop you dead in your tracks: a stencilled pilgrim here, a cloaked bodhisattva there.

Porto-born or -based artists include the startlingly prolific Hazul Luzah (a pseudonym), who works incognito under the cloak of darkness. His naturalistic, geometric-patterned, curlicue-embellished works dance across dilapidated city walls in the shape of flowers, exotic birds or religious motifs. Other home-grown talent includes Costah, known for his playful, brightly coloured murals; Frederico Draw, master of striking black-and-white graffiti portraits; and the ever-inventive MrDheo. Some of the artists are self-taught, others have backgrounds in architecture, digital art, illustration and design.

To plug into the scene today, arrange your own self-guided tour of Porto's must-see street art. High on any list should be the Travessa de Cedofeita and Escadas do Codeçal, as well as the car park at Trindade, with its large-scale murals. Lapa, just one metro stop north, is another hotspot, as is the gallery-dotted Rua Miguel Bombarda. On Rua das Flores, clever graffiti sits side by side with beautifully restored historic buildings – look out for vibrantly patterned works by Hazul, glowing neon portraits by Costah and 15 electric boxes – each with its own burst of street-art colour.

Coração Alecrim
ARTS & CRAFTS

(Map p372; www.coracaoalecrim.com; Travessa de Cedofeita 28; ⊗11am-7pm Mon-Sat) 'Green, indie, vintage' is the strapline of this enticing store, accessed through a striking doorway painted with woodland animals (crickets chirrup a welcome as you enter). It stocks high-quality handmade Portuguese products, from pure-wool blankets and beanies to one-off *azulejos,* shell coasters and beautiful ceramics.

Azulima
ARTS & CRAFTS

(Map p372; www.azulima.pt; Rua do Bolhão 124; ⊗9.30am-12.30pm & 2.30-7pm Mon-Fri, 10am-12.30pm Sat) Heaven for the *azulejo* obsessed, this shop does a fine line in tiles of every shape, size and colour – from geometric to naturalistic, from slick and modern to classic blue-and-white numbers.

Águas Furtadas
ART, FASHION

(Map p372; www.facebook.com/aguasfurtadas; Rua do Almada 13; ⊗10am-8pm Mon-Sat, 1-7pm Sun) This boutique is a treasure trove of funky Portuguese fashion, design, crafts and accessories, including born-again Barcelos cockerels in candy-bright colours and exquisitely illustrated pieces by influential Porto-based graphic designer Benedita Feijó.

Loja das Conservas
FOOD

(Map p372; Rua de Mouzinho da Silveira 240; ⊗10am-8.30pm Mon-Sat, 1-8pm Sun) An ode to the humble tinned fish, this store is stacked to the rafters with bold, retro-wrapped cans of tuna, *bacalhau* and sardines plain and spicy. It stocks popular brands such as Santa Catarina and Viana Pesca, which at between €2.50 and €4 a pop make funky gifts. Look out for the stuffed sardine as you enter.

Touriga
WINE

(Map p372; ☑225 108 435; Rua da Fábrica 32; ⊗11am-7pm Mon-Sat) Run with passion and precision by David Ferreira, this fabulous wine shop is a trove of well- and lesser-known ports and wines – many from small producers. Stop by for a wine or port tasting (€5 to €20). Shipping can be arranged.

A Vida Portuguesa
GIFTS & SOUVENIRS

(Map p372; www.avidaportuguesa.com; Rua Galeria de Paris 20; ⊗10am-8pm Mon-Sat, 11am-7pm Sun) This lovely store in an old fabric shop showcases a medley of stylishly repackaged vintage Portuguese products – classic toys, old-fashioned soaps and retro journals, plus those emblematic ceramic Bordallo Pinheiro *andorinhas* (swallows).

Casa Ramos
FOOD

(Map p372; Rua Sá da Bandeira 347; ⊗9am-7pm Mon-Fri, to 1pm Sat) Old-world grocery stores like this one are a dying breed. Besides beans, *bacalhau* and *alheira* sausages by the kilo, you'll find everything from traditional sweets to teas and charcuterie here.

Arcádia
CHOCOLATE

(Map p372; www.arcadia.pt; Rua do Almada 63; ◉9.30am-7pm Mon-Fri, to 5.30pm Sat) Purveyors of handcrafted chocolates, Arcádia has been reeling in the sweet-toothed locals since 1933. This gloriously old-fashioned shop rolls out gift-boxed pralines and flavoured bonbons, cocoa-rich bars, chocolates with Calém port or in the delicate form of hearts and flowers, and almond liqueur dragées – all made with care to traditional recipes.

🏠 Miragaia

CC Bombarda
MALL

(Map p372; Rua Miguel Bombarda 285; ◉noon-8pm Mon-Sat) Amid the galleries along Rua Miguel Bombarda, this small, unique shopping mall is a highlight. Inside you'll find stores selling locally designed urban wear, gourmet teas, organic cosmetics, jewellery, vinyl, bonsai trees, stylish home knick-knacks and other hipster-pleasing delights. There's a cafe serving light bites in an internal courtyard.

Armazém
ARTS & CRAFTS

(Map p372; Rua da Miragaia 93; ◉11.30am-8pm) Bang on trend with Porto's current thirst for creative spaces is the hipsterish Armazém, located in a converted warehouse down by the river. A gallery, cafe and store all under one roof, with an open fire burning at its centre, it sells a pinch of everything – vintage garb, antiques, vinyl, artwork, ceramics and funky Portuguese-designed bags and fashion.

CRU
ARTS & CRAFTS

(Map p372; www.cru-cowork.com; Rua do Rosário 211; ◉9.30am-8.30pm Mon-Fri, 10am-8pm Sat) Allowing Portuguese designers to give flight to their fantasy, this unique gallery space crackles with creativity. What's on offer changes frequently, but at any one time you might find understated fashion, ceramics, accessories, art and beautifully handcrafted jewellery.

🏠 Foz do Douro

Mercado da Foz
MARKET

(Map p384; Rua de Diu; ◉7am-7pm Mon-Sat) Stalls are piled high with fresh produce and flowers at this recently revamped covered market. There are plenty of food stands, where you can tuck into everything from

Trás-os-Montes cheeses and smoked sausage to Douro wines, gourmet burgers and hot dogs, and meltingly tender *leitão* (suckling pig) from the Bairrada region.

❶ Information

EMERGENCY
Police Station (☎222 092 000; Largo 1 de Dezembro)

Tourist Police (☎222 081 833; Rua Clube dos Fenianos 11; ◉8am-2am) Multilingual station beside the main city *turismo*.

MEDICAL SERVICES
Santo António Hospital (☎222 077 500; www.chporto.pt; Largo Prof Abel Salazar) Has English-speaking staff.

POST
Post Office (Map p372; Praça General Humberto Delgado 320; ◉8am-9pm Mon-Fri, 9am-6pm Sat) Across from the main tourist office.

Post Office (Map p372; Praça da Batalha 12; ◉9am-6pm Mon-Fri)

TOURIST INFORMATION
City Centre Turismo (Map p372; ☎300 501 920; www.visitporto.travel; Rua Clube dos Fenianos 25; ◉9am-8pm May-Jul & Sep-Oct, to 9pm Aug, to 7pm Nov-Apr) The main city *turismo* has a detailed city map, a transport map and the *Agenda do Porto* cultural calendar, among other printed materials.

iPoint Campanhã (Map p368; www.visitporto.travel; Estação de Comboio de Campanhã; ◉9.30am-6.30pm Jun-Aug) Seasonal information point run by the *turismo* at the Campanhã train station

iPoint Ribeira (Map p372; www.visitporto.travel; Praça da Ribeira; ◉10.30am-7pm Apr-Oct) Useful *turismo*-run information point on Praça da Ribeira, open seasonally.

Turismo (Map p372; ☎223 758 288; www.cm-gaia.pt; Av Diogo Leite 135; ◉9.30am-7pm Apr-Sep, 10am-6pm Mon-Sat Oct-Mar) Gaia's *turismo* dispenses a good town map and a brochure listing all the lodges open for tours.

Turismo (Map p372; ☎300 501 920; www.visitporto.travel; Terreiro da Sé; ◉9am-8pm May-Oct, to 7pm Nov-Apr) Handy tourist office right next to the cathedral. Offers a ticket and hotel booking service.

❶ Getting There & Away

AIR
Situated around 16km northwest of the city centre, the gleaming, ultramodern **Francisco de Sá Carneiro Airport** (☎229 432 400; www.aeroportoporto.pt; 4470-558 Maia) operates direct flights to major international hubs

including London, Brussels, Madrid, Frankfurt and Toronto.

TAP (www.flytap.com) has multiple daily flights to/from Lisbon. There are also low-cost carriers, such as easyJet (www.easyjet.com) and Ryanair (www.ryanair.com), with nonstop services to London, Madrid, Paris, Frankfurt, Amsterdam and Brussels.

BUS

As in many Portuguese cities, bus services in Porto are regrettably dispersed, with no central bus terminal. The good news is that there are frequent services to just about everywhere in northern Portugal, as well as express services to Coimbra, Lisbon and points south.

Domestic

Renex-Rede Expressos (Map p368; www. rede-expressos.pt; Campo 24 de Agosto) is the choice for Lisbon (€19, 3½ hours), with the most direct routes and eight to 12 departures daily, including one continuing on to the Algarve. They also have frequent services to Braga (€6, one hour). Buses depart from Campo 24 de Agosto.

For fast Minho connections, mainly on weekdays, three companies offer routes: **Transdev-Norte** (Map p368; ☎ 225 100 100; www. transdev.pt; Campo 24 de Agosto) runs chiefly to Braga (€6, one hour) and Guimarães (€6, one hour); **AV Minho** (☎ 222 006 121; www.avminho. pt; Rua Régulo Maguanha 46) runs four times daily via Vila do Conde (€2.45, one hour) to Viana do Castelo (€5.60, 2¼ hours); and **Rodonorte** (Map p372; www.rodonorte.pt; Rua Ateneu Comercial do Porto 19) has roughly hourly departures for Amarante (€7.80, 50 minutes), Vila Real (€9.50, 1½ hours) and Bragança (€14.30, three hours).

International

There are Eurolines (www.eurolines.com) departures from Interface Casa da Música (Rua Capitão Henrique Calvão). Northern Portugal's own international carrier, **Internorte** (Map p368; www.internorte.pt), departs from the same place. Most travel agencies can book outbound buses with either operator.

CAR & MOTORCYCLE

All major Portuguese and international car-hire companies have offices at the airport including **Cael** (☎ 229 964 269; www.cael.pt; Av Arquiteto Fernando Tavora 2021), while some, such as **Europcar** (☎ 222 057 737; www.europcar.com; Rua Antonio Bessa Leite 1478), also have offices downtown. Prices start at around €30 per day.

TRAIN

There are information points at both São Bento and Campanhã stations. Alternatively, call 707 210 220 or consult www.cp.pt.

Long-Distance Trains

Porto is the principal rail hub for northern Portugal. Long-distance services start at **Campanhã** (Rua Monte da Estação) station, 3km east of the centre.

Direct IC destinations from Porto include Lisbon (2nd class €24.70 to €30.80, 2½ to three hours, hourly).

Urbano, Regional & Interregional Trains

Most *urbano, regional* and *interregional* (IR) trains depart from the stunning indoor-outdoor **São Bento** (Praça Almeida Garrett) station, though all of these lines also pass through Campanhã.

For destinations on the Braga, Guimarães and Aveiro lines, or up the Douro Valley as far as Marco de Canaveses, take one of the frequent *urbano* trains. Don't spend extra money on *interregional, intercidade* (IC) or Alfa Pendular (AP) trains to these destinations as the *urbano* trains take around the same amount of time; Porto to Braga costs €14.50 by AP train, but around a fifth of that by *urbano*. Tickets are available for purchase on the day of travel.

ⓘ Getting Around

TO/FROM THE AIRPORT

➡ The Metro do Porto (http://en.metrodoporto. pt) violet line E (direction Estádio do Dragão) links the airport to downtown Porto; change at Trindade onto yellow line D (direction Santo Ovídio) for Aliados and São Bento stops. A one-way ticket costs €2 and the journey takes around 45 minutes.

➡ A daytime taxi costs €20 or €25 to/from the centre. Taxis authorised to run *from* the airport are labelled 'Maia' and/or 'Vila Nova de Telha'; the rank is just outside the Arrivals Hall. In peak-traffic time, allow an hour or more between the city centre and the airport.

➡ STCP (www.stcp.pt) runs a couple of public buses between the airport and the centre; the most useful is the 601 to Cordoaria, departing every 30 minutes from 5.30am to 11.30pm. A single costs €2.

BICYCLE

➡ Despite the narrow alleyways, steep hills and cobbled streets, cyclists are ubiquitous in Porto, and there are some particularly great rides along the Douro on dedicated bike paths from Ribeira to Foz or from Vila Nova de Gaia to Afurada and beyond.

➡ Bike rental outlets include **Fold 'n' Visit** (Map p372; ☎ 220 997 106; www.topbiketoursportugal.com; Rua Alferes Malheiro 139; rental per half/full day from €13/17), **L&L** (Map p372; ☎ 223 251 722; www.lopesrentabike.wix.com/porto; 2nd fl, Largo de São Domingos 13; bike hire per 1/24hr €2.50/15; ⏱10am-8pm) and

ℹ️ ANDANTE CARD

→ For maximum convenience, Porto's transport system offers the rechargeable Andante Card (www.linhandante.com), allowing smooth movement between tram, metro, funicular and many bus lines.

→ The card itself costs only €0.60 and can be recharged for one year. Once you've purchased the card, charge it with travel credit according to which zones you will be travelling in.

→ Purchase credit at metro ticket machines and staffed TIP booths at central hubs such as Casa da Música and Trindade, as well as the STCP office, the funicular, the electric tram museum and a scattering of other authorised sales points.

→ Your time begins from when you first enter the vehicle or platform: just wave the card in front of a validation machine marked 'Andante'.

→ Each trip allows you to move between methods of transport without additional cost.

Porto Rent a Bike (Map p372; 📞 913 104 024, 222 022 375; www.portorentabike.com; Av Gustavo Eiffel 280; bikes per half-/full day from €10/15; ⏱ 10am-2pm & 3-7pm). A full day's rental will set you back around €15. Many also offer guided cycling tours.

→ **Vieguini** (📞 914 306 838; www.vieguini.pt; Rua Nova da Alfandega 7; bikes per half-/full day €8/12; ⏱ 9am-7pm) has a great selection of high-quality mountain bikes and also rents motor scooters (around €25 per day).

BUS

→ Porto's transport agency **STCP** (Sociedade de Transportes Colectivos do Porto; 📞 808 200 166; www.stcp.pt) runs an extensive bus system with central hubs at Praça da Liberdade (the south end of Avenida dos Aliados), Praça Almeida Garrett (in front of São Bento train station) and Cordoaria.

→ Special all-night lines also run approximately hourly, leaving Aliados on the hour and returning on the half-hour from 1am to 5.30am.

→ City *turismos* have maps and timetables for day and night routes.

→ A ticket bought on the bus (one-way to anywhere in the STCP system) costs €1.95, or €1.20 with an Andante Card. (p397)

CAR & MOTORCYCLE

→ Driving in central Porto is stressful – avoid it if possible. Narrow one-way streets, construction and heavy traffic can turn 500m into half a morning.

→ Street parking is tight, with a two-hour maximum stay on weekdays. There is no limit on weekends, and parking spaces are more readily available.

→ Most squares have underground, fee-charging lots – follow the blue Ps. Be aware that opportunistic locals may guide you into places and then expect tips. They can be very disagreeable if you don't comply. They may also direct you into an illegal spot – be sure to double-check signs.

FUNICULAR

The restored **Funicular dos Guindais** (one-way adult/child €2.50/1.25; ⏱ 8am-10pm Sun-Thu, to midnight Fri & Sat Apr-Oct, to 8pm Sun-Thu, to 10pm Fri & Sat Nov-Mar) shuttles up and down a steep incline with tremendous river and bluff views from Avenida Gustavo Eiffel, opposite Ponte de Dom Luís I, to Rua Augusto Rosa, near Batalha and the cathedral. The funicular is part of the Andante Card scheme (www.linhandante.com).

METRO

Porto's newish **metro system** (http://en.metrodoporto.pt) is compact and fairly easy to navigate – though not comprehensive. Running from around 6am to 1am daily, it comprises six metropolitan lines that all converge at the Trindade stop.

→ Three lines – Linha A (blue, to Matosinhos), Linha B (red, to Vila do Conde and Póvoa de Varzim) and Linha C (green, to Maia) – run from Estádio do Dragão via Campanhã train station through the city centre, and then on to far-flung northern and western suburbs.

→ Linha D (yellow) runs north–south from Hospital São João to João de Deus in Vila Nova de Gaia, crossing the upper deck of Ponte de Dom Luís I. Key stops include Aliados and São Bento station.

→ Linha E (violet) connects Linha B with the airport.

→ Linha F (orange) links Senhora da Hora to Fânzeres.

Buy tickets from metro ticket machines, which have English-language menus. Tickets cost €1.20/1.60/2 for zone 2/3/4 with an Andante Card (p397). Zone 2 covers the whole city centre east to Campanhã train station, south to Vila Nova de Gaia and west to Foz do Douro.

For timetables, maps and fares, visit the metro website; all stations also have maps.

TAXI

There are taxi ranks throughout the centre, or you can call **Táxis Invicta** (📞 225 076 400; www.taxisinvicta.com). Count on paying around €5 to €7 for trips within the centre during the day, with a 20% surcharge at night. There's an extra charge if you leave the city limits, which includes Vila Nova de Gaia.

TRAM

➡ Only three Porto tram lines remain, but they're very scenic.

➡ The Massarelos stop, on the riverfront near the foot of the Palácio de Cristal, is the tram system's hub. From here, line 1 trundles along the river to nearby Praça Infante Dom Henrique (Ribeira). Line 1E (appears as a crossed-out '1') heads down the river in the opposite direction, towards Foz do Douro.

➡ Line 18 heads uphill to the Igreja do Carmo and Jardim do Cordoaria.

➡ Line 22 makes a loop through the centre from Carmo to Batalha/Guindais.

➡ Trams run approximately every 30 minutes from 8am to 9pm.

➡ One-way tickets cost €3; a two-day adult/ child pass costs €10/5.

Vila do Conde

POP 28,630

With its quaint historic heart, poetic folk hero, glassy river mouth, luscious beaches and salty past, you can understand why Vila do Conde is a popular weekend getaway for Porto residents. An important salt exporter during Roman times and a prime shipbuilding port during the Age of Discoveries, the town still drips history. Looming over it is the immense hilltop Mosteiro de Santa Clara, which, along with surviving segments of a long-legged medieval aqueduct, lends the town an air of monumentality. In addition to this, Vila do Conde's beaches are some of the best in northern Portugal, and a metro link makes getting here an easy afternoon jaunt from downtown Porto.

Vila do Conde sits on the north side of the Rio Ave, where it empties into the sea. From the Vila do Conde metro station, look for the aqueduct (about 100m away) and follow it towards the large convent (another 400m). From here it's a few steep blocks downhill to the town's historic centre. From the centre it's another kilometre via Avenida Dr Artur Cunha Araújo or Avenida Dr João Canavar-

ro to Avenida do Brasil and the 3km-long beach.

◉ Sights

Alfândega Regia Museu da Construção Naval MUSEUM

(Museum of Shipbuilding; Rua Cais da Alfândega; adult/reduced €1.10/0.55; ⊙10am-6pm Tue-Sun) Shipbuilding has been in Vila do Conde's bones since at least the 13th century. This museum on the Rio Ave's banks, just west of Praça da República, has exhibits on trade and models of hand-built *nau* (a sort of pot-bellied caravel once used for cargo and naval operations). The real attraction, however, is the replica of a 16th-century *nau* moored opposite the museum. Visitors can wander its various decks, peeking in rooms that provide a glimpse of 16th-century seafaring life.

Casa do Barco MUSEUM

(Cais das Lavandeiras; ⊙9am-6pm Jun-Sep, 9.30am-1pm & 2.30-6pm Oct-May) **FREE** On the lower level of Vila do Conde's glass-box riverfront tourist office, this small museum offers up models, photo displays, old fishing gear and one full-sized boat that provide a glimpse into the town's shipbuilding past.

Museu das Rendas de Bilros MUSEUM

(Museum of Bobbin Lace; Rua de São Bento 70; adult/reduced €1.10/0.55; ⊙10am-6pm Tue-Sun) It's no accident that seafaring fingers, so deft at making nets, should also be good at lacemaking. Vila do Conde is one of the few places in Portugal with an active school of the art, founded in 1918. Housed in a typical 18th-century town house in the town centre, the school includes the Museu das Rendas de Bilros, which displays eye-popping examples of work from Portugal and around the world.

Casa de José Régio MUSEUM

(Av José Régio; adult/reduced €1.10/0.55; ⊙10am-1pm & 2-6pm Tue-Sun) Religious art, antique furnishings, ceramics and early-20th-century contemporary art can be glimpsed at this museum, named after the distinguished local-born poet, playwright and healer José Régio (1901–69), who lived and worked here. Admission includes a guided tour through each floor of the town house. The stunning upstairs office and library, and the rooftop garden, are highlights.

☂ Beaches

Vila do Conde's two best beaches, **Praia da Forno** and **Praia de Nossa Senhora da**

Guia, are wide, blonde and picturesque even when the winds howl. Most of the year, seas are calm and suitable for young children. Buses marked 'Vila do Conde' from Póvoa de Varzim stop at the station and continue to the beach, about half-hourly all day from Monday to Friday (fewer on weekends).

Surfers can sometimes ride swells near the 17th-century Castelo de São João Baptista, at the river mouth. Once a castle, it's now a privately owned club with a glamorous, hard-partying reputation.

★ Festivals & Events

Festa de São João RELIGIOUS
(☉ Jun) The town's biggest event takes place during the three weeks leading up to 23 June, with fireworks, concerts, a traditional boat parade and a religious procession through the streets.

🛏 Sleeping

Pensão Patarata GUESTHOUSE €
(☎ 252 631 894; Rua do Cais das Lavandeiras 18; s/d €40/50; �) Off the southwest corner of Vila do Conde's grassy riverfront square, this family-run place has simple but sweet rooms with high ceilings, wooden furnishings and river views. There's a popular restaurant downstairs, where breakfast is served at extra cost.

Bellamar Hostel HOSTEL €
(☎ 252 631 748; www.facebook.com/bellamar hostel; Praça da República 84; dm €12-20, d €30-48; ☏) In a grand historic building opposite Vila do Conde's riverside plaza, this hostel offers budget travellers a home in the heart of the action. Doubles – some with river views – are complemented by two- to five-bed dorms, a guest kitchen and a small sitting area. Service isn't always the friendliest, and the meagre breakfast isn't worth the extra €7.

Hotel Brazão HOTEL €€
(☎ 252 642 016; www.hotelbrazao.pt; Avenida Dr João Canavarro 7; s/d/ste €50/66/82; P ✺ @ ☏) Set in a restored 16th-century nobleman's house 200m west of the Rua 25 de Abril *turismo,* this hotel is spacious and comfortable, albeit a bit faded. It's been added on to at various times over the years, making it a patchwork of old and new. Rates drop 25% between September and June.

✕ Eating & Drinking

Around the corner from the *turismo,* Praça José Régio, a rather ugly modern plaza in the middle of the quaint old town, has an assortment of outdoor cafes, bars and restaurants.

Adega Gavina SEAFOOD €€
(☎ 917 834 517; www.facebook.com/AdegaGavina; Rua do Cais das Lavandeiras 56; mains €7-20; ☉ 11.30am-3pm & 7.30-10.30pm Tue-Sat, 11.30am-3pm Sun) This long-standing riverfront favourite is first and foremost a seafood grill. Stroll into the kitschy interior and peruse the chalkboard menu, then choose your catch and watch the chef grill it perfectly on the street-side barbecue. Excellent-value lunch specials come with potatoes, rice and steamed greens.

O Cangalho SEAFOOD €€
(☎ 252 110 898; www.facebook.com/OCangalho; Rua do Cais das Lavandeiras; mains €8.50-17; ☉ 7.30-10.30pm Mon, noon-3pm & 7.30-10.30pm Tue-Sat) The funky, tricked-out vintage Land Rover parked out front may catch your eye, and as you come close you'll notice the stylish bistro interior and fresh fish on ice. Great style, great vibe, tasty seafood.

Forte São João Baptista CLUB
(☎ 918 806 989; www.facebook.com/fortesjoao; Avenida Brasil; ☉ Jul-Sep) The best party spot in Vila do Conde: think mighty, seasonal, blinged-out electronica throw-downs with international DJs, Bedouin tents, spinning disco balls and up to 2000 people spilling onto the windswept sands and dancing on the ancient fortress walls. Parties last until 6am. Make arrangements in advance to get on the door list.

ℹ Information

Loja Interativa de Turismo (☎ 252 248 445; turismo@cm-viladoconde.pt; Rua do Cais das Lavandeiras; ☉ 9am-6pm Jun-Sep, 9.30am-1pm & 2.30-6pm Oct-May) New tourist office on the riverfront, with a wealth of materials and helpful staff.

Turismo (☎ 252 248 473; turismo@cm-vila-doconde.pt; Rua 25 de Abril 103; ☉ 9.30am-12.30pm & 2-6pm Mon-Fri) Vila do Conde's original *turismo* occupies a cute little house in the historic centre.

ℹ Getting There & Away

Vila do Conde is 33km from Porto, and is a straight shot on the A28/IC1. It's served by Porto's Linha B (red) metro line to Póvoa de Varzim, stopping about 400m from the town centre. A one-way trip from central Porto costs €2.80 and takes about an hour – the trip is a little faster if you catch the express service.

Buses stop on Rua 5 de Outubro, near the *turismo*. AV Minho express buses run four times daily to Porto (€3.25, 55 minutes) and Viana do Castelo (€4.30, 80 minutes).

Amarante

POP 12.660

Set on a bend in the Rio Tâmega, the sleepy village of Amarante is dominated by a striking church and monastery, which sit theatrically beside a rebuilt medieval bridge that still bears city traffic. The willow-lined riverbanks lend a pastoral charm, as do the balconied houses and switchback lanes that rise quickly from the narrow valley floor.

The town enjoys a small degree of fame for being the hometown of São Gonçalo. Portugal's St Valentine, he is the target for lonely hearts who make pilgrimages here in the hope of finding true love. Surrounded by prized vineyards, Amarante is also something of a foodie mecca. As well as wine, the region produces excellent cheeses, *fumeiro* (smoked meats) and rich pastries.

History

The town may date back as far as the 4th century BC, though Gonçalo, a 13th-century hermit, is credited with everything from the founding of the town to the construction of its first bridge.

Amarante's strategically placed bridge (Ponte de São Gonçalo) almost proved to be its undoing in 1809, when the French lost their brief grip on Portugal. Marshal Soult's troops retreated to the northeast after abandoning Porto, plundering as they went. A French detachment arrived here in search of a river crossing, but plucky citizens and troops held them off, allowing residents to escape to the far bank. The French retaliated by burning down much of the town.

Amarante has also suffered frequent natural invasions by the Tâmega. Little *cheia* (high-water level) plaques in Rua 31 de Janeiro and Largo Conselheiro António Cândido tell the harrowing story.

⊙ Sights

Ponte de São Gonçalo BRIDGE

A symbol of the town's heroic defence against the French (marked by a plaque at the southeastern end), the granite Ponte de São Gonçalo is Amarante's visual centrepiece. The original bridge, allegedly built at Gonçalo's urging in the 13th century, collapsed in a flood in 1763; this one was completed in 1790.

Mosteiro de São Gonçalo MONASTERY

(Praça da República; ⊙9am-7pm Jun-Sep, to 5.30pm Oct-May) Founded in 1543 by João III, the Mosteiro de São Gonçalo and Igreja de São Gonçalo weren't completed until 1620. Above the church's photogenic, Italian Renaissance side portal is an arcaded gallery, 30m high, with 17th-century statues of Dom João and the other kings who ruled while the monastery was under construction: Sebastião, Henrique and Felipe I.

The bell tower was added in the 18th century. The best view of the royal statues is from the steep lane just west of the church entrance. Within the lofty interior are an impressive gilded baroque altar, pulpits, an organ casing held up by fishtailed giants, and Gonçalo's tomb in a tiny chapel (to the left of the altar). Tradition has it that those in search of a partner will have their wish granted within a year if they touch the statue above his tomb. Sure enough, its limestone toes, fingers and face have been all but rubbed away by hopefuls.

Museu Amadeo de Souza-Cardoso MUSEUM

(www.amadeosouza-cardoso.pt; Alameda Teixeira de Pascoaes; adult/child €1/free; ⊙10am-12.30pm & 2-6pm Tue-Sun Jun-Sep, 9.30am-12.30pm & 2-5.30pm Oct-May) Hidden in one of the Mosteiro de São Gonçalo's cloisters is this delightfully eclectic collection of modernist and contemporary art, a pleasant surprise in a town of this size. The museum is named after Amarante's favourite son, artist Amadeo de Souza-Cardoso (1889–1918) – one of the best-known Portuguese artists of the 20th century, who abandoned naturalism for homegrown versions of Impressionism and cubism. The museum is full of his sketches, cartoons, portraits and abstracts.

🏃 Activities

Rio Tâmega BOATING, WALKING

(boat hire per 30min/1hr €5/10; ⊙boat hire 9am-sunset) For an idyllic river stroll, take the cobbled path along the north bank. A good picnic or daydreaming spot is the rocky outcropping overlooking the rapids 400m east of the bridge. You can also potter about the peaceful Rio Tâmega in a paddle or row boat; boat hire is available along the riverbank.

🎊 Festivals & Events

Festas de Junho RELIGIOUS
Held during the first weekend in June, *festa* highlights include an all-night drumming competition, a livestock fair, a handicrafts market and fireworks, all rounded off with Sunday's procession in honour of the main man – São Gonçalo.

🛏 Sleeping

Parque de Campismo de Penedo da Rainha CAMPGROUND €
(📞255 437 630; www.ccporto.pt/parquecpenedor; Rua Pedro Alvellos; sites per adult/tent/car €2.50/3.20/4; ⊙Feb-Nov; ☲) A big, shady site that cascades down to the river, this campground has a *minimercado* (grocery shop) and bar. It's about 1km upstream (and uphill) from the town centre.

★ Hostel & Suites des Arts HOSTEL €€
(📞255 095 951; www.hosteldesarts.com; Rua Cândido dos Reis 53; dm €17-24, s €52-59, d €62-69; 🛜) This dynamic, perfectly placed new hostel occupies a grand old house in Amarante's picturesque town centre. Clean if spartan basement-level dorms are complemented by attractively appointed doubles upstairs and a spacious, artfully tiled kitchen where ample breakfasts are served each morning. Best of all is the cool attached bar (p401), with a terrace affording dreamy views over the Rio Tâmega.

Casa da Calçada HISTORIC HOTEL €€€
(📞255 410 830; www.casadacalcada.com; Largo do Paço 6; r €155-220, ste €250; 🅿✳🛜☲) Oozing class and boasting every creature comfort, this 16th-century palace (rebuilt following Napoleon's destructive campaign) rises royally above the Ponte de São Gonçalo. Past the antique-filled parlours lie elegantly furnished rooms with marble bathrooms. The Jacuzzi and pool overlook the hotel's vineyards. This Relais & Châteaux property is Amarante's most luxurious option.

🍴 Eating & Drinking

Open-air cafes and bars pop up every summer along the riverside on Avenida General Silveira, opposite the Mosteiro de São Gonçalo. For picnic supplies, browse the twice-weekly Mercado Municipal (Rua Capitão Augusto Casimiro; ⊙8am-1pm Wed & Sat).

Confeitaria da Ponte BAKERY €
(📞255 432 034; www.confeitariadaponte.pt; Rua 31 de Janeiro 186; pastries from €1.50; ⊙8.30am-8pm) Boasting a peaceful, shaded terrace overlooking the bridge, this traditional bakery has the best ambience for enjoying Amarante's famous pastries and eggy custards.

Adega Regional Quelha PORTUGUESE €€
(📞255 425 786; Rua de Olivença; mains €7.50-19.50; ⊙11.30am-2pm & 7-10pm Mon-Thu, 11.30am-10pm Fri-Sun) One of several low-key *adegas* (wine taverns) along the river's south bank, Quelha is a good place to sample regional delicacies such as Amarante's fine smoked meats and cheeses.

Zé da Calçada PORTUGUESE €€
(📞255 426 814; www.facebook.com/ZedaCalcada; Rua 31 de Janeiro 83; mains €11.50-13; ⊙noon-3pm & 7-10pm) Northern Portuguese fare is served in an elegant country-style dining room or on a verandah with idyllic views of the *moistero* and the bridge. Top picks here include duck rice and grilled goat. Weekday lunch specials are good value.

Bar do Hostel BAR
(📞255 095 951; Rua Candido dos Reis 53; ⊙10am-midnight) Attached to the Hostel des Arts, this vibrantly decorated bar serves a full lineup of coffee, local wines and mixed drinks to a young and artsy crowd. Grab a spot on the sofa in the high-ceilinged main room, or catch some rays on the welcoming riverview terrace. Tapas and well-priced daily lunch specials (€7.50) may tempt you to linger.

ℹ Information

Loja Interativa de Turismo (📞255 420 246; turismo@cm-amarante.pt; Largo Conselheiro António Cândido; ⊙9.30am-7pm Jun-Sep, 10am-1pm & 2-6pm Oct-May) Spiffy new tourist office south of the river.

ℹ Getting There & Away

If you have a car, you can use Amarante as an alternative base to explore the *quintas* (estates) of the Alto Douro.

There is free parking just east of the Museu Amadeo de Souza-Cardoso, where the *mercado municipal* is held. Avoid parking there overnight before crowded market days (Wednesday and Saturday).

At the small but busy **Estação Queimado** (Rua Antonio Carneiro), Rodonorte (www.rodonorte.pt) buses from Porto (€7.60, one hour) stop at least five times daily en route to Vila Real (€6.70, 30 minutes) and Bragança (€13.50, 2½ hours). There are also daily buses to Braga (€9, one to

1½ hours) and Lisbon (€20.40, 4¼ to 5¾ hours). Rede Expressos (www.rede-expressos.pt) runs buses to some of these same destinations.

Lamego

POP 11,190 / ELEV 550M

Most people come to Lamego – a prim, prosperous town 10km south of the Rio Douro – to see (and possibly to climb) the astonishing baroque stairway that zigzags its way up to the Igreja de Nossa Senhora dos Remédios. The old town centre itself has a mix of winding narrow lanes and tree-lined boulevards, with spotlit medieval landmarks looming from almost every angle. Connoisseurs also swear by Lamego's *raposeira*, the famously fragrant sparkling wine, which provides a fine break between bouts of port.

History

Lamego was an important centre even in the time of the Visigoths and has had a cathedral since at least the 6th century. The city fell to the Moors in the 8th century and remained in their hands until the 11th century. In 1143 Portugal's first *cortes* (parliament) was convened here to confirm Afonso Henriques as the country's first king. The little town grew fat thanks to its position on trading routes between the Douro and the Beiras and, thanks to its wine, was already famous in the 16th century.

◉ Sights

Igreja de Nossa Senhora dos Remédios   CHURCH
(⊙7.30am-8pm May-Sep, to 6pm Oct-Apr) One of the country's most important pilgrimage sites, this twin-towered, 18th-century church has a trim blue-and-white stucco interior with a sky-blue rococo ceiling and a gilded altar. The church, however, is quite overshadowed by the zigzagging monumental stairway that leads up to it. The 600-plus steps are resplendent with *azulejos* (hand-painted tiles), urns, fountains and statues, adding up to one of the greatest works in Portuguese rococo style.

It's a dramatic sight at any time, but the action peaks in late summer when thousands of devotees arrive and ascend the steps in search of miracles during the Festa de Nossa Senhora dos Remédios (p402). Most offerings are made at the rear altar where Mother Mary reigns supreme. If you can't face the climb by foot, a road (turn-off

1km out on the Viseu road) winds up the hill for about 3km before reaching the top.

Museu de Lamego   MUSEUM
(www.museudelamego.gov.pt; Largo de Camões; adult/reduced €3/1.50; ⊙10am-6pm) Occupying a grand 18th-century episcopal palace, the Museu de Lamego is one of Portugal's finest regional museums. The collection features five entrancing works by renowned 16th-century Portuguese painter Vasco Fernandes (Grão Vasco), richly worked Brussels tapestries from the same period, and an extraordinarily diverse collection of heavily gilded 17th-century chapels rescued in their entirety from the long-gone Convento das Chagas.

Sé   CATHEDRAL
(Largo da Sé; ⊙9am-1pm & 3-6.30pm) Older than Portugal itself, Lamego's striking *sé* has been declared a national monument. There is little left of the 12th-century original except the base of its square belfry. The rest of the structure, including the brilliantly carved Gothic triple portal, dates mostly from the 16th and 18th centuries. Arresting biblical frescoes and the high choir stalls are the work of 18th-century Italian baroque architect Nicolau Nasoni, who left his mark all over Porto.

✦ Festivals & Events

Festa de Nossa Senhora dos Remédios   RELIGIOUS
(www.aromariadeportugal.pt;) Lamego's biggest party runs from late August to mid-September. In an afternoon procession on 8 September, ox-drawn carts rattle through the streets carrying *tableaux vivants* (religious scenes represented by costumed people), and devotees slowly ascend the stairway on their knees. Less pious events in the run-up include rock concerts, folk dancing, car racing, parades and at least one all-night party.

🛏 Sleeping & Eating

Residencial Solar da Sé   GUESTHOUSE €
(☏254 612 060; Largo da Sé 7; s/d €34/45; ✳ 🖙) There are great deals to be had on rooms with French windows opening onto the *sé*. The carpet is a bit aged, but there's a funky modernist groove you might like. Or love.

Casa de Santo António de Britiande   GUESTHOUSE €€€
(☏254 699 346; www.casasantoantoniobritiande. com; Largo de São Sebastião, Britiande; r €115-130;

P✱🛜🞩) A stellar option just 5km south-east of Lamego in the village of Britiande, this lovely historic manor surrounded by fruit orchards has gorgeously landscaped gardens with a swimming pool. It's a great base for exploring the Alto Douro and tops for birdwatching tours. The friendly owner prepares delicious meals on request.

Trás da Sé
PORTUGUESE €

(📞254 403 996; www.facebook.com/restrasdase; Rua Virgilio Correia 12; mains €6.50-9; ⊙noon-3.30pm & 7-10pm Wed-Sun, noon-3.30pm Mon) Congratulations to the chef line the walls at this *adega*-style place, where the atmosphere is friendly, the menu short and simple, the food good and the local *vinho maduro* (matured wine) dirt cheap.

Mercado Municipal
MARKET €

(Avenida 5 de Outubre; ⊙7.30am-6pm Mon-Sat) Sells Lamego's famous hams and wines – ideal picnic food. Thursdays are especially busy.

🍷 Drinking & Entertainment

Old Rock Caffe
BAR

(Rua da Olaria 8; ⊙2pm-2am Mon-Sat, to midnight Sun) One of the town's most inviting bars, with an alternative vibe and great cocktails.

Teatro Ribeiro Conceição
THEATRE

(📞254 600 070; http://trc.cm-lamego.pt; Largo de Camões; tickets from €2.50) This handsomely restored theatre and cultural space hosts a wide range of programmes throughout the year, from children's puppet shows to classical concerts, orchestral concerts and ballets. There's also a cafe with outdoor seating.

ⓘ Information

Turismo (📞254 099 000; lojaturismo@cm-lamego.pt; Rua Regimento de Infantaria 9; ⊙10am-7pm Apr-Oct, 10am-1pm & 2-6pm Nov-Mar) Solid tourist office with knowledgeable, English-speaking staff.

ⓘ Getting There & Away

The most appealing route to Lamego from anywhere in the Douro valley is by train to Peso da Régua and by bus or taxi from there. A taxi from Régua costs about €15 to €20.

From Lamego's bus station, Rede Expressos (www.rede-expressos.pt) has daily bus service north to Peso da Régua (€6, 15 minutes), Vila Real (€6, 45 minutes) and Chaves (€11.90, two hours), and south to Viseu (€8.60, one hour) and Lisbon (€19.50, five hours). **Copy Print/Totola-mego** (📞254 619 447; Avenida Visconde Guedes

Teixeira 10; ⊙8am-8pm), a newsagent near the cathedral, sells tickets for these services.

Drivers take note: parking can be tight in Lamego.

Around Lamego

Lamego is a natural base for exploring the half-ruined monasteries and chapels in the surrounding environs, one of which dates back to the time of the Visigoths.

Capela de São Pedro de Balsemão
CHURCH

(www.culturanorte.pt/pt/patrimonio/capela-de-sao-pedro-de-balsemao; Balsemão; ⊙10am-1pm & 2-6pm Tue-Sun) FREE This mysterious little chapel was probably built by Visigoths as early as the 6th century. With Corinthian columns, round arches and intriguing symbols etched into the walls, it certainly pre-dates the introduction of even Romanesque architecture to Portugal. More ornate 14th-century additions were commissioned by the Bishop of Porto, Afonso Pires, who is buried under a slab in the floor.

Check out the ancient casket in the entrance chamber: supported by lions and intricately engraved, it depicts the Last Supper on one side and the Crucifixion on the other.

The chapel is tucked away in the hamlet of Balsemão, 3km northeast of Lamego above the Rio Balsemão. It's a pleasant downhill walk from Lamego through an old-world village, along a riparian corridor full of flowers, grapevines and wild shrubs, though it is a rather steep return trip. From the 17th-century Capela do Desterro at the end of Rua da Santa Cruz, head southeast over the river and follow the road to the left.

Mosteiro de São João de Tarouca
MONASTERY

(www.culturanorte.pt/pt/patrimonio/mosteiro-de-sao-joao-de-tarouca; Tarouca; adult/reduced €3/1.50; ⊙10am-1pm & 2-6pm Tue-Sun) The stunning, massive yet skeletal remains of Portugal's first Cistercian monastery, founded in 1124, stand eerily in the wooded Barosa valley below the Serra de Leomil, 15km southeast of Lamego. There is beauty in the decay, as a stream bisects the walls backed by a bowl of terraced hills. The monastery fell into ruin after religious orders were abolished in 1834.

Only the church, considerably altered in the 17th century, stands intact among the ghostly ruins of the monks' quarters. Its treasures include the gilded choir stalls, 18th-century *azulejos* (hand-painted tiles), and the church's pride and joy – a luminous *São Pedro* painted by Gaspar Vaz, contemporary and colleague of Grão Vasco.

From Lamego, Joalto/EAVT has several services each weekday (fewer on weekends) to Tarouca (€2.30).

Mosteiro de Salzedas MONASTERY
(www.culturanorte.pt/pt/patrimonio/mosteiro-de-santa-maria-de-salzedas; Salzedas; adult/reduced €3/1.50; ⊙10am-1pm & 2-6pm Tue-Sun) With picturesque pink stone arches, the Cistercian Mosteiro de Salzedas is located 3km up the Barosa valley from Ucanha in Salzedas. This was one of the grandest monasteries in the land when it was built in 1168 with funds from Teresa Afonso, governess to Afonso Henriques' children. The enormous church, which was extensively remodelled in the 18th century, is today a bit scruffy with decay, particularly its roofless cloisters next door; the faux crystal chandeliers are an odd sight, too.

Across from the church lies the old *judiaria* (Jewish quarter), with dark narrow lanes skirting around the gloomy centuries-old dwellings.

Peso da Régua
POP 9530

Gateway to the Alto Douro, the sun-bleached town of Régua abuts the Rio Douro at the western edge of the demarcated port-wine region. As the region's largest riverside town, it grew into a major port-wine entrepôt in the 18th century, and remains an important transport junction – thanks in part to the hulking IP3 bridge that soars overhead.

The town itself, set along a busy highway above the river, doesn't have a lot of charm. Most visitors stop in just long enough to visit the excellent Museu do Douro and get recommendations, maps and directions to nearby wineries. For those who linger, Régua makes a convenient base to visit the port-wine country, cruise the Rio Douro and take a scenic riverside train ride. Most tourists stick to the scenic riverfront, but the quaint old town one block uphill is an almost exclusively local scene, and well worth a wander.

◎ Sights & Activities

Museu do Douro MUSEUM
(www.museudodouro.pt; Rua Marquês de Pombal; adult/concession €6/3; ⊙10am-6pm Mar-Oct, to

5.30pm Nov-Feb) Bringing the Douro Valley's wine-producing history vividly to life, this wonderful museum has a wealth of artefacts and engaging displays, from a vast wall-size map of the river, annotated kilometre by kilometre, to old leather-bound texts, vintage port-wine posters and the remains of an old flat-bottomed port hauler. You'll find it all in a gorgeous converted riverside warehouse, with a restaurant and bar on-site. The gift shop, stocked with wine, handmade soaps, ceramics and jewellery, is also brilliant.

Comboio Histórico do Douro RAIL
(www.cp.pt; Estação CP, Largo da Estação; round-trip adult/child €42.50/19; ⊙Sat & Sun Jun-Oct) This restored steam train runs once daily on summer and autumn weekends along the Douro from Régua to Tua, making a 20-minute stop in Pinhão. For identical views without the vintage train flavour, hop aboard one of the five regular daily trains along this same route (each way €4.05, 45 minutes).

Tomaz do Douro CRUISE
(☑222 082 286; www.tomazdodouro.pt; Cais da Régua; cruises from €10) Offers different cruises along the Douro, including several that depart from Peso da Régua.

🛏 Sleeping

While lodging options in the town itself are rather uninspiring, the surrounding area has some of the best *quinta* (estate) accommodation you'll find anywhere in the Douro Valley, along with an exclusive five-star resort spa.

★ Casa do Romezal B&B €€
(☑919 866 186; www.casadoromezal.com; Calçada do Barreiro, Vilarinho dos Freires; d €90; ⊙Mar-Oct; ❋♿🐕🏊) Young brother-sister team Luis and Margarida run this charming B&B encircled by a small winery, set on a hillside that's been in their family since the 12th century. Three colourful, sunlit upstairs rooms share access to a swimming pool, a shaded front terrace with dreamy vineyard views, and a stone-walled library-lounge with wood stove, foosball table and vinyl record collection.

Guests enjoy free tours of the attached winery, along with tastings of the wine, olive oil and jams produced onsite.

Quinta de Marrocos GUESTHOUSE €€
(☑254 322 680; www.golddrink.pt/turismo; Estrada Nacional 222, Valdigem; s/d €72/80, with shared

bathroom €54/60; ❄️🛜) Housed in an old Franciscan monastery just 4km east of Régua on the left bank of the Douro, this estate has four comfortable rooms in a 17th-century house filled with family heirlooms. It is one of the oldest estates in the Douro, which has maintained viticultural activity for over four generations.

★**Six Senses Douro Valley**   HOTEL €€€
(📞254 660 600; www.sixsenses.com; Quinta de Vale Abraão, Samodães; r from €490; 🅿️❄️🛜🏊) European flagship of the luxury-minded Six Senses group, this gorgeously renovated, award-winning 19th-century manor house is nestled on an idyllic bend in the river 5km from Régua. The rooms, suites and villas are chic and sleek, the spa is extraordinary, and the restaurant is among the region's finest, with veggies from the on-site organic gardens and wine as the centrepiece.

Quinta da Pacheca   HERITAGE HOTEL €€€
(📞254 331 229; www.quintadapacheca.com; Rua do Relógio do Sol 261, Cambres; r €165-315; 🅿️🛜) One of the Douro's prime destinations for both wine tastings and overnight stays, Quinta da Pacheca sits in verdant countryside just south of Régua. It offers 15 rooms in a restored 18th-century manor, along with 10 brand-new rooms built inside giant wine barrels. Perks include a top-notch restaurant, guided wine tours and tastings, and complimentary bikes for guests' use.

Quinta do Vallado   HERITAGE HOTEL €€€
(📞254 318 081; www.quintadovallado.com; Vilarinho dos Freires; r €190-275; 🅿️❄️🛜🏊) This 70-hectare winery brings together five rooms in an old stone manor and eight swanky rooms in an ultramodern slate building, decked out with chestnut and teak wood, each complete with a balcony. They all share a gorgeous pool. Guests get a free tour of the winery, with a tasting. Cycling, hiking, fishing, canoeing – whatever your interest, just ask.

🍴 Eating

Tasca da Quinta   PORTUGUESE €€
(📞918 754 102; www.facebook.com/tascadaquinta; Rua Marquês de Pombal 42; mains €6.50-14.50; ⏱️7-11pm Tue-Fri, 12.30-3pm & 7-11pm Sat, 12.30-3pm Sun) This cosy, well-priced family-run restaurant offers small plates of well-prepared Portuguese classics, paired with a solid selection of local wines. It's best to book ahead.

A Tasquinha   PORTUGUESE €€
(📞254 318 070; Rua Branca Martinho; mains €9-17; ⏱️10am-10pm) Small and cosy, this tavern dishes out well-prepared regional mainstays with a focus on meat dishes. The portions are generous and the house wine of good quality.

Castas e Pratos   PORTUGUESE €€€
(📞254 323 290; www.castaspratos.com; Avenida José Vasques Osório; mains €20-35; ⏱️10.30am-11pm) The coolest dining room in town is set in a restored wood-and-stone railyard warehouse with exposed original timbers. You can order grilled *alheira* sausage or octopus salad from the tapas bar downstairs, or opt for green asparagus risotto or roasted kid goat and potatoes with turnip sprouts in the mezzanine.

ℹ️ Information

Loja Interativa de Turismo (📞254 318 152; www.cm-pesoregua.pt; Avenida do Douro; ⏱️9.30am-12.30pm & 2-6pm) Régua's high-tech tourist office, facing the Douro 1km west of the station, supplies information about the town and the region, including local accommodation and vineyards.

ℹ️ Getting There & Away

Rodonorte (www.rodonorte.pt) has at least two daily departures to Lamego (€5.90, 20 minutes) and Vila Real (€6.20, 25 minutes).

There are around 13 trains daily from Porto (€10, two hours); some continue up the valley to Pinhão (€2.80, 25 minutes) and Pocinho (€6.50, 1½ hours). If you've taken a train this far and want a car to visit the vineyards, your best bet is **Europcar** (📞254 321 146; www.europcar.com; Avenida João Franco; rental per day from €25).

To get to the *cais fluvial* (riverboat terminal) from the railway station, bear left at the traffic circle in front of the Império Hotel.

There is a public car park at the eastern end of the riverfront promenade.

ALTO DOURO

Heading upriver from Peso da Régua, terraced vineyards blanket every hillside, with whitewashed *quintas* (estates) perched high above the Douro. This dramatic landscape is the jaw-dropping by-product of over 2000 years of winemaking. While villages are small and architectural monuments few and far between, it's worth the trip simply for the panoramic ride itself (by car, train or boat).

Its allure has clearly not gone unnoticed. In 2001 Unesco designated the entire Alto Douro wine-growing region a World Heritage Site.

Further east towards Spain, the soil is drier, with the sculpted landscape giving way to more rugged terrain. But despite the aridity – and the blisteringly hot summers – the land around Vila Nova de Foz Côa produces fine grapes, olives and nuts.

Most recently, the construction of the Foz-Tua dam – completed in 2017 just metres from the Alto Douro – has sparked controversy among Portuguese environmental groups and the region's wine producers.

Pinhão & Around

Encircled by terraced hillsides that produce some of the world's best port – and some stellar table wines, too – pretty little Pinhão sits on a particularly lovely bend of the Rio Douro, about 25km upriver from Peso da Régua. Wineries and their competing signs dominate the scene. Even the delightful train station has azulejos (hand-painted tiles) depicting the grape harvest. The town itself, cute though it is, holds little of interest, but does makes a fine base for exploring the many surrounding vineyards.

In addition to drinking your fill, this is a good setting for country walks, and cruises along the river by boat or train.

🏃 Activities

Train to Pocinho   RAIL
(www.cp.pt) The most beautiful train trip in the area is this one-hour chug upriver along the Douro, leaving Pinhão for Pocinho five times daily (one-way €4.80, one hour).

Douro-a-Vela Boat Trips   BOATING
(☑918 793 792; www.facebook.com/douroavela; Folgosa; 2hr cruise €50) One of the sweetest thrills in the area demands that you simply lie back and cruise upriver into the heart of the Alto Douro aboard a sailboat. Catch the boat from the Folgosa do Douro pier, just outside DOC restaurant. The price listed is based on a six-person minimum (or pay €180 for two). Book ahead.

Quinta do Bomfim   WINE
(☑254 730 370; www.symington.com/visit-us; tours incl tasting from €17; ◷10.30am-7pm daily Mar-Oct, 9.30am-6.30pm Tue-Sun Nov-Feb) Conveniently located in downtown Pinhão, Symington's swanky *quinta* showcases a

small museum inside a restored historic winery. Multilingual guided tours (advance reservation required) offer views of the vineyards' ancient dry-stone terraces and visit the 19th-century lodge, where young wine is still aged in old wooden vats. Tours end in the gorgeous tasting room with its terrace overlooking the Douro.

Quinta Nova   HIKING, WINE
(☑254 730 430; www.quintanova.com; Covas do Douro; guided tour €16, incl tasting €20-110; ◷tours 10.45am, 12.15pm & 3.30pm year-round, plus 6pm Apr-Oct) Set on a stunning ridge, surrounded by luscious, ancient vineyards, overlooking the deep green Douro river with mountains layered in the distance, the Quinta Nova estate is well worth an in-depth exploration. The three hiking and biking trails (the longest is three hours) are the best in the region.

To get here, head 9km west of Pinhão, along the north bank of the Douro (EN322-2).

Quinta do Crasto   WINE
(☑254 920 020; www.quintadocrasto.pt; Gouvinhas, Sabrosa; tours incl tasting €20; ◷by appointment) Perched like an eyrie on a promontory above the Rio Douro and a spectacular ripple of terraced vineyards – amid the lyrical landscapes of the Alto Douro – Quinta do Crasto quite literally takes your breath away. Stop by for a tour and tasting (of four wines) or lunch (€65 with wine). Call ahead, as groups sometimes storm the place.

Quinta da Roêda   WINE
(☑220 109 830; www.croftport.com/en/visit-us/quinta-da-roeda-douro-valley; tours incl tasting €12-35; ◷10am-6pm) Just 1km east of Pinhão is this attractive *quinta* owned by the venerable Croft winery. Housed in old stables, it is traditional – all wood, stone and planks from the old lodges in Gaia – and surrounded by 110 hectares of vineyards. During harvest, it offers grape treading in three granite tanks called *lagares* (€24).

Quinta do Seixo   WINE
(☑254 732 800; www.sandeman.com/visit-us/douro/quinta-do-seixo; Tabuaco, Valença do Douro; tours from €13; ◷10.30am-1pm & 2-6.30pm) Worth visiting for its dizzying vistas alone, this gorgeous hilltop estate is the proud domain of Sandeman, one of the Douro Valley's oldest port producers. Visits begin with a propaganda-ish informational video, followed by a tour of the production facility,

but the real star here is the end-of-tour tasting, enhanced by mesmerising views across the vines to the sparkling Douro.

Quinta das Carvalhas WINE
(☑254 738 050; www.realcompanhiavelha.pt/pages/quintas/4; self-guided walk €10, bus/jeep tour €12.50/35, vintage tour incl premium wine tasting €90; ⊙10am-7.30pm Apr-Oct, to 6pm Nov-Mar) Just across the bridge from Pinhão, this *quinta* on the Douro's south bank welcomes visitors to its spiffy modern tasting room and wine shop, and offers a variety of vineyard tours climbing to a ridgeline with gorgeous views. Choose from a self-guided walk, an open-top bus tour, a jeep tour or a personalised vintage tour guided by the in-house agronomist.

Quinta do Tedo WINE
(☑254 789 165; www.quintadotedo.com; N222, Folgosa; tours incl 3-wine tasting €12, other tastings €22-60; ⊙10am-7pm Apr-Oct, 9am-5.30pm Nov-Mar) Blessed with sublime real estate carved by two rivers – the Douro and Tedo – this American-French-Portuguese–owned, 14-hectare estate offers short tours of their certified organic winery, followed by a tasting of port, table wine and organic olive oil. There's a lovely self-guided 3km hiking trail on the property that's wonderful for bird-watching.

Quinta do Panascal WINE
(☑254 732 321; www.fonseca.pt/en/visitors-centre; Valença do Douro; tours incl tasting €10-35; ⊙10am-6.30pm daily Easter-Oct, Mon-Fri rest of year) Producer of Fonseca ports, this lovely estate offers self-guided audio tours (in nine languages) through its beautifully sited vineyards, complemented by a variety of tasting options. It's about 15 minutes' drive west of Pinhão, well signed from the N222.

Quinta do Portal WINE
(☑259 937 000; www.quintadoportal.com; tours incl tasting €7.50; ⊙10am-1pm & 2-6pm) This award-winning vineyard produces ports, red and white table wines, and a little-known muscatel wine. The surrounding region is one of the only places in the country producing muscatel (the other is Setúbal). Tours include a visit to the cellar with a tasting of two wines.

Next door you'll find the quinta's popular **restaurant** (4-course menu incl wines €40; ⊙12.30-2pm & 7.30-9pm) and the Casa das Pipas guesthouse (doubles €120 to €160).

BIRD'S-EYE VIEW OF THE VINEYARDS

For jaw-dropping views of the Douro wine country, head for **Miradouro São Leonardo de Galafura** (Estrada São Leonardo, Galafura), a magnificent viewpoint between Peso da Régua and Pinhão. The N313-2 relentlessly switchbacks its way into the hills northeast from Régua, arriving a half-hour later at the overlook (640m), where the valley's full sweep spreads out before you, the Douro snaking off into the distance between kilometres of steeply terraced vineyards.

The winery lies about 12km north of Pinhão, along EN323, in the direction of Vila Real.

Sleeping

★Casa Cimeira INN €€
(☑914 550 477, 254 732 320; www.casacimeira-douro.com; Rua do Cimo do Povo, Valença do Douro; s/d €65/70; [P][※][@][☂][☀]) Set in a 200-year-old home at the top of the hilltop town of Valença – its cobbled streets wrapped with vineyards and olive tree groves and alive with old country warmth – this is the domain of the charming Nogueira family. Rooms are quaint and spotless, there's a small pool, a sun deck and family-style dinners featuring their own house wine.

Hotel Douro HOTEL €€
(☑254 732 404; www.hotel-douro.pt; Rua António Manuel Saraiva 39; s/d €50/65; [※][@][☂]) This cheery, well-kept hotel – the nicest of its kind in Pinhão – has spectacular Douro views from its river-facing front rooms, with other large rooms looking onto a quiet rear courtyard, and a delightfully shady terrace draped in flowering bougainvillea.

Quinta de Santo António INN €€
(☑254 789 177; www.quintasantoantonio.pt; N323, Adorigo; s/d €95/105; [P][※][@][☂][☀]) This stunning 25-hectare property is owned by the former winemaker for Sandeman. The drive up the steep, rutted dirt road is exciting, the perch high, the river and mountain views jaw-dropping, and the price fair. Don't leave until you've sipped their 25-year-old tawny. Get here via the road to Tabuaço.

DON'T MISS

SÃO SALVADOR DO MUNDO

A series of small chapels dotting the hillside, São Salvador do Mundo makes for a stunning diversion between Pinhão and Foz Côa. Follow the signs to these stone turnouts with scenic hill, vineyard and river views. Some have stone slab tables and benches that demand a picnic, surrounded by wildflowers and serenaded by birdsong. After lunch continue to the top of the road and stroll to the chapel on the pinnacle. Spectacular.

★ Quinta Nova INN €€€

(☑254 730 420; www.quintanova.com; Covas do Douro; s €185-280, d €195-290; 🛜🏊) Set on a ridge, surrounded by 120 hectares of ancient vineyards, overlooking the Douro river with mountains layered in the distance, Quinta Nova is simply stunning. Besides 11 plush rooms in a beautifully restored 18th-century manor, it offers romantic grounds, a pool, a restaurant, and wine tours and tastings.

Also on-site are some of the region's top walking trails – the longest of which is three hours – and a museum with a collection of vintage winemaking gear.

★ Morgadio da Calçada HERITAGE HOTEL €€€

(☑254 732 218, 915 347 555; www.morgadioda calcada.com; Rua Cabo de Vila 18, Provesende; r €120-140; 🅿✴🛜🏊) Housed in a 17th-century manor in the gorgeous hillside village of Provesende, a 20-minute drive from Pinhão, this welcoming guesthouse has eight minimalist rooms inside old stables, with skylights, pinewood floors and original details. Run by the 19th-generation owner, who also produces wine and soaps based on an old family recipe, this special hideaway serves up heritage and stories aplenty.

Casa de Casal de Loivos INN €€€

(☑927 283 122, 254 732 149; www.casa decasaldeloivos.com; Cabo da Rua, Casal de Loivos; s/d €150/170; @🏊) Nowhere in the Alto Douro will you find more magnificent river and vineyard views than at this elegant six-room house, owned by the same winemaking family for nearly 350 years. The halls are enlivened by museum-level displays of folkloric dresses, and the perch – up a steep cobbled road in the hilltop village of Casal de Loivos – is spectacular.

Perks include a swimming pool and sun terrace, trails through the vineyard just below and dinner (€27 excluding drinks, available upon request).

Quinta de la Rosa B&B €€€

(☑254 732 254; www.quintadelarosa.com; M590, Pinhão; d/ste from €135/195; 🅿🛜🏊) Gazing down over the banks of the Douro, the bright, appealing rooms at this riverside winery 2km west of Pinhão straddle different buildings, with private villas available for weekly rental. The attached restaurant, Cozinha da Clara, serves everything from tapas to multicourse meals perfectly paired with the *quinta's* own wines.

Vintage House Hotel HOTEL €€€

(☑254 730 230; www.vintagehousehotel.com; Rua António Manuel Saraiva; s/d from €185/245; 🅿✴@🛜🏊) Occupying a string of 19th-century buildings right on the palm-lined riverfront, this luxurious sleep has just been revamped by the team behind the Yeatman in Porto. The result is a clutch of 50 beautifully redone rooms and suites, 47 of which boast terraces or balconies with river views.

🍴 Eating

Papas Zaide PORTUGUESE €

(☑962 845 395, 254 731 899; Largo da Praça, Provesende; mains €8-10) A bit like wandering into your Portuguese grandmother's house, this quirky restaurant in Provesende village is all about simple, tasty home cooking. It often gets busy with tour groups, so call ahead to rustle up a table. The proprietress will ask if you prefer meat or fish; beyond that, everything is up to her whim – unpredictable, but always satisfyingly authentic.

★ DOC PORTUGUESE €€€

(☑254 858 123; www.ruipaula.com; Estrada Nacional 222, Folgosa; mains €31-34; ⊙12.30-3.30pm & 7.30-11pm) Architect Miguel Saraiva's ode to clean-lined, glass-walled minimalism, DOC is headed up by Portuguese star chef Rui Paula. Its terrace peering out across the river is a stunning backdrop. Dishes give a pinch of imagination to seasonal, regional flavours, from seafood *açordas* (stew) to game and wild mushrooms – all are paired with carefully selected wines from the cellar.

The restaurant is in Folgosa, midway between Peso da Régua and Pinhão, on the south side of the river.

Veladouro PORTUGUESE €€€

(☑254 738 166; Rua da Praia 3; mains €15-25; ⊙10am-midnight) Wood-grilled meats and fish are the speciality at this schist-walled restaurant by the riverfront. On sunny days, the vine-shaded front terrace is the place to be, with views of local fishermen under their umbrellas on the adjacent dock. From the train station, follow the main road left for 150m, then turn left again under a railway bridge to the river.

Cozinha da Clara PORTUGUESE €€€
(☑ 254 732 254; www.quintadelarosa.com/content/cozinha-da-clara; M590, Pinhão; tapas €2.50-15, mains €20-26, 3-course menu incl wine €50; ⊙ lunch 1-3pm, tapas 3-6pm, dinner 7-9.30pm) Whether you come for drinks, tapas and sunset over the river, or for one of the splendid three-course 'dinner parties' hosted by chef Pedro Cardoso, Quinta de la Rosa's (p408) recently launched restaurant is a delightful place to dine. Snag a table on the outdoor terrace if you can – views of the vineyards and the Douro flowing far below are breathtaking.

ⓘ Information

The tiny *turismo* in Pinhão is almost never open and doesn't have much information when it is. You're better off checking with the *turismo* in **Sabrosa** (☑ 259 937 130; turismo@cm-sabrosa. pt; Auditório Municipal, Rua do Loreto; ⊙ 10am-1pm & 2-7pm Mon-Fri, 10am-1pm Sat & Sun), 16km north, or Peso da Régua (p405), 29km to the west.

ⓘ Getting There & Away

Regional trains go to and from Peso da Régua (€2.80, 25 minutes, five daily), where you can catch an onward train to Porto.

It's best to have your own wheels if you want to explore the area independently, as some of the best spots are not accessible by public transport. Street parking is straightforward, except on high-season weekends; look around the train station or down by the river (first left after passing the train station).

Vila Nova de Foz Côa

POP 3030

In the heart of the Douro's *terra quente* (hot land), this once-remote, whitewashed town has been on the tourism map since the 1990s. That's when researchers – during an environmental impact study for a proposed dam – stumbled across an astounding collection of Palaeolithic art. These mysterious rock engravings, which number in the thousands, blanket the nearby Rio Côa valley. Archaeologists brought the petroglyphs to the world's attention, and the dam builders backed down when the whole valley was declared a Unesco World Heritage Site.

You may find the climate startlingly Mediterranean if you've just come from the mountains. Summers here are infernally hot, with temperatures regularly exceeding 45°C. But if you come in late March, you'll be treated to cooler climes, wildflowers and blooming almond trees.

◉ Sights & Activities

**Parque Arqueológico
do Vale do Côa** ARCHAEOLOGICAL SITE
(☑ 279 768 260; www.arte-coa.pt; Rua do Museu; each park site adult/child €15/5, museum €6/3; ⊙ museum & park 9.30am-6pm Tue-Sun Mar-May, to 7pm Jun-Sep, to 5.30pm Oct-Feb) Most visitors to Vila Nova de Foz Côa come for one reason: to see its world-famous gallery of rock art. Although the park is currently an active research zone, three sites are open to the public: Canada do Inferno, Ribeira de Piscos and Penascosa. While Penascosa has some of the most significant etchings, Canada do Inferno – which sits by the half-constructed dam – is the ideal place to understand just how close these aeons-old drawings came to disappearing.

Because the entire valley is a working archaeological site, all visitors must enter with a guided tour. Tours for Canada do Inferno depart at around 9.30am from the park museum in Vila Nova de Foz Côa; for Ribeira de Piscos at around 9.30am from the Muxagata visitor centre on the western side of the valley; and for Penascosa at around 9.30am from the Castelo Melhor visitor centre on the eastern side of the valley (which also offers €20 night tours departing from the museum).

Visitors gather at the various visitor centres, where they're taken, eight at a time, in the park's own 4WDs, for a guided tour of one of the sites (two hours at Canada do Inferno, which includes 1km of walking; one hour at Penascosa, with some walking; 2½ hours at Ribeira de Piscos, with 2km of walking). You can take in two sites in one day – one in the morning and one in the afternoon. There are guided bike tours (bring your own mountain bike) in similar-sized groups.

Visitor numbers are strictly regulated, so from July to September book a tour through the park office well in advance or you may miss out; reservations are accepted from

Tuesday through Sunday. You must book at least a few weeks ahead for bicycle trips at any time.

Make sure you bring comfortable shoes and a hat, sunscreen and water in summer months, as it gets extremely hot in the valley.

Old Town
AREA

The sleepy old quarter makes for a pleasant stroll in the early evening. Highlights include the Praça do Município, with its impressive granite *pelourinho* (stone pillory), and the elaborately carved portal of the Manueline-style parish church. Just east off the square is the tiny Capela de Santa Quitéria, once the town's synagogue.

Museu da Casa Grande
MUSEUM

(Rua Direita, Freixo de Numão; adult/reduced €2/1; ◎9am-noon & 2-6pm Tue-Sun) Archaeological finds from the Stone Age to the 18th century have been uncovered in the region around Freixo de Numão, 12km west of Vila Nova de Foz Côa. A good little display can be viewed in this baroque town house with Roman foundations. Some English and French is spoken. Guided tours are available by arrangement with the museum.

Miles Away
WINE, OUTDOORS

(☑938 749 528; www.milesaway.pt; Avenida Dr Artur Máximo Saraiva de Aguilar 8) This top-notch agency does tailor-made tours around the Douro and Côa valleys, focusing on wine, archaeology and nature. It can arrange visits to wine estates not normally open to the public, and lesser-known attractions such as the private Faia Brava Nature Reserve and the 200km-long Grande Rota do Vale Côa trail, along with close-to-nature lodging at its mobile 'Fly Camp'.

🛏 Sleeping & Eating

Pousada da Juventude
HOSTEL €

(☑279 764 041; www.pousadasjuventude.pt; Caminho Vicinal Currauteles 5; dm/d without bathroom €14/33, d €37; Ⓟ@◎) This hostel in a modern, pink-brick building is well worth the 800m walk north from the town centre (1.4km by road). Its basic but handsome doubles have views over a rugged valley; four-bed dorms are clean and well maintained. Amenities include a bar, open kitchen, laundry, cafeteria, games room and large patio with sweeping views.

Hotel Vale do Côa
HOTEL €€

(☑279 760 010; www.hotelvaledocoa.net; Avenida Cidade Nova; s/d €45/60; Ⓟ❄) This modern hotel near the tourist office offers comfortable, air-conditioned rooms with clean-swept wooden floors. Most rooms have verandas with views of the hilly countryside.

★ Casa do Rio
GUESTHOUSE €€€

(☑279 764 339; www.quintadovallado.com; Quinta do Orgal, Castelo Melhor; r/ste €250/350; Ⓟ❄◎≋) Set between the vineyards and the river, the all-wood Casa do Rio at Quinta do Orgal has a mix of rooms and suites offering stunning river views. Guests are welcomed with a full spectrum of amenities, from tours and tastings at the on-site winery to free use of bikes and fishing gear. There's a two-night minimum stay on weekends.

Restaurante Côa Museu
PORTUGUESE €€

(☑932 150 155; www.facebook.com/Coa MuseuRestaurante; Rua do Museu; mains €11-15; ◎10am-6pm Sun, Tue & Wed, to 11pm Thu-Sat) For lunch with a view, look no further than this contemporary Portuguese restaurant housed in Foz Côa's archaeological museum. Enjoy breathtaking perspectives on the Côa Valley while feasting on specialities such as grilled sea bass with local olives, or *posta de vitela mirandesa* (veal steak from nearby Miranda do Douro) served with wild mushrooms or apples in port wine.

Aldeia Douro
PORTUGUESE €€

(☑279 094 403; www.facebook.com/aldeiadouro; Rua Dr José Augo Saraiva de Aguilar 19; mains €7-15; ◎7-11pm Tue, 11.30am-3pm & 7-11pm Wed-Sat, 11.30am-3pm Sun) Great regional food is prepared with a twist at this friendly, contemporary restaurant with an attached wine bar. See their Facebook page for daily changing lunch specials.

❶ Information

Turismo (☑924 448 312; www.cm-fozcoa. pt; Avenida Gago Coutinho e Sacadura Cabral; ◎9am-12.30pm & 2-5.30pm)

❶ Getting There & Away

Long-distance coaches stop at the bus station about 150m north of the *turismo*. Rede Expressos (www.rede-expressos.pt) runs one bus daily from Vila Nova de Foz Côa to Bragança (€8.50, 1½ hours). Rodonorte (www.rodonorte.pt) has service to Miranda do Douro (€6.40, 2¼ hours), and to Viseu (€10.30, two hours) via Trancoso (€5.90, 40 minutes).

Five daily trains run to Pocinho, at the end of the Douro valley line, from Porto (€12.10, 4½ hours) and Peso da Régua (€6.50, 1½ hours), via

Pinhão (€4.80, one hour). A taxi between Pocinho and Vila Nova de Foz Côa costs around €10.

❶ Getting Around

Getting to the Foz Côa museum and visitor centres is much easier with your own wheels. In Vila Nova de Foz Côa, there is usually plenty of free parking near the *turismo* along Avenida Gago Coutinho.

A twice-daily bus passes the outskirts of Castelo Melhor (€2, 15 minutes); from there it's an easy walk to the Parque Arqueológico do Vale do Côa visitor centre. Alternatively, there is a taxi stand on the square in front of the park's office in Vila Nova de Foz Côa, and park guides often help organise carpools, too.

TRÁS-OS-MONTES

In Trás-os-Montes, despite its clutch of large towns, rural life is still the region's heart and soul, from the southwest's steep vineyard-clad hillsides, to the olive groves, almond orchards and rugged canyon-lands of the sun-baked east, and the chestnut-shaded, heathery highlands of the north.

Vila Real

POP 27,735 / ELEV 445M

Clinging to steep hillsides above the confluence of the Rios Corgo and Cabril, the university town of Vila Real is short on charm, although its historic centre, dotted with picturesque old churches, is pleasant enough. Its key attractions lie just beyond the city limits: the dramatically rugged highlands of the Parque Natural do Alvão; and the resplendent Casa de Mateus, one of Europe's most elegant country houses, surrounded by lovely vineyard country east of town.

◉ Sights

Vila Real's Gothic Sé (Travessa de São Domingos), once part of a Dominican monastery, has been restored to its 15th-century grandeur after a lengthy facelift. Other noteworthy churches in the historic centre include Capela Nova (cnr Ruas 31 de Janeiro & Direita) and Igreja de São Pedro (Largo de São Pedro), both resplendent with baroque architectural details and *azulejos* (hand-painted tiles).

★ **Casa de Mateus**　　　　PALACE
(☑ 259 323 121; www.casademateus.com; gardens €8.50, palace & gardens €12.50; ☺ 9am-6pm May-Oct, to 5pm Nov-Apr) Famously depicted on bottles of Mateus rosé, the 18th-century Casa de Mateus is one of Portugal's great baroque masterpieces – probably the work of Italian-born architect Nicolau Nasoni. Guided tours of the mansion (in English, French, Spanish and German) take you through the main quarters, which combine rusticity with restrained grandeur.

The palace's granite wings shelter a lichen-encrusted forecourt dominated by an ornate stairway and guarded by rooftop statues. Surrounding the palace is a fantasy of a garden, with tiny boxwood hedges, prim statues and a fragrant cypress tunnel that's blissfully cool on even the hottest days. (Don't miss the fanciful 5m-tall curved ladders used to prune the tunnel's exterior branches!)

Inside, the library contains one of the first illustrated editions of Luís Vaz de Camões' *Os Lusíadas,* Portugal's most important epic poem, while another room houses an unintentionally droll collection of religious bric-a-brac, including three dozen macabre relics bought from the Vatican in the 18th century: a bit of holy fingernail, a saintly set of eyeballs, and the inevitable piece of the true cross – each with the Vatican's proof of authenticity.

Near the guided tour starting point, the palace's *adega* (wine cellar) offers tastings of three locally produced ports (€5) or five DOP Douro wines (€4). Especially interesting is the Alvarelhão, which is essentially the same fine rosé originally bottled by Mateus in the 1940s.

The palace is 3.5km east of the town centre. Take Urbanos de Vila Real (www.urbanosvilareal.pt) bus 1 (€1.50, 15 minutes) towards the university (UTAD). It leaves from the Tribunal stop in Praça Luís de Camões, just north of the *turismo,* roughly half-hourly between 7.45am and 8.30pm, with fewer buses on weekends. Ask for 'Mateus' and the driver will set you down about 250m from the palace (if you don't ask, he may not stop).

Miradouro de Trás-do-Cemitério　VIEWPOINT
For a fine view across the gorge of the Rio Corgo and Rio Cabril, walk south to this panoramic viewpoint, just beyond a small cemetery and chapel.

Vila Real

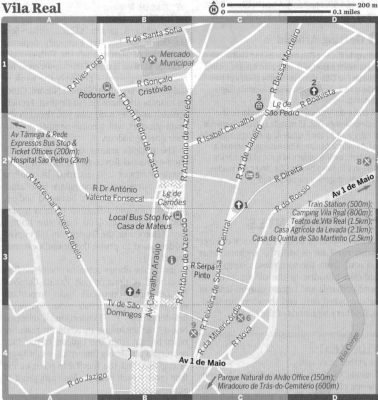

Vila Real

⊙ Sights

🛏 Sleeping

⊗ Eating

Museu Etnográfico de Vila Real   MUSEUM
(☑259 042 820; www.ccr-vilareal.pt; Largo de São Pedro 3; ⊙9am-noon & 2-5pm Mon-Fri) FREE This small museum documents the traditional culture of the surrounding highlands, with exhibits on linen-making, ceramics, games, musical instruments and local festivals.

🛏 Sleeping

Douro Village Hostel   HOSTEL €
(☑259 042 294; www.dourovillage.pt; Rua 31 de Janeiro 44; dm/d €15/35, breakfast per person €3 extra; ☜) With friendly service, plush dorms and a perfect downtown location, this recently opened hostel in a lovely old stone building fills a long-standing void in Vila Real's accommodation scene. The comfy upstairs lounge and pretty interior patio are just icing on the cake.

★ **Casa Agrícola da Levada**   INN €€
(☑259 322 190; www.casadalevada.com; Rua da Capela; s €58-75, d €68-85, 2-person studio €80, 4-person apt €140; 🅿☜▨) North of the centre at the end of a long, shady drive lies this ecofriendly gem. A collection of tastefully renovated old houses surrounds grounds that include rose gardens, grassy lawns, riverside paths and a swimming pool. The fabulous included breakfast abounds in locally sourced organic produce: freshly squeezed

OJ, homemade yoghurt and muesli, and outstanding olive oil.

The friendly, multilingual owners have deep roots in the region and are generous in sharing their knowledge of the area's highlights. Beautiful hand-drawn maps of local attractions including Casa de Mateus, Parque Natural do Alvão and the Douro Valley are available free, and there's an 'honesty shop' where guests can help themselves to glasses of wine, olive oil and other regional products throughout their stay.

Casa da Quinta de São Martinho   INN €€
(☑ 259 323 986; www.quintasaomartinho.com; Lugar de São Martinho, Mateus; d €65-80; P 🎅 ≋) Only 400m from the Casa de Mateus, this rambling granite-farmhouse-turned-inn is surrounded by pretty gardens. Rooms aren't fancy, but have wood-beamed ceilings and are traditionally furnished. Three-course dinners are served with advance notice.

✖ Eating

Numerous eateries are clustered in the historic centre, along the narrow streets just east of Avenida Carvalho Araújo. Self-caterers can stock up on local produce at the **Mercado Municipal** (Rua de Santa Sofia; ⊙ 8am-3pm Mon-Sat).

Transmontano   PORTUGUESE €
(Rua da Misericórdia 35-37; mains €6-13; ⊙ noon-3pm & 7-10pm Mon-Sat) Popular with locals, this plain-faced, family-run place in the central pedestrian zone serves delicious, belly-filling regional dishes.

Casa Lapão   CAFE €
(www.casalapao.pt; Rua de Misericórdia 53; pastries from €1; ⊙ 8.30am-7pm Wed-Mon) This spruce tearoom specialises in traditional local sweets, including *cristas de galo* (almond and egg paste in a flaky pastry dough) and *pitos de Santa Luzia* (made with pumpkin and cinnamon). For a savoury alternative, try the *covilhetes*, elegant swirls of pastry dough stuffed with veal.

Restaurante Cardoso   PORTUGUESE €
(☑ 259 325 329; Rua Miguel Bombarda 42; sandwiches €2.50-7.50; ⊙ noon-2am Mon-Fri, noon-2.30pm & 6.30pm-2am Sat) For late-night comfort food, Portuguese-style, this convivial downtown hole-in-the-wall is a perennial local favourite. The speciality here is Portugal's beloved *francesinha,* a toasted meat-and-cheese sandwich swimming in gravy,

best accompanied with fried potatoes and beer for the full-on, high-calorie effect.

Chaxoila   PORTUGUESE €€
(☑ 259 322 654; www.facebook.com/casadepasto chaxoila; EN2; mains €7-17.50; ⊙ 11am-11.45pm) A traditional roadside restaurant a little outside town on the EN2 towards Chaves, convivial Chaxoila serves up great daily specials such as *cabrito* (kid goat) and *açorda* (bread and shellfish stew) from the open-plan kitchen. With its vine-covered terrace, it is popular with locals, so book ahead. Many of the portions are fit for two.

☆ Entertainment

Teatro de Vila Real   PERFORMING ARTS
(☑ 259 320 000; www.teatrodevilareal.com; Alameda de Grasse) This slick, modern building, in a park-like area across the Corgo from the city centre, stages high-quality dance and theatre performances, along with classical, jazz and world music and frequent film screenings. At the back, the theatre's bright cafe overlooking the Corgo is popular with Vila Real's beau monde.

ℹ Information

Parque Natural do Alvão Office (☑ 259 302 830; pnal@icnf.pt; Largo dos Freitas; ⊙ 9am-12.30pm & 2-5.30pm Mon-Fri)

Turismo (☑ 259 308 170; www.portoenorte. pt; Avenida Carvalho Araújo 94; ⊙ 9am-1pm & 2-6pm) Located in a Manueline house in the town centre.

ℹ Getting There & Away

Several companies serve Vila Real. **Rodonorte** (☑ 259 340 710; www.rodonorte.pt) buses leave from a station on Rua Dom Pedro de Castro, 300m northwest of the *turismo*. **AV Tâmega** (☑ 259 322 928; www.avtamega.pt) and **Rede Expressos** (☑ 962 060 655; www.rede-expressos.pt) both operate from a lot slightly west of the Rodonorte station, at the corner of Rua Dom António Valente da Fonseca and Avenida Cidade de Ourense. Destinations served by these companies include Bragança (€10.50, 1¾ hours), Chaves (€7.60, 70 minutes), Lamego (€6, 45 minutes), Lisbon (€21.90, five to 5½ hours), Miranda do Douro (€12.80, 2¾ to 3¼ hours) and Porto (€9.50, 1½ hours).

Parque Natural do Alvão

With its rock-strewn highlands, schist villages, waterfalls and verdant pockets where cows graze in stone-walled pastures, the pristine Parque Natural do Alvão comes as a delightful revelation to travellers climbing from the hotter, drier country below. A drive of less than half an hour brings you from Vila Real to this extraordinary park straddling the central ridgeline of the Serra de Alvão, the highest peaks of which reach more than 1300m. The small (72 sq km) protected area remains one of northern Portugal's best-kept secrets and shelters a remarkable variety of flora and fauna, thanks to its position in a transition zone between the humid coast and the dry interior.

◉ Sights

The Rio Ôlo, a tributary of the Rio Tâmega, rises in the park's broad granite basin. A 300m drop above Ermelo gives rise to the spectacular Fisgas de Ermelo falls, the park's major tourist attraction.

★ Fisgas de Ermelo   WATERFALL
Just north of the town of Ermelo, on the N304 between Vila Real and Mondim de Basto, is a turn-off to the dramatic Fisgas de Ermelo waterfalls. From this junction, the road climbs 4km to an overlook with picture-perfect views of the falls and the rugged terrain surrounding them.

To see the falls from above, return to the main road and climb to a T-junction with a right-hand turn marked 'Varzigueto'. Follow the Varzigueto road a short distance and look for a pair of dirt roads on the right-hand side marked 'Piocas de Cima'. The first, signposted as '1.5km' is less rugged and more easily driven than the second, marked '600m'. Either entrance will eventually lead you to a footpath continuing down into the river gorge, where you'll find not only hair-raising views of the river plunging off a cliff face, but also (further up) a natural water slide and a series of pools perfect for cooling off on a hot day.

Ermelo   VILLAGE
The 800-year-old village of Ermelo is famous for its schist cottages capped with fairy-tale slate roofs. Once the main village of the region, it boasts traditional *espigueiros* (stone granaries), an ancient chapel, a sturdy granite *pelourinho* (pillory), a workshop that still practises the ancient local art of linen-making, and Ponte de Várzea – a Roman bridge rebuilt in medieval times.

The Ermelo turn-off is about 16km south of Mondim de Basto on the N304. The heart of town is about 1km uphill.

Lamas de Ôlo   VILLAGE
Set in a wide, verdant valley some 1000m above sea level, somnolent Lamas de Ôlo is the park's highest village, best known for its photogenic thatched roofs, as well as a nearby mill that was long driven by water from a crude aqueduct.

🏃 Activities

There are a number of fine hikes in the park. A 7km, three-hour jaunt around the southern village of Arnal is described in the Portuguese-language leaflet 'Guia do Percurso Pedestre', available at park offices. The signposted hike delivers views east beyond Vila Real to the Serra do Marão. While you're in Arnal, track down the slate-roofed centre for traditional handicraft techniques.

Another popular route is the 13km, five-hour loop through the high country starting just north of the Cimeira dam along the Vila Real–Lamas de Ôlo road. The trail, marked with red and yellow blazes, traverses the rock-strewn *planalto* (high plateau) for 8km to the village of Barreiro. From here, you can return 5km by road to your starting point, passing through Lamas de Ôlo en route.

The park's newest hike is a 12km loop to the impressive Fisgas de Ermelo waterfall. Inaugurated in 2018, it's clearly signposted opposite the village church in Ermelo.

🛏 Sleeping & Eating

Dona Benedita   GUESTHOUSE €
(☑ 255 381 221; s/d €25/50) In Ermelo, Dona Benedita rents out three rooms, one of which has an en suite bathroom.

Tasquinha d'Alice   PORTUGUESE €
(☑ 255 381 381; www.facebook.com/TasquinhaDAlice; Bobal; snacks €2.50-7; ⊙ 10am-9.30pm, closed Sep) In Bobal, halfway between Lamas de Ôlo and Mondim de Basto, Tasquinha d'Alice is recommended for its all-day snacks, such as great *alheira* (a light, garlicky sausage of poultry or game) as well as *salpicão* (small rounds of baked ham) omelette.

The open front porch, adorned with cow horns, saddles and sturdy wooden tables, is a delightful spot to relax, as is the back room with lovely vistas.

ℹ Information

Exploring the park on your own is not simple, as maps, accommodation and public transport are limited. Whether you plan to walk or drive in the park, it's worth visiting one of the park offices, located in Vila Real (p413) and Mondim de Basto (p415), beforehand. The Casa Agrícola da Levada (p412) in Vila Real is another excellent resource, providing free, beautifully hand-drawn maps of the park for overnight guests.

❶ Getting There & Away

Public transport within the park is extremely limited; having your own wheels is preferable.
Transcovizela (☐ 253 415 015) runs from Mondim de Basto to Lamas de Ôlo (€3.15, 50 minutes) twice on Tuesdays and Fridays.

Mondim de Basto

POP 7490 / ELEV 200M

Sitting in the Tâmega valley at the intersection of the Douro, Minho and Trás-os-Montes regions, Mondim de Basto has no compelling sights beyond a few flowery squares, but it makes an attractive base from which to explore the Parque Natural do Alvão. The vineyards surrounding town cultivate grapes used in the fine local *vinho verde*.

🏃 Activities

At **Senhora da Ponte**, 2km south of town on the N304, there's a rocky swimming spot by a disused watermill on the Rio Cabril. Follow the signs to the Parque de Campismo de Mondim de Basto and then take the track to the right.

Capela da Senhora da Graça   HIKING
Hikers wanting to feel a little burn in their thighs should consider the long haul up to the 18th-century Capela da Senhora da Graça on the summit of pine-clad Monte Farinha (996m). It takes about two hours to reach the top. The path starts east of town on the N312 (the *turismo* has a rough map).

By car, turn off the N312 3.5km from Mondim towards Cerva; from there it's a twisting 9.5km to the top.

Casa Santa Eulália   WINE
(☐ 255 386 111; www.casasantaeulalia.pt; Atei) **FREE** Eight kilometres north of town in Atei, the 17th-century Casa Santa Eulália, set amid 32 hectares of vineyards, offers free tastings of its refreshing local *vinho verde* with advance notice.

🛏 Sleeping & Eating

Quinta do Fundo   INN €
(☐ 255 381 291; www.quintadofundo.com; Vilar de Viando; r/ste €50/75; P❷❸❹) Rooms are

mostly tired-looking and unadorned at this spot 2km south of town just off the N304 – but the setting amid a sea of vineyards is lovely, with fine mountain vistas, a tennis court, bikes for rent and a swimming pool. The *quinta* (estate) also produces its own *vinho verde*.

Mondim Hotel & Spa   HOTEL €€
(☐ 255 381 062; www.mondimhotelespa.pt; Av da Igreja 19; d €55-75; P❋❷) Smack in the heart of town, this place offers a set of clean if soulless rooms with good amenities. The onsite spa has a Jacuzzi, sauna and gym. Ask about midweek discounts.

Adega Sete Condes   PORTUGUESE €€
(☐ 255 382 342; www.facebook.com/AdegaRegional7Condes; Rua Velha; mains €8-14; ⊙noon-3pm & 7.30-11pm Tue-Sun) Tucked into a tiny corner near the *turismo,* this rustic, granite-walled spot has a small menu of well-prepared traditional dishes, including locally raised *maronesa* beef, *bacalhau* (cod) and a very tasty *feijoada* (pork and bean stew).

❶ Information

Parque Natural do Alvão Office (☐ 255 381 209; www.natural.pt; Lugar do Barrio; ⊙9.30am-noon Tue-Thu, 9.30am-noon & 2.30-4.30pm Fri) About 700m west of the *turismo.*
Turismo (☐ 255 389 370; www.cm-mondim-debasto.pt; Praça do Municipio; ⊙9am-1pm & 2-5pm Mon-Fri, 9am-1pm Sat) Has loads of local information.

❶ Getting There & Away

Buses stop behind the *mercado municipal,* 150m east of the *turismo* and what remains of the old town. Transdev (www.transdev.pt) has six weekday and two to four weekend buses to Porto (€7, 2¼ hours) via Guimarães (€4.50, 1½ hours). For Vila Real (weekdays only), take a Transcovizela (p415) bus to Aveção do Cabo and change there for the short-hop Rodonorte bus to Vila Real (€4.85, 50 minutes, three daily).

Chaves

POP 22,360 / ELEV 340M

A spa town with a long and fascinating history, Chaves (*shahv*-sh) is a pretty and engaging place, straddling the mountain-fringed banks of the Rio Tâmega only a few kilometres south of the Spanish border. Its well-preserved historic centre is anchored at the edges by a 16-arched Roman bridge (p417) dating back to Trajan's reign, a

Chaves

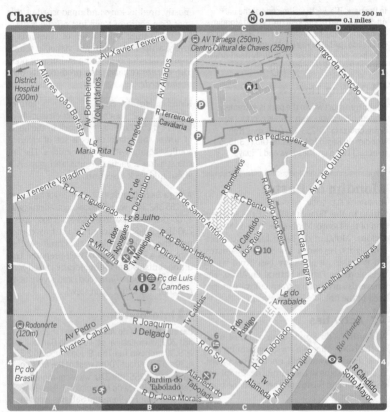

Chaves

◉ Sights
1 Forte de São Francisco	C1
2 Museu da Região Flaviense	B3
Museu Militar	(see 4)
3 Ponte Romana	D4
4 Torre de Menagem	B3

✦ Activities, Courses & Tours
5 Termas de Chaves	B4

🛏 Sleeping
Forte de São Francisco	(see 1)
6 Hotel Kátia	C4

✕ Eating
7 Carvalho	C4
8 Paprika & Cacau	B3
9 Pastelaria Maria	B3

◉ Drinking & Nightlife
10 Adega Faustino	C3

beautiful medieval tower and the rock-solid Forte de São Francisco.

All of these remnants testify to Chaves' earlier strategic importance in controlling the small but fertile plain that surrounds it. The Romans built a key garrison here, which was subsequently contested by the Visigoths, Moors, French and Spanish. The city saw particularly fierce fighting during the Napoleonic invasion, when it was at the forefront of the resistance against French domination.

Nowadays Chaves is a placid backwater, where the Portuguese come to pamper themselves in the natural hot springs that bubble up in the town's heart.

The backbone of Chaves' old town is Rua de Santo António, which runs northwest from the Roman bridge. The spa is near the river, just south of the centre.

There's plenty of free public parking below the Torre da Menagem and around Jardim do Tabolado.

Sights

Forte de São Francisco   FORT
Reached by a drawbridge and bordered by a park with floral designs, hedges and grand old oaks, the 17th-century Forte de São Francisco is the centrepiece of Chaves' old town. The fort, with its thick walls, was completed in 1658 around a 16th-century Franciscan convent. These days it's a top-end hotel (p418), though nobody minds if you snoop around inside the walls.

Ponte Romana   BRIDGE
Chaves' 140m-long Roman-era bridge makes a lovely place for a car-free stroll. The span was completed in AD 104 by order of Emperor Trajan (hence its other name, Ponte Trajano). It likely served as a key link on the important road between Braga and Astorga (Spain), as two engraved Roman milestones on the centre of the bridge indicate.

Museu da Região Flaviense   MUSEUM
(Praça de Luís Camões; ⊙9.30am-1.30pm & 2.30-6.30pm) FREE Small but interesting, this regional archaeological-ethnographic museum has lots of Roman artefacts, plus a collection of pre-Roman jewellery, bronze tools, grinding stones and menhirs, some dating back over 2500 years. There are also temporary art displays upstairs.

Torre de Menagem   TOWER
The lovely Torre de Menagem (castle keep) stands alone on a grassy embankment behind Chaves' main square, the only major remnant of a 14th-century castle built by Dom Dinis. Around the tower are attractive manicured flowerbeds and a stretch of old defensive walls, with views over the town and countryside. For even better views, visit the **Museu Militar** (€1; ⊙9.30am-1.30pm & 2.30-6.30pm), where a series of creaky staircases climbs past a motley collection of military gear to the tower's panoramic rooftop terrace.

Activities

Termas de Chaves   SPA
(☑276 332 445; www.termasdechaves.com; Largo das Caldas; 1-/2-/3-day spa packages from €60/79/99, additional treatments €10-60; ⊙9am-1pm & 2-7pm Mon-Sat, to 1pm Sun) The warm waters of the Termas de Chaves, which emerge from the ground at 73°C, are said to relieve a variety of ailments, from rheumatism to obesity. One- to three-day spa packages featuring everything from steam baths to massages are complemented by a plethora of additional treatments.

Sleeping

Budget accommodation is clustered along Rua do Sol in the historic centre. For a bit more character and charm, consider the slew of attractive rural inns in the hills surrounding town. Book ahead in summer, when the spa is in full swing. Most places offer big discounts from September to May.

Hotel Kátia   HOTEL €
(☑276 324 446; Rua do Sol 28; d/tr from €42/53; ❋ ❷) This family-run place offers small, stylish rooms – some with verandas – plus a decent restaurant downstairs. Get one of the rooms facing the street.

Quinta do Rebentão   CAMPGROUND €
(☑276 322 733; www.cccchaves.com; Vila Nova de Veiga; sites per adult/child/tent/car €3.20/2.20/2.60/3, 2-/4-person bungalows €40/52; ⊙Jan-Nov; @ ❷ ❄) Six kilometres southwest of Chaves, just off the N2, is this grassy, partly shaded suburban camping facility with free hot showers, pool access and basic supplies.

Quinta de Santa Isabel   INN €
(☑276 351 818; www.quintadesantaisabel.com.pt; Santo Estêvão; 2-/4-person apt €50/80; P ❷ ❄) This cluster of five lovely stone houses – some dating back to the 16th century and converted from haylofts or stables – sits at the foot of a vineyard-covered hillside in the tiny town of Santo Estêvão, 7km northeast of Chaves. Each kitchen-equipped unit features a fireplace or woodstove, and charming details such as ancient wood floors, stone walls and antique furniture.

Quinta da Mata   INN €€
(☑276 340 030; www.quintadamata.net; Estrada Nacional 213, Vilar de Nantes; d €65-80, ste €80-100; P @ ❷ ❄) This isolated, family-friendly country haven, 4.5km southeast of Chaves off the N213, centres on a lovingly restored, elegantly appointed 17th-century manor house with terracotta tile floors and stone walls. The grounds include tennis courts, a sauna and beautiful, flower-filled gardens on the lush hills overlooking the city. Breakfasts include local ham and other regional treats. Bikes are free for guests.

★Pedras Salgadas   BUNGALOW €€€
(☑259 437 140; www.pedrassalgadaspark.com; Bornes de Aguiar; d/q €180/190; P ❋ ❷ ❄) ✐

Fully equipped ecobungalows and a couple of treehouses are scattered around the woodlands of a spa park on the edge of Bornes de Aguiar, 30km south of Chaves. Shaded by tall trees, each spare and stylish cabin comes with grey slate-tiled walls, private decks and lots of glass surfaces.

Vidago Palace HOTEL €€€
(☎276 990 920; www.vidagopalace.com; Parque de Vidago, Vidago; r €225-370, ste from €400; P ❄ @ 📶 ≋) This salmon-pink grand palace in the spa town of Vidago, 12km south of Chaves, sits among the top rungs of Portugal's luxury hotels. The belle epoque grand dame showcases opulent rooms and suites, a gourmet restaurant in a ballroom, an 18-hole golf course, and a white-marble spa for taking in the natural spring waters.

Forte de São Francisco HISTORIC HOTEL €€€
(☎276 333 700; www.fortesaofrancisco.com; Rua do Terreiro da Cavalaria; s €65-110, d €80-150, ste €145-180; P ❄ @ ≋) For stylish digs in downtown Chaves, look no further than this remarkable historic inn. Housed in a 16th-century convent within the walls of the city's 17th-century fort, this extraordinary blend of four-star hotel and national monument has flawless rooms, as well as tennis courts and a sauna, plus a rare-bird aviary, centuries-old private chapel and an upscale restaurant and bar.

Eating & Drinking

Paprika & Cacau TAPAS €
(☎276 402 137; www.facebook.com/paprikaecacau; Rua da Infantaria 19; small plates €6-7; ⏲11am-3pm & 7-11pm Mon & Wed-Sat, 11am-3pm Tue) Right in the historic heart of Chaves, with views of the castle, this quaint Galician-owned restaurant serves up locally sourced Spanish-style treats in portions larger than normal tapas but smaller than full meals.

Pastelaria Maria BAKERY €
(☎276 324 139; www.facebook.com/MariaPasteis; Largo do Município 4; snacks from €0.60; ⏲7am-6.30pm Mon-Sat, to 1pm Sun) Look for the bright blue door of this tiny bakery, which whips up the best *pasteis de Chaves* (flaky turnovers filled with ground meat) in town.

Carvalho PORTUGUESE €€
(☎276 321 727; www.restaurante-carvalho.com; Largo das Caldas 4; mains €8.50-19; ⏲noon-3pm & 7-11pm Tue-Sat, noon-3pm Sun) Carvalho's top-notch regional dishes have earned recognition as some of Portugal's best. It is hidden away amid the cluster of parkside cafes opposite the Jardim do Tabolado.

Adega Faustino WINE BAR
(Travessa Cândido dos Reis; ⏲noon-3pm & 7-10pm Mon-Sat) Resembling a fire station from the outside, this cavernous ex-winery oozes atmosphere inside, with cobblestoned floors and gigantic wine casks lined up behind the bar. The menu features a long list of carefully prepared regional snacks (€4 to €9), from *salpicão* (sausage) to pig's ear in vinaigrette sauce, plus an excellent selection of quaffable local wines.

Entertainment

Centro Cultural de Chaves PERFORMING ARTS
(☎276 333 713; www.facebook.com/AuditorioCCChaves; Largo da Estação) Chaves' cultural centre stages regular concerts, plays and other events, most of them free of charge. For details on current shows, see the monthly *Agenda Cultural*, available at the *turismo*.

Information

Turismo (☎276 348 180; turismo@chaves.pt; Praça de Luís Camões; ⏲9.30am-1.30pm & 2.30-6.30pm Apr-Oct, to 6pm Nov-Mar; 📶) Helpful multilingual tourist office inside Museu Flaviense.

Getting There & Away

AV Tâmega (☎276 332 384; www.avtamega.pt; Largo da Estação) and **Rodonorte** (☎276 318 143; www.rodonorte.pt; Av de Santo Amaro) have terminals just north and west of the centre respectively. Both serve the following destinations: Bragança (€12, three hours), Coimbra (€16.60, 3¾ hours), Lisbon (€22.80, 6¼ hours), Porto (€13.60, 2½ hours) and Vila Real (€8.10, one hour, several daily).

Bragança

POP 23,190 / ELEV 650M

The historical capital of Trás-os-Montes, Bragança is at once a modern city of broad sterile avenues and suburban high-rises, and an overgrown medieval village from whose crenellated heights one can still survey the surrounding countryside and see small farms, fields and oak-chestnut forest. While many streets – especially some in the older *centro* – give the appearance of a town down on its luck, new construction and civic projects express Bragança's enduring

Bragança

Bragança

Sights
1 Centro de Arte Contemporânea Graça Morais	B1
2 Cidadela	D3
3 Domus Municipalis	D3
4 Igreja de Santa Maria	D3
5 Museu do Abade de Baçal	C1
6 Museu Ibérico da Máscara e do Traje	D2
Museu Militar	(see 8)
7 Pelourinho	D2
8 Torre de Menagem	D2

Sleeping
9 Arco da Velha	D2
10 Hotel Tulipa	A1
11 Pousada de São Bartolomeu	C3

Eating
12 Solar Bragançano	B2

Entertainment
13 Teatro Municipal	A1

pride and dynamism. Modern additions to the city's cultural life include a municipal theatre, museums dedicated to contemporary art and regional folk traditions, and eye-catching public sculptures such as the bronze postman outside the *correio* (post office) and the massive fighting bulls in the Rotunda do Lavrador Transmontano.

History

Known as Bragantia to the Celts and Juliobriga to the Romans, Bragança is an ancient city. Its location, mere kilometres from the Spanish border, made it an important post in the centuries-long battles between Spain and Portugal. The walled citadel was built in 1130 by Portugal's first king, Afonso Hen-

riques I. His son and successor, Sancho I, improved the fortifications by building Bragança's castle, with its watchtowers, dungeons and keep, in 1187, after reclaiming the city from the king of León.

In 1442 Afonso V created the Duchy of Bragança for his uncle, an illegitimate son of the first Avis king João I, thus launching one of Portugal's wealthiest and most powerful noble families. The Braganças assumed the Portuguese throne in 1640, ending Spain's 60-year domination of Portugal. The family went on to reign in Portugal until the dissolution of the monarchy in 1910, and held sway in Brazil through 1889, when the second Brazilian emperor Dom Pedro II was deposed in a military coup.

A PORCINE MYSTERY

Hundreds of crudely carved granite pigs, or boars, known as *berrões* are still scattered around the more remote parts of Trás-os-Montes and over into Spain. While they're widely acknowledged to be Celtic in origin, nobody knows for sure what purpose they served. Theories abound: they may have been symbols of fertility or prosperity, grave guardians, offerings to Iron Age gods, manifestations of the gods themselves or simply property markers.

You can see these mysterious pigs in museums in Bragança, Chaves and Miranda do Douro, or in situ in Bragança's citadel, where a weather-beaten porker supports a medieval pillory. The best-preserved example sits heavily atop a pedestal in the central square of tiny Murça, 30km northeast of Vila Real.

During the Napoleonic Wars, Bragança again served as an important strategic point against foreign invaders: it was from here that Sepúlveda launched his call to resistance against French forces.

◉ Sights

Cidadela
FORTRESS

Climb uphill from Largo de São Vicente and you'll soon set foot inside the astonishingly well-preserved 12th-century citadel. People still live in its narrow, atmospheric lanes, unspoilt by the few, low-key handicrafts shops and cafes that have crept in.

Within the ruggedly ramparted walls is the original castle – built by Sancho I in 1187 and beefed up in the 15th century by João I, then heavily restored in the 1930s. The stout Torre de Menagem was garrisoned up until the early 20th century. It now houses the Museu Militar (Military Museum; €2, Sun morning free; ⊙ 9-11.30am & 2-4.30pm Tue-Sun), the four floors of which are filled with swords, guns and suits of armour spanning several centuries, from medieval times to WWI and the Salazar dictatorship's colonial exploits. The price of admission is well worth the chance to climb to the top of the crenellated tower, with great views all around. In front of the *torre* is an extraordinary, primitive pelourinho atop a granite boar similar to the *berrões* found around the province.

Squatting at the rear of the citadel is an odd pentagonal building known as the Domus Municipalis (⊙ 9am-5pm Tue-Sun), the oldest town hall in Portugal (although its precise age is a matter of scholarly disagreement) and one of the few examples of civil Romanesque architecture on the Iberian Peninsula. Bragança's medieval town council once met upstairs in an arcaded room studded with weathered stone faces of man and beast, and scratched with symbols of the stonemasons.

Beside the Domus Municipalis is the early-16th-century Igreja de Santa Maria. Of particular interest are its brick Mudéjar columns, vividly painted ceiling, and a 17th-century Santa Maria Madalena at the high altar, with her traditional long hair and ragged garb.

Museu do Abade de Baçal
MUSEUM

(www.mabadebacal.com; Rua Abílio Beça 27; adult/reduced €3/1.50; ⊙ 9.30am-12.30pm & 2-6pm Tue-Sun) Set in a restored 18th-century bishop's palace, this is one of Portugal's best regional museums. Its diverse collections include local artefacts from the Celtic and Roman eras, along with objects, paintings and photographs depicting daily life in Trás-os-Montes from medieval times to the present.

Of particular interest are the handful of Iron Age stone pigs called *berrões*. The museum also features works by Portuguese naturalist painter Aurélia de Sousa and her contemporaries, as well as Christian pieces from India, which depict Jesus in a style highly influenced by Hindu and Buddhist art.

Museu Ibérico da Máscara e do Traje
MUSEUM

(Iberian Mask & Costume Museum; https://museudamascara.cm-braganca.pt; Rua Dom Fernão o Bravo 24/26; adult/child €1/0.50; ⊙ 9am-1pm & 2-5pm Tue-Sun) This visually appealing little museum displays a colourful and fascinating collection of masks and costumes from the ancient pagan-based solstice and Carnaval festivities celebrated in Trás-os-Montes and neighbouring Zamora (Spain). Costumes are displayed across three floors, with the upper exhibits dedicated to the work of local artisans.

Centro de Arte Contemporânea Graça Morais
MUSEUM

(https://centroartegracamorais.cm-braganca.pt; Rua Abílio Beça 105; adult/student €2/1, Sun morning free; ⊙ 10am-6.30pm Tue-Sun) This cross-border collaboration between Portugal and Spain has a permanent collection that features local painter Graça Morais' haunting portraits of Trás-os-Montes residents, alongside more abstract work. The modern annexe showcases rotating special exhibitions, and there's a cafe with a lovely patio.

🎊 Festivals & Events

Feira das Cantarinhas
FAIR

Bragança's biggest annual market, Feira das Cantarinhas, runs for three days in early May. It's a huge street fair of traditional handicrafts (a *cantarinha* is a small terracotta pitcher) held around the centre and Praça da Sé.

🛏️ Sleeping

Hotel Tulipa
HOTEL €

(☑273 331 675; www.tulipaturismo.com; Rua Dr Francisco Felgueiras 8-10; s/d €43/48; ❄️ 🛜) The Tulipa offers clean and comfortable contemporary rooms, most with flat-screen TVs, and some adapted for visitors with disabilities. An additional plus is the central location between the bus station and downtown. The downstairs restaurant serves great-value weekday lunch specials.

Ibis Bragança
HOTEL €

(☑273 302 520; http://ibis.accorhotels.com; Avenida das Forças Armadas, Rotunda Lavrador; r not incl breakfast from €38; P ❄️ 🛜) Just off the IP4 north of town, the Ibis is nicer than most hotels in the centre, despite its bland chain-hotel predictability. The rooms are small but bright and cheery, and the staff friendly.

Arco da Velha
APARTMENT €€€

(☑966 787 784; www.turismobraganca.com; Rua Dom Fernão o Bravo; 2-bedroom apt €130; P 🛜) The only place to stay within Bragança's atmospheric medieval citadel, this comfy split-level apartment sleeps up to five, allows pets and has its own parking spot just outside. Minimum stay two nights.

Pousada de São Bartolomeu
POUSADA €€€

(☑273 331 493; www.pousadas.pt; Estrada do Turismo; r €132-194; P ❄️ @ 🛜 🏊) This whitewashed modern affair may not be the most arresting *pousada* (upmarket inn) in Portugal, but its views over the Cidadela and countryside are way up there. It sits on a hilltop 1.5km south of the centre, and boasts a great restaurant and bright contemporary rooms with balconies overlooking the pool and castle.

🍴 Eating

Solar Bragançano
PORTUGUESE €€

(☑273 323 875; Praça da Sé 34; mains €8.50-14.50; ⊙noon-3pm & 7-10pm Tue-Sun) Upstairs in a manor house opposite the cathedral square, this elegant eatery boasts oak-panelled rooms, wide plank floors, a leafy and sun-dappled outdoor terrace, and a seasonal menu weighted towards local game, with specialities including wild boar, partridge with grapes, and pheasant with chestnuts.

O Geadas
PORTUGUESE €€

(☑273 326 002; www.facebook.com/RestauranteGeadas; Rua do Loreto; mains €13-19; ⊙noon-4pm & 7pm-midnight Tue-Sat, noon-4pm Sun) The unassuming roadside exterior can be deceptive: the food is stellar at this traditional restaurant with a spacious dining room. It has a long-standing tradition of hospitality and great service, with award-winning dishes like *couscous de cogumelos com perdiz estufada* (mushroom couscous with stewed partridge).

O Abel
PORTUGUESE €€

(☑273 382 555; www.oabel.pt; Rua do Sabor, Gimonde; mains €10-15; ⊙noon-2.30pm & 7.15-10pm Mon-Wed, Fri & Sat, noon-2.30pm Sun) Well-known for top-notch barbecues prepared by Mr Abel himself, this long-established, family-run restaurant 7km east of Bragança draws crowds from all over the region for delicious veal steaks, lamb, smoked sausage and other locally sourced grilled meats.

Dom Roberto
PORTUGUESE €€

(☑273 302 510; www.amontesinho.pt/restaurante-tipico-dom-roberto; Rua Coronel Álvaro Cepeda 1, Gimonde; mains €10-16; ⊙noon-2.30pm & 7-10pm) Catch a cab out to this traditional roadside tavern 7km from town, in the village of Gimonde en route to Montesinho. The ambience is down-home rural – think wooden beams and smoked hams hanging off the walls – and the food is the real deal.

Try the D Roberto steak, starters such as *alheira* (a light, garlicky sausage of poultry or game) and *salpicão* (pork sausage) and the delicious *milho doce* (sweetcorn) dessert.

⭐ Entertainment

Teatro Municipal
PERFORMING ARTS

(☑273 302 744; http://teatromunicipal.cm-braganca.pt; Praça Cavaleiro Ferreira) The boxy Teatro Municipal hosts high-quality music, theatre and dance shows, plus afternoon performances for children. There's a multiscreen cinema next door.

ⓘ Information

Parque Natural de Montesinho Office (☏ 273 329 135; www.icnf.pt; Parque Florestal de Bragança; ⊗ 9am-5.30pm Mon-Fri) Northeast of the *turismo*.

Turismo (☏ 273 381 273; www.cm-braganca. pt; Avenida Cidade de Zamora; ⊗ 9.30am-1pm & 2-5.30pm Mon-Fri) Helpful office north of the centre.

ⓘ Getting There & Away

BUS

Bragança's spiffy modern bus station, housed in the former train depot at the top of Avenida João da Cruz, is served by **Rede Expressos** (☏ 966 482 215; www.rede-expressos.pt) and **Rodonorte** (☏ 273 300 180; www.rodonorte.pt). Station offices tend to be open only at departure times.

BUSES FROM BRAGANÇA

TO	COST (€)	TIME (HR)	FIRM	DEPARTS
Braga	14.70	3	Rodo-norte (R)	daily
Guimarães	13.80	2¾	R	daily
Lisbon	22.80	7	R, Rede Expres-sos (RE)	3 times a week
Porto	14.30	3	R, RE	daily
Trancoso	10.90	2	RE	daily
Vila Nova de Foz Côa	8.50	1½	RE	daily
Vila Real	10.50	1¾	R, RE	daily
Viseu	14.70	3¼	R, RE	daily

CAR & MOTORCYCLE

Parking is generally not difficult. There are lots of paid spots in the square just south of the *sé*, with free overnight parking for motor homes in the lot just east of the Cidadela.

Parque Natural de Montesinho

The peaceful highlands along Portugal's northeastern border with Spain constitute one of Trás-os-Montes' most appealing natural and cultural landscapes – it's a patchwork of rolling grasslands, giant chestnut trees, oak forests and deep canyons, sprinkled with ancient stone villages, where an ageing population still ekes out a hard-scrabble existence.

The 750-sq-km Parque Natural de Montesinho was established to protect the area's 88 lean villages as much as their natural setting. This harsh, remote *terra fria* (cold land) inspired early Portuguese rulers to establish a system of collective land tenure and then leave the villagers to their own devices, allowing for a remarkably democratic, communal culture, which persists among older residents today.

◉ Sights

Unfortunately, remote villages of the park continue to be deserted by their young people, and many have not a single resident under the age of 60. However, these settlements – mostly just small clusters of granite houses roofed in slate and sheltering in deep valleys – retain an irresistible charm, especially in late April, when cherry and chestnut trees are in flower. In some towns, the government has helped preserve traditional slate-roofed stone houses as well as churches, forges, mills and the characteristic, charming *pombals* (dovecotes).

Villages that retain lashings of character include Pinheiro Novo, Sernande, Moimenta and Dine in the west, and Montesinho, Varge, Rio de Onor and Guadramil in the east.

Rio de Onor   VILLAGE

This lovely little town of 70 souls situated in the eastern half of the park is entirely unfazed by the Spanish–Portuguese border splicing it down the middle. It's interesting not just for its rustic stone buildings, the ground floors of which still house straw-filled stables for goats, sheep and donkeys, but also for its staunch maintenance of the communal lifestyle once typical of the region.

Spend an afternoon here and you'll see elderly locals trundling wheelbarrows from the well-tended community gardens surrounding town, pitchforking hay onto horse-drawn carts, stopping in at the local cafe – the communally shared proceeds of which are used to fund town festivals – or trading jobs with each other – one cousin staying to mind the store while the other goes to bring in the sheep. The twinned village also has one other claim to fame – a hybrid Portuguese–Spanish dialect known as Rionorês.

The border runs east–west through the middle of the village, while the Rio de Onor trickles along perpendicular to it. The road from Bragança continues north through

Parque Natural de Montesinho

town into Spain, branching right just before the border to cross an old stone bridge to the prettiest part of the village, where you'll find the community cafe.

From Bragança, STUB bus 5 heads to Rio de Onor (€2, one hour) two to three times daily.

Montesinho   VILLAGE

Hidden at the end of the road in a narrow valley wedged between forbidding granite heights, this tiny village is one of the park's best-preserved, thanks to a programme to restore old dwellings and stop construction of new ones. The village is also the jumping-off point for the 8km Porto Furado hiking trail through the rugged hills to a nearby dam.

STUB bus 7 runs from Bragança to Montesinho (€2, one hour) at least once daily.

Moimenta   VILLAGE

Moimenta has a lovely core of granite houses roofed in terracotta, plus a small baroque church – a rare dose of luxury in this austere corner of Portugal. The pretty 7km Calçada loop trail descends from town into the nearby river gorge, following sections of an old stone roadway across a remarkably well-preserved medieval bridge with a single impressive arch.

Dine   VILLAGE

One of the prettiest, best-preserved villages in the western half of the park, Dine is home to a tiny archaeological museum, which documents the 1984 find by a Danish diplomat of Iron Age remains in a nearby cave. The museum is usually locked, but just ask around and someone will rustle up the French-speaking caretaker, Judite,

who may also lead you around to the cave itself – pointing out traditional lime kilns and wild-growing medicinal herbs along the way.

Activities

There are plenty of cycling and hiking opportunities. Park offices in Bragança (p422) and Vinhais (p425) offer free brochures detailing 11 marked hiking trails around the park (downloadable online at www.cm-braganca.pt/pages/298). Additional trail info is available at www.natural.pt/portal/en/AreaProtegida/LigacoesPercurso/2.

If you come here in the summer, you can cool off in the park's plentiful (if chilly) rivers and streams. Look for signs pointing to *praias fluviais* (river beaches) throughout the park; one of the nicest such swimming spots is near the centre of the park, just northwest of the town of Fresulfe.

Sleeping

The natural base from which to explore the park is Bragança. Smaller villages within the park also offer accommodation, such as the numerous self-catering stone cottages in the village of Montesinho. Note that rooms book up in July and August. For a complete list of local sleeping options, check out the *alojamento* (lodging) section of the free *Nordeste Transmontano* booklet available from Bragança's tourist office (p422).

Eastern Park

Casinha Pequenina   RENTAL HOUSE €

(☑ 273 927 131; www.casinha-pequenina.ch; house €45) Swiss owner Marion Baldesberger rents

GHOST TOWNS: THE TRANSMONTANA EXODUS

Portugal is one of the few European countries to experience mass emigration well into the 21st century. In the 1970s alone, it's estimated that 775,000 people left the country – nearly 10% of the total population – with half a million more leaving between 2011 and 2014 as a result of the economic crisis. It's estimated that over 2 million Portuguese citizens now live abroad.

With difficult agricultural conditions and little industry, it's not surprising that Trás-os-Montes (along with neighbouring Minho) contributed more than its share to the exodus. The region's population shrank by nearly 33% between 1960 and 2001. To get an idea of the kinds of conditions they were fleeing, consider this: 60% of the region's workforce was engaged in agriculture into the 1990s – a figure higher than in many developing nations.

At the turn of the 20th century, the lion's share of emigrants headed to Brazil, which was undergoing a coffee boom. Later, many left for Portugal's African possessions, which received increased investment and interest during Salazar's regime. Then as Europe's postwar economy heated up in the 1960s and '70s, *transmontanas* began to stick closer to home, finding work as labourers in Germany, Belgium, Switzerland and especially France. Skilled workers such as nurses have joined the trend in recent years, heading to the UK, Germany and other northern European countries in search of higher pay.

The effect of this exodus is still visible, especially in rural areas. Many villages have been abandoned wholesale, left to a few widows and a clutch of chickens. Around others you'll find a ring of modern construction, almost always paid for not by the fruit of the land but by money earned abroad.

out this charmingly cosy two-storey house in the middle of Rio de Onor village, with a bedroom upstairs and a small living room/kitchen below. It's the perfect spot to settle into the slow-paced rhythm of life in this lovely little border town.

Casa de Onor INN €€
(☑ 273 927 163; www.casadeonor.com; Rio de Onor; s/d €40/70) In a pretty stone house overlooking the river in the centre of Rio de Onor, Senhora Rita Rego rents five rooms sleeping one to six people, each with private bathroom. Breakfast costs €5 extra, and other meals are available upon request for €20 per person.

★ A Lagosta Perdida B&B €€
(☑ 273 919 031; www.lagostaperdida.com; Rua do Cimo 4, Montesinho; s/d incl half board €77/117; P ⑳ ⑳) The region's most upscale accommodation is this refurbished stone-walled house, run by a friendly Anglo-Dutch family. It retains numerous period features, including high, beamed ceilings and an old stone water trough downstairs. The comfortable rooms come equipped with tea-making facilities, beautifully tiled modern bathrooms, flat-screen TVs and internet (though service can be spotty due to Montesinho's lack of fibre-optic cable).

🛏 Western Park

Parque de Campismo
Cepo Verde CAMPGROUND €
(☑ 273 999 371; www.montesinho.com; Lugar da Vinha do Santo, Gondesende; campsite per adult/child/tent/car €4.75/2.40/4.35/3, 2-/4-/5-person bungalow €50/55/60; ☉ camping Mar-Oct, bungalows year-round; P ⑳ ⑳ ⑳) This medium-sized rural facility is 9km west of Bragança near the tiny village of Gondesende on the park's southern border. Sixty campsites, some shaded and some in full sun, are set on a hillside above a central cafe and swimming pool (€3).

Casa da Bica INN €
(☑ 273 999 371; www.montesinho.com/casadabica; Rua do Lameiro 19, Gondesende; d/tr/f €45/55/90, entire house €200; P) In Gondesende, 13km northwest of Bragança, this schist cottage sleeps up to 11 people in five rather spartan rooms upstairs (only three have a private bathroom). Downstairs, there's a kitchen and a large living room with fireplace, where breakfast is served.

Casa dos Marrões INN €€
(☑ 273 999 550; www.casadosmarroes.com; Vilarinho; s/d €45/60, house €100; P ⑳) In Vilarinho, 17km northwest of Bragança, this small 18th-century home built of oak, chestnut and schist has lovely beamed ceilings and

exposed-stone walls. A spring-fed outdoor pool, plus nearby hiking trails and riverside beaches, enhance its appeal.

Casa de Casares
RENTAL HOUSE €€

(☑934 346 673; www.casas-de-casares.pt; Casares; 1-/2-bedroom house €75/85; P) Four lovingly restored traditional houses in the tiny village of Casares feature seven rooms and lots of original detail. Perfect if you're looking for a remote stay, with great countryside walks outside your door. There's a two-night minimum stay and breakfast is included.

Casa do Parâmio
COTTAGE €€

(☑273 999 371; www.montesinho.com/casa-do-paramio; Largo do Outeiro, Parâmio; house with/without breakfast €95/70) Right at the geographic heart of the park, this restored rural house features two doubles each with a private bathroom, a fireplace in the living room and a traditional wood oven in the kitchen. Owner Cristiana treats guests like friends, and with 48 hours' notice makes homemade breakfasts including traditional nut-and-honey tarts.

Moinho do Caniço
RENTAL HOUSE €€

(☑273 323 577; moinho@montesinho.com; N103, km 251, Castrelos; house €60; ☉Mar-Sep; P🐾) This tastefully refurbished watermill – complete with centuries-old kitchen and open fireplace – is 12km west of Bragança on the N103. The rustically furnished stone-floored cottage sleeps up to four people, with trout fishing in the Rio Baceiro just outside the door. STUB bus 2 (€2, 55 minutes) stops nearby.

✗ Eating

Café Montesinho
CAFE €

(Montesinho; snacks €3-12; ☉variable) A cosy spot in the hub of the village, stone-walled Café Montesinho serves snacks and drinks, and also rents an upstairs two-bedroom apartment (€50) that sleeps up to four people, complete with kitchen and a pleasant veranda. Hours are irregular.

O Careto
PORTUGUESE €€

(☑273 919 112; www.facebook.com/restaurante ocareto; Rua da Calçada, Varge; mains €10-15; ☉noon-3pm & 7-10pm Tue-Sun) Inside a traditional house in Varge village, the lovely Fátima presides over this family-run restaurant, which has been serving delicious dishes showcasing local beef, lamb and sausages for over 25 years.

Taberna do Capelas
PORTUGUESE €€

(☑273 999 086; N308, Parâmio; mains €10-14; ☉9am-midnight) This tavern in the tiny village of Parâmio is open all day long for coffee and drinks; at lunch and dinnertime it also serves simple meals featuring smoked sausages and local veggies, and tender meats such as lamb and cockerel (order ahead). Its homemade sweet rice is a great finale.

ⓘ Information

Parque Natural de Montesinho Office (Centro de Interpretação do Parque Natural de Montesinho; ☑273 771 416; cipnm@cm-vinhais.pt; Casa da Vila, Castelo, Vinhais; ☉9am-12.30pm & 2-5.30pm)

ⓘ Getting Around

Exploring the park is difficult without a car, a bike or sturdy feet. The free park map clearly indicates which roads are paved – unpaved roads can be dicey during and after rains.

Only some parts of the park are served by bus. For up-to-date schedules, check with Bragança's municipal bus company, STUB (Serviço de Transportes Urbanos de Bragança; ☑800 207 609; www.cm-braganca.pt/pages/114). Trips to towns within the park cost €2 and generally take an hour or less.

Miranda do Douro

POP 2085 / ELEV 560M

A fortified frontier town hunkering on the precipice of the gorgeous Rio Douro canyon, Miranda do Douro was long a bulwark of Portugal's 'wild east'. With its crumbling castle lending an air of medieval charm, modern-day Miranda has assumed a decidedly different role – receiving Spanish tourists on short breaks, as opposed to repelling Castilian attacks.

The town's beautifully hulking, 16th-century church (p426) may seem out of proportion to the rest of the town, but it once served as cathedral for the entire region. Visitors shouldn't miss Miranda's ethnographic museum (p426), which illuminates the region's cultural traditions, including ancient rites such as the 'stick dancing' of the *pauliteiros*.

Local street signs are written in the ancient language of Mirandês. Romance-language buffs will enjoy names such as Rue de la Santa Cruç, which read like a fantastical blend of French, Spanish and Portuguese.

SPEAKING MIRANDÊS

France has Provençal, Britain has Welsh and Gaelic, and Italy has dozens of distinct regional dialects. Portugal, by contrast, is one of Europe's most monolingual countries, thanks both to its long-stable borders (unchanged since the 13th century) and to the fact that it was conquered and consolidated within a very short period of time (less than 200 years).

The region around Miranda do Douro is a significant exception. Because of its proximity to Spain and long isolation from the rest of Portugal, residents of the towns and villages around Miranda still speak what linguists now recognise as an entirely distinct language. Closely related to Astur-Leonese – the regional language of the adjacent Spanish province – Mirandês is in fact closer to Iberian Latin, the language spoken during the Roman period, than it is to either Portuguese or Spanish.

While Mirandês has largely died out in the town of Miranda do Douro itself, it's still the first language of several thousand people in the surrounding villages. The Portuguese government officially recognised it as a second language in 1998, and increasingly the region's road signs are bilingual.

In 1882 Portuguese linguist José Leite de Vasconcelos described Mirandês as 'the language of the farms, of work, of home and love'. The same is true today.

Resurgent local pride in the language is evident in the window display of Miranda do Douro's **Papelaria Andrade** (Rue Mouzinho de Albuquerque 13), whose collection of Mirandês-language titles includes translations of *Asterix* comic books.

History

Miranda was a vital stronghold during Portugal's first centuries of independence, and the Castilians had to be chucked out at least twice: in the early days by Dom João I, and again in 1710, during the War of the Spanish Succession. In 1545, perhaps as a snub to the increasingly powerful House of Bragança, a diocese was created here – hence the oversized cathedral.

During a siege by French and Spanish troops in 1762, the castle's powder magazine exploded, pulverising most of the castle and killing some 400 people. Twenty years later, shattered Miranda lost its diocese to Bragança. No one paid much attention to Miranda again until the nearby dam was built on the Douro in the 1950s.

◉ Sights

Old Town AREA
The backstreets in Miranda's old town hide some dignified 15th-century facades. Some of the finest are along Rua da Costanilha, which runs west off Praça de Dom João III, ending in a Gothic gate.

Museu da Terra de Miranda MUSEUM
(Praça de Dom João III 2; €2; Sun morning free; ☉10am-1pm & 2-6pm Wed-Sun, 2-6pm Tue Apr-Oct; 9.30am-1pm & 2-5.30pm Wed-Sun, 2-5.30pm Tue Nov-Mar) This modest but attractive museum sheds light on a unique culture that has preserved age-old traditions into the 21st century. The handsome 17th-century building (formerly Miranda's town hall and jail) houses a fascinating collection of local artefacts: ceramics, textiles, furniture, musical instruments and tribal-looking masks, along with re-creations of a traditional kitchen and a blacksmith's forge.

Sé CATHEDRAL
(☉variable) Inside the right transept of this handsomely severe 16th-century cathedral, look for the doll-like Menino Jesus da Cartolinha, a Christ child in a becoming top hat whose wardrobe rivals Khloé Kardashian's, thanks to deft local devotees.

Barragem de Miranda LANDMARK
A road crawls across this 80m-high dam about 1km east of town, and on to Zamora, 55km away in Spain. Even dammed, the gorge is dramatic. You can take a one-hour boat trip through the gorge with **Europarques** (Crucero Ambiental Arribes del Duero; ☎273 432 396; www.europarques.com; adult/child under 10yr €18/9; ☉trips 4pm daily, plus 11am Sat & Sun).

⊨ Sleeping

Hotel Turismo HOTEL €
(☎273 438 030; www.hotelturismomiranda.pt; Rua 1 de Maio 5; s/d €30/45; ❄☎) Offering terrific comfort for a modest price, this place opposite the *turismo* features large, spotless

rooms – most including a separate sitting room – with cable TV, minibars and marble bathrooms. Front rooms have large windows with views across to the castle ruins, while the back rooms are quieter.

Hotel A Morgadinha   HOTEL €

(☑ 273 438 050; www.hotelmorgadinha.pt; Rua do Mercado 57/59; s/d €20/40; ❄ ⊠) This simple hotel – one of several budget options along the same street – features spacious rooms with parquet wood floors and bathtubs. There are nice river views from the upstairs breakfast area and from many of the rooms; avoid those facing the street, which are noisier and more claustrophobic.

Hotel Parador Santa Catarina   HOTEL €€

(☑ 273 431 005; www.hotelparadorsantacatarina.pt; Largo da Pousada; s/d/ste €58/78/88; P ❄ ⊠) Every guest gets a private veranda with spectacular views of the gorge at this luxurious hotel perched on the canyon's edge. The 12 rooms and suites are a handsome mix of traditional and contemporary, with hardwood floors, flat-screen TVs and large marble bathrooms. The attached restaurant is the most upmarket in town.

✖ Eating

São Pedro   PORTUGUESE €€

(☑ 273 431 321; Rua Mouzinho de Albuquerque 20; mains €8.50-14; ⊙ noon-3pm Sun, noon-3pm & 7-10pm Tue-Sat) Just in from the main old-town gate, this restaurant serves up a fine *posta á São Pedro* (grilled veal steak dressed with garlic and olive oil). The €13 *menu do dia* includes soup or salad, main course, dessert, wine and water.

O Mirandês   PORTUGUESE €€

(☑ 273 431 418; www.omirandes.net; Rua Dom Dinis 7; mains €7-14; ⊙ noon-3pm & 7-10pm Tue-Sat, noon-3pm Sun) Below the castle, just off the main road leading into the old town, this unassuming light-filled spot is popular with locals for its great-value lunch specials and tasty dinners.

Capa d'Honras   PORTUGUESE €€

(☑ 273 432 699; Travessa do Castelo 1; mains €11-17.50; ⊙ noon-2.30pm & 7-9.30pm) Named after the sinister-looking cape that is traditional to the region, this upmarket place just inside the old town gates serves local specialities such as *posta* (veal steak) as well as very good *bacalhau* (cod).

THE HILLS ARE ALIVE: STRANGE WAYS IN TRÁS-OS-MONTES

For centuries, the remoteness of Trás-os-Montes has insulated it from central authority, helping its people preserve nonconformist ways that sometimes raise eyebrows in other parts of Portugal.

A number of licentious – and blatantly pagan – traditions still survive in the countryside. Witness the antics of the Caretos of Podence (near Macedo de Cavaleiros) – where gangs of young men in *caretos* (leering masks) and vividly striped costumes invade the town centre, bent on cheerfully humiliating everyone in sight. Prime targets are young women, at whom they thrust their hips and wave the cowbells hanging from their belts. Similar figures are to be seen in Varge, in the Parque Natural de Montesinho.

Colourful festivals derived from ancient Celtic solstice rituals take place in many villages in the two weeks between Christmas Eve and Dia dos Reis (Epiphany). During the so-called Festa dos Rapazes (Festival of the Lads), unmarried men over 16 light all-night bonfires and rampage around in robes of rags and masks of brass or wood. Un-Christian indeed!

Then there are the *pauliteiros* (stick dancers) of the Miranda do Douro region, who look and dance very much like England's Morris dancers. Local men deck themselves out in kilts and smocks, black waistcoats, bright flapping shawls, and black hats covered in flowers and ribbons, and do a rhythmic dance to the complex clacking of *paulitos* (short wooden sticks) – a practice that likely survives from Celtic times. The best time to see *pauliteiros* in Miranda is during the Festas de Santa Bárbara (also called Festas da Cidade, or City Festival), which is held on the third weekend in August.

Finally, there are the region's so-called crypto-Jews. During the Inquisition, Jews from Spain and Portugal found that they could evade ecclesiastical authorities here. Many families continued to observe Jewish practices in secrecy well into the 20th century.

ℹ️ Information

Parque Natural do Douro Internacional Office (☎ 273 431 457; www.natural.pt; Largo do Castelo; ⊗ 8.30am-1pm & 2-4.30pm Mon-Fri) .
Turismo (☎ 273 430 025; www.cm-mdouro.pt; Largo do Menino Jesus da Cartolinha; ⊗ 9am-12.30pm & 1.30-6pm Mon-Sat May-Sep, to 5pm Oct-Apr)

ℹ️ Getting There & Away

BUS

Rodonorte (☎ 273 432 667; www.rodonorte. pt) offers service daily except Saturday to Mogadouro (€6.10, 45 minutes), with onward connections to Vila Nova de Foz Côa (€6.40, 2¾ hours), Vila Real (€12.80, three hours) and Porto (€15.20, 4¼ to 5¾ hours).

CAR & MOTORCYCLE

The quickest road from Bragança to Miranda do Douro is the N218, a winding 70km trip. The slower but lovelier 100km route (N216/N221) from Macedo de Cavaleiros via Mogadouro crosses a *planalto* (high plateau) dotted with olive, almond and chestnut groves and includes a dramatic switchbacking descent into the Rio Sabor valley. Miranda has plenty of free parking around Largo do Menino Jesus da Cartolinha.

Parque Natural do Douro Internacional

Tucked into Portugal's northeastern corner, this 870-sq-km, Chile-shaped park runs for 120km along the Rio Douro and the monumental canyon it has carved along the border with Spain. The canyon's towering, granite cliffs are the habitat for several threatened bird species, including black storks, Egyptian vultures, griffon vultures, peregrine falcons, golden eagles and Bonelli's eagles.

The human population is equally fragile. In the plains that run up to the canyon lip, there are some 35 villages, some inhabited by descendants of banished medieval convicts, as well as Jews who fled the Inquisition. The region's isolation has enabled its people to preserve even more ancient roots, such as the Celtic *dança dos paulitos*, a traditional dance accompanied by the complex clacking of *paulitos* (short wooden sticks). A few hundred villagers still speak Mirandês; you'll see town names written in Portuguese and Mirandês throughout the park's northern reaches.

👁 Sights

Miranda do Douro and Mogadouro are the most convenient places from which to explore the park. As you move south along the river, the terrain gains a distinctly Mediterranean air, with rolling orchards of olives and almonds and, in the southernmost reaches, land demarcated for port-wine grapes.

🏃 Activities

There are four marked trails in the park. The most convenient for nondrivers – and one of the most beautiful – is the 19km **Miranda do Douro to São João das Arribas loop**, starting and ending at Miranda do Douro's cathedral. The trail – open to hikers, cyclists and horses – passes through mixed oak woodlands and small villages, and includes striking vistas of the river at São João. Another stunning option is the **Vale da Ribeira do Mosteiro loop**, which passes through vineyards and rugged canyon country along a small tributary of the Douro.

☞ Tours

Without your own transport, the easiest way to see the Douro gorge is on an hour-long cruise from Miranda do Douro with Europarques (p426), or on the 2½-hour boat tours offered from Bemposta by **Naturisnor** (☎ 969 031 894; www.naturisnor.com; Cais Fluvial de Bemposta; 2½hr cruise €25; ⊗ Apr-Oct), which allow more time to appreciate the park.

From Miranda do Douro, **Douro Pula Canhada** (☎ 273 431 340; www.douropulacanhada.com; tours from €22) offers guided tours by jeep, mountain bike, donkey and on foot, as well as birdwatching.

🛏 Sleeping & Eating

With its impressive views of the river gorge, Miranda do Douro is the most attractive base for exploring the park. Mogadouro also offers tourist services, but at nearly 15km from the Douro, it's a far less scenic option. Several rural house rental options are also available; inquire at local tourist offices.

Casa dos Edras INN €€
(☎ 961 039 516; www.casadosedras.pt; Rua do Balhico, Aldeia Nova; r €75; P ❄ 🛜 🏊) This gorgeously restored country house sits within the park borders in Aldeia Nova, 7km northeast of Miranda do Douro. The eight pine-floored rooms come with garden or village vistas, and perks like a small swimming pool,

OFF THE BEATEN TRACK

MIRADOUROS: THE DOURO GORGE'S SCENIC OVERLOOKS

For fabulous, near-aerial views of the Douro gorge and its birdlife, it's well worth seeking out Parque Natural do Douro Internacional's seven spectacular *miradouros* (panoramic overlooks). North to south, with the nearest village in parentheses, these are:

Penha das Torres (Paradela) Opposite the Presa de Castro dam, about 12km upstream from Miranda do Douro near the village of Paradela, the park's easternmost viewpoint is famous as the first place in Portugal to see the sun rise.

São João das Arribas (Aldeia Nova) Just outside the village of Aldeia Nova, this viewpoint 8km northeast of Miranda do Douro sits adjacent to the clifftop chapel of São João das Arribas, with dramatic views down into the Douro canyon.

Fraga do Puio (Picote) Overlooking a horseshoe bend in the Douro just south of the village of Picote, this viewpoint is a prime spot to linger over sunset.

Carrascalinho (Fornos) Drive half an hour south of Mogadouro through the village of Fornos to find this remote viewpoint.

Penedo Durão (Poiares) Westernmost of the Rio Douro viewpoints, Penedo Durão commands views down towards the Presa de Saucelle dam. It's about 56km south of Mogadouro and 51km east of Vila Nova de Foz Côa.

Sapinha (Escalhão) This roadside pullout on the N221 highway 3km north of Escalhão is one of the park's most accessible viewpoints, with sweeping views of vineyard- and orchard-clad slopes dropping into the gorge of the Rio Águeda along the Spanish-Portuguese border.

Santo André (Almofala) The chapel of Santo André das Arribas, near Almofala, stands sentinel over the Rio Águeda gorge at this southernmost of the park viewpoints.

a lawn with outdoor seating and a fireplace for chilly nights. A hearty breakfast is included, and guests can use the bikes for free.

Casa de Campo I Bárrio RENTAL HOUSE €€
(☑273 738 088; www.casadelbarrio.com; Rua de I Bárrio 7, Picote; house for 2/3/5 people €80/100/140; P❄🛜) ⁄ This great rural option in the village of Picote, 17km southwest of Miranda do Douro, is run by a linguist and a biologist, who offer free guided nature walks for their guests. The cosy solarenergy–powered house sleeps up to five and features a fireplace and a small patio.

A Lareira PORTUGUESE €€
(☑279 342 363; Av Nossa Senhora do Caminho 58-62, Mogadouro; mains €8-14; ⊘noon-3pm & 7-10pm Tue-Sun) This recommended restaurant offers outstanding local beef, veal and mushrooms grilled on an open fireplace by the French-trained proprietor. The small, well-equipped rooms upstairs (single/double €25/30) are also excellent value.

ℹ Information

The most informative park office is in Miranda do Douro (p428), with another in **Mogadouro** (☑279 341 596; www.icnf.pt/portal/naturaclas/ap/p-nat/pndi; Rua Dr Francisco António Vicente 4, Mogadouro; ⊘10am-12.30pm & 2.30-5pm Mon-Fri).

ℹ Getting There & Away

Rodonorte (☑273 432 444; www.rodonorte. pt), **Santos** (☑279 652 188; www.santosviagensturismo.pt) and **Rede Expressos** (☑707 223 344; www.rede-expressos.pt) offer regular bus services to Miranda do Douro and Mogadouro from most major towns and cities in the region.

ℹ Getting Around

Public transport to smaller villages within the park is extremely limited, and mostly designed to serve schoolchildren; check with the park offices for current schedule information

The Minho

Best Places to Eat

➡ Casa de Pasto das Carvalheiras (p437)
➡ A Cozinha (p445)
➡ O Marquês (p451)
➡ O Abocanhado (p470)
➡ A Carvalheira (p460)

Best Places to Stay

➡ Dona Emília (p450)
➡ Quinta do Convento da Franqueira (p439)
➡ Mercearia da Vila (p459)
➡ Quinta do Ameal (p459)
➡ Collector's Hostel (p435)
➡ Casa do Adro (p466)

Why Go?

The Minho delivers world-class natural beauty with a knowing smile. Here are lush river valleys, sparkling beaches and granite peaks patrolled by locals – who, whether they are charging into 2m waves along the Costa Verde or shepherding their flock into high mountain meadows, seem particularly in tune with their homeland. This is, after all, the birthplace of the Portuguese kingdom, and it would be hard to find better-preserved landmarks than those lit up and on display in the Minho's gorgeous old cities.

Then there's the bold, sharp and fruity *vinho verde* to consider. This young wine is fashioned from the fruit of kilometres of vineyards that wind along rivers, over foothills and into Minho mountain villages. The crops are eventually crushed and bottled in community *adegas* (wineries), giving each destination its own flavour. Of course, if you sip enough along the way, they may all blend into one delicious memory.

When to Go
Braga

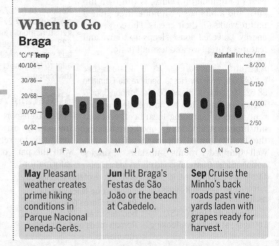

May Pleasant weather creates prime hiking conditions in Parque Nacional Peneda-Gerês.

Jun Hit Braga's Festas de São João or the beach at Cabedelo.

Sep Cruise the Minho's back roads past vineyards laden with grapes ready for harvest.

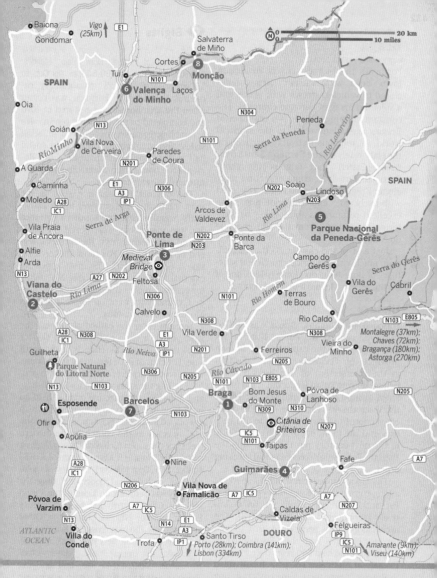

The Minho Highlights

1 Braga (p432) Visiting historic monuments, followed by dinner at a top restaurant.

2 Viana do Castelo (p446) Strolling the atmospheric streets then catching sunset on the beach.

3 Ponte de Lima (p457) Lounging at a cafe overlooking the medieval bridge and lush countryside beyond.

4 Guimarães (p440) Exploring the contemporary art and culture of this buzzing city.

5 Parque Nacional da Peneda-Gerês (p463) Hiking boulder-strewn peaks, ancient Roman roads and gorse-clad moorlands.

6 Valença do Minho (p453) Surveying Spain from the fortified heights.

7 Barcelos (p439) Mingling with locals at the Minho's largest outdoor market.

8 Monção (p455) Sampling Alvarinho wines and touring the grand neoclassical Palácio da Brejoeira.

Braga

POP 136,885 / ELEV 200M

Portugal's third-largest city is an elegant town laced with ancient narrow lanes closed to vehicles, strewn with plazas and a splendid array of baroque churches. The constant chiming of bells is a reminder of Braga's age-old devotion to the spiritual world. Its religious festivals – particularly the elaborately staged Semana Santa (Holy Week; ☉ Easter) – are famous throughout Portugal. But don't come expecting piety alone: Braga's upscale old centre is packed with lively cafes and trim boutiques, some excellent restaurants and low-key bars catering to students from the Universidade do Minho.

Just east of the city stands the magnificent, much-visited hillside church and sanctuary of Bom Jesus do Monte (p433), one of Portugal's most iconic tourist attractions.

History

Founded by Romans, Braga was settled in the 1st century BC, named Bracara Augusta and made the capital of the Roman province of Gallaecia. Braga's position at the intersection of five Roman roads helped it grow fat on trade, but it fell to the Suevi around AD 410, and was sacked by the Visigoths 60 years later. The Visigoths' conversion to Christianity in the 6th century and the founding of an archbishopric in the next century put the town atop the Iberian Peninsula's ecclesiastical pecking order.

The Moors moved in around 715, sparking a long-running tug of war that ended when Fernando I, king of Castilla y León, definitively reconquered the city in 1040. The archbishopric was restored in 1070, though prelates bickered with their Spanish counterparts for the next 500 years over who was Primate of All Spain. The pope finally ruled in Braga's favour, though the city's resulting good fortune began to wane in the 18th century when a newly anointed Lisbon archdiocese stole much of its thunder.

Not surprisingly, it was from conservative Braga that António de Oliveira Salazar, with his unique blend of Catholicism and fascism, gave the speech that launched his 1926 coup, introducing Portugal to half a century of dictatorship.

◉ Sights

★ Sé   CATHEDRAL

(www.se-braga.pt; Rua Dom Paio Mendes; ☉ 9.30am-12.30pm & 2.30-6.30pm Apr-Oct, to 5.30pm Nov-Mar) Braga's extraordinary cathedral, the oldest in Portugal, was begun when the archdiocese was restored in 1070 and completed in the following century. It's a rambling complex made up of differing styles, and architecture buffs could spend half a day happily distinguishing the Romanesque bones from Manueline musculature and baroque frippery.

The original Romanesque style is the most interesting and survives in the cathedral's overall shape, the southern entrance and the marvellous west portal, which is carved with scenes from the medieval legend of Reynard the Fox (now sheltered inside a Gothic porch). The most appealing external features are the filigree Manueline towers and roof – an early work by João de Castilho, who went on to build Lisbon's Mosteiro dos Jerónimos.

You can enter the cathedral through the west portal or via a courtyard and cloister that's lined with Gothic chapels on the north side. The church itself features a fine Manueline carved altarpiece, a tall chapel with *azulejos* telling the story of Braga's first bishop, and fantastic twin baroque organs (held up by formidable satyrs and mermen), which are played at mass every Sunday at 11.30am.

Connected to the church is the modern treasury museum (Cathedral Treasury Museum; adult/child €3/free; ☉ 9.30am-12.30pm & 2.30-6.30 Apr-Oct, to 5.30pm Nov-Mar), housing a goldmine of ecclesiastical booty, including the lovely Nossa Senhora do Leite of the Virgin suckling Christ, attributed to 16th-century French sculptor Nicolas Chanterène. Other highlights are the iron cross that was used in 1500 to celebrate the very first Mass in Brazil.

To visit the upper choir (Cathedral Chapels & Choir; adult/child €2/free) and outlying chapels, visitors must purchase a separate ticket and join a guided tour (some guides speak English). Follow your guide up the stone staircase for an up-close look at the mesmerising organs and gilded choir stalls, then continue downstairs into the cathedral's showpiece Capela dos Reis (Kings' Chapel), home to the tombs of Henri of Burgundy and Dona Teresa, parents of the first king of Portugal, Afonso Henriques. You'll also visit the *azulejo*-covered Capela de São Geraldo (dating from the 12th century

EASTER IN BRAGA

Braga hosts the most elaborate Easter celebrations in Portugal. Semana Santa (Holy Week) kicks off with Gregorian chants piped throughout the city centre and makeshift candlelit altars lighting the streets. The action heats up during Holy Thursday's Procissão do Senhor Ecce Homo, when barefoot, hooded penitents – members of private Catholic brotherhoods – march through the streets spinning their eerie rattles.

The Good Friday celebration in the cathedral is a remarkable, elaborately staged drama with silk canopies, dirge-like hymns, dozens of priests and a weeping congregation. On Saturday evening, the Easter Vigil Mass begins dourly, the entire cathedral in shadow, only to explode in lights and jubilation. Finally, on Sunday, the people of Braga blanket their thresholds with flowers, inviting passing priests to enter and give their home a blessing.

but reworked over the years) and the 14th-century **Capela da Glória**, whose interior was painted in unrepentantly Moorish geometric motifs in the 16th century.

⭐ Escadaria do Bom Jesus do Monte
CHRISTIAN SITE

(Monte do Bom Jesus) Climbing dramatically to the hilltop pilgrimage site of Bom Jesus do Monte, 5km east of Braga, is this extraordinary staircase, with allegorical fountains, chapels and a superb view. City bus 2 runs frequently from Braga to the site, where you can climb the 580 steps (pilgrims sometimes do this on their knees) or ascend by funicular (one-way/return €1.20/2).

⭐ Centro Interpretativo das Memórias da Misericórdia de Braga
MUSEUM

(www.scmbraga.pt/cimmb-palácio-do-raio; Rua do Raio 400; ☉10am-1pm & 2.30-6.30pm Tue-Sat) **FREE** Braga's newest museum is housed inside Palácio do Raio, whose exuberantly tiled rococo façade (by André Soares) is must-see material for any aficionado of the colour blue. The gorgeous interiors, also clad in *azulejos*, showcase works of sacred art, textiles, paintings, sculptures, jewellery, pottery and old medical instruments, all bearing witness to 500 years of the building's history.

GNRation
CULTURAL CENTRE

(☎253 142 200; www.gnration.pt; Praça Conde de Agrolongo 123; ☉9.30am-6.30pm Mon-Fri) **FREE** This spiffy modern cultural centre lives inside an 18th-century building that once housed police headquarters. Enter through the sliding glass doors and you're inside an incubator of the city's creative industry, with galleries, concerts, film screenings, workshops and theatre performances. Free guided tours are available with advance notice (call or contact info@gnration.pt).

Museu dos Biscainhos
MUSEUM

(www.culturanorte.pt/pt/patrimonio/museu-dos-biscainhos; Rua dos Biscainhos; adult/student €2/1, first Sun of the month free; ☉10am-12.30pm & 2-5.30pm Tue-Sun) An 18th-century aristocrat's palace is home to Braga's enthusiastic municipal museum, with a nice collection of Roman relics and 17th- to 19th-century pottery and furnishings. The palace itself – with its polychrome, chestnut-panelled ceilings and 18th-century *azulejos* depicting hunting scenes – and the gorgeously landscaped gardens out back are reason enough to visit. The ground floor is paved with deeply ribbed flagstones on which carriages would have once rattled through to the stables.

Fonte do Ídolo
RUINS

(Idol Spring; Rua do Raio; adult/student €1.85/0.95; ☉9.30am-1pm & 2-5.30pm Mon-Fri, 11am-5.30pm Sat) Tucked away below street level and concealed by a modern lobby is this evocative ancient spring, one of Braga's unexpected treasures. An essential community water source in the city's early days, the spring and its surrounding rock face were carved into a fountain during pre-Roman times by Celicus Fronto, an immigrant from the city-state of Arcobriga. One carving is of a toga-clad pilgrim thought to be holding the Horn of Plenty. An introductory video provides historical background.

Museu Dom Diogo de Sousa
MUSEUM

(www.culturanorte.pt/pt/patrimonio/museu-de-arqueologia-d-diogo-de-sousa; Rua dos Bombeiros Voluntários; adult/student €3/1.50, Sun free; ☉9.30am-6pm Tue-Sun Jun–mid-Sep, to 5.30pm mid-Sep–May) The archaeological museum houses a nicely displayed collection of fragments from Braga's earliest days. The four rooms feature pieces from Palaeolithic times (arrowheads, funerary objects and ceramics) through Roman rule and on up to the period

Braga

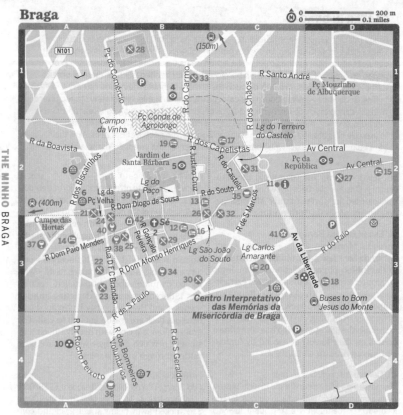

dominated by the Suevi-Visigoth kingdom (5th through 7th centuries). Especially fascinating are the huge *miliários* (milestones), carved with Latin inscriptions, that marked the Roman roads.

Termas Romanas do Alto da Cividade
RUINS

(☎ 253 278 455; Rua Dr Rocha Peixoto; adult/student €1.85/0.95; ⊙ 9.30am-1pm & 2-5.30pm Mon-Fri, 11am-5.30pm Sat) These ruins of an extensive bathing complex – with an attached theatre – dating from the 2nd century AD, were probably abandoned in the 5th century. See the seven-minute introductory video in English or Portuguese.

Museu da Imagem
MUSEUM

(☎ 253 278 633; Campo das Hortas 35-37; ⊙ 11am-7pm Tue-Fri, 2.30-6pm Sat & Sun) FREE In a beautifully minimalist medieval stone tower, outfitted tastefully with steel and wood stairs,

this museum shows off impeccably lit, international photography exhibits on three floors.

Praça da República
SQUARE

The cafes and restaurants on this broad plaza are a pleasant place to start or finish your day. An especially mellow atmosphere descends in the evening, when coloured lights spring up and people of all ages congregate to enjoy the night air.

The square-shaped, crenellated tower behind the cafes is the walled-up Torre de Menagem, which is all that survives of a fortified medieval palace.

Jardim de Santa Bárbara
GARDENS

(Rua Justino Cruz) FREE This 17th-century square has narrow paths picking their way through a sea of flowers and topiary. On sunny days the adjacent pedestrianised Rua Justino Cruz and Rua Francisco Sanches fill with buskers and cafe tables.

Braga

☞ Tours

Tourists' Affairs TOURS
(☏ 927 504 470; www.thetouristsaffairs.com) Excellent tour agency run by a pair of young, enthusiastic locals, an architect and an archaeologist, it specialises in all things Minho. Their focus is on tailor-made à la carte tours of Minho and beyond, but they also do walking tours of Braga – call ahead to reserve a spot and confirm a meeting point (often at Braga's tourist office).

✥ Festivals & Events

Festas de São João CULTURAL
(☉ Jun) A pre-Christian solstice bash dressed up to look like a holy day, this festival still bursts with pagan energy. Held for 10 days, it features medieval folk plays, processions, dancing, bonfires, fireworks – and little pots of basil, the symbol of São João (John the Baptist). Traditionally people write poems to loved ones and conceal them in their pots.

Locals also bust out squeaky plastic hammers and whack each other mercilessly.

🛏 Sleeping

★ **Collector's Hostel** HOSTEL €
(☏ 253 048 124; www.collectorshostel.com; Rua Francisco Sanches 42; dm €17-20, d/tr €44/62, s/d with shared bath €27/40) A delightful hostel, lovingly run by two well-travelled women who met in Paris (one of whom was born in the hostel's living room), restored the family house and all the furniture inside, and turned the three floors into a cosy hideaway where guests feel like they're in their grandparents' home, with a twist.

The downstairs floor has three four-bed dorms and a triple, while the upstairs has doubles, a lone single, a living room and a long balcony overlooking the town. The boat-like top floor is the hostel's funkiest part. Rates include breakfast and towels.

Just Go Hostel
HOSTEL €

(☑ 253 066 166; www.justgohostelbraga.com; Avenida da Liberdade 546; dm €17, tw €33-38; ❄ 🛜) Don't be deceived by the unassuming entrance to what appears to be an office building. Occupying the top two floors, this swanky, colourful hostel showcases well-appointed dorms and twins, and great city views from the shared living room and kitchen.

Each of the dorms has its own bathroom, along with lockers, light and plug for each bed, while two of the twins come with panoramic balconies. The hostel books excursions and activities, from surf lessons to hiking in Parque Nacional Peneda-Gerês. Breakfast is included; towels are for rent.

Casa de Santa Zita
GUESTHOUSE €

(☑ 253 618 331; www.osz.pt/braga; Rua São João 20; s/d €25/38; 🛜) This impeccably kept pilgrims' lodge has an air of palpable serenity. The sweet sisters offer bright, spotless rooms with hardwood floors and cherubic decor. Breakfast is served in a stone arched dining room. The only drawback is a midnight curfew.

Hotel dos Terceiros
HOTEL €

(☑ 253 270 466; www.terceiros.com; Rua dos Capelistas 85; s/d/tr €34/45/55; ⊘ closed Nov & Dec; ❄ 🛜) On a quiet pedestrian street near Praça da República, this simple hotel has recently updated rooms – including some with tiny balconies – overlooking a small square. Most rooms have one double and one single bed each, making them suitable for up to three people.

Domus 26
GUESTHOUSE €€

(☑ 917 339 095; www.domus26guesthouse.pt; Avenida São Miguel o Anjo 26; d €60-80; 🛜) Just outside the historic centre, this newly renovated guesthouse offers four plush, modern rooms in a 19th-century mansion, with frigobars (small fridges), coffee-makers and other homey touches. The best rooms have views up the street to Braga's cathedral.

Tea 4 Nine
GUESTHOUSE €€

(☑ 914 004 606; www.tea4nine.pt; Praça Conde Agrolongo 49; s/d from €75/100) This swish modern guesthouse has four stunning suites featuring clean-lined contemporary decor, pine floors and a full range of top-of-the-line amenities. Two face the square, two are out back and three more sit in another building facing the square. Note that there's no elevator. The sweet downstairs bistro with a garden does great lunch menus and a Sunday brunch.

Hotel Dona Sofia
HOTEL €€

(☑ 253 263 160; www.hoteldonasofia.com; Largo São João do Souto 131; s/d/tr €55/70/85; 🅿 ❄ @ 🛜) On a pretty central square, Dona Sofia has functional, if a bit dated, carpeted rooms of varying sizes; the best come with French windows overlooking the square. Limited free parking (first come, first served) is available, a rare perk in the city centre.

★ Vila Galé Collection Braga
LUXURY HOTEL €€€

(☑ 253 146 000; www.vilagale.com; Largo Carlos Amarante 150; r/ste from €144/195; 🅿 ❄ @ 🛜) Braga's newest luxury hotel is this magnificent former hospital and convent dating to 1508, adopted by the Vila Galé hotel chain and reopened in 2018. Abounding in vaulted ceilings, interior courtyards, baroque fountains and other grandiose architectural touches, it houses 123 palatial rooms and suites with five-star amenities, complemented by a spa, two outdoor pools, two restaurants and a bar.

Hotel Bracara Augusta
BOUTIQUE HOTEL €€€

(☑ 253 206 260; www.bracaraaugusta.com; Avenida Central 134; s/d/ste €99/129/199; 🅿 ❄ @ 🛜) This stylish, grand town house offers bright, modern rooms with parquet floors, classic decor and marble bathrooms. The suites have French doors opening onto decorative balconies. Its restaurant offers an excellent breakfast buffet, with open-air dining by a gurgling fountain out back.

✕ Eating

★ Livraria Centésima Página
CAFE €

(Avenida Central 118-120; snacks €3-5; ⊘ 9am-7.30pm Mon-Sat) Tucked inside Centésima Página, an absolutely splendid bookshop with foreign-language titles, this charming cafe serves a rotating selection of tasty quiches along with salads and desserts, and has outdoor tables in the pleasantly rustic garden. Its lunch specials are a steal.

Dona Petisca
TAPAS €

(☑ 253 052 480; www.facebook.com/donapetisca; Rua Dom Paio Mendes 32; sandwiches & snacks €3.50-5.50; ⊘ noon-midnight Tue-Thu, noon-1am Fri & Sat, 5pm-midnight Sun) This gourmet food shop with a narrow upstairs seating area sells all manner of sandwiches and snacks built around DOP and DOC Portuguese products – from ham and smoked sausage to cheeses, olives and wild mushrooms, all accompanied by quality wines. It's a great place to grab a bite any time of day or night.

Retrokitchen
PORTUGUESE €

(☑ 253 267 023; www.facebook.com/retrokitchen braga; Rua do Anjo 96; mains €9-12; ⊙ 10am-midnight Mon & Wed-Sat) A vintage theme runs through this funky, laid-back restaurant featuring tasty daily specials and a display of eclectic retro items curated by the friendly owner couple. The lunch menu is a steal (main course, bread and coffee for €5, or €6 with soup).

Taberna Velhos Tempos
PORTUGUESE €

(☑ 253 214 368; Rua do Carmo 7; mains €7.50-11; ⊙ noon-2.30pm & 8-10.30pm Mon-Sat) Under the motto 'rural cuisine for urban people', this wood-beamed tavern decorated with rustic bric-a-brac serves a tasty menu of traditional mainstays. Try the *bacalhau com natas* (baked codfish with potatoes and cream) or *arroz de pato com pinhão* (rice with duck and pine nuts). Full servings are huge; consider the half portions unless you've got a voracious appetite.

Spirito Cupcakes & Coffee
ICE CREAM €

(www.spiritocupcakes.com; Largo São João do Souto 19; cups & cones from €2; ⊙ 1.30-7pm Mon-Thu, 1.30-7pm & 9pm-midnight Fri & Sat) Don't miss the artisanal gelato at this always buzzing shop, where lines form out the door for a cup or cone of oatmeal-, cookie- or bubblegum-flavoured ice cream, and great cupcakes and coffees, too.

Anjo Verde
VEGETARIAN €

(☑ 253 264 010; Largo da Praça Velha 21; mains €8.50-9.50; ⊙ noon-3pm & 7.30-10.30pm Mon-Sat; ☑) This vegetarian offering serves generous, elegantly presented plates in a lovely, airy dining room. Vegetarian lasagne, soy stroganoff, risotto and vegetable tarts are among the specialities here. Mains can be bland, but the spiced chocolate tart is a superstar.

Silvas
PORTUGUESE €

(Largo do Terreiro do Castelo; mains €6.50-9; ⊙ noon-3pm & 7-11pm) A cosy little spot in the shadow of Torre de Menagem, this has a narrow glass-enclosed interior with a counter and a few tables outside. The well-prepared dishes change daily and include duck rice, rolled veal and always a fresh fish dish.

Frigideiras do Cantinho
CAFE €

(www.frigideirasdocantinho.pt; Largo São João do Souto 1; meat pies €1.65; ⊙ 8am-8pm Tue-Thu, to 10pm Fri-Sun) Set on a sweet, quiet plaza, with pleasant indoor and outdoor seating, this humble cafe is favoured by loyal locals for its *frigideiras:* meat pies with pork and veal, a tradition dating from 1796.

Mercado Municipal
MARKET €

(Praça do Comércio; ⊙ 8am-3pm Mon-Fri, 6am-1pm Sat) Packed with vendors of fresh produce, meats and cheeses, Braga's covered market buzzes on weekdays and Saturday mornings, and is ideal for self-caterers.

★Casa de Pasto das Carvalheiras
FUSION €€

(☑ 253 046 244; www.facebook.com/casadepasto dascarvalheiras; Rua Dom Afonso Henriques 8; small plates €5-15; ⊙ noon-3pm & 7pm-midnight Mon-Fri, noon-midnight Sat & Sun) This colourful eatery with a long bar serves up delectable, weekly changing *pratinhos* (small plates), from codfish confit with bok choy and noodles, to mushrooms with creamy polenta, to tasty concoctions of *alheira* (a light garlicky sausage of poultry or game) and turnip greens. Weekday lunch menus go for €9 or €12, depending on the number of dishes you order.

Pecado da Sé
PORTUGUESE €€

(☑ 919 990 990; Rua do Forno 22; mains €10-17; ⊙ noon-3pm Mon, noon-3pm & 8pm-midnight Tue-Thu, noon-3pm & 8pm-2am Fri & Sat) Down a side street from Braga's cathedral, this mod little hideaway mixes traditional Portuguese home cooking with international culinary influences, from classic *bacalhau com broa* (codfish with cornbread) and grilled Bisaro pork to fried chicken, prawn curry and Brazilian *picanha* (steak) with black beans. At lunchtime, it serves excellent all-inclusive menus (€10).

Brac
PORTUGUESE €€

(☑ 253 610 225; Campo das Carvalheiras; mains €14-17; ⊙ 11am-midnight Mon-Sat) This gourmet hotspot offers tasty *entradas* (appetizers) at the backlit bar, along with more elaborate dishes – Brazilian-style *moqueca* (seafood stew), rice with black pork and pleurotus mushrooms – in the swanky stone-columned dining room. Come at lunchtime for the all-you-can-eat buffet (€9 to €12.50 Monday through Saturday, €19.50 Sunday), best enjoyed on the front terrace overlooking a leafy park.

Cozinha da Sé
PORTUGUESE €€

(☑ 253 277 343; www.cozinhadase.pt; Rua Dom Frei Caetano Brandão 95; mains €12.50-18.50; ⊙ noon-3pm & 7.30-11pm Tue-Sat, noon-3pm Sun) Contemporary artwork hangs from the exposed stone walls at this intimate, cheery place. Traditional standouts include baked *bacalhau* (dried salt-cod) and *açorda de marisco* (seafood stew in a bread bowl).

Félix Taberna
PORTUGUESE €€

(☑253 617 701; Largo da Praça Velha 18-19; mains €10.75-21.50; ◔noon-3.30pm & 7.30pm-midnight Mon-Thu, to 1am Fri, 7.30pm-1am Sat) Savour terrific Portuguese dishes in this attractive country-style tavern with two cosy dining rooms showcasing lots of bric-a-brac. The menu is small but dishes are delicious, including breaded sardines, duck rice and *bacalhau à minha moda* (the chef's special codfish recipe).

Copo e Meio
PORTUGUESE €€

(☑253 070 175; www.facebook.com/restaurante copoemeio; Rua Dom Frei Cateano Brandão 118; tapas from €4.25, mains €9.50-19.50; ◔7pm-midnight Mon-Fri, noon-3pm & 7pm-midnight Sat) This swanky, gourmet tapas bar-restaurant with two cute upstairs stone dining rooms and a streetside deck gets packed with local mon-eyed types. Come for the tapas and wine.

🍷 Drinking & Nightlife

Pausa Cafeteria e Espaço de Livros
CAFE

(www.pausa-cafetaria.com; Praça Conde de Agro-longo 123; ◔9.30am-6.30pm Mon-Fri, from 10am Sat) Inside the GNRation cultural complex, this mural-clad industrial space creates a cool backdrop for Braga's alternative literary set. It's a chilled-out spot to peruse finds from the in-house book exchange while sipping cups of tea and nibbling on healthy snacks and baked goods.

Barhaus
BAR

(☑914 426 833; www.facebook.com/barhaus.net; Rua Dom Gonçalo Pereira 58; ◔3pm-2am Mon-Thu, 3pm-4am Fri & Sat, 7pm-1am Sun) This popular spot with two indoor bars and a huge open-air patio draws a crowd with posh pretensions for DJs and live shows.

Domus Vinum
WINE BAR

(Largo da Nossa Senhora da Boa Luz 12; tapas €4-7; ◔6pm-2am Wed-Mon) With Brazilian beats, a lantern-lit front patio and excellent wines by the glass, Domus Vinum draws a stylish crowd. The Portuguese and Spanish tapas are excellent. It's just west of the old-town entrance portal, Arco da Porta Nova.

Café A Brasileira
CAFE

(☑253262104;www.facebook.com/CafeABrasileira Braga; Largo Barão São Martinho 17; ◔8am-midnight Sun-Thu, to 2am Fri & Sat) A Braga classic, this 19th-century cafe is a converging point for old and new generations. Try the *café de saco* (a small shot of filtered coffee).

Mavy
BAR

(www.facebook.com/espacomavy; Rua D. Diogo de Sousa 133; ◔noon-2am Sun-Thu noon,-4am Fri & Sat) From early evening into the wee hours, a youthful crowd congregates at this bar in Braga's pedestrian zone for drinks, late-night comfort food and alternative music. There's a great selection of beers on tap, along with bargain-priced burgers, quiches and toasted sandwiches (€2 to €4).

Sé La Vie
BAR

(Rua Dom Paio Mendes 37; ◔3pm-2am Mon-Thu, to 3am Fri & Sat) A fun little cafe-bar with an alternative vibe that puts on great shows and has a good selection of beers and snacks.

Estúdio 22
BAR

(☑253 053 751; www.facebook.com/Estudio-22cafebargaleria; Rua Dom Paio Mendes 22; ◔2pm-2am Sun-Thu, to 4am Fri & Sat) Loungey cafe-bar on a bustling strip by the cathedral, great for sampling the speciality gin and tonics at night to the sound of live bands or DJs.

Taberna Svbvra
BAR

(Rua Dom Frei Caetano Brandão 101; ◔9pm-2am) Buzzy bar hidden behind a saloon-like wooden door, with a local low-key vibe and occasional live music.

Colinatrum
CAFE

(☑253 215 630; www.facebook.com/pages.colina trum; Rua Damião de Góis 11; ◔8am-12.30am Mon-Thu, 8.30am-2am Fri & Sat, 8.30am-12.30am Sun; 🛜) On a hill overlooking the countryside, this sleek glass-and-wood cafe is a fine meeting spot for a coffee or two, sunset cocktails or late-night bites. From the muslin-shaded outdoor terrace you'll have a splendid view of Bom Jesus do Monte.

☆ Entertainment

Teatro Circo de Braga
THEATRE

(☑253 203 800; www.theatrocirco.com; Avenida da Liberdade 697) One of the most dazzling theatres in the country, inside a grand fin-de-siècle building, where you can catch concerts, theatre and dance, with offerings ranging from the staid to the truly avant-garde.

🛍 Shopping

Som da Sé
MUSICAL INSTRUMENTS

(☑917 270 735; www.somdase.pt; Rua Dom Paio Mendes 77; ◔10am-7pm Mon-Sat) A vision of bliss for any music buff who's ever dreamed of owning a *guitarra portuguêsa* – the pear-shaped guitar used in fado music – this shop stocks a huge array of instruments made in Braga, which you can play on-site before choosing which to bring home. *Violas braguesas, cavaquinhos* (ukuleles) and other traditional Portuguese stringed instruments are also available.

❶ Information

The entire historical centre of Braga has free wi-fi.

Biblioteca Lúcio Craveiro da Silva (www.blcs. pt; Rue de São Paulo 1; ⊙9am-6pm Mon-Fri mid-Jul–mid-Sep, 9am-8pm Mon-Fri, 9.30am-12.30pm & 2-6pm Sat rest of year; ☏) Free wi-fi and internet access on public computers.

Hospital de Braga (☑253 027 000; www. hospitaldebraga.pt; Sete Fontes – São Victor) A block west of Avenida da Liberdade.

Police Station (☑253 200 420; Campo de São Tiago 6)

Post Office (Rua do Raio 175A; ⊙9am-6pm Mon-Fri) Just off Avenida da Liberdade.

Turismo (☑253 262 550; www.visitbraga. travel; Avenida da Liberdade 1; ⊙9am-6.30pm Mon-Fri, 9.30am-1pm & 2-5.30pm Sat & Sun) The helpful tourist office is in an art-deco–style building facing busy Praça da República.

❶ Getting There & Away

BUS

Braga has a centralised bus station that serves as a major regional hub.

Airport Bus (☑253 262 371; www.getbus. eu) About 10 buses daily do the 50-minute run between the Porto airport and Braga, in each direction. The one-way fare is €8 (€4 for children), return is €14 (€8 for children).

Empresa Hoteleira do Gerês (☑253 262 033; www.hoteisgeres.com/transports.html) Serves Vila do Gerês (€4.45, 1½ hours) about hourly during the week, five times on Saturday and three times on Sunday.

Rede Expressos (☑707 223 344; www. rede-expressos.pt) Has up to 15 daily buses to Lisbon (€21, 4½ hours).

Transdev (☑225 100 100; www.transdev.pt) Has at least eight buses per day to Viana do Castelo (€4.55, 1¾ hours), Barcelos (€2.70, one hour), Guimarães (€3.30, 50 minutes), Ponte de Lima (€4, one hour) and Porto (€4.85, one hour), plus four per day to Campo do Gerês (€4.30, 1½ hours). Service drops by half at weekends.

CAR & MOTORCYCLE

The A3 motorway makes Braga an easy day trip from Porto. The N101 from Braga to Guimarães is a good road for a slow ride.

Avic (☑253 203 910; www.avic.pt; Rua Gabriel Pereira de Castro 28; ⊙9am-7pm Mon-Fri, 9am-12.30pm Sat) An efficient agency for several car-rental companies.

TRAIN

Braga is at the end of a branch line from Nine and also within Porto's *suburbano* network, which means commuter trains travel every hour or so from Porto (€3.25, about one hour); the slightly faster Alfa Pendular (AP) train (€14.70, 37 minutes) is not worth the extra money.

Useful AP links include Coimbra (€21, 1¾ to 2¾ hours, four to seven daily) and Lisbon (€34, four hours, two to four daily).

Barcelos

POP 20,580

The Minho is famous for its sprawling outdoor markets, and the largest, oldest and most celebrated is the Feira de Barcelos, held every Thursday in this ancient town. Tour buses arrive by the dozen, spilling their contents into the already brimming marketplace. Even if you don't come on a Thursday, you'll find that Barcelos has a pleasant medieval core, with old stone towers perched over the river. It also harbours an ancient but still-thriving pottery tradition.

◉ Sights

★**Feira de Barcelos**   MARKET
(Barcelos Market; Campo da República; ⊙sunrise-sunset Thu) This market is held every Thursday in Barcelos on the banks of Rio Cávado. Despite attracting travellers, the market retains its rural soul. Villagers hawk everything from scrawny chickens to hand-embroidered linen, and Roma women bellow for business in the clothes section. Snack on sausages and homemade bread as you wander among brass cowbells, handwoven baskets and carved ox yokes.

Pottery is what most outsiders come to see. Especially popular is the yellow-dotted *louça de Barcelos* ware and the gaudy figurines à la Rosa Ramalho, a local potter known as the Grandma Moses of Portuguese pottery – her work put Barcelos on the map in the 1950s.

You'll need at least a couple of hours to see all the goods.

🛏 Sleeping & Eating

★**Quinta do Convento**
da Franqueira   INN €€
(☑253 831 606; www.quintadafranqueira.com; Carvalhal; s €80-95, d €100-115; ⊙Apr-Oct; ▣☏☒) Run by a delightful husband-wife duo, this remarkable *quinta* (estate) is housed in a 16th-century convent turned vineyard and inn, 6km southwest of Barcelos. If you've got

ROOSTER RESCUE

His colourful crest adorns a thousand souvenir stalls – and you will notice the great and brilliant cocks sprinkled along the Barcelos streets like bigger-than-life chess pieces – but just how and why did the proud Portuguese cockerel become a national icon? It seems that a humble pilgrim, plodding his way to Santiago de Compostela in the 16th (some say 14th) century, stopped to rest in Barcelos, only to find himself wrongfully accused of theft and then swiftly condemned to be hanged. The outraged pilgrim told the judge that the roast on the judge's dinner table would affirm the pilgrim's innocence. And, just as the judge was about to tuck in, the cooked cock commenced to crow. The pilgrim was set free.

time to linger, book ahead for one of the two fabulous self-catering apartments: the Cloister Flat, replete with charming historical details, or the more private Gatehouse, with its twin terraces affording splendid views.

Hotel do Terço HOTEL €€
(☑ 253 808 380; www.hoteldoterco.com; Rua de São Bento 7; s/d €52/62; P❄🕸) In the town centre, grab one of the stylish rooms at this sleek, modern option sitting atop its namesake shopping centre, a five-minute walk from the weekly market.

Galliano PORTUGUESE €€
(☑ 253 815 104; www.facebook.com/restaurantegalliano; Campo 5 de Outubro 20; mains €9-17; ⊙ noon-3pm & 7.30-11pm Mon-Sat, noon-3pm Sun) Head to this popular spot just northwest of the market for delicious regional delicacies like *barrosã grelhado* (grilled steak), along with good-value all-inclusive lunch specials (€9.90).

❶ Information

Turismo (☑ 253 811 882; turismo@cm-barcelos.pt; Largo Dr José Novais 27; ⊙ 9.30am-5.30pm Mon-Fri, 10am-1pm & 2-5pm Sat year-round, plus 10am-1pm & 2-4pm Sun mid-Mar–Sep) Hands out brochures and maps, and doles out useful info.

❶ Getting There & Away

Rede Expressos (p439) runs two express buses daily to Braga (€6, 25 minutes). **Transdev** (☑ 253 209 401; www.transdev.pt; Avenida Dr Sidónio País 445) has a more frequent but slower service to Braga (€2.70, one hour), with at least a dozen buses on weekdays and three to five on weekends. It also has services to Ponte de Lima (€3.75, one hour).

Barcelos' train station is on the Porto–Valença do Minho line. There are three to five direct trains a day to/from Porto (€5.30, 50 minutes), and commuter trains every hour or two that change at Nine (€4.20, 1¼ hours). There is similar service via Nine to Braga (€3.15, 35 minutes to 1¼ hours).

Guimarães

POP 47,590 / ELEV 400M

The proud birthplace of Afonso Henriques, the first independent king of Portugal (born here in 1110, he later used the city to launch the main thrust of the Reconquista against the Moors), and, thus, the Portuguese kingdom, Guimarães has beautifully preserved its illustrious past. Its medieval centre is a warren of labyrinthine lanes and picturesque plazas framed by 14th-century edifices, while on an adjacent hill stands a 1000-year-old castle and the massive palace built by the first duke of Bragança in the 15th century. Guimarães' glory was recognised in 2001, when Unesco declared its old centre a World Heritage Site. In 2012, the city was the European Capital of Culture, which has given it a more creative edge.

On top of the city's historical treasures, museums and cultural institutions, there are cafe-filled plazas, atmospheric guesthouses and delightful restaurants. Plus, Guimarães is a university town, lending much vitality to the place.

◉ Sights

Castelo CASTLE
(☑ 253 412 273; http://pdmas.guimaraes.pt/paco; adult/child €2/free; ⊙ 10am-6pm) FREE Built in the 11th century and still in fine form, the seven-towered castle is thought to be the birthplace of the great man himself, Afonso Henriques. Walk around the windswept ramparts and peruse multilingual exhibits on Portuguese history as you climb to the bird's-nest heights of Countess Mumadona's keep.

Penha VIEWPOINT
Some 7km southeast up a cobbled road – or a short ride on an ageing cable car – is the wooded summit of Penha (617m) overlooking Guimarães, the highest point for kilometres. Its cool woods make it a wonderful escape from the city and summer heat. Kids love

losing themselves amid the massive boulders, many cut with steps, crowned with flowers and crosses, or hiding in secret grottoes.

On the lower slopes of the hill lies the **Mosteiro de Santa Marinha da Costa**, 1.5km east of Penha's centre. It dates from 1154, when Dona Mafalda, wife of Afonso Henriques, commissioned it to honour a vow she made to the patron saint of pregnant women. Rebuilt in the 18th century, it's now a flagship Pousada de Portugal.

The easiest and finest route to the top of Penha is aboard the Teleférico de Penha (p446), which starts from Parque das Hortas, 600m east of Guimarães' old centre. You can also get there by taxi for about €10.

Plataforma das Artes e Criatividade
CULTURAL CENTRE

(Platform for Arts and Creativity; www.ciajg.pt; Avenida Conde de Margaride 175; adult/reduced €4/3, Sun mornings free; ⊙10am-1pm & 2-7pm Tue-Sun) For the 2012 European Capital of Culture, the old market square was revamped into a multipurpose cultural centre inside a shimmering three-floor metallic building that looks like a bunch of stacked-up boxes. Inside is a permanent exhibit by Portuguese painter José de Guimarães, with items from his private collection of pre-Columbian, African and Chinese art. Check out the room called Spells, with its impressive display of African masks.

Igreja de Nossa Senhora da Oliveira
CHURCH

(Largo da Oliveira; ⊙8.30am-noon & 3.30-7.30pm Mon-Sat, 9am-1pm & 5-8pm Sun) Founded by Countess Mumadona in the 12th century and rebuilt four centuries later, the beautiful Largo da Oliveira is dominated by this convent church.

The monument outside the church is a Gothic canopy and cross, reputedly marking the spot where the great Wamba the Visigoth, victorious over the Suevi, drove his spear into the ground beside an olive tree and refused to reign unless a tree sprouted from the handle. In true legendary fashion, it did just that.

Igreja de São Gualter
CHURCH

(Church of St Walter; Largo da República do Brasil; ⊙7.30am-noon & 3-5pm Mon-Sat, 7.30am-noon Sun) This slender 18th-century construction, with its 19th-century twin spires and blooming run-up from central Guimarães, has the most striking appeal of all the city's churches.

Museu Alberto Sampaio
MUSEUM

(☑253 423 910; www.culturanorte.gov.pt/pt/patrimonio/museu-de-alberto-sampaio; Rua de Alfredo Guimarães; adult/child €3/free, Sun morning free; ⊙10am-6pm Tue-Sun) Built around the serene Romanesque cloister of Igreja de Nossa Senhora da Oliveira, this museum has an excellent collection of ecclesiastical art and religious finery. Highlights include the tunic reputedly worn by João I at the Battle of Aljubarrota (1385).

Museu Arqueológico Martins Sarmento
MUSEUM

(www.csarmento.uminho.pt; Rua Paio Galvão; adult/reduced €3/1.50; ⊙10am-12.30pm & 2.30-5.30pm Tue-Sun) This fantastic collection of mostly Celtiberian artefacts is housed in a former convent and named after the archaeologist who excavated Citânia de Briteiros in 1875. Hefty stone artefacts, including thick Roman columns and milestones, and a mossy Celtic sarcophagus, are spread around the cloister.

Look for the impressive *pedras formosas* (beautiful stones) thought to have adorned Celtiberian bathhouses in the surrounding region, and the impressive case of Palaeolithic and Neolithic tools.

Paço dos Duques de Bragança
PALACE

(Ducal Palace; ☑253 412 273; http://pdmas.guimaraes.pt/paco; Rua Conde D Henrique; adult/child €5/free; ⊙10am-6pm) Looming over the medieval city on Guimarães' hilltop, with its crenellated towers and cylindrical brick chimneys, Paço dos Duques was first built in 1401 and later pompously restored as a presidential residence for Salazar. Today it's open to visitors, who can wander through the rooms, which house a collection of Flemish tapestries, medieval weapons, a chapel with glittering stained-glass windows, and enormous tapestries that relate various episodes in the Portuguese attempt to conquer North Africa.

Antigos Paços do Concelho
HISTORIC BUILDING

Guimarães' 14th-century former town hall sits above an arcaded portico providing a most graceful communication between cosy Largo da Oliveira and the more rambling Praça de Santiago.

Igreja de São Francisco
CHURCH

(Largo de São Francisco; ⊙9.30am-noon & 3-5pm Tue-Sat, 9.30am-1pm Sun) This 13th-century church has a brilliantly gilded and ornamented baroque interior, along with

Guimarães

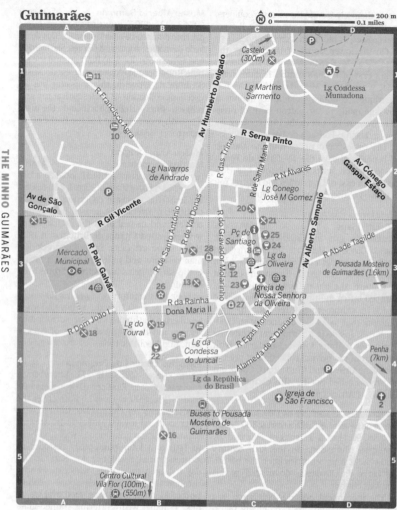

a lovely Renaissance cloister and 18th-century *azulejos* depicting scenes from the saint's life.

Tours

Quality Tours TOURS
(☎ 253 527 144; www.qualitytours.pt; Largo Martins Sarmento 89; bike/electric bike rental per 24hr €15/25; ☺ 9am-1pm & 2-6pm) Quality Tours rents bikes, scooters and four-wheelers, and organises a wide variety of tours in Guimarães and the surrounding area.

Festivals & Events

Guimarães Jazz MUSIC
One of the country's top festivals, this jazz extravaganza runs for 10 days in November.

Festas de Cidade e Gualterianas CULTURAL
(www.aoficina.pt) Marked by a free fair (held in Guimarães since 1452 to honour its patron saint), this festival features folk dancing, rock concerts, fireworks and parades. It takes place on the first weekend in August.

Guimarães

🛏 Sleeping

Santiago 31   HOSTEL €
(☏ 914 443 454; www.facebook.com/santiago
31hostel; Praça de São Tiago 31; dm €14-15, d/q
€40/80; 🛜) Boasting a fantastic location in
Guimarães' pedestrianised historic centre,
this hostel features bright dorms and private
rooms overlooking beautiful Praça de São Tiago or the spacious yard out back, along with
scrupulously clean, blue-tiled bathrooms.
Street noise at night is the main downside.

My Hostel   HOSTEL €
(☏ 253 414 023; www.myhostel-guimaraes.
webnode.pt; Rua Francisco Agra 135; dm €15-19, d
with shared/private bathroom €38/42; ❄🛜) This
stylish hostel has eight colourful, bright
dorms and doubles with swanky shared and
private bathrooms. There's a nice shared
kitchen/living room and a terrace overlooking the next-door neighbour's vast lawn.

1720 Quinta da Cancela   GUESTHOUSE €€
(☏ 919 199 299; www.quintadacancela.com; Rua
da Liberdade, S Lourenço de Sande; r/cottage
from €113/160; 🅿🛜🏊) Halfway between
Braga and Guimarães, this lovingly run
18th-century country wine estate has four
guest rooms filled with family antiques
and heirlooms, a cosy four-person cottage
and a natural pool onsite. Guests who book
directly receive breakfast and a bottle of
the estate's own *vinho verde*. Three-course
dinners (€30) are available on request, pre-

pared by the gracious, English-speaking
live-in owners.

Santa Luzia Arthotel   HOTEL €€
(☏ 253 071 800; www.santaluziaarthotel.com; Rua
Francisco Agra 100; s/d from €90/100; 🅿❄🛜🏊)
Embracing its motto, 'Inspired by art in
the heart of Guimarães', this stylish hotel
close to the city centre has ultracomfortable
rooms and suites, artfully done and with
four-star amenities. On-site facilities include
a homey lounge and bar area, a spa, a rooftop pool with deck chairs, an outdoor stage
and a welcoming foyer where piano concerts
are frequently held.

Hotel da Oliveira   HOTEL €€
(☏ 253 514 157; www.hoteldaoliveira.com; Rua de
Santa Maria 433; s/d €91/105, s/d ste €139/160;
❄🛜) With an unbeatable location in the
heart of town, this contemporary hotel in
a historic building has tastefully appointed
rooms jam-packed with amenities. The four
best suites overlook beautiful Praça da Oliveira, as does the breakfast room, whose front
terrace is a dreamy space to greet the day in
warm weather.

Casa do Juncal   GUESTHOUSE €€
(☏ 252 042 168; www.casajuncal.com; Rua Dr
Avelino Germano 65; s €90-120, d €105-135) This
gorgeously restored town house smack in
the heart of town features six swish suites,
each different in layout and with thoughtful original details. There's a beautiful little

WORTH A TRIP

CITÂNIA DE BRITEIROS

One of the most evocative archaeological sites in Portugal, Citânia de Briteiros (adult/child incl museum €3/1.50; ☉9am-6pm Apr-Sep, to 5pm Oct-Mar), 15km north of Guimarães, is the largest of a liberal scattering of northern Celtic hill settlements, called *citânias* (fortified villages), dating back at least 2500 years. It's also likely that this sprawling 3.8-hectare site, inhabited from about 300 BC to AD 300, was the Celtiberians' last stronghold against the invading Romans.

When archaeologist Dr Martins Sarmento excavated the site in 1875, he discovered the foundations and ruins of more than 150 rectangular, circular and elliptical stone huts, linked by paved paths and a water-distribution system, all cocooned by multiple protective walls. Highlights include two reconstructed huts that evoke what it was like to live in the settlement and, further down the hill, a bathhouse with a strikingly patterned stone doorway.

The Museu da Cultura Castreja (Museum of Pre-Roman Culture; Solar da Ponte; adult/child incl Citânia de Briteiros €3/1.50; ☉9.30am-12.30pm & 2-6pm Apr-Sep, to 5pm Oct-Mar), housed in Sarmento's 18th- and 19th-century manor house 2km down the hill towards Guimarães (in the village of Briteiros Salvadoralso), has important artefacts from various Celtiberian sites. Other artefacts are on display in the Museu Arqueológico (p441) in Guimarães.

From Guimarães, Transdev has about eight weekday buses that pass within 1km of the site; get off between the towns of Briteiros Salvador and Santa Leocádia. Check at the bus station for current schedule information.

back garden (though its chain-link fence detracts slightly from the view). Prices include breakfast and a welcome drink, and rental bikes are available.

Hotel Toural HOTEL €€
(📞253 517 184; www.hoteltoural.com; Lugar AL Carvalho; s/d €65/85; 🅿️ ❄️ @ 🛜) Accessed through a leafy alleyway entrance, this four-star hotel has 30 well-appointed rooms spread across two connected historic buildings. Some have views of the central patio or the distant mountains, but the nicest are the nine directly overlooking Largo do Toural.

Pousada Mosteiro de Guimarães POUSADA €€€
(📞253 511 249; www.pousadas.pt; Largo Domingos Leite de Castro, Lugar da Costa; s €130-190, d €140-200, ste €220-300; 🅿️ ❄️ 🛜 🏊) This former monastery overlooking the city from the slopes of Penha is a magnificent, sprawling structure. The gardens are stunning and you'll want to wander around the cloister, past dribbling fountains and masterful *azulejos*. The rooms inside the former monks' cells feel cramped, so book a room in the modern wing. Buses to the *pousada* run via Costa.

✗ Eating

Dan's Finger Food & Drinks BURGERS €
(www.facebook.com/dansfingerfood; Avenida de São Gonçalo 171; burgers €5-8; ☉noon-2.45pm & 7-10.45pm Tue-Sun) A young crowd queues up nightly at this trendy burger joint that does *picanha* (steak) burgers and tasty finger food like chicken and fish nuggets, all accompanied by great craft beer.

Danúbio Bar CAFE €
(Avenida Dom Afonso Henriques 15; sandwiches €5.50-9.50; ☉noon-11pm) This corner kiosk draws a local crowd for its delicious *pregos* (steak sandwiches), along with other simple but tasty snacks at low prices. Wash them down with beer either inside or on the tiny cobblestone square in front.

★ Résvés TAPAS €€
(📞253 067 491; www.facebook.com/resvesrestaurante; Rua de Santa Maria 39; tapas €7-9, mains €11-19; ☉11am-2.45pm & 7.30-9.45pm Tue-Sat) The upstairs restaurant and the downstairs bar are equally inviting at this newcomer opposite one of Guimarães prettiest squares. Feast on tapas or grilled meat on the 1st-floor terrace or sip drinks in the grassy back garden below. The wide-ranging menu features everything from garlic shrimp, mussels and clams to *picanha*, mushrooms with asparagus and pork belly gyozas.

Restaurante-Café Oriental PORTUGUESE €€
(📞253 414 048; Largo do Toural 11; mains €9-16; ☉noon-3pm & 7.30-11pm Sun-Thu, to 12.30am Fri & Sat) With tall windows gazing out over Largo do Toural, this historic restaurant under a

soaring ornamental stucco ceiling serves the full range of Portuguese classics, including fabulous *arroz de mariscos* (rice and seafood simmered in broth). At lunchtime, there's a good-value all-you-can-eat buffet (€11.40).

Histórico by Papaboa PORTUGUESE €€

(☑253 412 107; www.papaboa.pt; Rua de Val Donas 4; mains €12-20; ☺noon-2.30pm & 7-10pm) The setting – in a medieval fort with breezy courtyard seating and glassed-in stone dining room – is tremendous. Service is top-notch and the fare is dressed-up yet traditional, such as black pork with prawns and mustard sauce. The weekday *prato do dia* (lunch special) is a steal at €8.50. They have live music some nights.

Solar do Arco PORTUGUESE €€

(☑253 035 233; Rua de Santa Maria 48-50; mains €7.50-15; ☺noon-3.30pm, 7-11pm Wed-Mon; ✱) With a handsomely panelled dining room under a graceful arcade, this refined choice serves Portuguese classics made with straight-from-the-market ingredients. The location, smack in Guimarães historic centre, makes it popular with tourists, while the classy atmosphere draws in local families celebrating special events.

Cor de Tangerina VEGETARIAN €€

(☑253 542 009; www.cordetangerina.pt; Largo Martins Sarmento 89; mains €11-12; ☺noon-3pm Tue-Thu, noon-3pm & 7.30-10pm Fri & Sat; ☑) 🍃 This charming restaurant whips up a good selection of cuisine you won't find elsewhere in Guimarães. Changing art exhibitions decorate the walls, while the garden (with tangerine tree) produces many of the herbs used in the ancient stone kitchen. The chef is something of a herbal alchemist, capable of brewing all manner of teas and tonics, too.

★A Cozinha GASTRONOMY €€€

(☑253 534 022; www.restauranteacozinha.pt; Largo do Serralho 4; lunch menu €17.50, dinner mains €40-50; ☺7.30-11pm Mon, 12.30-3.30pm & 7.30-11pm Tue-Sat) Awarded a Michelin star in November 2018 after only two years in business, António Loureiro's intimate restaurant is Guimarães' newest go-to address. The parade of artfully presented amuse-bouches, market-fresh main courses and classic Portuguese desserts lives up to the hype, while the service – friendly, efficient and not the least bit overbearing – adds another stellar note.

Le Babachris PORTUGUESE €€€

(☑964 420 548; www.lebabachris.com; Rua Dom João 39; lunch €12, dinner €28-35; ☺1-2.30pm & 8-10.30pm Tue-Sat) The decor of this long and narrow two-floor restaurant is so simple and unassuming that you wouldn't expect such top-notch food to come out of its tiny kitchen. But top-notch it is – inventive, seasonal and market-fresh. They serve set menus only, featuring a meat and a fish option. Book ahead.

🍸 Drinking & Nightlife

Poncha's Madeira BAR

(☑967 292 146; www.facebook.com/ponchas madeirabar38; Rua de Santa Maria 38; ☺9pm-midnight Sun-Tue, to 2am Wed-Sat) This stone-walled bar with a small back garden makes an appealing stop for late-night cocktails.

Coconuts BAR

(☑253 047 207; Largo da Oliveira 1-3; ☺8am-midnight Tue, 8am-2am Wed-Sat, 9am-midnight Sun) A popular bar with *azulejo*-filled interiors and tables on the cobblestone square. It has coffee, snacks and a low-key vibe during the day. It turns into a happening hotspot at night, with DJs on Fridays and Saturdays.

Cervejaria Martins BEER HALL

(☑253 416 330; Largo do Toural 32-35; ☺10am-2am Mon-Sat) An always bustling cafe-bar where sport blasts on the TV and lots of men sit around the circular counter. A long-standing favourite, going strong since the 1950s. It serves food until late (cheaper if you eat at the counter).

El Rock BAR

(www.facebook.com/elrockbar; Praça de São Tiago 31; ☺2pm-2am) Dug into a narrow stone room and spreading onto the plaza is this funky beer bar. It hosts occasional live bands.

Tásquilhado BAR

(Rua de Santa Maria 42; ☺9pm-2am Mon-Sat) One of many bar-hopping venues in the historic centre, this cosy, ever-popular bar plays alternative sounds and offers enticing drink specials during the week.

★ Entertainment

Convívio Associação PERFORMING ARTS

(☑960 410 544; www.facebook.com/con viviogmr; Largo da Misericórdia 7-8; ☺3-7pm & 9pm-midnight Mon-Thu, to 2am Fri, 9pm-2am Sat) Started 52 years ago, this creative cultural association – also a jazz school – is still going strong.

Its programme includes classical music concerts, jazz sessions, exhibits, theatre and workshops. Fridays and Saturdays are the busiest nights, when an older boho crowd descends on the bar and small open-air patio.

Centro Cultural Vila Flor　ARTS CENTRE
(📞253 424 700; www.ccvf.pt; Avenida Dom Afonso Henriques 701) CCVF kick-started the city's cultural revival when it opened in 2005 in a striking modern building added on to a converted 18th-century palace. Events at this culture powerhouse include movie screenings, cafe concerts, theatre performances and art exhibits.

🛍 Shopping

Loja Oficina　ARTS & CRAFTS
(📞253 515 250; www.aoficina.pt/loja.php; Rua da Rainha Dona Maria II 132; ⊙10am-1pm & 2-7pm Mon-Sat) Guimarães is famous for its decorative needlework (known in Portuguese as *Bordado de Guimarães*), and this central shop keeps the tradition alive. Browse the display cases filled with fine embroidery and other local crafts up front or head to the back room to watch artists at work.

Oliva da Praça　FOOD
(📞916 075 920; www.facebook.com/olivadapraca; Rua Doutor António Mota Prego 13-15; ⊙12.30-7pm Tue-Sat) Opened by a young local couple in 2017, this shop specialises in award-winning extra-virgin olive oils from the neighbouring state of Trás-os-Montes, Enjoy free tastings and explore shelves stocked with other Portuguese foodie favourites such as sardines in decorative tins.

ⓘ Information

There's free wi-fi on the main squares in town.
Hospital da Senhora da Oliveira (📞253 540 330; www.hospitaldeguimaraes.min-saude.pt; Rua dos Cutileiros 114, Creixomil) Opposite the bus station.
Police Station (📞253 540 660; Alameda Dr Alfredo Pimenta)
Post Office (Rua Teixeira de Pascoais 307; ⊙8.30am-6.30pm Mon-Fri, 9am-12.30pm Sat)
Turismo (📞253 421 221; www.guimaraes-turismo.com; Praça de São Tiago; ⊙9.30am-7pm Mon-Fri, 10am-7pm Sat, 10am-5pm Sun Jun-mid-Sep, to 6pm Mon-Sat, 5pm Sun rest of year) The excellent, informative staff speak English, French and Spanish.

ⓘ Getting There & Away

BUS

Transdev (📞225 100 100; www.transdev.pt) has buses leaving at least hourly for Braga (€3.30, 50 minutes) Monday through Saturday, and eight buses on Sunday. It also has services to Porto (€3, 50 minutes) running approximately hourly on weekdays but less often on weekends.
Rodonorte (📞253 423 500; www.rodonorte.pt) heads for Amarante (€7.40, one hour), Vila Real (€8.30, 1½ hours) and Bragança (€13.80, 3½ hours).
Rede Expressos (📞707 223 344; www.rede-expressos.pt) has express service to Lisbon (€19.50, 4½ hours) daily.
Get Bus (📞253 262 371; www.getbus.eu) has six buses daily that do the 50-minute run between the Porto airport and Guimarães, in each direction. The one-way fare is €8 (€4 for children); return is €14 (€8 for children).

TRAIN

Guimarães is the terminus of a branch of Porto's wide *suburbano* network. Commuter trains potter out to Guimarães from Porto (€3.25, 55 to 75 minutes) 11 to 16 times daily. Avoid the much pricier, once-daily *intercidade* (express) train (€14.70, 55 minutes).

ⓘ Getting Around

There is street parking in front of the Convento do Carmo at the foot of the Paço dos Duques.

Quality Tours (p442) rents out bikes, scooters and four-wheelers, and organises guided walking tours.

From Parque das Hortas, 600m east of the historic centre, the **Teleférico de Penha** (Cable Car; 📞253 515 085; www.turipenha.pt; Rua Aristides Sousa Mendes; one-way/return €3/5; ⊙10am-7pm Mon-Fri, to 8pm Sat & Sun Jun, Jul & Sep, 10am-8pm daily Aug, shorter hours Oct-May) whisks visitors to the top of Penha (617m), a summit with fine views over Guimarães.

Viana do Castelo

POP 37,970

The jewel of the Costa Verde, Viana do Castelo is blessed with an appealing medieval centre, an attractive riverfront and lovely beaches just outside the city. The old quarter showcases leafy 19th-century boulevards and narrow lanes crowded with Manueline manors and rococo palaces, all dramatically presided over by the pearly white, neo-Byzantine Santa Luzia church (p447) on the hilltop high above town. The town's setting just by the Rio

Lima estuary makes Viana a handy base for exploring the lower Lima valley.

History

The remains of Celtic hill settlements on Monte de Santa Luzia, overlooking the contemporary town centre, convey Viana do Castelo's deep historical roots, while its Manueline mansions and monasteries recall its 16th-century prosperity as a major cod-fishing port. In fact, by the mid-17th century it had bloomed into Portugal's biggest overall port, with merchants trading as far afield as Russia.

More riches arrived in the 18th century, with the advent of the Brazilian sugar and gold trade. But with Brazil's independence and the rising importance of Porto, Viana's golden age stuttered and faded. These days Viana earns much of its living and reputation as the Minho's favourite resort town.

⊙ Sights

Monte de Santa Luzia   HILL
There are two good reasons to visit Viana's 228m eucalyptus-clad hill. One is the wondrous view down the coast and up the Lima valley. The other is the fabulously over-the-top, 20th-century, neo-Byzantine **Templo do Sagrado Coração de Jesus** (Templo Monumento Santa Luzia, Temple of the Sacred Heart of Jesus; www.templosantaluzia.org; admission to dome €2; ⊙9am-6.45pm Apr-Oct, to 4.45pm Nov-Mar). You can get a little closer to heaven by climbing to the *zimbório* (lantern tower) atop its dome, via a lift, followed by an elbow-scraping stairway – take the museum entrance on the ground floor.

Behind the Pousada do Monte de Santa Luzia is another attraction, the **Citânia de Santa Luzia** (www.culturanorte.pt/pt/patrimonio/citania-de-santa-luzia; adult/child €2/free; ⊙10am-1pm & 2-6pm Tue-Sun), ruins of a Celtiberian *citânia* (fortified village) from around the 4th century BC. You'll see the stones peeking above the wind-blown savannah. Most of the site is accessible via a boardwalk.

You can get up the mountain by the restored **funicular** (www.cm-viana-castelo.pt/pt/funicular-de-santa-luzia; Avenida 25 de Abril; one-way/return €2/3; ⊙9am-8pm Jun-Sep, 10am-noon & 1-5pm Oct-May, closed Mon Nov-Feb), which departs from near the train station every 15 minutes. You can also drive or take a taxi (3.5km) to the top or hike 2km of steps (only for the fit and/or penitent). The road starts by the hospital and the steps begin about 200m up the road.

Praia do Cabedelo   BEACH
This is one of the Minho's best beaches: a 1km-long arc of blonde, powdery sand that folds into grassy dunes backed by a grove of wind-blown pines. It's across the river from town, best reached on a five-minute **ferry trip** (one-way/return adult €1.40/2.80, child under 12yr/under 6yr half-price/free; ⊙9am-6pm May-Sep) from the pier south of Largo 5 de Outubro.

Gil Eannes   SHIP
(☑258 809 710; www.fundacaogileannes.pt; Doca Comercial; €4, children under 6 free; ⊙9.30am-7pm Apr-Oct, to 6pm Nov-Mar) Demanding attention on the waterfront near Largo 5 de Outubro is a pioneering naval hospital ship, the *Gil Eannes (zheel yan-*ish*)*. Now restored, the ship once provided on-the-job care for those fishing off the coast of Newfoundland. Visitors can clamber around the steep decks and cabins, though a scattering of old clinical equipment may make your hair stand on end.

Museu do Traje   MUSEUM
(Costume Museum; ☑258 809 306; www.cm-viana-castelo.pt/pt/mt-apresentacao; Praça da República; Tue-Fri €2, Sat & Sun free; ⊙10am-6pm Tue-Fri, 10am-1pm & 3-6pm Sat & Sun) This attractive museum houses the traditional wear used for farming, fishing and seaweed harvesting in centuries past. You'll see costumes worn during the Romaria de Nossa Senhora d'Agonia, and cool antique looms. The then-and-now mural-sized photos on the 2nd floor are pretty special, too.

Museu de Artes Decorativas   MUSEUM
(☑258 809 305; www.cm-viana-castelo.pt/pt/mad-apresentacao; Largo de São Domingos; Tue-Fri €2, Sat & Sun free; ⊙10am-6pm Tue-Fri, 10am-1pm & 3-6pm Sat & Sun) **FREE** The 18th-century Palacete Barbosa Maciel bears witness to Viana's affluent past. It houses this impressive collection of 17th- and 18th-century ceramics (especially blue Portuguese china) and furniture. Most impressive are three 2nd-floor rooms lined with *azulejos,* depicting scenes of hunting and palace life.

Praça da República   SQUARE
This fine hub of seven narrow laneways is at the heart of the old town's zone of mansions and monuments. An especially elegant example is the **Chafariz**, a Renaissance fountain built in 1554. The fountain is topped with Manueline motifs of an armillary sphere and the cross of the Order of Christ. The fortress-like **Antigos Paços do Concelho** is the old town

Viana do Castelo

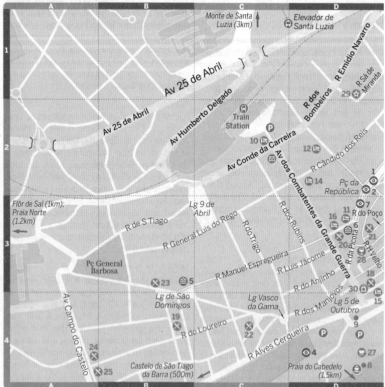

THE MINHO VIANA DO CASTELO

Viana do Castelo

⊙ Sights
1 Antigos Paços do Concelho	D2
2 Chafariz	D2
3 Fábrica do Chocolate	F1
4 Gil Eannes	D4
5 Museu de Artes Decorativas	B3
6 Museu do Traje	D3
7 Praça da República	D3

⊕ Activities, Courses & Tours
8 River Trips	D4
9 Viv'Experiência	D4

⊜ Sleeping
10 Casa Melo Alvim	C2
11 Dona Emília	D3
12 Enjoy Viana Guest House	D2
Fábrica do Chocolate	(see 3)
13 Hotel Jardim	E3
14 Hotel Laranjeira	D2
15 Margarida da Praça	D3
16 O Laranjeira	D3

⊗ Eating
17 À Moda Antiga	E2
18 Casa de Pasto Maria de Perre	D3
19 Casa Primavera	B4
20 Confeitaria Natário	D3
21 Dolce Vianna	D3
22 O Marquês	C4
23 O Pescador	B3
24 Taberna do Valentim	A4
25 Zefa Carqueja	A4

⊙ Drinking & Nightlife
26 Café da Sé	E3
27 Foz	D4
28 República	D3

⊕ Entertainment
29 Teatro Municipal Sá de Miranda	D1

⊕ Shopping
30 Arte Viana	D3

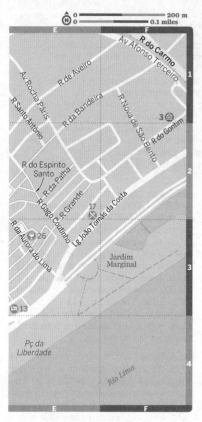

hall – a 16th-century creation that sometimes hosts contemporary art exhibitions.

Castelo de
São Tiago da Barra
CASTLE

(⊙ 9am-12.30pm & 2-5.30pm Mon-Fri) **FREE** You can still scoot around the ramparts of this squat castle, a short walk west of the centre, which began in the 15th century as a small-ish fort. It was integrated into a larger fort, commissioned by Felipe II of Spain (Felipe I of Portugal) in 1592, to guard the prosperous port against pirates.

🏃 Activities

Viana Locals
SURFING

(☑ 258 325 168; www.facebook.com/vianalocals; Praia do Cabedelo) A friendly, full-service board-sports outfitter and school right on Praia do Cabedelo. It has surfboards, kite gear and paddleboards for rent and sale, and also does overnight repairs.

Viv'Experiência
TOURS

(☑ 258 098 415; www.vivexperiencia.pt; Praça do Eixo Atlântico; ⊙ 10am-7pm Jul & Aug, 10am-1pm & 2-6pm Tue-Sun Sep-Oct & Mar-Jun, to 5pm Tue-Sun Nov-Feb) Operating from Viana's municipal tourist office, this agency offers food, wine and culture itineraries in the Minho and Douro; multilingual city tours; and a variety of activities, including canyoning, kayaking, surfing, hiking and bike rental.

Descubra Minho
TOURS

(☑ 969 220 704; www.descubraminho.pt; Montaria) Donkey tours, hikes and cycling trips to the nearby mountain of Serra d'Arga, just a 25-minute drive away, visit its eight scenic villages and protected nature that includes diverse fauna such as the Iberian frog and the Garrano horse. The local guides can even take you on full-moon night treks. Reserve ahead.

River Trips
TOURS

(☑ 962 305 595; www.passeiofluvial.com; ⊙ May-Sep) If there are enough passengers, boats run up and down the Rio Lima daily in summer from the pier south of Largo 5 de Outubro (the same dock where ferries depart to Praia do Cabedelo). The most common trip takes 40 minutes (adult/child €7.50/4).

Longer (90-minute) excursions (€12/6.50) take in the old shipyards; these must be booked at least a day ahead.

🎉 Festivals & Events

Carnaval festivities in Viana are considered northern Portugal's best. The town also goes a little nuts in mid-May during **Semana Académica** (or Queima das Fitas), a week of end-of-term student madness. The *turismo* has details of other annual events.

🛌 Sleeping

Enjoy Viana Guest House
GUESTHOUSE €

(☑ 914 668 475; Passeio Mordomas da Romaria 53-55; d/tr/q from €39/49/85) Friendly owner Bernardino rents out a variety of reasonably priced rooms at this simple guesthouse on a pedestrian street near the heart of town. Ranging from shared-bath twins to family suites, all are basic but immaculate, with crisp white sheets and bedspreads.

Orbitur
CAMPGROUND €

(☑ 258 322 167; www.orbitur.com; Rua Diogo Álvares, Praia do Cabedelo; per adult/child/tent/car €7.10/4.75/8.25/7.40; ⊙ Mar-Oct; 🛜🏊) Nestled on the inland side of lovely sand dunes, this shady site is within walking distance of the

SURFING & KITESURFING IN MINHO

Praia do Cabedelo (p447) is an excellent kitesurfing destination, with consistent onshore wind year-round. It's a great teaching site, but also fun for intermediate surfers thanks to the lagoon-like conditions created by the southern headland and harbour breakwater, which is a full kilometre north. There's good kiting and some traditional surfing at **Esposende** 17km south of Cabedelo, but conditions are iffy.

Among the fine beaches strung north along the 25km of coast between Viana do Castelo and Caminha, **Afife** has the best surf breaks, with waves topping out at 2m during peak swells. Four daily regional trains (€1.45, 12 minutes) make their way up the coast to Afife from Viana. Advanced kitesurfers will want to drive a bit further north to **Moledo**, where the wind and waves are at their fiercest and finest.

For tips and gear rental, stop by Viana Locals (p449) at Praia do Cabedelo.

ferry pier (and is a two-minute walk to the sea) and also has two- to six-person bungalows (€101 to €132). It heaves with holidaymakers in summer.

★Dona Emília GUESTHOUSE €€
(☎917 811 392; www.dona-emilia.com; Rua Manuel Espregueira 6; d with shared/private bathroom from €55/75;) This phenomenal new B&B in a 19th-century town house commands front-row perspectives of Viana's historical centre from its luminous, high-ceilinged common areas and six guest rooms. Second-floor units have shared facilities, while suites under the eaves have beautifully tiled private bathrooms. All abound in period details; two have terraces with views over Viana's elegant main square or the leafy backyard.

★Margarida da Praça GUESTHOUSE €€
(☎258 809 630; www.facebook.com/margaridadapracahotelrestaurante; Largo 5 de Outubro 58; s/d from €75/85; @) Down near the riverfront, this recently remodelled boutique inn offers plush rooms with three-star amenities in sober tones of grey, white and beige. The restaurant downstairs is popular for its all-inclusive weekday lunch menus (€9 to €11).

Staff are warm and helpful, and there's a TV room and a small top-floor terrace. The 3rd-floor suite (€10 more) is a charmer. Book ahead.

Casa Melo Alvim HOTEL €€
(☎258 808 200; www.meloalvimhouse.com; Avenida Conde da Carreira 28; d €90-120, ste €130-180; P@) Deluxe rooms in a stately 16th-century mansion, individually decked out with hardwood floors, four-poster beds, original stone accents and marble bathrooms. No two rooms are alike, but it is worth paying the extra €9 for the deluxe rooms, which have more space, huge ceilings and ornately carved beds.

Fábrica do Chocolate HOTEL €€
(☎258 244 000; www.fabricadochocolate.com; Rua do Gontim 70-76; r from €90) Housed in a former chocolate factory, this modern hotel sports 18 themed rooms and suites with a choco theme running throughout. The on-site cafe serves a full lineup of chocolatey treats, and the downstairs **museum** (☎258 244 000; www.fabricadochocolate.com; adult/child €8/6; ⊙10am-6pm Tue-Sun;) is free for hotel guests. It's all a little gimmicky (witness the gaudy, over-the-top decor in the Willy Wonka room) but fun for families.

O Laranjeira GUESTHOUSE €€
(☎258 822 258; www.olaranjeira.com; Rua Manuel Espregueira 24; s €40-64, d €48-71;) This bright town house is a fantastic choice in the old centre. It's a cosy family-run spot with eight small but soulful rooms, each with a theme and some with patios. There's an excellent restaurant on the ground floor, where guests enjoy special half-board rates (€19 extra per person).

Hotel Jardim HOTEL €€
(☎258 828 915; www.hoteljardimviana.pt; Largo 5 de Outubro 68; s €45-55, d €50-75; P@) In a stately 19th-century town house near the riverfront, this quirky two-star has spacious rooms with wooden floors, sizeable bathrooms and stone-framed French windows overlooking the historic centre or the river. For better views nab one of the rooms on the top floors.

Hotel Laranjeira HOTEL €€
(☎258 822 261; www.hotelaranjeira.com; Rua Cândido dos Reis 45; s €50-68, d €55-83; P) Smack in the historic centre, this modern hotel has 26 contemporary if poky rooms with pine floors and glass-partitioned bathrooms. Some have balconies and others great views of Santa Luzia.

Flôr de Sal BOUTIQUE HOTEL €€€
(☑258 800 100; www.hotelflordesal.com; Avenida de Cabo Verde 100, Praia Norte; s €125-145, d €145-195; P ✳ 🛜 ❄) Perched on a windswept stretch of rocky coastline 2km west of the centre, this sleek designer offering looks unpromising from the outside, but inside you'll find white-washed rooms with modern touches, and fine views from the huge balconies and the spacious bar-restaurant-lounge area downstairs. Sea-facing rooms are well worth the extra €20. There's also a spa, gym and indoor pool.

Pousada do Monte de Santa Luzia POUSADA €€€
(☑258 800 370; www.pousadas.pt/en/hotel/pousada-viana; Monte de Santa Luzia; d/ste from €140/220; P ✳ @ 🛜 ❄) This regal 1918 hotel sits squarely atop Monte de Santa Luzia, peering down at the rear of the basilica and beyond it to some of the best coastal views in Portugal. Common areas are splendid, while the rooms themselves are comfortable, if less inspired than the views.

🍴 Eating

Viana do Castelo whips up some excellent seafood – among the region's best. Although you can find fresh fish at restaurants throughout the old town, the best joints are around the old fishing quarter on the west side of town.

★ O Marquês PORTUGUESE €
(Rua do Marquês 72; meals from €6; ⊙noon-3.30pm & 7-10pm Mon-Fri, noon-3.30pm Sat) A tremendous backstreet find, this place is absolutely jammed with locals for the *platos do dia*. Think baked cod with white beans or roasted turkey leg with potatoes and salad. It's a friendly, satisfying, family-run affair.

Casa Primavera SEAFOOD €
(Taberna Soares; ☑258 821 807; www.facebook.com/TabernaSoares; mains from €7; ⊙10am-10pm Mon-Sat) At this authentic fishers' hole-in-the-wall decorated with framed pictures of boats, locals gather in the late afternoon for small plates of shrimp and other seafood snacks washed down with *champarrião*, a classic Viana concoction of *vinho verde* and beer dosed with sugar. Come nightfall, the menu expands to include full meals of codfish, potatoes, vegetables and other Portuguese staples.

À Moda Antiga PORTUGUESE €
(☑258 023 229; www.amodaantiga.pt; Largo João Tomás da Costa 63; mains €7-12; ⊙9.30am-7pm Tue-Thu & Sun, to 10pm Fri & Sat) On the water-front opposite the Jardim Marginal, this retro market and bistro serves great weekday lunch menus (soup, main dish, drink and coffee for just €7), along with all-day dishes such as handmade burgers. The industrial space has high ceilings and exposed stone walls and a curated selection of old-fashioned Portuguese brands, plus there are a couple of tables outside.

Confeitaria Natário BAKERY €
(☑258 822 376; Rua Manuel Espregueira 37; pastries from €1; ⊙9am-9pm Mon & Wed-Sat, 9am-1.30pm & 3.30-9pm Sun) This popular bakery is the place to try delicious *bolas de Berlim* (cream-filled doughnuts) – so good that you'll often have to wait in line. Get them warm from the oven at 11.30am and 4.30pm. Locals also convene here for *milfolhas* (flaky pastry filled with shrimp or meat), traditionally enjoyed with a glass of sparkling wine.

Dolce Vianna PIZZA €
(☑258 824 860; www.facebook.com/dolcevianna; Rua do Poço 44; pizzas €6.50-9; ⊙noon-3pm & 7-10pm) This popular pizzeria buzzes day and night, thanks to the endless variety of tasty, cheesy pizzas churned out of the wood-burning oven in the corner. Budget travellers will also appreciate the bargain-priced rooms for rent upstairs (singles/doubles from €20/30).

Casa de Pasto Maria de Perre PORTUGUESE €€
(☑258 822 410; www.casamariaperre.pt; Rua de Viana 118; mains €9.75-15.50; ⊙noon-3pm & 7-11pm Tue-Sat, noon-3pm Sun) This convivial two-floor restaurant with exposed stone walls in a tiny side street off the waterfront gets very busy at lunchtime. The focus is on daily

> ### CELEBRATION OF SORROWS
>
> Streets decorated with coloured sawdust, women decked out in traditional finery of scarlet and gold, men drinking till they keel over. Viana do Castelo's **Romaria de Nossa Senhora d'Agonia** (Festival of Our Lady of Sorrows) is one of the Minho's most spectacular festivals. It takes place for three or four days around 20 August. Accommodation is very tight at this time, so book well ahead.
>
> Expect everything from emotive religious processions to upbeat parades with deafening drums and lumbering carnival *gigantones* (giants) and *cabeçudos* (big heads).

specials featuring fresh fish dishes and also hearty meat options.

Taberna do Valentim
SEAFOOD €€
(☑258 827 505; Campo do Castelo 45; mains €9-12.50; ⊙12.30-3pm & 7.30-10pm Mon-Sat) Since 1939, this bright and buzzing seafood restaurant has been serving fresh grilled fish by the kilo and rich seafood stews such as *arroz de tamboril* (monkfish rice) and *caldeirada* (fish stew).

O Pescador
SEAFOOD €€
(☑258 826 039; www.opescadorviana.com; Largo de São Domingos 35; mains €12-18.50; ⊙noon-3pm & 7-10pm Tue-Sat, noon-3pm Sun) A simple, friendly, family-run restaurant admired by locals for its seafood and tasty lunch specials.

Zefa Carqueja
GRILL €€
(☑258 828 284; Campo do Castelo 46; mains €8-16; ⊙9.30am-3.30pm & 5.30-11.30pm) A decades-old Viana mainstay, this grill house does some of the best barbecue chicken and ribs in northern Portugal. You can also get barbecued seafood – including lobster. Dine in or line up at the grill and take it away.

Drinking & Entertainment

Café da Sé
WINE BAR
(☑258 824 895; www.facebook.com/saladestarviana; Largo do Instituto Histórico do Minho 16/18; ⊙8pm-2am Tue-Sun) Tucked below Viana's cathedral, this favourite nightspot draws a local crowd for caipirinhas, glasses of wine and nibbles of local charcuterie and cheeses from early evening onwards.

República
BAR
(Praça da Erva 17-19; ⊙9pm-2am Tue-Thu, to 3am Fri & Sat) This is where the action happens on weekend nights, at this cosy bar on the old town's main square. Tables spill out and crowds hang out till closing time.

Foz
CAFE
(☑258 808 060; www.facebook.com/fozzviana; Praça da Liberdade; ⊙11am-midnight Sun-Tue & Thu, to 2am Fri & Sat) This glass-box bar-cafe by the riverfront is a popular evening gathering point for locals. It's a prime spot for a sundowner, with full-on views of the water and the vast adjacent pedestrianised square.

Teatro Municipal Sá de Miranda
THEATRE
(☑258 809 382; www.cm-viana-castelo.pt/pt/teatro-municipal-sa-de-miranda; Rua Sá de Miran-

da) Viana do Castelo's cultural epicentre, this pink-washed neoclassical theatre hosts a regular lineup of music, theatre, dance and the occasional opera.

🛍 Shopping

Arte Viana
CLOTHING
(☑258 829 045; www.arteviana.pai.pt; Avenida Combatentes da Grande Guerra 24; ⊙9am-noon & 2-6pm) If Viana's Costume Museum (p447) leaves you lusting after your very own traditional Portuguese outfit, stroll a few blocks south to this main street boutique that sells a fabulous array of colourfully woven and embroidered dresses, scarves, slippers, handbags and jewellery. Even if you're not in the market to buy, the window displays alone are worth a look.

ℹ Information

Hospital (☑258 802 100; www.ulsam.min-saude.pt; Estrada de Santa Luzia; ▓) North of the train station.

Police Station (☑258 809 880; Rua de Aveiro)

Post Office (Avenida Conde da Carreira; ⊙9am-6pm Mon-Fri)

Viana Welcome Centre (p449) Centrally located down by the riverfront; offers tourist information, tours and activities.

ℹ Getting There & Away

BUS

Long-distance *expresso* buses operate from the shiny, centralised bus station, which is just across the tracks from the train station.

AV Cura (☑258 806 830; www.avcura.com) Runs up the Lima valley to Ponte de Lima (€3.60, one hour), Arcos de Valdevez (€4.55, 1½ hours) and Ponte da Barca (€4.75, two hours) at least hourly on weekdays (less at weekends).

AV Minho (☑258 800 340; www.avminho.pt) Runs a line from Porto (€6.50, two hours) at least four times daily, passing through Esposende (€3.70, 40 minutes); one to three daily buses run to Valença do Minho (€5, one hour) and Monção (€5.50, 1¼ hours).

Transdev (☑225 100 100; www.transdev.pt) Has at least eight weekday and four weekend runs to Braga (€4.55, 1¾ hours).

TRAIN

Daily direct services from Porto include five IR/international trains (€7.95, 1¼ to 1½ hours) and five regional services (€6.85, two hours). For Braga (€6.05, 1½ to two hours, 14 daily), change at Nine. There are also seven to 11 daily trains to Valença do Minho (€5.10, 45 minutes to one hour).

ℹ️ Getting Around

Parking can be a challenge – most locals opt for paid underground car parks sprinkled about the centre (including car parks on either end of Avenida dos Combatentes da Grande Guerra). There's ample free parking next to the Castelo de São Tiago da Barra. If you need wheels to hit the beaches north of Viana, **Orbita** (☑ 258 813 513; www.orbitaviagens.com; Rua Alves Cerqueira 216-218; ☺ 9am-6pm) rents cars down by the riverfront; reserve at least one day in advance.

To get up to Monte de Santa Luzia, take the funicular (p447), which departs from near the train station every 15 minutes.

Praia do Cabedelo is best reached via the ferry (p447) from the pier south of Largo 5 de Outubro.

Valença do Minho

POP 6540

Now you're really in the Minho, where all is green, fertile and rustling in shared Spanish–Porto winds and waters. And no place has a better view of it all than this atmospheric fort village occupying strategic heights above the picturesque Rio Minho.

Valença do Minho sits just a cannonball shot from Spain, and its impressive pair of citadels long served as the Minho's first line of defence against Spanish aggression. But history insists on repeating itself and these days the town is regularly overrun by Spanish hordes in search of bargain-priced Portuguese sheets and towels.

Walking tourism is also big in Valença. This is the spot where the Caminho Português (the Portuguese branch of the Camino de Santiago pilgrimage route) crosses into Spain for the final approach to Santiago de Compostela. You'll see plenty of backpackers following the scallop-shell symbols throughout town.

◉ Sights

The Spanish tourists come armed with wallets and make away with volumes of towels and linens from the high stacks that line the cobbled streets. The good news is that on even the busiest days (which tend to be Wednesdays and weekends), you can sidestep the towel touts and discover that Valença's two interconnected forts also contain a fully functioning village where locals shop, eat, drink and gossip among pretty squares and narrow,

medieval lanes. And when, in the evening, the weary troops retreat to Spain with their loot, the empty watchtowers return to silent contemplation of their ancient enemy – the glowering Spanish fortress of Tui just across the river.

Visitors can easily see the sights of the town as a day trip, but there are two atmospheric places to sleep within the fortress walls that allow you to see and feel peaceful Valença when it empties at sunset. That's when you can hear the footsteps of kittens in the laneways while birdsong echoes off ancient stone walls.

Fortaleza de Valença   FORTRESS

Valença's *fortaleza* is in fact two fortresses, bristling with bastions, watchtowers, massive gateways and defensive bulwarks, connected by a single bridge. The old churches and Manueline mansions inside testify to the success of the fortifications against several sieges, some as late as the 19th century. The earliest fortifications date from the 13th-century reign of Dom Afonso III, although largely what you see today was built in the 17th century, its design inspired by the French military architect Vauban.

Zip past the tacky gift shops and towel merchants and follow the cobbled lanes to the far end of the larger northern fortress, which incorporates Dom Afonso's original stronghold and contains almost everything else that's of interest. From Praça da República bear right, then left, into Rua Guilherme José da Silva (which turns into Rua Dr Pedro Augusto Dias). On the left, opposite the post office, is the **Casa da Eira**, with a handsome Manueline window somewhat marred by a horrendous corrugated tin roof that peeks above the crenellated walls. The 14th-century **Igreja de Santo Estevão**, with its neoclassical facade, is at the end of the street. From the church, take a left and you'll see the 1st-century **Roman milestone** from the old Braga–Astorga road.

From the milestone continue north to the end of Rua José Rodrigues and the now-decrepit Romanesque parish church, **Igreja de Santa Maria dos Anjos** (Church of St Mary of the Angels), dating from 1276. At the back is a tiny chapel with Romano-Gothic inscriptions on the outside. To the left of the parish church is the Capela da Misericórdia and beyond it the Pousada de São Teotónio (p454).

But the best fun can be had rambling on and around the series of exterior walls. In fact, if you turn right by the *pousada* you'll descend the atmospheric lane through one of the original gates, with a trickling stream running below and an impressive echo. Keep going and you'll pass through several thick, mossy layers to the outside world.

🛏 Sleeping

Residencial Portas do Sol GUESTHOUSE €

(☑ 965 851 667, 251 837 134; www.residencialportasdosol.com; Rua Conselheiro Lopes da Silva 51; s/d/tw not incl breakfast €30/40/45; ❋ @ 🛜) This spotless place in the heart of town (one of two options within the fortress walls) is set in an antiquated stone building refurbished and outfitted with all things IKEA-esque. High ceilings and old stone window frames lend old-world panache. It's in the north fort, a half block from the bridge. Rooms 6 and 7 upstairs have the best views.

Pousada de São Teotónio POUSADA €€€

(☑ 251 800 260; www.pousadavalenca.pt; Baluarte do Socorro; r €115-160; P ❋ 🛜) Perched on the outermost post of the fortress and surrounded by green ramparts, this bright, modern *pousada* has large, luxurious rooms, most with prime views overlooking the walls and river to Spain; a few have balconies.

🍴 Eating

The restaurants inside the fortress serve the usual menu of grilled meats and fish, some paired with lovely views of the surrounding countryside. In springtime, don't miss the river-eel specialities.

Fronteira Gastrobar PORTUGUESE €

(☑ 969 650 029; www.facebook.com/fronteira.gastrobar; Avenida de Espanha; lunch menu €7, tapas €4-12.50; ◷ 9am-2am Tue-Sun) Below the fortifications, near the bridge to Spain, this low-key place serves a wallet-friendly 'pilgrim's lunch' (€7) every weekday to recharge the batteries of Santiago-bound pilgrims. There's a lovely umbrella-shaded cobblestone terrace, gazing across fields towards the mountains and spires of Galicia. Occasional trains rumble by out front.

By night it's a tapas bar, with wines by the glass from €1.60.

Churrasqueira Valenciana PORTUGUESE €

(☑ 251 826 547; Rua Maestro Sousa Morais 6-8; mains €5.50-14; ◷ noon-3pm Tue-Sun) Come to this cavernous and always bustling dining room if you're looking for tasty and cheap grilled chicken. There's no patio dining, which means there's no view, but the local scene inside is worthy of your contemplation.

Fatum TAPAS €€

(☑ 251 818 140; www.facebook.com/fatumrestauranteefados; Casamata 2, Portas da Coroada; tapas €4-14, mains from €14; ◷ noon-3pm & 7-11pm Tue-Sat, noon-4pm Sun) Part wine and tapas bar, part swish restaurant and part entertainment venue – with frequent live fado concerts on Saturday evenings – Fatum is a class act. Sit under the tree-shaded terrace out front for a spot of people-watching or head inside under the barrel-vaulted stone ceiling; either way, this is Valença's most atmospheric place to dine.

Fortaleza PORTUGUESE €€

(☑ 251 823 146; Rua Apolinário da Fonseca 5; mains €10-16; ◷ noon-3.30pm & 7-9.30pm) Set in the south fortress, with tables inside and on a wide patio with views overlooking the edge of the fort, this place does decent grilled meats and fish, and rice with river eel in springtime. They have another more modern restaurant, Fortaleza 2, down the street at number 29.

ℹ Information

Turismo (☑ 251 823 329; www.visitvalenca.com; Portas do Sol; ◷ 9am-5pm Mon-Fri, 9am-12.30pm & 1.30-5pm Sat) Helpful tourism office in the old town gate at the eastern edge of Valença's historic centre.

ℹ Getting There & Away

BUS

AV Minho (☑ 258 800 340; www.avminho.pt) has three buses each weekday and two buses each on Saturday and Sunday, heading east to Monção (€3.70, 20 minutes) or south to Porto (€8.50, 2½ hours) via Viana do Castelo (€5, 1¼ hours).

TRAIN

Several trains run daily between Valença and Porto (€11.10, two to three hours), two of which continue as far as Vigo in Spain.

ℹ Getting Around

An uninspiring new town sprawls at the foot of the fortress. From the bus station it's about 1km north via Avenida Miguel Dantas (the N13) and Avenida dos Combatentes da Grande Guerra to the *turismo*. The train station is just east of Avenida Miguel Dantas.

There are free car parks just west of the fortresses, though they can fill to capacity at weekends. If you're spending the night inside the town, you should be able to find free street parking within the fort.

Monção

POP 2469

Like Valença do Minho to the west, Monção (mohng-*sowng*) was once an important fortification along the border with Spain. It has a modest but attractive historic centre – which includes the remains of its 14th-century fortifications still watching over the river – that sees far fewer visitors than Valença's. The town's big claim to fame is its fine *vinho verde* (wine), with signs touting Monção as the cradle of the refreshing Alvarinho wine (Spain's Galicia makes similar claims).

It is said that during a siege by Castilian soldiers in 1368, a local townswoman named Deu-la-Deu Martins managed to scrabble together enough flour from starving citizens to make a few loaves of bread, and in a brazen show of plenty tossed them to the enemy with the message, 'if you need any more, just let us know'. As the story goes, the disheartened Spaniards immediately withdrew to Spain.

◉ Sights & Activities

Old Monção   AREA

FREE The best part of Monção's old town is the utter lack of tourism. It's almost exclusively a local scene in chestnut-shaded **Praça Deu-la-Deu**, where a hand-on-breast statue of its namesake tops a **fountain** and looks hungrily down over the surrounding cafes.

The **Senhora da Vista** bastion at the northern end offers a gentle view across the sinuous Rio Minho into Spain. The **Capela da Misericórdia** at the square's southern end has a coffered ceiling painted with cherubs.

East of the square is the snug, cobbled old quarter. Two blocks along Rua da Glória is the pretty little Romanesque **igreja matriz** (parish church), where Deu-la-Deu is buried (look for the stone-carved alcove to the left of the entrance).

Palácio da Brejoeira   PALACE

(☎ 251 666 129; www.palaciodabrejoeira.pt; Quinta da Brejoeira, Pinheiros; guided tour of palace/grounds €7.50/5, wine tasting €2.50; ⊙ 9-11.30am & 2-5.30pm) On the N101, 5km south of Monção, this grand early 19th-century neoclassical palace has been open to the public since 2010. Visits are by guided tour only. Most interesting is the 45-minute palace tour, which runs every 30 minutes, taking in the opulent interiors, such as the Empire-furniture-filled king's room and the dining room where Franco and Salazar had a meeting in 1950, as well as the family's historic wine cellar, private chapel and gardens with 20 species of camellia.

Alternatively, opt for the hour-long tour of the grounds (offered at 11am and 4pm daily), which includes a forest, a plane-tree avenue, a romantic lake and a glimpse of the palace's vineyards – in total, the estate has 18 hectares planted with Alvarinho.

Museu Alvarinho   MUSEUM

(☎ 251 649 009; www.facebook.com/museualvarinhomnc; Praça Deu-La-Deu; ⊙ 9.30am-12.30pm & 2-5.30pm Tue-Fri, 10am-12.30pm & 2-5pm Sat & Sun) **FREE** This spiffy new museum in a beautiful old stone building on Monção's main square chronicles the history and production of Alvarinho wine through photos and Portuguese-only displays. Regardless of your language skills, you'll appreciate the free wine tastings offered onsite.

Termas de Monção   THERMAL BATHS

(☎ 251 648 367; www.tesal.com; Avenida das Caldas; €15; ⊙ 9am-7.45pm Mon-Sat, to 5.45pm Sun; ⊞) Monção's *termas* (thermal springs) have a large aquatic area with Jacuzzis, tiny waterfalls and a children's swimming area. In addition to dips in the warm springs, a wide variety of spa treatments (€27 to €85) are available.

Those wanting the aquatic experience without the fuss can head across the road to the *piscina municipal,* a handsomely designed 25m indoor pool, with a smaller pool for younger swimmers.

Adega Cooperativa de Monção   WINE

(☎ 251 656 120; www.adegademoncao.pt; Cruzes – Macedo; ⊙ 10am-12.30pm & 2.30-6pm Tue-Sat) Alvarinho is the delicious, tart and full-bodied variety of white *vinho verde* produced around Monção and neighbouring Melgaço. If you'd like to purchase it at the source, stop by this *adega* (winery) 1.8km south of Monção on the N101 to Arcos de Valdevez. Otherwise, the clutch of bars around Monção's principal squares will be happy to oblige.

✯ Festivals & Events

Feira do Alvarinho   CULTURAL

(Campo da Feira) The self-described cradle of Alvarinho, Monção hosts a three-day weekend festival honouring its wine in late June or early July. Highlights include music, folk dancing and much eating and drinking.

Festa do Corpo de Deus   RELIGIOUS

(Festa da Coca) The town's biggest party is held on Corpus Christi, the eighth Thursday

GOING GREEN IN VINHO VERDE COUNTRY

Outside Portugal, the Minho's beloved *vinho verde* (literally 'green wine') sometimes gets a bum rap, but often for good reason – exports tend to sit on shelves far too long. The stuff is made to be drunk 'green' – that is, while it is still very young, preferably less than one year old.

While the wine is made from fully ripe rather than still-green grapes, as is sometimes believed, the straw-coloured whites can indeed achieve greenish tints – a visual reminder of the green landscape from which they come. Served well chilled on a hot summer day, its fruity nose, fine bubbles and acidic bite make *vinho verde* one of the great delights of travelling in northern Portugal.

Vinho verde is grown in a strictly demarcated region of the Minho that occupies the coastal lowlands between the Rio Douro and the Spanish border. There are actually more vines here than in the Douro, but the *quintas* (estates) are subdivided to such a degree that most growers simply sell their fruit, or their wine, to community *adegas* (wineries).

Traditionally, the vines are trained high, both to conserve land and to save the grapes from rot, and you can still see great walls of green in the summer months. Like German wines, *vinho verde* tends to be aromatic, light-bodied and low in alcohol. There are red *vinho verdes*, though you may find them chalky and more of an acquired taste. White is both the most common and the easiest to appreciate. Alvarinho grapes, grown around Monção, are also used to make a delightful *vinho verde*.

For more information about the wine, its history and visiting particular regions and vineyards, check out www.vinhoverde.pt. Wine Tourism in Portugal (www.winetourismportugal.com) is another useful resource; it offers curated information about wine experiences all over Portugal, which can be booked on its website directly.

---

after Easter. Events include a religious procession and medieval fair, with a re-enactment of St George battling the dragon.

Festa da Nossa Senhora das Dores
RELIGIOUS

A big five-day celebration in the third week of August, headed by a pious procession.

🛏 Sleeping

Hospedaria Beco da Matriz
GUESTHOUSE €

(☎251 651 909, 967 304 788; hospedariabecomatriz@sapo.pt; Beco da Matriz; r €35) Sandwiched between the *igreja matriz* and the ramparts, this well-located place offers simple but impeccable rooms, with comfortable beds and spotless tile floors. Some rooms have excellent views over the ramparts to Spain. Check in at the Casa Copita bar downstairs if there's no answer at the door.

Solar de Serrade
INN €€

(☎251 654 008; www.solardeserrade.pt; Mazedo; d/ste €70/95; P🛜) One of two manor houses on area estates producing Alvarinho grapes and delicious wines, this magnificent 17th-century mansion sits in a sea of vineyards 3km south of town. Fronted by whimsical gardens, the stately main house has six doubles and four suites with elaborately furnished digs. Good for romantic getaways.

Fonte da Vila
BOUTIQUE HOTEL €€

(☎251 640 050; www.hotelfontedavila.com; Estrada de Melgaço; s/d/ste €55/70/90; P❋🛜) This remodelled manor house with a gurgling fountain on its front patio has cheerfully painted (if sometimes musty) rooms with wooden floors and a clean-lined contemporary look. There's an upscale seafood restaurant on the ground floor. The downside is its new-town location, on a busy road right across from the petrol station.

Convento dos Capuchos
BOUTIQUE HOTEL €€€

(☎251 640 090; www.conventodoscapuchos.com; Quinta do Convento de São António, Estrada de Melgaço; d €105-173, q €285; P🛜🏊) Monção's most captivating in-town property is this restored 18th-century hilltop monastery with a glimmering infinity pool overlooking the river below. Spring for one of the deluxe front rooms upstairs, with French doors opening onto small balconies above the splendid riverfront terrace. Less expensive rooms, in the newly constructed annexe, are large with chic furnishings, but lack the former's majesty and views.

The most unusual room is the Cella da Torre, built into the facade of the convent's former chapel, directly beneath the bell tower. The premises include a small spa and gym, as well as a restaurant.

✕ Eating & Drinking

Olmo
BURGERS €

(www.facebook.com/olmo.gastrobar; Largo do Loreto 155; burgers €6-10; ⊘noon-2am Tue-Sun) This corner gastrobar near the ramparts' edge has sidewalk seating with views towards Monção's main square and Spain. Burgers are the speciality, but it's also good for snacks, beers and cocktails any time of day. From the main square, go almost all the way to the river and look to your left.

Sete á Sete
PORTUGUESE €€

(☑251 652 577; www.restauranteseteasete.pai.pt; Rua Conselheiro João da Cunha; mains €8-22; ⊘noon-3pm & 7.30-10pm Tue-Sat, noon-3pm Sun) At the entrance to the old centre, this stone-walled dining room serves top-notch Minho specialities made with the finest, freshest ingredients, such as *foda à Monção* (local lamb roasted in the wood oven) and the seasonal river eel and *cabrito* (kid).

Cabral
PORTUGUESE €€

(☑251 651 775; Rua 1 de Dezembro 28; mains €9-18; ⊘noon-4pm & 7-10pm Sat-Thu) Cabral grills fresh fish and also does a tasty *arroz de marisco* (rice and seafood stew). It's all served in an attractive stone-walled dining room, almost always packed at lunch, down a narrow lane from Praça Deu-la-Deu.

Lés-a-Lés
CAFE

(☑251 653 090; www.facebook.com/les.a.les.moncao; Rua Dr Francisco Amaral; ⊘8.30am-midnight Mon-Thu, 9am-4am Fri & Sat, 2pm-midnight Sun) This whimsical, travel-themed cafe-bar, with globally inspired finger food and an airport-style Arrivals board for its international mixed drinks, makes a cosy stop day or night.

ℹ Information

Turismo (☑251 649 013; www.cm-moncao.pt; Praça Deu-la-Deu; ⊘9.30am-12.30pm & 2-6pm Jun-Sep, 9.30am-12.30pm & 1.30-5.30pm Oct-May) Adjacent to the Museu do Alvarinho, Monção's *turismo* also sells a small but high-quality selection of pottery and lacework from artisans of northern Portugal.

ℹ Getting There & Away

AV Minho (☑258 800 341) operates one weekend and two weekday buses that stop here en route from Melgaço (€3.70, 35 minutes) to Porto (€9, four hours) via Viana do Castelo (€5.50, 1½ hours).

ℹ Getting Around

From the bus station it's 600m east to the defunct train station, then another two blocks north up Rua General Pimenta de Castro to the first of the town's two main squares, Praça da República. Praça Deu-la-Deu and the heart of the old town lie just one block further.

You'll find street parking around Praça da República and Praça Deu-la-Deu.

Ponte de Lima

POP 5125 / ELEV 175M

This photogenic town by the sweet and mellow Rio Lima springs to life on weekends, when Portuguese tourists descend in droves, and every other Monday, when a vast market spreads along the riverbank. All the action happens within sight of Portugal's finest medieval bridge. Even if you can't make the market, Ponte de Lima's small, historic centre dotted with cafes and vast riverside gardens and greenways is well worth visiting. Even the outskirts are romantic: vineyards tumble to bustling avenues and at sunset swallows take flight, singing and diving until night finally falls.

◉ Sights

★ Ponte Medieval
LANDMARK

(Ponte Romana) FREE The city's *pièce de résistance*, this elegant 31-arched bridge across the Rio Lima is now limited to foot traffic. Most of it dates from the 14th century, though the segment on the north bank by the village of Arcozelo is bona fide Roman. Largo de Camões, with a fountain resembling a giant bonbon dish, makes a fine spot to watch the sun set over the bridge.

Museu do Brinquedo Português
MUSEUM

(☑258 240 210; www.cm-pontedelima.pt/pages/400; Largo da Alegria, Arcozelo; adult/child/family €3/1.50/6; ⊘10am-12.30pm & 2-6pm Tue-Sun; 🚹) In a gorgeous red mansion right after the Roman bridge in Arcozelo is this museum dedicated to Portuguese toys. The focus is on toys made from the late 19th century through to 1986. Displays in different rooms include raw materials and manufacturing techniques, and toys arranged by decade, from brightly painted wooden beach buckets to papier-mâché dolls and tinplate cannons.

There's also a play room and a toy workshop accessed through the garden.

Capela de Santo Ovídio
CHAPEL

For panoramic views up and down the Lima valley, climb 6km into the hills northwest of Ponte de Lima to this tiny, bizarre chapel dedicated to Santo Ovídio, patron saint of ears. Yes, you read that right. The interior is covered with ear-shaped votives offered in hope of, or as thanks for, the cure of an ear affliction. Take the steep 5km walking path from Arcozelo or drive up, following signs off the N201 4.5km northwest of Ponte de Lima.

Parque Temático do Arnado
GARDENS

(⊙10am-7pm) FREE West of the river, this small, intriguing green space with rose bushes and lemon-filled trellises next to a public swimming pool is notable for its annual Festival Internacional de Jardins (www.festivaldejardins.cm-pontedelima.pt; ⊙May-Oct), a competition in which 12 artists create temporary gardens built around a theme. The winning garden is chosen in October and remains rooted for the year.

Museu dos Terceiros
MUSEUM

(☑258 240 220; www.cm-pontedelima.pt/pages/401; Avenida 5 de Outubro; adult/child €2.50/1.25; ⊙10am-12.30pm & 2-6pm Tue-Sun) Downriver from Ponte de Lima's famous bridge, the 18th-century Igreja de São Francisco dos Terceiros houses a variety of ecclesiastical and folk treasures, but the highlight is the church itself, with its gilded baroque interior. The Renaissance-style Igreja de Santo António dos Frades, once a convent church, is now a wing of the museum.

Torre da Cadeia Velha
TOWER

(Old Prison Tower; ⊙9.30am-12.30pm & 2-6pm) FREE Two crenellated towers (part of the fortifications made in the 14th century) face the river at the end of Rua Cardeal Saraiva. The Torre da Cadeia Velha now houses temporary art exhibitions and the *turismo,* plus a host of pigeons on its window ledges.

Torre de São Paulo
TOWER

Along with the Torre da Cadeia Velha, this tower constitutes the only standing remains of Ponte de Lima's medieval walls. Note the somewhat bizarre *azulejo* (hand-painted-tile) image on its front wall, entitled *Cabras são Senhor!* (They're goats m'lord!) – a reference to a local story in which Dom Afonso Henriques almost attacked a herd of goats, apparently mistaking them for Moors.

Town Walls
LANDMARK

Fragments of the town walls survive behind and between the Torre da Cadeia Velha and the Torre de São Paulo.

Lagoas de Bertiandos e São Pedro de Arcos
NATURE RESERVE

(http://lagoas.cm-pontedelima.pt; Arcos; ⊙9am-12.30pm & 2-5.30pm Mon-Fri, 2.30-5.30pm Sat & Sun) FREE This 350-hectare nature reserve is set in a wildlife-rich humid zone just north of the Rio Lima. There's a wildlife interpretative centre and eight hiking trails, ranging from an easy lakeside loop (1.6km) to a longer 12.5km hike. Get there on the A27 4km west from Ponte de Lima, taking exit 3.

🏃 Activities

Ponte de Lima is a stop on the Caminho Português pilgrimage route from Porto to Santiago de Compostela, Spain. Day hikers can explore several charming walking paths through the surrounding countryside, past ancient monuments and along cobbled lanes trellised with vines. The *turismo* has literature on routes ranging from 5km to 14km. Pack water and a picnic – trailside eating options are few and far between.

Ecovia do Rio Lima
CYCLING

(www.ciclovia.pt) On both sides of the Rio Lima you'll find riverside bike paths – part of the Ecovia do Rio Lima network. For more info and maps, enquire at the *turismo* or check out the Ciclovia website.

Clube Náutico de Ponte de Lima
WATER SPORTS

(☑258 944 899; www.cnplima.com; São Gonçalo, Arcozelo; kayak & canoe per 1½ hr €3; ⊙9.30am-12.30pm & 2-8pm) Across the river and 400m downstream from town, this aquatic outfitter rents canoes and plastic kayaks for exploring the mellow river as it spreads over willowed sand bars, glistens blue in the sun and fades to deep green at dusk. It also rents bicycles (€5 per 1½ hours).

🎉 Festivals & Events

Vaca das Cordas & Corpus Christi
CULTURAL

The ninth Friday after Easter is the date for a tradition that probably dates back at least to Roman times and possibly has Phoenician origins. It features a kind of bull-running in which young men goad a hapless bull (restrained by a long rope) as it runs through the town.

It's followed the next day by the more pious Festa do Corpo de Deus, with religious processions and flowers carpeting the streets.

Feira do Cavalo
CULTURAL

(www.feiradocavalo.pt) Held annually over a long weekend in late June or early July, this four-day horse fair is one of the town's most raucous festivals, when the Expo Lima (the riverside fairground) becomes a race track and stage for horses, carriages and musicians.

Feiras Novas
CULTURAL

(www.feirasnovas.pt) Held here since 1125, this is one of Portugal's oldest ongoing events. Stretching over a long weekend in early September, it centres on the riverfront, with a massive market and fair, and features folk dances, fireworks, brass bands and all manner of merrymaking. Book accommodation well ahead.

🛏 Sleeping

★ Mercearia da Vila
GUESTHOUSE €

(☎ 258 753 562; www.merceariadavila.pt; Rua Cardeal Saraiva 34-36; s €45, d €55-60, ste €65-70; 🛜) Six rooms hide above a charming old grocery store in a perfect town-centre location. Each comes with a theme (from green tea to chocolate), as well as hardwood floors and original furniture. Some have balconies, while others such as the Sabão Amarelo room and the top-floor suite have windows with picture-postcard views over the historic centre and the river.

Quinta de Pentieiros
CAMPGROUND €

(☎ 258 240 202; http://lagoas.cm-pontedelima.pt; Rua de Pentieiros 570, Estorãos; site adult/child €6.75/5, 2-/4-person bungalows from €40/70, casas €90-100; 🅿 ⛲) Inside the Lagoas nature reserve, this estate has campsites and more comfortable bungalows and *casas* (houses) with kitchen units that work well for families. There's also an inviting swimming pool (€2/3 on weekdays/weekends), plus horse riding and bike rental. Prices are lower (and crowds fewer) on weekdays.

Residencial São João
GUESTHOUSE €

(☎ 258 941 288; Largo de São João 6; s/d/tr €30/35/40, s/d without bathroom €25/30) Septuagenarian owner Helena rents out six clean, serviceable and mostly bright rooms at this welcoming guesthouse a block from Ponte de Lima's famous bridge. Most have private bathrooms. Room 3, with views toward the river, is the best of the bunch. Quarters are tight and there's no TV, but the location can't be beaten.

> ### CROSSING THE RIVER OF OBLIVION
>
> When a Roman regiment first passed through Ponte de Lima in 137 BC, soldiers were convinced that the Rio Lima was Lethe itself – the mythical 'river of oblivion'. Alas, no such luck. Decimus Junius Brutus forced his men to plunge ahead, but they still remembered all their sins upon reaching the far side. The impressive Ponte Medieval (p457) – part of the Roman road from Braga to Astorga in Spain, and the town's namesake – supposedly marks their crossing. Though largely rebuilt in medieval times, it still contains traces of its Roman antecedent.

Casa do Arrabalde
INN €€

(☎ 258 742 442; www.casadoarrabalde.com; Arcozelo; s/d €65/80, 2-/4-person cottage €100/140; 🅿 🛜 ⛲) Just across the Ponte Romana in Arcozelo, this terrific option has huge verdant grounds and an inviting pool. The main quarters are still inhabited by the family who built the place in the 18th century. Rooms are grand and furnished with period antiques; the cottages out back are more contemporary. Book ahead, as the family is often away.

InLima Hotel & Spa
BOUTIQUE HOTEL €€

(☎ 258 900 050; www.inlimahotel.com; Rua Agostinho José Taveira 6; d €85-100; ✻ @ 🛜) Floating above the *ecovia* (greenway) like some whitewashed, frosted-glass pod from the future is the swankiest, most contemporary hotel in town. The 30 chic rooms all have woven floors, blonde-wood desks, lush linens, rain showers and wide terraces.

★ Quinta do Ameal
INN €€€

(☎ 916 907 016, 258 947 172; www.quintadoameal.com; Refóios do Lima; 2-/4-person ste €230/350; 🅿 🛜 ⛲) Known for its award-winning whites made with the local *loureiro* grape – featured in more than 40 Michelin-starred restaurants – this gorgeous estate just outside Ponte de Lima offers five luxurious kitchenette-equipped suites with a range of comforts and original details. Three suites are in the main house, with two more in a separate villa, with outside showers backed by bamboo forests.

The estate features lovely forest walks and kayaking options to Ponte de Lima. Wine tastings are included with the stay, as are generous breakfasts. Note the pretty natural pool surrounded by oak trees.

★Carmo's Boutique Hotel
BOUTIQUE HOTEL €€€

(☑258 938 743, 910 587 558; www.carmosboutiquehotel.com; Rua Santiago da Gemieira 10, Gemieira; d €210-260, ste €305-415; [P][※][⊛][≋]) Worth a splurge, this nouveau-romantic boutique hideaway in the village of Gemieira (6.5km east of Ponte de Lima) is all about casual and cosy chic. It has 15 sublime rooms, two pools, an intimate wine bar and a small basement spa inside a contemporary two-wing structure. The attached restaurant whips up great regional dishes, with breakfast served until noon.

✕ Eating

★A Carvalheira
PORTUGUESE €€

(☑258 742 316; Rua do Eido Velho, Eido Velho; mains €12-18; ⊙12.30-3pm & 7-10pm Tue-Sun; [P][※]) For superb food and an excellent wine list, head for this charming stone-walled restaurant in pretty countryside 5km southeast of town. Order ahead if you want the regional favourite – *arroz de sarrabulho* (stewed rice with pork and pork blood). Seafood options are also fabulous, from *pataniscas de bacalhau* (codfish fritter appetisers) to *espetada de lulas* (skewered squid and roasted peppers).

Açude
PORTUGUESE €€

(☑258 944 158; www.restauranteacude.com; Centro Náutico de Ponte de Lima, Arcozelo; mains €10.50-22; ⊙noon-3pm & 7-10pm Tue-Sat, noon-3pm Sun) A great option right on the riverfront in Arcozelo, a short walk from town, this boat-themed upstairs restaurant clad in wood serves tasty *posta à Açude* (veal steak) and great *lagareiro* octopus (with potatoes, garlic and olive oil).

Manuel Padeiro
PORTUGUESE €€

(☑258 941 649; www.manuelpadeiro.com; Rua do Bonfim 20; mains €7-16; ⊙noon-3pm & 7-10pm Mon & Wed-Sun) The speciality at this simple local tavern with a 60-year tradition is *arroz de sarrabulho*. Other dishes are well prepared too, including the daily weekday lunch specials, which are a steal.

Muralha
PORTUGUESE €€

(☑258 741 997; Largo da Picota 17-19; mains €7-13; ⊙noon-3pm & 7-10pm Wed-Mon) Tucked into an alcove behind one of the town's old towers, this somewhat divey dining room serves tasty octopus and meat dishes. It brags about its *cabrito* (kid), too.

Sabores do Lima
PORTUGUESE €€

(☑258 931 121; www.saboresdolima.com; Largo de António Magalhães 78; mains €8-13; ⊙noon-10pm Tue-Sun) A few steps from the river, the inviting Sabores do Lima has exposed stone walls that give a dash of style to its open dining room. The first-rate cooking features grilled meats, cod dishes and assorted seafood plates.

A Tulha
PORTUGUESE €€

(☑258 942 879; Rua Formosa 4; mains €10-16; ⊙noon-2.45pm & 7-9.45pm Tue-Sat, noon-2.45pm Sun; [⊛]) All dark wood, stone and terracotta tiles inside, this restaurant serves grilled meat and fish dishes – including the house speciality, *arroz de bacalhau* (codfish rice) – with plenty of vegetables. While food quality is good, service can be rather lackadaisical.

₮ Drinking & Entertainment

Chusso Bar
BAR

(www.facebook.com/chusso.bar.ptl; Rua Formosa; ⊙1.30pm-2am Tue-Thu, 2.30pm-4am Fri & Sat, 2.30pm-midnight Sun) Beloved for its prime people-watching terrace, perched above bustling Rua Formosa, this former umbrella factory also hosts occasional live music.

Arte e Baco
WINE BAR

(www.facebook.com/arteebaco; Rua Formosa 19; ⊙5pm-2am Sun-Thu, to 4am Fri & Sat) This black-floored, chalkboard-walled lounge features rotating art exhibitions, the finest wine from the Minho (mostly *vinho verde*) and Douro, fine cigars, better port and occasional live music.

Teatro Diogo Bernardes
THEATRE

(☑258 900 414; www.cm-pontedelima.pt/pages/410; Rua Agostinho José Taveira) Behind the Museu dos Terceiros, the galleried Teatro Diogo Bernardes, built in 1893, is the pride of the town, with interesting music and theatre performances throughout the year.

ⓘ Information

Hospital Conde de Bertiandos (☑258 909 500; Rua Conde de Bertiandos)

Police Station (☑258 900 380; Largo da Cadeia Nova 20)

Post Office (Praça da República; ⊙8.30am-5.30pm Mon-Fri)

Turismo (☑258 240 208; www.visitepontedelima.pt; Torre da Cadeia Velha; ⊙9.30am-1pm & 2-5.30pm) This exceptionally friendly and well-organised tourist office shares space with a small handicrafts gallery.

❶ Getting There & Away

There is free parking in a huge car park between the old town and the waterfront. On market days, when the car park is off-limits, look for street parking uphill from Praça da República.

Board long-distance buses on Avenida António Feijó (buy tickets on board) or at the bus station. All services thin out on Sunday.

AV Cura (☑ 258 806 830; www.avcura.com) has regular service to Ponte da Barca (€3, 40 minutes) and Viana do Castelo (€3.60, one hour).

Rede Expressos (☑ 258 942 870; www.rede-expressos.pt) also goes to Viana do Castelo (€6, 30 minutes). as well as Braga (€6, 30 minutes), Valença do Minho (€6.70, 25 to 65 minutes) and Lisbon (€21.90, five hours) via Porto (€7.60, 1¾ hours).

Transdev (☑ 225 100 100; www.transdev.pt) has regular service to Braga (€4, one hour) and Barcelos (€3.75, one hour).

Ponte da Barca

POP 2370 / ELEV 178M

Peaceful and friendly Ponte da Barca, named after the *barca* (barge) that once ferried pilgrims and others across the Rio Lima, has an idyllic, willow-shaded riverfront (perfect for cycling into the wooded valley), a handsome 16th-century bridge, a tiny old centre and the best source of information on the Parque Nacional da Peneda-Gerês.

The old town, just east of the bridge, is packed into narrow lanes on both sides of the main road, Rua Conselheiro Rocha Peixoto. Wednesday is market day.

◉ Sights & Activities

The riverfront is the focal point of the town (and a good place for a picnic), with picturesque weeping willows lining the banks of the Rio Lima and a green lawn that beckons sunbathers. The lovely, 10-arched **ponte** (bridge) originally dated from the 1540s. Beside it is the old arcaded marketplace and a little garden, **Jardim dos Poetas**, dedicated to two 16th-century poet brothers, Diogo Bernardes and Agostinho da Cruz, who were born here.

The *turismo* has a booklet called *Historia, Patrimonia & Cultura,* with regional information, including details of **hikes** in the surrounding valley, some of them punctuated with ancient sites. A simple stroll west for 4km leads to **Bravães**, a village famous for its lovely, small Romanesque **Igreja de São Salvador**. Its west portal is adorned with intricate carved animals, birds and human figures; its interior shelters simple frescoes of the Virgin and the Crucifixion.

★ Festivals & Events

Festa de São Bartolomeu   CULTURAL

(☉ Aug) Held from 19 to 24 August, this festival sees folk music and dancing aplenty, not to mention parades and fireworks.

🛏 Sleeping

Hotel Os Poetas   HOTEL €

(☑ 258 488 152; www.hotelospoetas.com; Rua Dr Alberto Cruz 9; s €40-50, d €50-60; P 🅿 🛜) A riverfront hotel close to the historic centre, with simple but lovely rooms; many – including No 104, whose small balcony makes it the best of the bunch – showcase views of the river.

Pensão Gomes   GUESTHOUSE €

(☑ 258 452 288; Rua Conselheiro Rocha Peixoto 13; s/d with shared bathroom €20/25) Welcome to your sweet Barca granny's house. Incredibly cheap, old-world rooms have worn wooden floors, sloping ceilings and tonnes of charm, and there are fabulous river and bridge views from the flowery rooftop terrace.

Casa Nobre do Correio Mor   INN €€

(☑ 919 440 801; www.laceme.pt; Rua Trás do Forno 1; d €65-120; 🛜 ⊠) Lovingly restored, this 17th-century manor house just above Ponte da Barca's parish church offers 10 gorgeous rooms, most with wide timber floors, antique furnishings and stone-framed French windows with city and river views.

✖ Eating & Drinking

Beside the old bridge is the old arcaded marketplace and a little garden, Jardim dos Poetas, which has a strip of occasionally happening bars with ample, shady riverside seating.

Cantinho do Parada   PORTUGUESE €€

(☑ 937 191 224; Largo 25 de Abril; mains €10-16; ☉ noon-2pm & 6.30-11pm Mon-Sat) The nickname 'Memórias de Mãe' (Memories of Mum) says it all at this backstreet hideaway specialising in traditional home-cooked fare. Tourist-pleasing steaks, codfish and octopus share the menu with earthier specialities like tripe, liver and chicken gizzards. It's best at lunchtime when *diárias* (daily specials) go for €6.50 including soup, fruit, wine and coffee.

Vai à Fava   PORTUGUESE €€

(☑ 258 027 769; Rua Dr Alberto Cruz 13; mains €9-15; ☉ 7.30-10pm Tue, 12.30-3pm & 7.30-10pm Wed-Sun) Dreamy river views from the open-air terrace are the star attraction at this trendy restaurant in the heart of town. Portuguese favourites like salmon poached in *vinho verde* are complemented by international fare (*chile con carne,* shrimp curry, burgers) and meat-free offerings such as vegetable strudel.

ℹ Information

ADERE Peneda-Gerês (☑ 258 452 250; www.adere-pg.pt; Rua Dom Manuel I; ⊙9am-12.30pm & 2.30-6pm Mon-Fri) Booking agent for many shelters and rural houses located in Parque Nacional da Peneda-Gerês.

Loja Interativa de Turismo (☑ 258 455 246; pit.pontedabarca@portoenorte.pt; Rua Conselheiro Rocha Peixoto 9; ⊙10am-1pm & 2-6pm Tue-Sat) About 100m from the medieval bridge, the tourist office has a town map and accommodation information.

Municipal Library (Rua Trás do Forno 33; ⊙9am-12.30pm & 2-5.30pm Mon-Fri, 9am-1pm Sat; 奈) Free internet access.

Post Office (Rua Com José Oliveira Bouças 8; ⊙9am-12.30pm & 2-5.30pm Mon-Fri)

ℹ Getting There & Away

You'll find free parking in the shady square at the western end of the bridge.

AV Cura (p452) buses run to Arcos de Valdevez (€1.45, 10 minutes), Ponte de Lima (€3, 40 minutes) and Viana do Castelo (€4.75, two hours) a number of times daily; they stop either in front of São João fountain on Rua Diogo Bernardes or in front of Churasqueira Barquense restaurant on Rua Dr Francisco Sá Carneiro.

Salvador (www.salvador-transportes.com) buses depart for Arcos de Valdevez regularly every day (€1.45, 10 minutes); they stop at Churasqueira Barquense restaurant. Enquire at the *turismo* for the current schedule. Salvador buses also travel to Braga daily (€4.05, one hour); buses stop next to Magalhães Hostel and the kiosk in the Bairro Santo António.

Rede Expressos (www.rede-expressos.pt) has three buses to Porto daily (€7.60, two hours); buy tickets beforehand at Varela cafe; buses stop on Rua Dr Carlos Araújo in front of the pink buildings.

Arcos de Valdevez

POP 1080 / ELEV 200M

Drowsy little Arcos de Valdevez is home to a couple of interesting old churches and several stately homes in a small, almost tourist-free old centre. It also has a vibrant, willow-shaded riverfront. While it doesn't merit a special trip, it's a handy gateway to the northern end of Parque Nacional da Peneda-Gerês.

🛏 Sleeping & Eating

Quinta da Breia COTTAGE €€
(☑ 258 751 751; www.casadabreia.com; Jolda São Paio; cottage €65-120; [P 奈 ⊛]) This sweeping 17th-century *quinta* (estate) nestled in a village just 10km from Arcos is owned by a sweet family who offer the charming, historic stone cottages (former staff quarters) to guests. The hosts have terrific tips for visiting the nearby national park. Minimum stay is two nights.

Hotel Ribeira HOTEL €€
(☑ 258 009 410; www.ribeiracollectionhotel.com; Largo dos Milagres; r €84-132; [P ⊛ @ 奈]) Except for its picturesque fairy-pink facade, this early-1900s town house has, unfortunately, been largely gutted of its original character, but it does have spotless, comfortable rooms with big windows, high ceilings and an excellent position by the river.

Churrasqueira O Braseiro GRILL €
(☑ 258 521 506; www.facebook.com/pg/obraseiro; Rua Soares Pereira; mains €7-11; ⊙9am-9.30pm Fri-Wed) Rain or shine, there's always a line at this unpretentious neighbourhood *churrasqueira*, which cooks up amazing grilled chicken and steaks, served at simple wooden tables or packed for takeaway.

Doçaria Central BAKERY €
(☑ 258 515 215; Rua General Norton de Matos 47; pastries from €1; ⊙9am-7pm Sun-Fri, 9am-1pm Sat) Founded in 1830, this wonderful confectioner stocks the town's favourite sweet, *rebuçados dos arcos* (enormous, jaw-breaking, hard-boiled sweets), and pastry, *charutos dos arcos* (preserved egg wrapped in a sugary dough). To get here take the street to the right of the tourist office, past the post office.

ℹ Information

Turismo (☑ 258 520 530; turismo@cmav.pt; Rua Prof Mário Júlio Almeida Costa; ⊙9.30am-12.30pm & 2-6pm Mon-Sat) This helpful, English-speaking tourist office is across from the town fountains.

ℹ Getting There & Away

The bus station is almost 1km north of the town centre, but regional buses will stop on request in front of the *turismo*.

AV Cura (p452) runs buses to Ponte da Barca (€1.45, 15 minutes), Ponte de Lima (€3.75, 50 minutes) and Viana do Castelo (€4.55, 1½ hours) eight times daily Monday to Friday, and once or twice on weekends.

Salvador (📞253 312 760; www.avic.pt) rolls once or twice on weekdays to Ponte da Barca (€1.45, 15 minutes), and to Soajo (€2.95, 40 minutes) in Parque Nacional da Peneda-Gerês. There is no weekend service into the park.

Parque Nacional da Peneda-Gerês

Spread across four impressive granite massifs in Portugal's northernmost reaches, this 703-sq-km park encompasses boulder-strewn peaks, precipitous valleys and lush forests of oak and fragrant pine. It also shelters more than 100 granite villages that, in many ways, have changed little since Portugal's founding in the 12th century. Established in 1971, Parque Nacional da Peneda-Gerês – Portugal's first and only national park – has helped preserve not just a unique set of ecosystems but also an endangered way of life for its human inhabitants.

Parque Nacional Peneda-Gerês can roughly be divided into four sections, each with its own entrance gateway. If your time is limited, you may get more out of your trip by focusing on a specific section of the park.

The northwestern corner, accessed via the Lamas de Mouro gateway, is a land of remote, rocky mountains and forested valleys, beloved for its photogenic pilgrimage site, Santuário de Nossa Senhora da Peneda (p464). The main villages here include Castro Laboreiro and Peneda.

The western sector, reached via the Mezio gateway, abounds in pretty stone villages, terraced agricultural fields and the evocative traditional granaries known as *espigueiros*. Lindoso castle near the Spanish border is another big draw here. Soajo is the best base for exploring this section of the park.

The more developed southern sector, with its headquarters at Campo do Gerês, offers the best variety of accommodation, along with beautiful waterfalls and fine boating opportunities on the reservoir at Rio Caldo. There's also some excellent hiking here – especially north of the spa town of Vila do Gerês, along the road through Mata da Albergaria forest to the Portela do Homem pass.

The eastern sector of the park, accessed via the Montalegre gateway, lies outside the Minho in the neighbouring state of Trás-os-Montes. It stands out for its austere middle-of-nowhere landscapes, and secluded villages such as Pitões das Júnias and Tourem.

❶ Information

Each of the park's gateways offers maps and information, along with thematic displays about a specific aspect of the park:

➡ Northwestern sector: **Lamas de Mouro** (📞251 465 010; www.cm-melgaco.pt/porta-de-lamas-de-mouro; ⏱9.30am-1pm & 2-6pm Apr-Sep, to 5pm Oct-Mar) gateway

➡ Western sector: **Mezio** (📞258 510 100; www.portadomezio.pt; ⏱9.30am-1pm & 2-8pm Jul & Aug, to 6pm Apr-Jun & Sep, to 5pm Oct-Mar) and **Lindoso** (📞258 578 141; portalindoso@cmpb.pt; ⏱10am-6pm Apr-Sep, 10am-12.30pm & 2-5pm Oct-Mar) gateways

➡ Southern sector: **Campo do Gerês** (📞253 351 888; museu@cm-terrasdebouro.pt; ⏱9.30am-12.30pm & 1.30-5pm Tue-Sun) gateway

➡ Eastern sector: **Montalegre** (📞276 518 320; www.icnf.pt/portal/ap/pnpg; Terreiro do Açougue; ⏱9am-1pm & 2-5.30pm Mon-Fri) gateway

The EU-assisted consultancy ADERE Peneda-Gerês (p462) in Ponte da Barca, formed to spur ecotourism in the region, is another excellent resource, with pamphlets on the park's natural, architectural and human landscapes, and detailed info on rental accommodation and village-to-village walks using marked trails.

❶ Getting There & Away

Parque Nacional Peneda-Gerês is larger than it looks on the map, and roads are notoriously curvy, so getting from point A to point B often takes longer than expected. While there's limited bus service to places like Campo do Gerês, Vila do Gerês, Soajo and Montalegre, you'll really need your own wheels to adequately explore the park.

The park's northwestern entrance (Lamas de Mouro) is the easiest starting point for travellers driving from Valença do Minho (47km, 55 minutes), Monção (32km, 40 minutes) or Galicia, Spain.

The western gateway at Mezio is the logical point of entry for travellers coming up the Rio Lima valley from Viana do Castelo (57km, 50 minutes), Ponte de Lima (36km, 35 minutes), Ponte da Barca (20km, 25 minutes) or Arcos de Valdevez (14km, 20 minutes).

The southern entrance to the park – via the historic spa town of Vila do Gerês and park headquarters at Campo do Gerês – is most convenient for travellers coming north from Braga (44km, 50 minutes) or Guimarães (48km, 65 minutes).

The Montalegre gateway is the best approach for travellers coming from Chaves (40km, 45 minutes) or other points east in Trás-os-Montes.

Parque Nacional da Peneda-Gerês

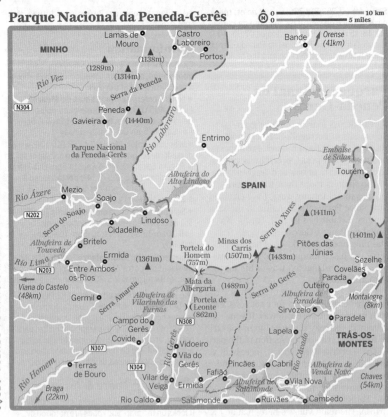

Northwestern Peneda-Gerês

The lesser-visited northwestern corner of the park, with rugged Serra da Peneda as its centrepiece, is ripe for exploration. Lower-lying forested hills fade into massive glacially formed peaks, some topped with powerful 21st-century windmills; others sit idly watching over vast boulder fields. Old stone houses huddle in the shadows, wild horses and cattle wander free, and stone fences sprout haphazardly, winding through wildflower prairies.

Aside from the small cluster of businesses around the park's northern gateway – Lamas de Mouro – the main settlements here are Peneda and Castro Laboreiro, respectively, 10km southwest and 7km southeast of the park entrance.

While Castro Laboreiro isn't much to look at, cheap accommodation makes it a good base for exploring the park's northernmost corner. The town is famous for its eponymous

endemic sheepdogs, and notable for the picturesque ruins of its 16th-century castle.

◎ Sights

**Santuário de Nossa
Senhora da Peneda** CHURCH

About 10km south of Lamas de Mouro, straddling a deep ravine, Peneda is one of the park's most stunning mountain villages, and the serra's namesake. Its centrepiece is the historic Santuário de Nossa Senhora da Peneda, backed by a domed mountain and gushing waterfall. Each year during the first week of September, pilgrims converge on the plaza in front of the church for candlelit processions and long nights of music, dance and prayer during the Festas de Nossa Senhora da Peneda.

🏃 Activities

Hiking is the principal activity in this end of the park. Maps and brochures with trail descriptions are available in Lamas de Mouro, but you can also download the brochures for many trails online.

Castro Laboreiro Loop HIKING

The picturesque ruins of Castro Laboreiro's 16th-century castle, built in 1505 on the foundations of a 12th-century Moorish castle, are easily accessible from town via this straightforward 1.6km loop (one hour). Leave the main road just east of the Miradouro do Castelo hotel in the town centre and head toward the massive rocky outcrop looming just south of you.

Following signs marked 'Accesso Sul', you'll soon climb to the castle's southern end and enter through an arched stone gateway with green wooden doors. Little of the original *castro* remains beyond the bases of a few massive granite external walls and the foundations of a square stone tower, but the mountain perspectives from within are magnificent. Exit the opposite (northern) end of the castle and follow the stone-cut steps and metal railings down to loop back to your starting point.

Trilho Castrejo HIKING

(www.icnf.pt/portal/turnatur/resource/doc/ap/pnpg/pr3castrejo-folh) Starting in Castro Laboreiro, this strenuous and spectacular 17km, seven-hour loop rambles over some of Peneda-Gerês' oldest footpaths, crossing between the high country *brandas* – the summer settlements where families traditionally travelled with their flocks in spring to plant potatoes and rye – and the lower-elevation *inverneiras*, where pigs were slaughtered and meats smoked during the chilly winter months.

Along the way the route, well-signposted with red and yellow blazes, crosses some beautiful old stone bridges, including the 1st-century Roman Ponte Cava da Velha and the later Ponte da Varziela.

Peneda Highlands HIKING

Hard-core climbers with their own gear can scale the face of Peneda's gorgeous domed peak, but mere mortals can feel a similar adrenaline rush on this steep 1km trail. Start directly behind Peneda's church and follow the zigzag path up, winding past and over the dome to an artificial lake high in the hills, where wild horses graze the savannah.

Stay on the trail past the lake to make an 8km loop back to the main highway uphill from Peneda.

Lamas de Mouro Interpretive Trail HIKING

Opposite the park's Lamas de Mouro gate, you'll find one of the Serra da Peneda's easiest walks, which offers a chance to learn a little about the region's history. The 4.5km interpretative trail winds past watermills, stone churches and community ovens, and alongside a stream before looping back to the start.

🛏 Sleeping & Eating

Miradouro do Castelo GUESTHOUSE €

(☑ 251 466 041; www.miradourodocastelo.com; Castro Laboreiro; s/d €25/45; P 🛜) The sweeping views from the simple rooms with hardwood floors steal the show at this guesthouse in Castro Laboreiro. Of the seven rooms, three have the 'wow' view. The downstairs restaurant serves good local staples (€8 to €15).

Parque Campismo
Lamas de Mouro CAMPGROUND €

(☑ 251 466 041; www.montesdelaboreiro.pt/parquecampismo.pdf; Lamas de Mouro; per adult/child/tent/car €4.20/2.80/3.70/3, 2-/4-/6-person bungalow €55/65/75) This tremendous private campground near boulder fields and flowering meadows has shady creekside tent sites plus four cosy pine-clad bungalows with kitchenettes. It rents out mountain bikes (€2.50/10 per hour/day) and offers treetop adventures, canyoning and hikes with shepherds. There are a couple of restaurants not too far away in the Lamas de Mouro village northwest of the park gate.

Peneda Hotel HOTEL €€

(☑ 251 460 040; www.penedahotel.pt; Lugar da Peneda; s/d/tr €70/75/100; P 🛜) Peneda village's only hotel sits right next door to the town's famous church. Once a nest for Igreja Senhora da Peneda's pilgrims, this mountain lodge features a waterfall backdrop, a gushing creek beneath and cosy rooms with blonde-wood floors, French windows and views of quaint Peneda village across the ravine. There's also a decent restaurant.

ℹ Information

Enter via Lamas de Mouro national park gateway (p463)

ℹ Getting There & Around

This is self-driving country. For a map of the region, visit the Lamas de Mouro park gateway.

Western Peneda-Gerês

POP 990 / ELEV 300M

Framed by the Serra do Soajo, western Peneda-Gerês rises from the Rio Lima valley to the Spanish border, with entrance gateways at either end.

THE MINHO PARQUE NACIONAL DA PENEDA-GERÊS

PROTECTED AREAS OF PENEDA-GERÊS

The government is working to ensure that Peneda-Gerês' largely undisturbed ecosystems remain that way. The park has a high-elevation inner zone, partly set aside for research and closed to the public, and an outer buffer zone, where development is controlled. Most villages, roads, tracks and trails are in the latter area.

The most assiduously protected area is the Mata da Albergaria, north of Vila do Gerês. Ironically, it's crossed by the N308 highway, which, because it serves an EU-appointed border crossing, cannot simply be closed. Motorised traffic is tolerated on a 6km stretch of road above Gerês but is forbidden to linger. Daily patrols ensure that motorists don't park on the road. Two side roads are also no-go areas for nonresidents: southwest down the Rio Homem valley and east from Portela do Homem into the high Serra do Gerês.

Campers must use designated sites or risk the wrath of park rangers. There are also restrictions on the type of boats allowed in the park's *albufeiras* (reservoirs), and no boats at all are allowed on the Vilarinho das Furnas and Paradela. Even swimming is prohibited in Vilarinho das Furnas.

Close to the park's western gateway at Mezio is Soajo (soo-*ah*-zhoo), a sturdy town high above the upper Rio Lima, best known for its photogenic *espigueiros* (p470). Soajo has splendid views over the surrounding countryside, with scenic walks providing a fine opportunity to take in the beauty of this protected region. Although it lacks the majesty of the Serra da Peneda high country, it's accessible by public transport and, thanks to village enterprise and the Turismo de Aldeia, you can stay in one of Soajo's restored stone houses and glimpse a vanishing way of life.

East into the mountains lies Lindoso, the park's other nearby gateway. A striking medieval castle here clings to its craggy perch, tempting travellers for a day visit but rarely an overnight stay.

◉ Sights & Activities

Castelo de Lindoso CASTLE
(Lindoso; €1.50; ◷10.30am-12.30pm & 2-5pm)
Built during the reign of Afonso III, this 13th-century castle 5km from the Spanish border long served as a key Portuguese military outpost. These days it's one of Peneda-Gerês' most photogenic attractions, with a vast collection of *espigueiros* spreading beneath its crenellated walls, all set against a dramatic mountain backdrop. You're free to walk around the castle perimeter; alternatively, a small admission fee grants access to a historical museum inside the main tower, with exhibits in Portuguese.

Caminhos do Pão &
Caminhos da Fé HIKING
Just off the M530, 250m north of Soajo's bus stop, is the signed trailhead for this 8.1km loop into the hills northeast of the

village. Initially paved with immense stones grooved by centuries of ox-cart traffic, it ascends though a landscape shaped by agriculture, taking in granite cottages, *espigueiros* and superb views of terraced fields.

Further up are three derelict watermills for grinding corn, stone channels that once funnelled the stream from one mill to the next, and the reservoir that fed them.

Trilho Pertinho do Céu HIKING
(http://trilhos.arcosdevaldevez.pt/activities/trilho-pertinho-do-ceu) Starting just above the idyllic village of Gavieira, this moderate 8km, 3½-hour loop climbs steadily up a two-lane dirt track before levelling out in bucolic high country between the old stone villages of Branda de Busgalinhas and São Bento do Cando. Along the way you'll enjoy plenty of picturesque stone walls, red-tile roofs and long vistas stretching across pastures to the Serra da Peneda's rocky peaks.

After admiring the church square in São Bento, begin a long descent east to the Rio Grande, which you'll then follow through Gavieira village back to your starting point.

⌂ Sleeping & Eating

★ Casa do Adro INN €
(☑258 576 327; Largo do Eiró; r €50; ℗ 🖰) This manor house (rather than a cottage), off Largo do Eiró by Soajo's parish church, dates from the 18th century. Rooms are huge, furnished with antiques and blessed with sweet vineyard and village vistas. There is a minimum two-night stay in August.

Casas de Soajo COTTAGE €
(☑258 576 165; www.casasdesoajo.com; cottage €50-135) About a dozen houses sleeping two

to eight are available for tourist accommodation in Parque Nacional Peneda-Gerês under Portugal's Turismo de Aldeia (village tourism) scheme. Three of these are in Soajo. Each of the houses has a fireplace or stove (with firewood in winter) and a kitchen stocked with breakfast food, including fresh bread on the doorstep each morning.

Book through ADERE Peneda-Gerês (p462) in Ponte da Barca or directly through the Casas de Soajo website.

Parque de Campismo
de Travanca   CAMPGROUND €
(☑ 258 522 285, 924 454 680; www.portadomezio.pt/parque-de-campismo; per adult/child/tent/car €4.20/2.80/3.70/3) High on a rocky hillside, 3km north of the park gateway at Mezio, this municipal campground has basic sites under the shade of stately, fragrant evergreens. A short downhill walk across the main road leads to a beautiful natural swimming hole.

Restaurante Videira   PORTUGUESE €€
(☑ 924 430 319, 258 576 205; Largo do Eiró, Soajo; mains for 2 €18-26; ⊙ noon-3pm Thu-Tue, 7-9pm Thu-Mon) Locals rave about Videira's authentic regional smoked meats and sausage and the homemade mainstays made with *cachena* veal. The shady, arched patio of this family-run tavern is fitted out with sturdy, polished wooden tables. Most dishes easily feed two; some are available in half portions. Videira is situated by the bus stop.

Saber ao Borralho   PORTUGUESE €€
(☑ 933 204 718, 258 577 296; www.saberaoborralho.com; Av 25 de Abril 1158, , Soajo; mains for 2 €24-27; ⊙ noon-2pm & 7-9pm Wed-Sun) This handsomely set place features excellent local dishes like the Minho *barrosã* steak as well as codfish dishes and a tempting dessert counter. Village house rentals are available here (€50 per night).

Espigueiro de Soajo   PORTUGUESE €€
(☑ 258 576 136; Avenida 25 de Abril 1425, Soajo; mains €9-16; ⊙ 11.30am-3pm & 7-9.30pm Tue-Sat, 11.30am-6pm Sun) This modern place serving terrific Minho meat has outdoor seating on a vine-covered terrace. Management is English-speaking (local by way of Boston) and very friendly. It's about 200m north of Soajo's centre on the N304.

❶ Information

There's an ATM below the parish council office, on the southeast corner of the main square, Largo do Eiró.

Enter via the Mezio national park gateway (p463) or Lindoso national park gateway (p463).

❶ Getting There & Away

Soajo is 21km northeast of Ponte da Barca via the N203 and M530, or the same distance from Arcos de Valdevez via the scenic N202. Buses stop along the M530, near Restaurante Videira in the heart of town. A few hundred metres east along the M530 towards Lindoso are Soajo's trademark *espigueiros*.

On weekdays there are one to two Salvador buses from Arcos de Valdevez (€2.95, 50 minutes). A taxi from Arcos or Ponte da Barca costs €20 to €25.

Southern Peneda-Gerês

ELEV 350M

Big nature rises in steep wooded pinnacles, gushes with cold streams, and pools into crystalline swimming holes at the southern end of Parque Nacional Peneda-Gerês. This is the park's busiest and most developed section, which in summer months sees droves of tourists, with car traffic sometimes jamming up the roads. Its beating heart is the spa resort town of Vila do Gerês, sometimes referred to as Caldas do Gerês, or more commonly as simply Gerês. The southern park is also a land of dams and reservoirs, providing summer boating and recreation opportunities not found elsewhere in Peneda-Gerês, with Rio Caldo serving as the hub.

The park gateway here is Campo do Gerês, a small village about 13km west of Vila do Gerês that houses an ethnographic museum documenting the village traditions of days gone by.

Vila do Gerês

POP 1290 / ELEV 350M

Sandwiched tightly into the Rio Gerês valley, this spa town has a rather charming fin-de-siècle core surrounded by a ring of less appealing, modern *pensões* (guesthouses).

The town is built on an elongated, one-way loop, with the *balneário* (spa centre) in the pink buildings on the lower road. The original hot spring and some baths are in the staid colonnade at the northern end (where the road takes a sharp U-turn).

◉ Sights & Activities

★ **Miradouro da Pedra Bela**   VIEWPOINT
For spectacular views over the Albufeira de Caniçada reservoir and the southern reaches

of Parque Nacional Peneda-Gerês, snake 6km uphill through the evergreen forest to this dramatically perched viewpoint east of Vila do Gerês.

Cascata do Arado   WATERFALL

This gorgeous waterfall is accessed from a bridge over the Rio Arado, just north of the village of Ermida. To see the falls from above, climb to the *miradouro* (viewpoint) via a signposted, 150m-long staircase from the parking area. Alternatively, boulder-hop your way upriver from the bridge past a series of natural pools to the base of the falls – a prime swimming spot in warm weather.

★ Via Geira Roman Road   HIKING

One of Peneda-Gerês' unforgettable hiking experiences is the Via Geira, an ancient Roman road that once stretched 320km between Braga and Astorga (Spain), and now has World Heritage status. The most beautiful stretch begins at Portela de Homem, where milepost XXXIV still stands.

From here you can walk southwest, following the Rio Homem downhill through the beautiful Mata de Albergaria forest. A 9.6km out-and-back trip brings you to milepost XXXI on the shores of the Albufeira do Homem reservoir.

This entire stretch is littered with Roman trail markers – some inscribed with the name of the emperor during whose rule they were erected. Ambitious hikers can continue another 4km southwest along the reservoir, turning south just before the Vilarinho das Furnas dam to reach milepost XXVII near Campo do Gerês. Another section of trail, further south in the Terras de Bouro region, leaves from São Sebastião, roughly 6km from Campo do Gerês. Throughout the region, the trail is signposted as 'Trilho da Geira'.

Trilho dos Currais   HIKING

The 'Corrals Trail' is a moderate 10km loop that takes four to five hours to complete. Along the way you'll wind beneath oak and pine and glimpse boulder fields, sublime valley views and – if you're lucky – resident wildlife. The trailhead is signposted on the east side of the N308, 1km north of Vila Gerês, directly opposite the Vidoeiro campground turnoff.

Trilho da Preguiça   HIKING

This park-maintained loop trail starts along the N308, on the mountainside about 4km north of Gerês. For 4.5km (2½ to three hours) it rolls through the valley's oak for-

ests. A leaflet about the walk is available from the park office (€0.75) or the tourist office (€0.10). You can also carry on to the Portela de Leonte, 6km north of Gerês.

Termas do Gerês   THERMAL BATHS

(www.aguasdogeres.pt; admission incl towel, robe & slippers €3; ☺8am-noon & 2.30-6pm May-Oct) After a long hike, finish the day by soaking away your aches and pains in the town's thermal springs. In addition to the sauna, steam bath and pool (available with basic admission), you can indulge in a full range of treatments, including massages and facials.

🛏 Sleeping

Hostel Gerês   HOSTEL €

(☎253 391 119; www.hostelgeres.com; Rua de Arnaçó 21; dm €15, s €35-40, d €70-80, s/d without bathroom €25/50; P🛜) Perched high on a hillside, but within easy walking distance of the centre, Gerês' hostel is a great base for active travellers, with its own private parking, a small in-house bar and young, friendly staff. The breakfast area enjoys fine views of the town and its mountain backdrop, as do some of the dorms and doubles.

Hotel Baltazar   HOTEL €

(☎253 391 131; www.baltazarhotel.com; Rua Lagrifa Mendes 6; s/d/tr €40/55/65; 🛜) In a fine old granite building, this friendly, family-run hotel just up from the hot springs has spacious rooms, many of which look onto a pleasant wooded park. For longer stays, half-and full-board plans are available at the excellent restaurant downstairs.

Adelaide Hotel   HOTEL €

(☎253 390 020; www.adelaidehotel.pt; Rua de Arnaçó 45; s €35-43, d €50-65; P🅰🛜🌊) High on a hillside at the southern end of town, this big, modern, lemon-yellow hotel wins for value. The rooms are spacious, with parquet floors and new beds. It's well worth paying the extra €5 for a room with a balcony and views. The hotel has a swimming pool on the other side of town, with a free shuttle to take you there.

Parque de Campismo de Vidoeiro   CAMPGROUND €

(☎966 615 645, 253 391 289; www.vidoeirogerescamping.com; per adult/child/tent/car €5/3.50/4.30/4.70; ☺mid-May–mid-Oct) This cool and shady facility is on a hillside next to the river, about 1km north of Vila do Gerês. Reception is open from 8am until noon and 3pm to 7pm. Avoid it in August, when screaming schoolchildren descend in droves.

Hotel Águas do Gerês
HOTEL €€

(📞 253 390 190; www.aguasdogeres.pt; Avenida Manuel F Costa 136; s €55-66, tw €69-96, d €75-102; 🅿️❄️🛜) In a grand, mansard-roofed, yellow-hued fin-de-siècle building, this recently renovated three-star has spacious, carpeted rooms with high ceilings and modern decor, although they don't live up to the exterior. The hotel also runs the hot springs and offers special packages.

✖ Eating

Lurdes Capela
PORTUGUESE €

(📞 253 391 208; Rua Dr Manuel Gomes de Almeida 77; mains €7.50-13; ⏱ noon-3pm & 7-10pm) Family-owned and operated, this restaurant offers top-end service and even better food served on a pleasant, open-air upstairs terrace. Look for it on the south end of town, just north of the tourist office.

O Churrasco
GRILL €€

(📞 253 467 871; Rua Tude de Sousa 21; mains €6.50-15; ⏱ noon-midnight) Enjoy mountain views from the picnic tables on the tree-shaded outdoor deck at this friendly *churrascaria* (barbecue) just north of Vila do Gerês. Grilled meat and fish are the stars of the show, all served with a smile at very reasonable prices.

Adega Regional
PORTUGUESE €€

(📞 253 390 220; Av 20 de Junho 4; mains €7.50-14; ⏱ noon-3pm & 7-10pm Tue-Sun) Set behind Hotel Universal, and just above a roaring stream, this historic stone *adega* (wine tavern) serves tapas and wine. Saturday-night karaoke kicks off at 10pm.

❶ Information

Park Office (Centro de Educação Ambiental do Vidoeiro; 📞 253 390 110; www.icnf.pt; Lugar do Vidoeiro 99; ⏱ 9am-1pm & 2-5pm Mon-Fri) About 1km north of the village on the track leading to the campground.

Turismo (📞 253 392 096; www.cm-terrasde-bouro.pt; Av Dom João V; ⏱ 9am-1pm & 2-5pm Sep-Jun, to 7pm Jul & Aug) By the roundabout at the southern entrance to town.

❶ Getting There & Away

Buses stop at a traffic circle just south of the loop.

Empresa Hoteleira do Gerês (📞 253 390 220; www.hoteisgeres.com/transports.html) runs between six and 10 buses daily from Gerês to Braga (€4.45, 1½ hours). Buy tickets at **Hotel Universal** (📞 253 615 896; www.hoteisgeres.com; Avenida Manuel F Costa 115; s €48-53, d €63-73; 🅿️❄️🛜🏊).

Campo do Gerês
POP 160 / ELEV 690M

Campo do Gerês (called São João do Campo on some maps, and just Campo by most) is a humble huddle of stone houses high in the mountains. It sees more hikers than shepherds once the weather turns warm, thanks to easy access to some spectacular trails.

◉ Sights & Activities

Nucleo Museológico de Campo do Gerês
MUSEUM

(cnr M533 & N307; adult/student €2/1; ⏱ 9.30am-12.30pm & 1.30-5pm Tue-Sun) At the main crossroads 1.5km south of Campo do Gerês village, this museum has exhibits on local flora and fauna – but its highlight is the section narrating the history of Vilarinho das Furnas, a neighbouring village that met its demise with the building of a dam just upstream in 1972. In anticipation of the town's submersion, villagers collected stories and objects to document their former way of life.

All exhibit descriptions are in Portuguese.

Equi Campo
HORSE RIDING

(📞 914 848 094, 253 357 022; www.equicampo.com; ⏱ 9am-7pm May-Sep, by arrangement Oct-Apr) One of two Campo-based outfitters located on the right just before you arrive in town. Guides lead organised hikes (per person half day/full day €7.50/12.50), horse-riding trips (one/two hours €21/40) and treetop adventures (€12). The wooden shack also has a few tables outside where snacks are served.

▣ Sleeping & Eating

Parque Campismo de Cerdeira
CAMPGROUND €

(📞 253 351 005; www.parquecerdeira.com; Rua de Cerdeira 400; per adult/child/tent/car €8/4/8/5, 2-/4-person bungalow €70/125; 🅿️🛜🏊) 🦮 In Campo do Gêres, this place has oak-shaded sites, a laundry, a pool, a minimarket and a good on-site restaurant. The ecofriendly bungalows open onto unrivalled mountain views.

Albergaria Stop
GUESTHOUSE €

(📞 253 350 040; www.albergariastop.com; Rua de São João 915; s €40-50, d €43-60, tr €62-80; 🅿️🛜🏊) This guesthouse has spotless rooms, wooden floors and mountain views. Most rooms have balconies, plus there is a pool and tennis courts. It's located just north of the village. There's a two-night minimum stay in high season.

HIKING PARQUE NACIONAL PENEDA-GERÊS

Parque Nacional Peneda-Gerês abounds in fantastic walks, suitable for every interest and fitness level, and offering access to the park's tantalisingly remote backcountry. Two of the finest leave from the village of Pitões das Júnias:

Mosteiro de Santa Maria das Júnias Loop

This moderate 2.5km, 1½-hour loop takes in some of the prime attractions in the countryside south of Pitões das Júnias, including a dramatic 30m waterfall and the ruined monastery of Santa Maria das Júnias. Tucked into a remote river valley, the church here was built by 12th-century Benedictine monks on the site of a 9th-century pre-Romanesque hermitage, then taken over to the Cistercians in the mid-13th century. The central shrine remains largely intact, surrounded by the ruins of several outbuildings.

The trailhead is about 1.2km south of Pitões das Júnias. Drive or walk 400m south of town to the village cemetery, then bear left and continue another 800m south to find two brown signs in a car park reading 'mosteiro 350m' (to the left) and 'cascata 950m' (to the right).

Turn right and follow the 'cascata' signs downhill along a dirt road, eventually turning right again onto a signposted wooden boardwalk and descending 217 steps to reach the Miradouro (viewpoint). Here, a wooden platform offers dramatic views across to the 30m waterfall, which crashes through a rocky cleft on the opposite side of the gorge.

Climb back up all 217 steps, then turn right at the top and zigzag southeast, following red-and-yellow blazes towards the monastery. After about 1km you'll arrive at a hilltop overlook, with the ruins of the Mosteiro de Santa Maria das Júnias spread out below you. It's a supremely peaceful spot, with the silence only broken by the rushing of the nearby stream and the rustling of leaves in the breeze. Leaving the monastery, stay on the near side of the stream and climb 350m up a dirt and gravel road to reach the car park where you started.

São João de Fraga Hike

This dramatic hike (10km, three hours round-trip) leads from Pitões das Júnias to the austere mountain chapel of São João de Fraga (1163m). After a long initial descent from town

---

Pousada da Juventude Vilarinho das Furnas   HOSTEL €
(🖋 253 351 339; www.pousadasjuventude.pt/pt/pousadas/geres; Rua da Pousada 1; dm/tw/d/bungalow €16/45/48/90; 🅿@🛜) Campo's woodland hostel offers a spotless selection of spartan four-bed dormitories, stylish doubles (with bathrooms) and roomier bungalows with kitchen units.

★ O Abocanhado   PORTUGUESE €€
(🖋 253 352 944; www.abocanhado.com; Brufe; mains €12-18; ⏰12.30-3.30pm & 7.30-9.30pm) With its stunning panoramic terrace high above the Rio Homem, this gorgeously situated restaurant is a temple to the finest ingredients that the surrounding countryside has to offer, including *javali* (wild boar), and *veado* (venison). Call ahead in low season.

🍷 Drinking & Nightlife

Geira Adega Regional   WINE BAR
(🖋 910 246 683; Rua da Geira 375) Overhung with vines, this charming wine bar in the stone-walled heart of Campo do Gerês village is a pleasant place to sip a glass or two.

ℹ Information

Campo do Gerês national park gateway (p463)

ℹ Getting There & Away

From Braga, Transdev (www.transdev.pt) has four daily buses (€4.30, 1½ hours, fewer at weekends) stopping at the museum crossroads and the village centre.

Rio Caldo

POP 890 / ELEV 160M

Just below Vila do Gerês, this tiny town sits on the back of the stunning Albufeira de Caniçada (Caniçada Reservoir), making it the park's centre for water sports.

🏃 Activities

Água Montanha Lazer   WATER SPORTS
(🖋 925 402 000; www.aguamontanha.com; Rua da Raposeira 31; per hr kayak/SUP/pedalo €6/10/12, motorboat €35-45; 4-/10-person cottage per day €80/160, per week €525/980) English-run Água Montanha Lazer rents out kayaks, stand-up paddleboards, pedal boats and a variety of motorboats. Family-oriented half-day water sports packages (per person €25 to €32) com-

(approximately 30 minutes), cross a bridge over a small river and begin climbing steadily into sparsely vegetated high country. After briefly levelling out on a high plateau, the climb resumes more steeply, reaching the final summit via a series of steps chiselled into the rock.

Near the top, spectacular views of the sawtooth peaks known as the Pitões begin unfolding to the northwest. To the south, your first glimpse of the whitewashed chapel of São João de Fraga peeking out from behind the boulders makes an equally strong impression. The chapel itself is usually closed, except on the first Sunday after the feast day of São João (24 June), when townspeople from Pitões das Júnias make their annual pilgrimage to this site, followed by a community picnic.

About half an hour into your return descent, it's well worth taking the 10-minute side trail that leads south along the high plateau to a *fojo de lobo* – an ancient stone corral traditionally used by shepherds to trap wolves and protect their flocks. From here, return to the main trail, turn east and retrace your steps to Pitões das Júnias.

Other Hikes

Want more? Other gems worth seeking out include:

Via Geira Roman Road (p468) Walk in the footsteps of the ancients, brushing up against dozens of intact Roman mileposts as you follow the Rio Homem downstream through the dense Albergaria da Mata forest.

Caminhos do Pão & Caminhos da Fé (p466) Experience first-hand the interplay between Portuguese mountain people and their natural setting on this loop through terraced fields and past ancient water mills.

Castro Laboreiro Loop (p465) Climb to the ruins of a medieval hilltop castle for spectacular views of the park's rugged northern mountains.

Trilho Pertinho do Céu (p466) Loop through some of the park's most picturesque stone villages as you traverse high pastures along the 'Close to Heaven Trail'.

bine kayaking, tubing and motor boating. AML also rents three attractively furnished cottages sleeping four to 10 people, all with verandas, kitchen units and water views.

Sleeping & Eating

Beleza Serra Guide Hotel GUESTHOUSE €€
(253 391 457; www.belezaserraguidehotel.com; Lugar do Bairro 25, Vilar da Veiga; s €54-65, d €64-79; P ❄ 🛜) A good base for hiking and kayaking, this guesthouse 4.5km south of Vila do Gerês has views of the Caniçada Reservoir across the highway out front, with simple, clean, comfortable rooms and a restaurant dishing up regional food.

Pousada do Gerês-Caniçada/ São Bento POUSADA €€€
(210 407 650; www.pousadas.pt; Av da Caniçada 1518, Caniçada; r €130-250; P ❄ 🛜 ≋) This lovely place has a spectacular setting. High above the Albufeira, it offers a splendid retreat at eagle's-nest heights. The rooms have wood-beamed ceilings and comfy furnishings; some have verandas with magnificent views. There's a pool, gardens, tennis court and an excellent restaurant serving local delicacies (trout, roasted goat). Take the N304 3km south from Rio Caldo, following signs for Caniçada.

Getting There & Away

Rio Caldo is 7km south of Vila do Gerês via the N308-1, or 12km south of Campo do Gerês via the N307 and N304. Empresa Hoteleira do Gerês runs between six and 10 buses daily from Rio Caldo southwest to Braga (€4.35, 1¼ hours) and north to Vila Gerês (€2.20, 15 minutes).

Eastern Peneda-Gerês

The eastern section of Parque Nacional da Peneda-Gerês – encompassing the Montalegre and Boticas municipalities in the remote Trás-os-Montes region – packs a punch, with pretty villages where time seems to have stood still for centuries; and endangered Iberian wolves still roam the thick oak forests.

Of these villages, Pitões das Júnias is the most scenic, set on a plateau surrounded by endless mountain vistas. It has an ancient monastery nearby, Santa Maria das Júnias, and a lovely waterfall, both an easy hike away.

Northeast of Pitões das Júnias, the village of Tourém, a stone's throw from the Spanish border, makes another attractive base.

Further south, the park gateway town of Montalegre has a more built-up feel, but makes an interesting stop nonetheless.

🛏 Sleeping & Eating

Casa do Preto INN €
(☑ 276 566 158; www.casadopreto.com; Largo do Salgueiro 3, Pitões das Júnias; s/d €40/50; P 🛜) This hotel in the heart of Pitões das Júnias has eight clean and spacious rooms with big bathrooms, the best commanding views over the village and surrounding mountains. The restaurant downstairs (mains €7.50 to €15) serves mean home-smoked *alheira* (sausage).

Casa dos Braganças INN €€
(☑ 276 579 138; www.casadosbragancas.com; Rua dos Braganças 8-10, Tourém; s/d €45/60; P 🛜) Casa dos Braganças in the village of Tourém is a delightful rural inn run by a friendly live-in family. The 18th-century house features 11 rooms and one suite with original details such as handpainted ceilings, stone walls, custom-made wood furniture and countryside views. Dinners on request.

Restaurante Ponte Nova PORTUGUESE €€
(☑ 253 659 882; Rua 25 de Abril 30, Cabril; mains €7-15; ⊙ noon-2pm & 7.30-9pm) At a picturesque spot next to the bridge in Cabril – 40km west of Montalegre on the way to Vila do Gerês – this place does good river trout and, if you order ahead, *cabrito* or *javali*

🍷 Drinking & Nightlife

Taberna Terra Celta BAR
(Rua dos Caldeireiros 2, Pitões das Júnias; ⊙ 9am-midnight Tue-Sun) For a cosy drink after a day on the trail, don't miss Taberna Terra Celta, in an old wooden and stone home with an upstairs fireplace on Pitões das Júnias' village square. On weekends it serves *fumeiro* (smoked meats), soups and salads.

ℹ Getting There & Away

Bus connections in the park's eastern reaches range from infrequent to nonexistent. You'll need your own wheels to properly explore this area.

Montalegre

POP 1815 / ELEV 1000M

Montalegre's small but particularly striking castle, part of Dom Dinis' 14th-century ring of frontier outposts, looms over the town

and the surrounding fertile plains fed by so many rivers. The future Duke of Wellington made use of it in his drive to rid Portugal of Napoleon's troops in 1809. Today visitors can only wander around its perimeter.

⊙ Sights

Barroso Eco Museu MUSEUM
(☑ 276 510 203; www.ecomuseu.org; Terreiro do Açougue 11; ⊙ 10am-1pm & 2-6pm) FREE Just downhill from Montalegre's castle, this museum hosts exhibits that showcase regional history, rural traditions and folklore.

🛏 Sleeping & Eating

Casa de Campo O Castelo GUESTHOUSE €
(☑ 935 663 060, 276 511 237; www.termontalegre. net; Terreiro do Açougue 1; r €50; ⊙ closed Mon & all of Sep; P 🛜) Directly beneath the castle, this simple family-run guesthouse features five rooms with hardwood floors and stone walls; two share a terrace with castle views. Owner John speaks perfect English.

Casa Zé Maria GUESTHOUSE €€
(☑ 276 512 457; Rua Dr Vitor Branco 21; s €50-60, d €55-65; P 🛜) This family-run, 19th-century granite manor features old-fashioned charm in its wooden-floored rooms with lacy bedspreads. It's located one block east and one block south of the *turismo*.

Tasca do Açougue PORTUGUESE €
(☑ 276 511 164; www.facebook.com/tascadoacou gue; Terreiro do Açougue 7; tapas €3-7, mains €7-11; ⊙ noon-3pm & 6-10pm Wed-Fri, noon-10pm Sat & Sun) In a charming stone cottage just below the castle, Tasca do Açougue serves tasty Iberian tapas dishes, including grilled octopus.

ℹ Information

Montalegre national park gateway (p463)

Turismo (☑ 276 510 205; www.cm-montalegre. pt; Terreiro do Açougue 11; ⊙ 10am-1pm & 2-6pm) Downstairs from the Barroso Eco Museu.

ℹ Getting There & Away

Transdev (☑ 225 100 100; www.transdev.pt; Rua General Humberto Delgado) runs three buses per day from Braga to Montalegre (€6.75, 2½ hours) from Monday to Thursday, and four on Friday; they run less frequently on weekends.

ℹ Getting Around

From the bus station it's 500m uphill on Rua General Humberto Delgado to a five-way roundabout. Turn right here, pass the town hall and continue uphill to reach the castle.

Understand
Portugal

Portugal Today

Bounding out of a dire recession with a rejuvenated mojo, Portugal is having a moment; indeed, cities like Lisbon and Porto are hotter than ever. A boom in tourism, improvements in quality of life thanks to quantifiable changes implemented by left-wing Prime Minister António Costa, and investment in green energy have been catalysts for this new-found swagger. The big issues now are how to address the country's shrinking population, and surging inner-city rents fuelled by mass tourism.

Best on Film

A Lisbon Story (1994) Wim Wenders' love letter to Lisbon.

Letters from Fontainhas (1997–2006) Pedro Costa's art-house trilogy set in Lisbon.

Capitães de Abril (Captains of April; 2000) Overview of the 1974 Revolution of the Carnations.

Best in Print

O Manual dos Inquisidores (The Inquisitors' Manual; António Lobo Antunes; 1996) Story about life under the Salazar dictatorship.

Memorial do Convento (Baltasar and Blimunda; José Saramago; 1982) Darkly comic 18th-century love story.

Livro do Desassossego (The Book of Disquiet; Fernando Pessoa; 1982) Literary masterpiece by Portugal's greatest poet.

Best in Music

Mariza (2018) Latest album by fado superstar Mariza.

Art of Amália Rodrigues (1998) Compilation by one of fado's greats, Amália Rodrigues.

Best of Rui Veloso (2000) Portugal's legendary rock-balladeer.

Left Foot Forward

When António Costa seized the reins as prime minister with his left-wing coalition in late 2015, the country seemed to give an audible sigh of relief – this was a new era in Portuguese politics. His objective was clear: achieve economic growth and reduce the deficit while reversing painful austerity measures – a daunting challenge, particularly given the fragile left-wing alliance holding his administration together. And yet he has largely been successful: the government has upped the minimum wage (to €700 per month in 2019), increased state pensions, cut taxes and improved welfare benefits. Unemployment has dropped substantially, at 6.8% in the first quarter of 2019 (markedly down from an all-time high of 17.5% in early 2013).

Population Crisis

It's been called a 'perfect demographic storm' that could have catastrophic effects on society and the economy. The population in Portugal has been shrinking – falling year on year since 2010 – and unless things change, demographers estimate that the population could fall from its 2019 mark of 10.25 million to just six million by 2060.

One key factor in the population decline is that the fertility rate has sunk to an all-time low, averaging 1.3 children per woman in 2018, compared to three per woman back in 1970. While there is no single reason for this, a major influence appears to be that women are choosing or needing to focus more on their careers – meaning that many are having children later or not at all. Families are also more dispersed than previously, leading to a lack of free childcare as a result (traditionally, grandparents would have fulfilled this role). According to European statistics office Eurostat, Portugal has the second lowest fertility rate (after Italy) in the EU.

At the other end of the spectrum, the ageing population is having an impact, slowing down productivity and threatening economic growth, pensions and public healthcare services. This is particularly visible in the small villages in Portugal's interior, where elderly residents are the norm and local children are a rare sight. Toy shops and schools are closing, while more businesses are being transformed into nursing homes.

In an attempt to redress the balance somewhat, Portugal has willingly opened its doors to refugees and migrants, as the country makes a bid to attract more work-age people to bolster its declining population. In 2018, Portugal made international news as the country that wants more migrants, and the latest statistics show it needs to attract 75,000 new residents every year to ensure a stable working population.

Going Green

Portugal has invested heavily in renewable energy in recent years, and it now meets more than 50% of its needs with sustainable power, making it one of the leaders in Europe (behind only Austria, Sweden, Iceland and Norway). The Alentejo is home to one of the world's largest solar farms, with 376,000 panels spread across a 130-hectare site, with a peak capacity of 46 megawatts.

This promising foundation in renewable energy took a leap forward in March 2018 when Portugal did something astonishing: for the first time in at least four decades, renewables exceeded the mainland power demand, generating 104% of the country's electricity supply – the majority of which came from wind turbines and hydropower.

Tourism: A Double-Edged Sword

When it comes to tourism, Portugal's star keeps rising, and the boom is visible: boutique hotels, restaurants and bars are popping up quicker than people can keep tabs on them. While the country continues to scoop up global tourism awards left, right and centre, tourism is spurring economic growth and setting national records, contributing €13.2 billion, or 6.8% of Portugal's GDP in 2017. So far, so positive, but Prime Minister Costa is aiming higher, seeking to increase tourism's total contribution to Portugal's GDP to the EU average of 10%, quipping 'you can never have too many tourists'.

But there is a flip side to the story. Some locals are lamenting the fact that short-term rentals are skyrocketing in cities such as Lisbon and Porto because of mass tourism, pushing residents and small businesses further and further out of the centre, as many apartments are now let through home-sharing services. In Lisbon, the local authorities are currently figuring out new legislation that will better control and protect apartments for local residential use. Whether this will actually work remains to be seen.

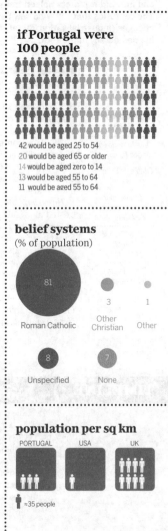

AREA: **88,323 SQ KM**

HIGHEST POINT: **TORRE (1993M)**

POPULATION: **10.25 MILLION**

UNEMPLOYMENT: **6.8%**

PER CAPITA GDP: **€27,300**

if Portugal were 100 people

42 would be aged 25 to 54
20 would be aged 65 or older
14 would be aged zero to 14
13 would be aged 55 to 64
11 would be aged 55 to 64

belief systems
(% of population)

81 Roman Catholic
3 Other Christian
1 Other
8 Unspecified
7 None

population per sq km

PORTUGAL USA UK

≈35 people

History

The small nation on the edge of Europe has seen a long line of conquerors and foreign rulers over the last 3000 years. Celts, Romans, Visigoths, Moors and Christian crusaders all made contributions to Portugal's early identity. In the 15th century, sea captains and intrepid explorers helped transform Portugal into the seat of a vast global empire. The centuries that followed saw devastation (the Lisbon earthquake of 1755) and great changes (industrialisation, dictatorship, decolonisation) before Portugal became a stable democracy in the 1980s.

Early Peoples

One of Europe's earliest places of settlement, the Iberian Peninsula was first inhabited many millennia ago, when hominids wandered across the landscape some time before 200,000 BC. During the Palaeolithic period, early Portuguese ancestors left traces of their time on earth in fascinating stone carvings in the open air near Vila Nova de Foz Côa in the Alto Douro. These date back some 30,000 years and were only discovered by accident, during a proposed dam-building project in 1992. Other signs of early human artistry lie hidden in the Alentejo, in the Gruta do Escoural, where cave drawings of animals and humans date back to around 15,000 BC.

Homo sapiens weren't the only bipeds on the scene. Neanderthals co-existed alongside modern humans in a few rare places like Portugal for as long as 10,000 years. In fact, some of the last traces of their existence have been found in Iberia.

Neanderthals were only the first of a long line of inhabitants to appear (and later disappear) from the Iberian stage. In the 1st millennium BC Celtic people started trickling into the peninsula, settling northern and western Portugal around 700 BC. Dozens of *citânias* (fortified villages) popped up, such as the formidable Citânia de Briteiros. Further south, Phoenician traders, followed by Greeks and Carthaginians, founded coastal stations and mined metals inland.

Prehistoric Sites

....

Vila Nova de Foz Côa (Douro)

....

Citânia de Briteiros (Minho)

....

Cromeleque dos Almendres (Alentejo)

....

Anta Grande do Zambujeiro (Alentejo)

....

Cromeleque do Xerez (Alentejo)

TIMELINE 〉	5000 BC 〉	700 BC 〉	197 BC 〉
	Little-understood Neolithic peoples build protected hilltop settlements in the lower Tejo valley. They leave behind stone monuments, including megaliths scattered around Évora in present-day Alentejo.	Celtic peoples, migrating across the Pyrenees with their families and flocks, sweep through the Iberian Peninsula. They settle in fortified hilltop settlements, known as *castros*, and intermarry with local tribes.	After defeating Carthage in the Second Punic War, the Romans invade Iberia, expanding their empire west. They face fierce resistance from local tribes, including the Lusitani, but eventually conquer them.

Roman Settlement

When the Romans swept into southern Portugal in 197 BC, they expected an easy victory. But they hadn't reckoned on the Lusitani, a Celtic warrior tribe that settled between the Rio Tejo and Rio Douro and resisted ferociously for half a century. Unable to subjugate the Lusitani, the Romans offered peace instead and began negotiations with Viriato, the Lusitanian leader. Unfortunately for Viriato and his underlings, the peace offer was a ruse, and Roman agents, posing as intermediaries, poisoned him. Resistance collapsed following Viriato's death in 139 BC.

For a vivid glimpse into Roman Portugal, you won't see a better site than Conímbriga, near Coimbra, or the monumental remains of the so-called Temple of Diana, in Évora.

By the 5th century, when the Roman Empire had all but collapsed, Portugal's inhabitants had been under Roman rule for 600 years. So what did the Romans ever do for them? Most usefully, they built roads and bridges. But they also brought wheat, barley, olives and vines; large farming estates called *latifúndios* (still found in the Alentejo); a legal system; and, above all, a Latin-derived language. In fact, no other invader proved so useful.

Moors & Christians

The gap left by the Romans was filled by barbarian invaders from beyond the Pyrenees: Vandals, Alans, Visigoths and Suevi, with Arian Christian Visigoths gaining the upper hand in 469.

Internal Visigothic disputes paved the way for Portugal's next great wave of invaders, the Moors – North African Muslims invited in 711 to help a Visigoth faction. They quickly occupied large chunks of Portugal's southern coast.

Southerners enjoyed peace and productivity under the Moors, who established a capital at Shelb (Silves). The new rulers were tolerant of Jews and Christians. Christian smallholding farmers, called Mozarabs, could keep their land and were encouraged to try new methods and crops, especially citrus and rice. Arabic words filtered into the Portuguese language, such as *alface* (lettuce), *arroz* (rice) and dozens of place names (including Fátima, Silves and Algarve), and locals became addicted to Moorish sweets.

Meanwhile, in the north, Christian forces were gaining strength and reached as far as Porto in 868. But it was in the 11th century that the Reconquista (the Christian reconquest) heated up. In 1064 Coimbra was taken and, in 1085, Afonso VI thrashed the Moors in their Spanish heartland of Toledo; he is said to have secured Seville by winning a game of chess with its emir. But in the following year, Afonso's troops were driven out by ruthless Moroccan Almoravids who answered the emir's distress call.

Roman Sites

....

Conímbriga (Beiras)

....

Milreu (Algarve)

....

Termas Romanas (Évora)

....

Núcleo Arqueológico (Lisbon)

....

Cidade de Ammaia (Alentejo)

AD 100	400	711	800
Romans collect taxes to build roads, bridges and other public works. They cultivate vineyards, teach the natives to preserve fish by salting and drying, and grant local communities much autonomy.	Rome crumbles as German tribes run riot in southern Europe. The Suevi, peasant farmers from the Elbe, settle in present-day Porto. Christian Visigoths follow suit, conquering the land in 469.	Visigoth King Witiza is assassinated. When his eldest son, Agila, is blocked from the throne he seeks help from North African Berbers. The Muslim force arrives, establishes peace and puts down roots.	The Umayyad dynasty rules the Iberian Peninsula. The region flourishes under the tolerant caliphate. The Arabs introduce irrigation, bring new crops (including oranges and rice) and establish schools.

Afonso called for help and European crusaders came running – rallying against the 'infidels'. With the help of Henri of Burgundy, among others, Afonso made decisive moves towards victory. The struggle continued in successive generations, and by 1139 Afonso Henriques (grandson of Afonso VI) won such a dramatic victory against the Moors at Ourique (Alentejo) that he named himself Dom – King of Portugal – a title confirmed in 1179 by the Pope (after extra tribute was paid, naturally). Afonso also retook Santarém and Lisbon from the Moors.

By the time he died in 1185, the Portuguese frontier was secure to the Rio Tejo, though it would take another century before the south was torn from the Moors.

The Burgundian Era

During the Reconquista, people faced more than just war and turmoil: in the wake of Christian victories came new rulers and settlers.

The church and its wealthy clergy were the greediest landowners, followed by aristocratic fat cats. Though theoretically free, most common people remained subjects of the landowning class, with few rights. The first hint of democratic rule came with the establishment of the *cortes* (parliament). This assembly of nobles and clergy first met in 1211 at Coimbra, the then capital. Six years later, the capital moved to Lisbon.

Afonso III (r 1248–79) deserves credit for standing up to the church, but it was his son, the 'Poet King' Dinis (r 1279–1325), who really shook Portugal into shape. A far-sighted, cultured man, he took control of the judicial system, started progressive afforestation programmes and encouraged internal trade. He suppressed the dangerously powerful military order of the Knights Templar, refounding them as the Order of Christ. He cultivated music, the arts and education, and he founded a university in Lisbon in 1290, which was later transferred to Coimbra.

Dom Dinis' foresight was spot on when it came to defence: he built or rebuilt some 50 fortresses along the eastern frontier with Castile and signed a pact of friendship with England in 1308, the basis for a future long-lasting alliance.

It was none too soon. Within 60 years of Dinis' death, Portugal was at war with Castile. Fernando I helped provoke the clash by playing a game of alliances with both Castile and the English. He dangled promises of marriage to his daughter Beatriz in front of both nations, eventually marrying her off to Juan I of Castile, thus throwing Portugal's future into Castilian hands.

On Fernando's death in 1383, his wife, Leonor Teles, ruled as regent. But she too was entangled with the Spanish, having long had a Galician lover. The merchant classes preferred unsullied Portuguese candidate João, son

Historic Collections

········

Museu do Oriente (Lisbon)

········

Museu Nacional de Machado de Castro (Coimbra)

········

Casa Museu Passos Canavarro (Santarém)

1147	1242	1297	1348
The Reconquista is under way as Christians attain decisive victories over the Moors. Portugal's first king, Afonso Henriques (crowned 1139), leads the attack, laying siege to Lisbon.	The last remaining Moors are driven out in the bloody battle of Tavira. Aided by Dom Dinis, some 50 fortresses are built to strengthen defences along the eastern frontier.	The boundaries of the Portuguese kingdom – much the same as they are today – are formalised with neighbouring Castile (Spain). The kingdom of Portugal has arrived.	The Plague reaches Portugal (most likely carried on ships that dock in Porto and Lisbon). As in other parts of Europe, the disease devastates, killing one in three.

INDIA AHOY!

Fed up with the Venetian monopoly on overland trade with Asia, Portuguese explorer Vasco da Gama set sail from Lisbon in 1497 for distant shores, with a motley crew aboard his handsome caravel. He skirted the coast of Mozambique and the port of Mombasa before finally washing up on the shore of Calicut, India, in May 1498. The bedraggled crew received a frosty welcome from the Zamorin (Hindu ruler) and, when tensions flared, they returned whence they came. The voyage was hardly plain sailing – monsoon tides were fraught with danger, scurvy was rife and more than half of Da Gama's party perished. For his success in discovering a sea route to India, Manuel I made him a lord when he returned in 1499 and he was hailed 'Admiral of the Indian Ocean'.

But, in 1502, mounting hostilities (with Muslim merchants, who considered Da Gama a rival) meant the Portuguese sea captain was forced to return to establish control. He seized an Arab ship and set it alight with hundreds of merchants on board, then banished Muslims from the port of Calicut. He returned to Europe with coffers full of silk and spices. Luís Vaz de Camões recounts the fascinating adventures of Portugal's *facundo capitão* (eloquent captain) in the epic poem *Os Lusíadas*.

(albeit illegitimate) of Fernando's father. João assassinated Leonor's lover, Leonor fled to Castile and the Castilians duly invaded.

The showdown came in 1385 when João faced a mighty force of Castilians at Aljubarrota. Even with Nuno Álvares Pereira (the Holy Constable) as his military right-hand man and English archers at the ready, the odds were stacked against him. João vowed to build a monastery if he won – and he did. Nuno Álvares, the brilliant commander-in-chief of the Portuguese troops, deserves much of the credit for the victory. He lured the Spanish cavalry into a trap and, with an uphill advantage, his troops decimated the invaders. Within a few hours the Spanish were retreating in disarray and the battle was won.

The victory clinched independence, and João made good his vow by commissioning Batalha's stunning Mosteiro de Santa Maria da Vitória (aka the Mosteiro da Batalha or Battle Abbey). It also sealed Portugal's alliance with England, and João wed John of Gaunt's daughter. Peace was finally concluded in 1411.

The Age of Discoveries

João's success had whetted his appetite and, spurred on by his sons, he soon turned his military energies abroad. Morocco was the obvious target, and in 1415 Ceuta fell easily to his forces. It was a turning point in Portuguese history, a first step into its golden age

Former Portuguese Colonies

Brazil, year of independence 1822

Goa, 1961

Guinea-Bissau, 1974

Angola, 1975

Cape Verde, 1975

Mozambique, 1975

São Tomé e Príncipe, 1975

East Timor, 1975

Macau, 1999

1385	1411	1415	1418
Intermarriage between Castilian and Portuguese royal families leads to complications. Juan I of Castile, claiming the throne, invades. The Portuguese, with English help, rout the invaders at Aljubarrota.	Newly crowned Dom João builds an elaborate monastery to commemorate his victory at Aljubarrota. João marries John of Gaunt's daughter, ushering in an English alliance lasting centuries.	Dom João's third son, Prince Henry the Navigator, joins his father in the conquest of Ceuta in North Africa. Thus begins the colonial expansion of Portugal.	Shipbuilding advances lead to the development of the caravel, a fast, agile ship that changes the face of sailing. Portuguese mariners put it to brilliant use on long voyages of exploration.

Exploration by the Portuguese

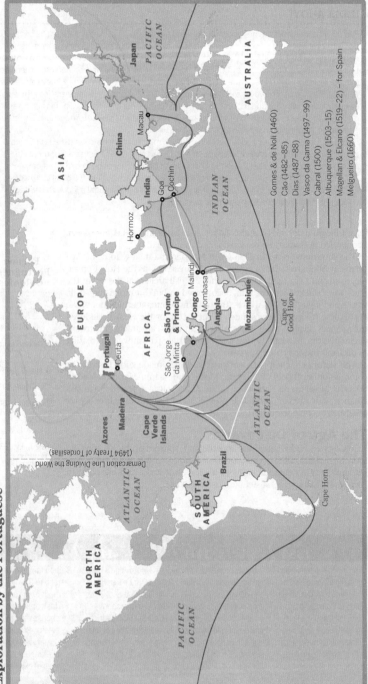

Gomes & de Noli (1460)
Cão (1482–85)
Dias (1487–88)
Vasco da Gama (1497–99)
Cabral (1500)
Albuquerque (1503–15)
Magellan & Elcano (1519–22) – for Spain
Melgueiro (1660)

Demarcation Line Dividing the World
(1494 Treaty of Tordesillas)

It was João's third son, Henry, who focused the spirit of the age – a combination of crusading zeal, love of martial glory and lust for gold – into extraordinary explorations across the seas. These explorations were to transform the small kingdom into a great imperial power.

The biggest breakthrough came in 1497 during the reign of Manuel I, when Vasco da Gama reached southern India. With gold and slaves from Africa and spices from the East, Portugal was soon rolling in riches. Manuel I was so thrilled by the discoveries (and resultant cash injection) that he ordered a frenzied building spree in celebration. Top of his list was the extravagant Mosteiro dos Jerónimos in Belém, later to become his pantheon. Another brief boost to the Portuguese economy at this time came courtesy of an influx of around 150,000 Jews, who had been expelled from Spain in 1492.

Spain, however, had also jumped on the exploration bandwagon and was soon disputing Portuguese claims. Christopher Columbus' 1492 'discovery' of America for Spain led to a fresh outburst of jealous conflict. It was resolved by the Pope in the bizarre 1494 Treaty of Tordesillas, by which the world was divided between the two great powers along a line 370 leagues west of the Cape Verde islands. Portugal won the lands east of the line, including Brazil, officially claimed in 1500.

The rivalry spurred the first circumnavigation of the world. In 1519 Portuguese navigator Fernão Magalhães (Ferdinand Magellan), his allegiance transferred to Spain after a tiff with Manuel I, set off in an effort to prove that the Spice Islands (today's Moluccas in Indonesia) lay in Spanish 'territory'. He reached the Philippines in 1521 but was killed in a skirmish there. One of his five ships, under the Basque navigator Juan Sebastián Elcano, reached the Spice Islands and then sailed home via the Cape of Good Hope, proving the earth was round.

As its explorers reached Timor, China and eventually Japan, Portugal cemented its power with garrison ports and trading posts. The monarchy, taking its 'royal fifth' of profits, became stinking rich – indeed the wealthiest monarchy in Europe, and the lavish Manueline architectural style symbolised the exuberance of the age.

It couldn't last, of course. By the 1570s the huge cost of expeditions and maintaining an empire was taking its toll. The final straw came in 1578. Young, idealistic Sebastião was on the throne and, determined to bring Christianity to Morocco, he rallied a force of 18,000 and set sail from Lagos. He was disastrously defeated at the Battle of Alcácer-Quibir (also known as the Battle of Three Kings): Sebastião and 8000 others were killed, including much of the Portuguese nobility. Sebastião's aged successor, Cardinal Henrique, drained the royal coffers ransoming those captured.

On Henrique's death in 1580, Sebastião's uncle, Felipe II of Spain (Felipe I of Portugal), fought for and won the throne. This marked the end of

The word Portugal comes from Portus Cale, a name the Romans gave to a town near present-day Porto. The word morphed into Portucale under Visigoth rule and expanded significantly in meaning.

Dom João II financed voyages by Vasco da Gama and others, but he is also known for rejecting Christopher Columbus. The Italian navigator approached Portugal first (in 1485) before turning to Spain.

1419	1443	1494	1497
Portuguese sailors discover Madeira. More discoveries follow, including those of the Azores in 1427 and the Cape Verde islands in 1460. Explorers also chart the west coast of Africa.	Explorers bring the first African slaves to Portugal, marking the beginning of a long, shameful era of slavery in Europe and later the New World.	The race for colonial expansion is on: Spain and Portugal carve up the world, with the Treaty of Tordesillas drawing the line 370 leagues west of Cape Verde.	Facing pressure from the church, Dom Manuel I expels commercially active Jews. Those staying must convert or face persecution. By 1536 the Inquisition is under-way, with thousands executed.

centuries of independence, Portugal's golden age and its glorious moment at the centre of the world stage.

Spanish Rule & Portuguese Revival

Spanish rule began promisingly, with Felipe vowing to preserve Portugal's autonomy and attend the long-ignored parliament. But commoners resented Spanish rule and held on to the dream that Sebastião was still alive (as he was killed in battle, some citizens were in denial); pretenders continued to pop up until 1600. Though Felipe was honourable, his successors proved to be considerably less so, using Portugal to raise money and soldiers for Spain's wars overseas and appointing Spaniards to govern Portugal.

An uprising in Catalonia gave fuel to Portugal's independence drive (particularly when the Spanish King Felipe III ordered Portuguese troops to quell the uprising) and in 1640 a group of conspirators launched a coup. Nationalists drove the female governor of Portugal and her Spanish garrison from Lisbon. It was then that the duke of Bragança reluctantly stepped forward and was crowned João IV.

With a hostile Spain breathing down its neck, Portugal searched for allies. Two swift treaties with England led to Charles II's marriage to João's daughter, Catherine of Bragança, and the ceding of Tangier and Bombay to England.

In return the English promised arms and soldiers; however, a preoccupied Spain made only half-hearted attempts to recapture Portugal and recognised Portuguese independence in 1668.

João IV's successors pursued largely absolutist policies (particularly under João V, an admirer of French King Louis XIV). The crown hardly bothered with parliament, and another era of profligate expenditure followed, giving birth to projects such as the wildly extravagant monastery-palace in Mafra.

Cementing power for the crown was one of Portugal's most revered (and feared) statesmen – the Marquês de Pombal, chief minister to the epicurean Dom José I (the latter more interested in opera than political affairs). Described as an enlightened despot, Pombal dragged Portugal into the modern era, crushing opposition with brutal efficiency.

Pombal set up state monopolies, curbed the power of British merchants and boosted agriculture and industry. He abolished slavery and distinctions between traditional and New Christians (Jews who had converted), and overhauled education.

When Lisbon suffered a devastating earthquake in 1755, Pombal swiftly rebuilt the city. He was by then at the height of his power, and he dispensed with his main enemies by implicating them in an attempt on the king's life.

The Treaty of Windsor (1386), which established a pact of mutual assistance between Portugal and England, began what is widely considered to be the oldest surviving alliance in the world.

Islamic Sites

Alcáçova (Mértola)

Núcleo Islâmico (Tavira)

Castelo de São Jorge (Lisbon)

Mouraria (Moura)

Museu Municipal de Arqueologia (Silves)

1497	1519	1572	1580
Following Bartolomeu Dias' historic journey around the Cape of Good Hope in 1488, Vasco da Gama sails to India and becomes a legend. Trade with the East later brings vast wealth.	Fernão Magalhães (Ferdinand Magellan) embarks on his journey to circumnavigate the globe. He is killed in the Philippines, but one of his ships returns, completing the epic voyage.	Luís Vaz de Camões writes Os Lusíadas, an epic poem that celebrates Da Gama's historic voyage. Camões dies poor and largely unrecognised, though he is later hailed as Portugal's greatest literary figure.	King Felipe II of Spain invades Portugal and becomes king. Spain will rule for 60 years, draining Portugal's coffers and ending its golden age.

A DEVASTATING EARTHQUAKE

Lisbon in the 1700s was a thriving city, with gold flowing in from Brazil, a thriving merchant class and grand Manueline architecture. Then, on the morning of 1 November 1755, a devastating earthquake levelled much of the city, which fell like a pack of dominoes, never to regain its former status; palaces, libraries, art galleries, churches and hospitals were razed to the ground. Tens of thousands died, crushed beneath falling masonry, drowned in the tsunami that swept in from the Tejo or killed in the fires that followed.

Enter the formidable, unflappable, geometrically minded Marquês de Pombal. As Dom José I's chief minister, Pombal swiftly set about reconstructing the city, true to his word to 'bury the dead and heal the living'. In the wake of the disaster, the autocratic statesman not only kept the country's head above water as it was plunged into economic chaos but also managed to propel Lisbon into the modern era.

Together with military engineers and architects Eugenio dos Santos and Manuel da Maia, Pombal played a pivotal role in reconstructing the city in a simple, cheap, earthquake-proof way that created today's formal grid, and the Pombaline style was born. The antithesis of rococo, Pombaline architecture was functional and restrained: *azulejos* and decorative elements were used sparingly, building materials were prefabricated, and wide streets and broad plazas were preferred.

Dom José I, for his part, escaped the earthquake unscathed. Instead of being in residence at the royal palace, he had ridden out of town to Belém with his extensive retinue. After seeing the devastation, the eccentric José I refused to live in a masonry building ever again, and he set up a wooden residence outside town, in the hills of Ajuda, north of Belém. What was known as the Real Barraca (Royal Tent) became the site of the Palácio Nacional de Ajuda after the king's death.

He might have continued had it not been for the accession of the devout Dona Maria I in 1777. The anticlerical Pombal was promptly sacked, tried and charged with various offences, though he was never imprisoned. While his religious legislation was repealed, his economic, agricultural and educational policies were largely maintained, helping the country back towards prosperity.

But turmoil was once again on the horizon, as Napoleon was sweeping through Europe.

The Dawn of a Republic

A French Invasion Unleashes Royal Chaos

In 1793 Portugal found itself at war again when it joined Britain in sending naval forces against revolutionary France. Before long, Napoleon gave Portugal an ultimatum: close your ports to British shipping or be invaded.

1640	1690	1703	1717
When Catalonia rebels against the oppressive monarchy, Felipe III sends Portuguese troops to quell the uprising. Portuguese nobles stage a coup and overthrow Spain. Dom João IV is crowned.	With the economy in tatters and the empire fading, the Portuguese pray for a miracle. The prayer is answered when gold is discovered in Brazil; incredible riches soon flow into the royal coffers.	France and Britain are at war. Facing (disastrous!) wine shortages, the English sign a new treaty with Portugal and become a major player in the Portuguese economy, with port production growing exponentially.	Brazilian gold extraction nears its peak, with over 600,000oz imported annually. Dom João V becomes Europe's richest monarch, lavishing resources on ostentatious projects like the Palácio Nacional de Mafra.

There was no way Portugal could turn its back on Britain, upon which it depended for half of its trade and the protection of its sea routes. In 1807 Portugal's royal family fled to Brazil (where it stayed for 14 years), and Napoleon's forces marched into Lisbon, sweeping Portugal into the Peninsular War (France's invasion of Spain and Portugal, which lasted until 1814).

To the rescue came Sir Arthur Wellesley (later Duke of Wellington), Viscount Beresford and their seasoned British troops, who eventually drove the French back across the Spanish border in 1811.

Free but weakened, Portugal was administered by Beresford while the royals dallied in Brazil. In 1810 Portugal lost a profitable intermediary role by giving Britain the right to trade directly with Brazil. The next humiliation was João's 1815 proclamation of Brazil as a kingdom united with Portugal – he did this to bring more wealth and prestige to Brazil (which he was growing to love) and, in turn, to him and the rest of the royal family residing there. With soaring debts and dismal trade, Portugal was at one of the lowest points in its history, reduced to a de facto colony of Brazil and a protectorate of Britain.

Meanwhile, resentment simmered in the army. Rebel officers quietly convened parliament and drew up a new liberal constitution. Based on Enlightenment ideals, it abolished many rights of the nobility and clergy, and instituted a single-chamber parliament.

Faced with this fait accompli, João returned and accepted its terms – though his wife and his son Miguel were bitterly opposed to it. João's elder son, Pedro, had other ideas: left behind to govern Brazil, he snubbed the constitutionalists by declaring Brazil independent in 1822 and himself its emperor. When João died in 1826, the stage was set for civil war.

Offered the crown, Pedro dashed out a new, less liberal charter and then abdicated in favour of his seven-year-old daughter, Maria, on the provisos that she marry her uncle Miguel and that uncle Miguel accept the new constitution. Miguel took the oath but promptly abolished Pedro's charter and proclaimed himself king. A livid Pedro rallied the equally furious liberals and forced Miguel to surrender at Évoramonte in 1834.

After Pedro's death, his daughter Maria, now queen of Portugal at just 15, kept his flame alive with fanatical support of his 1826 charter. The radical supporters of the liberal 1822 constitution grew vociferous over the next two decades, bringing the country to the brink of civil war. The Duke of Saldanha, however, saved the day, negotiating a peace that toned down Pedro's charter while still radically modernising Portugal's infrastructure.

A Hopeful New Era

The latter half of the 19th century was a remarkable period for Portugal, and it became known as one of the most advanced societies in southern

To 'relive' the Lisbon earthquake, visit the Lisbon Story Centre, located near the heart of where so much destruction occurred.

It was the Portuguese who started England's obsession with tea: their explorers introduced it to Europe in the mid-17th century, and tea enthusiast Catherine of Bragança did the rest.

1755	1770	1807	1815
Lisbon suffers what was Europe's biggest natural disaster in recorded history. On All Saints' Day, three massive earthquakes destroy the city, followed by a tsunami and ravaging fires that kill tens of thousands.	The king's powerful prime minister, the Marquês de Pombal, rebuilds Lisbon following a modern grid. He abolishes slavery, builds schools and develops the economy, crushing those in his way.	Napoleon invades Portugal. The Portuguese royal family and several thousand in their retinue pack up their belongings and set sail for Brazil. British warships guard their passage.	Having fallen hard for Brazil, Dom João VI declares Rio de Janeiro the capital of the United Kingdom of Portugal and Brazil and the Algarves, relegating Lisbon to second-class status.

SALAZAR & THE ECONOMY

When General António Carmona was named Portugal's president in 1926, he inherited a country in serious debt. Fearing economic catastrophe, Carmona called in an expert, a man by the name of António de Oliveira Salazar. At the time, Salazar was a 37-year-old bachelor, sharing spartan quarters with a priest (who would later become cardinal of Lisbon). Salazar himself was no stranger to religious life. He spent eight years studying to become a priest, and some residents of his small native village even called him 'father' on his visits. Only a last-minute decision led him to veer into law instead.

One of the country's first economists, Salazar garnered wide respect for his articles on public finance. When General Carmona approached him with the job of finance minister, Salazar accepted on one condition: that the spending of all government ministries fall under his discretion. The general agreed.

Salazar achieved enormous success in firing up the national economy. He severely curtailed government spending, raising taxes and balancing the budget during his first year. Unemployment decreased significantly. Salazar quickly became one of Carmona's star ministers. He also took on additional posts as other ministers resigned. In this way he consolidated power until Carmona eventually named him prime minister.

Salazar set a tone for civilian life that would last for many decades. Under his authoritarian rule, the country knew stability and prosperity, though at enormous cost: censorship, imprisonment and – in some cases – torture of political opponents. Among his most damning attributes was his attitude towards the working class. He believed in giving them a diet of 'fado, Fátima and football' to keep them happily compliant, but he had no intention of bettering their lot; at the end of his rule in 1968, Portugal had the highest rates of illiteracy and tuberculosis in Western Europe, and women were still not allowed to vote. Given the socially backward condition of the nation when Salazar relinquished power, the advancements of the last 50 years are all the more startling.

Europe. Casual visitors to Lisbon, such as Hans Christian Andersen, were surprised to find tree-lined boulevards with gas street lamps, efficient trams and well-dressed residents. The educational reformer João Arroio dramatically increased the number of schools, doubling the number of boys' schools and quadrupling the number of girls' schools. Women gained the right to own property; slavery was abolished throughout the Portuguese empire, as was the death penalty; and even the prison system received an overhaul – prisoners were taught useful trades while in jail so they could integrate into society upon their release.

Professional organisations, such as the Literary Guild, emerged and became a major force for the advancement of ideas in public discourse, inspiring debate in politics, religious life and the art world.

As elsewhere in Europe, this was also a time of great industrial growth, with a dramatic increase in textile production, much of it to be

1822	1832	1865	1890
In Brazil, Prince Regent Pedro leads a coup d'état and declares Brazilian independence, with himself the new 'emperor'. Dom João VI, his father, returns to Portugal to reclaim his crown.	Now king, Pedro I returns to Portugal, where he must contest his throne against his brother, Miguel. Two years of civil war end with Miguel's banishment. Dom Pedro's daughter becomes queen.	Portugal enjoys a period of peace and prosperity. Railways connect villages with Lisbon and Porto, now cities enriched by maritime trade. Advancements are made in industry, agriculture, health and education.	Portugal takes a renewed interest in its African colonies. Britain wants control of sub-Saharan Africa and threatens Portugal with war. Cowed, Portugal withdraws, causing a crisis at home.

exported. Other significant undertakings included the building of bridges and a nationwide network of roads, as well as the completion of major architectural works such as the Palácio Nacional da Pena above Sintra.

Dark Days & A King's Death

However, by 1900, discontent among workers began to grow. With increased mechanisation, workers began losing their jobs (some factory owners began hiring children to operate the machines), and their demands for fair working conditions went unanswered. Those who went on strike were simply fired and replaced. At the same time, Portugal experienced a dramatic demographic shift: rural areas were increasingly depopulated in favour of cities, and emigration (especially to Brazil) snowballed.

Much was changing, and more and more people began to look towards socialism as a cure for the country's inequalities. Nationalist republicanism swept through the lower-middle classes, spurring an attempted coup in 1908. It failed, but the following month Dom Carlos and Crown Prince Luís Filipe were brutally assassinated in Lisbon.

Carlos' younger son, Manuel II, tried feebly to appease republicans, but it was too little, too late. On 5 October 1910, after an uprising by military officers, a republic was declared. Manuel, dubbed 'the Unfortunate', sailed into exile in Britain, where he died in 1932.

The Rise & Fall of Salazar

After a landslide victory in the 1911 elections, hopes were high among republicans for dramatic changes, but the tide was against them. The economy was in tatters, an issue only exacerbated by a financially disastrous decision to join the Allies in WWI. In the postwar years the chaos deepened: republican factions squabbled, unions led strikes and were repressed, and the military grew more powerful.

The new republic soon had a reputation as Europe's most unstable regime. Between 1910 and 1926 there were an astonishing 45 changes of government, often resulting from military intervention. Another coup in 1926 brought forth new names and faces, most significantly António de Oliveira Salazar, a finance minister who would rise through the ranks to become prime minister in 1932 – a post he would hold for the next 36 years.

Salazar hastily enforced his 'New State' – a corporatist republic that was nationalistic, Catholic, authoritarian and essentially repressive. All political parties were banned except for the loyalist National Union, which ran the show, and the National Assembly. Strikes were forbidden and propaganda, censorship and brute force kept society in order. The sinister new Polícia Internacional e de Defesa do Estado (PIDE) secret police inspired terror and suppressed opposition using imprisonment and torture. Various attempted coups during Salazar's rule came to nothing.

The Portuguese were the first Westerners to reach Japan, in 1543. They founded Nagasaki, introduced the mosquito net and brought new words to the Japanese language, including *pan* (bread) and, possibly, *arrigato* (thank you).

Some historians believe Portuguese explorers reached Australia in the 1500s, 250 years before England's James Cook. For the inside scoop, read Kenneth McIntyre's *The Secret Discovery of Australia* (1977).

1900	1908	1910	1916
The republican movement gains force. The humiliating Africa issue is one among many grievances against the crown. Others include rising unemployment and growing social inequalities.	The royal family tries (and fails) to silence antimonarchist sentiment by shutting down newspapers, exiling dissidents and brutally suppressing demonstrations. Dom Carlos and his eldest son, Luís Filipe, are assassinated.	Dom Carlos' younger son, 18-year-old Manuel, takes the throne but is soon ousted. Portugal is declared a republic. Chaos rules, and the country will see 45 governments in 16 years.	Despite initial neutrality, Portugal gets drawn into WWI on the Allied side and sends 55,000 troops; nearly 10,000 perish. The war effort is devastating for the economy, creating a long postwar recession.

For a chilling taste of life as a political prisoner under Salazar, you could visit the 16th-century Fortaleza at Peniche – used as a jail by the dictator.

The only good news was the dramatic economic turnaround. Through the 1950s and 1960s, Portugal experienced an annual industrial growth rate of 7% to 9%.

Internationally, the wily Salazar played two hands, unofficially supporting Franco's nationalists in the Spanish Civil War and, despite official neutrality, allowing the British to use Azores airfields during WWII and engaging in illegal sales of tungsten to Germany. It was later discovered that Salazar had also authorised the transfer of Nazi-looted gold to Portugal – 44 tonnes, according to Allied records.

But it was something else that finally brought the Salazarist era to a close – decolonisation. Refusing to relinquish the colonies, he was faced with ever more costly and unpopular military expeditions. In 1961 Goa was occupied by India, and nationalists rose up in Angola. Guerrilla movements also appeared in Portuguese Guinea and Mozambique.

Salazar, however, didn't have to face the consequences. In 1968 he had a stroke, and he died two years later.

His successor, Marcelo Caetano, failed to ease unrest. Military officers sympathetic to African freedom fighters grew reluctant to fight colonial wars – the officers had seen the horrible conditions in which the colonies lived beneath the Portuguese authorities. Several hundred officers formed the Movimento das Forças Armadas (MFA), which on 25 April 1974 carried out a nearly bloodless coup in Lisbon, later nicknamed the Revolution of the Carnations (after victorious soldiers stuck carnations in their rifle barrels). Carnations are still a national symbol of freedom.

From Revolution to Democracy

Despite the coup's popularity, the following year saw unprecedented chaos. It began where the revolution had begun: in the African colonies. Independence was granted immediately to Guinea-Bissau, followed by the speedy decolonisation of the Cape Verde islands, São Tomé e Príncipe, Mozambique and Angola.

The transition wasn't smooth: civil war racked Angola, and East Timor, freshly liberated in 1975, was promptly invaded by Indonesia. Within Portugal, too, times were turbulent, with almost a million refugees from African colonies flooding into the country.

The nation was an economic mess, with widespread strikes and a tangle of political ideas and parties. The communists and a radical wing of the MFA launched a revolutionary movement, nationalising firms and services. Peasant farmers seized land to establish communal farms that failed because of infighting and poor management. While revolutionaries held

The Inquisitors' Manual (2003), by António Lobo Antunes, is a brilliantly written depiction of the dark days under Salazar, seen through the eyes of Faulknerian characters such as 'the minister', Senhor Francisco.

Officially neutral in WWII, Portugal was a major intersection of both Allied and Nazi spying operations. British secret-service agents based there included Graham Greene, Ian Fleming and double agent Kim Philby.

1932	1943	1961	1974
António de Oliveira Salazar seizes power. The Portuguese economy grows but at enormous human cost. Salazar uses censorship, imprisonment and torture to silence his opponents.	Portugal, neutral during WWII, becomes a crossroads for the intelligence activities of Allied and Axis operatives. Salazar works both sides, selling tungsten to the Nazis while allowing Britain the use of airfields.	The last vestiges of Portugal's empire begin to crumble as India seizes Goa. Independence movements are underway in Portugal's former African colonies of Angola, Mozambique and Guinea-Bissau.	Army officers overthrow Salazar's successor in the Revolution of the Carnations. Portugal veers to the left, and communists and moderates struggle for power in the unstable country.

sway in the south, the conservative north was led by Mário Soares and his Partido Socialista (PS; Socialist Party).

In the early post-Salazar days, radical provisional governments established by the military failed one after the other, as did an attempted coup led by General António de Spínola in 1975. A period of relative calm finally arrived in 1976, when Portugal adopted a new constitution and held its first elections for a new parliament. General António Ramalho Eanes was elected president the same year and helped steer the country toward democracy. He chose as his prime minister Soares, who took the reins with enormous challenges facing Portugal, including soaring inflation, high unemployment and downward-spiralling wages.

> Portugal only narrowly missed claiming Europe's first female prime minister: in 1979 Margaret Thatcher snatched the honour just three months before Maria de Lourdes Pintasilgo (1930–2004).

The Rocky Road to Stability

Portugal was soon committed to a blend of socialism and democracy, with a powerful president, an elected assembly and a Council of the Revolution to control the armed forces.

Mário Soares' minority government soon faltered, prompting a series of attempts at government by coalitions and nonparty candidates, including Portugal's first female prime minister, Maria de Lourdes Pintasilgo. In the 1980 parliamentary elections, a new political force took the reins: the conservative Aliança Democrática (AD; Democratic Alliance), led by Francisco Sá Carneiro.

After Carneiro's almost immediate (and suspicious) death in a plane crash, Francisco Pinto Balsemão stepped into his shoes. He implemented plans to join the European Community (EC).

It was partly to keep the EC and the International Monetary Fund (IMF) happy that a new coalition government under Soares and Balsemão implemented a strict programme of economic modernisation. Not surprisingly, the belt-tightening wasn't popular. The loudest critics were Soares' right-wing partners in the Partido Social Democrata (PSD; Social Democrat Party), led by the dynamic Aníbal Cavaco Silva. Communist trade unions organised strikes, and the appearance of urban terrorism by the radical left-wing Forças Populares 25 de Abril (FP-25) deepened unrest.

> Portugal: A Traveller's History (2004), by Harold Livermore, explores some of the richer episodes of the country's past, taking in cave paintings, vineyards and music, among other topics.

In 1986, after nine years of negotiations, Portugal joined the EC. Flush with new funds, it raced ahead of its neighbours with unprecedented economic growth. The new cash flow also gave Prime Minister Cavaco Silva the power to push ahead with radical economic plans. These included labour-law reforms that left many workers disenchanted. The 1980s were crippled by strikes – including one involving 1.5 million workers – though they were to no avail: the controversial legislation was eventually passed.

The economic growth, however, wouldn't last. In 1992 EC trade barriers fell and Portugal suddenly faced new competition. Fortunes dwindled as

1986	1998	1998	1999
In a narrow second-round victory, Mário Soares is elected president of Portugal, becoming its first civilian head of state in 60 years. The same year, Portugal joins the EC, along with Spain.	Lisbon hosts Expo '98, showcasing new developments, including Santiago Calatrava's cutting-edge train station and Europe's largest oceanarium and longest bridge (the Ponte de Vasco da Gama).	José Saramago, a lifelong communist, wins the Nobel Prize in Literature for his darkly humorous tales about ordinary characters facing fantastical obstacles; his work is condemned by the church.	Legendary *fadista* (performer of traditional song) Amália Rodrigues dies aged 79. Three days of mourning are declared. Her extraordinary 40-year career is credited with helping to revive the dying genre.

THE MYSTERY OF THE NEANDERTHALS

Scientists have never come to an agreement about the fate of the Neanderthals – stout and robust beings who used stone tools and fire, buried their dead and had brains larger than those of modern humans. The most common theory is that *Homo sapiens* drove Neanderthals to extinction (perhaps in some sort of genocidal warfare). A less accepted theory is that Neanderthals and humans bred together and produced a hybrid species. This idea gained credence when Portuguese archaeologists found a strange skeleton – the first complete Palaeolithic skeleton ever unearthed in Iberia – just north of Lisbon in 1999. The team, led by João Zilhão, director of the Portuguese Institute of Archaeology, discovered the 25,000-year-old remains of a young boy with traits of both early humans (pronounced chin and teeth) and of Neanderthals (broad limbs). The boy had been interred in what was clearly a ritual burial. Some believe this kind of relationship (love-making rather than war making) happened over the span of thousands of years and that some Neanderthal elements entered the modern human gene pool.

a recession set in, and disillusionment grew as Europe's single market revealed the backwardness of Portugal's agricultural sector.

Strikes, crippling corruption charges and student demonstrations over rising fees only undermined the PSD further, leading to Cavaco Silva's resignation in 1995. The general elections that year brought new faces to power, with the socialist António Guterres running the show. Despite hopes for a different and less conservative administration, it was business as usual, with Guterres maintaining the budgetary rigour that qualified Portugal for the European Economic & Monetary Union (EMU) in 1998. Indeed, for a while Portugal was a star EMU performer, with steady economic growth that helped Guterres win a second term. But corruption scandals, rising inflation and a faltering economy soon spelt disaster. Portugal had slipped into economic stagnation by the dawn of the 21st century. The next 10 years were ones of hardship for the Portuguese economy, which saw little or negative GDP growth, and rising unemployment from 2001 to 2010. As elsewhere in Europe, Portugal took a huge hit during the global financial crisis. Ultimatums from the EU governing body to rein in its debt (to avoid a Greece-style meltdown) brought unpopular austerity measures – pension reform, increased taxes, public-sector hiring freezes – that led to protests and strikes.

CR Boxer's classic text, *The Portuguese Seaborne Empire* (1969), is still one of the best studies of explorations by Portuguese mariners and the complex empire that unfolded as a result.

Hard Times

Portugal's economy wasn't particularly strong in the years before the economic crisis, making the economic fire all the more destructive. Lumped in with other economically failing eurozone nations, the group of them collectively known as PIIGS (Portugal, Italy, Ireland, Greece and Spain),

2001	2004	2007	2010
The Alto Douro wine region is awarded Unesco World Heritage status. Demarcated in 1756, it is one of the oldest vineyard regions in the world, with wine-growing origins dating back 2000 years.	Hosting the UEFA European Championship, Portugal makes it to the final only to suffer an agonising loss to Greece. Over €600 million is spent remodelling and constructing stadiums.	Portugal takes over the rotating EU presidency. The Treaty of Lisbon, an agreement that aims to give new coherence to the EU, is drafted.	Portugal legalises same-sex marriage, becoming the sixth country in Europe (and the eighth in the world) to do so. A media firestorm ensues as the church condemns the law.

Portugal – in dire financial straits – accepted an EU bailout worth €78 billion in 2011. The younger generation has borne the heaviest burden following the crisis, with unemployment above 40% for workers under the age of 25. In addition, there are the underemployed and those scraping by on meagre wages.

The EU bailout came with the stipulation that Portugal improve its budget deficit by reducing spending and increasing tax revenues. Austerity measures followed and the public took to the streets to protest against higher taxes and slashed pensions and benefits, in the context of record-high unemployment. Mass demonstrations and general strikes grew, with the largest attracting an estimated 1.5 million people nationwide in 2013 – an astounding figure given Portugal's small size. Those in industries most affected by government policy – including education, healthcare and transport – joined ranks with the unemployed and pensioners to amass in the largest gatherings since the Revolution of the Carnations in 1974.

Despite the bailout package, Portugal remained in its most severe recession since the 1970s. Every day, Portuguese were confronted with depressing headlines announcing freezes on public spending, cuts in healthcare, removal of free school lunches, curtailing of police patrols and rising suicides, among other issues. Pensioners living on 200-odd euros a month struggled to feed themselves without family financial support, and poverty and hunger affected untold millions; according to TNS Global, roughly three out of four people in Portugal struggled to make their money last through the month.

What began as a financial crisis soon turned into a political crisis, as successive government ministers failed to ameliorate the growing problems. With anger mounting on the streets, the public clamoured for the resignation of Prime Minister Pedro Passos Coelho. Indeed, his time in power would come to an abrupt end in 2015, with a left-wing Socialist Party government, led by António Costa, taking control and ushering in a new era in Portuguese politics.

2013	2014	2015	2017
Fed up with rising unemployment, soaring taxes and a proposed €4 billion in government spending cuts, 1.5 million protesters take to the streets of Portugal.	In an extraordinary turnaround, Portugal, buoyed by success in the private markets, exits its three-year, €78 billion international bailout programme without seeking an emergency backstop from its lenders.	The government approves a law granting citizenship to descendants of Jews who were expelled from the country five centuries ago. The new legislation enables Sephardic Jews to apply for dual nationality.	Portugal wins Eurovision for the first time with the song *Amar pelos dois* ('Love for Two'), making young Salvador Sobral a household name overnight.

Religion

Christianity has been a powerful force in shaping Portugal's history, and religion still plays an important role in the lives of its people. Churches and cathedrals are sprinkled about every town and city across the country, and Portugal's biggest celebrations revolve around religious events, with a packed calendar of colourful parades and concerts held on important feast days. Portugal is also home to a number of pilgrimage sites, the most important of which, Fátima, attracts several million pilgrims each year.

Church & State

Portugal has a deep connection to the church. Even during the long rule of the Moors, Christianity flourished in the north – which provided a strategic base for Christian crusaders to retake the kingdom. Cleric and king walked hand in hand, from the earliest papal alliances of the 11th century through to the 17th century, when the church played a role both at home and in Portugal's expanding empire.

Things ran smoothly until the 18th century, when the Marquês de Pombal, a man of the Enlightenment, wanted to curtail the power of the church – specifically that of the Jesuits, whom he expelled in 1759. He also sought to modernise the Portuguese state (overseeing one of the world's first urban 'grid' systems) and brought education under the state's control. State–church relations seesawed over the next 150 years, with power struggles including the outright ban of religious orders in 1821 and the seizing by the state of many church properties.

The separation of church and state was formally recognised during the First Republic (1910–26). But in practice the church remained intimately linked to many aspects of people's lives. Health and education were largely under religious auspices, with Catholic schools and hospitals the norm. Social outlets for those in rural areas were mostly church-related. And the completion of any public-works project always included a blessing by the local bishop.

In 1932 António de Oliveira Salazar swept into power, establishing a Mussolini-like Estado Novo (New State) that lasted until the 1974 Revolution of the Carnations. Salazar had strong ties to the Catholic church – he spent eight years studying for the priesthood before switching to law. His college roommate was a priest who later became the Cardinal Patriarch of Lisbon. Salazar was a ferocious anticommunist, and he used Roman Catholic references to appeal to people's sense of authority, order, and discipline. He described the family, the parish and the larger institution of Christianity as the foundations of the state. Church officials who spoke out against him were silenced or forced into exile.

Following the 1974 revolution, the church found itself out of favour with many Portuguese; its support of the Salazar regime spelt its undoing in the topsy-turvy days following the government's collapse. The new constitution, ratified in 1976, again emphasised the formal separation of church and state, although this time the law had teeth, and Portugal quickly transitioned into a more secular society. Today, only about half of all weddings happen inside a church. Divorce is legal, as is abortion (up to 10 weeks; the

Religious Events

....

Semana Santa (Braga)

....

Festa de São João (Porto & Braga)

....

Festa de Santo António (Lisbon)

....

Fátima Romaris (Fátima)

....

Romaria de Nossa Senhora d'Agonia (Viana do Castelo)

....

Festa de Nossa Senhora dos Remédios (Lamego)

LIFE UNDER MUSLIM RULE

The Moors opened schools and set about campaigns to achieve mass literacy (in Arabic, of course), as well as the teaching of mathematics, geography and history. Medicine reached new levels of sophistication. There was also a degree of religious tolerance, but this evaporated when Christian crusaders came to power. Much to the chagrin of Christian slave owners, slavery was not permitted in the Islamic kingdom – making it a refuge for runaway slaves. Muslims, Christians and Jews all peacefully coexisted, and at times even collaborated, creating one of the most scientifically and artistically advanced societies the world had ever known.

law went into effect following a 2007 referendum). In 2010 same-sex marriage was legalised, making Portugal the sixth European nation to permit it (with several other nations joining the ranks in recent years).

The Inquisition

One of the more unusual rituals celebrated around Easter is the *enterro do bacalhau* (burying of the codfish), which marks the end of Lent.

'After the earthquake, which had destroyed three-quarters of the city of Lisbon, the wise men of that country could think of no means more effectual to preserve the kingdom from utter ruin than to entertain the people with an auto-da-fé...' – Voltaire, *Candide*

One of the darkest episodes in Portugal's history, the Inquisition was a campaign of church-sanctioned terror and execution that began in 1536 and lasted for 200 years, though it was not officially banned until 1821. It was initially aimed at Jews, who were either expelled from Portugal or forced to renounce their faith. Those who didn't embrace Catholicism risked facing the auto-da-fé (act of faith): a church ceremony consisting of a Mass, a procession of the guilty, reading of the sentences and, later, burning at the stake.'Trials' took place in public squares in Lisbon, Porto, Évora and Coimbra in front of crowds sometimes numbering in the thousands. At the centre, atop a large canopied platform, sat the Grand Inquisitor, surrounded by a staff of aristocrats, priests, bailiffs, torturers and scribes, who meticulously recorded the proceedings.

The victims usually spent years in prison, often undergoing crippling torture, before seeing the light of day. They stood accused of a wide variety of crimes – such as skipping meals on Jewish fast days (signs of 'unreformed' Jews), leaving pork uneaten on the plate, failing to attend Mass or observe the sabbath, as well as blasphemy, witchcraft and homosexuality. No matter how flimsy the 'evidence' – often delivered to the tribunal by a grudge-bearing neighbour – very few were found not guilty and released. After a decade or so in prison, the condemned were finally brought to their auto-da-fé. Before meeting their judgement, they were dressed in a *san benito* (yellow penitential gown painted with flames) and a *coroza* (high conical cap) and brought before the tribunal.

The last auto-da-fé was held in 1765. Ironically enough, it was levied against 10 Jesuit priests who dared to oppose the autocratic and anticlerical Marquês de Pombal.

After the sentence was pronounced, judgement was carried out in a different venue. By dawn the next morning, for instance, executioners would lead the condemned to a killing field outside town. Those who repented were strangled before being burnt at the stake. The unrepentant were simply burnt alive. During the years of the Inquisition, the church executed over 2000 victims and tortured or exiled tens of thousands more. The Portuguese even exported the auto-da-fé to the colonies, burning Hindus at the stake in Goa, for instance.

As Voltaire sardonically suggested, superstition played no small part in the auto-da-fé. Some believers thought that the earthquake of 1755 was the wrath of God upon them, and that they were being punished – not for their bloody auto-da-fés but because the Holy Office hadn't done quite enough to punish the heretics.

Apparitions at Fátima

For many Portuguese Catholics, Fátima represents one of the most momentous religious events of the 20th century, and it transformed a tiny village into a major pilgrimage site for Catholics across the globe. On 13 May 1917, 10-year-old Lúcia Santos and her two younger cousins, Jacinta and Francisco Marto, were out tending their parents' flocks in the fields outside the village of Fátima. Suddenly a bolt of lightning struck the earth, and a woman 'brighter than the sun' appeared before them. According to Santos, she came to them with a message exhorting people to pray and do penance to save sinners. She asked the children to pray the rosary every day, which she said was key to bringing peace to one's own life and to the world. At the time, peace was certainly on the minds of many Portuguese, who were already deeply enmeshed in WWI. She then told the children to come again on the 13th of each month, at the same time and place, and that in October she would reveal herself to them.

Word of the alleged apparition spread, although most who heard the tale of the shepherd children reacted with scepticism. Only a handful of observers came to the field for the 13 June appearance, but the following month several thousand showed up. That's when the apparition apparently entrusted the children with three secrets. In the weeks that followed, a media storm raged, with the government accusing the church of fabricating an elaborate hoax to revive its flagging popularity. The church, for its part, didn't know how to react. The children were even arrested and interrogated at one point, but the three refused to change their story.

On 13 October 1917 some 70,000 people gathered for what was to be the final appearance of the apparition. Many witnesses there experienced the so-called Miracle of the Sun, where the sun seemed to grow in size and dance in the sky, becoming a whirling disc of fire, shooting out multicoloured rays. Some spoke of being miraculously healed; others were frightened by the experience; still others claimed they saw nothing at all. The three children claimed they saw Mary, Jesus and Joseph in the sky. Newspapers across the country reported on the event, and soon a growing hysteria surrounded it.

Only Lúcia made it into adulthood. Jacinta and Francisco, both beatified by the church in 2000, were two of the more than 20 million killed during the 1918 influenza epidemic. Lúcia later became a Carmelite nun and died at the age of 97 on 13 February 2005.

Three Secrets

Much mystery surrounds the three secrets told to the children at Fátima on 13 July 1917. Lúcia revealed the first two in 1941 at the request of the bishop of Leira, who was publishing a book on Jacinta. The first secret depicted a vision of demons and human souls suffering in the fires of hell. The second secret predicted that an even more disastrous war

Portugal's favourite holy man, Santo António, is the go-to for lonely hearts. Unmarried women and men light candles to him to find love, and on his feast day in June, Lisbon hosts free mass marriages for those too poor to spring for a private celebration.

Fátima Books & Films

The Fourth Secret of Fátima (2006), written by Antonio Socci

The 13th Day (2009), directed by Ian and Dominic Higgins

Miracle of Our Lady of Fátima (1952), directed by John Brahm

RELIGION APPARITIONS AT FÁTIMA

FAITH ON THE DECLINE

The percentage of Portuguese who consider themselves Catholics (around 81%) ranks among the highest in Western Europe. The number of the faithful, however, has been on a steady decline since the 1970s, when over 95% of the nation was Catholic. Today nearly half a million residents describe themselves as agnostic, and less than 20% of the population are practising Catholics.

Regional differences reveal a more complicated portrait: around half of northern Portugal's population still attend Sunday Mass, as do more than a quarter in Lisbon – with noticeably fewer churchgoers on the southern coast.

CRYPTO-JEWS

When Manuel I banned Judaism, most Jews fled or converted. Some, however, simply hid their faith from public view and wore the facade of being a New Christian (the name given to Jewish converts). Religious ceremonies were held behind closed doors, with the sabbath lamp placed at the bottom of a clay jar so that it could not be seen from outside. Within their Catholic prayer books Jews composed Jewish prayers, and they even overlaid Jewish prayers atop Catholic rituals (like the making of the sign of the cross). Clever food preparation – such as eating pork-free *alheiras* (seasoned garlicky sausages made of a mixture of chicken, rabbit, partridge or veal mixed with bread dough for consistency) – also helped hide their faith.

One Crypto-Jewish community in Belmonte managed to maintain its faith in hiding for over 400 years and was only revealed in 1917. Due to centuries of endogamy (inter-marriage), many of the 200 Jews in this community suffer from hereditary diseases. No longer underground (Belmonte now has its own synagogue and Jewish cemetery), members of the community remain quite secretive about the practices they maintained in hiding.

would follow WWI should the world – and in particular Russia – not convert. Disclosed months before the Bolshevik takeover in St Petersburg, this secret was considered particularly inflammatory, as it went on to say that, if Mary's call for repentance went unheeded, Russia would spread its terrors through the world, causing wars and persecution of the church. Lúcia was reluctant to reveal the third secret, claiming that she was told by the Virgin Mary never to reveal it. Stricken with illness and convinced she was going to die – and under pressure from the bishop of Leira – Lúcia finally agreed to write the secret down in 1944.

The bishop who received the secret then passed it on to the Vatican, who kept it hidden away for decades. Lúcia requested that the last secret be revealed in 1960 or upon her death, whichever came first. She picked 1960 as she figured that by then the secret would be more clearly understood. The Vatican, however, had other plans and announced in 1960 that the secret would probably remain sealed forever. Fátima followers, meanwhile, offered wild speculations on what the third secret might reveal – from nuclear holocaust to WWIII, catastrophic global financial crisis, famine, the apocalypse. The church kept them in suspense until 2000, when it was finally revealed.

The last secret was the most mystical and controversial of the three. Lúcia described seeing an angel holding a flaming sword who pointed at the earth and cried out 'penance'. Then she saw a ruined city full of corpses and beyond that a steep mountain, up which climbed a bishop dressed in white – whom she took to be the pope. At the top he knelt before a cross made of rough-hewn tree trunks and was killed by soldiers, who gunned him down.

Portugal still has a few good old-fashioned pagan celebrations. The most famous is the Festa dos Rapazes (Festival of the Lads), which features young men in rags and wooden masks rampaging around Miranda do Douro.

Some claim that this predicted the assassination attempt on Pope John Paul II in 1981. The attempt happened on 13 May – the anniversary of the first apparition – and the Pope himself claimed that the Virgin of Fátima saved him from death. (According to some reconstructions of the shooting, the assassin's bullet followed a bizarre elliptical path rather than a straight line, thereby avoiding the Pope's vital organs.) Conspiracy theorists claim that the church was hiding the 'real' third secret, which related to the apocalypse and a great apostasy within the church – a breakdown that would begin at the top. Recent scandals, including the Catholic sex-abuse cases in various parts of the world, have only fuelled speculation among some 'Fátimists' that the third secret has yet to be revealed.

Art & Architecture

Portugal has a long and storied art history. Neolithic tribes, Celtic peoples, Romans, Visigoths, Moors and early Christian crusaders have all left their mark here. The Age of Discoveries – a rich era of grand cathedrals and lavish palaces – began around 1500. In the 500 years that followed, Portugal became a showcase for a dizzying array of architectural styles – Manueline, mannerist, baroque, art nouveau, modernist and post-modernist. Meanwhile, painters, sculptors, poets and novelists all made contributions to Portugal's artistic heritage.

Palaeolithic Palette

The Cromeleque dos Almendres, a most mysterious group of 95 huge monoliths, forms a strange circle in an isolated clearing among Alentejan olive groves near Évora. It's one of Europe's most impressive prehistoric sites.

All over Portugal, but especially in the Alentejo, you can visit such ancient funerary and religious structures, built during the Neolithic and Mesolithic eras. Most impressive are the dolmens: rectangular, polygonal or round funerary chambers, reached by a corridor of stone slabs and covered with earth to create an artificial mound. King of these is Europe's largest dolmen, the Anta Grande do Zambujeiro, near Évora, with six 6m-high stones forming a huge chamber. Single monoliths, or menhirs, often carved with phallic or religious symbols, also dot the countryside like an army of stone sentinels. Their relationship to promoting fertility seems obvious.

With the arrival of the Celts (800–200 BC) came the first established hilltop settlements, called *castros*. The best-preserved example is the Citânia de Briteiros, in the Minho, where you can literally step into Portugal's past. Stone dwellings were built on a circular or elliptical plan, and the complex was surrounded by a drystone defensive wall. In the *citânias* (fortified villages) further south, dwellings tended to be rectangular.

Prehistoric Relics

Vila Nova de Foz Côa (Douro)

Citânia de Briteiros (Minho)

Cromeleque dos Almendres (Alentejo)

Romans

The Romans left Portugal their typical architectural and engineering feats – roads, bridges, towns complete with forums (marketplaces), villas, public baths and aqueducts. These have now largely disappeared from the surface, though the majority of Portugal's cities are built on Roman foundations. Today you can descend into dank subterranean areas under new buildings in Lisbon and Évora, and see Roman fragments around Braga. At Conímbriga, the country's largest Roman site, an entire town is under excavation. Revealed so far are city walls and some spectacular mosaics, along with structural or decorative columns, the original stone heating ducts for the thermal baths, the tunnels of the amphitheatre, carved entablatures and classical ornamentation, giving a sense of the Roman high life.

Portugal's most famous and complete Roman ruin is the Templo Romano, the so-called Temple of Diana in Évora, with its flouncy-topped

Roman Ruins

Conímbriga (Beiras)

Temple of Diana (Évora)

Teatro Romano (Lisbon)

Milreu (Algarve)

A SERENDIPITOUS DISCOVERY

In 1989 researchers were studying the rugged valley of the Rio Côa, 15km from the Spanish frontier, to understand the environmental impact of a planned hydroelectric dam that was to flood the valley. In the course of their work, they made an extraordinary discovery: a number of petroglyphs (rock engravings) dating back tens of thousands of years.

Yet it wasn't until 1992, after the dam's construction was under way, that the importance of the find began to be recognised. Archaeologists came across whole clusters of petroglyphs, mostly dating from the Upper Palaeolithic period (10,000 to 40,000 years ago). Local people joined the search and the inventory of engravings soon grew into the thousands. In 1998 the future of the collection was safeguarded when Unesco designated the valley a World Heritage Site.

Today Rio Côa (p409) holds one of the largest-known collections of open-air Palaeolithic art in the world. Archaeologists are still puzzling over the meaning of the engravings – and why this site was chosen. Most of the petroglyphs depict animals: stylised horses, aurochs (extinct ancestors of domesticated cattle) and long-horned ibex (extinct species of wild goat). Some animals are depicted with multiple heads – as if to indicate the animal in motion – while others are drawn so finely that they require artificial light to be seen. Later petroglyphs begin to depict human figures as well. The most intriguing engravings consist of overlapping layers, with successive artists adding their touches thousands of years after the first strokes were applied – a kind of Palaeolithic palimpsest in which generations of hunters worked and reworked the engravings of their forebears.

Corinthian columns nowadays echoed by the complementary towers of Évora's cathedral. This is the finest temple of its kind on the Iberian Peninsula, its preservation the result of having been walled up in the Middle Ages and later used as a slaughterhouse.

Architectural Movements

Great Gothic

Cistercians introduced the Gothic trend, which reached its pinnacle in Alcobaça, in one of Portugal's most ethereally beautiful buildings. The austere abbey church and cloister of the Mosteiro de Santa Maria de Alcobaça, begun in 1178, has a lightness and simplicity strongly influenced by Clairvaux Abbey in France. Its hauntingly simple Cloisters of Silence were a model for later cathedral cloisters at Coimbra, Lisbon, Évora and many other places. This was the birth of Portuguese Gothic, which flowered and transmuted over the coming years as the country gained more and more experience of the outside world after centuries of being culturally dominated and restricted by Spain and the Moors.

By the 14th century, when the Mosteiro de Santa Maria da Vitória (commonly known as Mosteiro da Batalha or Battle Abbey) was constructed, simplicity was a distant, vague memory. Portuguese, Irish and French architects worked on this breathtaking monument for more than two centuries. The combination of their skills and the changing architectural fashions of the times, from Flamboyant (late) Gothic to Renaissance and then Manueline, turned the abbey into a seething mass of carving, organic decorations, lofty spaces and slanting stained-glass light. A showcase of High Gothic art, it exults in the decorative (especially in its Gothic Royal Cloisters and Chapter House), and its flying buttresses tip their hat to English Perpendicular Gothic.

Secular architecture also enjoyed a Gothic boom, thanks to the need for fortifications against the Moors and to the castle-building fervour of 13th-century ruler Dom Dinis. Some of Portugal's most spectacular, huddled, thick-walled castles – for example, Estremoz, Óbidos and

Gothic Sites

Mosteiro de Santa Maria de Alcobaça (Estremadura)

Convento do Carmo (Lisbon)

Mosteiro de Santa Maria da Vitória (Estremadura)

Bragança – date from this time, many featuring massive double-perimeter walls and an inner square tower.

Manueline

Manueline is a uniquely Portuguese style: a specific, crazed flavour of late Gothic architecture. Ferociously decorative, it coincided roughly with the reign of Dom Manuel I (r 1495–1521) and is interesting not just because of its extraordinarily imaginative designs, burbling with life, but also because this dizzyingly creative architecture skipped hand in hand with the era's booming confidence.

During Dom Manuel's reign, Vasco da Gama and fellow explorers claimed new overseas lands and new wealth for Portugal. The Age of Discoveries was expressed in sculptural creations of eccentric inventiveness that drew heavily on nautical themes: twisted ropes, coral and anchors in stone, topped by the ubiquitous armillary sphere (a navigational device that became Dom Manuel's personal symbol) and the cross of the Order of Christ (symbol of the religious military order that largely financed and inspired Portugal's explorations).

Manueline first emerged in Setúbal's Igreja de Jesus, designed in the 1490s by French expatriate Diogo de Boitaca, who gave it columns like trees growing into the ceiling and ribbed vaulting like twisted ropes. The style quickly caught on, and soon decorative carving was creeping, twisting and crawling over everything (aptly described by 19th-century English novelist William Beckford as 'scollops and twistifications').

Outstanding Manueline masterpieces are Belém's Mosteiro dos Jerónimos, masterminded largely by De Boitaca and João de Castilho; and Batalha's Mosteiro de Santa Maria da Vitória's otherworldly Capelas Imperfeitas (Unfinished Chapels).

Other famous creations include Belém's Torre de Belém, a Manueline-Moorish cake crossed with a chess piece by Francisco de Arruda; his brother Diogo de Arruda's fantastical organic, seemingly

Manueline Sites

Mosteiro dos Jerónimos (Belém)

Torre de Belém (Belém)

Chapter House (Tomar)

Igreja de Jesus (Setúbal)

ART & ARCHITECTURE ARCHITECTURAL MOVEMENTS

TWO LEGENDARY ARCHITECTS

Porto is home to not one but two celebrated contemporary architects: Álvaro Siza Vieira (born 1933) and Eduardo Souto de Moura (born 1952). Both remain fairly unknown outside their home country, which is surprising given their loyal following among fellow architects and their long and distinguished careers. Both have earned the acclaimed Pritzker Prize, the Nobel of the architecture world (Siza Vieira in 1992, Souto de Moura in 2011). The two men are quite close, and they even have offices in the same building. They have collaborated on a handful of projects and, prior to going out on his own, Souto de Moura also worked for Siza Vieira.

On the surface, Siza Vieira's work may seem less than dazzling. Stucco, stone, tile and glass are his building materials of choice. Place means everything in Siza Vieira's work, with geography and climate carefully considered before any plans are laid, regardless of the size or scale of the project. Many of his works are outside the country, although the Serralves Museu de Arte Contemporânea in Porto and the cliffside Boa Nova Casa Chá near Matosinhos are two of his most famous works.

Like Siza Vieira, Souto de Moura spurns flashy designs. His works feature minimalist but artful structures that utilise local building materials. The Estádio Municipal de Braga, built for the 2004 European football championship, is set in a former granite quarry (granite from the site was used to make concrete for the stadium). The rock walls of the quarry lie behind one goal; the other side opens to views of the city. Better known is Souto de Moura's design for the Casa das Histórias Paula Rego in Cascais. The red-concrete museum is distinguished by its two pyramid-shaped towers, providing a modern reinterpretation of classic Portuguese shapes (which appear in chimneys, lighthouses, towers and old palaces such as the Palácio Nacional de Sintra).

barnacle-encrusted window in the Chapter House of Tomar's Convento de Cristo; and the convent's fanciful 16-sided Charola – the Templar church, resembling an eerie *Star Wars* set. Many other churches sport a Manueline flourish against a plain facade.

The style was enormously resonant in Portugal, and reappeared in the early 20th century in exercises in mystical romanticism, such as Sintra's Quinta da Regaleira and Palácio Nacional da Pena, and Luso's over-the-top and extraordinary neo-Manueline Palace Hotel do Buçaco.

Baroque

With independence from Spain re-established and the influence of the Inquisition on the wane, Portugal burst out in a fever of baroque – an architectural style that was exuberant and theatrical and fired straight at the senses. Nothing could rival the Manueline flourish, but the baroque style – named after the Portuguese word for a rough pearl, *barroco* – cornered the market in flamboyance. At its height during the 18th century (almost a century later than in Italy), it was characterised by curvaceous forms, huge monuments, spatially complex schemes and lots and lots and lots of gold.

Financed by the 17th-century gold and diamond discoveries in Brazil, and encouraged by the extravagant Dom João V, local and foreign (particularly Italian) artists created mind-bogglingly opulent masterpieces. Prodigious *talha dourada* (gilded woodwork) adorns church interiors all over the place, but it reached its extreme in Aveiro's Mosteiro de Jesus, Lisbon's Igreja de São Roque and Porto's Igreja de São Francisco.

The baroque of central and southern Portugal was more restrained. Examples include the chancel of Évora's cathedral and the massive Palácio Nacional de Mafra. Designed by the German architect João Frederico Ludovice to rival the palace-monastery of San Lorenzo de El Escorial (near Madrid), the Mafra version is relatively sober, apart from its size – which is such that at one point it had a workforce of 45,000, looked after by a police force of 7000.

Baroque Sites

....

Palácio Nacional de Mafra

....

Igreja de São Roque (Lisbon)

....

Igreja de São Francisco (Porto)

....

Casa de Mateus (Vila Real)

PESSOA'S MANY PERSONALITIES

'There's no such man known as Fernando Pessoa', swore Alberto Caeiro, who, truth be told, didn't really exist himself. He was one of more than a dozen heteronyms (identities) adopted by Fernando Pessoa (1888–1935), Portugal's greatest 20th-century poet.

Heralded by literary critics as one of the icons of modernism, Pessoa was also among the stranger characters to wander the streets of Lisbon. He worked as a translator by day (having learned English while living in South Africa as a young boy) and wrote poetry by night – but not just Pessoa's poetry. He took on numerous personas, writing in entirely different styles, representing different philosophies, backgrounds and levels of mastery. Of Pessoa's four primary heteronyms, Alberto Caeiro was regarded as the great master by other heteronyms Alvaro de Campos and Ricardo Reis. (Fernando Pessoa was the fourth heteronym, but his existence, as alluded to earlier, was denied by the other three.) Any one style would have earned Pessoa renown as a major poet of his time, but considered together, the variety places him among the greats of modern literature.

Pessoa for many is inextricably linked to Lisbon. He spent his nights in cafes, writing, drinking and talking until late into the evening, and many of his works are set in Lisbon's old neighbourhoods. Among Pessoa's phobias: lightning and having his photograph taken. You can see a few of the existing photos of him at the Café Martinho da Arcada, one of his regular haunts.

Despite his quirks and brilliance, Pessoa published very little in his lifetime, with his great work *Livro do Desassossego* (Book of Disquiet) only appearing in 1982, 50 years after it was written. In fact, the great bulk of Pessoa's writing was discovered after his death: thousands of manuscript pages lay hidden away inside a wooden trunk. Scholars are still poring over his elusive works.

Meanwhile, Tuscan painter and architect Nicolau Nasoni (who settled in Porto around 1725) introduced a more ornamental baroque style to the north. Nasoni is responsible for Porto's Torre dos Clérigos and Igreja da Misericórdia, and the whimsical Palácio de Mateus near Vila Real (internationally famous as the image on Mateus rosé wine bottles).

In the mid-18th century a school of architecture evolved in Braga. Local artists such as André Soares built churches and palaces in a very decorative style, heavily influenced by Augsburg engravings from southern Germany. Soares' Casa do Raio, in Braga, and much of the monumental staircase of the nearby Bom Jesus do Monte, are typical examples of this period's ornamentation.

Only when the gold ran out did the baroque fad fade. At the end of the 18th century, architects flirted briefly with rococo (best exemplified by Mateus Vicente's Palácio de Queluz, begun in 1747, or the palace at Estói) before embracing neoclassicism.

Modern Era

The Salazar years favoured decidedly severe, Soviet-style state commissions (eg Coimbra university's dull faculty buildings, which replaced elegant 18th-century neoclassical ones). Ugly buildings and apartment blocks rose on city outskirts. Notable exceptions dating from the 1960s are Lisbon's Palácio da Justiça in the Campolide district and the gloriously sleek Museu Calouste Gulbenkian. The beautiful wood-panelled Galeto cafe-restaurant is a time capsule from this era.

The tendency towards urban mediocrity continued after the 1974 revolution, although architects such as Fernando Távora and Eduardo Souto de Moura have produced impressive schemes. Lisbon's postmodern Amoreiras shopping complex, by Tomás Taveira, is another striking contribution.

Portugal's most prolific contemporary architect is Álvaro Siza Vieira. A believer in clarity and simplicity, he takes an expressionist approach that is reflected in projects such as the Pavilhão de Portugal for Expo '98, Porto's splendid Museu de Arte Contemporânea and the Igreja de Santa Maria at Marco de Canaveses, south of Amarante. He has also restored central Lisbon's historic Chiado shopping district with notable sensitivity, following a major fire in 1988.

Spanish architect Santiago Calatrava designed the lean, organic monster Gare do Oriente for Expo '98, architecture that is complemented by the work of many renowned contemporary artists. The interior is more state-of-the-art spaceship than station. In the same area lies Lisbon's architectural trailblazer the Parque das Nações, with a bevy of unique designs, including a riverfront park and Europe's largest aquarium. The longest bridge in Europe, the Ponte de Vasco da Gama, built in 1998, stalks out across the river from nearby.

Since the turn of the millennium, Portugal has seen a handful of architecturally ambitious projects come to fruition. One of the grander projects is Rem Koolhaas' Casa da Música in Porto (2005). From a distance, the extremely forward-looking design appears to be a solid white block of carefully cut crystal. Both geometric and defiantly asymmetrical, the building mixes elements of tradition – like *azulejos* hidden in one room – with high modernism, such as the enormous curtains of corrugated glass flanking the concert stage.

Literary Giants

In 2010 Portugal lost one of its greatest writers when José Saramago died at the age of 87. Known for his discursive, cynical and darkly humorous novels, Saramago gained worldwide attention after winning the Nobel Prize in 1998. His best works mine the depths of the human experience

ART & ARCHITECTURE LITERARY GIANTS

Portugal has few Renaissance buildings, but some examples of the style are the Great Cloisters in Tomar's Convento de Cristo, designed by Spanish Diogo de Torralva in the late 16th century; the nearby Igreja de Nossa Senhora da Conceição; and the Convento de Bom Jesus at Valverde, outside Évora.

Modern Sites

MAAT, Lisbon

Casa da Música (Porto)

Casa das Histórias Paula Rego (Cascais)

Gare do Oriente (Lisbon)

Torre Vasco da Gama (Lisbon)

and are often set in a uniquely Portuguese landscape. Sometimes his quasi-magical tales revolve around historic events – like the Christian Siege of Lisbon or the building of the Palácio Nacional de Mafra – while at other times he takes on grander topics (writing, for instance, of Jesus' life as a fallible human being) or even creates modern-day fables (in *Blindness*, everyone on earth suddenly goes blind). As a self-described libertarian communist, Saramago had political views that sometimes landed him in trouble. After his name was removed from a list of nominees for a European literary prize, he went into self-imposed exile, spending the last years of his life in the Canary Islands.

Memorial do Convento (Baltasar and Blimunda; 1982) is José Saramago's Nobel Prize–winning novel about the Mafra, a convent-palace dreamed up by size junkies and compulsive builders.

In the shadow of Saramago, António Lobo Antunes is Portugal's other literary great – and many of his admirers say the Nobel committee gave the prize to the wrong Portuguese writer. Antunes produces magical, fast-paced prose, often with dark undertones and vast historical sweeps; some critics compare his work to that of William Faulkner. Antunes' writing reflects his harrowing experience as a field doctor in Angola during Portugal's bloody colonial wars, and he often turns a critical gaze on Portuguese history – setting his novels around colonial wars, the dark days of the Salazar dictatorship and the 1974 revolution. Antunes is slowly gaining an international following, and many of his earlier novels have finally been translated into English.

Azulejos: Art of the Tile

Portugal's favourite decorative art is easy to spot. Polished painted tiles called *azulejos* (after the Arabic *al zulaycha*, meaning polished stone) cover everything from churches to train stations. The Moors introduced the art, having picked it up from the Persians, but the Portuguese wholeheartedly adopted it.

Portugal's earliest tiles are Moorish, from Seville. These were decorated with interlocking geometric or floral patterns (figurative representations aren't an option for Muslim artists for religious reasons). After the Portuguese captured Ceuta in Morocco in 1415, they began exploring the art themselves. The 16th-century Italian invention of majolica, in which colours are painted directly onto wet clay over a layer of white enamel, gave works a fresco-like brightness and kicked off the Portuguese *azulejo* love affair.

The earliest homegrown examples, polychrome and geometric, date from the 1580s and may be seen in churches such as Lisbon's Igreja de São Roque, providing an ideal counterbalance to fussy, gold-heavy baroque.

The late 17th century saw a fashion for huge panels depicting everything from saints to seascapes. As demand grew, mass production became necessary and the Netherlands' blue-and-white Delft tiles started appearing.

Portuguese tile makers rose to the challenge of this influx, and the splendid work of virtuosos António de Oliveira Bernardes and his son Policarpo in the 18th century springs from this competitive creativity. You can see their work in Évora, in the impressive Igreja de São João.

By the end of the 18th century, industrial-scale manufacture began to affect quality. There was also massive demand for tiles after the 1755 Lisbon earthquake. (Tiling answered the need for decoration and was cheap and practical.)

From the late 19th century, the art-nouveau and art-deco movements took *azulejos* by storm, providing fantastic facades and interiors for shops, restaurants and residential buildings. Today, *azulejos* still coat contemporary life, and you can explore the latest in *azulejos* in the Lisbon metro. Maria Keil (1914–2012) designed 19 of the stations, from the 1950s onwards – look out for her wild modernist designs at the stations

Gare do Oriente (p499), designed by Santiago Calatrava

of Rossio, Restauradores, Intendente, Marquês de Pombal, Anjos and Martim Moniz. Oriente also showcases extraordinary contemporary work by artists from five continents.

Fine Arts

Early Masters

As Gothic art gave way to more humanistic Renaissance works, Portugal's 15th-century painters developed their own style. Led by the master Nuno Gonçalves, the *escola nacional* (national school) took religious subjects and grounded them against contemporary backgrounds. In Gonçalves' most famous painting, the panels of Santo Antonio (in Lisbon's Museu Nacional de Arte Antiga), he includes a full milieu of Portuguese society – nobles, Jews, fisherfolk, sailors, knights, priests, monks and beggars.

Some of Portugal's finest early paintings emerged from the 16th-century Manueline school. These artists, influenced by Flemish painters, developed a style known for its incredible delicacy, realism and luminous colours. The most celebrated painter of his time was Vasco Fernandes, known as Grão Vasco (1480–1543). His richly hued paintings (still striking five centuries later) hang in a museum in Viseu dedicated to his work – as well as that of his Manueline school colleague Gaspar Vaz. Meanwhile, sculptors including Diogo de Boitaca went wild with Portuguese seafaring fantasies and exuberant decoration on some of Portugal's icons.

Star of Óbidos

The 17th century saw a number of talented Portuguese artists emerge. One of the best was Josefa de Óbidos, who enjoyed success as a female artist – an extreme rarity in those days. Josefa's paintings were unique in their personal, sympathetic interpretations of religious subjects and

THE EVOCATIVE WORLD OF PAULA REGO

The conservative Salazar years of the mid-20th century didn't create the ideal environment to nurture contemporary creativity, and many artists left the country. These include Portugal's best-known 20th-century artist, Paula Rego, who was born in Lisbon in 1935 but moved to the UK in 1951. Rego's signature style developed around fairy-tale paintings with a nightmarish twist. Her works deal in ambiguity and psychological and sexual tension, such as *The Family* (1988), where a seated businessman is either being tortured or smothered with affection by his wife and daughter. Domination, fear, sexuality and grief are all recurring themes in Rego's paintings, and the mysterious and sinister atmosphere, heavy use of chiaroscuro (stark contrasting of light and shade) and strange distortion of scale are reminiscent of the work of surrealists Max Ernst and Giorgio de Chirico.

Rego is considered one of the great early champions of painting from a female perspective and she has produced a substantial volume of work. Her acclaim is growing, particularly with the opening of the Casa das Histórias Paula Rego, in Cascais, which showcases her work.

for their sense of innocence. Although she studied at an Augustine convent as a young girl, she left without taking the vows and settled in Óbidos (where she got her nickname). Still she maintained close ties to the church, which provided many of her commissions, and remained famously chaste until her death in 1684. Josefa left one of the finest legacies of work of any Portuguese painter. She excelled in richly coloured still lifes and detailed religious works, ignoring established iconography.

Naturalism

In the 19th century naturalism was the dominant trend, with a handful of innovators pushing Portuguese art in new directions. Columbano Bordalo Pinheiro, who hailed from a family of artists, was a seminal figure among the Portuguese artists of his time. He played a prominent role in the Leã d'Ouro, a group of distinguished artists, writers and intellectuals who gathered in the capital and were deeply involved in the aesthetic trends of the day. A prolific artist, Pinheiro painted some of the luminaries of his time, including the novelist Eça de Queirós and Teófilo Braga (a celebrated writer who later became president of the early republic). One of his best-known works is a haunting portrait of the poet Antero de Quental, who later died by suicide.

20th Century

Building on the works of the naturalists, Amadeo de Souza-Cardoso lived a short but productive life, experimenting with new techniques emerging in Europe. Raised in a sleepy village outside Amarante, he studied architecture at the Academia de Belas Artes in Lisbon but soon dropped out and moved to Paris. There he found his calling as a painter and mingled with the leading artists and writers of the time, including Amedeo Modigliani, Gertrude Stein and Max Jacob. He experimented with impressionism, and later cubism and futurism, and created a captivating body of work, though he is little known outside Portugal.

José Sobral de Almada Negreiros delved even deeper into futurism, inspired by the Italian futurist Filippo Tommaso Marinetti. His work encompassed richly hued portraits with abstract geometrical details – an example is his famous 1954 portrait of Fernando Pessoa – and he was also a sculptor, writer and critic. He managed to walk a fine line during the Salazar regime, creating large-scale murals by public commission as well as socially engaged works critical of Portuguese society.

The Lisbon metro is not just about transport – it's an art gallery, showcasing the best of Portuguese contemporary art and architecture, with especially wonderful *azulejos*. Check out Metro Lisboa's website, www.metrolisboa.pt.

Saudade: the Portuguese Blues

The Portuguese psyche is complicated, particularly when it comes to elusive concepts like *saudade*. In its purest form, *saudade* is the nostalgic, often deeply melancholic longing for something: a person, a place or just about anything that's no longer obtainable. *Saudade* is profoundly connected to the seafaring nation's history and remains deeply intertwined with Portuguese identity. The emotion has played a starring role in some of Portugal's great works of art – in film, in literature and, most importantly, in music.

Roots of Saudade

Scholars are unable to pinpoint exactly when the term *saudade* first arose. Some trace it back to the grand voyages during the Age of Discoveries, when sailors, captains and explorers spent many months at sea, and the term gave voice to the longing for the lives they left behind. Yet even before the epic voyages across the ocean, Portugal was a nation of seafarers, and *saudade* probably arose from those on terra firma – the women who longed for the men who spent endless days out at sea, some of whom never returned.

Naturally, emigration is also deeply linked to *saudade*. Long one of Europe's poorest peoples, the Portuguese were often driven by hardship to seek better lives abroad. Until recently, this usually meant the men leaving behind their families to travel to northern Europe or America to find work. Families sometimes waited years before being reunited, with emigrants experiencing years of painful longing for their homeland – for the familiar faces and foods, and village life. Many did eventually return, but of course things had changed and so *saudade* reappeared, this time in the form of longing for the way things were in the past.

In Brazil, 30 January is set aside as the Dia de Saudade (Saudade Day). It's a fine day to engage in a bit of nostalgic longing for past lovers, distant home-lands and better days.

Nation of Emigrants

The great discoveries of Portuguese seafarers had profound effects on the country's demographics. With the birth and expansion of an empire, Portuguese settled in trading posts in Africa and Asia, but the colony of Brazil drew the biggest numbers of early Portuguese emigrants. They cleared the land (harvesting the Brazil wood that gave the colony its name), set up farms and went about the slow, steady task of nation building – with help, of course, from the millions of slaves brought forcibly from Africa. Numbers vary widely, but an estimated half-a-million Portuguese settled in Brazil during the colonial period, prior to independence in 1822, and over 400,000 flooded in during the second half of the 19th century.

By the 1900s, Portuguese had begun emigrating in large numbers to other parts of the world. The US and Canada received over half-a-million immigrants, with huge numbers heading to France, Germany, Venezuela and Argentina. The 1960s saw another surge of emigrants, as young men fled the country in order to avoid the draft that would send them to fight bloody colonial wars in Africa. The 1974 revolution also preceded a big

Goa, India, still has vestiges of its Portuguese colonial past. In Margão, on the street named Rua das Saudades, there are Christian and Muslim cemeteries and a Hindu cremation ground.

exodus, as those associated with the Salazar regime went abroad rather than face reprisals.

What all these emigrants had in common was the deep sadness of leaving their homeland to struggle in foreign lands. Those left behind were also in a world of heartache – wives left to raise children alone, villages deserted of young men, families torn apart. The numbers are staggering: over three million emigrants between 1890 and 1990; no other European country apart from Ireland lost as many people to emigration.

The most famous Portuguese emigrant to Brazil was the future king himself. When Napoleon invaded Portugal in 1807, the royal family and their extensive retinue fled to Brazil, where they installed themselves in Rio de Janeiro. Many royal retainers never returned home; Dom João VI returned only in 1822.

Saudade in Literature

One of the first great Portuguese works of literature that explores the theme of *saudade* is *Os Lusíadas* (The Lusiads; The Portuguese). Luís Vaz de Camões mixes mythology with historical events in his verse epic about the Age of Discoveries of the 15th and 16th centuries. The heroic adventurer Vasco da Gama and other explorers strive for glory, but many never return, facing hardships such as sea monsters and treacherous kings along the way. First-hand experience informed Camões' work: he served in the overseas militia, lost an eye in Ceuta in a battle with the Moors, served prison time in Portugal and survived a shipwreck in the Mekong (swimming ashore with his unfinished manuscript held aloft, according to legend).

The great 19th-century Portuguese writer Almeida Garrett wrote an even more compelling take on the Age of Discoveries. In his book *Camões*, a biography of the poet, he describes the longing Camões felt for Portugal while in exile. He also captured the greater sense of *saudade* that so many experienced as Portugal's empire crumbled in the century following the great explorations.

More recent writers also explore the notion of *saudade*, though they take radically different approaches from their predecessors. Contemporary writer António Lobo Antunes deconstructs *saudade* in cynical tales that expose the nostalgic longing for something as a form of neurotic self-delusion. In *As Naus* (The Return of the Caravels; 1988) he turns the discovery myth on its head when, four centuries after Da Gama's voyage, the great explorers, through some strange time warp, become entangled with the *retornados* (who returned to Portugal in the 1970s after the loss of the country's African empire) as Renaissance-era achievements collapse in the poor, grubby, lower-class neighbourhoods of Lisbon.

Saudade in Film

Portugal's most prolific film-maker, Manoel de Oliveira (1908–2015), was making films well past his 100th birthday. In a career that spanned 75

BRAZILIAN SAUDADE & BOSSA NOVA

Brazilian identity is also deeply connected to *saudade*, which isn't surprising given the influence Portugal has had on the country – nearly every inhabitant in Brazil can trace Portuguese roots somewhere in the family tree. In Brazil, *saudade* means much the same thing, and it has played a role in shaping the country's music – in particular, bossa nova. The 1958 hit 'Chega de Saudade' (often poorly translated as 'No More Blues'), by legendary songwriting team Tom Jobim and Vinícius de Moraes, is considered one of the first bossa nova songs ever recorded. In it, the singer pines for his lover, who has left him, and commands his sadness to go out and bring her back. Melancholic chords and a slow, wistful singing style are hallmarks here, as they are of nearly all bossa nova tunes. And even if you can't understand Portuguese, you'll still feel the sadness and deep sense of loss.

years, he became known for carefully crafted, if slow-moving, films that delve deep into the world of *saudade* – of growing old, unrequited loves and longing for things that no longer exist. In *Viagem ao Princípio do Mundo* (Voyage to the Beginning of the World; 1997), several companions make a nostalgic tour of the rugged landscapes and traditional villages of the north – one in search of a past that he knows only in his dreams (having heard of his ancestral land from his Portuguese-born father), another haunted by a world that no longer exists (the places of his childhood having been uprooted). Past and present, nostalgia and reality collide in this quiet, meditative film. It stars a frail, 72-year-old Marcello Mastroianni as Oliveira's alter ego; this was the actor's final film before he died.

One of the finest love letters to the capital is the sweet, meandering *Lisbon Story* (1994), directed by German film-maker Wim Wenders. The story follows a sound engineer who goes in search of a missing director, discovering the city through the footage his friend left behind. Carefully crafted scenes conjure up the mystery and forlorn beauty of Lisbon (and other parts of Portugal, including a wistful sequence on the dramatic cliffs of Cabo Espichel). *Saudade* here explores many different realms, inspired in large part by the ethereal soundtrack by Madredeus – band members also play supporting roles in the film.

Fado

'I don't sing fado. It sings me.' – Amália Rodrigues

Portugal's most famous style of music, fado (Portuguese for 'fate'), couldn't really exist without *saudade*. These melancholic songs are dripping with emotion – and they revel in stories of the painful twists and turns of fate, of unreachable distant lovers, fathomless yearning for one's homeland and wondrous days that have come and gone. The emotional quality of the singing plays just as important a role as technical skill, helping fado to reach across linguistic boundaries. Listening to fado is perhaps the easiest way of understanding *saudade*, in all its evocative variety.

Although fado is something of a national treasure – in 2011 it was added to Unesco's list of the World's Intangible Cultural Heritage – it's really the music of Lisbon. (In the university town of Coimbra, fado exists in a different, slightly more cerebral form: it's exclusively men, often students or alumni, who sing of love, bohemian life and the city itself.) No one quite knows fado's origins, though African and Brazilian rhythms, Moorish chants and the songs of Provençal troubadors may have influenced the sound. What is clear is that, by the 19th century, fado could be heard all over the traditional working-class neighbourhoods of Mouraria and Alfama, particularly in brothels and seedy taverns. It was the anthem of the poor, and it maintained an unsavoury reputation until the late 19th century, when the upper classes took an interest in the music and brought it into the mainstream.

Fado remained an obscure, mostly local experience until the 20th century, when it received national and later international attention. One singer who played a major role in its popularisation was Amália Rodrigues, the 'queen of fado', who became a household name in the 1940s. Born to a poor family in 1920, Amália took the music from the tavern to the concert hall, and then into households via radio and onto film screens, starring in the 1947 film *Capas Negras* (Black Capes). She had some of Portugal's best poets and writers of the day writing songs for her. Yet, along the way, she had her share of ups and downs – depression, illness, failed love affairs – and her heart-rending fado was more than an abstraction.

The national music of Cape Verde, a former Portuguese colony, is *morna*, a distant cousin of fado, with plaintive songs revolving around lost loves and homesickness. Renowned 'barefoot diva' Cesária Évora (1941–2011) produced many hits, including 'Sodade' (Creole for '*saudade*').

For more on Amália Rodrigues, check out the fine documentary *The Art of Amália* (2000), directed by Bruno de Almeida. The biopic *Amália* (2008), by Carlos Coelho da Silva, provides an in-depth portrait of a Rodrigues that few ever saw.

SAUDADE: THE PORTUGUESE BLUES FADO

SAUDADE OF THE JEWS

Until the end of the 15th century, Jews enjoyed a prominent place in Portuguese society. The treasurer of Dom Afonso V (1432–81) was Jewish, as were others who occupied diplomatic posts and worked as trade merchants, physicians and cartographers. Jews from other countries were welcomed in Portugal, including those expelled from Spain in 1492. Eventually, pressure from the church and from Spain forced the king's hand, and in 1497 Manuel I decreed that all Jews convert to Christianity or leave the country. A catalogue of horrors followed, including the massacre of thousands of Jews in 1506 by mobs running riot, and two centuries of the bloody Inquisition that kicked off in 1536.

Aside from a secretive Crypto-Jewish group in Belmonte that managed to preserve their faith, the Judaic community slowly withered and perished. Those who converted felt the heart-rending *saudade* of deep loss – essentially the loss of their identity. Once thriving Jewish neighbourhoods died as residents went into exile or perhaps suffered arrest, torture and even execution. The personal losses paralleled the end of a flourishing and tolerant period in Portugal's history and effectively ended the Jewish presence in Portugal.

Amália enjoyed wide acclaim, although her reputation was sullied following the 1974 revolution when she was criticised for tacitly supporting the Salazar regime (although there is little evidence of that). Fado's popularity slipped in the postrevolution days, when the Portuguese were eager to make a clean break with the past. (Salazar spoke of throwing the masses the three Fs – fado, football and Fátima – to keep them happily occupied.) The 1990s, however, saw a resurgence of fado's popularity, with the opening of new fado houses and the emergence of new fado voices. Amália's reputation was also rehabilitated. Upon her death at age 79 in 1999, Portugal declared three days of national mourning and suspended the general-election campaign in her honour. She is buried in the Panteão Nacional (National Pantheon).

While fado may bring to mind dark bars of the Salazar years, this is not a musical form stuck in time. Contemporary performers and exponents of a new fado style include the dynamic *fadista* Mísia, who experimented with full band instrumentation. The Mozambique-born singer Mariza has earned accolades for her extraordinary voice and fresh, eclectic approach. She continues to break new ground in albums like *Terra* (2008), *Mundo* (2015) and *Mariza* (2018) that bring in world music – African rhythms, flamenco, Latin sounds and jazz. Fado also runs deep in the veins of Carminho, a young singer with a powerful and mournful voice. Her mother was the owner of one of Lisbon's most traditional fado houses (now closed), where as a young girl she heard the best *fadistas* of the time. Another one to watch is Ana Moura, the youngest *fadista* to be nominated for a Dutch Edison Award. The men aren't outdone; one of the great male voices in traditional fado these days is Camané.

Fados are traditionally sung by one performer accompanied by a 12-string Portuguese *guitarra* (pear-shaped guitar). When two *fadistas* perform, they sometimes engage in *desgarrada,* a bit of improvisational one-upmanship where the singers challenge and play off one another. At fado houses there are usually a number of singers, each one traditionally singing three songs. Listening to *fado* today is a fast track to the Portuguese soul, allowing you to get a tangible sense of the nostalgic longing, or *saudade*, that so defines the character of the nation and its musical heritage.

The film *Fados* (2007) is Spanish director Carlos Saura's love letter to the great Portuguese music. The film features the singing of fado legends like Camané and Mariza as well as genre-defying singers not often associated with the art – Brazilian singers Caetano Veloso and Chico Buarque, among others.

Survival Guide

Directory A-Z

Accessible Travel

➡ The term *deficientes* (Portuguese for 'disabled') gives some indication of the limited awareness of disabled needs. Although public offices and agencies are required to provide access and facilities for people with disabilities, private businesses are not.

➡ Lisbon airport is wheelchair accessible, while Porto and Faro airports have accessible toilets.

➡ Parking spaces are allotted in many places, but are frequently occupied. The EU parking card entitles visitors to the same street-parking concessions given to disabled residents.

➡ Newer and larger hotels tend to have some adapted rooms, though the facilities may not be up to scratch; ask at the local turismo. Most campgrounds have accessible toilets, and some hostels have facilities for people with disabilities.

➡ Lisbon, with its cobbled streets and hills, may be difficult for some travellers with disabilities, but not impossible. The Baixa's flat grid and Belém are fine, and all the sights at Parque das Nações are accessible. Download Lonely Planet's free Accessible Travel guide from http://lptravel.to/AccessibleTravel, or for more information, contact one of the following organisations:

Accessible Portugal (☑211 338 693; www.accessibleportugal.com; Rua António Champalimaud, Lote 1) This Lisbon-based association promotes accessible tourism and is the brains behind the excellent TUR4all Portugal app (Android and iOS), which works like a database of accessible tourist resources and services throughout Portugal and Spain.

Secretaria do Nacional de Reabilitação (☑217 929 500; www.inr.pt; Av Conde de Valbom 63) The national governmental organisation representing people with disabilities supplies information, provides links to useful operations and publishes guides

(in Portuguese) that advise on barrier-free accommodation, transport, shops, restaurants and sights.

Accommodation

Seasons

In popular tourist destinations prices rise and fall with the seasons. Mid-June to mid-September are firmly high season (book well ahead); May to mid-June and mid-September to October are midseason; and other times are low season, when you can get some really good deals. Outside the resorts, prices don't vary much between seasons.

In the Algarve, you'll pay the highest premium for rooms from mid-July to the end of August, with slightly lower prices from June to mid-July and in September, and substantially less (as much as 50%) if you travel between November and April. Note that a handful of places in the Algarve close in winter.

We list July (high-season) prices in reviews.

Guesthouses

Guesthouses are small-scale budget or midrange accommodation, with a personal feel that can be lacking in larger hotels. Most are family-run places.

There are various types of guesthouses; prices typically range from €50 to €90 for

---

SLEEPING PRICE RANGES

The following price ranges refer to a double room with bathroom in high season. Unless otherwise stated breakfast is included in the price.

€ less than €60

€€ €60–120

€€€ more than €120

a double room with private bathroom (and as little as €35 for the simplest lodgings with shared bathroom).

Hostels

Portugal has scores of hostels, particularly in Lisbon and Porto. If you're thinking bare-bones, smelly backpacker lodging, think again: Lisbon's hostels are among the best in Europe, with stylish design, often in heritage buildings, and excellent amenities.

➡ High-season dorm beds typically cost around €20. Many hostels also offer simple doubles with shared bathroom, and some have small apartments.

➡ Bed linen and breakfast are usually included in the price. Standard features include kitchen, lounge with wi-fi access and computers for guest use.

➡ In summer reserve ahead, especially for doubles.

➡ Many of the hostels outside Lisbon are part of the Pousadas da Juventude network (www.pousadasjuventude.pt) affiliated with Hostelling International (HI).

➡ If you don't have an HI card, you can get a guest card, which requires six stamps (€2 per time) – one from each hostel you stay at – after which you have paid for your membership.

Pousadas

In 1942 the government started Pousadas de Portugal (www.pousadas.pt), turning castles, monasteries and palaces into luxurious hotels, roughly divided into rural and historic options. Today the *pousadas* are run by Pestana, a Portuguese company and member of Historic Hotels of Europe. July prices range from €120 to €250; prices in August are €10 to €20 more. Off-season, you can sometimes score deals as low as €75 a night. Most *pousadas* are cheaper during

BOOK YOUR STAY ONLINE

For more accommodation reviews by Lonely Planet authors, check out http://lonelyplanet.com/hotels/. You'll find independent reviews, as well as recommendations on the best places to stay. Best of all, you can book online.

the week; they have lots of discounts and deals, plus reduced prices for those aged over 55.

Turihab Properties

These charming properties are part of a government scheme, through which you can stay in a farmhouse, manor house, country estate or rustic cottage as the owner's guest.

High-season rates for two people, either in a double room or a cottage, range from €70 to €150. Some properties have swimming pools, and most include breakfast (often with fresh local produce).

There are three types of Turihab lodgings:

Aldeias de Portugal (www.aldeiasdeportugal.pt) Lodging in rural villages in the north, often in beautifully converted stone cottages.

Casas no Campo (www.casasnocampo.net) Country houses, cottages and luxury villas.

Solares de Portugal (www.solaresdeportugal.pt) Grand manor houses, some of which date from the 17th or 18th century.

Camping & Caravan Parks

Camping is popular in Portugal: there are many campgrounds, often in good locations and near beaches. Prices for sites are typically calculated per person, per tent and per vehicle – usually €5 to €6.50 for each. Keep in mind that many sites get crowded and noisy at busy times (especially July and August).

➡ Nearly all campgrounds have hot showers, electrical hookups and a cafe. The

best campgrounds also have a pool, restaurant, laundry service, children's playgrounds and perhaps a tennis court.

➡ Generally, campgrounds run by **Orbitur** (☑226 061 360; www.orbitur.pt) offer the best services. Some towns have municipal campsites, which vary in quality.

➡ For detailed listings of some 228 campsites nationwide, pick up the *Roteiro Campista* (€8.50; www.roteiro-campista.pt), updated annually and sold at turismos and bookshops. It contains details of most Portuguese campgrounds, with maps and directions.

Private Rooms

In coastal resorts, mostly in summer, you can often rent a *quarto* (private room) in a private house. These usually have a shared bathroom, are cheap and clean, and might remind you of a stay with an elderly aunt. Prices generally run from €35 to €45 per double.

Rental Accommodation

Plenty of villas and cottages are available for rent. Major sites like Airbnb list hundreds of private houses and apartments for rent.

Children

The great thing about Portugal for children is its manageable size and the range of sights and activities on offer. There's so much to explore and to catch the imagination, even for those with very short attention spans.

PRACTICALITIES

Weights & measures Portugal uses the metric system. Decimals are indicated by commas, thousands by points.

Newspapers Main newspapers include *Diário de Noticias*, *Público*, *Jornal de Noticias* and the tabloid bestseller *Correio da Manhã*. English-language newspapers include the long-running daily, the *Portugal News* (www.theportugalnews.com).

Radio National radio stations include state-owned Rádiodifusão Portuguesa (RDP), which runs the stations Antena 1, 2 and 3 and plays Portuguese broadcasts and evening music (Lisbon frequencies are 95.7, 94.4 and 100.3). For English-language radio there is the BBC World Service (Lisbon 90.2) and Voice of America (VOA), or a few Algarve-based stations, such as Kiss (95.8 and 101.2).

Television TV channels include Rádio Televisão Portuguesa (RTP-1 and RTP-2), Sociedade Independente (SIC) and TV Independente (TV1), with RTP-2 providing the best selection of foreign films and world-news coverage. Other stations fill the airwaves with a mix of Portuguese and Brazilian soaps, game shows and dubbed or subtitled foreign films.

DVDs Portugal uses the PAL system, incompatible with both the French SECAM system and the North American NTSC system.

Smoking Allowed in some restaurants and most bars. Restaurants that allow smoking are supposed to have separate smoking sections, but inadequate ventilation means nonsmokers will be breathing in the fumes. Many hotels still offer smoking rooms.

The Algarve has to be the best kid-pleasing destination in Portugal, with endless beaches, zoos, water parks, horse-riding outfits and boat trips.

Kids will also be happy in Lisbon and its outlying provinces. Attractions include: trams, puppet shows, a huge aquarium, a toy museum, horse-drawn carriages, castles, parks and playgrounds.

As for fairy-tale places, Portugal has these in spades. Some children enjoy visiting churches if they can light a candle, and they'll enjoy the make-believe of the castles and palaces sprinkled about the country.

In towns, hop-on, hop-off tours can be good for saving small legs, and miniature resort trains often cause more excitement than you would have thought possible.

Kids are welcome just about everywhere. They can even get literary: the late Nobel Prize–winning author José Saramago wrote a charming children's fable, *The Tale of the Unknown Island*, available in English.

For an entertaining guide packed with information and tips, turn to Lonely Planet's *Travel with Children*.

Practicalities

➡ The Portuguese are generally quite laid-back about breastfeeding in public as long as some attempt at discretion is made.

➡ Formula (including organic brands) and disposable nappies (diapers) are widely available at most pharmacies and grocery stores.

➡ Turismos, as well as most hotels and guesthouses, can recommend babysitters.

Discount Cards

➡ Portugal's network of *pousadas da juventude* (youth hostels) is part of the HI network. An HI card from your hostelling association at home entitles you to the standard cheap rates.

➡ A student card will get you reduced admission to almost all sights. Likewise, those aged over 65 with proof of age will save cash.

➡ If you plan to do a lot of sightseeing in the main cities, the Lisboa Card and Porto Card are for you. Sold at tourist offices, these offer discounts or free admission to many attractions and free travel on public transport.

Electricity

Type C
230V/50Hz

Type F
230V/50Hz

Embassies & Consulates

There's no New Zealand consulate in Portugal. The nearest New Zealand embassy is in **Madrid** (☑91 523 02 26; www.mfat.govt.nz; 3rd fl, Calle de Pinar 7, Madrid; Ⓜ Gregorio Marañon). The following embassies are in Lisbon; the Spanish consulate is in Porto and the UK Consulate is in Portimão.

Australian Embassy (☑213 101 500; www.portugal.embassy. gov.au; Av da Liberdade 200, 2nd fl)

Canadian Embassy (☑213 164 600; www.canadainternational. gc.ca; Av da Liberdade 198-200, Edifício Victoria)

French Embassy (☑213 939 294; www.ambafrance-pt.org; Rua Santos-o-Velho 5)

German Embassy (☑218 810 210; www.lissabon.diplo.de; Campo dos Mártires da Pátria 38)

Irish Embassy (☑213 308 200; www.embassyofireland.pt; Av da Liberdade 200, 4th fl)

Netherlands Embassy (☑213 914 900; http://portugal. nlembaixada.org; Av Infante Santo 43)

Spanish Embassy (☑213 472 381; www.exteriores.gob.es/ embajadas/lisboa/es/Paginas/ inicio.aspx; Rua do Salitre 1)

Spanish Consulate (☑225 363 915; Rua de Dom João IV 341, Porto; ⊙9am-2pm Mon-Fri)

UK Embassy (☑213 924 000; www.gov.uk/world/organisations/british-embassy-lisbon; Rua de Saõ Bernardo 33)

UK Consulate (☑213 924 000; www.gov.uk/world/organisations/british-vice-consulate-portimao; Avenida Guanaré, Portimão; ⊙9.30am-2pm Mon, Wed & Fri)

US Embassy (☑217 273 300; https://pt.usembassy.gov; Av das Forças Armadas)

Food

For detailed information about eating in Portugal, see the Eat & Drink Like a Local chapter.

Health

Portugal has a high-quality healthcare system, with pharmacies and doctors readily available countrywide.

Before You Go
RECOMMENDED VACCINATIONS

WHO recommends that all travellers should be covered for diphtheria, tetanus, measles, mumps, rubella and polio, regardless of their destination.

Since most vaccines don't produce immunity until at least two weeks after they're given, visit a doctor at least six weeks before departure.

HEALTH INSURANCE

Citizens of the EU are eligible for free emergency medical treatment if they have a European Health Insurance Card (EHIC), which replaces the no-longer-valid E111 certificate. It will not cover you for nonemergencies or emergency repatriation.

Citizens from other countries should find out if there is a reciprocal arrangement for free medical care between their country and Portugal. If you do need health insurance, consider a policy that covers you for the worst possible scenario, such as an accident requiring an emergency flight home. Find out in advance if your insurance plan will make payments directly to providers or reimburse you later for overseas health expenditures.

In Portugal
AVAILABILITY OF HEALTHCARE

Good healthcare is readily available, and for minor illnesses pharmacists can give valuable advice and sell over-the-counter medication. Most pharmacists speak some English. They can also advise when more specialised help is required and point you in the right direction.

HEAT EXHAUSTION & HEATSTROKE

Be mindful of heat exhaustion, particularly on hot summer days in the Algarve, and when engaging in vigorous outdoor activities anywhere in the country during the hottest months. Heat exhaustion occurs following excessive fluid loss with inadequate replacement of fluids

---

EATING PRICE RANGES

The following price ranges refer to a main course.

€ less than €10

€€ €10–20

€€€ more than €20

and salt. Symptoms include headache, dizziness and tiredness. To treat heat exhaustion, replace lost fluids by drinking water and/or fruit juice or an oral rehydration solution, such as Dioralyte, and cool the body with cold water and fans.

Heatstroke is much more serious, resulting in irrational and hyperactive behaviour and eventually loss of consciousness and death. Medical treatment should be sought. Rapid cooling by spraying the body with water and fanning is ideal. Emergency fluid and electrolyte replacement by intravenous drip is recommended.

JELLYFISH & SEA URCHINS

In general, jellyfish aren't a major problem in Portuguese waters, though there are rare sightings along the southern beaches. Stings from jellyfish are painful but not dangerous. Douse the wound in vinegar to deactivate any stingers that haven't 'fired'. Applying calamine lotion, antihistamines or analgesics may reduce the reaction and relieve the pain.

Watch for sea urchins around rocky beaches. If needles become embedded in skin, immerse the limb in hot water to relieve the pain. To avoid infection visit a doctor and have the needles removed.

RABIES

Rabies, though rare in Portugal, is a risk. It is transmitted via the bite of an infected animal. It can also be transmitted if the animal's saliva comes in contact with an open wound. If you've been bitten by a wild animal, begin a treatment of shots at once.

TAP WATER

Tap water is safe to drink in Portugal.

Insurance

Don't leave home without a travel-insurance policy to cover theft, loss and medical problems. You should get insurance for the worst-case scenario; for example, an accident or illness requiring hospitalisation and a flight home.

Check the small print as some policies specifically exclude 'dangerous activities' such as scuba diving, motorcycling or even trekking. If these activities are in your sights, either find another policy or ask about an amendment (usually available for an extra premium) that includes them.

Make sure you keep all documentation for any claims later on. Some policies ask you to call back (reverse charges) to a centre in your home country, where an immediate assessment of your problem is made.

Worldwide travel insurance is available at www.lonelyplanet.com/travel-insurance. You can buy, extend and claim online any time – even if you're already on the road.

Internet Access

Wi-fi access is widespread in Portugal. If you have your own laptop, most hotels, hostels and midrange guesthouses offer free wireless access. Many cafes and some restaurants also offer free wi-fi. Cybercafes are now rare.

We use the icon @ to indicate places that have a physical computer where guests can access the internet; the wi-fi icon indicates where wireless access is available.

Another option is using a biblioteca municipal (municipal library).

Legal Matters

➥ Fines for illegal parking are common. If you're parked illegally you'll be towed and will have to pay around €100 to get your car back. Be aware of local road rules, as fines for other transgressions will also be enforced.

➥ It's illegal in Portugal to drive while talking on a mobile phone.

➥ Narcotic drugs were decriminalised in 2001 in an attempt to clear up the public-health problems among drug users and to address the issue as a social rather than a criminal one. You may be brought before a commission and subject to fines or treatment if you are caught with up to 10 doses of a drug.

➥ Drug dealing is still a serious offence and suspects may be held for up to 18 months before coming to trial. Bail is at the court's discretion.

LGBT+ Travellers

In 2010 Portugal legalised gay marriage, becoming the sixth European country to do so. Most Portuguese profess a laissez-faire attitude about same-sex couples, although how out you can be depends on where you are in Portugal. In Lisbon, Porto and the Algarve, acceptance has increased, whereas in most other areas, same-sex couples would be met with incomprehension. In this conservative Catholic country, homosexuality is still outside the norm. And while homophobic violence is extremely rare, discrimination has been reported in schools and workplaces.

Lisbon has the country's best gay and lesbian network and nightlife. Lisbon and Porto hold Gay Pride marches, but outside these events the gay community keeps a discreet profile.

Maps

National and natural park offices usually have simple park maps, though these are of little use for trekking or cycling. The following offer a good range of maps:

East View Geospatial (www.geospatial.com) US company that sells excellent maps, including 1:25,000 topographic maps.

Stanfords (www.stanfords.co.uk) Good selection of Portugal maps and travel products in the UK.

Money

ATMs

ATMs are the best way to get cash in Portugal, and they are easy to find in most cities and towns. Tiny rural villages probably won't have ATMs, so it's wise to get cash in advance. Most banks have a Multibanco ATM, with menus in English (and other languages), that accepts Visa, Access, MasterCard, Cirrus and so on. You just need your card and PIN. Keep in mind that the ATM limit is €200 per withdrawal, and many banks charge a foreign transaction fee (typically around 2% to 3%).

Changing Money

Note that banks and bureaux de change are free to set their own rates and commissions,

so a low commission might mean a skewed exchange rate.

Credit Cards

Most hotels and smarter restaurants accept credit cards; smaller guesthouses, budget hotels and smaller restaurants might not, so it's wise to have cash with you.

Taxes & Refunds

Prices in Portugal almost always include 23% VAT (some basic foodstuffs and services carry reduced rates of 6% and 13%, respectively). Non-EU passport holders can claim back the VAT on goods from participating retailers – be sure to ask for the tax-back forms and get them stamped by customs. Refunds are processed at the airport or via post.

Opening Hours

Opening hours vary throughout the year. We provide high-season opening hours; hours will generally decrease in the shoulder and low seasons.

Banks 8.30am–3pm Monday to Friday

Bars 7pm–2am

Cafes 9am–7pm

Clubs 11pm–4am Thursday to Saturday

Restaurants noon–3pm and 7–10pm

Shopping malls 10am–10pm

Shops 9.30am–noon and 2–7pm Monday to Friday, 10am–1pm Saturday

Post

Post offices are called CTT (www.ctt.pt). *Correio normal* (ordinary mail) goes in the red letterboxes, *correio azul* (airmail) goes in the blue boxes. Automated red postal stands dispense stamps, saving you the hassle of waiting in line at the post office. Post to Europe takes up to five working days, and

up to seven for the rest of the world. Economy mail (or surface airlift) is about a third cheaper but takes a week or so longer.

Public Holidays

Banks, offices, department stores and some shops close on the public holidays listed here. On New Year's Day, Easter Sunday, Labour Day and Christmas Day, even turismos close.

New Year's Day 1 January

Carnaval Tuesday February/March – the day before Ash Wednesday

Good Friday March/April

Liberty Day 25 April

Labour Day 1 May

Corpus Christi May/June – ninth Thursday after Easter

Portugal Day 10 June – also known as Camões and Communities Day

Feast of the Assumption 15 August

Republic Day 5 October

All Saints' Day 1 November

Independence Day 1 December

Feast of the Immaculate Conception 8 December

Christmas Day 25 December

Safe Travel

➡ Compared with other European countries, Portugal's crime rate remains low, but some types of crime – including car theft – are on the rise. Crime against foreigners is of the usual rush-hour-pickpocketing, bag-snatching and theft-from-rental-cars variety. Take the usual precautions: don't flash your cash; keep valuables in a safe place; and, if you're challenged, hand it over – it's not worth taking the risk.

➡ Take care in the water; the surf can be strong, with dangerous ocean currents.

Telephone

To call Portugal from abroad, dial the international access code (00), then Portugal's country code (351), then the number. All domestic numbers have nine digits, and there are no area codes. Most public phones accept phonecards only – available at most newsstands – though a few coin-operated phones are still around. You can also make calls from booths in Portugal Telecom offices and some post offices – pay when your call is finished.

Long-distance and international calls are cheaper from 9pm to 9am weekdays, all weekend and on holidays.

Mobile Phones

Portugal uses the GSM 900/1800 frequency, the same as found in Australia, the UK and the rest of the EU. Mobile-phone usage is widespread in Portugal, with extensive coverage provided in all but the most rural areas. The main domestic operators are Vodafone, Optimus and TMN. All of them sell prepaid SIM cards that you can insert into a GSM mobile phone and use as long as the phone is not locked by the company providing you service. If you need a phone, you can buy one at the airport or at shops throughout the country with a package of minutes for under €20. This is generally cheaper than renting a phone.

Time

Portugal, like Britain, is on GMT/UTC in winter and GMT/UTC plus one hour in summer. This puts it an hour earlier than Spain year-round. Clocks are set forward by an hour on the last Sunday in March and back on the last Sunday in October.

Toilets

➡ Finding public toilets in major cities such as Lisbon and Porto can be difficult. Most towns and villages that draw tourists have free public toilets.

➡ The *mercado municipal* (municipal market) often has free toilets. These are generally fairly clean and adequately maintained.

➡ In more built-up areas, your best bet is to look for a toilet in a shopping centre or simply duck into a cafe.

Tourist Information

➡ Turismo de Portugal, the country's national tourist board, operates a handy website: www.visitportugal.com.

➡ Locally managed *postos de turismo* (tourist offices, usually signposted 'turismo')

are everywhere, offering brochures and varying degrees of help with sights and accommodation.

Visas

Nationals of EU countries don't need a visa for any length of stay in Portugal. Those from Canada, New Zealand, the USA and (by temporary agreement) Australia can stay for up to 90 days in any six months without a visa. Others, including nationals of South Africa, need a visa unless they're the spouse or child of an EU citizen.

The general requirements for entry into Portugal also apply to citizens of other signatories of the 1990 Schengen Convention (Austria, Belgium, Denmark, Finland, France, Germany, Greece, Iceland, Italy, Luxembourg, the Netherlands, Norway, Spain and Sweden). A visa issued by one Schengen country is generally valid for travel in all the others, but unless you're a citizen of the UK, Ireland or a Schengen country, you should check visa regulations with the consulate of each Schengen country you plan to visit. You must apply for any Schengen visa while you are still in your country of residence.

Volunteering

Online resources such as Global Volunteers (www.globalvolunteers.org/portugal), Go Abroad (www.goabroad.com) and Transitions Abroad (www.transitionsabroad.com) list opportunities for volunteers in Portugal – including teaching English and helping out on social projects.

World Wide Opportunities on Organic Farms (WWOOF; www.wwoof.pt) sometimes has opportunities in Portugal. In exchange for your volunteer help, you'll receive food and lodging, and learn about organic farming as well.

Women Travellers

➡ Women travelling alone in Portugal report few serious problems. Women should take the same precautions they'd take when travelling anywhere – be cautious where you walk after dark and don't hitch.

➡ If you're travelling with a male partner, people will expect him to do all the talking and ordering, and pay the bill. In some conservative pockets of the north, unmarried couples will save hassle by saying they're married.

➡ If you're a victim of violence or rape while you're in Portugal, you can contact the **Associação Portuguesa de Apoio à Vítima** (APAV, Portuguese Association for Victim Support; Map p92; ☎213 587 900; www.apav.pt; Rua José Estêvão 135), which offers assistance for rape victims. Visit the website for office locations nationwide.

Work

The most likely kind of work you will be able to find is teaching English, if you have Teaching English as a Foreign Language (TEFL) certification. If you're in the UK, contact the British Council, or get in touch with language schools in the area where you want to teach.

Bar work is a possibility in the Algarve, particularly in Lagos; ask around. You can also try looking in the local English press for job ads.

Transport

GETTING THERE & AWAY

An increasingly popular destination, Portugal is well connected to North America and European countries by air. There are also handy overland links by bus and train to and from Spain, from where you can continue on to other destinations on the continent.

Flights, cars and tours can be booked online at lonely-planet.com/bookings.

Entering the Country

From within Europe, you'll have no problems entering Portugal by land or air. If arriving from further afield, check if you need a visa before arrival.

Air

Most international flights arrive in Lisbon, though Porto and Faro also receive some. For more information, including live arrival and departure schedules, see www.ana.pt.

Airports & Airlines

TAP (www.flytap.com) is Portugal's international flag carrier as well as its main domestic airline. Major airports include the following.

Faro Airport (FAO; ☑289 800 800; www.aeroportofaro.pt; ☎)

Lisbon Airport (Lisbon Airport; ☑218 413 500; www.ana.pt/pt/lis/home; Alameda das Comunidades Portuguesas)

Porto Airport (☑229 432 400; www.aeroportoporto.pt; 4470-558 Maia)

Land

Portugal shares a land border only with Spain, and there are both bus and train services linking the two countries, with onward connections to the rest of mainland Europe.

Bus

The major long-distance carriers that serve European destinations are **Busabout** (www.busabout.com) and **Eurolines** (www.eurolines.eu); though these carriers serve Portugal, the country is not currently included in the multicity travel passes of either company.

For some European routes, Eurolines is affiliated with the big Portuguese operators **Internorte** (☑707 200 512; www.internorte.pt) and **Eva Transportes** (☑289 589 055; www.eva-bus.com).

CONTINENTAL EUROPE

Eurolines has services to Portugal from destinations all across Europe, typically running about twice a week. From Paris, hefty surcharges apply to one-way or return tickets for most departures from July to mid-August and also on Saturday year-round.

UK–Portugal and France–Portugal Eurolines services cross to Portugal via northwest Spain. The following Spanish lines offer services to Portugal:

Alsa (www.alsa.es)

Avanza (☑333 444 711; www.avanzabus.com)

Damas (www.damas-sa.es)

UK

Eurolines runs several services to Portugal from Victoria coach station in London, with a stopover and change of bus in France and sometimes Spain. These include two buses a week to Viana do Castelo (34 hours), five to Porto (33 hours), five via Coimbra to Lisbon (35 hours) and two via Faro to Lagos (38 hours). These services cost around £85 one-way.

Car & Motorcycle

If you're driving your own car or motorcycle into Portugal, you need the following.

➡ vehicle registration (proof of ownership)

➡ insurance documents

➡ motor vehicle insurance with at least third-party cover

CONTINENTAL EUROPE

Of more than 30 roads that cross the Portugal–Spain border, the best and biggest do so near Valença do Minho (E01/A3), Chaves (N532), Bragança (E82/IP4), Vilar Formoso (E80/IP5), Caia

(E90/A6/IP7), Serpa (N260) and Vila Real de Santo António (E1/IP1). There are no longer any border controls.

UK

The quickest driving route from the UK to Portugal is by car ferry to northern Spain. **Brittany Ferries** (www. brittany-ferries.co.uk) runs three routes, each of which depart twice weekly from mid-March through October.

➜ Portsmouth to Santander (from £850 return, 24 hours)

➜ Portsmouth to Bilbao (from £900 return, 24 to 32 hours)

➜ Plymouth to Santander (from £860 return; 20 hours) From Bilbao or Santander it's roughly 1000km to Lisbon, 800km to Porto and 1300km to Faro.

An alternative is to catch a ferry across the Channel, or take the Eurotunnel (www. eurotunnel.com) vehicle train beneath it, to France and motor down the coast. The fastest sea crossings are between Dover and Calais, and are operated by **P&O Ferries** (www.poferries.com).

Train

Trains are a popular way to get around Europe – comfortable, frequent and generally on time. But unless you have a rail pass the cost can be higher than flying.

You will have few problems buying long-distance tickets as little as a day or two ahead, even in summer. For those intending to do a lot of European rail travel, the European Rail Timetable (www.europeanrailtimetable. eu) is updated monthly and is available for sale as a

digital download on the website. Another excellent resource for train travel around Europe (and beyond) is the Man in Seat Sixty-One website (www.seat61.com).

CONTINENTAL EUROPE

There are several ways to travel to Portugal by train. The fastest way coming from Paris is to take the TGV Atlantique from Montparnasse station to Irún (in Spain). From there, change to the overnight Lisbon-bound train, which crosses into Portugal at Vilar Formoso (Fuentes de Oñoro in Spain), continuing to Coimbra and Lisbon; change at Coimbra for Porto. If heading south, change trains at Lisbon. You can also travel via Madrid and other parts of Spain, but aside from Galicia, all trains take the same journey into Portugal.

The only other train route into Portugal is via Vigo, Galicia, which heads on to Valença do Minho and Porto, where you can change to other destinations in Portugal. This latter route is handy if you're including a trip to Santiago de Compostela in your itinerary.

The train journey from Paris to Lisbon takes 21 hours and stops in a number of Spanish cities along the way. You can buy tickets direct from **SNCF** (www.oui. sncf).

If travelling by train from Spain, you can purchase tickets online through **Renfe** (www.renfe.com).

UK

The fastest and most convenient route to Portugal from the UK is with **Eurostar**

(www.eurostar.com) from London Waterloo to Paris, and then onward by TGV.

TRAIN PASSES

Many of the passes listed here are available through **Rail Europe** (www. raileurope.com); most travel agencies also sell them, though you will save a little by buying directly from the issuing authority. Note that even with a pass you must still pay for seat and couchette reservations and express-train supplements.

InterRail Pass (www.interrail.eu) Allows a certain number of travel days within a set time frame. The network includes 31 countries. A pass for five days of travel over one month costs €282 for 2nd class and €376 for 1st class. A month of unlimited travel costs €670 for 2nd class and €893 for 1st class. The InterRail Pass is available to European citizens and official residents residing in Europe for six months before starting their travels. You cannot use it in your home country (save for one outbound journey and one inbound one).

Eurail (www.eurail.com) Sells passes to non-European residents. The Global pass is valid for unlimited travel in 31 European countries, including Portugal, and ranges from five days (adult/under 28 €281/216) to three months (€897/689).

River

Transporte Fluvial del Guadiana (www.rioguadiana.net) operates car ferries across the Rio Guadiana between Ayamonte in Spain and Vila Real de Santo António in the Algarve every hour

TRAINS TO PORTUGAL

From	To	Cost (€)	Duration (hr)	Frequency
Madrid	Lisbon	60-95	10½	daily
Paris	Lisbon	152-220	21	daily
Vigo	Porto	15	3¼	twice daily

(half-hourly in summer) from 9am to 7pm Monday to Saturday, and from 10am to 5pm Sunday. Buy tickets from the waterfront office (€1.90/5.50/1.20 per person/car/bike).

Sea

There are no scheduled seagoing ferries to Portugal, but many to Spain. The closest North African ferry connections are from Morocco to Spain; contact **FRS** (www. frs.es) for details. Car ferries also run from Tangier to Gibraltar.

GETTING AROUND

Air

Flights within mainland Portugal are expensive and, for the short distances involved, not really worth considering. Nonetheless, TAP (www. flytap.com) has multiple daily Lisbon–Porto and Lisbon–Faro flights (taking less than one hour) year-round. For Porto to Faro, change in Lisbon.

Bicycle

Cycling is popular in Portugal, even though there are few dedicated bicycle paths. Possible itineraries are numerous in the mountainous national/natural parks of the north (especially Parque Nacional da Peneda-Gerês),

along the coast or across the Alentejo plains. Coastal trips are easiest from north to south, with the prevailing winds. More demanding is the Serra da Estrela (which serves as the Tour de Portugal's 'mountain run'). You could also try the Serra do Marão between Amarante and Vila Real.

Local bike clubs organise regular Passeio BTT trips; check their flyers at rental agencies, bike shops and turismos. Guided trips are often available in popular tourist destinations.

Cobbled roads in some old-town centres may jar your teeth loose if your tyres aren't fat enough; they should be at least 38mm in diameter.

Documents

If you're cycling around Portugal on your own bike, proof of ownership and a written description and photograph of it will help police in case it's stolen.

Hire

There are numerous places to rent bikes, especially in the Algarve and other touristy areas. Prices range from €10 to €25 per day.

Information

For listings of events and bike shops, buy the bimonthly Portuguese-language *Bike Magazine,* available from larger newsagents.

For its members, the UK-based Cycling UK (www. cyclinguk.org) publishes useful and free information

on cycling in Portugal, plus notes for half a dozen routes around the country. It also offers tips, maps, topography guides and other publications by mail order.

Transport

Boxed or bagged-up bicycles can be taken free on all *regional* and *interregional* trains as accompanied baggage. They can also go unboxed on a few suburban services on weekends or for a small charge outside the rush hour. Most domestic bus lines won't accept bikes on board.

Boat

Other than river cruises along the Rio Douro from Porto and the Rio Tejo from Lisbon, Portugal's only remaining waterborne transport is cross-river ferries. Commuter ferries include those across the Rio Tejo to/ from Lisbon and across the mouth of the Rio Sado between Setúbal and Tróia.

Bus

A host of small private bus operators, most amalgamated into regional companies, run a dense network of services across the country. Among the largest are **Rede Expressos** (☑707 223 344; www.rede-expressos.pt), **Rodonorte** (☑259 340 710; www.rodonorte.pt) and the Algarve-line **Eva Transportes** (www.eva-bus.com).

CLIMATE CHANGE & TRAVEL

Every form of transport that relies on carbon-based fuel generates CO_2, the main cause of human-induced climate change. Modern travel is dependent on aeroplanes, which might use less fuel per kilometre per person than most cars but travel much greater distances. The altitude at which aircraft emit gases (including CO_2) and particles also contributes to their climate change impact. Many websites offer 'carbon calculators' that allow people to estimate the carbon emissions generated by their journey and, for those who wish to do so, to offset the impact of the greenhouse gases emitted with contributions to portfolios of climate-friendly initiatives throughout the world. Lonely Planet offsets the carbon footprint of all staff and author travel.

Train Routes

Bus services are of four general types:

Alta Qualidade A fast, deluxe category offered by some companies.

Carreiras Marked 'CR'; slow, stopping at every crossroads.

Expressos Comfortable, fast buses between major cities.

Rápidas Quick regional buses.

Even in summer you'll have little problem booking an *expresso* ticket for the same or next day. A Lisbon–Faro express bus takes about four hours and costs around €20; Lisbon–Porto takes about 3½ hours for around €19. By contrast, local services can thin out to almost nothing on weekends, especially in summer when school is out.

Don't rely on turismos for accurate timetable information. Most bus-station ticket desks will give you a little computer printout of fares and services.

Car & Motorcycle

Portugal's modest network of *estradas* (highways) is gradually spreading across the country. Main roads are sealed and generally in good condition. The downside is your fellow drivers: the country's per-capita death rate from road accidents has long been one of Europe's highest, and drinking, driving and dying are political hot potatoes. The good news is that recent years have seen a steady decline in the toll, thanks to a zero-tolerance police crackdown on accident-prone routes and alcohol limits.

Driving can be tricky in Portugal's small walled towns, where roads may taper to donkey-cart size before you know it and fiendish one-way systems can force you out of your way.

A common occurrence in larger towns is people who lurk around squares and car parks, waving you into the parking space you've just found for yourself and asking for payment for this service. It's wise to do as Portuguese do and hand over some coins (€0.50) to keep your car out of 'trouble' (scratches, broken windows etc).

Automobile Associations

Automóvel Club de Portugal (ACP; ☎219 429 113, 24hr emergency assistance 808 222 222; www.acp.pt), Portugal's national auto club, provides medical, legal and breakdown assistance for its members. Road information and maps are available to anyone at ACP offices, including the head office in Lisbon and branches in Aveiro, Braga, Bragança, Coimbra, Évora, Faro, Porto.

If your national auto club belongs to the Fédération In-

ROAD DISTANCES (KM)

	Aveiro	Beja	Braga	Bragança	Castelo Branco	Coimbra	Évora	Faro	Guarda	Leiria	Lisbon	Portalegre	Porto	Santarém	Setúbal	Viana do Castelo	Vila Real	Viseu
Aveiro	---																	
Beja	383	---																
Braga	129	504	---															
Bragança	287	566	185	---														
Castelo Branco	239	271	366	299	---													
Coimbra	60	329	178	314	191	---												
Évora	305	78	426	488	191	251	---											
Faro	522	166	643	732	437	468	244	---										
Guarda	163	369	260	197	102	161	291	535	---									
Leiria	126	273	244	402	179	72	195	412	233	---								
Lisbon	256	183	372	530	264	202	138	296	402	146	---							
Portalegre	276	178	403	390	93	222	100	344	193	172	219	---						
Porto	71	446	58	216	308	123	368	585	202	189	317	339	---					
Santarém	188	195	309	464	181	134	117	346	295	78	80	147	251	---				
Setúbal	299	143	420	575	316	246	105	256	406	189	47	186	362	123	---			
Viana do Castelo	144	519	56	241	382	191	441	658	275	262	387	412	73	324	435	---		
Vila Real	169	528	94	120	261	199	450	683	159	282	412	352	98	349	460	150	---	
Viseu	86	415	185	228	177	86	366	554	75	158	288	268	127	220	331	241	113	---

ternationale de l'Automobile or the Alliance Internationale de Tourisme, you can also use ACP's emergency services and get discounts on maps and other products. Among clubs that qualify are the AA and RAC in the UK, and the Australian, New Zealand, Canadian and US automobile associations.

Driving Licences

Nationals of EU countries, the USA and Brazil need only their home driving licence to operate a car or motorcycle in Portugal. Others should get an International Driving Permit (IDP) through an automobile licensing department or automobile club in their home country.

Fuel

Fuel is expensive – about €1.60 for a litre of *sem chumbo* (unleaded petrol) at the time of writing. There are plenty of self-service stations, and credit cards are accepted at most. If you're near the border, you can save money by filling up in Spain, where it's around 20% cheaper.

Highways & Toll Roads

Top-of-the-range roads are *auto-estradas* (motorways), all of them *portagens* (toll roads); the longest of these are Lisbon–Porto and Lisbon–Algarve. Toll roads charge cars and motorcycles around €0.09 per kilometre (around €22 from Lisbon to Porto and €25 from Lisbon to Lagos). You can calculate prices at www.portugaltolls. com.

Nomenclature can be baffling. Motorway prefixes indicate the following:

A Portugal's toll roads.

E Europe-wide designations.

N Main two-lane *estradas nacionais* (national roads); prefix letter used on some road maps only.

IC *(itinerário complementar)* Subsidiary highways.

IP *(itinerário principal)* Main highways.

Note that Portugal's main toll roads now have automated tollbooths, meaning you won't be able to simply drive through and pay an attendant. Most car-rental agencies hire out the small electronic devices (for around €6 per week, less on subsequent weeks), and it's worth asking if one is available before renting a car.

Via Verde (707 500 900; www.viaverde.pt) For information on toll roads and details on where you can hire electronic tag devices throughout the country (useful if your car hire doesn't have them or you're driving your own vehicle).

Hire

➜ To rent a car in Portugal you should be at least 25 years old and have held your driving licence for more than a year (some companies allow younger drivers at higher rates). The widest choice of car-hire companies is at Lisbon, Porto and Faro airports. Competition has driven Algarve rates lower than elsewhere.

➜ Some of the best advance-booking rates are offered by internet-based brokers such as **Holiday Autos** (www. holidayautos.com). Other bargains come as part of 'fly/ drive' packages. The worst deals tend to be those done with international firms on arrival, though their prepaid promotional rates are competitive. Book at least a few days ahead in high season.

➜ The average price for renting the smallest and cheapest available car for a week in high season is around €300 (with tax, insurance and unlimited mileage) if booked from abroad, and a similar amount when booked through a Portuguese company.

➜ For an additional fee you can get personal insurance

through the rental company, unless you're covered by your home policy. A minimum of third-party coverage is compulsory in the EU.

➜ Rental cars are especially at risk of break-ins or petty theft in larger towns, so don't leave anything of value visible in the car.

➜ Motorcycles and scooters can be rented in larger cities and all over coastal Algarve. Expect to pay from €30/60 per day for a scooter/ motorcycle.

Insurance

Your home insurance policy may or may not be extendable to Portugal, and the coverage of some comprehensive policies automatically drops to third party outside your home country unless the insurer is notified.

If you hire a car, the rental firm will provide you with registration and insurance papers, plus a rental contract.

If you are involved in a minor collision with no injuries, the easiest way for drivers to sort things out with their insurance companies is to fill out a Constat Amiable (the English version is called a European Accident Statement). There's no risk in signing this: it's just a way to exchange the relevant information and there's usually one included in rental-car documents. Make sure it includes any details that may help you prove that the accident was not your fault. To alert the police, dial 112.

Parking

Parking is often metered within city centres but free on Saturday evening and Sunday. Lisbon has car parks, but these can get expensive (upwards of €20 per day).

Road Rules

➜ Despite the sometimes chaotic relations between drivers, there are rules. To begin with, driving is on the right, overtaking is on the left and most signs use international symbols. An important rule to remember is that traffic from the right usually has priority. Portugal has lots of ambiguously marked intersections, so this is more important than you might think.

➡ Except when marked otherwise, speed limits for cars (without a trailer) and motorcycles (without a sidecar) are 50km/h in towns and villages, 90km/h outside built-up areas and 120km/h on motorways. By law, car safety belts (seat belts) must be worn in the front and back seats, and children under 12 years may not ride in the front. Motorcyclists and their passengers must wear helmets, and motorcycles must have their headlights on day and night.

➡ The police can impose steep on-the-spot fines for speeding and parking offences, so save yourself a big hassle and remember to toe the line.

➡ The legal blood-alcohol limit is 0.5g/L, and there are fines of up to €2500 for drink-driving. It's also illegal in Portugal to drive while talking on a mobile phone.

Hitching

Hitching is never entirely safe, and we don't recommend it. Travellers who hitch should understand that they are taking a small but potentially serious risk.

In any case, it isn't an easy option in Portugal. Almost nobody stops on major highways, and on smaller roads drivers tend to be going short distances so you might only advance from one field to the next.

Local Transport
Bus
Except in Lisbon or Porto, there's little reason to take municipal buses, as most attractions are within walking distance.

Metro
Both Lisbon and Porto have ambitious metro systems that are still growing.

Taxi & Rideshare Services
➡ Taxis offer fair value over short distances and are plentiful in large towns and cities. Ordinary taxis are usually marked with an 'A' (which stands for *aluguer*, for hire) on the door, number plate or elsewhere. They use meters and are available on the street and at taxi ranks, or by telephone for a surcharge of €0.80.

➡ The fare on weekdays during daylight hours is about €3.25 *bandeirada* (flagfall) plus around €0.80 per kilometre, and a bit more for periods spent idling in traffic. A fare of €6 will usually get you across bigger towns. It's best to insist on the meter, although it's possible to negotiate a flat fare. If you have a sizeable load of luggage you'll pay a further €1.60.

➡ Rates are about 20% higher at night (9pm to 6am), on weekends and on holidays. Once a taxi leaves the city limits you also pay a surcharge or higher rate.

➡ In larger cities, including Lisbon and Porto, meterless taxis marked with a T (for *turismo*) can be hired from private companies for excursions. Rates for these are higher but standardised; drivers are honest and polite, and generally speak foreign languages.

➡ Uber is available in Lisbon and Porto.

Tram
Tram lovers shouldn't miss the charming relics rattling through the narrow streets of Lisbon and Porto.

Tours
If you're short on time, an organised tour can be a good way to take in the highlights of a destination.

Train
On weekends from June to October, you can ride the **Comboio Histórico do Douro** (www.cp.pt; Estação CP, Largo da Estação; round-trip adult/child €42.50/19; ⊘Sat & Sun Jun-Oct), a scenic steam train that operates between Regua and Tua in the Douro Valley.

Specialist Tours
For special-interest tours, try **Martin Randall Travel** (www.martinrandall.com), a UK cultural specialist that arranges first-rate escorted tours, including a historical and architectural tour of central Portugal, or **Naturetrek** (www.naturetrek.co.uk), which specialises in birdwatching and botanical tours and runs an eight-day excursion around southern Portugal.

Train
Portugal has an extensive railway network, making for scenic travel between destinations; see the **Comboios de Portugal** (✆707 210 220; www.cp.pt) website.

Discounts
➡ Children aged under five travel free; those aged five to 12 go for half price.

➡ A youth card issued by Euro26 member countries gets you a 20% discount on *regional* and *interregional* services on any day. For distances above 100km, you can also get a 20% discount on *intercidade* (express) services and a 10% discount on Alfa Pendular (AP) trains – though the latter applies only from Tuesday to Thursday.

➡ Travellers aged 65 and over can get 50% off any service by showing ID.

Information & Reservations

➡ You can get hold of timetable and fare information at all stations and from www.cp.pt.

➡ You can book *intercidade* and Alfa Pendular tickets up to 30 days ahead, though you'll have little trouble booking for the next or even the same day. Other services can only be booked 24 hours in advance.

➡ A seat reservation is mandatory on most *intercidade* and Alfa trains; the booking fee is included in the price.

Train Passes

The One Country Portugal Pass from **InterRail** (www.interrail.eu) gives you unlimited travel on any three, four, five, six or eight days over a month (2nd class costs per three/four/five/six/eight days €92/114/134/154/190; 1st class costs about 35% more; and if you're under 28, it costs about 15% less). It's available to all travellers who hail from outside Portugal and can be purchased from many travel agents in Portugal or in advance from the website.

Types & Classes of Service

There are four main types of long-distance service (note that international services are marked IN on timetables):

Regional (R) Slow, stop everywhere.

Interregional (IR) Reasonably fast.

Intercidade (IC) *Rápido* or express trains.

Alfa Pendular Deluxe Marginally faster than express and much pricier.

Only the Faro–Porto Comboio Azul and international trains such as *Sud-Expresso* and Talgo *Lusitânia* have restaurant cars, though all IC and Alfa trains have aisle service and most have bars.

Lisbon and Porto have their own *urbano* (suburban) train networks. Lisbon's network extends to Sintra, Cascais, Setúbal and up the lower Tejo valley. Porto's network takes the definition of 'suburban' to new lengths, running all the way to Braga, Guimarães and Aveiro. *Urbano* services also travel between Coimbra and Figueira da Foz. The distinction matters where long-distance services parallel the more convenient, plentiful and considerably cheaper *urbanos*.

Language

Portuguese pronunciation is not difficult because most sounds are also found in English. The exceptions are the nasal vowels (represented in our pronunciation guides by ng after the vowel), which are pronounced as if you're trying to make the sound through your nose; and the strongly rolled *r* (represented by rr in our pronunciation guides). Also note that the symbol zh sounds like the 's' in 'pleasure'. The stress generally falls on the second-last syllable of a word. In our pronunciation guides stressed syllables are indicated with italics. If you keep these few points in mind and read our coloured pronunciation guides as if they were English, you won't have problems being understood.

Portuguese has masculine and feminine forms of nouns and adjectives. Both forms are given in this chapter where necessary, and indicated with 'm' and 'f' respectively.

BASICS

Hello.	Olá.	o·laa
Goodbye.	Adeus.	a·de·oosh
How are you?	Como está?	ko·moo shtaa
Fine, and you?	Bem, e você?	beng e vo·se
Excuse me.	Faz favor.	faash fa·vor
Sorry.	Desculpe.	desh·kool·pe
Yes.	Sim.	seeng
No.	Não.	nowng
Please.	Por favor.	poor fa·vor

WANT MORE?

For in-depth language information and handy phrases, check out Lonely Planet's *Portuguese Phrasebook*. You'll find it at **shop.lonelyplanet.com**, or you can buy Lonely Planet's iPhone phrasebooks at the Apple App Store.

Thank you.	Obrigado.	o·bree·gaa·doo (m)
	Obrigada.	o·bree·gaa·da (f)
You're welcome.	De nada.	de naa·da

What's your name?
Qual é o seu nome?   kwaal e oo se·oo no·me

My name is ...
O meu nome é ...   oo me·oo no·me e ...

Do you speak English?
Fala inglês?   faa·la eeng·glesh

I don't understand.
Não entendo.   nowng eng·teng·doo

ACCOMMODATION

Do you have a single/double room?
Tem um quarto de   teng oong kwaar·too de
solteiro/casal?   sol·tay·roo/ka·zal

How much is it per night/person?
Quanto custa   kwang·too koosh·ta
por noite/pessoa?   poor noy·te/pe·so·a

Is breakfast included?
Inclui o pequeno   eeng·kloo·ee oo pe·ke·noo
almoço?   aal·mo·soo

air-con	ar condicionado	aar kong·dee·syoo·naa·doo
bathroom	casa de banho	kaa·za de ba·nyoo
bed	cama	ka·ma
campsite	parque de campismo	paar·ke de kang·peezh·moo
cot	cama de grades	ka·ma de graa·desh
guesthouse	casa de hóspedes	kaa·za de osh·pe·desh
hotel	hotel	o·tel
youth hostel	pousada de juventude	poh·zaa·da de zhoo·veng·too·de
window	janela	zha·ne·la

DIRECTIONS

Where's (the station)?
Onde é (a estação)?   ong·de e (a shta·*sowng*)

What's the address?
Qual é o endereço?   kwaal e oo eng·de·re·soo

Could you please write it down?
Podia escrever   poo·*dee*·a shkre·*ver*
isso, por favor?   ee·soo poor fa·*vor*

Can you show me (on the map)?
Pode-me mostrar   po·de·me moosh·*traar*
(no mapa)?   (noo *maa*·pa)

at the corner	*na esquina*	na *shkee*·na
at the traffic lights	*nos semáforos*	noosh se·*maa*·foo·roosh
behind ...	*atrás de ...*	a·*traash* de ...
in front of ...	*em frente de ...*	eng *freng*·te de ...
far	*longe*	*long*·zhe
left	*esquerda*	*shker*·da
near	*perto*	*per*·too
next to ...	*ao lado de ...*	ow *laa*·doo de ...
opposite ...	*do lado oposto ...*	doo *laa*·doo oo·*posh*·too ...
right	*direita*	dee·*ray*·ta
straight ahead	*em frente*	eng *freng*·te

EATING & DRINKING

What would you recommend?
O que é que   oo ke e ke
recomenda?   rre·koo·*meng*·da

What's in that dish?
Quais são os   kwaish sowng oosh
ingredientes   eeng·gre·dee·*eng*·tesh
daquele prato?   da·ke·le *praa*·too

I don't eat ...
Eu não como ...   e·oo nowng *ko*·moo ...

Cheers!
Saúde!   sa·*oo*·de

That was delicious.
Isto estava   eesh·too *shtaa*·va
delicioso.   de·lee·see·o·*zoo*

Bring the bill/check, please.
Pode-me trazer   po·de·me tra·*zer*
a conta.   a *kong*·ta

I'd like to reserve a table for ...	*Eu queria reservar uma mesa para ...*	e·oo ke·*ree*·a rre·zer·*vaar* oo·ma *me*·za pa·ra ...
(eight) o'clock	*as (oito da noite)*	ash (oy·too da *noy*·te)
(two) people	*(duas) pessoas*	(*doo*·ash) pe·so·ash

KEY PATTERNS

To get by in Portuguese, mix and match these simple patterns with words of your choice:

When's (the next bus)?
Quando é que sai   kwang·doo e ke sai
(o próximo   (oo *pro*·see·moo
autocarro)?   ow·to·*kaa*·rroo)

Where do I (buy a ticket)?
Onde é que eu   ong·de e ke e·oo
(compro o bilhete)?   (*kong*·proo oo bee·*lye*·te)

I'm looking for (a hotel).
Estou à procura de   shtoh aa proo·*koo*·ra de
(um hotel).   (oong o·*tel*)

Do you have (a map)?
Tem (um mapa)?   teng (oong *maa*·pa)

Please bring (the bill).
Pode-me trazer   po·de·me tra·*zer*
(a conta).   (a *kong*·ta)

I'd like (the menu).
Queria (um menu).   ke·*ree*·a (oong me·*noo*)

I'd like (to hire a car).
Queria (alugar   ke·*ree*·a (a·loo·*gaar*
um carro).   oong *kaa*·rroo)

I have (a reservation).
Eu tenho   e·oo ta·*nyoo*
(uma reserva).   (oo·ma rre·*zer*·va)

Could you please (help)?
Pode (ajudar),   po·de (a·zhoo·*daar*)
por favor?   poor fa·*vor*

Do I need (a visa)?
Preciso de   pre·see·*zoo* de
(um visto)?   (oong *veesh*·too)

Key Words

appetisers	*aperitivos*	a·per·ee·*tee*·voosh
bar	*bar*	baar
bottle	*garrafa*	ga·*rraa*·fa
bowl	*tigela*	tee·*zhe*·la
breakfast	*pequeno almoço*	pe·ke·noo aal·*mo*·soo
children's menu	*menu das crianças*	me·*noo* dash kree·*ang*·sash
cold	*frio*	*free*·oo
delicatessen	*charcutaria*	shar·koo·ta·*ree*·a
dinner	*jantar*	zhang·*taar*
food	*comida*	koo·*mee*·da
fork	*garfo*	*gar*·foo
glass	*copo*	*ko*·poo
hot (warm)	*quente*	*keng*·te
knife	*faca*	*faa*·ka

SIGNS

Aberto	Open
Encerrado	Closed
Entrada	Entrance
Fechado	Closed
Informação	Information
Lavabos/WC	Toilets
Proibido	Prohibited
Saída	Exit

lunch	almoço	aal·mo·soo
main course	prato principal	praa·too preeng·see·paal
market	mercado	mer·kaa·doo
menu (in English)	menu (em inglês)	me·noo (eng eeng·glesh)
plate	prato	praa·too
restaurant	restaurante	rresh·tow·rang·te
spicy	picante	pee·kang·te
spoon	colher	koo·lyer
vegetarian food	comida vegetariana	koo·mee·da ve·zhe·ta·ree·aa·na
wine list	lista dos vinhos	leesh·ta doosh vee·nyoosh
with/without	com/sem	kong/seng

Meat & Fish

beef	carne de vaca	kaar·ne de vaa·ka
chicken	frango	frang·goo
duck	pato	paa·too
fish	peixe	pay·she
lamb	cordeiro	kor·day·roo
pork	porco	por·koo
turkey	peru	pe·roo
veal	novilho	noo·vee·lyoo

Fruit & Vegetables

apple	maçã	ma·sang
apricot	alperce	aal·per·se
artichoke	alcachofra	aal·ka·sho·fra
asparagus	espargos	shpar·goosh
beetroot	beterraba	be·te·rraa·ba
cabbage	couve	koh·ve
capsicum	pimento	pee·meng·too
carrot	cenoura	se·noh·ra
celery	aipo	ai·poo

cherry	cereja	se·re·zha
corn	milho	mee·lyoo
cucumber	pepino	pe·pee·noo
fruit	fruta	froo·ta
grapes	uvas	oo·vash
lemon	limão	lee·mowng
lettuce	alface	aal·faa·se
mushrooms	cogumelos	koo·goo·me·loosh
nut	oleaginosa	o·lee·a·zhee·no·za
onion	cebola	se·bo·la
orange	laranja	la·rang·zha
peach	pêssego	pe·se·goo
peas	ervilhas	er·vee·lyash
pineapple	ananás	a·na·naash
plum	ameixa	a·may·sha
potato	batata	ba·taa·ta
prune	ameixa seca	a·may·sha se·ka
pumpkin	abóbora	a·bo·boo·ra
spinach	espinafres	shpee·naa·fresh
strawberry	morango	moo·rang·goo
tomato	tomate	too·maa·te
turnip	nabo	naa·boo
vegetable	hortaliça	or·ta·lee·sa
watermelon	melancia	me·lang·see·a

Other

bread	pão	powng
butter	manteiga	mang·tay·ga
cheese	queijo	kay·zhoo
egg	ovo	o·voo
honey	mel	mel
lentils	lentilha	leng·tee·lya
noodles	massas	maa·sash
oil	óleo	o·lyoo
pepper	pimenta	pee·meng·ta
rice	arroz	a·rrosh
salt	sal	saal
sugar	açúcar	a·soo·kar
vinegar	vinagre	vee·naa·gre

Drinks

beer	cerveja	ser·ve·zha
coffee	café	ka·fe
juice	sumo	soo·moo
milk	leite	lay·te
red wine	vinho	vee·nyoo

	tinto	teeng·too
tea	chá	shaa
(mineral) water	água (mineral)	aa·gwa (mee·ne·raal)
white wine	vinho branco	vee·nyoo brang·koo

EMERGENCIES

Help!	Socorro!	soo·ko·rroo
Go away!	Vá-se embora!	vaa·se eng·bo·ra
Call ...!	Chame ...!	shaa·me ...
a doctor	um médico	oong me·dee·koo
the police	a polícia	a poo·lee·sya

I'm lost.
Estou perdido.   shtoh per·dee·doo (m)
Estou perdida.   shtoh per·dee·da (f)

I'm ill.
Estou doente.   shtoh doo·eng·te

It hurts here.
Dói-me aqui.   doy·me a·kee

I'm allergic to ...
Eu sou alérgico/   e·oo soh a·ler·zhee·koo/
alérgica a ...   a·ler·zhee·ka a ... (m/f)

Where are the toilets?
Onde é a casa   ong·de e a kaa·za
de banho?   de ba·nyoo

SHOPPING & SERVICES

I'd like to buy ...
Queria comprar ...   ke·ree·a kong·praar ...

I'm just looking.
Estou só a ver.   shtoh so a ver

Can I look at it?
Posso ver?   po·soo ver

I don't like it.
Não gosto.   nowng gosh·too

How much is it?
Quanto custa?   kwang·too koosh·ta

It's too expensive.
Está muito caro.   shtaa mweeng·too kaa·roo

QUESTION WORDS

How?	Como?	ko·moo
What?	Quê?	ke
When?	Quando?	kwang·doo
Where?	Onde?	ong·de
Who?	Quem?	keng
Why?	Porquê?	poor·ke

Can you lower the price?
Pode baixar o preço?   po·de bai·shaar oo pre·soo

There's a mistake in the bill.
Há um erro na conta.   aa oong e·rroo na kong·ta

ATM	caixa automático	kai·sha ow·too·maa·tee·koo
credit card	cartão de crédito	kar·towng de kre·dee·too
internet cafe	café da internet	ka·fe da eeng·ter·ne·te
post office	correio	koo·rray·oo
tourist office	escritório de turismo	shkree·to·ryoo de too·reezh·moo

TIME & DATES

What time is it?
Que horas são?   kee o·rash sowng

It's (10) o'clock.
São (dez) horas.   sowng (desh) o·rash

Half past (10).
(Dez) e meia.   (desh) e may·a

morning	manhã	ma·nyang
afternoon	tarde	taar·de
evening	noite	noy·te
yesterday	ontem	ong·teng
today	hoje	o·zhe
tomorrow	amanhã	aa·ma·nyang
Monday	segunda-feira	se·goong·da·fay·ra
Tuesday	terça-feira	ter·sa·fay·ra
Wednesday	quarta-feira	kwaar·ta·fay·ra
Thursday	quinta-feira	keeng·ta·fay·ra
Friday	sexta-feira	saysh·ta·fay·ra
Saturday	sábado	saa·ba·doo
Sunday	domingo	doo·meeng·goo
January	Janeiro	zha·nay·roo
February	Fevereiro	fe·vray·roo
March	Março	maar·soo
April	Abril	a·breel
May	Maio	maa·yoo
June	Junho	zhoo·nyoo
July	Julho	zhoo·lyoo
August	Agosto	a·gosh·too
September	Setembro	se·teng·broo
October	Outubro	oh·too·broo

| November | *Novembro* | *no·veng·broo* |
| December | *Dezembro* | *de·zeng·broo* |

TRANSPORT

Public Transport

boat	*barco*	*baar·koo*
bus	*autocarro*	*ow·to·kaa·roo*
plane	*avião*	*a·vee·owng*
train	*comboio*	*kong·boy·oo*
tram	*eléctrico*	*ee·le·tree·koo*

I want to go to (Braga).
Queria ir a (Braga).   *ke·ree·a eer a (braa·ga)*

Does it stop at (Amarante)?
Pára em (Amarante)?   *paa·ra eng (a·ma·rang·te)*

What time does it leave/arrive?
A que horas sai/chega?   *a ke o·rash sai/she·ga*

Please tell me when we get to (Évora).
Por favor avise-me	*poor fa·vor a·vee·ze·me*
quando chegarmos	*kwang·doo she·gaar·moosh*
a (Évora).	*a (e·voo·ra)*

Please stop here.
Por favor pare aqui.   *poor fa·vor paa·re a·kee*

| aisle seat | *lugar na coxia* | *loo·gaar na koo·shee·a* |

NUMBERS

1	*um*	*oong*
2	*dois*	*doysh*
3	*três*	*tresh*
4	*quatro*	*kwaa·troo*
5	*cinco*	*seeng·koo*
6	*seis*	*saysh*
7	*sete*	*se·te*
8	*oito*	*oy·too*
9	*nove*	*no·ve*
10	*dez*	*desh*
20	*vinte*	*veeng·te*
30	*trinta*	*treeng·ta*
40	*quarenta*	*kwa·reng·ta*
50	*cinquenta*	*seeng·kweng·ta*
60	*sessenta*	*se·seng·ta*
70	*setenta*	*se·teng·ta*
80	*oitenta*	*oy·teng·ta*
90	*noventa*	*no·veng·ta*
100	*cem*	*seng*
1000	*mil*	*meel*

cancelled	*cancelado*	*kang·se·laa·doo*
delayed	*atrasado*	*a·tra·zaa·doo*
platform	*plataforma*	*pla·ta·for·ma*
ticket office	*bilheteira*	*bee·lye·tay·ra*
timetable	*horário*	*o·raa·ryoo*
train station	*estação de caminhos de ferro*	*shta·sowng de ka·mee·nyoosh de fe·rroo*
window seat	*lugar à janela*	*loo·gaar aa zha·ne·la*

a ... ticket	*um bilhete de ...*	*oong bee·lye·te de ...*
1st-class	*primeira classe*	*pree·may·ra klaa·se*
2nd-class	*segunda classe*	*se·goong·da klaa·se*
one-way	*ida*	*ee·da*
return	*ida e volta*	*ee·da ee vol·ta*

Driving & Cycling

I'd like to hire a ...	*Queria alugar ...*	*ke·ree·a a·loo·gaar ...*
bicycle	*uma bicicleta*	*oo·ma bee·see·kle·ta*
car	*um carro*	*oong kaa·rroo*
motorcycle	*uma mota*	*oo·ma mo·ta*

bicycle pump	*bomba de bicicleta*	*bong·ba de bee·see·kle·ta*
child seat	*cadeira de criança*	*ka·day·ra de kree·ang·sa*
helmet	*capacete*	*ka·pa·se·te*
mechanic	*mecânico*	*me·kaa·nee·koo*
petrol/gas	*gasolina*	*ga·zoo·lee·na*
service station	*posto de gasolina*	*posh·too de ga·zoo·lee·na*

Is this the road to ...?
| *Esta é a estrada para ...?* | *esh·ta e a shtraa·da pa·ra ...* |

(How long) Can I park here?
| *(Quanto tempo) Posso estacionar aqui?* | *(kwang·too teng·poo) po·soo shta·see·oo·naar a·kee* |

The car/motorbike has broken down (at ...).
| *O carro/A mota avariou-se (em ...).* | *oo kaa·rroo/a mo·ta a·va·ree·oh·se (eng ...)* |

I have a flat tyre.
| *Tenho um furo no pneu.* | *ta·nyoo oong foo·roo noo pe·ne·oo* |

I've run out of petrol.
Estou sem gasolina.   *shtoh seng ga·zoo·lee·na*

GLOSSARY

For terms for food, drinks and other culinary vocabulary, see p531.

adegas – wineries

Age of Discoveries – the period during the 15th and 16th centuries when Portuguese sailors explored the coast of Africa and finally charted a sea route to India

albergaria – upmarket inn

albufeira – reservoir, lagoon

aldeia – village

alta – upper

anta – see dolmen

arco – arch

armillary sphere – celestial sphere used by early astronomers and navigators to chart the stars; a decorative motif in Manueline architecture and atop *pelourinhos*

arrayal, arraiais (pl) – street party

artesanato – handicrafts shop

avenida – avenue

azulejo – hand-painted tile, typically blue and white, used to decorate buildings

bairro – town district

baixa – lower

balneário – health resort, spa

barcos rabelos – colourful boats once used to transport port wine from vineyards

barragem – dam

beco – cul de sac

biblioteca – library

bilhete diário/turístico – day pass/tourist ticket

câmara municipal – city or town hall

caldas – hot springs

Carnaval – Carnival; festival that takes place just before Lent

casa de hóspedes – boarding house, usually with shared showers and toilets

casais – huts

castelo – castle

castro – fortified hill town

cavaleiro – horseman

CCI – Camping Card International

Celtiberians – descendants of Celts who arrived in the Iberian Peninsula around 600 BC

centro de saúde – state-administered medical centre

cidade – town or city

citânia – Celtic fortified village

claustro – cloisters

concelho – municipality, council

cortes – Portugal's early parliament

CP – Caminhos de Ferro Portugueses (the Portuguese state railway company)

cromeleque – circle of prehistoric standing stones

cruz – cross

direita – right; abbreviated as D, dir or Dta

dolmen – Neolithic stone tomb (*anta* in Portuguese)

Dom, Dona – honorific titles (like Sir, Madam) given to royalty, nobility and landowners; now used more generally as a very polite form of address

elevador – lift (elevator), funicular

espigueiros – stone granaries

esplanada – terrace, seafront promenade

estação – station (usually train station)

estalagem – inn; more expensive than an *albergaria*

expressos – comfortable, fast buses between major cities

estradas – highways

fadista – singer of *fado*

fado – traditional, melancholic Portuguese style of singing

feira – fair

festa – festival

fortaleza – fortress

GNR – Guarda Nacional Republicana, the national guard (the acting police force in rural towns without PSP police)

guitarra – guitar

gruta – cave

hospedaria – see *casa de hóspedes*

IC (intercidade) – express intercity train

ICEP – Investimentos, Comércio e Turismo de Portugal, the government's umbrella organisation for tourism

igreja – church

igreja matriz – parish church

ilha – island

IR (interregional) – fairly fast train that doesn't make too many stops

jardim – garden

judiaria – quarter in a town where Jews were once segregated

largo – small square

latifúndios – Roman system of large farming estates

litoral – coastal

livraria – bookshop

Lisboêtas – Lisbon dwellers

loggia – covered area or porch on the side of a building

lugar – neighbourhood, place

Manueline – elaborate late Gothic/Renaissance style of art and architecture that emerged during the reign of Dom Manuel I in the 16th century

mantas alentejanas – handwoven woollen blankets

marranos – 'New Christians', ie Jews who converted during the Inquisition

menhir – standing stone monument typical of the late Neolithic Age

mercado municipal – municipal market

mesa – table

minimercado – grocery shop or small supermarket

miradouro – viewpoint

Misericórdia – derived from Santa Casa da Misericórdia (Holy House of Mercy), a charitable

GLOSSARY

institution founded in the 15th century to care for the poor and the sick; it usually designates an old building that was founded by this organisation

moliceiro – high-prowed, shallow-draft boats traditionally used for harvesting seaweed in the estuaries of Beira Litoral

mosteiro – monastery

mouraria – the quarter where Moors were segregated during and after the Christian *Reconquista*

museu – museum

paço – palace

parque de campismo – camping ground

parque nacional – national park

parque natural – natural park

pelourinho – stone pillory, often ornately carved; erected in the 13th to 18th centuries as symbols of justice and sometimes as places where criminals were punished

pensão, pensões (pl) – guesthouse, the Portuguese equivalent of a B&B, though breakfast is not always served

planalto – high plain

pombal – dovecote, a structure for housing pigeons

ponte – bridge

portagem – toll road

pousada – government-run upmarket inn, often a converted castle, convent or palace

pousada da juventude – youth hostel; usually with kitchen, common rooms and sometimes rooms with private bathroom

praça – square

praia – beach

PSP – Polícia de Segurança Pública, the local police force

quinta – country estate or villa; in the Douro wine-growing region it often refers to a wine lodge's property

R (regional) – slow train

Reconquista – Christian reconquest of Portugal (718–1249)

reservas naturais – nature reserves

residencial, residenciais (pl) – guesthouse; slightly more expensive than a *pensão* and usually serving breakfast

ribeiro – stream

rio – river

romaria – religious pilgrimage

rua – street

saudade – melancholic longing for better times

sé – cathedral

sem chumbo – unleaded (petrol)

senhor – man

senhora – woman

serra – mountain, mountain range

solar – manor house

tasca – tavern

termas – spas, hot springs

terra quente – hot country

torre de menagem – castle tower, keep

Turihab – short for Turismo Habitação, a scheme for marketing private accommodation (particularly in northern Portugal) in cottages, historic buildings and manor houses

turismo – tourist office

vila – town

FOOD GLOSSARY

a conta – the bill

açorda – bread-based stew, usually served with mixed *mariscos* (shellfish) or *camarão* (prawn)

agua – water, usually offered *sem gas* (still) or *com gas* (bubbly)

amêijoas – clams

arroz – rice

arroz de marisco – rich shellfish and rice mixture

arroz de tamboril – monkfish rice

atum – tuna

azeite – olive oil

azeitonas – olives

bacalhau – salted codfish

bacalhau à brás – shredded fried cod with potato and scrambled egg

bacalhau com – shredded cod with cream and potatoes

bica – espresso

bife – steak

borrego – lamb

caldeirada – fish and shellfish stew, not unlike bouillabaisse

camarão/camarões – prawn/prawns

carapau – a type of (small) mackerel

carne – meat

carne de porco – pork

carne de vaca – beef

cataplana – seafood stew cooked in a copper pot

cerveja – beer

choco – cuttlefish

choriço – smoked pork sausage

couvert – bread, cheese, olives brought to you table before your meal

cozido à portuguesa – stew of sausages, meats and vegetables

dose – a portion, usually big enough for two

ementa – menu

entradas – appetizers

espadarte – swordfish

especialidade da casa – house speciality

espetada – kebab

feijoada – bean and sausage stew, usually made with white beans

frango – chicken

frutos do mar – seafood

galão – tall weak coffee with milk

lula – squid

mariscos – shellfish

meia de leite – coffee with milk

meia dose – half-portion, usually serves one

migas – fried breadcrumbs flavoured with sausage

pão – bread

pastel de nata – custard tart

pastelaria – pastry shop and bakery

peixe – fish

pernil no forno – roast leg of pork

petiscos – small (tapas-sized) plates

piri piri – spicy chilli sauce

polvo – octopus

prato do dia – plate of the day

prato principal – main course

queijada – cheesecake

queijo – cheese

salmão – salmon

sandes – sandwiches

sardinhas – sardines

sobremesa – dessert

vinho – wine

vinho blanco – white wine

vinho tinto – red wine

vinho verde – semi-sparkling young wine

vitela – veal

Behind the Scenes

SEND US YOUR FEEDBACK

We love to hear from travellers – your comments keep us on our toes and help make our books better. Our well-travelled team reads every word on what you loved or loathed about this book. Although we cannot reply individually to your submissions, we always guarantee that your feedback goes straight to the appropriate authors, in time for the next edition. Each person who sends us information is thanked in the next edition – the most useful submissions are rewarded with a selection of digital PDF chapters.

Visit **lonelyplanet.com/contact** to submit your updates and suggestions or to ask for help. Our award-winning website also features inspirational travel stories, news and discussions.

Note: We may edit, reproduce and incorporate your comments in Lonely Planet products such as guidebooks, websites and digital products, so let us know if you don't want your comments reproduced or your name acknowledged. For a copy of our privacy policy visit lonelyplanet.com/privacy.

OUR READERS

Many thanks to the travellers who used the last edition and wrote to us with helpful hints, useful advice and interesting anecdotes:

Aliaksandr Roussak, André Rousseau, Andrea Casella, Anthony O'Toole, Bill Cooke, Bruce Crow, Caryn Lesko, David Muir, David Willett, Dawn Simpson, Eric Wallbank, Esther McClelland, Evelien van Delft, Fiona Daniel, G Frank, Gayle Taylor, Gordon Winocur, Gwyneth Graham, Irving Levinson, Jean-Francois Berthiaume, Jim Martin, Jody Hoffmann, John Briggs, John Docker, John Robinson, Keith Clay, Kevin Boreham, Kirk Siang Yeo, Lis Lindskov, Marco Crombeen, Margaret McAspurn, Marianna Bebu, Mariella Abdilla, Meltem Kılıçcı, Michelle Charrette, Peter Tudor, Philippe Jolicoeur, Rachel Armitage, Renato Maserati, Ricardo Antunes, Seb Neylan, Sharon Malleck, Stephanie Park, Vitor Passarinho, Yvon Lemieux

WRITER THANKS

Gregor Clark

Muito obrigado to all the Portuguese people who generously shared their local knowledge – especially Inês Albuquerque in Vila Real; Alice Braga in Parque Nacional Peneda Gerês; Pedro Mendes in Guimarães; Francisca, Rita and Roberto in Amarante; Nuno in Viana do Castelo; Margarida and Luis in Peso da Régua; and Yvonne in Foz Côa. Back home, *abraços* to Gaen, Meigan and Chloe, who always make coming home the best part of the trip.

Duncan Garwood

Thank you to everyone who helped me on this project, starting with Tom Stainer in London. In Portugal, *obrigado* to Edoardo Queiroz; Joana Sequeira; Margarida Salavessa; Samuel Pereira; João Maltes; the team at Idanha-a-Velha *turismo*, Carla Regio; Claudia Figueira; Kirk Mitchell; Cristina Baía; Patricia Santos; Martha at Praia de Mira; and the folks at Gouveia *turismo*. Most of all, a heartfelt *grazie* to Lidia, Ben and Nick.

Catherine Le Nevez

Muitíssimo obrigada first and foremost to Julian, and to all of the locals, fellow travellers and tourism professionals throughout the Algarve who provided insights, information and great times. Huge thanks too to Destination Editor Tom Stainer and the Portugal team, and everyone at LP. As ever, *merci encore* to my parents, brother, *belle-sœur*, *neveu* and *nièce*.

Kevin Raub

Thanks to Tom Stainer at Lonely Planet. On the road, thanks to Carolina Cardoso, Rui Matias, Jayme Simões, Filipa Achega, Hugo Ferreira, Francisco Gomes and Inês Oliveira.

Regis St Louis

I am grateful to Nina in Évora; Mitch and Vicki in Evoramonte; Filipa in Estremoz; Lina, Eduardo and Lenny in Beirã; and countless others who shared tips and insight along the way. Thanks also to my co-authors for all their hard work. Special thanks to my family, who make coming home the best part of travelling.

Kerry Walker

A big thank you goes to all the people who helped make this book what it is, not least the team at Porto Visitor & Conventions Bureau. I am *muito obrigada* to 'gourmet guru' André Apolinario at Taste Porto Food Tours, Diogo at Prova and David at Touriga for their insight into Portuguese wine, as well as Nuno and Rita at Workshops Pop Up for their excellent tips.

ACKNOWLEDGEMENTS

Climate map data adapted from Peel MC, Finlayson BL & McMahon TA (2007) 'Updated World Map of the Köppen-Geiger Climate Classification', *Hydrology and Earth System Sciences*, 11, 1633–44.

Cover photograph: Decorated *moliceiros* boats, Aveiro, Olimpio Fantuz./4Corners Images ©

THIS BOOK

This 11th edition of Lonely Planet's *Portugal* guidebook was curated by Gregor Clark and researched and written by Gregor, Duncan Garwood, Catherine Le Nevez, Kevin Raub, Regis St Louis and Kerry Walker. The previous edition was written by Regis, Kate Armstrong, Kerry, Marc Di Duca, Anja Mutić and Kevin.

This guidebook was produced by the following:

Destination Editor
Tom Stainer

Senior Product Editors
Genna Patterson, Jessica Ryan

Regional Senior Cartographer Anthony Phelan

Cartographer Hunor Csutoros

Product Editor Ronan Abayawickrema

Book Designer Mazzy Prinsep

Assisting Editors Melanie Dankel, Sarah Reid, Rosie Nicholson, Katie Connolly, Kellie Langdon, Amy Lynch, Lorna Parkes, Sam Wheeler

Cover Researcher
Naomi Parker

Thanks to Paul Harding, Sandra Henriques Gajjar, Sandie Kestell, Charlotte Orr, Kathryn Rowan, Saralinda Turner, Amanda Williamson

Index

Map Legend

Sights

- Beach
- Bird Sanctuary
- Buddhist
- Castle/Palace
- Christian
- Confucian
- Hindu
- Islamic
- Jain
- Jewish
- Monument
- Museum/Gallery/Historic Building
- Ruin
- Shinto
- Sikh
- Taoist
- Winery/Vineyard
- Zoo/Wildlife Sanctuary
- Other Sight

Activities, Courses & Tours

- Bodysurfing
- Diving
- Canoeing/Kayaking
- Course/Tour
- Sento Hot Baths/Onsen
- Skiing
- Snorkelling
- Surfing
- Swimming/Pool
- Walking
- Windsurfing
- Other Activity

Sleeping

- Sleeping
- Camping
- Hut/Shelter

Eating

- Eating

Drinking & Nightlife

- Drinking & Nightlife
- Cafe

Entertainment

- Entertainment

Shopping

- Shopping

Information

- Bank
- Embassy/Consulate
- Hospital/Medical
- Internet
- Police
- Post Office
- Telephone
- Toilet
- Tourist Information
- Other Information

Geographic

- Beach
- Gate
- Hut/Shelter
- Lighthouse
- Lookout
- Mountain/Volcano
- Oasis
- Park
- Pass
- Picnic Area
- Waterfall

Population

- Capital (National)
- Capital (State/Province)
- City/Large Town
- Town/Village

Transport

- Airport
- Border crossing
- Bus
- Cable car/Funicular
- Cycling
- Ferry
- Metro station
- Monorail
- Parking
- Petrol station
- S-Bahn/Subway station
- Taxi
- T-bane/Tunnelbana station
- Train station/Railway
- Tram
- U-Bahn/Underground station
- Other Transport

Routes

- Tollway
- Freeway
- Primary
- Secondary
- Tertiary
- Lane
- Unsealed road
- Road under construction
- Plaza/Mall
- Steps
- Tunnel
- Pedestrian overpass
- Walking Tour
- Walking Tour detour
- Path/Walking Trail

Boundaries

- International
- State/Province
- Disputed
- Regional/Suburb
- Marine Park
- Cliff
- Wall

Hydrography

- River, Creek
- Intermittent River
- Canal
- Water
- Dry/Salt/Intermittent Lake
- Reef

Areas

- Airport/Runway
- Beach/Desert
- Cemetery (Christian)
- Cemetery (Other)
- Glacier
- Mudflat
- Park/Forest
- Sight (Building)
- Sportsground
- Swamp/Mangrove

Note: Not all symbols displayed above appear on the maps in this book

Regis St Louis

The Alentejo Regis grew up in a small town in the American Midwest. He spent his formative years learning Russian and a handful of Romance languages, which has served him well on journeys across much of the globe. Regis has contributed to more than 50 Lonely Planet titles, covering destinations across six continents. When not on the road, he lives in New Orleans. Regis also wrote the Plan section.

Kerry Walker

Porto Kerry is an award-winning travel writer, photographer and Lonely Planet author, specialising in Central and Southern Europe. Based in Wales, she has authored/co-authored more than a dozen Lonely Planet titles. An adventure addict, she loves mountains, cold places and true wilderness. Kerry's insatiable wanderlust has taken her to all seven continents and shows no sign of waning. She features her latest work at its-a-small-world.com and tweets @kerryawalker. Kerry also wrote the Understand section.

OUR STORY

A beat-up old car, a few dollars in the pocket and a sense of adventure. In 1972 that's all Tony and Maureen Wheeler needed for the trip of a lifetime – across Europe and Asia overland to Australia. It took several months, and at the end – broke but inspired – they sat at their kitchen table writing and stapling together their first travel guide, *Across Asia on the Cheap*. Within a week they'd sold 1500 copies. Lonely Planet was born.

Today, Lonely Planet has offices in Franklin, London, Melbourne, Oakland, Dublin, Beijing and Delhi, with more than 600 staff and writers. We share Tony's belief that 'a great guidebook should do three things: inform, educate and amuse'.

OUR WRITERS

Gregor Clark

The Douro & Trás-os-Montes, the Minho Gregor is a US-based writer whose love of foreign languages and curiosity about what's around the next bend have taken him to dozens of countries on five continents. Chronic wanderlust has also led him to visit all 50 US states and most Canadian provinces on countless road trips through his native North America. Since 2000, Gregor has regularly contributed to Lonely Planet guides, with a focus on Europe and the Americas. Titles include *Italy*, *France*, *Brazil*, *Costa Rica*, *Argentina*, *Portugal*, *Switzerland* and *Mexico*.

Duncan Garwood

The Beiras From facing fast bowlers in Barbados to sidestepping hungry pigs in Goa, Duncan's travels have thrown up many unique experiences. These days he largely dedicates himself to the Mediterranean and Italy, his adopted homeland, where he has been living since 1997. He's worked on more than 30 Lonely Planet titles, including *Rome*, *Sardinia*, *Sicily*, *Spain* and *Portugal*, and has contributed to books on food and epic drives.

Catherine Le Nevez

The Algarve Catherine's wanderlust kicked in when she roadtripped across Europe from her Parisian base aged four, and she's been hitting the road at every opportunity since, travelling to some 60 countries and completing her Doctorate of Creative Arts in Writing, Masters in Professional Writing, and postgrad qualifications in editing and publishing along the way. Over the past decade-and-a-half she's written scores of Lonely Planet guides and articles covering Paris, France, Europe and far beyond. Her work has also appeared in numerous online and print publications. Topping Catherine's list of travel tips is to travel without any expectations.

Kevin Raub

Lisbon, Greater Lisbon, Estremadura & Ribatejo Atlanta native Kevin Raub started his career as a music journalist in New York, working for *Men's Journal* and *Rolling Stone* magazines. He ditched the rock 'n' roll lifestyle for travel writing and has written over 70 Lonely Planet guides, focusing mainly on Brazil, Chile, Colombia, USA, India, the Caribbean and Portugal. Kevin also contributes to a variety of travel magazines in both the USA and UK. Along the way, the self-confessed hophead is in constant search of wildly high IBUs in local beers. Follow him on Twitter and Instagram (@RaubOnTheRoad).

OVER PAGE MORE WRITERS

Published by Lonely Planet Global Limited
CRN 554153
11th edition – Nov 2019
ISBN 978 1 78657 801 3
© Lonely Planet 2019   Photographs © as indicated 2019
10 9 8 7 6 5 4 3 2 1
Printed in China